THE QUICKWAY
CROSSWORD DICTIONARY

Twelfth edition

Compiled and revised by
Henry W. Hill and Rowland G. P. Hill

PENGUIN BOOKS

PENGUIN BOOKS

Published by the Penguin Group
Penguin Books Ltd, 80 Strand, London WC2R 0RL, England
Penguin Putnam Inc., 375 Hudson Street, New York, New York 10014, USA
Penguin Books Australia Ltd, Ringwood, Victoria, Australia
Penguin Books Canada Ltd, 10 Alcorn Avenue, Toronto, Ontario, Canada M4V 3B2
Penguin Books India (P) Ltd, 11 Community Centre, Panchsheel Park, New Delhi – 110 017, India
Penguin Books (NZ) Ltd, Cnr Rosedale and Airborne Roads, Albany, Auckland, New Zealand
Penguin Books (South Africa) (Pty) Ltd, 24 Sturdee Avenue, Rosebank 2196 South Africa

Penguin Books Ltd, Registered Offices: 80 Strand, London WC2R 0RL, England

www.penguin.com

First published by Frederick Warne & Co. Ltd 1953
Twelfth edition published by Penguin Books 1998
2

Copyright © Frederick Warne & Co. Ltd, 1998
All rights reserved

Set in 8/8½ Monotype Ehrhardt
Typeset by Rowland Phototypesetting Ltd, Bury St Edmunds, Suffolk
Printed in England by Clays Ltd, St Ives plc

CONTENTS

'Open Locks, Whoever Knocks'

PREFACE

This Dictionary has been specially compiled to meet the exacting needs of modern crossword enthusiasts. All the distinctive features of *The Quickway Key* – of which over 100,000 copies have been sold – have been retained; but notable additions have been made. These include a far greater number of CLUE words, a wide range of synonyms, and a complete vocabulary of the Eight-Letter Words.

The distinctive features are:
1. All CLUE words having the same number of letters are grouped together.
2. Every line begins with a possible CLUE word.
3. All CLUE words are printed in capital letters.
4. Classification code letters, such as *ar* = architecture, *md* = medicine, etc. are placed at the extreme right-hand edges of the lines, on the basis of the equivalents. A detailed list is given on page xi.
5. A very wide range of the latest words has been recorded, of which few may be found in any other one dictionary. Words in brackets indicate, not synonyms or equivalents, but areas in which the word in question is to be encountered.
6. Participles and past tenses of verbs have frequently been recorded, especially when in the passive they form adjectival phrases.

These distinctive features materially reduce the time that has to be spent in the search for interesting clues.

A large number of dictionaries have been consulted; these include *The Shorter Oxford Dictionary*, *The Century*, *Chambers's*, *Nuttall's*, *Webster's Collegiate Dictionary*; also etymological and classical dictionaries, Roget's *Thesaurus* and Nuttall's *Synonyms and Antonyms*. Clue words have been taken from encyclopaedias, *The Statesman's Year Book*, Dr Brewer's *Reader's Handbook*, and authoritative books on Glass, China, Pewter, Curios, etc.

Words such as **CRITH, HELITE, CHENAR, LIBIDO, ZYGOTE**, etc., have been collected from scientific books and reports dealing with Modern Chemistry, Electricity, Physics, Zoology, Botany, Engineering, Physiology, etc., also from books on Theosophy and New Thought. Store catalogues and the special catalogues referring to wireless apparatus, tools, seeds, drapery, and other trades have been ransacked. A wide range of terms dealing with sports and pastimes has been included, as for example: **SCRUM, CAPPED, STANCE, DORMY, ROQUET, BURNED, GOLD, HYPE, OXER, CRAPS**.

Australian, South African, Canadian, Indian, American, and foreign words, such as **COOEE, TREK, MUSH, BHYLE, PRONTO, DUCE, TCHEKA**, are represented.

The mythological names include many Greek, Roman, Norse, Egyptian, Chaldean, and Hindu Gods.

Nearly all English words have in the course of centuries passed through many variations in their spellings. For example, in Murray's *New English Dictionary* the spelling of the word 'POWDER' has between the thirteenth and seventeenth centuries passed through the following variations, *poudre, pudre, puder, powdre, powdir, powdyr, pouder, powdere, poudire, pouldre, pulder, poulder, powlder*; and to these might be added the Scots variations of *pouther* and *powther*. A number of variations in spelling have been collected, but the range of variations recorded in different dictionaries is so large that those now given should not be regarded as exhaustive.

The selection of suitable definitions or synonyms for the words of three or four letters seldom presents any difficulty; in fact, these short words often have so many completely different meanings that more than one line is required to indicate possible clue solutions. For example, **BOX** may refer to a receptacle, a shrub, a driver's seat, a box at the theatre, an affair of fisticuffs, or to some occult nautical rite in which a compass is involved.

The longer words are usually more definite in their meanings; but **BESTED** and **WORSTED** may in some cases be synonymous terms, whilst **CLEAVE** may imply either 'adhere to' or 'split asunder'. Crossword setters, however, have a somewhat similar outlook to that master of the English language, Humpty Dumpty, who declared that: 'When *I* use a word, it means just what I choose it to mean – neither more nor less'. And further, being bound by no inhibition of compunction in splitting up words to suit the nefarious purpose, the setter may insist that **BOOKS-HOP** is a voluminous dance in spite of any exact or meritorious definition while evolving his uncanny mystification.

Similarly, there are those who insist upon providing a clue such as 'five o'clock disappointment' for 'no tea' (spelt 'NO-T' i.e. 'NOT'), or 'up to his neck in the sea' for the philosopher Seneca (SE-NEC(K)-A) and, recently, that two auxiliaries acting correctly thus BE/HAVE.

This particular aspect of crosswords has been delightfully epitomized in the sonnet commemorating the 5,000th Crossword in *The Times*, reproduced on page xi by the kind permission of its author.

The various items enumerated under the heading *GENERAL INFORMATION* will frequently be found of special value in elucidating clues without the necessity of delving into a selection of reference books.

The compiler wishes to express his thanks to those numerous correspondents who so kindly forwarded valuable suggestions. It is his hope that this new volume will be found to fulfil the multifarious requirements of earnest crossword solvers and setters and so enhance the pleasures of the crossword hour.

H. W. HILL

Postscript

For this 12th edition, our fourth further revision, many more amplifications of definitions, meanings and usage, as well as new words have been added throughout this volume.

To the General Information section we have added the chronology of the founding and spread of the European Union, and the memberships within the Russian Commonwealth of Independent States (C.I.S.), the Länder of reunified Germany, communities in Federal Spain, as well as Metropolitan and older counties of England and Wales, and the Regions in Scotland. We are indebted to Dr David Hill for the much longer list of Chemical Elements.

The History of the Crossword Puzzle and our Miscellany of verses and quotations from letters and wordy articles is retained for your pleasure.

Once again we thank the generous-minded crossword enthusiasts for sending in words and suggestions, as well as corrections, welcomed and incorporated whenever possible.

R.G.P.H. and I.E.H.

Publisher's Note

The preparation of this, the 12th Edition has once again been undertaken by the author's son Rowland G. P. Hill and also Ingrid Hill for this fourth revision. Nevertheless, this resulting, greatly enlarged, volume remains substantially in the style of the 8 editions compiled (1923–51) by the late Col. H. W. Hill.

A HISTORY OF THE CROSSWORD PUZZLE

What is a fifteen-letter definition of one of the two or three most popular inventions of the twentieth century?

The answer, of course, is 'crossword puzzle'. On 21 December 1913, the first crossword puzzle ever set appeared in the *New York World* and the craze spread like wildfire. By 1925 it had crossed the Atlantic and Britain rapidly became a nation of crossword addicts. That bastion of dignity, *The Times*, however, was characteristically cautious. It was not until 1930, after a lively debate in the letters column, that it finally succumbed. The crossword was here to stay. Today 99 per cent of the world's daily newspapers and most Sunday papers carry a crossword and regular solvers are counted in multi-millions.

While the shape of the crossword puzzle derives from the word-square, with its repetition in both directions, the notion of differentiated verticals and horizontals probably derives from the acrostic: Greek 'akros' (at the end), and 'stichos' (line of verse). The sybils or prophetesses of ancient Greece used this form of riddle as fortune-telling devices and Cicero records this in De Divinatione. This led in due course to the double acrostic form favoured by our Queen Victoria.

However, it was in 1913 that Arthur Wynne of Liverpool, England, then with the *New York Sunday World*, was determined to introduce something fresh; so he began on a geometric shape – a diamond-shaped 'word-hanger' and gave it the name 'word-cross'.

Soon, the name was transposed to 'crossword', from the subtitle 'find the missing *cross words*', and the enthusiastic public began to send in their own creations; Wynne began to change a word here and there – the right of the crossword editor to suit the readers. It was the solvers, however, who insisted on rules: such as no obscure abbreviations; minimum use of (only well known) foreign words; definitions in dictionary form; that the grid pattern shall interlock all over; a set minimum of squares shall be black; a limit to the number of letters in isolation (unkeyed); and that the design be symmetrical.

This, in turn, led to a greater familiarity with all the shortest words; so much so that the **ZOO** was regarded as home for the **EMU** and animals from **AI** to **YAK**; the most important river was the **PO**, and Egypt was only famous for **IBIS** and **ISIS**, while **ERSE** was the celebrated language of all time!

Not long after this, the then editor of *The Bookman* found that the crossword had actually brought back many dying but acceptable words, to the extent that those previously unfamiliar with specific terms like **APSE** and **NAVE** in a cathedral, or more general words such as **AVER**, **IRE**, **NEE**, **EMIT**, **ERR**, **ELATE** etc. had now become aware of these words. Such was the comeback of vocabulary and usage that this new vehicle for wordpower had brought about, even if cliché use was a resultant hazard.

Reaction soon set in with the urge to discard 'limited vocabulary', make use of reference books, and for an undeniable educational value to bring the standard to a great art worthy of its exalted ancestors.

By 1925 there were about 10 million fans in America. Schools began to make use of them and university psychologists compared crossword ability with IQ tests and found parallel results. Further, a new national habit was revealed in changed situations, in everyday life.

To take one instance. The Baltimore and Ohio Railroad installed dictionaries in each carriage of commuter trains for the convenience of passengers, many of whom took crossword books when on long journeys; and one witness said that 'everyone is going about with knobs of knowledge sticking out on their foreheads like the buffers on a railway engine'.

One New York magistrate was faced with the frustrating task of distracting an intent group of twenty-one solvers; when one defendant pleaded innocent of failure to appear to the charge by explaining he had a longstanding engagement with a crossword, the judge promptly sentenced him to ten days in the workhouse!

Another incident related the effect on a would-be solver who was joined by two others in a noisy restaurant. When closing time had passed none of the three would budge, so the police had to threaten arrest of the first of the three. Thereupon that guilty party expressed delight at the prospect of further, uninterrupted, solitary solving being offered to him!

In the third printing of *The Times Crossword Puzzle Book* in 1925 – that vintage year for solvers – the following warning was given to solvers to alert readers to the possible two symptoms that might result once the contagion set in:

1. If you want to do any more work the rest of the day, put down this book now. If you insist on going ahead, say goodbye to everything else.
2. This is your problem: Do you want to own a book which will delight and distract you (and perhaps shatter the serenity of your home) for at least one hundred hours?

Again, a Broadway revue, 'Puzzles of 1925', included a skit on a Sanatorium for crossword fans seeking a cure, and in that year England reeled with horror as collectively 5 million working hours a day in America – most of them in office time – were spent on poring over a puzzle. 'But that couldn't happen here!'

However, Arthur Wynne had already sold six puzzles to the *Sunday Express*, and thereby earned the title of Crossword Originator and Constructor on both sides of the Atlantic. Soon, in that year, *The Times* was forced to eat its words. 'Who would have thought . . . that the crossword puzzle had come to stay? To most of us it looked like a transatlantic craze which could not be expected to take root in solid, unimaginative English minds.'

What a comeback for those, knowledgeable in the classics and such mysteries, to make use of a mine of 'irrelevance' and so-called 'useless information'.

It only remains to add that, just as everything stops for tea, so, even with newsprint rationing in wartime, the crossword remained a feature which many brains felt to be a necessity, for balance of mind and outlook.

Thus, in its inimitable, modest, way the crossword has invaded the international scene leaving a trail of possessed solvers in its wake.

Abridged and adapted from 'A History of the Crossword Puzzle' by Michelle Arnot; Papermac. This book also contains samples of not only the first, but other famous crosswords, as they originally appeared.

During the 1920s the first edition of this book – in pocket diary format, with a pencil – was already in evidence, especially among those travelling to and from the City. Later editions were enlarged to the present size.

R.G.P.H.

CROSSWORD MISCELLANY

To the Editor of The Times

SIR,

Much have I travelled in another life,
Taken the golden road to Samarkand,
Rolled down to Rio, wandered down the Strand
(Bananaless), asked after Laban's wife.
I swore, 'I will not cease from mental strife
Nor shall my pencil slumber in my hand
Till I have re-discovered Penguinland
And found a cricketer's Malayan knife.'

In vain; the tangled clues still tantalize
And synonyms elude, like runic rhymes.
So would-be solvers with lack-lustre eyes,
Confronted with the anagram for limes,
Look at each other with a wild surmise
Silent, upon a crossword in *The Times*.

    Yours faithfully,
    ELTON EDE

The Crossword Cure
To The Times Crossword Editor

O nameless coiner of the cryptic clue,
  O master of delusive definition,
Embracing in your panoramic view
  A world of miscellaneous erudition,
Once more I pay the homage due
  To your wise conduct of your Inquisition,
Bringing a daily boon and breathing space
To the tired runners in a mad world's race.

You leave no fruitful avenues unexplored
  That minister to innocent hilarity,
But never strike a harsh or jarring chord,
  Or find a virtue in unveiled vulgarity.
Rumour and gossip are by you ignored;
  You season ridicule with kindly charity,
Yet on occasion with unerring eyes
Transfix malicious folly as it flies.

You jog my memory with your mental jerks;
  To you, in fine, I owe a double debt
For while the old machinery still works
  And shows no sign of breaking down as yet –

Thanks to the stimulus of your quips and quirks –
   You teach me to remember, and forget.
For Hell's most grisly gangsters have no power
To crash the gate that guards the Crossword hour.

   C. L. GRAVES

The above poem, which appeared in *The Times* of 23 July 1941, is reproduced by the kind permission of the author's son.

Wordy Might-have-beens

Many of us think that words mean what we can remember we thought they meant, in the manner that two famous historians described history as being not what we thought but what we can remember. We have done just that, as other methods are self-defeating.

Reader's Digest tells us that 'it pays to increase your word power' and this was clear to Sir Winston Churchill, who roused, cajoled, admonished and conciliated people of all nations during an era of unparalleled tribulation. He used strong words to convey his vigorous thoughts, such as imponderable, vitiate, ignoble, verbiage, juncture, brazen, subventions, and bemused.

We therefore dwell on the unknown weightlessness implicit in imponderable as a unit of slimming, as well as lack of seriousness or gravity in astronautical travel. Vitiate suggests a graduate of avoidance, according to the Boolean law of credibility, applied to hyper non-existensialism, or missing evidence.

Ignoble must rank as democratic in opposition to the Lords, and verbiage as a screen in the Dunsinane tradition of foliage rather than the modern smoke version. But then Shakespeare wrote all his plays on words, and depended on pitprops and malaprops to uphold his staging.

Likewise Brunel found himself in the position of King Lear's Gloucester in having his observant eyes outgauged at a juncture near Clapham Heath, and thereby losing his foresight together with his broad-minded, western, lines of development.

Further, while showing arrears or being topless may be the rule for nudists, these could be actionable matters for the Queen's Bench over which the royal motto proclaims 'My God, and I'm right', despite the questionable exposure of a thigh and a garter long ago at Court.

After the bronze age we find few brazen images or artifacts until horse brasses became popular, and top brass denoted support for an iron lady, and her generals. We hope that the discovery through scientific subventions encompassing nuclear magnetics will lead to chips with everything. How much can a polar bear?

Thus, in conclusion, we are bemused artistically by the Three Graces comprising Faith with Hope, and, as any vintner knows, the greatest of the three is Clarity.

   E. & O.E.

50 years ago
From the Manchester Guardian Weekly, 12 December 1924

The world is a puzzling place, but man is not to be deterred from the delights of additional and self-inflicted bewilderment. At one time he found his pleasure in the manipulation of bits and pieces in a jig-saw. Then came the more intellectual diversion of acrostics. Now we are asked to revel in an import from America called 'cross words'. The acrostic in its time must have done valuable work for the Bible Society, since the more obscure names of the Old Testament have a knack of beginning and ending with the vowels that otherwise defy the puzzle-maker, while they are also fairly hard to remember. The new pastime must be a great comfort to the salesmen of dictionaries, glossaries, and the like, and the old complaint that the average man's vocabulary is limited to some five or six hundred words out of the treasury that is open to him may be dissipated by the present quest of verbal oddities. The complete 'cross word' enthusiast is led up hills of chemistry into dales of botany, he must even put his nose to the English grammar and be quite sure where the species 'adverb' begins and ends. The thing beneath the word need not excite him; it is the raiment of letters that he seeks, and he must be sure to get them in their proper order. The young lady who thought that to write was human but to spell divine might profit by the new pastime, but people who are more deeply interested in things than in words will wonder, like the charity boy confronted with the alphabet, whether it is worth going through so much to learn so little. However, the nominalists appear to be a large, happy, and busy faction, but this only increases one's fears as to the fate of a family in which there should be a lonely realist railing at all this quest of the shy noun or dim elusive epithet. May not the result of such a clash become upon occasion – cross words?

Our Mellifluous Bard

Together with his contemporaries (Chaucer,
Spencer, Dryden, Obs and Trad) our own
William Shakespeare once again appears
in this volume, introducing a unit of honeyed
sound/capacity. This arose from
the Tudor delight in gardens, leafy
bowers and walks, mells and malls –
a setting lending a counter point of interest to enhance
consorts of viols, recorders and gambas (and nightingales too).
While they were concerned to fill a mell
with melody, nowadays we would employ
garden orchestras and transistor radios.
This unit of pleasant sound bordering on the herbaceous,
appears as 'PHILOMEL' and, as
such, treads dainty a measure among the bulk of more weighty items.

THE ARDENT CHRONICLER

The Enthusiast – Christopher Robin

And finally, after dinner, almost a ritual, there was *The Times* crossword, with my mother (to give her a slight advantage) reading out the clues and my father trying not to be too quick with the answers.

My father had a passion for crosswords. We shared *The Times*: this was the rule. It was fairly easy. It took about half an hour and, though he would get most of the answers (including all the quotations), my mother and I would be able to manage a few contributions. On Sunday we took the *Observer* and so on Sunday evening we did the 'Everyman' crossword. This left my father free to wrestle single-handed with his favourite Torquemada.

How many Torquemada solvers survive today? Any that do will surely agree that his were the most difficult crosswords and he the most brilliant composer of them all; and that even Ximenes, good though he was, was never quite in the same class.

Solving crosswords is immensely satisfying. In a way it is the same sort of satisfaction you get from solving mathematical problems. Pencil, paper and brains: that's what you need. And you wrestle away until at last the answer comes. Or you can describe it as fitting words into an exact, interlocking pattern of squares. You can't alter the pattern: that is fixed. You juggle with the words, juggle with the letters, until at last it all fits, until the last letter falls neatly, satisfyingly into place. 'Got it!' and with a happy sigh you put your pencil back in your pocket. In this respect it resembles the writing of light verse.

from *The Enchanted Places* by CHRISTOPHER (ROBIN) MILNE

Breakfast Peace
From Mr and Mrs John Beeching

Sir, We were delighted this morning to find our crossword puzzles printed on separate sheets of paper, allowing a blissful return to the period of companionable silence after breakfast when we each apply ourselves to the puzzle most suited to our talents.

Thank you for your efforts in bringing this about.

JOHN BEECHING
CICELY BEECHING
The Times, 20 Feb 1987

Ready Solution
From Mr John Ruffle

Sir, On a recent visit to Egypt a friend purchased a copy of *The Times* for £E2.50 (approx. £1.25p) and was (I think) delighted to find that the crossword had been accurately completed.

I have tried asking my supplier what he will charge for this remarkable service. Mr and Mrs Beeching (20 February) might also be interested if you could provide details of how it can be arranged.

JOHN RUFFLE
The Times, 27 Feb 1987

Cryptic   5 March 1976

Sir, Returning home from my local **hammam** I was somewhat **esurient** and so visited our **spence** and set the table complete with **ortolan** but my fear was **adipose**, so I stopped eating and performed a quick **antiphon** with my wife, before retiring to bed.

All the words in bold appeared in this week's crossword puzzles, and if they are known and understood by your average reader I will eat my **zucchetta**.

W. L. FRASER,
GLASGOW

Royal Gravity

William Rufus was hunting one day in the New Forest, when William Tell (the memorable crackshot, inventor of the crossbow puzzle) took unerring aim at a reddish apple which had fallen on to the King's head, and shot him through the heart.

W. C. SELLAR and R. T. YEATMAN

Due to lack of space, Mary Poppin's favourite panegyric word will not appear in this edition. It has 34 letters and is 'Supercalifragilisticexpialidocious'. For a sample, please apply to your nearest chemist, with prescription.

(as printed on film posters)

'Open Locks, Whoever Knocks'

We wish to acknowledge with thanks and express our appreciation of kind and helpful letters suggesting the adoption of various new words or listings for the GENERAL INFORMATION section or items for our miscellany.

These are all welcomed and carefully considered as contributions to the worldwide community linked by crosswords and various word games and contents.

R. G. P. HILL and I. E. HILL

CATEGORY CLASSIFICATION

ac	acoustics	*fr*	forestry	*nv*	navigation
ae	aeronautics	*ga*	games	*oc*	oceanography
ag	agriculture	*gl*	geology	*pb*	plumbing
am	automation	*gn*	genetics	*pc*	psychology, psychiatry
ar	architecture	*go*	geography	*pg*	photography
as	astronomy	*gp*	geophysics	*pl*	physiology
au	automobiles	*gs*	glass	*pm*	pharmaceutics
ba	bacteriology	*hd*	heraldry	*pp*	paper
bc	biochemistry	*hr*	horology	*pr*	printing
bd	building	*hy*	hydraulics	*ps*	physics
bl	biology	*jn*	joinery	*pt*	paints, painting
br	brewing	*le*	leather-working	*rd*	radar
bt	botany	*lt*	light	*rl*	religion
ce	civil engineering	*lw*	law	*ro*	radio
cf	combining form	*ma*	mathematics	*rw*	railways
ch	chemistry	*md*	medicine and medical	*sp*	space
ck	cookery	*me*	measurements	*sv*	surveying
cn	cinema	*ml*	metallurgy	*tc*	telecommunications
cp	computers	*mn*	mining	*to*	tools
cr	carpentry	*mo*	mountaineering	*tv*	television
cy	cytology	*mt*	meteorology	*tx*	textiles
ec	ecology	*mu*	music	*vt*	veterinary
eg	engineering	*nc*	nuclear (physics)	*wv*	weaving
el	electrical, electronics	*nm*	numismatics, coins	*zo*	zoology
fd	foundry	*nt*	nautical		

Note: Language and nationality abbreviations are found closer to the definition, within parenthesis, but not in italic type, which is reserved for the above classifications.

Ass.	Assyrian	Hung.	Hungarian	Rus.	Russian
Aus.	Australian	Ind.	Indian	S. Am.	South American
Bab.	Babylonian	It.	Italian	Sc.	Scottish
C. Am.	Central American	Jap.	Japanese	Scand.	Scandinavian
Ch.	Chinese	Jew.	Jewish	Sem.	Semitic
Eg.	Egyptian	Lat.	Latin	Sp.	Spanish
Fin.	Finnish	N. Am.	North American	Sum.	Sumerian
Fr.	French	NZ	New Zealand	Turk.	Turkish, etc.
Ger.	German	Pers.	Persian		
Gr.	Greek	Rom.	Roman		

Various literary abbreviations are also given:

obs.	obselete
Shak.	Shakespeare
sl.	slang
Spens.	Spenser

Groups of a Kind

Terms of the Chase

3 NAG of colts
NYE of pheasants
POD of seals, whales
RAG of colts
4 BEVY of roes, quails
BITE of mites
CAST of hawks
CETE of badgers
CLAT of worms
COIL of teal
DOWN of hares
DULE of turtles
FALL of woodcock
GANG of elks
HERD of cranes, curlew, deer, cattle
HILL of ruffs
HIVE of bees
KNOB of wild duck
LEAP of leopards
NEST of rabbits
PACE of asses
PACK of hounds
ROUT of wolves
SEGE of herons
SORD of mallards
STUD of stallions
SUTE of mallards
TAKE of fish
TEAM of oxen
TRIP of goats
WISP of snipe
5 BROOD of hens
CHARM of goldfinches
COVEY of partridges
DOYLT of tame swine
DROVE of kine
FLOCK of sheep
HOVER of crows
PLUMP of wild fowl
PRIDE of lions
SEDGE of herons
SHOAL of fish
SIEGE of herons
SKEIN of geese (flying)
SKULK of foxes
5 SLOTH of bears
SWARM of bees
TRIBE of goats
TROOP of monkeys
WATCH of nightingales
WEDGE of geese (flying)
BARREN of mules
COLONY of gulls
COVERT of coots
DOGDOM of dogs
GAGGLE of geese
GAMBLE of lambs, casinos
HARRAS of horses
FLIGHT of doves
KENNEL of raches
KINDLE of kittens
LABOUR of moles
LITTER of whelps
MUSTER of peacocks
SCHOOL of porpoises, whales
SPRING of teal
TROGLE of snakes
UPPING of swans
7 BUZZING of bees
CLOWDER of cats
COMPANY of widgeon
DOPPING of sheldrake
FLITTER of bats
SOUNDER of swine
8 BUILDING of rooks
BUSINESS of ferrets, flies
DABBLING of ducks
FESNYING of ferrets
MUTATION of thrushes
RICHNESS of martens
SINGULAR of boars
STINGING of wasps
9 BATTERING of rams
BIRTHRATE of rabbits
COWARDICE of curs
10 CHATTERING of choughs
EXALTATION of larks
SHREWDNESS of apes
UNKINDNESS of ravens
11 CONCOVATION of eagles
LAMENTATION of swans
MURMURATION of starlings
12 CONGREGATION of plovers

Miscellaneous

3 ACE of spades, disaster
BAG of mail
BED of nails
BOX of delights
JAM of traffic
PIT of disgrace, miners
SEA of troubles
SEE of diocese
4 AREA of surfaces
BALE of hay
BANK of reserves, money
BEVY of buxom wenches
BODY of corporations, authorities
BUZZ of barflies
CAMP of allegations
CASK of beer, anglers
CREW of seamen
CURE of doctors
DISC of information
FOLD of highlanders
GANG of thieves, crooks
GIST of arguments
KNOT of sea-speeds, entanglements
LACK of principles
LAWN of grass
LEAP of lovers
LOAD of bricks
MASS of catholics
MESS of potage
MILE of distance
NEST of machineguns, pickpockets
NOOK of cookery
PACK of cards
PACT of agreements
PARK of artillery
PECK of popcorn
POOL of typists
REAM of paper
ROLE of supporters
ROPE of pearls
RUCK of stones
SACK of redundants, coals
SOLE of unitarians
STAB of bayonets
TALE of Two Cities
TANK of liquids
TEAM of players
TUFT of grass
WARD of patients
WIND of change
YARD of ships, ale, space
ZONE of influence
5 BATCH of mail
BENCH of bishops
BERRY of holes
BLAST of explosions, hunters

5 BLUSH of boys
BREAK of tea
BURKE of peers
CAPER of dancers
CASTE of ranks, religions, societies
CHAOS of regulations
CHOIR of choristers
CLUMP of trees
CROWD of people
DRIFT of fishers
DRUCK of people
FEAST of brewers
FIELD of interest
FLEET of cars, warships
HAREM of concubines
HORDE of insurgents, savages
HOUSE of cards, Commons, Lords,
   iniquities
LYING of pardoners
METER of consumption
ORBIT of spheres
PINCH of snuff
POINT of decimals
POSSE of police, savages
QUIRE of paper
RANGE of investments
ROUTE of knights
SCALE of wages, maps
SHEAF of corn, wheat
SKEIN of silk, wool
SLATE of candidates
SQUAT of daubers
STAND of arms, one night
STATE of princes
SYNOD of clergy
TRUSS of hay
TRUTH of barons
VAULT of architects
WINDS of uncertainties
6 BABBLE of barbers, brooks
BASKET of currencies
BORDER of the herbaceous
BOTTLE of drinks, hay
BOXING of compasses
BUDGET of exchequers, papers
BUMBLE of dignitaries
CELLAR of wines
CHARGE of entries, cavalry
COLUMN of gossip
COMEDY of errors
CONVOY of ships
CURACY of clerics
FLIGHT of angels, aeroplanes
GALAXY of beauty, stars
GARAGE of cars, buses
GIGGLE of comedians, schoolgirls
HATFUL of medals
LEAGUE of nations

6 **LITTER** of garbage
MARINA of pleasure craft
MEDLEY of tunes
MELODY of makers, harpers, songs
MOTION of meetings
NUDITY of naturists
PALATE of recipes
PAPACY of popes
PUNNET of strawberries
RECORD of events, LP music
SAVOUR of cookery
SPLASH of Baptists
TARTAN of Scots
THRAVE of threshers
THRONG of angels
TRIPOD of triangles
TROUPE of actors, vaudeville artistes
7 **ACRONYM** of organizations
BATTERY of guns
BLARNEY of bartenders
BOREDOM of briefs
BRIGADE of Guards, firemen
CABINET of curiosities, ministers
CLUSTER of stars
COMPANY of chairmen, actors
CONCERT of music
CONSORT of viols
DISCORD of tuners
DRAUGHT of beer
FRAUNCH of millers
HENPECK of husbands
HISTORY of remembrances
LIBRARY of books, information
PALETTE of artists
PEEPING of toms
POVERTY of beggars, pipers
SCUTTLE of coals
TABLOID of scandals
TOLLING of church-bells
WASSAIL of carollers
WORSHIP of writers
8 **ALLIANCE** of interests, nations

8 **ALPHABET** of indexes
BELCHING of drunks, smoke
CONCLAVE of cardinals
CREDENCE of sewers
EXCHANGE of stock, addresses, phones, ideas
FIGHTING of pugilists, beggars
FLATNESS of steppes
HATCHING of eggs, plots
LAUGHTER of ostlers
PLANNING of bureaucrats
REGIMENT of women, soldiers
SEQUENCE of events
SHOUTING of sergeants
SPECTRUM of light, politics, sex
SQUADRON of cavalry, aeroplanes
STRADDLE of athletes
STRIKING of clocks, off-rolls
SUBTILNE of sergeants
TERMINUS of trains, buses
TWANGING of harpists
9 **ANTHOLOGY** of verse, literature
BLOCKHEAD of dunces
CAVALCADE of horsemen, songs
COMMUNITY of saints
CONFUSION of initials
ELOQUENCE of lawyers
GATHERING of the clans
GEOGRAPHY of situations, surroundings
HASTINESS of cooks
MORBIDITY of majors
PORTFOLIO of shares
SAFEGUARD of policies, porters
SYMBIOSIS of life-styles
10 **BLACKSLACK** of handymen
CONFESSION of sins
DISCRETION of priests
IMPATIENCE of wives
INFIDELITY of boyfriends
SENTENCING of convicts
11 **CONSPIRACY** of authorities

The Chemical Elements

	Name	Atomic No.	Symbol		Name	Atomic No.	Symbol
3	TIN	50	Sn	**8**	CHLORINE	17	Cl
4	GOLD	79	Au		CHROMIUM	24	Cr
	IRON	26	Fe		EUROPIUM	63	Eu
	NEON	10	Ne		FLUORINE	9	F
	LEAD	82	Pb		FRANCIUM	87	Fr
	ZINC	30	Zn		HYDROGEN	1	H
5	ARGON	18	A		LUTETIUM	71	Lu
	BORON	5	B		NITROGEN	7	N
	RADON	86	Rn		NOBELIUM	102	No
	XENON	54	Xe		PLATINUM	78	Pt
6	BARIUM	56	Ba		POLONIUM	84	Po
	CARBON	6	C		RUBIDIUM	37	Rb
	CERIUM	58	Ce		SAMARIUM	62	Sm
	COBALT	27	Co		SCANDIUM	21	Sc
	COPPER	29	Cu		SELENIUM	34	Se
	CURIUM	96	Cm		TANTALUM	73	Ta
	ERBIUM	68	Er		THALLIUM	81	Tl
	HELIUM	2	He		TITANIUM	22	Ti
	INDIUM	49	In		TUNGSTEN	74	W
	IODINE	53	I		VANADIUM	23	V
	NICKEL	28	Ni	**9**	ALUMINIUM	13	Al
	OSMIUM	76	Os		AMERICIUM	95	Am
	OXYGEN	8	O		BERKELIUM	97	Bk
	RADIUM	88	Ra		BERYLLIUM	4	Be
	SILVER	47	Ag		GERMANIUM	32	Ge
	SODIUM	11	Na		LANTHANUM	57	La
7	ARSENIC	33	As		MAGNESIUM	12	Mg
	BISMUTH	83	Bi		MANGANESE	25	Mn
	BROMINE	35	Br		NEODYMIUM	60	Nd
	CADMIUM	48	Cd		NEPTUNIUM	93	Np
	CAESIUM	55	Cs		PALLADIUM	46	Pd
	CALCIUM	20	Ca		PLUTONIUM	94	Pu
	FERMIUM	100	Fm		POTASSIUM	19	K
	GALLIUM	31	Ga		RUTHENIUM	44	Ru
	HAFNIUM	72	Hf		STRONTIUM	38	Sr
	HOLMIUM	67	Ho		TELLURIUM	52	Te
	IRIDIUM	77	Ir		UNUNUNIUM	110	Uun
	KRYPTON	36	Kr		YTTERBIUM	70	Yb
	LITHIUM	3	Li		ZIRCONIUM	40	Zr
	MERCURY	80	Hg	**10**	DYSPROSIUM	66	Dy
	NIOBIUM	41	Nb		GADOLINIUM	64	Gd
	RHENIUM	75	Re		LAWRENCIUM	103	Lr
	RHODIUM	45	Rh		MOLYBDENUM	42	Mo
	SILICON	14	Si		PHOSPHORUS	15	P
	SULPHUR	16	S		PROMETHIUM	61	Pm
	TERBIUM	65	Tb		TECHNETIUM	43	Tc
	THORIUM	90	Th	**11**	CALIFORNIUM	98	Cf
	THULIUM	69	Tm		EINSTEINIUM	99	Es
	URANIUM	92	U		MENDELEVIUM	101	Md
	YTTRIUM	39	Y		UNNILENNIUM	109	Une
8	ACTINIUM	89	Ac		UNNILHEXIUM	106	Unh
	ANTIMONY	51	Sb		UNNILOCTIUM	108	Uno
	ASTATINE	85	At	**12**	PRASEODYMIUM	59	Pr

Name	*Atomic No.*	*Symbol*		*Name*	*Atomic No.*	*Symbol*
12 PROTACTINIUM	91	Pa	**12**	UNNILQUADIUM	104	Unq
UNNILPENTIUM	105	Unp		UNNILSEPTIUM	107	Uns

Gaseous Emanations

5 NITON from Radium

6 IONIUM from Uranium
8 ACTINIUM from Thorium
POLONIUM from Radium

Weights and Measures
With some approximate English equivalents

1 A acre, ampere, electric current *Int.*
B bel, power comparison unit *Int.*
C colomb, charge *Int.*
F farad, capacitance *Int.*
G magnetic flux density, gram = 0.035 oz *Int.*
H henry, inductance *Int.*
J joule, energy *Int.*
K kelvin, temperature *Int.*
L litre = 1 qt (liq.) *Int.*
M metre, length = 39.37 ins *Int.*
N newton, force *Int.*
S second, time, angle, lat., long. *Int.*
T tesla, magnetic flux density, tonne, metric ton *Int.*
V volt, voltage *Int.*
W watt, power *Int.*
2 AP apothecaries' measure *Int.*
AV avoirdupois (avdp), weight *Int.*
BU bushel, 4 pecks (2219.3 cu ins); 0.036 cu m (Br. Imp.) *Britain*
BU TSUBO = 3.306 sq m (area) *Japan*
CD candela, luminous intensity *Int.*
CI curie, unit of activity of radioactive substance *Int.*
CM centimetre = 0.394 ins *Int.*
DB decibel (dB), unit of noise *Int.*
DL decilitre (10 dl = 1 litre) *Int.*
DR dram, 27.34 grains, 0.06 oz, 1.771 gram *U.S.*
EL 1 metre (old EL = 27.08 ins) *Netherlands*
FT foot = 12 ins, 0.33 yds, 30.48 cm *Int.*
GB gilbert (Gb), magnetomotive force (magnetic potential) *Int.*
GI gill (Br. Imp.), 5 fl oz, 8.66 cu ins, 142.06 cu cm *Britain*
GI gill (liq.), 4 fl oz, 7.21 cu ins, 118.29 ml *U.S.*
GO 0.18 litre *Japan*
GR grain, 0.036 dram, 0.002 oz, 0.06 gram *Int.*

2 HZ hertz (Hz), frequency *Int.*
HU 51.77 litres *China*
IN inch, $\frac{1}{12}$ foot, $\frac{1}{36}$ yard, 2.54 cm *Int.*
KG kilogram, 2.2 lb *Int.*
KM kilometre, 0.6 mile *Int.*
KW kilowatt, 1.3 horsepower; kilowatt-hour/KWh. *Int.*
LB pound, 16 oz, 7000 grains, 0.453 kg *Int.*
LI ¾ mile = 360 pu *China*
LM lumen, luminous flux *Int.*
LX lux, illumination *Int.*
MI mile, 5280 ft, 320 rods, 1760 yds, 1.609 km *Int.*
ML millilitre *Int.*
MM millimetre, 0.04 in *Int.*
NT nit, luminance *Int.*
OE oersted (Oe), magnetic field strength *Int.*
OZ ounce, 28 grams, 16 drams, 437.5 grains *Int.*
PE ¾ metre *Portugal*
PK peck (dry), 8 qt, 537.605 cu in, 8.809 litres *U.S.*
PK peck (Br. Imp.), 2 gals, 554.8385 cu ins, 0.009 cu m *Britain*
PT pint (liq.), 4 gi, 28.875 cu ins, 0.473 litre *U.S.*
PT pint (dry), ½ qt, 33.600 cu ins, 0.550 litre *U.S.*
PT pint (Br. Imp.), 4 gi, 34.677 cu in, 568.26 cu cm *Britain*
PU 70.5 ins = 5 ch'ih *China*
QT quart (liq.), 2 pts, 57.75 cu ins, 0.946 litre *U.S.*
QT quart (dry), 2 pts, 67.20 cu ins, 1.101 litres *U.S.*
QT quart (Br. Imp.), 2 pts, 69.35 cu ins, 1.136 litres *Britain*
RD rod, 5.50 yds, 16.5 ft, 5.029 m *Int.*
RI 2.440 miles *Japan*
SB stilb (Sb), unit of luminance *Int.*
SE 118.615 sq yds (0.9918 are) *Japan*
SR steradian, solid angle *Int.*
ST stokes, kinematic viscosity *Int.*
TO 18.03 litres = 4.77 U.S. gals *Japan*

2 TU 100.142 miles = 250 li *China*
WA WAH, 2 m *Thailand*
WB weber, magnetic flux *Int.*
YD yard, 3 ft, 36 ins, 0.914 m *Int.*

3 AAM 30–35 gals *E. Indies*
ARE 100 sq m, 119.6 yds *Int.*
AUM 31 Imp. gal *S. Africa*
BAT BAHT, TICAL, 15 grams
   (231.5 grains) *Thailand*
BEL power comparison unit *Int.*
CAB 3 pts *Hebrew*
CHO 1815 sq ft (3000 bu/area;
   360 shaku/length) *Japan*
COR 8½ bushels *Hebrew*
CWT hundredweight; 45.35 kg (short),
   50.80 kg (long) *Britain*
DWT pennyweight *Britain*
ELL (Eng.) 45 ins, (Sc.) 37 ins,
   (Jersey) 4 ft *Britain*
ERG unit of energy; 1 erg =
   10^{-7} joules *Int.*
FEN 5.76 grains (silver weight) *China*
FOD 0.3138 m, 1.029 ft *Denmark*
FOT 11.689 ins; 10 fot = 1 stäng *Sweden*
FOU bushel *Scotland*
FUT FOUTE 1 Eng. ft *Russian Fed.*
GAL gallon (liq.), 4 qt (231 cu ins),
   3.785 litres *U.S.*
GAL gallon (Br. Imp.), 4 qt
   (277.4 cu ins), 4.545 litres *Britain*
GIN KATI, CATTY 1¼ lb *Malaysia*
GUZ GUDGE 27–36 ins *E. Indies*
GUZ GUEZA, ZER 1 m
   (40.95 ins) *Iran*
HIN 6 qts *Hebrew*
KAN 1 litre; 1¾ lb (Hong Kong)
   Netherlands
KEN 1.82 m, 5.96 ft *Japan*
KIN 0.600 kg, 1.32 lb *Japan*
KON CATTY 1¾ lb *Korea*
KUP 10 ins *Thailand*
LOG ¼ pt *Hebrew*
LOT 10 grams (new),
   ½ oz (old) *Germany*
LUX unit of light (lx); 1 1m over an
   area of 1m squared *Int.*
MIL one thousandth of an inch *U.S./G.B.*
MIL MILL 1.000 archins
   (new mil) *Turkey*
MIN minim, $\frac{1}{60}$ fluidram, 0.0591 cu cm
   (Br. Imp.) *Britain*
MIN minim, $\frac{1}{60}$ fluidram, 0.0616 cu cm
   U.S.
MNA 1½ kg = 1.172 oke *Greece*
MOU 806.65 sq yds (or 920.41 sq yds)
   China
MUD 1 hectolitre *Netherlands*
NIN $\frac{10}{12}$ in *Thailand*

3 NIT (nt) luminance; 1 candela per m
   squared *Int.*
NIU 1 in *Thailand*
OCK 1 kg; (1881) 1 ock =
   100 drachmas; new batman =
   10 ocks, kantar = 10 batmans *Turkey*
OHM resistance V/A *Int.*
OKA 3 lb *Egypt*
OKE 1.28 l (liq.); 1.28 kg (old); 2.8 lb
   Bulgaria
OKE 400 drams *Cyprus*
ONS 100 grams *Netherlands*
PIC PIk 2 ft (Greece picki 0.64 m)
   Cyprus
PIE 11.73 in *Rome*
PIK DIRAA 0.58 m *U.A.R.*
PIN half a firkin *Britain*
POT 0.966 litre *Denmark*
RAD radian, plane angle; radiation
   absorbed dose, 0.01 joule/kg
   (100 ergs/gramme) *Int.*
RAI ¾ acre *Thailand*
REM roentgen equivalent man; 1 rem =
   1 rad Q.F. *Int.*
RIO ounce *Japan*
ROD 5.50 yds, 16.5 ft, 5.029 m *Int.*
SEN 40.6 m, 44 yds *Thailand*
SHO 1.804 litres *Japan*
SUN 1 in *Japan*
TAN 133 lb *China*
TOD 2 stone *Britain*
TON 20 cwt, 0.907 m/tons (short),
   1.016 m/tons (long) *Int.*
TOU 10 litres *China*
TUN 252 gals *Britain*
VAT 1 hectolitre *Netherlands*
WAH WA 2 m *Thailand*
WEY 13 stone *Britain*
ZAK 1 hectolitre *Netherlands*
ZAR 1 m *Iran*
ZER GUZ, GUEZA 1 m (40.95 ins)
   Iran

4 ACRE 4840 sq yds, 0.405 hectare,
   4046 sq m *Britain*
ATTO (a) 10^{-18} *Int.*
AUNE 1 m, (France 1.18 m),
   (Jersey 4 ft) *Belgium*
BAHT BAT, TICAL, 15 grams
   (231.5 grains) *Thailand*
BALE 10 reams *Britain*
BATH 6 gals *Hebrew*
BUTT 108 gals *Britain*
CHEE TAHIL 1¾ oz = 10 chee =
   100 hoon *Malaysia*
CHEK 14⅜ ins *Hong Kong*
CH'IH 14.1 ins (customs), 5 ch'ih =
   1 pu *China*
CHIN CATTY 1¾ lb (customs) *China*

4 CHUO 1.815 sq ft (customs) *China*
COSS 1.82 km, 1¾ miles *India*
CRAN ca. 750 herrings *Britain*
CU CM 0.06 cu in *Int.*
CU FT 1728 cu ins, 0.0370 cu yd,
  0.028 cu m *Int.*
CU IN 0.00058 cu ft, 16.387 cu cm *Int.*
DECI (d) 10^{-1}; 1 dm = 0.1 m *Int.*
DEKA DECA 10; 1 dekametre =
  10 metres *Int.*
DITO 1 cm *Italy*
DOLA DOLIA, 96 doli = 1 zolotnick
  Russian Fed.
DOSE quantity of radiation (absorbed
  energy), see rad, rem
DRAH 22 ins *Morocco*
DRAM 27.343 grams, 0.0625 oz,
  1.7718452 grains *Int.*
DUIM 1 in *Russian Fed./Netherlands*
DYNE unit of force; 1 dyne =
  10^{-5} newton *Int.*
ELLA 1 yd *Sabah/N. Borneo*
ELLE 60 cm; (Latvia) 0.53 m *Switzerland*
EPHA bushel *Hebrew*
FL DR fluidram, 60 minims
  (0.22 cu in), 29.572 ml *U.S.*
FL DR fluidram, 60 minims
  (0.21 cu in), 3.5516 cu cm *Britain*
FL OZ fluid ounce (Br. Imp.),
  8 fluidrams, 28.413 cu cm *Britain*
FOOT 12 ins, 0.333 yd, 30.48 cm *Int.*
FUNT FOUNTE 0.90 lb (U.S.S.R.),
  405.5 grams *Poland*
FUSZ 12 zolls = 1.037 ft (Vienna),
  1¾ fusz = 1 m *Switzerland*
GIGA (G) 10^9; 1 GHz = 10^9 hertz *Int.*
GILL 4 fl oz (7.218 cu ins), 118.29 ml
  U.S.
GILL 5 fl oz (Br. Imp.), 8.669 cu in,
  142.0652 cu cm *Britain*
GRAM 0.035 oz *Int.*
GRAO 0.769 gr, 0.18 in *Portugal*
HAND (horses) 4 in *Britain*
HAT'H MOOLUM, CUBIT, 18 ins
  India
HIDE 120 acres *Britain*
HOON TAHIL, CHEE, 1¾ oz =
  10 chee = 100 hoon *Malaysia*
IMMI 1.5 litres *Switzerland*
INCH 0.083 ft, 0.027 yd, 2.540 cm,
  25 mm *Int.*
JOCH 57.55 ares = 1.422 acres *Austria*
KATI CATTY, GIN 1¾ lb *Malaysia*
KELA ½ bushel *Egypt*
KHAT 1 cm *Turkey*
KILO (k) 10^3; 1 km = 1000 m; comput.:
  2^{10} = 1 kilobyte = 1024 bytes *Int.*
KILO kilogram, 2.2 lb *Int.*

4 KNOT 6.080 ft; 1 nt mile/hour =
  0.514 4444 m/s *Britain*
KOKU 180.39 litres (see TO) *Japan*
KOSS 2000 yds *India*
KUNG 78.96 ins (customs) *China*
KWAN KUWAN, 3.75 kg, 8.26 lb *Japan*
KYAT 16.33 grams *Burma*
LAST 30 hectolitres *Netherlands*
LINE LIGNE, 2.26 mm *Paris*
LINK 7.92 in *U.S./G.B.*
MACE 93¾ gr (Sabah/N. Borneo),
  58¾ gr *China*
MARC MARK 0.2448 kg (old) *France*
MEGA (M) 10^6; 2^{20} 1 megabyte =
  1048576 bytes *Int.*
MIJL 1 int. nautical mile *Netherlands*
MILE 5280 ft, 320 rods, 1760 yds,
  1.609 km *Int.*
MILE nautical, 6080.20 ft (formerly)
  U.S.
MILE nautical/admiralty, 6080 ft *Britain*
MILE nautical/international, 1853 m
  Int.
MILE postal, 4714 ft *Austria*
MOIO 2¾ qts *Portugal*
MUDD 1 bushel *Morocco*
NAIL 2¼ ins *Britain*
NANO (n) 10^{-9}; 1 nm = 10^{-9} m *Int.*
NATR 2 lb *Ethiopia*
OKET 1 oz avoirdupois (av) *Ethiopia*
ONCA 28.68 grams *Portugal*
ONCE 30.59 grams (old) *France*
PAAL 1½ m *Indonesia*
PACK 240 lb *Britain*
PALM 1 decimetre (dm) *Netherlands*
PARA 90 lb *Sabah/N. Borneo*
PECK 2 gals *Britain*
PHOT intensity of illumination
  (1 1m/sq cm), 1 phot = 104 lux *Int.*
PICO (p) 10^{-12}; 1 pF = 10^{12} farad *Int.*
PIED 11.81 ins = 10 pouces (Belgium),
  12.79 ins *Canada*
PIED de roi 0.3248 m *Paris*
PINT (liquid) 28.875 cu ins, 0.473 litre
  U.S.
PINT (dry) ½ qt (33.67 cu ins),
  568.260 cu cm *Britain*
PINT (Br. Imp.) 4 gi (34.67 cu ins),
  568.260 cu cm *Britain*
PIPA 500 litres, 429 litres (old) *Portugal*
PIPE 126 gals *Britain*
POLE 16½ ft *Britain*
POND ½ kilogram *Netherlands*
POOD 36.113 lb *Russian/Fed.*
PUND 500 grams, (Sweden
  425.1 grams) *Scandinavia*
REAM 20 quires (of 24 sheets: paper)
  Britain

4 REED 152 ins *Hebrew*
RODE 3.138 m *Denmark*
ROOD 40 perches, ¼ acre *Britain*
ROTL ROTTOLA, RATEL, 0.9905 lb (customs) *U.A.R.*
SACK 2 weys *Britain*
SAWK 20 in *Thailand*
SEAH 14 pts *Hebrew*
SEAM (glass) 24 stone *Britain*
SEER 1.061 lb (Sri Lanka), 2.057 lb (government) *India*
SIHR 16 miseals, 1136 gr weight *Iran*
SHIH 157.89 lb *China*
SKOT low-intensity lighting *Int.*
SQ IN 0.007 sq ft, 6.4516 sq cm *Int.*
SQ MI 640 acres, 102 400 sq rods, 2.589 sq km *Int.*
SQ RD 30.25 sq yds, 0.006 acre, 25.293 sq m *Int.*
SQ YD 1296 sq ins, 9 sq ft, 0.836 sq m *Int.*
STAB 1 m (3¾ old fuss) *Germany*
TAEL 1¾ oz (Hong Kong), 936¼ grams *Thailand*
TAEL 10 momme (Japan), 1¾ oz (silver weight) *China*
TANK 68.1 grams (72 tanks = 1 seer) *Bombay*
TENG (basket) 2218.2 cu ins (varies) *Burma*
TERA (T) 10^{12}; 1 Tm = 10^{12} m *Int.*
TOLA 180 grains; legal weight of rupee *India*
TORR unit of pressure (vacuum), 133.322 newtons/sq m *Int.*
T'SUN 1.41 ins *China*
VARA 83.5 cm–1 m, 33–43 ins (varies) *S. America/U.S.*
VISS 3.60 lbs (3.65 old) *Burma*
VOLT (V) W/A voltage *Int.*
WATT kilowatt, 1.3 horsepower *Int.*
X-RAY unit of length, 1.002×10^{-13} m *Int.*
YARD 3 ft, 36 ins, 0.9144 m *Int.*
YLEM hypothetical density (10^{16} kg m^{-3}) *Int.*
ZOLL 3 cm (ca. 1 in. old) *Switzerland*

5 ANKER 7½ gals *S. Africa*
ANKER 38.25 litres (or 30 stoof) *Latvia*
ARDEB 5.61 bushels = 100 sq m = 119.6 sq yds *Egypt*
ASSAY ton, 29.16 grams *U.S.*
BAHAR BEHAR 450 lb *Arabian Peninsula*
BARYE unit of pressure (old); 1 barye = 0.1 pascal *Int.*
BERRI 1.67 km, 1.04 miles (old) *Turkey*
BRACA 2.20 m *Portugal*

5 BRAZA 1.732 m *Argentina*
CABLE 100 fathoms *Britain*
CABOT 10 pots (19.75 litres) *Jersey*
CANCH 6 cubits *Hebrew*
CANDY 500 lb (560 lb Bombay) *India*
CANNA 2 yds *Malta*
CARAT metric, 200 milligrams *Int.*
CATTY 1¾ lb *China*
CAWNY 1 acre *India*
CENTI (c) 10^{-2} *Int.*
CHAIN 66 ft, 22 yds *Britain*
CHANG 10 ch'ih = 11 ft 9 ins (1200 grams/3 lb Thailand) *China*
CHEKI 509 lb *Turkey*
CH'IEN (1 lb), 58¾ grains (silver weight) *China*
CHING 121 sq ft *China*
CH'ING 72 600 sq ft *China*
CLOVE 7 lb *Britain*
COOMB 4 bushels *Britain*
COVID CUBIT 18–21 ins (Tamil Nadu/Madras) *India*
CUBIT 18 ins *Britain*
CURIE (Ci) unit of activity of radioactive substance *Int.*
DEBYE 10^{-18} e.s.u.; 1 d = $3.335\ 64 \times 10^{-30}$ coulomb metre *Int.*
DIRAA PIK 0.58 m *Egypt*
DOLIA DOLA 96 doli = 1 zolotnick *Russian Fed.*
DUCAT 58.873 grains (gold weight) *Vienna*
EIMER 29–30.7 litres *Germany*
EPHAH bushel *Hebrew*
FADEN 4.077 steres *Latvia*
FANAN THANAN 1 litre *Thailand*
FARAD (F) capacitance *Int.*
FEMTO (f) 10^{-15} *Int.*
FOUTE FUT, 1 Eng. ft *Russian Fed.*
GAUSS (G) magnetic flux density; 1 G = 10^{-4} tesla *Int.*
GISLA 360 lb of rice (Tanzania) *Zanzibar*
GRAIN 0.0365 dram, 0.002 oz, 0.06 grams, $\frac{1}{24}$ pennyweight *Britain*
GRANO 0.757 grain *Rome*
GREIN 0.065 gram *Netherlands*
GROSS 12 dozen *Britain*
GUDGE GUZ, 27–36 in *India*
GUEZA GUZ, ZER, 24–44 ins; 1 m (government) *Iran*
HECTO (h) 10^{2} *Int.*
HENRY (H) inductance *Int.*
HERTZ (Hz) frequency *Int.*
HOMER 8 bushels *Hebrew*
JOULE heat, energy (1 joule = 1 watt second) *Int.*
KANEH 6 cubits *Hebrew*

5 KANNA 2.62 litres *Sweden*
KANNE 1 litre (formerly 1.06 liq./ 0.91 dry qt U.S.) *Germany*
KERAT 1⅛ ins (old), 3.09 grains weight (old) *Turkey*
KETTE CHAIN 10 m *Germany*
KIKEH ca. 1 bushel (varies) *Turkey*
KODDI 7.58 litres *Arabian Peninsula*
KOUZA 9 Br. Imp. qts *Cyprus*
KOYAN 5333¾ lb *Malaysia*
KRINA 20 litres *Bulgaria*
KUWAN KWAN, 3.75 kg = 8.267 lb *Japan*
LATRO 1.917 m *Czech Rep.*
LIANG LEANG, 1¾ oz, 16 liang = 1 chin = ¾ lb *China*
LIBRA ca. 1 lb *S. America/Malta*
LIBRA ARRATEL, 1.012 lb *Portugal*
LIGNE 2.26 mm *Paris*
LIPPY ½ gal *Scotland*
LITRE 1.057 liq./0.908 dry qt *U.S.*
LITRE 2 pts (1 qt/liq.) Br. Imp. *Britain*
LIVRE 1 kg (Greece 1 lb) *Belgium*
LOKET ca. 0.59 m *Czech Rep.*
LUMEN (lm) luminous flux; 1 lm = (¼ pi) cd. *Int.*
MAAS 1.837 litres (Switzerland 1.5 l) *Germany*
MAHND 2.04 lb *Arabian Peninsula*
MARCO 8 oncas, 229.5 grams *Portugal*
MARCO 3550 grains *Spain*
MAUND 82.286 lb (government) *India*
METRE 3.3 ft, 1.1 yds *Int.*
METZE 61.5 litres *Austria*
MICRO (μ) 10⁻⁶ *Int.*
MILHA 1.297 miles *Portugal*
MILLI (m) 10⁻³; 1 mm = 10⁻³ m *Int.*
MINIM (min) ¹⁄₆₀ fl. drams (0.003 cu ins), 0.061 mm *Int.*
MKONO 45.72 cm *E. Africa*
MOMME ¹⁄₁₀₀₀ kwan = 10 fun, 3.75 grams *Japan*
OBOLE 10–12 grams *Greece*
OCQUE 3 lb *Greece*
OKIEH 1 oz *Egypt*
ONCIA 436.165 grains *Rome*
PALMO 0.22 m (Spain 0.20 m) *Portugal*
PARAH 25.4 litres, (China 15 gals) *Sri Lanka*
PECUL 133 lb *China*
PERCH POLE, 1 rod (U.S.); 30¼ sq yds (5½ yds) *Britain*
PIEDE 11 ins *Malta*
PFUND 500 grams (zollpfund) Switzerland, Austria *Germany*
PFUND 419 grams *Latvia*
PICKI PIK, PIC, 0.64–0.67 m *Greece*

5 PICUL 132.3–133 lb (ca.) Malaysia, Hong Kong *Japan*
PICUL 180 lb weight of water *Sabah/ N. Borneo*
PINTE 0.931 litre *France*
POIDE de marc 0.2448 kg = 8 oz *France*
POISE dynamic viscosity; 1 poise = 0.1 pascal second *Int.*
POUCE 27.07 mm, 1.066 ins (old) *France*
POUND 0.45 kg, 16 oz, 7000 grains *Int.*
QIRAT 209 sq yds *Egypt*
QUART (Br. Imp.) 2 pts (69.35 cu ins), 1.136 litres *Britain*
QUART (liq.) 2 pts, 57.75 cu in, 0.946 litre *U.S.*
QUART (dry) 2 pts, 67.20 cu in, 1.101 litres *U.S.*
QUIRE 24 sheets of paper *Britain*
RATEL 1.014 lb *Iran*
RATEL ROTL, ROTTOLO, 0.9905 lb (customs) *Egypt*
ROEDE 1 dekametre *Netherlands*
SAJEN 7 ft *Russian Fed.*
SHAKU ¹⁰⁄₃₃ m, 12 ins, 3.306 sq dm, 18.039 cu cm *Japan*
SHENG 1.035 litres *China*
STERE 1 cu m *Netherlands/France*
STILB (sb) luminance; 1 candela/ sq cm; 1 sb = 10⁴ nits *Int.*
STONE 14 lb *Britain*
STOPA 0.288 m *Poland*
TAHIL 1¾ oz = 10 chee = 100 hoon *Malaysia*
TESLA (T) magnetic flux density (1 weber per m squared) *Int.*
THERM unit of heat (gas), 100.000 btu *Int.*
TOISE 1.949 m *France*
TONDE 131.4 litres (liq.), 139.1 litres (dry) *Denmark*
TONNE (t) metric ton = 1000 kg (Br. Imp. ton = 1016 kg) *Int.*
TONOS 3307 lb *Greece*
TOVAR 128.2 kg *Bulgaria*
TSUBO 4 sq yds *Japan*
UNGUL 1 in *India*
VEDRO 10 schtoffs, 12.3 litres (Bulgaria 10 l), 3 gals *Russian Fed.*
VERST VERSTA 0.66288 mile, 1166 yds *Russian Fed.*
WISSE 1 stere *Netherlands*
YOJAN ca. 5 miles *E. Indies*
6 ALMUDE 16.7 litres *Portugal*
AMPERE electric current, force = 2 × 10⁻⁷ newton/m of length *Int.*
ANOMAN AMMOMAM, AMOMAM, 5.77 U.S. bushels *Sri Lanka*

6 ARCHIN ARSHIN, ARSIN, (cloth) 27 ins; 1 m (39.37 ins) *Turkey*

ARPENT 100 sq perches, 51.07 m.ares (Quebec 180 Fr. ft) *France*

ARROBA 14.68–15 kg, 32 lb *Portugal/Brazil*

ARSHIN 28 ins, 0.7112 m *Russian Fed.*

ARTABA 66 litres *Iran*

BANDLE 2 ft *Eire*

BARILE 58.34 litres *Rome*

BARREL 36 gal cask *Britain*

BATMAN 6½ lb (varies) *Iran*

BRASSE 1.62 m *France*

BUNDER 1 hectare *Netherlands*

BUNDLE 2 reams *Britain*

BUSHEL 8 gals *Britain*

CANTAR KANTAR, 124.45 lb (old weight) *Turkey*

CAWNIE 1.322 acres (Tamil Nadu) *India*

CENTAL 100 lb *U.S.*

CHAPAH 1.8 lb *Sabah/N. Borneo*

CHARKA 0.123 litre *Russian Fed.*

CHOPIN quart *Scotland*

CHUPAH 3.125 lb of water at 62°F (as a measure of capacity) *Singapore*

CHUPAH 36 oz of water *Malacca*

COVADO 0.66 m *Arabian Peninsula*

COVIDO 19 ins *Arabian Peninsula*

DECARE 1000 sq m *France*

DENARO 1 gram; (old/Rome 18.17 grams) *Italy*

DIRHEM 1.761 dr (customs); (Cairo 3.12 grams) *Egypt*

DJERIB 1 hectare, 2½ acres *Turkey*

DOENUM DONUM, 25 acres *Turkey*

DRACHM (fluid) 0.961 U.S. fluid dram *Britain*

ENDAZE 25½ ins *Turkey*

FANEGA ca. 55.5 litres (Argentina 137 litres) (Costa Rica 11 bu) *S. America/Portugal*

FATHOM 6 ft *Britain*

FEDDAN 1.038 acres *Egypt*

FIRKIN 9 gals *Britain*

FOUNTE 0.90282 lb *Russian Fed.*

FRASCO 2⅜ litres *Argentina*

GALLON (gal) 0.004 cu m *U.S./Britain*

KANTAR CANTARO, 99.049 lb = 100 rotls; 45 kg/cotton *Egypt*

KANTAR 100 lb *Ethiopia*

KARWAR 100 batmans *Iran*

KEDDAH 2.0625 litres *Egypt*

KELVIN (K) temperature, 1 K = 1°C *Int.*

KOILON 33.12 litres *Greece*

KORREL 0.1 gram *Netherlands*

KULMET 10.93 litres *Latvia*

KWARTA 1 litre *Poland*

LIBBRA 1 kg; 339 grams (old) *Italy*

6 LINIYA 0.1 in; 1 archine = 280 liniyas *Russian Fed.*

MAATJE 0.1 litre, 1 dl *Netherlands*

MICRON millionth part of a metre *France*

MIGLIO 0.925 mile *Rome*

MISCAL 10 grams; 71 grains (old) *Iran*

MUSCAL 1½ drams *Turkey*

NEWTON (N) force; 1 kg with acceleration of 1 m/s per s. *Int.*

NOGGIN small cup, ¼ pt *Britain*

PARMAK 1 arsin (1 m) = 10 parmak = 100 khats (cm) *Turkey*

PARSEC (astron.) 3.2616 light years *Int.*

PASCAL (Pa) 1 newton per sq m (air pressure) *Int.*

POTTLE 4 pts *Britain*

RADIAN (rad) plane angle; (1 rad = 57.296° = 57°17′45″ *Int.*

RATTEL ROTLLE, 1.02 lb *Arabian Peninsula*

ROTOLO 1¾ lb *Malta*

ROTTOL 1.6 ltres (old) *Turkey*

SAGENE 7 ft *Russian Fed.*

SCHENE 7½ miles *Egypt*

SECOND (s) second 60th of an hour (¹⁄₆₀ of a min.) *Int.*

SEIDEL 0.354 litre *Austria*

SHTOFF 1 qt *Russian Fed.*

SKEPPE 17.39 litres *Denmark*

STOKES (St) kinematic viscosity; 1 St = 10⁻⁴ m squared/s *Int.*

STREEP 1 mm *Netherlands*

STRICH 1 mm *Germany*

STUNDE 4.8 km *Switzerland*

TALBOT luminous energy *Int.*

THANAN FANAN, 1 litre *Thailand*

TIERCE 42 gals *Britain*

TOMAND 187.17 lb of rice *Arabian Peninsula*

VERSTA VERST, 0.66288 mile, 1166 yds *Russian Fed.*

VISHAN 3 lb *India*

YOJANA ca. 5 miles *India*

7 BRACCIO d'ara, 0.7 m (a cubit) *Italy*

CALORIE unit of heat; 1 calorie = 4.1868 joules *Int.*

CANDELA (cd) luminous intensity *Int.*

CANTARA 1 arroba *Spain*

CANTARO KANTAR, 99.0492 lb = 100 rotls; 44.5 kg *Egypt*

CAPICHA 263 litres *Iran*

CELSIUS thermometer, 0°C = 32F (30°C = 85F, 100°C = 212F) *Int.*

CENTNER 50 kg *C. Europe/Denmark*

CENTRAD ¹⁄₁₀₀ of a radian (rad) plane angle *Int.*

7 **CHALDER** 96 bushels *Britain*
CHENICA 1.359 litres *Iran*
COULOMB (C) electric unit of charge *Int.*
DARIBAH 15.84 hectolitres *Egypt*
DECIARE $\frac{1}{10}$ are *France*
DECIBEL (dB) unit of noise; $\frac{1}{10}$ of a bel (B) *Int.*
DIOPTER optical measure *Greece*
DRACHMA 3.906 grams approx (Netherlands); 3.21 (Turkey) 3.2 grams *Greece*
ESTADIO 258 m (old) *Portugal*
FALTCHE 143.22 ares *Moldavia*
FURLONG 220 yds *U.S./Britain*
HECTARE 2.5 acres *Int.*
GANTANG 1 Br. Imp. gal (Malaysia); 144 oz weight of water as measure of capacity *Sabah/N. Borneo*
GARNETZ 3.28 litres *Russian Fed.*
GILBERT (Gb) magnetomotive force; 1 Gb = 10/4π ampere-turns *Int.*
KLAFTER 2.0740 yds; (Switzerland 1.9685 yards) *Austria*
KULIMET 11.48 litres *Estonia*
LAMBERT unit of brightness (obs.) *Int.*
MEGA-ERG a million ergs *Greece*
MILLIER 1000 kg *France*
OERSTED (Oe) magnetic field strength; 1 Oe = 10¾π Am⁻¹ *Int.*
PECHEUS 0.648 m *Greece*
PERSAKH 6000 guz, 3.88 miles *Iran*
POUNDAL unit of force *Int.*
PULGADA 0.914 in *Spain*
QUANTAR 99 lb *Egypt*
QUARTER 28 lb; 8 Br. Imp. bu (8.257 U.S. bu) *Britain*
QUINTAL 100 libras, 101.4 lb (France 1 cwt) *Spain*
QUINTAL 58.752 kg, 129.5 lb *Portugal*
QUINTAL (metric) 100 kg = 220.46 lb *Int.*
ROTTOLO ROTH, RATEL, 0.9905 lb (customs) *Egypt*
SCHEPEL 1 decalitre *Netherlands*
SCRUPLE (s ap) 20 grains, 0.3333 dram, 1.295 grams *Int.*
SIEMENS (s) electric conductance *Int.*
SKJEPPE 17.37 litres *Norway*
STREMMA 10 ares *Greece*
THERMIE unit of heat/calory *France*
VERCHOK 1.75 ins *Russian Fed.*
VIERTEL 7.73 litres (Switzerland 15 litres) *Denmark*
VIRGATE a quarter of a hide *Britain*
WICHTJE 1 gram *Netherlands*
8 **ANGSTROM** unit, 1 angstrom = 10⁻¹⁰ m *Int.*

8 **APOSTILB** unit of luminance, 10⁻⁴ lambert *Int.*
ASSAY-TON 29.167 grams *U.S.*
BOISSEAU 15 litres *Belgium*
BOUTYLKA 1.625 U.S. liquid pints *Russian Fed.*
CENTIARE a square metre *France*
CENTIBAR meteorological measure *France*
CHALDRON 25 cwt of coal *France*
CHITTACK 5 tolas, 900 grains *Bengal*
DAKTYLOS 25.4 mm *Greece*
DECAGRAM 10 grams *Int.*
DECIGRAM $\frac{1}{10}$ gram *Int.*
FLUIDRAM 60 minim (0.2255 cu in) 29.572 ml *U.S.*
FLUIDRAM (Br. Imp.) 60 minim (0.2167 cu in) 3.55 cu cm *Britain*
FOOT-RULE a 12 in measure *Britain*
HIYAKA-ME 5 797 198 grains *Japan*
HIYAK-KIN 132½ lb *Japan*
HOGSHEAD a large cask *France*
KASSABAH 3.8824 yds *Egypt*
KILODYNE 1000 dynes *France*
KILOGRAM 1000 grams; 2.2 lb *Int.*
KILOWATT 1000 watts; 1.3 horsepower (1 h.p. = 0.75 kw) *Int.*
KORTONDE 138.97 litres *Norway*
MUTCHKIN about a pint *Scotland*
NEUTRINO 7 × 10⁻³² grams, beam without mass *Int.*
PARASANG PERSAKH, 6000 guz, 3.99 miles *Iran*
PASSEREE 5 seers *Bengal*
PHAROAGH 10 mills (10 000 km); 2 hours' journey (old) *Turkey*
PHILOMEL unit of sound capacity (Shakespeare) *Britain*
POLEGADA 27.77 mm *Portugal*
PUNCHEON a large cask *France*
QUADRANT an arc of 90° *France*
QUARTERN a gill; 4 lb *Britain*
SCHEFFEL 50 litres (old 16 metzen/ Prussia) *Germany*
SCHOPPEN ½ litre (Switzerland 0.375 litre) *Germany*
SERPLATH 80 stone *Scotland*
SKALPUND (skaal-pund) ½ kg (Sweden 425 grams/0.937 lb) *Norway*
SULTCHEK cu m (whose sides equal a parmak/dm) *Turkey*
THANGSAT 21.3 litres *Thailand*
THORLAND unit of illumination *Int.*
TONELADA 793.15 kg *Portugal*
YARDLAND usually 30 acres *Britain*
ZOLOTNIK 65.8306 grains, 96 doli *Russian Fed.*

Coins and Monies: Ancient and Modern

2 AS Roman bronze coin

AT Laotian monetary unit (1 kip = 100 at)

BU 17/18 cent. Japanese (¼ of a ryo)

LI old Chinese monetary unit ($\frac{1}{100}$ of a tael)

PU ancient Chinese currency

XU Vietnamese monetary unit (1 dong = 100 xu)

3 AES Roman money (Grave, Rude, Signatum)

AKA Ceylonese gold piece (Sri Lanka)

ATT Siamese (Thailand) copper coin ($\frac{1}{64}$ of the tical)

BAT BAHT, TICAL Thai monetary unit (100 satangs = 1 baht)

BIT West Indian money of a/c

BOB British shilling (obs.)

BUN penny, British late 19 cent.

COB Spanish monetary unit

DAM DAWM, Indian copper coin

DUA Malayan 19 cent. hat money (2 ampat)

ECU French five-franc piece

FEI Oceanian monetary unit, see YAP

FEN Chinese monetary unit (100 fen = 1 yuan)

FIL Iraqi monetary unit (1000 fils = 1 ID); Jordanian; Yemeni (Aden); Bahraini; Kuwaiti

FUN Korean copper coin, late 19 cent.

HAO Vietnamese monetary unit (10 hao = 1 dong)

HAT money, coinage of Pahang/Malay, 19 cent.

JOE Portuguese Joao (in English)

JON North Korean monetary unit (100 jon = 1 won)

KAS 17 cent. copper coin for Tranquebar/India (Danish col.)

KIP Laotian monetary unit (1 kip = 100 at)

LAT Latvian monetary unit; 17/19 cent. Siamese (Thailand) silver tongue money

LEK Albanian monetary unit (1 lek = 100 qindars)

LIS French 17 cent. gold and silver coin

LEU Romanian monetary unit, pl. LEI (1 leu = 100 bani)

LEV Bulgarian monetary unit, pl. LEVA (1 lev = 100 stotinki)

3 MAS Indonesian (Sumatra) 13/18 cent. small gold coin

MIL proposed coin, 1/1000

ORE Scandinavian monetary unit (100 öre = 1 krona)

PIE Indian monetary unit ($\frac{1}{12}$ of the anna)

PUL Russian and Georgian copper coin 15/19 cent.

PYA Burmese monetary unit (100 pyas = 1 kyat)

REE REI, Portuguese money of a/c

RIX 19 cent. Ceylonese dollar

RYO Japanese monetary unit (10 ryos = 1 oban)

SEN Japanese monetary unit (100 sen/ 1 yen); Indonesian (100/1 rupiah); Cambodian (100/1 riel)

SHU old Japanese coin ($\frac{1}{16}$ of a ryo)

SOL Peruvian monetary unit (1 sol = 100 centavos); old French halfpenny

SOU French five-centime piece

WON N and S Korean monetary unit (1 won = 100 jon/chon)

YAP Micronesian (Caroline I.) stone discs used as currency (Fei)

YEN Japanese monetary unit (1 yen = 100 sen)

4 ADLI ADLEA, old Indian silver coin, Tripoli (20 cent.)

AKÇE AKÇA (OTMANI), first Ottoman silver coin (¾ of a para)

ANGE D'OR, French 14 cent. gold coin

ANNA Indian copper coin ($\frac{1}{16}$ of a rupee) from 17 cent. onwards

ATIA 18 cent. copper coin of Portuguese India (6⅛ Port. reis)

AURA Icelandic monetary unit (100 aurar = 1 krona)

BAHT Thai monetary unit (1 baht = 100 satangs)

BANU Romanian monetary unit, pl. BANI (100 bani = 1 leu)

BEKA Hebrew monetary unit (½ shekel)

BELL money: Chinese copper coinage; French Revolution

BIRR Ethiopian monetary unit (1 birr = 100 cents)

BONK colloq. for Javanese old copper coins (½ stuiver, 8 stuivers)

BUCK the US dollar (colloq.)

CASH 2000 years old Chinese bronze currency ($\frac{1}{1000}$ of a tael)

CEDI Ghanian monetary unit (1 cedi = 100 pesewas)

4 CENT decimal coinage of various countries

CHIP a counter; a sovereign

CHON South Korean monetary unit (100 chon = 1 won)

DALA late 19 cent. Hawaiian silver coin

DAWM DAM, Indian copper coin

DEKA 10 cent. small Ceylonese (Sri Lanka) gold coin

DEMY late 14 cent. half-piece of Scottish gold coin

DIME US 10-cent piece

DOIT Dutch half-farthing 16–19 cent.

DONG Vietnamese monetary unit (old 60 dong = 1 tien/tael)

DURO Spanish monetary unit (5 pesetas)

EURO common European unit

FALS copper coin of Persia and Umayad and Abbasid caliphates

FYRK Swedish monetary unit (¼ of an öre)

GANI Italian 14 cent. token currency (dodkin)

GELD ancient tribute; Ger. for money

GROS French 13 cent. silver coinage (gros tournois)

HVID 15 cent. Danish silver coin

HWAN WON Korean monetary unit

ISAR other name for 17–19 cent. German river gold ducats (Flussgelddukaten)

JOAO 18–19 cent. Portuguese gold coin (6400 reis)

JOEY 4d. piece (Joseph Hume); later 3d. piece

KASU 18 cent. Indian (Mysore) copper coins

KINA Papuan (New Guinea) monetary unit; (Australian dollar)

KOBO Nigerian monetary unit (1 naira = 100 kobo)

KRAN 19 cent. Persian silver coin (1000 dinar)

KYAT Burmese monetary unit (100 pyas = 1 kyat)

LAKH Indian monetary unit, 100 000 rupees

LARI Indian/Maldive Islands monetary unit (100 lari = 1 rupee); old Persian silver wire money

LIRA Italian monetary unit (pl. LIRE); Turkish monetary unit (100 kurus = 1 lira)

MAHE BICHE, French for pice

MARK German monetary unit (100 Pfennige = 1 Mark)

4 MERK Scottish 13s. 4d. (thistle merk); money of a/c

MITE a very small coin

MOCO late 18 cent. San Domingo coin; centre piece of Sp. dollar

OBAN Japanese oval gold coin (1 oban = 10 ryos)

OBOL B.C. Greek silver coin (⅙ of a drachm); Charon's ferry fee, 1½d.

ONZA Sp. and Latin American 8 escudos gold piece

PALA Ceylonese (Sri Lanka) deka

PARA Yugoslavian monetary unit (1 dinar = 100 paras); money in Turkish and old coin (¹⁄₄₀ of the piastre)

PEÇA PEZA, 18 cent. Portuguese gold coin (4 escudos)

PESO Filipino monetary unit (1 peso = 100 centavos); monetary unit of Mexico, Cuba, and various S. American countries; former piece of eight

PICE Indian monetary unit, Nepalese monetary unit (100 pice = 1 rupee) (¼ of an anna)

PITI old Indonesian tin coin (1 Spanish real = 4000 piti)

POGH ancient Armenian copper coin

POND S. African pound (Eng. gold sovereign)

PULS Afghani monetary unit (1 afghani – 100 puli)

PUNT Irish monetary unit

QUID a sovereign; a pound (colloq.)

RAND monetary unit of S. Africa and various nearby countries

REAL old Spanish (¼ of a peseta) and Portuguese monetary unit; Dominican Rep. monetary unit (8 reales = 1 peso)

REIS plural of REAL

RIAL Persian monetary unit (1 rial = 100 dinars); Moroccan (old)

RIEL Cambodian monetary unit (1 riel = 100 sen)

RING money, first coins of Australia

RUBA 10 cent. Sicilian monetary unit (¼ dinar)

RYAL gold coin; the rose noble

SALT money, primitive African currency

SENT Estonian monetary unit (100 sent = 1 kroon)

SKAR Tibetan copper coin

SPUR RYAL, colloq. for ½ ryal

4 SYLI Guinean monetary unit (1 syli = 100 cauris)

TAEL old Chinese monetary unit (1000 bronze cash = 1 tael)

TAKA Bangladeshi monetary unit (1 taka = 100 paisa)

TARO 16–18 cent. Maltese silver coin (12 tari = 1 scudo); early Sicilian gold coin

VELD POND, S. African (Boer) gold coin

WARK Ethiopian 19 cent. gold coin

WIRE money, Persian Lari (thin bars of silver)

YANG 19 cent. Korean silver coin

YUAN Chinese monetary unit (Yuan Shi Kai)

5 ABBEY CROWN, 16 cent. 20 shillings gold piece

ACKEY 18/19 cent. silver coin (Gold Coast)

ADLEA ADLI, old Indian silver coin; Tripoli (20 cent.)

AGNEL 13 cent. French gold coin (mouton d'or)

ALBUS German 'Weisspfennig' (grossus albus/white groat) 14/15 cent.

ALTUN Turkish 15 cent. gold coin

ALTYN Russian (Tartar) silver coin 17 cent. (3 kopeks)

AMANI early 20 cent. Afghani gold coin (1 amani = 30 afghani)

AMPAT Malay hat money

ANGEL old English gold coin

ASPER 13/15 cent. Middle Eastern base silver coin

AUREI Roman gold coins

BAIZA Omani monetary unit (1000 baizas = 1 rial/R.O.)

BELGA Belgian coin

BETSO small Venetian coin

BICHE French for 18 cent. pice

BRASS money (colloq.)

BRICK TEA, ancient Chinese and Tibetan currency (2½ lb = 1 tael)

BRIOT CROWN for Charles I

BUTUT Gambian monetary unit (100 butut = 1 dalasi)

CANOE DOLLAR, Canadian silver dollar

COLON Costa Rican monetary unit (1 colon = 100 centimos); El Salvadorian monetary unit

CROWN five-shilling piece

DALER Scandinavian Thaler (riksdaler)

5 DARIC gold coin of Darius (Persia) (1 daric = 20 sigloi)

DENGA 14/15 cent. Russian coin (silver penny)

DINAR Yugoslavian monetary unit (1 dinar = 100 paras); various Moslem countries; ancient Arab gold coin

DOBLA a number of old gold coins; 16 cent. double scudo

DOBRA 14 cent. Portuguese gold coin

DUCAT Italian old gold coin

EAGLE former US gold coin (10 dollars)

FANAM Indian monetary unit, gold (ancient), silver (modern) (⅛ of a rupee)

FUANG 19 cent. Siamese (Thai) monetary unit (⅛ of a Baht)

FUGIO CENT, first US coin

FRANC monetary unit of various countries

GERSH Ethiopian monetary unit, silver (¹⁄₁₀ of a talari)

GIGOT 16 cent. Brabantian copper coin (Flemish negenmanneke)

GRAMO late 19 cent. Spanish private gold coin

GRANO Maltese monetary unit; old copper coin of Naples and Sicily

GROAT silver 4d. piece

GROOT 13 cent. Dutch silver gros

HARDI 14 cent. gold and silver piece of England and dominion of France

HECTE Greek monetary unit (⅙ of the statar)

HENRI D'OR French gold coin, 16 cent.

HOLEY DOLLARS, ring money

HUSUM DALER, 16 cent. Danish daler

IMADI Yemeni precursor to the riyal

JUSTO 15 cent. Portuguese gold coin (= 2 cruzados)

KAIKI SHOHO, ancient Japanese gold coin

KAKIM ancient Siamese (Thai) bars currency

KARAN KRAN, Persian silver piece

KNIFE money, simple B.C. Chinese bronze coinage

KOBAN 16/19 cent. Japanese gold coin (¹⁄₁₀ of the oban)

KOPEK Russian monetary unit (100 kopeks = 1 rouble)

KRONA Scandinavian monetary unit (1 krona = 100 öre)

KRONE Austrian monetary unit, gold or silver

5 KROON Estonian monetary unit
LEONE 17 cent. Venetian silver coin
(= 10 lire)
LEPTA Greek monetary unit
LIARD old French farthing
LIBRA 19 cent. Peruvian monetary
unit; Roman pound
LITAS Lithuanian monetary unit,
pl. LITU
LITRA 6 cent. B.C. Sicilian monetary
unit
LIVRE old French franc (20 sols =
1 livre)
LOCHO Venezuelan monetary unit
LOUIS D'OR, 20-franc piece
MASSE D'OR, 14 cent. French gold
coins
MEDIO Venezuelan monetary unit
MINIM tiny Roman bronze coins
MOHUR 15-rupee gold coin
MOKKO East Indian islands drum
currency
MONGO Mongolian monetary unit
(100 mongos – 1 tugrik)
NAIRA Nigerian monetary unit
(1 naira = 100 kobo)
NGWEE Zambian monetary unit
(100 ngwee = 1 kwacha)
NOBLE old English coin, 6s. 8d.
ONCIA 14 cent. Italian money of a/c;
gold coin
ONLIK old Turkish silver coin
(= 10 paras)
ORTUG old Swedish silver coin
PADMA TANKA, S. Indian B.C. gold
coin
PAISA PICE, Indian monetary unit
(100 paisa = 1 rupee); Bangladeshi
monetary unit (100 paisa = 1 taka);
Bhutani monetary unit
PAOLO Italian cities
PENCE plural of penny, British
PENGO Hungarian silver unit
PENNI Finnish monetary unit
(100 penniä = 1 markka)
PENNY British copper coin
PIECE OF EIGHT = peso
PLACK Scottish 15/16 cent. billion
coin
PLATE money, Swedish copper plates
(platmynt)
POUND monetary unit of Britain and
various countries
QUART D'ECU, French silver coin
(= 15 sols)
RIYAL Sudanese monetary unit
(1 Sud. pound = 10 riyals);
monetary unit of Arabian Peninsula

5 ROYAL D'OR, French Louis IX gold
coin
RUPEE Indian monetary unit
(1 rupee = 100 paisa); Nepalese,
Pakistani, Mauritian monetary unit
RUPIA Portuguese rupee (Goa and Diu)
SAIGA 7 cent. Merovingian coin
SALUT D'OR European medieval gold
coin
SAUDI Arabian gold sovereign
SCEAT SCEATT 7 cent. English coin,
base silver or copper
SCUDO old Italian 'shield' currency,
gold or silver; pl. SCUDI
SEMIS half a Roman as
SENGI Zairean monetary unit
(10 000 sengi = 1 zaire)
SHAKI Persian silver coin
(= 10 kazbegi)
SICCA RUPEE, colloq. for E. India
Co. rupee
SOLDI old Italian gold coin; pl. of
soldo
SOLDO Italian sol or sou (halfpenny)
SPADE money, Chinese B.C. coinage
SRANG early 20 cent. Tibetan silver
currency
STICA STYCA, small Saxon coin
SUCRE Ecuadorian monetary unit
(1 sucre = 100 centavos)
SWORD DOLLAR, 16 cent. Scottish
silver ryal
SYCEE boat-shaped Far Eastern silver
ingot
TAKOE ⅛ of an ackey (Gold Coast)
TALAR a special 19 cent. thaler
TANGA 17 cent. Portuguese East Indian
coin
TARIN old Sicilian silver coin
THIRD GUINEA, old English gold
coin
THREE PENCE, British coin from
16 cent. (obs.)
TICAL Thai monetary unit (bar or
baht); old Burmese monetary unit
TICCY S. African 3d. piece
TIGER tongue money, old weight-
related silver bar currency of
Indochina
TILLA old Afghani and Turkestani gold
coin
TOMAN Persian gold unit
TRIME US 3-cent silver piece
UNCIA ancient Roman monastery unit
($\frac{1}{12}$ of the as)
UNITE English/Scottish 17 cent. gold
piece; 'Faciam Eos in Gentem
Unam'

5 VLIES old Dutch gold or silver coin

WITTE special 14 cent. albus

ZAIRE Zairean monetary unit (1 zaire = 100 makuta = 10 000 sengi)

ZLOTY Polish monetary unit (1 zloty = 100 groszy)

6 ABACIS old Portuguese Indian and E. African silver coin

ABBASI old Persian coin (base metal) and Georgian coin (silver)

ABDERA ancient Thracian coins

ADOLFS D'OR, Swedish 5-thaler coin, gold

AGOROT Israeli monetary unit (100 agorot = 1 Israeli pound)

AMANIA Afghani monetary unit

ANCHOR money, 19 cent. British silver coins

AUREUS Roman precursor of the solidus, gold

BALBAO Panamanian monetary unit (1 balboa = 100 centesimos)

BAMBOO money, inscribed Chinese 'stick' currency

BAUBEE BAWBEE, Scottish billion coin

BEZANT Byzantine gold coin (Nomisma)

BONNET PIECE, Scottish 16 cent. gold coin

BULLET money, 14/19 cent. Siamese (Thail) monetary unit, gold or silver

BUKSHA old Yemeni monetary unit

CANOPY type penny, William the Conqueror era

CARLIN 13 cent. Sicilian monetary unit, gold or silver

CARLIN D'OR, old English monetary unit, pure gold (salute)

CAURIS Guinean monetary unit (100 cauris = 1 syli)

CEITIL old Portuguese copper coin

CHO-GIN 18 cent. Japanese silver bar

CONDOR old Chilean monetary unit

COPANG Japanese gold coin

COPPER old penny (colloq.)

COWRIE shell money, Far East and Africa

CUARTO old Bolivian half-peso; ¼ of a Real

DALASI Gambian monetary unit (1 dalasi = 100 butut)

DECIME S. American 10-centavos

DENARO Italian denier, 8 cent.

DENIER Carolingian silver penny (12 deniers = 1 solidus)

6 DINERO old Spanish silver penny; Peruvian 10-centavo coin; Spanish for money

DIOBOL ancient Greek silver coin (¾ of a drachma)

DIRHAM Moroccan monetary unit (1 dirham = 100 M. francs); Iraqi (20 dirhams = 1 dinar); monetary unit Arab Emirates

DIRHEM ancient Arab and Ottoman coin

DIZAIN old French decimal coin (10 deniers)

DOBLON old Uruguayan coin, gold

DODKIN old coin of poor metal

DOLLAR monetary unit of the USA and various countries

DOPPIA 18 cent. Sardinian gold unit

DRACHM DRACHMA, Greek monetary unit, both ancient and modern

EIRAKU SEN, cash-type Japanese bronze coins

ESCUDO Portuguese monetary unit (1 escudo = 100 centavos); Chilean monetary unit (100 centesimos); old Spanish monetary unit

FALUCE Ceylonese (Sri Lanka) monetary unit, ¼ of a fanam

FILLER Hungarian monetary unit (100 filler = 1 forint)

FLORIN silver 2-shilling piece

FOLLIS Byzantine bronze coin

FORINT Hungarian monetary unit (1 forint = 100 filler)

GADHYA PAISA, old Indian base silver coin

GEORGE D'OR, 18 cent. five thaler coin, gold

GEORGE NOBLE, 16 cent. English gold coin (6s. 8d.)

GIULIO papal 'grosso largo'

GOTHIC CROWN, Victorian

GOTHIC FLORIN, superseded godless florin, 19 cent.

GOURDE Haitian 19 cent. silver coin

GRINNA Russian monetary unit, silver (= 10 kopeks); money of a/c

GROSSO Italian monetary unit, pl. GROSSI

GROSZY Polish monetary unit (100 groszy = 1 zloty)

GUINEA 21 shillings

GULDEN Dutch monetary unit, German (old) monetary unit

GYLLEN 16 cent. Swedish gulden

6 HALALA Yemeni monetary unit, bronze and copper (obs.)

HALERU Czechoslovakian monetary unit (100 haleru = 1 koruna), (Heller)

HALLER HELLER

HEAUME D'OR and d'argent, 14 cent. Flemish

HELLER German, Austrian, Swiss monetary unit (penny)

ICHIBU GIN, 19 cent. Japanese coin (= 1 bu)

JAITIL Indian 14 cent. (50 jaitils = 1 tankah)

KAPANG KEPING

KENGEN DAIHO, ancient Japanese bronze sen

KEPING 18/19 cent. Malay & Sumatran copper coins

KHOUMS Mauritian monetary unit (5 khoums = 1 ouguiya)

KORONA Hungarian monetary unit, silver (Austrian kronc)

KORUNA Czechoslovakian monetary unit (1 koruna = 100 haleru)

KURUSH Turkish monetary unit (100 kurus = 1 lira)

KWACHA Zambian monetary unit (1 kwacha = 100 ngwee); Malawi monetary unit (1 k. = 100 tambala)

LAUREL 17 cent. twenty-shilling piece

LEPTON Greek coin, copper ($\frac{1}{7}$ of an obol)

MACATA old Guatemalan monetary unit

MACUTA Portuguese African monetary unit 18/19 cent. (= 50 reis)

MAKUTA Zairean monetary unit (100 makuta = 1 zaire)

MANCUS European designation of old Arab gold dinar

MARKKA Finnish monetary unit (1 markka = 100 penniä)

MATONA Ethiopian monetary unit, copper or nickel

MAUNDY money, British royal 'give aways'

MAZUNA Moroccan monetary unit, 19 cent.

MISCAL 18 cent. Spanish silver piastre; monetary unit of Chinese Turkestan

NICKEL US 5-cent piece

OCTAVO OCHAVO, old Spanish silver coin; Mexican copper coin

OSELLA 16 cent. Venetian gift coin

6 OTMANI Ottoman monetary unit, silver (see AKÇE)

OBOLUS OBOL, ancient Greek coin

PAGODA Indian gold coin

PAHANG Malay hat money

PARDAO Portuguese Indian monetary unit, xeraphim

PATACA 17 cent. Arab silver and money of a/c; old Brazilian monetary unit

PATACA 18 cent. Brabantian and Westphalian monetary unit, silver

PATACA 18 cent. Algerian money of a/c; African name for Maria Theresa thaler

PATACA Macauan monetary unit (1 pataca = 100 avos)

PATARD 15 cent. Dutch silver piece

PERPER early 20 cent. Montenegran silver unit; old Ragusan monetary unit

PESETA Spanish monetary unit

PLAQUE old Dutch billion coin

PRAGER GROSCHEN, late 13 cent. Bohemian coin, silver

PRUTAH old Indonesian monetary unit

QINDAR Albanian monetary unit (100 qindars = 1 lek)

QUARTO old Spanish monetary unit (¼ real)

QUIRSH Saudi Arabian monetary unit (20 quirsh = 1 Saudi riyal)

RAPPEN Swiss monetary unit (100 rappen = 1 Swiss francs)

ROUBLE Russian monetary unit (1 rouble = 100 kopek)

RUPIAH Indonesian monetary unit (1 rupiah = 100 sen)

SANESE D'ORO, 14 cent. North Italian (Sienna) coin, gold

SATANG Thai monetary unit

SEQUIN Venetian gold coin (Zecchino); Ottoman monetary unit

SESINO 18 cent. Italian copper or billon coin (½ soldo)

SHEKEL Jewish half crown

SIERRA LEONE, late 18 cent. silver coin

SIGLOS ancient Persian silver piece ($\frac{1}{20}$ of a gold daric)

SIXAIN old French monetary unit (= 6 deniers)

SOMALO old Somali monetary unit

SOOKOO SUKU, old Malayan coin, silver

SOVRAN poetical sovereign

STATER ancient Greek gold or silver coin

6 STIVER West Indian Dutch Stuiver
SUELDO 19 cent. Bolivian coin, silver (8 sueldi = 1 peso)
TALARI Abyssinian coin, silver
TALBOT 15 cent. Anglian, gold
TALENT old Hebrew monetary unit; ancient weight unit
TANGKA 18 cent. Tibetan monetary unit, base silver
TANKAH various old Indian coins
TANNER British sixpence (obs.)
TESTER Henry VIII shilling
TESTON TESTONE/TESTOON, 16 cent. shilling; Italian silver coin
THALER 15/20 cent. German monetary unit, silver (Guldengroschen)
TICKEY S. African 3d. piece
TOMAUN Persian gold coin
TORNEZ 14 cent. Portuguese coin, silver (French gros tornois)
TOSTAO 16 cent. Portuguese coin, headless
TRIENS small Byzantine gold coin (¾ of a solidus)
TRIPLE UNIT, largest English Civil War gold coin, 17 cent.
TUGRIK Mongolian monetary unit (1 tugrik = 100 mongos)
UNGARO Italian for the Hungarian 17 cent. ducat
VIERER old Swiss coin, silver (2 vierer = 2 rappen)
VINTEM 15 cent. Portuguese silver coin (= 20 reis); old Brazilian copper coin
WOLSEY GROAT, English, 16 cent. special coin
YUZLIK large, old Turkish silver coin equal to 100 paras
ZECHIN SEQUIN, Venetian monetary unit

7 ACRAGAS ancient Greek monetary unit (Sicily)
AFGHANI Afghani monetary unit (1 afghani = 100 puli)
ALTILIK 19 cent. Ottoman 6-piastre piece, base silver
ANGELET half an angel, 17 cent.
ANGELOT a Louis XI gold coin
ANGOLAR Angolan escudo
ANGSTER 14/19 cent. Swiss coin, silver or copper
ASHRAFI 15/18 cent. Persian coin, gold (replaced by the toman)
BAIOCCO Italian papal coin (¹⁄₁₀₀ of the scudo)

7 BARHINA Portuguese coin, gold (1 bahrina = 400 reis)
BOLIVAR Venezuelan monetary unit (1 bolivar = 2 reales = 100 centimes)
BRILLEN DUKAT, 17 cent. Danish coin, gold
BRILLEN THALER, 16 cent. German monetary unit
BRIQUET French for Dutch vuurijzer, 15 cent. silver coin
BULLION pieces, gold or silver objects valued on carat-mass content
BUQSHAH (Sana) Yemeni monetary unit (40 buqshahs = 1 riyal)
CADIERE late 15 cent. gold piece; silver coin of Charles V and VI
CAROLIN old Swedish coin, gold or silver
CAROLUS gold coin of Charles V (Spanish) Habsburg Emperor
CAVALLO 15 cent. Sicilian copper coin (¹⁄₂₀₀ of a ducat)
CENTAVO S. American monetary unit, various countries
CENTIME one-hundredth of a franc (various countries)
CHALKOS Greek monetary unit (Alexander the Great), copper (¹⁄₄₈ of the drachm)
CORDOBA Nicaraguan monetary unit (1 cordoba = 100 centavos)
CORONAT KWARTNIK, 14/15 cent. Polish monetary unit (½ groschen)
CRUSADO old Portuguese monetary unit
CRUZADO 15 cent. Portuguese gold coin; new Brazilian monetary unit
DAALDER Dutch thaler; Charles V silver coin
DENARII pence
DENNING 17 cent. Danish equivalent of Russian denga
DHARANA Indian old punch-marked coins (Ceylonese purana)
DOBLONE Italian 4 or 8 scudi gold pieces
DOUZAIN old French shilling (12 deniers)
DRACHMA Greek monetary unit (1 drachma = 100 lepta), ancient and modern
DUPLONE 18/19 cent. Swiss gold coin (16 francs)
ENRIQUE 15 cent. Spanish gold coin
ESCALIN 17 cent. Dutch silver coin
ESPADIN 15 cent. Portuguese ½ justo
ESPHERA Goan (Portuguese) 16 cent. gold coin

7 EKPWELE Equatorial Guinean peseta
(1 ekpwele = 100 centimos)

FERDING Swedish silver farthing,
16 cent.

FILIPPO 16/18 cent. Spanish coin,
silver

FOLLARO Italian Byzantine copper
coin

GAZETTA old Venetian copper coin

GODLESS FLORIN (Victoria/Britain)
omitting 'Dei Gratia', not valid in
heaven

GUARANI Paraguayan monetary unit
(1 guarani = 100 centimos)

GUERCHE 19 cent. Ethiopian coin,
silver ($\frac{1}{6}$ of the talari)

GUILDER Dutch florin

HIBERNO Viking coin, Ireland

JACOBUS gold coin of James I

KAZBEGI Persian Safavid copper
coin

LEMPIRA Honduran monetary unit
(100 centavos); old Brazilian
monetary unit

LEOPARD 14 cent. English 3-shilling
gold coin

MANCHIR first Ottoman copper coin,
14 cent.

MANILLA W. African copper coin

MARENGO Napoleonic 20 franc gold
piece

MATAPAN 13 cent. Venetian grosso

MILREIS old Brazilian and Portuguese
coin

MOIDORE Portuguese 4-cruzado piece
(= 4000 reis); 18 cent. Brazilian
monetary unit

NOMISMA Byzantine gold coins; Greek
for money

NONSUNT 16 cent. Scottish
12-penny groat; Northumberland
shillings

NOVODEL Russian coins
(or imitations)

NUMMIUM Byzantine bronze unit,
pl. nummia

ORMONDE money, minted in Ireland
1643

OUGUIYA Mauritanian monetary unit
(1 ouguiya = 5 khoums)

PAHLEVI former Persian gold unit,
superseded the toman

PAOLINO Italian silver scudo, 15/16
cent.

PARISIS D'OR, 11 cent. French gold
coins

PATAGON Dutch early 17 cent., silver
(= 48 stuivers)

7 PEACOCK RUPEE, 19 cent. Burmese
coin, gold or silver

PESEWAS Ghanaian monetary unit
(100 pesewas = 1 new cadi)

PFENNIG German copper coin

PHOENIX 18 cent. Sicilian gold coin;
19 cent. Greek silver coin
(= 100 lepta)

PIASTRE PIASTER, Egyptian
monetary unit
(100 piasters = 1 E. pound);
Sudanese monetary unit;
old European name for Spanish
peso and variations

PISTOLE DOUBLOON, old Spanish
double escudo, gold

POLTINA Russian ½ rouble

QUARTER US quarter of a dollar

QUETZAL Guatemalan monetary unit
(1 quetzal = 100 centavos)

QUINTAR QINDAR, Albanian
monetary unit

ROYALIN 18 cent. Danish colonial
monetary unit (Tranquebar/India);
silver

RUSPONE 18 cent. Florentine monetary
unit, gold (= 3 ducats)

SANTIMS early 20 cent. Latvian (100
santims = 1 lats)

SAN TOME THOME, Portuguese
Indian 16 cent. gold piece

SAPEQUE Indochinese dong

SESTINO 15 cent. Neapolitan billion
piece

SEXTANS ancient Roman bronze coin

SILIQUA Byzantine silver coin
($\frac{1}{24}$ of a solidus)

SOLIDUS old Roman gold coin
(= 72 Roman libra)

SOSLING 15 cent. Danish six-penny
coin, silver

SOVRANO SOUVERAIN D'OR, old
Dutch gold coin

STAMPEE French W. Indies 18 cent.
sous

STOOTER 16 cent. Dutch coin, base
silver ($\frac{1}{20}$ of a daalder)

STUIVER 15 cent. Dutch coin, base
silver

TALLERO old Italian thaler; 20 cent. It.
Eritrean

TAMBALA Malawian monetary unit
(100 tambala = 1 kwacha)

TAMPANG Malay hat money

TESTOON old Italian silver coin

TESTRIL tester; a sixpence

THISTLE crown, dollar, merk, British
16/17 cent.

7 THISTLE NOBLE, 16 cent. British large gold piece

THRYMSA 6 cent. Anglo-Saxon monetary unit (¾ of a solidus)

TRIBUTE penny, Judaean Roman denarius

TRIOBOL day-money for a judge in ancient Greece (½ drachm)

UGORSKY Russian name for Hungarian 15 cent. gold coin

UNICORN Scottish 15 cent. gold piece

ZLATNIK first Russian gold coins

ZOLOTYE Russian gold coins; Crimean campaign reward, 17 cent.

8 ADELAIDE TOKENS, Australian one pound gold tokens

AGNUS DEI type of penny of Aethelred II

ALBERTIN 16 cent. Dutch (Spanish) gold coin

AMBROSIN Milanese coin

ASSIGNAT paper currency, French Revolution

BAZARUCO Portuguese Indian 16 cent. coin, base metal

CAROLOUS KAROLUS, French dizain

CENTIMOS Equatorial Guinean monetary unit (100 centimos = 1 ekpwele)

CHUCKRAM Indian 18/20 cent. (4 chuckrams = 1 gold fanam)

CLEMENTI papal silver coin (15 baiocchi)

CROSAZZO Genoese 17 cent. silver coin

CRUZEIRO Brazilian monetary unit (1 cruzeiro = 100 centavos)

DENARIUS main silver coin of the Roman Empire

DIDRACHM ancient Greek 2-drachma

DINHEIRO 12/14 cent. Portuguese billon denier

DOHOZARI 19 cent. tiny Persian gold coin

DOUBLOON Spanish monetary unit (2 pistoles)

DREILING 15 cent. German 3 pfennig. billon

DUCATONE Italian 16/18 cent. silver coin

DUCATOON Venetian silver coin

FARTHING a quarter of a penny

FLORENCE Edward III gold florin

FLORETTE variations of French 15 cent. gros

FREDERIK D'OR, Danish 19 cent. gold coin

8 GENOVINO 12 cent. Genoese gold coin

GIGLIATO 14 cent. silver coin of Charles II of Naples

GIUSTINA 16 cent. Venetian silver coin (8 lire)

GORY-OBAN 19 cent. Japanese ½ oban gold coin

GROSCHEN Austrian monetary unit (100 groschen = 1 schilling); monetary unit of Holy Roman Empire, silver

GROSSONE papal 14/18 cent. silver coin

GULDINER GULDENGROSCHEN, 15 cent. European silver coin (before thaler)

HALFMARK old English coin, 6s. 8d.

HATPIECE 16 cent. English monetary unit, gold (80s.)

HEMIOBOL ancient Athenian and Corinthian ½ obol

HEXAGRAM Byzantine silver coin

IMPERIAL Russian 10-rouble gold coin, 18 cent.

JOHANNES old Portuguese coin

KAHAVANU 9 cent. Ceylonese (Sri Lanka) gold coin

KREUTZER old Austrian copper coin

KWARTNIK Polish 14/15 cent. ½ groschen

MAGDALON Provençal 15 cent. gold florin

MARAVEDI MARABOTINO, old Spanish copper coin

MILLIMES Tunisian monetary unit (1000 millimes = 1 dinar)

MOCENIGO a kind of 15 cent. Italian lira

MURAJOLA Italian billon coins of low silver content

NAPOLEON French 20-franc gold coin

NGULTRUM Bhutani monetary unit (1 ngultrum = 2 tikchung = 100 paisa)

PAVILLON D'OR, 14 cent. French gold coin

PHILIPPI 4 cent. B.C. Macedonian (Black Sea) currency

PICCIOLO old Maltese copper coin

PLAPPART 14 cent. Swiss billon coin (15 Heller)

QUADRANS Roman copper coin (temncius), ¼ as

QUATRUNX Roman 4 oz coin (triens)

QUINCUNX Roman 5 oz coin

ROSE-RYAL English gold coin of James I (30s.)

SCELLINO Somalian monetary unit

8 SCYPHATE Byzantine monetary unit
SEMUNCIA Roman ½ uncia
SEQUENCE marks, Roman B.C. denarii
SESTERCE Roman silver coin
SHILLING old English 12 pence;
monetary unit of Austria and
various other countries
SIXPENCE old English silver coin
SKILLING old Scandinavian shilling
SPINTRIA old porno tokens (tesserae)
SREBENIK 10 cent. Russian silver coins
STAMENON Byzantine solidus
STERLING gold or silver purity of
British coinage

8 STOTINKA Bulgarian (100 stotinki =
1 lev)
TESSERAE old Roman tickets or tokens
TIKCHUNG Bhutani monetary unit
(2 tikchung = 1 ngultrum)
VIRGINIA Virginian 18 cent. copper
coin
XERAPHIM Portuguese Indian silver
coin
ZECCHINO old Italian ducat
ZERMABUB early 18 cent. Ottoman
gold coin

Alphabets

Greek

ALPHA
BETA
GAMMA
DELTA
EPSILON
ZETA
ETA
THETA
IOTA
KAPPA
LAMBDA
MU
NU
XI
OMICROM
PI
RHO
SIGMA
TAU
UPSILON
PHI
CHI
PSI
OMEGA

Hebrew

ALEPH
BETH
GIMEL
DALETH
IIE
VAU
ZAIN or ZAYIN
CHETH or HETH
TETH
JOD or YOD
CAPH or KAPH
LAMED
MEM
NUN
SAMECH or SAMEKH
AIN or AYIN
PE
TZADDI or ZADE
KOPH
RESH
SCHIN or SHIN
TAU

French Revolutionary Calendar

French Republic 1794

VENDEMIAIRE Vintage *Sept.*
BRUMAIRE Fog *Oct.*
FRIMAIRE Sleet *Nov.*
NIVOSE Snow *Dec.*

PLUVIOSE Rain *Jan.*
VENTOSE Wind *Feb.*
GERMINAL Seed *Mar.*
FLOREAL Blossom *Apr.*
PRAIRAL Pasture *May*
MESSIDOR Harvest *June*
THERMIDOR, FERVIDOR Heat *July*
FRUCTIDOR Fruit *Aug.*

The 12 Signs of the Zodiac

Spring
ARIES Ram
TAURUS Bull
GEMINI Twins

Summer
CANCER Crab
LEO Lion
VIRGO Virgin

Autumn
LIBRA Balance
SCORPIO Scorpion
SAGITTARIUS Archer

Winter
CAPRICORNUS Goat
AQUARIUS Water Carrier
PISCES Fishes

The 9 Planets and their Satellites

MARS Deimos, Phobos
EARTH Luna
VENUS
NEPTUNE Triton, Nereid

SATURN Rhea, Dione, Mimas, Titan, Phoebe, Tethys, Janus, Iapetus, Hyperion, Enceladus
PLUTO
URANUS Ariel, Titania, Oberon, Umbriel, Miranda
JUPITER Io, Europa, Callisto, Ganymede
MERCURY

Constellations in the Heavens

3 ARA
LEO
4 CRUS
CRUX
LYRA
URSA MAJOR
URSA MINOR
5 ARIES
CETUS
DRACO
HYDRA
INDUS
LEPUS
LIBRA
LUPOS
MUSCA
ORION
VIRGO
AQUILA
AURIGA
BOOTES
CANCER
CARINA
CORONA
CORVUS
CRATER
CYGNUS
DORADO
FORNAX
GEMINI

6 PUPPIS
TAURUS
TUCANA
7 CENTAUR
CEPHEUS
COLUMBA
PEACOCK
PEGASUS
PHOENIX
PERSEUS
SCORPIO
SERPENS
8 AQUARIUS
ERIDANUS
HERCULES
PLEIADES
9 ANDROMEDA
CENTAURUS (Alpha & Beta Centauri)
DELPHINUS
OPHIUCHUS
10 CANIS MAJOR
CANIS MINOR
CASSIOPEIA
TRIANGULUM
URSUS MAJOR
URSUS MINOR
11 CAPRICORNUS
SAGITTARIUS

CANES VENATICI
CORONA BOREALIS
PISCIS AUSTRALIS
TRIANGULUM AUSTRALIS

Major Stars

4 **BETA** Centaurus
  ENIF Pegasus
  KAUS Sagittarius
  MIRA Cetus
  VEGA Lyra
5 **ACRUX** Crux
  ALGOL Perseus
  ALPHA Centaurus
  ANKAA Phoenix
  AVIOR Triangle
  DENEB Cygnus
  DUBHE Ursus Major
  HADAR Centaurus
  HAMAL Aries
  MIZAR Ursus Major
  NUNKI Sagitarrius
  RIGIL (KENT) Centaurus
  SABIK Ophiuchi
  SPICA Virgo
6 **ACAMAR** Eridanus
  ADHARA Canis Major
  ALIOTH Ursa Major
  ALKAID Ursa Minor
  ALNAIR Crux
  ALTAIR Aquila
  CASTOR Gemini
  DIPHDA Cetus
  ELNATH Taurus
  GACRUX Crux
  GEINAH Corvus
  HYADES Taurus

6 **KOCHAB** Ursa Minor
  MARKAB Pegasus
  MENKAR Cetus
  MIMOSA Crux
  MIRFAK Perseus
  POLLUX Gemini
  SHAUFA Scorpio
  SIRIUS Canis Major
  SUHAIL Velori
7 **AINILAM** Orion
  ALPHARD Hydra
  ANTARES Scorpio
  CANOPUS Carina
  CAPELLA Aurga
  ELTANIN Draco
  MENKENT Centaurus
  POLARIS Ursa Minor
  PROCYON Ursa Minor
  REGULUS Leo
  SCHEDAR Cassiopeia
8 **ACHERNAR** Eridanus
  ALPHECCA Corona Borealis
  ARCTURUS Bootes
  DENEBOLA Leo
  ZUBENUBI Libra
9 **ALDEBARAN** Taurus
  ALPHERATZ Andromedra
  BELLATRIX Orion
  FOMALHAUF Pisces
10 **RASALHAGUE** Ophiuchi
11 **BETELGEUSE** Orion
  MIAPLACIDUS Carina

Months of the Jewish Year

TISHRI
HESHVAN
KISLEV
TEBET
SHEBAT

ADAR or **VEADAR**
NISAN or **ABIB**
IYAR
SIVAN
TAMMUS
AB
ELUL

Books of the Bible

Old Testament (39)

GENESIS
EXODUS
LEVITICUS
NUMBERS
DEUTERONOMY
JOSHUA
JUDGES
RUTH
1st SAMUEL
2nd SAMUEL
1st KINGS
2nd KINGS
1st CHRONICLES
2nd CHRONICLES
EZRA
NEHEMIAH
ESTHER
JOB
PSALMS
PROVERBS
ECCLESIASTES
SONG OF SOLOMON (SONG OF SONGS)
ISAIAH
JEREMIAH
LAMENTATIONS
EZEKIEL
DANIEL
HOSEA
JOEL
AMOS
OBADIAH
JONAH
MICAH
NAHUM
HABAKKUK
ZEPHANIAH
HAGGAI
ZACHARIAS
MALACHI

The Apocrypha (13)

ESDRAS
TOBIT
JUDITH
ESTHER
THE WISDOM OF SOLOMON
ECCLESIASTICUS
BARUCH
EPISTLE OF JEREMY
SONG OF THE THREE HOLY CHILDREN
HISTORY OF SUSANNA
BEL AND THE DRAGON
THE PRAYER OF MANASSES
MACCABEES

New Testament (27)

GOSPEL OF ST MATTHEW
GOSPEL OF ST MARK
GOSPEL OF ST LUKE
GOSPEL OF ST JOHN
ACTS OF THE APOSTLES
EPISTLE FO THE ROMANS
1st EPISTLE TO THE CORINTHIANS
2nd EPISTLE TO THE CORINTHIANS
EPISTLE TO THE GALATIANS
EPISTLE TO THE EPHESIANS
EPISTLE TO THE PHILIPPIANS
EPISTLE TO THE COLOSSIANS
1st EPISTLE TO THE THESSALONIANS
2nd EPISTLE TO THE THESSALONIANS
1st EPISTLE TO TIMOTHY
2nd EPISTLE TO TIMOTHY
EPISTLE TO TITUS
EPISTLE TO PHILEMON
EPISTLE TO THE HEBREWS
1st PETER
2nd PETER
1st JOHN
2nd JOHN
3rd JOHN
JAMES
JUDE
THE REVELATION

The 7 Major Ecumenical Councils (in Asia Minor)

NICEA (Iznik) *A.D. 325*
CONSTANTINOPLE (Istanbul) *A.D. 381*
EPHESUS (Efes) *A.D. 431*
CHALCEDON (Kadikoy) *A.D. 451*
CONSTANTINOPLE (Istanbul) *A.D. 533*
ISTANBUL *A.D. 680–681*
NICEA (Iznik) *A.D. 787*

British Prime Ministers

From 1770

Lord NORTH
Lord ROCKINGHAM
Lord SHELBURNE
Duke of PORTLAND
William PITT
Henry ADDINGTON
William PITT
Lord GRENVILLE
Spencer PERCEVAL
Lord LIVERPOOL
George CANNING
Lord GODERICH
Duke of WELLINGTON
Lord GREY
Lord MELBOURNE
Sir Robert PEEL
Lord MELBOURNE
Sir Robert PEEL
Lord John RUSSELL
Lord DERBY
Lord ABERDEEN
Lord PALMERSTON
Lord DERBY
Lord PALMERSTON
Lord John RUSSELL
Lord DERBY
Benjamin DISRAELI
W. E. GLADSTONE
Benjamin DISRAELI
Lord BEACONSFIELD

W. E. GLADSTONE
Lord SALISBURY
W. E. GLADSTONE
Lord SALISBURY
W. E. GLADSTONE
Lord ROSEBERY
Lord SALISBURY
A. L. BALFOUR
Sir H. CAMPBELL-BANNERMAN
H. H. ASQUITH**
David LLOYD GEORGE
A. BONAR LAW
Stanley BALDWIN
J. R. MACDONALD
Stanley BALDWIN
J. R. MACDONALD**
Stanley BALDWIN
Neville CHAMBERLAIN**
W. Spencer CHURCHILL**
Clement ATTLEE**
Sir W. CHURCHILL
Sir Anthony EDEN
Harold MACMILLAN**
Sir Alec DOUGLAS-HOME
Harold WILSON**
Edward HEATH
Harold WILSON**
James CALLAGHAN
Margaret THATCHER***
John MAJOR**
Tony BLAIR

** and *** signify the number of consecutive terms of office

Presidents of the United States

George WASHINGTON
John ADAMS
Thomas JEFFERSON
James MADISON
James MONROE
John Quincy ADAMS
Andrew JACKSON
Martin van BUREN
William HARRISON
John TYLER
James Knox POLK
Zachary TAYLOR
Millard FILLMORE
Franklin PIERCE
James BUCHANAN
Abraham LINCOLN
Andrew JOHNSON
Ulysses GRANT
Rutherford HAYES

James GARFIELD
Chester ARTHUR
Grover CLEVELAND
Benjamin HARRISON
Grover CLEVELAND
William McKINLEY
Theodore ROOSEVELT
William TAFT
Woodrow WILSON
Warren HARDING
Calvin COOLIDGE
Herbert HOOVER
F. D. ROOSEVELT
Harry TRUMAN
Dwight D. EISENHOWER
John F. KENNEDY
Lyndon B. JOHNSON
Richard M. NIXON
Gerald R. FORD
James E. CARTER
Ronald REAGAN
George BUSH
Bill CLINTON

Nobel Prize Winners in Literature

Since 1901

1901 Sully PRUDHOMME *Fr.*
1902 Theodor MOMMSEN *Ger.*
1903 B. BJORNSON *Nor.*
1904 Frédéric MISTRAL & J. ECHEGARAY y EIZAGUIRRE *Fr. & Spain*
1905 H. SIENKIEWICZ *Pol.*
1906 Giosue CARDUCCI *Italy*
1907 Rudyard KIPLING *Brit.*
1908 Rudolf EUKEN *Ger.*
1909 Selma LAGERLOF *Sweden*
1910 Paul von HEYSE *Ger.*
1911 Maurice MAETERLINCK *Belg.*
1912 Gerhart HAUPTMANN *Ger.*
1913 Sir R. TAGORE *India*
1914 no award
1915 Romain ROLLAND *Fr.*
1916 V. von HEIDENSTAM *Sweden*
1917 Karl GJELLERUP & H. PONTOPPIDAN *Den.*
1918 no award
1919 Carl SPITTELER *Switz.*
1920 Knut HAMSUN *Nor.*
1921 Anatole FRANCE *Fr.*
1922 J. BENAVENTE y MARTINEZ *Spain*
1923 William Butler YEATS *Ire.*
1924 Wladyslaw REYMONT *Pol.*
1925 George Bernard SHAW *Ire.*
1926 Grazia DELEDDA *Italy*
1927 Henri BERGSON *Fr.*
1928 Sigrid UNDSET *Nor.*
1929 Thomas MANN *Ger.*
1930 Sinclair LEWIS *U.S.*
1931 Erik Axel KARLFELDT *Sweden*
1932 John GALSWORTHY *Brit.*
1933 Ivan BUNIN *U.S.S.R.*
1934 Luigi PIRANDELLO *Italy*
1935 no award
1936 Eugene O'NEILL *U.S.*
1937 Roger MARTIN du GARD *Fr.*
1938 Pearl BUCK *U.S.*
1939 Frans Eemil SILLANPAA *Fin.*
1940–
1943 no awards
1944 J. V. JENSEN *Den.*
1945 Gabriela MISTRAL *Chile*
1946 Hermann HESSE *Switz.*
1947 André GIDE *Fr.*
1948 T. S. ELIOT *Brit.*

1949 William FAULKNER *U.S.*
1950 Bertrand RUSSELL *Brit.*
1951 Pär LAGERKVIST *Sweden*
1952 François MAURIAC *Fr.*
1953 Sir Winston CHURCHILL *Brit.*
1954 Ernest HEMINGWAY *U.S.*
1955 Halldor LAXNESS *Ice.*
1956 Juan Ramon JIMENEZ *Spain*
1957 Albert CAMUS *Fr.*
1958 Boris PASTERNAK (declined award) *U.S.S.R.*
1959 Salvatore QUASIMODO *Italy*
1960 Saint-John PERSE *Fr.*
1961 Ivo ANDRIC *Yugos.*
1962 John STEINBECK *U.S.*
1963 George SEFERIS *Gr.*
1964 Jean-Paul SARTRE *Fr.*
1965 Mikhail SHOLOKHOV *U.S.S.R.*
1966 Shmuel Yosef AGNON & Nelly SACHS *Isr. & Sweden*
1967 Miguel Angel ASTURIAS *Guat.*
1968 Kawabata YASUNARI *Japan*
1969 Samuel BECKETT *Ire.*
1970 Aleksandr SOLZHENITSYN *U.S.S.R.*
1971 Pablo NERUDA *Chile*
1972 Heinrich BOLL *Ger.*
1973 Patrick WHITE *Austr.*
1974 Eyvind JOHNSON & Harry MARTINSON *Sweden*
1975 Eugenio MONTALE *Italy*
1976 Saul BELLOW *U.S.*
1977 Vicente ALEIXANDRE *Spain*
1978 Isaac Bashevis SINGER *U.S.*
1979 Odysseus ELYTIS *Gr.*
1980 Czeslaw MILOSZ *U.S.*
1981 Elias CANETTI *Bulg.*
1982 Gabriel Garcia MARQUEZ *Colombia*
1983 William GOLDING *Brit.*
1984 Jaroslav SEIFERT *Czech.*
1985 Claude SIMON *Fr.*
1986 Elie WIESEL *U.S.*
1987 Joseph BRODSKY *U.S./U.S.S.R.*
1988 Negbeh MAHFOUZ *Egypt*
1989 Camilo José CELA *Spain*
1990 Octavio PAZ *Mexico*
1991 Nadine GORDIMER *S.A.*
1992 Derek WALCOTT *St Lucia*
1993 Toni MORRISON *U.S.*
1994 Kenzaburo OE *Japan*
1995 Seamus HEANEY *Ire.*
1996 Wislawa SZYMBORSKA *Poland*
1997 Dario FO *Italy*

Counties of the British Isles

England and Wales

Metropolitan Counties

GREATER MANCHESTER
MERSEYSIDE
SOUTH YORKSHIRE
TYNE & WEAR
WEST MIDLANDS
WEST YORKS

Non-Metropolitan Counties

3 MON* is GWENT
4 AVON
BEDS
CAMS
GLAM* now S. GLAM, W. GLAM
GLOS
KENT
OXON
TYNE & WEAR
5 BERKS
BUCKS
CARDS* in DYFED
CARMS* in DYFED
CLWYD
DERBY
DEVON
DYFED
ESSEX
FLINT* in CLWYD
GWENT
HANTS
HERTS
HUNTS*
LANCS
LEICS
LINCS
NOTTS
PEMBS* in CLWYD
POWYS
SALOP** now SHROPSHIRE
WILTS
WORCS in HEREFORDSHIRE & WORCS
YORKS
6 BRECON* in POWYS
DORSET
DURHAM
LONDON
OXFORD
RADNOR* in POWYS
STAFFS
SURREY
SUSSEX now E. SUSSEX, W. SUSSEX
7 BEDFORD
CUMBRIA

7 DENBIGH* in CLWYD
GWYNEDD
LINCOLN
NORFOLK
RUTLAND in LEICESTERSHIRE
SUFFOLK
WARWICK
8 ANGLESEY* in GWYNEDD
CARDIGAN* in DYFED
CHESHIRE
CORNWALL and SCILLY
HEREFORD in HEREFORD & WORCS
HERTFORD
MONMOUTH* is GWENT
PEMBROKE* in DYFED
SOMERSET
STAFFORD -shire
9 CAMBRIDGE -shire
CLEVELAND formerly North Yorkshire
NORTHANTS NORTHAMPTON-shire
WILTSHIRE
YORKSHIRE
10 GLOUCESTER -shire
HUMBERSIDE SOUTH RIDING YORKS
+ part of NORTH LINCOLNSHIRE
HUNTINGDON in CAMBRIDGE
LANCASHIRE
NOTTINGHAM -shire
12 LINCOLNSHIRE
14 NORTHUMBERLAND

Scotland

9 Regions (53 districts)

3 AYR*
4 BUTE*
FIFE
ROSS*
5 ANGUS*
BANFF*
ELGIN*
MORAY*
NAIRN*
PERTH*
6 ARGYLL*
FORFAR*
LANARK*
7 BERWICK*
BORDERS
CENTRAL
ISLANDS (Orkney, Shetland, Western)
KINROSS*
LOTHIAN
PEEBLES*
RENFREW*
SELKIRK*
TAYSIDE

7 WIGTOWN*
8 ABERDEEN*
  AYRSHIRE*
  CROMARTY*
  DUMFRIES
  GALLOWAY
  GRAMPIAN
  HIGHLAND
  ROXBURGH*
  STIRLING*
11 STRATHCLYDE

Ireland

4 CORK†
  DOWN
  LEIX†
  MAYO†
5 CAVAN†
  CLARE†
  KERRY†
  LOUTH†
  MEATH†
  SLIGO†
6 ANTRIM

6 ARMAGH
  CARLOW†
  DUBLIN†
  GALWAY†
  OFFALY†
  TYRONE
  ULSTER (P)
7 DONEGAL†
  KILDARE†
  LEITRIM†
  MUNSTER (P)†
  WEXFORD†
  WICKLOW†
8 KILKENNY†
  LAOIGHIS
  LEINSTER (P)†
  LIMERICK†
  LONGFORD†
  MONAGHAN†
9 FERMANAGH
11 LONDONDERRY

* Counties which no longer exist after local
government reorganization in 1974.
** Name for Shropshire from 1974 to 1980.
† Counties of the Republic of Ireland.

The 50 United States of America

State/Abbreviation	Joined/no.	Approx. Population	Capital
4 IOWA *Ia.*	1846/29th	2.8 mill.	DES MOINES
OHIO *O.*	1803/17th	10.8 mill.	COLUMBUS
UTAH *Uh.*	1896/45th	1.5 mill.	SALT LAKE CITY
5 IDAHO *Id., Ida.*	1890/43rd	1.0 mill.	BOISE
MAINE *Me.*	1820/23rd	1.2 mill.	AUGUSTA
TEXAS *Tex.*	1845/28th	17.0 mill.	AUSTIN
6 ALASKA *Alas.*	1959/49th	0.5 mill.	JUNEAU
HAWAII	1959/50th	1.1 mill.	HONOLULU
KANSAS *Kan.*	1861/34th	2.4 mill.	TOPEKA
NEVADA *Nev.*	1864/36th	1.2 mill.	CARSON CITY
OREGON *Ore., Oreg.*	1859/33rd	2.8 mill.	SALEM
7 ALABAMA *Ala.*	1819/17th	4.0 mill.	MONTGOMERY
ARIZONA *Ariz.*	1912/48th	3.6 mill.	PHOENIX
FLORIDA *Fla.*	1845/27th	13.0 mill.	TALLAHASSEE
GEORGIA *Ga.*	orig. 13	6.5 mill.	ATLANTA
INDIANA *Ind.*	1816/19th	5.5 mill.	INDIANAPOLIS
MONTANA *Mont.*	1889/41st	0.8 mill.	HELENA
NEW YORK *N.Y.*	orig. 13	18.0 mill.	ALBANY
VERMONT *Vt.*	1791/14th	0.6 mill.	MONTPELIER
WYOMING *Wyo.*	1890/44th	0.5 mill.	CHEYENNE
8 ARKANSAS *Ark.*	1836/25th	2.3 mill.	LITTLE ROCK
COLORADO *Colo.*	1876/38th	3.3 mill.	DENVER
DELAWARE *Del.*	orig. 13	0.6 mill.	DOVER
ILLINOIS *Ill.*	1818/21st	11.5 mill.	SPRINGFIELD
KENTUCKY *Ky., Ken.*	1792/15th	3.7 mill.	FRANKFORT
MARYLAND *Md.*	orig. 13	4.8 mill.	ANNAPOLIS
MICHIGAN *Mich.*	1837/26th	9.3 mill.	LANSING
MISSOURI *Mo.*	1821/24th	5.1 mill.	JEFFERSON CITY

State/Abbreviation	Joined/no.	Approx. Population	Capital
8 NEBRASKA *Neb.*	1867/37th	1.6 mill.	LINCOLN
OKLAHOMA *Okla.*	1907/46th	3.1 mill.	OKLAHOMA CITY
VIRGINIA *Va.*	orig. 13	6.2 mill.	RICHMOND
9 LOUISIANA *La.*	1812/18th	4.2 mill.	BATON ROUGE
MINNESOTA *Minn.*	1858/32nd	4.4 mill.	ST PAUL
NEW JERSEY *N.J.*	orig. 13	7.7 mill.	TRENTON
NEW MEXICO *N.M.*	1912/47th	1.5 mill.	SANTA FE
TENNESSEE *Tenn.*	1796/16th	4.9 mill.	NASHVILLE
WISCONSIN *Wis.*	1848/30th	4.8 mill.	MADISON
10 CALIFORNIA *Cal.*	1850/31st	29.7 mill.	SACRAMENTO
WASHINGTON *Wash.*	1889/42nd	4.9 mill.	OLYMPIA
11 CONNECTICUT *Conn.*	orig. 13	3.2 mill.	HARTFORD
MISSISSIPPI *Miss.*	1817/20th	2.6 mill.	JACKSON
NORTH DAKOTA *N.D., N.Dak.*	1889/39th	0.7 mill.	BISMARCK
SOUTH DAKOTA *S.Dak., S.D.*	1889/40th	0.7 mill.	PIERRE
RHODE ISLAND *R.I.*	orig. 13	1.0 mill.	PROVIDENCE
12 NEW HAMPSHIRE *N.H.*	orig. 13	1.1 mill.	CONCORD
PENNSYLVANIA *Penn.*	orig. 13	12.0 mill.	HARRISBURG
WEST VIRGINIA *W.Va.*	1863/35th	1.8 mill.	CHARLESTON
13 MASSACHUSETTS *Mass.*	orig. 13	6.0 mill.	BOSTON
NORTH CAROLINA *N.C.*	orig. 13	6.6 mill.	RALEIGH
SOUTH CAROLINA *S.C.*	orig. 13	3.5 mill.	COLUMBIA
COLUMBIA *(District) D.C. (site of the capital of the U.S.)*			WASHINGTON D.C.

The 12 Provinces of Canada

State	Population	Capital
YUKON Territory	ca. 30,000	WHITEHORSE
QUEBEC	ca. 7.3 mill.	QUEBEC
ALBERTA	ca. 2.7 mill.	EDMONTON
ONTARIO	ca. 11.1 mill.	TORONTO
MANITOBA	ca. 1.1 mill.	WINNIPEG
NOVA SCOTIA	ca. 0.9 mill.	HALIFAX
NEW BRUNSWICK	ca. 0.7 mill.	FREDERICTON
NEWFOUNDLAND	ca. 0.6 mill.	ST JOHN'S
SASKATCHEWAN	ca. 1.0 mill.	REGINA
BRITISH COLUMBIA	ca. 3.8 mill.	VICTORIA
PRINCE EDWARD ISLAND	ca. 0.2 mill.	CHARLOTTETOWN
NORTHWEST TERRITORIES	ca. 65,000	YELLOWKNIFE
District of Franklin		
District of Keewatin		
District of Mackenzie		

The 15 Union Republics of the Former Soviet Union

State	Population	Capital
UZBEK S.S.R* (Uzbekistan)	ca. 12 mill.	TASHKENT
KAZAKH S.S.R. (Kazakhstan)	ca. 14.5 mill.	ALMA-ATA
KIRGIZ S.S.R. (Kirgizstan, Kirghiz/Kirgiziya)	ca. 3 mill.	FRUNZE
LATVIAN S.S.R.	ca. 2.4 mill.	RIGA
RUSSIAN SOVIET FEDERATED S.R.	ca. 134 mill.	MOSCOW

State	Population	Capital
TADZHIK S.S.R. (Tajikistan, Tadzhikstan)	ca. 3.5 mill.	DUSHANBE
TURKMEN S.S.R. (Turkmenistan, Turkmeniya)	ca. 2.5 mill.	ASHKHABAD
ARMENIAN S.S.R.	ca. 3.1 mill.	YEREVAN
ESTONIAN S.S.R.	ca. 1.4 mill.	TALLINN
GEORGIAN S.S.R. (Sakartvelo, Gruziya)	ca. 5 mill.	TBILISI (Tiflis)
MOLDAVIAN S.S.R.	ca. 3.9 mill.	KISHINYOV
UKRAINIAN S.S.R. (Ukraine)	ca. 50 mill.	KIEV
AZERBAIJAN S.S.R. (Azerbaydzhan)	ca. 5.8 mill.	BAKU
LITHUANIAN S.S.R.	ca. 3.3 mill.	VILNIUS
BELORUSSIAN S.S.R. (Byelorussia, Belorussia/White Russia)	ca. 9.1 mill.	MINSK

* S.S.R. = Soviet Socialist Republic

C.I.S. The Commonwealth of Independent States
(formerly the Soviet Union) now is comprised of the founders and 9 other Republics

State	Population	Capital
BYELORUSSIA	ca. 10 mill.	MINSK
UKRAINE	ca. 51.5 mill.	KIEV
***THE RUSSIAN FEDERATION**	ca. 148 mill.	MOSCOW
and 9 other Republics:		
ARMENIA	ca. 3.8 mill.	YEREVAN
AZERBAIJAN	ca. 7.5 mill.	BAKU
GEORGIA	ca. 5.5 mill.	TBILISI
KAZAKHSTAN	ca. 17 mill.	ALMA-ATA
KYRGYZSTAN	ca. 4.4 mill.	BISHKEK
MOLDAVIA	ca. 4.4 mill.	KISHINEV
TAJIKISTAN	ca. 5.1 mill.	DUSHANBE
TURKMENISTAN	ca. 4.5 mill.	ASHKHABAD
UZBEKISTAN	ca. 21.2 mill.	TASHKENT

* Divided into 2 cities of Federal
Status (MOSCOW and St
Petersburg), 21 Republics, 6
Territories (Krai), 49 Provinces
(Oblast), 10 Autonomous Areas + 1
Jewish Autonomous Region.
CHECHENIA is within the
Russian Federation.
The 3 Baltic Republics ESTONIA,
LATVIA, LITHUANIA were recognized
as Independent in 1991.

The Former 6 Socialist Republics of Yugoslavia (Jugoslavia)

State	Population	Capital
SERBIA (Srbija) (includes the 2 Autonomous Provinces of Vojvodina and Kosovo/Kosmet)	ca. 9.3 mill.	BELGRADE
CROATIA (Hrvatska)	ca. 4.8 mill.	ZAGREB
SLOVENIA (Slovenija)	ca. 2.0 mill.	LLUBLJANA
MACEDONIA (Makedonija)	ca. 1.9 mill.	SKOPJE
MONTENEGRO (Crna Gora)	ca. 0.6 mill.	TITOGRAD
BOSNIA AND HERZEGOVINA (Bosna i Hercegovina)	ca. 2.9 mill.	SARAJEVO

SERBIA & MONTENEGRO are
  now one State
CROATIA – Independent
BOSNIA & HERZEGOVINA is
  divided into Independent
  BOSNIA (capital SARAJEVO)
SERBIAN BOSNIA (SRPSKA)
  (temporary capital PALE)
MACEDONIA – Independent

Germany (Reunited 1991)

The 15 Länder, semi-autonomous provinces (incl. 3 cities)

Länder	Population	Capital
BADEN-WÜRTTEMBERG	ca. 10.2 mill.	STUTTGART
BAYERN (Bavaria)	ca. 11.8 mill.	MÜNCHEN (Munich)
BERLIN	ca. 3.5 mill.	BERLIN, the city
BRANDENBURG	ca. 2.5 mill.	POTSDAM
BREMEN, Freie Hansestadt	ca. 683,000	BREMEN, the city
HAMBURG, Freie Hansestaat	ca. 1.7 mill.	HAMBURG, the city
HESSEN	ca. 5.9 mill.	WIESBADEN
NIEDER SACHSEN (Lower Saxony)	ca. 7.6 mill.	HANNOVER
MECKLENBURG-POMMERN (Pomerania)	ca. 1.8 mill.	SCHWERIN
NORDRHEIN-WESTFALEN	ca. 17.6 mill.	DÜSSELDORF
RHEINLAND-PFALZ (Rhineland-Palatinate)	ca. 3.9 mill.	MAINZ
SAARLAND	ca. 1 mill.	SAARBRÜCKEN
FREISTAAT SACHSEN (Saxony)	ca. 4.6 mill.	DRESDEN
SACHSEN-ANHALT (Saxony)	ca. 2.7 mill.	MAGDEBURG
SCHLESWIG-HOLSTEIN	ca. 2.7 mill.	KIEL
THURINGEN (Thuringia)	ca. 2.5 mill.	ERFURT

Spain
Autonomous Communities and Provinces

Province	*Population*	*Capital*
ANDALUCÍA	ca. 6.9 mill.	SEVILLA
ARAGÓN	ca. 1.2 mill.	ZARAGOZA
ASTURIAS	ca. 1 mill.	OVIEDO
BALEARES (Balearic Islands)	ca. 709,000	PALMA de MALLORCA
BASQUE	ca. 2.1 mill.	VITORIA
Islas CANARIAS		
(Canary Isles) 2	ca. 1.5 mill.	1) LAS PALMAS
		2) SANTA CRUZ de TENERIFE
CANTABRIA	ca. 527,000	SANTANDER
CASTILLA-La MANCHA	ca. 1.6 mill.	TOLEDO
CASTILLA-LEÓN	ca. 2.5 mill.	VALLADOLID
CATALUÑA	ca. 6 mill.	BARCELONA
EXTREMADURA	ca. 100,000	MÉRIDA
GALICIA	ca. 2.7 mill.	SANTIAGO de COMPOSTELLA
MADRID	ca. 5 mill.	MADRID
MURCIA	ca. 1 mill.	MURCIA & CARTAGENA (jointly)
NAVARRA	ca. 520,000	PAMPLONA
La RIOJA	ca. 263,000	LAGRONO
VALENCIA	ca. 3.8 mill.	VALENCIA

Enclaves in North Africa (Morocco)

CEUTA	3750
MELILLA	4054

European Union (EU)
(from the Iron & Steel Union: France, Germany & Luxembourg)

1950 **BELGIUM, FRANCE, W. GERMANY, ITALY, LUXEMBOURG, NETHERLANDS** (The Six)
1973 **DENMARK, IRELAND, UNITED KINGDOM** joined
1981 **GREECE** joined
1985 **GREENLAND** autonomously opted out of Denmark's membership of the EEC
1986 **SPAIN** and **PORTUGAL** joined
1995 **AUSTRIA, FINLAND** and **SWEDEN** joined

Association Agreements (for future membership)

1991 **CZECHOSLOVAKIA, HUNGARY, POLAND**
1992 **CZECH REPUBLIC, ROMANIA, SLOVAKIA**

Applicants for Membership

1987 **TURKEY**
1991 **CYPRUS**
1994 **POLAND, HUNGARY**

European Free Trade Association (EFTA)
(Prior to these countries entering the European Union)

1960 **AUSTRIA, DENMARK, FINLAND, ICELAND, LICHTENSTEIN, NORWAY, SWEDEN, UNITED KINGDOM** – also **SWITZERLAND** (not in EU)

African Countries
With Present & Former Names

Country	Capital
4 CHAD/TSCHAD	N'DJAMENA (Fort-Lamy)
MALI (col. French Soudan)	BAMAKO
TOGO (col. Togoland)	LOME
5 BENIN (col. Dahomay)	PORTO-NOVO
CONGO (Brazzaville)	BRAZZAVILLE
CONGO (Kinshasa) (Zaire)	KINSHASA (Leopoldville)
EGYPT (Arab Republic of Egypt)	CAIRO
GABON (col. part of French Equatorial Africa)	LIBREVILLE (Freetown)
GHANA (col. Gold Coast & part of Togoland)	ACCRA
KENYA	NAIROBI
LIBYA	TRIPOLI
NIGER	NIAMEY (Zinder/Damagaram)
SUDAN, The	KHARTOUM
6 ANGOLA (col. Portuguese West Africa)	LUANDA
GAMBIA, The	BANJUL (Bathurst)
GUINEA	CONAKRY
MALAWI (col. Nyasaland)	LILONGWE (Zomba)
RWANDA (Kinyarwanda) (col. Ruanda)	KIGALI
UGANDA	KAMPALA
ZAMBIA (col. Northern Rhodesia)	LUSAKA
7 ALGERIA	ALGIERS
BURUNDI (Kirundi) (col. Ruanda & Urundi)	BUJUMBURA
COMOROS islands (Grande Comore & Moheli & Anjouan)	MOCONI (Moheli & Anjouan)
ERITREA	ASMARA
LESOTHO Kingdom (Sesotho) (col. Basutoland)	MASERU
LIBERIA	MONROVIA
MOROCCO	RABAT
NAMIBIA (col. South West Africa)	WINDHOEK (national)
	SWAKOPMUND (summer)
NIGERIA Federal Republic (col. British protectorates of Northern & Southern Nigeria)	ABUJA
SENEGAL (together with Gambia: Senegambia)	DAKAR
SOMALIA (col. Br. & It. Somaliland)	MOGADISCIO
TUNISIA	TUNIS
8 BOTSWANA (col. Bechuanaland)	GABORONE
CAMEROON (Col. Kamerun)	YAOUNDE
DJIBOUTI (col. Afars & Issas, Fr. Somaliland)	DJIBOUTI
ETHIOPIA (ancient Abyssinia)	ADDIS ABABA
MALAGASY/MADAGASIKARA (col. Madagascar)	ANTANANARIVO
TANZANIA (col. Tanganyika & Zanzibar)	DAR ES SALAAM
ZIMBABWE (col. Southern Rhodesia)	HARARE (Salisbury)
9 CAPE VERDE islands (Windward & Leeward groups)	PRAIA

9 MAURITIUS (in the Indian Ocean, incl. islands of Rodrigues, Cargados Carajos Shoals, Agalega)	PORT LOUIS	
SWAZILAND Kingdom	MBABANE (administrative)	
	LOBAMBA (royal & legislative)	
10 BOKINA FASO (col. Upper Volta)	OUAGADOUGOU	
IVORY COAST	ABIDJAN	
MAURITANIA	NOUAKCHOTT	
MOZAMBIQUE (col. Portuguese East Africa)	MAPUTO	
SEYCHELLES (archipelago of ca. 85 islands)	VICTORIA	
	FREETOWN	
11 SIERRA LEONE	CAPETOWN (legislative)	
SOUTH AFRICA	PRETORIA (administrative)	
	BLOEMFONTEIN (judicial)	
GUINEA-BISSAU (col. Portuguese Guinea)	BISSAU	
WESTERN SAHARA (col. Spanish Sahara, divided 1976 between Morocco and Mauritania; Southern region: Rio de Oro; Northern region: Saguia el Hamra)	EL AAIUN (chief town, formerly capital)	
EQUATORIAL GUINEA (col. Spanish Guinea) incl. Macias Nguema Biyogo (Fernando Po/Poo) and Pagolu islands	MALABO (Santa Isabel)	
SAO TOME E PRINCIPE (islands)	SAO TOME	
CENTRAL AFRICAN REPUBLIC (col. Oubangui–Chari)	BANGUI	

Note: French-speaking Central Africa today comprises the territories of Central African Republic, Congo/Brazzaville, Gabon and Congo/Kinshasa

Other Recent Changes of Name

Country	Status	Capital
5 YEMEN (formerly South Yemen)	People's Democratic Republic	ADEN
YEMEN (Yemen P.D.R. & Yemen (San'a) formed the Yemen Republic 1972)	Republic	SAN'A
6 BELIZE/BELICE (formerly British Honduras)	self-governing	BELMOPAN
BRUNEI (Negeri Brunei) (formerly Sarawak)	British protected sultanate (N. Borneo)	BANDAR SERI BEGAWAN
GUYANA (col. British Guiana)	Republic	GEORGETOWN
TAIWAN (formerly Formosa)	Republic	TAIPEI
7 MYANMAR (formerly Burma)	Republic	YANGON/Rangoon
8 SRI LANKA (formerly Ceylon)	Republic	COLOMBO
SURINAME (col. Dutch Guiana)	Republic	PARAMARIBO
9 IRIAN JAYA (Irian Barat, West Irian or West New Guinea) (formerly part of Dutch East Indies)	Province of Indonesia	DJAJAPURA
10 BANGLADESH (formerly East Pakistan)		DHAKA

Country	Status	Capital
10 KALIMANTAN (Indonesian name for Borneo) divided into West, Central, South & East Kalimantan	Provinces of Indonesia	PONTIANAK (W) PALANGKARAJA (C) BANDJARMASIN (S) SAMARINDRA (E)
PAPUA NEW GUINEA (formerly Australian Papua & UN Territory of New Guinea)	Australian territory admin. as part of Territory of Papua & New Guinea	PORT MORESBY
SARAWAK & SABAH	States of E. Malaysia on N. Borneo	KUCHING KOTA KINABULU
THE UNITED ARAB EMIRATES (formerly Trucial States or Trucial Oman) include:		
OMAN (Sultanat Uman) (formerly Muscat and Oman)	Sultanate	MUSCAT
DUBAI (Dubayy) (incl. exclave Hajarayn)	Emirate	DUBAYY (Dubai)
QATAR (Dawlat Qatar)	State of Qatar	ad-DAWHAH (Doha)
SHARJAH (Ash-Shariqah) (incl. exclaves Dibbah, Khwar al-Fakkan, Khwar al-Kalba)	Emirate	ash-SHARIQAH (Sharjah)
ABU DHABI (Abu Zaby)	Sultanate	ABU ZABY

Polynesia

Islands	Status	Capital or admin. headquarters
4 FIJI (borders on Melanesia) main islands: Viti Levu, Vanua Levu, Lau group	Independent	SUVA (on Viti Levu)
5 SAMOA main islands: Tutuila, Manu'a, Rose Island	Dependency of US	PAGO PAGO (on Tutuila)
TONGA or PULE'ANGA TONGA (Kingdom of Tonga, also called Friendly Islands) main islands: Tongatapu/Tongatabu, Vavau, Haapai	Independent 1970	NUKUALOFA (on Tongatapu/ Tongatabu)
6 HAWAII includes Mauna Kea, highest island in Polynesia	50th state of US	HONOLULU
TAHITI or OTAHEITE includes Tahiti Nui & Tahiti Iti; largest island of the Windward Group (Society Islands)	French Polynesia	PAPEETE (on Tahiti, capital of French Polynesia)
TUBUAI ISLANDS (Austral Islands) main islands: Tubuai, Rurutu Raevavae, Rimatara, Rapa	French Polynesia	MATAURA (on Tubuai)
TUVALU (col. Ellice Islands) (formerly part of the British crown colony of Gilbert & Ellice islands) largest island: Vaitupu	Independent 1978, constitutional monarchy	FUNAFUTI (on Funafuti)
7 EASTER ISLAND – RAPANUI (Great Rapa) or **TE PITO TE HENUA** (Navel of the World) main islets: Motu-Nui, Motu-Iti, Motu-Kaokao	Dependency of Chile	HANGA-ROA (on Easter Island)
TOKELAU ISLANDS (Union Group) main islands: Nukunono, Atafu, Fakaofu	New Zealand territory	NUKUNONO (unofficial capital)

TUAMOTU ARCHIPELAGO or **PAUMOTU** main islands: NW = Rangiroa, Makemo, Raroia (Kon-Tiki!), centre: Anaa, Amanu, Hao, SE = Mururoa, Fagataufa, Tureia	French Polynesia	APATAKI (on Apataki)
MANGAREVA/MAGAREVA ISLANDS (Gambier Islands) main islands: Mangareva/Magareva, Taravai, Aukeua, Akamaru	French Polynesia	RIKITEA (on Mangareva/ Magareva)
CLIPPERTON ISLANDS (uninhabited)	French Polynesia	
NEW ZEALAND (North & South)	Independent	WELLINGTON (on North Island)
COOK ISLANDS S (Lower) Cooks: Rarotonga, Atiu Takutea, Mauke, Mitiaro, Manuae, N (Manuhiki) Cooks: Penrhyn, Manihiki, Danger (Pukapuka), Palmerston, Rakakanga, Suvorov, Nassau	Dependency of New Zealand	AVARUA (on Rarotonga)
WESTERN SAMOA main islands: Savaii, Upolu	Independent 1962	APIA (on Upolu)
SOCIETY ISLANDS Windward group: Tahiti, Moorea, Leeward group: Bora-Bora, Raiatea Motu-Iti, Huahine	French Polynesia	PAPEETE (on Tahiti)
MARQUESAS ISLANDS main islands: Hiva Ova (largest), Tahuata, Nuku Hiva/ Nukahiva, Hatutu	French Polynesia	HAKAPEHI (TAI-O-HAE) (on Nuku Hiva/ Nukahiva)

Melanesia

Islands	*Status*	*Capital or admin. headquarters*
FIJI – see Polynesia		
LOYALTY ISLANDS main islands: Mare, Uvea, Lifou	French New Caledonia	TADINOU (on Mare)
VANUATU (col. New Hebrides) main islands: Espiritu Santo (largest), Efate, Banks, Ambrim	Republic	VILA (on Efate)
BISMARCK ARCHIPELAGO main islands: New Britain, New Ireland, the Admiralties, Mussau, Lavongai (New Hanover), Duke & York Islands, Vitu Islands	Papua New Guinea	RABAUL (on New Britain)
ADMIRALTY ISLANDS main islands: Manus (largest), Hermit & Ninigo groups	extension of Bismarck Archipelago	LORENGAU (on Manus)
NEW CALEDONIA main islands: New Caledonia, Belep, Pins, Walpole, Hunter, Huon	French Overseas Territory	NOUMEA (on New Caledonia)
D'ENTRECASTEAUX ISLANDS main islands: Normanby, Fergusson, Goodenough (Morata), Sanaroa (Welle), Dobu	Papua New Guinea	VIVIGANI (on Goodenough)

Micronesia

Islands	Status	Capital or admin. headquarters
GUAM – (largest & southernmost of the Mariana Islands)	self-governing territory of US	AGANA
*BANABA (col. Ocean Island)	Republic	Tapawa?
NAOERO/NAURU (col. Ger. Marschall Islands protectorate: UN Trust Territory under Australia)	Republic	YAREN (on Naoero/Nauru)
MARIANA ISLANDS (North) main islands: Saipan, Tinian Agrihan (highest), Rota	UN Trust Territory under US jurisdiction	SAIPAN (on Saipan – also territory capital)
CAROLINE ISLANDS main islands: Ponape, Yap, Truk, Kusaie, Nukuoro, Kapingamarangi	UN Trust Territory under US jurisdiction	SAIPAN
KIRIBATI (col. Gilbert Islands, or Kingsmill) stretching from Washington to Flint Islands & Christmas atoll to Banaba; main islands: Tarawa Butaritari (Makin), Abemama, Abaiang (the former British crown colony included Ocean Island, Central & Southern Line Islands, Phoenix I.)	Independent 1979	TARAWA (on Tarawa)
MARSHALL ISLANDS main islands: Radak Chain (Sunrise): Mili, Majuro, Bikar, Utirik Ralik Chain (Sunset): Kwajalein, Jaluit, Bikini, Wotho, Eniwetok	UN Trust Territory under US jurisdiction	SAIPANTHE
TRUST TERRITORY OF THE UN under US jurisdiction includes: Mariana & Caroline Islands, Marshall Islands, the Federated States of Micronesia (Ponape, Kusaie, Truk & Yap) and the district of Palau	under US jurisdiction	

* Population resettled on Rambi/Fiji

The 12 Caesars and later Roman Emperors

Name	Manner of death	Born	Rule
Gaius **JULIUS CAESAR** (wife **CORNELIA**)	Murdered 15/3	12/7 100 B.C.	60–44 B.C.
Caesar **AUGUSTUS** (Octavian/ Gaius Octavius/Gaius Julius Caesar Octavius) (wife **LIVIA**)	Old age (77) on 19/8	23/9 63 B.C.	27 B.C.–A.D. 14
TIBERIUS (Claudius Nero Caesar Augustus) (wife **JULIA**)	Natural 16/3 on Capri	23/9 63 B.C.	A.D. 14–37
CALIGULA (Gaius Caesar) (wife **CAESONIA**)	Murdered 24/1	31/8 12 B.C. in Antium/ Anzio/Italy	37–41
CLAUDIUS I (Tiberius Claudius Drusus Nero Germanicus) (wife & niece **AGRIPPINA**)	Poisoned 13/10	1/8 10 B.C. in Lugdunum/Lyon	41–54

Name	Manner of death	Born	Rule
NERO (Lucius Domitius Achenobarbus) (wife: a) **OCTAVIA**, b) **POPPAEA SABINA**, first wife of Otho)	Suicide	15/12 37 in Rome	54–68

End of Caesar's line

GALBA (Servius Sulpicius)	Murdered 15/1	24/12 3 B.C.	68–69
OTHO (Marcus Salvius Otho) (wife **POPPAEA SABINA**)	Suicide 16/4	A.D. 28/4 32	69–69
VITTELLIUS (Aulus)	Murdered 20/12	A.D. 15	69–69

Flavian House

VESPASIAN (Titus Flavius Vespasianus)	Natural 24/6	A.D. 9	69–79
TITUS (Titus Flavius Vespasianus) (wife **AGRIPPA II BERENICE**, wife of Herod)	Murdered? 13/9	A.D. 30/12 39	79–81
DOMITIAN (Titus Flavius Domitianus)	Murdered 18/9	A.D. 24/10 51	81–96

End of Flavian line & the 12 Caesars

Five Good Emperors

NERVA (Marcus Cocceius Nerva)	Natural	A.D. *c.* 30	96–98
TRAJAN (Marcus Ulpius Traianus, Germanicus) (wife **PLOTINA**)	Natural 8/8 in Selinus/Selindi (TR)	15/9 53 in Italica (Santiponce/Spain)	98–117
HADRIAN (Publius Aelius Hadrianus) (wife **VIBIA SABINA**)	Natural 10/7	24/1 76 in Rome?	117–138
ANTONINUS PIUS (Titus Aurelius Fulvius Boinonius Arrius Antoninus) (wife **FAUSTINA**)	Natural 7/3	19/9 86 Lanuvium	138–161
LUCIUS VERUS (Lucius Aurelius)	Natural	15/12 130	161–169

Roman Emperors

MARCUS AURELIUS (Antoninus) (co-ruler with Antoninus Pius & Lucius Verus 140s–169)	Natural 17/3	A.D. 26/4 121	169–180
COMMODUS (Lucius Aelius Aurelius) (mistress **MARCIA**)	Murdered 31/12	31/8 161 in Rome	180–192
PERTINAX (Publius Helvius)	Murdered 28/3	1/8 126 (Liguria)	193–193
MARCUS DIDIUS (Julianus)	Murdered 1/6	*c.* 135 in Milan	193–193
***SEPTIMIUS SEVERUS** (Severus Lucius Septimius) (wife **JULIA DOMNA**)	Illness Febr. in Eburacum/York, Engl.	146 in Leptis Magna, Libya	193–211

* 198–211 Septimius Severus ruled with his son Caracalla

Name	Manner of death	Born	Rule
GETA (Publius Septimius) (together with his father Septimius Severus & brother Caracalla)	Murdered Febr.	189 in Milan	209–212
CARACALLA (Marcus Aurelius Antoninus) sole ruler 212–217 (wife **FULVIA PLAUTILLA**)	Murdered 8/4 in Carrhae (Harran/TR)	4/4 188 in Lugdunum/ Lyon	198–217
MACRINUS (Marcus Opellius)	Executed June (TR)	c. 164 (Caesarea/ Algeria)	217–218
ELAGABALUS (HELIOGABALLUS) (Varius Avitus Bassianus)	Murdered	204 (Emesa/Homs)	218–222
SEVERUS ALEXANDER (Marcus Aurelius Severus Alexander)	Murdered in Gaul	208 (Phoenicia/ Lebanon)	222–235
MAXIMINUS/MAXIMIN (Caius Julius Verus Maximinius)	Murdered March		235–238
GORDIAN I (Marcus Antonius Gordianus) together with his son **GORDIAN II**	Suicide Apr. Killed in battle	c. 157	238 for 3 weeks
*GORDIAN III (Marcus Antonius Gordianus)	Murdered in Zaitha	225	238–244

* May 238–Aug. 238 GORDIAN III
ruled with the elderly senators
Maximus and Balbinus, both
murdered

Name	Manner of death	Born	Rule
PHILIP THE ARABIAN (Marcus Julius Philippus)	Murdered		244–249
DECIUS (Gaius Messius Quintus Trajanus)	Killed in battle	c. 201 (Budalia/ Pannonia/Yu)	249–251
GALLUS (Gaius Vibius Trebonianus) co-rulers: Hostilian (son of Decius, died early) & Volusianus (his own son)	Murdered		251–253
AEMILIAN (Marcus Aemilius Aemilianus) ruled 3 months	Murdered	Mauretania/Africa	253–253
VALERIAN (Publius Licinus Valerianus); his son Gallienus ruled the West	In Persian captivity		253–260
*GALLIENUS (Italy & the Balkans only); fought usurper **AUREOLUS**	Murdered		260–268

* While GALLIENUS ruled Italy
& the Balkans POSTUMUS
(258–268) was independent
emperor in Gaul; he was
succeeded by VICTORINUS

Name	Manner of death	Born	Rule
CLAUDIUS II GOTHICUS (Marcus Aurelius Claudius)	Of plague	May 214 (Dardania Yu)	268–270

Name	Manner of death	Born	Rule
QUINTILLUS (brother of Claudius II)	Murdered?		270 for 3 months
***AURELIAN** (Lucius Domitius Aurelianus)	Murdered in Caenophrurium (TR)	*c.* 215	270–275

* TETRICUS ruled Spain, Gaul & Britain, but went over to Aurelian's side

Name	Manner of death	Born	Rule
ULPIA SEVERINA (Widow of Aurelian)	Natural		275 for 6 months
TACITUS (Marcus Claudius)	Murdered Apr. in Tyana/Cappadocia	*c.* 200	275–276
FLORIAN (Florianus) half-brother of Tacitus	Murdered June		276–276
PROBUS (Marcus Aurelius Probus)	Murdered Nov.		276–282
DIOCLETIAN (Gaius Aurelius Valerius Diocletianus) in the East; co-emperor in the West:	Abdicated 1/5; died 313 or 316	245 (Dalmatia)	284–305
MAXIMIAN (Marcus Aurelius Valerius Maximanus)	Abdicated 1/5; murdered or suicide 308		286–305
CONSTANTIUS I CHLORIUS (Aurelius Valerius Constantius) of the West (wife: a) **HELEN** b) **THEODORA**, stepdaughter of Maximian), father of Constantine the Great	Natural		305–306
GALERIUS (Gaius Valerius Maximianus) of the East	Disease	Sardica/Sofia	305–311
FLAVIUS VALERIUS SEVERUS declared emperor in West by Galerius (his friend)	Murdered by Maxentius, son of Maximian		306–306
MAXENTIUS (Marcus Aurelius Valerius) proclaimed Augustus of the West 28/10 306	Killed by Constantine in battle		306–312
MAXIMINUS (Gaius Galerius Valerius) nephew & friend of Galerius who proclaimed him Augustus of the East 308; died in Tarsus/TR shortly after having invaded dominion of Licinius & been defeated	Disease		308–313

Name	Manner of death	Born	Rule
LICINIUS (Valerius Licinianus Licinius) 11/11 308 Galerius declared Maxentius a usurper & appointed Licinius Augustus of the West; Constantine defeated Licinius at Adrinople 324	Executed 325		308–324
CONSTANTINE THE GREAT (emperor of the West from 312; Licinius emperor of the East 308–324); declared Constantinople the capital of the East Roman Empire (wife **FAUSTA**, daughter of Maximian)	Natural 22/5	27/2 late 280s	324–337
CONSTANTIUS II (Flavius Julius Constantius) co-emperor with his brothers, **CONSTANTINE II** (murdered 340) and **CONSTANT I** (murdered 350); sole ruler 353–361	Illness	7/8 317 (Sirmium, Yu)	337–361
JULIAN THE APOSTATE (Flavius Claudius Julianus)	Died in battle June	331/332	361–363
JOVIAN (Flavius Jovianus)	Natural 17/2	c. 331 (Singidunum/ Belgrade)	363–364
VALENTINIAN I (Flavius Valentinianus) (wife/2nd **JUSTINA**) 28/3 he appointed his younger brother Valens as co-ruler (East)	Illness March	321	364–375 (West)
***VALENS** (uncle of Gratian)	Killed in battle 9/8	c. 328	364–378 (East)
* The pagan PROCOPIUS proclaimed himself Emperor in Constantinople in September 365, but he was killed by Valens on 27/5 366			
GRATIAN (Flavius Gratianus) proclaimed co-emperor on 24/8 367 by his father Valentinian I and from that date also shared his office with his uncle Valens till 378		359 (Sirmium, Yu)	367–383 (West)
VALENTINIAN II (Flavius Valentinianus) half-brother of Gratian and son of **JUSTINA & VALENTINIAN I**; recognized as co-ruler of West (Italy, Africa, Illyrium) by Gratian; 387–388 in exile in Thessalonica; a caesar compared to Theodosius I	Murdered?	371 (Treveri/Trier)	375–392 (West)

Name	Manner of death	Born	Rule
THEODOSIUS (I) THE GREAT (son of Valentinian I's general Theodosius) one of the last to reign over both East & West Roman Empire; appointed his sons Honorius (West) & Arcadius (East) to succeed him	Illness 17/1	11/1 347 (Cauca/Coca/ Spain	379–395 (East & West)
MAGNUS MAXIMUS Spanish usurper who ruled Britain, Gaul & Spain; he and his son **FLAVIUS VICTOR** as co-ruler recognized for a short time as co-emperor by Theodosius I & Valentinian II	Executed by Theodosius		383–388 (West)
***HONORIUS FLAVIUS**, co-ruler with his father Theodosius I 23/1 393–17/1 395 then sole ruler until 409 and again from 411–423 (wives: 1) **MARIA**, 2) her sister **THERMANTIA**)	Natural	9/9 384	393–423 (West)

* ATTALUS (Priscus Attalus), a usurper elevated to emperor by the Visigothic leaders Alaric & Ataulphus (409–410 & 414), was exiled by Honorius

Name	Manner of death	Born	Rule
ARCADIUS, ruled jointly with his father Theodosius I 383–395, solely 395–402, together with his son Theodosius II 402–408 (wife **EUDOXIA**)	Natural	377	383–408 (East)
CONSTANTINE III (Flavius Claudius Constantinus) usurping emperor of Britain & Gaul, recognized by Honorius 409 as joint ruler but threatened Italy; had made his son **CONSTANS** caesar 407	Executed by Honorius' generals		407–411
CONSTANTIUS III, Honorius' master of the soldiers who helped to overthrow Constantine III; in 417 married **PLACIDIA**, half-sister of Honorius; appointed co-emperor 8/2 421 but died soon afterwards, still unrecognized by the Eastern Emperor	Natural		421–421 (West)

Name	Manner of death	Born	Rule
*VALENTINIAN III (Flavius Valentinianus) son of Constantius III and Placidia who controlled the government till 437; married **LICINIA EUDOXIA** 29/10 437 (daughter of Theodosius II)	Murdered 16/3	2/7 419 in Ravenna	425–455 (West)
* JOHN, a usurper, ruled briefly in the West (423–425) on death of Honorius			
MAXIMUS PETRONIUS, proclaimed Western Emperor 17/3 455 and forced Valentinian's widow **EUDOXIA** to marry him	Killed by the people 31/5	396	455–455 (West)
THEODOSIUS II, son of Arcadius who made him co-emperor 402 (wife: **EUDOCIA**)	Of injuries from hunting accident	10/4 401	408–450 (East)
MARCIAN, ruled together with his nominal wife Empress **PULCHERIA** (d. 453), sister of Theodosius II	Natural	396	450–457 (East)
AVITUS (Eparchius Aritus) proclaimed Emperor by the Goths of Toulouse, but forced to abdicate by the 'kingmaker' Ricimer on 17/10 456			455–456 (West)
MAJORIAN (Julius Majorianus) helped to overthrow emperor Avitus (455–456)	Executed 7/8		457–461 (West)
LEO I, a Thracian who recognized Majorian in the West 457, but not his successor Libius Severus in 461; vacant throne in the West for 2 years until he installed Anthemius 467 as West Roman Emperor	Natural		457–474 (East)
LIBIUS SEVERUS, installed by the 'kingmaker' Ricimer, but never recognized by Leo I	Natural 15/8		461–465 (West)
ANTHEMIUS, son-in-law of Eastern Emperor Marcian (wife **EUPHEMIA**); his daughter **ALYPIA** married to Ricimer	Beheaded 11/7		467–472 (West)

OLYBRIUS, installed by Ricimer and emperor from April to Nov. (wife **PLACIDIA**, daughter of Valentinian III)	Natural 2/11		472–472 (West)
GLYCERIUS, installed as emperor 5/3 472 by Gundobad (nephew of Ricimer); never recognized by Leo I who sent a fleet commanded by **JULIUS NEPOS** against him	Natural		473–474 (West)
JULIUS NEPOS, proclaimed himself emperor on landing in Italy; Glycerius surrendered without a struggle	Murdered		474–475 (West)
ZENO, father of Leo II (474–474 who died 7 years old); in exile 475–Aug. 476 when **BASILISCUS** (brother-in-law of Leo I) ruled in Constantinople; appointed Theodoric to replace Odoacer as king of Italy (489)	Natural	Isauria	475–491 (East)
ROMULUS AUGUSTULUS, usurper and last of the Western Roman Emperors; installed on the throne 31/10 475 after his father Orestes (who ruled Italy in his young son's name) had deposed Julius Nepos; German warrior **ODOACER** captured & executed Orestes 28/8 476	Unknown		475–476

End of Western Roman Empire

CLASSICAL MISCELLANY

The Sevens

The seven against Thebes

The seven military leaders in the civil war between Oedipus' twin sons Eteocles and Polyneices

6 TYDEUS
8 CAPANEUS
  ETEOCLUS
10 AMPHIBRAUS
  POLYNEICES (or ADRASTUS)
  HIPPOMEDON (or ADRASTUS)
13 PARTHENOPAEUS

The seven deadly sins

4 ENVY
  LUST
5 ANGER
  PRIDE
  SLOTH
8 GLUTTONY
12 COVETOUSNESS

The seven Epigoni

The seven sons of the seven chieftains against Thebes

8 ALCMAEON
  DIOMEDES
  EURYALUS
9 AEGIALEUS
  PROMACHOS
  STHENELUS
11 AMPHILOCHUS

The seven hills of Rome

7 CAELIAN
  VIMINAL
8 AVENTINE
  PALATINE
9 ESQUILINE
  QUITRINAL
10 CAPITOLINE

The seven Pleiades

(stars)

Daughters of Atlas & Pleione

4 MAIA
6 MEROPE
7 TAYGETE
  ALCYONE (brightest)

7 CELAENO
  ELECTRA
8 ASTEROPE (faintest)

The seven senses

5 SIGHT
  SMELL
  TASTE
6 SPEECH
7 FEELING
  HEARING
13 UNDERSTANDING

The seven sleepers of Ephesus

Western tradition

4 JOHN
5 DENIS
7 MALCHUS
  MARCIAN
8 MAXIMIAN
  SERAPION
11 CONSTANTINE

Eastern tradition

4 JOHN
6 MARTIN
8 ANTONIUS
9 DIONYSIUS
10 JAMBLICHUS
  MAXIMILIAN
11 CONSTANTINE

The seven wise men

(according to Plato)

4 BIAS
5 MYSON
  SOLON
6 CHILON
  THALES
8 PITTACUS
9 CLEOBOLUS

The Seven Wonders of the World

1 The **PYRAMIDS** of Egypt
2 The **TOMB of MAUSOLOS in Bodrum**
3 The **COLOSSUS** at Rhodes
4 The **HANGING GARDENS** of Babylon
5 The **TEMPLE OF ARTEMIS** at Ephesus
6 The **STATUE OF ZEUS** by Phidias
7 The **PHAROS of Alexandria** or
The **PALACE OF CYRUS** cemented with gold

The Threes

The Cyclops

Three round-eyed sons of Uranus & Gaia who forged the thunderbolts for Zeus; one-eyed cannibal giants (Homer) who built walls of ancient cities.

5 ARGES Bright
7 BRONTES Thunderous
8 STEROPES Lightener

The Furies

Avenging deities – ERINYES or EUMENIDES – sent from Tartarus to avenge wrong and punish crime.

6 ALECTO Unceasing in Anger
7 MEGAERA Jealous
9 TISIPHONE Avenger of Murder

The three Gorgons

Winged female creatures with hair of snakes; daughters of Phorcys and his sister-wife Ceto who were children of Gaia and Pontus, the sea.

6 MEDUSA The Queen
7 EURYALE The Far Springer
   STHENNO The Mighty

The three Gorgon sisters

with only one eye between them

4 DINO
   ENYO
9 PEMPHREDO

The three Graces

Goddesses of fertility and charm, associated with Aphrodite; daughters of Zeus by Hera or Eurynome (daughter of Oceanus) or of Helios and Aegle.

6 AGLAIA Brightness
   THALIA Bloom
10 EUPHROSYNE Joyfulness

The Greek fates

6 CLOTHO spins the thread of life
   The Spinner
7 ATROPOS cuts it off
   The Inflexible One
8 LACHESIS controls its destiny
   The Disposer of Lots

The Hecatoncheires

Hundred-handed giants, children of Uranus and Gaia/Ge.

4 GYES
6 COTTUS
8 BRIAREUS

The Seasons (Horae)

Three daughters of Zeus and Themis or of Helios (sun) and Selene (moon)

4 DIKE Justice
6 EIRENE Peace
7 EUNOMIA Good Order

The Fours

The Harpies

Malignant monsters with birds' wings and claws who snatched away the souls of the dead.

5 AELLO Stormswift
7 OCYPETE Swiftwing
   CELAENO Dark one
   PODARGE Swiftfoot

The four primary divine beings

From whom Erebus (the dark void) and Night were born.

4 EROS Love
4/6 GAIA/GE Earth
5 CHAOS Space
8 TARTARUS Hell

The pyramids of Egypt

5 ZOSER
6 CHEOPS
   KHAFRE
8 HENKAURA

Some Others

Sixteen nymphs

4 ECHO repulses Pan
5 THETIS mother of Achilles
6 AEGINA wife of Zeus
CALYCE mother of Endymion
DAPHNE of a mountain
MEROPE wife of river god Asopos
RHODAS mated with the sun Helios
THOOSA mother of Polyphemus
7 ASTERIA mother of Hecate
CLYMENE wife of Helios, mother of Phaethon
GALATEA of the sea
8 ARETHUSA one of the Hesperides
CASTALIA excited Apollo
ECHENAIS loved by Daphnis
PENELOPE mother of Pan, wife of Odysseus, wife of Hermes
PERIBOCA mother of Penelope

Groups of nymphs by habitat

6 DRYADS of the trees
NAIADS of caves and springs
7 NEREIDS of the sea
10 HAMADRYADS of trees

The six wives of Hermes

5 HERSE son Cephalus, a hero
6 CHIONE son Autolycus
8 AGLAUCUS son Ceryx, first high priest of Eleusis
PENELOPE son Pan
DEIANIRA
10 PERSEPHONE son Eleusis, eponymous hero

The nine Muses

4 CLIO History
5 ERATO Erotic Poetry
6 THALIA Comedy
URANIA Astronomy
7 EUTERPE Lyric Poetry
8 CALLIOPE Epic Song
9 MELPOMENE Tragedy
10 POLYHMNIA Hymns
11 TERPSICHORE Dance

The twelve Titans

(Children of Heaven/Uranus & Earth/Ge/Gaia)

4 RHEA
THEA
5 COIUS
CRIUS
6 CRONUS
PHOEBE
TETHYS
THEM1S
7 IAPETUS
OCEANIIS
8 HYPERION
9 MNEMOSYNE

The Hesperides

Guardians of Golden Apples; variously daughters of Erebus & night, Atlas & Hesperis, or Phorcys & Ceto

5 AEGLE
8 ARETHUSA
ERYTHEIA
HESPERIS or
12 HESPERETHUSA

Offspring of Zeus

(the son of Cronus & Rhea)

3 ATE (d) evil; evicted from Olympus by Zeus
ARES (s) god of war; warlike spirit; mother: Hera
4 HEBE (d) mother: Hera; goddess of youth; married Heracles
5 AEGLE (d) wife of Helios (sun god); sometimes claimed as mother of the Three Graces
ARCAS (s) mother: Callisto; ancestor of the Arcadians
BELUS (s) mother: Io; father of Danaus & Aegyptus

5 HELEN (d) mother: Leda of Sparta; wife of Tyndareus
MINOS (s) mother: Europa; King of Crete
6 AEACUS (s) mother: nymph of Aegina
AGLAIA (d) one of the Three Graces
APOLLO (s) mother: Leto; god of divine distance, crops & herds; Averter of Evil (Alexikakos); common to Greece & Rome
ATHENE (d) mother: Metis; virgin goddess of war & good counsel
CLOTHO (d) one of the Three Fates
HERMES (s) mother: Maia; fertility & messenger god born in a cave
POLLUX (s) mother: Leda; twin-brother of Castor (the Dioscuri)

6 THALIA (d) one of the Three Graces
ZETHUS (s) mother: Antiope
7 AMPHION (s) mother: Antiope
ARTEMIS (d) mother: Leto; goddess of
wild nature; sister of Apollo
PERSEUS (s) mother: Danae; founder
of Mycenae; King of Argos
ZAGREUS (s) mother: Persephone;
killed as a child by the Titans
8 DARDANUS (s) mother: Electra;
founder of Troy; grandfather of
Tros
DIONYSUS (s) mother: Semele; wine
god
ENDYMION (s) mother: nymph Calyce;
King of Elis
HERACLES (s) mother: Alcmene; of the
12 Labours

8 LACHESIS (d) one of the Three Fates
SARPEDON (s) mother: Europa; leader
of Lycian forces in Trojan War
TANTALUS (s) punished by eternal
thirst & hunger; ancestor of
Pelopids
10 HEPHAESTUS (s) mother: Hera; smith
god
PERSEPHONE (d) mother: Demeter;
wife of Hades; as Kore, grain
goddess
11 EUPHROSYNE (d) one of the Three
Graces
12 RHADAMANTHUS (s) mother: Europa;
King of the Cyclades islands

Consorts of Zeus

2 IO daughter of Inachus (river god of
Argos); priestess Callithyia
4 HERA sister & wife of Zeus; Queen of
Heaven; as Eileithyia, birth goddess
LEDA daughter of Thestius (King of
Aetolia); Zeus swanned around and
so she leda-'n-egg hatching Helen &
Pollux
LETO daughter of Coeus & Phoebe
(Titans); goddess of fertility
MAIA eldest of the 7 daughters of Titan
Atlas (the Pleiades) by Pleione
5 DANAE daughter of Acrisius, King of
Argos
METIS (wise counsel); Zeus mated with
Metis by mouth and Athene was his
brainchild
6 AEGINA daughter of river god Asopus
& nymph Merope
CALYCE a nymph; mother of
Endymion who was loved by moon
goddess Selene
EUROPA daughter of Phoenix who rose
from the ashes to take Zeus, the
bull, by the horns to Crete
SEMELE daughter of Cadmus (founder
of Thebes) and Harmonia; niece of
Europa
SELENE moon goddess; daughter of Eos
THEMIS steadfast daughter of Gaia;
prophetess; mother of the Seasons &
the Fates
7 ALCMENE daughter of Electryon, king
of Mycenae; wife of Amphitryon
who killed his uncle Electryon

7 *ANTIOPE daughter of Nycteus (one of
the Spartoi) raped by Zeus in the
guise of a satyr
DEMETER sister & consort of Zeus;
goddess of agriculture, health, birth
& marriage & divinity of the
underworld
****ELECTRA** daughter of Atlas &
pleione; mother of the Cabeiri
(Cabiri), protectors of seafarers &
promoters of fertility
8 CALLISTO handmaiden of Artemis who
changed her into a she-bear; later,
by courtesy of Zeus, she stars as
Ursa Major and her son (Arcas) as
Arcturus
EURYNOME daughter of Oceanus;
together with Hera & Aegle
variously regarded as mother of the
Three Graces
GANYMEDE son of Tros (or
Laomedon), King of Troy; Latin
Catamitus; kidnapped by Zeus in
the guise of an eagle
10 PERSEPHONE daughter & consort of
Zeus; as Persephassa goddess of the
dead

* not to be confused with the daughter of Ares,
god of war, or a queen of the Amazones.
** not to be confused with the mother of the
Harpies Aello & Okypete, or the daughter of
Agamemnon and Clytemnestra

Brothers & Sisters of Zeus

4 HERA Queen of Olympus; mother of
Ares (god of war), Hebe (goddess of
youth & cupbearer to the gods),
Hephaestus

5 HADES ruled the underworld together
with his queen Persephone

7 DEMETER goddess of agriculture; bore
Plutus (Wealth) by her consort
Iason, and Persephone by Zeus; also
known as Ioulo

8 POSEIDON god of sea, water, earthquakes;
also worshipped as 'Hippios' (of
horses); divine ancestor of rulers of
Thessaly & Messenia

Offspring of Poseidon

(brother of Zeus)

5 ARION/AREION by DEMETER; swift horse
who saved the life of Adrastus, King
of Argos

ORION son of EURYALE, one of the
Gorgons

6 NELEUS son of TYRO; father of Nestor,
Pero, etc.

PELIAS brother of Neleus

TRITON son by AMPHITRITE; minor sea god

7 ANCAEUS son by TEGEA; King of the
Leleges of Samos

ANTAEUS son by GAIA; wrestling giant
of Libya, crushed by Heracles

BUSIRIS son by LYSSIANASSA; King of
Egypt (Usire/Osiris); killed by
Heracles

***GLAUCUS** gleaming son, in love with
sea god Melicertes; merman covered
with shells and seaweed; sea god

7 PEGASUS by the monster MEDUSA;
winged horse

8 EUMOLPUS sweet-singing son by
CHIONE, daughter of Boreas (North
Wind); King of Thrace

NAUPLIUS son by AMYMONE, one of
Danaus' 50 daughters

10 AMPHIMARUS son; father by Linus (the
musician killed by Apollo) by the
Muse Urania

POLYPHEMUS son by the nymph
THOOSA; sea god and one of the
Cyclopes; made Odysseus his
prisoner

* not to be confused with a) son of Sisyphus
(King of Corinth) by Merope: father of
Bellerophon; b) the honeyed son of King Minos
(Crete) and Pasiphae; c) 'gold for bronze' Lycian
prince, ally of Priam in the Trojan War; grandson
of Bellerophon

Trojan War

*Besiegers of Troy and ancestors &
offspring*

4 AJAX colossal son of Telamon (king of
Salamis); took on Hector
single-handed; rescued body of
Achilles from the Trojans

AJAX small son of Oileus (king of
Locri); violated Cassandra; drowned
by Poseidon

5 CREON father of Lycomedes of Scyros
who hosted Achilles, and killed
Theseus, Attic hero

6 ATREUS father of Agamemnon &
Menelaus by Aerope; son of Pelops;
later married Pelopia, daughter &
wife of Thyestes

DANAOI besiegers of Troy

MOPSUS seer and son of Manto by
Carian king Rhacius (or Apollo);
challenged Calchas after fall of Troy

6 NESTOR son of Neleus (brother of Pelias,
son of Poseidon by Tyro); Achaean
leader; sailed home after the war

PELEUS father of Achilles; husband of
Thetis (one of the Nereids)

TEUCER half-brother of Ajax; famous
archer; defended Achaean camp;
founded city of Salamis on Cyprus

7 ARGEIOI besiegers of Troy

CALCHAS seer of the Achaean forces;
son of Thestor; priest of Apollo

ORESTES son of Agamemnon &
Clytemnestra

PROTEUS helped Menelaus to reach
Sparta; assistant to Poseidon

8 ACHAEANS besieged Troy together
with the Danaoi & Argeioi

ACHILLES son of Peleus (king of the
Myrmidons) & Thetis; handsome
warrior of Agamemnon's army;
killed Hector

8 DIOMEDES commander of 80 Argive ships and important leader; son of Tydeus (one of seven against Thebes); wounded Aphrodite; took the Trojan Palladium

MENELAUS brother of Agamemnon; husband of Helen

ODYSSEUS (also known as ULYSSES) captured Troy by means of the wooden horse; suitor of Helen; king of Ithaca and son of Laertes & Anticleia; father by Penelope of Telemachus

TELEPHUS wounded by Achilles; guided Achaean fleet to Troy; son of Heracles & Ange

9 AGAMEMNON commander-in-chief of the forces against Troy; brother of Menelaus; kin of Mycenae or Argos and son of Atreus and Aerope; husband of Clytemnestra (daughter of Tyndareus, king of Sparta); murdered by their son Orestes; his daughters: Iphigeneia/Iphianassa (sacrificed to Artemis), Electra/Laodice, Chrysothemis

PATROCLUS cousin of Achilles and allowed to impersonate him; killed by Hector

10 ANTILOCHUS son of Nestor; killed by Memnon

TELEMACHUS son of Odysseus by Penelope; welcomed by Nestor when searching for his father

Defenders of Troy and ancestors & offspring

4 ILUS ancestor of Priam; one of the three sons of Tros

TROS grandson of Dardanus; father of Ilus, Ganymede & Arsaracus

5 HELEN daughter of Zeus by Leda or Nemesis; sister of Clytemnestra; wife of Menelaus of Sparta; after death of Paris wife of his brother Deiphobus whom she betrayed; indirect cause of the war

PARIS son of Priam; stole Helen and caused the Trojan War

5 PRIAM King of troy (VII) son of Laomedon; also known as Podarces; father of Hector, Paris, Cassandra, Polyxena, Helenus, Polydorus, Troilus

6 AENEAS cousin of Hector; leader of Trojan survivors; founder of Rome; son of Trojan Anchises by Aphrodite

HECTOR chief Trojan warrior; eldest son of Priam

HECUBA wife of Priam

MEMNON hero and brother of Priam; son of Eos (dawn); King of Ethiopia; killed Antilochus and was killed by Achilles

7 ANTENOR elder of the city of troy; advised the Trojans to return Helen to Menelaus, and Agamemnon to give up girl he stole from Achilles

GLAUCUS ally of Troy; leader of the Lycian forces

HELENUS son of Priam and Hecuba

HESIONE daughter of Laomedon

TROILUS son of Priam; killed early by Achilles

8 ANCHISES father of Aeneas by Aphrodite; king of Dardanus on Mt Ida

ASTYANAX son of Hector

DARDANUS founder of Troy; grandfather of Tros; son of Zeus & Electra; father of Erichtonius

GANYMEDE one of the three sons of Tros

LAOMEDON father of Priam and Hesione; refused to pay Apollo and Poseidon for building the walls of Troy; he and all his sons (except Priam) killed by Heracles

POLYXENA daughter of Priam and Hecuba

SARPEDON ally of Priam; leader of the Lycian forces

TITHONUS son of Laomedon, king of Troy, and brother of Priam; father of Memnon by Eos; made immortal but not ageless by Zeus

9 ARSARACUS one of the three sons of Tros

POLYDORUS son of Priam and Hecuba

ANDROMACHE wife of Hector

Argonautica, on Board and Ashore

3 INO second wife of ATHAMAS who hated his children by NEPHELE and wanted PHRIXUS sacrificed

5 AESON father of JASON deprived of the throne of Iolcos by his half-brother PELIAS

5 CIRCE witch-goddess & sister of the king of Colchis (or daughter of HELIOS, the sun god, & nymph PERSE); freed MEDEA & JASON from the guilt of murdering ABSYRTUS

CREON king of Corinth whose daughter caught JASON's fancy and drove MEDEA mad with rage

HELLE daughter of JASON's uncle ATHAMAS by NEPHELE, the cloud goddess; tried to escape by sea with her brother PHRIXUS on the ram with the golden fleece; drowned in the Hellespont

JASON son of AESON who had been told by his uncle PELIAS to fetch the Golden Fleece of Colchis if he wanted to regain the throne of Iolcos, his rightful inheritance; assembled fifty heroes on board 'Argo' and set sail to find this fleece washed in a gold-carrying stream of the Caucasus; met MEDEA and married her on the return voyage

MEDEA enchantress of JASON who escaped with him and the Golden Fleece from Colchis; killed PELIAS on their return and turned murderous in jealousy towards the daughter of CREON, killing both, and her own children by JASON; later became Queen to AEGEUS of Athens and when attempting to poison her stepson THESEUS was exiled; eventually reached Colchis and restored her father AEETES as king; by some accounts her Athenian son MEDUS later gave his name to the country of the Medes (Media) who later joined with the Persians

TALOS rock-throwing bronze giant; a creation of the god Hephaestus; invulnerable to fire, but made drunk by MEDEA who by prising out the bronze nail in his foot killed him

6 AEETES King of Colchis and father of MEDEA; refused to give up the Golden Fleece and placed many obstacles in the way of JASON & MEDEA

AEGEUS king of Athens who received the refugee MEDEA and married her

AMYCUS ruler in Bithynia of the savage Bebryces; killed by POLYDEUCES

6 CHIRON king of the CENTAURS (half man half horse); educator of JASON, ACHILLES & ASCLEPIUS (god of medicine, son of APOLLO and the nymph CORONIS)

MOPSUS seer (one of two); sailed on 'Argo'; died of snake bite in Libya

PELIAS king of Iolcos and uncle of JASON; usurper

SIRENS daughters of the river god ARCHELOUS; spurned by the Argonauts

TIPHYS navigator of the Argonauts

TRITON minor sea god, son of POSEIDON by AMPHITRITE; assisted JASON

7 ANCAEUS navigator of the Argonauts after TIPHYS

ATHAMAS uncle of JASON; king of the MINYANS in Boeotian city of Orchomenus; father of PHRIXUS & HELLE by NEPHELE; later consort of jealous INO

CYANEAN ROCKS (the Symplegades) two moving cliffs at the mouth of the Bosphorus that crushed whatever sought to pass

CYZICUS king of the DOLIONES who was killed by JASON

HARPIES supernatural winged beings; tormentors of king PHINEUS

MINYANS the tribe of JASON whose most prominent members took part in the expedition

NEPHELE first wife and cloud goddess of ATHAMAS who bore him HELLE and PHRIXUS

ORPHEUS musician and husband of EURYDICE, a dryad

PHINEUS aged and blind king whose food was spoilt by the HARPIES; he told the Argonauts the course to Colchis and how to clear the CYANEAN ROCKS

PHRIXUS son of ATHAMAS and brother of HELLE who escaped to Colchis on the ram with the Golden Fleece; on arrival he killed the ram and hung up the fleece in the grove of ARES there to be guarded by a dragon which MEDEA later put to sleep

8 ABSYRTUS son of AEETES and younger brother of MEDEA

ALCIMEDE perhaps the wife of AESON and mother of JASON

DOLIONES the tribe ruled by CYZICUS

10 POLYDEUCES one of the Argonauts who defeated the Bithynian king AMYCUS in a fist fight

A Sweep around the World in Mythology

Ass. Assyrian Fin. Finnish Jap. Japanese
S.Am. South American Bab. Babylonian
Ger. German N.Am. North American Scan.
Scandinavian C.Am. Central American Gr.
Greek N.Z. New Zealand Sem. Semitic Ch.
Chinese Hung. Hungarian Pers. Persian
Sum. Sumerian Eg. Egyptian It. Italian
Rom. Roman

1 I (Ch.) the Excellent Archer; husband of **CH'ANG-O**, Moon goddess

2 AN ANU (Sum/Sem.) supreme sky god; see **BEL/BAAL/MARDUK & EA**

AN (Brazil/Tupinamba Indian) the Soul

BA (Eg.) 'soul', immortal element (**KA**)

DA (Africa/Benin) assistant to the creator-god **MAWU** of the Fon people

EA ENKI (Sum./Sem.) 'House of the Water', god of the **APSU** & supreme wisdom; see **BEL/BAAL**

EC (Siberia) Yeniseian high god who swallowed souls

EL Creator & chief god of the Sem./ Ugaritic pantheon; see **BEL/BAAL, ALEYIN & MOT**

FU SHEN (Ch.) 'the bat', dispenser of Happiness; see **SHOU HSING & TS'AI-SHEN**

GE GAEA/GAIA (Gr.) Mother Earth born of **CHAOS**; mother of **URANUS** & the 12 **TITANS**

HU (Ch.) deity of creative will; emperor/god of the North Sea

HU (Eg.) crew member, with **SHIA**, of the solar barque of **RE**

IO (Gr.) mistress of cloud-disguised **ZEUS** who turned her into a white heifer; equated with Eg. **ISIS**

IO (N.Z./Maori) supreme being with eternal abode in the highest of 12 heavens

JE (Ch.) the Sun

KA (Eg.) 'spirit', immortal element (**BA**)

KA (India) Who? Indefinable Absolute (Brahma)

LI (Ch.) the Earth

LU HSING (Ch.) deer-mounted god of prosperity

MA Hittite/Hurrian **HEBAT**, goddess of war (Rom. **BELLONA**)

NU (Eg.) frog-headed male or female aquatic god, waist-high in water; see **NUN**

NU & KUA (Ch.) incestuous couple

whose relationship resulted in the human race

OM sacred syllable; eternal soul; penetrator & cause of the universe (India/Brahman)

OT Mongolian Queen of fire

PO (Polynesia) the Void (Chaos) from which the world evolved; place of the dead; see **HINA**

RA RE/PHRA (Eg.) supreme celestial & solar god & creator; son of **GEB** (Earth) and **NUT** (Sky); see **HAPI & MAAT**

SA (Eg.) hieroglyphic sign & magic, vital fluid of every divine 'Lord of the City'

TU (Polynesia) chief warrior god

UL (Oceania) lord of the moon and spirit of night

UO (C.Am.) trusted frog-mates of Mayan rain gods **CHAAC**

VE (Norse) son of **BOR & BESTLA**; brother of **ODIN**; (Ger.) sacred places

WO (Africa/Cameroon) the chimpanzee son of **ZAMBA** (God)

YU (Ch.) monster & great tamer of the flood

ZU (Sum./Sem.) thieving storm-bird from whom **MARDUK** recovered the Tablets of Fate, token of the all-powerful supreme gods

3 AER Air, pure intelligence, born of Desire & Darkness (Phoenician cosmology); begat cosmic Egg with **AURA** (breath)

AHI IHI (Eg.) sistrum-playing son of Hethor & Horus of Edfu

AHU (Polynesia) raised shrine for offerings within the marae

AMA (Jap.) Japan-like Heaven linked to Earth by a heavenly bridge

AMA TSU-KAMI gods of the Earth (Jap.)

ANU (Sem.) see **AN, ANSHAR**

ANU Celtic mother-goddess (**ANA/DANU**)

APO (India) 'the Water' (Vedic apas); see **APSU**

ASK ASH/ASKR (Norse) forefather of man by his wife **EMBLA**; son of **ODIN**

ASO holy mountain in S. Japan

ATE (Gr.) malevolent daughter of **ERIS** or **ZEUS** who led gods & men astray; exiled by **HERACLES** & followed by her limping sisters, the **LITAE**

AYA (Ass./Bab.) wife of **SHAMASH**, sun-god & soothsayer who revealed the future

AZI (Altaic) forest and mountain spirit

BAU (Sum.) she gave the kiss of life to

man; daughter of **AN/ANU** & wife of **NINGURSU/NINURTA**

BEL (Sum.) **BAAL** ('Lord', a title conferred on a number of gods by the Phoenicians) god of War & Rain; son of **EL**; see **MARDUK, ENLIL**

BES BISU (Eg.) large-headed dwarf with bushy tail; god of recreation

BOR (Norse) father of **ODIN** by **BESTLA**; see **MIDGARD, VILI, VE**

COU CU CHULAINN (Ulster Cycle) tribal hero; father of **FINN**

DIA (Gr.) was seduced by **ZEUS** disguised as a horse; wife of **IXION** (king of the Lapiths) who, as punishment for casting eyes on **HERA**, was bound to a fiery wheel rolling ceaselessly through the sky

DIS Roman **HADES**, divinity of the Netherworld

DON DANU (Welsh/Irish) god of fertility & the forge; fiend of the Children of Darkness (**LLYR**); father of **GWYDION**

EOS (Gr.) the Dawn & mother of the winds **ZEPHYRUS, NOTUS, BOREAS** and **HESPERUS** (the evening star) & all stars, and **PHAETHON** by **CEPHALUS**; sister of **HELIOS & SELENE**; daughter of **HYPERION & THEIA** (Titans) (Rom. **AURORA**)

FAL (Irish/Celtic) stone of Fal which gave a cry when stepped on by the rightful king of Ireland; one of 4 magical treasures (**DAGDA**/cauldron; **LUG**/spear; **NUADA**/sword) possessed by the chieftain gods of the Irish Tuatha De Danann

FAM (Africa/Bantu) an Adam, created by an invisible father; see **NZAME**

GEB KEB/SEB (Eg.) goose or male with head surmounted by a goose (ideogram of his name); earth god

HAP (Eg.) see **HAPI**

HEH NEHEH (Eg.) Infinity, Happiness & Long Life; husband of **HEHET**

HEL (Norse) Queen of Niflheim (nine worlds of Darkness); goddess of death and daughter of **ODIN**'s rogue **LOKI**

HAP HEP (Eg.) see **HAPI**

HOD (Norse) killer of **BALDR**; see **HODUR**

IAB (Samoyed) spirit of nature

IDA mountain on Crete & birthplace of **ZEUS**; Mt in Asia Minor near Troy; ancient Germanic temples

IFA (Nigeria/Yoruba) the Great Truth

INO (Gr.) mother of Melicertes who was carried by a dolphin to Corinth; sister of **SEMELE** whose baby, **DIONYSUS**, she had cared for, much to the annoyance of **HERA**; nymph Leucothes

ION (Gr.) forefather of the Ionian people; prince of Athens; son of **CREUSA & APOLLO**

ITI (Oceania) the Moon; see **VATEA**

KEB GEB/SEB separated from his sister & spouse **NUT** by their father **SHU**

KUA see **NU**

KUL (Siberia/Ostyaks) genie that haunted big lakes & deep waters

KUU (Fin.) father of Kuutar; 'moon' in Finnish

LAR LARES (plur.) (Rom.; Etruscan 'chief' or 'prince') the juvenile family guardian of the household whose altar was the hearth

LHA (gods) & **DRE** (demons) Tibetan supernatural beings; Buddhist deities

LIR Irish sea god; father of **MANANNAN**

LOA (Oceania/Marshall I.) creator of the world

LUG (Irish/Celtic) **LAMFOTA** intellectual father of Ulster hero **CU CHULAINN/ COU**; Welsh **LLEU/LLAW/GYFFES**, uncle of **GWYDION** & son of virgin **ARANRHOD**; also Lugnasad fertility feast (1 August)

MAH MAO (Pers.) moon god and assistant of **VOHU MANAH**

MAO MAHOU (Africa/Dahomey) superior being

MEN Hittite/Hurrian mounted lunar god associated with **ATTIS** and Thracian **SABAZIUS**; (Pers. **MAH/MAO**)

MIN AKHMIN (Eg.) son of **RA**; ithyphallic Pan-god of fertility & travellers

MOT (Sem.) god of the Dead, harvest deity; son of **EL**; killed by **BAAL** (who was helped by his sister/wife **ANATH/ ANAT**)

MUT (Eg.) as **HERA**, wife of **AMON-RA**, becoming Queen of the Gods; also appears as **BAST/BASTET** or cat or lioness-headed goddess **TEFNUT** or Pekhet, patron of music and festivals

NIO (Jap.) Herculean spirits

NUM (Siberia) sky god, like **TORUM** and **EC**

NUN (Eg.) primordial ocean; see **NU**

NUT NUIT/NEUTH (Eg.) mother of **OSIRIS, HORUS, SETH, NEPHTHYS, ISIS**; goddess of the sky; (Gr. **RHEA**)

NYX (Gr.) (Night) son of **CHAOS**; brother of **EREBUS** (shadows)

ONI (Jap.) malevolent forces/devils;

Oni of Hell have red or green bodies
& heads of oxen or horses

OPS Roman goddess of crops; wife of
SATURN

ORO Tahitian deity who rules the
Underworld

PAN (Gr.) son of **HERMES & PENELOPE**
& part of the cult of **DIONYSUS**;
shepherd god of woods & pastures,
worshipped as phallic he-goat (Satyr)
in grottoes by Arcadians; great
nymph chaser, one, Syrinx, became a
reed so he cut several to make Panpipes; also surprised lone travellers
causing 'panics'; known as Priapus in
Asia Minor.

PAN NYAMIA (Africa) son of the Earth;
god of the sky and cultivation

QAT (Siberia) spirits residing on high
mountain tops

QAT QUAT (Australia/New Hebrides)
chief god, hero or spirit; rel.
TANGAROA

RAM (Eg.) most sacred Ram Ba Neb
Djedet (see **BANADED**); (Celtic) cult
animal associated with ram-headed
serpent god Cernunnos

RAN (Norse) 'the ravisher' wife of
AEGIR who used a (drag)net to capture
men; her 9 daughters were also
temptresses

ROT Lappish deity of the Netherworld

SEB KEB/GEB father of the Osirian gods

SET SETH (Eg.) brother or son of **OSIRIS**
whom he killed & rival of **HORUS**;
incarnation of evil & the arid desert

SHU (Eg.) god of light & air, supporter
of the sky; unisexually created by **RA**;
brother & husband of **TEFNUT** (1st
couple of the Ennead) who bore him
GEB & NUT

SIF (Norse) Thor's faithful wife

SIN NANNA (Bab./Sum.) moon god and
Lord of the Second Cosmic Triad;
see ISHTAR

SOL INDIGES Rom. sun god (Gr.
HELIOS)

SUN Hittite weather god; father of
TELEPINU

TYR TIW (Norse) an **AESIR** and one-
handed god whose other hand was
severed by the hideous wolf **FENRIR**;
(Rom. **MARS**); (Tuesday)

ULL (Norse) AESIR enchanter & stepson
of **THOR**; patron of snowshoes

UNO (Hung.) female deer/heifer;
ancestor of the Hungarians

UTU (Sum.) god of sun & justice with
head of buffalo; son of **NANNA/SIN &
NINGAL**; see ISHTAR

YIN (Ch.) the Earth, moon being the
essence of **YIN; YIN**/fem.–**YANG**/masc.,
theory of opposite & complementary
forces in nature

YUE (Ch.) the Moon and the lunar
month

4 ABUK (Africa/S.Sudan) spirit & fem.
name of one of the first Dinka; see
DENG

ACIS (Gr.) Sicilian shepherd crushed
under a rock by jealous Polyphemus,
the main Cyclops, blinded by
ODYSSEUS; see **GALATEA**

ADAD (Bab.) see HADAD

ADAM Persian-Mazdean first man, after
JINNS; also Gayomart-Adam

ADAT (N.Borneo) governs the Cosmos
acc. to Dayak/Iban belief; 'custom' in
Arabic

AEON ancestor of the first inhabitants
of Phoenicia, Genos & Genea; see
BAAU

AGNI (India/Hindu) two-faced, many-
tongued mouthpiece of the gods; god
of fire & lightning (Gr. Hephaestus);
see **RUDRA**

AHTO AHTI (Fin.) chief water god;
husband of **VELLAMO** (Kalevala)

AJAX (Gr.) see Trojan War, besiegers

AKKA RAUNI (Fin.) sacred mountain
ash; 'old woman' in Finnish; see **UKKO**

AKNA (C.Am.) divinity of childbirth;
wife of **AKANCHOB**

AMMA (Bokina Faso/Dogon) chief god
& creator among 8 sacred pairs;
(Sudan) father of Yurugu & Nommo

**AMON AMMON, AMEN, AMANA, AMON-
RA, AMOM** (Eg.) King of the Gods,
18th-dynasty conqueror of Thebes;
the phallic, or Ram, **AMON**
represented regeneration, fertility,
harvests & was patron of the Pharaoh;
husband of **MUT** (mother) with
adopted son **KHONS**

ANAT ANATH (Sem.) sister & wife of
BAAL

ANPU (Eg.) see ANUBIS

APEP APEPI (Eg.) swallower of solar
barque

APET OPET/TAUERET (Eg.)
hippopotamus deity of maternity &
household

APSU (Ass./Bab.) earth-encircling
sweet water; united with **TIAMAT**, salt
water, to bring forth all beings (Gr.
OCEANUS); see **EA, APO & MARDUK**

ARES (Gr.) spear-brandishing warrior from Thrace; companions: **ERIS, ENYO, DEIMOS, PHOBOS**

ASET ISIS (Eg.) member of the Osirian Triad

ASHA (Persia) 'universal law', born of **AHURU MAZDA**, king of Nature

ASIA (Gr.) rivals Oceanid Clymene as mother of **ATLAS**; (Africa/Guinea) Earth goddess; (Siberia) see **MAMALDI**

ATAR (Persia) Mazdean-Zoroastrian FIRE, comforting & wise; accompanies the Sun's chariot

ATEA (Oceania/Marquesas I.) creator & father of Dawn/**ATANUA**; rel. **RANGI**, sky-god (N.Z.)

ATEN ATON (Eg.) solar disk whose rays end in hands; Atenism introduced by Akhenaten/Amenophis **IV**, married to Nefertiti

ATRI (India) son of **BRAHMA**; father of **SOMA**

ATUA (Polynesia) the gods

ATUM ATUM-RA/RE/TUM (Eg.) mongoose-headed, self-fertilizing creator (ichneumon) god; the setting Sun, father of **SHU & TEENUT**

AUGE priestess of **ATHENE** seduced by **HERCULES**

AURA (Phoenicia) 'breath'; see **AER**

BAAL (Sem./Rom. Jupiter) Lord of the Earth & chief Ugaritic warrior, rain & fertility god; son of **EL**; husband of **ISHTAR**/Asherat; see **BEL, MARDUK, MOT**

BAAU (Sem.) wife of Kolpia & mother of **AEON**

BADB war goddess in the Celtic Triad of 'Valkyries'; see **MORRIGAN & MACKA**

BAST BASTET (Eg.) cat-headed goddess in Bubastis of music & dance & spouse of Ptah of Memphis

BIAS (Gr.) brother of **MELAMPUS**, seer & descendant of **AEOLUS** (son of **HELLEN**)

BISU (Eg.) see **BES**

BOUS (Norse) son of **ODIN & RINDA** who killed the blind **HODUR/HOD**

BRAN (Celtic) the blessed giant & poet who waded across the Irish Sea; child of **LLYR**

BRES (Celtic/Irish) King of the Tuatha Dé Dannan (people of goddess **DANU**) who married **BRIGIT**, daughter of the chieftain **DAGDA**; forced to abdicate which resulted in a war fought with magical weapons between the Tuatha & the Fomorians

BULL Universal symbol of power & strength (**EL**/Canaan); (Persia) Gosh/ Bull & Gayomart/first man, the animal/human pair which produced all life; Bull of Mithraism; emblem of the Great God (Crete)

BUNI (Siberia) chief of the Netherworld

BURI (Norse) grandfather of **ODIN, VILI & VE**, the 3 brothers who killed **YMIR** and formed the earth, named Midgard, from his body; see **AUDUMLA**

BUTO (Eg.) nurse of **HORUS**; cobra-goddess; she & **NEKHEBET**, the **NEBTI**, appeared on royal documents or on Pharoah's forehead

CAGN (Africa) omnipotent creator and chief Bushman deity whose abode is known only to antelopes; husband of Coti

CETO (Gr.) daughter of Pontus & Gaia with a heart of steel; mother of the Gorgons, the dragon Ladon (father of Syrinx & **DAPHNE**) & perhaps also of the Hesperides

CEYX (Gr.) & wife Alcyone turned into birds for comparing themselves to **ZEUS & HERA**; changed by **APOLLO** into a sparrow-hawk

CHIN (C.Am./Yucatan) Mayan god of Vice

CLIO (Gr.) Muse of History, with trumpet & clepsydra

DANU Irish Celtic mother goddess

DENG (Africa/S.Sudan) weather god; with **ABUK** & Garang founder of the Dinka religion

DEUS Latin for divinity; Sanskrit Dyaus (Zeus)

DEVA happy Buddhist heavenly being; Devas are opposed to Asuras who encourage evil

DEVS (Persia) Mithratic demons

DJOL (Samoyed) spirit of nature

DWYN DWYNWEN Welsh god of love; son of **DAGDA**

ECHO (Gr.) a nymph; mother of **IAMBE** by **PAN**; (N.Am.) with Thunder (Hino) & Wind (Ga-oh/a) member of Iroquois Triad of giants & magicians

ENKI (Sum./Sem.) **EA** god of liquid elements, revered in Eridu, holy city at the mouth of **APSU**. See **MARDUK**

ERIS (Gr.) 'Strike', daughter of Night & sister of **ARES**; mother of **ATE**

EROS (Gr.) god of love; son of **HERMES** & Aphrodite; beloved of Psyche ('soul')

ESUS wood-cutter & part of Celtic Triad acc. to Lucan

FINN (Celtic) mac Cumal, of the Ossianic Cycle; hero, warrior & poet of the fiana band; see **COU**

FREY see **FREYR**

GAEA GAIA (Gr.) see **GE** and **RHEA**

GARM GARMR (Norse) wolf destined to kill and be killed by **TYR** in Ragnarök; son of **ODIN** (or a giant)

GERD GERDA/GERDR (Norse) of the Netherworld & giant **GYMIR**'s daughter; wife of **FREY/FREYR**

HAPI HAP/HEP (Eg.) bearded fertility god of the Nile & consort of **NEKHBET**; as a bull, reincarnation of **PTAH**

HELL (Ch.) 18 hells, reserved for torture & dispersed among 10 law-courts, each ruled by a king; (Jap.) underground kingdom of the dead with soldiers; deep land (Soko no Kuni) home of ugly female & male demons

HARE (Ch.) producer of the drug Immortality; stopped I, who shot down 9 suns, from punishing his wife, the moon goddess **CH'ANG-O/** Heng-o

HEBE (Gr.) **DIA** goddess of eternal youth; a female Ganymede, dispenser of nectar to the gods; married **HERCULES** on his deathbed

HERA (Gr.) Olympian Queen of the sky, jealous of other goddesses; much deceived by brother & husband **ZEUS**; see **MUT**

HERO (Gr.) priestess of Aphrodite and beloved of **LEANDER**

HINA HINE (Polyn.) guardian of **PO** & women; see **TANE**

HIRO Tahitian chief of the Netherworld

IDUN (Norse) wife of divine poet **BRAGI**; keeper of apple trees for longevity; see **AESIR**

ILMA (Fin.) weather god whose daughter Luonnotar (Nature), mother of Väinämöinen, was associated with creation

INTI APU-PUNCHAU Inca sun god & ancestor of the Incas with the face of a disk of gold

IREJ (Persia) inherited Iran from his father **FERIDUN**; murdered by his brothers Selm (of Rum) & Tur (of Turkestan)

IRIS (Gr.) winged water-carrier for the gods; messenger & rainbow goddess

ISIS ASET/ESET (Eg.) Queen of the gods & the Osirian Triad; wife of **OSIRIS** & mother of **HORUS** & great mother goddess; see **IO**

JADE (Ch.) 'Jade Emperor Lord on High', 2nd in supreme Triad whose heavenly court was modelled on that of earthly Emperors

JORD FJORGYN (Norse) mother of **THOR**; beloved of **ODIN**; see **AESIR**

JOVE (Gr./Rom.) one of the 12 chief gods of Gr./Rom. pantheon: **JUNO, VESTA, MINERVA, CERES, DIANA, VENUS, MARS, MERCURIUS, NEPTUNUS, VOLCANUS, APOLLO**

JUNO (Rom.) deity of state & protectress of women (a female **JUPITER**)

JUOK (Africa/Nile) supreme being; creator of all men on earth

KADI (Ass./Bab.) symbol of the creative earth & goddess of justice

KALA (India) weather, an epithet of **YAMA**

KAMI (Jap.) Shinto deities

KAPO (Hawaii) deity of fertility and abortion

KARA (Norse/Iceland) a sweet-singing swan-maiden Valkyrie; beloved of warrior Helgi who wounded her in flight

KINK (C.Am./Maya) 'Time', worship of; also 'sun' or 'day'; a 260-day calendar was intermeshed with a 365-day one & renewed every 52 years; end of Universe set for year A.D. 2011

KORE (Gr.) **DEMETER**'s beloved flower-gathering daughter abducted by **HADES** near Nysa, or, as Persephone, by Enna in Sicily

KUSA (India) the plant from which **RAMA** made his bed & rested when **HANUMAN** brought him news of his wife **SITA**, abducted to the kingdom of Lanka

LARA (Rom.) talkative nymph (Mania); mother of the **LARES & MANES**; lost her tongue to **JUPITER** (hence 'Muta')

LEDA (Gr.) conceived **POLLUX & HELEN** by the seducer **ZEUS**, & **CASTOR** & Clytemnestra by husband Tyndareus in the same night!

LETO (Gr.) another of **ZEUS**'s conquests; jealous **HERA** made sure she underwent many misadventures before giving birth to **APOLLO & ARTEMIS**

LEZA LESA (Africa/Zambia) God & Creator to many people, including Bantu tribes

LLEW LLAW GYFFES (Celtic/Welsh) 'Llew of the strong hand', wielding a spear & a sling; see Irish **LUG**

LLYR (Welsh) children of Llyr, deities of the underworld as opposed to the children of **DON**, sky deities; god of fertility & craftsmanship; brother of **BRAN** the Blessed (Bendegeit Bran)

LOKI (Norse) the evil flame, son of giant **FARBAUTI** (fire raiser) & Laufey (tinder wood); the mischief-maker among the gods, causing also the death of **BALDR** using the blind **HOD/HODUR** (of the shadows); Loki was bound to a rock, but escaped to fight the **AESIR** gods at **RAGNAROK**, being killed by **HEIMDALL**; father of **ANGRBODA** (Anguish) & 3 evil offspring: **HEL**/Death, **JORMUNGUND**/evil serpent surrounding the world & **FENRIR**/wolf; see **HOENIR**

LOTA (Tahiti) divine bird; (burbot fish)

LUNG WANG (Ch.) dragon kings

MAAT MAYET (Eg.) patroness of law & order & counterweight on a divine scale to the hearts of the dead; daughter of **RA**; wife of **THOTH**

MAIA (Rom.) wife of **VULCAN**, oldest of gods; pre-Jupiter goddess of the waters & earth mother (as also **VESTA**)

MAMI (Ass./Bab.) goddess of child-labour thus mankind; see **NINTUD**

MANA (Polynesia) all-penetrating dynamic force

MANU (India) ancestor of mankind; see **SURYA**

MARA (India) demon defeated by **BUDDHA**

MARS MASPITER/MARSPITER/MAMAR/MAVORS Rom. spirit of plants who grew to become god of war, subordinate only to **JUPITER**, receiving woodpeckers & wolves as sacrifice

MAUI (Polynesia) fished for the Earth and lifted up the Sky and made it his tutor; gave fire to mankind

MAWU (Africa) see **DA**

MENG (Ch.) guardian of exit from Hell; gave compulsory soup of Oblivion & Forgetfulness to souls en route to Transmigration

MILK Altaic satans

MIRU (Polynesia) ruler of the Netherworld

MO-LI (Ch.) 4 brother gods, guardians of Buddhist temples

MONT MENTHU (Eg.) Thebes, sun god, of war, deposed by his son **AMON** (later, King of Gods)

NAGA Buddhist serpent deities

NIKE (Gr.) as **ATHENA** a portable, wingless owl, but as herself a winged goddess of victory & daughter of **PALLAS** (Giant) & **STYX**; (Rom. **VICTORIA**)

NINA fire god of the Incas

NUIT (Eg.) see **NUT**

ODIN WODEN/WOTAN (Norse) sovereign & magician of the gods; also Lord of wisdom, poetry, heroism, fate, war, victory, and husband of **FRIGG/FRIJA**, father of Volsungs; helped by his brothers **VILI & VE** he killed **YMIR**, first of all living beings & father of all giants; dwelled in **VALHALLA**; made an Adam & Eve (**ASKR & EMBLA**) out of trees & lifted the earth from the sea; grandson of **DURI** & son of **BOR** by **BESTLA**; see **YMIR**

OGUN (Africa/Nigeria) god of the Yoruba tribe

OPET (Eg.) see **TAURT**

PAHA (Fin. 'bad') one of 3 evil spirits, with **HIISI & LEMPO** (Kalevala)

PAPA (N.Z.) the Earth; see **RINGI & VATEA**

PASI or **VARUNA** (India) the all-seeing god regulating oaths, civil order, movements of the heavens, rains, waters; also King of the Dead, father of **AGASTYA**, the ascetic, & brother of partner **MITRA**

PTAH PHTHAH (Eg.) of Memphis, mummified maker of things, incl. the universe; god of fertility; patron of fine arts; husband of **SEKHMET**; father of **NEFERTUM**; see **BAST & HAPI**

PENG (Ch.) gigantic bird causing huge waves when rising from the sea

POIA (N.Am./Indian) the Scar-face & orphaned son of disobedient **SOATSAKI**, who found a way to his grandfather, the Sun, and was relieved of his scar as reward for slaying 7 monstrous birds threatening his father, the Morning Star

P'O-P'O (Ch.) Mrs Wind riding a tiger in the clouds; once male **FENG PO**

PURA (Oceania) originally sky god, later minor hero

QUAT (Polynesia) celestial deity

RAKI (Maori) the Heaven in Polynesia and New Zealand

RAMA (India/Hindu) popular deity and a model of reason, with a devoted monkey **HANUMAN**; husband of **SITA**; as **RAMACANDRA** 7th incarnation of **VISHNU**

RHEA (Gr.) mother goddess (Phrygian **CYBELE**); daughter of **URANUS & GAEA**; sister and consort of **CRONUS** and mother of **ZEUS**; see **NUT**

RIGI (Polynesia) butterfly who separated the earth from the sea

RIGR (Norse) another name for **HEIMDALL** as father of three classes (bond-man, free citizen, royal) by three women

RITA (India) guardian of fire

ROHE (N.Z.) ruler of the middle world

RONA (N.Z./Maori) mother of **TANE** who ate the moon

SATI (Eg.) goddess of the Cataracts of the Nile & the archer who released its flood force; together with **ANUKET** she was a wife of **KHNUM**

SATI (India) wife of **SIVA** & daughter of **DAKSA** (Sage); places of pilgrimage sprung up where bits of her body, murdered by divine hands, fell

SETH see **SET**

SHEN (Ch.) gods

SHOU HSING (Ch.) patron of longevity

SIGI (Norse) son of **ODIN?**; founder of the **VOLSUNG** tribe

SITA (India) see **RAMA & HANUMAN**

SIVA SHIVA (India) three-eyed ambiguous lord of Saiva sects; Vedic **RUDRA** (destruction), Agni (fire) & Prajapati (creator) absorbed by him; father of six-headed **SKANDA** & elephant-headed **GANESA**; bull **NANDI** was the mount for this half male, half female; husband of **SATI**; see **BRAHMA**

SOMA (India) Vedic holy plant & ambrosia conferring immortality; the golden nectar of the gods assuming many different forms; **HAOMA** of the **AVESTA**

SPOR Slav deity guarding stables and fields

STYX River of Death; see **CHARON, NIKE & TETHYS**

T'AI-I (Ch.) took the place of **SHANG TI** as Supreme god

TANE (Polynesia) coloured Heaven red and separated it from the Earth; mixed sand & clay to create **HINA/HINE**, an Eve, and then married her;

creator of **TIKI**, messenger & guardian spirits; son of **RONA**

TARA (Himalayas/Mongolia) multi-eyed, multi-coloured Buddhist divinity dispensing relief from suffering and protecting travellers both on their earthly journeys and spiritual explorations

THAT (India/Hindu) the Absolute; Brahman

THOR THUNOR/DONAR (Norse) thunder & war god (armed with the 'boomerang' hammer **MJÖLLNIR**), the most worshipped of all (Rom. **JUPITER**), with very ornate temples & travelling in chariot drawn by goats; his mother was **JORD** (earth), his faithful wife **SIF** & sons Magni (strength) & Modi (anger); he fell at **RAGNARÖK** having slain the undersea evil serpent of **MIDGARD** but dying of its venom

TIKI Polynesian protective spirits; see **TANE & HINA**

TILO (Mozambique) god of the sky, thunder & rain

TI-MU (Ch.) Earth, Mother

T'U-TI (Ch.) divine old couple & popular gods of Place

TYRO (Gr.) nymph & mother of **NELEUS & PELIAS** (enemy of **JASON**) by **POSEIDON**

UKKO (Fin.) sky god who supported the world and ruled the heavens; controlled rainfall & fertility; husband of **AKKA/RAUNI**

UMAI (Siberia/Orkhon) goddess of cradles and the hearth

VALI VELI/VILE (Norse) unkept son of **ODIN** waiting for his battle

VELA Lithuanian realm of the Dead

VILI (Norse) son of **BOR**; brother of **ODIN & VE**

YAMA (India) red-eyed inventor of mortality astride a buffalo, with many-eyed dogs protecting his realm of the Dead; first of eight steps to full concentration, with him as judge; see **SURYA**

YAMM YAM (Sem.) hydra-like serpent ruler of the waters of the earth who was killed by **BAAL**

YANG (Ch.) Sky, and square (hence royal domain square); active masculine principles that permeate all being

YIMA (Pers.) son of the Sun; first man and father of the human race; accused by Zoroaster of causing the end of the golden age; replaced as first man by **GAYOMART**

YMIR AURGELMIR (Norse) first living being; father of all the giants & dwarfs emanating from his corpse; great-grandfather of **ODIN** who killed him; see **MIDGARD & AUDUMLA**

YOMI (Jap.) the Netherworld to which **IZANAGI** descended to look for his wife **IZANAMI**

ZEUS (Gr.) was the omnipotent lord of the skies & of wisdom, and protector; son of **CRONUS** (the cannibal, later exiled) & he overcame the revolts of the **TITANS** (see Classical Miscellany) & **GIANTS & GAEA**; he married Metis (wisdom), Themis (law), **HERA**, & seduced many more

5 AEGIR (Ger./Scan.) giant monster of the sea

AESIR (Norse) family of gods, enemies of the **VANIR**; together with **BALDER, BRAZI/BRAGI, IDUN, JORD, HEIMDALL, LOKI**, etc. the gods of battle **ODIN, FRIGG, TYR, THOR** inhabited **ASGARD/ VALHALLA**, the top celestial abode

AESON (Gr.) son of **TYRO** and father of **JASON**; see **ENIPEUS**

AGAVE (Gr.) aunt of **DIONYSUS** who, escaping from **PENTHEUS'** prison, struck her & the other women of Thebes with madness; as the Maenads they held orgies on Mount Cithaeron; her father **PENTHEUS**, in pursuit, was riven apart by her (Euripides' drama Bacchae)

AHURA MAZDA/AURAMAZDA (Pers.) Zoroastrian creator of the universe and the twin spirits of evil and good fighting it out on Earth

AMANA (Eg.) see **AMON**

AMMON (Eg.) see **AMON**

ANATH ANAT (Sem.) sister & consort of **BAAL** whom she rescued from the Netherworld; goddess of war and patron of love who later merged with **ASTARTE** and was called Atargatis; see **MOT**

ANNWN (Celtic) the Netherworld; see **PRYDERI**

ANSUD (Sum.) **NINURTA** as a thunderbird

ARTIO (Celtic/Helvetii) bear-goddess of the Bern region

ARURU (Sum.) mother-goddess & wife of **ENKI**

APEPI APEP/APOPHIS/REREK (Eg.) huge serpent; god of darkness & evil; enemy of **RA**

ARION (Gr.) swift horse, son of **POSEIDON & DEMETER**

ASHUR ASSHUR (Ass.) Lord of the gods of Assyria and its capital Ashur; similar to **ANSHAR** (father of **AN**) or Sum. **ENLIL**

ASIAQ (Eskimo) protectress of the weather and the atmosphere

ATIRA (N.Am.) held court in heaven together with husband **TIRAWA**

ATLAS (Gr.) a Titan condemned by **ZEUS** to support the pillars that separated Heaven & Earth; turned into a rocky mountain by **PERSEUS**; son of **ASIA?**

ATTIS ATTS (Gr.) Phrygian husband of **CYBELE** (Magna Mater); son of twin-sexed **AGDISTIS** who killed him; solar divinity of the Roman Empire; see **MEN & LYCUS**

AYWIL (Africa) father of **DENG**

BALDR BALDER (Norse), the Sun god killed by **LOKI**

BALOR Irish divinity with an evil eye

BENNU (Eg.) heron-like sacred bird; soul of **OSIRIS**; (Gr. **PHOENIX**)

BINGO (Africa/Bantu) son of **NZAME**

BRAGI (Norse) like **ODIN**, a poet & scald; husband of **IDUN**

BRESS (Celtic) husband of **BRIGIT/ BRIDGET**, pastoral poetic goddess

CACUS Roman cattle-thief and bandit who was killed by Hercules; son of fire god **VULCAN** and brother of **CACA**

CHAAC (C.Am.) Mayan rain god; see **UO & TLALOC**

CHONS see **KHONS & MUT**

CERES Roman goddess of crops associated with Gr. **DEMETER**

CH'UNG (Ch.) celestial administrator

CIRCE (Gr.) goddess of debased love, enchantments & evil spells who poisoned her husband & transformed whoever landed on her island into an animal

CREON (Gr.) King of Thebes whose city **OEDIPUS** freed from a monster, the **SPHINX**

CUNTI (India) mother of seven hundred thousand Buddhas

CUPID Roman arrow-shooting son of **VENUS**; roguish good spirit; (Gr. **EROS**)

DAGDA DAGDE/EOCHAID (Irish/Celtic) all-knowing pot-bellied father-figure, with a wheel-mounted outsize club;

with one end he could crush the enemies of his people, with the other restore them to life – hence master of life & death, & symbol of fertility & owner of a magic cauldron that never became empty; see DWYN & BRIGIT

DAITI (Pers.) river which flows from the centre of the world

DAKSA DAKSHA (India) father-in-law of SIVA & husband of 27 lunar stations

DANAË (Gr.) ACRISIUS, king of Argos, was father of DANAË, whose future son, said the oracle, would cause the king's death; so ACRISIUS built an underground prison for DANAË & her nurse; but ZEUS, already attracted by the charms of DANAË, entered as a shower of gold to become her lover; the result was PERSEUS, and the fulfilment of the fate as foretold

DATAN a Polish god of the fields

DEIVA Lithuanian werewolves

DELKA Lithuanian divine baby-minder

DIANA Roman huntress and helper of women; sister of APOLLO; (Gr. ARTEMIS)

DIEVS Baltic sky god

DOMFE (Sudan) aquatic spirit

DONAR (Ger.) see THOR

DURGA (India) another of the characters assumed by SIVA's wife when called on to annihilate a demon; she mounts a lion & has 10 arms, each with a weapon, to overcome the monster; see GANESA

DYAUS (India) Vedic father in the sky; (Gr. ZEUS/Rom. JUPITER)

DYLAN (Celtic) divinity of darkness and the sea; son of GWYDION and ARANRHOD

ECHUA (C.Am.) god of travellers

ELVES ALFAR (Ger./Scan.) water (wood & mountain) creatures

EMBLA (Norse) wife of ASK/ASH and thus mother of mankind

EMMA-O (Jap.) (Indian YAMA) King of Hell from which only the supplication of the living could release you; left the judgement of female souls to his sister

ENECH (Hung.) see HUNOR

ENLIL BEL (Sum.) god of sky & wind; second in the divine assembly of AN/ ANU; husband of NINLIL, grain goddess; see ASHUR

EPONA AUGUSTA (Celtic/Rom.) mounted goddess connected with horses & donkeys; patroness of riders; see MACHA

ERLIK (Siberia/Altaic) father figure and an Adam; master of Death; sometimes in bird disguise

FATUA FAUNA, see FAUNUS

FAUNS (It.) see SATYRS

FLORA FERONIA Roman divinity of flowers

FREYR YNGRI (Norse/Swedish) a VANIR and son of NJORD and divine forefather of the Ynglingar kings of Sweden; bestower of fertility and guardian of crops; husband of GERD (daughter of giant GYMIR)

FRIGG FRIJA/FREA ('Friday') (Norse/ Ger.) beloved wife of ODIN/WODAN; mother of BALDR/BALDER

FU-HSI (Ch.) with serpent's tail, one of 3 legendary emperors & in Triad of medicine gods

GAMAB (Africa) vicious divinity

GANAS (India) attendants of SIVA

GARMR (Norse) see GARM

GAUNA (Africa/Bushmen) vicious divinity

GANGA GANGES (India) sacred river & deity

GYMIR (Norse) see GERD & FREYR

HADAD ADAD (Ass./Bab.) controlled rainfalls & tempest; withheld rains on orders of ENKI, causing famine

HADES (Rom. PLUTO, Gr. TARTARUS) son of CRONUS & RHEA; King of the Netherworld with queen Persephone; 3-headed CERBERUS, guardian dog, stolen from him by HERCULES; allowed the Furies (Erinyes) to torment the wicked

HAKEA (Hawaii) chief of the Netherworld

HAOMA (Pers.) see SOMA

HALDI chief Urartian god depicted standing on a lion

HEBAT Hurrian Queen of gods; see MA

HEHET (Eg.) see HEH

HEKET (Eg.) frog-headed goddess

HELEN (Gr.) wife of MENELAUS won by shepherd PARIS; see Trojan War

HIISI (Fin.) vicious spirits

HODUR HODER/HOD (Norse) blind son of ODIN, tricked by LOKI into slaying BALDR; see BOUS

HORON (Sem.) god of the Netherworld

HORUS HOR (Eg.) falcon-like sky god with solar & lunar vision & son of ISIS; each Pharaoh a HORUS incarnate; HORUS succeeded OSIRIS by defeating SETH

HOU T'U (Ch.) supreme Earth

HSI-HO (Ch.) wife of TI CHUN/SHANG TI; gave birth to ten suns whom she polished by bathing them every morning

HUACA Incan mystic forces and guardian spirits

HUNOR ENECH (Hung.) horned forefather of the Hungarians

HYLAS (Gr.) a partner of HERCULES who was drowned by a naiad

IAMBE (Gr.) inventor of iambic verse; see ECHO

INARI (Jap.) rice god

INDRA (India) storm, rain & sky god who gained mastery over the sun and killed the monsoon-preventing dragon VRTRA; chief thousand-eyed Vedic warlike god, rival of KRISHNA; husband of INDRANI; father of ARJUNA

INNUA (Eskimo) SILAP INNUA, master of the air; powers of the Universe/Yua

INUAT (Eskimo) souls and spirits

IRENE EIRENE (Gr.) goddess of peace and one of the Horae (Seasons)

IXION (Gr.) see CENTAURS & DIA

JANUS (Rom.) keeper of the universe and all beginnings who faced both the future and the past

JASON (Gr.) leader of the Argonauts in the quest for the Golden Fleece; see TYRO

JINNS (Oriental) genii spirits

JUMNA YAMUNA (India) river sacred to Hindus at its confluence with the Ganges

KALKI (India) giant with horse's head; AVATAR/VISHNU incarnation still to come

KALMA (Fin.) goddess of death; see SURMA

KAMSA (India) see KRISHNA

KARMA (India) see SURYA

KAU-FU (Ch.) giant or composite animal; son of KUNG-KUNG (horned monster)

KENOS (S.Am.) great forefather; an Adam

KHNUM KHNEMU (Eg.) elephantine lord of the cataracts and potter-god; shaped and gave life to his god models; husband of the sisters SATI (fertility) and ANUKET

KHONS (Eg.) moon god and adopted son of MUT and AMON-RA

KINGU (Sum.) husband of TIAMAT from whose blood ENKI/EA made Man; see MARDUK

KINTU (Mozambique) initially the only man on earth

KISIN (C.Am./Maya) the 'earthquake' who assisted evil Usukun & his brother HAPIKERN, all enemies of mankind locked in eternal war with the god of creation

KURKE Baltic divinity of the crops

KWOTH (Sudan) supreme god

LADON (Gr.) river god & father of SYRINX whom he transformed into a reed; dragon who guarded the entrance to the garden of the Hesperides & was killed by HERCULES; see PAN

LAHMU & LAHAMU/Lakhmu & Lakhamu (Sum.) a pair of hideous serpents & parents of ANSHAR

LAIUS (Gr.) ruler of Thebes and father of OEDIPUS by IOCASTE/JOCASTA, sister of CREON

LARES Roman household genii; see LAR & PENATES

LAUME Baltic protective goddesses

LEMPO (Fin.) vicious spirit; see HIISI

LESKY Slav sylvan spirit and guardian of flocks & herds

LETHE (Gr) river and spring of oblivion in the Netherworld; daughter of ERIS (Strife); sister MNEMONYME (Spring of Memory)

LIBER (It.) divinity of rural settlements, vines & fertility who, on his festival day LIBERARIA, presided over boys entering manhood

LINUS (Gr.) may have invented melody & rhythm; killed by APOLLO after challenging him to a song contest; music-teacher to HERCULES who killed him in anger

LITAE (Gr.) daughters of ZEUS; old, limping Prayers who blessed those showing them respect

LODUR (Norse) fellow-traveller with ODIN, LOKI & HODUR on an unpopulated earth; gave warmth & colour of life to trees

LOTAN LEVIATHAN (Sem.) primeval serpent

LOUHI (Fin.) goddess in the land of the dead, MAAN-ALA (MANALA)

LUGUS LUG (Irish/Celtic) see NUADU

MACHA MORRIGAN/BADB/NEMAIN (Celtic) three war goddesses: a) mother of twins and guardian of MACHA's fortress (Emain Macha/ Ulster), b) wife of NEMHED, c) similar to Gallic EPONA (mare goddess)

MADER ATCHA (father) & **MADER AKKA** (mother) Lappish gods of Creation

MAHOU (Africa) see **MAO**
MAIRA (Brazil) Indian paradise, a land
with no evil
MANES (Rom.) good, protective objects
of a popular cult culminating in the
festivals of Parentalia & Feralia; see
LARA
MANNA Lappish Earth Mother
MAYET (Eg.) see **MAAT & THOTH**
MBOIA (Africa/Bantu) see **NZAME**
MEDEA (Gr.) murderous enchantress
who helped **JASON** to overcome the
obstacles to secure the Golden Fleece
placed in their way by her father,
king **AEETES** of Colchis; see **AEGEUS**
MIDAS (Gr.) son of **GORDIUS & CYBELE**,
wished for the touch of gold, was
granted it & repented; he was later
asked to choose between **APOLLO** &
Marsyas on lyre or flute playing;
APOLLO, not being chosen, gave him
the ears of an ass, whereupon **MIDAS**
ended his life by consuming the blood
of a bull
MIMIR (Norse) giant wise water spirit
of **AESIR** tribe; guardian of the
fountain of knowledge
(Mimisbrunnar); often consulted by
ODIN whose eye lay in **MIMIR**'s well;
also a smith
MINOS (Gr.) lover of **SCYLLA** who
drowned; enemy of the Athenians
who killed his son Androgeus; son of
ZEUS and **EUROPA**
MITRA (India) maintains universal
order together with **VARUNA**, a dyad;
see **PASI**; (Pers. Mithra)
MOIRA (Gr.) Fate that supersedes the
gods
MOMUS (Gr.) symbol of guilt and son
of Night
MONJU BOSATSU (Jap.) guide of all
Buddhas; supreme wisdom
MUMMU (Sum.) male attendant of **APSU**
MUSUN (Samoyed) spirit of nature
NANDI (India) divine bull; mount of
SIVA
NANNA (Sum.) see **SIN & ISHTAR**
NEBTI (Eg.) vulture and cobra goddess
NEHEH see **HEH**
NIOBE (Gr.) wife of **AMPHION** (Thebes)
and sad mother of a dozen; see
SIPYLON
NJORD (Norse) a **VANIR** and father of
fertility deities **FREYR & FREYJA**
NUADU (Irish) came before **LUG** as King
of the gods; fisherman
NUSKU (Sum.) lunar god of fire & light

who wards off the demons of night;
shows himself when the Moon (**SIN**),
his father, is new
NZAME (Africa/Bantu) invisible
divinity who made **FAM**, an Adam;
husband of **MBOIA** and father of
BINGO
OMARA (Africa/Nile) descended from
the sky & became the first man;
ancestral god of the Shilluks tribe
OPHIS (Eg.) see **OPHOIS**
ORION (Gr.) a giant, son of **POSEIDON**
who could walk on the seabed; went
hunting with **ARTEMIS** & then swam
far out to sea; **APOLLO** challenged his
sister to hit this target on the waves &
she killed **ORION**; alternatively, set a
scorpion on **ORION** who was then
tended by Asclepius, struck by a
thunderbolt from Zeus & ended up as
a bright constellation in the heavens
OTAVA (Fin.) or **TAPIO**, sky god as a
Great Bear
PAIVA (Fin.) the sun and mother of
Päivätär; 'day' in Finnish
PALES (Rom.) rural festival spirits
(Parilia)
PARIS (Gr.) awarded **ERIS**'s golden
apple to Aphrodite on Mt. Ida, much
to the annoyance of **HERA & ATHENE**;
see **HELEN**
PEMBA (Sudan) created all beasts &
plants on earth and made the first
woman
PERUN PERKUNAS (Slav/Lithuanian)
spirit of the sky governing lightning;
Russian war god; see **VARPULIS**
PICUS (Rom.) woodpecker god of
agriculture sacred to **MARS**; as myth.
king, son of **SATURN**; father of **FAUNUS**
and unwilling husband of sorceress
CIRCE
PINGA (Eskimo) protectress of game
PLUTO (Gr.) see **HADES**
PWYLL (Celtic) see **PRYDERI**
RADHA (India) beloved of **KRISHNA**
RANGI (N.Z./Maori) sky god
RAUNI (Fin.) see **UKKO**
RAVEN (N.AM./Indian) important hero
associated with **COYOTE**
REMUS founder of Rome with his twin
brother **ROMULUS**; later killed by him;
adventurous sons of **MARS** and the
vestal virgin **RHEA SILVIA**, daughter of
the ruler **NUMITOR** whose brother
AMULIUS wanted **ROMULUS & REMUS**
drowned in the Tiber
REREX (Eg.) see **APEPI**

RERIR (Norse) husband of **FREYJA**; see **VOLSUNG**

RINDA RENDI (Norse) mother of **BOUS** who was raped by **ODIN**

RINGI (N.Z.) the Sky, in love with **PAPA**, the Earth

ROBUR Gallic divinity of the oak tree

RUDRA (India) destructive ancestor of **SIVA**, causing death & disease with his arrows; father of the storm gods **MARUTS/RUDRAS**

SAKTI (India) chief Hindu goddess and wife of **SIVA**

SATYR (Gr.) wood genii; monkey/he goat, sensual companions of **DIONYSUS** at his orgy festivals

SEBEK SEBEQ/SEBEK-RE/SOBK-RE/ SUCHOS (Eg.) crocodile or crocodile-headed man; protector of reptiles

SEIDA SAITI/SEJDA is found in the mountains as the head-like rock resembling some animal, and as such was worshipped & sacrificed to by the Lapps (Saami people)

SEDMA (Eskimo) goddess of marine animals

SEKER SOKAR/SOKARIS (Eg.) hawk or hawk-headed mummy; god of Darkness and Decay

SHAIT (Eg.) goddess of destiny

SHEDU (Ass./Bab.) good demons

SHEOL Hebrew Hell

SHERI KHURRI, the bulls of the Hurrite storm-god **TESHUP**

SIBYL one of ten Roman female prophets

SILAP INUA (Eskimo) master of the air

SKADI (Norse) wife of **NJORD** after his defection to the **AESIRS**

SUANU (Africa) deity of sudden death

SURMA (Fin.) monster guarding the abode of **KALMA**; personification of Death

SURYA (India) important Hindu solar divinity and dissipator of Darkness who fathered the Aswin twins (heavenly horsemen), **SURGIVA** (ruler of monkeys), **KARMA** (fighter), **YAMA** (god of Death) and **MANU** (ancestor of mankind)

TAGES (Rom./Etruscan) self-appointed grandson of **JUPITER** who possessed magic and wisdom

TAPIO (Fin.) dark-bearded, with cloak of moss; spirit of the woods together with his family; see **OTAVA**

TAURT APET/OPET/TAWERET/THOUERIS (Eg.) pregnant hippopotamus

standing on his hind legs; deity of maternity & household

TELLA Hittite bull

THEIA (Gr.) mother of **SELENE**

THOTH DJHOWTEY (Eg.) ibis-headed god of the moon & learning; created the languages and was the scribe of the gods; protector of **ISIS**; husband of **MA'AT/MAYET**; representative of **RA** on earth; (Gr. **HERMES**)

TORUM (Siberia) Ugrian sky god (like **NUM & EC**)

TUONI (Fin.) hellish river god and resident of **TUONELA**; husband of **TUONETAR** and father of **LOVIATAR**

TUPAN (S.Am.) spirit of lightning & thunder who rejects prayers

TYCHE (Gr.) goddess of fortune & abundance (Rom. **FORTUNA**)

VANIR (Norse) family of gods (**NJORD**, **FREYR**, **FREIJA**, etc.), enemies of the **AESIR**; associated with fertility & riches

VARUA (Polynesia) the spirits

VATEA (Occania) perhaps father of **PAPA**; from his eyes emerged the Sun (**TONGA**) and the Moon (**ITI**)

VELNS Baltic/Teutonic devil

VENUS charming Roman goddess of gardens associated with Gr. **APHRODITE**; divine ancestor of the Roman Caesars through **AENEAS** (son of Aphrodite); beloved of **ADONIS**

VESTA Roman goddess of the hearth fire & patroness of bakers; her assistants, the six Vestal Virgins (priestesses)

VIDAR (Norse) son of **ODIN** who killed the monstrous wolf **FENRIR**

VOLKH VOLGA (Slav) werewolf; white bull with golden horns

VOLOS VYELYES (Slav) divinity of cattle

VRTRA (India) see **INDRA**

WEN-TI WEN CH'ANG (Ch.) god of literature

WODAN WODEN/WOTAN (Ger.) see **ODIN**; (Wednesday)

YAKSA (India) tree demon

YU-TZU (Ch.) rain maker with a magic sword

ZAMBA (Cameroon) god and creator, father of the Learned (**N'KOKON**), the Idiot (**OTUKUT**), the Gorilla (**NGI**) and the Chimpanzee (**WO**)

ZEMIS Haitian heroes and spirits

ZETES (Gr.) Argonaut & son of **BOREAS**, the North Wind

ZORYA (Slav) female triad of protectors of the whole universe

ZOSIM (Slav) patron of bee-keepers

6 ABNOBA Gallic goddess of hunting (Black Forest)

ADONIS (Gr.) beautiful lover of APHRODITE/VENUS (ATARGATIS/ ASTARTE) and son of SMYRNA (MYRRHA) by her father THEIAS, ruler of Syria; claimed also by Persephone; originally associated with plant life and the Babylonian couple TAMMUZ & ISHTAR

AEGEUS (Gr.) King of Athens; like POSEIDON, claimant to fatherhood of THESEUS (Attic hero) by AETHRA from Argolis; husband of exorcist MEDEA of Colchis who tried to poison his son THESEUS

AEOLUS (Gr.) wind god (Aeolian harp) who tried to help ODYSSEUS; eponymous ancestor of Aeolis; see BIAS, ALCYONE, MELAMPUS

AEROPE (Gr.) see ATREUS

AESHMA (Pers.) incarnation of rage & devastation; Asmodeus in Book of Tobit

AETHER (Gr.) see EREBUS

AETHRA (Gr.) suicidal mother of THESEUS and guardian & slave of HELEN; see AEGEUS

AGENOR (Gr.) see CADMUS & PERSES

AH-PUCH (C.Am./Maya) god of Death & the ninth hell; skeleton-like

AKHMIN MIN (Eg.) Pan-god of fertility, travellers

ALEYIN (Sem.) son of BAAL

ANANDA (India) favourite disciple of BUDDHA

ANANTA VASUKI (India) serpent; as 'infinite' another name for VISHNU

ANSHAR (Bab.) supreme ruler of heaven above (an-), twin brother and husband of earth below (Ki-shar); both children of APSU (the waters around the earth) & TIAMAT (the sea) or their twins LAHMU & LAHAMI; each a parent of AN/ANU

ANUBIS ANPU (Eg.) son of RA or OSIRIS; god of the dead, funerals etc.; Lord of the mummy; black-skinned, with head of jackal or dog

ANUKET ANQET/ANQUET (Eg.) goddess of the Nile and the Cataracts; second wife of KHNUM; sister of SATI, his first wife

APOLLO (Gr. & Rom.) deity of light and later sun god; also associated with healing & prophecy & herds; see DIANA, IASO, ION, LINUS, MIDAS

ARAWAN (Gr.) see PRYDERI

AREMHA (Polynesia) spirits of ancestors, as gods

ARJUNA (India) see INDRA

ASGARD (Norse) the abode of the AESIR gods

ASHMAN (Sum.) grain goddess

ASHTAR Phoenician patron goddess of Carthage, as Venus

ASOPUS (Gr.) river god; husband of nymph MEROPE; father of AEGINA

ASSHUR (Ass.) see ASHUR

ATABEI (Haiti) father of JOCA-HUVA, god in heaven

ATANUA (Oceania) see ATEA

ATHENA ATHENE (Gr.) unmarried & childless goddess of war; protectress of Athens and wise counsellor; see NIKE, CECROPS

ATREUS (Gr.) son of PELOPS of Mycenae & Hippodamia; father of Agamemnon & MENELAUS; his son Pleisthenes by AEROPE was killed by ATREUS' younger brother THYESTES, father of PELOPIA

ATUGAN Mongolian mother goddess

AUGEAS (Gr.) King of Elis whose manure-filled stables were cleaned in one day – one of the labours of HERCULES who directed the rivers Alpheus & Peneius to flush out these stables for him

AURORA (Rom.) the dawn wind; see EOS

AVATAR (India) bestial or human incarnation on earth of a god (VISHNU)

BACABS (Yucatán/Maya) four wind gods and brothers, placed by their supreme god at the four points of the compass to support the sky; patrons of bee-keepers

BAIAME (Australia) omnipotent father & hero

BALDER (Norse) see BALDR

BANNIK (Slav) spirit of the baths

BASTET see BAST

BENDIS (Gr.) moon-goddess wife of DIONYSUS

BESTLA (Norse) wife of BOR; see ODIN

BICUDO (Brazil/Indian) fish with beaklike jaw

BOREAS (Gr.) winged North Wind who kidnapped Oreithyia (daugher of the King of Athens) and had two sons by her, CALAIS & ZETES; see EOS

BRIGIT BRIGANTIA (Celtic) poetic

goddess of arts & crafts (confused with DANU) who had three namesakes, daughters of DAGDA (Rom. MINERVA)

BRIXIA (Celtic) wife of LUXOVIUS

BRAHMA (India) Hindu four-faced creator god who emerged from a lotus of VISHNU's navel (or from a golden egg) to become part of the trinity after SIVA; identified with Vedic Prajapati (creator); married to SAVITRI and SARASVATI (or SATARUPA)

BROMIO (Gr.) DIONYSUS when roaring

BUDDHA Bodhisattva (India) whose mother, Queen Maya, dreamt he entered her womb as a little white elephant; founder of Buddhism

CADMUS (Gr.) son of AGENOR (King of Tyre) who founded Thebes and married HARMONIA, and brought writing to Greece

CALAIS & ZETES, sons of BOREAS, later slain by HERCULES & changed into NE winds 'Prodromes' (ahead of the rising Dog Star); an ARGONAUT

CASIUS (Gr.) mountain abode of myth. Khazzi people; near Antioch/Antakya

CASTOR & POLLUX (Rom.) (Etruscan Kastur & Pultuke) prominent deities of the Roman cavalry & protectors of sailors & travellers

CAUTES (Pers.) symbol of dawn

CH'ANG-O (Ch.) the Moon

CHARON ferryman for the underworld

CHASCA Inca male page to the Sun

CH'IH YU CHI-YOU (Ch.) monster with iron head

CHI-LIN (Ch.) friendly unicorn and, like the stork, herald of babies; patron of the saintly and wise

CONSUS Italian deity of agriculture whose festival days spelt a holiday for horses & mules; colleague of OPS

COYOTE (N.Am.) greatest hero of N.Am. Indian tribes; clever trickster; see RAVEN

CREUSA (Gr.) see ION

CRONUS (Gr.) son of URANUS & GAIA and father of ZEUS; see RHEA & HADES

CURCHE (Baltic) see KURKE

CUYCHA Inca rainbow god

CYBELE (Gr.) goddess of caverns & earth; married ATTIS, then GORDIUS (of the knot); their son MIDAS succeeded

DAEMON (Gr.) supernatural evil power

DAEVAS (Pers.) evil power, as devil

DANAUS (Gr.) father of fifty murderous daughters & twin brother of AEGYPTUS; see AMYMONE

DAPHNE (Gr.) nymph, daughter of river Peneius; desired by APOLLO, she barely escaped, called for help from GAEA & disappeared into a new chasm from which a laurel soon grew; APOLLO made this sacred to her memory

DEIMOS Fear; see ARES

DEVANA a Czech DIANA

DOGODA (Slav) the West Wind

DUMUZI (Sum.) presided over fertility & regeneration in many forms; as wild bull, son of NINSUN; as DUMUZI-ABZU, god of the marshland

EREBUS (Gr.) Darkness born of Chaos and incestuous brother of NYX (Night), fathering Day and AETHER (Sky)

EUROPA (Gr.) daughter of PHOENIX or of AGENOR, King of Phoenicia (Lebanon) & Telephasso; captivated & captured by new bull in her herd, ZEUS, who when she climbed onto him plunged into the sea to reach southern Crete where she gave birth to MINOS, Rhadamanthus & Sarpedon, each adopted by EUROPA's new husband, King Asterius

FAUNUS (It.) prophetic divinity of the countryside; father or husband of FAUNA/FATUA; (Gr. PAN); see MAIA, PICUS

FENG-PO (Ch.) releaser of winds from goatskin sack; transformed into female P'O-P'O

FENRIR (Norse) wolf-giant son of LOKI, once chained but escaped for RAGNARÖK (Armageddon) where he swallowed ODIN, whose son VIDAR in turn killed FENRIR

FREYJA (Norse) many-sided goddess with magic powers presiding over fertility, wealth, love & death; produced golden tears; wife of hammer-snatcher THRYM; daughter of NJORD

GANESA (India) elephant-headed son of SIVA and PARVATI; ejects barriers

GARUDA (India) god and bird; mount of VISHNU

GAUNAB (Africa) Hottentot vicious demon

GEFION (Norse) fertility goddess & patroness of virgins whose sons were cloaked as oxen & ploughed out (Danish) Zealand (as an island) from Sweden, leaving empty lake Vänern

GRAIAE (Gr.) the three grey sisters of

the Gorgons with only one eye to
share – taken from them by Perseus
(DINO, ENYO, PEMPHREDO)

GRI-GRI (Sudan) clan spirit

GURUHI (Africa) vicious god able to
poison humans

HAEMUS (Gr.) one of the mountain
abodes (Thrace) of the hundred-
headed monster TYPHON, son of
TARTARUS & GAIA

HARITI KISHI-MOJIN (Jap.) Buddha
changed her from child-eating
monster to protectress of children;
female counterpart of KAN-NON

HATHOR ATHYR (Eg.) mother goddess
with cow's horns in attendance at the
birth of a pharaoh; associated with
festivity & love; daughter of NUT
(Sky) and RE; linked with Aphrodite,
ARTEMIS, DIANA, JUNO and Sem.
ASTARTE

HECATE (Gr.) Carian divinity of
fertility & witchcraft; daughter of
PERSES (Titan) & ASTERIA (nymph);
promoter of wealth & influential over
heaven, earth and the sea; famous for
her pillars (Hecataea) and protection
of doorways & crossroads; see SCYLLA

HELIOS (Gr.) the Sun god who sailed to
Rhodes in a crescent moon bowl
where he mated with the nymph
RHODAS and became the ancestor of
the Rhodosians; see EOS

HELLEN (Gr.) ancestor of all the Greeks
(named after his sons AEOLUS &
DORUS, and grandsons ION &
ACHAEUS); King of Phthia and
grandson of PROMETHEUS

HEPATU Hittite Queen of gods standing
on a panther; Hurrian HEBAT

HERMES (Gr.) bearded messenger and
fertility god from Arcadia, linked
with the Cabeiri and Roman MERCURY

HOENIR (Norse) fellow-traveller with
ODIN, LOKI and LODUR who gave a soul
to the trees

HUN-TUN (Ch.) Chaos, depicted as
long-haired dog

ICARUS (Gr.) flew too high on
homemade wings and drowned near
Icaria island; son of DAEDALUS,
sculptor and architect (Labyrinth/
Crete)

IKTOMA (N.Am./Sioux) invisible being
who formed the world

INANNA (Sum.) goddess of the
Netherworld

INTOTA (N.Am.) Sun god

IOLAUS (Gr.) helped his labouring
uncle HERCULES with the killing of
the Hydra

ISHTAR (Ass./Bab.) (Sum. INANNA)
variously described as goddess of the
morning & evening star VENUS, as a
warrior & as goddess of love, harlots
& courtesans; daughter of ANU or SIN;
as the 'star of lamentation' stirring up
quarrels & breaking friendships;
threatened the release of the dead
back to earth if thwarted; left her
lovers worse off, but was revered as
the omnipotence of love; see ASTARTE

ITZANA (N.Am.) the Great God of the
Lacandones Indians

IXCHEL (N.Am.) moon goddess and
vicious woman

JUMALA (Fin.) ancestor of UKKO; 'god'
in Finnish

KAN-NON (Jap.) protective deity

KAUKIS Baltic dwarfs and guardians of
homes

KEELUT (Eskimo) dog-like vicious earth
demon

KHEPAT Hurrian wife of TESHUP

KHEPER KHEPRI (Eg.) sun-pushing
scarab or man with a scarab on his
head; the rising sun RA

KHNEMU (Eg.) see KHNUM

KHONSU (Eg.) see KHONS

KHURRI (Hurrian) see SHERI

KOSHAR KOTHAR (Bab.) divinity of arts
& crafts; palace-builder to BAAL

KRICCO (Slav) guardian of orchards

KRIMBA Bohemian house divinity

KUBABA Hittite CYBELE

KUPALA (Slav) associated with herbs &
trees

KVASIR (Norse) a man of surpassing
wisdom created by the saliva of the
AESIR & the VANIR; killed by 2 dwarfs
who mixed his blood with honey; this
became the mead of the gods, hydromel,
dispensed by ODIN to poets in favour

LAKSMI SRI (India) wife of VISHNU

LAUFEY (Norse) see LOKI

LOTHIA (Fiji) ruler of the Netherworld

LYCAON (Gr.) Mountain and king of
Arcadia whose family was turned into
wolves by ZEUS

MANALA TUONELA/POHJOLA (Fin.) home
of LOUHI, goddess of the dead – like
TUONELA of TUONI; entered over
bridge or by boat

MANNUS (Ger.) son of giant TUISTO;
sired the forefathers of 3 main
Germanic tribes

MARAWA (Australia) strong, forceful spirit

MARDUK (Ass.) oldest son of **EA & APSU**; personified creation & fertility & the growth of Babylon, becoming leading god; he defeated **TIAMAT**, goddess of the sea, floods & primitive chaos & organized the world, regulating the heaven & the stars; see **LAHMU**

MARICI MARISHI-TEN Buddhist and Tibetan three-headed sunrise god

MARUTS RUDRAS (India) young storm gods of the clouds; rain-givers

MASAYA Nicaraguan lord of volcanoes

MEDUSA (Gr.) one of the 3 Gorgons; seduced by **POSEIDON** in the temple of Athene who revenged herself by turning **MEDUSA**'s hair into snakes; decapitated by **PERSEUS**, her blood gave birth to the horse **PEGASUS**

MEGARA (Gr.) wife of **HERCULES**

MEIDEN Baltic hare god

MEMNON (Gr.) Lord of Ethiopia; son of Tithonus & **EOS**, supporter of Priam; killed Antilochus, son of Nestor, but in turn died by the hand of Achilles at Troy

MENTHU (Eg.) see **MONT & BUKHE**

MERWER (Eg.) bull sacred to Ra-Atum (Gr. **MNEVIS**)

METION (Gr.) see **DAEDALUS**

MEULER (Chile) god of waterspout (and whirlwinds & typhoons)

MINEPA (Mozambique) evil spirit

MITHRA (Pers.) Creator who killed the bull from whose blood life sprang; trusted helper of **AHURA MAZDA**; bestower of rain and patron god of the Roman army; sun god; see **RASHNU**

MNEVIS (Eg.) see **MERWER**

MOKADI (Cameroon) a spirit

MOKOSH (Slav) divinity of domesticated animals

MOTRES MATRONAE (Gaul) Mother Goddess

MULUKU (Mozambique) the highest being

MYRRHA (Gr.) see **ADONIS**

NAREAU (Oceania/Gilbert I.) maker of Heaven & Earth

NANSHE (Ass./Bab.) goddess of springs & canals; daughter of **ENKI/EA**

NEMHED (Celtic) see **MACHA**

NEREUS (Gr.) old Aegean sea god, son of **PONTUS**; father of the sea nymphs **NEREIDS**

NERGAL (Sum.) ruled the Kingdom of

the Dead, whom he could recall to life, with his consort Allatum

NGAHUE (N.Z.) Lord of the dead & thunder

NINHAR (Sum.) rain & weather god & roaring bull responsible for the greening of the desert; son of **NANNA & NINGAL** (or **ENKI & NINHURSAG**); husband of **NINIGARA**

NINIGI (Jap.) divine ancestor of the emperors of Japan whose grandmother was Amaterasu (sun goddess); her gifts, the jewel, mirror and sword, are Imperial emblems

NINLIL BELTIS (Ass./Bab.) fertility goddess; see **ASHUR/ASSHUR, ENLIL & BEL**

NINSUN (Ass./Bab.) all-knowing mother of all-seeing Gilgamesh, the hero of the Babylonian 'national' poem

NINTUD (Sum.) see **MAMI**

NOMIOS (Gr.) **APOLLO** as lord of herdsmen

NYAMIA (Guinea) supreme god

OENEUS (Gr.) King of Calydon, Actolia who neglected to make **ARTEMIS** a due offering of his fruit harvest & therefore saw his domains ransacked & his family perish by the fury of a monster bull; see **ALTHAEA & DEIANIRA**

OENGUS (Irish) son of **DAGDA**; an Irish **EROS**

OILEUS (Gr.) see **AJAX**

OLOFAD (Micronesia) ascended to Heaven; divides his time between it & the Earth

ONATHA (N.Am./Iroquois) goddess of Wheat, for ever sacred of searching for the Dew after being kidnapped by the evil spirit

OPHOIS Wepwawet (Eg.) see **UPUAUT**

ORENDA (N.Am./Iroquois) divine force and vigour in Nature

ORMAZD OHRMAZD (Pers.) omnipotent first man who sprang from **ZURVAN**

OSIRIS (Eg.) father of **HORUS**; supreme god & ruler of the Dead; son of **NUT & GEB**; see **ISIS, UPUAUT & BENNU**

PADURI (Siberia/Altaic) lord of the reinder

PALLAS (Gr.) four namesakes: a) son of **EVANDER**; b) a giant killed by **ATHENE**; c) a Titan; d) Attic idol, brother of **AEGEUS**; (Pallantids, his sons)

PANDIA (Gr.) beautiful daughter of **SELENE**

PELEUS (Gr.) father of **ACHILLES** by

nereid Thetis; he inadvertently killed his father-in-law & caused his wife ANTIGONE to hang herself believing she had been deceived

PELOPS (Gr.) son of TANTALUS whom Poseidon befriended; uncle of Agamemnon

PERSES (Gr.) son of PERSEUS (King of Argos) & Andromeda; perhaps myth. founder of Persia

PHANES (Gr.) first divinity, born from an egg; married Night and begat Heaven & Earth

PHOBOS (Gr.) see ARES & DEIMOS

PHOEBE (Gr.) bright titaness & daughter of URANUS & GAIA; mother of LETO; associated with the moon

PILLAN (Chile/Araucanians) thunderbolt

PLUTUS (Gr.) wealthy son of DEMETER & the Titan IASION

POLLUX (Rom.) see CASTOR

POMONA Roman divinity of orchards

PONTUS (Gr.) most ancient divine embodiment of the sea (Black Sea) and waters; incestuous son of GAIA; father of NEREUS, EURYBIA, THAUMAS, PHORCYS and CETO

PURUSA (India) primal man from whose body the universe emerged

RAGANA Lithuanian werewolves

RASHNU (Pers.) one of a trio of judges (Mithra, Sraosha) deciding the fates of the souls of the deceased

RESHEF (Eg.) god of war with head of gazelle

RHODAS (Gr.) see HELIOS

RUDRAS (India) storm gods; see RUDRA & MARUTS

SATURN SATURNUS Roman grain god and patron of sowing; colleague of OPS and CONSUS; (Gr. CRONUS); see LUA & PICUS

SATYRS (Gr.) creatures of the wild, part man, part goat; male counterparts of nymphs; (It. FAUNS)

SCYLLA (with Charybdis) female monster of Straits of Messina, devoured sailors; though killed by HERCULES, she was revived by Phorcys, her father

SEKHET (Eg.) see SEKHMET

SEKUME (Africa) second after FAM, the first man; made MBONGWE, his wife from a tree

SELENE (Gr.) moon goddess whom PAN lured into the forest with white fleece; wife of ZEUS; mother of PANDIA; daughter of HYPERION & THEIA (Titans); sister/daughter of HELIOS & EOS; (Rom. LUNA)

SEMELE (Gr.) daughter of CADMUS immolated when forced to witness her lover ZEUS in all his glory by jealous HERA; ZEUS carried her child DIONYSUS until the destined time of birth

SHAKAN (Sum.) see UTU

SILENI Phrygian river genii, waterhorse beings, including Marsyas; see SATYRS

SIRENS (Gr.) 2 female-faced hawks, sometimes mermaids, on the rocks of Straits of Messina, sang to lure seamen into shipwreck & massacre; Ulysses/ODYSSEUS was warned by CIRCE, stopped the ears of his crew while he was tied to the mast to listen to Alerta and Alclara, and so his ship passed unharmed; see ACHELOUS

SKANDA (India) see SIVA

SMYRNA (Gr.) see ADONIS; now modern Izmir, port of Turkey

SPHINX (eg.) body of lion (or ram or goat), head of lion, later replaced by that of Pharaoh; (Gr.) a monster; lion with female's face & breast & bird's wings, guarded the way to Thebes, famous for challenging wayfarers with tricky questions, with death for failure; OEDIPUS solved the riddle 'what has 4 legs, then 2 legs & finally 3 legs?' as man (infancy, maturity, old age); thereupon the SPHINX jumped to death into the sea

SVAROG (Slav) god of the sky; father of Svarogich, a fire god

TAATOA (Oceania/Society I.) made the earth and the sea

TAKARO (New Hebrides) he organized cosmos

TAMMUZ TAMMUZI (Sum.) forerunner of DUMUZI; pastoral grain god & shepherd with a large following; son of ENKI & DUTTUR; husband of INANNA/ISHTAR; see ADONIS

TARHUN TARHUND (Hittite) see TELEPINU & WURUSEMU

TAWALS Polish divinity in charge of the welfare of fields

TEFNUT TEFNET (Eg.) lioness or lion-headed woman with solar disc; diety of dew & moisture; sister and wife of SHU

TELLUS Roman earth divinity receiving pregnant cow as sacrifice

TENGRI (Siberia) both good and bad demons

TESHUB TESUP Hittite weather god victorious over **KUMARBI**; see **SHERI**

TETHYS (Gr.) incestuous mother of the Oceanids & **STYX**; sister & wife of **OCEANUS**; daughter of **URANUS & GAIA**; see **TYCHE**

THEIAS (Gr.) see **ADONIS**

THEMIS (Gr.) consort of **ZEUS**; mother of the Seasons & the Fates; daughter of **GAIA**; prophetess

TIAMAT (Sum.) primeval salt water & sea who gave birth to the gods; wife and mother of **KINGU** (or **APSU**); killed by **MARDUK**

T'IEN-MU (Ch.) goddess of lightning with blazing mirrors

TINNIT Carthaginian chief goddess of fertility; consort of **BAAL HAMMON**; Sem. **ASTARTE**

TIRAWA (N.Am.) the Great Chief; see **ATIRA**

TITYUS (Gr.) son of **GAIA** by a giant; tried to assail **LETO** and was killed by her children **APOLLO & ARTEMIS** (or **ZEUS**); ended as a square meal of liver for vultures

TLALOC (C.Am./Aztec) god of rain, thunder & lightning

TODOTE Samoyed divinity of Death and illwill

TORANN (Irish) Thunder; (Gallo-Roman **TORANIS/TARASUS**)

TRITON (Gr.) sea-god, son of **POSEIDON** & Amphitrite; a merman with crayfish claws who lived near Libya & enjoyed blowing his conch (shell) trumpet to terrify enemies; **TRITON** also appeared in a sea-chariot drawn by Centaurs with crawfish claws; he also lasciviously ravished women on shore

TUISTO (Ger.) giant father of **MANNUS**, the hermaphrodite first man

TUNGAT TUMRAT (Eskimo) spirits of locality

TUWATA (Hittite) see **KAL**

TYDEUS (Gr.) brain-eater & brother of Melanippus; father of **DIOMEDES**

TYPHON (Gr.) hundred-headed winged monster, half man, half serpent, with thunderous voice who threw **ZEUS** (later rescued by **HERMES & PAN**) into a cave in Cilicia; fled to Sicily and was crushed under Mt Etna by **ZEUS**; son of **GAIA & TARTARUS**; husband of **ECHIDNA**; see **HAEMUS**

UPUAUT (Eg.) wolf- or jackal-headed conqueror of the world together with **OSIRIS & ANUBIS**; he was at the head of the procession at Osirian festivals

URANUS (Gr.) god of an incestuous heaven; made his chaotic wife and mother **GAIA** fertile with rain; she gave birth to the Titans, Ceclopes and hundred-handed Hecatoncheires; attacked and overthrown by his son **CRONUS**; the giants and ash-tree nymphs arose from the blood of **URANUS'** testicles, and from the genital foam in the sea came Aphrodite, goddess of love; see **RHEA & PHOEBE**

USUKUN (C.Am./Maya) hater of humans & brother of **HAPIKERN**

VAHRAM (Pers.) bull, white horse, camel, ram, bird, wild goat; also youth and a warrior

VARUNA (India) Sky, one supreme being

VASUKI (India) see **ANANTA**

VISHNU (India) Hindu guardian of the world known through **RAMA, KRISHNA** and other incarnations (avatars); renewer of moral order; husband of **LAKSMI/SRI** and Bhumidevi; see **ANANTA & GARUDA**

VULCAN VULCANUS (Rom.) one of earliest gods (pre-dating Jupiter); married **JUNO**, earth goddess **MAIA**, & **VESTA**, father of **CACUS**, a **SATYR** killed by **HERCULES**, & in turn Servius Tullus, King of Rome; **VULCAN** was sun god, the thunderbolt & power of fire, later warmth, heating

VU-NUNA (Ugric/Votyak) water deity

VU-VOLO (Ugric/Votyak) water deity

XOLOTL (C.Am./Aztec) dog-headed god who created present mankind out of bloodied dried bones; twin of chief deity the Feathered Snake (Quetzalcoatl)

YANTHO (C.Am./Maya) brother of **USUKUN & HAPIKERN**

YARILO (Slav) deity of love and happiness

YASODA (India) mother of **KRISHNA** by adoption

ZETHUS & Amphion (Gr.) twins born in a thicket to **ZEUS** & Antiope & for a while cared for by shepherds; attacked Thebes & killed Lycus & his wife Dirce; see **NIOBE**

7 ABELLIO Gallic divinity of the apple tree

ACHERON (Gr.) river of Woe in HADES near Epirus

ADMETUS (Gr.) ZEUS punished APOLLO for the murder of the Cyclopses, makers of the thunderbolt that had killed APOLLO's son Asclepius (father of medicine), by sending APOLLO to serve at the court of ADMETUS; there APOLLO (Nomios) played the lyre & looked after the king's mares & ewes

AHRIMAN (Pers.) evil spirit; see GAYOMART

ALCYONE (Gr.) one of the 7 Pleiades & daughter of AEOLUS, god of the winds

ALTHAEA (Gr.) mother of MELEAGER & wife of OENEUS, King of Calydon

AMYMONE (Gr.) fountain & spring; mother of NAUPLIUS by POSEIDON; one of fifty murderous daughters of DANAUS

ANDARTA ANDRASTA (Celtic) warrior goddess

APOPHIS (Eg.) see APEPI

ARIADNE (Gr.) daughter of King Minos of Crete; took pity on THESEUS, sent by Athens to kill the cannibal MINOTAUR; she, with DAEDALUS, gave THESEUS the thread-spinning spider that showed THESEUS the way out of the Labyrinth by retracing his steps; when he had killed the MINOTAUR, she escaped with THESEUS to Naxos where he left her; later DIONYSUS claimed her, resulting in the sons Oenopion, Euanthes & Staphylus

ASTARTE (Sem.) great goddess of fertility associated with ISHTAR/ ATHTAR, ARTEMIS, DIANA, JUNO & Aphrodite, and also Hebrew ASHTORETH, and Atargatis; see ANATH and ADONIS

ASTERIA (Gr.) see HECATE

ATAKSAK (Eskimo) joyful spirit living in Heaven

AUDUMLA (Norse) cow and wet-nurse (made of molten hoar frost) of the giant AURGELMIR's (YMIR's) six-headed son; she formed BURI (grandfather of ODIN and his brothers who later killed Aurgelmir) by passing her tongue over stones; created the sky and the earth from his corpse

AUGUSTA (Celtic/Rom.) see EPONA

AUMANIL (Eskimo) land-based guide of whales

BACCHUS Roman wine god; (It. LIBER) (Gr. DIONYSUS)

BALANZA (Africa) lord of the trees

BANADED (Eg.) ram, incarnation of the soul of OSIRIS; (Gr. MENDES)

BELENUS (Celtic) connected with the sun & fire; widely revered pastoral god; (Gr. APOLLO)

BELLONA DUELLONA Roman goddess of war; perhaps sister or wife of MARS; see MA

BHARATA (India) see RAMA

BRIDGET (Celtic) see BRESS & BRIGHT

BUXENUS Gallic divinity of the box-tree

CABEIRI (Gr.) major divinities of Samothrace

CALYPSO (Gr.) daughter of ATLAS & TETHYS, who was told by ZEUS to let ODYSSEUS/ULYSSES go after her 7 years of bliss with him on her isle of Ortygia where he had been cast ashore by a storm

CAMENAE (Rom.) prophetic nymphs, a.o. Antevorta (the past), Postvorta (the future) & Carmenta, mother of Evander by Mercury

CAMILLA (Rom.) huntress taught by her father METABUS; warrior and friend of DIANA

CAMULON (Celtic) see COU

CECROPS (Gr.) cultured, dragon-like arbitrator between ATHENA & POSEIDON and first King of Attica

CHU-LUNG CHU-YING (Ch.) reptile with human face whose eyes when open brought daylight and, when shut, made night fall, and whose changing breath brought on the seasons

CLYMENE (Gr.) Oceanid & mother of Prometheus & perhaps ATLAS; see ASIA

COCYTUS (Gr.) tributary of ACHERON (NW Gr.) & one of the rivers of HADES

CORONIS (Gr.) mother of Asclepius (god of healing) who was shot by ARTEMIS

CUMHALL (Celtic) see COU

CURETES (Gr.) young protectors of the baby ZEUS

CYLLENE (Gr.) sacred mountain in Arcadia where HERMES was born in a cave to ZEUS & MAIA

DAPHNIS (Gr.) shepherd son of HERMES born near Etna

DAZBORG DAZHBOG Russian sun god

DEMETER (Gr.) daughter of CRONUS & RHEA; corn maiden & goddess of fertility, harvests, marriage & laws; her Megara temples in the forest were centres of orgies: Eleusinian mysteries; POSEIDON, as a stallion, seduced her & she bore the speaking horse ARION & daughter Despoena; after the kidnap of her daughter KORE by HADES, all natural growth on earth ceased until her parents RHEA & ZEUS made a compromise, claiming her daughter's presence 2/3 of the year, granting HADES 1/3 – hence the seasons

DIIWICA Serbian DIANA

DOMOVOI (Slav) hairy spirit of the house in human shape, sometimes with horn & tail; silky fur even on palms of hands

DWYNWEN (Welsh) see DWYN

ECHIDNA (Gr.) half woman, half snake; wife of TYPHON; mother of CERBERUS, the Hydra, the CHIMAERA & the Nemean lion

EK-CHUAH (C.Am./Maya) divine patron of cacao growers & traders; also connected with war and death

EMAKONG (Australia) a traveller in the Netherworld of ophidian men who took back fire and the night

ENIPEUS (Gr.) river god of Elis; loved by TYRO; mother of AESON

ERIGONE (Gr.) suicidal daughter of the Athenian ICARIUS

EURYALE (Gr.) see ORION

EURYBIA (Gr.) with heart of steel; daughter of PONTUS

EVANDER (Gr.) son of HERMES associated with PAN; see CAMENAE

FERIDUN (Pers.) see IREJ

FERONIA Roman/Etruscan divinity of springs and fertility

FJORGYN (Norse) see JORD

FORTUNA Roman TYCHE (Gr.)

FU-HSING (Ch.) see FU

FYLGJUR female Germanic protective spirit

GALATEA (Gr.) sea nymph who preferred ACIS (son of FAUNUS) to large one-eyed Polyphemus

GLAUCUS (Gr.) a) son of King MINOS by PASIPHAË & brother of ARIADNE; b) sea god, son of POSEIDON

GOIBNIU Irish smith; (Welsh GOFANNON)

GORDIUS (Gr.) Phrygian king who tied the Gordian knot (cut by Alexander the Great); father of MIDAS

GUMONGO (N.Am./Guacure Indians) rules the northern half of the sky

GWYDION (Welsh) cultured son of the sky god DON and brother & husband

of ARANRHOD (Fertility); father of the twins DYLAN (Sea) and LLEU (Irish LUG) for whom he made a wife out of flowers

HANUMAN (India/Jap.) red-faced monkey in human shape, born of the wind and a nymph; adventurous – on solo flight to the Himalayas to collect healing herbs; giant jumper across to Ceylon, or clever spy to retrieve RAMA's wife SITA from the clutches of the demon RAVANA

HARPIES (Gr.) these tempest-goddesses, Podarge, the ravisher, Aello & Ocypete were winged & as fast as the wind; later these appear as monsters, birds with bear's ears, old hags & as birds with strong claws stealing food from the table; attacked & defeated by the Argonauts, they finally fled

HELICON (Gr.) highest mountain in Boeotia (Gulf of Corinth); favoured place of the Muses where PEGASUS gave them a fountain by stamping with his hoof

HIPPIOS (Gr.) POSEIDON when associated with horses

HUNAB-KU (C.Am./Maya) father of ITZAMNA

HURAKAN (C.Am./Maya) divinity of thunder and tornado

IACCHUS (Gr.) son of ZEUS & DEMETER (or DIONYSUS & KORE/Persephone) welcomed at the Eleusinian Mysteries)

IAPETUS (Gr.) a Titan and son of URANUS & GAIA; father of ATLAS, Prometheus, Epimetheus and Menoetius

ICARIUS (Gr.) king of Attica & host to DIONYSUS; murdered by his intoxicated shepherds; father of ERIGONE who found his grave

INDRANI (India) wife of INDRA

INTONAN (C.Am.) Aztec Earth goddess

IOCASTE JOCASTA (Gr.) wife of LAIUS

ITZAMNA (C.Am./Maya) four-fold cultured lord of heaven who introduced writing and the calendar to mankind and patronized medicine; decided the points of the compass were Red in the East, White/North, Black/West and Yellow/South, and had a skilful female colleague in the moon goddess IXCHEL; married to Ix Chebel Yax (Weaving)

IZANAGI & **IZANAMI** (Jap.) eighth incestuous couple after the separation of Heaven & Earth who used a gem-studded spear to stir the primordial soup to create terra firma to stand on instead of their drifting bridge of heaven; on taking a bath, the sun (Amaterasu) sprang from **IZANAGI**'s left eye, the moon from his right one and out of his nose came the storm god **SUSANOVO**; see **YOMI**

JOCASTA **IOCASTE** (Gr.) mother of **OEDIPUS**; sister of **CREON**

JUPITER **JOVIS** Roman protector of the state & war god; chief of the triad with **JUNO & MINERVA**; also sky god (Gr. **ZEUS**) whose divine presence was welcomed at harvest & wine festivals; called **FULGUR** as master of the thunderbolt and **LATIARIS** when lording it over the Latin League; often busy with oaths & treaties; god of light & weather & of the Roman Games, chariot races, athletic contests; see **TAGES**

KANTAKA (India) the horse of **BUDDHA**

KIVUTAR (Fin.) divinity of illness and pain

KHOVAKI SAVAKI (Siberia) creator and protective spirits of the shaman

KRISHNA (India) born of **VASUDEVA & DEVAKI** (sister of **KAMSA**, vicious king of **MATHURA**) but cared for by a cowherd (**NANDA**) and his wife **YASODA**; this eighth incarnation of **VISHNU** humiliated the storm god **INDRA**; in love with **RADHA**, but married **RUKMINI**

KUEI-HIU (Ch.) unfathomable crater into which all the waters of the world flow or emerge from

KUKUKAN (C.Am./Maya) feathered serpent divinity

KUMARBI Hurrian heir to **ANU** who was defeated by **TESHUB**; fathered monstrous stone **ULLIKUMMI**; depicted standing on the shoulders of **UPELBURI** (Atlas)

LAELAPS (Gr.) hound of **CEPHALUS**

LAMASSU or **SHEDU** (Ass./Bab.) good, protective genii, often depicted as winged bulls with human heads

LAPITHS (Gr.) see **CENTAURS**

LEANDER (Gr.) see **HERO**

LEI-KUNG (Ch.) lord of thunder and Taoist gruesome divinity who punishes men guilty of hidden crimes

LIBANZA (Congo) God of the Upotos,

who gave immortality & 2 days' rest each month to the moon

LOPEMAT Latvian protectress of cattle

LYNCEUS (Gr.) see **AEGYPTUS**

MAAN-ENO Estonian fertility deity and consort of **UKKO**

MAMALDI (Siberia/Amur) wife of **KHADAU** with whom, as the first human couple, she brought **ASIA & SAKHALIN** into existence before he killed her; shamans

MAMMITU (Ass./Bab.) bestower of Destiny on the new-born; see **MAMI**

MANITOU MANITOUS (N.Am./ Algonquins) mystical & clever forces of nature

MARSABA (Oceania) divinity of the Netherworld and vile spirit

MARSYAS (Gr.) river god & satyr; defeated **APOLLO** in flute contest and was flayed alive by him; (tributary of the Meander river)

MELQART most important god of Tyre and chief of the Carthagean pantheon; (Rom **HERCULES**)

MERCURY Roman patron of traders; son of **MAIA**; (Gr. **HERMES**)

METABUS Roman; see **CAMILLA**

MEZAMAT Latvian protectress of wood

MICHABO (N.Am./Algonquin) the Great Hare spirit

MICTLAN (C.Am.) Aztec Netherworld with 9 rivers that the souls of the dead must negotiate, & 9 hells

MIDGARD (Norse) the middle abode where humanity dwelt, situated halfway between Niflheim (for the dead) & Muspellsheim (for the giants); made by the sons of **BOR** from **YMIR**'s body

MINERVA Roman divinity of the arts, war & victory; (Gr. **ATHENA/NIKE**)

MODEINA Polish god of the forest

MORRIGU (Celtic) see **MORRIGAN**

NEKHBET NEKHEBET (Eg.) vulture or vulture-headed goddess of childbirth; winged serpent protecting the pharaoh; daughter of **RE**; wife of **HAPI**; associated with **MUT**; counterpart of **BUTCE**/Lower Egypt

NEPTUNE (Rom.) god of water and the sea, perhaps of Etruscan origin

NEREIDS see nymphs and daughters of **NEREUS**

NERTHUS Germanic peaceloving island-based mother goddess revered by several tribes, including invaders of England, the Angles

NINMAKH NINTUR/ARURU/NINHURSAG
(Sum.) guardian of animal birth &
bestower of desert wildlife

NINURTA NINGURSU/IMDUGUD/ANZU
(Sum.) god of rain, floods & thunder;
son of ENLIL & NINLIL and husband of
BAU/NINNIBRU

NYIAMIA NYAMIA (Guinea) chief god

NYIKANG (Africa/Nile) his grandfather
OMARA came from Heaven as the first
man – or his ancestry traced to the
first cow

OCEANUS (Gr.) the river surrounding
the flat earth and forefather of the
gods as son of URANUS & GAIA;
husband of TETHYS (Titaness) &
father of thousands of stream spirits
& sea nymphs; see STYX

OEDIPUS (Gr.) incestuous son of LAIUS
(King of Thebes) & JOCASTA who
unknowingly killed his father &
married his mother; see SPHINX

OGYRVAN Arthurian giant; father of
Guinevere

OHDOVAS (N.Am.) midgets below the
earth who control poisonous monsters

OHRMAZD (Pers.) see ORMAZD

OLUKSAK (Eskimo) divinity of lakes

OLYMPUS (Gr.) site of the throne of
ZEUS; abode of gods; highest
mountain in Greece (2917 m/
9370 ft); one of many namesakes in
Greece & Asia Minor

ONUPHIS (Eg./Gr.) together with
Mneuis/Merwer (Ra Atum) &
Buchis/Bukhe (Menthu) sacred bull
& soul incarnate of OSIRIS

ORPHEUS (Gr.) skilful musician and son
of CALLIOPE (a Muse) and OEAGRUS,
Thracian river god (or APOLLO);
joined the Argonauts; killed by
Thracian women; see EURYDICE

PARVATI (India) the charming lover
wife GANESA of SIVA enjoying
discoursing metaphysics when so
required

PEGASUS (Gr.) winged horse born of
dying MEDUSA; see HELICON &
SISYPHUS

PELOPIA (Gr.) wife of ATREUS

PENATES (Rom.) the guardian deities of
the household, as images, normally 2
to look after the food & wine; shared
a place on the hearth by the altar of
VESTA. At every meal the first helping
was offered to them, see LARES

PERSEUS (Gr.) son of ZEUS & DANAË; he
cut off the head of the Gorgon

MEDUSA & later rescued Andromeda
from being sacrificed to a monster &
took her as his wife, retiring to
Mycenae; forefather of the Perseids;
see ATLAS

PHEBELE (Congo) divine father who by
MEBELI begat MAN, a son

PHOENIX (Eg./Gr.) as a sun-eagle
immolates itself in fire & flies
upwards with life renewed

PHORCYS (Gr.) see PONTUS

POLEVOI POLEVIK (Slav) grass-covered,
black lord of the field

POUNTAN (Micronesia) ingenious
divinity of cool, light winds

PRIAPUS (Gr.) son of DIONYSUS &
Aphrodite, a satyr variation of PAN,
with superphallus to fertilize both
animals & plants; guardian of
seafarers & garden gnome

PROCRIS (Gr.) see CEPHALUS

PROTEUS (Gr.) a prophetic, aged sea-
god, son of OCEANUS & TETHYS, was
the protector of POSEIDON's seals;
(Eg.) king of Egypt who gave
protection to Paris & Helen (of Troy)

PRYDERI (Celtic) song of RHIANNON and
PWYLL, king of Dyfed (myth. land of
abundance) who swopped home with
his friend ARAWAN, the ruler of
ANNWN (Netherworld)

PYRAMUS & THISBE, Babylonian couple
who killed themselves under a
mulberry tree (referred to in
Midsummer Night's Dream/
mechanicals' play)

ROBIGUS Roman divinity of corn rust
and mildew

ROMULUS twin brother of REMUS and
co-founder of Rome

RUKMINI (India) see KRISHNA

RUSALKA (Slav) aquatic & sylvan
divinity; drowned maiden

SAVITRI (India) see BRAHMA

SEKHMET SEKHET (Eg.) lioness or lion-
headed goddess of war; wife of PTAH
and mother of NEFERTUM, lotus deity;
see BAST

SEMARGL (Russia) wind god

SHAMASH (Sem.) (Sum. UTU) a
bestower of life and mounted sun god
who belonged to the second cosmic
triad together with his father SIN and
sister & wife ISHTAR/AIA; sirened
Justice & Right

SHANG-TI TI CHUN (Ch.) husband of
HSI-HO and father of ten suns

SHIKOME (Jap.) demons

SHIVENI Urartian sun god with winged solar disc

SIGMUND (Ger./Scan.) son of VOLSUNG with magic weapon

SIPYLON (Gr.) Lydian mountain on which NIOBE (daughter of TANTALUS) turned into rock after APOLLO & ARTEMIS had killed her children

SOKARIS (Eg.) see SEKER

SRAOSHA (Pers.) see RASHNU

STRIBOG STRIBORG Russian wind god

SURGIVA (India) see SURYA

T'AISHAN FUCHUN (Ch.) ruler of Mt T'ai where sacrificial ritual ceremonies and prayers for good crops were held; spiritual fountain of life

TARANIS Welsh thunder & sky god; (Rom. JUPITER)

TARHUND TARHUN Hittite weather god; see TELEPINU & WURUSEMU

TAUERET APET/OPET (Eg.) divinity of childbirth

TELAMON (Gr.) father of AJAX

TELAVEL Baltic heavenly smith who made the sun and the skies

T'EN-LUNG (Ch.) heavenly dragon who may have produced the Universe and all life

TESHEBA bull-mounted Urartian weather god

THAUMAS (Gr.) see PONTUS

THAUNAS (Gr.) see PONTUS

THESEUS (Gr.) Attic hero & son of AEGEUS, ruler of Athens, and AETHRA (or of POSEIDON & AETHRA); assailed the fire-breathing bull MARATHON & the Cretan MINOTAUR; fathered Hippolytus (partaker in the Argonautic expedition) by captured Amazon ANTIOPE; see ARIADNE

TOOTEGA (Eskimo) little woman on island who can walk on water

TORTALI (New Hebrides) ruler of the sun and mate of mortal AVIN

TUONELA (Fin.) the Netherworld and home of TUONI & TUONETAR, his wife

TUPURAN (N.Am.) killed by NIPARAYA; his disciples, absorbed with witchery & magic, were imprisoned in a subterranean cave

VEJAMAT Latvian patroness of the wind

VELLAMO (Fin.) wife of AHTO/AHTI

VIZ-ANYA (Hung.) water mother

VIZETOT Nicaraguan divinity of famine

VOLSUNG (Ger./Scan.) saga dynasty of the line of ODIN, through 2 generations (Sigi & Rerir) to VOLSUNG; thence Sigmund & his son Sigurd/Siegfried are the heroes in Wagner's Ring Cycle

VOSEGUS protective divinity of the forest-covered Vosges

WAKONDA (N.Am./Sioux) great life force and father figure in the sky

YEN-WANG YEN-LO-WANG (Ch.) highest judge in hell; (Indian YAMA)

YU-HUANG (Ch.) divine Jade Emperor

YUM-KAAX (C.Am./Maya) god of the forests and maize

YUN T'UNG (Ch.) a youth stirring up the clouds

ZIPACNA (C.Am./Maya) twin brother of CAPAKRAN

8 ACHELOUS (Gr.) river god; father of the SIRENS (killers, deceptive birds)

ACHILLES (Gr.) son of PELEUS & the nereid Thetis, a sea nymph, who bathed him in fire for invulnerability but omitted the heel – later the cause of his death in the fall of Troy where he had already killed Hector

AEGYPTUS (Gr.) twin brother of DANAUS whose daughters killed all their cousins except LYNCEUS

AGDISTIS (Gr./Rom.) great mother goddess; see CYBELE

AGLOOLIK (Eskimo) lives under ice; good spirit of the seal cave

AITVARAI Baltic winged spirits

ALCESTIS (Gr.) wife of ADMETUS

AMAETHON (Welsh) god of agriculture and third son of DON

AMALTHEA AMALTHEA (Gr.) she-goat (or nymph) and foster-mother of ZEUS whom she suckled in a cave on Crete

ANGRBODA (Norse) daughter of LOKI

ANTICLEA (Gr.) mother of ODYSSEUS

ANTIGONE (Gr.) daughter of JOCASTA by her son & husband OEDIPUS

ARDUINNA Gallic goddess of hunting; DIANA of the Ardennes

ARICONTE Brazilian divinity blamed for the deluge

ASTRAEUS (Gr.) see ZEPHYRUS

AULANERK (Eskimo) lives nude in the sea; cause for gladness

AWIKWAME North American Indian sacred mountain

BAGBARTU BAGMASHTU Urartian gods

BALARAMA (India) wine-loving, strong serpent-like (Sesa) incarnation of VISHNU; half-brother of KRISHNA

BHUSANDI (India) crow which flew into RAMA's mouth

CAPAKRAN (C.Am./Maya) divinity of earthquakes and mountains; twin brother of ZIPACNA

CATEQUIL Inca deity of thunder & lightning

CENTAURS (Gr.) part man, part horse anarchic mountain denizens and children of IXION, king of the LAPITHS; chariot-pullers for DIONYSUS; mounts for EROS

CENTEOTL (C.Am./Aztec) young maize gods

CEPHALUS (Gr.) beloved of EOS who made him kill his wife PROCRIS, who had given him a magic spear and the hound LAELAPS

CERBERUS (Gr.) venomous watchdog of HADES, son of the giant Typhoeus & ECHIDNA, had 3 heads & welcomed all the dead to HADES, to enter but not leave; however, HERMES with his flute & ORPHEUS with his lyre charmed him, as did also honeycakes; as a labour HERCULES lifted him up to earth to make a show of him

CERCOPES (Gr.) twin sons of OCEANUS & THEIA; thieves of Ephesus

CHIMAERA CHIMERA (Gr.) fire-breathing female monster (part lion, part goat, part dragon) of Caria & Lycia, killed by BELLEROPHON; see ECHIDNA

CIPACTLI (C.Am./Aztec) alligator-like divinity

CUKULCAN (Yucatán) the bird-snake & law-giver who came from the West with 19 followers and, after 10 years, sailed away again into the rising sun

DAEDALUS (Gr.) father of ICARUS; son of METION & descendant of Hephaestus; sculptor, & architect of the Labyrinth in Crete

DARZAMAT Latvian protectress of the garden

DEIANIRA (Gr.) 2nd wife of HERCULES who caused his death; sister of MELEAGER & daughter of OENEUS

DIOMEDES (Gr.) Thracian king whose horses fed on human flesh; see TYDEUS

DIONYSUS (Gr.) son of ZEUS & SELENE; married ARIADNE on Naxos; as god of fecundity, warmth & lust, herds, fruits & wine, often in love with nymphs, he was much associated with Bacchantes, rustic Satyrs, goat-god PAN, PRIAPUS & the CENTAURS in the woods

DIVIRIKS Baltic rainbow deity

DZIEWONA Polish DIANA

ECALCHOT Nicaraguan wind god

ENDYMION (Gr.) shepherd son of ZEUS & nymph CALYCE (or of AETHLIUS, ruler of Elis) fathering fifty daughters in his sleep in a cave on Mt Latmus (Caria) with the mood goddess SELENE

EURYDICE (Gr.) wife of ORPHEUS killed by a snake bite

FARBAUTI (Norse) giant father of LOKI

GAHONGAS (N.Am./Iroquois) dwarfs who live in water rocks

GAYOMART (Pers.) creative force dormant for three thousand years whose golden sperm became mankind after his losing battle with the evil spirit AHRIMAN; see YIMA

GLUS-KABE GLUS-KAP (N.Am./Algonquin/Micmac) unselfish killer of a frog monster

GOFANNON Welsh smith; (Irish GOIBNIU)

GUCUMATZ (Guatemala) a plumose snake and maker of life who can take the form of different animals as he pleases

HAPIKERN (C.Am./Maya) fiend of the human race; see YANTHO & USUKUN

HARMONIA (Gr.) married CADMUS with all the gods in attendance; daughter of ARES and Aphrodite

HEIMDALL (Norse) an AESIR god, guarded the Bifrost (Rainbow bridge) that linked the Asgard gods to mankind & sounded the last trumpet call commencing the final battle of RAGNARÖK (Twilight of the Gods) in which he killed LOKI, although he died too; born of 9 mothers!

HELLOTIS (Gr.) see EUROPA

HERACLES (Gr.) strong son of ZEUS & ALCMENE (grandchild of PERSEUS) who had to labour for his half-brother Eurystheus; husband of MEGARA whom he killed together with their children

HERCULES (Rom.) 12 Labours: 1. to kill the Nemean Lion & obtain the skin of invulnerability; 2. the destruction of the 9-headed Lernaean Hydra; 3. capturing the wild boar of Erymanthus; 4. dispersing the Stymphalian Birds; 5. the Ceryncian Hind; 6. cleaning the Augeian Stables; 7. the Cretan Bull; 8. the mares of DIOMEDES; 9. Girdle of

Hippolete; 10. the cattle of Geryon;
11. the golden apples of the
Hesperides; 12. the journey to the
Underworld

HESPERUS (Gr.) he & his brother
Phosphorus appear (as sons of **EOS**)
jointly as **VENUS** the morning or
evening star; he was also perhaps a
son of **ATLAS**; his sons were Daedelion
& Ceyx & his daughters (3 or 4) were
the **HESPERIDES** (see Classical
Miscellany); they were the clouds, or
celestial flocks, in the West, near the
setting sun, who lived in their garden,
watching over the Golden Apples

HUECUVUS (Chile) demon readily able
to assume any other form

HYPERION (Gr.) a Titan, ancestor of
man; father (with **THEIA**) of **HELIOS**
(the Sun) **SELENE** (the Moon), **CIRCE**
(debased love) & **EOS** (Dawn/Aurora)

IPHICLES (Gr.) father of **IOLAUS** and
mortal half-brother of **HERACLES**

ISMENIUS (Gr.) river god; his son
LINUS killed by **HERCULES** for trying
to teach him how to play the lyre

JELPIN-JA (Ugric/Vogul) sacred rivers
and lakes

JOCA-HUVA (Haiti) lord in heaven; see
ATABEI

JURASMAT Latvian mother of the sea

JUVENTAS Roman goddess of youth;
(Gr. **HEBE**)

KAKA-GUIA (Guinea) bull-headed
deliverer of the souls of the dead to
the chief deity **NYAMIA**

K'RACOCHA Inca high god

KULLERVO (Fin.) shepherd and evil
spirit

KUMARBIS Hurrite father of the gods;
see **KUMARBI & ANUS**

KUNG-KUNG (Ch.) horned monster
whose power-struggle with **SHANG-TI**
put heaven askew; see **KAM-FU**

KUSANAGI (Jap.) the sword **SUSANOO**
found in the snake-god's tail & which
later became one of the 3 emblems of
Imperial power

LATIARIS (Rom.) see **JUPITER**

LAUKAMAT Latvian protectress of the
field

LOMPSALO Lappish wizard

LOVIATAR (Fin.) black-faced creature
with horrible skin, goddess of illness,
who gave birth to nine monsters; see
TUONI

LUKELONG (Oceania) female creator of
heaven and earth

LUXOVIUS (Celtic) god of the baths and
healing married to **BRIXIA**

MAMA-QORA Inca sea mother

MANANNAN MANAWYDAN (Celtic/
Welsh) deity of the sea; see **LLYR &
LER**

MARATHON (Gr.) fire-breathing bull
assailed by **THESEUS** (son of **AEGEUS**)

MARZANNA Polish patron of orchards

MELAMPUS (Gr.) seer who could
understand the talk of animals;
descendant of **AEOLUS** (son of
HELLEN); see **BIAS**

MELEAGER (Gr.) descendant of **AEOLUS**
who killed his uncles; see **ALTHAEA**

MENELAUS (Gr.) son of **ATREUS &
AEROPE**; brother of **AGAMEMNON**; see
PROTEUS

MESHKENT (eg.) brick-shaped goddess
with human head sprouting long
palm shoots & symbol of crouching
mothers-to-be

METSABOK (C.Am./Lacandones) divine
master of rain and clouds

MEZAVIRS Latvian divinity of forest

MINOTAUR (Gr.) half human, half bull
monster of Crete; offspring of
PASIPHAE & POSEIDON's white bull;
killed by **THESEUS & ARIADNE**

MORPHEUS (Gr.) patron of dreams
about humans; see **PHOBETOR**

MORRIGAN MORRIGU (Celtic) war
goddess & consort of Irish **DAGDA**; see
MACHA

MYRTILUS (Gr.) charioteer of
OENOMAUS (King of Pisa killed by his
son-in-law **PELOPS**) and thrown into
the Myrtoan sea by **PELOPS**

NAUPLIUS (Gr.) see **AMYMONE**

NEFERTUM NEFERTEM/NEFERTEMU (Eg.)
lion-headed man; lotus god; son of
PTAH & SEKHMET (or **BAST**)

NEKHEBET (Eg.) see **BUTO, NEKHBET**

NINGURSU NINURTA/IMDUGUD/ANZU
(Sum.) as a rain cloud huge lion-
headed bird with a thunderous roar;
deity of tilling & ploughing

NINIGARA (Sum.) cream and butter
goddess and spouse of **NINHAR**

NIPARAYA (California/Indian) bodyless
omnipotent god of heaven & earth;
dispenser of food to all beings; father
of **QUAAYAYP**

NYALITCH NYALIC (Africa/Nile) chief
god of the Dinka people

ODYSSEUS ULYSSES (Gr./Rom.) the
hero of a great wandering saga tale of
the victor of the siege of Troy,

interlaced with connections with the
Greek gods, magic, Cyclops etc.; son
of Laertes & Anticleia (or of
SISYPHUS); King of Ithaca; brave &
wise wanderer married to PENELOPE;
consort of CIRCE, CALYPSO etc.

OENONAUS (Gr.) see MYRTILUS

ORAMATUA Tahitian 'forefathers';
spirits

OSSIANIC Cycle (Celtic) tells about the
superhuman exploits of a band of
young heroes (the fiana); named after
Ossian, their greatest poet & son of
FINN

PACA-MAMA Inca Earth Mother

PASIPHAË (Gr.) see GLAUCUS &
MINOTAUR

PELOPIDS (Gr.) see TANTALUS

PENELOPE (Gr.) mother of PAN; wife of
ODYSSEUS or Telegonus, his son by
the sorceress CIRCE; daughter of
ICARIUS of Sparta and nymph
PERIBOCA

PENTHEUS (Gr.) King of Thebes, from
whose prison DIONYSUS escaped, to
strike Pentheus' mother, AGAVE, & all
the other women of Thebes with
madness

PHAETHON (Gr.) killed by a
thunderbolt (ZEUS) while searching
for his father HELIOS; son of nymph
CLEMENE; see EOS

PHILEMON & BAUCIS senior hospitable
Phrygian couple who received ZEUS
and HERMES

PHOBETOR (Gr.) provider of dreams
about animals; see MORPHEUS

PORTUNUS Roman god of harbours
(and city gates)

POSEIDON (Gr.) major sea god; brother
of ZEUS; see TYRO

QUAAYAYP see NIPARAYA

QUIATEOR Nicaraguan rain god

QUIRINUS Roman war and state god

RAGNARÖK (Norse, 'the final fate of the
powers'); the final battle between the
AESIR gods & the Giants when the
Sun will be devoured & a terrifying
winter spread over the earth
(Götterdämmerung)

RHIANNON (Welsh) Gallic mare goddess
EPONA; Irish MACHA; wife of king
PWYLL; mother of PRYDERI whom she
killed

ROSMERTA (Celtic) goddess of
abundance; (Rom. MERCURY)

SABAZIUS (Thrace) see MEN

SAKHALIN (Siberia) see MAMALDI

SATARUPA (India) see BRAHMA

SHARRUMA son of HEBAT, Hurrian
Queen of gods

SILVANUS Roman god of untilled earth
associated with PAN

SISYPHUS (Gr.) trickster husband of
MEROPE and son of AEOLUS; grandfather of Bellerophon, the hero who
fought the CHIMAERA with PEGASUS

SLEIPNIR (Norse) magical, eight-legged
horse of ODIN, born of trickster LOKI
(as a mare) and swift & clever
Svadilfari

SOATSAKI (N.Am.) beloved wife of
Morning Star (a heavenly power &
daughter of the Sun & Moon) whose
disobedience relating to a turnip
caused the Sun to expel her from
heaven; see POIA

STRIBORG STRIBOG Russian wind god

SUCELLUS Dis Pater (Celtic) often
depicted with wooden hammer
(mallet) & drinking cup

SUSANOWO SUSANOO (Jap.) who sired
8 children, revered as princes, with
his sister Amaterasu; their first-born
male child was the ancestor of the
Emperors; on one of his exploits he
killed the man-eating 8-headed snake
& thunder god with his sword; see
KUSANAGI

TANGAROA (Polynesia, N.Z.) made the
earth and lesser gods and mated with
HINE, but sprouted mankind from
himself

TANTALUS (Gr.) son of ZEUS (or
TIMOLUS of Lydia) and ruler of
Sipylus in Lydia/Phrygia who abused
his friendship with the gods and
suffers never-ending hunger and
thirst in HADES as a result; cursed
ancestor of the PELOPIDS; father of
PELOPS & NIOBE

TARTARUS (Gr.) see HAEMUS

TELEPINU son of Hittite weather god
TARHUNT/TARHUND; his disappearance
caused life on earth to retreat but the
sting of a bee made him reappear &
life resumed

TEUTATES (Celtic) god of the clan &
messenger; (Rom. MARS, MERCURY/
Gr. ARES, HERMES); see ESUS &
TARANIS

THOUERIS (Eg.) see TAURT

THUNNUPA (Chile/Aymara) bearded
white puritan from the North who
said No to polygamy and chica
(popular drink)

THYESTES see AEGISTHUS

TONATIUH (C.Am.) Aztec sun god of the fifth age connected with the eagle

TPEREAKL (Micronesia) with his wife Latmikaik (who emerged from a sea-lashed rock) they rule the world & are the source of life

T'SAI-SHEN (Ch.) divine lords of wealth

T'SAO-SHEN (Ch.) divine lords of the kitchen

UPELBURI (Hurrian) see KUMARBI

VAMMATAR (Fin.) diety of illness and pain

VARPULIS (Slav) wind god and follower of PERUN

VASUDEVA (India) father of KRISHNA

VODYANOI (Slav) huge fish and fearsome water deity covered with moss

WURUSEMU Hattic sun goddess (Hittite Arinnitti) and wife of TARHUN/TARHUND, the weather god

YUNCEMIL (C.Am.) death deity; see ECHUA & BACABS

ZEPHYRUS (Gr.) the West Wind, suitor of Hyacinthus; son of EOS by ASTRAEUS

ZUTTIBUR (Slav) sylvan god

TWO-LETTER WORDS

A

gl, go **AA** volcanic lava; river (Scand.)
AB, AV a Hebrew month
AB- as prefix (from; away; off)
el, ch **AC** alternating current; Actinium
AD a short advertisement; Anno Domini
ch **AG** silver (Argentum)
AH exclamation of Satisfaction
zo **AI** South American three-toed sloth
cp **AI** Artificial Intelligence
ch, pc **AL** Aluminium; adaptation level
AL AZ, 'The' in Arabic
ch **AM** 1st person sing. to be; Americium
ps **AM** Anno Mundi; amplitude modulation
AN if; ornate box; Actinium; Acton
rl **AN** indefinite article; deity (Anu)
AO any other; essential (alpha & omega)
bt **AP** son of (Welsh); arboreal pollen
pm, me **AP** apothecaries' measure
ch **AR** Argon, inert gas
me, nm **AS** Roman pound & bronze coin
ma, ch **AS** integer; Arsenic
nm **AT** preposition of location, scale; coin
ch **AT** Astatine, radioactive element
ch, mn, as **AU** gold; element; astronomical unit
me **AV, AB** Jewish month; (avdp) weight
AW interjection
to **AX** axe
AY, AYE yes, yeah; more so
AZ, AL 'the' in Arabic

B

ch, rl **BA** Barium; the soul (Egypt)
BE 2nd letter; exist; Chinese language
ch **BE** Beryllium; Japanese bread-winner
ch **BI** Bismuth
BI- bisexual; both of; double
ch **BK** Berkelium
bt **BO** sacred tree of Buddha
ch **BR** Bromine
me **BU** bushel; tsubo, Jap. measure
BY preposition of agent

C

ch **CA** Calcium; ca' canny (Sc.); alert
me **CC** cubic centimetre (liquid)
ch, me **CD** Cadmium; candela (luminance)
CD corps diplomatique
ch **CE** Cerium; letter 'C'
ch **CF** Californium
me **CI** curie (radioactivity)
me **CL** chlorine; centilitre
me **CM** centimetre
ch **CO** Cobalt; company
ch **CR** Chromium; credit
ch **CS** Caesium
md **CT** computer (axial) tomography (CT)
ch **CU** Copper

D

DA father; knife; yes (Rus.)
me **DB** decibel
el **DC** direct current
mu **DE** musical note; Liberian tribe (KRU)
DE letter 'D'
mu **DI-** of both; pair; musical note (di)
me **DL** decilitre
mu **DO** act; ditto, perform; 1st note (doh)
me **DR** dram; debit; doctor
ch, ec **DY** Dysprosium; plant detritus (lake)

E

go **EA** inlet; drainage canal in Fens
rl **EA** Chaldean fish god (Enki)
me **EB** Epstein-Barr virus
rl **EC** Yeniseian (Siberia) deity
EE eye (Sc.); letter 'E'
EF letter 'F'
EG for example; ancient pyramid
EH exclamation
EL 'the' (masc.) in Sp.; letter 'L'
el, me, rl **EL** electricity; Dutch metre; deity
'EM them (colloquial); letter 'M'
pr **EM** printing unit of space
pr **EN** half the width of an em
cf **EP-** outside; extra; above

ER interjection

rl **ES** letter 'S'; soul (Finno–Ugric & Hung.)

ch **ES** Einsteinium, element

as **ET** Ephemeris Time (celestial mechanics)

ch **EU** Europium, element; European Union

EX late; out of

cf **EX-** formerly

F

mu **FA** 4th note (major key)

ch, mu **FE** Iron; 4th note (minor key)

mu **FI** musical note

rl **FO** Chinese Buddha

ch **FR** Francium, element

me **FT** foot

rl **FU** Ch. lit. form; prefecture; pot; god

FY, FIE denoting disgust

G

ch **GA** Gallium; people (S. Ghana)

me **GB** Gilbert; Great Britain

ch **GD** Gadolinium, element

ch, rl **GE** Germanium; Mother Earth, Gaea (Gr.)

GE S.Am. Indian tribe & language

tx **GI** judo, karate garment

GO proceed; depart; fare

me, ga **GQ** Japanese measure & board game (i–go)

mu **GU** violin; rainy season (Somalia)

H

ch **HA** Hahnium; exclamation

ch **HE** Helium; male pronoun

ch **HF** Hafnium, element

ch **HG** Mercury

HI exclamation; North Am. greeting

HM, HUM perhaps; disbelief

ch, tx **HO** Holmium; exclamation; Jap. dress

HO, HUO Chinese wine storage vessel

HO tribe & language of Bihar (India)

rl **HU** ancient invaders of China; vessels; gods

me **HZ** hertz, radio wave frequency

I

pc **ID, IDE** fish (carp); instinctive impulses; hedonist (Fr.)

rl **ID** (Syriac ida), Arabic festival

IE that is; pine tree

IF supposing that

IL male pronoun, definite article (lit.)

I'M I am

me **IN** prep. within, inside; inch

rl **IO** beloved of Jupiter; Zeus' beloved heifer

ch **IR** Iridium, element

rl **IS** being; existing; soul (ES)

cf **-IS** of abnormal condition, disease (Gr.)

IT personality, a thing; sex appeal

J

rl **JE** the Sun (China)

rl **JI** Japanese Buddhist sect ('times')

JO a sweetheart (Sc.)

K

zo, bt **KA** jackdaw (Sc.); tropical tree

rl, me **KA** spirit; Babylonian measure, Qa

me **KG** kilogram

me **KM** kilometre

KO knock out; Jap. floral art school

ch **KR** Krypton

KU ancient Chinese wine beaker

me **KW** kilowatt

zo **KY, KYE** kine, cattle (Sc.)

L

LA 'the' (Fr., It., Sp.: fem.)

mu, ch **LA, LAH** 6th note; Lanthanum

LE 'the' (Fr. Masc.)

mu **LE** musical note

md **LH** luteinizing hormone

me **LI** Ch. character; mile; food vessel

nm **LI** coin; Hainan island people (Ch.)

rl, ch, mu **LI** Ch. 'the Earth'; Lithium; note

lt, me **LM** lumen (light)

LO and behold!'; look – a surprise for you!

ch **LR** Lawrencium, element

ps **LS** -coupling (nuclear physics)

ch, rl **LU** Lutetium; Chinese deity

lt, me **LX** lux (luminance)

M

rl, eg **MA** mother; goddess; mechanical
  advantage
    MC son of (Sc., Irish)
mu **ME** 1st-person pronoun; musical
  note
ch **MG** Magnesium
mu, me **MI** 3rd note (sol-fa scale); mile
me **ML** millilitre
me **MM** millimetre
md **MO** moment; Medical Officer
ch **MO** Molybdenum; Modus Operandi
    MO -ho, Tungus tribe in Manchuria
    MP Member of Parliament;
  legislator
md **MS** abbr. for Mrs or Miss; multiple
  sclerosis
    MU letter of Greek alphabet
    MY of me, mine

N

ch **NA** Sodium (Natrium); negative
  reply
ch **NB** Niobium, element
ch **ND** Neodymium, element
ch **NE** Neon; negative reply
ch **NO** Nobelium; negative reply
ch **NP** Neptunium, element
lt, me **NT** nit (luminance)
    NU Gr. letter; minority population
  (Ch.)
rl **NU** Nun, Kua, deities (Eg., Ch.)

O

lw **OB** objection
    OD magnetic force
me **OE** grandchild; oersted (magnetic)
    OF preposition of possession; af
  (Sc.)
    OG King of Basan (Old Test.)
    OH exclamation; surprise
    OK all correct (Americanism)
mu, ri **OM** Hindu mantra chant
    ON preposition of location
mu **OP** opus (musical or artistic work)
hd **OR** alternatively; heraldic gold
pl, ch **OS** bone; mouth; Osmium
cf, rl **OT-, OTO-** (Gr.) of the ear; deity Ot
    OU OW, exclamation of pain
zo **OX** a bull (cattle)
me **OZ** ounce; (Australia)

P

ch **PA** Protactinium; Maori fort
ch **PD** Palladium, element
me **PE** Portuguese measure
    PH acid/alkaline content value
pr **PI** mixed type (circle); Gr. letter
    PI ritual jade (China)
me **PK** peck
ch **PM** Promethium; afternoon; Prime
  Minister
ch **PO** Polonium; people (Min-chia)
rl **PO** chamber-pot; Ch. earthly soul
rl **PO** Maori 'night'; the Void
  (Polynesia)
ch **PR** Praseodynium; public relations
me **PT** pint
ch, nm, me **PU** Plutonium; Ch. money &
  measure

Q

me **QA, KA** Mesopotamian liquid
  measure
me **QT** quart

R

ch, rl **RA** Radium; Eg. sun god (Re, Phra)
ch **RB** Rubidium, element
me **RD** rod
mu, rl **RE** 2nd note; concerning; (Ra, Phra)
ch **RE** Rhenium, element
md **RH** rhesus blood type
me **RI** Japanese miles
ch **RN** Radon, element
ch **RU** Ruthenium, element

S

me **SB** stilb
ch **SC** Scandium, element
ch, mu, me **SE** Selenium; musical note; Jap. me
ch, mu **SI** Silicon; 5th note (minor)
me, rl **SI** Intern. System of Units; Inca
  Moon
ch **SM** Samarium, element
ch **SN** Tin, element
mu **SO** thus, therefore, then, 5th note
  (sol)
    SO language (Laos, Thailand)
ch, me **SR** Strontium; steradian
me **ST** street; saint (abbreviation);
  stokes

T

ch **TA** thanks; Tantalum, element
ch, md **TB** Terbium; element; tuberculosis
ch **TC** Technetium, element
ch, mu **TE** Tellurium; 7th musical note (ti)
ch **TH** Thorium, radioactive element
bt **TI** tree-lily (Asia, Polynesia)
ch, mu **TI** Titanium; Ch. flute; 7th note (te)
rl **TI** Ch. people, concept & deity
     (T'ien)
ch, md **TM** Thulium; me of glucose in man
me **TO** prep. of direction; Jap. liquid me
me, rl **TU** Ch. miles; chief warrior
     (Polynesia)
     TV (television)

U

mu **UD, OUD** Islamic stringed instrument
     UG UH, ugh, exclamation of horror,
     disgust
rl **UL** Lord of the moon (Oceania)
     UM sound of pensive understanding
cf **UN-** negative, not
rl **UO** Mayan 2nd month; rain god
     acolytes
     UP preposition, adverb (above)
rl **UR** of the Chaldees
cf **UR-** prehistoric; original; primitive
     (Ger.)
     US objective of 'we'
mu **UT** 1st note; Universal Time

V

mu **VA** go on
rl **VE** sacred place; brother of Odin
go **VO, VOE,** vae, firth; creek

W

me **WA** exclamation; unit of length
     (wah)
nt **WA** Pacific outrigger canoe
me **WB** weber
     WC toilet; (bog)
     WE plural pronoun
     WO WHOA! stop!
     WU Ch. dialect; -chin, Ch. pottery
     glaze
rl **WU** deepest contemplative Buddhist
     experience (Ch.)

X

ch **XE** Xenon, element
nm **XU** Vietnamese monetary unit

Y

     YA yes, exclamation
ch **YB** Ytterbium, element
me **YD** yard
     YE you (plural, obs.); the (obs.)
     YI Chinese philosophy
     YO exclamation of surprise
mu **YO** basic Japanese scale
rl **YU** precious jade; wine vessel;
     monster (Ch.)

Z

     ZA abbr. of pizza (N. Am.)
     ZA guilds of feudal Japan
ch **ZN** zinc, element
zo **ZO** Himalayan cattle; Jap. image
ch **ZR** Zirconium, element
     ZZ slumber (cartoon indication)

THREE-LETTER WORDS

A

rl **AAH** the Moon-God of Egypt
me **A-AK** Dutch liquid measure
ABA Eastern camel-hair fabric
ABB yarn for the warp
ABC a railway guide; alphabet
ABP abbr. for Archbishop
ABS anti-lock braking system (cars)
ABU father (Arabic)
ABY atone; pay penalty; retribution
ACE aviator; particle; (cards); great, terrific
lw, pc **ACT** deed in writing; do; perform
ADD join; tag; annex; append; tot
ADO stir; fuss; commotion; hubbub
ADS advertisements
to, ag **ADZ** adze; wood-shaping; tilling
nm **AES** Roman money
nt **AFT** abaft; astern
rl **AGA, AGHA** oriental title; (Khan) Ismaili spiritual leader
AGE era; period; epoch; senility
AGO past; gone
AHA! exclamation of discovery
rl **AIA** Sumerian god
AID succour; help; subsidy; assistant (-fatigue, -burn out)
-AID funds, events for charity
AIL suffer; pain; peak; pine
AIM object; direct; intend; purpose
AIR mien; ventilate; display; tune
AIT river or lake islet; eyot
bt **ALA** wing or side petal of blossom
rl **ALB** white linen clerical vestment
ALE mead; beer
ALK resin from turpentine tree
ALL entirely; whole
go **ALP** pasture land; (high mountain)
md **ALS** serum
mu **ALT** high notes in the scale
rl **AMA** holy wine or vessel
me **AMP** electrical unit (abbr. for ampère)
rl **ANA** Celtic goddess; equal parts
cp **ANA-** prefix; up; back; again
cp **ANA-** without-; interference
pr **AND** the ampersand, &
cp **AND** logic element; binaries
lw **ANN** annat (Sc.)
zo **ANT** emmet; pismire; termite
ANU Celtic goddess; Babylonian sea-god

ANY some (in questions, negatives)
zo **APE** imitate; copy. mimic; monkey
APT appropriate; pertinent; prone
ARB dealer in take-over bids (Am.)
el, ma **ARC** luminous bridge; curve; (lamp)
me **ARE** hectare (2.5 acres)
ARG abbreviation for chemical silver
rl, nt **ARK** chest; coffer; place of refuge; floating zoo
ARM equip; limb; estuary
bt **ARN** elder tree
ART skill; dexterity; craft
md **ARV** Aids related virus
bt, rl **ASA** gum; Norse God (Valhalla)
pg **ASA** colour system
ASE Peer Gynt's mother
bt, gl, go **ASH** cinder, forest tree; wood; volcanic
ASK interrogate; invite; sue
zo **ASP** viper; snake (Cleopatra)
zo **ASS** moke; burro; donkey
ATE Goddess of Mischief; eaten
AUF fool; oaf; simpleton
zo **AUK** flightless sea bird; garefowl
me **AUM** Afrikaans liquid measure
AVA kava; Hawaiian palm-lily drink
rl **AVE** prayer; hail
AWE reverential veneration
to **AWL** the cobbler's tool; bradawl
bt **AWN** beard in chaff
to **AXE** to cut down; hatchet
cf **AXO-** of nerve fibre projection (Gr.)
AYE yea; for ever
rl **AZI** Altaic spirit

B

zo **BAA** to bleat (sheep)
BAB fishing bob
BAC ferry; brewing tub
BAD evil; depraved; detrimental; baneful
ga **BAG** hand-; sack; steal; score
BAH! a derogatory exclamation
BAM bamboozle; hoax
BAN muslin; bar; interdict; outlaw
ck **BAP** small soft bread loaf (Scotland)
lw **BAR** pub; ban; except; hinder; law
mu, hd **BAR** musical notation division; fess
go, nv **BAR** (sand-); rod; glazing; window
BAR ingot (gold); (prison, zoo)

cf **BAR-** of weight, pressure (Gr.)
BAT spree; batsman; vampire
bed **BAT** striker; brick-; lead wedge
me, nm **BAT** Thai measure and monetary
unit
bt **BAY** bark; laurel; (sick-)
go, bd **BAY** cove; bight; wing; mill-dam
gl, bt **BED** -rock; couch; berth; layer;
plant-
zo, hd **BEE** insect; emblem of Fr. Empire
BEG crave; implore; entreat; petition
BEG BEY, Ottoman title
rl, tc **BEL, BAAL** god; circuit amplifier
ma **BEL** logarithmic unit
bt **BEN** winged seed of ben-tree
BET lay; wager; stake; gamble
BEY, BEG Ottoman title
BIB sip; tipple; baby's napkin
zo, ga **BIB** whiting pout; (fencing)
BID order; direct; invite
BID tender, offer (auction)
BIG huge; swollen; pregnant
BIN receptacle (wine, corn, bread,
litter-)
cf, bl **BIO-** organic, of life (Gr.)
BIS encore
to **BIT** piece; fragment (lathe); cutter
cp, nm **BIT** harness; binary digit; account
zo **BOA** snake; fur collar
nm **BOB** style of hairdressing; Br.
shilling
ga **BOB** dog-sleigh; (racing)
BOG sog; morass; swamp; marsh;
(WC)
zo **BOK, BUCK** a South African deer
zo **BOM, BOMA** snake (anaconda)
BOO cry down; decry; hoot; execrate
zo **BOT** the larva of the bot-fly
nt **BOW** tie; prow; knot; bend, defer
(squash)
ga, mu **BOW** arc; archery; (violin stick)
el **BOX** encase; chest; container; (TV)
cp, rw **BOX** flowchart; signal; connection
bt **BOX** seat (theatre; driver); shrub
ga, nt **BOX** cuff; fight; spar
ga **BOX** close-rank (cycling); rugby
scrum)
ga **BOX** abdomen protector (cricket,
baseball)
BOY lad; page; stripling; Champagne
BOZ Charles Dickens' non-de-
plume
BRA woman's garment; brassière
me **BTU** Br. Thermal Unit as joules
BUB yeast; strong drink; boy (USA.
Ger.)
bt **BUD** sprout; blossom; graft; chum
(Am.)

zo **BUG** -bear; insect; secret mike
BUM bailiff; loafer; backside
ct, nm **BUN** coiffure style; penny; (baker's-)
BUR, BURR rough edge
bt, to **BUR** chestnut shell; drill bit (lathe)
cp, el **BUS** omnibus; trunk route for
signals; -bar
BUT yet; except; nevertheless; unless
BUY purchase; bribe; corrupt
ga **BYE** (cricket); (golf); (tournament
draw)

C

me **CAB** cabriolet; taxi-; Heb. 3 pints
cf **CAC-** degenerate and diseased;
(cacaphony)
CAD vulgar rascal; cheat; deceiver
cp **CAL** Conversational Algebraic
Language
CAM oval wheel; (machinery)
CAN able to; preserve (food);
pannikin
ar **CAP** out-do; headgear; roof of
windmill
CAP explosive; cover
CAR vehicle
nt, zo **CAT** tackle; whip; rig; puss; mouser
mt **CAT** clear-air turbulence (aviation)
md **CAT** computerised axial
tomography, X-ray, CT
CAW KAW, bird sound
CAY kay; key; shoal; reef; islet
CEE a shape of spring
rl **CER, KER** Gr. destructive spirit
ma, rl **CHI** Gr. letter; -square; Ch. breath
of life
me **CHO** Jap. unit of length; commodity
of tax
CID (el-), Spanish warrior
CIG cigarette (fag)
CIT citizen
CLY to steal
bl **CNS** Central Nervous System
zo **COB** pony; male swan; spider
bt, ck **COB** a head; spike of maize; nut
nm **COB** harbour; clay; basket; dollar
zo **COD** pod; husk; deceive; codfish
COG toothed wheel; humble status
bd **COG** rib (roof tile); wooden bowl
cr, nt **COG** tenon (locking joint); small
boat
COG coax; cajole; cheat; wheedle
go, gl **COL** mountain pass; neck; arête (Fr.)
nv, mu **CON** (pro and con); steer; swindle;
with
CON study; memorize; a convict

cf **CON-** prefix: conjoint
COO dove's voice of peace
ga **COP** hill; head; tuft
COP policeman; arrest; (ice hockey)
mu, me **COR** heart; horn; Hebrew bushels
bt **COS** lettuce
nt **COT** cottage; crib; small boat
zo **COW** bovine; browbeat; intimidate;
depress
rl **COU** Celtic and Gallic god
ga **COX** coxswain; steersman (rowers)
COY shy; bashful; demure; diffident
COZ cousin (obs.)
CRI the crackle of pewter
ck **CRU** yield; produce; wine/
champagne (Fr.)
CRY sob; yell; bawl; blazon
zo **CUB** enclosure for cattle; young
animal
CUB scout
CUD food for re-chewing (bovine)
CUE signal; stimulus; shuffleboard
ga **CUE** (billiards); (acting)
CUP bleed; succeed anew; prize;
(drink)
bd **CUP** a beverage; warp in plank
zo **CUR** mongrel; pariah; dog
CUT incision; gash; wound; channel
CUT chop; sever; carve; avoid;
shorten
go **CWM, CWYM** steep rounded hollow
(Welsh)
CWT a hundredweight (50kg)
cf **-CYT, -CYTE** of the cells

D

zo, ck, ga **DAB** fish; expert; trial effort; touch
ground (motorcycling); apply
paint
DAD a blow; to thrash; to scatter;
father
DAG shred; cut; dagger; pistol
to **DAH, DHAR** Burmese curved knife
ar **DAK** post; bungalow (Ind.)
bt **DAL** lentil
bd, zo, nm **DAM** barrier; brood mare with foals;
Indian coin (dawm)
DAN tub; a title; Israeli tribe
(Danites); martial arts expert
DAP to fish with a may-fly
zo **DAR** dace (fish)
DAW idiot; jackdaw
DAY epoch; era; 24 hours
ch **DDT** pesticide
DEB a debutante
el **DEE** die (Sc.); electrodes

nc, me **DEL** nabla; differential operator
DEN cave; lair; haunt; snuggery
DEW an aqueous precipitation
DEY dairymaid
DIB dip; make holes
DID diddled; performed
pr **DIE** embossed metal block; (dice);
dee (Sc.)
ar **DIE** perish (death); pedestal dado
ga **DIG** excavate; delve; appreciate
(slang); scoop; (volleyball)
zo **DIK** -dik, small African antelope;
trouble
DIM obscure; vague; tarnish
pt, me **DIN** clamour; row; paper size
pg **DIN** colour system
DIP dop; duck; douse; souse; swim
ce, ck **DIP** descent; magnetic angle;
(fondue)
gl **DIP** (strike); (pole); lower; immerse
cf, md **DIS-** neg. prefix; disjoint (disease);
fail
rl **DIS** Pluto, the underworld (Gr.)
DIT a ditty (Spenser); (verse)
rl **DIV** (dividend); evil spirit (Persia)
ga **DIX** lowest trump (card game)
nv, me **DME** distance measuring equipment
bl **DNA** deoxyribonucleic acid; genetic
heredity code
md **DOC** doctor
DOD clip; poll; lop
zo **DOE** female of fallow-deer, hare,
rabbit
zo, ml, to **DOG** canine; (firedogs); to trail;
spike; dressing iron; nippers
zo **DOG** -day cicada; (-winkle, a snail)
mu **DOH** first note of tonic sol-fa scale
me **DOL** pain intensity unit
DOM Portuguese title (lord, prince)
rl **DON** put on; assume; Sp. title; Danu
(a god)
DOP to dip; duck; Cape brandy
DOR befool; mock; mockery; bedim
zo **DOR, DORR** dung-beetle; drone
mu **DOT** decimal point; full stop; speck;
lengthened note
DOW fit and able
mt **DRY** parch; desiccate; (freeze-)
go, tx **DRY** (forest); (gas); (spinning)
nm **DUA** Malaysian money
cn **DUB** to name; substitute sound track
DUB to smooth; rub; confer
knighthood
DUD worthless; defective
DUE owing; proper; becoming; (tax)
mu **DUE** expected; two parts shared
DUG udder; nudged; exhumed;
excavated

md, nt **DUM** dum fever; Dutch fishing boat
DUN mound; sand-brown; gloomy
DUN to cure fish; to demand payment
bl **DUN** mayfly development; pupa of imago
mu **DUO** song in two parts; partnership
DUP to open
mu **DUR** major key (Ger.)
DUX a leader (Lat.); (duke)
me **DWT** pennyweight
DYE colour; tinge; stain
md, cf **DYS-** (dysfunction), failure

E

ma, me, ps **EAN** to produce; effective atomic number
ag, pl **EAR** plough; till; lug; heed; hearing organ
EAT chew; consume; devour; erode
EAU -de-Cologne, anti-odour water
EBB recede (tide); wane; subside
el **ECM** electronic counter measures apparatus
el, md **ECT** electroconvulsive (shock) therapy
nm **ECU** 5-franc coin; European currency unit
EDO last trad. Jap. period (Tokugawa)
EEC European Economic Community
md **EEG** electroencephalography (neurology)
zo **EEL** snake-like fish
pl **EEN** eyes (Sc.)
E'EN even
E'ER ever
EFE a Pygmy people
zo **EFT** a newt; forthwith (obs.)
bl, ck **EGG** ovum; (hen's, new laid-); incite
ar **EGG** oval (-shape); -and dart; esteem
pc **EGO** I, the self; conscious subject
pc **EGO-** -tism; -centric; self-centred aspect
vt **EIA** equine infectious anaemia
ma **EIK, EKE** add; addition (Sc.)
EKE increase; likewise; extra income
ELD old age; olden times; decrepitude
rl **ELF** sprite; gnome; imp; pixy/pixie
zo **ELK** moose; the whooper swan
me **ELL** cloth length; elbow; pipe-fitting
bt **ELM** stately tree
ELO mask and show of Nupe tribe (Nigeria)

el **EMF** electromotive force
zo **EMU** Australian bird, cassowary type
ps, me **EMU** electromagnetic unit
END conclude; finality; terminate; death
mu **END** aim; -s and means; -piece (encore)
gl, bl **END** moraine; -plate (illustration)
ENE once (Sc.)
fr **ENG** durable dark Burmese wood
ENS entity; (realissimum, perfect being)
EON, AEON an age; eternity
rl **EOS** dawn goddess (Aurora) (Gr.)
cf **EPI-** outer-; skin (-dermis); epicentre
bl **EPP** end-plate potential
ps **EPR** electron paramagnetic resonance
ERA age; period; epoch; cycle; time
ERE before; sooner than
ERF small garden in S. Africa
me, pc, go **ERG** unit of work; 1 dyne; force; purpose; sand dune desert (Arab)
me, md **ERG** electroretinogram (retina)
zo **ERN** sea eagle
ERR offend; sin; wander; tresspass
bt **ERS** vetch
ESS the letter 'S'
ps, me **ESU** electrostatic system of units
ETC et cetera, and so forth
vt **EVA** equine viral arteritis (disease)
rl **EVE** evening (ere an event); Adam's mate
zo **EWE** fem. sheep; people (SE Ghana, Toto)
cf, ar **EXO-** exterior of; (exogamy); (exonarthex)
pl, mt **EYE** visual organ; (needle); (cyclone)
EYE observe; watch; view; bud; island

F

FAD whim; craze; crochet; hobby
bl **FAD** flavinco enzyme 'D'
FAG knot; -end (cigarette)
FAG drudge; fatigue; a bore; pupil servant
mu **FAH** spoken sol-fa note (4th)
rl **FAM** the hand (slang); Bantu god (Africa)
FAN air cooler; flutter; blower
ae **FAN** admirer; agitate; inflame; -jet
go, ag **FAN** alluvial; spread out; thresher
ag, ga **FAN** belt; winnower; (Am. football)
FAP drunk; fuddled (Shak.)

pc **FAP** fixed action pattern (ethology)
bt, ck **FAR** distant; remote; buck-wheat
ck, pr **FAT** obese; grease; vat; printing term
lw **FAS** free alongside ship (commerce)
FAW gypsy
tc **FAX** electronic facsimile transmission
FAY, FEY clean out; fairy; elf; fit closely
FEB the shortest month, February
FED ate; subsisted; supplied (means)
FEE remuneration; pay; reward; toll
nm **FEI** yap, Micronesian monetary unit
go, nm **FEN** marsh lands; Ch. weight and money
FET get; fetch (obs.)
lw **FEU** tenure; lease; tax (Sc.)
FEW scant; rare; scarce
FEY, FAY spiritual exaltation; fated
tx **FEZ** cap with tassel (Moslem)
FIB petty falsehood; white lie
FIE add; insult (obs.)
ht **FIG** fruit; excrescence; tobacco
FIG costume (obs.); small trifle
nm **FIL** Middle Eastern monetary unit
zo, mu **FIN** organ of locomotion (fishes); end
ae **FIN** metal piece; rudder; tail-
ht **FIR** cone-bearing tree, conifer
FIT appropriate; qualified; suitable
md **FIT** spasm; healthy; adjust; befit
FIX repair; correct; quandary; dilemma
ce, nv **FIX** hitch; tie; ground control
md **FLU** influenza
FLY coach (obs.); sly; observant
nt **FLY** abscond; flee; Dutch coastal sailboat
pr, ae, zo **FLY** pr. term; decamp; winged insect
FOB watch pocket; impose; delude
lw **FOB** free on board (commerce)
me **FOD** Danish unit of measure (foot)
FOE antagonist; opponent; enemy
bt, mt **FOG** moss; rank grass; thick mist
FOH Buddha (Chinese)
FON people (Dahomey, Nigeria)
FOP a dandy; a 'nut'; beau; coxcomb
FOR dative prep., direction; purpose
FOR on this account, reason
me **FOT** Swedish unit of measure (foot)
me **FOU** tipsy; full; a bushel (Sc.)
zo **FOX** deceive; baffle; reynard
FOX N. Am. Indian tribe (Mesquakie)
nt **FOY** parting feast; assistance boat
rl **FRA** brother; friar
FRO from; away; (to and fro)

ck, zo **FRY** cook; swarm; small-; smolt (fish)
FUB fat man; cheat
zo **FUD** hare's tail
FUG frowsty warmth; un-aired room
rl **FUM** Chinese phoenix
nm **FUN** merriment; enjoyment; Korean coin
FUR incrustation; a pelt; winter wear
FUR people (Sudan)
me **FUT** foute; Russian unit of measure

G

GAB talk; gas; mouth (gam); hook
GAD rod; goad
rl **GAD** to rove; prophet, OT; Israeli tribe
GAE go (Sc.)
GAG wheeze; to silence; (reflex)
ps, me **GAL** girl; unit of gravity; gallon
GAM gossip, talk; mouth; leg
zo **GAM** school of whales
gl **GAP** fissure; opening; gat; interval
zo **GAR** to compel (Sc.); a fish (bowfin)
ch **GAS** chat; gab; poison-; gasoline
mu **GAT** pistol; strait; gap; Ind. music form
GAU ancient Ger. community (Lat. *pagus*)
rl **G'AU** Tibetan reliquary
GAY, GEY lively; merry; homosexual
rl **GEB** Keb, Seb, Egyptian god
zo **GED** pike or luce (fish)
GEE surprise cry (Am.); (-up, hasten) (horse)
GEG Albanian dialect
GEL viscous colloidal; lubricant
bt **GEM** jewel; precious (stone); a leaf-bud
GEN detailed information; manna (Heb.)
ge, gl **GEO** gio; creek; voe; vae; firth; frith
cf, ps **GEO-** ge-, earth-related (geophysics)
rl, ga **GET** obtain; fet; breed; divorce (Jew.); return of ball
GEY GAY; fairly; rather (Sc.)
zo, cr **GIB** cat; the Rock; iron or steel packing band; cotters'-
GID sheep-disease; sturdy
GIE give (Sc.)
GIF if (Sc.)
GIG whirl; cloth machine; vehicle
GIM neat
bt, ck **GIN** machine; snare; juniper-flavoured spirits
me **GIN** Malaysian measure

ck, zo **GIP** cleaned herring
zo **GIR** Indian cattle breed
GMT Greenwich Mean Time
zo **GNU** bovine-like antelope (S. Africa)
zo **GOA** Tibetan antelope
GOB mouthful; coal (left-overs)
GOB worked out mine; mouth (sl.)
GOD Deity; idol; image
rl **GOG** and Magog; evil force (Bible)
GOT seized; procured; achieved
rl **GOY** gentile, Christian (Jew.)
GRU ice
mu **GUE** Shetland violin
mn **GUF, GUFA, GOPHER** reed ships
mn **GUG** inclined mine tunnel
nt **GUL** sail; outrigger; dugout (Papua)
bt **GUM** stick; mucilage; resin; -tree
rl **GUN** artillery; pistol; African god
GUP idle chatter; rumour
me **GUR, KOR, COR** Mesopotamian
measure
pl **GUT** narrow channel; intestine;
(intuition)
nt **GUY** rope; effigy; burlesque; man
me **GUZ** a measure (E. Indies and Iran)
G'WI Kalahari bushmen
ga **GYM** gymnastics-hall (gymnasium)
fr **GYN** timber-loading device
md **GYN-** of woman; (gynaecology)
GYP college servant; bedmaker
GYR- rotate; gyrate; revolve

H

HAD befooled; caught; kept; owned
HAE have (Sc.)
HAG parasite fish; virago; beldam;
witch
HAH! exclamation
rl **HAL** Sufi Moslem state of mind
(ahwal)
rl, ck **HAM** a heavy actor; amateur radio
operator; meat (pork)
ar **HAN** Ottoman inn (Turkish)
HAN -jen, CH. people; Jap. fief
nm **HAO** Vietnamese money
rl **HAP** chance; luck; accident; fortuity;
god
HAS (he) owns, possesses; (have)
rl, nm **HAT** dignity of Cardinal; bonnet;
coin
bt **HAW** hawthorn berry; hedge;
boundary
bt **HAY** hedge; fence; harvested grass
rl **HEH** Neheh, Hu, Sia, Eg. god
rl **HEL** Norse goddess of death
HEM a cough; to sew (edge); confine

zo **HEN** a fowl
bt **HEP** hip; berry of the dog-rose
rl **HEP** Hapi, Hap, Eg. god
HER 'she' as object
bl **HET** hot and bothered; heterosexual
HEW chop; hack; fell; cut rocks
cf, me **HEX-** a group of six (Gr.); magic
spell; (hexameter)
HEY! exclamation to call attention
mu **HEY** English country dance
(traditional)
HIC! a small hiccup
HID secreted; concealed
HIE to hasten; a cry; greeting (Am.)
HIM 'he' as object
me **HIN** 6 quarts (6.8 litres) (Heb.)
pl, bt **HIP** -hurray; -joint; rafter; berry; hep
HIS belonging to him
cp **HIT** computer answer; data record
mu **HIT** strike; success; pop song
HOB part of grate; hub; peg or stake,
target for quoits
HOB a rustic; a fairy
rl **HOD** a coal scuttle; Hoder, Hodur, a
god
to **HOE** a promontory; to weed; cutter
zo **HOG** boar; pig; glutton; scrubbing
broom
HOG act selfishly; monopolize road-;
trim horses' manes
HOO! hold! stop!
bt, ga **HOP** plant; tree; dance; step; jump
rl **HOR** Horus, Egyptian god
ck **HOT** violent; acrid; fervid; ardent;
spicy
pc **HOT** heated; highly radioactive
go **HOW** glen; dell; low hill
HOW in what manner, condition?
HOX to hamstring
HOY ahoy, hoa! sailor's cry;
(exclamation)
nt **HOY** sailing coaster; smack; sloop
rl **HSI** Ch. deity; Ch. Imperial seal
rl **HSU** of Chinese and Japanese faiths
(Tao)
ga **HUB** centre; wheel cap; (quoits)
HUB plug socket; cover; hilt (sword)
HUE and cry; tint, colour shade
HUG embrace; enfold; clasp
HUH! exclamation (surprise or
contempt)
HUI hui-hui, Moslems of NW China
mu **HUM** bee-sound; Pooh song;
wordless sound (tune); workshop
sound
el **HUM** extraneous elements from
other circuits in amplifier
gl **HUM** limestone outcrops (karst)

HUN nomadic pastoral Cossack
rl HUN Taoist superior soul
HUP! a horse hastener; hiccup
HUT hovel; shed; cabin; cot
HUX method of fishing
HYP depression; hip

I

rl IAB spirit of nature (Samoyed)
cp IAL International Algebraic Language
IAT International Atomic Time (TAI)
IBN son of (Arabic) title
IBO native and lang. (Igbo), E. Nigeria
ICA Indian people of Colombia (Arhuaco)
go, ck ICE frozen water; gru; coat with sugar
hd ICH (Ich Dien) 'I serve' (Prince of Wales)
ICY cold; frigid; chilling; frosty
rl IDA birthplace of Zeus (Crete)
zo IDE kind of carp (orfe)
IDO artificial language
rl IFA the Great Truth (Nigeria)
ILK clan; category; that same (Sc.)
ILK each, every (Sc.); (OE: gaelic)
ILK ailing; evil; bad; sick
IMP extend; strengthen; graft; sprite
INK writing, printing fluid
INN caravanserai; tavern; hostelry
el ION electrically charged particle
rl ION forefather of the Ionians
I.O.U. (I owe you) debt agreement; note of hand
IPA International Phonetic Alphabet
IRE rage; fury; resentment; passion
IRK make weary or bored; (irksome)
ISE I shall (Sc.)
cf ISH exit; issue (Sc.); -ish (-like, adj.)
cf ISM ideological preference
cf, mt ISO- equal; same (Gr.); -bar (pressure)
ISO new colour system
ITS belonging to it
md IVP intravenous pyelogram
bt IVY a creeper sacred to Bacchus

J

ga JAB prod; poke; stab; a thrust; injection; punch (boxing); stroke (hockey)

JAD a quarrying cut
JAG a notch; a binge; to stab
JAH Jehovah
bt JAK bread-fruit tree
ck, tx, ro JAM A conserve; child's garment; radio block; non-function
ga JAM tightly packed, congested (traffic); pitch inside (baseball)
mu, ga JAM jazz-session; impede (Am. football)
JAP Japanese
JAR discord; jolt; jangle; pot (glass)
JAT Indo-Aryan
pl, go, ga JAW the mouth; gossip; entrance; corner (billiards); to splash
zo JAY bird; nitwit; (-walker)
JEE to move; to budge (Sc.)
rl JEN Confucian supreme virtue
mn, ae JET spray; black lignite; -propel
ga JEU a game (Fr.); (gambling call)
JEW A Hebrew, Israeli (yehudi)
nt JIB to baulk; shy; a sail; lifting arm, boom (cranc); insult, sly remark
to JIG tune; dance; apparatus
cp JOB stab; profession; work; unit of runs
nm JOE a sweetheart (Sc.); Port. 'joao' coin
JOG push; nudge; -trot; rog; run slowly (memory); (cattle driving)
nm JON N. Korean monetary unit
JOT an iota; to note briefly
JOW to toll; a stroke of a bell (Sc.)
JOY rapture; ecstasy; delight; (-ride)
me JUD a mass of coal
ck JUG ewer; pot (drinks); to stew; prison
bt JUR earth-nut
JUT protrude; extend
rl JUZ the 30 sections of the Koran (Quran)

K

zo KAA (jungle) rock python (Kipling)
zo KAE jackdaw (Sc.)
KAF fountain conferring immortality
pr K'AI shu, standard Ch. script and print model
KAM crooked (Shak.)
me KAN Dutch and Hong Kong measure
nm KAS, KAST Dutch wardrobe, chest; Ind. coin
me KAT Egyptian weight
KAW, CAW bird sound
go, gl KAY, CAY, KEY shoal; reef (bed)

zo **KEA** parrot that kills sheep (NZ)
zo, rl **KEB** ewe; sheep louse, Eg. god
(Geb)
KEF drugged stupor
KEG small cask or barrel
bt **KEI** an apple (Indian plum)
me **KEN** know; recognize; knowledge;
Jap. unit of length
KEP shaft-hoist stop; to catch (Sc.)
rl **KER** destructive spirit (Gr.)
KET carrion; matted wool; a fleece
(Sc.)
me **KEV** 1000 electron-volts
bt **KEX** fool's parsley; dried stalks
mu **KEY** code; (crib); solution; legend;
wedge; clamp; (lock); -board
(music); opener; reef
rw, cp, ga **KEY** signal; identification digit;
penalty area (baseball)
le **KID** faggot; bundle of sticks; tub;
deceive; hoax; pliable leather
zo **KID** young goat; a boy; infant
bt **KIF** Indian hemp; drug (cannabis)
KIN relationship. affinity; kindred
me **KIN** Japanese unit of weight
rl **K'IN** Mayan Sun god (C. America)
eg **KIP** nap; unit of force (1000lb/
454kg)
le **KIP** small untanned hide; (sleep)
mu **KIT** tub; (army-); violin; gear;
accessories
bt **KOA** acacia (Sandwich Islands)
zo **KOB** water antelope; target (quoits)
KON catty, Korean unit of weight
go **KOP** hill (S. Africa)
me **KOR, COR, GUR** Mesopotamian
measure
KRI Hebrew marginal direction
KRU KRoo; a Liberian
KRU, KROO De, Liberian Kawa-
speaking people
rl **KUA** Nu, progenitors of humanity
(Ch.)
KUL, KULA the family (India)
rl **KUL** water-haunting genie (Siberia)
KUN Turkic nomads (Cumans)
rl **KUN** soil magician; whale monster
(Ch.)
me **KUP** Thai unit of length (10 ins)
rl **KUU** (moon), father of Kuutar
(Finland)
KWA subgroup of Niger-Congo
language
KYA native hut (S. Africa)
zo **KYE, KY, KINE** cattle (Sc.)

L

mn **LAC** dye; shellac; transparent resin
LAD youngster; stripling; boy; kid
LAG convict; dawdle; loiter; dally
LAG delay; insulate; cover; wrap
mu **LAH** spoken sol-fa 6th note
mu **LAI, LAY** ballad, poem (Sd.)
LAM to thrash; weaving device;
Arabic letter
LAO Thai people
LAP fold; wrap; polish; circuit; drink
zo **LAR** white-handed gibbon
rl **LAR** Roman household god
LAT inscribed pillar (India)
mn **LAT** Latvian and Thai money
LAV wash; (toilet); lavage
lw, ps **LAW** statute; canon; rule; (gravity)
LAX slack; loose; remiss; careless
LAY, LAI ballad; put down; (egg)
(table)
LAY person; non-professional
egghead
LAZ, LAS E. Black Sea people and
language
ga **LBW** leg before wicket (cricket)
me, go **LEA** measure of yarn; meadow; lee;
lay; open land; pasture
LED induced; helped; conducted
go **LEE** sheltered (wind); lea; meadow
nt, nv **LEG** lower limb; stage; tack in sailing
cp, ga **LEG** section of route; path in routine
walk; square- (cricket); gam
ga **LEG** division of turns (skittles)
nm **LEI** garland (Hawaii); Romanian leu
nm **LEK** bird courtship; Albanian coin
as **LEO** lion; 5th sign of Zodiac
rl **LER, LIR** Irish sea god
ga **LET** permit; allow; lease; hire;
(badminton, tennis)
LET hindrance; prevent; delay
nm **LEU** Romanian money (plur. lei)
nm **LEV** Bulgarian money (ley)
LEW luke-warm; tepid
lw **LEX** an enactment
nm **LEY** lev; lea; pasture; common
pewter
rl **LHA** -mo, city goddess of Lhasa
(Tibet)
LIB ad lib.; extemporize (acting)
LID top; cover; coverlet
LIE falsehood; rest; recline; repose
ga **LIE** shape of landscape; (golf)
rl **LIF** male survivor of chaos (Norse)
rl **LIL** lelek, 'soul' (Finno-Ugric)
go, nt **LIN** pool, port (Celtic); to cease
LIP touch the edge; rim; mouth
rl **LIR, LER** Irish sea god

lw **LIS** litigation
bt, hd **LIS** fleur-de-lis; heraldic lily (Fr.)
LIT lighted; kindled; ignited
rl **LOA** creator, ritual drama (Guatemala)
ga **LOB** worm; clumsy throw (underarm) (cricket) (badminton)
cp, nt **LOG** record; diary; tree-trunk
ma **LOG** Hebrew pint; (logarithm tables)
ga **LOO** toilet; card game
LOP truncate; amputate; dock (tails)
me **LOT** to catalogue; fate; portion; (choose); unit of weight (Ger.)
LOW base; vile; abject; depressed
LOW bellow; moo; to flame; to blaze (Sc.)
LOW first of group (jump) (parachuting)
LOY narrow spade
LSD money (Libra; Solidus; Denarius)
md **LSD** hallucinatory drug
rl **LUA** Roman deity
LUD King Lud patron of anti-automation
rl **LUD** sacred fir tree grove (Votyaks)
LUE to sift
nt **LUG** ear; tug; haul; drag; handle; (sail)
rl **LUG** Celtic deity
rl **LUL** 'soul', lelek (Finno-Ugric)
LUM chimney (Sc.)
LUO kavironda, people (Kenya, Uganda)
mu **LUR** Scand. prehistoric bronze horn
LUR native mountain people (Iran, Luristan)
me **LUX** unit of light
LUZ a legendary bone
ch **LYE** alkaline solution
zo **LYM** dog on leash
go **LYN** waterfall (Celtic)

M

MAB the queen of the fairies
as **MAC** son of (Sc.); 13th month, Mayan cal.
MAD crazy; demented; raving; insane (angry)
zo **MAG** chatter; steal; magpie
nm **MAG** halfpenny; magazine (journal)
rl **MAH** Mao, Persian moon god
cf **MAL-** faulty; wrong; imperfect
MAM Madame, ma'am (respected lady); (brothel)

MAN mankind; husband; employee; male human
MAN Bantu people (Yao), Africa
zo, rl **MAO** the peacock; Persian god Mah
go **MAP** delineate; chart; plan
MAR spoil; deface; impair; disfigure
nm **MAS** Indonesian gold coin
pg, wv **MAT** dull surface; weave; interlace
ar, wv, ga **MAT** carpet; raft; slab; foundation floor (boxing) (wrestling)
zo **MAW** craw; crop; (stomach)
MAX a kind of gin; (trap); maximum
MAY have permission, possibility
bt **MAY** hawthorn blossom; 5th month
me, mu **MEL, Mell, Mall** honey; unit of pitch; leafy bower; promenade
MEL language group (Sierra Leone)
rl **MEN** humanity; lunar god (Asia Minor)
MEO Miao, mountain dwellers, SE Asia, Ch.
me **MET** METROPOLITAN; bushel; came together
me **MEV** million electron-volts
zo **MEW** sea-gull; moult
MEW cage; confine; cat-speech
me **MHO** electrical unit of conductivity
MID central; amid; middle
me, nm **MIL** unit of measure; thousand
MIM prim; demure; precise
me, rl **MIN** liquid measure; Eg. fertility god
MIR Russian commune; space station
cf **MIS-** hatred of (Gr.); wrong act (mistake)
MIX blend; combine; jumble; mingle
nm **MNA** mina; 50 shekels
zo **MOA** extinct bird, emu type (N.Z.)
MOB cap; rabble; populace; crowd
MOD assembly; meeting; (mod con)
mu **MOD** modern; Gaelic choral contest
MOE mow; grimace; mop
MOG move away
as **MOL** 8th month of Mayan calendar
MOM, MUM, BAMUM people (Cameroon, Africa)
nt **MON** canoe (Solomon Islands, Pacific)
MON people (Talaing) and lang., SE Asia
MOO when a cow lows
MOP swab; grimace; moe; -of hair
fr **MOR** type of humus layer
rl **MOT** bon mot; witticism; god of ME
me **MOU** Chinese unit of area
MOW stack; pile of hay; cut down (lawn)

MOW facial expression; moe
MRS married woman; (mistress)
MUD mire; sludge; slime; Dutch measure
MUG fool; face; cup; assault; injure
MUM mother (Mom); silence; beer brew
MUN man (dialect)
rl. **MUT** Egyptian goddess
MUX to spoil; a mess
zo **MYA** shellfish

N

nt **NAB** seize; grab; knoll; shoal
NAE none (Sc.)
NAF unfashionable; unsuitable
zo **NAG** harass; pester; horse
lw **NAM** distraint (obs.)
bt,ga **NAP** doze; forty winks; cherry; card; game
bt,ga **NAP** non-aubacial pollen; racing tip
NAY contrariwise; vote against; no (obs.)
N.C.O. non-commissioned officer (army)
NEB beak; nose; nib; a point
NEE born (Fr.) (maiden name)
nt **NEF** silver model ship; cadenas; casket; salt cellar
go **NEK** a pass (S. Africa); a col
cf,ar **NEO** old style revived (Gr.)
bt **NEP** catmint; knot in cotton fibre
rl **NER** tamid, Hebrew holy lamp (synagogue)
NET neat; nett; snare; capture; (fishing-)
NEW novel; recent; fresh; modern
NIB beak; point; neb; (pen)
NIL nihil; zero; nothing
NIM steal; (nick)
me **NIN** Thai inches (Niu)
rl **NIO** Japanese herculean spirits
NIP squeeze; pinch; bite; sip; a dram
NIS not so; imp; hobgoblin; mix
zo,me **NIT** egg of louse; light unit
me **NIU** Thai inches
rl **NIX** nothing; water elf; nixy (Ger.)
NOB aristocrat; knave at cribbage; head
NOD head gesture; assent; -off (doze); on the -(auction, bid)
me **NOG** small pot; tree nail; peg; wooden brick; noggin, ale cup
NOK ancient Nigerian culture
NOM de plume (Fr.), writer's pseudonym

cf **NON-** negative; not; without (Lat.)
NOR logic; not (neither here nor there)
cp **NOT** negating; Boolean logic of false and true
NOW at this time or instant; the present
lt,me **NOX** measure of illumination
rl **NOX** Nyx; personification of night
ac,me **NOY** unit of perceived noise
NUB shove; hang; knob; gist
rl **NUM** sky god (Siberia)
rl **NUN** a religieuse; a sister; -Nu, Eg. god
NUR knot in wood
rl **NUT** dandy; eccentric person; sky goddess; screwed bolt end
mu **NUT** boss on anchor; bridge (holding strings above soundbox – violin)
bt **NUT** single-seeded fruit in shell
md,bt **NUX** (vomica)
zo **NYE** brood of pheasants
rl **NYX, NOX** night goddess (Erebus) (Gr.)

O

OAF fool; idiot; dolt; changeling; oof
OAK outer door (university)
bt **OAK** hardwood tree; heart of- (seaman)
OAR narrow paddle; to row; an oarsman
bt,mu **OAT** a grain; pan-pipe; (wild-s)
OBI, OBY magic; a fetish (West Indies)
OBI Japanese sash; karate belt
OBO annual Mongolian festival (5th month)
bt **OCA** potato (South Africa)
OCA pal-leaf book (Sri Lanka)
OCH! oh! or ah! (Sc. & Ir.)
me **OCK** unit of weight (Turkey).
ODD singular; peculiar; quaint; droll
ODE celebratory poem
O'ER poetical over
OES Os; circlets
OFF away; gone (switched-)
OFT often; frequently; repeatedly
el,me **OHM** unit of electrical resistance
OHO! exclamation
cf **-OID** of resemblance, similarity (Gr.)
OIL anoint; lubricate; petroleum
zo,bt,ck **OIL** (plant-) (fish-) (blubber-)
me **OKA** 3lb in Egypt
me **OKE** unit of dry and liquid weight
OLD antique; archaic; pristine; aged

OLI Buli, African people (Congo)
zo OLM a blind lizard
ONA S. Am. Indians (Tierra del Fuego)
ma ONE indivisible number; pronoun; single ae, ane (one and own) (Sc.)
me ONS 100 grams in Netherland
OOF, OAF silly fellow
OOM uncle (Afrikaans)
OPE open (obs.)
cf, bt, ck OPO- derived from juice
OPS Goddess of Wealth; wife of Saturn
OPT to choose; elect; pick
cf -OPY, -OPIA of visual defect (Gr.)
pl ORA mouths, orifices (Lat.)
ORB globe; -weaver (spider); emblem of royal power; 'Imperial apple'
zo ORC killer whale; ogre; eagle
ORD edge; beginning
mn ORE metal-bearing earth; (iron-)
nm ORE Scand. coin (öre, øre)
rl ORO Tahitian deity
ORT a bit; refuse; a crumb
OSH oblost, admin. region (Russian)
mu OUD, UD Islamic lute
OUR ¾ of an –; belongs to us
OUT outside; expose; get out!
zo, ck OVA eggs; cod's roe; (caviare)
OWE run up an account; to be in debt
zo OWL night bird; to smuggle (by night)
OWN possess; admit; concede
ch OXO organic compound radical
me OZS ounces

P

zo, tc PAD cushion; stuff; paw; data; packet; (factory-); (floor); spare bed
el PAD attenuator; electrical network
PAH! exclamation of disgust; stockade (NZ)
PAI Po (Min-chia), people of Yunnan, Ch.
PAL staunch friend; mate; palooka
ga PAM knave of clubs at loo (card game)
ck PAN small pool; (frying); (-gold); Ch. bowl
rl PAN goat-like god; African sky god
ga, go, zo, PAN film camera motion; Mexican
mu   card game; saline flats; ape; -pipes
PAN- all-embracing unity (Gr.)

PAO authorized court circular; gazette (Ch.)
go, pl, ck PAP conical hill; nipple; mushy food
zo, ga PAR, PARR young salmon; equality (golf)
PAS pace, ballet step
PAT dab; tap; rap; caress; aptly
zo PAU bustard (S. Africa)
zo PAW fury foot; handle roughly
rl PAX kiss of peace; era of –; hold! osculatory (marriage)
PAY expend money; (wages) (compliment) (respects); (stipend); (debts)
bt, ck PEA flower; pod vegetable
mu PED pack-saddle; basket; pedal; organ
PEE to urinate; (piss)
ga PEG short drink; spigot; wooden nail; rod; dowel; spike; (croquet)
PEG secure; fasten; (tent) (violin); (prices); a scale
to, zo PEN impound. write (quill-); indite; female swan; squid shell
go PEN mountain; headland (Celtic)
PEP energy; drive (USA)
PER by means of; (price – amount)
PES hind-limb equestrian pedestal
zo PET fondle; favourite; kept animal
rl PEW row of seats in church
ma PHI binary listing
bt PIA arrowroot (Polynesian)
me PIC, PIK picki, diraa, units of length
ma, ck PIE, PI, PYE pastry-covered flan; tart
pr, nm PIE mixed print; Rom. inches; Ind. money
zo, ml PIG hog; (savings) (-gy bank); to guzzle; (-lead); (-iron)
me PIK, PIC picki, diraa, inches (Medit.)
ga -PIK high lob (pelota, Sp.)
me, ga PIN half a firkin; transfix; wedge; pile; (point); (-down, wrestling)
jn PIN peg; nail; to fasten; dowel; dovetail; tenon; (tailoring)
ga PIP to black-ball; overtake (racing)
bt, vt PIP fruit seed; fowl disease; depression; code signal; dice spots; chirp
mn PIT mine; abyss; oppose; (theatre)
ga PIT set; match (tennis); (cock-); (motor racing-)
mu PIU little more (or less) (It.)
rl PIX holy box; coin box; pyx
md PKU gene disorder (phenylketonuria)
fr, nt, tx PLY fold; layer; veneer; roofing felt; to ferry; yarn; (career)
bt POA a genus of grass

bt **POD** husk; to swell; group unit; room

zo **POD** a shoal of whales or seals

zo **POE** parson bird (NZ)

POH! exclamation

bt, ck **POI** Polynesian fermented taro starch

zo **POM** Pomeranian dog; Briton in Australia

mu **POP** sound burst; explode; (weasel)

as **POP** 1st month of Yucatán Mayan year

POT vessel (flower-); (tea-); tankard

ga **POT** random shot (billiards) (bowls)

POT (home-distilled) (poteen) (drugs)

me **POT** Danish litre

POW Prisoner of War

md **POX** disease; small-; cow-; syphilis

POY balancing-pole; a grant

POZ positive; certain

cf **PRE-** before (pre-war) (Lat.)

PRO for (argument); professional

cf **PRO-** in favour of (on account of) (Gr.)

PRY peer; snoop; examine

PSI Greek letter

md **PSP** test of blood flow through kidney

md **PTH** parathyroid hormone

PUB licensed public drinking house

zo **PUD** paw; pad; pudding

zo **PUG** dog; fox or monkey

nm **PUL** Russian and Georgian coin

PUN same-sound words; (humour); homophone; paronomasia

zo **PUP** whelp; young dog or seal

zo **PUR, PURR,** curr, hoot (cat or owl sounds)

md **PUS** septic discharge (infection)

PUT game at cards; rustic; (throwing the weight/shot)

PUT place; -down; demote; quell; install; -off; delay, evade; -through; connect

PUT -up; construct; -up with, tolerate; -up for (election)

PUT -and call (Stock Exchange)

gl **PUY** volcanic formation

ch **PVC** synthetic resin, polyvinyl chloride

nm **PYA** Burmese money

rl **PYE** rule for determining Easter date

zo **PYE** pie; magpie; thief

PYO Burmese verse, type

rl, nm **PYX, PIX** holy box; coin box at the Mint

Q

rl **QAT** mountain spirits (Siberia); Melanesian and Australian deities

QUA as (Lat.)

QUI who (Lat.)

QUO whither (Lat.); status quo; as it is

R

me **RAD** radical; afraid (Sc.); radiation dose

mu **RAG** worn garment; (-paper) (-stone); (-time jazz); prank; (-week) (student's-)

mu **RAG** torment; tease; Hindi scale

me **RAI** Thai acre; ethnic group (orig. Nepal)

RAJ British power (India)

bt **RAK, Arak** Ar. desert shrub; (toothbrush)

zo, nt **RAM** male sheep; butt; (prow); (power-press); cram; engine

RAN raced; scurried; flowed; melted

mu **RAP** snatch; tap; music; reprimand

nm **RAP** counterfeit Irish halfpenny

RAS vizier (Abyssinia/Ethiopia)

zo **RAT** to desert; rodent; betray

cp **RAW** bleak; crude; uncooked; painful; unprocessed data; (-deal)

RAX reach; strain (Sc.)

zo, mu **RAY** the skate; spoken sol-fa note (re)

vt, zo **RAY** sheep scab; (-spider) (light-) (X-)

RED disentangle; revolutionary; colour

nm **REE** hen-bird of ruff; riddle; tipsy; Portuguese unit of account; rei

md **REF** reference; a hormone factor (renal)

go **REG** gravel, desert plain (Arabia)

go **REH** saline efflorescence (India)

nm **REI** Portuguese unit of account, ree

me **REM** ionizing radiation dosage (roentgen)

cf, md **REN-** of the kidney (renal)

REP debauchee; rip; fabric; agent; repetition; repertory (theatre)

lw **RES** a thing; a point

RET to rot flax; hemp or jute

rl **REV** to speed up; Reverend; increase revolutions, accelerate

REV revise, revision; revert, reverse

zo **REX** a king; cat breed

go **RIA** inlet of the sea (funnel-shaped)

ck **RIB** bone (-cut, spare); border band
go, bd, bt **RIB** ridge; petiole; frame; watercress
RID to free; clear; expel; destroy
bt **RIE, RYE** a grain; (-whisky)
RIF, RIFF riffi, riffians, Berber tribe
nt **RIG** wanton; manipulate; fit out; sail
go **RIM** brim; border; edge; lip
me **RIO** a tael; ounce (Japan)
RIP tear; rend; -saw, -cord (safety); (speed); lose control
ga **RIP** rest in peace; famous sleeper; seaward current (surfing)
RIP fish-basket; a Lothario
mu **RIT** strike; tear (Sc.); ritardando, repeat
nm **RIX** Ceylonese (Sri Lankan) dollar
ch **RNA** ribonucleic acid (genetic code)
ROB rook; fleece; strip; fruit syrup
zo **ROC, ROK** fabulous bird (Sinbad)
me **ROD** pole or perch; cane; twig; gad
nc, ga, md **ROD** metal bar (piston); (fishing-); retinal nerve; gun (Am.)
zo **ROE** deer; fish ova (caviare)
ROG to jog; to shake
zo **ROK** roc; fabulous bird
ROM gipsy; a Romany
RON King Arthur's ebony spear
zo **ROO** a kangaroo
rl **ROT** to decay; putrefy; nonsense; Same god
ROW line; brawl; din; (oars); quarrel
cp **ROW** cards; punched cards
ROY a king (obs.)
rl **RTA, RITA** Hindu cosmic order (Vedas)
RUA storage pit (NZ); 'street' (Port.)
RUB chafe; abrade; dilemma
zo **RUC** rok; roc; a fabulous bird
RUD rub; polish; flush; ochre
RUE lament; regret; suffer; sorrow
bt **RUE** herb of grace
RUG mat; coverlet; a drink; shaggy dog
RUM Rummy card game; Moslem term for Roman Empire and its people
RUN hurry on foot; race; (-away), escape; manage; propel; trip; long- (theatre)
ga **RUN** score (cricket, baseball etc.)
cp **RUN** route; series (track); chicken coop; sequence; performances
RUT wheel track; groove; desire
ga **RUT** (mating season); deep piste (skiing); monotony of routine
RYA a wall-rug

vt **RYE, RIE** (-bread); a bird disease
RYE rie; (whisky)
me **RYO** Japanese monetary unit

S

SAB sob (Sc.)
md **SAC** bag, often fluid-containing; N. Am. Indian tribe (Sauk)
SAD sorry; downcast; gloomy; dismal
SAE so (Sc.); stamped addressed envelope
SAG droop; settle; bend
zo **SAI** Brazilian monkey
bt, ch **SAL** Indian timber tree; salt
SAM together; to collect; to curdle
bt, zo **SAP** undermine; juice; egghead; moisture; (stone); (-beetle)
SAT seated; perched; settled
to **SAW** a saying; adage; seen; toothed cutter
to, mu **SAX** knife, slate-cutter's hammer; (o-phone)
SAY tell; declare; utter; allege
SAZ guitar (Turk.)
go **SEA** basin; ocean; wave surge
rl **SEB, KEB, GEB** Egyptian deity
SEC dry (flavour)
SED (fish-hook); a fillet
rl **SEE** watch; heed; holy- (Vatican)
bt, zo **SEG** sedge; bullock
SEL self (Sc.)
me, nm **SEN SE** Asian unit of length and money
bt **SEP** sepal, outer leaf of flower (calyx)
ma, zo **SET** group; clique; fix; prepare; (-out); (-sail); badgers' den
nt **SET** wave flow (surfing) (tennis); (-sail) (hair-) (stage-)
rl **SET, SETH** god of darkness (Eg.)
SEW stitch; hem; baste
SEX gender
zo **SHA** shapo; wild sheep
SHE female pronoun
SHE Miao-Yao speaking people (Ch.)
mu, me **SHO** Jap. mouth organ; unit of capacity
nm, rl **SHU** old Jap. coin; god of Eg. and Ch.
SHY coy; bashful; jib; wary
SIB, SYB akin to (sibling), brother, sister
SIC as written (Lat.)
SIK to seek (Sc.)

SIL ochre pigment
rl **SIM** a Simeonite; low churchman
SIN transgress; wickedness; inquity; err
rl, ma **SIN** Nanna, moon god; (trig. sine)
SIP, SUP taste
SIR sire; master; knight
SIS girl; sweetheart; sister
cf **-SIS** (analy-sis); abstract results
SIT brood; incubate; rest; repose
SIX sax (Sc.)
ga **SKI** gliding on snow; winter sport
ga **SKY** the heavens (weather); rowing fault
SLY artful; wily; astute; fly
SNY upward curve
SOB cry; blubber; weep; snivel
lw **SOC** privilege; sac; society
SOD turf; lawn; grass; pervert
go **SOG** morass; marsh; to saturate; bog
mu **SOH** spoken 5th note of sol-fa scale
nm, mu **SOL** old Fr. halfpenny; 5th note (so, soh); monetary unit (Peru)
rl **SOL** Indiges, Roman sun god; gold
mu **SON** male offspring; disciple; Fr. sound
SOP to soak; to steep; a bribe
SOS help! Save our Souls!
SOT drunkard
nm **SOU** French mite; sol
ag, zo **SOW** disseminate; plant; seed; fem. pig
tx **SOX, SOCKS** stockings; hose
bt, ck **SOY** bean, sauce; oriental footwear
SPA spring; health resort; hydro
SPY espy; behold; detect; observe
md **STY, STYE** pig pen; eye ailment
SUB subscription; money gift; substitute; junior officer
cf **SUB-** beneath, inferior, under (Lat.)
rl **SUD** Mesopotamian goddess (Ninlil)
lw **SUE** prosecute; plead
zo **SUG** a kind of worm
SUK Nilotic language
ma, cp **SUM** total; amount; addend and augend
as, rl **SUN** centre of solar system; -gods
me **SUN** Japanese inches
SUP to take super; imbibe
lw **SUS** arrest on suspicion
zo **SUS** silicon unilateral switch; wild pig
SYB, SIB akin to; (sibling)
SYN syne; since (Sc.)
cf **SYN-** joined, together, along with (Gr.)

T

TAB flap; tally; check; pull-strip
TAB protector for bow (archery) (theatre)
TAD a little (USA); street boy (USA)
ga **TAG** catchword; touch; label; game; wedge; append
cp, ga **TAG** identification symbols; digits; expel (baseball)
zo **TAI** Japanese bream; Thai people
ar, tx **TAJ** Mahal; headdress (Ind.)
TAN to beat; brown colour
me **TAN** boat people (Tanka); a weight (Ch.)
rl **TAO** 'heavenly way' (Ch.)
to, pb **TAP** rap; pat; knock; broach; exploit; faucet; (screw) (stopcock)
nt **TAR** pitch; bitumen; sailor
tx, zo **TAT** needlework; native cloth; pony
zo **TAU** bug; toad-fish
rl **TAU** Egyptian or St Anthony's cross
TAW a marble; game
TAY SE Asian people
lw **TAX** levy; tariff; (accuse); strain
bt, ck **TEA** beverage; bohea; (cannabis)
TEC teck; detective
TED spread
mu **TEE** (golf); hinge; 7th note (te, ti)
zo **TEG** deer; sheep; tag
ch **TEL** tetraethyl lead
rl **TEM, ATUM** Egyptian god
TEN a net drawn up; number
TER thrice
TEW gear; iron chain; scourge
me **TEX** weight in grams of 1000m of yarn
THE definite article
THO' though; SE Asian people
THY of thee; thine
zo **TIB** a courtesan; gib; cat
me **TIC** nervous twitch; spasm
TIE dead-heat; bind; unite; (neck-)
ga **TIG** game; cup; equal scores (games)
mn, ga **TIN** can; preserve; receptacle; money; metal; wall strip (squash)
rl **TIN** Tinia, Tina, Etruscan and Gr. gods
TIP gratuity; vails; cant; tilt; incline
TIR Transport International Routing
'TIS it is
zo, pl **TIT** small bird; pony; teat or nipple
TIV N. Nigerian farming people
rl **TIW, TYR** Germanic god
me, bt, zo **TOD** 28lb of wool; bush; fox
pl **TOE** foot-finger; on -s; readiness
tx **TOG** to dress; garment

zo **TOK** nesting place of capercaillies (Sc.)

TOL take away; Bengali school of humanities

TOM male cat; -boy (girl)

me **TON** measure of weight (2240lb/ 1000kg)

me **TON** 20 cwt; (displacement) (cargo space)

ga **TON** hundred runs (century, cricket)

TOO also; as well; – much; – many (overdone)

TOP toy; vertex; zenith; acme; excel; lid

gl, ar **TOR** granite outcrop on a hill; (tower)

TOT child; to total

me **TOU** Ch. unit of capacity (10 litres)

bt **TOW** haul; flax, hemp, jute, bast fibres

mu **TOY** trifle; plaything; (instrument); lute

cf **TRI-** of three together (Gr.); (-angle)

TRY test; essay; attempt; endeavour

ga **TRY** rugby football score

nt **TUB** basin; container, boat, kit, kid

TUG tow; (-ship); pull; (-of war); gliding (aircraft)

zo **TUI** parson-bird (NZ)

me **TUN** barrel; large cask; 252 gals

zo, to **TUP** ram; to mate (of sheep); hammer

zo **TUR** Caucasian goat

TUT! deprecating exclamation

TUT piece-work; a hassock

TWA two (Sc.); Pygmy people

TWI Niger-Congo lang. subgroup (Kwa)

TWO a pair; brace; couple; deuce (cards)

TYE ore washing buddle; tie

TYG tall china cup; mug

TYO Teke, Bateke, Ato, Bantu people (Congo/Kinshasa)

rl **TYR** Norse (Engl. Tiw), one-handed war god

mu **TZ'U** speech-like trad. songs (Ch.)

U

zo **UCA** fiddler crab

UDA purplish brown glaze

bt **UDO** Jap. vegetable; universal language

UGH! UG, UH, exclamation of disgust

bt **ULE** gum (Mexico)

ULL Norse patron of snow-shoes

ULT ultimo, the latest

rl **UMA** Parvati, wife of Siva/Shiva (Ind.)

nt **UNA** gat-boat with centreboard for deltas

cf **UNI-** treat as one, singular (Lat.)

rl **UNO** United Nations Organization; ancestor of the Hungarians

UPS peak occasion; (– and downs)

zo **URE** wild ox; aurochs

URF stunted child (Sc.)

URN jar; vase; receptacle

URU S. Am. Indians (Lake Titicaca)

USE usage; avail; employ; apply; usury

zo **UTA** American lizard

UTO Aztecan languages

UTU blood money; requital (NZ); sun god

bt **UVA** a bunch (of grapes)

V

VAC vacation; holiday

VAD Voluntary Aid Detachment (Women's); war worker

go **VAE, VOE** gio; creek; firth; fjord

VAG peat (Sc.)

VAI, VEI tribe (Liberia and Sierra Leone)

VAN fan; forefront; vehicle; wind vane

el, me **VAR** unit of reactive power of A/C

pl **VAS** blood vessel; vesicle, glandular tubes

me **VAT** fat; vessel; tank; value-added tax; Dutch liquid measure

VEI, VAI Mande-speaking African tribe

me **VEL** (wind) velocity; speed + force (of impact)

vt **VET** animal doctor; examine; check

VEX harass; fret; chafe; make angry

VIA by way of; route detail

VIE strive; contend; contest

mu **VIF** lively (Fr.)

VIM force; (vim and vigour)

VIS -a-, facing; comparison

VIZ namely

go **VLY** vlei, pool (S. Africa)

VOE vae; geo; gio; fiord; estuary; firth

hd **VOL** two wings coinjoined at base; crest

VON in names of nobility (of) (Ger.)

nv **VOR** navigational ranging system

VOW promise; dedicate; oath
mu **VOX** voice; song part; public opinion
gl **VUG** rock cavity (Cornish)
VUM boom (cannon noise) (USA)

W

mn **WAD** manganese ore; stuffing; pile of paper; (cottonwool)
WAE woe (Sc.)
WAG vibrate; wit; humorist; (tailing)
me **WAH, WA** Thai unit of length
WAN pale; sickly; languid
WAP whop; a bundle; swat; wrap; copulate; beat
WAR strife; enmity; hostilities; (price-)
WAS past of 'be' (sing.)
zo **WAT** hare; drunken (Sc.)
WAX increase; grow; beeswax (seal)
WAY route; method; track
WEB a textile fabric; cobweb
WED a pledge; to marry; unite
WEE diminutive; urinate (sl.)
ga **WEI** chi-go board game (Ch.)
md **WEN** tumour; wart; metropolis
WET humid; watery; drench; moisten
me **WEY** various weights, salt, corn, etc
WHO which person?
WHY for what reason (purpose?)
WIG vallancy; toupee; periwig; peruke
WIG berate; scold; lecture; upbraid
ga **WIN** gain; acquire; achievement
WIS, WIT know (obs.)
WIT wag; quick thinker; humorist; (half-)
WOE affliction; sorrow; grief; anguish
nm **WON** to dwell; abode and money (Korea)
WON came first (race); earned; got; swayed; persuaded
WOO to court (for marriage or gain)
WOP, WHOP whip; (Sc.)
WOT known (obs.)
WOW event; sound change
WRY awry; askew; crooked; distorted
WUM aghem, African tribe (Cameroon); vum
pb **WYE** a person (Sc.); Y-branched pipe

Y

YAB jabber (Sc.); confused chattering
YAH! exclamation of derision
zo **YAK** Tibetan ox
rl, bt, ck **YAM** sweet potato; Semitic deity
YAO pottery ware and Ch. legendary emperor
YAO mountain people of Ch. and SE Asia
nm **YAP** yell; cry; bark; money (fei) Pacific stone-disc currency
nt **YAW** deviate; sideways heaving; head movement of horse (gliding)
YEA, AY, AYE yes; verily
nm **YEN** a gold or silver Japanese coin
YEP yeh; yes (Amer.)
YES yea; aye; ay
YET a gate (Sc.)
YET still; further; besides; however
bt **YEW** wood for the bow; (cemetree)
YEX hiccough
rl **YIN** -yang, life's complementary forces (Ch.)
YIP pert forward girl (Sc.)
YOD phonetic sound 'y' (yon)
YON yonder
YOU 2nd-person pronoun
zo **YOW** ewe (Sc.)
rl **YUE** Moon and lunar month (Ch.)
YUG an age of the world (Hind.)

Z

nt, me **ZAK** Kashmir raft; Dutch measure
rl **ZAM** Persian earth spirit (djin)
me **ZAR** Iranian 1 metre
to **ZAX** slate cutter; sax
ZED, ZEE letter 'Z' (Engl., USA)
mu **ZEL** cymbal
rl **ZEN** sect and school of Buddhism (Jap.)
me **ZER** guz, gueza, gudge, measure (Iran)
zo **ZHO** zobo; hybrid yak and cow
ZIP liveliness; fastener (trousers); a ping sound; postcode
zo **ZOO** zoological garden
cf **ZOO-** of animal classification (Gr.)
nm **ZUZ** an ancient Jewish coin

FOUR-LETTER WORDS

A

rl **ABBA** Chaldean or Coptic divine; father

rl **ABBE** French abbot; priest

ABED in bed

ABER river mouth (Celtic)

ABET aid; incite; favour; countenance

ABIB 1st month of the Jewish year

ABLE skilful; adroit; expert; competent

ABLY masterly; powerfully; cleverly

nt **A-BOX** opposite bracing of yards

ABUT ABUTT; adjoining; terminate

bt **ACER** the maple-tree

ACES (spot); dice game

ACHE pain; pang; agony; anguish

ch **ACID** vitriolic; sour; tart; (rain) (-drop, sweet)

ACME zenith; apex; pinnacle; pitch

md **ACNE** a skin disease

md **ACOR** acidity

me **ACRE** area of space (land)

cf **ACRO-** topmost; first (Gr.)

lw **ACTA** proceedings in a court

ch **ACYL** carboxylic acid radical

ADAM the first man; a gaoler

ADAR 12th month of the Jewish year

bd **ADDS** overall quantities, extras

ADIT opening or passage; entrance

to **ADZE** adz; a mattock

AEON an age; era; cycle; period; eon

cf **AERO-** air or gas

AERY ethereal; visionary

AFAR away; distant; remote; aloof

AFER the South-West wind

AGAR ploughman of playing fields, Eton

bl, ck, md **AGAR** seaweed; mucilage; gel

AGED elderly; ancient; antiquated

rl **AGHA AGA**, ruler of sect, estates owner

AGIO premium; discount; brokerage

ÅGNI Hindu fire-god and protector

AGOG astir; eager; excited

ck **AGON** sardine-like Alpine fish

ga **AGON** contest; struggle; (antagonist) (Gr.)

zo **AGUA** South American toad

md **AGUE** malarial fever; chilliness

AHEM! exclamation

nt **AHOY!** exclamation (nautical)

AIDE helper; assistant; coadjutor

md **AIDS** acquired immune deficiency syndrome

ga **AIDS** last three fingers of sword hand (fencing)

AIN'T (am not, are not)

AINU aboriginal (Jap.)

bt **AIRA** hair-grass

AIRE an altar; Irish freeman

AIRY blythe; breezy; ethereal; spacious

AJAR slightly opened

bt **AKEE** West Indian fruit tree

AKIN sib; agnate; similar; related

ALAR winged, pertaining to wings

ALAS alack; welladay

zo **ALCA** sea-auk genus

nt **ALEE** on the lee-side

bt **ALFA** esparto grass

bt **ALGA** seaweed

cf, md **ALGO-** pain

pr **ALIF** 1st letter Arabic alphabet

ALLY ALLEY; a marble of real alabaster

ALLY unite; marry; confederate; friend

ALMS oblations; gifts; bounty

ALOD allod; freehold

bt **ALOE** a large genus of bitter herbs

go **ALPS** mountain range; (-pastures)

ALSO in like manner; further

mu **ALTO** male voice of highest pitch

ch **ALUM** mordant mineral salt

AMAH ayah; Indian nurse

md **AMBE** ancient surgical instrument

AMBO high reading desk

rl **AMEN** prayer affirmation (Hebrew)

zo **AMIA** bow-fin or mud-fish (N. Amer.)

ch **AMIC** ammoniac; friend

AMID betwixt; between; amongst

ch **AMIN** ammoniate (acid)

AMIR EMIR; Arab ruler

rl **AMMA** a truss; Syrian abbess

AMMO ammunition

AMOK AMUCK; in a frenzy; berserk

AMOR Roman cupid; Eros

AMOY language (Formosa)

ch **AMYL** a tar product

ANAK a giant of Palestine

pl, zo **ANAL** of the anus

zo **ANER** male ant
ANEW again; freshly; repeatedly
cf, md **ANGI-** of blood vessels
bt **ANIL** the indigo plant; dye
ANKH life symbol (Egypt)
nm **ANNA** 16 annas to the rupee
zo **ANOA** wild ox of Celebes
ANON unknown; hidden; at once; again
ANSA decorated vase-handle
ar **ANTA** a pilaster
ANTE a stake at poker
cf **ANTE-** before
pl **ANUS** excremental orifice
APED copied; imitated; mimicked
APER an impersonator
APEX acme; zenith; pinnacle; ticket
APIS sacred bull (Egypt)
zo **APOD** fish without ventral fins
ar, rl **APSE** polygonal recess; behind altar
rl **AQUA** water; solution
ARAB Saracen; Moor
ARAF Mohammedan purgatory
bt **ARAK** oriental palm sap spirit; areca nut
bt **ARAR** North African timber tree
ARBA covered wagon (Tartar)
rl **ARCA** chest or coffer
ar **ARCH** roguish; cunning; portal
mu **ARCO** bow of stringed instrument
cp, me **AREA** of space; zone; yard; topic
ARES Mars, the God of War
nt **ARGO** the Argonauts' ship
mu **ARIA** air; tune; melody (opera)
ARID dry; parched; sterile; barren
bt **ARIL** outer seed cover
ARMS armorial emblems
ARMY host; array; throng; force
mu **ARPA** harp (It.)
'ARRY HARRY; Cockney names
nt **ARSE** backside; tail of block
ARTS crafts; guiles
ARTY spuriously aesthetic
bt **ARUM** lily genus
ch **ARYL** aromatic hydrocarbon radical
ASAR eskar; gravel ridges
bt **ASCI** bags of spores
ASHY ashen; wan; pallid; hueless
ASIA largest continent
zo **ATKA** type of mackerel
ATLI a Norse king (Atle)
ATOM jot; tittle; whit; particle
ATOP acop; on top (obs.)
cp, ma **ATTO** one million million millionth 10^{-18}
cf **AUDI-** of hearing
AULA a hall; a court
AUNT (Aunt Sally)

nm **AURA** a zephyr; emanation
rl **AUTO** da fé, act of faith (burning of heretics)
cf **AUTO-** (-car) (-matic)
AVAL an endorsement on a bill
bt **AVEL** an awn of barley
go, gl **AVEN** subterranean; sinkhole
AVER avouch; confirm; authenticate
zo **AVES** birds, collectively
AVID eager; greedy; voracious
AVON river (Celt.)
AVOW own; aver; admit; confess
AWAY afar; distant; abroad; absent
AWED inspired by reverence, cowed
bt **AWNY** bearded
AWRY askew; oblique; crooked
AXED discharged; sacked; cut down
AXEL freestyle jump (ice skating); (optional)
bt **AXIL** angle between branch and trunk
AXIN cochineal ointment
zo **AXIS** the chital; Indian spotted deer
AXLE axis; spindle; shaft
zo **AXON** nerve cell impulse-carrying process
AYES supporting votes (Parliament)
mu **AYRE** AIR; old English verse song
AZAN polychrome microanalytical
AZER AZERI; Azerbaijani (Asian)

B

BAAL Phoenician god; false god; idol
BAAS the boss; master (Cape Dutch)
rl, ck **BABA** PAPA, Pope, Patriarch; (rum-, cake)
BABE infant; suckling
BABU Hindu clerk
BACK help; support; posterior; wager; trim sails to windward; reverse; retreat
nt, ga, ar **BACK** (-pay); fall-; (wrestling) (football); extrados of arch; (-sail)
BADE (bid); commanded
BAFF BIFF, BUFF; smite
BAFT abalt; an oriental fabric
nm **BAHT** Thai monetary unit
lw **BAIL** (cricket); hoop; handle; surety
BAIT worry; badger; a lure; refreshment
go **BAIU** plum rains; Japan
BAKE harden; parch
BALD bare; hairless; prosaic; unadorned
ag **BALE** BANE; harm; misery; bundle; hay

ga, nt **BALK BAUK, BAULK,** impede; refuse; timber; (baseball) (-head)

BALL party; rout; globe; bullet

BALM salve; unguent; fragrance; soothing

BANC bench; office place (obs.)

lw, mu, bd **BAND BOND,** unite; a troupe; a coterie; musicians; brace; (elastic-)

cp, ro **BAND** magnetic; zone; wavelength

ch, bt, zo **BANE** poison; ruin; sheep-rot

BANG explosion; a fringe of hair

BANG bhang; the assassin's drug

ck **BANG** a drink (beer, cider, nutmeg, ginger)

nm **BANI** Romanian monetary unit

go, cp **BANK** bench of rowers; deposit and loan office; tilt ridge; obstacle; layer; (river-)

BANT adopt a slimming diet

BARB to shave; thorn; spike; (fish-hook)

zo **BARB** horse

BARD a poet, playwright; minstrel

BARE naked; nude; exposed; bleak

cf **BARI- BARY-;** low (baritone) (Gr.)

bt, nt **BARK** cortex; yelp; yap; a ship; cork

BARM yeast; ferment; leaven

BARN granary; store; out-building; (-dance)

me **BARN** nuclear cross-section unit 10^{-18} metres

cf **BARO-** of weight, pressure (barometer)

BART Bartholomew, baronet

bt **BARU** fluffy fibre

cp **BASE** basis; abject; vile; sordid; starting point; foundation; data; radix

nt, ga **BASE** (naval-); (baseball)

BASH smite; baff; wallop; buffet; attempt

cf **BASI- BASO-;** depth (bassoon) (Gr.)

BASK luxuriate; revel; yap; (sunbathing)

mu **BASS** low voice; deep, grave

bt, zo **BASS** American linden tree; perch

bl **BAST** bass; fibre of that tree

ri **BAST** cat-headed Egyptian goddess

BATE abate; decrease; lessen; tease

BATH basin; pool; (mud-)

me **BATH** Jewish liquid measure

me, cp, tc **BAUD** telegraphic transmission;

rd pulse rate (modulation)

BAUK BAULK, BALK, beam; ridge; hinder

zo **BAWD** whore; hare

BAWL howl; yawl; yell; shout

BAWN fort; cattle-pen

zo **BAYA** the Indian weaver bird

bt **BAYS** laurels of distinction

cp **BEAD** bubble; globule; a moulding; module

BEAK magistrate; prow; bill; mandible

nt, ga **BEAM** rafter; ray; shine; emit; smile; plank (gymn.) (fencing) (baseball)

nt **BEAM** radio directional system; width

bt **BEAN** leguminous plant

zo **BEAR** carry; uphold; suffer; produce

ck, pl, mu **BEAT** spent; exhausted; batter; throb; (heart-); rhythm; notation

nt **BEAT** a policeman's walk; patrol route; sail to windward; punish (corporal)

BEAU fop; dandy; gallant; coxcomb

BECK beckon; a small stream

ck **BEEF** meat of cattle; grumble (USA), strength

mu **BEEN** the vina; Indian guitar

BEEP telephone signal

BEER ale; lager; swipes

bt **BEET** the beetroot

BEIN comfortable; well found (Sc.)

BEJA tribe (Africa)

nm **BEKA** Hebrew monetary unit

mu **BELL** model of soundness; to bellow; alarm-; telephone-; resonant musical peals

mu **BELL** (church-s)

nm **BELL** monetary unit (Fr. Revolution); Ch. coin

BELT zone; girdle; band; thrash

rl **BEMA** judge's seat; pulpit

BEND stoop; incline; a spree; sag; curve

hd, ga **BEND** diagonal band on a shield; ball to swerve in flight (soccer)

bt **BENE** the oil-plant

bt **BENT** curved; crooked; withered grass

bt **BERE** bear; barley (Sc.)

mo **BERG** mountain; iceberg

BERM a ledge; slanting bank

BEST worst; defeat; overcome

nc **BETA** ray; function; 2nd ltr of Gr. alphabet

BEVY swarm; flock; throng

bt **BHEL** Bengal quince

BHIL a Dravidian race (Ind.)

cp **BIAS** prejudice; (bowls); error; partiality

el, ps **BIAS** voltage applied to determine characteristics of device

tx **BIBS** uniform for babies and netballers

BICE pale blue or green
BIDE await; tarry; stay; dwell
BIER a conveyance for the dead; hearse
BIFF BAFF; BUFF; smite; crash
BIGA two-horsed Roman chariot
BIGG bere; a kind of barley (Sc.)
zo **BIKE** bicycle; wasp's nest; a swarm
md **BILE** bitter liver secretion; ill-humour
BILK balk; cheat; decieve; thwart
lw, zo **BILL** fondle; account; placard; poster; invoice; law; beak; -hook
go **BILL** narrow headland; peninsula
BIND tie; fasten; restrain; secure
ga, lw **BIND** seizing prey in flight (falconry); (fencing) agree; hindrance
bt **BINE** hop-stems; (wood-)
BING a heap of corn or alum
BINK bench; bank; shelf (Sc.)
BINT a girl (Arabic)
bt **BION** plant capable of separate life
ch **BIOS** yeast-growth promoter
zo, ga **BIRD** a fowl; shuttlecock (badminton); prison term; magistrate; girl
bt **BIRK** the birch-tree
BIRL spin; whirl (Sc.)
BIRR impetus; violent thrust; a whirr
nm **BIRR** Ethiopian monetary unit
zo **BIRT** the turbot
BISE cold dry wind (Swiss)
ck **BISK** bisque; soup; pottery style
BITE a nibble; etch; nip; grip; grasp
nt, cp **BITT** (to bitt a cable)
BLAB divulge; disclose; tell tales
BLAD fragment; lump; stain; batter (Sc.)
bt **BLAE** blue (Sc.); (-berry)
zo **BLAY BLEY,** a river fish; the bleak
bt **BLEA** inner bark of tree
md **BLEB** transparent blister; bubble
BLED past tense of bleed
BLEE complexion; colour
bt **BLET** spot on decayed fruit; to rot
BLEW sounded, puffed; panted; past of to blow
rd **BLIP** radar reflection spot
BLOB viscous globule
BLOC political/economic grouping
BLOT blur; mar; tarnish; erase
ga, mu **BLOW** sound (horn); puff; pant; (baseball); (bowling); strike (boxing)
bd **BLUB** sob; cry; blubber; blistering (USA); hole in plastercast

BLUE navy; azure; sapphire; (Oxford)
mu **BLUE** cobalt-; ultramarine; glum; jazz
BLUR dim; sully; obscure; blot
zo **BOAR** male hog
nt **BOAT** craft; bark; skiff; vessel
BOCK light beer
BODE portend; presage; augur
BODY corpse; carcass; substance; torso; horse (gymn.)
BOER Afrikaaner (ex-Dutch)
ga **BOGU** kendo armour of Kendoka
BOGY bogey; bugbear; hobgoblin
pr **BOIL** seethe; rage; fume
BOKO nasal organ (sl.)
pr **BOLD** brave; valiant; daring; strong
bt **BOLE** a tree-trunk; recess
bt **BOLL** pod; capsule
ga **BOLO** Filipino knife; uppercut blow (boxing)
BOLT abscond; flee; gulp; missile; fasten; sift; lock (door) (nuts and —s); (-hole)
zo **BOMA** boa; anaconda
BOMB petard; block-buster; bombard; charged explosive; success
ga **BOMB** (basketball); (lacrosse); surfing)
BOND link; band; chain; contract; (bricks)
zo **BONE** steal; (china); skeletal
sp **BONK** knock; extreme fatigue (cycling); sexual intercourse
BONT many-coloured (S. Africa)
BONY full of bones; strong; stout
BOOB BOOBY, blockhead; dune; mistake
BOOH! a derisive interjection; sadness
BOOK tome; volume; manual; reserve
nt **BOOM** boost; resound; barrier; vum (Am.); spar attached to mast; dhow; economic upthrust
BOON benefit; merry; jovial
BOOR clodhopper; lout; lubber
ga **BOOT** gain; to eject; luggage recess; footwear; kick; dismiss
ar **BOOT** facing brickwork base
BORA cold Adriatic wind
BORD coal face (mining)
to, mu **BORE** tidal wave; tire; drill; calibre, North Wind
BORN née; begotten
to **BORT BOART,** low-quality diamond for drills

BOSA a Persian liquor
BOSH tosh; inane chatter; bunkum
BOSK bosket; thicket; grove
pb, gl **BOSS** foreman; stud; protuberance; keystone; boxwood cone; hole plug; rock dome
ga **BOSS** (archery, butt)
lw **BOTE** compensation; reparation
BOTH all of two
zo **BOTS** botts; the larvae of the botfly
zo **BOUD** insect in grain; weevil
BOUN to dress; prepare; set out (Sc.)
rl **BOUS** Norse deity, son of Odin and Rinda
BOUT contest; conflict; turn
nt **BOVO** Genoese fishing boat
mn **BOWK** large iron barrel; kibble
BOWL beaker; goblet; dish; (pipe); heavy ball; stadium, show centre
ga **BOWL** throw (cricket); (Am. football)
nt **BOWS** the fore-end of a ship; fancy knots
BRAD small nail
go **BRAE** hill overlooking valley (Sc.)
BRAG boast; vaunt; a game of cards
bt, rl **BRAN** husk of grain; Celtic deity
BRAT urchin; gamin; child
BRAW fine; brave; showy (Sc.)
BRAY braise; pound; clamour; blare; donkey talk
BRED reared; raised; nurtured
BREE eyebrow; liquor
BREN sub-machine gun
BRER brother; (brer-rabbit)
zo **BRET** a fish of the turbot kind
BREW concoct (beer); devise; plot
ck **BRIE** a creamy cheese
nt **BRIG** two-masted sailing ship; bridge (Sc.)
me **BRIL** unit of brightness
BRIM verge; marge; border; to coast
BRIN a fan-stick
mu **BRIO** vivacity
zo **BRIT** whitebait (fish); a citizen of UK
BROB a wooden wedge
BROC pewter wine measure
to **BROG** an awl; to pierce
BROW rim; edge; brink; forehead
zo **BUBO** the eagle owl
zo, nm **BUCK** talk; jump; deer (bok); dollar
BUDE a gas burner
BUFF baff; biff; strike; yellow; devotee
BUFF pliant leather; the bare skin
BUHL brass and tortoiseshell inlay
mn **BUHR** burr-stone; a millstone

bt **BULB** (electric); corm; tuber
cp **BULK** mass; volume; magnitude; storage
zo, ga, rl **BULL** male animal (deer) (walrus); deck game; centre of target; papal decree
zo, ga **BUMP** fall; the call of the bittern; noise of rocks; volleyball pass
BUND league; association
BUNG barrel-stopper; large cork
rl **BUNI** chief of the Netherworld (Siberia)
rl **BURI** Odin's grandfather (Norse)
nt **BUNK** sleeping berth; run away
nt, ga **BUNT** butt; part of a sail; (baseball)
nt **BUOY** cheer; sustain; floating mooring; (light-)
ar **BURG** borough; burgh; bury; castle
BURK burke; murder; smother; hush up
BURL a knot in thread or wood
ps, md **BURN** a brook; char; glow; set on fire; combustion; (sun-)
ga, md **BURN** (bowls) (Am. football); injury
BURR rough edge; the burdock; dialect tone
bt **BURR** growth on tree-trunk, root
zo **BURT** flat-fish, turbot type
BURY burgh; clump of trees; inter
bt, zo **BUSH** thimble; (bearings); a shrub; (-baby)
go **BUSH** outback; wild scrubland
BUSK to entertain in the street
nt **BUSS** to kiss; a fishing boat
BUST bosom; sculpture; broken; bankrupt
BUSY sedulous; officious; industrious; engaged
rl **BUTO** nursing deity (Eg.)
BUTT log end; meet exactly; abut
BUTT thrust; a mound; bottom; fag-end; (rifle); bum
BUZZ rumour; a whispered report; wasp noise
BYRE a cow-house
cp **BYTE** data or data transfer unit

C

CABA cabas; work-basket; pannier
cf **CACO-** degenerate; diseased; (cacophony)
zo **CADE** cask of herrings; pet lamb
CADI CAID, KADI, Ottoman ruler; judge; (alcaide, mayor)
CAER camp; fort (Welsh)
ck **CAFE** coffee-house; snackbar

CAGE confine; cabin; lift (mine); road crossing
nt CAIC CAIQUE, Turkish coastboat
lw, zo CAIN rent (in kind); a weasel
ck CAKE (baked); solidify; piece of soap
zo, pl CALF young of cow; part of leg
nt CALK CAULK; spike; calkin
CALL (name); summon; visit; (-girl)
me, cp, tc CALL conversation time unit
CALM tranquil; still; windless
mn CALP shale bed (Irish)
mn CALX chalk or lime
zo CAMA South African hartebeest
bd CAME arrived; reached; attained; lead for lights fixing
CAMP pitch a tent; outdoor living place
CAMP exaggeratedly stylized; gay
bt CANE rattan; bamboo; beat
CANG Chinese pillory
CANT incline; thieves' patter; hypocrisy; tilt
bd CANT to cut waste from a log
CANY made of cane
CAPA Spanish cloak
tx, go CAPE CAPA, COPE, cloak; headland
mu CAPO (da-); device on guitar fingerboard
tx, ga, cp CARD woolcomb; personality; game; (wool); (credit); (punched); (score)
lw CARE tend; concern; worry; heed
cr CARF groove made by a carpenter
CARK care; trouble; fret; anxiety
CARL churl; clown
zo CARP cavil; censure; goldfish
CARR reclaimed bog land
CART van; wagon; transport
bd, md, lw CASE box; enclose; plight; facing (brick); patient; law
nm CASH ready money; Chinese coin
CASK casque; helmet; barrel; tub; cade
CAST mien; shed; toss; mould; tint; throw; direct, arrange, performers; (eye); (angling)
ga CAST swift, clean-shooting bow (archery)
cf CATA- KATA-, from; against (catapult)
CATE dainty food
CAUF live-fish box
mn CAUK sulphate of baryta
bd CAUL net; membrane; aluminium or plywood sheet
gl CAVE cavern; grotto; den; beware!
zo CAVY genus of rodents; guinea-pig
mn CAWK heavy spar

CEDE yield; relinquish; apportion; forego
bd CEIL ciel; roof; ceiling
el, bl CELL cavity; dungeon; nucleus + protoplasm
me CELO unit of acceleration
CELT Kelt; early Aryan
nm CENT 10 cents make one dime
CERE to wax; to wrap in cerecloth
CERT alleged certainty; a snip
CEST cestus; a belt or girdle
rl CHAC CHAAC, C. Am. (Mayan) rain gods
zo, cp CHAD shad; sea-bream; punched hole
CHAI gipsy girl
CHAL gipsy man
CHAM CHAMOIS, -leather (cleaning)
CHAP jaw; cleft; fellow; guy; chapman
zo, ck CHAR a lake fish; tea; to scorch; to burn
zo CHAT talk; gossip; warbler; wheatear
CHEF expert cook
CHEW ruminate; munch
CHIC charmingly correct
CHID scolded; rated; rebuked
pl CHIN part of lower jaw
ga CHIP fruit basket; cut; to chaff; stake; golf shot
ck, cp CHIP (potato); semi-conductor; (microchip data)
cf CHIR- the hand (chiromancy, palmistry)
CHOP the jaw; veer; vary; change
ga CHOP cut; meat; strike; (cricket); (table tennis)
CHOU ornamental ribbon
zo CHOW Chinese dog
zo CHUB the cheven; a freshwater carp
CHUG throb of motor
CHUI Judo referee's rebuke
CHUM pal; palooka; buddy; messmate
CHUT a peevish cry
bd CIEL ceil; plaster; wainscot
bd CILL SILL, wall window frame base
ar CIMA CYMA, ogee moulding of cornice
CIRC prehistoric stone circle
tx CIRE polished silk fabric (Fr.)
zo CIRL a species of bunting
CIST CYST, stone chest; tomb
lw CITE quote; summon; adduce
CITY cathedral town
CLAD garbed; dressed; clothed
nt CLAG smokescreen (naval)
zo CLAM bivalve shellfish; to clog

CLAN family; coterie; clique; set
zo CLAP beak of hawk; applaud; cheer
cr CLAW tear; scratch; lacerate; talon; nail extractor
mn CLAY alumina; fine grained earth; (ceramics)
mu CLEF key; (treble; bass); score
zo CLEG horse-fly
CLEM to starve
nt CLEW clue; trace; brail; truss; aft corner of windsail
zo CLIO Muse of History; molluscs
CLIP cut; trim; prune; curtail; embrace
ga CLIP fasten; (film); speed; club; (Am. football)
CLIP coloured marker (croquet)
CLOD sod; turf; lump; yokel; rustic
CLOG obstruct; hamper; trammel
md CLOT curdle, thicken; coagulate; idiot
CLOY glut; pall; satiate; surfeit
CLUB cudgel; bludgeon; combine; set
CLUE clew; hint; guide; ball of string
COAK a dowel-pin; metal bush
mn COAL fossil fuel
COAT cover; lay; spread; vesture
COAX cajole; allure; wheedle
bt COCA the cocaine plant (Peru)
zo, pl COCK rooster; cockerel; penis
bd COCK (hay-) (stop-) (-a pistol) (-a snoot)
bt COCO coconut palm (fruit)
mu CODA finale
lw, cp CODE digest of laws, rules; cypher; (genetic)
CODY trampoline somersault
CO-ED mixed school
lw COIF hairstyle; judge's black cap
el COIL wind up; (dynamo)
nm COIN of currency; invent; counterfeit
nv COIR cordage; coconut fibre
bt COIX a grass; Job's tears
COKE processed coal; (Coca-Cola)
COLD icy; polar; gelid; passionless
bt COLE kale; cabbages generally
COLL fondle; embrace
zo COLT young horse; camel or ass
COLT gun; young cricketer
md COMA stupor; drowsiness
bt COMA tuft of follicles; (comet)
COMB cock's comb; crest; wave; (bees) (hair-dressing)
COMB combe; coomb; dell; valley
COME reach; attain; ensue; arrive
mu COME as, like; (come prima); as at first

COMS malt-dust
nt COND to navigate
bt, nt CONE (fir-cone); buoy; navigation mark; doubles badminton
CONK the nose
nt CONN con; cond; steer; navigate
CONS arguments again; cf. pros
zo CONY CONEY, hyrax; rock-rabbit
ck, lw COOK chef; to falsify accounts etc.
COOL calm; collected; allay; indifferent
COOM soot; axle dirt; coal-dust
zo COON sly fellow; raccoon
CO-OP co-operative, idealistic stores
CO-OP add to governing board
COOP hen-coop; cask; cage; confine
zo COOT old idiot, a water-fowl
tx, rl, ar COPE manage matters; cloak; wall mouldings
rl COPT Egyptian Christian
COPY model; ape; mimic; transcribe
CORB CORF, iron, coal, (alms)-basket
CORD line; rope; braid; cut wood
pl CORD (vocal); (spinal); (umbilical)
bd CORE centre; heart; kernel; (solid) base; (steel, brick)
bt CORK a stopper; bung; bark of cork oak
bt CORM a kind of bulb
bt CORN preserve; an excrescence; grain
COSH police baton; to slug
me COSS about 1¾ miles (2.8 km) (Ind.)
COST price; charge; outlay; detriment
COSY tea-pot cover; cozy; snug
COTE (sheep-); enclosure
COUP (-d'état); overturn; gain
bd COVE bay; bight; harbour; a fellow; moulding
COWL a monk's hood; chimney-pot
pl, zo COXA the hip-joint; leg of insect
COZY COSY, snug; comfortable
bt CRAB bitter apple; peevish person
zo CRAB a portable winch; crustacean
gl, mo CRAG steep, ragged, rockface
CRAM ram; stuff; glut; study
me CRAN about 750 herrings
CRAW maw; crop; fowl's stomach
zo CRAX S. American bird; curassow
CREE to soften grain
nt CREW mob; gang; crowd; crowed
bt CREX the white bullace
ce, rl CRIB manger; cot; coop; copy; grillage; (Xmas)
CRIS creese; Malay knife; kris
CROP reap; an ox-hide; whip; craw

zo **CROW** brag; vaunt; crowbar; croak
CROY embankment; fish-trap
CRUD hardening crust of snow (skiing)
CRUP the buttocks; brittle
bt **CRUT** a dwarf; shaggy oak-bark
mo **CRUX** the crucial point; mountaineering
ma **CUBE** shape of dice; the third power
CUFF sleeve-end; buffet; slap; a stroke
lc **CUIR** leather
CULL reduce numbers (of herds)
bt **CULM** coal-dust; corn or grass stalk; peak
CULT ritual; worship; system; ism
CURB check; restraint; kerb
ck **CURD** (lemon-); coagulated milk
CURE remedy; antidote; panacea; heal
rl **CURE** care of souls; priest (Fr.)
ga **CURL** wind; wave; ringlet; ripple; (Am. football); wave-top (surfing)
CURT abrupt; terse; brief; laconic
zo **CUSK** burbot, an eel-like fish
as **CUSP** point of change (curves) (moon) (zodiac)
CUSS a curse; cross-grained fellow
CUTE shrewd; clever; adroit; chic
CWYM steep rounded hollow (Welsh)
pl **CYAR** the ear-hole
CYMA moulding of a cornice; ogee
bt **CYME** young; shoot; inflorescence
pl **CYST** water-bag; bladder; growth
cy **-CYTE** CYTO-, of cells (cytology
CZAR TSAR, TZAR, ruler (caesar) (Russia)

D

zo **DACE** small river fish; dare; dart
DADA anarchic artistic non-style
DADE hold child by leading-strings
DADO decorative skirting
DAFT idiotic; absurd; ridiculous
nt **DAGO** felucca; lateen-rig vessel
DAIL Irish Parliament
DAIS raised platform; a canopy
DALE vale; valley; dingle
bt **DALI** Brazilian timber-tree
DALL incised tile; cow-dung fuel
DALT a foster-child
DAME the wife of a baronet
DAMN doom; condemn; ruin
DAMP dank; humid; depress; discourage

zo **DANE** man of Denmark; (great-) dog
DANK moist; clammy; humid; damp
pl **DANT** soft or fine coal
DARE defy; venture; challenge; presume
bt **DARI** Indian millet
DARK ebon; murky; Cimmerian
DARN to mend by stitching; curse (damn)
DART rush; run; hurl; a missile
DASH throw; onset; elan; frustrate
DATA accepted inferences; premises; facts
cp, tc **DATA** available coded information
bt **DATE** period; epoch; age; a fruit
DAUB smear; sully; smirch; plaster
lw **DAVY** safety-lamp; affidavit
nm **DAWM** a fortieth of a rupee (Ind.)
DAWN cock-crow; dayspring; gleam
DAZE stun; amaze; astound; confuse
D-DAY invasion day (6 June 1944)
DEAD exactly; directly; defunct; late
DEAF heedless; inattentive; (no kernel)
DEAL pinewood; allot; treat; bargain
rl **DEAN** guild president; church dignitary
DEAR beloved; costly; expensive
DEBT liability; arrears; obligation
cf **DECA-** ten times (decade)
cf **DECI-** one tenth (decilitre)
nt, cp, tc **DECK** adorn; array; (cards); floor, sound centre; (surfing)
lw **DEED** feat; exploit; document
DEEM opine; judge; imagine; believe
DEEP the ocean; profound; recondite
zo **DEER** a solid-horned ungulate
DEEV devil; (spirit) (Persia)
DEFT dextrous; adroit; handy; skilful
DEFY flout; spurn; brave; dare
ck **DELI** (delicatessen) food shop
DELL dale; dene; dingle; vale
bl **DEME** possible interbreeders
DEME Greek township; tribal division
DEMO demonstration (political)
DEMY a size of paper
DENE dell; dune; sandhill
DENT niche; notch; dint; indentation
DENY contradict; gainsay; refute
md **DERM** the skin
DERN durn; secret; dreadful; gatepost
DERV diesel oil
ga **DESI** (designated) baseball hitter
DESK writing table; a lectern
rl **DEVA** a benign spirit (Hindu)
rl **DEVI** the wife of Siva (Hindu)

DEWY spangled with dew
nt **DHOW** Arab ship; lateen sail
ch **DIAD** divalent atom; social (dyad)
DIAL (telephone); face; indicator disc
DICE game; sometimes loaded
lw **DICK** sworn declaration; detective
DIDO antic; caper; queen of Carthage
zo **DIEB** North African jackal
DIED perished; expired; departed
to **DIES** days; screwtaps
DIET assembly; viands; sustenance
DIGS lodgings
bt **DIKA** West African mango
DIKE ditch; rine; rhine; mortarless wall; lesbian
bt, md, ck **DILL** medicinal herb; condiment
nm **DIME** a ten-cent piece (USA)
DINE give a dinner to; eat
DING ring; urge; enforce; dash; sea-damage to surfboard
ga **DINK** a hit (tennis) (volleyball)
DINT in skilled manner
DIRE awful; disastrous; calamitous
DIRK dagger; poniard (Sc.)
DIRT mud; mire; dust; muck; grime; soil
bt **DISA** S. African orchid
cp, tc **DISC** disk; record; flat round plate; recording plate (gramophone)
DISH a culinary conception; frustrate
bt, cp **DISK** disc; any flat round token; magnetic computer storage device
bt **DISS** an Algerian grass
mu **DIVA** a prima donna
DIVE plunge; descent; a gambling hell
DOAB alluvial land (India)
bt **DOCK** curtail; lessen; deduct; a weed
nv, lw **DOCK** basin for shipping; (law court)
zo **DODO** extinct bird (Mauritius)
DOER agent; executive; performer
DOFF daff; take off; divest
DOGE Duke of Venice
bt **DOHL** pulse; (dried peas)
nm **DOIT** Dutch or Scotch half-farthing
DOJO martial arts centre
DOKE a dint; a dimple
DOLE an allowance; dispense; share
DOLL to dress up; a toy
DOLT dunce; booby; dullard
gl **DOME** a cupola; round roof; similar rock formation
DONE ended; finished; transacted
nm **DONG** Vietnamese monetary unit
DON'T prelude to a prohibition

bt **DOOB** an Indian grass
zo **DOOD** camel or dromedary
DOOM kismet; condemn; last judgment; fate
DOOR portal; entrance; access; egress
ch **DOPO** source of adrenalin
DOPE drug; narcotic; doctor; varnish
mu **DOPA** after(wards)
DORA Defence of the Realm Act
zo **DORN** the thorn-back skate
DORP burg; town; village
zo **DORR** the dor-beetle
zo, nt **DORY** golden-coloured fish; skiff; dinghy
DOSE draught; drench; physic
DOSS a shake-down; a hassock
DOST thou doest
DOTE love tenderly; talk trash; (infatuation)
DOTH a poetical 'do'
DOTS grains, insulting material
DOTY decayed; half-rotten
zo **DOUC** a highly coloured monkey
bt **DOUM** the doom-palm
tx **DOUP** weaving half-haeld
DOUR stem; grim; relentless; obstinate
DOUT extinguish
mu **DOUX** sweet (Fr.); also billet doux love notes
zo **DOVE** emblem of peace
DOWD woman's nightcap; scruffy
DOWN fluff; pasture; hill; prone
DOXY loose woman; moll
DOZE nap; slumber; forty winks
DOZY drowsy; sleepy; dreamy; date; timber; decay
DRAB khaki colour; a cloth; a trull
ga **DRAG** (billiards); (snooker); (coaching); (net)
bd **DRAG** a hunt; haul; pull; steel plate smoother; linger
DRAG uneven painting; men got up as women
me **DRAM** drachm; a tot of spirits
DRAT a mild expletive
DRAW depict; attract; raffle; lottery
nt **DRAW** tie; (curling); taking in sails
DRAW iron; chimney draught
DRAY strong cart for heavy goods
DREW drafted; depicted; extracted
zo **DREY** a squirrel's nest
DRIB purloin small pieces; inveigle
ar **DRIP** ooze; dribble; trickle; percolate; cornice projection
ar **DROP** globule; bead; sink; quit; lower newel stair-post projection; overtake; discontinue

DROW trow; troll; cave elf
(Shetland)
DRUB maul; thrash; beat; pound
md **DRUG** medicinal; narcotic etc.
mu **DRUM** ridge of hills; tambour
cf **DRUM** base of dome; recording
centre
DUAD union of two
DUAL twofold
DUAN a division of a poem; a canto
DUCE leather, dictator (It.)
zo,ga **DUCK** cloth; dive; dip; underplay;
bird; zero score (cricket)
DUCT tube; canal; pipe; conduit
DUDE a dandy; fop; nut
DUDS clothing; rags; useless ones
DUEL single combat (of honour)
mu **DUET** composition for two voices
mn **DUFF** low-calory fine-grain coal
DUFF muff; a pudding; refurbish;
useless
DUKE (strawberry leaves); peer
DUKW amphibious army vehicle
DULL benumb; blunt; abate; stolid
DULY properly; regularly; exactly
DUMA Russian Parliament
nt **DUMB** mute; inarticulate; soundless;
lighter
ga **DUMP** (bawling); (drag racing);
(trotting); (ice hockey); (Am.
football)
DUMP unload; rubbish-heap; storage
program; slovenly place
DUNE dene; sandy ridge
DUNG manure; droppings
ck **DUNK** dipping bread into soup, etc.
DUNT staggering affection; heavy
blow
DUPE gull; delude; outwit;
hoodwink
bt **DURA** an Indian grass
DURE endure; harden; severe
DURN dern; a door-post
DUSE deuce; demon; evil spirit
DUSK eventide; twilight; eve
DUST pulverulence; a disturbance
DUTY obligation; excise; tariff
ch **DYAD** cf. monad; pair (team of 2)
DYAK a native of Borneo
DYED stained; tinted; tinged
DYER dye-worker
bd **DYKE** DIKE, ditch; fosse; lesbian
me **DYNE** the unit of force

E

EACH both; every one
EARL JARL, lord; peer
EARN win; gain; merit; acquire
EASE allay; still; assuage; relief
EAST a cardinal point
EASY facile; affluent; flowing
ar **EAVE** roof overhang; (-s dropping)
listening
EBON of ebony; black
bt **ECAD** habitat-adapted plant form
ECHO repeat; resound; reverberate
tc **ECHO** delayed reflected sound
ECRU pale yellowish brown
cf **ECTO-** external
EDAM spherical Dutch cheese
EDDA Scandinavian saga
EDDY ripple; swirl; vortex
EDEN garden of delight
EDGE brink; fringe; zest; sharpness
EDGY on edge; nervous
cp **EDIT** revise; annotate; arrange data;
(newspaper)
EGAD a refined expletive
EGIS AEGIS, patronage; shield
EIRE Republic of Ireland
bt **EJOO** the sago palm
EKED existed on small pittance
ELAN dash; impetuosity; vivacity
ELIA Charles Lamb
ELMO Elmo's fire; electrical flame
bt **ELMY** abounding with elms
ELSE other; otherwise; besides
ELUL 12th month of the Jewish year
EMIR amir; Eastern title
EMIT vent; eject; exhale; discharge
zo **EMYS** terrapin genus
cf **ENDO-** internal (Gr.)
ENTE heraldic engraftment
cf **ENTO-** internal (Gr.)
ENVY ill-will; malice; covet; grudge
EOAN dawning; eastern
ga **EPEE** sharp-pointed duelling sword
(Fr.) (fencing)
me **EPHA** ephah; Hebrew bushel
EPIC heroic; historic; saga-like
EPOS epic poem (Homeric)
ERGO therefore
cf **ERGO-** of work (Gr.)
ERIC eriach; blood-money (Irish
Law)
ERIN the Green Isle, Ireland
zo **ERNE** the sea-eagle
EROS God of Love; Cupid
ERSE the Gaelic language
bt **ERSH** stubble
ERST formerly; whilom

zo **ESOX** the pike
ESPY discover; observe; perceive; notice
ESSE mere existence
ETCH engrave; draw; cropped ground
ETNA volcano (Sicily)
ETON a returnable note
ETUI needle case; container; etwee
EVEN level; uniform; steady; impartial
EVER aye; always; eternity
zo **EVET** eft; newt; ewft
EVIL harm; malice; baneful; malign
EVOE a Bacchanalian cry
EWER pitcher; jug with handle
EWRY scullery; place of ewers, pots
EXAM examination
EXES expenses
EXIT way out; a stage departure
EXON an officer; Yeoman of the Guard
EXPO exposition; exhibition
zo **EYAS** nyas; young hawk
EYED observed; watched; espied
EYER a watcher
EYES visual organs; discs on bowls
EYOT ait; river or lake islet
zo **EYRA** S. American cat
lw **EYRE** journey; circuit; court

F

bt **FAAM** Indian orchid
zo **FAAP** the garfish
bt, ck **FABA** broad Windsor soup bean
ga **FACE** defy; dare; surface; confront; dial; forward side of stick; wave; (hockey); (surfing)
FACT incident; actuality; truth
FACY impudent
FADE wither; dwindle; insipid; ball off course; lose colour
mu **FADO** lament of the heart (Port.)
FAEX dregs
FAIL wane; flag; decline; neglect
FAIN willingly; gladly; readily
FAIR market; just; equitable; blond
FAIX by my faith
ga **FAJA** coloured sash (pelota)
FAKE a cable coil; counterfeit; pretence
mu **FALA** old madrigal
nt **FALL** autumn; the Fall; drop; cascade; part of halyard sail
md **FALX** a membrane
FAMA the goddess of rumour

FAME renown; repute; lustre; celebrity
rl **FANE** vane; temple; church
FANG tooth; claw; talon
FARE manage; victuals; passenger (ticket)
ck **FARL** Scottish oatcake
FARM ferm; till; cultivate; lease
ck **FARO** card game; sour beer
FART puff of wind; flatus
ga **FAST** astain from solid food; firm; rapid; (stand-); stop (archery)
FATA Morgana; a mirage; perfect knight
FATE kismet; doom; destiny; lot
FAUN woodland deity; Pan
FAUX pas; offensive false step
ck **FAVA** faba; bean puree
zo **FAWN** cringe; a colour; fallow-deer
FAZE disconcert; worry
FEAL faithful; constant; loyal
FEAR awe; alarm; dread; anxiety
FEAT exploit; deed; trick
FEED cater; sustain; provender
FEED thickening paint; (-pipe); consume; (cattle)
FEEL sense; touch; experience
FEET paws, hoofs
FELL hew; cut; tumbled; barren hill
FELL cruel; deadly; spirited; skin
lw **FELO** de se; suicide
lw **FELT** fabric; sensed; handled; touched
FEME a woman
FEND parry; ward off, make shift
bt **FERN** vascular cryptogamous plant
hd **FESS** FESSE, broad heraldic band
FETE gala; festival; carnival; holiday
FEUD clan warfare; strife; a fief
lw **FIAR** freeholder, not a life-renter
lw **FIAT** decree; command; ukase
bt **FICO** a snap of the fingers; a fig
lw **FIEF** land held on fuedal tenure
mu **FIFE** a variety of flute
FIFF dress required to play pipes
FIKE fidget; trivial detail
cp **FILE** list; dossier; smoothing tool; data set to
tc **FILE** arrange in order; available stored information
bd **FILL** sate; glut; replenish; earthwork
FILM thin skin; scum; thread; pellicle; cine
FIND discover; discovery; decide
mu **FINE** forfeit; delicate; tenuous; exact; end (It.)
FINN a Finlander

FINS stabilizers on ships, aircraft (surfing)
FIRE discharge; kindle; ignite; blaze
FIRM fast; tight; compact; a company
FIRN nerve; granular glacier snow
FISC state treasury; revenue; purse
zo **FISH** to angle; search by sweeping
FIST neif; the clenched hand; to punch
FIST calligraphy
FITZ son of
FIVE the pentad
FIZZ hiss; champagne
nt **FLAG** banner; ensign; to signal
bt **FLAG** droop; weary; a stone; a plant
FLAK anti-aircraft gunfire (German)
FLAM 2-note side-drum flourish
ck **FLAN** open tart; savoury quiche
ck **FLAP** flop; wave; vibrate; cover; pastry
FLAT smooth; level; insipid; residence
mu **FLAT** level; (platform); sandbar; lowered pitch
FLAW blemish; defect; crevice
bt **FLAX** linum; the linen plant
FLAY skin; excoriate; strip; criticise
zo **FLEA** pulex irritans
FLED ran; bolted; retreated
FLEE escape; abscond; decamp
FLEW fled; the chap of a hound
FLEX to bend; an electric lead
FLEY flay; frighten; cause to fly
FLIP a joy ride; (egg-flip)
FLIT fly; dart; flicker; migrate
zo **FLIX** fur; beaver-down
FLOC accumulation of solids in liquid
FLOE floating arctic ice
FLOG lash; scourge; whip
FLOP flap; a failure; a fiasco; high jump
FLOT stratified ore
FLOW run; emanate; abound; circulate
FLUE smoke pipe; light down; fluff
FLUX flow; mutation; change; (soldering)
zo **FOAL** colt or filly
bd **FOAM** spume; froth; spray; rage; lightweight concrete
FOHN warm mountain wind (N. Alpine)
FOIE liver (Fr.)
ga **FOIL** track of game; baffle; outwit; (table tennis)
ga **FOIL** thin metal; fencing rapier
FOIN a thrust with spear or sword

gl **FOLD** lap; wrap; furl; double; envelop; bend in rock strata; (sheep)
FOLK kindred; relations; people
pr **FOND** loving; attached; archive unit
rl, pr **FONT** fount; source; spring; type
FOOD viands; victuals; rations
FOOL gull; beguile; hoodwink; ninny
pl, me, mu **FOOT** pay; discharge; settle; walking base of body; lower edge; measure of pitch
FORD wade; a river crossing
FORE a warning cry at golf
FORK branch; divide; divaricate
FORM bench; formula; mould; fashion
FORM bed of hare; mode; ceremony
FORS force; fortitude; fortune (Ruskin)
FORT keep; citadel; fastness
FOSS ditch or moat
FOUD magistrate or bailiff (Orkney)
FOUL noisome; ribald; unfair; sullied
ga **FOUL** infringement of rules in games, sports
ga, ck **FOUR** 4; cricket boundary worth four runs score; (petit)
zo **FOWL** poultry; game birds
FOXY sly; wily; sour; a colour
FRAP to bind; to strike
FRAU a German married woman
FRAY rub; brush; quarrel; skirmish
nv **FREE** rid; loose; clear; informal; wind from the beam or abaft; available, unmarked player (netball)
FRET fray; fume; chafe; abrade; grieve
cr, mu **FRET** (swa); (work); geometrical ornament; wood slats for fingers on guitar-like instruments
zo **FRIT** glass material; a wheat-fly
FRIZ frizz; to curl; to crisp
to **FROE** woodcutter's cleaver
zo, rw **FROG** a batrachian; horse's foot; rail crossings
bd **FROG** cloak or coat button or tassel; brick indentation
FROM preposition of source
to **FROW** tool or lathe splitting
FUEL combustibles
mu **FUGA FUGUE**, contrapuntal composition
FUGH exclamation of abhorrence
FULL replete; copious; ample; thicken
FUME smoke; vapour; exhalation; reek

FUMY vaporous; fumous; fussy
FUND reserve; store; supply; capital
zo **FUNG** mythical Chinese pheasant
FUNK terror; fear; shirk; touchwood
cr **FUOR** decayed-rafter strengthener
FURL fold; roll; stow; wrap
FURY frenzy; rage; turbulence; shrew
FUSE melt; liquefy; blend
FUSE electric safety cut-off
FUSS ado; stir; fume; fidget; fret
FUST shaft of column; musty smell
FUZE quickmatch; a timing device
FUZZ fluff; light particles; police
FYKE bagnet for fishing
FYRD pre-Conquest Saxon military array

G

GABY a simpleton; nitwit
to **GADE** gaid; gad; goad; graver
GAEL Celtic
nt **GAFF** low theatre; a hook; a spar
bt **GAGE** a pledge; stake; wager; plum
to **GAID** gade; gad; spike on gauntlet
GAIN get; win; acquire; profit
tc, cr **GAIN** increase of message signal power; mortise; notch
GAIR field of lush grass
GAIT walk; bearing; step; pace
bt **GAIT** pasturage; charge; sheaf of corn
GALA festival; festivity; pomp; show
bt **GALE** high wind; rent; a bog plant
GALL vex; torment; provoke; rancour
GALL bile; malignity; glass scum
GALT gault; clay; marl; brick-earth
mu **GAMB** leg; shank; (viol de-) cello
GAME lame; plucky; dauntless; pastime
cf **GAMO-** marital, sexual union
GAMP an umbrella
GAMY high in flavour
hd **GANG** crew; band; horde; coterie
ga **GANT** sports glove; basket pelota
GAOL jail; prison; objective
GAPE stare; to yawn
GARB dress; costume; heraldic sheaf
GASH slash; score; slit; wound
GASP pant; puff
zo **GATA** tropical Atlantic shark
ga **GATE** (slalom); (canoeing); (skiing); (water skiing)
GATE entrance; barrier; attendance; ban

ga, cp **GATE** goal; portal; electrical switch
GATE (flood-); valve); (lock)
bt, nt **GAUB** an Indian tree; guy-rope
GAUD a gewgaw; showy ornament; gawd
pt **GAUL** old France; hollow in a finishing coat
GAUM to smear; to daub
GAUP gawp; gape
zo **GAUR** a wild Indian ox
GAVE presented; granted; yielded
GAWD gaud; a piece of finery
zo **GAWK** gowk; simpleton; a cuckoo
GAWN small tub; a ladle
GAZE stare; view; regard; contemplate
GEAL to congeal; pert. to earth
bt **GEAN** wild cherry
GEAR tackle; harness; dress; mechanism
GEAT hole for metal casting
GECK dupe; mock; simpleton
zo **GEDD** the pike
GEED went faster
GEEZ archaic Semitic dialect
GELD gold; tribute; castrate; spay
GELT geld; gilt; money; emasculated
md **GENA** the cheek
md **GENE** heredity factor
GENS Roman class; patrilineal kin, sib
GENT a would-be gentleman
GENU nerve-tract bend
cf, bl **-GENY** of origin; cause; generation
md **GERM** ovule; nucleus; a bacillus
GEST an exploit; feat; bearing
bt **GEUM** avens and herb-bennet genus
GHAT Indian mountain; landing-stair; funeral pyre
GHEE Indian oil or butter
nt **GIBE** jibe; sneer; deride; taunt
GIFT boon; bounty; gratuity; faculty
ma, mu **GIGA** one thousand million 10^9; jig (It.), folkloric dance form
cp **GIGO** garbage in, garbage out; data unreliability
GILD guild; trade's union; add lustre
bt, go **GILL** a flirt; a ravine; ground ivy; mountain stream
zo, me **GILL** breathing organ; ¼ pint
zo **GILT** gilded; aureate; a young sow
GIMP smart; spruce; a trimming
GING gang or company
GINN jinn; djinn; demon; spirit
GIRD bind; reproach; gibe; spasm
zo **GIRL** young roe-buck; young woman
GIRO payment transfer system
nt **GIRT** tightly moored; bound; girth

cr **GIRT** surround rail; beam
GIST essential point; pith
ga **GITE** bed or an abode (Fr.);
(mountaineering)
GIVE yield; confer; grant; present
GLAD (eye); joyous; elated;
delectable
GLEE hilarity; merriment; mirth
mu **GLEE** squint; part song
GLEN vale; dale; dell; dingle; valley
bl **GLIA** supportive cells (neuroglia)
GLIB voluble; fluent; ready; facile
GLIM a light; a glimmer
GLOW fervour; shine; burn; gleam
GLUE cement; an adhesive
GLUM grum; crestfallen; downcast
GLUT surfeit; surplus; cloy; satiate
G-MAN gun-man; bandit
GNAR knar; yarr; snarl
zo **GNAT** insect (mosquito)
GNAW bite; corrode; erode; champ
GOAD spur; rouse; incite; an ankus
GOAF worked-out mine; slag
ga **GOAL** end; aim; ambition; object;
score-portal
GOAN Indian; E. African Indian
zo **GOAT** Capricornus; horned animal
cn **GOBO** sound-absorbing panel
GO-BY evasion
zo **GOBY** fish having nests of seaweed
GODS lofty theatrical supporters
GOEL an avenger of blood (Heb.)
GOER a mover; a go-between
GOLA a cyma; cyme; a moulding
GOLD or; money wealth; bull at
archery
ga **GOLF** goff; gowf; for 9, 18, or 19
holes
GOME black cart-grease
bl **GONA- GONO-**, of genitals; offspring;
seed
GONE hied; wended; fared; left;
parted
cy **GONE** group of 4 nuclei or cells
mu **GONG** prelude to a meal; percussion
instrument, oriental
GOOD weal; virtuous; upright;
proper
GOOF simpleton; silly cuckoo
GOOR coarse sugar from the date-
palm
GORE clotted blood; wedge of cloth
GORM sheen; shine of varnish
GORY sanguinary; ensanguined
GOSH an ejaculation
GOTH Teutonic barbarian
GOUL GOWL, howl; yowl
GOUM native Algerian soldier (Fr.)

GOUT a drop; taste; relish
md **GOUT** paroxysmal form of arthritis
zo **GOWK** gouk; simpleton; oaf; cuckoo
GOWN robe; garment
GRAB snatch; seize; grip; a card
game
nt **GRAB** two-masted vessel (Malabar)
GRAF German title; a count
bt, me **GRAM** misery; chick pea; weight
cf **-GRAM** written; drawn; result
GRAY grey; ash-coloured
GREE a step; degree; goodwill
GREW thrived; raised; progressed
GREY gray; a neutral tint
el **GRID** frame; network; box layout of
crossing lines
zo **GRIG** sand-eel; grasshopper; cricket
GRIM stern; dire; hideous; grisly
GRIN girn; smirk; a snare
GRIP clutch; handbag; small ditch
gl **GRIT** endurance; courage; quartz-
rock (sand)
GROG rum and water
GROS silken fabric
GROT a grotto
GROW wax; develop; expand; raise
zo **GRUB** caterpillar; food; (cricket);
root out
GRUM glum; surly; morose; guttural
mn **GUAG** space left by mineral
extraction
zo **GUAN** Brazilian game bird
nt **GUFA** Tigris ferry boat
mn **GUHR** loose earth found in rocks
zo **GUIB** the harnessed antelope
GULF chasm; abyss; bight; bay
zo **GULL** beguile; hoax; deceive; sea-
bird
cp **GULP** as many bytes as digits;
swallow; choke
hd **GULY** coloured red in heraldry
GUNK semi-solid material from
synthesis
GURU Hindu teacher
GUSH rush; spout; stream; an
outburst
pc **GUST** squall; burst of passion; relish;
taste unit
zo **GYAL GAYAL**, E. Indian ox
nt **GYBE** gibe; sneer
GYLE to ferment; a brew
zo **GYNE** ant
cf, pl **GYNE- GYNO-, -GYNY**, of females
GYRA embroidered border
GYRE a circular motion
GYRO a gyroscope
GYVE fetter; shackle; handcuff; bond

H

HAAF deep-sea fishing ground (Shetland)
HAAK sailing lighter (North sea)
HAAR harr; a cold sea mist
to **HACK** notch; gash; kick; chopper
zo **HACK** literary drudge; sorry; jade (horse)
ga **HACK** mattock; blow; foothold (curling)
HADE slope of mineral vein or fault; hole in the ice
rl **HADJ HAJI,** a pilgrimage to Mecca
md **HAEM** iron pigment in haemoglobin
HAFF river mouth, lagoon (Ger.)
HAFT heft; hilt; handle; to haggle
HA-HA haw-haw; sunken fence; laughter
HAIK hyke; haick; an Arab wrap
HAIL health; greeting; frozen rain
HAIR jot; iota; quality; character
HAKA native dance (NZ)
zo **HAKE** a pot-hook; loiter; sea fish
HALE haul; drag; healthy; robust
ga **HALF** a moiety; a half-back; draw (tie); golf; term (netball)
ar **HALL** manor house; a college; aula
ag **HALM HAUM, HAULM,** cornstalk at harvest time
rl, as **HALO** a saintly aura; solar, lunar ring of light
HALT to stop; to limp; crippled; waver
HAME bar for trace attachment
HAND manual labour; assistance
me **HAND** proffer; (cards); 4 in (horses); serve (badminton)
HANG suspend; hover; slope; drift; long jump technique
nt **HANK** skein; coil; hoop; ring
HARD firm; compact; arduous
zo **HARE** to speed; puss
HARK hear; listen; attend (nostalgia)
HARM hurt; scathe; wrong; injury
lw **HARO** an appeal (Channel Islands)
mu **HARP** reiterate; lyre, plucked instrument
HARR haar; a storm; an eagre
zo **HART** male red-deer
ck, cp **HASH** chop; mangle; mince; a jumble; mess-up; unwanted data
jn **HASP** clasp or fastening; staple; clip
HAST (thou) havest
HATE abhor; loathe; enmity; odium
HATH has
HAUL tug; pull; drag; draw; heave
HAVE own; possess; hold; contain

zo **HAWK** rapacious bird or person
HAWK intentional cough; to peddle
to **HAWK** plasterer's mortar board
HAWM to lounge about
HAZE fog; mist; pall; miasma; to bully
HAZY vague; obscure; indistinct; murky
HEAD top; chief; steer; (bowls); (beer)
cp, tc **HEAD** acme; (black-); electromagnetic
HEAL cure; remedy; assuage; compose
HEAP pile; mound; amass; collect; jack and live bowls
lw **HEAR** heed; hark; try judicially
ga **HEAT** rage; passion; ardour; excite; qualifying round in sports; to warm
HEBE an Olympian cup-bearer
HECK fish-weir; a rack; river bend
HEED mind; mark; obey; regard; caution
jn **HEEL** submit; low fellow; twerp; underfoot; spur
HEFT hilt; handle; heaved
HEIR inheritor; offspring
HELD grasped; adhered; restrained
HELL Hades, Gehenna; gambling house
nt **HELM** tiller; steering gear; steer
HELM helmet; crown; top; guide; direct
HELP aid; abet; back; second; relieve
cf, pl **HEMA- HEMO-,** of blood (Gr.)
bt **HEMP** rope-fibre; a plant
HEND to seize; to apprehend (obs.)
HERA (Juno), wife of Zeus
bt **HERB** a simple; an annual plant
HERD drove; rabble; tend; collect
HERE at this place
HERL harl; barb of feather
ar, rl **HERM** (Hermes') head or bust on decorative pillar
zo **HERN** heron (obs.)
HERO a priestess of Aphrodite
HERR German gent
HERS HERN, of her
HEST behest; command (Shak.)
HEWN cut; felled; chiselled
HICK bucolic; country cousin (USA)
me **HIDE** about 100 acres (41 hectares)
HIDE a skin; pelt; secrete; cache
HIED set off
HI-FI high-fidelity sound
HIGH eminent; lofty; arrogant; shrill; pressure; drug-induced state

HIKE to carry; to ramble; long distance walk; (price rise) (Am. football)

bt HILA the eyes of beans

bt,go HILL to earth up plants; midget mountain; (mole-)

HILT haft; heft; handle

zo HIND a rustic; backward; a deer

to HINK a reaping hook

HINT imply; insinuate; innuendo

HIRE rent; charter; lease; salary

HISK to breathe with difficulty

HISS also HISH and HIZZ

HIST! hush!

HIVE to collect; store up; a skep

HOAR hoary; rime; venerable

HOAX gammon; spoof; dupe; delude

HOBO a tramp; a vagrant (USA)

HOCK Rhenish wine; a joint; the hough

HOED weeded

HOER manipulator of a hoe

zo HOGG hog; a two-year old sheep

HOIK hike; an upward turn

HOIT to leap; to caper

cp,nt HOLD grasp; contain; keep; cargo space; order a halt

HOLE cavity; lair; burrow; pierce; (golf)

cp HOLE orifice; punched-card system

bt HOLM evergreen oak; holly

HOLM flat land; an islet (Scand.)

HOLT woodland; a copse; a burrow

HOLY sanctified; consecrated; divine

HOME habitat; seat; institution; residence

cf HOMO- of same; alike; (homosexual) (Gr.)

HOMY homelike

HONE to pine; to moan; a whetstone

HONG Chinese factory

HONK to hoot

HOOD cowl; cover; to blind

zo HOOF horse's foot; to walk

HOOK promontory; snare; sickle

to HOOK to bend; to steal; seize; connect; strike; curved device; to hit (boxing) (bowls) (baseball) (rugby) (football) (cricket); (rug making); hold

HOOP a whoop; a band; a toy; (baseball)

HOOP the basket and its rim (basketball)

HOOT honk; boo; decry; execrate

HOPE expect; anticipate; confidence

bt HOPS beer flavouring

go,pl,zo, HORN cornucopia; drinking cup;

mu wind instrument; antler; phallus; pyramidal moutain peak

ck HORS out of; beyond (hors-de-combat); (-d'oeuvres)

HOSE stockings; hosiery; to sprinkle

HOSH courtyard of Arab house

HOST multitude; consecrated wafer

HOUR always passing

HOVA a Malagasi; from Madagascar

HOVE past tense of heave; raised

HOWL growl; yowl; wail; yell; squall

HOYA genus of climbing plants

rl HUAN jade Chinese ritual object

zo HUCK a German trout

HUED coloured; tinted

HUEL a wheal; a Cornish mine

HUER fish-scout watching for shoals

HUFF swell; bluster; anger; (draughts)

HUGE vast; colossal; gigantic; immense

zo HUIA New Zealand starling

nt HULK old ship used as store, prison, etc.

bt,nt HULL husk; pod; to pierce; ship

pc HUMP hillock; to carry; depression

HUNG dangled; draped; hovered

HUNK chunk; lump; large slice

HUNT pursue; hound; search; chase

HURL cast; pitch; fling; whirl

HURT pain; offend; mar; an injury

HUSH quiet; calm; still; silence

bt HUSK hull; rind; coating

zo HUSO the great sturgeon

HUTO native of Rwanda (Africa)

nm HWAN (Korea) monetary unit

HWYC emotional fervour; intonation (Welsh)

HYKE haik; loose Arab garment

mu HYMN panegyric; paean; song of praise

HYPE a wrestling throw

ch,md HYPO diluted; syringe (sl.); injection

cf HYPO- of lesser, smaller (Gr.)

I

zo IBEX mountain wild goat

IBID in the same place (Lat.)

zo IBIS a wading bird, sacred in Egypt

ICED frozen; congealed

rl ICON IKON, sacred picture; image

IDEA notion; fantasy; conceit; insight; scheme; plan; vision

lw IDEM the same

cf IDEO- of mental image; idea

IDES Roman date

cf **IDIO-** personal; self produced; distinct
IDLE inert; lazy; inactive; unused
IDLY indolently
IDOL hero; pet; image
IDYL idyll; pastoral poem
IEIE Hawaiian palm tree
IGEL squat tumbler glass (Ger.)
wv **IKAT** pattern dye and wave technique (Indonesia)
bt **ILEX** evergreen oak
rl **IMAM** Mohammedan priest
rl **IMAN** Moslem faith
IMPI Zulu regiment
INBY inbye; inwards (Sc.)
INCA ancient king or prince of Peru
INCA an Indian of Peru area
me **INCH** measure of short length; creep
INCH creep forward
INFO information (centre)
INKY black; blotted
INLY inward; secret
INRO Japanese comfit box
INTO preposition of direction
IOTA a jot; tittle; whit; particle
cf **IPSA-** IPSO-, one's own, of self (Gr.)
pl **IRIS** Rainbow Goddess, messenger of Zeus; eye membrane
mn **IRON** golf club; metal; to smoothe
IRON gyve, fetter; strength
bt **ISCA** excrescence on oak or hazel
ISIS Moon Goddess; mother of Horus
ISLE ait; eyot; islet
md **ITCH** constant teasing desire
ITEM detail; entry; innuendo
zo **ITER** canal or duct
md **ITIS** undiagnosed disease
ar **IWAN** Islamic vaulted hall
IWIS ywis; certainly
bt **IXIA** South African iridaceous plants
IBZA Russian arctic log hut

J

bt **JACA** the bread-fruit tree
zo, nt **JACK** (cards); flag; lifter (car); pike
nt, cp **JACK** appliance; sailor; (bowls); plug
mu **JACK** harpsichord plucking device
zo **JADE** sorry nag; mean woman
mn **JADE** to fatigue; Chinese gemstone
JAIL gaol; to imprison
JAIN Indian religious sect
JAMB a door-post; to wedge; stick
nm **JANE** jean; twilled cloth; Genoese
JANN jinn; Moslem demon

JANT jaunt; ramble
JAPE jibe; joke; jest; quip
JARL earl (Norse)
JAWY with jaws
mu **JAZZ** rag-time music
JEAN jane; twilled cloth
JEEP American general purposes vehicle
JEER mock; scoff; taunt; deride
JEFF dicing with quadrants; circus rope
JEHU a coachman
JERK yerk; jolt; pluck; twitch; a good-for-nothing; (weight-lifting)
JESS a leg-strap in falconry
JEST jape; quirk; raillery; banter
JETE leap from one foot to another (gymn.)
bt **JHOW** Indian grass
JIAO Chinese coin
JIFF a jiffy; a moment
JILL a flirt; Jack's girl friend
JILT deceive, delude; to discard
JINK a sharp turn; to dodge
JINN ginn; djinn; Moslem spirit
JINX bad joss
JIVE jazz dance (swing)
JOCK a Scotsman; college athlete (USA); -strap (genital support)
zo **JOEY** small kangaroo
nm **JOEY** small drinking glass; 4d. piece
bt **JOHN** a variety of pink
JOIN link together; associate
JOKE jest; banter; witticism
JOLE jowl; jaw; jolt
JOLT jar; jog; jerk; shake
JOSH to rag; ridicule
JOSS Chinese idol; luck; incense; perfume (wooden stick)
JOTA (Sp.) dance, with castanets
JOUK jook; duck; dodge; bow (Sc.); perched hawk (falconry)
JOVE Jupiter; alchemist's tin
JOWL dewlap; the cheek
JUBA negro dance
rl **JUBE** rood-loft
JUDO advanced form of Jap. wrestling
JUDY Mr Punch's wife
bt **JUGA** leaflets in a pinnate leaf
JU-JU W. African black magic
JUKE a head movement; -box (gramophone); feint (Am. football)
JULY seventh month
JUMP leap; skip; bound; purloin; escape; recoil of guns; sprint (cycling)
JUNE sixth month

nt **JUNK** scrap-metal; trash; Chinese
    ship
JUNO Queen of Heaven
lw **JURY** twelve persons; makeshift
JUST true; exact; impartial; barely
bt **JUTE** sack and twine fibre

K

rl **KABA** sacred stone of Mecca and all
    Islam
KADI cadi; Moslem judge
nt **KAEP** dugout canoe (sail)
    (Philippines)
KAGO Japanese palanquin
zo **KAGU** crane of New Caledonia
KAIF KEIF, drugged stupor
nt **KAIK** CAIQUE, sailing vessel (Med.)
KAIL a ninepin
KAIN cain; tribute in kind
zo **KAKA** New Zealand parrot
bt, ck **KAKI** the Chinese date-plum;
    persimmon fruit
KALA time; destiny; death (Sanskrit)
bt **KALE** kail; colewort; curly cabbage
bt **KALI** prickly saltwort or glasswort
KALI wife of Siva; goddess of
    destruction
KAMA Hindu cupid
gl **KAME** glacier-outwash mound
KAMI Japanese god or title
KANA Japanese handwriting
KANG Chinese water-jar
bt **KANS** Indian sugar-cane grass
KAON 1 of class of mesons
KART midget racing car
KAST KAS, Dutch wardrobe
tx **KATA** Tibetan cloth or scarf
cf **KATA-** CATA-, against; down (Gr.)
bt **KAVA** ava; Polynesian drink; plant
bt **KECK** to retch; dried hemlock; type
    of grass
KEEL ruddle; flat-bottomed barge
    (coal) (-over, to capsize)
nt **KEEL** undermost part of ship;
    projecting fin; main frame of
    airship; (balancer)
KEEN acute; eager; sharp
mu **KEEN** funeral song (Irish)
KEEP stronghold; provender; retain
KEIF kaif; drugged stupor
KEIR bleaching-vat
KELK a blow; to beat; large stone
KELL caul; cobweb; film; network
KELP kilp; seaweed; wrack
zo, tx **KELT** Celt; salmon; woollen cloth
KEMB to comb

KEMP coarse rough hairs of wool
mu **KENT** pole; pike; bugle with keys
KEPI military cap (Fr.)
KEPT held; stored; retained; endured
KERB curb; edge of pavement
KERF a saw-cut; a swath
to **KERN** QUERN, a hand-mill for grain
KERN KIRN, Irish footsoldier
zo **KETA** a caviare fish
KHAN Oriental ruler
KHEL a clan (Afghanistan)
KHOR wadi-like riverbed (Sudan)
KHUD Indian ravine
md **KIBE** chilblain
KIBY affected with chilblains
KICK resist; rebel; spurn; boot; punt
KIEF keif; kef; stupor; drowsiness
KIER keir; bleaching-vat
KILL slay; destroy; despatch;
    consume
KILN furnace; oven
me **KILO** unit of 1000 (metric system)
    10^3
KILP kelp; calcined ashes of seaweed
KILT a philbeg; pleated skirt; tuck
    up
KIND class; type; genus; benign;
    gentle
zo **KINE** cows
cf **KINE-** of moving; movies; cinema
    (Gr.)
KING monarch; sovereign; ruler; a
    card
KINK bend; knot; curl; loop; whim
KINO a mixture of gums; catechu
KIPE basket for catching fish
KIRI knobkerrie; Kaffir throwing
    stick
rl **KIRK** a church (Sc.)
KIRN kern; last sheaf; harvest image
KISH wicker turf basket; impure
    graphite
KISS buss; touch gently; (billiards)
KIST chest; coffer
zo **KITE** accommodation bill; a toy; a
    bird
KITH kindred; acquaintances; friends
KIVE a mashing vat
zo, bt **KIWI** apteryx, NZ flightless bird;
    fruit
KNAB to bite; to gnaw
KNAG knot in wood; peg; a wart
KNAP to snap; a swelling; a hillock
KNAR gnar; snarl; growl; a knarl
pl, ma **KNEE** leg-joint; graphic curve
KNEW understood; perceived
KNIT draw together; weave; wrinkle
KNOB a bunch; boss; door-handle

KNOP knob; hilltop (S.A.); button

go, nv, zo **KNOT** knag; small sandpiper; 1 sea mile (200 yards, 1.85 km) per hour

KNOW comprehend; discern; be familiar with

KNUB knob; a small lump

KNUR knar; gnarl; wooden ball

KNUT a nut; a dandy

zo **KOBA** kob; African water antelope

zo **KOEL** Indian cuckoo

nt **KOFF** Dutch sailing vessel

KOHL black antimony eye pigment

bt **KOLA** African nut tree; a beverage

KOOK novice surfer; inept person

pc **KORO** fear of penis retraction

mn **KOTH** volcanic mud (S. America)

mu **KOTO** Japanese stringed instrument

KRIS creese; Malay dagger

KROO an African race

zo **KUDU** a large African antelope

KUEI food vessel; bronze age; (China)

KUFI calligraphy (Mid. East)

KUNA Panamanian Indian

KURD native of Near East

ck **KVAS** rye beer (Rus.)

nm **KYAT** (Burma) monetary unit

KYLE narrow strait or sound (Sc.)

L

LACE tie; fasten; (boot-); intermix

LACE intricate thread tracery

LACK need; deficiency

LACY LACEY, lace-like texture

LADE load; burden; ladle; bale

LADY gentlewoman

LAIC layman

LAID deposited; ribbed; prostrate

LAIN rested; reclined; reposed

LAIR den; form; burrow; quagmire

LAIS a courtesan

pt **LAKE** mere; pool; crimson colour; inland water

nm **LAKH** lac; 100,000 rupees

LAMA Tibetan priest

zo **LAMB** baby sheep

LAME halt; crippled; feeble; imperfect

LAME gold- or silver-threaded material

LAMP lantern; shine

bt **LANA** the genipap tree of Demerara

ae **LAND** realm; tract; disembark; (fish); (bowls)

LANE narrow way; passage; by-road; subdivision of track (running); (traffic)

LANG long (Sc.)

LANK lax; loose; drooping; thin

LANX Roman platter

LAPP a Laplander; Saami

LARD bacon fat; smear; flatter

rl **LARE** Roman household god

zo **LARK** frolic; prank; spree; skylark

LASH whip; scourge; satirize; (eye-)

LASS girl; a sweetheart

to **LAST** final; boot-maker's anvil

LAST continue; endure; a cargo

LATE overdue; past; recent; deceased

LATH a narrow strip of wood; batten

LAUD extol; praise; eulogy; panegyric

mn, gl **LAVA** plutonic rock matter; magma

LAVE to wash; bathe; bath

LAWN fine linen or cambric; greensward

LAZE to idle; relax

LAZY torpid; slothful; sluggish

el, pb, nt **LEAD** surpass; guide; precede; plummet; conductor, plumbing metal; bullets; (swing the —)

bt **LEAF** thin plate; lamina; page of book; leaf foliage

LEAK ooze; drip; percolate

LEAL loyal; true; faithful (Sc.)

LEAN rest; rely; depend; incline; lank

LEAP spring across; (-clear); caper; (-year)

LEAR an unlucky king

LEAT watercourse to a mill

rl **LEDA** beloved of Zeus (disguised as swan)

hd, bt **LEEK** an emblem of Wales; onion genus

LEER ogle; smirk; smile with contempt

LEES the dregs; open lands (park)

lw **LEET** court of record; list of candidates

LEFT sinister; abandoned; bequeathed

LEHR glass annealing oven (King Lear)

LEND (loan); furnish; grant an advance

LENE unaspirated

tx **LENO** a fabric like muslin

pg **LENS** optical glass (camera) (spectacles) (tele-, microscope)

rl, mu **LENT** loaned; inclined; a fast; slow music pace (It.)

LESS smaller; inferior; minor; fewer

LEST for fear that

LETO mother of Apollo and Artemis

LETT Baltic people of Latvia, Lettland
LEUD Frankish vassal
LEVY tribute; exact; muster; impose
LEWD licentious; rude; pornographic
LIAR an economizer of truth
mn **LIAS** argillaceous limestone
zo **LICE** insect carriers of typhus; bedbugs; skin, hair parasites
LICH LYCH, corpse; (funeral gate)
LICK to tongue; to lap; defeat; overcome
LIDO a bathing pool with sunbathing area
LIED stated falsely; German ballad
LIEF gladly; willingly; beloved
lw **LIEN** right of retention; cylindrical bronze vessel (China)
LIEU place; stead
LIFE vitality; duration; existence; (memoir); -style; -sentence
ga **LIFT** exalt; raise; elevate; steal; underarm stroke (badminton); drug-serenity
LIFT thermal current (gliding); hitchhiking
LIKE prefer; enjoy; cognate; match
mu **LILT** cheerful song or air; ditty
hd, bt **LILY** fleur-de-lis; (water-)
pl, zo **LIMB** extension to torso; edge; border; branch; an imp
bt **LIME** to ensnare; citrus fruit
LIMN to paint; draw; illuminate
LIMP walk lamely; slack; flaccid
LIMY glutinous; viscous
LINE link; ancestry; (business-); rope; (air-); (life-); note; row
LING small bronze bell (China)
zo, bt **LING** sea-fish; common heather
me **LINK** connect; chain; torch; nexus; circuit; (route); (missing-); 7.92 in/20cm
LINN pool; waterfall
LINO linoleum floor covering; (-cuts)
md **LINT** surgical linen; loose fibre dust
LINY streaky; wrinkled
zo **LION** cat; predator; King of Jungle
zo **LIPP** a crimson fish
nm **LIRA** LIRE, Italian, Turkish money
mu **LIRE** LYRE, harp
LIRK a fold; to hang in creases (Sc.)
nt **LISI** canoe, S. Pacific
LISP make th of s
LIST register; roll; elect; (catalogue)
LITH joint; segment
LIVE exist; survive; active; alive; dwell; appearing in person; mortal

rl **LLEW LLEU, LLAW,** Gyffes, Irish/Celtic deity
rl **LLYR** (Irish LIR), Celtic deity
LOAD lade; charge; encumbrance; burden
LOAF lounge; dawdle; (bread)
ag **LOAM** rich mould; soil
pl, bt, ga **LOBE** projecting part of ear; a cotyledon; arc of skating
LOCH lake; arm of the sea (Sc.)
cp **LOCK** close; seal; bolt; hug; ringlet (hair); entwine
rw, mu **LOCO** locomotive; stand-in; playing at a certain pitch (It.)
LODE vein in ore; drain; open ditch
LO-FI opp. of Hi-Fi
ga **LOFT** upper room; attic; striking angle (golf)
LOGE a box in a theatre
LOGO symbol for services, organizations
cf **-LOGY** science of, knowledge; speech
pl **LOIN** pubic, genital zone; groin; crutch; (-cloth)
LOKE grassy road (East Anglia); cul-de-sac
rl **LOKI** Norse Aesir deity, enemy of Odin
LOLL sprawl; lounge
LOLO SW China aboriginal tribe
LOMA lobe; fringe
zo **LOMP** the lump fish
LONE isolated; solitary; secluded
LONG prolix; lengthy; crave; aspire
tx **LONK** north-Engl. mountain wool
LOOF the palm of the hand
LOOK scan; gaze; peer; seem; mien
LOOM approach menacingly; weaving device; lighthouse rays; midpoint of oar (rowing)
zo **LOON** Great Northern Diver (water bird); rascal, loafer
cp, zo **LOOP** bight; bend; loophole; closed circuit feedback; continuous tape; flank of horse
LOOT booty; plunder; sack; ransack
LOPE run with easy strides
zo **LOPH** molar cusp crest
LORD dominate; master; ruler; a peer
LORE wisdom; erudition; doctrine
LORN forlorn; lost; forsaken; undone
zo **LORY** Australian parrot
LOSE mislay; waste; squander; fail
cp, el, tc **LOSS** defeat; reverse; deprivation; reduction of power; lose out; bereavement
LOST missing; astray; vicious; dreamy

bt **LOTE** lotus; water-lily
LOTH averse; unwilling; allergic
ga **LOTO** lotto; a game (now lottery)
LOUD clamorous; noisy; stentorian
LOUP loop; to leap
LOUR scowl; frown; glower
LOUT boor; clod; booby; yokel
LOVE adore; affection; courtship
   (-birds); zero score (lawn tennis)
LOWN sheltered; tranquil (Sc.)
ck **LUAU** traditional roast-pig feast
   (Hawaii)
zo **LUCE** full grown pike
LUCK hap; fate; hazard; fortune;
   chance
ga **LUDI LUDUS**, public games (Rome)
ga **LUDO** a game (dice and counters)
LUES poison; plague; disease
nt **LUFF** the weather-gauge; leading
   edge of a sail
LUGE toboggan
LULL calm; assuage; an interim
LUMP chunk; projection; hunk
hd **LUNA** the moon; heraldic argent
LUNE half-moon shape
pl, rl **LUNG** respiratory organ; Ch. deity
LUNT a light; a slow-match
LURE entice; decoy; bait; recall
   (falconry)
LURE dummy bird (falconry);
   mechanical hare, rabbit
   (greyhounds)
LURK skulk; lie in wait
bt **LUSH** juicy; luscious; richly verdant
LUSK a sluggard; to laze
LUST desire; cupidity; covet
mu **LUTE** tenacious composition; guitar
mu **LUTH** lute (Fr.)
LUTZ jump (ice-skating) technique
LUXE luxuriousness (Fr.)
LYAM leam; dog-leash
bt **LYME** a coarse grass
zo **LYNX** sharp-eyed cat
hd **LYON** Heraldic Court (Sc.)
LYRA a constellation
zo **LYRA** brain psalterium in mammals
mu **LYRE LYRA**, early harp (It.)
md **LYSE** make undergo lysis

M

MA'AM marm; madame (the Queen)
gl **MAAR** a crater
bt **MACE** staff of authority; spice
MACH supersonic speed
MACK MAIK, make (Sc.)
MADE formed; fashioned; compelled

rl **MAGI** wise men of the East;
   (magicians)
nm **MAHE** biche, French pice
rl **MAIA** Roman deity
MAID lass; damsel; virgin
MAIL the post; chain-armour
   (-order)
MAIM cripple; mutilate; disable
MAIN at dice or cockfighting;
   essential
pb **MAIN** the ocean; might; power;
   (pipe)
MAKE do; gain; form; cause; reach
zo **MAKI** a Malagasy lemur
zo **MAKO** Australasian shark
zo **MALA** -lobe in insects
bl **MALE** masculine gender; virile
MALL mallet; to bruise; public walk
mn **MALM** calcareous loam
bt, ck **MALT** steeped grain
MAMA MAMMA, mammy; mother
rl **MANA** magical influence (Maori);
   Polynesian divine force
zo **MANE** neck hair on lions, horses
rl **MANU** mankind's ancestor (India)
MANX curtailed (cat); of Isle of Man
MANY sundry; divers; manifold
me **MARC** oil-cake refuse; old Fr.
   measure
zo **MARE** female horse
nm **MARK** (letters of); brand; stigma;
   coin (Ger.); catch (football); strike
   (bowls)
cp **MARK** (post); symbol; character;
   code pulse; signature
MARL mixture of clay, sand and
   lime
MARM ma'am; madame (the Queen)
MARS God of War; a planet
MART market; bazaar; emporium;
   hammer (Sc.)
MASH mix; crush; knead; compound
MASK veil; cloak; revel; disguise;
   visor
cp **MASK** (gas-); conceal; isolating bits
rl **MASS** bulk; whole; heap; (church)
ae, bt, nt **MAST** beech-nuts, etc.; supporter of
   sails, aerials, airships
bt, ck **MATE** comrade; checkmate; tea plant
MATH a mowing
pg, pt **MATT** roughened; glass; non-glossy
   photographs, paint
tx **MAUD** shepherd's woollen plaid
   (Sc.)
rl **MAUI** Polynesian divine fire maker
to **MAUL** mall; hammer; to molest;
   melée (rugby football); tear (flesh)
zo **MAWK** a maggot

MAXI larger than standard
MAYA people and language of C. Am.
MAZE daze; bewilder; a labyrinth
MAZY winding; intricate
ck, go **MEAD** fermented honey; meadow; field
bt, ck **MEAL** a repast; ground grain; flour
MEAN middle; average; intend; signify
MEAT food; flesh
MEDE native of Media (Medes and Persians)
MEED reward; recompense
MEEK mild; lowly; pacific; unassuming
MEER mere; pool; lake (obs.)
MEET fit; proper; encounter; join; competition (athletics); (hunting)
cf, ma, me **MEGA-** one million times
cf **MEIO-** decrease in size or numbers (Gr.)
MELD fuse; merge; face-up (cards)
MELT dissolve; fuse; thaw; soften
MEMO memorandum; note; jotting
MEND repair; patch; amend; correct
mu **MENO** less tempo; slower (It.)
ck, cp **MENU** bill of fare; optional facilities
MERE pool; lake; marsh; boundary
MERE unmixed; simply; alone; only
MERI Maori war club
nm **MERK** an old Scots silver coin
tx **MERV** silk dress material
MESA broad; flat; rocky; tableland (Sp.)
MESH net-work; brewery grains; ensnare
cf **MESO-** middle; intermediate secondary (Gr.)
ck **MESS** muddle; jumble; dish of food; eat; (-table) military
mu **META** Roman racing pylon; half-speed (tempo) (It.)
cf **META-** between; beyond; change (Gr.)
METE measure; limit; boundary
rl **MEUM** and tuum (liturgical me or thee)
MEWL to squall
MEWS stables; cages for hawks
MEZE hors d'oeuvres (Gr.)
MIAN Ind. title of respect
MIAU a cat-call
mn **MICA** a silicate used as glass
zo **MICE** small rodents
MICH lie hid; skulk; sneak; play truant
zo **MIDA** the larva of the bean-fly

MIEN air; bearing; deportment; aspect
MIFF annoyance; resentment
MIKE shirk; loiter; microphone; tease; (take the −)
MILD suave; bland; placid; soothing
me **MILE** 1760 yards (1.609 km)
rl **MILK** cat-lap; (dairy); Altaic devils
nm **MILL** grind; factory; fight
zo **MILT** the spleen; roe; spawn
MIME mimic; ape; copy
zo **MINA** 50 shekels; Indian bird
MIND mark; heed; dislike; intention; (brain)
MINE pit; colliery; sap; of me
MING Chinese porcelain; (dynasty)
cf **MINI-** small; of compact size
zo **MINK** furry animal, weasel type
MINO Japanese raincoat
nm **MINT** coin factory; unused, fresh
bt **MINT** aromatic plant; to invent
zo **MINX** pert selfish girl; she-puppy
MINY subterraneous
go **MIRE** mud; swampy ground; bog
MIRK MURK, gloom; darkness
rl **MIRU** Polynesian ruler of Netherworld
MIRY muddy; marshy
lw **MISE** cost; expense; a treaty
MISS fail; want; need; (spinster)
MIST fog; haze; obscurity
mn **MISY** MYSY, impure iron ore
nm, zo **MITE** widow's donation; (cheese-)
MITT mitten; a covering for the wrist
MIXT mixed; mingled; blended
MOAN bewail; lament; deplore
MOAT protective ditch; (− in the eye)
MOCK taunt; flaunt; deride; imitate
zo, nm **MOCO** rock cavy; coin (San Domingo)
MODE style; form; way; vogue
el, mu **MODE** method; wave frequency; (scales)
MODI methods; (modus)
mu **MODO** style of playing required (It.)
mu **MODO** system of major, minor scales
MODS first B.A. examination, Oxford
tx **MOFF** Caucasian silk fabric
cf **MOGI-** effort, difficulty, defect (Gr.)
gl, go **MOHO** earth crust/mantle boundary
zo **MOHR** West African gazelle
MOIL toil; soil; daub
me **MOIO** Portuguese measure
zo **MOKE** burro; ass; donkey
MOKO Maori tattooing

MOLD MOULD, shape
MOLE jetty; artificial harbour; skin blemish
zo MOLE the gentleman in velveteens
MOLE unit of substance, betrayer of secrets; birthmark
mu MOLL courtesan; gangster's sweetheart; minor key (Ger.)
bt MOLY a countercharm; garlic
MOME a dullard; buffoon
rl, pr MONK friar; ink-stain in printing
el MONO single; transmission path
rl MONT Mentu, Mont-Re, war god (Upper Eg.)
MOOD humour; temper; vein; disposition
MOON wander aimlessly; a satellite
MOOP to nibble; to browse (Sc.)
MOOR fasten; berth; heath; (Othello)
MOOT an assembly; debate; discuss
MOPE to be dull and listless
zo MOPS a pug-dog
MOPY downcast; dejected; sad
bt MORA finger game; tree; short syllable
MORE additional; further; again
MORN morning; tomorrow
MORT death tune; a quantity
bt MOSS a cryptogamic plant
MOST more than more; superlative
MOTE particle; speck; blemish
MOTE moot; assembly; to debate (obs.)
zo MOTH large-winged insect
mu, cf MOTO- of creating movement (Gr / It.)
MOUL MOOL, mouldy (Sc.)
MOVE shift; stir; budge; propose
MOWN scythed; cut
bt, md MOXA a cauterizer
mn MOYA volcanic mud
MOZE to raise the nap on cloth
MUCH plenteous; greatly; largely
MUCK refuse; dirt
me MUDD Moroccan measure
MUFF a duffer; hand-warmer; spoil
me MUID hogshead; dry measure for corn
MUIR moor (Sc.)
zo MULE machine; slipper; a hybrid
go MULL snuff-box; headland; mistake
MULL to heat wine, punch; to ponder; err
pr MULL cotton book-cover
MULT multure; fee for grinding corn
MUMM to mask; act; masquerade
MUMP nibble; grin; deceive; beg
nc MUON heaviest known lepton

MURE immure; a wall
MURK mirk; darkness; obscurity
bt MUSA banana genus
MUSE meditate; ponder; contemplate
MUSE poets (source of inspiration)
MUSH pulp; dog-sled command
zo MUSK a scent; a deer
MUSS a mess; scramble; disarrange
MUST obliged; necessitated
MUST mould; unfermented grape juice
MUST elephant frenzy
mu MUTA change; (style of playing) (It.)
mu MUTE dumb; still; a sordine
MUTT a fool
zo MYNA the Indian starling
MYTH legend; fable; invention
zo MYXA beak extremities

N

bt NABK a petal in the crown of thorns
rl, zo NAGA sacred Hindu and Buddhist snakes
NAIF naive; artless; ingenuous
me NAIL spike; secure; pin; 2¼ inches (57 mm)
zo NAJA venomous snake; a cobra
NAME term; nominate; renown; (called)
NANA benteak skill
cp NAND logic; NOT-AND (Boolean)
ma NANO- one thousand millionth 10^{-9}
me NANO- second and light advances one foot
NAOS a shrine (Greek)
NAPE the back of the neck
NAPO (ne plus); finish
zo NAPU the musk-deer of Java
nt, md, ga NARD spikenard; an unguent; Arab backgammon
zo NARE nostril
NARK police spy; a squealer
NARY neither; nor any
cf NASO- nasal, of the nose
pl NATE buttock
me NATR Ethiopian measure
rl NAVE (wheel); hub; main aisle
nt NAVY fleet of ships
NAZE cape; mull; headland; ness
NAZI German national socialist
NEAL anneal; to temper (metal)
nv NEAP a small-measure tide
NEAR nigh; close by; stingy; miserly
zo NEAT trim; tidy; gim; simple; cattle
NECK col; an isthmus

NEED want; lack; require; poverty
bt, md **NEEM** (medicinal) shrub; (margosa oil)
bt **NEEP** a turnip
NE'ER never (poetic)
NEMO nobody
ch **NEON** an inert gas; (lighting)
NEPE flannel footwear
NERD untidy, good-for-nothing, person
NERF car bump (motor racing)
NERO a tyrant; imperial fiddler (Rome)
NESH soft; crumbly; tender
NESS naze; cape; promontory
NEST abode; resort; store (-egg)
NETT NET, without discount; price after tax
mu **NEUM NEUME**, a musical phrase
NEVE firm, dry glacial snow
NEWS tidings; word; report
zo **NEWT** an eft; amphibian
NEXT close to; bordering; adjacent (of kin)
zo **NIAS** nyas; eyas; a young hawk
NIBS His Nibs; home ruler
NICE precise; fine; finical; pleasant
NICK notch; reckoning; winning throw
ga **NICK** steal; prison; Satan; shot (squash)
zo **NIDE** a brood of pheasants
NIGH near; impending; almost
rl **NIKE** winged goddess of victory (Gr.)
nc **NILE** reactivity unit
ma **NILL** unwilling; incandescent sparks
rl **NINA** fire god of the Incas
NINE one over the eight (drunk)
bt **NIPA** Indian palm tree; toddy
lw **NISI** prius; unless previously
NIXY nixie; malignant water-spirit
NIZY dunce; simpleton
NOCK the notch of an arrow
bt, cp **NODE** knot; knob; information site; junction (stem)
tc, mu **NODE** drama plot; difficulty; retransmission; border-point of second
rl **NOEL** Xmas; Yule
NOES opposition votes
NOIL a knot of combed wool
NOLL NOUL, **NOWL**, the head; poll; crown
md **NOMA** mouth gangrene
NONE not one
NOOK cranny; corner; recess; arbour
NOON mid-day; meridional

cp **NO-OP** do nothing instruction
NOPE American negation
NORM rule; model; standard behaviour; output
rl **NORN** one of the three Norse fates
pl **NOSE** sagacity; scent; pry; projection; beak
NOSY NOSEY, inquisitive; (busy body)
NOTE heed; mark; record; letter; fame
NOTE single musical sound; ultimatum
NOUN a substantive
NOUS talent, sharp wit, intellect
zo **NOUT** neat; cattle (Sc.)
as **NOVA** a newly exploding star
NOWT nothing (slang)
hd **NOWY** knotted
NUDE bare; naked; undraped; stark
NULL void; invalid; nugatory
cp **NULL** ineffectual; no-op
NUMB torpid; deadened; paralysed
NUNG a bale of cloves
NURL to mill; to indent
zo **NYAS** nias; eyas; young hawk

O

OAKS a race for fillies at Epsom
OAKY hard; tough; strong
OAST hop-kiln; (-house)
OATH vow; pledge; curse; expletive
nm **OBAN** Japanese gold coin
OBEX a barrier; an obstacle
OBEY heed; mind; comply; submit
rl **OBIT** R. C. funeral service
mu **OBOE** the hautboy
nm **OBOL** Charon's ferry fee over Styx
lw **ODAL** udal; absolute tenure in land
ODDS chances; probabilities
ODIC odylic force
rl **ODIN** Norse father of heaven
ODOR ODOUR, stink; smell
ps **ODYL** magnetic force
OFFA King of Mercia; (-'s dyke); (trench fortification)
OGAM ogham; ancient Irish writing
ar **OGEE** a double curve in architecture
OGLE side glance; leer; smicker
rl **OGMA** Ogmios, Irish/Celtic deity
OGPU Soviet secret police
rl **OGRE** monster; giant
rl **OGUN** Yoruba deity (Nigeria)
OILY greasy; unctuous; oleaginous
OKAY perfectly correct
me **OKET** Ethiopian measure

bt, ck **OKRA** gumbo vegetable; mallow
mt **OKTA** ⅛ of sky area
cf **OLEO** oleomargarine; oleograph
OLID evil-smelling
ck **OLIO** mess; medley; mixture; stew
OLLA olio; jar; urn; cooking pot
OLPE Grecian jug
OMAR Arab title
OMEN sign; portent; presage; augury
me **OMER** a Hebrew unit of capacity
OMIT miss; skip; exclude; neglect
me **ONCA** Portuguese measure
me **ONCE ONST**, old Fr. measure; ene
(Sc.)
cf **ONCO-** of mass; swelling; tumour
(Gr.)
tx **ONDE** fabric using shades for effect
hd **ONDY** wavy; ondine
ONER singular; a single; an adept
ONLY sole; alone; singly; barely; but
ONST once
cf **ONTO-** of origin; development (Gr.)
ONUS burden; load; responsibility
zo **ONYM** special or zoological group
ONYX agate streaked with
chalcedony
nm **ONZA** old Spanish–Latin Am. gold
piece
OOCH illegal mooring method
(yachting)
OOFY wealthy; opulent; plutocratic
OOID egg-shaped
OOZE slime; mire; exude; leak; drip
OOZY viscous; slimy
zo **OPAH** the king-fish or sunfish
nm **OPAL** iridescent precious stone
OPEN access; overt; candid; undo;
commence
rl **OPET APET**, Taweret, Thoueris,
deity (Eg.)
cf, md **-OPIA -OPY**, sight defect (Gr.)
O-PIP observing station
mu **OPUS** a composition; a work
ORAL by word of mouth
zo **ORCA** the whale genus
zo **ORFE** a gold fish; ide
ORGE drunken revelry
ORGY sensual, sexual excess
ar **ORLE** fillet under an ovolo
nt **OROU** trading vessel; canoe (Papua)
ORRA odd; worthless (Sc.)
zo **ORYX** antelope; legendary unicorn
cf, md **-OSIS** of pathology; diseased
(Gr.)
cf **OSMO-** liquid balance pressures
mu **OTEZ** remove! (usually the mutes)
(Fr.)
pl **OTIC** receptor cells in ear

OTTI attar; an essential oil; perfume
(It.)
OUFE phonetic word for 'woof'
OURS OURN, belonging to us
OUSE bark for tanning
OUST evict; eject; expel; dislodge
OUZO aniseed spirits (Gr.)
OVAL elliptical
OVEN kiln; heated container
ga **OVER** above; besides; very; (cricket)
zo **OVID** horned ruminant; Roman poet
md, zo **OVUM** egg, female reproductive cell
OWED due; outstanding; indebted
zo **OWRE** the wild ox
OWSE tan vat liquor
zo **OXEN** kine; cattle; neat
OXER a stiff fence
lw **OYER** authority to hold courts
(hearings)
OYES OYEZ, Hear! (call of the public
crier)

P

me **PAAL** Indonesian metric measure
zo **PACA** South American rodent
PACE speed; step; walk; peace
PACK stow; crowd; bale; load;
(cards)
cp **PACK** group (cubs, wolves); store
data; secret influence
me, ga **PACK** forwards (rugby); bringing in
supporters; 240 lb (Br.)
zo **PACO** the alpaca; Peruvian camel
PACT bond; agreement; contract
PADS body protection (cricket)
PAFF piff-paff; jargon
ce, cp, tc **PAGE** bell-hop; attendant (boy);
wooden wedge; leaf (books);
screen display; paginate
PAID requited; defrayed; settled;
(− a visit)
PAIK a beating (Sc.)
PAIL bucket
PAIN vex; fret; ache; rack; torment;
injure
PAIR two; twain; brace; couple
lw **PAIS** a jury list
zo **PALA** South African antelope
PALE wan; sallow; paling; district
hd **PALE** vertical division; frontier;
(beyond the −)
rl **PALI** Buddhist sacred language
PALL mantle; cloak; cloy; sate;
surfeit; funerary cloth cover
bt **PALM** to conceal; a token of victory
zo **PALP** jointed feeler (insects)

PALT rubbish (Dutch)
hd **PALY** ashen; divided vertically
PAND narrow curtain over a bed (Sc.)
PANE window glass; a patch
PANG throe; paroxysm; to cram
PANT gasp; puff
rl **PAPA** Gr. parish priest; a bishop
rl **PAPA** the Earth (NZ)
nm **PARA** paragraph; monetary unit of Turkey and former Yugoslavia
me **PARA** measure of weight (Sabah/Indonesia)
bt **PARA** Brazilian rubber
cf **PARA-** irregular; beyond (Gr.)
cf **-PARA** bring forth; (parent) (Gr.)
zo **PARD** leopard; panther
PARE cut; peel; lessen; diminish
PARK train of artillery; an enclosure; (cars); public garden; sportsfield (Sc.)
zo **PARR** young salmon
PART sever; divide; quit
PASS exceed; overstep; enact; (time); discharge; satisfy examiners
ga **PASS** length of inviting gesture; water-ski course; (football)
go **PASS** narrow mountain route (via col)
PAST gone; done; over; former; bygone
PATE top of head; pie, patty, meat paste
PATH way; track; trail; access
cp **PATH** route (transmission); sequence
nt **PAUL PAWL**, a check stop; gadget
zo **PAUW** the South African bustard
PAVE smooth; prepare; facilitate
PAVE the cobbled roads, of stone
zo **PAVO** peacock; southern constellation
PAWK trick; a cunning device (Sc.)
ga **PAWN** pledge; a chessman
PAYA Honduran Indian
PAYE pay as you earn
mo **PEAK** top; acme; apex; zenith; upper aft corner (sail)
PEAL clang (bells); echo; resound; thunder
mu **PEAN PAEAN** song of triumph
bt **PEAR** juicy cousin of apple
bt **PEAS** vegetables in a pod; sweet- (flowers)
PEAS fine gravel for parachuters' landings
PEAT turf used for fuel
zo **PEBA** armadillo; the black tatou
nm **PECA PEZA**, Portuguese gold coin

PECH PEGH, to pant (Sc.)
me **PECK** strike with beak; 2 gal. (9 litres)
cf, md **PEDI-** of the feet (Gr.)
cf **PEDO- PAEDO-**, of children, infants (Gr.)
PEEK to peep (Sc.)
mo **PEEL** skin; pare; rind; bark; flay; fall; (croquet) (jumping)
PEEL a shovel; a fort; to pillage
to **PEEN** mason's hammer with cutting face
PEEP sly look; cry of a chicken; (-show)
PEER to peep; to appear; a nobleman; equal status group
zo **PEKE** a Pekinese dog
PELA white wax from a scale-insect
PELF money; riches; filthy lucre
PELL skin; hide; parchment
PELT raw hide; throw; rain heavily
PEND hang; impend; an enclosure
rl **PENG** gigantic bird (Ch.)
PENT enclosed; confined; shut up
PEON day-labourer; bondsman; police
PEON foot-soldier; serf (Mex.); messenger
bt **PEPO** a fruit of the gourd type
rl **PERI** fairy (jinn); peeress (Iolanthe)
PERK smarten up; trim; spruce
PERM a permanent wave
zo **PERN** the honey-buzzard
PERT saucy; forward; impertinent
nm **PESO** monetary unit (Latin Am., Philippines)
PEST plague; pestilence; scourge
PHEW! exclamation of exertion
PHIZ face; visage; physiognomy
me **PHON** a decibel; unit of loudness
me **PHOT** unit of illumination
rl **PHRA RE, RA**, supreme deity (Eg.)
PHUT broken; out of order; (go-)
pl **PIAL** spinal cord membrane
PIAT anti-tank gun
pr **PICA** magpie; size of type
md **PICA** depraved appetite
nm **PICE** Indian and Nepalese monetary unit
to **PICK** cull; select; choice; peck; charge forward (basketball)
cf, ma **PICO-** one million millionth 10^{-12}
PICT early Scottish race
ck **PIDE** unleavened bread (Turk.)
PIED spotted
PIER jetty; mole; sea promenade
zo **PIET** the magpie; dipper; water-ousel

mu **PIFA** piffero; rustic shawm (It.)
zo **PIKA** small rodent; guinea-pig type
zo **PIKE** peak; a turnpike; a weapon; fish; posture
bd **PILA** Roman javelin; pile column
el, wv **PILE** nap; heap; mass; stake; projecting carpet threads (velvet, knots)
zo **PILI** hairs on bacteria
md **PILL** to rod; plunder; blackball
cf **PILO-** of body hair (Gr.)
PIMP procurer for immoral purposes
bt **PINE** to wilt; pine-apple; fir-tree
PING the noise of a bullet
bt, nt **PINK** rose colour; a flower; to pierce; to knock; mast-carrying sail ship
me **PINT** measure of capacity; 4 gills (0.5 1)
bt **PINY** full of pines
me **PIPA** Portuguese measure
pb **PIPE** long tube; (hose-) (drain-); calumet
mu **PIPE** to call, cask; bosun's whistle
me **PIPE** exchequer roll; 126 gallons
le **PIPI** pods for tanning
PIPY tubular
PIRN reel; bobbin; thread on a reel
PISE rammed clay
PISH exclamation of contempt
PISS to pee; urinate
bt **PITH** quintessence; gist; marrow
cy **PITS** (coal mines); cell cavities; scars
ga **PITS** despair; (arm-); (auto racing)
PITY ruth; condolence; compassion
PIXY pixie; a small fairy
PIZE term used in execration
PLAN plot; scheme; design; sketch
PLAP plop; plash; splash
PLAT to plait; piece of ground; dish
zo **PLAX** flat platelike structure
ga **PLAY** act; romp; game; frolic; farce; (match); umpire's command; theatre
PLEA excuse; prayer; claim; argument
PLED pleaded; argued; disputed
PLIM to swell
PLOD jog along; toil; moil; drudge
PLOP to fall into water
PLOT plan; conspiracy; outline; allotment
PLOW a plough; to plough
PLOY employment; a frolic (Sc.)
PLUG a stopple; stop; plod; peg; pipe-fitting; promote; (angling)
bt **PLUM** £100,000; a fruit
PLUS in addition; more
PNYX Athenian meeting place

ga **POCH** card game (half pack) (4 persons)
md **POCK** a pustule; pox-scar mark
mu, md **POCO** little; rather (It.); slightly
POEM ode; lyric; elegy; lay
POET bard; balladmonger
nm **POGH** ancient American copper coin
POKE bag; bonnet; nudge; prod; jab
POKY POKEY, small; cramped; confined; stupid
nt, me, ps **POLE** a mast; 5½ yds (5m/16½ ft); native of Poland; (magnetic-)
zo **POLL** clip; lop; election; head; parrot
ga, mu **POLO** 4-a-side mounted game (ball and sticks); Sp. dance with song
POLT a blow; a hard knock; a club; (bolt)
cf **POLY-** of many (Gr.)
bt **POME** an apple; a ball of dominion; orb
POMP pageantry; ceremony; display
POND pool; mere; to ponder
me **POND** Dutch ½ kg; S. African pound
ck **PONE** bread made from Indian corn
ga **PONE** who cuts dealt cards
md **PONS** medical link or bridge
zo **PONY** £25; nag; tit; palfrey
me **POOD** Russian weight, 36 lb (16 kg)
POOH exclamation of contempt; (bear)
ga **POOL** mere; pond; tarn; merge; combine; billiards
bt **POON** East Indian tree; wood for spars
nt **POOP** nincompoop (idiot); stern of ship; a push
POOR scant; meagre; sterile; needy
rl **POPE** the Bishop of Rome
nt **POPO** outrigger; sail dugout
rl **POPO** Po'po, tiger riding wind (Ch.)
md **PORE** con; study; small orifice
PORK swine flesh
PORN pornography
ck **PORT** haven; gate; entry; (-wine)
nt, mu **PORT** larboard (bearing); bagpipe music
mu **PORT** bagpipe music; mien; bearing
cp, tc **PORT** gateway for information retrieval
PORY porous; pervious
POSE puzzle; nonplus; feign; a posture
POSH very superior
cp **POST** mail; (-station); appoint (job); pillar; record
ga **POST** passing (football) (basketball)
cf **POST-** after, after, behind; (-war)

bt **POSY** motto or verse; nosegay
pp **POTT** size of hand-cut paper
POUF pouffe; large cushion; gauze
POUR gush; flow; emit; stream; rush
zo **POUT** to register pique; whiting
PRAD a horse (slang)
nt **PRAM** perambulator; Baltic coasting vessel; dinghy with transoms
nt **PRAO PRAU**, vessel of East Indies
PRAY beg; crave; implore; entreat
PREE to prove; to taste (Sc.)
cf **PREP-** preparation; prepatory; (-school)
PREX college president (USA)
PREY despoil; pillage; devour; quarry
PRIG pilfer; a coxcomb; a fop
bt **PRIM** formal; precise; mim; privet shrub
nt **PROA** Malay sailing canoe
PROD goad; poke; nudge; prick
PROG proctor; (university police)
mu **PROM** promenade concert
PROP support; uphold; buttress
PROS arguments for; cf. cons
nt **PROW** the cutwater; ram; bow
PROX proximo; next month
PSHA! pshaw
rl **PTAH** Phthah, god of fertility, creation (Eg.)
PUCE pink colour
PUCK ice hockey ball; an imp
zo **PUDU** a small deer of the Andes
PUFF fuff; pant; blow; flatter; (smoke)
PUGH interjection of disgust
PUJA Hindu ritual; obeisance
PUKE to vomit
zo **PUKU** Central African antelope
PULE to whine; to cry
PULK Laplander's sledge
PULL draw; drag; haul; pluck; pick; handle (sash lift) sidestroke (polo)
PULP any soft uniform mass
nm **PULS** Afghan monetary unit
PULT Germ. orchestral music stand
bt **PULU** Haaiian tree-fern fibre
zo **PUMA** mountain lion
ga **PUMP** raise water; inflate; compressor; dance shoe; interrogate; (angling)
nm **PUMY** pumice-stone
PUNA Andean plateau
me **PUND** Dutch pound; weight
PUNK tinder; dud; worthless
nt, nm **PUNT** gamble; kick; flat-boat; Irish money
PUNY tiny; weak; petty; Lilliputian

zo **PUPA** a chrysalis, dormant stage
PURE chaste; unsullied; unmixed; neat
rl **PURE** Oceanian deity
PURL knit; row; ripple; mulled ale; fine wire worked round silk thread
PURR curr (cat or pigeon noise)
ga **PUSH** a gang; urge; jostle; press; (badminton); jog
zo **PUSS** cat or hare
ga **PUTT** to hole the ball (golf)
zo **PUXI** North Amer. edible caterpillar
rl **PYES** calendar for calculating Easter
md **PYIC** discharging plus
rl **PYRE** a funeral pile (for cremation)
ch **PYRO** pyrogallic acid

Q

ar, zo, pr **QUAD** quadrangle; quadruped; prison
go **QUAG** quagmire; morass; swamp
QUAT TWAT, TWERP, a nonentity; a nobody
nt **QUAY** wharf; landing place; jetty
QUIB jibe; quibble
nm **QUID** chew of tobacco; sterling pound
zo **QUIN** a kind of scallop; (quintuplet)
QUIP sally; retort; taunt; joke
QUIT leave; desert; retire
QUIZ puzzle; chaff; an enquiry
QUOB quab; tremble
QUOD prison
QUOP quap; throb

R

RAAD South African parliament
bt **RABI** the grain crop of Hindustan
RACA a term of contempt
nv, mt **RACE** tidal high seas by headlands; current (mill) rapids; human
ga **RACE** compete; run (horse); groove (ball)
zo **RACH** dog; pointer or setter
RACK torture; stretch; anguish; harass
RACK a grating; wrack; cloud; to amble
RACK toothed rail (cog); shelf
RACY spirited; piquant; pungent
RAFF riff-raff; rabble; rubbish
nt **RAFT** a floating framework; (mat)
RAGE fume; fury; craze; ire
mn **RAGG** ragstone; siliceous sandstone

bt **RAGI** species of millet
rl **RAHU** the dark planet in Hindu Myth
RAID foray; inroad; invasion; irruption
zo **RAIL** fence; scold; genus of birds
rw **RAIL** sleeping on sleepers
mt **RAIN** pitter-patter; a downpour
RAIS Arab chief, captain
RAJA RAJAH, Indian ruler
to, nt **RAKE** roué; inclination; gardening; streamline angle of mast (funnel)
rl **RAKI** aniseed brandy (Turkey); heaven (NZ)
RAKU tea ceremony pottery Japan
md **RALE** rattling sound in the lungs
mu **RALL** rallentando, slow down (It.)
rl **RAMA** heroic incarnation of Vishnu
zo **RAMI** appendage ends in collembola
RAMP a slope; a swindle; climb; spring
zo **RANA** amphibian genus, frogs, etc.
RANA a Rajput prince or chief
nm **RAND** mountain; S. African monetary unit
RAND edge; border; margin; inner sole
RANG past tense of ring
RANI ranee; the wife of a rajah
RANK row; grade; foul; musty; nasty; set of organ pipes
RANT rave; orate; spout; declaim
mu **RANT** corranto, dances
mu **RANZ** alphorn for cowherds (Swiss)
bt **RAPE** land division in Sussex; oil seed
RAPE ravish; violate; outrage
RAPT enthralled; absorbed; fascinated
ck **RARE** choice; unusual; precious; part-raw
RASE erase; expunge; level
md **RASH** hasty; headlong; skin eruption; to slice
to, bt, ck **RASP** to file; abrade; (-berry)
bt **RATA** ironwood (NZ); instalment
RATE scold; assess; appraise; speed
RATH Burmese state carriage
RATH RATHE, early; soon; Irish fort
RAVE rant; enthuse wildly
RAZE RASE, gut; demolish; overthrow
READ peruse; decipher; study; understand (radio); evaluate conditions; (curling)
lw **REAL** true; genuine; (-estate)
nm **REAL** a monetary unit
me **REAM** expand a hole; 20 quires (paper)

REAP gain; crop; gather; harvest
REAR raise; breed; erect; end; behind
RECK to care for; regard; heed
REDD to tidy; to arrange; to clear
REDE counsel; advise; advice
bt, me **REED** rush; watergrass; inches (Isr.)
mu **REED** to thatch; a pipe
go, nt **REEF** rocky ledge; shoal; lode
REEK smoke; vapour; fume; stink
to **REEL** sway; whirl; totter; a bobbin
mu **REEL** a quick folkdance pattern
zo **REEM** unicorn of the Bible (oryx)
REFT bereft; left destitute
REIN govern; restrain; check
nm **REIS** plural of real (coins)
RELY depend; lean; confide; trust
REND rip; tear; sunder; sever; rupture
tx **RENT** hire; let; lease; schism; torn
tx **REPP** ribbed fabric
vt **RESP** a sheep disease
REST repose; lean; recline; sit; respite
bl **RETE** a plexus; network of vessels
lw **REUS** a defendant; debtor
zo **RHEA** the South American ostrich
rl **RHEA** mother of Zeus; nature-goddess (Gr.)
bt **RHEA** the ramie plant or fibre
cf, md **-RHEA** -RHEO, flowing, fluidity (Gr.)
RHOM parellelogram; brick
bt **RHUS** cashew-nut genus
nm **RIAL** RYAL (Iran) (Morocco); English gold
bt **RICE** a cereal
RICH opulent; wealthy; fertile; luscious
ag **RICK** stack; wrench; sprain
RIDE domineer; control; mount (horses)
nm **RIEL** Cambodian monetary unit
le **RIEM** REIM, leather strap (S. Africa)
RIFE prevalent; current; abundant
mu **RIFF** a Moroccan (mountain Berber); jazz
gl **RIFT** fissure; cleft; gap; split
go **RIFT** rif, a Berber tribe; valley
RIFT disagreement
bt **RIGA** deal; balsam; (-hemp)
rl **RIGI** Polynesian butterfly deity
rl **RIGR** Heimdall, Norse deity
RILE vex; anger; provoke; irritate
go **RILL** rivulet; brook; streamlet
bl **RIMA** narrow cleft
RIME hoar-frost; rhyme; poem
bt **RIND** peel; bark; external cover
go **RINE** rone; rune; rean; water-course

RING encircle; hoop; arena; siege
nm RING (old) Australian coin; (wedding-)
ga RINK a sheet of ice for curling; ice hockey, skating
RIOT orgy; broil; uproar; tumult
RIPE mature; ready; mellow; fit
RISE soar; mount; tower; rebel
RISK chance; hazard; peril; speculate
bt RISP to rasp; branch of green stalks
rl RITA guardian of fire (India)
rl RITE form; usage; observance
RIVA rift; cleft
gl RIVE tear apart; rend; pierce
zo RIXY quarrelsome; the sea-swallow
ROAD route; thoroughfare; highway
ROAM rove; ramble; meander; saunter
ROAN a colour; sheepskin binding
ROAR yell; shout; bellow; howl
ROBE clothe; invest; drape; dress
ROCK a distaff; oscillate; sweetmeat
gl, mu ROCK hard earth-crust; (-'n roll)
me RODE travelled; a roadstead; Danish me
pl, nc RODS retinal receptors (eye); (reactors)
ROER elephant gun
rl ROHE ruler of the middle world (NZ)
ROIL rile; to stir up; to vex
ROKY foggy; reeky; smokey
ROLE part; function; character
nt, ga mu ROLL reel; lurch; enfold; scroll; tilting movement (gliding); mini-loaf sandwich; stroke (croquet); linked drum notes
rl ROME Holy See (Rome)
ROMP sport; frisk; caper; gambol
pl RONA Maori (NZ) deity
RONE rine; rune; rean; gutter
RONT RUNT, stunted; a stump
rl ROOD The Cross; church screen
me ROOD a quarter of an acre
ar, mo ROOF cover; canopy; shelter; overhang
zo ROOK cheat; defraud; gregarious bird; chariot (Arab); castle (chess)
ROOL to ruffle; to raggle
ROOM chamber; accommodation; space
ROOM roum; a deep-blue dye
bt ROOT fix; implant; origin; radix
mu, ma, cr ROOT lowest note of a chord; tenon; (square-) (cubic-)
nt ROPE tie; secure; bind; tether; (guy)
ROPY stringy; viscous; adhesive
bt, mu ROSE arose; colour; (ceiling); flower; sound vent of lute

bt ROSS the refuse of plants
ROSY roseate; blooming; blushing
rl, mu ROTA roster; R.C. court; wheel of life; perpetual musical round; canon
ROTE mechanical repetition; order of work
ck ROTI the joint (Fr.)
me ROTL rottola, ratel, Arab measure
ROUE rake; debauchee; libertine
bt ROUM a deep-blue dye; pod
ROUT vanquish; defeat; disorder; cut a groove
ck ROUX sauce of melted butter, flour
ROVE roam; ramble; stray; range
nm RUBA Sicilian monetary unit
RUBE a rustic (USA)
mn RUBY a size of type; a gem
ga RUCK wrinkle; fold; crease; sprain; 3 players in football
zo RUDD freshwater fish; the red-eye
RUDE boorish; churlish; rough; raw
RUED regretted; repented
zo RUFF a frill; to trump; a bird
RUGA fold; corrugation
RUIN wreck; demolish; subvert
go RUKH the jungle (India)
RULE control; sway; precept; custom; regime
pl RUMP survivors of previous parliament; behind
RUNE incised writing of the Norsemen
RUNG ladder step; toiled
go RUNN low-lying land in India
zo RUNT dwarf; stump; a pigeon
zo RUSA Indian deer; the sambar
bt RUSA Indian grass; (geranium oil)
RUSE wile; trick; artifice; stratagem
bt RUSH dash; fly; career; sally; a reed
ck RUSK a biscuit
RUSS a Russian (slang)
RUST fust; must; corrosion
bt RUTA genus of plants; rue
RUTH mercy; pity; sorrow; misery
nm RYAL RIAL, rose-noble, old English coin
RYND iron millstone support
RYOT Indian cultivator

S

ck SACK sherry; container; pillage; pouch
me SACK dismiss; container (wool); 2 ways
bt SADR the lote-bush

SAFE sure; secure; reliable; certain
SAFE strongbox; guaranteed secure
SAGA heroic Norse history
bt SAGE a Solomon; genus salvia
bt SAGO edible palm pith
SAGY seasoned with sage
nt SAIC Levantine ketch
SAID stated; declared; alleged
nt SAIL cruise; glide; depart; jib
(rig)
SAKE cause; regard; reason
ck SAKI Japanese wine from rice
zo SAKI South American monkey
genus
SALE market; vending; auction
zo SALP swimming tunicate
SALT mariner; wit; pungent;
salacious
ch, nm SALT (sea-); primitive African
currency
SAME ditto; identical; exactly similar
ck SAMP porridge made from Indian
corn
mn SAND grit; (seashore)
SANE rational; sound; normal; lucid
hd SANG chanted; blood red
SANK foundered; subsided; dug
SANS without (Fr.)
zo SAPO the toad-fish
mn SARD a precious stone; agate
ga SARE pelota game
tx SARI Indian garment; scarf
tx SARK a shirt or chemise
SARN a pavement
tx SASH window frame; ribbon for
order
SASS impudence; sauce
SATE cloy; glut; surfeit
rl SATI suttee (self-immolation); deity
(Ind.)
bt, mu SAUL Indian tree; an oratorio
SAVE except; rescue; to husband;
retain
me SAWK 20 inches (Thailand)
SAWN cut with a saw
SAXE a kind of paper; light blue
md SCAB a blackleg; a sore-scar
zo SCAD horse-mackerel
SCAN view; examine; scrutinize;
poetic metre
cp SCAN check records; test
communication channels
gl SCAR mark; blemish; steep rock
SCAT a tax; scare away; be off
zo SCAT animal waste
go SCAW SKAW, a promontory
SCON SCUN, skim; skip
SCOT a Scotsman; a tax

nt SCOW flat-bottomed boat; dumb-
barge
SCUD wrack; hasten; bustle
mt SCUD small low clouds
SCUG skug; shelter; expiate
SCUM dross; froth; refuse; scoria
SCUN SCON, skim
zo SCUP a swing; the porgy fish
SCUT a short tail
tx SCYE armhole of a garment
me SEAH Jewish dry measure 14 pt
zo, pb SEAL fasten; a pinniped; drainwater;
seadog
me SEAM joint; vein; stratum; 24 stone
SEAN SEINE, a drag-net
SEAR burn; scorch; a pawl; dry
SEAT chair; residence; abode; See
SEAX Celtic sword
SECT faction; schism; party
bt, zo SEED sow; germ; embryo; progeny;
selected player (tennis)
SEEK try; ask; hunt; search; court
SEEL to close the eyelids; good
fortune
SEEM appear; look; pretend
SEEN observed; regarded; perceived
SEEP to ooze; to trickle; to sipe
SEER augur; prophet; soothsayer
me SEER Sri Lankan and Indian
measure (kg)
bt SEGO an American plant
SEID a descendant of Mohammed
SEIL sile; strain; a sieve (Sc.)
cf SELF- of ego (-centred) (-ish) (DIY)
SELL vend; barter; hawk; betray
pr, hd SEME heraldic printing design
detail; strewn with stars, etc.
cf SEMI- (demi-) (hemi-); a prefix of
half
SEND transmit; propel; eject
SENT forwarded; despatched; flung
nm SENT Estonian coin
zo SEPS reptile genus; lizards
SEPT a clan in Ireland; (one of 7)
md SERA a lock of any kind; pl. of
serum
SERB native of Serbia
bt SERE succession of plant
communities
SERF thrall; villein; slave
SESS CESS, tax
SETA bristle; prickle
rl SETH SET, Setekh, Setesh, god of
death (Eg.)
SETT squared block; packing piece;
pile driving
SETT badger's home, (mining)
SEVE wine's distinctive bouquet (Fr.)

SEWN stitched
mu **SEXT** musical interval
zo **SHAD** a fish of the herring type
zo **SHAG** tobacco; green cormorant; rape
SHAG coarse hair; roughen; deform
SHAH Persian monarch
SHAM deceive; substitute
SHAN Burmese borderer
go **SHAP** a steep hill
SHAW a grove; a thicket
bt **SHEA** African butter-tree
SHED emit; cot; shack
rl **SHEN** Chinese gods
SHEW show; exhibit; parade
me **SHIH** Chinese measure
SHIM brake-plate; to wedge up; packing tool
rw **SHIN** to climb; tramp; trudge; fishplate (track)
nt **SHIP** to export; seagoing vessel
SHIR SHIRR, to pucker
SHIT to defecate; faeces; nonsense; insult
SHOD provided with shoes
el, rw **SHOE** footwear; fitting; (-horn); socket; pick-up
SHOO be gone! scare away
SHOP emporium; store; jargon
ga **SHOT** (marksman); pellets; report; injection; dose; attempt; winner (bowls)
SHOT putting the weight/shot (throwing)
rl **SHOU** Hsing, patron of longevity (Ch.)
SHOW flaunt; blazon; expound; pomp
SHUG to crawl
SHUN avoid; evade; eschew; elude
SHUT lock; bar; close; slam; secure
gl **SIAL** granitic earth shell
SICE the six at dice
SICE SYCE; groom (India)
SICK poorly; ailing; disgusted; ill
bt **SIDA** genus of mallows
SIDE verge; border; cause; behalf; facet
SIDI Afr. Moslem title of respect
SIDY aloof and pretentious
SIFT separate; sort; search out
pc **SIGH** a heavy sad breath
rl **SIGI** Norse deity
SIGN beckon; endorse; emblem; portent
cp, ms **SIGN** arithmetical or instructional pointer
go **SIKE** SYKE, Arctic stream

rl **SIKH** sect; a Punjabi military tribe
SILE sieve; colander
tx, lw, pt **SILK** coccoon thread; Queen's Counsel; eggshell gloss
bd, gl **SILL** doorstep; window frame (lock) igneous rock plate
SILO fodder storage; ensilage
gl, go **SILT** sediment; ooze; mud
gl **SIMA** basaltic earth shell
SIMP a simpleton; a mutt
SINE SYNE, since; then (Sc.)
mu, rl **SING** relate in verse; chant; (hymn)
SINK flag; droop; subside; founder; descending air mass (gliding)
mu, rl **SINK** point where lines of flux end; (kitchen-); (geology)
SINN Fein (Irish party)
SIPE ooze; to seep; percolate
SIRE progenitor; father; 'My Lord' (liege)
lw **SIST** summon; delay; stay (Sc.)
rl **SITA** wife of Rama (India)
SITE location; place; position
bt **SIUM** the water parsnip
rl **SIVA** SHIVA, the Destroyer (India)
SIZE glue; varnish; bulk; volume
SIZY sticky; viscous
nm **SKAR** Tibetan copper coin
go **SKAT** a card game
go **SKAW** SCAW, a promontory
bt **SKEG** stump; branch; wild plum
SKEG fin-keel of surfboard; rudder fastening (yachting)
SKEP beehive; wicker basket
SKEW SKUE, awry; oblique; a squint
SKID heavy timber; drag shoe; side-slip
SKIM graze; touch; skirt; brush
SKIN peel; pare; flay; hide; pelt; veneer; film
SKIO SKEO, a hut in the Orkneys
SKIP skipper; large tub; omit; leap; kibble
cp **SKIP** (-rope); jump to next instruction
SKIP captain of team; rink (ice sports)
SKIT a lampoon; burlesque
lt, me **SKOT** unit of low-intensity lighting
zo **SKUA** the pirate gull
zo **SKUG** SCUG, shelter; expiate; squirrel
zo **SKYE** terrier
SKYR curds (Iceland)
SLAB chunk; block; mat; thick; mud
gl, ga **SLAB** flat rock shelf; pitcher's mound (baseball)
bt **SLAE** sloe (Sc.); blackthorn
SLAG scoria; debris; mine waste

SLAM bang; shut with violence
ga SLAM illegal lift (wrestling) (bridge)
SLAP spank; a cleft; a gap in a fence
SLAT strip; lath; slate; sharp blow
SLAV European ethnic grouping
SLAW sliced cabbage used as salad
SLAY kill; destroy; despatch; murder
SLED sledge; sleigh; snow vehicle on runners
SLEW to twist; turn round; killed
wv SLEY the reed of a weaver's loom
cp SLIC Selecting Listing in Combination
SLID slipped; skidded; glided; tripped
SLIM slight; slender; lithe
SLIP trip; fall; slide
rw, el, pa SLIP (-carriage); ring; escape; let go; garment; mistake
nt SLIP launch (way); (factor); (scraper); paint
ga SLIP ceramic decor base; fielding position (cricket)
SLIT rip; rend; tear; slash; sever
SLOB muddy ground
bt SLOE SLAE, blackthorn
SLOG smite; swipe; work doggedly
SLOP a policeman; night soil; a spill
SLOT track of deer; slit; groove; fixture
rw, ga SLOT reserved future; tackle; (timetable); (-machine); position on wave (surfing) (Am. football)
cp SLOW tardy; dilatory; dull; (-down)
SLUB to twist whilst spinning
SLUD sludge; ooze; mud
SLUE to revolve
SLUG a pellet; homeless snail
me, pr, nm SLUG pound; unit of acceleration of mass; typecast; strike; token coin
SLUM a purlieu; squalid neighbourhood
mu SLUR stigma; stain; aspersion; sully
SLUT a slattern; a jade; prostitute
SMEE widgeon; pintail
SMEW migratory sea duck
SMIT to infect; a stain; infection
SMOG chemicals as fog
SMUG self-satisfied; to confiscate
SMUT soot; a plant disease
SNAG projecting stump; a hindrance
SNAP bite; nip; snip; crack; break
bt, ga SNAP a snap-shot (photo); (cards); break; grab; sudden action; (-dragon)
SNEE a large knife (Dutch)
zo SNIG to cut; an eel

ga SNIP clip; piece; snippet; a certainty (racing)
SNOB proud social climber
mt SNOW frozen vapour flakes; (cocaine)
SNUB slight; give offence; (of tickets)
SNUG cosy; compact; sheltered; pub
SOAK steep; drench; saturate
SOAP to flatter; washing agent; (box); (opera)
SOAR rise; mount; tower; aspire
SOCK plough-share; hose
ch SODA an alkali
SOFA couch; divan; ottoman
rl SOFI SUFI, Moslem mystic; dervish
SOFT pliable; plastic; yielding; dulcet
SOHO London quarter
SOIL loam; stain; sully; tarnish
lw SOKE privilege; (East Anglian)
bt SOLA hat-plant; sponge-wood; pith
SOLD retailed; paddled; deceived
zo SOLE a fish; unique; solitary; only; under-surface of shoe
ga SOLE ski, golf club; curling stone
ga, mu SOLO card game; lone performer
ck SOMA an intoxicating drink
zo SOMA animal body
cf SOMA- some-, somatic of the body (Gr.)
SOME several; indefinite; (much, slang)
ac, me SONE unit of loudness
mu SONG lay; carol; ballad; lullaby
SOON anon; early; willingly; lief
SOOT grime (coal-smoke)
SOPH sophomore; a student
zo SORA Carolina rail
bt SORB mountain ash; service tree
SORE raw; tender; grievous; painful
bt SORI fern spore-cases
SORN to cadge board and lodgings
SORT arrange; classify; kind; race; character
ch SORY sulphate of iron
SO-SO indifferent; moderate
SOSS a mess; a puddle; plump
SOUK bazaar; Eastern market stall
SOUL spirit; fervour; essence
ch SOUP broth; consommé; muddle; mix-up; laboratory medium for cultures
ga SOUP broken wave foam (surfing)
SOUR tart; acid; rancid; caustic; bitter
SOWN disseminated; scattered; strewn

bt, ck **SOYA** Korean protein bean
  bt **SPAD** SPUD, potato; surveyor's nail (USA)
  ck **SPAM** spiced ham
  me **SPAN** yoke; to bridge; wholly; (spick and −)
mu, cp **SPAN** interval; difference in value range
nt, mn **SPAR** to box; rafter; pole
  zo **SPAT** the spawn of shellfish; a slap
  SPAY to render unfertile; geld; castrate
  SPEC on speculation (slang)
  SPED fled; hurried; hastened
  SPEW vomit; eject violently
  SPIN turn; twist; twirl; prolong
  go **SPIT** eject saliva; tongue of land (shoal)
  ck **SPIT** rod for impaling meat over fire (barbecue); (-and polish) (-image)
  SPIT express contempt; spittle; froth
  SPIV felonious speculating parasite
  SPOT blot; stain; patch; mark; site
  SPOT hand punch (cards); treated carbon paper
  SPOT aiming point; billiard balls; (leopard); observe
  SPRY alert; brisk; nimble; lively
bt, jn **SPUD** narrow spade; potato; plumb bob nail; weight; dowel
  tx **SPUN** whirled; woven; extended; told
  rw **SPUR** goad; urge; impel; prick; siding
  SPUR wing dam; griffe (decor); (dyke)
  me **STAB** pierce; spear; gore; Ger. measure
  me **STAG** male deer; share pusher; (-party, men only)
  STAM to confound; confusion
  STAR an asterisk; a heavenly body
  lw **STAY** stop; check; curb; tarry; abide
  nt **STAY** support (rope, wire); remain; (put); stamina
  bt **STEM** dam; hold; resist; stock; stalk
  nt **STEM** bowsprit (-rudder bearing)
  STEN a tommy-gun
  STEP pace; tread; rung; stage; - dance
  nt **STEP** fixture for securing base of movable mast
  STET let it stand (Lat.), instruction to printers
  ck **STEW** ragout; simmer; jug; fishpond
  STIR spur; stimulate; tumult; prison
  ar **STOA** covered colonnade
  STOB stub; stump; wedge

STOG to stir up mud
STOP block; impede; cease; desist
zo **STOT** young ox; steer
STOW pack; arrange; place
bt **STUB** fag-end; counterfoil record; tree stump
bd **STUC** stucco; stone-like plaster coat
ck **STUD** knob; nail; breeding place; collar fastener; headless bolt (gun) weld)
STUM unfermented wine; must
STUN bewilder; amaze; dumbfound
md **STYE** an inflamed eyelid
rl **STYX** river to Hades
SUCH so; like; similar; sic
SUCK imbibe; chew; absorb; engulf
SUDD flood debris; dense mat of aquatic vegetation (Nile)
nt **SUDS** soapsuds; the wash
SUED entreated; prosecuted; high and dry
lw **SUER** a plaintiff
ck **SUET** meat fat for cooking
SUEZ canal; (Lesseps, the engineer)
SUFI Islamic mystic; Moslem sect
SUIT gratify; beseem; action; case
SULK glower; be sullen; silent anger
SUMA Nicaraguan Indian
SUMO Japanese wrestling and martial art
SUMP pit; morass; tank for remainders
SUNG chanted
SUNK immersed; engulfed; dug
bt **SUNN** Indian plant; its fibre
SUPE a supernumerary; a toady
SURA a chapter of the Koran
bt **SURA** the sap of the coco-palm
SURD an irrational number; (ab surdum)
SURE certain; secure; reliable; safe
SURF foaming waters
SWAB swob; mop up
SWAD pod; podgy person; clump
SWAG plunder; festoon
SWAM swim (past tense)
zo **SWAN** the Swan of Avon, Shakespeare
SWAP SWOP, to barter; exchange
SWAT a fly-killer; a smart blow
bd **SWAY** rock; roll; reel; influence; power; (thatching)
SWIG gulp down; pulley gear
SWIM float; overflow; be dizzy
SWIN sea river or channel
SWOB SWAB, mop
SWOP SWAP, exchange; barter
SWOT SWAT, an earnest student

SWUM swim (past participle)
SYBO cibol; onion
nm **SYLI** Guinean monetary unit
SYNE SINE, syn (Sc.); since

T

. **TABI** Japanese sock (with separate toe)
TABU TABOO, ban; veto; (against mores)
mu **TACE** be silent
nt **TACK** a nail; navy food; hasten; change course; (zigzag) sailing
ck **TACO** fried tortilla/salad dish (Mex.)
TACT diplomacy; finesse
nm, me **TAEL** money of account, weight (Asia)
TA'EN taken
TAFT a plumbing joint
zo **TAHA** African weaver-bird
zo **TAHR** Himalayan goat
TAIC THAIC, Indo-Chinese lang. group
rl **TAI'I** supreme deity (China)
TAIL extremity; queue; trail; entail
nm **TAKA** Bangladeshi monetary unit
TAIN mirror silver
TAKE grasp; seize; adopt; carry
mn, md **TALC** mica; baby powder
TALE story; fable; narration
TALK parley; speech; lecture; (small-)
TALL towering; elevated
TAME docile; dull; domesticate
TAMP pack earth solidly; thump
rl **TANE** Polynesian deity
me **TANK** cistern; reservoir; refuel; armoured vehicle; weight (Ind.)
cp **TANK** mercury delay line
zo **TANT** small scarlet spider
tx **TAPA** Polynesian fibre cloth
TAPE to bind; ribbon; to measure; (red)
cp **TAPE** magnetic strip for recording data
TARA old Irish Convocation
bt, rl **TARA** edible NZ fern; Buddhist deity
bt **TARE** gross weight; a weed
go **TARN** mountain pool; a marsh
bt **TARO** edible plant of the arum type
nm **TARO** Maltese, Sicilian coin
TART sharp; small pie; call girl
TASH Indian silk fabric with gold thread

TASK toil; drudgery; labour
TASS pouch; thigh-armour
TA-TA good-bye; a short walk
TATE a London art gallery
TATH cattle dung; to manure
zo **TATU** tatou; peba; armadillo
TAUT tense; strained; stressed
TAWA N. Zealand hardwood
ae **TAXI** motor-cab; move on runway
TAYO apronlike garment (S. Am.)
T-BAR drag ski-lift
bt **TEAK** hardwood tree; (wood)
zo **TEAL** small waterfowl; a duck
TEAM group; harnessed animals
TEAR rip; rend; lacerate; sob
TEAT a nipple
TEDE tead; torch; flambeau
TEED ball mounted for driving off (golf)
TEEM swarm; to abound; be prolific
gs **TEEM** pour molten glass
TEEN grief; affliction; allot (obs.)
TEER to stir; to sieve
bt **TEFF** Abyssinian cereal grass
bt **TEIL** the lime tree
bl **TELA** weblike tissue
cf, tc **TELE-** of wired communications
TELL recite; divulge; reckon
TEND incline; verge; nurture; minding
me **TENG** Burmese measure of weight
TENT probe; a pavilion, canvas, bivouac
me **TERA** International unity of quantity
ar **TERM HERM,** dub; entitle; phrase; period; a pedestal supporting a bust
zo **TERN** sea-bird (gull-type)
ch, md **TEST** essay; assay; try; (-tube)
TEST attest; proof; ordeal; criterion
cp **TEST** probe; examine; check data element; competition
TETE head; (-a-), secret
TEXT writing; (-book); theme; sermon
tc **TEXT** the message for transmission
THAI (Siamese); language; people
THAN conjunction of comparison
zo **THAR** goat-antelope of Nepal
THAT pronoun (demonstrative)
ml **THAW** melt; liquefy in heat
THEE objective of thou
THEM objective of they
THEN adverb of past time
THEY Kipling's pronoun; the bosses who decide
THIN lean; fine; lank; sparse
THIS pronoun (demonstrative)

THOR the God of Thunder (Norse)
rl **THOU** familiar pronoun; (God)
THUD a dull sound
THUG violent criminal
THUS like this; as a result
bt **THUS** Frankincense, form of resin
nm **TIAO** Chinese money of account
TIBU Saharan tribe
zo **TICK** credit; mark; (clock); bug
zo **TICK** blood-sucker, cattle disease
   carrier
nt **TIDE** season; course; sea movement
TIDY neat; spruce; trim; orderly
TIED united; constrained; fastened
nt **TIER** row; rank; mainsail to boom
   canvas link
TIFF quarrel; peevishness
ar **TIGE** the shaft of a column
rl **TIKI** Maori charm or amulet; spirits
bd **TILE** roof brick; a hat
mn, gl **TILL** cash drawer; cultivate; tillite;
   boulder clay; moraine boulders;
   until
rl **TILO** god of the sky (Mozambique)
TILT incline; lean; slant
TIME era; term; date; (-switch)
cp **TIME** single channel with multiplex
   signals
rl **TI'MU** Earth Mother (Ch.)
TINE point of antler; spike; to
   enclose
TING ring; tinkle; food vessel (Ch.)
TINT hue; dye; stain; tinge
TINY pygmy; wee; puny; minute
TIRE tyre; iron hoop; attire
TIRE weary; harass; vex; fatigue
zo **TITI** South Amer. squirrel monkey
TIVY with speed; tantivy (bugle/
   call)
zo **TOAD** an amphibious batrachian
cr **TOAT** handle of bench plane
zo **TOBY** beer-mug; Punch's pet dog
TO-DO ado; bustle; excitement
zo **TODY** green humming bird
cr **TOED** of obliquely fastened timber
pl **TOED** having toes; (-the line)
TOFF fop; dandy; swell
lw **TOFT** grove
ck **TOFU** soya curd (China)
tx **TOGA** Roman garment
tx **TOGS** garments for a purpose
TOIL snare; travail; pains; strive
TOIT a cushion
TOLA Indian weight; 180 grains troy
TOLD narrated; related; recounted
TOLL tribute; road fee; (funeral bell)
bt **TOLU** oleo-resin; balsam
TOMB grave; sepulchre; mausoleum

TOME book; volume; work
cf, md **-TOMY** of surgery, removal (Gr.)
TONE cadence; inflection; tint
nt **TONY** a simpleton; genteel; posh
TOOK grabbed; gained; captured
nt **TONY** Indian sailing canoe
to **TOOL** cat's paw; utensil (artisan's)
bt **TOON** Indian cedar
TOOT a wastrel; the devil; honk
zo **TOPE** shark known as the penny-dog
TOPE Buddhist monument
TOPE clump of trees; to booze
TOPO fishing boat, (Venice)
cf **-TOPY** of location, habitat (Gr.)
TORE rent; split; a moulding
ar **TORI** mouldings at the base of
   columns
TORN lacerated; ripped
me, ps **TORR** unit of low pressure
lw **TORT** redress of wrongs
TORY a Conservative
TOSH bosh; twaddle; boloney
TOSS pitch; hurl; cast; throw of coin
   (matches/sport)
TOTE to carry; totalizator
TOUR trip; round; jaunt; ramble
TOUT paid agent; tipster
TOWY like tow; hempen
TOYE lute music
TOZE to pluck; pull by the ears
TRAM a beam; tramcar
gl, mn **TRAP** U-shaped bend (pipe);
   igneous rock; (-door)
el **TRAP** adorn; ambush; ensnare; pony
   carriage; switch
cp **TRAP** automatic branch switch for
   emergencies
TRAY salver; carrying board
TREE the Cross; decoder; (family-)
TREK travel by ox-wagons (S.
   Africa)
TREK blue, black outlines on tin-
   glazed earthenware (Holland)
TRET a trade allowance
TREY a three at cards or dice
TREZ third; the third tine of antler
TRIG trim; tight; secure; a dandy
TRIG wedge; skid; boundary line
bd **TRIM** neat; tidy; clip; adjust; edging,
   skirtings
TRIM correct level of vessel in water;
   speeds of surfing; balance (gliding)
mu **TRIO** composition for 3 instruments
TRIP tour; err; slip; stumble; dance;
   'high' period of drug influence
TROD trampled; walked
TROT to run; gait of a horse
TROW to trust; believe; suppose

me **TROY** weights used for gold, etc.
TRUE loyal; staunch; straight; exact
TRUG hod for mortar; gardening basket
TSAR Czar; Ksar; Tzar; Zsar; ruler of Russia
me **TSUN** Chinese inch; ritual jade (Ch.)
TUAN title of respect (China and Malay)
mu **TUBA** bass trumpet; transmitter
rw **TUBE** pipe; telescope; Underground; cathode (television); (follicle); hollow part of wave (surfing)
TUCK fold; net; thrust
TUCK beat of drum; food; to cram; body posture (athletic)
mn, gl **TUFA** calcareous deposit; volcanic dust
mn **TUFF** volcanic rock–debris
TUFT knot; bunch; clump; tuffet
bt **TULE** Californian bulrush
TUMP hillock; to earth up
bt, zo **TUNA** prickly pear; great tunny fish
mu **TUNE** air; melody; strain
TURF sod; sward; earth; peat; (racing track)
TURK citizen of Turkey; Ottoman; (young-)
cp **TURN** spin; bend; divert; curdle; hinge; act; output
mu **TURR** three-stringed Burmese violin
zo **TUSK** pointed tooth; sea-fish cod type
bt **TUTU** short ballet skirt; shrub (NZ)
rl **TUUM** (meum and tuum); thine (Latin)
zo **TUZA** tucan; Mexican pouched rat
TWAS it was
TWEE precious; overly cute
bt **TWIG** observe; understand; sprig
TWIN double; duplex
TWIT taunt; ridicule; upbraid; ass
zo **TYKE TIKE**, dog; cur
TYMP mouth of blast furnace's hearth
TYPE kind; sort; class; species; emblem
TYPO a compositor; (typographer)
TYRE rubber outer wheel of vehicle
TYRE tire; attire; dress
TYRO tiro; novice; recruit; neophyte
TZAR Tsar; Czar; Ksar; Zsar (Rus.)

U

nt **UCHE** 2 mast, passenger vessel
lw **UDAL ODAL**, freehold estate
UGLY hideous; unsightly; hateful
bt **ULEX** furze genus
md **ULNA** an arm-bone
UMBO boss of a shield; a knob
zo **UMBO** the point of a bivalve shell
zo **UNAU** S. American two-toed sloth
UNDO open; untie; nullify
zo **UNIO** genus of freshwater mussels
UNIT a standard quantity; measure
UNTO preposition of direction
bt **UPAS** the deadly antiar tree
UPON on, preposition of situation
hd **URDE** pointed, variated
URDU a language (India, Pakistan)
md **UREA** a crystalline compound, or gas
URGE push; drive; impel; incite; spur
zo **URIA** a genus of sea-birds, guillemots
ch, md **URIC** the acid (of urea)
mn **URRY** blue clay near a coal seam
as **URSA** a constellation (Great Bear)
zo **URUS** the European wild ox
zo **URVA** an ichneumon (India)
USED habituated; employed
cp, tc **USER** consumer; spender; subscriber
lw **USUS** act, right of making use of something
UTIE wall tie (USA)
UVAE grapes, raisins, etc
pl **UVEA** part of the iris of the eye

V

VAIN empty; conceited; unavailing
hd **VAIR** heraldic fur
nt **VAKA** outrigger, sailing canoe
VALE dale; valley; farewell
VALI provincial governor (Turk)
VAMP boot-uppers; to patch
VAMP cinema character (parody)
mu **VAMP** improvise accompaniment
VANE weathercock; nag; blade; fane; feather-fletching of arrow (archery)
nt **VANG** mast-peak steadying brace
me **VARA** S. Amer. yd of 33 in (84 cm)
zo **VARI** monkey (Madagascar?)
VARY alter; change; alternate; differ
VASE urn (flowers)
cf, md **VASO-** of canal, duct, blood-vessel
VAST huge; spacious; colossal

ce **V-CUT** wedge cut, tunnelling
technique

ck **VEAL** dinner for prodigal son; (calf)

rl **VEDA** sacred Hindu books

nv **VEER** vary; turn; shift (of wind)

as **VEGA** star

tx **VEIL** mask; cloak; screen; cover

gl, pc **VEIN** lode; seam; ledge; mood;
humour

bt, pl **VEIN** blood vessel; (vascular) bundle
(leaf)

nm **VELD** Boer gold coin (S. Africa)

ag **VELL** rennet; to cut turf

me **VELO** speed of 1 ft (30 cm) per sec.

VEND sell; hawk; peddle

VENT utter; discharge; orifice; wind

VERB part of speech denoting action

lw **VERT** the greenery of the forest

hd **VERT** heraldic green

nt **VERY** a signal light; (-much)

lw, tx **VEST** endow; endue; clothe; a
garment

VETO ban; forbid; embargo

hd **VETU** lozenge

VIAL phial; ampulla; level tube;
bubble

to **VICE** vise; a screw-press

VICE sin; iniquity; in place of

VIDE see (Lat.)

VIED contested; competed; strove

VIEW eye; scan; survey; prospect;
opinion

lw **VILE** base; ignoble; paltry; cheap

mu **VINA** East Indian banjo

bt **VINE** climbing grape plant

VINT Russian card game, to make
wine

VINY producing grapes or vines

mu **VIOL** antique violin

hd **VIRE** crossbow bolt; heraldic amulet

VISA permit; authorization

me **VISS** 3.60 lb (Burma and India)

VIVA long live! (It.) (Sp.) (Ptg.)

VIVE long live! (Fr.)

mu **VIVO** lively; with animation

go **VLEI** artificial lake (S. Africa)

VOCE the voice; (sotto-voce) (It.)

VOID null; invalid; empty; vacant;
emit

mu **VOLA** rapid series of notes

zo **VOLE** genus of rodents; water-rats,
etc.

me **VOLT** electrical unit

VOLT a turn; sudden leap; (fencing)

VOTE suffrage; ballot; elect; poll

nt **VOYA** anchor cable

hd **VULN** to wound (heraldic)

ar, bd **VYSE** spiral staircase

W

mm **WADD** manganese ore

WADE to ford

go **WADI** desert river bed (often dry)

WAFT float; convey; beckon

nt **WAGA** outrigger sail canoe (Papua)

WAGE pay; hire; stipend; salary

WAIF a stray vagabond; (ownerless)

WAIL cry; weep; deplore

as **WAIN** wagon; constellation

mu **WAIT** bide; tarry; linger; serve;
minister; carol singer; shawm

nt **WAKA** Maori canoe

WAKE funeral vigil; rouse; trail;
wash

WALE weal; raised streak; ridge;
bruise

ga **WALK** hike; saunter; gait; career;
(police beat); (baseball)

bd **WALL** dividing construction; rock
face; alignment of players (soccer);
obstacle (jumping)

ga **WAND** rod; staff; baton; (magic);
target (archery)

bt **WANE** ebb; fail; decline; droop;
(moon)

WANT need; crave; wish; penury

nt **WAPP** shroud-tightener; yachting

lw **WARD** fend; repel; custody; a minor

ar **WARD** hospital dormitory; bailey,
courtyard

bt **WARE** a caution; seaweed

nm **WARK** bulwark; Ethopian coin

WARM ardent; fervid; keen; zealous

WARN caution; admonish; notify

nt, tx **WARP** twist; haul; carpet thread base

md **WART** a verruca; body blemish;
(character)

WARY canny; cautious; vigilant

WASE straw head-pad

nt **WASH** lave; rinse; cleanse; wake

zo **WASP** stinging insect

rl **WAST** preterite of 'to be' (thou-)

me **WATT** unit of electrical horsepower

WAVE sway; beckon; brandish;
ripple

WAVE swell; billow; comber; roller

WAVY curly; sinuous; billowy

WAXY pliant; yielding; wrathful

WEAK frail; insipid; watery; fragile

WEAL prosperity; state; stripe
(beating)

WEAN alienate; detach; grow up

WEAR bear; don; sport; impair

nv **WEAR** alter course stern to wind

bt **WEED** a cigar; to root out; eradicate;
hoe

WEEK unit of time (7 days)
WEEN to think; consider; guess; judge
WEEP sob; bewail; lament
tx WEFT threads crossing warp
WEIR a low dam across a river
zo WEKA Maori hen
bt WELD join together; mignonette
ar, bd WELL fount; source; origin; hale; staircase area
bd WELT shoe-edging; to flog; metal roofing seam
WEND wander; a Slavonic race
WENT left; departed; decamped
WEPT cried; lamented; sobbed
WERE past of 'to be'
rl WERT 'thou' form
WEST cardinal direction
WHAP WHOP, WHIP, chastise
WHAT interrogative pronoun
WHEN adverb of time
WHET sharpen; heighten; rouse
WHEW exclamation of exertion
WHEY skimmed milk
WHIG Liberal; sour whey
WHIM caprice; notion; idea
gl WHIN doleritic igneous rock
bt WHIN gorse, furze
mu WHIP quirt; flog; driver; coachman; V-shaped woodwind instrument
WHIP official controlling group (MPs) (cyclists)
WHIR whirl; spin; revolving rapidly
WHIT jot; iota; speck; scintilla
WHIZ WHIZZ, a noise of speed
WHOA! exclamation 'to halt'
WHOM object of who
WHOP WHAP, WHIP, wop; chastise
WICK (candle); creek; quick; alive
ga WICK stone against stone (curling)
ga WIDE broad; rife; distant; (cricket)
WIEP fascine; part of Dutch mattress
WIFE spouse; to marry
WILD rash; disorderly; savage; untamed
WILE ruse; stratagem; dodge; chicanery
WILL wish; desire; bequeath; testament
rl WILT to droop; to wither (thou of to be)
WILY sly; artful; crafty; insidious
WIND coil; twist; turn; breeze; blow
bt, ck WINE fermented grape or other juice
WING to fly; aerofoil; (stage); (chair); flank

ga, bd WING flanker (football) fielder (baseball, lacrosse); annexe
WINK an eye signal
WINO an excessive alcohol drinker
WINY having the flavour of wine
WIPE rub; clean; polishing rag
tc, nm WIRE bind; snare; telegram; Persian money
WIRY flexible and strong, but thin
WISE sagacious; sage; sapient
WISH will; want; desire; behest
rl WISP (of snipe); small broom; a whisk
WIST knew (thou)
WITH in company (preposition)
bt WOAD plant yielding a blue dye (Druids)
fr WOLD wood; a weald downland (forested)
zo WOLF devour; wild canine; jarring howl
WOMB uterus
WONT habit; custom; practice; use
bt WOOD timber; grove; forest
tx WOOF the weft
tx WOOL fleece; a staple product
WOOM beaver fur
WORD term; news; advice; pledge; (pass-)
cp WORD remark; rumour; data units
WORE bore; sported; donned; lasted
WORK toil; operate; endeavour; a job
zo WORM a groveller; to insinuate; creature
WORN rather the worse for wear
bt WORT malt after mashing a plant genus
wv WOVE intertwined; matted; knitted
WRAP wind; swathe; enfold; muffle
WREN member of WRNS (Women's Royal Naval Service, 2nd World War
zo WREN a bird
rl WRIT summons; formal document; (holy-)
me WROT wrought timber abbrev.
WYND a lane; narrow alley (ancient)

X

zo XEMA genus of gulls
cf XERO- of being dry (Gr.)
rl XMAS Christmas; Noel; Yule
md X-RAY Roentgen ray
XYST gymnasium

Y

YAFF WAFF, to bark (Sc.)
YALD YAULD, active; supple (Sc.)
rl **YAMA** Hindu underworld god
nm **YANG** Korean silver coin
YANK an American; to heave; hoik; extract with a twist
le **YAPP** limp leather binding
me **YARD** 36 in/91 cm
YARD (court-); (Scotland-)
nt **YARD** (lan-) rope; lugsail; (-arm)
YARE dexterous; quick; prompt
tx **YARN** spun thread; sailor's story
bt **YARR** to snarl; the spurrey plant
zo **YAUP** yelp; hungry; blue titmouse
nt **YAWL** yowl; howl; fishing-boat
YAWN gape
md **YAWS** tropical disease
YEAH yes (USA) (slang)
zo **YEAN YEEN**, to lamb; to produce
YEAR 12 months
YEEN WEEN, to know (suspect) something
YEGG hobo; cracksman; safe-breaker
YELD barren, not giving milk
YELL bawl; scream; screech
YELP yap; cry of pain; bark
YERK jerk; rouse; excite
YEST yeast
zo **YETI** abominable snowman
YILL ale (Sc.)
YIPS nervousness (golf)
zo **YITE** the yellow bunting
nc **YLEM** theoretical neutron substance
YMIR the Frost Giant (Scand.)
YOGA Hindu philosophy and exercises
YOGI ascetic yoga practitioner (Ind.)
YO-HO exclamation (piratical)
zo **YOIT** the yellow bunting
YOKE team together; enslave; restrain
YOKE shoulder crosspiece harness, also of rudder
YOKO Japanese wood block
ck **YOLK** heart of egg; wool oil
YOOP an onomatopoeic sob
YORE in olden times (former ages)
YOTE board-game (West Africa)
YOUR of you
YOWL howl; yawl; gowl; bawl
YO-YO a toy; a bandalore
nm **YUAN** Chinese monetary unit
YUCK to itch; the itch
rl **YUGA** one of the Hindu ages of the world
YUKO score in judo
rl **YULE** Xmas; Noel; winter solstice
ga **YUMP** bump or collision (motor racing)
zo **YUNX** the wryneck bird
YURT a Siberian house or tent

Z

ZANY buffoon; merry-andrew; mimic
ZARF zurf; metal coffee-cup holder
zo **ZATI** an Indian parrot
gl **ZAWN** cavern
bd **Z-BAR** building fixture
ZEAL fervour; intensity; enthusiasm
zo **ZEBU** humped domestic ox (India)
bt **ZEIN** zeine; a protein found in maize
ZEND a Persian dialect
ZENO- of strangeness, foreign (Gr.)
ae **ZEPP** zeppelin; airship
nm **ZERO** cipher; nought; nothing; nil
ZEST peel-flavouring; gusto; relish
ZETA the Greek Z
ar **ZETA** sexton's room over porch
rl **ZEUS** Olympian deity
zo **ZIMB** Abyssinian tse-tse fly
ch **ZINC** a metallic element
ZING pep (USA)
mo **ZION SION**, a hill (mount) in Jerusalem
ZOAR a place of refuge
zo **ZOBO** zhobo; dsomo; hybrid yak-cow
gl, bl **-ZOIC** pertaining to life; (mesozoic)
me **ZOLL** Swiss measure; toll; customs-duty (Ger.)
ZONA zone; belt
zo **ZONA** patch; strip; area
cp **ZONE** belt; girdle; district; (category)
pg **ZOOM** aerobatic manoeuvre; change focal length
bl **ZOON** the product of a fertilized ovum
ac **ZOOP** extraneous noise
ZOOT fashionable; gaudy
ZSAR TZAR, TSAR, CZAR, ruler (Russia)
ZULU native people of Kwa-Natal, S. Africa
zo **ZUNA** Angola sheep
ZUNI Mexican Indians
ZUPA Serbian village confederation
ZURF zarf; metal coffee-pot holder
bl, md **ZYME** (en-) a ferment; a disease germ

FIVE-LETTER WORDS

A

AAZIZ Queen of Sheba; also Balkis
bt **ABACA** Manila hemp
ar **ABACI** counting frames; column crowns
nt **ABACK** aft; behind; backwards; (taken-)
nv **ABACK** sails set for wrong side wind
ABADA rhino (15th cent.)
nt **ABAFT** aft; astern
ABASE lower; reduce; disgrace
ABASH awe; confound; disconcert
ABATE wane; diminish; lessen
rl **ABBEY** a monastery
rl **ABBOT** the head of an abbey
ABCEE an abc; an alphabet
nt **ABEAM** abreast; on the beam
bt **ABELE** the hoary poplar
bt **ABHAL** the fruit of the cypress
ABHOR hate; loathe; abominate; detest
ABIDE lodge; tarry; tolerate; sojourn
bt **ABIES** the fir genus
zo **ABLEN** a freshwater fish; the bleak
ABLER more competent; more expert
zo **ABLET** ablen; the bleak
ABODE house; dwelling; home; lived
me **ABOHM** electro-magnetic unit
ABOIL on the boil; boiling
zo **ABOMA** boa–constrictor (S. Amer.)
A-BOMB nuclear weapon
cp, md **ABORT** to miscarry; sterile; break off
ABOUT almost; around; near
ABOVE aloft; over; before; exceeding
ch **ABRIN** toxic protein
ABUSE misuse; defame; traduce; revile
ABUZZ buzzing; humming
ABYSS ABYSM, chasm; bottomless pit; gulf
zo **ACARI** mites and ticks
ck **ACCRA** Caribbean batter fritters
zo **ACERA** bubble–shell genus
ACERB sour; bitter; acid; harsh
ck **ACHAR** acid pickles; salt relishes (Pers.)
ACHED pained; sorrowed; grieved
md **ACHOR** dandruff
md, bt **ACINI** granulations; berries

bt **ACKEE** Jamaican fruit
ACLIS spiked club; javelin
zo **ACONE** insects' coneless compound eyes
bt **ACORN** oak seed; cord–end
ACRED lavishly landed
ACRID sour; pungent; bitter; mordant
zo **ACRON** head of embryonic insect
ACTED performed; simulated; deputized
bl **ACTIN** muscle protein
ACTON padded jerkin
ACTOR player; trouper; histrion
md **ACUTE** keen; sharp; accent (illness)
ma **ACUTE** closed geometrical angle
ADAGE proverb; dictum; maxim; saw
ADAPT adjust; accommodate
ma **ADDED** summed; combined; appended
cp, zo **ADDER** viper; snake; asp; calculator
ADDLE confuse; putrid; muddled
lw **ADEEM** to revoke a legacy
md **ADEPS** fatty tissue
ADEPT adroit; expert; proficient
AD-HOC for a set purpose
ADIEU farewell; goodbye
ADIOS farewell (Sp.)
md, mu **AD-LIB** extemporize; natural body weight
ADMAN advertising pundit
ADMIT acknowledge; concede; own
ADMIX infuse; blend; mingle
ADOBE sun–dried brick
ck **ADOBO** braised stew (Philippines)
ADOPT accept; assume; espouse; father
ADORE worship; revere; idolize; love
ADORN decorate; deck; enrich; garnish
ADSUM (present at a roll-call)
ADULT a grown–up; mature; ripe
rl **AEGIS** Minerva's shield; protection
AESOP a fabulist; parable teller
AFFIX add; fasten; subjoin; attach
AFOOT astir; happening
AFTER later; in imitation of
AGAIN anew; afresh; moreover
zo **AGAMA** genus of lizards; saurians
zo, ck **AGAMI** game bird, edible when young (S. Am.)

AGATA shaded coloured glass (N. Am.)

mn **AGATE** a quartz; ruby type

pr **AGATE** type printing measure

AGATY like an agate

bt **AGAVE** aloe; cactus drink; drug

rl **AGAVE** daughter of Cadmus

lw **AGENT** doer; factor; deputy; proxy

AGGER a mound

AGILE nimble; spry; alert; brisk

AGING AGEING, growing old

lw **AGIST** pasture rate

AGLOW glowing; gleaming; shining

nm **AGNEL** French gold coin (lamb)

rl, zo **AGNUS** Dei; pascal lamb

AGONY pangs; anguish; torment; throe

AGORA Greek, Roman market place

AGRAS sweet Algerian drink

AGREE accede; engage; conform; concur

AHEAD leading; onward; in front

nt **AHOLD** close to the wind

nt **AHULL** hove to

AIDED abetted; seconded; succoured

AIDER helper; assistant; acolyte

AILED afflicted; peaked; pined

AIMED directed; pointed; trained

AIMER purposeful person

AIRED ventilated; spread abroad

AIRER dryer; ventilator

rl **AISLE** passage; walk

AITCH (H); aitch-bone

bt **AJUGA** bugle genus of plants

AKALI Sikh fanatic

zo **AKELA** Kipling's lone wolf

ALACK alas; lackaday; woe is me

ALALA Anc. Gk. battle cry

hd **ALANT** heraldic mastiff

ALARM fear; scare; dismay; a tocsin

zo **ALARY** alar; having wings

ALATE winged; of late; lately

mn **ALBIN** an opaque white mineral

ALBUM book for photos or stamps

zo **ALCES** the elk; moose (N. Am.)

bt **ALDER** a hardwood tree

ALERT wary; watchful; vigilant

bt **ALGAE** the seaweeds

md **ALGID** cold; chilly

ALGIN seaweed extract for iodine

cp **ALGOL** a star; language-data

md **ALGOR** unusual coldness

bt **ALGUM** almug; sandalwood

ALIAS otherwise; an assumed name

lw **ALIBI** proof of absence

ALIEN strange; exotic; remote; foreign

ALIGN ALINE, adjust; rectify; arrange; regulate; conform

ALIKE similar; analogous; equal

ALISH resembling beer

ch **ALITE** ground clinker from sintering

ALIVE vital; quick; alert; brisk

ALKYD glyptal resins; polyesters

ch **ALKYL** aliphatic radicals

rl **ALLAH** Moslem word for the Deity

ALLAY lull; calm; relieve; repress

ALLEY large marble; taw; passage

ALL-IN exhausted; insurance policy; inclusive

zo **ALLIS** the allice shad; a fish

ALLOD freehold estate

ALLOO halloo

ALLOT distribute; apportion; assign

ALLOW admit; own; concede; grant

ALLOY a base admixture

ch **ALLYL** organic radicle

bt **ALMUG** algum; sandal-wood

bt **ALOED ALOID, ALOIN,** aloes bitter fruit

bt **ALOES** bitter purgative drug

ALOFT above; overhead; skyward

ALONE only; sole; single; isolated

ALONG by; beside; together

ALOOF apart; away; distant

zo **ALOSE** allis; shad-fish

ALOUD audibly; loudly; clamorously

ALPHA the first or beginning (Gr. letter)

bt **ALPIA** bird-seed

nt, rl **ALTAR** shrine; sanctuary; receding step in drydock

ALTER vary; change; turn; transform

zo **ALULA** bastard wing

AMASS heap; gather; accumulate; pile

mu **AMATI** violin (Cremona)

AMAZE daze; astound; perplex

mn **AMBER** fossilized resin

AMBIT precinct; extent; compass

AMBLE dawdle; saunter; stroll

cf, md **AMBLY-** dysfunction (Gr.)

rl **AMBON** lectern; pulpit

rl **AMBRY** alms-box; niche; almonry

AMEND emend; better; rectify; correct

bt **AMENT** a catkin

tx, rl **AMICE AMICT,** pilgrim's linen cloak

ch **AMIDE AMINE,** ammonia compounds

AMISS wrong; faulty; erroneously

AMITY friendship; fellowship; harmony

zo **AMMON** Tibetan sheep

AMONG emong; amidst; amongst

AMORT halfdead; dejected; spiritless

AMOUR an affair; a love intrigue
cf AMPHI- of double function
AMPLE ointment-box; wide; capacious
AMPLY plentifully; bountifully
AMPUL ample; oil-jar; flask
zo AMSEL AMZEL, blackbird
AMUCK madly; in murderous frenzy
AMUSE entertain; cheer; charm; divert
bt ANANA the pineapple
md ANCON the elbow; a console
cf ANDRO- of the male
rl ANEAL ANELE, anoint; unction
zo, nm ANGEL divine messenger; fish; old English coin
ANGER ire; rage; choler; passion
cf ANGIO- of blood vessels
ga ANGLE a corner; to entice; to fish; (tennis)
ANGOR acute pain or anxiety
ANGRY irate; wroth; piqued; riled
pc ANGST anxiety; anguish; pain (Gc.)
pc ANIMA living personality; soul
bt ANIME resine; fiery
ANION electro-negative ion
bt ANISE plant furnishing aniseed
ANISO unequal
me ANKER European liquid measure
pl ANKLE foot-leg joint
ANKUS elephant goad
ri ANNAL a Mass
rl ANNAT an Ecclesiastical levy
zo ANNET the kittiwake
ANNEX add; append; join; unite
ANNOY badger; worry; affront; molest
ANNUL cancel; quash; revoke
el ANODE positive electrical pole
pc ANOIA idiocy; anoesia
pc ANOMY urban isolation syndrome
ANOMY lawlessness; miracle
bt ANONA custard-apple genus
ANTIC prank; lark; caper
ANTRE a cave; a cavern
zo ANURA frogs; toads; batrachians
zo, md ANVIL ossicle, ear bone for sound
mu ANVIL blacksmith's forge block; operatic percussion
ANZAC Australian, NZ Army Corps
AOGAI lacquer inlaid with mother-of-pearl (Haliotis), Japan
pl AORTA the great artery; coronary
APACE rapidly; swiftly; at speed
APART aloof; asunder; separately
zo APERY monkey-house
zo APHID APHIS, green-fly; ant-cows
zo APIAN relating to bees

APING copying; mimicking; imitating
zo APISH ape-like
bt APIUM the celery genus
md APNEA cessation of breathing
zo APODA eels, etc.
zo APODE limbless creature
ce A-POLE wooden A frame
nt APOOP astern
nt APORT to port
APPAL scare; daunt; shock; astound
ga APPEL stop-call (fencing); appeal
bt, ga APPLE the award of Paris; fruit; (Adam's); ball (baseball); orb; big city
APPLY bestow; use; employ; refer
APPUI APPUY, support; reciprocal action
APRIL 4th month
rl APRON short cassock; protective garment
to APRON wedge; lathe; sea defence
APRON aircraft parking area
ar APRON lead sheet dam slope; panel
APSIS extreme point in an orbit
APTLY fittingly; appositely; apropos
go ARABY Arabia
bt, ck ARACK ARRACK, fermented palm juice
bt ARBOR tree; bower; spindle; axis
zo ARDEA the heron genus
me ARDES 5½ bushels, Egyptian
bt ARDIL fibre from groundnuts
bt ARECA betal-nut palm
AREFY dry up; shrivel; wither
ARENA ring; stage; battlefield
bt ARENG the sago palm
ARETE knife-edge mountain ridge (Swiss)
ch ARGAL crude tartar
mn ARGIL potter's earth
ch ARGOL argal; crude tartar
ch ARGON a light gas
ARGUE plead; dispute; reason; debate
zo ARGUS watchful; a pheasant
rl ARIAN heretic sect (Christian)
zo ARIEL a sprite; a gazelle
ARIES the Ram of the Zodiac
ARISE ascend; soar; emerge; rebel
ARLES earnest money on engagement
ARMED equipped protected
ARMET medieval helmet
ARMIL insignia of royalty
ARNEE Indian buffalo
bt ARNOT pig-nut; earth-nut
bt AROID a plant allied to the sun

AROMA scent; perfume; fragrance; odour

AROSE got up; began; sprang; revolted

bt, ck **ARRAH** Indian lentil; Irish expletive

ARRAS tapestry; hangings

cp **ARRAY** range; marshal; contents

lw **ARRET** decree; arrest

ARRIS sharp edge; arete

ARROW bolt; shaft; dart; reed

ARSIS vocal inflection; emphasis

lw **ARSON** fire-raising; pyromania

ARTEL a Russian guild

ARYAN Indo-European

ck **ASADO** saddle (meat) (Sp.)

ASCII dwellers on the equator; computer code

ASCOT fashionable race meeting

bt **ASCUS** spore case

nt **ASDIC** submarine-detector

ASHEN wan; pale; hueless; pallid

ga **ASHES** results of cricket on the hearth

ASHUR Assyrian god

ASIAN Asiatic

ASIDE apart; away; aloof; laterally

ASKED invited; demanded; requested

zo **ASKER** a newt; petitioner; suitor

ASKEW awry; aslant; askance; oblique

bt **ASPEN** the trembling poplar

nm **ASPER** a small silver Turkish coin

ck **ASPIC** savoury meat jelly; sap

bt **ASPIC** 12-pounder cannon; lavender

mu **ASSAI** enough; very

ASSAY essay; test; try; analysis

ASSER rafter; thin lath

ASSES mokes; donkeys; burros

ASSET a possession

ASTEL a dam; a splinter

bt **ASTER** flowering plant

ASTIR alert; awake; agog; excited

md **ATAXY** functional disorder; (Ataxia)

zo **ATCHI** Caucasian ibex

cf **ATELO-** incomplete; imperfect

ATILT on edge; slanting

ATIMY dishonour; disgrace

zo **ATLAS** a Titan; a moth; a bound collection of maps

ATMAN the Buddhist ego

ATOLL coral island

ATOMY atom; skeleton; a pygmy

ATONE expiate; satisfy; propitiate

md **ATONY** debility; off colour

nt **ATRIP** anchor clear; aweigh

ATTAR otto; fragrant rose oil

ATTIC Athenian; (salt); garret; loft

ATTLE refuse from mines; rubbish

AUBIN Canterbury gallop

cf, tc **AUDIO-** related to hearing

cp **AUDIT** examine accounts; review of patients; record

ga **AUFIN** bishop (chess)

to **AUGER** a drill

AUGET explosive charge for mines

AUGHT zero; ought; naught; 0

AUGUR seer; soothsayer; portend

AULAE Roman halls or courts

AULIC (royal court)

mu **AULOS** ancient Gr. oboe-like instrument

AUNTY auntie

AURAL of the ear

AURIC golden

ch **AURIN** golden red dye

ch **AURUM** gold; chemical element

ch **AUXIN** growth-affecting substance

AVAIL benefit; help; suffice; use

nt **AVAST** stop; stay; cease

bt **AVENS** the herb bennet

AVERT avoid; divert; forfend; parry

zo **AVIAN** AVINE, of birds

AVION air (by air) aircraft (Fr.)

nt **AVISO** a dispatch boat (Sp.)

AVOID shun; elude; forsake; eschew

lw **AVOUE** French lawyer, advocate

AWAIT tarry; bide; stay; pause

AWAKE alert; ready; alive; vigilant

AWARD give; grant; adjudge; prize

AWARE mindful; conscious

nt **AWASH** nearly submerged

AWFUL dire; dread; fearful; imposing

bt **AWNED** bearded like barley

AWNER grain separator

AWOKE bestirred; roused; incited

AXIAL AXILE, sharing same axis

AXIOM truism; assumed truth

pl **AXION** brain/spinal cord

AXITE a propellant

AXLED having a spindle

AXMAN chainman (USA)

AXOID axoidean

ch **AZIDE** hydrazoic acid salt

AZOIC devoid of life

ch **AZOTE** nitrogen

AZOTH the alchemist cure-all; panacea

ch **AZOXY** potash/nitro-affected

AZTEC extinct Mexican-Indian

AZURE AZURN, sky-blue; the sky; vault of heaven

AZURY blue; cerulean

ro **AZUSA** missile tracking system

AZYME unleavened bread

B

BAARD transport ship
BABEL (tower), multilingual
 confusion
bt BABUL gum-arabic tree
bt BACCA a berry
pl,ga BACKS dorsals; defence (football)
ar BACKS riverside of colleges
 (Cambridge)
ck BACON gammon; to be saved
hd BADGE emblem (for recognition)
BADLY corruptly; wickedly;
 imperfectly
BAFFY an old golf club
ck BAGEL hard glazed doughnut roll
 (Jew.)
BAGGY loose fitting; bulging
me BAHAR 3½ cwt (197 kg), East Indian
tx BAIZE BAYZE, coarse (curtain/
 billiard) cloth
ck BAKED oven-cooked (sundried)
BAKED parched; hardened; dried up
ck BAKER bread/pastry maker
mn BALAS orange ruby
ae BALED in bundles
nt BALER a bowl; scoop (small boats)
BALKY apt to stop suddenly
mt BALMY relaxing air, climate;
 soothing
as BALOO the Bear; (hulla-)
bt,nt BALSA Peruvian raft; a tree
tc BALUN balance/unbalance
 transformer
zo BAMBI faun
bt BANAK American tree
BANAL commonplace; trivial; trite
BANAT Transylvanian district
nt BANCA outrigger sail canoe
 (Philippines)
lw BANCO bench; bank money
ga BANDY ice hockey; crooked; dispute
mu BANJO job an octaroon would like;
 5-string fretted, plucked stringed
 instrument
lw,rl BANNS public notice of marriage
zo BANNY a minnow
BANTU African tribe
BARBE war-horse armour; nun's
 kerchief
zo BARBS jagged tip of feathers
BARED naked; unadorned; stripped
rl BARET BIRETTA, cardinal's cap
BARGE shove; jostle
nt BARGE cargo craft
mn BARIA BARYTA
mt,ch BARIC of weight/pressure
 (barometer); barium

bt BARKY pertaining to tree bark
BARMY foolish; dotty
ck BARON lord; (-of beef) sirloin
mu BARRE single finger chord on guitar
hd BARRY divided by horizontal bars
me BARYE unit of pressure dynes
BASAL basic; fundamental source
BASED founded on
le BASEL tanned skin
cp BASIC basal; fundamental source
bt,ck BASIL chisel edge; a herb
ga,pl BASIN pond; dock; reservoir; bowl;
 trough
BASIS ground work; first principle
BASON a basin
zo BASSE bass; fish like a perch
mu BASSO a bass singer (It.)
mu BASTA stop! enough (It.)
BASTE cook; sew; stitch; thrash
ga BASTO ace of clubs (cards)
BATAK Mayo-Polynesian language
BATAK people in Sumatra
cp BATCH lot; amount; crowd; series
BATED restrained; repressed;
 reduced
BATEY gold and silver embroidery
BATHE immerse
cf BATHY- deep (bathysphere)
tx BATIK method of dyeing (Ind.)
zo BATIS wattle-eye flycatcher
mu,ck,ga BATON staff; wand; sceptre; rod;
 (relay) athletics; truncheon; bread
BATTA Indian grant
BATTY bat-like; dotty
tx BAUGE cloth; drugget
ga BAULK deliberate fault (badminton);
 hinder; refuse (horse-jumping)
ga BAULK timber beams; thwart
 (billiards)
nt BAULK (-head) ship's watertight
 section walls
bt,nt BAVIN faggot of brushwood
BAWDY lewd; immoral (-house)
BAYED recessed; howled like a dog
BAYOU channel, outlet of river/lake
BAZAR bazaar; mart; souk; exchange
BEACH shore; strand; sands; margin
rl BEADS necklace rosary, (prayer-)
BEADY small and bright; (-eyed)
BE-ALL sum and substance; ultimate
BEAMY shining; radiant; broad;
 smile
BEANO jamboree; beanfeast; spree
BEARD defy; oppose; confront
BEAST brute; ruffian; animal
mu,pl,ps BEATS (heart); (drum); fluctuations
 in sound intensity; strokes
BEAUX gallants (Fr.)

mu **BEBOP** dissonant jazz
to **BECHE** drill extractor
lt **BECKE** of microscope juncture light
BEDAD! Irish interjection
bt **BEECH** a hardwood tree
BEEFY stolid; powerful
to **BEELE** pickaxe
BEERY maudlin; fuddled
BEFIT suit; become
BEGAD! exclamation of surprise
BEGAN started; initiated; originated
BEGAT bred; sired; engendered
BEGET sire; become father
BEGIN start; initiate; commence
BEGOT procreated; gave rise to
BEGUM Moslem princess
BEGUN originated; opened
bt **BEHEN** sea-lavender
BEIGE fabric; yellowish grey
BEING existence; actually
zo **BEISA** oryx; unicorn
nm **BEKAH** half shekel (Hebrew)
nt **BELAY** make fast (rope) (sails)
BELCH a report (from stomach)
nm **BELGA** Belgian currency
BELIE prove an accusation was
    wrongly held
BELLE beauty queen
BELLY stomach; abdomen; (-laugh)
mu, ga **BELLY** (-flop) flat dive; to swell;
    topside of string instrument;
    bottom of surfboard
BELOW under; beneath; Hades
ce **BENCH** seat; form; court; tribunal;
    form of quarry
md **BENDS** cramps, pains (deepsea
    divers)
hd **BENDY** divided into bends
bt **BENNE BENE** an oil plant
bt **BENTH** ground ivy
tx **BERET** round (Basque) cap
bt **BERRY** fruit; barrow; mound
nt **BERTH** cabin bed; ship at quay;
    situation
mm **BERYL** a gem
zo **BERYX** perch-like sea fish
ck **BESAN** Indian lentil flour
BESET assail; encircle; surround
ga **BESOM** a broom of twigs (ice
    curling)
BESOT assot; get fuddled, or drunk
bt **BETEL** nut of the areca palm
BETON a kind of concrete
nm **BETSO** a small Venetian coin
ck **BETTY** flask; jemmy; sweet pastry
BEVEL BEZEL, glass ornamentation
    groove
BEWIT leather strap in falconry

tx **BEZAN** Bengali cotton cloth
BEZIL metal groove for glass
BEZIL clock gem
bt **BHANG** hashish; Indian hemp
zo **BHYLE** Indian ox
nt **BIBBS** wooden brackets
rl **BIBLE** The Scriptures
zo **BIDDY** a fowl; a chicken; farm girl
zo **BIDET** genitals bath; small horse
me **BIDON** about 5 qt (5.6 litres)
BIDRI Indian metal-ware
BIELD shelter; protection
bt **BIFER** twice-yearly flowering/
    fruiting
BIFID two-clefted
nt **BIGHT** cove; bay; coil; loop
BIGLY ostentatiously
BIGOT zealot; fanatic; dogmatist
BIJOU pretty trinket (gift)
BILBO Spanish rapier
nt **BILGE** waste-space between deck
    and hull
nt **BILGE** underwater curve of hull;
    nonsense
BILIN BILE, intestinal enzyme; anger
cp **BILLI** giga; one thousand million 10^9
zo **BILLY** Australian cooking can, goat
    (male)
BINAC Binary Automatic Computer
BINAL twin; double
BINGE a carousal
BINGO brandy; gambling pastime
zo **BINNY** a Nile fish
ec **BIOME** largest land community area
ec **BIOTA** a region's fauna/flora
zo **BIPED** two-footed animal
BIPOD (cf. tripod) two-legged
bt **BIRCH** to flog; forest tree
BIRTH genesis; nativity; origin
zo **BISON** American buffalo
ce **BITCH** female dog; wolf; disagreeable
    woman; spike
BITER wild dog; insect; cheat
nt **BITTS** a cable attachment
BITTY incomplete; fragmentary
mu **BIWAR** Japanese lute-form
ch **BIXIN** annatto
BLACK ebon; inky; dusky; sombre
bt **BLADE** roisterer; leaf; flat edge (bat,
    club, (golf), knife, oar, sword)
mm **BLAES** hardened shale
md **BLAIN** blister; blotch
BLAME chide; rebuke; reproach
BLAND soft; suave; mild; benign
BLANK lacuna; vacant; empty; void;
    (cartridge); no score
BLARE blazon; proclaim; clangour
BLASE cloyed; surfeited (Fr.).

BLASE immune to novelty or impressions
BLAST gust; explode; (shrivel); cell; noise
cp BLAST release memory areas
BLAZE horse mark; flame; proclaim
BLAZE path mark (trees)
zo BLEAK drear; desolate; river-fish
BLEAR dim; rheumy; watery
BLEAT the cry of a sheep
zo BLECK coal-fish
BLEED exude; secrete; impoverish
BLEEP radio signal
BLEND mix; unite; knead; coalesce
BLENT blended; amalgamated
BLESS laud; exalt; praise; extol
BLEST endowed with blessings
BLIMP small airship; (reactionary Colonel)
BLIND ruse; feint; curtain; sightless
BLINK glance; flicker; ignore
nt BLIRT blore; squall; gust
BLISS ecstasy; rapture; felicity
bt BLITE the plant Good King Henry
BLITZ sudden total bombardment; lightning war (Ge.)
ck BLOAT BLOTE, cure by smoke, dilate
cr, nt BLOCK bar; obstruct; mass; (tackle) building; hoist
cp, me, tc BLOCK unit of data
ga BLOCK foul (badminton); (Am. football); (basketball)
BLOKE a fellow; a man
BLOND fair; flaxen
BLOOD cruor; gore; kindred; lineage
ce, bt, pt BLOOM bud; blossom; prime; thrive; film on old paint, iron, steel block
cn BLOOP sound-track joint thud
BLORE blirt; violent gust
BLOWN winded; trumpeted; exposed
BLOWY breezy; gusty; windy
BLUED tempered; squandered
BLUER more blue; gloomier
mu BLUES Royal Horse Guards; sad American-negro songs
BLUEY blanket; bundle (Australia)
go BLUFF sheer; brusque; spoof; headland; cliff
BLUNT blont; dull; abrupt
BLURB recommendation; description (bk. cover)
BLURT utter hastily
BLUSH flush; colour; redden
BOARD embark; victuals; council; non-gem diamond drill
to BOART BORT, square-sawn timber; pressed wood; (squash) platform; stage; plank

ga BOAST brag; crow; vaunt; angle stroke (squash)
BOBBY policeman
BOCAL glass beaker
BOCHE a Hun, also a German
BODED portended; presaged; augured
BODGE BOTCH, bungle; fail
bt BODHI Buddhist sacred tree
nm BODLE farthing (Sc.)
ga BOGEY min. golf score; hobgoblin
BOGGY soggy; swampy; marshy
rw BOGIE railway axle; truck
BOGLE bugbear; scarecrow
BOGUS sham; spurious; false
bt BOHEA inferior tea
BOIAR BOYAR, Slavonic nobleman
BOITE night-club, disco
BOLAR pertaining to clay
BOLAS S. American missile
nt BOLIN bowline
me BOLUS large pill
BOMBE swollen Rococo style decor
ga BONCE marble game, head (slang)
BONED seized; stole; purloined
bl BONER sharp blow; erection
tx BONES of skeletons; bobbins (lace)
mu BONGO African antelope; percussion single small drum; head injury from fall (skateboarding)
BONNE French nurse
ml BONNY bonnie; ore pocket
BONUS award; premium; subsidy
rl BONZE Buddhist priest
BOOBY looby; dunce; simpleton
zo BOOBY water bird
BOOED hooted; noisily objected
BOOER vociferous interrupter
zo BOOPS humpbacked whale
BOORT (diamond polishing)
BOOST boom; push; eulogize
BOOTH market stall; voting cubicle; (toilet)
BOOTS last joined; shoe cleaner
BOOTY loot; spoil; plunder
BOOZE BOOZY, alcoholic drink; tipsy
BORAK banter; chaff (Australia)
ch BORAX tincal; borate of soda
BORED drilled; wearied
BOREE French peasants' dance
zo BORER an insect; seaworm
ch BORIC boracic
BORNE narrow-minded; carried
ch BORON a non-metallic element
BOSKY busky; shady; thickly wooded
BOSOM breast; confidential

nc **BOSON** elementary particle (photons, mesons)

nt **BOS'UN** boatswain (leader)

BOSSY dictatorial; domineering

BOTCH to patch; worthless

BOTHY hut; cottage (Sc.)

zo **BOTTS** larvae; worms

BOUCH to bush; to debouch

bt **BOUGH** branch; limb; offshoot

BOULE (buhl); inlay work; hardwood log

ga **BOULE** Greek Parliament; roulette; French bowls

BOUND limit; pale; leap; spring

BOURG a town; burgh; borough

BOURN BURN, stream; border

BOUSE BOWZE, BOWSY, drunk; tipsy

mn **BOVEY** a kind of coal

BOWED bent; curved; subdued

pl **BOWEL** rectum

nt **BOWER** arbour; shelter; anchor

ga **BOWER** the knave at euchre (cards)

BOWIE a large knife

ga **BOWLS** skittles; a game

nt **BOWSE** to heave; bouse

nt **BOW-TO** to face the wind

BOXED crated

BOXEN made of boxwood

BOXER a pugilist

pr **BOX-IN** surrounding type with rule

ck **BOXTY** Halloween dish (Ir.)

BOX-UP mistake; error

BOYAR boiar; Russian nobleman

BOYAU ditch; trench (Fr.)

nt **BOYER** Flemish sloop

ga, to **BRACE** pair; couple; stiffen; anti-capsize stroke (canoeing); stirrup-stand (polo); support; tauten; string a bow (archery)

zo **BRACH** bitch-hound

tx **BRACK** a flaw in cloth

bt **BRACT** specialized leaf

cf, go **BRADY-** of slow (river)

tx **BRAID** brede; broid; weave; entwine

ga, nt **BRAIL** (falconry); to furl sails

BRAIN cerebellum; intellect

mn **BRAIT** rough diamond

BRAKE thicket; harrow; wagonette

bt **BRAKY** overgrown with ferns

BRAND brond; stigma; mark; torch

bt **BRANK** buckwheat

BRANK bridle for scolds

zo **BRANT** a goose

BRASH hasty; brittle; loose rock

ml, mu **BRASS** (top) money; impudence; effrontery; alloy of copper and zinc; metal wind instrument

tx **BRAUL** striped cloth

BRAVE to dare; heroic; valiant

BRAVO well done!; an assassin (It.)

BRAWL struggle; fight; quarrel (drunk)

BRAWN muscular strength

BRAXY splenetic sheep disease

BRAZE to solder

ck **BREAD** food; fare; aliment

mu **BREAK** interval; smash; shatter; successful sequence; separate; sprint; voice-change; tone quality; short solo

zo **BREAM** a fish; to clean

go **BREDE** slow river

BREED farm; beget; race

BRERE brother (-Rabbit: Mark Twain)

zo **BRENT** lofty; smooth; a goose

mu **BREVE** a long note

bt **BRIAR** a pipe; wild rose

BRIBE pass money (inducement); graft

BRICK building unit; a loyal friend

BRIDE (betrothed) banned but beloved

lw **BRIEF** short; concise; a writ

bt **BRIER** briar; wild rose

zo **BRILL** prill; type of turbot

BRINE salt water; the sea; tears

BRING fetch; convey; produce

BRINK brim; brow; verge; margin

BRINY the sea; salty

BRISK agile; alert; nimble

BRITE over-ripe

bt **BRIZA** totter-grass

zo **BRIZE** the gadfly

go **BROAD** wide; spacious; liberal; stretch of fresh water (inland); woman

BROCH early stone hut

zo **BROCK** badger; a brocket

ck **BROIL** quarrel; affray; roast

BROKE broken; ruined; penniless

BROOD incubate; progeny; meditate

BROOK beck; rill; tolerate; allow

BROOL a deep murmur

bt **BROOM** brush; gorse (plantagenet)

BROSE Scottish porridge

ck **BROTH** soup; a concoction

BROWN tan; ecru; russet; sorrel

zo **BRUIN** a bear

BRUIT to noise abroad; a rumour

BRUME fog; mist; vapour

BRUNT shock; impulse

BRUSH skirmish; scrap; sweep; conductor; grooming; touch lightly

BRUTE savage; senseless; rough

zo **BUCCO** puff-bird genus

bt **BUCHU** African medicinal plant
BUCKO a bully (USA)
BUDDY a partner; blooming
BUDGE lambskin fur; pompous; to stir
mu **BUFFA** comic opera (It.)
BUFFO comic actor
BUFFS a famous regiment
BUFFY buff colour
BUGGY a gig; a vehicle
mu **BUGLE** jet bead; horn
bt **BUGLE** genus of flowering plants
BUILD erect; construct; raise
BUILT fabricated; established
BULGE swell; belly
BULGY protuberant
BULKY vast; massive; voluminous
rl, zo **BULLA** Papal seal; edict; mollusc
pl **BULLA** bone cover of ear
ga **BULLY** hector; intimidate; splendid; salt beef; race off (hockey)
BULSE a bag of diamonds
BUMBO rumbo; a drink
BUMPS Cambridge and Oxford rowing event
BUMPY uneven
BUNCH set; lot; lump; batch; group of people (associated interest)
zo **BUNNY** a rabbit
BUNTY wheat disease; purge
mt **BURAN** or **purga** westerly tundra wind (Siberia)
BURGH town; borough
to **BURIN** engraving tool
BURKE murder; hush up
BURLY stout; lusty; portly
BURNT charred; parched; tanned
zo **BURRO** donkey; moke
bt **BURRY** having burs; prickly
md **BURSA** a sac; a pouch
BURSE BOURSE, PURSE, money container; treasury
BURST split; exploded; rent asunder
BUSBY bearskin headdress
BUSES vehicles
BUSHI kerido; samurai (Japanese knight)
BUSHY overgrown; bosky (tail)
BUSKY bosky; woody; shady
go **BUTTE** hill with flat top; ridge
BUTTS rifle range
BUTTY mining partner; deputy; barge
BUXOM (of females) comely; lively; jolly
BUYER purchaser; shopper
BUZZY muzzy; dazed
BWANA master; boss (Swahili)
BYARD miner's hauling strap

ce **BYATT** walkway; timber support
BY-END subsidiary aim
lw **BY-LAW** municipal bye-law
lw **BY-WAY** (indirect route) by-path

C

CABAL clique; junto; set
CABAS rush-basket
CABBY coach or taxi-driver
ga **CABER** tossing a treetrunk (Scots)
nt **CABIN** hut; shed; room in ship
CABIR nature worship (Lemnos)
me, nt **CABLE** wire; 100 fathoms
CABRE aero-stunt
bt **CACAO** the chocolate-tree
CACHE a hide; store
CADDY porter (golf); tea container
CADET younger son; trainee
CADGE peddle; sponge; portable perch (falconry)
CADGY frolicsome; wanton
CADRE nucleus; framework
CAGED captive; mewed
CAGEY cautious; irritable; secretive
CAGOT Pyrenees pariah race
CAIRD tinker; gipsy
zo **CAIRN** heap of stones; terrier
CAKED clotted; plastered
CALID hot; fiery; ardent; glowing
rl **CALIF CALIPH, KALIF,** Moslem governor
CALIN a Chinese alloy
bt **CALIX** calyx; cup
bt **CALLA** bog-arum
zo **CALVE** give birth
bt **CALYX** flower's outer whorl, calix
zo, nt **CAMEL** ship of the desert; caisson
CAMEO small relief carving in colour-layered gem stone
tx **CAMIS CAMISE, CHEMISE,** loose garment (Fr.)
go **CAMPO** Savanna (Brazil)
CANAL channel; duct; waterway
ga **CANAS** form of jousting
CANDY a sweetmeat; to crystalize
CANED thrashed; tanned
fr **CANEY** with unduly narrow growth rings
bt, ck **CANNA** arrowroot; thickening starch
CANNE walking cane; quarter staff (fencing)
CANNY shrewd; cautious; knowing
nt **CANOE** dug out, river vessel (N. America)
rl **CANON** precept; rule; church dignitary

mu **CANON** repetitive part song
mu **CANTO** sung contrapuntal poem
CANTY cheerful; talkative
rl **CAPEL CAPLE**, composite stone; church (Welsh)
zo **CAPEL CAPUL**, a horse
bt **CAPER** dance; gambol; a plant
nt **CAPER** Dutch privateer
zo **CAPLE** capel; capul; a horse
bt **CAPOC** kapok; Indian cotton
zo **CAPON** fish; letter; fowl
ga **CAPOT** to win all tricks at piquet
zo **CAPRA** she-goat
md **CAPUT** head; distal-end swelling; broken
bt, me **CARAT** gold weight (carob seed)
CARED heeded; recked; minded
CARET the mark ⅄
bt **CAREX** sedge; reed; grass
nt **CARGO** load; freight
CARIB a Caribbean
CARLE rude strong man
CARNY blarney; flattery
bt **CAROB** locust or algaroba tree, bean
mu **CAROL** lay; ditty; warble; hymn
ga **CAROM** cannon in French billiards
CARRY convey; urge; accomplish; transfer (sound, golf); sustain
go **CARSE** low-lying land
ga **CARTE** (fencing score); card
md **CARUS** unconsciousness
CARVE cut; hack; slice; engrave
bt **CARVY** caraway plant
CASAL belonging to a case (grammar)
nt **CASCO** Manila barge
CASED boxed; packed; enveloped
CASSE broken paper
CASTE class; rank; lineage
mu **CATCH** latch; clutch; ensnare; seize; crab (rowing); a round (song); canon
CATER provide food, etc
CATES viands; dainties
CATTY feline; spiteful
nt **CAULK** make water-tight
CAUSE reason; object; source
CAVED CAVERNOUS, (-in), fallen; collapsed
gl, go **CAVES** grottoes; caverns
CAVES darts; table quoits (East Anglia)
CAVIE hen-coop or cage
CAVIL carp; censure; criticize
CAVIN covered approach
CAWED crowed
ch **CAWKY** of baryta; of barium oxide
CAXON hairy wig

· **CEASE** cesse; end; stop; desist
zo **CEBUS** S. American monkey
bt **CEDAR** a Lebanon tree
CEDED granted; allotted; yielded
mu **CEDEZ** restrain the tempo (Fr.)
CELLA central body of temple
mu **CELLO** violoncello
rl **CENSE** burn incense
cf **CENTI-** 100th; (centimetre)
mu **CENTO** a medley
CEORL churl; a freeman
CERED covered with wax
rl **CERES** harvest goddess
rl **CERGE** altar candle
CERIC wax-like
ch **CERIN** a constituent of wax
ga **CESTA** curved basket (pelota)
zo **CETIC** (spermaceti)
CETYL a radical in spermaceti
CHACK the toss of a horse's head
CHAFE rub; heat; vex; gall
CHAFF husks; deride; raillery
go **CHAIN** line of mountains, of islands
me **CHAIN** necklace; tether; fetter; measure of distance; (-stores)
rw **CHAIR** seat of profession; preside; rail-track binding
ga **CHALK** white limestone pencil; record; touch-mark (bowls)
zo **CHAMA** large oyster
CHAMP (horses); chew; crunch
CHAMP potato dish (N. Ire.)
zo **CHANK** species of conch-shell
mu **CHANT** intone; carol
CHAOS anarchy; disorder; confusion
CHAPE the catch of a buckle
ck, md **CHAPS** the jaws; chops; cold-sores
CHAPS cowboy's leather leg overalls
bt, ck **CHARD** kale-like vegetable
CHARE chore; daily work
CHARE narrow street or court
CHARK char; charcoal
CHARM spell; allure; amulet
CHARM nuclear behaviour
zo **CHARR** char; (trout)
nt **CHART** sea-map; weather map, graph, diagram
CHARY frugal; circumspect; wary
ga **CHASE** pursue; hunt; follow; race; forest; (baseball)
CHASE engrave; frame; type-case
CHASM gap; cleft; rift; abyss
zo **CHAUS** Ind./Afr. wild cat
CHEAP mean; common; paltry
lw, ga **CHEAT** dupe; fraud; swindle; deceive; (iceskating) (surfing)
ga **CHECK** curb; stay; control (of king) chess

pl, bd, cr **CHEEK** insolence; sauce; jaw;
    mortise; tenon lock; dormer side
    CHEEP pipe; bird song
    CHEER gaiety; hearten; encourage
zo **CHELA** lobster claw
rl **CHELA** a Buddhist disciple
cf **CHEMO-** chemical action
mu **CHENG** Chinese reed instrument
    CHERI darling (masc., Fr.)
nt **CHERT** flint; hornstone
ga **CHESS** a matey game
mu **CHEST** coffer; coffin; breast; set of 6
    viols
    CHEVY chivy; chase; scamper
    CHIAN of Chios
ck **CHICA** orange-red dye; liquor; girl
    (Sp.)
zo, bt, ck **CHICK** to sprout; child; chicken;
    (-peas)
    CHICO youth (Sp.)
    CHIDE scold; rebuke; reprove
    CHIEF boss; head; prime; principal
    CHILD babe; nursling; offspring
bt, ck, mt **CHILI** pod of cayenne pepper; hot
    southerly sirocco wind (Tunisia)
    CHILL cold; frigid; depress
    CHIMB edge of cask
    CHIME harmonize; strike; agree
    CHINA porcelain; Celestial Empire
md, go **CHINE** cleft; ravine; backbone
    CHINK gap, rift; cranny; clink
ck **CHIPS** a carpenter (potato) software
    CHIRK chirp; cheep; cheerful
    CHIRM bird noises
cf **CHIRO-** hand; (chiromancy,
    palmistry)
    CHIRP chirr; chirl; to trill; bird call
    CHIRT to squeeze
bt, ck **CHIVE** a type of onion
    CHIVY chevy; chase; pursue
    CHOCK wedge; block; a log
ar, rl, mu **CHOIR** the chancel; a group of
    singers
    CHOKE gag; stifle; burke; strangle;
    stutter
el **CHOKE** (carburettor); waveguide
    groove; inductor
pl, ck **CHOPS** chaps; the jaws; cutlets
mu **CHORD** harmonious sound
    combination; wing-width (hang-
    gliding)
    CHORE chare; household toil
    CHOSE selected; picked; culled
mo **CHOSS** scree or shale climb
pg, mu **CHROM-** **CHROMATIC** colours; scale
to **CHUCK** jerk; throw; cluck;
    instrument
    CHUFF to feel better

ga **CHULA** rebound from wall (pelota)
    CHUMP lump of wood; blockhead
ck **CHUNK** lump or bit (marmalade)
    CHURL ceorl; freeman; clodhopper
    CHURN stir strongly (milk-)
go **CHUTE** waterfall; sloping channel
bt **CIBOL** variety of onion; shallot
bt **CICER** chick-pea
ck **CIDER** cyder; fermented apple-juice
    CIGAR a Havana
md **CILIA** filaments; eye-lashes
    CIMAR cymar; simar; scarf
zo **CIMEX** bed-bug
    CINCH girth; a certainty
    CIRCA about, approximately (Lat.)
rl **CIRCE** a glamorous witch (Ulysses)
    CIRRI tendrils; clouds
zo **CISCO** American char
    CISSY effeminate youth
lw **CITAL** summons; accusation
    CITED quoted; adduced; mentioned
    CIVET cat; perfume; fur
    CIVIC municipal; corporate
    CIVIL polite; courteous; suave
    CIVVY a civilian
    CLACK click; clink; clatter; prate
zo **CLAIK** the barnacle goose
    CLAIM right; privilege; usurp
cr, to **CLAMP** vice; fasten; joining device
to, zo, ck **CLAMS** pincers; seafood
mu **CLANG** (characteristic) sound of
    church bells
    CLANK clatter; clangour
rl **CLARE** a nun of St Clare
    CLARO milk in taste (cigars)
bt **CLARY** sweet-herb
    CLASH jar; differ; contend; collide
    CLASP hasp; catch; grip
    CLASS set; grade; category
zo, bt **CLAVA** club-shaped swelling; fungi
    CLAVE clove; cleft; clung
    CLEAN immaculate; pure; scour;
    innocent; penalty free (contests,
    events)
cp **CLEAR** serene; free; lucid; to empty
nt **CLEAT** a wedge; slat; T-shaped
    fitting for rope
    CLEEK golf club; hook; peg
    CLEFT clift; split; rift; cranny
    CLERK scribe; scrivener; recorder
    CLEVE a cliff; a valley
    CLEVY draught-iron of a plough
    CLICK klick; tick; a latch
bt **CLIDE CLITE,** burweed
    CLIFF crag; headland; precipice
    CLIMB scale; ascend; surmount
    CLIME region; place; climate
bt, zo **CLINE** ecological life assessment

CLING hold; cleave; embrace
CLINK prison; chink; jingle
gl **CLINT KLINT**, limestone ridge
CLOAK cape; cover; pretext; (-room)
nt **CLOCK** chronometer; horologe;
    timepiece
CLOFF cleft; a weight allowance
CLONE asexual; duplicated life
bt **CLONE** plant stock; pure line
rl, mu **CLOSE** estop; end; grapple; cadence;
    shut; near; familiar
ga **CLOSH** skittles
rl, tx **CLOTH** woven fabric; the clergy
CLOUD haze; vapour; obscure;
    billowy aerial mass; gloom
CLOUR to knock; a bump
CLOUT dish-cloth; nail; buffet;
    clothing; influence
bt, me **CLOVE** a spice; a weight
CLOWN jester; fool; buffoon; dunce
ga **CLUBS** suit (cards); (juggling);
    apparatus (gymnastics)
CLUCK the call of a hen
CLUMP cluster; group; patch
CLUNG clasped; adhered; held
CLUNK a gurgle
CLUNY pillow-lace
go **CLUSE** gorge, Jura mountains (Fr.)
COACH teach; trainer; vehicle
CO-ACT co-operate; aid; abet
CO-AID helper; assistant
COALY resembling coal
rl **COARB** bishop or abbot
COAST shore; strand; seaside
zo **COATI** American racoon
COBBY stout; brisk
nt **COBLE** fishing boat
zo **COBRA** hamadryad snake
COCKY conceited
bt, ck **COCOA** beverage from cacao
bt **COCUS** green ebony
CODAN carrier-operated-device-anti-
    noise
CODED in code; in cipher
CODEX ancient manuscript
md, pl **CODON** triplet DNA bases fixing
    genetic codes
ar **COIGN QUOIN**, corner-stone; (wedge)
COKED coal converted in gasworks
md **COLIC** flatulence
zo **COLIN** American partridge
COLLY coal-smut
COLON punctuation; money
pl **COLON** large intestine
bt **COLZA** cabbage; rape oil
go **COMBE COOMB**, hollow in hillside
COMBO small jazz/dance band
COMER an arrival; (new-)

as, ga **COMET** card game; nebulous body
COMFY comfortable
COMIC droll; farcical; ludicrous
zo **COMMA** a butterfly; punctuation
    mark; posture (skiing)
ar, ck **COMPO** (-site); stucco; soldier's
    ration
COMUS God of Revelry; a masque
mu, rl, ar **CONCH** seashell; trumpet;
    semicircular niche
CONED tapering
CONES fine flour; retina; pigments
    (eye)
zo **CONEY CONY**, hamster
mu **CONGA** dance (Afro-Cuban)
CONGE leave; dismissal (Fr.)
bt **CONGO** black tea
bt **CONIA** hemlock
CONIC conical; tapering
bt **CONIN CONINE**, hemlock
CONTO KONTO, money account
COOED (doves) made love
COOEE cooey; Australian bush-call
ck **COOKY** a cook; a small cake
CO-OPT to select extra committee
rl **COPAL** a resin; a varnish
nm **COPEC** kopeck; a Russian copper
COPED vied; contended; overcame
COPER dealer
COPOS lassitude
bt **COPRA** dried coconut kernels
COPSE coppice; grove; thicket
zo, cp **CORAL** lobster roe; language
bt, mn **CORAL** marine growth reef; gem
mu **CORDA** string; soft pedal (It.)
CORED centre removed, bored
CORER fruit/earth-sample cutting
    device
zo **CORGI** small breed of dog (Wales)
CORKY lively; skittish
mu, zo **CORNO CORNU**, Fr. horn; deer
CORNY horny; (humour) trite (slang)
CORPS staff; contingent; troops
mn **CORVE** tram used in mines
COSEY COSY, snug; teapot-cover
lw **COSTS** expenses; prices; fees
rl **COTTA** a surplice
bt **COUCH** sofa; divan; squat; grass
pl **COUGH** to clear throat, lungs
COULD was able (past of can)
ga **COULE** a thrust (fencing)
COUNT compute; number; reckon;
    lord
COUPE car with adjustable roof
lw **COURT** woo; (homage); tribunal
COURT (-yard); enclosed area; cards
ga **COURT** of palace; (-favour) (tennis-)
COVEN group of witches

COVER wrap; cloak; shroud; invest
COVET desire; hanker after
zo **COVEY** a brood; a bevy
lw **COVIN** collusive fraudulence
COWAN uninitiated freemason
COWED daunted; overawed; abashed
COWER fawn; quail; cringe; shrink
COWLE written agreement (Ang.-Ind.)
COWRY small shell used as money
md **COXAE** hip-joints
COXED commanded; steered
COYLY bashfully; demurely; shyly
zo **COYPU** nutria; S. American rodent
COZEN cheat; deceive; sponge
CRACK gap; rift; rent; crevice
nt **CRAFT** skill; dexterity; guile; vessel
gl **CRAIG** CRAG, rocky outcrop
zo **CRAKE** the corncrake
CRAME booth; covered stall
bd **CRAMP** a spasm; hinder; impede; joining device; metal; tool
zo **CRANE** hoisting machine; wader
CRANK handle; bend; twist; quirk
CRAPE transparent gauze; to curl
ga **CRAPS** a dice game (gambling)
CRASH (-course); shatter; smash
CRASS gross; dense; stupid
CRATE hamper; packing case
CRAVE beg; yearn; implore
CRAWL fish-pen; creep; abase
CRAZE mania; insane passion; fad
CRAZY mad; idiotic; rickety
CREAK grate
CREAM to mantle; top of milk
zo **CRECK** the corncrake
rl **CREDO** CREED, belief; tenet; dogma
CREEK bay; cove inlet; bight
CREEL fish-basket
ce **CREEP** crawl; cringe; grovel; heat stress expansion/shrinkage of steel/concrete
hd **CREME** cream-like substance
CRENA a furrow; a notch
ck **CREPE** wrinkled fabric; rubber; pancake (Fr.)
CREPT crawled; fawned; glided
bt **CRESS** watercress, etc.
ht **CREST** top; apex; summit; device
CREWE CRUSE, earthenware pot
CRICK cramp; spasm; convulsion
CRIED wept; sobbed; lamented
CRIER proclaimer; howler
CRIES yells; shrieks; shouts
CRIME felony; enormity; misdeed
CRIMP corrugated surface; decoy
ck **CRISP** curl; brittle; friable; (potato-)
me **CRITH** unit weight of a gas

CROAK throaty speech; (raven) (frog)
CROAT inhabitant of Dalmatia, Croatia
CROCK antique; invalid; earthenware plate
CROFT a small farm; a pasture; small writing table
mu **CROMA** CROME, a quaver; cromb; crook; hook
CROME cromb; crook; hook
CRONE old woman; a ewe
CRONY familiar friend
rl, mu **CROOK** crome; bend; crosier; detachable section of horn
CROOL to mutter
to **CROOM** a pitchfork
CROON chromatic singing
nm **CRORE** 100 lacs of rupees
CROSS crusty; sullen; thwart
rl **CROSS** hybrid; symbol; burden
mu **CROUD** Welsh violin
md **CROUP** rump; throat disease
CROUP pommel or side-horse (gymn)
ck **CROUT** (sauer-) pickled cabbage (Ger.)
CROWD mob; throng; herd; swarm
nm **CROWN** diadem; garland; 5 shillings (25p)
to **CROZE** cooper's tool; groove
ar **CRUCK** medieval oaken roof; crossbeam
CRUDE raw; rough; immature
CRUEL fell; dire; brutal; inhuman
ck, rl **CRUET** pepper; salt; eucharistic flagon
ck **CRUMB** soft part of a loaf
CRUMP crooked; wrinkled; a bang
CRUSE vial; small bottle
CRUSH squeeze; subdue; pulverize
CRUST incrustation; coating
mu **CRWTH** Welsh violin
rl **CRYPT** vault; tomb; catacomb
cf **CRYPT-** secret; hidden (cryptic, coded)
CUBAN a native of Cuba
bt, ck **CUBEB** dried pepper-berry
CUBED raised to third power
me **CUBIC** volumetric
me **CUBIT** length of 18 or 22 in (45 or 55 cm)
zo **CUDDY** cabin; rent; donkey
CUFIC an Arabic script
CUISH cuisse; thigh-armour
CULCH rubbish
CULET lower facet of a diamond
zo **CULEX** a gnat genus

CULLS brick or timber rejects (USA)
CULLY silly dupe; to deceive
me **CUMEN** a cubic metre per sec. (flow)
bt, ck **CUMIN** CUMMIN, caraway; spice
CUPEL assaying vessel
CUPID Eros; the god of love
tx **CURCH** KERCHIEF, scarf; hankie
ck **CURDY** coagulated; (lemon-, tofu curd)
CURED healed; remedied; preserved
CURER healer; (fish, ham) (smoker)
rl **CURIA** Vatican papal court
me **CURIE** unit of radiation
CURIO rare bric-à-brac
CURLY wavy; sinous; twisty
zo **CURRE** golden-eye duck
CURRY to dress leather; thrash
ck **CURRY** Indian spiced dish
CURSE anathema; execrate; maledict
CURST tormented; plagued
CURVE turn; bend; inflict
me **CUSEC** cubic flow per second
CUSHY easy and well-paid
bt **CUTCH** catechu; couch grass
CUTER more cunning; sharper
bt **CUTIN** in plant cuticle
ga **CUT-IN** football; motoring; intrude
md **CUTIS** true skin
to **CUTTO** cuttoe; large knife
CUTTY short; curtailed; clay pipe
CUT-UP carved out; criticized adversely; distressed; (rough); high spin-shot (golf)
CUVEE blend of wine (Fr.)
bt **CYCAD** a palm
CYCLE period; age; era; circle
cp **CYCLE** series of repeating sequences
CYMAR CIMAR, SIMAR, scarf; loose dress
CYMRY Cymric; Welsh
CYNIC misanthrope; captious; morose
CZECH Bohemian; of Czech Republic

D

DACHA weekend villa (Rus.)
DADDY dadda; papa; father; (sugar-)
DAFFY stunt riding; aerial skiing; crazy
DAGON Philistine Fish-God
DAILY diurnal; quotidian
DAIRI (Japan) Mikado's palace
DAIRY milkshop; creamery
bt **DAISY** sometimes ox-eyed
zo **DAKER** corncrake; crake

DAKIR daker; dicker; half-a-score
rl **DALAI** Lama; Tibetan Priest-King
nm **DALER** a dalesman; coin dollar (Sw.)
DALLY sport; wanton; toy; dawdle
zo **DAMAN** coney; Syrian hyrax
bt **DAMAR** dammar; resin
DAMON and Pythias
DAMPS exhalations; humidity
DAMPY dejected; moist; humid
DANCE hop; caper; prance; pirouette
nt **DANDY** fop; beau; swell; coxcomb; ketch or yawl; sailship
mn **DANTY** broken coal
mu **DANZA** dance (It., Sp.)
el **DARAF** elastance unit
to **DARBY** plasterer's float
me **DARCY** permeability coefficients unit
DARED braved; ventured; presumed
nm **DARIC** gold coin of Darius
bt **DAROO** sycamore
ga **DARTS** target game (mini-javelins) (blow)
DASHY showy; ostentatious; gaudy
DATED of an era
cp **DATUM** something given
ck **DAUBE** braised meat in wine (Fr.)
DAUBY sticky; viscous; glutinous
DAUNT cow; appal; scare; intimidate
nt **DAVIT** ship's crane for lifeboats
DAYAK DYAK, river people (Borneo)
DAZED mazed; dazzled; bewildered
DEADS ore débris
DEALT (cards); trafficked; traded
DEARN mournful; lonely; solitary
DEARY a dear
DEATH demise; decease
DEBAG remove trousers forcibly
DEBAR ban; deny; prevent; stop
DEBIT due; arrears; liability
cp **DEBUG** de-program; error removal
cp **DEBUG** cleansing of vermin, microphone
DEBUS get off a bus
DEBUT first appearance
me, ps **DEBYE** unit of dipole moment
DECAY rot; putrify; wither
DECAY decline, decompose, disintegrate
cp **DECAY** decrease of voltage
nc **DECAY** transformation of radioactive nuclide
cf **DECEM-** DECIM, DECEN, of ten (prefixes)
DECOR of decorative effect
DECOY lure; ensnare; inveigle
DECRY censure; vilify; disparage
DEDAL daedal; intricate
DEEDE Devil (17th cent.)

DEEDY illustrious; active
DEFER delay; adjourn; postpone
DEIFY idolize; apotheosize
DEIGN condescend; vouchsafe
rl DEISM belief in a god
DEIST a free-thinking believer
rl DEITY god; divine providence
DEKKO reconnoitring inspection
DELAY dally; retard; impede
DELFT glazed earthenware (from Holland)
DELPH delf; pottery
go DELTA multiple river mouth; 4th letter (Gr.)
ae, gl DELTA (wing) alluvial deposits
DELVE dig; scoop; excavate
DEMIT release; resign
DEMOB demobilize
DEMON imp; goblin; devil; troll
DEMOS the common people
DEMUR pause; object; waver
DENIM twilled cotton goods
DENSE compact; close; solid
DEPOT depository; storehouse
DEPTH profundity; abyss
DERAY to disarrange
DERBY a race; a hat
DERIC pertaining to skin
cf, md, pl DERMA- of the skin
DERRY a prejudice (Aust.)
DETER prevent; restrain; dissuade
ga DEUCE the Devil; score; two; (cards) (tennis)
DEVIL imp; to drudge; Lucifer
DIAMB 2-iamb verse foot
rl DIANA moon-goddess; Artemis
DIARY journal; chronicle; record
pr DIAZO reproduction process paper
tc DIBIT 2 binary units of information
ck DICED cut in cubes; bookbinding decoration
DICER dice-player
cf, bt, pl DICHO- combining in two parts (-tomy)
DICKY open back-seat; apron; shirt-front
DICTA pronouncements
go DIDOT typographical measurement
DIDST (thou) did
zo DIDUS the dodo genus
ch, ps DIENE unsaturated hydrocarbons
DIGHT adorned; arrayed
cp, ma, pl DIGIT finger; toe; integer; data symbol
DIGUE water-advance-prevention seawall
DIKED banked; ditched
DILDO artificial penis

DILLY native bag (Aus.)
bt DILLY diligence; the daffodil
mn DILSH inferior-coal layer
ch DIMER 2-like-molecule-based species
DIMLY obscurely; vaguely
nm DINAR coin (Iran, Jordan, Yugoslavia)
DINED and wined, replete
rw DINER restaurant car
zo DINGO Australian dog
DINGY dull; sullied; squalid
DINIC dizzy; vertiginous
DINKY elegant; miniature
el DIODE thermionic valve; one-way circuit
DIOTA two-handled jar
DIPPY a little insane
DIPUS the jerboa
DIRGE elegy; requiem; lament
DIRTY foul; sordid; mean; paltry
DISCO recorded-music dancehall, discothèque
DISME a tithe; a tenth; a dime
mu DITAL guitar tuning key
DITCH moat; trench; rine, drain
DITTO the same again
DITTY refrain; sonnet; ode; lilt
DIVAN council; saloon; sofa; couch
DIVED plunged; fathomed; explored
zo DIVER a sea-bird; underwater descendant
DIVES the rich man in the Bible
DIVOT a piece of turf
DIVVY dividend; share; divide
DIXIE camp-kettle; Southern USA
DIZEN to dress gaudily
DJINN genie; demon; afrit
DO-ALL factotum
DOBBY a dotard; part of a loom
zo DODDY hornless cow
DODGE evade; avoid; shuffle
DODGY artful; tricky; risky
DOGAL of the Doge of Venice
DOGGO to be hidden; concealed
DOGGY fond of dogs
DOGMA tenet; doctrine; maxim
tx DOILY ornamented cake cloth
DOING performing; swindling
DOLCE softly, sweetly
DOLED (-out) (benefit money)
tv, ce DOLLY camera carriage; grommet (washer); hardwood block; corn-; tee marker (curling)
ck DOLMA rice-filled leaf
DOLOR dolour; grief; sorrow
ar DOMAL DOMED, upper vaulting
mu DOMRA Russian plucked instrument

ar **DOMUS** patrician's house (Roman)
DONAH coster's sweetheart
DONAT donet; grammar-book; primer
DONEE the recipient
DONNA my lady in Spain
ps **DONOR** giver; bestower; (blood); semi-conductor
DOPED drugged; covered with varnish
DOPER dauber; horse-doper
DOPEY slow-witted; dull
rd **DORAN** missile-tracking system
zo **DOREE** dory; golden-yellow fish
ar **DORIC** Greek architecture
DORMY unbeatable at golf
zo **DORSE** Baltic cod; coal-fish
DORSE reverse side
DOSED physicked; drenched
tx **DOSEL DOSER**, tapestry cloths
DOTAL referring to a dowry
DOTED loved; drivelled
DOTTY barmy; silly; deranged
DOUAR dowar; Arab camp
DOUAY a Bible edition
DOUBT distrust; indecision; demur
DOUCE dulce; sweet
DOUGH money; the kneadful
bt **DOURA** millet
DOUSE dowse; slacken suddenly; drench
DOWDY slovenly; untidy; slatternly
bd **DOWEL** a wooden pin; steel rod (stairs); slate; cramp
lw **DOWER** bequest (-house)
DOWLE fluff; downfibre
DOWNY feathery; filamentous; knowing
DOWRY wedding endowment for bride
DOWSE water-divining art
DOYEN senior member
DOZED snoozed; drowsed; slumbered
DOZEN apostolic number
DOZER nap taker
DOZER (bull-), earth mover, tractor
DRACO a constellation
DRAFF dregs; residue
DRAFT outline; sketch; prepare
DRAIL to trail; to draggle
el **DRAIN** empty; tap; a gutter; sewer; (brain-); transistor electrode
zo **DRAKE** male duck
DRAMA histrionic art; play
DRANK quaffed; caroused; imbibed
DRANT to drone; to drawl
DRAPE cover; array; deck

DRAWL lag; drag; drone
DRAWN hauled; sketched; eviscerated
DREAD awe; fear; apprehension
DREAM reverie; hallucination
DREAR bleak; dismal; gloomy
DREGS lees; draff; sediment
DRESS garb; guise; apparel
DREST DRESSED
DRIED aerified; parched; desiccated
DRIER desiccator; dryer
to, ga, gl **DRIFT** wander; intention; surface
go water; glacial; continental; meaning; float; (archery) (motor-racing)
zo, to **DRILL** cloth; ape; bore
DRILY dryly; sarcastically
to **D-RING** 'D'-shaped ring
DRINK potion; draught; absorb
DRIVE urge; impel; coerce; motivate; private access road; hit
cp **DRIVE** operate; pulsating circuit
DRIVE mechanical power transmitter
lw, hd **DROIT** ancient right; title
DROLL odd; rummy; whimsical
DROME racecourse; aerodrome
DRONE idler; hum; dawdle
mu, zo **DRONE** bagpipes' tone; male bee
DROOL salivate before eating; drivel (pleasure)
DROOP sag; fade; wilt; languish
md, ae **DROPS** small doses; gouts; pastilles (sweets); (rain) (ear/eye); guttae carvings; globular earrings
DROSS scum; dregs; scoria
DROVE has driven; led cattle
DROWN flood; drench; lose life
rl **DRUID** Celtic priest; bard
DRUNK crapulous; tipsy; quaffed
bt **DRUPE** a stone fruit
mn, rl **DRUSE** mining cavity; a sect
mn **DRUSY** having cavities
DRUXY partly decayed timber
DRYAD wood-nymph
bt **DRYAS** mountain avens
DRYER drier
DRYLY drily; insipidly; aridly
zo **DSOMO** zhomo; a hybrid
DUCAL with strawberry leaves; duke's
nm **DUCAT** Italian gold or silver
DUCHY a dukedom of land
DUDDY ragged; in tatters
DUKEY wheeled platform; inclined-road train
DULCE soft; sweet; douce
rl **DULIA** angel adoration (RC)
DULLY stupidly; inertly; languidly

bt **DULSE** edible seaweed
zo **DUMBA** fat-tailed sheep
mu **DUMKA DUMKY**, laments; songs
(Rus., Cz.)
cp **DUMMY** doll; (bridge); model for
practice
pb, to **DUMMY** mallet head; mason's
hammer
DUMPS low spirits; dejection
DUMPY short and thick
DUNCE dolt; dullard; booby
DUNCH punch; jolt; to gore
zo **DUNNE** the knot-sandpiper
DUNNY deaf; dull of apprehension
rl, ar **DUOMO** Italian cathedral
DUPED deluded; gulled; hoaxed
DUPER trickster; dodger; sharper
DUPLE double; twofold
rl **DURGA** wife of Siva
DURGY undersized; dwarf
bt **DURIO** Malay tree; (durian fruit)
DUROY corduroy; figured serge
bt **DURRA** molasses/sugar-source
sorghum grass
bt **DURRA** semi-tropical grain sorghum
DURST dared
bt, ck **DURUM** hard wheat for pasta
DUSKY swarthy; shady; dark; dim
DUSTY powdery
DUTCH of Holland; (go-) share
DUVET eiderdown; for bed or jacket
hd **DWALE** heretic; heraldic sable
bt **DWALE** the deadly nightshade
DWARF imp; pygmy; midget;
stunted
DWELL abide; reside; linger
DWELT stayed; tarried; sojourned
DWINE to pine; to fade
DYING moribund; expiring; demise
me **DYNAM** work unit

E

EAGER keen; ardent; avid; zealous
nm **EAGLE** (golf); 10-dollar; gold piece
zo **EAGLE** lectern; standard; erne; bird
EAGRE AIGRE, tidal bore (wave)
EARED having lugs (ears)
EARLY betimes; before usual
EARST ERST, formerly
el **EARTH** world; soil; humus; ground;
base; end of flow
EASED allayed; soothed; assuaged
EASEL canvas carrier
EASLE hot ashes (Sc.)
EATEN masticated; corroded
EATER consumer; devourer

ar **EAVES** overhanging roof-edges
EBBED waned; receded; declined
EBLIS a djinn; evil spirit
bt **EBONY** black wood
rl **ECHAL** synagogue cupboard for ark,
law
ECLAT splendour; brilliance;
panache
ECTAL ectad; outer; external
EDDER top binding of a hedge
md **EDEMA OEDEMA**, dropsy;
waterlogged body
EDGED keen; bordered; fringed
EDGES curving; skating technique
EDICT ukase; decree; order
EDIFY uplift; enlighten; instruct
EDILE Roman magistrate
EDUCE elicit; draw; extract
EDUCT deduction
EERIE eirie; uncanny; weird
EGEST throw out; eject; cast
zo **EGGAR** egger; silkworm moth
EGGED incited; urged; impelled
EGGER an egg collector; inciter
zo **EGRET** heron
zo **EIDER** sea-duck
EIGHT twice four; figurative (ice-
skating)
EIGNE eldest son; first born (Sc.)
lw **EIGNE** entailed and inalienable
EIRIE eerie; weird; unaccountable
EJECT evict; expel; oust; emit
EKING prolonging
EKKER exercise (an old word)
ELAIN clarified oil or fat
zo **ELAND** antelope (S. Africa)
zo **ELAPS** venomous coral snake
ELATE exult; rouse; animate
pb **ELBOW** jostle; nudge; a bend; pipe-
fitting, gate-joint
ELCHI Turkish envoy
bt **ELDER** older; ancestor
ELECT cull; select; chosen
ELEGY dirge; threnody; lament
ELEVE pupil (Fr.)
ELFIN small elf; puckish; pixy
ELGIN (marbles)
ELIDE contract; curtail
ELITE the elect; very select
bt **ELMEN** made of elm
ELOGY EULOGY, funeral speech;
panegyric
ELOPE run away; abscond; decamp
ELUDE evade; baffle; escape
ELUTE cleanse; purify by washing
mn **ELVAN** Cornish rock; elvish
bt **ELVAS** prune; plum (Port.)
zo **ELVER** young eel

EMAGE area of text block in square ems
EMBAR prevent; bar; shut; stop
EMBAY to shelter; to landlock
EMBED to plant; enclose
EMBER glowing fuel
EMBOG engulf
EMBOW to arch; to vault
EMBOX encase; pack
EMBUS to put in a bus
EMEER Ameer; Emir
EMEND amend; rectify; correct
mn **EMERY** carborundum
EMOTE register emotion
EMPTY void; vacant; vacuous; inane
ENACT ordain; decree; authorize
ENATE growing out
ENDED finished; concluded; ceased
ENDER a finale; a cropper
END-ON abutting
ENDOR home of a witch
ENDOW endue; indue; endew
ENDUE grant; endow; invest
md **ENEMA** a clyster; rectal douche
ENEMY foe; rival; antagonist
ENGLE ANGLE, early English people
ENJOY relish; appreciate
ENMEW to put into; contain; cage
ENNUI weariness; boredom (Fr.)
ENODE jointless; knotless
ENROL list; enlist; chronicle
tx **ENSOR** levers net
ENSUE pursue; result; follow
ENTER invade; record; insert
ENTRY adit; inlet; portal; note
ENURE inure; accustom
ENVOY diplomat; postscript
ch **ENZYM** ENZYME, ferment yeast
rl **EOLIC** EOLUS, EOLIAN, AEOLIAN, god of the Winds
ch **EOSIN** red dye or ink
EPACT moon's age at new year
me **EPHAH** Hebrew bushel
rl **EPHOD** vestment; surplice
EPHOR Greek magistrate
EPOCH era; cycle; remarkable period
EPODE part of an ode
EPOPT an Eleusinian initiate
EPOXY oxygen fixed to 2 different atoms; epoxide resin
md **EPSOM** salts
EQUAL peer; competent; equable
EQUES Roman Knight
EQUIP rig; arm; accoutre; array
zo **EQUUS** the horse genus
cp **ERASE** delete; cancel; use null data
ERATO Muse of lyric poetry
ERECT build; upright; vertical

cf, pc **-ERGIC** of work, function, purpose
pc **-ERGIC** purposive; of innate drive
el **ERGON** quantum of oscillator energy
bt **ERGOT** parasitical fungus
bt **ERICA** the heath genus
lw **ERICK** a blood-fine (Irish)
ERODE eat away; corrode; consume
bt **EROSE** gnawed-looking (of leaves)
cf **EROTO-** of sexual love
ERRED strayed; sinned; wandered
cp **ERROR** mistake; fault; fallacy
bt, zo **ERUCA** the salad plant; a larva
ERUPT eject; eruct; burst forth
bt, ck **ERVUM** the lentil
gl **ESCAR** ESKER, glacial gravel ridge
ESCOT scot; an ancient tax
ESSAY discussion paper
ch **ESTER** ethereal salt
ESTOC short cavalry sword (Fr.)
lw **ESTOP** stop; bar; impede
go **ETANG** lake amid sanddunes (Fr.)
ETAPE stage point, esp. cycle races
ch **ETHER** upper air; volatile gas
ETHIC ethical; moral
ETHOS guiding spirit of a group or nation
ch **ETHYL** alcohol radical
mu **ETUDE** a composition (Fr.)
ETWEE étui; pocket-case
ga **EULER** jump (ice-skating); card-game
mt **EURUS** the East wind
EVADE elude; avoid; foil; dodge
EVENS fifty-fifty
cp **EVENT** incident; outcome; occurrence
EVERT turn inside out
EVERY all; each
EVICT eject; dislodge; dispossess
EVITE evade; avoid; shun
EVOKE arouse; excite; summon
EXACT precise; extort; mulct
EXALT raise; extol; magnify
EXCEL outvie; surpass; exceed
EXEAT a short leave
EXERT strive; try; endeavour
EXILE refugee; banish; proscribe
bt **EXINE** outer pollen-grain wall layer
EXIST be; live; endure; last
zo **EXITE** limb-lobe in arthropoda
lw **EX-LEX** outlaw
EXODE dramatic climax
EXPEL eject; dislodge; oust
EXTOL exalt; laud; glorify
EXTRA supernumeracy; additional
EXTRA- EXTRO-, outside of the usual
EXUDE ooze; percolate; sweat
EXULT crow; gloat; triumph

EYING watching; observing
EYRIE eagle's nest

F

FABLE myth; legend; allegory
bd **FACED** defied; confronted; covered
FACER opponent; a blow
FACET small polished surface
FACIA control panel; shop name-
board
FADDY crotchety; particular
rl **FAERY FAIRY**, elf
FAGIN beech mast; (Oliver Twist)
(Dickens)
mu **FAGOT FAGGOT**, bundle of sticks;
bassoon (It.)
bt **FAGUS** the beech tree
bt **FAHAM** Indian orchid
FAINT swoon; dim; indistinct
FAIRY FAERY, peri; elf; pixie
FAITH tenet; dogma; belief
FAKED spurious; counterfeit
FAKER forger; cheat; swindler
FAKIR monkish mendicant; magician
FALSE sham; erroneous; untrue
FAMED illustrious; renowned
FANCY whim; idea; caprice
md **FANGO** radioactive mud
el **FAN-IN** convergence; inputs to
circuit
nt **FANNY** messdeck kettle; underparts
(female)
rl **FANON** napkin; scarf
el, me **FARAD** unit of electrical capacity
ck **FARCE** hilarious comedy; parody;
travesty
ck **FARCE FARCI**, forcemeat; stuffed;
filled
FARCY glanders; equine malady
FARED fed; travelled; prospered
FARLE oatcake (Sc.)
rl **FARSE** biblical extract
FARSI PARSI (Persian) language
FASTI Roman calendar of festivals
FATAL lethal; baneful; ruinous
FATED doomed; destined
FATES Clotho, Lachesis & Atropos
FATTY adipose; pudgy; plump
rl **FATWA** Islamic edict
cp, el, ga, **FAULT** blemish; mistake; (blame)
gl misfunction (electric); tectonic
crust break; infringement of rules;
tennis; badminton
zo **FAUNA** animal life
FAUST a drama by Goethe
md **FAVUS** scalp disease

FEAST banquet; carousel; delight
FEAZE TEAZE, unravel (knots)
FECIT FACIT, maker (signature) (arts)
FED-UP disgruntled; browned off
FEEZE to twist; worry
FEIGN pretend; simulate; assume
ga **FEINT** stratagem; artifice; trick;
pretence; capillary break (fencing)
zo **FELID** one of the cat tribe
zo **FELIS** the cat tribe
FELIX the cartoon cat
FELLY felloe; part of rim of wheel
FELON criminal; miscreant; outlaw
FEMTO one thousand million
millionth 10⁻¹⁵
md, pl **FEMUR** thigh bone
bd **FENCE** receiver of stolen goods,
border; palisade; duel
FENDY shifty
FENKS finks; blubber refuse
FENNY marshy; swamp; boggy
lw **FEOFF** a fief; grant of land
zo **FERAE** wild animals
FERAL wild; deadly; funereal
me **FERMI** very short length unit
bt **FERNY** fernlike, covered with fern
nt **FERRY** river-crossing craft; transport
hd **FESSE** heraldic band
FESTA FIESTA, festival (Saint's day)
FETAL FOETAL, of the unborn;
embryonic
nv, mt **FETCH** bring; carry; storm distance;
wind
FETED partied; honoured; lionized
FETID noxious; stinking; noisome
FETOR offensive odour
lw, rl **FETWA FATWA**, judgement; sentence
(Arab)
lw **FEUAR** a lease-holder (Sc.)
md **FEVER** ardour; passion; (heated)
FEWER rather less
pl **FIBER** neuron; nerve tissue
FIBRE staple; cellulose; filament;
toughness
FICHE chit, official note form
FICHU small lace or muslin shawl
bt **FICUS** the fig
FIELD glebe; arable acre, (sports)
(racing)
cp **FIELD** (magnetic) stored data
FIEND imp; demon; monster; wretch
lw **FIERI** facias; a writ
FIERY ardent; fierce; igneous
mu **FIFED** fluted
FIFER fife-player
mu **FIFTH** ordinal of 5; harmonic
interval
FIFTY L

FIGHT fray; brawl; combat; contest
FILAR threadlike; filamentous
FILCH steal; pilfer; purloin
to **FILED FILER** (smoothed) (archivist)
zo **FILLY** girl-foal
FILMY diaphanous; see through
FILTH dirt; muck; impurity
FINAL last; ultimate; terminal
zo **FINCH** a passerine
FINED mulcted; amersed
FINER refiner; keener; smaller
lw **FINES** penalty payments; mechanical
   particles
FINIS the end; conclusion
FINOS merino wool
go **FIORD FJORD**, arm of the sea
   (Scand.)
FIRED discharged; kindled; sacked
FIRER an incendiary; igniter
bt **FIRRY** full of pines
FIRST chief; premier; primeval ·
go **FIRTH FRITH**, wide inlet, estuary
FISHY questionable; unreliable
FISTY of fisticuffs (fight)
zo **FITCH** pole-cat; fur-brush
bt **FITCH** vetch; chick-pea
FITLY aptly; properly; seemly
FITTE FYTTE, verse of a ballad
cp **FIT-UP** casing shutter, form work
nm **FIVER** £5 bank note
ga, vt **FIVES** wall ball game; horse disease
FIXED secured; placed; settled
FIXER builder, mason, fraudster
FLAFF flutter; be fussy
to **FLAIL** threshing whip; to skin (an
   animal)
FLAIR natural aptitude
FLAKE hurdle; hanging platform
nt **FLAKE** scale; lamina; to peel off
   (corn-); (snow-) hook bait
   (angling); coil a rope serpentine
   fashion
FLAKY FLAKEY, fissile
FLAME ardour; blaze; flare; lover
FLAMY FLAMEY, lambent
to **FLANG** miner's pick
FLANK side; border; touch (Am.
   football)
FLARE a signal light; glare
FLARE flame; dress spread; talent
FLARY flaming; flickering
el **FLASH** glint; sparkle; showy; mark;
   display (electric)
FLASK ampulla; vial; phial
ck **FLAWN** custard; pancake
FLAXY FLAXEN, hemp linen colour
FLEAD pork fat for lard
FLEAK a small lock

md **FLEAM** surgical knife
FLECK dapple; speckle; variegate
zo **FLECK** the flounder
nt **FLEET** a creek; swift; flotilla
FLESH mankind; to accustom
FLEWS bloodhound's chaps
ga **FLICK** flip; fleece; wound; lifting
   stroke (hockey); silent movie
bd **FLIER FLYER**, aeronaut; poster;
   shoring post
ga **FLIER FLYER**, fast mover; (high-);
   ball out of play
zo **FLIES** stage screens; (angling);
   (trouser fastening); insects
FLING hurl; dance; escapade
mn **FLINT** variety of quartz
FLIRT philander; coquet; flip
FLISK FRISK, comb; hand search;
   caper
nt, tx **FLOAT** drift; raft; buoy; weaving
   technique
bd **FLOAT** (procession); (cash); memory;
   WC ball valve
zo, wv **FLOCK** herd; multitude; unspun
   wool
FLONG stereotyping paper; brick
   made with moist paper and glue
FLOOD spate; downpour; deluge
FLOOK FLUKE, lucky shot
FLOOR stumping ground; nonplus;
   throw down
bt **FLORA** flowers collectively
bd, nt **FLORY** fleury; boat
FLOSS silklike; slag; dental debris
FLOUR ground grain meal
FLOUT scoff; mock; taunt; jeer
FLOWN flew; (high-) insolence;
   rotted
FLUFF make mistake; lint; unspun
   wool; girl
FLUID liquid; unsettled; gaseous
zo **FLUKE** parasite worm; (whale)
nt **FLUKE** (anchor); fortunate shot
FLUKE unaverage
FLUKY FLUKEY, accidentally
   fortunate
FLUME a water-chute
FLUMP plump down
FLUNG tossed; hurled; pitched
mn **FLUOR** calcium spar
pr **FLUSH** blush; poker term; level,
   even; margin
FLUSH chase out, surge; (hot-);
   (toilet)
nt, mu **FLUTE** kind of boat; wind
   instrument
FLYER FLIER, aviator; bird
FOAMY frothy; spumy

FOCAL converging
FOCUS point of convergence
mt FOEHN a hot wind in the Alps
FOGEY old-fashioned person
FOGGY obscure; hazy; indistinct
FOGLE silk handkerchief (slang)
rl FOISM Chinese Buddhism
FOIST impose; thrust; palm
md FOLIC acid in vitamin-B complex
FOLIO a sheet of paper; play; edition
FOLLY inanity; absurdity; fatuity
FOMES absorbent substance
tx FONDU colour blending in calico
ck FONDU cheese and wine dip (Swiss)
FORAY raid; inroad; sally; invasion
FORBY adjacent
cp FORCE power; energy; army; coerce;
   intervene
gl, go FORCE fors; foss; waterfall (Scand.)
FORDO undo; ruin; destroy
pr FOREL heavy parchment book cover
to FORET a drill
FORGE smithy; falsify; fabricate
FORGO renounce; go without
FORKY branching
pr FORME bed of type
mu, ga FORTE outstanding skill; loud;
   handguard of sword (fencing)
FORTH forward; onward; ahead
FORTY two score
FORUM tribunal; court; market-place
FORUM open discussion; public-
   speaking
zo FOSSA Malagasy civet cat
FOSSE ditch; moat; canal
FOUND to cast; establish; start
pr, cp FOUNT spring; well; source; type
md FOVEA pit; a pock mark; centre of
   vision in retina
FOXED baffled; deluded; yellow;
   damp stain
FOYER lobby; fire grate; (theatre
   interval)
FRACK FRECK, eager; bold; hale
FRAIL weak; infirm; rush basket
FRAME fashion; concoct; mood
ga, lw FRAME a game of snooker; unit of
   film; tv; display; (snooker) chassis
   surround; conspire; entrap; falsify
nm FRANC 100 centimes
zo FRANK candid; open; gannet
rl FRATE FRATER, brother; friar
rl FRATI friars; brethren
FRAUD guilt; imposture; deception
FREAK monstrosity; quirk; vagary
FREED emancipated; exempted
FREER deliverer; more lavish
FREMD strange; a stranger (Sc.)

FRESH novel; recent; unsalted; bold
FRETT ore refuse
rl FREYA wife of Odin
rl FRIAR FRIER, FRATE, wandering
   monk
ck FRIED simmered in fat
FRILL ruffle; border; mannerism
FRISK romp; search
FRITH FIRTH, estuary
ck FRITO FRITES, crisp potato (tortilla)
   mix
FRITZ a German
FRIZZ to curl; to crisp
FROCK smock; costume
bt FROND fern leaf
md FRONS part of skull
mt FRONT van; face; assurance; weather;
   cover; (war)
ag FROST (hoar-); rime; iciness; a
   failure
FROTH spume; foam; effervesce
FROWN glower; scowl
FROWY rank; musty
FROZE became ice; stopped still;
   acted coldly
bt, ck FRUIT produce; crop; issue
   (ripeness); offspring; edible plant
   seed flesh coating
FRUMP a joke; dowdy woman
FRUSH brittle; broken; thrush
FRYER a frying pan
bt FUCUS dye; disguise; seaweed
FUDER large wine cask (Moselle)
ck FUDGE fake; nonsense; sweetmeat
mu FUGAL like a fugue
mu, pc FUGUE polyphonic composition;
   escape from sanity
FULLY amply; entirely; completely
ck FUMET bone/veg. essence for sauce;
   deer dung
FUMID smoky; vaporous
bt FUNDI a West African grain
bt FUNGI mushrooms; toadstools, etc.
md FUNIS umbilical cord
FUNKY nervous; timid; cowardly
nt FUNNY droll; comical; boat
mu FUOCO with fire (It.)
zo FURCA forked structure
FUROR wave of enthusiasm
FURRY incrusted
FURZE gorse; whin
FURZY whinny; horse-call
FUSED melted; merged; blended
FUSEE vesuvian; firelock fuzee
FUSIL fusible; a musket
FUSSY fidgety; bustling
FUSTY musty; rank; mouldy
FUZED provided with a fuze

FUZEE fusee
FUZZY wooly; shaggy; blurred
FYTTE FITTE, verse of a ballad

G

ar **GABLE** roof/window construction
GADGE instrument of torture
zo **GADUS** the cod genus
GAFFE a social solecism
GAGED pledged; pawned; engaged
GAGER one who pawns his goods
GAILY gayly; blithely; lively
bd **GAIZE** friable sandstone
zo **GALAH** Australian cockatoo
ar **GALBE** elegant sweep; contour
bt **GALEA** helmet-shaped
tx **GALON** scalloped-edge narrow lace
mu **GALOP** lively round dance
mu **GAMBA** ancient cello
GAMMA letter (Gr.); radioactive ray
mu **GAMUT** range; scope; entire series;
    notes and scales
GANAT KANAT, QANAT, tunnelled cliff
    irrigation (Oman, Iran)
GANCH execution by throttling
    (Turk.)
mn **GANIL** limestone
GANJA Indian drink made of hemp
zo **GANZA** a wild goose
GAPED wide open; yawned
GAPPY crannied
ck **GARNI GARNISH,** addition of
    vegetables to a dish
GARNI bed and breakfast only
    (hotel)
GARTH Celtic fort; yard; fish-weir
mt, go **GARUA** winter precipitation mist in
    W. Peru
GARUM fish sauce
GASSY gaseous; aerated
GATED confined (school)
GAUDY garish; tawdry; flashy
rw, to **GAUGE** estimate; measure; track
    width; (rain)
mn **GAULT** clay
GAUMY dauby; smeary
GAUNT lean; lanky; emaciated
me **GAUSS** unit of magnetic intensity
tx **GAUZE** transparent fabric; bandage;
    mesh
GAUZY filmy
to **GAVEL** mason's hammer; mallet
GAVEL sheaf of corn
GAWKY awkward; ungainly; clumsy
zo **GAYAL** wild ox
GAYER merrier; brighter

GAZED looked intently
GAZER starer; rubber-neck
GEBUR neighbour (Ang. Sax.)
zo **GECKO** lizard
cp **GECOM** automatic computer code
zo **GEESE** plural of goose
gl, go **GEEST** heath; sandy region
    (glaciated)
GEIST ghost; (polter-) mental
    phantom
GELID cold to freezing
GEMEL twin; coupled vessels/bottles
bt **GEMMA** leaf-bud
GEMMY JEMMY, glittering; wood-
    pole
GENET civet-cat fur
cf **-GENIC** genetic; caused by genes;
    focus or origin
rl **GENIE GINIE,** Arabian apparition
GENII men of genius
ck, nt **GENOA** a cake; large jib-sail
gn **GENOM** gamete nucleus chromosome
    content
GENRE speciality (artistic)
zo **GENUS** group of a species
zo **GENYS** lower jaw in vertebrates
mn **GEODE** crystalline cavity
GEOID globe; shape of this earth
nm **GERAH** twentieth of a shekel
GESTE generous act of honour
GET-UP style of dress
GHAZI Arab fanatic; conqueror
GHOST spook; spectre; phantom
GHOUL a gruesome fiend
GHYLL goyal; ravine; gully
GIANT Cyclops; colossus; huge
ce **GIANT** monitor; nozzle; water gun
GIBED JIBED, taunted; jeered
GIBER JIBER, scoffer; joker; derider
bo, mt **GIBLI** hot sirocco wind (Libya)
GIBUS an opera hat
GIDDY dizzy; fickle; mutable
GIGOT leg of mutton (Fr.)
mu **GIMEL GYMEL,** vocal music
ga **GIMME** very short putt (golf)
GIPSY gypsy; zingaro; a Romany
GIRTH girdle; thong; cinch; tummy
    belt of horse; holds on saddle
GIVEN GIVER, conceded; bestowed;
    donor; granter
ck **GLACE** polished; sugar-surfaced
GLADE woodland avenue
GLAIR eggwhite; varnish
pl, pb **GLAND** a secretory organ; seal
pl **GLANS** the acorn of the penis
GLARE glower; frown; glitter
GLARY dazzling; lustrous
GLASS mirror; telescope; tumbler

GLAVE keylike halberd
GLAZE GLAZY lustre; burnish; shiny
zo **GLEAD GLEDE,** buzzard; kite
GLEAM ray; beam; glimmer; shine
GLEAN cull; collect; harvest
bt **GLEBA** spore-bearing tissue in truffles
rl **GLEBE** sod; church land
GLEED glowing ember
ga **GLEEK** three-handed card game
ga **GLIMA** ancient Icelandic wrestling .
GLINT gleam in the eye, or in a gem
GLOAM dusk; darkening
GLOAT exult; crow; revel
GLOBE orb; sphere; ball; earth
ck **GLOGG GLUGG,** spiced, mulled wine (Scan.)
bt **GLOME** globular head of flowers
GLOOM sadness; depression; darkness
GLORY exult; honour; renown
GLOSS comment; polish; veil
gl **GLOUP** subterranean blowhole; cave
GLOUT to be sulky
GLOVE gauntlet; mitten
GLOZE wheedle; flattery; adulation
GLUED stuck together; adhered
GLUER a user of mucilage
GLUEY adhesive; viscous; glutinous
bt **GLUME** husks
el **GLUON** hypothetical particle binding two quarks
ar **GLYPH** vertical fluting
GNARL snarl; growl; grumble
GNARR a knot in wood; a snag
GNASH to grind the teeth
GNOME dwarf; a maxim
bt **GOBBO** okra; a fruit
tx **GODET** dress gusset (flare); open cup
rl **GODLY** holy; pious; devout
GOETY black magic
GOFER gauffre; wafer; errand boy
GOING wending; faring; elapsing; road conditions
GOING horizontal nosings (stairs); departure
zo **GOLDY** goldfish
GOLLY exclamation
pl **GONAD** reproductive gland
zo **GONAL** forming a gonad
GONER irretrievably lost
GOODS chattels; effects
GOODY a sweet
GOOFY crazy stunt; goofy foot on skateboard (Disney dog)
to, zo **GOOSE** tailor's iron; poultry bird
GO-OUT sluice in embankment
GORAL indian antelope
GORED run through (bull-fighting); (tailoring)
go **GORGE** gulch; defile; gulp; cram; narrow canyon
bt **GORSE GORSEY,** ginst shrub
ck **GOUDA** a Dutch cheese
to **GOUGE** to scoop out; circular chisel
bt, ck **GOURD** pumpkin (as container)
md **GOUTY** acidic; oedemic swelling
bt **GOWAN** a daisy
GOYAL ghyll; kloof; coombe
GRACE adorn; embellish; favour
GRADE step; rank; slope; degree
GRAFF graft; ditch; moat
GRAFT intrigue; swindle; engraft
rl **GRAIL** Holy Grail; sacred chalice
bt, me **GRAIN** corn; response; flow; grist
to **GRAIP** dung-fork
go **GRAMA** pasture land (USA)
GRAME gram; misery
nm **GRAND** lordly; £1,000
GRAND granolithic screed; jointless cement floor
GRANT cede; confer; gift; largesse
bt **GRAPE** fruit of the vine
ma **GRAPH** a diagram showing related factors
GRASP clasp; clutch; hold; scope
bt **GRASS** herbage; pasture; to turf; to betray others
GRATE abrade; rasp; jar; fireplace
mu **GRAVE** solemn; engrave; tomb; slow tempo
ck **GRAVY** meat juice
ga **GRAZE** skim; browse; touch lightly; pre-attack (fencing)
GREAT eminent; bulky; huge
zo **GREBE** web-footed bird
GREED voracity; avidity; gluttony
GREEK Attic; Doric; Hellenic
ga **GREEN** raw; fresh; inexperienced; outdoor range (archery)
ga **GREEN** verdant; (village); (golf); (bowls); unbroken wave (surfing); ecology party supporter
GREET hail; welcome; greit (Sc.)
GREYS cavalry regiment
bt **GRIAS** species of pear
zo **GRICE** young wild boar
GRIDE GRYDE, to grate
GRIEF woe; anguish; mishap
gl **GRIKE** limestone-rock fissure
GRILL broil; grid-iron; question
GRIME dirt; soil; sully; befoul
GRIMY filthy; smutty; unclean
GRIND abrade; pulverize; sharpen
GRIPE grasp; squeeze; ditch
GRIST corn for milling; provision

ck **GRITS** coarse oatmeal porridge
GRIZE grece; grees; staircase
GROAN moan; complain; grumble
nm **GROAT** Joey; fourpenny piece
GROCK a kindly clown
ar, ce **GROIN** breakwater; under abdomen; intersection edge (vault)
GROOM syce; equerry; bridegroom
GROPE search by feeling
me **GROSS** coarse; 12 dozen
cp **GROUP** clump; cluster; arrange; index reference
tc **GROUP** multiple channels on one path
cp **GROUP** sequence of data storage stations
GROUT coarse meal; mortar
GROVE wood; thicket; spinney
GROWL snarl; grumble; complain
GROWN raised; waxed; extended
ck **GRUEL** thin porridge
GRUFF surly; rude; churlish
GRUNT snort like a pig
GRYDE gride; grate
bt **GUACO** plant; snake-bite antidote
GUANO bird's manure
GUARD shield; watch; bulwark
cp **GUARD** fire-; safety barrier between circuits; protect; soldier; linesmen; vigilante
bt **GUAVA** pear-shaped fruit
GUESS surmise; conjecture; divine
GUEST visitor; lodger
nt **GUFAH** GOPHER, reeds for Ra ships
cp **GUIDE** pilot; signpost; control; -line; edge; information
GUILD trade's union; fraternity
GUILE craft; duplicity; cunning
lw **GUILT** proof or sense of wrong
mu **GUIRD** Cuban instrument
GUISE garb; aspect; manner
GULCH gully; gorge; ravine
hd **GULES** heraldic red
GULFY full of whirlpools
GULIX fine linen (Dutch)
GULLY water-worn channel; (cricket); rift between rocks (mountaineering)
ck, ga **GUMBO** a stew; okra soup; muddy course; (horse racing)
GUMMY viscous, sticky
GURRY fish offal; Indian fortress
mu **GUSLA** GUSLI, Slavonic zither
GUSTO zest; relish; enjoyment
GUSTY squally; stormy; puffy
GUTSY deep voice; of the intestine; greedy
ar **GUTTA** Doric ornament; drop

GUTTY old type golf ball
GUYED mocked; ridiculed; derided
gl, go **GUYOT** submarine mountain
zo **GYALL** gayal; jungle bull
nt **GYBED** (a sailing manoeuvre)
zo **GYGIS** tern genus (water birds)
mu **GYMEL GIMEL**, 14th C. vocal music
GYPSY GIPSY, zingaro; Romany
GYRAL revolving; whirling
hd **GYRON** heraldic device
md **GYRUS** convolution of the brain

H

HABIT dress; usage; wont; custom
rl **HADES** the abode of the dead
rl **HADJI HAJJI**, pilgrim (Arab)
cf, pl **HAEMA- HAEMO-**, concerning the blood (Gr.)
HAFIZ knowledge of the Koran
HAIRY furry
HAJIB Moslem court chamberlain
HAKIM wise man; physician (Arab)
HALED hauled; dragged along
bt **HALFA** esparto grass
HALLO! hello! hillo!
HALMA a board game of leapfrogging
ck **HALVA** ground sesame sweetmeat
HALVE bisect; divide
HAMAL porter (Turk.)
HAMAM Turkish bath
HANAP pewter goblet
HANDY near; dexterous; adroit
HANIF orthodox Moslem
HANKY handkerchief
HANSA of North German mercantile league, Hanseatic
cf **HAPLO-** single; simple (Gr.)
HAPLY perchance; peradventure
HAPPY joyous; lucky; opportune
rl **HARAM** the inviolable, Islam
HARDS HURDS, refuse of flax, cornstems etc.
HARDY bold; intrepid; robust
HARED sprinted; sped; ran
bd **HAREM** seraglio; zenana; ladies' quarters
bt, tx **HARLE HARL**, flax fibre
zo **HARPY** fabulous monster; vulture
zo **HARPY** golden eagle; extortioner
HARRY harass; ravage; raid
HARSH raucous; strident; caustic
HASTE alacrity; speed; hustle
HASTY swift; reckless; headlong
HATCH to plot; doorway; to shade
HATED loathed; abominated

HATER abhorrer; detester
zo HATHI wild Indian elephants
HATTO bishop eaten by rats
bt HAULM halm; stubble (harvest); stem
HAUNT frequent; importune; resort
HAURL harl; rough-cast
HAUSA Northern Nigerian
HAVEN port; refuge; asylum
HAVER to drivel; blather
HAVOC waste; carnage; devastation
nt HAWSE bow anchor pipe
bt, ck HAZEL a colour; nut-tree; nut
ga HAZER steer riding, wrestling for cowboys (rodeo)
nt HEADS or tails; toilets (bows); chief; source; foam; endpoint; tool edge
HEADY rash; hasty; wilful; intoxicating
HEALD warp guide in a loom
HEARD listened to; tried
HEART core; centre; spirit
go HEATH heather- or ling-covered acid soil or scrubland
ga HEATS preliminary qualifying races
nt, gl HEAVE to raise; push; haul; (rock strata)
HEAVY weighty, serious, ponderous, of gravity, massive
cf, me HECTO- multiplied by 100; of units (Gr.)
HEDGE lay off; enclose; fence
pc HEDGE guarded reservation (speech)
HEFTY heavy; strong; powerful
HEIGH! exclamation
HEKIM judge (Arab.)
HELIO a heliograph
zo HELIX screwthread form; snail
HELLO! hallo! hillo! hollo!
HELOT Spartan slave; serf
ag HELVE axe-handle; haft; shaft
HEMAL HAEMAL, concerning blood
HE-MAN virile; butch
HEMPY like hemp
HENCE henceforth; away; therefore
bd HENCH chimney shaft side
bt HENNA a dye; a shrub
me HENRY electrical induction unit
ch HEPAR a sulphur compound
HERBY herbaceous; herbous
HEROD a tyrant
zo HERON a wading bird
HERSE a portcullis
me, tc HERTZ unit of signals frequency
HERUT political party (Israel)
HET-UP hot and bothered, aroused
bt HEVEA rubber-tree
HEWED axed; hacked; fashioned

HEWER cutter; sculptor; miner
HIDER one who conceals
HIKED HIKER, tramped as rambler
go HILLY undulating
bt HILUM the eye of a bean
HINDI Indian dialect
rl HINDU practiser of Ind. religion
HINGE depend; turn; hang
zo HINNY whinny; a mule; mule call
cf, zo, go HIPPO- (horse) (of rivers) (-potamus)
HIRED chartered; leased; rented
HIRER an employer of labour
cf, pl HISTO- of tissue (Gr.)
HITCH fasten; catch; obstacle; knot; (baseball)
HITHE HYTHE, haven; port
HIVED bees accommodated; stored
HIVER a bee keeper, apiarist
md HIVES bee homes; nettle-rash; croup
HOARD amass; garner; save; secrete
HOARY venerable; ancient; silvery
zo HOBBY recreation; horse; falcon
HOBIT mortar; short gun
mu HOBOY HAUTBOIS, the oboe; (high) woodwind
HOCUS (-pocus); to cheat; drug; conjure
HODGE codged; a rustic
HOGAN hooch; a strong liquor
to HOIST heave; elevate; pulley
HOLEY holed; riddled
bt HOLLY an evergreen
cf HOMEO- of sameness (Gr.) (-pathy)
zo HOMER homing pigeon; boomerang
HOMER guide signal arrangement; home run (baseball)
mu HONDO sad Andalusian song (Sp.)
HONED whetted; sharpened
HONEY sweetness
HOOCH fire-water
HOOEY HOO HA, balderdash; nonsense
HOOKA hookah; narghile; hubble-bubble pipe
HOOKY full of barbs
ck HOOSH a stew; a mixture
vt HOOVE a cattle disease
HOPED desired; anticipated
HOPPY flavoured with hops
HORAL horary; hourly
HORDE clan; throng; gang; crew
HORNY callous; spikey; lustful
zo HORSE steed; palfrey; nag; cob
HORSE cavalry; flogging frame
HORSY HORSEY, equuscentric
HORUS son of Osiris (Egypt)
HOSED drenched; watered

HOTEL inn; tavern; hostel
HOTLY eagerly; ardently; fervidly
HOUGH hamstring; the ham
zo **HOUND** pursue; chase; hunting dog
HOURI a nymph of paradise; peri
HOUSE mansion; domicile; lineage;
(curling)
HOVEL shelter; hut; cabin; shed
HOVER hang; vacillate; wave
to **HOWEL** barrel maker's tool
HOWSO howsoever; although
HUBBY husband
HUFFY petulant; irritable
HULCH hunch; bump; bunch
HULKY unwieldy; clumsy
HULLO! hallo!
HULLY husky
HUMAN mortal; cosmic; rational
hd **HUMET** abbreviated fesse
HUMIC wet; dank; mouldy
HUMID damp; moist
md **HUMOR** bodily fluid (eye)
HUMPH! exclamation of
dissatisfaction
HUMPY Australian native hut
HUMUS decomposed organic soil
enrichment
ck **HUMUS** chick pea/garlic puree
HUNCH presentiment; hump; lump
HUNKS miser; niggard
HUNKY rugged masculine physique
zo **HUNYA** fighting rams
HURDS hards; flax refuse
HURLY confusion; flurry (-burly)
HURRY hasten; expedite; speed
HURST a grove; a wood
zo **HUSKY** Canadian sled-dog
HUSKY hoarse; raucous; guttural
HUSSY housewife; brazen girl
HUTCH coop; (chicken-); bin
HUZZA Bravo; Hurrah!
as **HYADS HYADES**, cluster of stars
HYDRA water monster; source of
trouble
HYDRO a spa; a hotel
cf, md **HYDRO-** of water; spa (Gr.)
zo **HYENA** a carnivore (2nd hand)
nt **HYLAM** form of junk (Thailand)
HYLEG ruling planet in horoscope
HYLIC materialistic
rl **HYMEN** God of Marriage
pl **HYMEN** maidenhead; vaginal
membrane
md **HYOID** tongue-bone
cf **HYPER-** above normal; excessive
(Gr.)
HYPHA a fungus filament
zo **HYRAX** rock-rabbit; cony

bt **HYSON** green tea (China)
HYTHE HITHE, haven; port

———

I

cf, md **-IASIS** abnormal; diseased (Gr.)
cf, pc, md **-IATRO -IATRY**, of healing (Gr.)
ICENI Ancient British tribe
md **ICHOR** a god's blood; a fluid
ICIER ICILY, colder; frostily; frigidly
ck **ICING** a sugar-coating
cf, pc **ICTAL-** of transitory emotions (Gr.)
ICTIC abrupt; sudden
ICTUS a stroke; accentuation
IDEAL Utopian; fanciful; visionary
cf, pc **ID-EGO-** single but divided entity
(Gr.)
IDIOM lingo; peculiar phraseology
IDIOT moron; subnormal; foolish
person
IDIST Ido linguist
IDLED IDLER, slacked; lounger; drone
IDOLA fantasies; apparitions
IDOSE monosaccharide
IDRIS mythical Welsh giant; (water)
IDYLL pastoral poem of ideal dreams
IGLOO Eskimo snow-hut
md **ILEAC ILEUM, ILEUS**, of intestine;
colic
md **ILEUM** (intestine)
md **ILEUS** intestinal obstruction, colic
ILIAC pertaining to loins
ILIAD epic poem; (siege of Troy)
md **ILIUM** part of hip-bone
gl **ILLAM** gem-bearing Sri L. gravel
cp **IMAGE** ikon; idol; copy; likeness
(mirror) stored (public relations)
zo **IMAGO** perfect state of insect
mt **IMBAT** cool Near-Eastern wind
zo **IMBER** the great northern diver
IMBOW to arch
IMBUE dye; steep; stain; permeate
ch **IMIDE** acid anhydride compound
IMPEL urge; drive; incite; actuate
IMPEN to pen; to write
IMPLY mean; hint; signify; involve
bt **INAJA** Brazilian palm
INANE fatuous; empty; void; vapid
INAPT unfit; inapposite; clumsy
INARM to encircle
mn **INBYE** mine direction
INCOG incognito; disguised
lw **INCUR** (debt); become liable for;
arouse
md **INCUS** ear-bone like an anvil
pr **INCUT** inset; side note let into text
INDEX pointer; forefinger; exponent

INDRA Hindu God of Rain
zo **INDRI** babakoto; large lemur
INEPT inane; futile; pointless
bt **INERM** without prickles
INERT slack; dull; torpid; inactive
INEYE to graft
INFER deduce; gather; surmise
cp **INFIX** implant; ingraft; instil;
    notational graft
cf **INFRA-** below; inferior; (-red); (Gr.)
ar, bd **INGLE** fireside; (nook); (seat)
mn **INGOT** lump of gold, metal
md, pl **INION** the nape of the neck; occiput
INKER recording device
INKLE broad linen tape
INKOS Zulu chief
lw **IN-LAW** of spouse's relatives
INLAY (buhl) tesselate
cp, el, go, **INLET** bay; bight; creek; entrance;
ro   intake opening; valve
INNER interior; within; (mind);
    (soul); central
tc, el **INPUT** capital investment; charge;
    work done
cp **INPUT** program; data signal fed in
ga **IN-RUN** pre ski-jump start
INSET an insertion; implant
INTER bury; inhume; entomb
cf **INTER-** (-national) (-racial)
    combined
INUIT an Eskimo
bt **INULA** herb
INURE harden; toughen; train
INURN bury; entomb
zo **INUUS** Barbary ape (Gibraltar)
INVAR an alloy of nickel and steel
INWIT intuition; conscience
ch, md **IODAL IODIC,** containing iodine
ar **IONIC** of IONIA (Asia Minor)
lw **IRADE** Turkish written decree
IRAQI IRAKI, dwellers in Iraq
IRATE wroth; ireful; angry; incensed
IRENE Roman goddess of peace
md **IRIAN** relating to the iris
IRISH Hibernian
mn **IRITE** an iridium compound
IRKED bored; wearied; jaded
fr **IROKO** African utility timber
ch **IRONE** smell constituent of violets
IRONS prisoners' chains; golf clubs
IRONY satire; sarcasm; mockery
ISIAC referring to Isis
rl **ISLAM** (Mohammedanism)
    submission to Allah
ISLET isle; eyot; atoll
pr **ISSUE** outcome; result; publication;
    vent
bt **ISTLE IXTLE,** aloe fibre

ITCHY scratchy; desirous; uneasy
zo **IVORY** dentine; elephant tusk
IVRIT modernized Hebrew
    (language)
IXION wheel-bound king; (Hell)
zo **IZARD** Pyrenean ibex or chamois

J

go **JABAL JEBAL, JIBAL** (Arab)
    mountain, Gibraltar (Jabal Tariq)
JABOT lace frill; neck ruffle
JACKS wooden wedges
JADED weary; tired; fagged;
    exhausted
tx **JADOO** artificial silk
bt, ck **JAFFA** orange (type)
zo **JAGER** the great skua; pirate gull
JAGGY uneven; serrated; notched
bt, md **JALAP** a cathartic root
JAMBE a part of leg armour
bt **JAMBU** rose apple tree
JAMES a flunkey
JAMMY smothered in jam
JANTU Indian water-raising device
JANTY jaunty; airy; showy
JANUS god of doorways
JAPAN varnish; lacquer; enamel
vt **JARDE** tumour on a horse's leg
JASEY worsted wig
mn **JASPE** veined jaspar
JAUNT trip; outing; excursion
JAWED talked; lectured
tx **JEANS** overalls; denim trousers
rl **JEHAD JIHAD,** Islamic Holy War
ck **JELLY** gelatin; aspic (-fish) (wobble)
to **JEMMY** gemmy; spruce; lever
JENNY spinning machine; billiard
    shot
JERID Turkish javelin
JERKY spasmodic; convulsive;
    irregular
ck **JERKY** beef biltong
JERRY a German; (chamber) -night-
    pot
rl **JESSE** candlestick; stained window
nt **JETTY** jut; projection; a pier
JEWEL gem; trinket
JEWRY Judaea; the Jews
go **JHEEL** Indian marsh
JHOOM jungle cultivation
nt **JIBED** gibed; sneered; taunted
JIFFY a moment; an instant
to **JIMMY** jemmy; a lever for break-ins
rw **JINTY** locomotive type
JINGO ultra-militarist; nationalist
JINKS high jinks; merry-making

JIPPO jupon; vest

zo JOCKO a chimpanzee

cp JOINT splice; seam; united;
concerted

ck JOINT meat roast; marijuana
'cigarette'

bd JOIST log or plank supporting floor/
roof

JOKED JOKER, jested; wag; humanist

nt JOLLY mirthful; cheerful; (-boat)

JONAH bad luck bringer

tx JORIA East Indian wool

JOTUN Norse giant

JOUGS iron neck-ring; pillory

me JOULE electrical unit of work

JOUST tilt; encounter; tournament
(knights)

bt JUDAS traitor; spy-hole; tree

lw JUDGE decide; arbiter; critic

pl JUGAL malar; (cheek-bone)

bt JUGUM pair of opposite leaves

JUICE sap; fluid extract; petrol

JUICY succulent; moist; lush

ck JULAP JULEP, cordial cocktail (Am.)

zo JULIS a wrasse; a small fish

zo,bt JULUS IULUS, catkin; wire-worm

mo JUMAR movable clamp on rope

zo JUMBO elephant; locomotive;
airliner (jet); drill carriage

JUMPS nervous apprehension;
obstacle (horse racing)

zo JUNCO North American snow-bird

JUNTA cabal; govt. by rebel clique

JUNTO coterie; clique; faction

JUPON jippo; surcoat; petticoat

lw JURAL legal; lawful

lw JURAT an alderman; (affidavit)

lw JUROR a juryman

tx JUSSI Manila textile fabric

JUTES people of Jutland (Danes)

cf JUXTA- (-position) (in front or
behind)

K

rl KAABA sacred stone in Mecca

zo KAAMA hartebeest; S. Afr. antelope

KADIR (cup for pig-sticking)

nt KAFIR Turkish/Greek lateen ship

zo KALAN sea otter of North Pacific

rl KALIF Calif; Caliph; ruler of Islam

rl KALPA calpa; a day of Brahma

mn,go,gl KAMES glacial deposits

KAMIS Eastern tunic

KANAT ancient tunnel network
(irrigation) (Oman)

me KANDY S. Indian weight

me KANEH CANEH, 6 cubits (Hebrew)

bt,ck KANYA Afr. shea tree; its butter

bt,tx KAPOK fibre of silk-cotton tree

fr KAPUR Indonesian wood

KARMA destiny based on each
incarnation

me KAROB 24th part of a grain

go KAROO South African plateau

fr KARRI dense Australian wood; tree

gl,go KARST limestone caves (Yugoslavia)

cf,pl KARYO- nucleus (Gr.)

tx KASHA dress material

ck KASHA cracked-buckwheat meal
(Rus.)

KASHI enamelled Islamic tiles
(Persia, India)

bt,ck KASSA catechu made from betel-nut

bt KAURI New Zealand fir tree

nt KAYAK covered seal-skin canoe
(Eskimo)

ga KAYLE ninepin; skittle

mu KAZOO children's 'hum' instrument

ck KEBAB meat dish (Turk.)

bt KECKS fool's parsley

nt KEDGE small anchor; using anchor
rope to move boat (sailing)

KEDGE KEDGY, brisk; lively; happy

KEEPS permanent possession

mn KEESH carburet of iron

ck KEEVE vat; fermenting tub

ck KEFIR fermented milk

tx KELAT short springy Asian wool

mn KELLY top pipe of drill string;
Manxman

KEMPO martial art (China)

KEMPS the plantain

KENDO swordsmanship (Japan)

ps,nc KERMA kinetic movement energy
released in matter

KERNE Irish foot-soldier; boor

nt KETCH two-masted vessel

ch KETEN colourless gas

nt KEVEL belaying pin

zo KEVEL young gazelle

cr,jn KEYED wedged; beam; (typewriter);
solvable; tensed

tc KEYER frequency-change device

KHAKI olive-drab; army uniform
colour

KHEDA elephant enclosure

KHMER people and language
(Cambodia)

zo KIANG Tibetan wild horse

KIBED chapped with cold

zo KIDDY youngster; goatling

KIDEL KIDDLE, fish-trap

KIDGE brisk; pot bellied

KILEY KYLEY, boomerang

KILIM woven carpet without pile (Turk.)
KINGS two biblical books; monarchs
KINKY crotchety; entangled; bizarre; unconventional
to KINSH stone-mason's lever
ar KIOSK covered stall; booth (telephone); open pavilion (Moslem)
zo, ga KITTY kitten; common cash; jack (bowls)
mu KLANG complex musical tone
KLICK click
KLONG canal; waterway; floating market (Thai)
go KLOOF S. African ravine
KLOPS German meatballs
KNACK skill; dexterity; faculty
KNARL gnarl; a knot in wood
bt KNAUR swollen tree-trunk outgrowth
KNAVE rascal; rogue; caitiff
KNEAD mix; blend; incorporate
KNEED (baggy-); (knock-)
KNEEL bend knee, submit; (prayer)
KNELL toll; ring; sound; (bells)
KNEPH an Egyptian deity
to KNIFE to stab; to lance; blade (cut)
KNOCK rap; beat; buffet
KNOLL knell; hillock; mound
KNOSP ornamental flower-bud
KNOTE (rope-making)
zo KNOUD the grey gurnard
KNOUT Russian whip
KNOWN understood; recognized
tx KNUBS waste silk
KNURL knob; milled edge
KNURR knot in wood
zo KOALA Australian bear
nt KOBIL cobble; small boat
ck KOFTE KOFTA, meat rissole
zo KOKOB venomous serpent
bt KOKRA wood used for flutes
nt KOLEH racing canoe (Malay)
KONDO bronze-gilt finish
nm KOPEC KOPEK, Russian farthing
go KOPJE S. African hillock
KORAN Moslem Sacred Book
nt KOTIA Indian dhow
KOWTOW kow-tow; make obeisance
KRAAL native village
zo KRAIT venomous snake
KRANG KRENG, whale flesh
zo KRILL plankton; whale food
nm KRONA KRONE, Scandinavian coin
KUDOS credit; prestige; fame
KUFIC early Arab alphabet
KUKRI Gurkha knife

KULAK Russian peasant proprietor
bt KUNDA lawyer-vine
KVASS Russian beer
KWELA tin whistle (African)
KYACK American pack saddle
KYLEY kiley; boomerang
KYLIN Chinese or Japanese dragon
KYLIX Greek drinking vessel
zo KYLOE Hebridean cattle
KYOTO Japanese pottery
bt KYPOO extract of catechu; (couch grass)
rl, mu KYRIE orthodox Mass (response)
KYUDO mounted archers (Japan)

L

LABBA S. Am. guinea-pig
hd LABEL badge. adhesive sticker; address tag
cp LABEL coded information signal
bt, pl LABIA lips of orifice
rl LABIS cochlear; eucharistic spoon
LACED twined; stiffened; (straight)
cp LACED fortified drink; final punched card
tx LACET lace-work
LACIS filet lace; network
LADAS a classic runner
LADED LADEN, loaded; burdened (freight)
LADIN Swiss Latin
LADLE scoop; bale; dole
lw LAGAN LIGAN, (flotsam)
ck LAGER light beer; storage area
gl LAHAR volcanic mud avalanche
tx LAINE woollen fabric
LAIRD Scottish landowner
LAITY laymen
LAKIN ladykin; small damsel
LAMED crippled
LAMIA sorceress; witch
LAMMY sailor's quilted jumper
LANCE lancet; spear; pierce
go LANDE sterile tract (Fr.)
LANKY lean; tall; gaunt
nt LANTY lightbuoy to aid navigation
LAPEL upper folds on face of a coat
mn, tx LAPIS stone; (calico-printing)
LAPSE slip; slide; indiscretion
bt LARCH species of trees; softwood; tamarack (USA)
ck LARDY full of lard; (-cake)
LARES Roman household gods
mu LARGE massive; bulky; copious; longest note
mu LARGO slowly

LARKY sportive; frolicsome

to **LARRY** mortar-mixing tool

LARUM alarm

LARUS aquatic bird

zo **LARVA** caterpillar; grub; maggot

md **LASER** resin; searing ray

LASSO rope with running noose

mu **LASSU** slow section of a csardas Hung. dance

jn **LATCH** catch; fasten (door); attach oneself; comprehend

LATER tardier; more recent

bt **LATEX** sap; untreated rubber

to **LATHE** county division; machine

LATHI bamboo cudgel

LATHY thin; long and slender

LATIN Roman; of Latinium; tongue

rl, mu **LAUDA LAUDE**, religious praise, concert poems

rl **LAUDS** liturgical office after matins; praises

LAUGH guffaw with mirth; (-at) deride

LAUTA royal Inca badge

LAVED washed; bathed

LAVER brazen washing basin

bt **LAVER** edible seaweed

LAXLY loosely; slackly; remissly

LAY-BY halting place beside road

zo **LAYER** seam; stratum; bed; hen

LAY-IN maternity; extended sleep

ga **LAY-UP** shot near basket (b-ball)

LAZAR leper

LAZED idled; reposed

LEACH to wash by percolation

LEADY leaden

LEAFY leavy; full of leaves

LEAKY not watertight; tattling

LEANT inclined; reposed; trusted

LEAPT jumped; sprang

LEARN acquire; hear; memorize

LEARY old mine-shaft

LEASE let; hire; tenure

LEASH three; bind; thong

LEAST smallest; minutest

LEAVE forsake; quit; depart

LEAVY leafy

LEDGE shelf; ridge; layer

LEDGY full of ridges

nt, zo **LEECH** blood-sucker; hanger-on; (limpet); leecher (doctor); sail

nt **LEECH** edge of a sail

LEERY sly

lw **LEGAL** lawful; licit; proper; correct

LEGER a race; light; small

LEGGY lanky

LEG-IT proceed on foot; walk; hike

mu **LEGNO** wood (It.), drumstick

LEMAN lover; gallant; paramour

bt, ma **LEMMA** grass glume; subsidiary theorem

LEMMA summary preceding a tome

cf **-LEMMA-** of subsidiary theorem; (true data logic)

bt, ck **LEMON** citrus fruit; the answer

zo **LEMUR** ghost; nocturnal monkey

LENCA Honduran Indian

mu **LENTO** slowly

LEPER lazar

LEPID jocose; pleasant

zo **LEPIS** a scale

md **LEPRA** leprosy

cf, md **-LEPSI** of seizure, collapse (Gr.)

nm **LEPTA** (Greece)

cf, md **LEPTO-** small, thin, fine, weak (Gr.)

mt **LESTE** dry African South wind

LETCH to separate by percolation

LETHE the river of oblivion

LET-IN admission; note added to text

LET-UP an alleviation

cf, md **LEUKO-** white; (blood); colourless

ch **LEVAN** polymerized grass fructose

LEVEE embankment; reception

LEVEL raze; plane; even; flush; grade

to **LEVER** a jemmy; prise

LEWIS masonry grip; machine gun

bt **LIANA LIANE**, tropical climbing plant

me **LIANG** Chinese ounce

LIART LIARD, LYART, dapple-grey

lw **LIBEL** slander; defame; traduce

LIBER bast; inner bark; a book

LIBRA the Balance (Zodiac)

LICIT lawful; permissible

mt **LIDAR** cloud pattern detector

LIEGE one bound by oath

LIFER prisoner sentenced for life

lw **LIGAN** lagan; (flotsam)

mu **LIGHT** kindle; illume; buoyant; easy; featherweight; music

hr **LIGNE** watch-movement measure unit

LIKED enjoyed; relished

LIKEN to compare

LIKIN Chinese transport duty

bt **LILAC** a colour; a shrub

LIMBO hell; paradise of fools

LIMED cemented; ensnared; treated

pc **LIMEN** threshold

LIMER fibre brush for limewashing

LIMIT restraint; bound; border

mu **LIMMA** a semitone

LINCH ledge; projection; cliff

LINED care-worn; with lines

tx **LINEN** flax cloth; underwear; bed sheets

nt **LINER** a shim; a vessel; layer of paint
LINGO speech; language
wv **LINGO** jacquard harness weight
LINGY active; limber; heathery
LININ (cell nucleus)
ga **LINKS** (cuff); golf course; chains;
shackles; connections; back players
(hockey)
ch, md **LIPID** living-tissue fat/wax
tx **LISLE** thread
LISSE warp threads in tapestry
LISTS the combat-ground
nm **LITAS** Lithuanian currency unit
LITHE blithe; active; supple
LITHY pliable; bendable; limber
pr **LITHO-** (-graph), printed picture
technique
me **LITRE** nearly 1¾ pints
LIVED dwelt; abode; survived
LIVEN enliven; animate; vivify
md **LIVER** internal organ
LIVID ghastly pale
nm **LIVRE** old French franc
LLAMA S. American camel
go **LLANO** S. American plain
zo **LOACH** loche; a river-fish
LOAMY of sand-clay mix tilth; soil
LOATH reluctant; unwilling
LOBAR LOBATE, LOBED, rounded
projection
ar, bd **LOBBY** passage; to seek votes;
pressure group; tambour entry hall
LOCAL an inn; topical; regional
zo **LOCHE** a loach; a river-fish
md **LOCUM** locum tenens; a deputy
LOCUS locality; position; area
nv **LODAR** special loran system, radar
LODGE reside; sojourn; deposit;
dwelling; masons' workshop
gl **LOESS** alluvial deposits
LOFTY stately; imposing; towering
bt **LOGAN** poised rock; a berry
zo **LOGGE** miller's thumb; small fish
LOGIA oracles; dicta
cf **-LOGIA** of speech
LOGIC reasoning; dialectics
LOGIE sham jewels
LOGON provision for new group to
be added
cp, tc **LOG-ON** check-in for new users of
computers
LOGOS the Divine Word
LOKAL tavern, club, assembly place
ck **LOKUM** Turkish delight (sweetmeat)
LOLLY lollipop; a lump; money
LOLOS aboriginal race (China)
bt **LOOFA** luffa; flesh-brush
LOONY mad; lunatic

LOOPY kinky; dotty
ga **LOOSE** liberate; slack; vague; lax;
free; puck, ball (ice hockey); let fly
(archery)
LOPED ran with easy strides
nt, nv **LORAN** radio-navigation system
LORDS cricket ground
LORIC corset (13th cent.)
zo **LORIS** Cingalese monkey
LORRY larry; truck; vehicle
zo **LORUM** mandibular plates in
hemiptera
LOSEL worthless; scoundrel;
ne'er-do-well
LOSER also ran; (billiards)
LOSSY of energy-dissipating
equipment
ec **LOTIC** of running water
ga **LOTTO** a game
bt **LOTUS** water lily
go **LOUGH** loch; an arm of the sea; ria;
or inland lake
nm **LOUIS** obsolete French gold coin
mu **LOURE** French bagpipe; dance;
technique applied to violin playing
zo **LOUSE** parasitic insect
LOUSY mean; louse-infected
tx **LOVAT** close tweed
LOVED adored; liked; esteemed
LOVER a Romeo; admirer; swain
LOWER depress; degrade; frown;
(under)
LOWLY meek; humble; modest
zo **LOXIA** cross-bill birds
LOYAL leal; true; devoted
LUBBA coarse grass in Orkneys
LUCID clear; limpid; sane; pure
LUCKY fortunate; auspicious
LUCRE gain; profit; wealth; (gold)
cf, pc **LUDIC-** amusing play; (-rous) absurd
(Gr.)
LUGER automatic pistol; sleigh
driver
me **LUMEN** unit of luminous flux
LUMPY coagulated
LUNAR of the moon
ck **LUNCH** luncheon; midday repast
mu **LUNGA LONGO,** prolonged sounds
(It.)
ga **LUNGE** thrust forward (fencing);
equitation
LUNIK artificial moon satellite
bt **LUPIN** a flower
tx **LUPPA** cloth of gold or silver
md **LUPUS** skin disease
. **LURCH** stagger; sway; roll; toss
LURED enticed; decoyed; inveigled
LURID glowing; sensational

LUSHY tipsy
LUSTY robust; vigorous; sturdy
LUSUS a freak; an exception
LUTED sealed with luting
mu LUTER lute-player
LYART liart; liard; dapple-grey
LYASE double-bonding enzyme
LYCEE high school (Fr.)
LYING mendacious; recumbent
md LYMPH a fluid; vaccine
LYNCH mob law; kill
LYRIC a short poem; tuneful
LYRID meteor from Lyra
zo LYRIE Manx shearwater gull
md LYSIN disintegratory antibody
md LYSIS recovery
LYSSA hydrophobia; rabies
zo LYTHE the pollack
LYTHE LITHE, flexible; agile
cf, pc, md LYTIC -LYTTIC, pertaining to lysis;
opposing action (drugs) (Gr.)
zo LYTTA rod of tongue cartilage

M

zo, bt MACAW parrot; palm
lw MACER a court usher
MACHE materials for papier mâché
mn MACLE double crystal
cf MACRO- of major, large (Gr.)
MADAM MADAME, lady; manageress
(boss) (bordel)
zo MADGE leaden hammer; magpie
bt MADIA the tar-weed; oil-plant
MADLY deliriously; insanely
MAFIA Sicilian secret society
gl MAFIC non-felsic strata in igneous
rock
zo MAGAR Indian crocodile
mu MAGAS stringed-instrument bridge
MAGIC witchery; sorcery; charm
mn MAGMA plutonic rock
rl MAGOG legendary giant (and Gog)
rl MAGOT Barbary ape (as oriental
monster)
rl MAHDI Moslem prophet (dervish)
bt MAHWA butter-tree
bt MAIZE Indian corn
MAJOR a rank; greater
MAKER creator; manufacturer
MAKWA Chinese jacket
md MALAR cheek-bone
MALAX soften by kneading/diluting
MALAY of Malaysia
bt MALIC (apples)
MALIK village headman (Ind.)
MALTY malt-flavoured

zo MAMBA S. African snake
mu MAMBO dance
pl MAMMA mother; mammary gland
(lactation)
MAMMY negro nurse
MANAL pertaining to the hand
ch MANEB chemical fungicide
MANED having a mane
nm MANEH mina; 50 shekels
MANES ghosts; departed souls
MANET stage direction 'remain'
MANGA covering for a cross
vt MANGE MANGY, scabrous; parasitic
bt MANGO tropical fruit
MANGY scabrous
MANIA frenzy; delirium; craziness
zo MANIS the scaly ant-eater
MANLY hardy; intrepid; bold
bt MANNA food; a form of sap
MANOR freehold estate
MANSE priest's house
zo, rl MANTA ox ray; a sea fish; prayer
chant
zo MANUS mane; of the hand
MAORI first colonizers (New
Zealand)
MAPES ice skating jump
bt MAPLE sugar-tree
bt MAQUI Chilean evergreen shrub
MARCH advance; walk; border land;
3rd month
MARDY spoilt; naughty
pr MARGE margin; verge; edge
rl, as MARIA virgin; lunar seas
MARID powerful jinn
MARLY clay-like
MARRY unite; wed; espouse; join
go MARSH bog; swamp; fen; morass
MASAI African tribe
el MASER microwave amplifier
MASHY mashie; a golf club
MASON stone-worker
MASSA master
ga MASSE a billiard stroke
MASSY massive; bulky
bt MASTY full of beech-mast
cp, ga MATCH suit; tally; agree; lucifer;
equivalence; contest; best of 3
games (tennis)
MATED (chess); married; matched
MATER mother
MATEY be friendly, chummy
MATIN morning (Fr.)
mn MATTE crude black copper
ck MATZO thin unleavened Passover
bread
bt MAULS marsh mallow
me MAUND an Eastern weight

MAUVE a mallow colour
zo MAVIS the thrush
MAWKY crotchety; maudlin
MAXIM gun; adage; saw; precept
MAYAN native of Honduras, Mexico
MAYBE perhaps
MAYOR town chief
rl MAZDA Supreme Deity (Zend-Avesta)
MAZER goblet; bowl
ck MEALY farinaceous; flour mix
MEANS mode; agency; method; wealth
MEANT signified; purposed
me MEASE a group of 500
MEATY fleshy
ck MEBOS salted apricots (S. Africa)
rl MECCA desired objective; heart of Islam
MEDAL decoration; award of honour
MEDIA communications (TV, radio, press etc.)
md, bt MEDIC doctor; clover lucerne etc.
MELEE fray, brawl; scuffle; mixture
zo MELES badger genus
bt MELIC lyric; a grass
ck MELLA honey mixtures
bt MELON a gourd
pl, pc MENSA of brain genius; table; tooth surface
MERCY pity; lenity; clemency; grace
MERGE coalesce; immerse; submerge
MERIT desert; worth; credit; earn
zo MERLE the blackbird
zo MERON posterior of certain insects
ar MEROS triglyph channel surfaces
bt MERRY the English wild cherry
ga MERRY blithe; jocund; lively; too strong a stroke (golf) (bowls)
ma MESAL of geometric measures
bd MESHY netted; reticulated; structure
lw MESNE intermediate
MESON cosmic ray constituent
rl MESSA MISSA, MASS, MESSE (musical setting) (liturgy)
MESSY untidied; disordered; unclean
mu MESTO sadly (It.)
ch, mn METAL bullion; ore; (element)
METAL broken stone for roads
METED measured; apportioned
bt METEL thorn apple
ma METER counting instrument; (taxi-)
cf -METIC alien; (cos-) make-up (Gr.)
METIF METIS, person of mixed race
ch, pg METOL 4-methylaminophenol
ma METRA a measuring instrument

me METRE measured rhythm (prosody, verse, music)
me METRE 39.37 inches per metric system base unit
rw METRO metropolitan underground railway
mu METRO- of regular beat; (-nome)
MEUTE MEW, cage for hawks, falcons
mu, ar MEZZO middle voice; storey
MIAOW miaul; caterwaul
md MIASM miasma; effluvia
zo MICKY Irish lad; young bull; microphone
cf, ma MICRO- tiny; one millionth 10^{-6}
MIDAS had a golden touch
nt MIDDY a midshipman
zo MIDGE dwarf; gnat
ga MID-ON (cricket) fielding position
MIDST among; middle
MIGHT indefinite subjunctive of verb
zo, ag MILCH milk-cow
MILER relative to mile (high, run in a minute etc.)
as MILKY lacteal; (-way) heavenly dairy
cf, ma MILLI- one thousandth 10^{-3}
MIMED mimicked; acted
MIMIC ape; copy; mime; mock
MINCE chop fine; palliate
MINED dug; undermined
MINER sapper; (coal-)
mu MINIM dwarf; single drop; note
MINIM down-stroke of pen
mu MINIM 2 crochets of ½ semi-breve
MINOR pretty; lesser; under-age
MINOS King of Crete
MINUS less; lacking; wanting
me MIRED bogged; unit of colour temperature
MIRTH glee; gaiety; hilarity
MIRZA a Persian title
MIS-DO sin; do wrong
to MISER skinflint; hoarder; stingy niggard
cr MISER hand-auger; marline spike for drilling holes
MISSY young lady
MISTY dim; obscure; cloudy
rl MITRA MITHRA, god of Persians, Gr., Romans
rl MITRE bishop's hat; 45 degrees
tx MITTS MITTENS, fingerless gloves
MIXED blended; mingled; confused; atypical
MIXEN MIDDEN, dunghill
ro MIXER a good companion; kitchen; compatible; frequency changer
MIX-UP mêlée; scuffle; brawl; muddle

MIZZY bog; swamp; quagmire
pc MNEME effect of memory
persistence
ck MOCCA chocolate/coffee mixture
mn MOCHA agate; gem
tx MOCHE packet of spun silk
mu MODAL logic; music; grammar
general structure
MODEL example; pattern; copy;
miniature; design; art
tc MODEM varying speed links to
tranmission lines
nv MODER matrix of astrolabe
lv MODUS style; a method
rw MOGUL ex-Mongolian empire
builder in India; type of steam
locomotive; mound on ski slope
nm MOHUR Indian gold coin
tx MOIRE watered silk
MOIST dark; clammy; humid
MOLAR grinding; tooth; holistic
phenomena
pc MOLAR purposive behaviour;
learning situations
nc, ps MOLAR volume of unit of substance
bd MOLER diatomaceous earth
zo MOLLY the wagtail bird; she-man
mu MOLTO very; much (It.)
rl MOMUS God of Ridicule
zo MONAD primitive organism; minimal
matter units
zo MONAL a pheasant
MONDE MONDANE, worldly society
(Fr.)
MONEL an alloy
nm MONEY cash; coin; currency; wealth
bt MONOX the crowberry
ga MONTE gambling game like faro
MONTH lunar cycle
MOOCH slouch; loiter
MOODY sullen; morose; glum;
captious
MOOED lowed (cow-speak)
MOONY dreamy; distraight
MOORE movement in gymnastics
MOORY sterile; boggy
zo MOOSE the elk
MOPED pined; motorized bicycle
MOPPY tipsy; fuddled
MOPSY mopsey; untidy woman
MORAL ethical; virtuous; 'right-
minded'
MORAT mulberry juice
zo MORAY MURAY, variety of tropical
eel
bt MOREL cherry; nightshade
MORES social norms, behaviour,
standards

bt MORIL morel; mushroom
MORMOR bugbear
MORNE blunt head of a lance
MORON mental defective; retarded;
stupid
ro, zo, rl MORSE signalling (code); the walrus;
cope or cloak clasp (metal)
bt MORUS mulberry
MOSES a law-giver
mu MOSSO (It.) moving; animated;
lively
bt MOSSY cryptogamous; lichenous
MOTED of dust particles
MOTEL motorists' hotel
mu MOTET sacred melody
MOTHY moth-eaten
mu, ar, MOTIF theme; feature
hd, wv, le,
cr
MOTIF repeated pattern in art, music
eg MOTOR automobile; engine; prime
mover
pl MOTOR stimulator of movement
ar MOTTE MOTE, castle mound (keep)
MOTTO pithy maxim; slogan; theme
MOUCH mooch; skulk; slouch
bl MOULD shape (in form); create;
fungus blight
MOULT to cast feathers
MOUND knoll; tumulus; hillock
MOUNT climb; scale; ascend; tower
MOURN bewail; lament; deplore
MOUSE MOUSY, of small quiet
rodents
MOUTH opening; orifice; declaim;
(river); (utterance); pompous
speech
MOVED shifted; budged; roused
MOVER proposer
MOWED scythed; cut
MOWER grass-cutting machine
MOYEN means; influence
MPRET Albanian ruler
nt MTEPI canoe dugout, sail (East
Africa)
ch MUCIC an acid
MUCID musty; mouldy; slimy
MUCIN viscous proteins/
carbohydrates
MUCKY dirty; filthy; muddy
bt MUCOR mould; fungus
bt MUCRO stiff sharp point
pl MUCUS slime (nasal)
bt MUDAR MADAR, medicinal herb
MUDDY impure; without clarity (of
water, ideas)
rl MUFTI Moslem high authority
MUFTI civilian clothing

MUGGY damp and warm
zo MUGIL the mullet fish
MULCH soil condition; manure
lw MULCT fine; penalize
MULSE mulled wine
MULSH mulch; litter; manure
cf MULTI- many-sided; of uses; much (Lat.)
MUMMY embalmed corpse (Eg.); mother
md MUMPS glandular epidemic
MUNCH chew; crunch; masticate
tx MUNGO shoddy; inferior cloth
MURAL fixed to a wall
zo MURAY cf. moray; murry
MURED walled in; immured; pent
zo MUREX Tyrian dye; molluscs
MURID Moslem disciple
MURKY lurid; dark; lowering
mn MURRA fluorspar
zo MURRE razorbill or guillemot
MURUT language of N. Borneo
MUSAL pert. to poetry/Muses
zo MUSCA fly genus
bt MUSCI the mosses
MUSED pondered; contemplated
MUSER ruminator; non-active thinker
MUSHY pulpy
mu MUSIC melody; harmony
MUSKY fragrant like musk
MUSTY mucid; fusty; mouldy
mu MUTED muffled; pianissimo
gn MUTON smallest mutable gene element
MUZZY dazed; confused
bt MYALL Australian hard-wood tree
md MYOID like muscle
md MYOMA muscle-fibre tumour
MYOPE MYOPS, of short-sightedness
MYOPY MYOPIA, of short-sightedness
bt MYRRH labdanum with aromatic gum (scent)
zo MYSIS the opossum shrimp
zo MYXON fish of mullet family

N

NABIT crushed candy
NABOB Indian ruler (wealthy)
NACRE mother-of-pearl
NADIR opposite to zenith
md NAEVE a birthmark
NAGGY querulous; quarrelsome
zo NAGOR Senegal antelope
NAIAD water-nymph
NAIVE artless; ingenuous; candid

NAKED stark; open; bare; denuded
mu NAKER a kettle-drum
NAKIR examiner of the dead (Koran)
NAMED yclept; specified; dubbed
NAMER nominator; god-parent
zo NANDU rhea; American ostrich
zo NANNY children's nurse; female goat
gl NAPPE mountain-chain structure
ce NAPPE normal surface overflow of dam
NAPPY drowsy; a dish
NAPPY napkin; baby's diaper; horse refusing orders
cf NARCO- of sleep, numbness, stupor (Gr.)
pl NARES NARIS, of the nostrils
md NASAL of the nose, phonetics, errhine
NASIL conflict-inhibiting social signal
NASTY foul; loathsome; ribald
NATAL nascent; initial
NATTY neat; spruce; matching, trim
NAVAL nautical; maritime; marine
pl NAVEL centre (meditation); belly-button
bt NAVEW wild turnip
NAWAB Indian governor, nobleman
NAZIR Indian bailiff
nt NEAPS shortfall tides
NEATH beneath
mu NEBEL the Jew's harp
cf NECRO- of the dead (Gr.)
zo NEDDY donkey; moke; burro
NEEDS perforce; necessarily
NEEDY poor; indigent; penniless
NEELE NEELD, needle; sharp point
NEESE neeze; sneeze
NEGRE NEGRO, black
NEGUS Abyssinian King
NEGUS a drink; hot punch
NEIGH to whinny
me NEPER power ratio unit
md, pl NERVE pluck; hardihood; neural; fibres
pc NERVY anxious; apprehensive; excitable
NETTY meshy; reticulated
mu NEUME a musical phrase (Gr.)
pc NEURO- of the nerves; nervosity (Gr.)
NEVER not at any time
pl NEVUS birthmark; discolouration of skin
NEWEL finial of a staircase
NEWLY recently; freshly
NEWSY chatty; gossipy

lw, tc **NEXUS** interconnecting series; ideas; bonds
NICER more pleasant; more exact
ar, bd **NICHE** nook; corner; recess
NICOL (polarizing light)
NIDGE to dress stones
NIDOR odour of cooking
md **NIDUS** nest; a breeding place
NIECE daughter of brother or sister
NIFFY smelly
NIFTY classy; stylish
NIGHT darkness; obscurity
NIHIL nil; zero; nothing
bt **NIKAU** New Zealand palm
NINES elaborate party clothes
cp **NINES** complement representing negative values
NINNY simpleton; nitwit; coward
NINON dress material
mu **NINTH** ordinal number 9th; chord
NIOBE a weeper
NIPPY a waitress; alert; parsimonious
NISAN Jewish April
NISUS an effort; an endeavour
NITID gleaming; shining
ch **NITON** gaseous element
ch **NITRE** saltpetre
zo **NITTY** full of nits; lice eggs
NIVAL nivose; niveous; snowy
NIXIE water-elf
NIZAM Indian prince
NOBBY smart; ornate; snobby
NOBEL invented dynamite; prize
nm **NOBLE** patrician; obsolete gold coin
NOBLY grandly; splendidly
mu **NODAL** knotty
zo **NODDY** fool; sea-mew
NODUS knotty point
ga **NO-HIT** noscore for striking games
NO-HOW in no way
mu **NOIRE** quarter note; crotchet (Fr.)
cp, mu **NOISE** din; clamour; uproar; digit mode fixed
NOISY blatant; vociferous; riotous
NOMAD migrant herder (seasonal)
NOMEN name title description (Lat.)
NOMIC customary
NOMOS Greek province
NONCE the present; time; now
NONES (Roman calendar)
mu **NONET** piece for 9 singles
bt **NOOPS** the cloudberry
NOOSE loop; lasso; lariat
bt **NOPAL** Mexican cactus
NORIA Persian water-wheel
NORMA NORM, fixed rule; model style

NORNS Scandinavian Fates
NORSE Viking; early Scandinavian
mt **NORTE** northerly wind in Central America (Sp.)
NORTH (to Polestar); septentrion (Shak.)
NOSED advanced carefully; snooped
NOSEY inquisitive
md, pl **NOTAL** dorsal; of the back
NOTCH natch; dent; nick; incision
NOTED famous; recorded; remarked
zo **NOTUM** back of a bug
mt **NOTUS** southerly wind
NOVEL recent; new; book of fiction
NO-WAY in no manner; no-how
hd **NOWED** coiled; in knot
fd **NOWEL** foundry loam
ck **NOYAU** almond cordial
pl **NUCHA NUQUE**, nape; back of neck
NUDGE jog; jostle; elbow
ga **NULLO** a game
NURSE tend; sickbed attendant
ck **NUTTY** nut-like; -flavoured
zo **NYALA** African antelope
tx **NYLON** artificial fibre
zo **NYMPH** maiden; development stage of insect
zo **NYULA** parasite insect

O

bt **OAKEN** made of oak
nt **OAKUM** picked tarred rope
nt **OARED** rowed; oar-bearing
OASIS fertile spot in desert
ck **OATEN** made of oats
OAVES (OAFS), idiots; changelings
nm **OBANG** old Japanese gold coin
OBEAH obi; West African magic
OBESE abnormally fat; corpulent
me **OBOLE** weight of 10 or 12 g
OCCUR happen; befall; chance
go **OCEAN** the broad sea; main
OCHER OCHRE, OCHRY, browny yellow pigment
bt, zo **OCREA** armoured shin-guard
OCTAD series of eight
OCTAL notation system based on 8
OCTAN happening every 8 days
mu, tc **OCTET** group of eight; packet signal
ch **OCTYL** organic radical
bt **OCUBA** vegetable wax
cl, pl **OCULO-** of the eye (Gr.)
ODDLY queerly; quaintly
mu **ODEON ODEUM**, ancient Grecian music hall
ODIUM obloquy; hatred; enmity

ck **ODOUR** smell; stench
ODYLE mesmerism
bt **OFBIT** devil's bit; a scabious
OFFAL edible entrails; garbage
OFFER bid; tender; proposal
OFTEN oft; frequently; repeatedly
cf **OGAMY** of marital relationship
OGGLE to quiver
OGHAM Irish alphabet
ar **OGIVE** pointed arch (Gothic)
OGLED OGLER, leered; voyeur
(contempt)
OILED OILER, lubricated; oil can; oil
man
zo **OKAPI** animal related to giraffe
OLDEN OLDER, ancient times; more
elderly
ch **OLEIC** OLEIN, OLEON, fatty acid;
(glycerine)
ch **OLEUM** fuming sulphuric acid
cf **OLIGA-** OLIGO-, of the clique (Gr.)
bt **OLIVE** (branch), emblem of peace
OLLAM Irish doctor
cf **-OLOGY** study, science of (Gr.)
OMAHA a Sioux Indian of Nebraska
OMATI a Mexican Indian
ga **OMBRE** a card game
tx **OMBRE** colour-shaded woven stripes
OMEGA last letter of Greek alphabet
OMLAH N. Ind. court officers
OMRAH Moslem court lord
ONCER he did not do it again
bt **ONION** a shallot
ON-OFF control and keying electron
ONSET assault; attack; storm
ONTAL pert, to reality/noumena
cf **-ONYMY** group nomenclature (Gr.)
OOMPH magnetic personality
OOPAK black pea
OOZED seeped; percolated
go **OPACO** OPAC, shadow side of
mountain slope (It.)
mu **OPERA** drama set to music, voices;
works
zo **OPHIC** pertaining to snakes, serpents
OPIHI Hawaiian limpets
OPINE suppose; surmise; ween
bt, md **OPIUM** a narcotic drug
bc **OPSIN** rhodopsin protein
OPTED chosen; elected
md **OPTIC** optical; the eye
bt **ORACH** a kind of spinach
rl **ORALE** Papal veil
zo **ORANG** -UTAN, primate (Indonesia)
ORANT worshipper
ORATE declaim; harangue
ORBED globular; spherical
ORBIT ambit; heavenly path; circuit

md **ORBIT** the eye-socket
zo **ORCIN** killer whale
ORDER group; decoration; bid;
decree; enact; ukase
ORDER rank; (working);
(purchasing); (tall) purpose
OREAD mountain nymph
ch **ORGAL** argal; crude tartar
mu **ORGAN** medium; means; instrument
(govt); keyboard instrument with
bellows
bl **ORGAN** differentiated, function
structure
zo **ORIBI** South African antelope
ORIEL mullioned window
as **ORION** a constellation
ORIYA (Orissa, India) language
tx **ORLON** artificial textile fabric
nt **ORLOP** a ship's deck
zo **ORMER** ear-shell
zo **ORNIS** avifauna; a bird
ORPIN yellow pigment
ORRIS gold or silver lace
bt **ORRIS** astringent root
cf **ORTHO-** correct, straight (Gr.)
zo **ORTYX** American quail
bt **ORVAL** the herb clary
bt **ORYZA** grass genus; rice
OSCAN early Italic tribe
OSCAR film award
bt **OSHAC** gum-plant
bt **OSIER** a willow
OSMIC relating to smell
ch **OSONE** oxidation product of osazone
ch **OSRAM** osmium and wolfram
mu **OSSIA** alternative version (It.)
zo **OTARY** genus of seals
OTHER different
OTTAR attar; aromatic oil
zo **OTTER** fishing device; water weasel
OUGHT aught; nought; a cipher
zo, me **OUNCE** small snow-leopard; weight
OUNDY ONDY, of the waves;
scalloped
zo **OUSEL** OUZEL, blackbird
OUTDO exceed; surpass; eclipse
OUTED exposed as gay; expelled
OUTER exterior; external; outside
OUTRE odd; bizarre; strange
bt, pl **OVARY** seed-vessel; (of female)
OVATE OVAL, OVOID, eggshaped
lw **OVERT** open to view; apparent
zo **OVINE** sheep-like
gn **OVISM** ovum germ theory
ar **OVOLO** a moulding; wide & convex
bt **OVULE** small seed
OWCHE ouch; jewel socket
OWING due; outstanding

OWLER smuggler (by night)
zo **OWLET** young owl
OWNED admitted; confessed; allowed
nt **OWNER** the captain
zo **OWSEN** oxen
OWSER tan vat liquor
zo **OX-BOT** bot-fly
OXBOW part of yoke
go,gl **OX-BOW** lake; former meander of
river
bt **OX-EYE** daisy; marguerite
zo **OX-FLY** bot-fly
ch **OXIDE** oxygen compound
ch **OXIME** aldehyde/ketone compound
ch **OXINE** metal analysis reagent
bt **OXLIP** species of primrose
md **OZENA** an ulcer
OZONE doubled oxygen (surrounds
Earth)

P

PACED stepped; walked; hurried
ga **PACER** speed setter; (heart ticker);
runner; trotting horse; (bowls)
ck **PADAR** coarse flour meal
bt **PADDY** Irishman; temper; rice
bt **PADMA** lotus
bt **PADRA** black tea (China)
rl **PADRE** army chaplain; priest
PAEAN chant of praise, joy, triumph
cf **PAEDO-** of children, infants (Gr.)
PAEON a poetical foot
PAGAN paynim; heathen idolator
PAGED found by the bell-hop
bt **PAGLE PAIGLE**, cowslip
md **PAINS** meticulous care; discomfort
pt **PAINT** depict; portray; pigment;
colour medium (art)
ga **PAIRS** couples; 2-person teams
(tennis) (rowing) etc.
bt **PALEA** inner husk; chaff
PALED blanched; encompassed
cf,zo **PALEO-** of ancient; prehistoric life
(Gr.)
PALES Goddess of cattle
cf **PALIN-** of repetitive, reverse (Gr.)
PALMY of oasis; flourishing; thriving
zo **PALPI** jointed feelers
md **PALSY** oedema; waterlogging
go **PAMPA PAMPAS**, grazing land S.
America
bt **PANAX** ginseng; medicinal plant
nt **PANCH** thick mat; fender
zo **PANDA** giant (bear) and lesser
(raccoon)
PANDY a slap on the open hand

PANED variegated; glazed
lw **PANEL** list; board; schedule; wall
carving
PANIC fear; fright; terror; alarm
bt **PANSY** flower; effeminate man
cf **PANTO-** of all, everything
(pantomime) (Gr.)
PANTS undershorts; short breaths
(panting)
rl **PAPAL** popish; pontifical
bt,ck **PAPAW PAWPAW**, fruit (S. Am.)
PAPER journal; sheet; essay
PAPPY succulent; juicy; easy
PARCH dry; scorch; shrivel
PARED PARER, cut (nails); trimmer
tx **PAREU** Polynesian wrap
PARGE to apply plaster; whitewash
PARKA Alaskan fur coat with hood
PARKY cold; chilly
PAROL oral; by word of mouth
PARRY avert; evade; prevent; move
(fencing)
PARSE analyse grammatically
PARSI Parsee; Indo-Persian
PARTS abilities; talents; (spare-)
lw **PARTY** eligible suitor; (3rd-)
PARTY faction; clique; (political-)
PARTY social occasion; feast
PASCH Passover (Hebrew); Easter
PASEO promenade (Sp.)
PASHA Turkish governor
PASHM under-fur of Cashmere goat
PASSE faded; out of date; old-
fashioned (Fr.)
ga **PASSE** 17 to 36 at roulette
PASTE to stick; an adhesive
ck **PASTY** glutinous; patty; a pie
PATCH cobble; botch; mend; small
area; (eye) (ice-skating)
cp **PATCH** routine for correcting
mistakes
rl **PATEN** eucharistic plate
PATER father
cf **PATHO-** suffering; diseased;
abnormal (Gr.)
-PATHY ditto; also treatment
PATIO courtyard
tx **PATTE** ash-band (Fr.)
ck **PATTY** a small pie; dumpling-shaped
concoction
PAUSE rest; hesitate; interval
(concert)
mu **PAUSA** break in music (It.)
PAVAN a dance (Sp.); a dream;
fantasy
PAVED tesselated
PAVER pavier; pavement layer
PAVID timid

PAVON lance pennon
PAWED fingered; scraped
PAWKY sly; crafty; shrewd
PAYED moored (by ropes) (covered
 with pitch)
PAYED remunerated; paid (in cash)
PAYEE receiver of payments
PAYER rewarder; liquidator
pr PAYNE decorative floral printing
 style
PEACE harmony; concord; repose
bt PEACH to divulge
bt PEACH fruit; sweetheart
PEAKY sickly
pr PEARL a gem (oyster); mother
 (shell); fall; wave for surfing; a size
 of type
PEASE peas as pudding
PEATY like peat
to PEAVY lumberman's hook
bt PECAN American nut
me PECUL Chinese weight, 133 lb (60
 kg)
PEDAL to cycle
cf PEDIA- concerning children, infants
 (Gr.)
PEDUM shepherd's crook
ga, mu PEELS equal shots (curling); rounds
 of bells
PEERY peg top
zo PEGGY a warbler; bird
zo PEKAN the fisher-marten
PEKOE black tea (China)
PELLS records; rolls of parchment
md PELMA sole of foot
PELTA light shield or buckler
PENAL punitive; disciplinary
nm PENCE pennies; (Peter)
pl PENIS male reproductive organ;
 phallus
zo PENNA a feather
nm PENNY a denarius
bt PEONY piony; a plant
me PERCH pole; 5½ yd (5 m)
zo, bt, pc PERCH fish, roost; seat; fixation
 pause
PERIL risk; hazard; danger; jeopardy
PERKY smart; lively; brisk
PERMA- Siberian/Arctic continuous
 -frost
tx PERMO lustre; dress fabric
PERRY fermented pear juice
tx, nv PERSE dark blue; a cloth
PESKY irksome; trying; vexatious
bt PETAL a flower leaf
nt, rl, ga PETER blue flag; rock (cards)
PETIT mignon; petty; trivial
ch PETRE saltpetre

nt PETTY trivial; unimportant; -officer
PHARO FARO, a game of chance
cp, el PHASE stage of development;
 (moon); aspect; guise; periodic
 operation quantity; electrical cyclic
 motion; conduct a planned series
 on scheduled basis
PHEON the broad arrow
PHIAL VIAL, ampulla (flask for a
 potion)
PHILO- -PHILE, fond of; loving;
 freindly towards (Gr.)
bt PHLOX flowering plant
cf -PHOBE hater of; averse to; anti-
 (Gr.)
zo PHOCA genus of seals (seadogs)
tc, cf -PHONE speech, sound (telephone);
 lingual factor (Gr.)
cf PHONO- science of sound, speech,
 word phonetics (Gr.)
cf -PHOTO PHOTO-, of light reactions,
 pictures, transmission (Gr.)
pl PHREN the head, brain, mind;
 mentality; psychology
cf PHYLA PHYLO-, classifications of
 kind, genus (Gr.)
md PHYMA tubercle
mu PIANO softly; keyboard
bt PICEA spruce genus
PICOT little lace loop
md PICRA powdered aloes
me PICUL pecul; Chinese weight
zo PICUS woodpecker
ck PIDAN preserved duck egg
zo PI-DOG Indian pariah dog; stray;
 scavenger
PIECE part of (theatre, music etc.)
 (-together)
mu PIENO all performing (It.)
rl PIETA holy picture
PIETY holiness; sanctity
me PIEZE pressure unit
PIGMY small race (Africa)
PIKED armed with pikes
ck PILAV PILAU, PILAFF, savoury rice
 dish
PILCH fur or flannel gown
PILED amassed; heaped; erected
PILER gatherer
nt, nv, ga, PILOT guide; steer; direct; (-boat);
cp croquet; experimental; effort;
 processing representative; sample
PILUM heavy javelin
bt PILUS a botanical hair
ck PINCH squeeze; grasp; (-of salt)
PINED languished; drooped
go, gl PINGO frozen hill (tundra) (Eskimo)
ch PINIC an acid

nt **PINKY** small boat; dinghy
zo **PINNA** wing-like structure
md **PINNA** bone in ear/nose
PINNY pinafore
md **PINTA** tropical Amer. skin disease
zo **PINTO** spotted American bean; piebald horse
PIN-UP cut-out romantic wall picture
PIOUS devout; godly; religious
PIPED canalized; shouted
mu **PIPER** (bagpipes)
zo **PIPIT** tit-lark
PIQUE vexation
PISTE track; footprint; ski-way
mu **PITCH** toss; hurl; locate; tar; emphasis; acoustics; voice
gl **PITCH** angle of inclination of axis in fold
nt **PITCH** heaving of ship in storm; camping
ga **PITCH** play area; sports ground (baseball); position of ball (croquet, fencing)
PITHY terse; concise; laconic
mo **PITON** iron spike for ropes (climbing); peak tapering to a point
PITOT tube recording air speed
PIVOT hinge; axle; axis; centre
PIXIE pixy; a fairy; elf
ck **PIZZA** Italian savoury 'pie'
cp **PLACE** site; scene; post; assign; digit position in ordered set
as **PLAGE** spectroheliogram spot
PLAGE continental seaside resort
tx, wv **PLAID** a tartan; a maud; clothing (Sc.)
go **PLAIN** prairie; obvious; simple; grass lands; steppes; unelaborate
PLAIT weave; twine; braid
to, bt **PLANE** level; flat; smooth; a tree; slide specimen
PLANK sawn timber; lay down
bt **PLANT** inculcate; sow; machinery; place in reserve; evidence (frame-up)
PLASH plesh; pool; weave; splash
PLASM mould or matrix
ch **PLATE** silver ware; to overlay; wrought silver & gold; electro-plated silver
PLATE accumulator electrode; ceramic; window glass; dish
PLATE competition prize (money); (quantity plateful)
PLATO Greek philosopher
PLATT ore dump

cf **PLATY-** of broad, flat shape (platypus) (Gr.)
go **PLAYA** beach; dryable wetlands (Sp.)
PLAZA public square; market place
PLEAD argue; reason; entreat
PLEAT fold
PLEBS common people; proletariat
mu **PLEIN** full organ stops mixed max (Fr.)
cf **PLEIO-** of more; increase
zo **PLEON** abdominal region in crustacea
PLIED folded; carried on; ferried
PLIES (plural) ply, laminate (wood)
PLUCK pick; cull
PLUCK valour; daring; mettle; courage
PLUFF to puff
PLUMB vertical; to fathom level
PLUME feather; crest; to pride (nom de)
PLUMP stout; chubby; corpulent
PLUMY feathered
wv, tx **PLUSH** a material long-pile cut velvet
PLYER transport worker
me **PMEST** formula; personality; matter; energy; space; time
ck **POACH** coddle (eggs); steal animals (game)
POCKY pitted
zo **PODEX** anal region
PODGE a fat man; a puddle
PODGY short and fat; pudgy
POESY poetry; a posy
zo **POGGE** armed bull-head fish
POILU French soldier; unshaven
lw **POIND** distrain
cp, mu **POINT** aim; tip; apex; sharpen; remark; fixed; floating; decimal; identify; pedal; organ; score
me **POISE** deportment; balance; viscosity
POKAL a drinking cup; prize (Ger.)
POKED thrust; jabbed; prodded
POKER cards; (red hot-)
el **POLAR** opposite (magnetic) (current flow)
md **POLIO** infantile paralysis
gl **POIJE** large limestone depression
mu **POLKA** a dance (Polish); (Bohemian)
zo **POLLY** parrot
md, zo **POLYP** coral; sea; anemone; a growth in humans
zo **PONGO** orang-utan, primate of Indonesia
gl **PONOR** vertical downshaft in karst sink-hole caves

rl **POOJA** Hindu ritual; obeisance
go **POORT** col or pass (S. Africa)
bt **POPPY** (opium) flower
PORCH portico; entrance; stoa
PORED examined diligently
PORER student
pl, gl **PORES** sweat excretion glands (skin);
granular soil cavities
zo **PORGY** porgie; a sea-fish (Bess)
PORKY fat (super piglet)
md **PORTA** transverse fissure; liver
PORTE (sublime) Ottoman
government
POSED perplexed; masqueraded
POSER an attitudinizer
POSIT to affirm; postulate
POSSE power; force of constables
zo **POTTO** West African sloth
POTTY petty; small; dotty
POUCHE cortex particles in flax
roughing
POUCH bag; wallet; sack; steal
zo **POULP** a cephalopod
ck **POULT POULTRY** fowl (edible)
zo, nm, **POUND** to crush; strike repeatedly;
me enclosure; money; unit of weight
POUZE refuse of crushed apples
zo **POWAN** Loch Lomond fish
zo **POWER** force; faculty; control
zo **POYOU** armadillo
nt **PRAAM** a barge; small cargo coaster,
Northern Europe
PRADO art gallery, Madrid
nt **PRAHU** Malay boat
PRANG a crash landing; destroy
PRANK practical joke; caper; frolic
mn **PRASE** green quartz
PRATE babble; chatter; jabber
zo **PRAWN** a crustacean
nt **PREDY** ready for action
PREEN to clean the feathers
PRESS crush; urge; crowd; hurry;
burden; newspapers; linen; juice
extractor; press-ups (gymn)
(fencing) basketball
PREXY college president (USA)
PRICE cost; charge; rate; reward
pl **PRICK** perforate; mark; penis
PRIDE arrogance; hauteur; conceit
PRIED peeped; spied; snooped
PRIER pryer; a nosey parker
PRIMA first; leading; (-donna)
pr **PRIMA** repeated, resumption mark
pt, ps **PRIME** chief; principal; zenith; first
quality; prepare by charging (oil
stoves, explosives, gas lamps); pre-
paint coating; prize cycling
mu **PRIMO** leading part

PRINT stamp; brand; impress
rl **PRIOR** previous; earlier; cf. abbot
PRISE to lever
PRISM refracting glass
PRIVY private; outdoor toilet; parts
(genitals); councillor
PRIZE esteem; reward; booty (ship,
-money); salvage; premium; sports
cup; (boxing) (racing)
PROBE scrutinize; examine; prove
PRONE face downwards; apt to;
rifleman's firing position; with
tendency to
to **PRONG** the tine of a fork
lw, ck, cp, **PROOF** test; ordeal; impenetrable;
pr evidence (whisky); (water-); study;
first print; control
PROPS theatrical properties (scenery
etc.)
PROSE non verse writing
cf **PROSO-** of matters ahead; future
(Gr.)
PROSY prolix; tedious; vapid
cf **PROTO-** of beginning, original,
primitive (Gr.)
PROUD vain; imperious; stately
PROVE evince; verify; examine
PROWL prey; stalk; rove; slink
PROXY substitute; deputy; agent
PRUDE person of intolerant modesty
ck **PRUNE** dried plum
gs **PRUNT** applied glass badge mass
mn **PRYAN** felspathic clay
PRYER prier; snooper
mu **PSALM** sacred song sung to a harp
PSHAW! belittling exclamation
md **PSOAS** tenderloin
md **PSORA** the itch
zo **PTERE** a wing (-dactyl)
pl **PUBES** genital zone of abdomen
pl **PUBIC** of genital/loin region
md **PUBIS** pelvic bones
PUDGY podgy; fat; fleshy
PUFFY tumid; swollen; bombastic
PUGIL a pinch of
PUKKA veritable; genuine (Hindu)
PULED whined
PULER a whimperer
zo **PULEX** the flea
PULKA Lapland sledge
PULPY soft; succulent
ck, md, bt, **PULSE** a lentil; to throb; beat;
ps, el transient disturbance
PUMPS evening shoes (dancing)
(men's)
PUNCH pummel; pierce; horse;
chisel; (Mr puppet)
nt **PUNGY** Chesapeake Bay schooner

PUNIC Carthaginian; faithless
PUNKA punkah; Indian fan
mu PUNTA with the point of the bow of violin (It.)
ga, mu PUNTO fencing; Cuban dance
to PUNTY glass blower's iron
zo PUPAL in the chrysalis state
pl PUPIL learner; tyro; alumni; (eye); alumnus
zo PUPPY whelp; novice
ck PUREE thick soup; strained pulp
PURER cleaner; more chaste
mt PURGA BURAN, NW tundra wind (Siberia)
PURGE cleanse; absolve; shrive
PURIM Jewish feast
zo PURRE the dunlin bird
PURSE to wrinkle; money-bag
PURSY fat and asthmatic
bt, zo PUSSY willow catkin; tame cat
PUTID putrid; worthless
ck PUTOO nut-meal
PUTTI chubby-Baroque child image
PUTTY cement with linseed oil
PUT-UP preconcerted
ga PUTZI Chinese game
go PUZTA Pannonian plain (Hungary)
PYGAL related to backsides
PYGMY pigmy; midget; Lilliputian
PYLON gateway; turning mark; tower; tow-rope hitch (water-skiing)
md PYOID pus-like
PYRAL (funeral pyre)
ch PYRAN cyclic carbon/oxygen compound
bt PYRUS apple or pear genus
rl PYXIS pyx; sacred box

Q

QANAT GANAT, KANAT, underground irrigation system (Oman)
nt Q-BOAT disguised armed ship
ar QIBLA mihrab wall, mosque
QUACK charlatan; humbug; empiric; cry
QUADS quadruplets
QUAFF gulp; swallow; drink deep
mu, zo QUAIL cower; flinch; small bird; toy musical instrument with birdsong
gl QUAKE QUAKY, tremble; quiver; unstable; shaky; (earth-)
QUALE having independent existence
QUALM scruple; pang; throe
QUANK sound a rhino makes
QUANT punt or jumping pole

QUARK hypothetical sub-atomic entity
ck QUARK curd cheese (Ger.)
QUARL a segment of fireclay
zo QUARL jellyfish
me QUART (cards); 2 pints (1.13 litres)
QUASH nullify; annul; override
QUASI as it were; virtually; pretence; false
cp QUASI excess data
cf QUASI- seemingly; resembling (Gr.)
QUASS KVASS, Russian beer
QUEAN transvestite; gay
ga QUEEN (cards); (chess); (royal); (bee); gay
QUEER odd; rummy; curious; strange; gay
QUELL suppress; crush; quench
QUERK to throttle; to grunt
QUERL to twirl; a coil
QUERN primitive stone handmill
QUERY question; dispute; ask
QUEST search; pursuit; inquiry
QUEUE a hopeful tail
QUICK fleet; agile; brisk; alive
QUIET still; calm; lull; pacify
QUIFF a curly lock
QUI-HI Anglo–Indian
zo QUILL a feather; a pen
QUILP a hideous dwarf
QUILT twilt; counterpane
md QUINA quinne
QUINS quintuplets
mu QUINT sequence of five; organ stop
QUIPO QUIPU, mnemonic Inca language; coloured and knotted cords
me QUIRE choir; 24 sheets
QUIRK twist; subterfuge; evasion
QUIRT riding whip
QUITE fully; exactly; entirely
QUITS acquittance; clear of debt
QUOAD as far as
QUOIT discus
QUOTA share; portion; allotment
QUOTE cite; mention; adduce
QUOTH spake; said; remarked
rl QURAN KORAN, Moslem Holy Book

R

rl RABBI Jewish religious teacher
md, zo RABID furious; violent; result of rabies bite
RABOT marble polisher
RACED ran; hurried; competed
RACER that races; competes

RACON remote-object identifying beacon
RADAR radio-location
zo RADGE rodge; grey duck; gadwall
RADII plural of radius
nc, ro RADIO telegram; wireless (-active)
ma, bt RADIX (logarithms); a root
ch RADON radioactive element
nt RAFFE three-cornered sail
RAFTY damp; musty
RAGED raved; fumed; stormed
rw RAILS safety fence; iron road; surrounds (surfing)
RAINY showery
RAISE erect; uplift; exalt; breed
RAJAH Indian prince
RAKED enfiladed; searched; combed
RAKER ransacker; scraper
bd RAKER inclined tubular scaffolding
RALLY arouse; recover; (tennis); banter
RALLY mass meeting (motor sports; party)
zo RALPH a mischievous raven
RAMAL branching
nt RAMED framed on the stocks
RAMET asexual offspring of clone
md RAMEX hernia; rupture
nt RAMIE ramee; rope fibre
tx RAMIE Chinese grass for banknotes, textiles
RAMMY strongly scented
bt RAMUS branch; twig; spray
RANCE a rocket trough
RANCH stock-farm; (dude); estate
RANDY sexually rampant
RANDY a virago; a romp; a beggar
RANEE rani; Indian queen
RANGE array; align; scope; roam; distance; habitat
RANGE variation limits; mountain chains; (kitchen)
RANGY long-limbed and slender
RANTY boisterous; vociferous
RAPED violated; outraged; ravished
RAPID fast; fleet; swift; hasty
hd RAPIN devouring animal
RARER scarcer; more uncommon
mu RASCH (Ger.) rushed/rushing/in a rush
RASED RAZED, erased; effaced; demolished; blotted out
RASPY rough; scratchy; abrasive
zo RASSE small civet
RATAL rate value
zo RATAN rattan; cane
RATCH pawl; ratchet; rack

RATED assessed; chid; scolded; valued
RATEE a person being rated
zo RATEL honey-badger
nt RATER assessor; (yachting)
RATIO proportion; rate; quota
RATTY irascible; irate; angry
RAVED raged; ranted; drivelled
RAVEL entangle; twist together
zo RAVEN large crow-like bird
RAVER a maniac
RAVIN raven; prey; plunder; rapine
RAWLY unskilfully; immaturely
RAYAH Ottoman non-Moslem
RAYED shone; arrayed
tx RAYON artificial silk
RAZOR shaving device
REACH expanse; stretch; scope
REACT recoil; resist; repeat
READY prompt; alert; willing
REALM kingdom; domain
tx REAMY novely yarn
RE-ARM re-equip (defence)
mu REBEC REBECK, Moorish fiddle (violin)
REBEL revolt; rise; insurgent
REBID (auction)
REBUS a pictorial puzzle
REBUT confute; disprove; rebuff
RECAP redescribe briefly
RECCE reconnaissance
go, nv RECIF reef or bar (S. Africa)
mu RECIT swell of organ
RECTO right-hand page
RECUR reappear; revert; resort
REDAN earthwork; redoubt
mu REEDY a thin tone (woodwind)
nv REEFY full of rocks
REEKY smoky; vaporous
lw REEVE steward; sheriff; rope
zo REEVE the female ruff; a bird
REFER submit; relate; advert
REFIT repair; re-equip
mu REGAL royal; kingly; princely; a reed-organ portable, for churches
REGET regain; recover
REGIE government monopoly; control
bt REGMA botanical capsule
REICH German realm
REIFY to materialize
REIGN rule; govern; control
REIVE REAVE, to ravage
RELAX abate; slacken; loosen
RELAY team race; pass on
RELET to offer on hire again
RELIC memento; souvenir; keepsake; survival from past

RELIT rekindled; re-illuminated
ae, nt **REMAN** get a fresh crew
REMIT send by post; release; postpone
pl, md **RENAL RENES**, of the kidneys
RENEW renovate; refurbish, restore
REPAY refund; recompense; avenge
REPEL repulse; parry; withstand
md **REPET** repeat; the same again
REPLY echo; answer; respond
REPOT transplant
cp **RE-RUN** repeat; commence again; restart after error or fiasco
RESAW saw again; revisualized
pr **RESET** reprint with alterations; adjust
bt **RESIN** rosin; conifer gum
ch **RESOL** synthetic resin
ag **RE-SOW** to sow again
md **RETCH** attempt to vomit; strain
cf **RETRO-** predated, from the past (Gr.)
lw **RE-TRY** try again; new trial
REVEL feast; carouse; luxuriate
mu **REVUE** variety entertainment
REWET part of a wheel-lock
REWIN regain
cf, md **-RHAGE** of bleeding; discharge (Gr.)
bt **RHEIC** (rhubarb)
ch **RHEIN** chrysophanic acid
RHEMA word, verb (Gr.)
md **RHEUM** water mucous discharge
RHINE wine; ditch; (-stone) gem
cf, pl, zo **RHINO-** of the nose (Gr.)
ma **RHOMB** a rhombohedron; geometrical shape
bd **RHONE RONE**, eaves gutter
nt, as **RHUMB** sky compass; (stars)
RHYME rime; poetry; metre
bt **RHYNE** Russian hemp
bt **RIBES** currant genus
ck **RICER** machine for mincing food
ch **RICEN** castor bean albumin
RIDER horseman; added clause
go **RIDGE** ledge; crest; weal; range
RIDGY furrowed; corrugated
RIFLE ransack; strip; to groove
RIGEL a star in Orion
RIGHT due; equity; privilege
RIGID staunch; unbending; strict
RIGOL a diadem; crown; coronet
md **RIGOR** rigour; rigidity
md **RIGOR** shivering, chill (of death)
RILED angered; annoyed
RILLE lunar valley
RIMED frosted
to **RIMER** an enlarging tool
RINGE heather whisk

RINGS pair for hanging gymnasts
ga **RINKS** fours (bowls); ice floors (skating)
RINSE lave; clean; wash
RIOJA Spanish wine
RIPEN mature; develop; perfect
RIPER further advanced
RIPON a spur
RISEL support for a vine
RISEN ascended; mounted; revolted
RISER rebel; stair-board; handle, centre of bow (archery); early bird
RISHI poet; Vedic seer
RISKY hazardous; speculative
zo **RISSA** kittiwake genus
go **RITHE** small stream
RITZY luxurious; presumptuously; sham
RIVAL vie; emulate; match; equal
RIVEL to wrinkle; shrivel
RIVEN rived; rent; split
RIVER stream; torrent; tributary
RIVET fasten; metal bolt
nm **RIYAL** Sudanese coin
bt **RIZOM** head of corn or oats
nt, zo **ROACH** part of sail; a fish
ROAST parch; chaff outrageously
ROBED garbed; attired; arrayed
zo **ROBIN** national bird; circular appeal
bt **ROBLE** Californian white oak
ROBOT an automaton
ROCKY stony; shaky; unsteady
mu **ROCTA** ancient violin
RODEO cattle round-up; competitive spectacle
zo **RODGE** radge; grey duck; gadwell
ro **ROGER** wireless call – over
ROGUE knave; rascal; scamp
bl, pc **ROGUE** genetic variant/exception (-elephant, wild, dangerous mood)
bt **ROHAN** red-wood mahogany tree
ROIST to bluster; to swagger
zo **ROKER** thornback; ray; skate
ROMAL kerchief; raw hide whip
ROMAN citizen of Rome; (-Empire)
ROMEO a lover
ROMER (Rhineland) broad wine glass
ROMIC a phonetic notation
hd **ROMPU** heraldic fracture
pr **ROMPY** rampageous
RONDE round-hand type (Fr.)
mu **RONDE RONDO**, dance; music in several strains
ROOKY new recruit
ROOMY spacious
ROOST a fowl support; to perch
ck **ROOTY** radical; bread (India)

ROPED tied; lashed; bound
ga ROQUE a form of corquet (Fr.)
 RORAL RORIC, ROSCID, moist with
   dew
bt, ck ROSIN RESIN (conifer gum) (wine)
ROTAL according to roster
ps ROTON quantum of rotational energy
ROTOR a machine; airfoil; wind
   turbulence (aeronautics)
ga ROUGE (Eton wall game); cosmetic;
   point for Can. football
ROUGH rugged; crude; coarse; long
   grass areas on golf course
mu ROUND convex; rotund; period
   (tour); canon; (visits); (a table)
ROUND shot; in a circle; (drinks);
   (contest); cut; series
ROUSE awaken; annoy; disturb
ROUTE way; course; itinerary
ROVED roamed; wandered; rambled
ga ROVER nomad; pirate; (croquet);
   (Australian football)
bt ROWAN mountain ash
ROWDY ruffian; rough; boisterous;
   drunk and disorderly; noisy
ROWED sculled; upbraided
ROWEL spurwheel (riding)
ROWEN second hay crop
ROWER oarsman
ROYAL regal; superb; august
ROYLE to rile; to salt fish
RUADE parallel turn (skiing)
nt RUATA junklike craft (Siam)
bt RUBIA madder genus
nm RUBLE ROUBLE, Russian monetary
   unit
bt RUBUS bramble genus
RUCHE plaited trimming
RUDDY rubicund; red
RUDER coarser; cruder
zo RUDGE a partridge
zo RUFFE ruff; freshwater perch
ga RUGBY (football); (school)
RUING regretting; lamenting
RULED lined; governed; decided
RULER monarch; regent; dictator
RUMAL -romal; shawl (Hindu)
mu RUMBA Cuban dance
RUMBO rum punch
RUMEN paunch of ruminant
bt RUMEX sorrel genus
ga RUMMY odd; queer; card game
bt RUNCH crunch; the wild charlock
RUNER bard
RUNIC ancient Scandinavian script
me, lw, pr RUN-IN the finish in racing; to train
   a new motor; arrest (police); merge
   paragraphs

RUNNY liquid
pr RUN-ON process of continuing;
   unbroken
pr RUN-UP gold band; binding;
   approach run (jump); last
   preparations before event; sew a
   garment rapidly; hoist a flag;
   accumulate debts
nm RUPEE 16 annas
md RUPIA skin disease
RURAL Arcadian; sylvan; pastoral
RUSHY full of rushes
RUSTY corroded; out of practice
RUTTY uneven; furrowed; grooved

S

bt SABAL a fan palm genus
SABER cavalry sword (USA)
ac SABIN unit of acoustic absorption
zo SABLE antelope; marten; fur
hd SABLE black; dusty; sombre
SABOT wooden shoe; (-age)
SABRA SABRE, native of Israel;
   cavalry sword
SADHU Hindu ascetic
SADLY gloomily; dismally;
   mournfully
SAFER surer; more secure
rl SAGAN Jewish priest
SAGER wiser; cleverer
zo SAGRA bettle genus
SAGUM Roman cloak
SAHIB boss (white) (India)
zo SAIGA puff-nosed antelope
rl SAINT to canonize; one venerated
rl SAITH SAYS, Biblical usage
rl SAIVA votary of Siva
zo SAJOU American monkey
SAKIA Persian water-wheel
ck SALAD mixed cold dish
bt SALAL evergreen shrub
zo SALDA a bug genus
bt, ck SALEP SALOP, orchis root beverage
lw SALIC male succession; law
ch SALIN saline; a salt
bt SALIX willow genus
SALLE salon; hall (Fr.)
pr SALLE paper-sorting room
SALLY bell-rope tufting, outburst;
   wit
zo SALLY a stone-fly; a wren
ck SALMI hashed game
zo SALMO salmon genus
SALON saloon; hall
zo SALPA genus of sea-squirts
gl, go SALSE volcanic mud

md **SALTS** saline draughts
SALTY witty; briny; saline
SALVE save; rescue; heal; a remedy
SALVO an exception; a volley
mu **SAMBA** dance (S. American)
ga **SAMBO** official Fila-style (wrestling)
zo **SAMIA** silk-worms genus
SAMMY American Tommy; G.I.,
footsoldier (N. Amer.)
SANDY yellowish red
SANER less idiotic; more normal
mu **SANSA** tambourine
SAPID savoury; affected; palatable
SAPOR SAVOUR, flavour; taste
SAPPY juicy; succulent; weak
zo **SARDA** mackerel; tunny genus
mu **SAROD** SAROH, Indian guitar
as **SAROS** an astronomical cycle
SARSE a fine sieve
SARUM Salisbury; (rotten borough)
zo **SASIA** pigmy woodpeckers (Ind.)
zo **SASIN** antelope; Indian blackbuck
SASSE Dutch weir with flood-gates
rl **SATAN** Devil; Lucifer; Beelzebub
SATED replete; surfeited; cloyed
tx **SATIN** glossy fabric
SATIS enough (Latin)
rl **SATYR** goat-like sylvan deity; Pan
SAUCE impudence; a condiment;
relish
SAUCY pert; bold; malapert; flippant
nm **SAUDI** gold sovereign (Arabia)
go **SAULT** a rapid (Canadian)
SAUNA Finnish steam-bath
zo **SAURY** skipper-fish
ck **SAUTE** boiled, then fried
SAVED rescued; freed; redeemed;
kept
SAVER a hoarder; an economist
bt **SAVIN** evergreen conifer
SAVOR savour; taste; odour; relish
bt **SAVOY** curly cabbage
SAVVY commonsense; nous;
gumption
SAWED cut with a saw; sawn
SAXON of Saxony
SAYER a speaker; an assayer
SAYON medieval peasant's jacket
SAY-SO a dictum
md **SCALA** a surgical instrument
bt **SCALD** the dodder-plant; a burn
SCALD skald; Scandinavian bard
zo, mu **SCALE** climb; balance; flake; lamina;
(fish-); proportion and size; exact
drawing; sol-fa application
md **SCALL** leprosy; a scab; mean
SCALP skin + hair of the head;
trophy

SCALY encrusted; shabby; mean
SCAMP rogue; knave; stint
SCANT to stint; scarcely sufficient
bt **SCAPE** leafless peduncle bearing
flowers
SCAPE shaft; stem; fault
SCARD shard; sherd; fragment
SCARE alarm; appal; dismay; daunt
SCARF neckerchief; a carpenter's
joint
zo **SCARF** cormorant; scart; skart
hd **SCARP** heraldic scarf; rampart slope
SCART to scratch; scrape; a niggard
SCARY timid; frightening; windy
SCATT SCAT, tax; (-free)
zo **SCAUP** a sea-duck
go **SCAUR** river bank; rocky cliffs; scar
mu **SCENA** stage of an ancient theatre;
operatic unit of aria; duet etc
SCENE show; pageant; sight; view
SCENT perfume; odour; redolence;
trail
SCHUT cattle-pound (South Africa)
SCION offshoot; branch; descendant
SCOAT scote; to scotch; to wedge
SCOBS shavings; sawdust; dross
zo **SCOBY** SCOBBY, the chaffinch
SCOFF sneer; mock; deride
SCOLD rate; upbraid; censure; chide
ck **SCONE** coronation stone; a
confection
SCOON skim along the water
SCOOP dig; hollow; excavate; ladle
pr **SCOOP** gliding singing; journalists'
(-)
SCOOT decamp; bolt; run
zo **SCOPA** stiff hairs of moths
SCOPE room; space; liberty; object
cf **-SCOPE** viewing instrument (Gr.)
zo **SCOPS** screech-owl
cf **-SCOPI -SCOPY**, viewing scrutiny
(Gr.)
mu **SCORE** record; mark; furrow;
scratch; music in parts form;
printed
SCORN spurn; deride; mock; disdain
cf **SCOTO-** of darkness (Gr.)
SCOTS of Scotland; Scottish
SCOUR scrub; scrape; purge
SCOUT to explore; reconnoitre
zo **SCOUT** the guillemot; razor-bill
SCOVE to tamp; to poise
SCOVY smeared; blotched
SCOWL frown; lower; glower
bt **SCRAB** crab-apple; to scratch; scrape
SCRAG to throttle; odd lean bit
SCRAM! clear off! get out!
nc **SCRAM** emergency plant shutdown

SCRAN skran; scraps of food
SCRAP bit; atom; particle; tussle
SCRAT a devil; a goblin; monster
SCRAW a turf; a sod (Irish)
zo SCRAY sea-swallow
gl, mo SCREE slope of loose rock face (talus)
SCREW twist; copulate
tx SCRIM strong muslin lining for walls
SCRIP wallet; purse; satchel
lw SCRIP (receipt for) share certificates
zo SCROD to shed; young codfish
go SCROG stunted bush; thicket
bt, go SCRUB clean; scour; maquis; stunted growth land
SCRUM (rugby football)
SCUBA underwater breathing apparatus
nm SCUDO Italian silver dollar
SCUFF scurf; a scale; to shuttle
SCUFT SCRUFF; the nape of the neck
nt SCULL an oar; a cockboat; to row
zo SCULL skua-gull; a shoal of fish
SCULP to carve; to engrave; to flay
zo SCURF dandruff; scum; bull-trout
zo SCUTE a shield; scale of fish
SEAMY dark; sordid; nasty
zo SEA-OX the walrus
SEAVE a wick made of a rush
bt SEAVY overgrown with rushes
SEBAT 5th month of the Jewish year
zo SEBUM sebaceous gland excretion
mu SECCO a fresco; unaccompanied
SEDAN carrying chair
bt SEDGE SEDGY, reeds; overgrown grass; flock of herons
SEEDY shabby; run to seed; unwell
ga SEEGA board game (Egypt, Somalia)
mu SEGNO repetition
mu SEGUE follow on at once (It.)
SEINE large fishing net
SEISM an earthquake
SEITY personality; selfhood
SEIZE grasp; clutch; grapple; impound
SEKOS Greek sanctuary
SELAH a pause in the Psalms
go SELVA tropical rainforest (Brazil)
zo SEMEN fluid containing spermatozoa
SEMIC pertaining to a sign
nm SEMIS Roman bronze coin, half an as
SENAL a landmark (South America)
SENCH to cause to founder
zo SENEX S. American hawk; a swift
md SENNA dried cassia leaves
SENOR Spanish title of address

pc SENSE wisdom; reason; receptive perception; detect; notice
cp SENSE (common); (intuition); perception system
mu SENZA without
bt SEPAL calyx segment
zo SEPIA genus of cuttlefish; pigment
SEPIC done in sepia
SEPOY native Indian soldier
gl, go SERAC glacial ice
SERAI caravanserai; Seljuk Turkish inn
tx SERGE twilled fabric
SERIC Chinese; silken
pr SERIF short cross-line in typography
zo SERIN song-bird; canary
gl SERIR gravel desert (reg), Libya
SERON bale of exotic produce
zo SEROW Asiatic goat
gl SERRA SIERRA, saw (serrated) mountain ridge
mu SERRE tightened, with tension, speed
SERRY to crowd together
md SERUM antibody for inoculation
SERVE do; act; suit; aid; obey; attend
ga SERVE put ball into play (court games)
au, cp SERVO braking system; difference minimizer
rl SESHA Serpent-King (Hindu)
zo SESIA clear-wing moths
SESSA hurry!
bt, zo SETAE bristles; cat's whiskers
md SETON a dressing
SET-TO an affray
SET-UP scheme; plot; locate; unit
SEVEN cardinal number
SEVER cut; part; sunder; detach
SEWED stitched; threaded
SEWEL a scarecrow
zo SEWEN sewin; salmon type
SEWER drain
rl SEXTE sixth hour service
SEXTO a size of book
S'FOOT by Jesus' foot! an imprecation
SHACK a shed; to tramp; a vagabond
SHADE hue; tint; veil; cover; screen
SHADY shadowy; obscure; doubtful
SHAFT arrow; missile; handle; pit
nm SHAHI Persian copper coin
mu SHAKE jar; jolt; agitate; quiver; dance; shudder; trill (ornamental)
SHAKO chako; military cap
SHAKY tottering; unstable; loose
mn SHALE shaly clay; husk

SHALL future auxiliary verb
SHALT future auxiliary verb
SHALY laminated and friable
zo, bt SHAMA Indian song-bird; cereal
SHAME abash; mortify; infamy
SHAND shame; base coin; worthless
pl SHANK (golf); the tibia
SHAPE mould; fashion; form; image
zo SHAPO wild sheep of Tibet
SHARD SHERD, fragment; wing case
SHARE divide; quota; (stocks & –s)
SHARK predatory fish or financier;
    cheat
mu SHARP fine; thin; keen; caustic
SHAVE pare; clip; shear; skim; graze
SHAWL a wrap
mu SHAWM SHALM, proto-oboe
ag SHEAF bundle of harvested wheat
SHEAL to shell; to husk
SHEAR clip; cut; fleece; strip; force;
    retreat
SHEEN gloss; lustre; shine; polish
zo SHEEP a woolly ruminant
SHEER absolute; precipitous; turn
    aside
tx SHEET a bed-cloth; wide expanse;
    rope
SHEIK Arab chief
SHELF ledge; shoal; sandbank
nt SHELL case; husk; projectile;
    bombard; racing rowing boat
    (universities)
SHETH part of plough
SHEVA (Hebrew vowel point)
SHEWN SHOWN, displayed; revealed;
    taught
rl SHIAH Moslem sect
ga SHIAI tournament (judo)
SHIED (coconuts); (horses)
SHIEL SHIELING, sheep shelter
ma, cp, ga SHIFT chemise; vary; alter; trick;
    wile; change place; working hours;
    flexible arithmetic; realignment of
    forwards (Amer. football)
rl SHIKO prostrate veneration (Burma)
SHINE SHINY, radiate; glitter;
    polished
SHIRE county; draught-horse
SHIRK evade; avoid; neglect;
    malinger
SHIRL to slide
SHIRR to pucker; to wrinkle
SHIRT a blouse; distinctive garment
SHIVE a slice; a wooden bung
mn SHOAD fragments of ore
nv, nt, zo SHOAL swarm; throng; bank; bar;
    fishes
zo SHOAT young hog

ag SHOCK STOOK, pile of corn sheaves
SHOCK onset; disturbance; to disgust
SHOER a farrier; blacksmith
ga SHOGI chess variant (Japan)
SHOLA a wood; a thicket (Ind.)
SHOLE ground plank
SHONE radiated; sparkled; flashed
SHOOK cask staves; trembled;
    quaked
bt SHOOT emit; dart; fire; spout
go SHORE prop; brace; strand; beach
mn SHORL tourmaline
SHORN shaven; fleeced; clipped
SHORT terse; abrupt; laconic; pithy;
    wee
go SHOTT seasonal salt lake
SHOUT cry; cheer; call; bellow
SHOVE jostle; push; press; elbow
SHOWN presented; paraded; revealed
SHOWY gay; garish; loud; gaudy
ck SHRED cut into small pieces; scrap
SHREW dormouse; virago; scold
bt SHRUB a cordial; dwarf tree
SHRUG to draw up; contract
bt SHUCK a husk; shell or pod
el, rw SHUNT electrical diversion; sort a
    train
SHYLY shily; coyly; bashfully
SIBBE sibling; close of kin
SIBYL prophetess; witch; sorceress
mn SICCA newly coined; a rupee
SIDED flattened; biased
SIDER partisan; protagonist
SIDLE to go crabwise
SIEGE besiege; invest; city
SIEUR SIRE, title of respect
SIEVE to sift; to strain; a temse
cp SIGHT see; view; observe; scene;
    visual scan check
SIGIL signature; occult mark; seal
SIGMA a Greek letter; reactor circuit
ml SILAL high-silica cast iron
mn SILEX silica
SILKY silken
SILLY inane; inept; unwise; stupid
bt, fr SILVA SYLVA, forest area
tx SIMAR CYMAR, CIMAR, scarf; loose
    dress
zo SIMIA genus of apes
pl SINAL pertaining to sinus
SINCE after; subsequently; because
md, pl SINEW a tendon
SINGE sear; burn; scorch
SINIC Seric; Chinese
rl SINTO shinto; ancestor-worship
    (Jap.)
pl SINUS a cavity; a bay; nasal duct
SIOUX Dakota Indian

SIPED oozed; exuded; percolated
SIRED fathered; generated
SIREN syren; seducer; hooter
bt SIRIH betel-leaf (Malay)
bt SISAL fibrous plant, (ropemaking)
bt SISON stone parsley
SISSY sweetheart; a weakling
mu SITAR Indian long-necked lute
SITED placed, situated
SIT-IN demonstration by occupying premises
zo SITTA the nut-hatch
SIVAN Jewish month
mu SIXTH ordinal number; harmonic interval
SIXTY cardinal number
SIZED SIZER, graded; cut to size (-machine)
SIZEL SCISSEL, metal clipping
SKALD SCALD, Scandinavian bard
gl SKARN silicate-gangue mineral
zo SKATE scate; the ray; a roller-skate
zo SKEET the pollack; a long scoop
zo SKEIN coil of yarn; group of geese
bd SKIDS short planks; load-taking rail; unsinkable tube
SKIED SKIER, skied in the crowd; tourer on skis
SKIES the firmament
nt SKIFF a light boat; to skim; sculling (university) boat
SKILL knack; address; art; facility
SKIMP stint; scamp; scanty
zo SKINK African lizard; a shin-bone
SKIRL a shrill cry or sound
SKIRR scurry; hasten; scour
SKIRT hem; border; skim; edge; part of target (archery); garment (ladies'); canvas cover of canoe; feathers on shuttle (badminton)
SKISH competiton (angling)
zo SKITE the yellow bunting
SKOAL Hail! a toast! (Scand.)
SKULK lurk; slink; cower; sneak
SKULL the sconce; the noddle
SLACK lax; loose; lazy; sluggish
SLACK shallow dell; small coal
SLADE valley; spade
SLAIE weaver's reed
SLAIN killed; despatched; murdered
SLAKE quench; extinguish; allay
SLANG argot; to scole; to abuse
SLANT tilt; list; lean; slope
SLASH cut; gash; slit; swipe
SLATE SLATY, roofing stone; reprimand
SLAVE serf; thrall; drudge; menial
ro, tc SLAVE (-stations of signal network)

SLEEK smooth; soft; glossy; silken
SLEEP doze; slumber; nap; siesta
SLEET snow mingled with rain
SLEPT drowsed; slumbered; rested
SLICE fire-shovel; cut; sever; piece; dip oar too deep; cause a ball to spin (golf) (cricket); (bread-)
nt SLICK plausible; efficient; oil spill
SLIDE skid; glide; transparency
mu SLIDE grace notes; trombone
SLIDE sliding seat (rower); microscope
S'LIFE God's Life imprecation
SLIME SLIMEY, ooze; mire; viscous; clammy
SLING hang; hurl; drink
SLINK move away secretly; lurk
SLIPE SLYPE, mining skip
SLIPS men's bathing trunks
SLIPS (theatre); (shipbuilding)
mn SLOAM clay between coal-beds
SLOAT slot; bar; bolt
nt SLOOP escort ship, yacht
SLOPE slant; shelve; grade; a ramp, (ski-), sneak off
SLOPS ready-made clothes; nightsoil (prison)
SLOSH slush; sludge; sentimentality
zo SLOTH torpor; tree bear; laziness
SLOYD Swedish handicrafts training
SLUED turned round; tipsy
SLUGS half-roasted ore
SLUMP collapse; sudden fall; marsh
SLUNG flung; thrown; suspended; cast
SLUNK lurked; cowered; skulked
SLUSH slosh; sludge; mire; bathos
SLYLY SLYER, more craftily; artfully
gl SLYNE face of a jointed rock
SLYPE narrow passage
nt SMACK coastal fishing vessel
SMALL tiny; petty; trivial; minute
SMALT blue glass; blue pigment
SMART rankle; pungent; trim; witty
SMASH crash; crack; disrupt; ruin
ga SMASH hard strokes (in ball games)
SMAZE smog and haze (N. Am. & Aus.)
SMEAR daub; plaster; sully begrime
SMELL scent; aroma; odour; perfume
zo SMELT stank; melt ore; small fish
SMIFT a fuse
SMILE smirk; grin; simper
SMIRK an affected smile
SMITE hit; buffet; knock; chasten
SMITH a metal worker; blacksmith
SMOCK a chemise; pastoral garment

ck **SMOKE** fume; (fire-); cure; tobacco-

zo **SMOLT** young river salmon

SMOTE struck (in battle)

zo **SMOUT** speckled trout

zo **SMUCK** a crowd of jellyfish

SNACK hasty light repast; a share

zo **SNAIL** spiral cam; mollusc

zo **SNAKE** serpent; reptile; currency link-up

SNAPE to bevel

SNARE gin; net; toil; wile; trap

SNARL gnarl; growl at; entangle

SNATH SNEAD, crooked

SNEAK lurk; slink; skulk; blab

SNEER gibe; mock; jeer; scoff

SNIDE spurious; dishonest; counterfeit

SNIFF to smell; inhale; scent; snuff

zo **SNIPE** to shoot from ambush; bird

zo **SNOEK** S. African fish; barracouta

SNOOD hairnet; a fillet

SNOOK lurk; snoop; derisive action

SNOOP to pry

SNORE loud breathing during sleep

SNORT loud exhalation through nostrils

gl **SNOUT** nose; nozzle; proboscis; glacial valley

SNOWY pure; unblemished; niveous

SNUFF sniff; (tobacco)

SOAPY unctuous; emollient; flattering

mu **SOAVE** sweetly

SOBER staid; sedate; steady; grave

zo **SOBOL** the Russian sable

cf **SOCIO-** of social; societal nature

SOCKS a drubbing; foot covers

SOCLE plinth

SODDY covered with sod; turfy

nv **SOFAR** underwater navigation system

SOFTA Moslem student

SOGGY boggy; marshy; wet; saturated

SOKEN socage district

bt **SOLAH** solar; sola; sponge-wood

as **SOLAR** concerning the sun (light, heat)

ar, bd **SOLAR** sunshine parlour; solarium

nm **SOLDO** Italian copper coin

ar **SOLEA** raised pathway

SOLED (boots)

zo **SOLEN** razor-fish genus

mu **SOL-FA** the major octave as sung

SOLID hard; dense; stout; stable

cp, bd **SOLID** (-state) electronic devices; door; floor; etc.

SOLON wise legislator; wiseacre

SOLUM piece of ground; soil

lw **SOLUS** alone; sole right, agreement

SOLVE elucidate; unravel; interpret

mu **SOMMA SOMMO**, highest; utmost

nt, nv **SONAR** underwater sound ranging

SONDE upper atmospheric probe; long tube

ae **SONIC** relating to sound; (super-)

cp **SONIC** acoustic delay line

SONNY term of endearment to son

SOOTH truth; reality; true; indeed

SOOTY begrimed

SOPOR deep sleep; moral lethargy

SOPPY moist; wet; silly; weak-minded

mu **SOPRA** above

SORAL pertaining to sorus

SORBO porous rubber

mu **SORDA** damped with a mute

md **SORDE** lips/teeth crust during fever

zo **SOREL** a buck of the third year

SORER more grieved; tenderer

zo **SOREX** a genus including shrew-mice

SORRY sad; dejected; regretful; abject

bt **SORUS** cluster of capsules on ferns

SOUGH low moan; whine; drain

SOUND probe; fathom; hale; valid

tc **SOUND** (music) audible waves, ethereally sent

go, nt **SOUND** narrow sea passage; inlet

SOUPY like soup

SOUSE pickle; sauce; douse; swoop

SOUTH the Southern regions

SOWED strewn; spread; cast

SOWER propagator; disseminator

cp **SPACE** extent; capacity; duration; (universe); a blank

cp **SPACE** area; line conditions in a spiral

to, ga **SPADE** for a dig; (suit of cards)

SPADO spade; eunuch; a sword

SPAHI Algerian cavalryman

SPAKE discoursed; declared; told

SPALL break; split; clip

SPALT a flux; brittle

SPANK a blow; a slap on the bottom

SPARE save; hoard; store; frugal

ga **SPARE** full-pins score on 2 balls (bowling)

SPARK to flash; bright lad

SPASM tic; throe; twitch; paroxysm

SPATE a sudden flood

zo **SPAWN** offspring; ova; sperm

SPEAK express; declare; talk

SPEAR a lance; to pierce

hd **SPEAR** male descent (cf. **DISTAFF**)

SPECK stain; blemish; blubber; lard
SPECS spectacles; reading glasses
SPEED haste; urge; célerity; rate
SPELD chip; splinter
SPELK rod; switch
SPELL write correctly; charm; period
bt **SPELT** spelled; German wheat
SPEND lavish; disburse; exhaust
SPENT consumed; worn; wasted
ar **SPERE** screen of open hall
zo **SPERM** spawn; semen
SPEWY wet; boggy
zo **SPHEX** the wasp genus
md **SPICA** spur; spike; bandage
SPICE to season; flavour; relish
SPICK spike; nail; tidy; fresh
ck **SPICY** aromatic; piquant; racy
SPIED observed; beheld
SPIES secret agents
bt **SPIKE** large nail; lavender; disarm (gun); impale; peak; (fence); volleyball
SPIKY spiny; sharp; pointed
SPILL (woodpile) (wood shed)
SPILL upset (liquid); shed; matchstick
SPILT diffused; scattered; dropped
md **SPINE** spina; spike; back-bone; thickness of arrow (archery); axis of book
zo, bt **SPINK** chaffinch; primrose
SPINY thorny; spiky; difficult
bt **SPIRE** steeple; a curl; sedge
SPIRT spurt; spout; gush; jet
SPIRY spiral
SPITE gall; pique; hatred; malice   *◀*
zo **SPITZ** Pomeranian dog
zo **SPIZA** a finch genus
SPLAT part of a chair-back
SPLAY to widen; spread out
SPLIT divulge; rent; cleave
SPODE china-ware
zo **SPOIL** mar; booty; snake's skin
SPOKE orated; spouted; said
SPOOF hoax; humbug; bamboozle
SPOOK phantom; ghost; spectre
cp **SPOOL** reel; bobbin; small wheel (tape); (film)
nv **SPOOM** to scud down wind (sailing)
SPOON ladle; to court; metal lure (angling); golf club
SPOOR track or trail of an animal
SPORE reproductive cell
SPORT play; gambol; romp; frolic
zo **SPOTS** blemishes; markings (leopard)

SPOUT gush; issue; nozzle
bd **SPRAG** a check-stop; young salmon; pipe or timber wedge
zo **SPRAT** small sea-fish
SPRAY foam; spring; diffuse
SPREE a carousal
SPRIG shoot; twig; a brad
nt **SPRIT** a sprout; boom; spar
zo **SPROD** a second-year salmon
md **SPRUE** a disease
SPUME froth; spray
SPUMY foaming
SPUNK pluck; courage; tinder; semen
SPURN scorn; scout; slight; disdain
SPURT spout; sprint; rush; speed; sudden increase; spray
SQUAD band; gang; crew; bevy
SQUAT crouch; cower; dumpy; stocky; occupy empty house; technique (weight-lifting)
SQUAW Native American woman
SQUIB firework; skit; lampoon
zo **SQUID** cuttlefish; a calamary
SRUTI Hindu tradition
cp, mo **STACK** to pile; chimney; (cards); store; (hay); data; rock (sea)
STADE stadium; arena
mu **STAFF** rod; pole; stick; personnel; (stave) notation system
STAGE produce; present; platform; set up; so far; rig; (motor race)
STAID steady; grave; sedate
STAIN sully; taint; tarnish; soil
STAIR a step; a stairway
STAKE picket; wager; risk; hazard; target (horse-shoe pitching)
nv **STAKE** pole; sea mark; share
STALE dried out; unappetizing; out of date
bt, ag **STALK** hunt; strut; stride; stem; haulm
rl **STALL** (flying); stop; halt; booth; carved seat (church)
STAMP impress; brand; (postage-)
STAND sustain; tolerate; arena seating; fair; defence; upright
ga **STAND** cricket partnership; lacrosse etc.
STANK STUNK, reeked corruption
zo **STARE** gape; gaze; the starling
STARK (naked); scared; severe
lw, rl **STARR** Jewish deed; bond
START begin; entry point (races)
STATE nation; officialdom; condition; (control); status; declare; (of war, alert) period of time; (circumstances)

ar, mu **STAVE** staff; stick; ladder rung; musical notation; (–church; Scand); -dance

md, ae, nt **STAYS** abdominal supports; visits; struts (aircraft); guy ropes (sails, masts, boats)

STEAD substitution; bed frame; use; help

ck **STEAK** thick slice of meat

STEAL (hearts); (shows); quick scores (cricket); rob; move silently; seize; gain

rw, ck, ps **STEAM** (power); (engines); light cookery; water vapour

STEED warhorse; palfrey; mount

STEEL blade; metal; braze; nerve; strength; hardness; determination; resolution

STEEP imbue; dip; soak; excessive; uphill gradient

zo **STEER** guide; pilot; bullock

STEIN earthenware beer tankard (Ger.)

STELA STELE inscribed column; tablet; sap system

STEPS ladders; grades; stages; (dance-) (ice)

nt **STERE** cubic metre

nt **STERN** dour; grim; rigorous

STEVE to stow

nm **STICA** Saxon farthing

mu **STICH** stave; a verse

STICH a row of trees

STICK adhere; attach (loyal); stab; endure

STICK (parachutist); punishment; (walking-)

STIED penned like pigs

STIFF stark; erect; prim; starchy

STIFF not easy; also-ran (horse-racing); corpse

me **STILB** unit of luminance

STILE the gnomon of a sundial

STILE steps in wall or fence (footpath)

STILL not sparkling; calm; distil

zo **STILT** a pole (pole-walking); a snipe

STING prick; wound; hurt; afflict

STINK stench; odour; smell

STINT allotted task; limit; scrimp

zo **STINT** sandpiper; dunlin

bt **STIPA** the feather grasses

bt **STIPE** stalk; stem

zo **STIRK** young ox or cow

STIRP line of descent

ck **STIVE** to stew

STIVY stuffy; close

me **STOAK** to stop; to choke

zo **STOAT** ermine; weasel

STOCK cravat; store; gamer; fund

STOCK log (-house); ski-stick; (-in trade); seat (live-); (-anchor); procure

STOCK wooden chest; stocks (penalty)

ar **STOEP** stoop; verandah (S. Afr.)

STOIC Zenonist; suffers silently (Gr.)

STOKE replenish; refuel

STOLA Roman lady's dress; shawl

bt **STOLE** peculated; plagiarized; a sucker

STOLE robbed; priest's vestment

bt **STOMA** breathing pore

STOMP move importantly (heavily)

STONE boulder; weight 14lb/6.3kg

STONY hard; flinty; obdurate; broke

STOOD allowed; brooked; bore

bt **STOOK STOUK,** 12 sheaves (of corn)

STOOL a seat without a back; ramify

STOOM stum; renew fermentation

STOOP flagon; condescend; yield

STOOR stour; dust; commotion

STOPE mining ledge; to excavate

bd, mu, lw **STOPS** projecting stones; (organ); delays, hindrances

cp **STORE** hoard; garner; stock; supply

zo **STORK** infant conveyor; bird

mt **STORM** fume; rage; scold; turmoil

pr **STORY** narrative; novel; (news-)

STOUP stoop; flagon; tankard

md **STOUR** tumult; paroxysm

ck **STOUT** wide-girthed; robust; a drink (porter)

STOVE oven; kiln; to heat; (-in) smashed

mu **STRAD** a Stradivarius violin

STRAP belt; binding; (safety-)

bt, bd **STRAW** dried cereal stalk; thatch; trifle; (last-)

STRAY err; rove; wander; deviate; lost

STREW scatter; spread; broadcast

STRIA stripe; streak; small channel

bt **STRIG** stalk; footstalk

STRIP peel; divest; dismantle; shred

STRIP (air-); marked line; ribbon

zo **STRIX** screech-owl

STROB measure of angular velocity

le, nt **STROP** sharpening leather; rope

mu **STRUM** thrum; (guitar)

STRUT support; brace; walk; swagger

STUCK set; fixed; adhered; stabbed

STUDS wall timber; collar fasteners; men

STUDY con; scan; reflect; learning; den

STUFF cram; pack; cloth; fabric

mn STULL cross-timber in a mine

mn STULM shaft used to drain a mine

STULP a stump (cricket)

ga STUMP log; block; stub; (cricket)

STUNG pricked; afflicted; deceived

STUNK STANK, of ill odour

STUNT to dwarf; (arrested); breakneck risks

cp STUNT box in teleprinter controlling operation

STUPA Buddhist monument; a dagoba

md STUPE hot bandage; fomentation

STURT strife; wrath; vexation

ga STUTZ parallel bars swing (gymn.)

nm STYCA Saxon half-farthing

STYLE pen; dub; entitle; mode; distinction; (life-)

cp STYLE constant; recognization script for viewing

STYLO a pen; a stylograph

SUAVE bland; pleasant; polite

SUBAH province; viceroyship (Ind.)

zo SUDAK the pike-perch

SUDRA the lowest Hindu caste

le SUEDE unglazed leather

SUENT neaty and tidy

ck SUETY of suet fat

rl SUFIC Islamic mysticism

ck SUGAR sweetening; flattery

lw SUING legal prosecution

SUITE retinue; series; train; apartment

cp SUITE sequence of interrelated programs

SULKS SULKY, grumpiness; morose

ga SULKY chariot for trotting races

SULLY soil; taint; stain; defame

bt, ck SUMAC SUMACH, plant used in dyeing

SUNCK female chief of Native American tribe

rl SUNNA SUNNI, of Moslem traditions; orthodox sect

SUNNY bright; brilliant; unclouded

SUN-UP sunrise; dawn; cock-crow

SUPER a supernumerary; extra special

cf SUPER- superior; above; (-market)

cf SUPRA- transcending; (supranational)

tx, rl SURAH Indian silk; chapter of Koran

md SURAL (calf of the leg)

tx SURAT coarse Indian cotton

SURER more certain; safer

SURGE roll; swell; heave; a billow; advance

SURLY churlish; morose; crusty; gruff

SURMA Ind. eyeshadow

rl SURYA Hindu sun-god

ck SUSHI bean–curd rice dish (Jap.)

SUTOR a cobbler

rl SUTRA Brahmin exercises

SWAGE drill-bit shaping tool

SWAIN a peasant; a country lover

SWALE shady spot; vale; channel

rl SWAMI religious instructor (Hindu)

SWAMP flood; inundate; fen; slough

SWANG swamp greensward

SWANK brag; swagger

SWAPE handle; oar; sconce

SWARD turf; bacon rind

SWARE testified; deposed; cursed

SWARF to faint; to swoon; grit

zo SWARM throng; teem; cluster; bevy; (bees)

SWAZI of Swaziland (S. Africa)

SWEAR affirm; vow; vouch; blaspheme

SWEAT exude; ooze; perspire; (toil)

bt, ck SWEDE a turnip

SWEEP (chimney); brush; lottery

nt SWEEP a blend; scope; curve; oar

SWEET luscious; honeyed; dulcet

mu, nt SWELL expand; dilate; amplify; bulge; undulating sea

SWEPT brushed

zo SWIFT fleet; quick; sudden; prompt

SWILL quaff; wash; rinse

zo SWINE pig; evil-doer; (foul); deceiver

SWING sway; dangle; hang; turn round

mu SWING movement; pendulum; 1930s' easy music

ga SWING of golf; oar (strokes); punch (boxing)

SWIPE smite; slog; steal

go SWIRE a col; a hollow between 2 hills

SWIRL whirl; gyrate; eddy

SWISH to birch; thrash; posh; fine

SWISS of Switzerland; Helvetian

md SWOON to faint (with shock)

SWOOP rush; stoop (eagle); descent

SWORD (-blade); rapier; cutlass

SWORE oaths; blasphemies

lw SWORN under oath; affirmed

SWUNG rocked; vacillated; dangled

SYCEE silver in small ingots (China)

rl SYLPH SYLPHIDE, an airy fairy; (Pope); Cupid's beloved

fr **SYLVI** (–culture) forestry
management
rl **SYNOD** ecclesiastical Council
mu **SYREN SIREN**, alarm hooter; love
songs; enticer
ck **SYRUP** strongly sweetened liquid

T

TABAC snuff-colour; (tobacco)
tx, zo, wv **TABBY** brindled; watered silk; a cat;
earliest plain weave
md **TABES** emaciation; atrophy
md **TABID** consumptive; phthisical
cp **TABLE** index; list; schedule; board;
array of data
TABOO ban; bar; prohibit; interdict
mu **TABOR** camp; laager; small drum
bt **TACCA** tropical plant genus
mu **TACET** be silent!
TACHE moustache; catch; freckle;
loop
cf **TACHY-** rapidity, speed (Gr.)
TACIT silent; implicit; inferred
TACKY viscous; gummy; sticky
TAFFY a Welshman; toffy; blarney
TAFIA Malay rum
TAGAL Filipino
zo **TAGMA** region of metameric animal
TAHLI Hindu gold ornament
go **TAIGA** coniferous region (Siberia)
tx **TAILS** men's evening dress; (heads
or–)
TAINT stain; tarnish; sully; defile
zo **TAIPO** taepo; vicious animal (NZ)
TAKEN seized; captured; won;
assumed
TAKER grasper; acceptor
ro **TALBE** air/sea rescue system
TALES stories; equals in kind;
(jurors)
TALLY agree; correspond; match;
count; score; (wag)
cp **TALLY** printout from adding
machine
TALMA loose cloak
TALON claw; concave; moulding
zo, md **TALPA** on the mole genus; a wen
TALUK Indian subdistrict
gl, md **TALUS** steep scree slope; knuckle
bone, dice; earthwork; ankle bone
TAMED docile; domesticated; curbed
TAMER subjugator; subduer
TAMIL a Dravidian language (Sri
Lanka)
TAMIN glazed worsted stuff
TAMIS tammy; straining cloth

TAMMY tamis; a tam-o'-shanter
(Scots hero)
bt **TAMUS** black bryony
mu **TANGO** Argentine dance
TANGY piquant; sharp in taste
bt **TANIA** African farinaceous tuber
TANKA Canton boat population
TANNA tana; Indian police station
ck, bt **TANSY** Easter cake; bitter herb
mu **TANTO** so; so much
TAPAS side-snacks in a bar (Sp.)
TAPED measured; sized up; bound
together; (red-)
TAPER wax-candle; slender and
conical
TAPET tapestry; tapis
zo **TAPIR** related to pig (South Amer.)
TAPIS TAPET, of tapestry; wall
decoration
TAPIS hidden; under consideration
bt **TAPPA** tapa; fibre for mats
mu **TARDO** slowly
TARDY late; sluggish; dilatory
TARED macadamized (road); freight
weighed
bt **TARFA** tamarisk; (exudes manna)
zo **TARIN** the siskin
TAROT divining cards (78)
TARRY stay; linger; sojourn; loiter
md **TARSE** the tarsus; foot; ankle
zo **TARSI** feet of insects
TARUS projection between roof
surfaces
TASSE thigh armour; drinking cup
(Fr./Ger.)
TASTE savour; experience;
preference
mu **TASTO** It. finger board of stringed or
keyboard instrument
TASTY piquant; savoury; appetising
TATAR Turkic native within CIS
zo **TATOU** tatu; peba; armadillo
TAT-TA goodbye; a stroll
bt **TATTA** Indian screen; of cuscus
grass
TATTY tattered; worn out; shabby
nt **TAUNT** deride; revile; high-masted
TAWED treated with alum
TAWER a leather-dresser
TAWNY fulvid; brown; tanned
TAWSE taws; leather strap (Sc.)
TAXED burdened; accused
zo **TAXEL** N. American badger
TAXER inspector of taxes
bt **TAXIN** yew extract
TAXIS taxi-cabs (hired cars)
-TAXIS tropism; species responses
bt **TAXUS** yew genus

TAZZA wine cup with shallow bowl
TEACH coach; edify; instruct
TEASE vex; annoy; plague; harass
ar,rl **TEBAM** dais; rostrum in synagogue
zo **TEDDY** a bear; Pooh's cousin
TEENS thirteen to nineteen
TEENY wee; tiny; minute
TEETH dentures; snowcomb (curling)
TE-HEE titter; snigger
TEIAN Ionian, (Anacreon)
TELAR web-like; woven; spun
cf **TELEO-** far, distant, end (Gr.)
tc **TELEX** teleprinter universal system
TELIC final; conclusive
zo **TELUM** last abdominal somite in insects
rl **TEMPE** the Gods' amusement park, Thessaly
mu **TEMPO** (cards); relative rapidity
TEMPT allure; lure; decoy; entice
TEMSE sieve; to sift
zo **TENCH** a fish
TENET rigid doctrine; dogma; belief
ar **TENIA** moulding on architrave
TENNE an orange-brown colour
TENON of mortise lock (doors)
mu **TENOR** purport; trend; course; high male voice
TENSE taut; tight; intent; strained
TENTH a tithe; ordinal number
TENTY attentive; alert; (tenter hooks)
TEPAL a perianth leaf
TEPID TEPOR, lukewarm; moderate
me **TERCE** about 42 gal (191 litres)
zo **TEREK** a sandpiper
md **TERES** a muscle
bt **TERFA** edible fruit-body of terferia
md **TERMA** terminal lamina of brain
TERNE inferior tin-plate
TERRA earth
tx **TERRY** a fabric
TERSE abrupt
me **TESLA** magnetic-flux density
bt **TESTA** husk; integument
TESTY techy; fretful; irritable
cf **TETRA-** of four parts (Gr.)
TEWEL chimney flue
THANE Scottish baron
THANK express gratitude
THAWY inclined to thaw
bt **THECA** seed or spore case
THEFT larceny; robbery; pilfering
THEIC tea-pot devotee
bt **THEIN** tea
THEIR of them
THEMA subject for discussion

mu **THEME** melodic/topical motif repeated
THERE at that place
me **THERM** thermal unit of gas
THESE pl. of this
THETA a Greek letter
THEWY muscular; strong
THICK dense; solid; stupid; friendly
THIEF pickpocket; an Autolycus
pl **THIGH** upper part of leg; (hams)
THILL shaft of a cart; fire-clay
rl **THINE** of Thee, Thy, of God
THING object; article; entity
THING TING, Scandinavian Parliament
THINK deem; muse; cogitate
mu **THIRD** ordinal number, 3rd; melodic interval
mm **THIRL** to cut through workings
THIRL a restriction; to pierce
THOFT a rowing bench
nt **THOLE THOWL,** rowlock
le **THONG** length of leather; lash; whip
bt **THORN** prickle; spine; (in flesh)
THORP homestead; hamlet; dorp
THOSE pl. of that
THOTH Egyptian god of wisdom
zo **THOUS** African jackal genus
nt **THOWL** thole; pin for an oar
THRAP to fasten
THREE cardinal number; a leash
THREW flung; hurled; projected
md **THROB** regular beat; palpitation
THROE pang; agony; anguish
THROW cast; toss; fell; pitch; (dice); (fit); (party)
mu **THRUM** yarn; fringe; to strum
THULE Ultima Thule; (Greenland)
THUMB that odd large finger; turn pages
THUMP knock; bang; punch; pommel
THURL thirl; passage in a mine
bt **THUYA** arbor vitae
bt,ck **THYME** fragrant savoury plant
cf **THYMO-** of emotion; temper; soul (Gr.)
THYMY fragrant
TIARA ornamental head-dress
zo **TIBBY** cat
tx **TIBET** heavy goat-hair fabric
md **TIBIA** the large shinbone
nm **TICAL** Siamese rupee
nt **TIDAL** of ebb and flood
zo **TIDDY** the wren
TIDED surmounted; managed to survive

TIE-IN tubular scaffolding; interior grip
nt TIFFY an artifer
zo TIGER jungle cat; diminutive groom
TIGHT taut; tense; close; compact; tipsy
ga TIGNA forward somersault (gym.)
bt TIKUL Indian tree
TILDE diacritical mark
TILED tesselated
TILER Masonic doorkeeper
bt TILIA lime-tree
TILKA Hindu caste mark
ag TILTH good soil condition for cultivation
TIMED measured, finite
cp TIMER time-fixed, -ing device
TIMES the newspaper
TIMES durations
TIMID shy; fearful; diffident
TIMON Athenian misanthrope
zo, md TINEA moth genus; ringworm
TINED pronged
TINGE hue; tint; stain; dye
bt TINGI Brazilian soap-tree
TINNY like tin; sharp in sound
TINTY crudely tinted
TIPSY tight; drunk; fuddled
tx TIRAZ Moorish silk fabric
TIRED weary; harassed; attired
T'IRON a webbed bar
TISRI Hebrew month
TITAN giant; Cyclops; Goliath
rl TITHE a tenth; a tax
lw TITLE claim; right; (due); ownership; deeds; rank
ba TITRE quantity of antibody
TITUP tittup; skip; canter
TIVER ochre sheep dye
nm TIZZY a sixpence
TOADY a sycophant
TOAST scorch; health proposal
TOBAS S. American native race
TOBIT Apocryphal book
TODAY this day
me TODDE 28 lb weight (obs.)
TODDY a cordial; mixed drink (India)
au TOE-IN front-wheels adjustment
TOGGY arctic coat made from beaver
TOGED arrayed in a toga
zo TOGUE mackinaw; lake-trout
tx TOILE twill; linen-silk mixture
TOILS a snare
me TOISE old French linear unit
TOKAY Hungarian wine
TOKEN sign; symbol; mark; badge
nm TOMAN Persian gold coin

me TOMIN a weight of 12 grains
to TOMMY Atkins; soldier; lever
mu TONAL accented; harmonious notes
TONDO circular relief sculpture
TONED moderated; shaded; tinted
pt TONER organic dye
TONGA Eastern cart
ck TONIC strengthening; bracing; quinine drink
mu TONIC keynote of octave
bt TONKA tree whose seeds contain coumarin
mu TONUS state of persistent excitation; minor scale; Gregorian tone
bt, ar, pl TOOTH prong; fang; tusk (cog) (comb) (dog-)
zo TOPAU rhinoceros-bird
mn TOPAZ a gem
TOPEE sun helmet
TOPER toss-pot; sot; tippler
zo TOPET crested titmouse
zo TOPHI ear cartilage nodules
TOPIA Roman mural decoration
md TOPIC theme; subject; a remedy
TOPOS cliché description
tx TOQUE Canadian knitted cap
TOQUE woman's twisted silk turban
lw TORAH the Mosaic law
rl TORAN Buddhist porch
TORCH flambeau; link; fire-brand
TORIC type of lens
ar TORII Jap. gateway
hd TORSE heraldic wreath
zo TORSK a cod
md TORSO body trunk
ar TORUS an architectural moulding
TOSSY contemptuous
TOTAL all; sum; whole; gross
TOTED carried; borne; transported
TOTEM symbol of local guardian spirits (from 'ototeman') N. Am.
TOUCH contact; handle; concern; effect
TOUGH tenacious; strength
TOUSE tousle; haul; tease
nt TOWED hauled; dragged; tugged
tx TOWEL an altar or drying cloth (bathroom)
TOWER soar; mount; turret
TOWNY a townsman
TOXIC TOXIN
TOYED played with (idea) (ball) etc.
TOYER dilettante; trifler
TRACE vestige; remains; copy; sketch
TRACE trail; elements; figures
TRACK spoor; (rail-); (racing-); follow

pr **TRACT** region; pamphlet; homily
pl **TRACT** bundle of nerve fibres
go **TRADE** exchange; barter; swap;
  (-winds)
   TRAIL path; route; tow; haul; follow
rw **TRAIN** drill; school; retinue
   TRAIT characteristic
bt **TRAMA** agaric-gill hyphae
nt **TRAMP** hike; vagrant; hobo; (-ship)
   TRAPE TRAIPSE, move around
  vaguely
   TRAPS snares; luggage etc.
   TRASH worthless refuse; poor whites
  (USA)
mn **TRASS** volcanic earth
   TRAVE beam; wooden frame
   TRAWL a drag-net
   TREAD trample; step; press
   TREAT offer; occasion; cure; deal
fr **TREED** up-a-tree; in refuge
  (cornered); forested
   TREEN wooden; collectors' term for
  household objects
   TREND popular fashion; (inclined to)
   TRESS ringlet; lock of hair
tx **TREWS** Scottish trousers
el, ps **TRIAC** silicon-controlled rectifier
tv, mu **TRIAD** a trinity; 3-colour phosphor
  dot pictures; chord
cp **TRIAD** 3 binary digits, symbols, data
  units
lw **TRIAL** test; ordeal; case; (court)
mn **TRIAS** sandstone
   TRIBE clan; race; class; order
nt **TRICE** an instant; to haul
   TRICK dupe; cheat; artifice; (cards);
  duty turn; device
lw **TRIED** essayed; attempted
   TRIER experimentalist
ga **TRIES** (Rugby football, 3 or 4
  points)
mu **TRILL** warble; quaver; shake
as **TRINE** triple; threefold; a triad;
  astrology
as **TRINE** favourable planet aspect
lw **TRIOR** an examiner
ck **TRIPE** stomach offal; nonsense
   TRIST sorrowful; sad
   TRITE hackneyed; obvious; worn
ga **TROCO** a ball game
   TROIC Trojan
   TROLL to fish; sing; cave-elf
  (Scand.)
mn **TRONA** Egyptian soda
   TRONC distribution of pooled tips
me **TRONE** steelyard; a drain
   TROOP march (army); throng; crowd
   TROPE metaphor; figure of speech

mu **TROPE** 12-note technique
   TROTH to plight; confidence; faith
zo **TROUT** fish of Salmo genus
   TROVE something found; (treasure-)
   TRUCE lull; respite; armistice
   TRUCK a wheel; barter; a vehicle
nt **TRUCK** wagon; mast-head
   TRUER more worthy of belief
   TRULL vagrant; a drab
   TRULY verily; exactly; veritably
ga **TRUMP** (the last trump); to ruff;
  leading suit (cards) (bridge)
mu **TRUMP** a trumpet; Jew's harp
   TRUNK torso; butt; stem; saratoga
cp **TRUNK** highway; interface channel
md, ar **TRUSS** bind; fasten; framework of
  timbers
   TRUST credit; reliance; merger
ma **TRUTH** probity; fact; honesty;
  reality; (Boolean)
bt **TRYMA** a stone fruit; a drupe
   TRY-ON a bluff
mu, rl **TRYST** rendezvous: (Lutheran carol)
   TSUBA Japanese sword hilt
rl **TSUNG** ritual jade (China)
mu **TUBAL** of tuba; tubular construction
   TUBBY fat; obese; dull
   TUBED piped
bt **TUBER** bulbous growth
zo **TUCAN** Mexican pouched rat
bt **TUCUM** S. American palm
   TUDEH political party (Iran)
   TUDOR a royal house
   TUFTY feathery
   TUILE TUILLE, TUILLERY, armour
  plating
   TUISM a curious theory
bt **TULIP** showy flower
tx **TULLE** a delicate fabric
mu **TUMBA** instrument S. Domingo
   TUMID swollen; bombastic
   TUMPY lumpy; uneven
   TUNED attuned; harmonized;
  adapted
mu, ro, tv **TUNER** sound adjuster; channel
  selector
md **TUNIC** surcoat; a membrane
zo **TUNNY** large fish, mackerel type
mu **TURBA** chorus of the people in
  opera
zo **TURBO** whelk and winkle genus
ae **TURBO-** jet engine
   TURCO Ottoman soldier
   TURFY swardy; grassy; cespitose
   TURNS rotation; artistes' acts;
  pirouettes; virtuoso tricks (ice
  skating) (water-skiing)
   TURPS turpentine

zo, pl **TUSKS TUSKY, TUSSES,** elephant's ivory; teeth
TUSKY with long teeth
bd **TUSSE** wall-face projecting stone
TUTOR coach; instruct; guardian
TUTSI native of Burundi (Africa)
mu **TUTTI** all in (It.)
ch **TUTTY** impure oxide of zinc
TUZZY tuft; tuffet; cluster
TWAIN a couple; brace; pair
zo **TWAIT** species of shad
TWANG tang; flavour
TWEAK pinch; twist; twitch
tx, wv **TWEED** twilled cloth
TWEEN between; twixt
TWEER TWIER blast-furnace
TWERP nasty nitwit
TWICE twofold; doubly; encore
wv, tx **TWILL TWEEL,** woven fabric
TWINE ENTWINE, bind together; cord; winding
TWIRL whirl; rotate; revolve
TWIST writhe; hunger; (tobacco)
zo **TWITE** mountain linnet
TWIXT betwixt; between
pr **TWO-ON** doing 2 jobs at once
pr **TWO-UP** printing, processing twin series
TWYER TWEER, blast furnace; jet
rl **TYCHE** Greek goddess of fortune
TYING fastening; shacking
TYLER tiler; Masonic doorkeeper
fr **TYLER** tight-line gorge system
TYPAL typical; representative
pr **TYPED** typewritten; given a classification
bt **TYPHA** bulrush
TYPIC emblematic; symbolic
TYRED wheeled, pneumatic
rl **TYTHE** tithe; a tenth; church tax

U

nt **U-BOAT** a submarine
UBYKH language
zo **UDDER** mammary gland
bd **U-DUCT** gas heater ventilator
UGRIC Finns, Magyars, Turks, etc.
UHLAN Prussian cavalryman
UHURU freedom (Swahili)
UKASE Russian decree
md **ULCER** open sore
ULEMA Turkish hierarchy
bt **ULMIC ULMUS,** of elms; (exudations)
ULMIN humus; a brown pigment
bt **ULMUS** elm genus
pl **ULNAD ULNAR,** of the forearm bone

md **ULOID** like a scar
cf **-ULOUS** of tendency towards
el **ULTOR** anode
ULTRA extreme
cf **-ULTRA** of extreme, beyond excessive
bt **UMBEL** inflorescence flower
UMBER brown pigment
as **UMBRA** a shadow; (total solar eclipse)
zo **UMBRE** the grayling
nt **UMIAK** Eskimo boat
pc **UMWEG** detour to goal, round about (Ger.)
UNAPT inept; irrelevant
UNARM disarm
ch, cp **UNARY** consisting of 1 component; monadic operation
UNBAR open; permit
UNBAY to open up
UNBED arouse
UNBID uninvited; spontaneous
UNBIT not bitten
ar **UNBOW** to unbend
UNBOX uncase; unpack
UNCAP unhat; uncover; open
UNCLE pawnbroker; relation
UNCLE Sam; Tom; Remus
zo **UNCUS** hook or claw
UNCUT untrimmed; book before guillotine process
UNDAM release
UNDER below; lower; subject to
UNDID untied; nullified
UNDUE excessive; inordinate
UNFIT unqualified; improper
UNFIX detach; undo; loosen
UNGUM unstick
UNHAT uncover; uncap
rl **UNIAT** Russian Christian
UNIFY unite; combine
lw **UNION** linked; marital; coalition; guild
pb **UNION** league; joint organization; junction (pipes, el., gas)
UNITE bind together; federate; (concerted)
UNITY concord; harmony; accord
UNLAP unfold
UNLAY untwist; unravel
UNLED without guidance
UNLET vacant; tenantless
UNMAN dishearten; unnerve
UNMEW release from confinement
ma **UNODE** a geometric conception
UNSAY retract; disavow; (cancel previous pacts)
ck, bd **UNSET** unmounted; still liquid or sticky; virgin

cp **UNSET** for computers as reset
md, vt **UNSEX** geld; castrate; spay
lw **UNTAX** declare free from tax
UNTIE undo; unbind; unknot
UNTIL till; to such time as
UNWED not yet married
UNZIP undo patent fastening
mu **UP-BOW** violin bow position in play
UP-END tilt; place in vertical
position
nt **UPPER** superior; higher; part of shoe
above sole; (-works of ship)
md **UPSET** capsize; overturn; disconcert;
spill; (stomach)
zo **UPUPA** hoopoe genus
ch **URATE** UREIC, of uric acid
URBAN of the city
bt **UREDO** fungus genus
UREIC pertaining to urea
bt **URENA** Indian mallow
URGED URGER, pleaded; impelled;
prompter; agitator
zo **URIAL** Asiatic wild sheep
zo **URILE** cormorant
md **URINE** liquid body waste
URNAL URNED, of the urn
(cremation)
zo **URSON** Canadian porcupine
zo **URSUS** the bear genus
zo **URUBU** American turkey-buzzard
USAGE habit; wont; custom
lw **USHER** court official; precede
USING applying; employing
USUAL normal; ordinary; habitual
USURP arrogate; assume; seize
USURY exorbitant; interest
UTTER declare; enunciate; total
md **UVULA** (soft palate)
UZBEG UZBEK, Turkish Tatar; of
Uzbekistan region

V

VAGAL of the vagus nerves
VAGUE dim; indistinct; indefinite
md **VAGUS** a cranial nerve
hd **VAIRE** VAIRY, charged with heraldic
fur
VALET gentleman's gentleman
VALID cogent; substantial; strong
mu **VALSE** waltz; dance
VALUE worth; price; cost; utility
el, pl, mu, **VALVE** electron tube; regulator
rw device; (heart); (horn); steam
VANED having vanes or blades
VANIR three Norse deities
VAPID insipid; feeble; jejune

VAPOR vapour; miasma; steam
bt **VAREC** seaweed; kelp
VARIA miscellany
md **VARIX** uneven dilation
md **VARUS** pigeon-toed
gl, go **VARVE** clay; silt sediments in lake or
sea
md **VASAL** (blood-vessel)
rl **VATIC** prophetic; oracular; (Vatican)
VAULT leap; cell; tomb; crypt
VAUNT boast; exult; swagger
rl **VEDAS** VEDIC, of Hindu sacred
writings
zo **VEERY** American thrush
VEGAN total vegetarian
VEINY full of veins
ar **VELAR** cupola or dome
VELDT grass lands (S. Africa)
zo **VELIA** water-bugs
md **VELUM** soft palate
VENAL mercenary; corrupt; sordid
ga **VENEW** VENEY, fencing thrust
VENOM virus; poison; rancour; gall
VENUE location of an event
VENUS Aphrodite
VEREY signal light
cp, rl **VERGE** edge; staff; mace; margin
(punched card)
VERSE poetry; stanza; stich; stave
pr **VERSO** left-hand page
me **VERST** Russian; ⅔ of a mile (1 km)
VERTU VIRTU, rarity in art
VERVE energy; vigour; inspiration
zo **VESPA** wasp genus
VESTA goddess of the hearth
bt **VETCH** ers; the tare
VEXED VEXER, annoyed; bothered;
provoker
bt **VEXIL** a banner; a petal
VIAND food
md **VIBEX** a blood spot
rl **VICAR** parish parson
cp **VIDEO** recorded television film;
visual display unit
ck **VIFDA** VIVDA, dried meat
VIGIL watch; wake; eve
VILER more degraded
ar **VILLA** country residence (Roman)
md, bt **VILLI** small fibres
bt **VIMEN** slender shoot
bt **VINCA** periwinkle
VINED with tendrils
VINIC of wine making; alcoholic
VINYL plastic fibre
bt, mu **VIOLA** plant genus; stringed
instrument
zo **VIPER** adder; asp
zo **VIREO** American song-birds

as **VIRGO** (Zodiac); a constellation; the Maiden
md **VIRUS** mini-transmitter of infection
VISIT frequent; call; drop in
zo **VISON** American mink
VISOR VIZOR, movable part of a helmet; a mask
VISTA view; scene; prospect
VITAL essential; animate; living
bt **VITEX** verbena
bt **VITIS** the vine
VITTA a headband; garland
bt **VITTA** stripe; oil cavity
VIVAT (applause)
ck **VIVDA VIFDA** dried meat
vt **VIVES** a disease of horses
VIVID intense; brilliant; graphic
zo **VIXEN** female fox; hussie
zo **VIZEN** scold; shrew; termagant
VIZIR vizier; vezir; minister (Ottoman)
VLACH a Wallachian; (Romanian)
VOCAL articulate
tc **VODAS** echo-suppression device
ac **VODER** synthetic-speech device
ck **VODKA** Russian spirits; drink
VOGAD telephony
VOGUE fashion; mode; practice
mu **VOICE** express; declare; utter; sound production; (vocal)
tc **VOICE** human speech as electrical signals
VOIDS ratio of solids to spaces occupied by air or water
tx **VOILE** gauzy material
md **VOLAR** (palm of the hand)
mu **VOLEE** rapid phrase
VOLET part of triptych
mu **VOLTA VOLTE**, old dance turn; repeat
VOLTE 2-legged turn (horsemanship)
mu **VOLTI** turn over
md **VOMER** ploughshare; nose-bone
VOMIT spew; eject; disgorge
VOTED VOTER, polled; balloted; elector
VOUCH VOWED, VOWER, swore; dedicated; pledger
VOWED swore; pledged; dedicated
VOWEL open speech sound
VOWER pledger; promiser; swearer
VROUW woman; wife (Dutch)
VULGO VULGATE, in popular style (language)
pl **VULVA** female genitals; orifice
mu **VUOTA VUOTO**, pause, interval (It.)
VYING striving; competing

W

mn **WACKE** basalt; trap-rock
WADDY Australian war club
WADED forded
zo **WADER** long-legged bird
WADEX word/author index for computers
ck **WAFER** crisp cake
WAGED pledged; conducted; salaried
zo **WAGEL** black gull
WAGER bet; hazard; stake; gamble
WAGES stipend; remuneration
WAGON wain; lorry; truck
md, bt **WAHOO** cascara sagrada
pl **WAIST** narrows above hips
WAITS Yule minstrels
WAIVE remit; forego; relinquish
WAKED kept vigil; stimulated
WAKEN awaken; excite; animate
bt **WALAN** amboyna tree
nt **WALAP** outrigger sail canoe (S. Pacific)
zo **WALER** Australian horse
nt, rd **WALTY** unstable; radar
mu **WALTZ** valse; dance
WANED ebbed; decreased; declined
WANLY sickly; languidly
WANTY a loading strap
WARES merchandist; commodities
WARTY with excrescencs; blemishes
WASHY watery; thin; feeble
WASTE dissipate; squander; fritter away
WASTE industrial-; household-; rubbish (-paper)
WASTE infertile; unusable area; (-land)
nt **WATCH** guard; tend; mark
WATCH small timepiece; (wrist-)
ch, go **WATER** liquid of life; (rain-) (drinking-)
WATER irrigate; flood; sprinkle; moisten
WAVED fluctuated; brandished; hand-greeted
WAVER sway; totter; vacillate
zo **WAVEY** rough sea; (design); snow-goose
WAXED cered; sealed; grew; increased (moon)
WAXEN of ceruminous secretion; (bees-); images
fr, go **WEALD WOLD**, woodland
WEARY jaded; spent; fatigue; tire
wv **WEAVE** plait; mat; entwine; interlace
ga **WEAVE** figure of 8 movement (basketball) (lacrosse) (football)

WEBBY filmy; reticulated
me WEBER magnetic flux
ga WEDGE tapered wood blocker; golf club
bt, tx WEEDS unwanted plants in garden, crops, lawns; widow's mourning costume
bt WEEDY weak and lanky
WEELY wicker fish trap
WEEPY lacrimose; oozy
nt WEIGH balance; ponder; (anchor)
WEIRD eerie; uncanny; supernatural
WEISM excessive use of 'we'
WELCH WELSH, people of Cymru; of Wales
WELCH WELSH, fail a promise
WENCH maid; damsel
WHACK THWACK, beat; smite; defeat
zo WHALE the orc; a cetacean
WHALL wall-eye
zo WHAME the burrel-fly
WHARE Maori hut
WHARF quay; dock; pier
zo WHAUP curlew
WHEAL weal; bruise mark after blow
mn WHEAL mine (Cornish)
bt WHEAT a cereal
WHEEL a revolving frame; to turn; whirl
WHEEL of tactics (– & deal) (roulette) (fate)
zo, ck WHELK edible gastropod; seafood
zo WHELP puppy; cub; pup; to litter
WHERE the place concerned
WHICH the item concerned
nt, ga WHIFF puff; outrigger boat, strike-out (baseball); smell; cigarette
WHIFT a breath; a snatch; glimpse
WHILE at concurrent time; pass the time
zo WHILK the scoter; sea duck
WHINE whimper; snivel; cry
WHIRL twirl; spin; gyrate; eddy
WHISK a brush; stir; hasten; rush
WHIST keep silence; (cards)
WHITE pale; wan; pallid; chalky
WHIZZ whiz; rush past; flash by; of fireworks (-king)
WHOLE entire; intact; total
WHOOP a shout of joy
WHORL convolution; spiral; medieval furniture motif
bt WHORT whortleberry
WHOSE the owner of item concerned
WHOSO he who
bt WICKY mountain ash
WIDEN extend; enlarge
WIDER broader; more remote

zo WIDOW a bereaved wife; (black-, spider)
WIDTH span; amplitude; beam
WIELD control; exert; ply; brandish
tx WIGAN stiff canvas
WIGHT a creature; strong; nimble
WILED beguiled; let time pass
WILLY wool cleaning machine; penis
WINCE flinch; blench; shrink
WINCH hoisting machine
WINDY stormy; breezy; pneumatic (Sc.); afraid
WINED drank wine
ga WINGS boundary players (football) (bowls) (flying) (theatre)
WINGY rapid
WINZE ventilating shaft; a curse
WIPED rubbed; mopped; cleansed
WIPER cleaner-dryer; (windscreen-)
el WIRED telegraphed; snared; connected
WISER sager; more expedient
WISPY flocculent; nebulous
WITAN Witenagemot (Anglo-Saxon); moot; council
WITCH hag; crone; sibyl
bt WITHE willow twig
bt WITHY species of willow
WITTY droll; facetious; humorous
WIVES spouses
WIZEN shrivelled; dried up
rl WODEN Odin; Wotan
WOMAN female human
WOMEN pl. of woman
zo WONGA Australian pigeon
fr WOODS tree area; wooden-head clubs (golf)
WOODY of tree products; sylvan
WOOED WOOER, courted; lover; swain
WOOER a lover; a swain
ga WOOFS variation in handicapping (golf)
WOOFY dense; close in texture
bt WOOLD twist; dyer's weed
zo WOONT the mole
WORDY verbose; prolix; garrulous
WORLD universe; globe; earth
zo WORMY vermigerous
WORRY fret; chafe; fidget; badger
WORSE comparative of bad
WORST the most bad; to defeat; conquer
WORTH value; cost; merit; desert
rl WOTAN Odin; Woden
WOULD conditional auxil. verb
WOUND harm; hurt; lacerate
wv, tx WOVEN plaited; interlaced

bt **WRACK** (– and ruin); seaweed
tx **WRANG WRUNG**, twisted to squeeze water out
WRATH ire; rage; fury; passion
WREAK avenge; inflict havoc
nt **WRECK** ruin; blight; shatter; (ship-)
WREST to twist; obtain by violence
WRICK to sprain
WRING extort; wrest; writhe
WRIST hand/arm joint
cp **WRITE** indite; scrawl; scribble; (pen); transcribe data
WRONG injure; falsify; error; tort
WROTE inscribed; penned; engrossed
WROTH wrathful; angry; furious
WRUNG tormented; racked
WRYLY in a distorted manner
bt **WYTHE** willow twig

X

nt **XEBEC ZEBEC**, Algerian pirate ship
bt **XENIA** pollen effect on young plant
ch **XENON** a gas
ec **XERIC** adapted to dry conditions
cr **X-MARK** face-mark
X-RING innermost target (shooting)
md **X-UNIT** X-ray unit
XYLEM woody tissue
ch **XYLIC** benzoic acid
XYLOL aromatic fluid
ch **XYLYL** xylene

Y

bt **YACCA** Jamaican tree
nt **YACHT** pleasure ship
zo **YACOU** guan, a game bird
ga **YAGLI** traditional oiled wrestling (Turkey)
YAHOO hooligan
YAMEN YAMUN, mandarin's office, house (Ch.)
zo **YAPOK** S. American water-opposum
bt **YAPON** evergreen shrub; cassino
YAQUI Mexican Indians
rl **YASHT** Zend-Avesta prayer book
nt **YAWED** slithered in rough sea
YEARN crave; hanker; desire
YEAST leaven; balm; ferment
YELEK a long vest (Turk.)
bt **YERBA** Paraguay tea
bt **YEWEN** made of yew
YEXED hiccupped
YIELD submit; render; supply
YODEL yodle; Tyrolese singing

YOICK encourage; Lappish chants
me **YOJAN** about 5 miles (8 km) (E. Ind.)
YOKED coupled; linked; paired
YOKEL rustic; churl; clodhopper
YOLKY egg-yolk consistency
mm, bd **YORKY** slate with curved cleave
YOSHI order to continue judo contest
YOUNG boyish; juvenile; recent
YOURS of you; ending of a letter
YOUTH lad; stripling; heyday of life
el, me **YRNEH** unit of reciprocal inductance
bt **YUCCA** lily genus
YUCKY itchy
bt **YULAN** Chinese magnolia
nt **YULOH** aft-oar for sculling
YUSHO Chinese rice disease

Z

nt **ZABRA** Spanish coasting vessel
ZAMBO cross-bred Indian
bt **ZAMIA** a palm genus
ZANJE irrigation canal (S. Amer.)
bt **ZANTE** satin-wood
nt **ZARUG ZARUK** Yemeni dhow
ZAYAT Burmese inn
nt **ZEBEC XEBEC**, Algerian ship
zo **ZEBRA** a horse in pyjamas
zo **ZEBUS** Abyssinian tsetse–fly
bt **ZEINE** the gluten of maize
zo **ZEMNI** the blind mole-rat
ZENER semi-conductor current
ZERDA African fox
zo **ZHOBO ZHOMO**, yak and cow hybrid
rl **ZIARA** Moslem shrine
zo **ZIBET** Asiatic civet
ga **ZIMBA** Am. Indian and Eskimo game
zo **ZIMBI** cowry used as money
ZINCO zincograph
mu **ZINKE** old type of comet
zo **ZIZEL** marmot; ground-squirrel
nm **ZLOTY** Polish money
ar, ma **ZOCCO ZOCLE**, square base
zo **ZOEAL** early crustacean life
zo **ZOFRA** Moorish carpet
ZOGAN Japanese inlay work
rl **ZOHAR** sacred Jewish book
ZOISM theory of life origin
ZOIST a believer in zoism
ZONAL ZONAR, of regional areas
ZONIC ZONES, of girdle divisions, 5 belts
ZONDA the dry wind of the Andes
zo **ZOOID** polyp; polypide

ZOOKS gadzooks; exclamation
mu **ZOPPA** limping syncopation
zo **ZORIL** African skunk
zo **ZORRA** American skunk
zo **ZORRO** S. American fox-wolf

ZUPAN Serbian rural council
ZYGAL like an 'H'
ZYGON connecting bar
ZYMIC relating to fermentation
zo **ZYMIN** ex-enzyme

SIX-LETTER WORDS

A

ABACOT bycoket; hat of state (15th cent.)

ma, ar **ABACUS** ancient hand computer; sandstone (capital)

ABALYN synthetic resin; lacquer

ABASED demoted; humbled; put down

md **ABASIA** uncoordination in walking

lw **ABATED ABATER**, tension; moderated nuisance

ABATIS abattis; obstacles

ck **ABATTE** heavy meat-flattening knife

rl **ABBACY** office of abbot

rl **ABBATE** a title

rl **ABBESS** head of nuns' abbey

ABDALS Moslem fanatics (Pers.)

ABDEST Mohammedan rite

ABESSE thin, long pastry

rl **ABDIEL** seraph; 6-winged angel

ABDUCE separate; retract

ABDUCT remove; kidnap

ABIDED ABIDER, sojourned; dweller; accepted decision

pc **ABIENT** avoidance reflex

ABJECT servile; base; ignoble

ABJURE renounce; recant; repudiate

ABLAUT vowel pronunciation mark

ABLAZE on fire; flaming; excited

ABLEST most competent; cleverest

bt **ABLOOM** thriving; flowering

ABLUSH blushing; flushing

nt **ABOARD** on/within a ship; (transport)

ABOLLA black cloak in Anc. Rome

pl **ABORAL** remote from the mouth

ABOUND verb of plentifulness (abundance)

ABRADE erode; scrape a surface

ABROAD overseas; far and wide

ABRUPT steep; hasty; brusque; curt

mo **ABSEIL** rapid twin-rope descent technique

pc **ABSENT** not present; evading; (-minded)

ABSORB assimilate; engulf; merge

ABSURD irrational; asinine

md, pc **ABULIA** atrophy of reasoning

ABUSED ABUSER, violated; ravager

bt **ACACIA** flowering tree

bt **ACACIO ACAJOU**, cashew nut

ACADIA Nova Scotia

bt **ACAJOU** gum; acacio

zo **ACARUS** insect genus

ck **ACATES** food; nourishment

ACCEDE assent; agree; comply

ACCENT tone; stress; cadence

ACCEPT take; receive; admit

cp **ACCESS** entry; approach; retrieval

ACCITE to cite

ACCLOY to cloy; satiate; surfeit

ACCORD mutual agreement; text guide

ACCOST confront; hail; greet

ck **ACCOUB** edible thistle

ACCREW ACCRUE, accumulate; bank interest; result

ACCUSE charge; cite; censure

md, zo **ACEDIA** torpor; fish

ACERIC (Maple)

ch **ACETAL** plastic; cosmetic base

ck **ACETIC ACETYL**, the acid in olive oil

bt **ACHENE** seeded fruit

ACHING continued pain; sorrowing

ck, bt **ACHIRA** edible canna; ginger, america herbs

mu **ACHTEL** eighth note; quaver

bt, mn **ACICLE** bristle; sharp crystal

ch **ACIDIC** containing acid

bt **ACINUS** berry

ACK-ACK anti-aircraft guns; (defence)

mn **ACLIDE** spiked club

mn **ACMITE** pyroxene rock

ma **ACNODE** in double point tangets

md **ACOPIC** curative of fatigue

md **ACORIA** morbid appetite for food

bt **ACORUS** sweet flag; calamus root

ACQUIT absolve; release; exonerate

ACRACY anarchy

ACRISY poor judgement

zo **ACRITA** sponges

ACROSS athwart; transversely

ACTING performing; pretending

lw, md **ACTION** doing; function; deed; (legal-)

cp **ACTIVE** operator; busy; self-adjusting

cp **ACTUAL** real; true; definite; topical

ACUATE ACUITY, pointed; sharp (perception)

bt, zo **ACULEI** prickles; thorns

ACUMEN keenness of perception

mu **ADAGIO** leisurely
ADAMIC pertaining to Adam
ADDEEM judge
cp, ma **ADDEND** an increase
ADDICT habituate (hooked) (drugs) (hobby)
ADDING totting; summing
ADDLED deranged; rotten; (eggs)
ADDUCE offer proof; analysis
ch **ADDUCT** product of molecular reaction
md **ADENIA** enlargement of glands
ADHERE cohere; cling; cleave
ADIENT tending to expose to stimulus
ADIEUS ADIEUX, farewells
ADIPIC fatty; adipose
ADJECT to add to; extend
ADJOIN abut; annex; link
ADJURE exhort; urge; beg; pray
ADJUST arrange; trim; rectify; fit
ADMASS common consumers; the masses
ADMIRE esteem; prize; revere; respect
ADNATE joined to another organ
zo **ADNEXA** appendages; close structures
ADNOUN noun derived from adjective
ADONAI lord (Hebrew)
ADONIC species of short verse
zo **ADONIS** perfect boy; eye of bird
zo **ADORAL** adjacent to the mouth
ADORED ADORER, worshipped (lover)
cf **ADRENO-** of adrenalin
ADRIFT afloat; distracted; loose
ADROIT expert; skilful; masterly
ADSORB to condense a gas
ADVENE come to agreement
rl **ADVENT** arrival; approach; coming; (Xmas)
ADVERB manner; time of an action
ADVERT to notice; printed offer; (notice) (ad.)
ADVICE ADVISE, ADVISO, recommend; bulletin
ar, rl **ADYTUM** chancel; in a church
ck **ADZUKI** red Japanese bean
bt **AECIAL** spore-producing part of fungi
AEDILE Roman magistrate
rl **AENEAD AENEID**, epic of Aeneas (Lat.)
AEOLIC Aeolian dialect (Gr.)
rl, mu **AEOLUS** god of the wind (aeolian harp); wind operated

AERATE expose to air action
ro, tv **AERIAL** etherial; empyreal; airy; transits (leaps); antenna
AERIFY aerate
md **AEROBE** an organic growth
AEROSE coppery; brassy
AERUGO verdigris; patina
AFFAIR incident; concern; skirmish; (love-)
AFFEAR to be terrified
AFFECT assume; feign; influence; mood
lw **AFFEER** settle a price
ma **AFFINE** similar curves of variables
AFFIRM vouch; endorse; allege; oath
AFFLUX incoming flow; influx
AFFORD produce; impart; confer; spare
AFFRAY onset; brawl; strife; fracas
AFFRET effray; broil; startle; frighten
AFFUSE sprinkle; pour upon
zo **AFGHAN** native of Afghanistan; (-hound)
AFIELD in the open, away from base
AFLAME blazing; on fire; (set −)
nt **AFLOAT** on the sea; drifting; unfixed; lost
pg **AFOCAL** without focal length
AFRAID timid; fearful; anxious; scared
ce **A-FRAME** two sloping legs joined at top
AFREET evil spirit (Arab.)
AFRESH anew; again
AFRIDI Afghan tribe NW Frontier
AFSHAR rug-making nomadic tribe
ck **AFTERS** sweet or dessert course
AGALMA impression of a seal
bt **AGAMAE** cryptogamic plants
AGAMIC assexual
bt **AGARIC** fungus; mushroom
AGEING maturing; mellowing (process)
AGEISM discrimination against elderly people
pc **AGENCY** trading office; go-between
AGENDA items of business
AGHAST appalled; astounded
md **AGNAIL** a whitlow
AGNAME nickname
AGNATE (relationship) akin; allied
AGNISE acknowledge; confess
AGNOSY ignorance
AGOING going on; current; topical
AGONIC zero declination
zo **AGOUTA** Haitian rat
zo **AGOUTI AGOUTY**, guinea-pig; S. American rodent

ck **AGRAFA** Greek cheese
AGRAIL narrow-gauge railway
AGREED consented; (same aim)
md **AGUISH** shivering; chilly
AHIMSA sacredness of life (Hindu, Jain)
AIDING assisting; succouring
zo **AIGLET AGLET,** young eagle; pendant
zo **AIGRET AIGRETTE-EGRET,** white plume
AIKIDO ancient Japanese martial art
AILING sick; unwell; indisposed
AIMING pointing (gun); endeavouring
AINHUM chronic disease causing digit loss
AIR-ACE super-airman
AIR-BED inflated mattress
AIRDOX coal-mining process using air
AIR-DRY dry to parity with atmosphere
AIR-GUN air-operated weapon
AIRILY buoyantly; gaily
AIRING stroll; ventilation
AIR-LOG linear travel recorder
AIRMAN aeronaut
AIR-SAC air-cell
AIRWAY AIRLINE, route; transport company
ar, rl **AISLED** having (processional) corridors; (church; hall)
AJOURE perforated metalwork
AKIMBO arched; bent arms
md **ALALIA** loss of speech
ALALIA decorative script (Sp.); Moresque ceramic wares
ALARUM ALARM, danger signal; panic; (-clock)
zo **ALATED ALATE,** winged (birds, insects, aircraft etc.)
ALBATA an alloy
ALBEDO light reflective power
ALBEIT although; despite all; even though
ALBERT a watch chain
gl **ALBIAN** cretaceous rock stage
zo **ALBINO** white (genetic exception)
ALBION England (Morte D'Arthur)
mn **ALBITE** (felspar)
md, bt **ALBUGO** eye-trouble; fungus
ALCADE ALCAID, judge; mayor (Sp.)
ALCAIC poetic metre
zo **ALCEDO ALCYON,** kingfisher
ALCLAD an aluminium alloy
ALCOVE a bower; arbour; recess tree
bt **ALDERN** wood of alder tree

ALDINE 16th-century books printed by Aldus
ALECTO a Fury
ALEGAR sour ale
ALEGER lively; cheerful
bt **ALERCE** cedar wood
ar **ALETTE** pilaster
zo **ALEVIN** salmon fry
md **ALEXIA** inability to read
md **ALEXIN** defensive protein
ALGATE always; nevertheless
bt **ALGOID** (seaweeds)
bt **ALGOUS** (algoid)
ALIBLE nourishing
ALIGHT descend; ignited; flaming
ar, pr **ALINED ALIGNED,** brought into line; layout
ALIPED having winged feet
ch **ALKALI** opposite to acid
ch **ALKANE** methane series
ch **ALKENE** ethylene series
ALLEGE assert; maintain
gn **ALLELE** alternative form of gene
zo **ALLICE** Severn shad; fish
ALLIED united; related; cognate; akin
ALLIES affinities; associates
ALL-OUT top speed
ALLUDE refer; imply; hint; insinuate
ALLURE tempt; decoy; seduce; cajole
mu **ALMAIN ALMAND-ALLEMANDE,** Ger. dance form
ALMIRA storage furniture (Ind.)
ALMOIN alms; alms-chest (tenure)
bt, ck **ALMOND** dessert nut; (oil)
ALMOST nearly; approximately
ALMUCE amice or furred hood
me **ALNAGE** measuring by the ell
ALNICO permanent magnet alloy
ALOGIA mental deficiency speech defect
tx, zo **ALPACA** llama; Peruvian camel (mohair)
md **ALPHUS** leprosy; psoriasis
ALPINE of the Alps
ALPINI Italian mountain troops
bt **ALPIST** bird-seed
bt **ALSIKE** Swedish clover
ALTERN alternata
bt **ALTHEA** rose of Sharon
ch **ALUDEL** distilling apparatus
ALUMNA a woman graduate
ALUMNI collegiates; pupils; scholars
md **ALVINE** pert. to belly, intestines
ALWAYS continually; eternally
AMADOU dried fungus; tinder
ch **AMATOL** explosive
AMAZED astounded, nonplussed

md **AMAZIA** mammary non-
development
AMAZON female warrior; virago;
shrew
AMBAGE circumlocution; subterfuge
mn **AMBERY** stone-like Baltic resin
(gem)
ga **AMBIGU** French version of poker
AMBLED AMBLER, sauntered; casual
walker
bt **AMBURY** ANBURY, turnip disease
AMBUSH surprise trap attack
md **AMELIA** congenital limb absence
AMENDS recompensate; apology;
adjustment; (make-)
AMENED ratified
md **AMENIA** menstrual disorders
bt **AMENTA** catkins
AMERCE to fine arbitrarily
ch **AMIDIN** starch solution
pg **AMIDOL** developing agent
pc, md **AMIMIA** loss of sign ability
ch **AMINOL** an explosive
ml, zo **AMNION** embryonic habitat
md **AMNOIS** membrane
zo **AMOEBA** protozoa
bt **AMOMUM** cardamom; aromatic
shrub; seeds as spice
AMORAL against customary mores
AMORCE toy detonator; percussion
cap
AMORET sweetheart; love knot
ar **AMORPH** altogether shapeless
AMOUNT sum; total; aggregate;
attain
el, me **AMPERE** unit of current intensity
AMPLER more copious; fuller; richer
AMREET water of immortality
AMRITA nectar; ambrosia
AMULET charm; talisman; safeguard
AMURCA olive-oil extract
AMUSED diverted; beguiled;
enlivened
md, pc **AMUSIA** loss of musicality
ch **AMYLIC** AMYLUM, of starch
md **AMYOUS** lacking muscle; muscular
weakening
zo **ANABAS** tree-climbing fish
ANADEM garland; chaplet
ANALET précis of an analysis
cp **ANALOG** system behaviour
comparison
bt **ANANAS** pineapple
ANANYM name written backwards
ANARCH ANARCHIST, against all
forms of government
ck **ANNATO** ANOTTO, orange dye in
cheeses

nt **ANCHOR** ship's brake; (sheet-)
(-bolt)
md **ANCOME** a boil; a whitlow
zo **ANCONA** a fowl
go **ANDEAN** of the Andes (S. Am.)
cf, pc **ANDRON** ANDROS-, men's meeting
room; of males (Gr.)
ANELED anointed (extreme unction)
md **ANEPIA** loss of power of speech
ANERGY failure of energy; immunity
mu **ANESIS** tuning to lower pitch
md **ANESIS** abatement of symptoms
ANGARY angaria; war-rights
md **ANGINA** quinsy (pectoris)
zo **ANGLED** ANGLER, fished; schemed;
fisher; frog
ANGLES corners; aspects; (– and
Saxons)
tx **ANGORA** cloth (mohair) of camel,
goat, cat
zo **ANHIMA** horned screamer bird
ANICUT dam for irrigation (Ind.)
ANIGHT at night, nocturnal
ch, tx, md **ANILIC** of dyes (anil/indigo)
zo **ANIMAL** creature; beast; carnal
ANIMUS spirit; soul; animosity (ill
will)
ANKLED having ankles
ANKLET ornament or fetter
cf, md **ANKYLO** fusion; bent
ANLACE dagger
ANNALS historical records
rl **ANNATE** ANNATS, first fruits
ml **ANNEAL** to temper; strengthen metal
ANNONA year's produce
pr, bt **ANNUAL** yearly (book) (occasion)
(plants)
bt **ANODAL** genetic spiral upward
ANODIC anodal; positively polar
ANOINT anele; consecrate
zo **ANOLIS** lizard genus (Amer.)
pc **ANOMIA** ANOMIC, inability to recall
names
pc **ANOMIE** crash of social values
ANONYM purposely without
signature
md **ANOPIA** defective vision
ANORAK hooded windproofer
ANOTIA absence of ears
zo **ANOURA** frog genus
md **ANOXIA** deficiency of oxygen
ANSATE handled
ANSWER reply; response; refute
zo **ANT-COW** arphis (fly)
ANTERO before; previously; prior to
ANTHEM ANTIPHON, church
(national) hymn
bt **ANTHER** part of stamen

ANTHUS meadow pipit
bt **ANTIAR** upas tree
zo **ANTLER** sheddable deer horn
zo **ANTLIA** proboscis of insects
md **ANTRUM** cavity; cave; den
rl **ANUBIS** jackal-headed Egyptian
   deity
md **ANULUS** ring-shaped structure
zo **ANURAL** tailless
md **ANURIA** absence of urine secretion
ANYHOW in any case; in any way
ANYWAY anyhow
AONIAN (Muses)
AORIST a past tense (Gr.)
pl **AORTAL AORTIC**, of great heart artery
AOSMIC free from odour
APACHE Parisian assassin; American
   Indian
APATHY show of disinterest; torpor
APEDOM apishness
md **APEPSY** poor digestion
APERCU a précis; a summary
md **APHONY** loss of voice; dumbness
md **APHTHA** thrush disease
APIARY art of beekeeping
APICAL topmost
APICES culminations; highest points
APIECE to each
APINCH pinching
gl **APLITE** quartz-feldspar microgranite
APLOMB self-possession; poise
mn **APLOME** garnet
pl, md **APNOEA** breaks in breathing rhythm
zo **APODAL APODEL**, footless, 'fin-less'
as **APOGEE** furthest distance of other
   orbit from earth
APONIA painlessness
APORIA rhetorical doubt
md **APOSIA** absence of thirst feeling
bt **APOZEM** a decoction
lw **APPEAL** entreat; implore; invoke
APPEAR seem; emerge; dawn; look
APPEND add; fasten; subjoin
APPORT object produced by
   medium
APPOSE to seal; superimpose
zo **APTERA** wingless insects
APTOTE indeclinable noun
APULSE pulsing
zo, rl **AQUILA** eagle; bird of prey (lectern,
   bible holder)
mt **AQUILO** N, N-E wind (Lat.)
ARABIC language; race
bt **ARABIN** gum arabic
bt **ARABIS** rock-cress
ARABLE tillable; cultivable
mn **ARANGO** cornelian
ARBOUR bower; garden; retreat

bt **ARBUTE ARBUTUS**, strawberry tree
ar **ARCADE** arched gallery; (shopping
   passage)
rl **ARCADY** mythical pastoral paradise
   (Gr.)
rl **ARCANA ARCANE** (astrological)
   mysteries
ar **ARCATE ARCHED**, bow-shaped;
   vaulted; concave
as **ARCHER** bowman; (Zodiac
   Sagittarius)
bt **ARCHIL** violet dye
ARCHLY roguishly; merrily;
   shrewdly
ARCHON Greek magistrate
el **ARCING** electrical leap; diversion;
   sparking
ARCTIC northern; boreal; cold
ARDENT fiery; fervent; intense
ARDOUR warmth; heat; passion; zeal
bt, md **AREOLE AREAOLA**, cell nucleus;
   . minimal space
zo **ARGALA** adjutant bird (Hindu)
zo **ARGALI** wild sheep of Asia
ARGAND (burner); (diagram)
md **ARGEMA** optical ulcer
hd **ARGENT** silver
ARGIVE (Argos); Greek
nt **ARGOSY** richly laden vessel
ARGUED reasoned; implied; mooted
ARGUER disputed; debated; pleaded
ARGUFY wrangle
ARGUTE subtle; ingenious
tx **ARIDAS** East African taffeta
ARIGHT correctly; properly
mu **ARIOSE ARIOSO**, melodious, aria-
   recitation
ARISEN reappeared; origin; arose
   (cropped up)
bt **ARISTA** beard of corn
ARKITE Noachian
nt **ARMADA** invasion fleet
ARMING preparing for war
go, hd **ARMLET ARMULET**, arm decoration;
   creek; armour
ar **ARMOUR** metal wear (knight's);
   foundation protection
md **ARMPIT** the axilla
tx **ARMURE** embossed-appearing cloth
ARNAUT Albanian mountaineer
bt **ARNICA** a plant genus
AROINT AROYNT, be gone from here!
AROUND about; encompassing
ma **AROURA** 100 square feet (Egyptian)
AROUSE excite; stir; provoke
me **ARPENT** 100 square perches
bt, ck **ARRACH ARRACK**, orache herb;
   fermented toddy

ARRANT errant; unmitigated
ARREAR ARREARS, unfinished; overdue (debts)
ARRECT erect; intent; alert
ARREST stem; curb; detain; capture
ARRIDE to please; to laugh at
ARRIVE reach; attain; land; come
me ARROBA Spanish 25 lb (11 kg) weight
ARROWY like an arrow
go ARROYO ravine; gully (Sp.)
me ARSHIN 30 in (76 cm) (Rus.)
ch ARSINE poison gas
md ARTERY blood vessel
ARTFUL sly; wily; subtle; astute
cf, md ARTHRO- joint; articulation
pt ARTIST painter; master; adept
bt ARUNDO reed genus
ASALTO assault (fox & geese game) (It.)
ASCEND climb; scale; mount
ASCENT rise; elevation; eminence
ASCIAN equator dweller
ASEITY self-origination
pc ASEMIA symbol comprehension inability
ASGARD abode of Norse gods
ASHAKE ashiver; aquake
ASHAME to feel shame (obs.)
ASHERY ash-heap
ASHIER more ashen; pale grey
ar ASHLAR ASHLER, hewn stone (building)
nt ASHORE stranded; aground; on land
ASH-PAN dust-pan; trash pan
rw ASH-PIT fire refuse tip (locomotive)
md ASITIA off one's oats
ASKANT askance; obliquely
ASKARI African soldier
ASKING requesting; begging; inviting
ASLAKE to slake; to mitigate
ASLANT ASLOPE, obliquely; askew; awry
ASLEEP dormant; slumbering
ASNORT snorting
mu ASONIA inability to distinguish pitch
ASPECT facial expression; view; outlook
bt, zo ASPICK lavender; asp
ASPIRE aim; seek to attain; yearn for
zo ASPOUT blowing-off (whales)
ASQUAT squatting
ASSAIL attack; defame; asperse
ASSART to grub up trees, etc
nm ASSARY ancient Roman coin
ASSENT concur; agree; accord

ASSERT declare; maintain; allege; aver
ASSESS compute; tax; rate; value
ASSETS possessions; effects
lw ASSIGN allot; appoint; adduce; transfer
ASSIST aid; help; succour; abet
lw ASSIZE county court
ASSORT group; arrange; classify
ASSUME to take as fact; feign; take office
ASSURE aver; guarantee; warrant
ASTARE staring
ASTART suddenly
nt ASTERN aft; abaft; in reverse
ASTERT astart; suddenly (Spens.)
md ASTHMA breathing disorder
ASTRAL starry; stellar; sidereal
ASTRAY erring; wandering; missing
ASTRUT puffed up (obs.)
ASTUTE artful; subtle; wily
ASWARM swarming
ASWING asway
ASWOON in a swoon
ASYLUM a sanctuary; refuge
mu ATABAL Moorish drum
ATAMAN Cossack chief
ATAVIC inherent; heriditary
ATAVUS remote ancestor
md ATAXIA paralysis
md ATAXIC irregular
pc ATELIA retaining childish traits
rl ATHENE goddess of wisdom and war
AT-HOME a reception; open house
ATHROB throbbing
ATHYMY melancholy
ATKINS British private soldier (Tommy)
md ATOCIA female sterility
ch, ps ATOMIC of minimal particle (energy)
mu ATONAL lacking tone
ATONED reconciled; propitiated
ATONER an expiator
md ATONIC unaccented; debilitated
md ATOPIC allergic; misplaced
ATRIAL pertaining to atrium
ar ATRIUM Roman hall; (patio)
zo ATRIUM cavity (sinus); fish gills
ATROUS jet black
ATTACH annex; adhere; cement
ATTACK storm; charge; assail; impugn
ATTACK sudden onset of battle or disease
ATTAIN acquire; achieve; reach; grasp
ATTASK to task
ATTEND serve; guard; hearken; heed
ATTENT intention; attentive (Spens.)

ATTEST ratify; confirm; endorse
ATTIRE garb; rig; accoutre; outfit
lw ATTORN transfer (homage)
  (property)
ATTRAP array; adorn
ATTUNE harmonize; accord; adapt
ATWAIN in sunder
ATWEEM between
ATWIXT betwixt
md ATYPIC unclassified; unusual
AUBADE dawn; concert; morning
  song
AUBURN carroty; Titian; hair
  (colour)
AUDILE who prefers auditory images
  to visuals
ro AUDION wireless amplifier
AUGEAN foul; arduous (stables)
  (Hercules)
cp, ma AUGEND sum to be added to
mn AUGITE volcanic rock
AUGURY omen; portent; sign;
  presage
AUGUST majestic; venerable;
  imposing
mu AULETE flautist
rl AUMBRY ambry; cupboard
AUMUCE amice; furred hood
AUNTIE aunty; prude
ar AURATE having ears; gilded (design)
AUREAT gilded; golden; auric
nm AUREUS Roman gold coin
AURIFY change into gold
AURIGA a constellation; the
  Charioteer
AURINE dye-acid
md AURIST ear specialist
AURORA goddess of dawn; northern
  lights
AUROUS golden; aureate
AUSPEX seer; diviner; prophet
AUSSIE an Australian
mt AUSTER South wind
AUSTIN Augustine
AUTHOR writer; creator; cause; agent
AUTISM self-absorption
AUTUMN the fall
AVALON a western legendary isle
bt AVANCE avens; herb bennet
AVANTI forward (It.)
rl AVATAR incarnation of Brahma
AVAUNT be off with you!
AVAUNT AVENER, AVENOR, feudal
  master of the Horse
AVENGE retaliate; to take revenge
AVENUE entry; access; approach; fine
  road
AVERSE loath; allergic; reluctant

zo AVIARY a large bird-cage
AVIATE to fly (aircraft pilot)
ch AVIDIN protein in egg
AVIDLY voraciously; greedily;
  eagerly
AVISED hue; complexion
AVITAL hereditary; ancestral
lw AVOCAT advocate (Fr.)
zo AVOCET AVOSET, wading bird
AVOUCH maintain; guarantee
AVOURE confession; justification
  (Spens.)
lw AVOWAL AVOWED, open admission;
  on oath
lw AVOWEE (advowson)
lw AVOWRY (replevin)
AVULSE to grab
AWAKEN rouse; stir up; kindle
AWASTE wasting
AWATCH watching; alert
AWEARY tired; faded; spent
nt AWEIGH atrip; apeak (raise anchors)
AWHEEL cycling; motoring
AWHILE sometime; briefly; soon
ar AWNING tent-like shelter; canopy
md AXENIC free from parasites
ar, nt AXICLE pulley wheel in sheave;
  (tackle)
md AXILLA armpit
AXUNGE hog's lard; wheel-grease
zo AYE-AYE squirrel-like lemur
bt AZALEA plant, rhododendron type
ch AZARIN brilliant crimson dye
AZAZEL Satan's standard-bearer
tx AZMURE semi-embossed cloth
AZONAL recent formation (soil)
AZONIC not local
AZOTIC lifeless
AZRAEL destroying angel
AZURED coloured light blue; (sea)
ch AZURIN blue dye
AZYGOS occurring singly

B

BAAING bleating; (sheep & lambs)
BAALIM false gods (Baal)
BABBIT Babbit metal
BABBLE noise (babies) (crowds)
  (chatter)
BABBLE (Eco-, Euro-) etc. jargon
BABIES newborn, of human &
  wildlife
bt BABLAH acacia-rind
zo BABOON dog-like herd monkeys
BACKED BACKER, reversed (cars);
  aided (finance); abetted

BACKET coal box; hod; coal scuttle
cp BACK-UP supporting service; assistance
zo, to BADGER animal (-teasing; -baiting) tool; pester
bt BADIAN tree with anise-flavoured fruit
bd, ce BAFFLE balk; thwart; acoustics; slat; plate
tx BAFTAS cotton; muslin
BAGFUL contents; capacity of a bag
BAGGED obtained (first); stolen; shot (wildlife)
zo BAGGIT salmon after spawning
BAGMAN commercial traveller; tramp
bd BAGNIO bath-house (It.)
mt BAGUIO tropical cyclone; Philippines
BAGWIG an 18th-century wig
go BAHADA BAJADA, alluvial plain (Piedmont)
lw BAILED BAILEE, obtains pre-trial freedom
lw BAILER BAILOR, deposits securities as bail, on trust
nt, ce BAILER who pumps out water (sump); sand pump
ar BAILEY courtyard in castle
lw BAILIE alderman in council (Scots)
BAITED teased; provoked; (bear-) (badger-)
bt BAJREE Indian grass
BAKERY bake-house
ck BAKING cooking in oven; heat drying
BALAAM unimportant newsprint
mn BALASS a ruby
bt BALATA rubberlike gum
nm BALBOA coin of Panama
rl BALDER less hirsute; Nordic sungod
BADLY inelegantly; plainly
zo BALEEN whalebone
BALING bundling; emptying
nt BALIZE sea mark
go BALKAN of S.E. Europe (peninsula)
BALKED refused; frustrated
BALKER fish-spotter
BALKIS Queen of Sheba; also Aaziz
mu BALLAD narrative poem; epic song
BALLED clogged; ill done; (black-); vetoed
BALLET art dance
BALLOT voting; (election); rote paper
bt BALSAM aromatic balm
go, nt, lw BALTIC European sea; (-shipping exchange)
bt BAMBOO tree-like grass

ck BAMMIE Caribbean cassava cake
bt, ck BANANA fruit; (republic); (can split)
nm BANCOR monetary unit
BANDED united; bound
BANDIT outlaw; brigand; footpad
me BANDLE 2 ft (60 cm) (Irish)
zo BANDOG ferocious (banned) dog
BANGED with hair cut square
ck BANGER a cooked sausage
BANGHY Ind. porter's shoulder-yoke
BANGLE bracelet; armlet; ring
BANGUE bhang; a narcotic
BANG-UP slap-up; stylish
bt BANIAN Hindu caste; fig-tree
BANISH exile; expel; eject
bd, rw BANKED deposited; road; rail; dyke
ga BANKER lender; pushing locomotive; cards
BANKER mason's table; fishing boat; (gambling)
gl BANKET auriferous rock (Transvaal)
BANNED barred; tabooed; vetoed
bt BANNER petal; flag; standard
zo BANTAM carved work; small hen; (boxing)
BANTER cheerful; witty repartee; bandy
bt BANYAN Indian fig; banian
ga BANZAI! Japanese hurrah; drag-racing
bt BAOBAB African tree
ga BARANI BARONI, gymnast's somersault (It.)
BARBED bearded; hooked; pointed
zo BARBEL carp
BARBER hairdresser (men)
zo BARBET bird; dog
bt BARCOO grass (Aust.)
BARDIC poetic; epic
tx BAREGE fabric
BARELY only just
ga BAREME rules for show-jumping
BAREST bleakest; baldest; shoved
BARGED charged into; shoved
BARGEE bargeman
BARING uncovering; (-teeth)
BARISH rather bare
ch BARIUM metallic element
BARKED grazed (shins); helped
BARKEN to become like bark
BARKER shop-tout
bt, ag, ck BARLEY a cereal for beer
BARMAN pot-man; bar-tender
BARNED stored
BARNEY humbug; prize fight
BARONY a baron's holding
nt BARQUE BARQUA-BARK, three-masted sailing ship

bt **BARRAS** resin
BARRED barricaded; forbidden;
ostracized
me, ck **BARREL** cask for beer, wine, oil; 36
gal.
ar **BARREL** part of a gun; vaulting
BARREN bare; sterile; unfertile
rl **BARRET** beret; cap
BARROW street seller's cart; ancient
mound
BARTER trade; exchange; traffic
BARTON domain lands; farmhouse
ps **BARYON** heavy subatomic particle
ch **BARYTA** barium oxide
mn **BASALT** igneous rock
BASELY spuriously; corruptly
BASIAL osculatory
BASIFY make into a salifiable salt
BASING founding; establishing
BASKED warmed by the sun
BASKET pannier; creal; punnet; trug;
goal (basketball)
BASNET helmet; bassinet
BASQUE Biscayan
zo **BASSET** outcrop; (cards); hound
BASTED oiled while roasting;
patched; thrashed
hd **BASTON** heraldic baton
BASUCO BAZUCO, crack; cocaine
waste (S. Am.)
BASUTO African
ch **BASYLE** radicle
bt, ck **BATATA** sweet potato; yam
nt **BATEAU** boat (French)
nt **BATELO** small dhow (Arabian
coasts)
BATHED laved; suffused
BATHER swimmer; laver
BATHIC pertaining to sea depths
BATHOS anti-climax; bombast
BATING except; abating; deducting
BATLET linen-beater
BATMAN an officer's servant (valet)
BATOON baston; bar; staff;
truncheon
ga **BATTED** (cricket)
BATTEL Oxford kitchen account
nt, bd **BATTEN** slat used for sails,
tarpaulins; hatches
BATTEN BATTON on someone
(become dependent) (parasitic)
ck, ar **BATTER** pancake mix; beat to
destroy; sloping wall; player with
striker (cricket, baseball)
BATTLE military encounter (armies);
contest; fight
BATTUE a beat; slaughter
nm **BAUBEE** BAWBEE, halfpenny (Sc.)

BAUBLE showy trinket (gee-gaw);
jester's wand
nt **BAURUA** rapid outrigger canoe
(Polyn.)
zo **BAVIAN** poetaster; baboon
BAWLED clamoured; shouted; yelled
BAWLER a howler
nt **BAWLEY** Thames fishing-boat
zo **BAWSON** BAWSIN, a badger
zo **BAWTIE** a hare; a dog
BAYING in full cry; sound of
foxhounds (hunting); wolves
BAYRAM Mohammedan festival
BAZAAR mart; emporium; exchange
gl **BEACHY** pebbly (of shoreline)
nt **BEACON** signal-fire; lighthouse; sea
mark
rl **BEADED** strung together; (necklace)
(prayer-s)
BEADLE public order officer
ro, zo **BEAGLE** a hound; jammer
nt **BEAKED** of birds; of ships; rammer
bow
BEAKER drinking cup, mug
ar, bd, nt **BEAMED** smiled; (lighthouse);
supported (wood); guided by radar
ga **BEAMER** head line bowling (cricket)
(foul)
BEARER porter; joist; (cheque)
(funerals)
ck **BEATEN** punished (bodily); defeated;
whisked (eggs); hammered
BEATER striker; whisker; knocker;
(fire-) (gamebirds-)
BEAUTY grace; comeliness; fairness
zo **BEAVER** water rodent; (-dam); hard
worker; (-hat)
BECAME grew into; graced
nt **BECKET** an eye in a knot
BECKON call; wave; signal; invite
BECOME BECAME, suit; changed;
grown into
zo **BED-BUG** cimex; (bed-louse)
bt **BEDDED** planted out; (hotel room);
(laid)
bt **BEDDER** millstone; a plant;
bedmaker
BEDECK array; gild; adorn
to **BED-KEY** bedstead tightener
BEDLAM mad-house; uproar
BEDLOCK WEDLOCK, matrimony;
marriage
BEDUIN BEDOUIN, nomadic Arab
ae **BEEPER** remote-controlled aircraft
zo **BEETLE** insect; maul; heavy mallet;
(to speed)
BEFALL betide; happen; chance
BEFANA Epiphany present; a fairy

BEFORE formerly; above (texts); in front of
BEGGAR pauper; to bankrupt; beyond imagination
BEGGED implored; entreated; cadged
BEGONE! go away; avaunt!
BEGUNK piece of deception
BEHALF benefit; interest; advantage
BEHAVE act; comport; demean
BEHEAD decapitate; execute
BEHELD saw; surveyed; contemplated
BEHEST command; mandate; order
pl **BEHIND** abaft; following; buttocks
BEHOLD regard; discern; look
BEHOOF profit; advantage; benefit
BEHOVE befit; suit; beseem
BEHUNG draped; well-endowed
BELACE adorn with lace; beat
BELATE delay; retard; hinder
BELAUD overpraise; bepuff
BELDAM a hag; beldame
BELFRY bat habitat; bell-tower
BELGIC Belgian; of Belgium
BELIAL a low and profligate devil
BELIED falsified; counterfeited
BELIEF faith; creed; dogma; tenet
BELIER confidence criminal; liar
BELIKE likely; perhaps; maybe
BELIVE speedily; ere long (Sc.)
BELLED bellowed
bt **BELLIS** the daisy
md **BELLOW** lead colic
BELLOW roar; bawl; clamour
nt **BELLUM** Iraqi long canoe
BELOCK to fasten; to lock
zo **BELONE** garfish
BELONG to appertain
BELTED girt; zoned; girdled
zo, ck **BELUGA** sturgeon; source of caviare
BEMASK to conceal
zo **BEMBEX** genus of sand-wasps
BEMOAN lament; bewail; mourn
BEMUSE daze; bewilder
BENDER spree; a stretcher
tx **BENGAL** fabric; (Lancer)
BENIGN kindly; amiable; friendly
nv **BENITO** navigation system
bt **BENNET** herb
bt **BEN-NUT** oil-nut of horse-radish tree
rl **BENSHI BANSHEE**, Irish fairy; house ghost
BENUMB stupefy; deaden; blunt
ch **BENZOL** benzene
BERATE rate; scold; chide; reprove
BERBER Moroccans of Atlas mountains
BERBER a Barbary language

BEREAN extinct Scottish sect
BEREFT stripped; deprived; destitute
BERLIN a vehicle; wool
BERTHA big Hun gun (1st World War)
hd, nm **BESANT BEZANT**, Byzantine gold; circlet
BESIDE near; close by; alongside
BESTED overwhelmed; worsted
BESTIR hasten; rouse; strive
BESTOW confer; grant; give; award
BESTUD to stud
BETAKE BETOOK, remove oneself; go away; leave
BETEEM produce; shed
rl **BETHEL** a chapel; sect
BETIDE befall; happen; chance
BETIME betide; befall
BETISE stupid act (Fr.)
bt **BETONY** a plant
BETRAY divulge; reveal; entrap
BETTED wagered
BETTER superior; amend; rectify; gambler
BETTOR punter; wagerer
BEVIES flocks; crowds
hd **BEVILE** heraldic device
BEWAIL moan; lament; grieve; deplore
BEWARE achtung! heed; mind
zo **BEWTER** bittern
BEYLIK a Bey's province
BEYOND over; past; farther
nt **BEZAAN BEZAN**, Dutch ketch
nt **BEZANT BESANT**, Dutch sailing vessel
BEZOAR a stony concretion
zo **BHARAL** wild sheep (Tibet)
BHISTI Indian water-carrier
ch **BIACID** of a base
BIASED prejudiced
BIAXAL BIAZAL, having two optical axes
BIBBER wine-bibber; toper
bt **BIBLUS** papyrus; paper-reed
pl **BICEPS** upper arm muscle
BICKER bowl; quarrel; nipple
hd, zo **BICORN** having 2 horns (ungulates)
BIDALE a benefit
BIDDED (auction) offered
BIDDER tenderer
BIDENT two-pronged
BIDING waiting; sojourning
BIDOUS lasting 2 days
BIFFED coshed; bashed
BIFFIN apple pie; dried apple
BIFLEX double curve
bt **BIFOIL** two-blade plant

BIFOLD two-fold; double
BIFORM having two shapes
BI-FUEL propelled with two fuels
BIGAMY plural marriage
BIG-END crank end of connecting rod
BIGGEN BIGGIN, child's cap; small wooden bowl
BIGGER larger; greater; bulkier
el **BIGRID** double-control-grid thermionic
BIG-WIG important person
BIKING cycling
BIKINI minimal 1- or 2-piece bathing-suit
BILBAO wall mirror (N. Amer.)
BILDAR Indian camp servant
nt **BILGED** double-bottomed (broad) boat
BILKED BILKER, defrauded; absconder
BILLED advertised; debited
ar **BILLET** a log; note; lodgings; ticket; romanesque moulding; thumbpiece on a tankard
zo **BILLIE** tin can; billy; male goat
BILLON an alloy
BILLOT gold or silver bar
BILLOW rolling, heaving (waves); glider wing fullness
BIMANA BIMANE, both handed
BIMBOY male bimbo
ma, cp **BINARY** mathematical system; 2 digits
mu **BINARY** sonata form in 2 keys
BINATE double; in pairs; twosome; twin
pr, bd, ce **BINDER** loose cover; bandage; (book); cement
BINGHI Australian aborigine
BINGLE base hit (baseball)
ga **BINGLE** base hit (baseball)
el **BINODE** 2-electrode thermionic tube
BINOUS binate; double
md **BIOPSY** tissue examination
zo **BIOSIS** life; distinguishing organisms
md **BIOTIC** biological
BIOTIN B vitamin
BIPACK two-film colour photography
pr **BIPONT** bipontine
BIRDED snared
BIRDER bird catcher
ga **BIRDIE** one under bogey at golf
nt **BIREME** cf. trireme; 2-banked oared galley (Mediterranean)
BIRKEN made of birch-wood

BIRKIE BIRSIE, lively lad (Sc.)
BIRLER a carouser
BIRSLE to scorch; to toast (Sc.)
BISECT to halve
rl, ga **BISHOP** church dignitary; chess; (horse-faking)
BISQUE croquet handicap; glazeless firing
ck, ga **BISQUE** lobster soup; extra stroke (golf)
BISTER BISTRE, sombre brown pigment
BISTRO small eating house (Fr.)
BITING mordant; champing
BITTED (horse's bit)
BITTEN tricked; corroded; (once-)
BITTER acrimonious; sour; tart; (beer); severe; (grief); (pill)
BITTLE flat club; beetle
zo **BITTOR** the bittern
ch **BIURET** urea product
BIZARD carnation
BLADED having a blade
BLAGUE blarney; swagger
BLAMED reproached; censured
BLANCH bleach; whiten; fade
BLARED trumpeted; pealed
BLASHY watery
BLAZED proclaimed; (trees)
BLAZER bright-coloured sports jacket
hd **BLAZON BLASON**, to display; blare; bear (crest); (mark)
BLEACH blanch; whiten
BLEAKY bleak; cheerless
BLEARY blear-eyed; tired-looking
BLEBBY blubby; blistered
BLENCH blink; shrink; flinch
mn **BLENDE** an ore of zinc
zo **BLENNY** fish
bt **BLEWIT** mushroom
bt **BLEYME** inflammation
bt **BLIGHT** mildew; disease; shrivel
BLINDS camouflage; screens; deceit
bt **BLINKS** chickweed
BLINKY blink-eyed
BLITHE merry; vivacious; joyous
BLONDE silk lace; fair lady
BLOODY sanguinary
BLOOMY blooming
BLOTCH a blemish; pustule; (ink-)
BLOTTO fuddled
BLOUSE loose outer garment
au **BLOW-BY** piston-leakage gas
BLOWED blasted; confounded
zo **BLOWER** a whale; telephone; voice pipe
BLOWTH bloom; blossoms

BLOWZE coarse woman
BLOWZY fat; tawdry; unkempt
BLUISH of blue colour
BLUEST most blue; gloomiest; (films)
BLUFFY an act of deceit (bluffing)
BLUING tempering steel
BLUISM (blue-stocking); female intellectual
BLUNGE (clay mixing)
BOARDS theatre stage; ice rink wall
BOATEL botel; boating hotel afloat
BOATER straw hat
BOBBED short hairstyle; moved up & down
cp BOBBIN spool; reel; magnetic core
BOBBLE bauble; trinket; ripple; decoration
BOBBLE regain lost balance (water-skiing); fumble (baseball)
ga BOBLET 2-man bob; sled
BOBWIG wig of short hair
bt, ag BOCAGE boscage; leafy underwood; small fields and large hedges (Fr)
BOCKEY bowl made from a gourd
BODEGA wine-shop (Sp.)
BODGER pedlar; botcher
BODICE woman's upper body garment
BODIED real, live persons; (able-)
pl BODIES organizations; corpses; torsos
BODILY corporeally
BODING an omen; portending
BODKIN dagger; needle for tape
BODKIN three people crowded up
BOECKL figure skating, jump and turn
nt BOEIER Dutch merchantman
BOFFIN back-room scientist
BOGGLE to be amazed, stupified
BOGLET a small bog
bt BOG-OAK near-fossil wood
mn BOG-ORE limonite found in marshes
BOILED heated to evaporation point
BOILER hot-water heater
zo BOIOBI green snake
BOLARY clay-like
BOLDER more daring; saucier
BOLDLY confidently; valiantly
mu BOLERO Spanish dance; rhythm
BOLIDE meteor
BOLLED BOLLEN, swollen; podded
BOLTED barred; escaped; ate rapidly
BOLTER bran shredder
bt BOMBAX cotton-tree
BOMBED blitzed
zo BOMBIC BOMBYX, silkworm

BON-BON sugar-plum; Xmas cracker
BONDED warehoused (customs-free)
BONDER binding stone or brick
zo BONGAR poisonous Indian snake
mu BONGOS Conga twin drums
BONING levelling; removing bones
zo BONITO (tunny) (Sp.)
BONKED BONKER, performed sexual intercourse
BON-MOT witticism
nt, ar, bd BONNET women's cap; car casing; sail; bay window roofing; chimney cowl
BONNIE blithe; fair; joyous; pretty
tx BONTEN woolen stuff
BON-TON chic; good style; fashionable
zo BONXIE skua-gull
BONZER lucky strike (Aust.)
BOODLE loot; stolen money; as bribe
BOOHOO weep aloud
BOOING noisily disapproving; hooting
BOOKED entered; recorded; reserved; (copped)
BOOKIE bookmaker (betting)
BOOMED advertised; resounded
zo BOOMER born in baby boom; surfwave; kangaroo
BOOSED BOOZED, drank lustily
BOOTED wearing boots; dismissed
BOOTEE short boot
BOOTES constellation
BO-PEEP (sheep) hide and seek; (game)
bt BORAGE a plant
ch BORATE boric oxide
to BORCER rock-drill
BORDAR cottage
BORDEL sex-workers' den; bawdy-house
BORDER margin; boundary; edge
mt BOREAL BOREAS, of North wind
BOREEN Irish lane or track
BORING tedious; drilling
nt BORLEY BAWLEY, Thames barge
ma BORROW copy; assume; feign; obtain a loan; linguistic absorption; (arithmetical device)
ck BORSCH beetroot soup (Rus.)
zo BORZOI Russian hound
go BOSCHE wood; bush (S. Afr.)
bt BOSKET a grove; small wood
BOSSED controlled; dominated
BOSSED ornamented with round knobs
zo BOSSET rudimentary antler
BOSTAL hill road

mu **BOSTON** a dance

tx, bt **BOTANY** Australian wool; of plants

BOTCHY of ineptly bungled repair

zo **BOT-FLY** gad-fly

BOTHER pother; pester; worry

BOTHIE a house; a hut (Sc.)

hd **BOTONE** heraldic budding

bt **BO-TREE** sacred tree; pipal

nt **BOTTER** sea yacht

BOTTLE container; (-bank); courage; (-out, funk)

nt, pl **BOTTOM** basis; foot; foundation; buttocks; dell; (sea-); ship's; lowest rank; alluvial plain

ga **BOTTOM** unjumpable ditch (horse riding); last innings (baseball)

BOTTOM time a diver spends under water

BOUCAN dried meat

BOUCHE metal plug

wv, tx **BOUCLE** billowy woven cloth

BOUFFE farcical (Fr.)

BOUGHT purchased; bribed; bond deals (N. Am.)

mu **BOUGIE BOOGY,** form of jazz music

BOULET sloping pastern

zo, ga **BOUNCE** dog-fish; rebound (bad cheque); of ball games

BOUNDS (out of bounds)

BOUNTY gift; reward; liberality

go **BOURNE** destination; burn (Sc.); intermittent stream (often dry)

BOURSE Stock Exchange (Fr.)

cy **BOUTON** axon arborization end

me **BOVATE** peasant holding (20 acres; 8 hectares)

BOVINE cow-like (character); dull

BOW-BOY Cupid; Eros

BOW-CAP an extreme bow of airship

BOW-DYE scarlet

pl **BOWELS** colon & rectum, undermost parts

BOWERY shady; (New York)

zo **BOWESS** a young hawk

zo **BOWFIN** mudfish (N. Am.)

BOWING fiddling; submitting (respect)

ga **BOWLED** ball cast (cricket; bowls)

pl **BOW-LEG** crooked leg (knock-kneed)

ga **BOWLER** hard hat; cricketer (thrower)

BOWMAN archer

BOW-NET lobster-pot

BOW-OAR No. 1 of a racing crew

BOW-PEN a drawing instrument

to **BOW-SAW** narrow saw

nt **BOWSIE** cleat; knot on wood

tx **BOW-TIE** male neckwear

zo **BOW-WOW** jocular word for dog

cp, rw **BOXCAR** data converter; goods truck

ce **BOX-DAM** surrounding coffer-dam

lw **BOX-DAY** day for lodging papers

BOXING pugilism; packaging; cased frame (in window)

ce, bd **BOXING** (Christmas box); stone ballast under/between sleepers; boarding

BOYISH youthful; puerile; young

zo **BOYUNA** serpent

BRACED supported; propped

BRACER pick-me-up; support; protector; arm guard (archery)

cf **BRACHY-** short

BRAINY intellectual; clever

bt **BRAIRD** germination

ck **BRAISE** to stew

zo **BRAIZE** red pandora fish

BRAKED put on the brake; halted

BRANCH bough; off-shoot; agency; division

cp **BRANCH** change of direction; sequence

BRANDY strong distilled spirit

BRANKS scold's bridle

BRANKY showy (Sc.)

mu **BRANLE BRANSLE,** dance movement (Fr.); gavotte

BRANNY like bran

BRASEN BRAZEN, made of brass; impudent

BRASHY fragmentary

bt **BRASIL BRAZIL,** Brazil wood; sappan tree

zo **BRASSE** perch

BRASSY brassie; a golf club

BRAVED dared; defied; challenged

BRAVER nobler; more daring

BRAWLY bravely; excellently

BRAWNY hefty; lusty; sturdy; robust

BRAYED ground in a mortar

to **BRAYER** (printing) roller

BRAYLE hawk leash

BRAZED soldered

BREACH rupture; crack; rift; quarrel

ga **BREAST** chest; bosom; (-plate); oppose; (-high); -stroke; riser of stairway (-wall)

pl **BREATH** air for lungs; -of life; (-less)

BREECH the hinder part of a gun (loader)

BREEKS trousers

bd, zo **BREESE BREEZE,** soft wind; even pace (horses); cinder-brick; gad fly

BREEZY gusty; windy; hearty

md **BREGMA** part of skull

lw **BREHON** Irish judge

BRETON of Brittany
ck BREVET a patent; nominal rank
mu, rl BREVIS short; mass setting
ck BREWED plotted; concocted
ck BREWER a brewster; maltster (beer)
bt BRIARY BRIERY, set with brambles
BRIBED paid for wrong doing
BRIBER a corrupter
bd BRICKY of brick
BRIDAL nuptial; conjugal
ce, ga, mu BRIDGE card game; span; surmount;
loan; violin; billiards; (bowls);
(gym); (wrestling); transition;
convert; link between passages
BRIDLE curb; control; restrain;
check; harness; track; path (horses)
BRIGHT vivid; shining; gay; merry
BRIGUE intrigue; cabal; strife
BRILLS eye-lashes (horse)
bt BRIONY bryony; a plant
BRISKY brisk; effervescing
BRITON ancient British inhabitant
to BROACH hint; suggest; tap; clasp;
pointed chisel
go, nv BROADS waterways
BROCHE brocade; embroider
BROGAN leather shoe
BROGUE decorated shoe; Irish accent
BROKEN fractured; snapped;
smashed
BROKER dealer
BROLLY umbrella
ch BROMAL oily fluid
ch BROMIC containing bromide
zo BRONCO unbroken horse (Amer.)
BRONZE an alloy of copper and tin
BRONZY bronze-like
BROOCH ornamental clasp
BROODY pensive; hen
BROOKY abounding with streams
bt BROOMY full of broom (gorse)
BROUGH town; burgh; borough
BROWNY of brown colour
BROWSE nibble; crop; feed
zo BRUANG Malayan bear
md BRUCIA a poison
BRUISE batter; crush; contuse; wale
zo BRUMBY unbroken horse
ck BRUNCH combined breakfast-lunch
BRUSHY rough; shaggy
BRUTAL inhuman; ruthless; savage
BRUTUS a kind of wig
to BRUZZE V-shaped woodturning tool
bt BRYONY BRIONY, a plant
BUBBLE trapped air; (blowing–s)
(-bath); (S. Sea-); gurgle
BUBBLY champagne; effervescent
pl BUCCAL (cheek); cavity; mouth

ck BUCCAN dried meat
BUCKED bleached; exhilerated
ce, cp BUCKET water pail; container; (seat);
(mill wheel); goal
zo BUCKIE large whelk
BUCKLE thatcher's spar; bootclasp;
wrinkle
BUCKRA white man
BUDDED grafted
rl BUDDHA founder of religion
BUDDLE (ore-washing)
BUDGER a stirrer; a mover
BUDGET package (finance); tiler's
pocket
bt BUDLET a little bud
BUFFED buffeted; polished
zo BUFFEL an American duck
BUFFER concussion absorber; old
fool
cp BUFFER limited memory storage
BUFFET cuff; smite; sideboard
BUFFET self-service meal
cn, nt BUG-EYE wide-angle; N. Am. fishing
boat
BUGGER active sodomite
tc BUG-KEY faster transmission key
mu BUGLER horn blower
BUGLET a small glass bead
zo BUGONG a moth
nm BUKSHA Yemeni coin
BUKSHI tip; percentage (Ind.)
bt BULBED BULBAR, bulbi form
bt BULBIL bud developing into a plant
ck, zo BULBUL nightingale; Turkish sweet
bt BULBUS a corm; a bulb
ck BULGAR Bulgarian
BULGED protruded
BULGER a golf club
ck BULGUR cracket wheat (Levant)
md BULIMY morbid appetite; voracity
BULKED in bulk
BULKER street thief
BULLED (Stock Exchange)
BULLER torrential turmoil
BULLET projectile; slug
BUM-BAG hip pouch on waist belt
nt BUMKIN short broom
BUMMED loafed; idled around
BUMMEL meander; cycle seat
BUMMER camp follower; man of
trade
BUMMLE to blunder; an idler
ga BUMPED knocked into; (-off);
(oarsman's race)
BUMPER buffer; full; generous;
bouncer; (cricket)
BUNCHY clustered; tufty
BUNDLE parcel; package; packet; roll

BUNGED blocked up; (pipes)
BUNGLE miss; fail; botch
md BUNION a swelling
BUNKED bedded in tiers; decamped; gone away
ga BUNKER defence shelter; coal depot; (golf)
BUNKUM blather; nonsense
ch BUNSEN laboratory gas burner
BUNTED butted
mn BUNTER mottled sandstone
BUOYED moored; sustained (-up); uphold
BUPPIE black urban Yuppie
BURBLE confusion; trouble
zo BURBOT eel-pout; fish
BURDEN load; incubus; onus
BUREAU office; department
nt, mn BURGEE pennant; flag; coal
BURGLE rob premises
ck BURGOO savoury mess
zo BURHEL Asiatic goat
BURIAL BURIED, interment; hidden; (funeral)
BURKED hesitated; hushed up; avoided (-issue)
BURLAP coarse canvas
BURLED with knots removed
BURLER cloth-dresser
BURMAN native of Burma; Burmese
BURN-BAG container for disposal of scandal
BURNED BURNT, scorched; charred; (sun-)
BURNER controlled flame; (balloon); (welding)
bt, zo BURNET plant; moth
BURN-UP damage by excess; nuclear combustion
BURRED roughened surface
BURROW tunnel; mine; excavate
md BURSAL BURSAE, cavity
BURSAR treasurer; cashier; (college)
BURSCH German student
nt BURTON a tackle
BURYAT Central Asian Turkmens
el BUS-BAR metallic rod link; contact
BUSHED lost in the bush
me BUSHEL 8 gallons (36 litres)
BUSIED actively employed
BUSIES detectives (sl.)
BUSILY diligently; assiduously
BUSKED wearing a busk; corseted
BUSKER tragedian; street entertainer
BUSKIN kind of boot; cothurnus
BUSMEN transport workers
BUSSED transported; osculated; kissed

BUSTED gone bust (sl.); bankrupt; caught
BUSTER frolic; a roisterer
BUSTLE busy street crowd; stir; tumult
BUST-UP violent quarrel
ch BUTANE bottled gas for households
BUTLER male household steward
BUTTED trammed; bunted
ck BUTTER milk fat spread (bread and −)
ck BUTTIE sandwich
el BUTTON switch; (press-); fastening; (-mushroom)
ch BUXINE (alkaloid)
BUYING purshasing; bribing; corrupting
BUYOUT obtaining control of shareholdings
BUZZED spread abroad; bruited
el BUZZER electric sound signal (intercom, phone)
BYE-BYE (golf); adieu
BYE-LAW subsidiary law
BY-FORM a variant
BYGONE past; of yore
BY-LANE BYROAD, side road
mu BYLINA Rusian poem; song
ga BY-LINE goal area line (soccer)
BYNAME nickname
md BY-PASS a shunt (heart etc.); major ring road
BY-PATH hidden path
BY-PLAY significant acting in dumb show
BY-PLOT subsidiary plot
BY-ROAD secondary road
BY-ROOM small ante-chamber
tx BYSSUS fine linen cloth
zo BYSSUS a tuft of filaments
BYWORD maxim; proverb
BY-WORK by-time work
nm BYZANT BEZANT, gold coin (Byzantine)

C

rl CABALA Jewish traditional doctrine
CABANA beach house; shack
ae CABANE pyramidal strut system
CABBLE smash into small pieces
tx CABECA Indian silk
CABIRI ancient Semitic divinities
el, ro, tc CABLED telegraphed
CABLET tow-rope
CABMAN cabby (taxi-driver)

zo **CABRIE CABRIT**, prong-horn antelope
CABURN spun-yarn
mu **CACCIA** the chase, hunt (It.); oboe form
CACHED hidden; concealed; (stores depot)
CACHET seal of prestige; distinctive merit
bt, ck **CACHOU** a sweetmeat; cashew nut
pl **CACKIE** faeces (human waste)
zo **CACKLE** of hens' egglaying chorus
bt **CACOON** bean
bt **CACTAL** of a cactus plant
bt **CACTUS** prickly plant
CADDIE caddy (golf); porter
zo **CADDIS** tape; a worm
mu **CADENT** falling tones; speech inflection
CADGED sponged; begged; importuned
CADGER huckster; beggar; mendicant
ch **CADION** chemical detection reagent
ch **CADMIA** sulphide of cadmium
md **CAECUM** a blind sac
CAESAR an autocrat; tsar; shah
go **CAFARD** Algerian desert; melancholia
zo **CAFFRE** Caffrarian; wild tabby cat
CAFTAN kaftan; Persian vest
CAGING confining (zoos); framework; enclosing
CAGMAG meat unfit for food
CAHIEN notebook (reports)
CAHOOT partnership
zo **CAIMAN** alligator (S. Am.)
nt **CAIQUE KAIK**, skiff
CAJOLE persuade; coax; wheedle
CAKING clotting; precipitating; coagulating
ps **CAKRAS CHAKRAS**, psychic body centre (Asia)
CALADE fairground horseshow circus
CALASH vehicle; hood
CALCAR glass furnace
CALCED wearing shoes; shod
ch **CALCIC** containing calcium
ga **CALCIO** 17th-century football, Florence
tx **CALICO** cotton cloth
md **CALIGO** dimness of sight
mt **CALINA** dusty haze in Med. region
rl **CALIPH CALIF**, sheik of Islam
nt **CALKED CAULKED**, hull made watertight; refitting

nt **CALKER CALKING**, ship's bottom painter
CALLED visited; named; shouted for; phoned
CALLER representative; referee; ringer
CALLID skilled; expert; shrewd
CALL-IN transfer control; main to sub
CALLOW immature (of character, growth)
CALL-UP military induction
pl, bt **CALLUS CALLOUS**, wart; hardening (skin, bark)
CALMED lulled; soothed; sedated; allayed
CALMLY sedately; serenely; placidly
me **CALORY CALORIE** thermal energy unit
CALPAC Eastern cap
bt **CALTHA** king-cup
CALVER iceberg beginning to break up
zo, go **CALVES** pl. of calf; give birth to (deer) (icebergs)
bd **CALYON** wall construction stone
CAMAIL chain-mail
bt **CAMASS** lily (edible bulbs)
bt **CAMATA** acorns
ar, ga **CAMBER** cross-slope; tie-beam; convexity; ski-flexibility; arching position
lw, pg **CAMERA** closed courtroom; image-recorder
tx **CAMESE CAMISE-CAMISOLE**, woman's blouse (or bodice)
CAMION motor truck; waggon
tx, wv **CAMLET** Angora goat hair fabric
CAMPER tent dweller; lives rough
el **CAMP-ON** electronic telephone connector
go **CAMPOS** Savannah (Brazil)
CAMPUS college grounds
ck **CANAPE** cocktail delicacy; sofa or settee
CANARD hoax; news spoof
zo, ck **CANARY** caged finch; dance; wine
CANCAN a dance
CANCEL quash; annul; blot
as, md **CANCER** the Crab (Zodiac); malignant cell growth
ga **CANCHA** court for playing pelota
CANDID frank; honest; sincere
me **CANDIE** 500 lb (226 kg) (Ind.)
CANDLE light; taper
CANGUE Chinese criminal yoke
CANINE doggy
CANING thrashing

CANKER corrupt; infection/infestation

mu **CANNED** preserved; pre-recorded (ro, tv)

mn **CANNEL** bituminous coal

CANNON (artillery); (billiards); (croquet)

CANNOT unable to

ar **CANOPY** awning; umbrella/shade; cover (firmament) (parachute); ceiling décor

CANTAB Cambridge; university; (degree)

me **CANTAR** about 1 cwt (50 kg) (Syrian)

CANTED cross-sloped; tilted; oblique

CANTER slow relaxed gallop (horses)

md **CANTHI** corners of the eye

CANTLE (saddle); fragment

go **CANTON** autonomous province (Swiss)

mu, rl **CANTOR** Precentor; leading church singer

mu **CANTUS** chant

CANUCK Canadian

nt, ga **CANVAS** sails; tent covering (linen); winning length (rowing)

CANVAS CANVASS, list voting intentions

CANYON deep ravine; gulch; rift

me **CAPFUL** the quantity to fill a cap

lw **CAPIAS** writ

lw **CAPITE** royal tenant, feudal

md **CAPIVI** balsam; copaiva

zo **CAPLIN** small smelt

eg **CAP-NUT** end-sealed nut

CAPOTE long cloak (Fr.)

CAPPED covered; limited (finances); decorated; exceeded (record)

ch **CAPRIC** acid

zo **CAPRID** of goats

CAPRIN an acid found in butter

CAPTOR capturer

nt **CARACK CARRACK**, sailing vessel (of the Discoveries)

CARACT mark; sign; character

CARAFE glass water-jug

zo **CARANX** mackerel

bt **CARAPA** crab-wood tree (S. Am.)

ch **CARBOL** (carbolic)

ch **CARBON** charcoal

CARBOY glass jar

pg **CARBRO** carbon/bromide printing

lt **CARCEL** French luminous-flux unit

CARDED combed (wool); indexed

cf, md **CARDIO-** of the heart

ck **CARDOL** cashew-nut oil

nt **CAREEN** heel over; trim; nit picking

CAREER move swiftly; professional lifestyle

CARESS embrace lovingly; fondle

CARFAX CARFOX, crossroads, four forked

bt **CARICA** paw-paw tree

pl, md **CARIES** dental decay

bt, zo **CARINA** keel-like structure

CARING tending; nursing; feeling; committed concern

CARKED worried; perplexed

CARLOT churl; peasant

CARMAN van driver

CARMEN carriers; an opera

CARNAL of the flesh; sensual; sexual

CARNET motorcar passport

CARNEY horse-disease

eg **CARNOT** thermal-efficiency unit

pl **CARPAL** of the wrist

CARPED cavilled; grumbled

bt **CARPEL** seed vessel

CARPER censurer; critic

CARPET floor fabric

md **CARPUS** the wrist

me **CARRAT CARAT**, gold measure

CARREL cross-bow arrow; quarry

bt, ck **CARROT** root vegetable; incentive; (donkeys)

CARTED removed (by transport)

CARTEL price fixers' ring; league; cabal

CARTER wagoner

CARTON strengthened cardboard box

ga **CAR-TOW** automobile rescue (police station); glider-launching method

CARVED CARVEN, cut, shaped, engraved

CARVEL CARAVEL, the Discoverer's sailing vessel; jelly fish

CARVER sculptor; a knife

bt **CASABA** yellow winter melon

ck **CASEIC CASEIN-CASEUM**, of cheese (protein)

CASERN army barracks

CASHED converted into money (specie)

bt **CASHEW** tropical nut

bt **CASHOO CATECHU**, an astringent

bd **CASING** cover; packing; box; lining

ga **CASINO** gaming saloon; 15th-century card game

CASKET jewel case; reliquary

CASQUE a helmet; morion

bt **CASSIA CASSIS**, the black currant

zo **CASSIN** snail's helmet shell

pr, cp **CASTER** cruet; furniture wheel; type casting

ar **CASTLE** citadel; fortress; stronghold

ga **CASTLE** (chess move); wicket (stumps) (cricket); (home)
md **CASTOR** beaver gland scent; purgative oil
pr **CAST-UP** vomit; job content
CASUAL chance; informal; (-partner)
rl **CASULA** a chasuble; vestment
CATCHY deceptive; infectious
CATENA a chain; a series
CATENA doctrinal writings
zo **CATGUT** cord; violin string
CATHAY China; (Marco Polo)
el **CATION** electro-positive element cathode
bt **CATKIN** pendulous inflorescence
CAT-LAP tame tipple
CATLOG catalogue
CATNAP forty winks; doze
bt **CATNIP** mint; catmint
ck **CATSUP** a relish; ketchup
nt **CATTED** the anchor well slung
zo **CATTLE** kine; oxen
CAUCUS powerful, inner political group
zo **CAUDAD** towards the tail
zo **CAUDAL** tail-like; inferior
bt **CAUDEX** palm-stem
CAUDLE hot spice wine
CAUGHT trapped; entangled
CAUKED CAWKED, hull made water tight
CAUKER CAWKER, oakum picker's yarn; drink
bt **CAULIS** stem
CAUSAL producing; resulting
CAUSED occasioned; created; effected
CAUSER instigator; prime mover
CAUSEY pavée; causeway (obs.)
CAUTEL craft; wariness (obs.)
CAUTER searing-iron
lw **CAVEAT** suspension of court hearting
CAVERN cave; grotto; den
zo **CAVIAR** fish-roe of the sturgeon
zo **CAVIES** guinea-pig
ce **CAVING** exploring caves; (-in); collapse quarrying & mining method
CAVITY void; empty hole; (teeth)
CAVORT prance; buck; leap
pr **CAXTON** a book in block letters
zo **CAYMAN** alligator; caiman
zo **CAYUSE** Wild West bronco; nag
CEASED stopped; desisted; terminated
mu **CEBELL** old English gavotte
ck **CECILS** rissoles

md **CECITY** blindness
bt **CEDARN CEDARY**, cedar wood; colour
CEDING yielding; giving way
CEDRAT CEDRATE, citrous
lw **CEDULA** S. American mortgage
bt **CELERY** crisp vegetable
md **CELIAC** coeliac; abdominal
CELLAR underground cold storage; low purchase prices
CELLED honeycombed; alveolate
CELTIC KELTIC, Gaelic language; culture
CELURE decorated route; wagon roof
bd, md **CEMENT** cohese; adhere; concrete; hold together (friendship) (teeth)
CENSED redolent with incense
rl **CENSER** urn for burning incense
CENSOR to control secrecy, morals etc.; official who vets books, films
CENSUS official counting (population)
me **CENTAL** 100 lb (45 kg)
ga **CENTRE CENTER**, middle point; official head office; (-forward)
cf **CEPHAL-** of the brain (Gr. pl)
zo **CEPOLA** snake-fish
bt **CERAGO** pollen
md **CERATE** an ointment
CERCAL caudal, of the tail
bt **CEREAL** grain; corn
bt **CEREUS** a cactus genus
mn **CERINE** an ore of cerium
CERING covering with wax
pr **CERIPH SERIF**, style of lettering
CERISE cherry-colour
ch **CERITE** cerium silicate
ch **CERIUM** metallic element
ml **CERMET** metal-ceramic alloy
CEROON seroon; a bale
bt **CERRIS** the bitter oak
ch **CERUSE** white-lead
zo **CERVID** with antlers (deer)
md **CERVIX** neck of womb
zo **CERVUS** the stag genus
lw **CESSIO** an assignment
lw **CESTUI** a beneficiary
CESTUS a girdle; boxing glove
mu **CESURA CESURE**, pause interruption
zo **CETINE** spermaceti
zo **CHACMA** baboon
CHAFED fretted by rubbing; galled
zo **CHAFER** a beetle; cockchafer
CHAFFY light; worthless; jovial
CHAGAN a Khan; oriental ruler
CHAISE horse drawn vehicle
CHALET Swiss cottage
CHALKA Zulu king
CHALKY of chalk, pasty

CHANCE happen; betide; fortune
CHANCY hazardous; risky; fortuitous
cp CHANGE alter; vary; shift; veer;
    printout
nt, mu CHANTY SHANTY, sea songs
rl CHAPEL a printer's association;
    (church)
CHAPPY cleft; chinky
el, lw CHARGE fee; trust; command;
    (cavalry-); (electrical-); indict
CHARKA small cup with silver
    handle (Rus.)
CHARON ferryman of Styx
CHARRY like charcoal
CHASED followed; tracked; engraved
CHASER hunter; pursuer; a
    neutralizing drink; steeple-chasing
    horse
CHASMY gaping; yawning
CHASSE a liqueur; dance step (ice
    skating); (badminton)
CHASTE pure; virginal; incorrupt
CHATON the head of a ring (Fr.)
ar CHATRI umbrella-shaped dome
    (Hindu)
CHATTA umbrella (Ind.)
CHATTY talkative; gossipy
CHAWED CHEWED, gnawed;
    crunched; masticated
CHECKY chequered (chess-board)
CHEEKY insolent; impudent
CHEERY buoyant; merry; blithe
CHEESE CHEESEY, of milk, fatty
CHEESY tacky
mn CHEKOA porcelain-clay
CHEQUE order to pay (banking);
    (bouncer)
bt CHERRY a tree fruit; ruddy colour
mn CHERTY flinty
CHERUB angel; child
CHERUP chirp; to urge
mn CHESIL CHISIL, gravel; shingle
pl CHESTY of bronchials; low-pitched
    voice
ga CHEUCA Argentine Indian's game
    like hockey
CHEVAL a frame
zo CHEVAN chevin; chub
ar CHEVET an apse
zo CHEWET chough (bird); chatterer
md CHIASM (optic nerve)
ck CHICHA liquor from maize (S. Am.)
CHICHI 'precious'; over-decorated
bt CHICLE chewing gum
CHICLY fashionably; modishly
CHICOT jester to Henri III
CHILDE chylde; nobleman's son
    (Harold)

bt CHILLI CHILLY-CHILI, cayenne pepper
CHILLY bleak; frigid; cold
mu, rl CHIMED CHIMES, clock music;
    church bells; (-in)
rl CHIMER bishop's robe
mu CHIMES bell tunes (clocks)
zo CHINCH grain insect; bed-bug; cimex
go CHINED ravined; cleft to the back-
    bone
CHINEE a Chinaman
CHINKY gaping; chappy
nt CHINSE to caulk
tx CHINTZ floral cotton cloth
CHIPPY off colour
pl CHIRAL pertaining to the hand
CHIRPY chatty; cheerful; cheery;
    (bird)
to CHISEL carpenter's planing tool; to
    cheat
mn CHISIL chesil; gravel
zo CHITAL spotted deer
zo CHITIN horny material
zo CHITON a mollusc; Greek tunic
CHITTY disrespectful; infantile;
    order note
mu CHIUSO closed horn notes (It.)
bt, ck CHIVES onion-like salad plant
CHIVVY hasten; nag; pester
CHOICE select; dainty; option;
    election
CHOKED stifled; throttled;
    suppressed
CHOKER a tie; a neckerchief
CHOKEY prison
CHOKRA office boy (Ind.)
CHOLER anger; ire; spleen; rage
md CHOLIC (bile); bilious
CHOOSE pick; elect; adopt; prefer
CHOOSY pernickety; fastidious
CHOPPY irregular; of sea waves
mu CHORAL chanted; sung
md CHOREA St Vitus' dance; the shakes
cf CHOREA- dance; (choreography)
CHOREE trochee; poetic metre
bt CHORIA external membranes
mu CHORIC of a choir
mu CHORUS group of voices
CHOSEN elected; selected; picked
CHOUAN Breton guerilla
zo CHOUGH cliff bird
CHOUSE to cheat; a trick
rl CHRISM Holy oil
cf, mu CHROMA- CHROMATIC, highly
    coloured all-note scale
ml CHROME pigment of chromium
    metal
bc, cf, md CHROMO -somes, genes in DNA
    protein

cf **CHRONO-** -meter (time)
CHUBBY plump; buxom
CHUFFY puffy; surly
ga **CHUKKA** period of play at polo
CHUMMY sociable; matey
mn **CHUNAM** lime; stucco (Ind.)
CHUNKY with lumps (marmalade)
rl **CHURCH** temple; kirk
CHURLY churlish; surly; sullen
ck **CHUTNY CHUTNEY**, fruity pickle
(India)
CHYLDE churlish; sullen; surly
ch **CHYMIC** chemical
CHYPRE a perfume
zo **CICADA CICALA, CIGALA**, a chirping
insect
bt **CICELY** a genus of plants; myrrh
pr **CICERO** type fount; guide; (orator)
bt **CICUTA** hemlock; cow-bane
rl **CIERGE** wax candle
zo **CIGALE** cigala; cicada
ar **CILERY** carving; carved foliage
CILICE hair-cloth
bt, zo **CILIUM** whip-like hair
zo **CIMBEX** the saw-fly
ar **CIMBIA** a fillet
CIMIER crest of helmet (Fr.)
zo **CIMISE** bed-bug; cimex
CIMNEL simnel; saffron cake
CINDER ember; ash
CINEMA kinema; movies; talkies
CINGLE surcingle; girth; cinch
ga **CINQUE** five (cards) (dice) (ports);
(-foil)
ar **CINTRE** centering
ma **CIPHER CYPHER**, the zero; secret
writing system
CIPHER an unimportant person
CIPIER Swiss jailer
CIPPUS funereal column
CIRCAR district (Hindu)
CIRCLE ring; compass; circuit; set
cf **CIRCUM-** around; (circumference)
CIRCUS round; (acrobatics, riding
etc.)
gl, go **CIRQUE CORRIE, COOMBE**, deep,
rounded glacier hollow
bt **CIRRUS** tendril; cloud
CISLEU a Jewish month
bt **CISSUS** wild vine
CISTIL pewter box
bt **CISTUS** rock-rose
mu **CITHER** zither (guitar)
CITIED with many cities
CITING quoting; summoning
mu **CITOLE** a dulcimer; psaltery
ch **CITRIC** (lemons)
zo **CITRIL** song bird; a finch

CITRIN vitamin P
bt **CITRON** a fruit; lemon
bt **CITRUL** the pumpkin
bt **CITRUS** plant genus
CIVICS science of citizenship
CIVIES mufti; civilian clothes
CIVISM good citizenship
CLAGGY sticky; cloggy; cledgy
CLAMMY dank; viscous; sticky
CLAQUE hired applause (theatre)
ck **CLARET** dark red wine colour
CLARTY miry; muddy
CLASSY superior; (upper-); high-
toned
CLATCH botch; daub
CLAUSE paragraph; proviso;
condition
mu **CLAVES** Cuban percussion
CLAVIS a translation; a key
md **CLAVUS** toga stripe; corn; callus
CLAWED lacerated; torn; extorted
CLAYES hurdles; wattles
CLAYEY like clay; cledgy
nt **CLEATS** herb coltsfoot; rope holders
CLEAVE cling; cohere; split; rend
hd **CLECHE** a cross voided
mn **CLEDGE** fuller's earth (clay)
CLEDGY clayey; tenacious
CLENCH clinch; secure; fasten;
grapple
rl **CLERGY** the cloth; priesthood
rl **CLERIC** clerical; a clerk; church
officer
CLEVER able; adroit; gifted;
dexterous
CLEVIS draught-iron of plough
nt **CLEWED** coiled; trussed
CLICHE artist's proof; trite phrase
CLIENT customer; dependant
gl **CLIFFY CLIFTY**, craggy; (broken)
ec, bl **CLIMAX** acme; culmination; orgasm
ga **CLINCH** clench; grasp; (agreement);
(boxing) (fencing)
CLINGY adhesive; sticky
md **CLINIC** health centre; hospital
zo **CLIONE** 'whales' food'; small fish
CLIQUE coterie; junto; cabal; set
zo **CLOACA** a sewer; reproductive canal
CLOCHE bell-glass; (hat)
CLOCHE protective glass cover for
plants
CLODDY clodly; earthy; gross;
boorish
CLOGGY adhesive; clingy
CLOKED cloaked; concealed;
disguised
CLONIC convulsive
md **CLONUS** muscular spasm

CLOSED united; grappled; shut
CLOSER nearer; tighter
ar **CLOSET** small room; wardrobe; (WC)
CLOTHE attire; drape; invest; robe
ck **CLOTTY** like thick cream; curd
CLOUDY dim; overcast; gloomy;
  murky
CLOUGH ravine; cleft; chine
CLOUGH trade allowance
zo **CLOVEN** cleft; hooved (ungulates);
  split asunder
bt **CLOVER** trifolium
CLOYED satiated; cumbered;
  surfeited
CLUMPS a numskull; nitwit; dullard
CLUMPY massive; shapeless
CLUMSY awkward; heavy-handed
mn **CLUNCH** marl; clay
zo **CLUPEA** sprat genus
CLUTCH (of eggs); grasp; clench;
  grip
CLUTCH (motoring); (in the –es of);
  critical situation
COACHY a coachman
md **COAGEL** gel made by coagulation
zo **COAITA** S. American monkey; coati
COALED stoked (stocked with coal)
COARSE crude; impure; rough; rude
COATED spread; covered
COATEE coat with short tails
COAXED persuaded; allured; seduced
COAXER cajoler; flatterer; wheedler
mn **COBALT** element; blue
mn **COBBLE** a stone; to repair (shoes)
COBCAL sandal
bt **COBNUT** hazel-nut
bt **COBRES** S. American indigo
zo **COBRIC** cobra-type
tx **COBURG** a twilled fabric
COBWEB flimsy fly-trap; spider's
  web
md, bt **COCCUS** seed-vessel; microbe
md **COCCYX** terminal bone of spine
zo **COCHIN** a fowl
COCKAL the game of knuckle-bones
COCKED erect; drunked; (-hat); (gun)
zo **COCKER** a spaniel
COCKET customs seal; a certificate
bt **COCKLE** a weed
zo **COCKLE** shellfish; to pucker
COCKSY bumptious; conceited
COCK-UP blunder; mistake; fiasco
zo, tx **COCOON** silk casing; to isolate
CODBER pillow-slip
CODDED in a pod; hoaxed
CODDER a gatherer of peas
ck **CODDLE** pamper; humour; indulge;
  (eggs)

CODGER an eccentric old man
lw **CODIFY** regulate; reorganize;
  systematize (law making)
cp **CODING** sorting; putting into cipher
cp **CODIST** summarist; programmer
bt **CODLIN** an apple
md **COELOM** the body cavity
COERCE force; impel; constrain
COEVAL contemporaneous
ck **COFFEE** beverage; of Kaffe, Ethiopia
ce, nt **COFFER** chest; box; lock chamber
  (-dam)
pr **COFFIN** burial case; printing frame
COFFLE a slave gang
COGENT potent; urgent; forcible;
  convincing; persuasive
COGGED toothed; cheated
COGGIE small bowl
nt **COGGLE** small boat
COGNAC brandy from that district
COHEIR joint heir
COHERE cleave; unite; join; stick
COHORN obsolete trench-mortar
COHORT tenth part of a legion;
  group (army)
bt **COHUNE** palm
COIGNE enforced billeting (Irish)
COILED spiral; wound
COINED invented; minted
COINER counterfeiter; inventor
COITUS sexual intercourse;
  copulation
CO-JOIN join together; unite
COKING making coke from coal (gas)
COLDER chillier
COLDLY frigidly
ar **COLLAR** neckband; (clothing);
  harness; pipe joint cover; tie beam
COLLED embraced; hugged
COLLET collar; setting of a jewel
zo **COLLIE** colley; sheep-dog
ck **COLLOP** a slice of meat
bt **COLLUM** lowest part of stem
bt **COLMAR** pear
zo **COLMEY** the coal-fish
COLONY a settlement (dominion)
COLOUR tint; hue; dye; shade
COLTER ploughshare
zo **COLUGO** flying lemur
pr **COLUMN** pillar; (army movement);
  file; (agony-) (newspaper-)
as **COLURE** intersecting celestial circle
rl **COMARB** abbot; coarb
COMART an agreement
COMATE comose; hairy; hirsute
COMBAT contest; war; resist; oppose
COMBED brushed; carded;
  straightened

COMBER foaming billow; searcher (beach)

md COMEDO a blackhead

COMEDY a light play (theatre)

COMELY seemly; graceful; shapely

ck COMFIT sweetmeat; confit

bt COMFRY comfrey; wild plant

COMING approach; future; expected

COMITY courtesy; civility

COMMIT entrust; enact; consign

COMMIX to mix; mingle

COMMON shared; (-land); usual; vulgar

mu COMODO easily flowing, leisurely (It.)

COMOPT cine-film with optical soundtrack

COMOSE hairy; downy; comate

COMPEL coerce; force; oblige

COMPLY agree; submit; yield; conform

ck COMPOT a preserve

pl, zo CONCHA CONCH, ear cavity; sea shell (spiralled)

CONCHY conscientious objector

CONCUR agree; harmonize; help

CONNED navigated; steered

CONDER pilot; fish-scout

md CONDOM safe-sex sheath

zo CONDOR vulture

CONFAB pow-wow; conference

CONFER bestow; grant; consult

ck CONFIT comfit; sweetmeat

CONFIX fasten; attach; append

CONGEE confee; dismissal; farewell

zo CONGER eel

bt CONGOU black tea

CONICS geometry of the cone

zo CONIES CONEYS, rabbits; pikas; hyrax genus

bt, ch CONIIN CONIUM, hemlock extract

bt CONIMA gum resin

ch CONINE an alkaloid

ck CONJEE CONGEE, rice-water

CONKED petered out

bt CONKER chestnut

CON-MAN trickster; swindler

nt CONNED CONNER, studied; deceiver; steered; (-ing tower)

pl CONOID pineal gland; a paraboloid

nv CONSOL Government bond; long-range navigational system

CONSUL Government official (abroad)

CONTRA against; opposite; contrasting; guerrilla in Nicaragua

cf, mu CONTRA -lower in pitch; anti

CONVEX protuberant lens; (mirror) (shape)

CONVEY carry; transport; transfer

nt CONVOY an escorted group (ships) (motorcade)

bt CONYZA fleabane

COOING (and billing); dovetalk

ck COOKED heated food; falsified accounts (books)

ck COOKER stove; range; processor (factory)

ck COOKIE super-heavy bomb; a bun

COOLED calmed; allayed; moderated

COOLER a drink; colder; (jail)

COOLIE labourer (China)

COOLLY calmly; placidly; impudently

COOMBE combe; rounded valley

bt COONTY arrowroot (Florida)

COOPED cabined and confined

COOPER a mixed drink; cask-maker; casked

COOTIE feathered legs (Sc.)

nm COPANG Japanese gold coin

nm COPECK KOPEK, 1/100th part of rouble

COPIED transcribed; aped

COPIER copyer; scribe; plagiarist

COPIES reduplications; imitations

COPING top course of a wall; striving

COPPED caught; run in; arrested

mn, nm COPPER metal; penny; policeman; laundry bowl

COPPIN ball of thread

COPTIC (Egyptian Christianity)

COPULA a link

COQUET to flirt

ar CORBEL stone bracket

zo CORBIE a raven; carrion crow

bt CORCLE embryo seed

CORCUR purple dye

CORDED ribbed; furrowed

CORDON a ribbon of honour; a guard

COREAN KOREAN, of Korea

to CORERS geological specimen collectors (oil)

to CORING boring; drilling (oil-fields)

md CORIUM true skin

CORKED sealed (bottle)

CORKER a poser; a finisher

CORKIR red or purple lichen dye

bt CORMUS stem

md CORNEA eye-membrane

CORNED preserved; granulated; salted

bt CORNEL dog-wood

ga CORNER angle; bend; nook; monopolize; (football)

mu **CORNET** an officer; trumpet
zo **CORNUA** horns
CORODY an allowance; a pension
el **CORONA** a crown; (solar); (aura); discharge
bt **COROZO** vegetable ivory
md **CORPSE** carcass; cadaver; dead body
CORPUS governing body; association
CORRAL cattle-pen; to round up
go **CORRIE CIRQUE**, a hollow; a valley
zo **CORSAC CORSAK**, fox (Central Asia)
CORSET a bodice; stays
CORTES Spanish Parliament
pl, bt **CORTEX** skin tissue; treebark; covering
pm **CORTIN** extract of adrenalin
CORVET CURVET, leap; frolic; jump about
zo, nt **CORVUS** a crow; grappling iron
bt **CORYMB** a panicle; a raceme
md **CORYZA** snuffly cold
COSHED bashed; mugged; set upon
COSHER to pamper; to chat
COSIER more cosy; a botcher; cobbler
COSILY snugly; comfortably
ma **COSINE** sine of complement of angle
COSMIC cosmical; orderly
COSMOS universe; order ·
rl **COSSAS** Indian Muslims
zo **COSSET** a pet lamb; to pet
md **COSTAL** (rib)
CO-STAR actors cast together
COSTER costermonger; apple-seller
COSTLY dear; sumptuous; rich
hd **COTISE** a bendlet
COTTAR COTTER, a cottager
COTTER wedge; pin
bt, tx **COTTON** yarn; oil; (-on, learn)
zo **COTYLA** a sucker
md **COTYLE** bone-cavity; cup
zo **COUGAR** puma
COULEE ravine; couloir
COUPED bartered for; cut off
COUPEE an antic; a salute
COUPER a dealer
COUPLE pair; brace; connect; mate
COUPON a voucher
md **COURAP** disease (E. Ind.)
COURSE circuit; orbit; series (lecture-)
COURSE (river-); flow; direction; hunt
COUSIN a kinsman
nm **COUTER** £1 (sl.)
tx **COUTIL** strong cotton fabric
rl **COVENT COVEN, CONVENT**, ladies' home

COVERT concealed; secret; thicket
COVESS female cove or chap
bd **COVING** (fireplace); moulding
bt **COWAGE** a leguminous plant
COWARD craven; dastard; recreant
COW-BOY cattle herder; erratic cyclist
bt **COWDIE** cowrie-pine
COWING intimidating; browbeating
COWISH like a cow
COWLED hooded
COW-MAN cow-herd
bt **COWPEA** herb, source of black-eye peas
vt **COW-POX** cow-teat disease
zo **COWRIE** sea-shell; cowry
COYISH coy; rather reserved
zo **COYOTE** prairie wolf
zo **COYPOU** coypu; rodent (S. Am.)
COZIER tramp; cosier
CRABBY perplexing; peevish; nit-ridden
zo **CRABER** water-vole
zo **CRABRO** hornet genus
ga **CRADLE** crib; holder; (cats'-); (lacrosse) (wrestling)
CRAFTY artful; deceitful; cunning
CRAGGE the neck
CRAGGY rugged; rough; jagged
ga **CRAMBO** a game; a rhyme
CRAMPY affected with cramp
CRANCH crunch; chew
CRANED with neck out-stretched
md **CRANIA** skulls (cranium)
CRANKY eccentric; crotchety
CRANNY chink; fissure; cleft; rift
nt **CRANSE** boom iron to take stay-sails
CRANTS funeral garlands
CRAPED curled
md **CRASIS** temperament
CRATCH hay-rack; manger
CRATED boxed; encased
gl **CRATER** bomb-hole; funnel of volcano
CRAVAT necktie; neckscarf
CRAVED entreated; desired
CRAVEN coward; recreant; dastard
CRAVER beggar; an addict
nt **CRAYER** small trading ship
CRAYON coloured pencil; blackboard chalk
CRAZED decrepit; loony; deranged
CREAKY crepitative, groaning voice; (wood)
CREAMY like cream
CREANT forming; creative
CREASE Malay dagger; creese; kris

ga **CREASE** a fold; wicket limit (cricket); goal area (ice hockey)
CREASY crumpled
CREATE cause; fashion; invent
CRECHE a day-nursery
CREDIT trust; loan; merit; belief
CREEKY winding
CREEPY CREEPS, eerie; horrific
CREESE Malay dagger; crease; kris
CREESH grease (Sc.)
CREMOR creamy juice
CRENEL loophole or notch
ck **CRENIC** acid
ck **CREOLE** descendant of people of mixed races; West Indies cookery
tx **CREPON** crêpe fabric
ch **CRESOL** tar product (creosote)
ch **CRESOL** resin/plastic phenols
bt **CRESSY** like water-cress
CRESTA the ice-run at St Moritz
me **CRETIC** a metric foot
CRETIN deformed; idiot; moron
CREVET goldsmith; crucible
CREWEL embroidery
CRIKEY exclamation of surprise
lw **CRIMED** charged with (framed)
CRIMPY frizzy, waved
CRINAL comate; hirsute; hairy
CRINGE fawn; stoop; cower
CRISES decisive moments
CRISIS emergency; turning point
ck **CRISPY** crisp
pl **CRISTA** a crest; balance organ in ear
CRITIC arbiter; reviewer; judge
CROAKY harsh; guttural (voice)
CROATS Croatia (Yugoslavia)
mu **CROCHE** eighth note, quaver (Fr.)
bt **CROCUS** the saffron
ga **CROISE** attack on blade; cross-swords (fencing)
CRONET horse-hoof hair
mu **CROOKS** tubular devices
CROPPY crop-eared
CROSSE lacrosse stick
pl **CROTCH** a crutch; a fork; the groin
CROTON oil plant
CROUCH cringe; stoop; cower
md **CROUPY** affected with croup
CROUSE lively; pert (Sc.)
ck **CROWDY** gruel (Sc.); thin porridge
CROWED exulted; boasted; (cocks)
ar **CRUCKS** tree-trunk framework
CRUDER rougher; coarse; harsher
CRUISE ocean travel; economical speed; patrol
CRUISE search for partner; (street patrol)
CRUIVE fish trap

CRUMBY in crumbs; crummy
zo **CRUMMY** cow with crumpled horn
CRUNCH cranch; munch; bite
pl **CRURAL** of the thighs
CRUSET crucible; crevet
CRUSIE lamp with rush wick (Sc.)
CRUSTA engraved gem; a shell
ck **CRUSTY** of bread; surly; morose
pl **CRUTCH** walking support; the groin
CRYING weeping; calling out; notorious; clamour
cf **CRYPTO-** hidden; secret; (cryptogram); coded
CUBAGE solid content
tx **CUBICA** shallon cloth
CUBING raising to third power
CUBISM modern artistic geometry
CUBIST geometrical daubist
CUBOID (cubical)
CUBSHA Indian drug
zo, mu **CUCKOO** migratory bird; simpleton; (clock); toy (instrument)
zo **CUDDIE** a donkey; a silly ass
CUDDLE hug; embrace; fondle
CUDDLY easily fondled; lovable
to, ga **CUDGEL** heavy club; bludgeon; batter
ga **CUE-BID** (contact bridge)
zo **CUE-OWL** scops-owl; a migrant owl
gl **CUESTA** gently sloping ridge (Sp.)
CUISSE thigh-armour
CUITER fondle; pamper
rl **CULDEE** order of monks
CULLED numbers reduced selectively; altered
CULLER group reducer
CULLET scrap-glass
ck **CULLIS** broth; jelly; gutter; groove
go **CULMEN** summit; highest point
zo **CULTCH** oyster-spawn
CULTUS a cult
zo **CULVER** pigeon; wood-pigeon
CUMBER encumber; impede; clog
tx **CUMBLY** harsh woollen cloth (Ind.)
CUMMER KIMMER, godmother; gossip
bt, ck **CUMMIN CUMIN**, spice (seed); anti-colic
CUNEAL wedge-shaped
nt **CUNNER** Chesapeake oyster boat
me **CUPFUL** filling a cup
CUP-MAN boon companion
ar, ml **CUPOLA** dome; furnace
md **CUPPED** hollowed; bleeding process
CUPPER cup-bearer
ch, ml **CUPRIC** of copper
CUP-TIE annual football competition

bt **CUPULA CUPULE**, acorn-cup; husk; crusta body
rl **CURACY CURATE**, vicar's assistant
bt **CURARE CURARI-CURARA**, arrow poison used by S. Am. Indians
rl **CURATE** assistant to parish priest
CURBED restrained; held back
bt **CURCAS** a nut
ck **CURDLE** coagulate; congeal; (curds)
lw **CURFEW** general prohibition to leave house
md **CURING** healing; preserving (leather); (food)
CURLED wavey; twisted; (hairstyle)
CURLER ice skating technique; hair-holder
zo **CURLEW** wading bird
CURRED purred; cooed
bt, ck **CURRIE CURRY**, hot spice mix (Asia); horse comb
CURSED CUSSED, sworn at; damned as evil
CURSER vituperator
cp **CURSOR** a slide-rule adjunct; space indicator
mu **CURTAL** early bassoon
CURTER CURTLY, in more brusque style; briefly
CURTSY CURTSEY, a woman's courtesy knee bow
CURULE Roman chair
CURVED arched; bent; bowed
CURVET CORVET, leap; frolic; jump about
ck **CUSCUS COUSCOUS**, millet dish (N. Africa)
zo, bt **CUSCUS** flying squirrel; cereal fibre
zo **CUSHAT** ring dove
md **CUSPID** a canine tooth
CUSTOM habit; usage; wont; tax
CUSTOS university official
CUTEST most alluring; cunning; slyest
CUTLER a dealer in knives etc.
ck **CUTLET** meat sliced wtih bone; chop
go, el **CUT-OFF** end process; cessation of power
el **CUT-OUT** automatic process or power stoppage
tx, nt, bd **CUTTER** tailor; fast yacht; rubbed brick
pr **CUTTER** author's abbreviation marks
zo **CUTTLE** squid
CUTTOE large knife (US)
bt **CYANIN** colouring of rose/cornflower
CYCLED repeated sequence of operations

cp **CYCLIC** periodic; closed-loop data
CYCLUS a bicycle or tricycle
CYESIS pregnancy
zo **CYGNET** young swan
zo **CYGNUS** swan genus
mu **CYMBAL** metal clashing instrument
md **CYMENE** (camphor)
CYMOID having a waving profile
CYMOSE CYMOUS, inflorescence quality
CYMRIC Welsh
bt **CYNARA** artichoke genus
CYNICS Athenian philosophical sect
CYNOID dog-like
bt **CYPHEL** flowering shrub
ma, pr **CYPHER CIPHER**, zero; non-entity; code
zo **CYPRIS** shrimp species
tx **CYPRUS** black fabric
md **CYSTIC CYSTIS**, of bladder; cyst (body capsule)
md **CYTASE** an enzyme
CYTOID cell-like
zo **CYTULA ZYGOTE**, fertilized ovum

D

DABBED touched repeatedly; daubed
bd **DABBER** dome-shaped brush; inking ball
DABBLE mix; meddle; sprinkle
zo **DABOIA** venomous snake
fr **DABREY** latex collection tray
DACOIT pirate; robber (Burma)
tx **DACRON** polyester fibre
DACTYL finger or toe
DADDLE walk totteringly
DAEDAL intricate; mazy; complex
DAFTLY idiotically; crazily
DAGGED cut into slips
pr **DAGGER** dirk; stiletto; poniard († mark)
DAGGLE bedraggle; defile; sully
rl **DAGOBA** Buddhist shrine
bt **DAHLIA** a flower genus
bt **DAIKON** Japanese radish
DAIMIO Japanese noble
DAINTY choice; exquisite; tasty; chic
ch, me **DALTON** of oxygen (atomic mass)
DAMAGE mar; hurt; impair; injury
tx **DAMASK** patterned linen fabric
DAMIER large-squared pattern
DAMINE like a fallow deer
bt **DAMMAR** resin; damar
ce **DAMMED** embanked; blocked; (rivers)
DAMNED condemned; doomed

DAMPED moderated; deadened
DAMPEN moisten; discourage; depress
DAMPER (ironing); a regulator
pr DAMPER printing roller (lithography)
DAMPLY unenthusiastically
DAMSEL lass; maiden; girl
bt DAMSON small plum
DANCED capered; frisked; hopped
DANCER ballerina; rhythmic artist
DANDER saunter; anger
zo DANDIE terrier (dog)
DANDLE pet; fondle; caress
DANGER risk; peril; hazard; jeopardy
DANGLE to fondle; swing; suspend
DANISH of Denmark
DANITE (Mormon sect)
DANTON to daunt; to subdue (Sc.)
bt DAPHNE evergreens
DAPPED fished with a mayfly
DAPPER neat; nimble; sprightly
pt DAPPLE to variegate with spots (horse)
DARING lark snaring; audacious
DARKEN darkle; cloud
DARKEN obscure; perplex
DARKER blacker; duskier
DARKLY opaquely; mysteriously
tx DARNED repaired; mended; accursed
bt DARNEL rye grass; tares
tx DARNER special thread; needle; sewing machine
DARTED sprang out; shot; flew
zo DARTER Brazilian pelican
md DARTRE skin-disease; herpes
DASHED cast; sped; rushed; shattered
tx DASHER gadabout; (haber-) (clothing)
zo DASSIE badger; hyrax
DATARY papal officer
ps DATING courting; (post); age estimate
DATION act of giving
DATIVE prepositions of giving; for, to
bt DATURA thorn-apple
DAUBED smeared; plastered; stained
DAUBER inferior painter
bt DAUCUS the carrot
mn DAVINA volcanic substance
DAWDLE amble slowly; idle; dally
DAWISH like a jackdaw
DAWNED sunrise; began to appear; (ideas)
DAY-BED a sofa; couch
DAY-BOY non-resident schoolboy

zo DAY-FLY an ephemeral insect
DAZING sunshine direct into eyes
DAZZLE daze; confuse; bewilder
rl DEACON church official
DEADEN benumb; blunt; obtund
DEADLY fatal; mortal; baneful; lethal
DEAFEN overwhelm with loud noise
DEAFLY unhearingly
DEALER vendor; monger; trader
DEARER costlier; fonder
DEARIE term of endearment
DEARLY affectionately; expensively
DEARTH scarcity; lack; shortage
DEBASE degrade; lower; humble
DEBATE dispute; contest; argue
DEBRIS broken bits & pieces
DEBTED indebted; owed
lw DEBTEE the lender
lw DEBTOR the borrower
DEBUNK expose; unmask; reveal
cp DECADE ten of (years); data locations
DECAMP abscond; bolt; fly
ar, rl, mu DECANI deans-side; southside (choir) of cathedral
DECANT to pour gently
me DECARE 1000 sq. metres
DECEIT guile; fraud; chicanery
DECENT proper; seemly; suitable (clean)
DECERN to judge; to decree
DECIDE settle; determine; resolve
ma, as DECILE aspect; deci-intervals
mu, nm DECIMA DECIME, a tenth
nt DECKED DECKER, with floors (double bus); adorned
pr DECKLE paper (-frame; -edge; -gauge)
ck DECOCT boil; concentrate the essence
DECODE decipher; translate; solve
DECREE ordain; ukase; fiat; edict
DECURY squad of ten (Roman)
ga DEDANS gallery (tennis)
DEDUCE infer; gather; conclude
DEDUCT subtract; withdraw
lw DEEDED conveyed by deed
DEEMED believed; determined; judged
DEEPEN darken; dredge; make obscure
DEEPER DEEPLY, further down; profoundly
DEESHY very small (Irish)
DEFACE disfigure; injure; sully
DEFAME asperse; vilify; traduce
DEFEAT rout; frustrate; overwhelm
DEFECT flaw; blemish; faul (traitor)

DEFEND ward; protect; guard
DEFIED challenged; braved
DEFIER scorner; challenger (opponent)
DEFILE violate; taint; vitiate; a gorge
DEFINE specify; explain; limit
pl DEFLEX unflex; relax (muscles)
md DEFLUX a discharge
DEFORM distort; deface; spoil
DEFRAY pay; meet; liquidate; bear
DEFTLY adroitly; skilfully
me DEGREE grade; rank; class; order; units of measurements
DEHORN remove horns from cattle
ch DE-ICER windscreen, wing-ice remover
DEIFIC divine; godlike
DEIXIS linguistic context limits
DEJECT cast down; depress; dishearten
DELETE erase; obliterate; efface
DELICE DELOUSE, remove louse invasion
DELUDE dupe; beguile; trick
DELUGE flood; cataclysm; inundate
DELVED dug; excavated; searched
DELVER a digger; miner
lw DEMAIN DEMESNE, DOMAIN, private land
cp DEMAND claim; exact; require; request
DEMEAN behave; lower; degrade
DEMENT madden; derange
DEMISE a death; to bequeath
DEMODE not fashionable; out of date
DEMOTH take out of storage (armaments)
DEMURE modest; grave; discreet
DENARY ten
DENIAL dementi; refutation; refusal
DENIED refused; contradicted; refuted
wv, tx DENIER disowner; gainsayer; silk; nylon quality
DENNET light two-wheeled carriage
DENOTE signify; imply; indicate
DENSER more compact; thicker; closer
DENTAL of teeth
DENTED DINTED, bent after bumping
ar DENTEL DENTIL, dogtooth pattern (arches)
zo DENTEX sea perch
pl DENTIN DENTINE, tooth ivory
DENUDE strip; bare; divest
DEODAR sacred tree
DEPART start; vanish; retire; die
DEPEND rely; hang; hinge; rest

DEPICT sketch; limn; portray; draw
DEPLOY open; expand; extend; unfold
lw DEPONE to testify under oath
DEPORT banish; expel; behave
DEPOSE oust; divest of office; depone
DEPUTE delegate; authorize; change
DEPUTY envoy; proxy; agent
rw DERAIL upset; leave rail track
DERAIN vindicate; prove; justify
DERATE reduce; devalue; demote
zo DERBIO a green sea-fish
nm DERHAM dirhem; Moroccan coin
DERIDE ridicule; mock; lampoon; scorn
DERIVE obtain; draw; trace; receive
pl DERMAL dermic; relating to skin
pl DERMIS DERMIC, of layer of skin
DESCRY to espy; detect; discern
DESERT quit; abandon; forsake; merit
ck DESERT a Sahara; fruit, etc
ar DESIGN plan; devise; scheme
DESIRE covet; crave; want; passion
DESIST stay; stop; forbear; pause
zo DESMAN musk-rat
bt DESMID river-weed
DESPOT dictator; tyrant; autocrat
DETACH sever; divide; part; disengage
DETAIL delineate; recount; relate; item
DETAIN retain; keep; hold; confine
DETECT discover; reveal; unmask
DETEST hate; abhor; loathe
lw DETORT to pervert
DETOUR deviation; circumambulation
ro DETUNE adjust resonant circuit
DEUCED devilish; confounded
rl DEUNME Jew turned Moslem
DEVICE gadget; ruse; bomb; emblem
lw DEVISE scheme; plan; bequeath
DEVOID lacking; vacant; empty
DEVOIR politeness; duty
DEVOTE dedicate; give; resign
DEVOUR gorge; gobble; consume
DEVOUT pious; saintly; sincere
mt DEWING morning precipitation
DEWLAP pendulous neck-flesh
DEXTER on the right-hand side
ch DEZINK (zinc extraction)
rl DHARMA law of Buddha
DHOBIE Indian washerman
DIADEM crown; coronet; tiara
tx DIAPER a napkin for incontinent babies

bt **DIATOM** algae with silica shells
zo **DIAXON** with 2 axes, in sponges
to **DIBBED DIBBER**, pointed tool (garden)
DIBBLE dibber; to make holes
DICING gaming
DICKER ten; to barter
DICTUM maxim; precept; wise words
lw **DICTUM** precept; award
DIDDER to shiver
DIDDLE cheat; totter; dodder
DIESEL heavy oil (motor)
pr **DIESIS** printing mark
ck **DIETAL DIETED-DIETER**, of food regime
DIFFER deviate; vary; wrangle
DIGAMY second marriage
DIGENY sexual reproduction
DIGEST assimilate (summarized material)
DIGGED delved; dug; mined
DIGGER Australian
DIGRAM double picture
DIKAST diccast; Athenian judge
zo **DIK-DIK** S. African antelope
bd **DIKING** making floor barriers (dikes)
DIKKAH tribune in a mosque
zo **DIKKOP** bustard (S. African)
DIKTAT enforced settlement
md **DILATE** amplify; expand; enlarge
DILOGY double-entendre
DILUTE water down; weaken a solution
tx **DIMITY** figured cloth; strong cotton
DIMMED obscured; clouded; dulled
DIMMER light-fading device (cars)
DIMMER fainter; darker
DIMOUT partial black-out
DIMPLE cheek depression
DIMWIT fool; weak-minded
mu **DIN-DIN** Indian cymbals
DINGED hurled; enforced; urged
DINGER home-run (baseball)
DINGES what's its name (S. African)
nt **DINGHY** dingey; open, ballasted sailing craft
DINGLE dell; dale; vale; glen
DINGUS gadget; contraption
DINKUM honest; genuine (Aust.)
DINNED persistently repeated
DINNER principal meal
DIONYM name containing 2 terms
md **DIOTIC** affecting both ears
DIPLEX simultaneous tranmission
md **DIPLOE** skull tissue
zo **DIPNOI** fish with lungs and gills
pl **DIPODY** two-footed
el, ro **DIPOLE** type of radio aerial

DIPPED immersed; doused; soused
zo **DIPPER** waterbird; ousel; ladle
me **DIP-ROD** oil gauge
me **DIPSAS** serpent
mn **DIPYRE** a silicate of alumina
DIRECT straight; bid; order; address
DIREST most calamitous; cruellest
nm, me **DIRHAM DIRHEM**, coinage (Morocco); ancient weight (silver)
DIRKED stabbed by dagger
DISARM to remove guns, weapons etc.
lw **DISBAR DEBAR**, expel a professional from practice
bt **DISBUD** remove buds (gardening)
mu **DISCAL** of discs
bt **DISCUS** flower centre; quoit
ga **DISCUS** a thrown weight
DISEUR DISEUSE, raconteur (Fr.)
DISHED frustrated; thwarted
DISMAL dull; doleful; lugubrious
DISMAN to castrate; render impotent
DISMAY appal; scare; daunt; alarm
DISOWN deny; disclaim; reject
DISPEL banish; scatter; dismiss
bt **DISTAL** terminal; furthest from axis
DISTIL vaporize; drip; emanate
DISUSE desuetude; neglect
DITHER didder; tremble; hesitate
mu **DITONE** notation interval
zo **DIURNA** insects; ephemerae (of a day)
DIVERS diverse; different; sundry
DIVERT distract; amuse; relax; deflect
DIVEST divest; strip; denude; bare
DIVIDE separate into parts; share; sever
go **DIVIDE** watershed; continental-; cleave
DIVINE sacred; angelic; defect
rl **DIVINE** (water); augur
DIVING plunging; penetrating; swooping
mu **DIVISI** separation of strings for part playing (It.)
mu **DIVOTO** solemnly; in devotion (It.)
DIZAIN poem in ten stanzas
zo **DIZOIC** with 2 sporozoites
DJIBBA Eastern garment
DOABLE practical
DOBBIE a dotard; a brownie
zo **DOBBIN** old horse
DOCENT reader/teacher in University
DOCILE pliant; amenable; compliant
nt, sp, vt **DOCKED** without tail; safe in harbour
DOCKER dock-labourer; stevedore

lw **DOCKET** doquet; a summary

zo **DOCTOR** a fish; medico; to falsify

vt, zo **DODDED** de-horned

bt **DODDER** parasitic plant; didder; shake

bt, zo **DODDLE** a pollard

DODGED evaded; quibbled; avoided

DODGER trickster; shifter; evader

nm **DODKIN** a doit

zo **DODMAN** a snail

DOFFED removed; took off (cap)

DOFFER carding mechanism (wool)

DOGANA DOUANE, customs house (It/Fr.)

zo **DOG-BEE** a drone

DOG-BOX enclosure for dogs

DOG-EAR broken/damaged book corner

zo **DOG-FOX** renard

mn **DOGGAR** ironstone

DOGGED sullen; obstinate; determined

nt **DOGGER** fishing boat (North Sea)

DOG-LEG crooked hole shot (golf)

DOG-MAD rabid; crazy; insane

DOIGTE finger play (fencing)

DOINGS multifarious activities

DOITED crazy; stupid

DOLING distributing (to needy)

DOLING (small portions)

zo **DOLIUM** molluscs

nm **DOLLAR** 100 cents

DOLLED prinked up; overdressed

ck **DOLLOP** viscous mass; helping

DOLMAN hussar's jacket

DOLMEN ancient grave; cromlech

DOLOSE fraudulent; deceitful

DOLOUR anguish; sorrow; pain

lw **DOMAIN** demesne; dominion; sway

ps **DOMAIN** borders of strong magnetic force on ferromagnetic crystals

DOM-BOC Saxon book (judgments)

tx **DOMETT** shroud fabric

ga, rl **DOMINO** priest's cape; cloak; game

mn **DOMITE** variety of trachyte

DONARY DONATE, gift; give (money etc.)

ar **DONJON** castle keep (above dungeon)

zo **DONKEY** burro; moke; ass

DONZEL budding knight; a page

DOODLE a simpleton; a trifler; drawing

DOOMED destined; condemned

DOONGA flat-bottomed house-boat (Indian)

DOPING administering drugs

DOPING sniffing varnish

mu **DOPPIO** increase speed to double (It.)

as, zo **DORADO** constellation; a dolphin

zo **DORBIE** heath bird; dunlin

DORCAS charitable society

ar **DORIAN** Doric scroll motif (capitals) (Gr.)

DORING lark-catching

DORISM Doricism

ar **DORMER** window in the roof

ar **DORMIE** dormy; unbeatable at golf

bt **DORMIN** hormone controlling dormancy

tx **DORNIC** figured linen

pl **DORSAL** nerves of touch; limbs

pl, zo **DORSAL** spinal, back fin

DORSEL pannier

rl **DORTER** dormitory

md **DOSAGE** DOSING, medicine amount prescribed

rl **DOSSAL** DOSSEL, altar cloth in church

md **DOSSIL** pledget; slug

DOTAGE DOTANT, DOTART, DOTISH, senility

DOTERY drivel spoken by senile

DOTING infatuated; madly fond of

DOTTED stippled; speckled

pt **DOTTER** birds'-eyes graining brush

DOTTLE pipe-ash

DOUANE custom-house (Fr.)

mu, ga **DOUBLE** twofold; dual; score; trill

DOUCHE shower (bath)

ck **DOUGHY** soft consistency like dough

zo **DOUKAR** dabchick

DOURLY grimly; sternly; obstinately

DOUSED drenched; extinguished (fire)

DOWSED DOWSER, water found by diviner

DOUTER extinguisher

ar **DOWELL** metal pin; cramp

lw **DOWERY** DOWER, widow's share of assets

tx **DOWLAS** coarse cloth

DOWNED floored

DOWSER water-diviner

tx **DOYLEY** DOILY, lacement (dining room)

DOZING somnolent; drowsy

DRABBY sluttish; unkempt

nm **DRACHM** drachma; a dram

DRAFFY dreggy; waste; worthless

DRAFTS preliminary texts

DRAFTS cheques (bank-); recruits

DRAGEE sweetmeat

zo **DRAGON** monstrous saurian

DRAPED dressed; robed; clothed

DRAPER haberdasher
DRAPET coverlet
DRAPPY a wee drop (Sc.)
DRAWEE (Bill of Exchange) payee
DRAWER cheque-payer; (chest of); artist
DRAZEL a slut
DREAMT DREAMY, imagined visions
DREARY dismal; lonely; dull; gloomy
DREDGE use dragnet; deepen a channel
lw **DRENCH** (tenure); soak; imbrue
DRESSY dapper; dandified
DRIEST very dry
DRIVEL prate; twaddle; balderdash
DRIVEN urged; compelled; overworked
DRIVER chauffeur (taxi-); (pile-)
ga **DRIVER** club (golf)
nt **DROGER** a coaster; drogher; (Irish Sea)
DROGUE sea anchor; wind sleeve; target
DROMIC DROMOS, of aerodrome; racecourse
nt **DROMON** medieval warship; galley
DROMOS Greek race-course
DRONED buzzed; drawled; idled
zo **DRONGO** king crow
cp **DROP-IN** computer error; visit; party
md **DROPSY** condition of retention of fluids
DROSKY Russian horse-cab
DROSSY impure; foul; worthless
DROUGE harpoon drag
DROUTH DROUGHT, dryness (climate)
DROVER cattle-driver
DROWSE nap; slumber; doze
DROWSY lethargic; comatose; soporific
DRUDGE menial; scullion; toil; slave
rl **DRUIDS** a sacred order
bt **DRUPEL** a stone-fruit; a drupe
DRUSED crystalline
rl **DRUSES** Moslem sect (Lebanon, Syria)
DRY-BOB non-rower (Eton)
DRY-FLY (fishing) (angling)
DRYING parching; desiccating
DRYISH rather dry; very dull; sarcastic
mn **DRYITE** fossil wood
DRY-ROT wood decay
DRY-RUB massage; rub down
DUBBED DUBBER, sound film translator
DUBBED greased
DUBBIN a leather grease; dubbing

DUCKED bobbed; immersed
zo **DUCKER** a plunger; bird
DUDDER to shake; to deafen
DUDEEN Irish clay pipe
DUELLO duelling (It.)
DUENNA chaperone
mu **DUETTO** a duet
DUFFED stole cattle (Aust.)
tx **DUFFEL DUFFLE**, coarse felt cloth coat
DUFFER a pedlar; muff; stupid person
zo **DUGONG** sea-cow; halicore; manatee
ga, nt **DUG-OUT** canoe; shelter; (baseball)
DUG-OUT retired officer
zo **DUIKER** duyker; cormorant
DUKERY seat of a duke
mu **DULCET** melodious; honeyed (sounds)
DULLED blunted; assuaged; softened
DULLER more listless
DUMBLY silently; mutely
DUM-DUM soft-nosed bullet
DUMPED unloaded; deposited; corpse
ga **DUMPED** surfer (Australia)
DUMPER track with unloading chute
ga **DUMPER** mighty wave surfing
DUMPLE to cook a dumpling
zo **DUN-COW** species of ray
gl **DUNITE** olivine igneous rock
DUNKER tunker; baptist; dipper
zo **DUNLIN** sandpiper
ck **DUNLOP** a cheese; –type
DUNNED importuned
DUNNER debt-collector
bd **DUNTER** monumental mason or polisher
DUPERY deception; gulling
DUPING confidence tricks
zo **DUPION** double cocoon
ps **DUPLET** electrons bonding atoms
mu **DUPLET** of equal time notes
el **DUPLEX** two-room flat; two-way flow
DUPLEX double-sided emulsified photo paper
mn **DURAIN** type of coal
DURANT glazed fabric
mu **DURATE** harsh to the ear
DURBAR Grand Audience; festival (Ind.)
DURDEN a thicket; a copse
DURDUM dirdum; an uproar
DURESS restraint; imprisonment
rl **DURGAH** Moslem saint's shine (Ind.)
DURGAN dwarf
zo **DURHAM** breed of cattle

bt **DURIAN** Malay fruit
DURING throughout; pending
bt **DURION** see durian
DURITY hardness; firmness
tx **DURRIE** Indian cotton fabric
DUSKEN to grow dark
DUSKLY duskily; gloomily
tx **DUSTER** dry house cloth (cleaning)
DUST-UP quarrel; fisticuffs; fight; brawl
DUTIED posted to other duties (army)
DUTIED charged; taxed (excise)
DUTIES obligations (work) (excise)
zo **DUYKER** duiker; African antelope
ch **DYADIC** (two); characteristic of things paired
cp **DYADIC** binary operation
DYEING colouring; staining
el **DYNAMO** energy converter
DYNAST ruler (in family line)
el **DYNODE** valve
zo **DZEREN** DZERON, Mongolian antelope

E

EADISH aftermath; second crop
zo **EAGLET** a young eagle
EAR-BOB an earring
EAR-CAP ear-muff
EARFUL a diatribe; (explosion of anger)
nt **EARING** ploughing; rope
md **EARLAP** tip of ear
EARNED merited; won; deserved
EARNER wage taker; breadwinner
EARTHY material; gross; unrefined
EAR-WAX cerumen
zo **EAR-WIG** informer; insect
ce **EASERS** relief holes (prior to tunnelling)
EASIER more tranquil; more pliant
EASILY tranquilly; calmly
EASING relieving; calming; soothing
rl **EASTER** Resurrection
rl **EASTER** EOSTRE (goddess); Saxon Spring
EATAGE cattle food
EATING food intake; devouring; eroding
EBBING waning; declining; subsiding
ga **ECARTE** card game
bl **ECESIS** unviable-species invasion
bt **ECHARD** non-usable soil water
ECHOED repeated sound
ECHOES resounded reverberations

ECHOIC aural copycat; mimic
ECLAIR a cream-filled pastry
md **ECLEGM** oil and syrup
cf, md **-ECTOMY** (surgical) removal
ar **ECTYPE** a cast; a copy
md **ECZEMA** a skin disease
EDDIED swirled; rippled; whirlpool
EDDISH eadish; aftermath
bt **EDDOES** W. Indian potatoes
rl **EDENIC** of the garden of Eden
EDGING border; frill; rim; nearing
EDIBLE eatable; esculent
pr **EDITED** prepared for publication
EDITOR corrector; reviser; annotator
EDUCED extracted; elicited; derived
EEL-POT an eel-trap
EERILY wierdly; uncannily
EFFACE erase; expunge; delete
EFFECT achieve; cause; create
EFFETE spent; worn; barren; abortive
rl **EFFIGY** image; statue; likeness
EFFLUX flow; effusion; discharge
EFFORT essay; trial; striving; strain
EFFUSE emanate; issue; pour; spill
EGENCE exigence
mn **EGERAN** garnet
EGERIA spiritual adviser
ck **EGG-CUP** container for boiled egg
EGGERY nesting-place
EGGING inciting
EGGLER an egg-dealer
ck **EGG-NOG** a drink; egg and rum
pc **EGOISM** conceit; vanity; self-praise
EGOIST egoist; not an altruist
EGOITY identity
pc **EGOTIC** essence of personality
EGRESS emergence from shade; exit
bt **EGROIT** a sour cherry
EIDOLA apparitions
mu **EIGHTH** a quaver ⅛ note
ga **EIGHTS** carmanship; (the boat race)
EIGHTY four-score
zo **EIRACK** young hen (Sc.)
EITHER one of two
EKEING ekeing; adding; stretching
bt **ELAEIS** African oil palm
ELAINE the lily-maid of Astolat
ELANCE throw out; launch
zo **ELANET** insectivorous kite
ELAPSE intervene; pass; slip
ELATED exalted; proud; excited
zo **ELATER** click-beetle genus
ELATOR a rouser
ELDEST oldest
lw **ELEGIT** writ
ELEMIN oil from resin
ELEVEN a cricket team

ae **ELEVON** hinged wing-control surface
ELFISH puckish; impish; mischievous
ELICIT deduce; evoke; extract
ELIDED cut off a syllable
lw **ELISOR** (jury selection)
ELIXIR a cordial; quintessence; (potion)
bt **ELK-NUT** oil-nut
zo **ELLECK** red gurnet
md **ELODES** sweating sickness
rl **ELOHIM** the Creator (Hebrew)
ELOIGN to carry away
ELOPED bolted; absconded; disappeared
ELUDED evaded; dodged; foiled
mn **ELVANS** felspar veins
ELVISH elfish; elf-like; tricksy; –pixie
me **ELWAND** an ellwand
ELYTRA chitinized forewings in coleoptera
EMBALE to pack; to bundle
EMBALL encircle; ensphere
EMBALM perfume; to preserve
EMBANK confine by banks
nt **EMBARK** start; enter; board
EMBERS live cinders
EMBLEM badge; token; device; symbol
EMBODY imbody; incorporate; include
zo **EMBOLY** pushing or growing in
EMBOSS cover with raised decoration (gems)
pl **EMBRYO** fertilized ovum; rudiment
EMERGE emanate; appear; issue
md **EMESIS EMETIC**, vomiting (causing this)
EMEUTE riot; disorder; insurrection
EMIGRE French royalist abroad
EMMESH immesh; enmesh; entrap
EMPALE EMPARK, enclose with a fence
EMPAWN pawn; impawn; pledge
EMPERY empire; power
EMPIRE commercial, financial dominions
EMPLOY make use of (workers, methods etc.)
rl **EMPUSA EMPUSE**, ghost or goblin (Hecate)
EMUCID mouldy
ENABLE allow; permit; empower
md **ENAMEL** durable paint; crown cover (teeth)
ENCAGE hold captive (hen coop) (zoo)

ENCAMP camp; pitch; settle
ENCASE pack in box; (set jewels)
ENCASH convert from cheque to cash
ENCAVE to cache; to store away
cp, tc **ENCODE** convert into cyphers or symbols
cp **ENCODE** data as digits for processing
md **ENCOPE** an incision
ENCORE call for repeat (threatre)
pl, md **ENCYST** form capsule in living body
END-ALL finish; conclusion; ultimate
ENDEAR captivate; charm; win
ENDING finale; closing; finis
zo **ENDITE** phyllopodium lobe in crustacea
bt **ENDIVE** species of chicory
ENDOSS ENDORSE, sanction; ratify
nt **ENDROL** dugout canoe sailing outrigger (S.W. Pacific)
END-SAC coelomic vesicle in arthropoda
ENDUED indued; endowed; supplied
ENDURE tolerate (pain, disaster, hunger)
md **ENECIA** fever
me **ENERGY** vigour; power; (Joule)
md **ENESIS** vomiting
ar **ENFACE** decorate a surface (art)
ENFOLD wrap up; cover (protective)
ENGAGE contend; agree; promise
ENGINE machine; device; method
ENGLYN 4-line stanza (Welsh)
ENGOBE ceramic technique
ENGULF surround; overwhelm
ENIGMA mystery; puzzle; code; rebus
ENJOIN bid; direct; command
mu **ENKOMO** small Cuban drum
ENLACE enfold; entwine
ENLIST engage; enrol; secure (ally) (army) (association)
ENMESH entrap (in net); (involved)
ENMITY animus; hatred; aversion
ENNEAD group of nine
zo, bt **ENODAL** without joints, knobs
ENOSIS political fusion (Cyprus) (Gr.)
ENOUGH ample; adequate; sufficient
ENRAGE incense; infuriate; madden
rw **ENRAIL** to transport by train
ENRAPT in an ecstasy
ENRICH fertilize; endow; adorn
ENROLL enlist
ENROOT enrace; implant
bt **ENSATE** sword-shaped
lw **ENSEAL** (documents, laws etc.); legalize

ENSIGN National Flag (ships)
ENSIGN officer (US Army)
ag ENSILE fodder storage (silage)
ENSPAN to yoke up (S. Africa)
ENSUED followed; resulted; accrued
ENSURE guarantee; secure; fix
lw ENTAIL leave; bequeath; involve
md ENTERA intestines
ENTICE seduce; allure; decoy; cajole
ENTIRE complete; perfect
ga ENTIRE stallion (racing)
ENTITY being; essence; existence; unit
ENTOMB bury; inter; inhume
ENTRAP inveigle; ensnare; entangle
ck, mu ENTREE dish; menu; arrival (theatre)
ENVIED grudged; coveted
ENVIER rival
bt, ch ENZYME ferment; catalyst; leavening
EOCENE a geological period
mu EOLIAN AEOLIAN, EOLIC, Aegean harp (Gr.)
to EOLITH prehistoric flint implement
pc EONISM transvestism (d'Eon)
EOSTRE Saxon goddess; (Easter)
EOTHEN from the East
gl, mn EOZOIC EOZOON, rock containing fossilized foraminifera
EPACME vigorous period in a life-history
EPARCH Greek governor
ar EPAULE bastion-shoulder
zo EPEIRA genus of spiders
EPHEBE young Athenian
EPHORI Spartan magistrates
as EPIGEE APOGEE, furthest point of orbit from Earth
zo EPIZOA parasites
EPODIC lyric
EPONYM name derived from a person
EPOPEE epic poem
md EPULIS gum disease
EQUANT imaginary circle
EQUATE to equalize; to average
EQUINE horsey
EQUITY impartial justice
ERASED expunged; cancelled; deleted
ERASER a scraper; a mark remover
ml ERBIUM rare metal
EREBUS darkness; son of Chaos
EREMIC pertaining to sandy desert
ERENOW before this time
zo ERGATE sterile female ant, worker
lw ERIACH a fine; blood-money (Irish)
bt ERINGO ERYNGO, sea-holly
ERINYS one of the Furies

tc, me ERLANG unit of telephone traffic flow
ERMINE the stoat's winter coat
gl ERODED worn away (by climate, water)
EROTIC amatory; sexual; libidinous
ERRAND mission; change; message
ERRANT roving; rambling; wandering
ERRATA errors; mistakes
ERRING straying; mistaking
ERSATZ substitute (food etc.) (Ger.)
bt ERYNGO sea-holly genus
ga ESCAPE break free; flee; wrestling
bt ESCAPE (fire-); a non-weed in wild
ESCARP steep slope
ESCARS gravel ridges
md ESCHAR burnt wounds; scab
ESCHEW to shun; avoid; miss
ESCORT protect; guard; convoy
hd ESCROL ESCROW, deed; heraldic scroll
nn ESCUDO Porguguese coin
ESKIMO an Inuit; arctic dweller
lw ESNECY privilege of choice
ESPADA bull-fighting sword (Sp.)
ESPIED discovered unexpectedly
ESPRIT wit; sprightliness; (de corps)
rl ESSENE ascetic Hebrew
md ESSERA skin eruption
lw ESSOIN excuse for absence
ml ESTAIN French pewter
lw ESTATE condition; rank; property; (landed)
ESTEEM deem; consider; value
ESTRAY to stray; a stray; lost
bl ESTRUS (oestrus) heat; rut
lt ETALON an interferometer
er ETCHED engraved; corroded by acid
pr ETCHER an engraver
ch ETHANE odourless paraffin gas
ETHICS moral science; philosophy; code
ETHIOP an Ethiopian
mu ETHNIC racial
mo ETRIER portable stirrup
ETYMON derivation; meaning
ETYPIC unique
md EUCAIN drug similar to cocaine
ga EUCHRE card game
ma EUCLID geometer (laws)
zo EUCONE of insect compound eyes
mn EULITE an orthopyroxene
EULOGY panegyric; encomium
EUNOMY good government
EUNUCH a castrated man
EUONYM a suitable name
bt EUPION vegetable oil

zo **EUPODA** beetles
EUREKA Found! (Archimedes)
mn **EURITE** a granite
EUTAXY regularity
EUTONY pleasantness of wood sound
EVADED eluded; dodged; avoided
EVADER sidestepper of law, tax, etc.
EVANID faint; evanescent
to, cr **EVENER** leveller; roller; plane
EVENLY smoothly; fairly; uniformly
EVILLY wickedly; maliciously
EVINCE display; show; exhibit
EVOKED reminded; recalled;
   reroused
EVOLVE unfold; unroll; develop
EXAMEN a disquisition; an enquiry
rl **EXARCH** a title; viceroy; Gr. bishop
EXCEED cap; outdo; surpass;
   transcend
EXCEPT bar; ban; exclude; omit
EXCESS surplus; glut; balance
md **EXCIDE EXCISION**, to cut off
EXCISE duty; impost; tax; (Walpole)
EXCITE rouse; incite; kindle
EXCUSE acquit; pardon; exempt
EXCUSS to decipher; shake off
lw **EXCUSS** to seize
ar, bd **EXEDRA** a hall; a recess
EXEMPT free; released; immune
EXEQUY OBSEQUY, funeral rites; gifts
EXEUNT all quit the stage
EXHALE breathe out; emanate; emit
EXHORT urge; encourage; counsel
EXHUME unearth; disinter
EXILED banished; outlawed
EXILIC (Jewish) exile
lw **EXITUS** yearly rent; issue
EXODIC (Exodus); migratory
EXODUS departure
bt **EXOGEN** a class of plant
EXOMIS Greek sleeveless tunic
EXOTIC not native; extraneous;
   foreign
EXPAND spread; dilate; swell; extend
EXPECT hope; await; forecast
EXPEND disburse; consume; exert
EXPERT apt; adroit; skilful; able
EXPIRE end; die; stop; finish
EXPIRY conclusion; extinction
EXPORT sell & send goods abroad
   (ship)
EXPOSE an exposure; reveal; unmask
EXPUGN take by assault; conquer
EXSECT to cut away; cut out
zo **EXSULE** apterous life-cycle form in
   hemiptera
EXTANT existent; current
EXTASY ecstasy; rapture; trance

EXTEND stretch; reach; expand
EXTENT amount; scope; range; field
EXTERN day-boy (non resident)
EXTERN not inherent
bt **EXTINE** (pollen grain)
EXTORT exact; extract; wrench; elicit
EXUDED sweated; oozed; percolated
zo **EXUVIA** cast-off skins, shells
md **EYE-CUP** (used for eye lotion)
EYEFUL a glance
EYEING watching
EYELET loop-hole
pl **EYELID** eye skin cover
zo **EYRANT** bird of prey on nest

F

FABIAN policy of patiently waiting
   for opportune moment
FABLED renowned; fictionalized
FABLER an Aesop; parable teller
FABRIC structure; texture; web
ar **FACADE** front view; face; masking
cp **FACE-UP** confront; position of
   printing
md **FACIAL** frontal; of the face
lw **FACIES** external appearance; the face
FACILE easy; dexterous; plaint
ar, ce **FACING** confronting; opposing;
   covering; forward looking; surface
   finish
FACTOR broker; middleman
FACTOR agent or manager of estate
ma **FACTOR** causal influence; component
lw **FACTUM** memorandum; deed; point
   of controversy
as **FACULA** sun-spot
FADDLE to trifle; to play
FADGED suited; prospered
ro **FADING** diminishing; withering;
   reducing speed at end of race
FAECES human excrement
FAERIE fairy; fairyland; (Spens.)
FAFFLE to stammer
FAG-END butt (cigarette)
FAGGED tired
bd, mu **FAGGOT FAGOT**, bundle of sticks;
   fascine bassoon; facing brick
mn **FAIKES** shaly sandstone
FAILED did not succeed; missed
   (fiasco)
FAILLE nun's veiling
FAINTY feeble; languid
FAIRER more equitable; beautiful;
   blonde
FAIRLY moderately; passably
FAITOR rogue; imposter; evil-doer

FAKEER Indian beggar
FAKING forging; doctoring; feinting
ga FAKING pretending; (badminton etc.)
zo FALCON hawk; missile
mv, tx FALLAL finery; streamer
FALLEN cast down; disgraced; lapsed
FALLOW untilled; idle; dormant
FALSER more fallacious
FALTER totter; waver; vacillate
gl FALUNS Miocene deposits
pl FAMBLE the hand (sl.)
FAMILY household; race; lineage
FAMINE dearth; scarcity; starvation
FAMOUS renowned; eminent
FANGED toothed; taloned
FANGLE a contraption; (new-); novelty
FANGOT a quantity of wares
FANNED inflamed
FANNEL FANNON, flag; banner; splint
FANNER winnower
ps, el FAN-OUT multiple outputs (circuit)
ga FAN-OUT fanlike scattering (football)
ga FANTAN Chinese gambling game
FANTOM phantom; spook; ghost
FAQUIR religious mendicant
FARCIN glanders; farcy
FARDEL a bundle; burden; load
ck FARFEL kosher dumplings; doughy grains
ck FARINA flour; cereal meal; polenta
FARING experiencing; feeding
FARMED leased
FARMER tiller; cultivator
FARROW litter of pigs
FASCES Roman badge
ar, pl FASCIA a band; name-board; connective tissue
FASHED vexed; worried (Sc.)
FASTED abstained from food
FASTEN bind; secure; tie; latch
FASTER quicker; speedier
FASTLY firmly
bt FAT-HEN goose-foot
FATHER adopt; beget; sire
nt FATHOM 6ft (1.8 m); comprehend
FATTED fattened
FATTEN grow plump
FATTER more obese
FAUCAL throaty; guttural
md FAUCES (mouth)
FAUCET a tap; fosset
FAULTY defective; blameworthy
zo FAUNAL relating to animals
FAUNUS Pan
FAUTOR a supporter
FAVOSE honeycombed; cellular

FAVOUR gift; patronize; bias
FAWNER sycophant; clinger; parasite
nt FAYING fitting closely
FEALTY fidelity; loyalty; homage
FEARED apprehended; dreaded
FEATLY neatly; dexterously; adroitly
FEAZED untwisted; unravelled
rl FECIAL Roman priest; fetial
FECKET waistcoat (18th cent.)
bt, ck FECULA (plants); starch
FECUND prolific; fertile; fruitful
FEDARY a confederate
FEDORA trilby hat (USA)
FEEBLE faint; frail; weak; without strength
FEEBLY languidly; without strength
FEEDER a bib; inflow channel
cp FEED-IN programming data
FEEING hiring; recompensing
zo FEELER antenna; tentacle
zo FEELER organ of touch; (put out a-)
FEELER tentative suggestion
zo FELINE catlike; catty
FELLAH a peasant; worker (Arab)
FELLER wood-cutter
md FELLIC (bile)
FELLOE felly; rim of wheel
FELLOW peer; mate; equal
lw FELONY crime; misdemeanour
FELTED covered with felt
FELTER to mat together
FELTRE cuirass
FEMALE feminine
FENCED walled; equivocated
FENCER hedger; dealer in stolen goods
ga FENCER swordsman
nt FENDER protective rope mat; firescreen
FENIAN an Irish conspirator
FEN-MAN fen-lander; (East Anglian)
zo FENNEC African fox
bt, ck FENNEL vegetable
FEODAL feudal
FERASH lowly servant (Ind.)
FERGIE double-side kick (skiing)
FERIAE Roman holidays
FERIAL (holidays)
FERINE wild; savage; untamed; fierce
FERITY wildness
zo FERRET polecat; silk ribbon
FERRIC (iron)
FERULA fennel
FERULE a rod; cane
FERVID fervent; eager; ardent
bt FESCUE a pointer; a grass
FESTAL joyous; gay
FESTER rankle; rot; putrefy

rl **FETIAL FECIAL**, Roman priest
FETISH talisman; amulet; charm
FETISH idol; object of sexual fantasy
el **FETRON** junction; field-effect
transistor
FETTER manacle; shackle; bond;
gyve
FETTLE good condition; fitness
FEUDAL vassal-lord polity
FIACRE French cab
FIANCE betrothed man
FIASCO total failure, breakdown;
flask
FIBBER a liar
FIBRED having fibres
FIBRID synthetic fibrous bonding
particle
FIBRIL small fibre; slender thread
bt, md **FIBRIN** gluten; clot formative
md **FIBULA** ancient brooch; leg bone
FICKLE volatile; mercurial; unstable
FICTOR a modeller
mu **FIDDLE** a railing; violin; ruse; touch
FIDGET nervous movement; fret,
worry
FIERCE savage; cruel; violent
rl **FIESTA** carnival; Mardi Gras (S.
Am.)
FIGARO a barber; schemer
FIGGED all dressed up
cp **FIGURE** reckon; digit; (father-);
ground
bd, mu **FIGURE** diagram; timber markings
FIJIAN (Fiji Islands)
FIKERY fuss (Sc.)
bt **FILAGO** cudweed
FILFOT fylfot; a swastika; (Nazis)
FILIAL dutiful, as a son; branch
office
FILING particle; documents; rasping
FILLED replete
nm **FILLER** Hungarian coin; (complete)
bd **FILLER** extenders; (stopgap); paste
ck **FILLET** hair-ribbon; boneless fish/
meat
to **FILLET** band; plain lines on book;
tool
pg **FILL-IN** shadow technique
FILLIP to flip; an incitement
FILOSE thread-like
tc **FILTER** strain; selective process
el **FILTER** limited band network output
FILTHY foul; dirty; corrupt
ck **FILTRE** coffee-brewing method (Fr.)
bt **FIMBLE** hemp
mu **FINALE** climax; conclusion; finis; last
movement
FINDER discoverer

ck **FINDON** dried haddock
FINEER (fraudulent credit)
FINELY excellently; delicately
tx **FINERY** splendour; trappings; fallals
FINEST keenest; sharpest; purest;
best
FINGER digit; pilfer; touch
ar **FINIAL** a pinnacle; decorative acorn,
knob
FINING refining
FINISH end; terminate; accomplish
bt **FINISH** final coat of paint; fixed
joinery
FINITE limited; restricted
zo **FINLET** small fin
zo **FINNAN** Findon haddock
FINNED bearing fins
zo **FINNER** fin-back whale; torqual
FINNIC Finnish-related (peoples
etc.)
zo **FINNOC** white trout
bt **FIORIN** bent-grass
mu **FIPPLE** wood block in recorder
mouthpiece
FIRING igniting; kindling; expelling
me **FIRKIN** 9 imperial gallons
me **FIRLOT** a quarter boll
FIRMAN Ottoman decree; licence
(Turk.)
FIRMED confirmed; established
FIRMLY steadily; compactly;
strongly
lw **FISCAL** monetary; financial
nt **FISHED** strengthened; caught
(angled) (compliments)
FISHER (-man); (weasel; black fox)
zo **FISHES** alternative pl. of fish
FISSLE rustle; whistle (Sc.)
FISTED struck with the fist
ga **FISTIC** (-cuffs); fight; (boxing)
hd **FITCHE FITCHY**, pointed
FITFUL off and on; irregular;
unreliable
FITTED apt; seemly; adjusted
ce **FITTER** an artificer; more seemly;
engine assembler
FIXING repairing; deciding; settling
FIXITY permanence; fastness
FIXIVE gummy; adhesive; glutinous
FIZGIG fisgig; a flirt; damp squib
FIZZED hissed; effervesced
ga **FIZZER** a fast one; ball
FIZZLE a fiasco; (-out); splutter
FLABBY lacking body firmness;
flaccid
FLACON scent-bottle; small flask
(Fr.)
FLAGGY drooping; weak

FLAGON a flask; later beer tankard
FLAITH Anc. Irish chief
FLAKED peeled off
ck **FLAMBE** ignited brandy dish; uneven pottery glaze (Fr.)
FLAMED on fire; excited; glazed
FLAMEN Roman official of rites
FLANCH a flange
rw, ce **FLANGE** projecting rim (wheel); pipe disc; chord (girder)
bd **FLANKS** haunches (horse); sides; intrados of arch
FLARED burnt unsteadily
FLASHE a sluice
FLASHY gaudy; impulsive; vapid
FLATLY positively; plainly
FLATTY puncture (tyre)
FLATUS body-wind; fart
FLAUNT vaunt; parade; display; (nudity)
mu **FLAUTO** modern traverse flute (It.)
FLAVIN yellow dye
FLAWED defective; wrongly designed
FLAXEN pale yellow; (linen)
FLAYED skinned
FLAYER skinner
ga **FLECHE** arrow; slender spire; running attack (fencing)
FLEDGE grow feathers; become air-worthy (birds)
FLEDGY feathery; downy
FLEECE to strip; plunder; sheepskin
FLEECH flatter; coax (Sc.)
tx **FLEECY** woolly; flocculent
FLENCH FLENSE, to cut up the blubber of a whale
FLESHY carnal; corporeal
FLETCH to feather an arrow (archery)
hd **FLEURY** (fleur-de-lis); dilly-flower; lily
FLEWED deep-mouthed
FLEXED bent; extended (of muscles)
pl **FLEXOR** joint-bending muscle
FLICKS movies
ar **FLIGHT** retreat; exodus; rout; stairs; aerial journey; escape (high-diving) (badminton)
FLIMSY frail; trivial; weak
FLINCH wince; blench; quail
gl **FLINTS** nodules of silica (fossil sponges); flocculation
FLINTY obdurate; hard; miserly
bd **FLITCH** a side of bacon; stack of veneer panels
FLITTY flighty; unstable
nt **FLOATS** (paddle-wheels); mobile platforms (processions); rafts

FLOATY buoyant; light
FLOCCI woolly filaments
tx **FLOCKS** waste wool
FLOCKY downy
FLOPPY flaccid; drooping
FLORAL flowery
mn **FLORAN** tin ore
bt, pr, ar **FLORET** flowerlet; decoration for spacing
FLORID ornate; meretricious
nm **FLORIN** once coined at Florence
FLOSSY silky
FLOURY like flour
to **FLOUSE FLOUSH**, to turn the edge of a tool; to splash (Sc.); (flush)
bt **FLOWER** bloom; blossom
ch **FLUATE** fluoride
mn **FLUCAN** clay
FLUENT flowing; voluble; fluid
FLUFFY downy; fluey
bd **FLUING** of splayed window jambs
FLUKED was fortunate
FLUNKY a lackey; snob
FLURRY agitation; bustle; perturb
FLUSHY reddish
mu, ar **FLUTED** channelled; grooved
mu **FLUTER** flutist; flautist
FLUXED melted; purged
FLUXES fusible substances for soldering
bd **FLY-BOX** receptacle for bait (angling)
FLYING aviation; fleeing; soaring
FLYMAN cabman
FLY-NET morquito curtain
FLY-NUT winged nut
FLY-ROD fishing rod for flies (angling)
FOAMED spurned; frothed
FOBBED imposed on; tricked
pl **FOCILE** a bone (arm or leg)
mu **FOCOSO** spiritedly
nt **FO'C'SLE** forecastle; bows
me **FODDER** a weight; animal food
FOEMAN foe; antagonist; enemy
bl **FOETAL FETAL**, of the unborn (embryonic)
FOETOR a stench; offensive odour
md **FOETUS** life in embryo
FOG-BOW white rainbow
FOGGED blurred; overcast
FOGRAM antiquated; a fogey
FOIBLE faible; weak point; defect
ga **FOIBLE** sharp half of sword (fencing)
FOILED baffled; thwarted; balked
FOILER a frustrator
FOISON plenty; autumn
FOLDED doubled; wrapped; furled

FOLDER leaflet; brochure
FOLIAR (leaves); laminar
FOLIER goldsmith's foil
FOLIOT goblin
gl, pl **FOLIUM** striatum; thin stratum; brain cover
FOLKSY imitation rustic
mu **FOLLIA** (composition)
FOLLOW succeed; chase; pursue; heed
FOMENT fan; excite; stimulate
FONDER tenderer; (preference) (love)
FONDLE pet; caress; dandle
FONDLY affectionately; lovingly
ck **FONDUE** melted cheese/wine dish (Swiss)
FONDUS calico-printing
FONTAL primary; baptismal
FOOLED duped; hoodwinked; hoaxed
FOOLEN (embankment)
FOOTED walked; paid; kicked
ga **FOOTER** football (sl.)
FOOTLE twaddle; bunkum
FOOZLE bungle; mis-hit
FORAGE fodder; search; pillage
FORBID ban; inhibit; taboo; veto
FORBYE besides; hard by
FORCED unnatural; compulsory
FORCER compeller
FORDED crossed by wading
FORE-BY besides (Sc.)
FOREGO yield; resign; relinquish
FOREST woodland; grove; boscage
to **FORFEX** scissors
FORGAT forgot
FORGED fabricated; spurious; welded
FORGER falsifier; hammerman
FORGET overlook; slight
FORGOT neglected; (oversight)
nm **FORINT** Hungarian currency
FORKED bifurcated
FORLAY to ambush; lie in wait for
FORMAL precise; exact; stiff; set
cp, pr **FORMAT** style; layout; size; (printing); data
FORMED arranged; moulded; shaped
FORMER prior; previous; bygone
ch **FORMIC** (acid)
ch **FORMYL** organic radical
md **FORNIX** (shell); (brain)
FORPET FORPIT, a fourth part; a quarter (Sc.)
FORREL forel; parchment
FORRIT forward (Sc.)
zo **FORROW** not with calf (Sc.)
FORSAY forbid; renounce
FORTED guarded; castellated

mn **FOSSIL** petrified
FOSTER cherish; nourish; encourage; (-parent)
nt **FOTHER** leak-stopping
me **FOTMAL** 70 lb (31.7 kg) of lead
FOUDRE large storage/transport wine cask
FOUGHT strove; contended; warred
FOULED polluted; sullied
FOULLY scurvily; unfairly; basely
FOURBE a cheat; trickster
mu **FOURTH** ordinal number; 4th; interval (harmonic)
FOWLER bird-shooter
zo **FOX-BAT** flying fox
FOXING deceiving; duping; deluding
FOXISH cunning; sly; shrewd
FOYBLE part of sword-table
FRACAS an uproar; brawl; riot
FRACID overripe; rotten
FRAGOR a crash
FRAISE defence of pointed stakes
FRAMED constructed; devised
FRAMER contriver; frame-maker
nt **FRANCO** free of expense; in bond (storage); duty-free
FRANZY crotchety (dial.)
FRAPPE chilled with ice (Fr.)
FRATCH a quarrel; a brawl (dial.)
rl **FRATER** refectory; brother; friar
FRAYED worn; chafed; fretted
FRAZIL anchor-ice; spicular ice
FREELY unimpeded; willingly; readily
FREEZE chill; numb; congeal; (statues); (golf); (basketball)
FRENCH Gallic
pl **FRENUM** a ligament
FRENZY delirium; madness; fury
FRESCO drink; paint; refreshment
FRESCO coolness; wall painting; (al fresco: out of doors)
mu **FRETTA** increase the pace (It.)
ar **FRETTE** a strengthening band
FRETTY ornate
FRIARY monastery
FRIDAY (Robinson Crusoe); assistant
FRIDGE ice-box; refrigerator
FRIEND ally; chum; intimate
ar **FRIEZE** rough stuff; decorative border
rl **FRIGGA** wife of Odin
FRIGHT alarm; dismay; panic; dread
FRIGID icy; cold; formal
pg **FRILLY** fluted; overdressed
FRINGE border; edge
FRINGY adorned with fringes
FRISKY gay; lively; sportive

FRIVOL to trifle
FRIZEL (flint-lock)
FROGGY abounding in frogs
ck **FROISE** pancake; fraise (Fr.)
FROLIC romp; gambol; play; lark
FRONDE political party (Fr.) 17th
    cent
FROSTY chilling; wintry
FROTHY empty; unsubstantial;
    foamy
FROUZY rank; musty; rancid
to **FROWER** a cleaver
FROWST stuffy and hot
FROWSY frowzy; unkempt;
    disorderly
FROZEN froren; frosty; iced
FRUGAL thrifty; saving;
    parsimonious
FRUITY fruitful; luscious
FRUMPY dowdy
bt **FRUTEX** a shrub
FRYING cooking with fat
ar **FUCATE** painted; a sham
mn **FUCOID** a fossil seaweed
FUDDLE muddle; inebriate
FUDGED cheated; faked; bungléd
FUFFED puffed
mu **FUGATO** like a fugue
md **FUGILE** ear trouble
pc **FUGUES** memoryless wandering
FUHRER Hitler-type dictator; leader;
    guide; (Ger.)
FULANI tribe (South Sahara)
FULFIL meet; effect; satisfy
FULGID fulgent; flashing; steaming
FULGOR splendour
FULHAM FULLAM, FULLAN, a die
    loaded at one corner, to throw high
zo **FULICA** coot genus
FULLED scoured and thickened
to **FULLER** hammer
zo **FULMAR** sea-fowl; the petrel
FULVID tawny; yellow
FUMAGE chimney tax; hearth money
FUMBLE grope; bungle; stammer
FUMILY sulkily; smokily
pg **FUMING** ammonia process
zo **FUMMEL** funnel; mule
FUMOUS (fumes); vaporous
FUNDED endowed; financially secure
FUNDIE fundamentalist
ar **FUNDUQ** caravanserai fort (Arab.)
FUNDUS back part
FUNEST doleful; lamentable
bt **FUNGAL** FUNGIN, (fungi) mushrooms
zo **FUNGIA** genus of corals
bt **FUNGUS** plant
FUNKED played the coward

bt **FUNKIA** a lily genus
FUNNEL fummel; smoke-stack
md **FURFUR** dandruff
FURIES avenging deities
FURLED closely rolled
FURORE outburst of excitement
    anger
FURRED animals bearing winter coat
ag **FURROW** rut; groove; seam;
    corrugate; track of the plough
bt **FURZEN** furzy; whinny
mn **FUSAIN** friable coal
bt **FUSEAU** macroconidium of
    dermatophytes
el **FUSING** liquid metals merging;
    (short circuit)
FUSION melting; amalgamation
bt **FUSOID** wide-middled and end-
    tapered
FUSSED worried; fretted; fidgeted
FUSTED mouldy; rancid; malodorous
bt **FUSTET** shrub; the sumac
bt **FUSTIC** tropical American tree
FUSURE smelting; fusion
FUTILE bootless; vain; useless
FUTTAH FUTTER, rat-proof raised
    store-house (NZ)
FUTURE hereafter; prospective
FUZZED ground to powder
FUZZLE intoxicate; fuddle

G

GABBED talked; prattled
GABBLE jabber; prate; chatter
mn **GABBRO** (felspar)
ce **GABION** net frame holder for rocks
    as wall
bt **GABLED** having gables
GABLET small gable
fr **GABOON** African mahogany-like
    wood
GADDED wandered about
GADDER a gadabout; a rover
zo **GADFLY** horse-fly
GADGET a cunning device;
    contraption
zo **GADINE** gadean; cod-type
zo **GADOID** codfish type
GADUIN part of cod liver oil
GAELIC Scottish-Highland dialect;
    Celtic
GAFFED (fishing)
GAFFER rustic; foreman
GAFFLE spur (cock-fight)
mu **GAGAKU** Japanese court orchestral
    music

GAGGED silenced; joked
_to_ GAGGER an interpolator
_zo_ GAGGLE a flock of geese
GAGMAN joke-writer; comic
GAIETY gayety; merriment; vivacity
GAINED acquired; reached; won
GAINER winner; beneficiary
GAINLY comely; conveniently
GAINST against
GAITED having a distinctive walk
GAITER garnash
_cf_ GALACT- of milking
_zo_ GALAGO lemur (Madagascar)
_mu_ GALANT courtly dance
GALAXY Milky Way; brilliant
  assembly
_bt_ GALBAN a gum used in medicine
_nt_ GALEAS galley
_bt_ GALEGA goat's rue
_ch_ GALENA lead sulphide
_nt_ GALIOT brigantine
_bt_ GALIUM bed-straw genus
GALLED chagrined; fretted; vexed
GALLET stone splinter
_nt_ GALLEY ship; boat; cook-house
_ch_ GALLIC French; an acid
GALLIO insouciance personified
_me_ GALLON 4 quarts (4.5 litres)
GALLOP a dance; full speed of a
  horse; fast canter
GALLOW to terrify
GALLUP poll (public opinion); voting
  system
_tx_ GALOON galloon; silk fabric
GALOOT lout
GALORE galore; in abundance
GALOSH GALOSH, waterproof
  overshoe
GAMASH gaiters
_zo_ GAMBET a bird; red-shank
_ga_ GAMBIT opening move (chess)
GAMBLE stake; hazard; risk; wager
GAMBOL frolic; romp; caper; jump
  about (lambs)
GAMELY pluckily
_pl, zo_ GAMETE mature reproductive cell
_tx_ GAMGEE absorbent wool/gauze
GAMING gambling
GAMMER old woman
GAMMON (bacon); hoax; cozen
_zo_ GAMONT gamete-bearing individual
_cf_ -GAMOUS marital, sexual, union
_zo_ GANDER a glance (USA); male goose
_rl_ GANESA Hindu elephant god
GANGER foreman; overman
_mn_ GANGUE veinstone
_zo_ GANNET solan goose
_zo_ GANOID sturgeon type of fish

GANOIN fish dermis secretion
_rw_ GANTRY travelling crane; signal
  frame
GAOLED imprisoned; incarcerated
GAOLER jailer; prison warder
GAPING yawning; staring; gazing
_mu_ GAPPED pentatonic scale
GARAGE motor shed; repair shop
GARBED clothed
GARBLE misquote; distorted;
  confused speech
GARCON waiter (Fr.)
GARDEN a pleasance; park;
  (horticult.); (flowering)
_zo_ GARDON roach; ide (Fr.)
GARGET throat inflammation
_vt_ GARGIL goose disease
GARGLE a mouth wash
_vt_ GARGOL swine disease
_zo_ GARIAL gavial; crocodile
GARISH gaudy; ornate; florid
_bt_ GARLIC genus of plants
GARNER to store; collect; hoard
_mn_ GARNET carbuncle, precious stone
_ck_ GAROUS garum; a fish sauce
_zo_ GARRAN horse; galloway (Sc.)
GARRET loft; attic
GARRON (see garran)
GARROT a tourniquet; execution;
  (-cord)
_zo_ GARROT ocean duck
_bt_ GARRYA flowering evergreen
GARTER stocking supporter
_rl_ GARUDA Asian (Hindu) birdgod
_nt_ GARVEY small sailing boat (N. Am.)
_zo_ GARVIE the sprat
GAS-BAG a blimp; airship;
  chatterbox
GASCON of Gascony
GASHED severely stabbed
GASHLY ghastly; frightful
GASIFY convert into gas
GAS-JET a burner; flame
_bd_ GASKET leafproof joint (materials)
GASKIN cord for lashing sails to
  yards; hemp fibre
GAS-MAN gas company employee
GASPED panted; blew; puffed
GASPER cigarette; fag (sl.)
GASSED poisoned by gas
GAS-TAR coal-tar
_zo_ GASTER hymenoptera abdomen
_ck_ GATEAU cake (Fr.); layer cake
GATHER assemble; muster; fold
GATING a university restriction
_el_ GATING circuit switching; sensory
  intake
_bt_ GATTEN dogwood

GAUCHE boorish; bad mannered
(Fr.)
GAUCHO cowboy rider (S. Am.)
ck GAUFRE honey-cake; wafer (Fr.)
GAUGED measured; estimated
to GAUGER excise officer; width, size
checker
GAUPUS a silly person
vt GAVAGE forced bird-feeding
zo GAVIAL garial; crocodile (Asia)
GAWPUS a silly person
GAYEST liveliest; merriest; blithest
GAY-YOU fishing boat (Annam.)
GAZEBO garden summer house
GAZING reviewing; gaping; regarding
GAZUMP organize house deal price
rises
GEARED harnessed
GEBBIE the stomach (Sc.)
GEEZER man in charge; elder
nt GEHAZI dhow; Arab sailboat
GEIGER radioactivity counter
GEISHA mousmee; dancing girl
(Jap.)
GELDED castrated; enfeebled
zo GELERT Llewellyn's faithful hound
ch GELTER one chemical to remove
another
rl GEMARA (Talmud) (Heb.)
GEMINI Castor and Pollux; (Zodiac)
bt GEMMAE leaf-buds
GEMMAN gentleman
GEMMED jewelled; budded
me GEMMHO inverse meg-ohm
GEMOTE GEMOT, witenagemot,
Saxon Council
GENDER sex; (grammar)
GENERA plural of genus; (kinds)
GENIAL hearty; kindly; cordial
GENIUS adept; gift; talent; djinn
zo GENNET jennet; small Spanish horse
gn GENOME gamete nucleus
chromosome
cf -GENOUS producing
GENTLE mild; tender; courteous
zo GENTLE maggot; larva of fly
(angling)
GENTLY tenderly; gradually
zo GENTOO a Hindu; a penguin
GENTRY 'the nobs'; 'the upper ten';
(class)
GENUAL of the knee; (curtsey)
(-flect)
mn GEODIC (crystalline cavity)
GEOGEN environmental factor
zo GEOMYS rodents (USA)
nm GEORGE a jewel
GERANT gerent; manager

zo GERBIL a rodent
GERMAN Teutonic; of Germany
bt GERMEN GERMIN, an ovary; a germ
GERUND verbal noun
bt GERVAO West Indian shrub
bt GERVAS plant (W. Indies)
GESTIC legendary
GETTER a sire; obtainer; achiever;
collector
ck GEUSIS tasting
GEW-GAW GEE-GAW, bauble, trinket,
gaud
gl GEYSER hot spring; steam fountain;
water heater (gas)
GHARRY gharri; Indian cart
zo GHAZAL GHAZEL, a form of Persian
verse; gazelle
rl GHEBER GHEBRE, GUEBRE,
Zoroastrian
GHETTO exclusively Jewish quarter;
area of a minority
nt GHOBUN outrigger sail dugout
(Papua)
GHURKA Ghurka; native of Nepal
GHURRY clock; time interval (Ind.)
GIAOUR unbeliever (Turk.)
GIBBER jabber; gabble; babble
GIBBET hanging post
zo GIBBON an ape
GIB-CAT wornout cat
nt GIBING scoffing; jibing
GIBLET internal part of a fowl
GIFTED intellectual; able; talented
GIGGIT to move rapidly (USA)
GIGGLE snigger; titter; cackle
GIGLET GIGLOT, a giddy girl; a
wanton
nt GIGLIO trawler (sail)
(Mediterranean)
GIGMAN would-be gent
GIGOLO dancing partner; kept man
GILDED covered in gold; gilt
nm GILDER GUILDER, Dutch coin
GILLIE attendant; game-keeper (Sc.)
GILPEY boisterous boy or girl (Sc.)
zo GILPIN the coal-fish
nt GIMBAL compass steadier
to GIMLET a boring tool
GIMMAL (machinery)
zo GIMMER 2-year-old ewe
bt GIMPED crenated
GINETE Spanish trooper
GINGAL Indian musket; swivel gun
bt, ck GINGER sandy; reddish; spice
bt GINGKO GINKGO, Chinese yew;
maiden-hair tree
GINGLE jingle; Irish car
tx GINNED snared; processed cotton

zo **GINNET** a nag; a jennet
GIRDED reproached; braced; surrounded
ar **GIRDER** a cross-beam (construction)
GIRDLE belt; zone; enclosure
bt **GIRKIN** gherkin (cucumber)
GIRNEL granary; meal-chest
GITANA Spanish; gipsy woman
GITANO Spanish gipsy man
mu **GIUSTO** in time; regular (It.)
GIVING yielding; allowing
GIZZEN to wither; leaky
ar **GLACIS** slope in front of fortress
GLADLY with pleasure; joyously
GLAGOL Slavonic alphabet
GLAIRY viscous; semi-fluid; anti-flow; glue-like
GLAIVE broadsword or falchion
GLANCE glimpse; look; ricochet
GLARED stared; glowered; frowned
GLASSY GLAZED, vitrified; smooth, shiny or mirrorlike surface
GLAZER polisher; calico-smoother
GLEAMY casting rays of light
GLEDGE cunning look; to squint
GLEETY limpid; ichorous
GLIBLY volubly; oily tongued
GLIDED skimmed; skated
GLIDER powerless aeroplane; (towed)
md **GLIOMA** nervous-tissue disease
GLITZY glistery; showiness; sham
GLOBAL globular; world-wide
md **GLOBIN** (haemoglobin)
GLOCAL global and local trade etc.
zo **GLOMUS** capillary-mass glomeruli
GLOOMY dim; dismal; obscure
rl **GLORIA** a hymn; halo
cf **GLOSSO-** of tongue; words
GLOSSY smooth; sheeny; bright; (surface)
GLOVED wearing gloves
GLOVER glove-maker
GLOWED showed warmth; shone; gleamed
GLOWER scowl; frown; glare
GLOZED palliated; wheedled
GLOZER flatterer; sycophant
ch **GLUCIC** (glucose)
GLUING cementing; uniting
GLUISH (glue); sticky; viscous
bt **GLUMAL** of the husk
GLUMLY sulkily; suddenly
GLUMPS the sulks
ck **GLUTEN GLUTIN**, starch free; wheat gum
ch **GLYCIN** gelatin-sugar
ch **GLYCOL** a liquid

GNARLY GNARRY, knotted; crabbed; gnarled
GNAWED fretted; tormented
zo **GNAWER** a rodent; masticator
mn **GNEISS** laminated; metamorphic rocks
bt **GNETUM** plant (E. Indies)
GNOMIC didactic
GNOMON sundial; shadow-caster
cf **-GNOSIA** (of knowledge)
GNOSIS esoteric knowledge
GOADED impelled; spurred; stung
ga **GOALIE GOALER**, goalkeeper (ice hockey) (polo) (football)
zo **GOANNA** iguana (Aust.)
GOATEE a beard
ga **GO-BANG** a game
GOBBET lump; swallow; mouthful
GOBBIN coal refuse
GOBBLE to swallow; bolt; (turkey)
GOBLET tumbler; glass cup; rummer
GOBLIN sprite; gnome; spectre
ga **GO-CART** two-wheeled cart; (racing)
GO-DOWN warehouse; kneel
GODSON protégé
zo **GODWIT** bird of passage
GOETIC (black magic)
GOFFER to plait; to crimp
GOGGLE to roll the eyes; eye piece (tv.)
GOGLET porous vase
GOIDEL Celtic; Gael
md **GOITER GOITRE**, a tumour; bronchocele
GOLDEN gilt; auric; (-handshake etc.)
GOLFER golf player
GOLIAS medieval nom de plume
GOLLAR to scold; speak loudly
GOLORE abundance; galore
GOLOSH GALOSH, waterproof overshoe
ck **GOMMER** soup ingredient
bt **GOMUTI GOMUTO**, sago palm; black fibre
GONGED signalled to stop by police (USA)
md **GONION** angle (of lower jaw)
GOODLY fair; comely; seemly
ga **GOOGLY** a strange delivery (bowling) (cricket)
el **GOOGOL** 10 to the 100th power
zo **GOORAL** Asiatic goat
rl **GOOROO GURU**, Hindu teacher
GOPACK HOPAK, Russian folkdance
zo **GOPHER** American rodent; a short drink
bt, nt **GOPHER** 'timber' of the Ark, reeds and bitumen coracle (Tigris)

GOPURA Hindu temple tower
ar, zo GORAMY gourami; fish
hd GORGED glutted; stuffed
GORGET throat armour; lady's ruff
md GORGET instrument
GORGIO gipsy term for a non-gipsy
GORGON ugly monster (Gr. myth.)
zo GORHEN hen grouse
GORIER more blood-stained
GORING a pricking; puncture
rl GOSHEN land of plenty (for
 Israelites)
GOSPEL glad tidings; (New
 Testament)
mn GOSSAN GOZZAN, ferruginous rock
GOSSIP chatter; boon companion
ar, pt GOTHIC language (story); style
GOTTEN got; acquired
GOUDIE GOWDIE, goldfinch; jewel;
 gold lace
GOUGED scooped out
nm GOURDE coin (Haiti)
vt GOURDY swelling (horse)
GOVERN rule; sway; control; restrain
bt GOWANS dandelion
GOWNED robed; arrayed
GOWPEN a handful (Sc.)
gl GRABEN land-subsidence structure
GRACED virtuous; chaste
rl GRACES 3 goddesses of charm &
 fertility
GRADED classified; arranged
ce GRADER road-making implement;
 blade; sorter
GRADIN raised step or seat
GRADUS dictionary of prosody
GRÄFIN German countess
GRAINS malt husks; prongs;
 harpoons
GRAINY granulated
GRAITH accoutrements; equipment
 (Sc.)
zo GRAKLE starling
me GRAMME weight (Fr.); (1 cu.cc.
 water)
GRANGE manor house with farm
nt GRANNY grandmother; knot
rl GRANTH Sikh Scriptures
bt GRANUM pigment globule
cf GRAPHO- of drawing; recording
GRAPPA strong spirit from grape
 refuse
GRASSY green lawn
to GRATER kitchen implement;
 shredder
mn GRATHE to repair coal-mine plant
ck GRATIN oven-browned (cheese
 topping)

GRATIS without payment
nt GRAVED cleaned; chiselled; cut
md GRAVEL disease; embarrass; puzzle
ce GRAVEL granular material (stones);
 fragmented rock
GRAVEN engraved; carved
to GRAVER (entraver); more sedate
GRAVES wine
GRAVID pregnant
GRAZED scratched; brushed
zo GRAZER browser; herbivore
mu GRAZIA GRAZIOSO, elegantly;
 gracefully
GREASE to oil; lubricate; bribe
GREASY unctuous; sebaceous;
 slippery
GREATS final exam, in classics, Ox.
 B.A.
GREAVE GREEVE, leg armour
GREECE GREESE, GRIECE, flight of
 steps; staircase; a degree
GREEDY eager; voracious; grasping
ck, bt GREENS leafy vegetables
GREENY GREENISH (colour)
GREEVE GREAVE, steward; a reeve
GREGAL gregarious
rw GRICER train-locomotive-spotter,
 fan
GRIDED grated; pierced
GRIEVE GREEVE, sadden; lament
wv GRIFFE horizontal frame knives
bd, ar GRILLE iron grating (tennis); gate
zo GRILSE young salmon
GRIMED begrimed; dirtied; foul
GRIMLY fiercely; dourly
GRINGO Yankee in S. America
GRIPED furrowed; trenched
GRIPER extortioner; oppressor
GRIPPED influenza (Fr.)
GRISLY grim; ferocious; fierce; dire
zo GRISON weasel (S. Am.)
to GRITER teasel spade
GRITTY coarse sand; the intimate
zo GRIVET Abyssinian monkey
GRIZEL meek patient wife
GROATS hulled oats
GROCER provisioner; (-shop)
GROGGY tipsy; staggering; unwell
pl GROINS loins; between the thighs
bt GROMEL gromil; gromwell; a plant
nt GROMET a rope ring
cr GROOVE furrow; rut; cutting
GROPED searched; picked; sought
bt GROSER gooseberry
nm CROSZY Polish coin
GROTTO cavern; cave
GROUND earth; clod; domain; cause
zo GROUSE complaint; game bird

ck **GROUTS** coarse meal; groats
GROUTY thick; muddy; sulky
GROVEL crawl; cringe; fawn
GROWER husbandman; gardener
(commercial)
GROWTH increase; progress
ar, bl **GROYNE** GROIN, arches; breakwater;
sea wall
GRUBBY grimy; dirty; dishonest
GRUDGE envy; covet; enmity; dislike
zo **GRU-GRU** edible insect
GRUMLY morosely; surlily
GRUMPH grunt (Sc.)
GRUMPY surly; sullen; churlish
GUACHE style of painting
GUANIN GUANO, bird excrement;
fertilizer
GUDDLE to tickle trout (Sc.)
(angling)
GUEBRE Gueber; Parsee fire-
worshipper
GUELPH Royal (Hanoverian) House
zo **GUENON** African monkey
GUFFAW boisterous laugh
GUGGLE to gurgle
GUIDED regulated; instructed;
steered
GUIDER a director; leader; pilot
GUIDON flag; signal (Fr.)
GUILED beguiled; treacherous
bt **GUILLS** corn marigold
GUILTY criminal; culpable; sinful
nm, zo **GUINEA** gold coin; game fowl; (-pig);
stable groom; worm
GUISER mummer; strolling actor
mu **GUITAR** type of lute
nm **GULDEN** GILDER, florin (Dutch)
GULLED duped; tricked; hoaxed
GULLER a cheat; imposter
md **GULLET** throat (of bird); trench
GULLEY large knife (Sc.); earth cleft
ch **GULOSE** aldohexose monosaccharide
GULPED swallowed; bolted
GUMLAC resinous matter
GUMMED stuck; cemented
eg **GUNITE** fine cement concrete
GUNMAN armed bandit
GUNMEN gangsters; assassins
zo **GUNNEL** a blenny; butterfish
nt **GUNNEL** ship's side; gunwale
GUNNER artillery-man
GUN-SHY fearful of firearms
nt **GUNTER** emergency sail; instrument
GUNYAH Australian native hut
GUPPIE green or gay yuppie
GURGLE purl; ripple; murmur
GURKHA a native of Nepal
bt **GURJUN** Indian balsam

bd **GURLET** type of pickaxe
el, me **GURLEY** cylinder fall speed
zo **GURNET** fish; gurnard
GURRAH Indian earthen jar
GUSHED rushed; spurted; spouted
GUSHER spurting oil well; voluble
person
tx **GUSSET** an insertion (clothing)
GUTNIK swallowable transistor radio
ar **GUTTAE** Doric ornamentation
GUTTED plundered; eviscerated; fed
up
hd **GUTTEE** bedewed
ar, bd **GUTTER** trough; drainage; run off
pr **GUTTER** inner margins of book
GUTTLE to guzzle
GUZZLE swill; swallow greedily
nt **GYBING** jibing
ch **GYPSUM** lime sulphate
GYRATE spiral; revolve; spin
bt **GYROSE** like a crook

H

mt **HABOOB** Sudan line-squall
HACKED mangled; hired; kicked
zo **HACKEE** chipmunk; American
squirrel
HACKER pirate within computer data
storage
zo **HACKET** kittiwake
HACKLE cock's neck feathers
HACKLE fly (angling); comb
HACKLY rough
zo, ck **HADDIE** haddock (Sc.)
HADDIN a holding; residence (Sc.)
gl **HADING** geological fault
rl **HADITH** Moslem oral tradition
nc **HADRON** elementary particle class
pl **HAEMAD** on same side as heart
md **HAEMAL** HAEMIC, relating to blood
ch **HAEMIN** hydrochloride of haematin
HAFFET the temples (Sc.)
HAFFLE to lie; prevaricate
HAFTED handled
HAGBUT arquebuse; hackbut
(ancient gun)
zo **HAGDEN** shearwater gull
zo **HAGEEN** dromedary; camel
HAGGED ugly; lean; haggish
ck **HAGGIS** Scottish dish
HAGGLE to mangle; higgle; bargain
zo **HAGLET** shearwater gull
HAIDUK Hungarian yeoman
mt **HAILED** acclaimed; greeted;
originated from; iced snow fall
HAIQUE Arab wrap

HAIRDO hairstyle; coiffure
HAIRED hairy; hirsute; comate
HAIRST harvest (Sc.)
HAKEEM physician (Arabic)
zo **HALFER** fallow deer
HALIDE compound of halogen and other radical
HALING hauling
zo **HALION** skipper fish
HALLAN a partition (Sc.)
rl **HALLEL** Passover feast
HALLOA hallo!
HALLOO a hunting cry
HALLOW to reverence
zo **HALLUX** hind toe of bird
HALOED sainted
ch **HALOID** (salt)
HALSED embraced by the neck
nt **HALSER** hawser
HALTED limped; hesitated; stopped
HALTER cord head harness (horses); hesitant; faltering; uncertain
HALVED bisected; fifty-fifty
HALVES moieties
HAMATE set with hooks
HAMBLE mutilate the foot
HAMITE fossil; native (E. Africa)
HAMLET cluster of cottages
HAMMAL HAMAL, Turkish porter
HAMMAM HAMAM, Turkish bath
to **HAMMER** forge; a gavel
ga, pl **HAMMER** throwing (athletics); a shot (squash); bones in ear
bt **HAMOSE** HAMOUS, hooked
HAMPER basket; impede; embarrass
bd **HANDED** served; conducted; led on; right– or left–; tool
HANDLE touch; feel; manipulate
HANGAR aircraft shed
HANGED dangled; depended
HANGER broadsword; wood on hillside
HANGER (clothes); steel bar; stirrup strap; baseball
HANG-UP unexpected hiatus; breakdown
HANJAR Persian dagger
nt **HANKED** skeined; jibbed
HANKER desire; crave; yearn; want
HANSEL earnest penny; handsel
HANSOM a horse-cab
HANTLE considerable number (Sc.)
HAPPEN occur; betide; chance; befall
HAPTIC pert. to sense of touch
HARASS annoy; tire; vex; worry
HARDEN nerve; steel; brace; injure
HARDER stiffer; firmer
HARDLY barely; scarcely; narrowly

HARD-UP impecunious; indigent
zo **HARELD** sea-duck
HARING speeding; rashly
HARISH like a hare
HARKED listened; hurried; -back (recalled)
HARKEN hearken; listen; attend
HARLED covered with rough-cast
HARLOT strumpet; moll; trollop
HARMAN policeman; a copper
HARMED damaged; injured
bt **HARMEL** Syrian rue
mu **HARPED** iterated; dwelt
mu **HARPER** lyrist; harpist
HARRIS a tweed
ag **HARROW** lacerate; tear; furrow (plough)
HARTAL Indian boycott
ck **HASHED** chopped; mixed; recooked
HASLET roasting meat; pig's fry
HASTED hastened; hurried
HASTEN hurry; speed; despatch; urge
HAT-BOX for hat transport
HATFUL maximum score in an end (bowls)
HATHOR goddess of love (Egypt)
HATING detesting; loathing; abhorring
HAT-PEG place to hang hat
HAT-PIN woman's hat fixer
HATRED odium; enmity; rancour
HATTED wearing a hat
HATTER hatmaker; (mad-); (hats); independent miner (Aus.)
HAULED dragged; tugged; towed
HAULER haulier; carter
ar, pl **HAUNCH** part of an arch; hip to thigh
HAUSSA West African race
zo **HAUTIN** sea-fish in fresh water
mn **HAUYNE** a silicate
HAVERS twaddle; empty talk
HAVING holding; possessing
ar **HAWHAW** HAHA (sunk fence); guffaw
HAWKED peddled; streaked
HAWKER pedlar; retailer; falconer
zo **HAWKEY** HAWKIE, dark cow with white streaked face (Sc.)
nt **HAWSER** halser; cable
ck **HAY-BOX** cooking method
HAYMOW hay in barn
HAYSEL hay-makers' festival
ga **HAZARD** obstacle; risk; chance; peril; jeopardy; old dicing game
HAZILY obscurely; foggily; mistily
HAZING bullying; brutal horse-play
HEADED titled; (direction)

ga **HEADED** (cask); (football)
cp **HEADER** (brick); (diving); headline; identity label
HEAD-ON directly; straight; (collision)
HEALED cured; remedied
HEALER doctor; restorer
HEALTH soundness; hygiene; haleness
HEAPED massed; accumulated; piled
HEARER one of an audience
HEARSE funeral car
HEARTH fireplace; fireside; home
HEARTY robust; sincere; cordial
HEATED agitated; excited; hectic
HEATER warmer
bt **HEATHY** heavy helmet
HEAUME heavy helmet
HEAVED hoisted; dilated; panted
HEAVEN Elysium; Paradise; bliss
HEAVER a lever; strong man
vt **HEAVES** disease (horse); broken wind
HEBREW a Jew; Semitic language
rl **HECATE** goddess of witchcraft
HECKLE to question; to barrack
HECTIC feverish; heated; hot
HECTOR intimidate; bully; a swaggering
wv **HEDDLE** heald shaft in handloom
bt **HEDERA** ivy
HEDGED skulked; avoided; (betting)
HEDGER a trimmer of fences
HEEDED attended; noticed
HEE-HAW to bray (donkey)
HEELED armed; equipped; leant; (well-)
HEELER hanger-on (USA)
rl **HEGIRA HEJIRA**, Mohammed's flight from Mecca to Medina, A.D. 622
zo **HEIFER** young cow
HEIGHT altitude; acme; zenith
as **HELIAC** heliacal; (sun)
HELION virago; shrew; hell-cat
ch **HELITE** an amalgam
ch **HELIUM** a gaseous element
HELLAS ancient Greece
nm **HELLER** German copper coin
HELMED with a helmet; directed
HELMET part of retort; head armour
md **HELOMA** corn on foot
HELPED prevented; aided; succoured
HELPER assistant; abettor; ally
HELVED having a handle; hafted
mn **HELVIN** mineral
me **HEMINA** about 10 oz (283 g)
HEMMED bordered; enclosed
HEMMER a stitcher; a sewer

bt **HEMPEN** made of hemp
bt **HENBIT** dead nettle
HENISM philosophical belief
HEPTAD series of seven
HERALD harbinger; crier; proclaim
HERBAL book describing plants
HERDED tended; massed
HEREAT at this point
HEREBY by this (means) (document) (moment)
HEREIN in this (document) (situation)
HEREOF of this (before-mentioned)
HEREON on this (occasion)
HERESY schism; heterodoxy; recusancy
HERETO in addition
bt **HERIFF** butweed
lw **HERIOT** a fine
HERMAE sculptured busts
rl **HERMES** Mercury (Gr.) the messenger
HERMIT anchorite; recluse
md **HERNIA** rupture
HEROES demi-gods
HEROIC bold; intrepid; valiant
md **HEROIN** a drug
md **HERPES** skin disease; shingles
hd **HERSED** in harrow form
rl **HESPER** evening star; vesper; prayer
HESVAN HESHVAN, Jewish month
cf **HETERO-** of unlike, different (sex) (Gr.)
HETMAN Cossack chief
HEWING hacking; shaping; (digging); (coal)
HEXADE series of six
ch **HEXANE** paraffin
HEXODE a thermionic valve
ch **HEXOSE** monosaccharide subgroup, a sugar
HEYDAY frolic; period of vigour; zenith
md **HIATUS** a chasm; gap; lacuna
md **HICCUP HICCOUGH**, temporary breakdown of breathing
go, ce **HICKEY** pipe-bending tool (USA)
lw **HIDAGE** a tax
HIDDEN latent; covert; recondite
HIDING a beating; screening; masking
HIEING going along; hiking
HIEMAL wintry; hyemal
HIGGLE to bargain; haggle
HIGHER superior; nobler (above)
HIGHLY eminently; loftily
HI-JACK kidnap; rob; armed take-over of transport

HIJRAH Hegira; flight from Mecca
HIKING walking; foot-slogging
lw **HILARY** Law Court session; Oxford term
HILLED earthed up
zo **HILSAH** fish (Ganges)
HILTED hafted; helved
HINDEE North Indian tongue
HINDER delay; interference with flat of ball (handball) (paddle ball)
HINGED depended on; swing on (door)
HINTED implied
HINTER suggester
ar **HIPPED** melancholic; roof
HIPPIC horsy; equine
HIPPIE unkempt wanderer
md **HIPPUS** clonic spasm of iris
HIRAME gold, silver leaf on lacquer (Jap.)
HIRCIN mutton suet
zo **HIRCUS** the goat
HIRING bribing; engaging
rl **HIRMOI** HIRMOS, hymns; ode (Gr. church)
zo **HIRSEL** HIRSLE, flock of sheep (Sc.); a throng; to slide
HISPID bristly
HISSED hizzed; booed; (snake)
HISSER disapprover
HITCHY catchy
HITHER to this place
ga **HIT-OUT** aim blows; verbal attack; aggressive action by players or fans (boxing); starting shot in hockey
ga **HITTER** smiter; slogger; striker
HIVING storing; clustering (bees)
HOARSE guttural; husky; raucous
HOAXED tricked; gulled; gammoned
HOAXEE the victim
HOAXER practical joker
zo **HOAZIN** (S. Am.) pheasant
ga **HOBBER** touching the kob (quoits)
HOBBIT denizen of Middle Earth; (Tolkien)
HOBBLE halt; limp; shackle; clog; leg harness (farm)
HOBJOB an odd job
HOBNOB to be familiar; associate; chat
mu **HOCKET** hiccup (Fr.); extra rests in vocal parts
ga **HOCKEY** 11-a-side stick and ball game
HOCKLE to mow; hamstring
tx **HODDEN** grey cloth
HODMAN mason's labourer

HOEING weeding
HOGGED clipped; bent
HOGGER miser; selfish monopolist; (road-)
zo **HOGGET** young sheep; colt or boar
HOGGIE fishing craft (Brighton)
HOGGIN sand and gravel mixture
HOGPEN hogsty (USA); pigsty
pp **HOG-PIT** waste paper stock pit
HOGSTY pig pen; pigsty
HOIDEN hoyden; a romp; rude; rustic
ga **HOLANI** early form of hockey (Turk.)
bt **HOLARD** whole of soil water
la **HOLDER** a tenant; possessor (-stand) (-case)
HOLD-UP robbery under arms
HOLIER more sacred
HOLILY piously
HOLISM treatment of the body and mind as one entity
HOLLER HOLLOA, shout (distress)
bd **HOLLOW** empty; void; cavity-wall; vacuum; dell
ch **HOLMIA** oxide of holmium
ch **HOLMIC** (holmium)
HOMAGE fealty; devotion; loyalty
HOMELY plain; simple; domestic
HOMILY sermon; address; discourse
ae **HOMING** (pigeons); aerial navigation; returning to base
ck **HOMINY** boiled maize
HONEST fair; just; trusty; sincere
HONING whetting
HONKED tooted (motoring)
HONOUR exalt; dignify; fame; renown
HOODED cowled; cloaked
zo **HOODIE** carrion-crow (Sc.)
rl **HOODOO** VOODOO, witchcraft (W. Indies); column of boulders & earth
HOOFED ungulate (twin-toed)
HOOKAH water smoking pipe; narghile
HOOKED (golf); hamate; addicted (drugs)
nt, ga **HOOKER** fishing boat; prostitute; scrum player (Rugby football)
HOOKUM command; instructions (Ind.)
cp, ro, tc, **HOOK-UP** radio connections; (-link)
tv
HOOPED encircled; with handle; whooped
HOOPER (tubs); a cooper
ga **HOOP-LA** game at fairs

zo **HOOPOE** HOOPOO, crested birds, horn-bill type
HOOTED honked
HOOTER a siren
zo **HOOVED** ungulate
vt, zo **HOOVEN** (cattle-disease)
HOOVER dust-removing appliance
zo **HOOVES** pl. of hoof; cleft feet
zo **HOPDOG** pale tussock moth
zo **HOP-FLY** plant louse
HOPING wishing; desiring; trusting
HOPPED jumped; danced; bounced
nt **HOPPER** wooden trough; hop-picker; lighter (dredging)
zo, cp **HOPPER** locust; truck; punched card feeder
rw **HOPPET** hand-basket
ce **HOPPIT** kibble; sinking bucket; skip
rl **HORARY** book of hours (prayers)
HORNED with horns; butted
zo **HORNER** dealer in horns; sand-eel
zo **HORNET** stinging insect
HORNIE the devil; old Nick
HORRID horrific; terrible; dreadful
HORROR terror; panic; alarm; dismay
HORSED mounted (rider)
HOSIER dealer in stockings
HOSTEL an inn; lodging house
bt **HOT-BED** earth-bed; breeding place
ck **HOT-DOG** sausage sandwich
ck **HOT-POT** meat-stew
HOT-ROD supercharged car
HOTTER more ardent; warmer
HOUDAH howdah; seat on an elephant
zo **HOUDAN** breed of fowls
nt **HOUNDS** (mast head)
HOURLY at every hour (trains)
HOUSED resided; sheltered; stored
rl **HOUSEL** the Eucharist
HOUSTY a sore throat (dial.)
HOWDAH houdah; seat on an elephant
HOWDIE midwife (Sc.)
nt **HOWKER** hooker; vessel (Dutch)
HOWLED yowled; cried; lamented
zo **HOWLER** (monkey); grievous error
zo **HOWLET** (owlet); fledgling owl (dial.)
HOYDEN hoiden; tomboy; romp
ck **HRAMSA** garlic-flavoured cheese (Sc.)
HUBBLE an uproar; hubbub
HUBBLY rowdy
HUBBUB disorder; noise; uproar; din
HUCKLE the hip; a haunch
ga **HUDDLE** crowd; confuse; jumble; counsel before line-up (Am. football)

ag **HUDDUP** get up!; fertile; irrigated, 2 crops land
ga **HUFFED** blustered; (draughts) forfeited
HUFFER a bully; blusterer
HUGELY enormously; immensely
nt **HULLED** pierced; husked; (ship's side)
HULLER hulling machine
HUMANE kind; benign; merciful
HUMBLE degrade; abash; meek; lowly
HUMBLY unobtrusively
HUMBUG quackery; charlatan; untruth; peppermint
HUMECT HUMIFY, HUMEFY, to moisten; dampen
md **HUMERI** bones of the upper arm
hd **HUMETE** abbreviated fesse
tx **HUMHUM** coarse cloth (Ind.)
HUMIAN philosophy of David Hume
HUMINE black ground powder; humus
mn **HUMITE** limestone
HUMMED buzzed; droned
HUMMEL hornless; awnless
HUMMER a sledge-runner
HUMMIE small bulge
ck **HUMMUS** HUMMUZ, HUMOUS, chick-pea purée
md **HUMOUR** indulge; pamper; wit
zo **HUMPED** shouldered; hunchback; (camel)
HUMPEN drinking glass (Ger.)
HUMPER meat-porter; carrier
HUNGER hanker; desire; crave
HUNGRY ravenous; famishing
HUNKER to squat down; old fogey
HUNTED searched; sought; hounded
zo **HUNTER** chaser; stalker
bt **HURBUR** burdock
HURDLE wattle fence
HURLED flung; heaved; slung; cast
HURLER a thrower; pitcher
HURLEY shinty; the stick used in hurling (-burley)
HURRAH HURRAY, shout of triumph
HURTER a buffer plank
HURTLE to whirl; to crash
HUSHED quietened; calmed; stilled
HUSKED hulled
HUSKER a remover of husks
HUSSAR light cavalryman
HUSSIF (housewife); a holdall for needles, thread etc.
HUSTLE bustle; jostle; elbow; rush
HUTTED in huts
HUZOOR Indian title of respect

as **HYADES** 5 stars in Taurus
zo **HYAENA** hyena
cp **HYBRID** cross-bred; mongrel; analog; digital mix
HYDRIA Grecian water-vase
ch **HYDRIC** (hydrogen)
ch **HYDRID** hydrogen compound
md **HYDROA** itching skin disease
HYDRON dry/rigid, wet/soft plastic
as, zo **HYDRUS** constellation; water-snake
HYEMAL hiemal; wintry
HYETAL (rainfall)
HYGEEN dromedary
HYGEIA Goddess of Health
HYKSOS Egyptian dynasty
HYLISM materialism
HYMNAL collection of hymns
HYMNED celebrated in song
HYMNIC of hymns
bt **HYPHAE** fungoid filaments
HYPHEN word-join stroke
bt **HYPNUM** a moss genus
bt **HYSSOP** aromatic herb

I

IAMBIC rhythmic
IAMBUS Greek satiric metre
cf, md **-IATRIC** of healing, medical (Gr.)
bt **IBERIS** candytuft
zo **IBEXES** mountain goats (Alps)
IBIDEM in the same place
ICARUS an early aeronaut
ICE-AGE period of icing over
to **ICE-AXE** ice-breaking, -cutting device
ICE-CAP earth ice layer
ICE-MAN ice deliverer
to **ICE-SAW** ice-cutting device
ICICLE frozen water stalactite
ICIEST frostiest; most frozen
ICONIC illustrative
pc, rl **ICONIC** brief visual experience; of sacred portrayal
pc **IDEATE** to fancy; project fantasy
IDIASM a peculiarity
IDIOCY lunacy; dementia; craziness
IDLING nothing doing
IDOLUM IDOLON, mental picture
I'FAITH indeed; truly; verily
cp **IF-THEN** conditional indication operation
IGNAVY laziness; idleness
IGNITE kindle; inflame; fire
cp **IGNORE** disregard; overlook; skip (agent)
zo **IGUANA** lizard; a saurian

bt **ILEXES** holm-oaks
ILL-GOT ill-gotten; (stolen)
ILLISH somewhat unwell
mn **ILLITE** monoclinic clay material
ILLUDE to deceive; conceal; (conjuring)
ILL-USE mistreat
IMAGED imagined; fancied; sculpted
IMBIBE drink; assimilate; absorb
IMBREX pantile; curved roof-tile
IMBRUE to moisten; to drench
IMBUED dyed; inspired; steeped
IMMASK to cover; disguise
md **IMMUNE** secure against attack; (virus)
IMMURE enclose; incarcerate; confine
IMPACT shock; stroke; collision
bd **IMPAGE** horizontal part of door-frame
IMPAIR mar; injure; harm; vitiate
zo **IMPALA** South African antelope
IMPALE cause death on a spear
IMPARK enclose
IMPARL to hold mutual discourse
IMPARL parley
IMPART bestow; confer; divulge
IMPAVE to pave
IMPAWN to pledge
IMPEDE obstruct; hinder; thwart
IMPEND threaten; hover; approach
IMPEST infect with plague
IMPING ekeing; extending; grafting
IMPISH puckish; mischievous
IMPLEX complicated
IMPONE to stake; to wager
IMPORT imply; purport; gist; drift
IMPOSE lay; inflict; charge; dictate
ar **IMPOST** a tax; a duty; a cess; bracket-like base for arches
IMPUGN attack; contradict; question
IMPURE unclean; sullied; tarnished
IMPUTE charge; ascribe; imply
INARCH to graft
bd **INBAND** header stone
bd **INBOND** brick-laying
INBORN innate; inherent; congenital
INBRED in-tribe parentage
INCAGE encage; confine
INCARN to incarnate
INCASE encase; enclose; enshrine
INCASK to put in a cask
INCAST a bonus; thrown in
INCAVO incised stone (cameo)
INCEPT to begin; to commence
INCEST prohibited co-habitation among close kin
INCHED advanced by inches

INCISE engrave; scribe
INCITE stir; goad; foment; rouse
INCLIP to grasp; enclose; surround
INCOME revenue; annual receipts
INCULT uncultivated
INCUSE INCUSS, to stamp; forge
INDABA native council (S. Afr.)
INDEED really; truly; verily; actually
ch INDENE liquid coal-tar hydrocarbon
ar, lw INDENT to notch; order; make a
deed; stonework design
INDIAN of India; native American
lw INDICT to charge in writing
INDIGN unworthy
INDIGO a blue dye
INDITE endite; write; pen; dictate
ch INDIUM metallic element
ch INDOLE benzpyrrole
INDOOR within the house
INDUCE urge; actuate; incite
INDUCT introduce; install; initiate
INDUED endued; invested with
INDUNA Zulu chief
INEUNT cusp; fold; tooth; point
joint; all enter the stage (theatre)
INFALL an inroad
INFAME defame
INFAMY shame; obloquy; disgrace
INFANT babe; suckling; minor
INFECT taint; spread disease
cp INFECT (computer virus)
lw INFEIF INFEFT, (land transfer)
INFELT heart-felt
INFEST enfest; overrun; throng; beset
INFIMA end species in classification
list
INFIRM frail; weak; decrepit
INFLOW that which flows in
INFLUX importation in abundance
INFOLD enfold; embrace
INFORM tell; notify; apprise
rl INFULA Roman priestly badge
INFUSE instil; inculcate; steep
INGATE aperture in a mould
INGEST absorb; swallow
ga IN-GOAL Rugby football
INGULF engulf; overwhelm
INHALE breathe in; (smoking)
nt INHAUL drag in (ropes)
INHERE to be innate
INHIVE to hive (bees)
INHOOP to confine
nc INHOUR reactivity unit
INHUME to inter; to bury; entomb
md INJECT pump in; interpolate; insert
INJURE harm; hurt; mar; impair
lw INJURY ill; detriment; wrong;
damage

zo INK-BAG (cuttle-fish)
INKING marking with ink
INKNIT to knit in
INKNOT to knot
INKOSI Zulu chief, king
INK-POT ink container
zo INK-SAC (cuttle-fish)
INLACE to lace
INLAID fitted flush to surface
INLAND remote from the sea
gl INLIER geological formation
pr INLINE white-relieved black-letter
print
cp IN-LINE (traffic) programme
instructions
INLOCK enlock
INMATE resident; guest; denizen
INMOST innermost; deepest
INNATE inherent; congenital; inborn
INNING harvest grain
nt INRAIL enclose with rails; fencing
INROAD raid; foray; incursion
INRUSH invasion; irruption
INSANE mad; crazy; deranged
INSEAM mark with a seam
INSECT mean; contemptible
zo INSECT six-legged invertebrate
INSERT inject; introduce; infix
INSHIP embark; to ship
INSIDE inner; internal; interior
INSIST maintain; demand; urge
INSOLE inner sole
INSPAN to yoke
INSTAL install; induct; invest
INSTAR adorn with stars
pl INSTEP part of the foot
INSTIL infuse; ingraft; implant
INSTOP make fast; to stop
pl INSULA part of cortex (brain); island
ar INSULA middle-class house (Roman)
INSULT abuse; affront; ridicule
INSURE ensure; assure; guarantee
INTACT inviolate; integral; scatheless
INTAKE inlet of a pipe; consume
INTEND mean; purpose; contemplate
INTENT set; bent; eager; attentive
INTERN confine; segregate
zo INTIMA innermost organ layer
INTIME private; home-like
bt INTINE inner coat of pollen grain
INTOED with toes turned in
INTOMB entomb; bury; inter
mu INTONE to chant
INTORT to twist; to wreathe; to wind
ga IN-TURN curved sliding shot
(curling)
md INTUSE a bruise (Spens.)
bt, ck INULIN vegetable base (elecampane)

INUNCT anoint
lw **INURED** hardened; accustomed
INVADE raid; infringe; assault; violate
INVENT devise; contrive; create; make
INVERT reverse; upset; overturn; gay
INVEST apply money to purpose
INVITE ask; bid; call; request; solicit
INVOKE adjure; conjure; implicate
INWARD direction inside
INWICK curling cannon
INWORK penetrative work
INWORN inwrought
INWRAP to perplex; enwrap
zo **INYALA** nyala; bushbuck
ch **IODATE** (iodic acid)
ch **IODIDE** salt of hydriodic acid
ch **IODINE** medicinal element
IODISM morbid state
IODIZE treat with iodine
mn **IOLITE** a translucent silicate
ar **IONIAN** scrollshaped pillar capital (Gr.)
IONISM relating to ions, atoms without electrons
ch **IONIUM** (radium)
ps **IONIZE** convert into ions
ch **IONONE** terpene compound
IRANIC Iranian, from Iran
IREFUL angry; wroth; incensed
IRENIC pacific; peaceful
IRIDAL prismatic; iridian
pl, zo **IRIDIN** active principle of iris; (the eye)
IRISED like a rainbow
md **IRITIC** (iritis); inflamed
md **IRITIS** (eye disease)
IRKING irksome; tedious; wearying
IRONED in irons; smoothed
IRONER a laundry operative
IRONIC satirical; sarcastic
IRRUPT rush in; break in
ISABEL brownish yellow
ISAGON equi-angular figure
bt **ISATIC** woad-like
ch **ISATIN** an indigo product
bt **ISATIS** plant providing woad dye
ISLAND isle; isolate; (traffic-)
ISOBAR line of equal barometric prssure
rl **ISODIA** Jewish sacred feast
ps, el **ISOGAM** line of constant acceleration of free fall
ISOGON an isagon
mt **ISOHEL** sunshine comparison map
lt **ISOLUX** same-light-intensity line
ch **ISOMER** (similar substance)

ISONYM paronym
gl **ISOPIC** contemporaneously formed
zo **ISOPOD** (crustaceans)
ISRAEL Jacob and his offspring
ISSUED distributed; emitted; emerged
ISSUER publisher (source)
pr **ITALIC** Italian; semi-cursive script
ITCHED wanted to; craved; hankered
ITSELF reflexive pronoun
zo **IVIGAR** sea-urchin
IZZARD zeta, zee, zed, Z

J

JABBED poked; prodded
JABBER much talk; effusive prattle
JABBLE rough sea; splash (Sc.)
zo **JABIRI** Brazilian stork
zo **JACANA** wading bird
JACENT lying at length
zo **JACKAL** doglike carnivore
JACKED lifted with a jack (motor car)
JACKET cover; jerkin; coat
JADERY tricks of prankster
JADISH worn-out; unchaste
zo **JAEGER** gull; huntsman (Ger.)
JAGGED rough (rocky); uncouth; uneven
JAGGER brass wheel; pastry
JAGHIR a reward (Hindu)
zo **JAGUAR** S. American leopard
JAILED gaoled; incarcerated
JAILER JAILOR, gaoler; warder (prison)
ck **JALEBI** saffron batter sweetmeat (Ind.)
JAMBEE a cane; walking-stick
JAMBOK sjambok; hide whip
bt **JAMBUL** Indian evergreen
JAMMED crushed; squeezed
JAMMER radio interferer; competitor blocking Roller Derby race
JAMPAN sedan chair (Ind.)
JANGLE wrangle; clash; bicker
JANKER log-transporter (Sc.)
JARGON routine instruction code; (shop)
bt **JAROOL** Indian blood-wood
bt **JARRAH** tree (W. Australia)
JARRED wrangled; grated; disturbed
JARVEY Irish coach driver (jaunty)
rl **JASHER** lost Hebrew book
bt, ck **JASMIN** shrub; flower; scented tea
mn **JASPER** quartz

rl **JATAKA** nativity (Buddha)
JAUNTY open horse-drawn cart for lovers
JAW-BOX a sink (Sc.)
JAWING scolding
JEAMES a flunkey
JEERED mocked; derided; taunted
JEERER scoffer; sneerer
zo **JENNET** gennet; small Spanish horse
zo **JERBOA** a jumping rodent
JEREED jerid; blunt javelin
JERKED twitched; flipped; jolted
JERKER underhand thrower
le **JERKIN** a leather jacket
zo **JERKIN** a hawk; gyrfalcon
JERQUE examine ship's papers
zo **JERSEY** cow; knitted garment
ch **JERVIN** alkaloid (hellebore)
hd **JESSED** heraldic ornamentation
JESTED joked; made merry; quizzed
JESTER joker; buffoon; wag; fool
JET-LAG disturbance of body time change
lw, nt **JETSAM JETSOM**, goods thrown overboard; jetson; jettisoned
ar **JETTEE** projection
JEWESS female Jew
JEWISH Hebrew
JEZAIL Afghan trifle
tx **JIBBAH** jubbah; Eastern garment
JIBBED refused to go; baulked
zo **JIBBER** restive horse
JIBING sneering; quizzing; taunting
zo **JIBOYA** boa-constrictor; snake
JIFFEY an instant
mu **JIGGED** danced
me **JIGGER** liquid measure; mechanical device
ga, zo **JIGGER** golf club; insect; chigger
JIGGLE wriggle; joggle; jolt
JIGJOG jolting; trotting
ga **JIG-SAW** fret-saw; a puzzle (pictorial)
JILLET a flirt; a wanton
JILTED discarded
bt **JIMSON** thorn-apple
JINGAL Eastern cannon
JINGLE Irish covered car; tinkle; rhyme
JINKER dodged; eluded; turned sharply
JINKER timber-cart (Aust.)
el **JITTER** instability; fear
cp, el **JITTER** cathode ray tube signals
JOBBER stockbroker; book stocker/dealer
bd **JOBBER** builder's handyman

JOB-LOT odds and ends (auction) (sale)
JOCKEY horse race rider; disc–; coax to more favourable position
JOCOSE facetious; humorous; waggish
JOCUND sportive; merry; cheerful
JOGGED travelled slowly; shook
JOGGER slow runner; exerciser
JOGGLE a notch; to jar; to shake
cp **JOGGLE** agitate; punched cards
JOHNNY life and soul of a party
JOINED united; coupled; connected
JOINER a carpenter
ar **JOISTS** floor-board supports
JOKING jesting; bantering; rallying
gl, go **JOKULL** glacial ice-cap
JOLTED jogged; shook; jounced
JOLTER hustler
JORDAN a river; chamber pot (Shak.)
pr **JOSEPH** riding habit; unsized paper
JUSKIN yokel; clown
JOSSER a fellow; a chap; a palooka
JOSTLE push; approach closely; barge
JOTTED noted; recorded
JOTTER memorandum book
JOUNCE to jolt; shake
JOVIAL genial; convivial; blithe
JOVIAN (Jupiter) of Jove
JOWDER JOWTER, fish hawker
zo **JOWLER** hunting dog
JOYFUL happy; pleased; glad; blithe
JOYOUS merry; jocund; happy
JUBATE maned; having a fringe
tx **JUBBAH** Eastern garment
JUDAIC Jewish; Hebrew; Israelitish
cp **JUDDER** shudder; jar; screen scan blurs
JUDEAN native of Judea
JUDGED considered; sentenced
JUDGER a judge; umpire; arbitrator
rl **JUDICA** Passion Sunday
bt **JUGATE** coupled; yoked
me **JUGFUL** filling a jug
JUGGED (hare); imprisoned
JUGGLE conjure; shuffle; swindle
JUG-JUG meat in aspic; nightingale's song
JUICER machine for extracting fruit juice
bt, ck **JUJUBE** shrub; lozenge
JULIAN calendar; system
zo **JUMART** hybrid animal (Fr.)
ck **JUMBAL** crisp sweet cake
JUMBLE confuse; mix; muddle
zo **JUMBUK** a sheep (Aust.)

zo **JUMENT** a mare
JUMPED leapt; bounded; (grabbed)
to **JUMPER** chisel
rl **JUMPER** religious sect; over-blouse
bt **JUNCUS** plants (rush)
go **JUNGLE** tropical wild forest;
(concrete-)
JUNGLY jungli; unsophisticated
JUNIOR younger; a son
JUNIUS anonymous writer
JUNKER Prussian landowner,
aristocrat
ck **JUNKET** a sweetmeat; to feast; regale
bt **JUPATI** palm yielding raffia fibre
lw **JURANT** swearing
lw **JURIST** a lawyer
JUSTER more equitable
JUSTLE jostle; nudge; elbow
JUSTLY fairly; impartially; rightly
JUTTED projected; protruded
JUZAIL Afghan heavy rifle
JYMOLD gimmal; gimbal

K

KABAKA former ruler of Buganda
(Uganda)
rl **KABALA** Moslem Holy of Holies
mn **KABOOK** iron-stone (Sri Lanka)
KABOON backward somersault
(trampoline)
KABUKI realistic dramatic art (Jap.)
KABYLE Algerian Berber
KACHIN Burmese borderer
KAFFIR African native
KAFILA caravan; train of camels
tx **KAFTAN** robe (Turk.)
pc **KAIROS** critical moment of decision
for changes
KAISER German emperor
zo **KAKAPO** New Zealand parrot
ch **KALIUM** potassium
bt **KALMIA** American laurel
zo **KALONG** Malay fox-bat
tx **KALPIS** Grecian water-vase
KAMEES KAMIS, Eastern garment
bt **KAMELA KAMILA**, orange dye (E.
India)
KAMERA CAMERA, private room;
secret
KAMMER salon; drawing room
(Ger.)
mu **KAMMER** chamber (orchestra)
mt **KAMSIN** a hot wind of the Sahara
KANAKA South Sea islander
wv **KANARA** Persian runner carpet in
pairs

bt **KANTEN** a seaweed
KANUCK a Canadian
KAOLIN China day
bt **KARAKA** NZ food tree
ga **KARATE** open-handed fighting (Jap.)
KARMIC relating to Karma
tx **KAROSS** skin blanket (S. Africa)
gl **KARREN** grooved limestone (karst)
go **KARROO** tableland (S. Africa)
bl **KARYON** cell-nucleus
KASBAH Arab town, fort (N. Africa)
KATION cation
zo **KATIPO** Austr. venomous spider
ga **KAYLES** early form of skittles
(English)
KAYMAK clotted cream (Turk.)
ps **KAYSER** wave-number unit
KEBBIE a cudgel (Sc.)
rl **KEBLAH KIBLAH**, towards Mecca
KECKLE CACKLE, (rope protection)
bt **KECKSY** dried stalks
KEDDAH kheda; elephant trap
nt **KEDGED** warped; towed into dock
nt **KEDGER** a kedge; small anchor
KEEKER mine inspector (Sc.)
nt, nv **KEELED** carinated; navigated; (-over,
capsized)
nt **KEELER** tub; bargee
zo **KEELIE** kestrel; street Arab (Sc.)
KEENER professional mourner
KEENLY sharply; acutely; astutely
KEEPER warden; (zoo-); (time-)
el **KEEPER** guard-ring; magnet;
armature
KEEVED tubbed
ck **KELKEL** dried sole
md **KELOID** of scar tissue
KELPIE water spirit; seaweed
gatherer
nt **KELSON KEELSON**, inner keel
KELTIC Celtic
zo **KELTIE** kittiwake gull
me **KELVIN** thermo-dynamic
temperature
to **KENCHI** ivory carving tool
KENNED recognized; knew; surmised
KENNEL channel; gutter; a haunt;
(dog-)
me **KENTLE** 100 lb (45 kg); quintal
gl **KENYTE** fine-grained igneous rock
md **KERION** hair disease
KERITE insulating material
zo **KERMES** crimson dye; cochineal
KERMIS kermess; Dutch fair
pr **KERNED** letter with projecting face
bt, cp **KERNEL** inner nut; heart; set of
procedures
bt **KERRIA** Japanese rose

KERRIE knob-kerrie
tx KERSEY woollen cloth
ch KETENE acetone-based compound
ch KETONE KETOSE, acetone;
 –monosaccheride
KETTLE water-boiling pot
mn KEUPER sandstone
KEYAGE quayage
el KEYING signals by modulation
KEY-MEN the indispensables
cp KEYPAD symbols and digit entry to
 computer
KEY-PIN key-pivot
eg KEY-WAY longitudinal key-slot cut
KHALIF Calif; Caliph; chief of Islam
ar KHANAT ancient hill tunnels for
 water supply
wv KHILIM KILIM, woven rug (Turk.)
KIBBLE cudgel; hand-mill; hound
me KIBBLE iron-ore bucket; coal
 measure
KICHEL cake
KICKED hacked; objected; punted
ga, ar, ce KICKER footballer; thrill-giver;
 (horse); rebel; base of wall; column
ga KICKUP football practice; small
 dance
tx KIDDER a corn cornerer; a carpet
KIDDER forestaller; huckster; con-
 man
KIDDLE weir
zo KIDDOW guillemot
zo KID-FOX young fox
KIDNAP abduct; capture; steal
md KIDNEY kind; humour
bt KIEKIE New Zealand shrub
KIKUYU tribe (Kenya)
me KILERG 1000 ergs
fr KILHIG tree-pushing pole
mn KILLAS slate
KILLED slaughtered; neutralized
zo KILLER shark; murderer
mn KILLOW a black earth
tx KILLUT Indian robe of honour
tx KILTED wearing Scots kilt
KILTIE kilted soldier (Sc.)
KIMMER woman neighbour
tx KIMONO Japanese robe
bc KINASE activator of the true
 enzymes
ch KINATE salt
tx KINCOB Indian thread work
KINDER more benevolent
KINDLE provoke; animate; ignite
KINDLY congenial; benevolent
KINEMA cinema; body movement
 linguistics
zo KINETY structure unit in protozoa

KINGLY regal; imperial; august
KINKED snarled; twisted
wv KINKLE a kink; twist; ruck
zo KIPPER a salmon after spawning
ck KIPPER smoked herring
KIRBEH Arab water-skin
rl KIRKIN church attendance (Sc.)
KIRPAN Sikh 3 ft (0.9 m) knife
ck KIRSCH wild-cherry spirit
tx, me KIRTLE a gown; a mantle; (unit of
 –); weight of flax
ck KISHKA Yiddish/Polish sausage
KISMET fate; destiny
ga KISSED bussed; (billiards)
ga KISSER mouth (sl.); bow-string knot
 (archery)
KIT-BAG army bag (uniforms etc.)
ga KIT-KAT rounders for boys
zo KITTEN baby cat
KITTLE ticklish; intractable (Sc.)
KITTLY ticklish; sensitive
KLAXON a motor horn
KLEPHT Greek bandit
ps K-MESON KILO-MESON, elementary
 particles
KLOOCH Indian squaw
KNACKY cunning; (know the knack)
KNAGGY knotty; rough in temper
KNARRY knotty; rugged
bt KNAWEL a plant
KNICKS knickers; undergarment;
 (female)
KNIFED stabbed
KNIGHT a chess-man; a paladin;
 hereditary title
KNITCH faggot (dial.)
KNOBBY knotty; stubborn
KNOTTY intricate; difficult
KNOWER an erudite man
ch KOBALT cobalt
mn KOBANG old Japanese gold coin
KOBOLD goblin; gnome
ga KOLVEN club and ball game
 (Holland)
zo KOODOO antelope (S. Africa); kudu
mn KOPECK KOPEK, Russian farthing
KOREAN COREAN, of Korea
bt KORKIR corkir; purple dye
mn KORUNA crown (Czech)
ck KOSHER of food; ritually prepared
 (Jew.)
as KOSMOS COSMOS, universe
KOTWAL Indian police officer
bt KOUSSO plant (Abys.)
bt KOWHAI Maori trees
KOW-TOW salutation; obeissance
 (China)
KOZUKA knife beside a sword (Jap.)

KRAKEN sea monster (Danish)
go KRANTZ rocky summit (S. Africa);
crown
rl KRASIS Eucharistic wine with
water
KREESE creese; Malay dagger; kris
rl K-THIBH (Hebrew Scriptures)
zo KUKANG lemur or loris (Malay);
monkey
ck KULICH Orthodox Easter cake (Rus.)
KULTUR education; German culture
bt KUMBAR Indian coarse wood
bt KUMBUK E. Indian tree
ck KUMISS koumiss; drink (Tatar)
ck KÜMMEL a liqueur
gl KUNKUR Indian limestone
KURKEE coarse blanket
nm KURUSH (Turkey) small coin
ga KUSHTI national wrestling (Iran)
bt, ck KUSKUS COUSCOUS, millet dish
(Arab); fibre pasta (Indian)
KUTTAR short Indian dagger
K-VALUE thermal conductivity of
material
KWAART clear lead glaze (Holland)
KYBOSH insurmountable obstruction
zo KYLOES Highland cattle

L

LAAGER Boer wagon encampment
LABEFY impair; weaken
pl LABIAL lip (sounds); labia (vagina)
LABILE unstable; liable to err
bt, pl LABIUM a lip; fold; (vagina)
LABOUR toil; drudge; industry
md LABOUR in birth throes
LABRET lip ornament
pl LABRUM upper lip
ch LACCIC (a resinous dye)
LAC-DYE (dye); shellac; (plastic)
lw LACHES negligence
tx LACING twining; beating;
intermixing
LACKED short of; needed; wanted
LACKER one in want
LACKEY flunkey; footman; attendant
ch LACMUS litmus; lichen-dye
ch, ck LACTIC acid, milk, products
LACUNA a void; gap; blank; hiatus
LADDER rent in stockings; climbing
aid
ce LADDER mud bucket; (snakes and-)
LADDIE youngster; lad; boy (Sc.)
LA-DI-DA (of speech and manners);
(superior)
LADIES gentlewoman

LADING freight; cargo; burden; (bill
of-)
LADINO Spanish dialect of exiled
Jews
to, bd LADKIN LATTERKIN, wooden tool to
open leaded panes
LADLED spooned; dispensed
LAGENA amphora; vase
LAG-END the bitter end; (the last)
LAGGED loitered; apprehended;
(insulated)
LAGGER laggard; loafer; idler
go LAGOON LAGUNE, lake; nearly
enclosed sea inlet (bayou) (atoll);
pool
LAICAL (laity)
pr LAID-IN note of inclusion of extra
item
LAIDLY loathly; clumsy (dial.)
LAID-ON available; made ready for
use
LAID-UP ill; out of action;
(mothballs)
zo LAITHE pollack fish
LAKIST (Lake school of poetry)
LALLAN lowland (Sc.)
LAMBDA Gr. letter; warmth and
energy; gay symbol
LAMBED yeaned
zo LAMBIE small lamb (Sc.)
LAMELY haltingly
mu LAMENT deplore; wail; a jeremiad;
dirge; piece for bagpipes
LAMINA thin plate; ply (laminated)
LAMING crippling; disabling
LAMISH somewhat lame
LAMMAS 1 August
LAMMED thrashed; drubbed
LAMMER amber (Sc.)
tx LAMMIE quilted jumper; lammy
vt LAMPAS swelling in horse's palate
tx LAMPAS damask figured cloth
ch LAMPIC (alcohol)
LANARY wool store
tx LANATE woolly
LANCED cut open; pierced
LANCER a cavalry-man
md LANCET a cutting instrument
ar LANCET window
LANDAU a carriage
LANDED disembarked; owning
estates
LANDER a miner
tx LANGET coarse Dutch lace
LANGUE tongue (linguistics)
zo LANGUR Indian monkey
LANKLY ungracefully; clumsily
zo LANNER hawk; falcon

zo **LANUGO** prenatal hair in mammals
zo **LAPDOG** small pet dog
LAPFUL load in one's lap
gl **LAPIES** grooved limestone rock
(karst)
LAPPED gem cutting; racing;
covered
LAPPER folder
LAPPET loose flap; a lobe
LAPSED slipped; become void;
(below par)
LAPSUS slip; memory failure; (of
pen, tongue) (Lat.); mistake; error
ck **LARDED** smeared with lard; made
enticing
LARDER storehouse; cold pantry
ck **LARDON** slice of bacon
LARGER bigger; wider; greater;
bulkier
LARIAT lasso; rope with noose
zo **LAROID** pertaining to gulls
LARRUP to beat; to flog
zo **LARVAE** caterpillars; grubs; maggots
zo **LARVAL** (larva)
pl **LARYNX** throat; vocal cord
LASCAR East Indian sailor
LASHED secured; scourged; buffetted
LASHER rope; pool below a weir;
whipper
LASHES thongs; eye-lashes; whip
strokes
nt **LASKET** loop line in a sail
mn **LASQUE** flat diamond
zo **LASSIE** damsel; maid; lass; collie
dog
LASTED endured; remained;
continued
LASTER bootmaker; cobbler
LASTLY ultimately; finally; endwise
nt **LATEEN** triangular sail (dhow)
LATELY recently; latterly
LATENT dormant; concealed;
potential
cf **LATERO-** lateral, to the side,
sideways on (Gr.)
LATEST most up-to-date
LATHEN made of laths
LATHER soapy froth; foam
LATISH somewhat late
rl **LATRIA** highest kind of worship
LATTEN sheet brass
LATTER modern; recent; previous
LAUDED praised; extolled; magnified
LAUDER eulogist; encomiast;
panegyrist
zo **LAUNCE** a balance; an eel
LAUNCH hurl; inaugurate; start; float
nt **LAUNCH** craft; lifeboat

bt **LAUREL** the bay-tree
ck **LAURIN** an extract from laurel
rl **LAVABO** ritualistic washing
md **LAVAGE** washing
LAVING bathing
LAVISH squander; dissipate;
luxurious
LAVOLT medieval dance; lavolta
lw **LAW-DAY** day of open court
LAWFUL legal; legitimate; rightful
lw **LAWING** litigation; tavern-bill
LAWYER solicitor; counsel; advocate
LAXIST amoral philanderer
LAXITY slackness; latitude; neglect
LAXMAN lacrosse player
nt **LAY-DAY** final loading
LAYING placing; betting; imputing
LAYMAN not a cleric; unprofessional
LAY-OFF dismissal (industrial)
LAY-OUT set out; plan; format
LAZILY slothfully; drowsily; supinely
LAZING idling
mn **LAZULI** blue spar
LEADED set in lead
LEADEN heavy; dully
LEADER head; chief; guide; director
cp **LEADER** (editorial); preceding signal
cp **LEAD-IN** wire connecting an aerial;
(TV); computer
bt, pr **LEAFED** having leaves; book binding
LEAGUE combine; union; cabal;
distance
LEAKED oozed; percolated;
(published)
LEALTY loyalty; fidelity
zo **LEAMER** dog on lead
LEANED relied; leant; inclined
LEANER thinner; skimpier
LEANLY lankly; slenderly; scantily
ar **LEAN-TO** a shed beside a wall
LEAPED sprang; skipped; gambolled
zo **LEAPER** jumper; vaulter; chaser
cp **LEASED** let out; reserved for user
ag **LEASER** gleaner; post-harvester
bt, pr **LEAVED** interleaved; bookbinding
LEAVEN yeast; balm; ferment; imbue
LEAVER a forsaker; quitter; deserter
bc **LECTIN** antibody-like substance
LECTOR reader (university title)
ar **LEDGER** account book
LEERED ogled; gloated
nt **LEEWAY** arrears of work; sideways
movement of boat
lw **LEGACY** bequest; gift; (amount
devised)
LEGATE ambassador; envoy; delegate
mu **LEGATO** smoothly
LEG-BYE (cricket); penalty

LEGEND myth; fable; fiction; caption
LEGGED dashed off; ran quickly; (four-)
LEGION host; multitude; horde; army
lw **LEGIST** skilled in law; jurist
bt **LEGUME** seed vessel; pod; vegetable
zo **LEIPOA** Australian game-bird
LENDER loaner; creditor
LENGTH extent; duration; reach
LENIFY assuage; mollify
LENITY clemency; leniency
rl **LENTEN** (Lent); sparing; during fast
ec **LENTIC** of standing water
bt **LENTIL** a bean; pulse
· **LENTOR** slowness; tenacity; viscosity
LENVOY postscript
as **LEONID** a meteor from Leo
LEPCHA native of Sikkim
zo, ga **LEPPER** LEAPER, steeplechase horse
LEPPEY soft, kind work
cf, md **-LEPSIA** of seizure, epilepsy (Gr.)
nm **LEPTON** hundredth of a drachma
nc **LEPTON** nuclear particle
zo **LEPTUS** larval form of acarina
ar **LESENE** pilaster-strip moulding (Saxon)
md **LESION** injury; wound
lw **LESSEE** (lease); tenant
LESSEN reduce; mitigate; decrease
LESSER lower; minor; inferior; temporary owner
mu, rl **LESSON** task; precept; warning; Bible reading; short keyboard piece
lw **LESSOR** lease holder
LETHAL fatal; deadly; mortal
LET-OFF a reprieve
LET-OUT release
LETTER note; epistle; missive; initial
LETTIC LETTISH, Latvian language group
LEUCOL coal-tar product
ag **LEVADA** descending irrigation channel (Madeira)
LEVADE horse dressage movement
LEVANT to decamp; the East
LEVIED mustered; taxed
rl **LEVITE** Jewish tribe; priest
LEVITY frivolity; flippancy; giddiness
ck **LEVURE** flour water paste for sealing pot-lids
mn **LEVYNE** zeolite
LEWDLY lustfully; indecently
el **LEYDEN** electrical jar
LIABLE accountable; likely; obnoxious

LIAISE to form a liaison; link-up
LIBANT sipping
LIBATE to make a libation; taste (drink)
LIBIDO life force; sexual urge
go **LIBYAN** of Libya; desert
bt **LICHEN** reindeer moss
md **LICHEN** skin disease
LICKED lapped; lammed; defeated
LICTOR Roman officer
LIDDED having lids; (eyes)
mu **LIEDER** German ballads
pl **LIENAL** of the spleen
ar **LIERNE** cross-rib
LIFTED elevated; stole; upraised
LIFTER raiser; thief; (weight-) (shop-)
ch **LIGAND** outlying ion
ch **LIGASE** catalysing enzyme
md **LIGATE** to tie up
LIGGER thatch ridge stick; bedspread; night-line
LIGHTS (ancient); (Northern); offal; lamps
LIGNIN wood-fibre
bt **LIGNUM** hardwood
bt **LIGULA** LIGULE, grass; petal
mn **LIGURE** precious stone
LIKELY probable; credible
LIKING fondness; regard
LILIED adorned with lilies
LILITH Adam's first wife
mu **LILTED** verse sung rhythmically
LIMBEC a still; a distilling vessel
zo **LIMBED** with limbs; (animal); (furniture)
LIMBER flexible; pliant; supple
pr **LIMBIC** bordering; marginal
LIMBUS limbo; paradise of fools
LIMING snaring; treating with lime
zo **LIMMER** mongrel; idler; jade
LIMNED painted; illuminated
LIMNER artist; delineator
LIMOUS muddy; slimy; sticky
LIMPED walked with disability
LIMPER a lame man
zo, ce **LIMPET** univalve mollusc; leech caisson (for docks); hanger on
LIMPID clear; pellucid; pure
pr **LINAGE** (cost per line) advert rate
bt **LINDEN** lime tree
LINEAL in a direct line (graph) (diagram)
cp **LINEAR** slender; graph; key to combinations
ga **LINE-UP** show of unity; order of batting (cricket); horses at start of race; wave break point (surfing)

rl **LINGAM** sacred symbol (Hindu);
   penis
LINGEL waxed thread (Sc.)
LINGER lag; loiter; dawdle; tarry
ml **LINGET** LINGOT, an ingot; metal
   block
LINHAY farm shed
bd **LINING** aligning; inner cover; first
   coating; ease; painting defect
LINKED connected; united; coupled
cp **LINKED** subroutine, outside program
   path
zo **LINNET** bird; lintie
tx **LINSEY** mixed wool and linen cloth
bd **LINTEL** LINTOL, joist beam over a
   doorway, window
tx **LINTER** cotton fibre
zo **LINTIE** linnet; a song-bird (Sc.)
el **LINVAR** linear variometer resolver
zo **LIONEL** LIONET, young lion
ch **LIPASE** enzyme
LIPLET little lip
ch **LIPOIC** an acid regulating oxidation
md **LIPOID** fatty; sebaceous
md **LIPOMA** a fatty tumour
ga **LIPPED** labiate; (gentle golf shot)
LIPPED (tight-)
LIPPEN to reply; to trust (Sc.)
LIPPER a rippling; surface roughness
me **LIPPIE** quarter of a peck (Sc.)
LIQUID fluid; fluent; melting; dulcet
LIQUID (cash); flowing speech
   sounds 'r' and 'l'
LIQUOR (alcohol); (cooking liquid)
LISPED couldn't pronounce 's'
   sounds
LISPER person who lisps
LISSOM lithe; agile; pliant; supple
LISTED enlisted; canted over;
   registered
ar **LISTEL** fillet
LISTEN hark; attend; eavesdrop
LISTER arranger; recorder
rl **LITANY** solemn supplication
   (repentance)
bt **LITCHI** LYCHEE, fruit (China)
LITHER lazy; worthless; smooth
md **LITHIA** oxide of lithium
ar, md **LITHIC** (stone)
ch **LITMUS** acid-test dye
zo **LITTER** scatter; the newborn;
   bedding
LITTLE tiny; pygmy; brief; trivial
LITUUS augur's staff
LIVEDO blueness of skin from
   congestion
LIVELY joyful; active; vigorous;
   quick

tx **LIVERY** uniform; costume
lw **LIVERY** writ of possession
rl **LIVING** livelihood; animate; alive
zo **LIZARD** saurian reptile
go **LLANOS** plains of South America
LOADED laden; filled; cumbered
LOADER one of the gun's crew;
   stacker
cp **LOADER** input memory routine
LOAFED lounged
LOAFER idler; vagrant; flâneur;
   drone
LOANED lent; advanced; borrowed
LOATHE hate; detest; abhor
ck **LOAVES** of bread
pl **LOBATE** (lobes); (of the ear)
LOBBED pitched; gently threw
LOBING gadrooning
LOBOLA wife-purchase (S. Africa)
bt **LOBOSE** lobate
LOBULE small lobe
LOCALE meeting place (hall) (Fr.)
LOCATE fix; place; settle; find
LOCHAN a pond; a loch (Sc.)
LOCKED grappled; embraced;
   clasped
LOCKER a cupboard; a drawer
LOCKET an ornament; a fastening
LOCK-UP jail-cell, garage with lock
bt **LOCULI** cells
bt, zo **LOCUST** acacia tree; insect
LODGED deposited; dwelt; harboured
LODGER temporary resident
LODORE a cataract
LOFTED skied
LOFTER (golf)
LOGGAN rocking stone; logan
ga **LOGGAT** LOGGET, medieval ninepin;
   heavy wooden pole
nt **LOGGED** recorded
cp **LOGGER** jumberman; recorder of
   events
ar **LOGGIA** semi-exposed gallery, arcade
bd **LOG-HUT** log-cabin
ma **LOG-LOG** logarithm of a logarithm
LOGMAN woodman; logger
cp **LOG-OFF** check-out; (register
   departure)
ce **LOGWAY** chute route beside dam
md **LOHOCK** syrup
md **LOIMIC** (plague)
LOITER linger; dawdle; delay; tarry
zo **LOLIGO** cuttle-fish; squid
bt **LOLIUM** genus of grass
LOLLED hung out; reclined
LOLLER lounger; flâneur
LOLLOP to lounge
bt **LOMENT** a type of legume

LONELY solitary; remote; forlorn
bt **LONGAN** Chinese fruit tree
LONGED craved; desired
LONGER more extensive; taller
bt **LOOFAH** sponge; skeleton; gourd
LOOKED examined; observed;
  glanced
LOOKER onlooker; spectator
LOOK-IN hasty visit; glance; short
  participation (Am. football)
cp **LOOK-UP** seek information; select
  data
nt **LOOMED** came into view
LOOPED encircled; knotted
zo **LOOPER** a caterpillar; wave over
  surfer; short pass (Am. football)
LOOSED set free
LOOSEN slacken; release; untie;
  relax
LOOTED ransacked
LOOTER plunderer; pillager;
  despoiler
zo **LOP-EAR** a lop-eared rabbit
LOPING running easily
LOPPED trimmed; truncated
LOPPER to curdle; trimmer; a
  cutting
bt **LOQUAT** Chinese fruit
LORATE thong-shaped
nt **LORCHA** junk-rigged Portuguese
  ship
LORDED domineered
LORDLY noble; magnificent; arrogant
LORICA a cuirass
zo **LORIOT** golden oriole
LOSING mislaying; squandering;
  failing
LOSSES casualties; damages;
  privations
LOTION a wash
LOUDER noisier; more stentorian
LOUDLY uproariously; clamorously
LOUNGE open sitting room;
  (reception-)
LOURED frowned; scowled
LOUSED infested with lice
LOUVER louvre; ventilator
ar **LOUVRE** open turret (Fr.)
bt **LOVAGE** genus of herb; angelica type
LOVELY beauteous; delectable
LOVING adoring; esteeming
LOWBOY low chest of drawers (N.
  Am.)
LOWERY gloomy; overcast; murky
LOWEST most debased; deepest
LOWING bellowing; mooing
LUBBER heavy; clumsy fellow;
  (land-)

LUBRIC slippery; lewd
bt **LUCAMA** fruit (Chile)
LUCENT bright; shining; clear
LUCINA Diana or Juno
LUCKIE elderly woman (Sc.)
LUCUMO Etruscan title
md **LUETIC** pestilential
ar **LUFFER** (see Louvre); open turret
LUGGED tugged; hauled; dragged
nt **LUGGER** small sailing ship
LUGGIE vase with ears
LULLED soothed; assuaged; calmed
LUMBAL LUMBAR, of lower backbone
LUMBER walk awkwardly
LUMBER accumulated property
  (bulk)
lt, me **LUMERG** unit of luminous energy
LUMPED heaped up
LUMPER stevedore
ck **LUMPIA** oriental egg roll
LUNACY mania; dementia; craziness
bt **LUNARY** lunar; moonwort fern
LUNATE like a crescent-moon;
  (shape)
LUNGED thrust
LUNKAH Indian cheroot
LUNULA LUNULE, crescent-like
LUPINE wolf-likel; wolfish
bt **LUPINE** lupin; a fodder plant
LURING enticing; inveigling;
  decoying
LURKED hid; lay in wait
LURKER skulker
LUSIAD Portuguese epic poem
LUSTED eagerly desired (sexually)
LUSTIC lusty; vigorous
LUSTRA periods of five years
LUSTRE Roman purification
  ceremony
LUSTRE gloss; splendour; glory
zo **LUTEAL** of the corpus luteum
ck **LUTEIN** egg yellow
LUTINE (Lloyd's bell) (marine
  disaster)
LUTING a composition; clay; joining
  clay pieces using slip
mu **LUTIST** lute player
LUTOSE miry; unsafe; swampy
LUXATE dislocate
LUXURY epicurism; super-comfort
bt **LUZULA** a rush genus
LYCEUM lecture hall; (college)
ck **LYCHEE** Chinese dessert fruit
LYDIAN effeminate
mn **LYDITE** black slate; touchstone
md **LYMPHY** (lymph)
LYRATE lyre-shaped
mu **LYRISM** playing the lyre

LYRIST lyrical writer
ch **LYSINE** diamino-caproic acid

M

bt **MABOLA** Philippine tree
bt **MACACO** a tropical tree
MACHAN platform for tiger-shooting
md **MACIES** emaciation; wasting away
pr **MACKLE** macule; a blur in printing
MACKLE spot, blotch, stain
MACLED spotted
MACRON a mark showing long vowel
pl **MACULA** retinal vision area (eye)
md **MACULE** spot symptom; (small-)
  (chicken-) pox
MADCAP hair-brained; frolicsome
MADDEN enrage; infuriate
bt **MADDER** a plant; a red dye
MADMAN maniac; bedlamite
tx **MADRAS** bright kerchief; cotton
  fabric
MAENAD a frenzied woman
MAFFIA MAFIA, Sicilian secret
  gangsters
zo **MAGGOT** worm; grub; larva; a whim
MAGIAN Wise Men of the East
pt **MAGILP** megilp; painters' varnish
MAGISM Persian philosophy
MAGNET lodestone; attraction; lure
nc **MAGNON** spin-wave energy quantum
ch **MAGNOX** magnesium alloy
me **MAGNUM** 2 quart (2.2 litre) bottle
zo **MAGPIE** (target shooting) (nil); bird
bt **MAGUEY** Mexican aloe
MAGYAR Hungarian
MAHOUN mahound; evil spirit
  (Arabic)
MAHOUT elephant driver
zo **MAHSIR** mahseer; an Indian fish
MAIDAN Indian parade ground; a
  plain
MAIDEN lass; damsel; virgin
MAIDEN untaken; non-winner
  (horse-racing); non-scoring
  (cricket)
MAILED posted; (clad in chain-mail)
MAILED (fan-); (black-)
MAIMED crippled; disabled;
  mutilated
MAINLY chiefly; principally; largely
lw **MAINOR** stolen goods; theft
MAJLIS parliament of Iran or Egypt
MAJOON narcotic drug mixture
  (Hindu)
MAKE-UP fiction; facial
  embellishment

MAKING forcing; compelling;
  reaching
bt **MAKORE** African mahogany wood
MALADY ailment; disorder;
  complaint
MALAGA a Spanish wine
ch **MALATE** a salt of malic acid
MALAWI central African country
MALAXE to rub, knead plaster
ch **MALEIC** obtained from malic acid
MALGRE maugre; in spite of
MALICE spite; rancour; malevolence
MALIGN defame; slander; traduce
MALISM pessimistic belief
MALKIN scarecrow; mawkin
bt **MALLEE** Australian tree
to, ga **MALLET** wooden hammer (croquet)
  (polo)
rw, zo **MALLET** maul; beetle
bt **MALLOW** plant (marsh); herb
bt **MALTED** malt added (in process)
MALTHA petroleum
zo **MAMMAL** genus of breast-feeders
bt **MAMMEE** West Indian fruit
MAMMER stammer; hesitate; hover
MAMMET puppet; scarecrow
MAMMON god of riches; wealth
MANAGE contrive; control; regulate
MANANA tomorrow or perhaps later
  (Sp.)
hd **MANCHE** sleeve; the channel (Fr.)
MANCHU former ruling class in
  China
MANDOM humanity
MANEGE riding school; equitation
MANFUL virile; courageous; bold
MANGAL charcoal brazier (Turk.)
MANGER a trough
MANGLE pre-ironing (laundry)
MANIAC madman; lunatic; fiend
bt **MANILA** Manila cheroot
bt **MANIOC** tapioca; cassava
MANISM belief in nature cult
rl **MANITO** Great Spirit (American
  Ind.)
MANJAK Barbados asphalt
ch **MANNAN** anhydride of mannose
nt **MANNED** provided a crew
MANNER behaviour; style;
  deportment
MANQUE 1 to 18 in roulette; missed
  career
MANTEL a beam; mantel-shelf
MANTIC inspired; prophetic; vatic
zo **MANTID** pertaining to mantis
zo **MANTIS** a praying insect
gl **MANTLE** cloak; hood; covering;
  suffuse; rock layer between crust

and core of earth; (-piece) (gas-)
MANTON Spanish shawl
rl, pc **MANTRA** a Vedic hymn;
    meditational prayer, sound ritual
MANTUA lady's cloak or gown
mu **MANUAL** handbook; organ key-board
MANURE compost; fertilizer;
    dressing
mn **MANWAY** underground ladderway
MAOISM ideas of Mao Zedong
MAOIST follower of Mao Zedong
MAPPED charted; drew; delineated
MAQUIS (resistance movement)
bt **MAQUIS** rough shrub
MARACA Latin-American percussion
MARAUD raid; plunder; pillage
gl, bd, mn **MARBLE** decorative metamorphic
    rock; balls; famous friezes
MARBLY like marble
MARCEL a hair wave; style of
    coiffure
mu **MARCIA** (often marcial); (women's
    name)
MARCID wasting
md **MARCOR** marasmus; weight loss
zo **MARGAY** American tiger-cat
MARGED bordered; edged
MARGIN verge; brim; brink; reserve
zo **MARGOT** fish (perch)
MARIAN concerning the Virgin
    Mary
rl **MARIAN** Virgin Mary (year)
bt **MARIET** violet campanula
nt **MARINA** yacht-mooring basin
nt **MARINE** nautical; naval; maritime
MARISH a marsh; swamp
MARIST sect, follower of Virgin
    Mary
nt **MARKAB** dhow, Egypt
MARKED unmistakable; notable
nt **MARKER** examiner; buoy; signpost
tc **MARKER** device determining call
    paths
MARKET mart; emporium; sale; vend
zo **MARMOT** ground squirrel
MAROON claret-colour; firework
    (alarm signal)
MAROON runaway slave
MARQUE accredited; boundary;
    model
bt **MARRAM** sand dune; bent grass
MARRED disfigured; impaired
MARRER spoiler; bungler; botcher
bt, ck **MARRON** chestnut (Fr.); hue, shade
zo **MARROT** guillemot
bt, pl, ck **MARROW** medulla; essence; pith;
    (veg) (bone)
MARSHY boggy; fenny; paludal

zo **MARTEN** (weasel)
zo **MARTIN** swallow
MARTYR victim; sacrifice; persecute
MARVEL wonder; prodigy; miracle
MARVER iron or stone block
gs **MARVER** glass blower's table
hd **MASCLE** heraldic lozenge
as **MASCON** moon high-gravity region
MASCOT charm; talisman; halidom
MASHAQ Persian goatskin water-bag
MASHED bruised; pulped; kneaded
MASHER fop; dandy; lady-killer
MASHIE a golf-club
nt **MASHVA MUCHVA**, mini-dhow (E.
    Africa)
rl **MASJID** masjed; a mosque (Arabic)
MASKED disguised; cloaked;
    screened
MASKER masquerader; mummer
ck **MASLIN** rye-bread
MASORA Hebrew traditions
MASQUE mask; a play; revel
MASSED collected; heaped; lumped
MASSES the proletariat
go **MASSIF** central mountain-mass (Fr.)
zo **MASTAX** gizzard in rotifera
nt **MASTED** having masts
bt **MASTEL** maple tree
MASTER maestro; tutor; teacher;
    expert
bt, bd **MASTIC** resin; coating with proofing;
    (pitch); (bitumastic)
ck **MASTIC** liquorice-like flavour
bt **MATHES** may-weed
bt **MATICO** Peruvian astringent plant
zo **MATIES MATJES**, (Dutch); herring;
    wrasse
zo **MATING** pairing; check-mating
    (chess)
rl **MATINS** morning service
pr, cp **MATRIX** original die; mould; cavity;
    array of items; numbers (discs)
MATRON head nurse; dame
MATTED entangled; interlaced
MATTER signify; import; stuff; affair
MATURE ripen; mellow; full grown
MAUDIT one pursued by bad luck
MAUGRE in spite of
MAULED hammered; mangled;
    bruised
MAUMAU Kenyan nationalists
MAUNDY Thursday before Good
    Friday
MAUSER rifle
MAWMET maumet; mammet; puppet
MAXIMA highest or top limits
mu **MAXIXE** dance (Brazil)
zo **MAY-BUG** cockchafer

tc **MAYDAY** verbal distress call
MAY-DEW spring
zo **MAY-FLY** a species of ephemera;
(angling)
MAYHAP perhaps
lw **MAYHEM** criminal mutilation;
maiming
MAYING spring festival (blossom)
bt **MAZARD** skull; cherry
rl **MAZDAH** supreme deity (Zend
Avesta)
MAZILY confusedly; distractedly
ch **MAZOUT** petroleum extract
MEABLE easily penetrable
MEADOW mead; lea; sward; field
MEAGRE thin; skinny; lean; gaunt;
lank; mean; emaciated
zo **MEAKER** a minnow
MEALER (out-boarder)
ck, bt **MEALIE** maize dish (Africa)
MEANLY ignobly; basely; sordidly
MEASLY stingy; miserly; meagre
ck **MEATHE** mead; a liquor
pl **MEATUS** passage in the body
MEDDLE muddle; intrude; interfere
MEDIAD MESIAD, toward median axis
MEDIAL average; mean; mediocre
as **MEDIAN** traversal; a Mede
bt **MEDICK** lucerne or clover
md **MEDICO** doctor or student
MEDISM Grecian treachery
MEDIUM moderate; means; psychic
pl **MEDIUS** the middle finger
bt **MEDLAR** fruit
mu **MEDLEY** farrago; jumble; olio
MEDLEY mixed selection
zo **MEDUSA** jellyfish; a gorgon
MEEKEN to humble; to abase
MEEKLY lowly; submissively
MEETLY fitly; suitably; correctly
cf **MEGALO-** of great size, power (Gr.)
MEGASS bagasse; cane refuse
me **MEGERG** million ergs
ps **MEGGER** insulation recorder
MEGILP magilp; linseed-oil and
varnish
me **MEGOHM** a million ohms
md **MEGRIM** neuralgic pain; migraine
zo **MEGRIM** flat fish; witch/lemon sole
zo **MEHARI** racing dromedary; camel
MEHTAR Ind. house-servant, groom
mu **MEHTER** battle band (Turk.)
MELINE canary-yellow
MELLAY mêlée; affray; broil; brawl
MELLEY scuffle; contest; conflict
vt, zo **MELLIT** a horse-scab
MELLOW mature; ripe; genial; soften
mu **MELODY** air; tune; descant; theme

MELTED molten; dissolved; relaxed
MELTER liquefier
tx **MELTON** woollen cloth
. **MEMBER** part; limb; component
MEMNON desert crier
MEMOIR life; biography; journal
cp **MEMORY** remembrance; recollection;
access store
MENACE threat; alarm; intimidate
MENAGE housekeeping; household
(group)
MENALD speckled
MENDED restored; rectified;
improved
MENDER repairer; restorer
MENHIR obelisk; long grave stone
MENIAL slave; flunky; degrading
(chore)
pl **MENINX** a brain-membrane
zo **MENNAD** the minnow
MENSAL monthly
pl **MENSES** menstruation
MENTAL intellectual; psychical
MENTOR guide; monitor; counsellor
zo **MENURA** lyre-bird
MERCER a dealer in silks and cloths
MERELY simply; solely; only; purely
MERESE wine-glass stem flange
MERGED sunk; absorbed; immersed
MERGER an amalgamation
tx, zo **MERINO** sheep; wool
bt **MERISM** development of like
members
MERKIN false hair; a mop
zo **MERLIN** falcon; small hawk
ar **MERLON** projecting part of
battlement
MERMAN cf. mermaid
zo **MERONT** phase in neosporidia
zo **MEROPS** bird; bee-eater
cf **-MEROUS** of number of parts (Gr.)
zo **MERULA** thrush; blackbird
MESAIL vizor of helmet
MESCAL Mexican drink
go **MESETA** tableland (Spain)
MESHED reticulated; engaged
MESIAL MESIAN, middle; median
bt **MESLIN** maslin; mixed grain
MESODE part of an ode
MESPOT Mesopotamia
MESSED mussed; confused; ate
together
zo **MESSIN** a mongrel (Sc.)
MESTEE mixed race; octoroon
me **METAGE** measurement
METEOR aerolite; shooting star
METHAM chemical insecticide;
weedkiller

METHER vessel for mead
METHOD order; system; process
ch **METHYL** spirit
METIER role (Fr.); profession (vocational)
METING measuring
ar **METOPE** forehead; sculptural frieze
METRIC decimal system of weights and measures
cf **-METRIC** (isometric) of measure
METTLE courage; ardour; pluck
MEWING caterwauling; confining
MEWLED yowled; squalled
MEWLER a crying child
MIASMA bad air; exhalation
MICHED concealed; played truant
MICHER skulker; beggar; pilferer
MICKLE muckle; great; much
MICMAC an American Indian
me **MICRON** millionth part of metre
MID-AGE middle time of life
MID-AIR up in the air
MIDDAY noon; meridian
MIDDEN dunghill
MIDDLE centre; intermediate; medial
zo **MIDGET** sand-fly; dwarf
ga **MID-LEG MID-OFF**, cricket, fielding position
bt **MIDRIB** largest leaf vein
nt **MID-SEA** at sea
MIDWAY halfway
MIFFED ruffled; annoyed
MIGHTY puissant; potent; dynamic
MIGNON dainty; pretty
rl **MIHRAB** mosque niche facing Mecca
MIKADO Emperor of Japan
MILADY my lady
MILDEN to mollify; make mild
MILDER calmer; softer; gentler
bt **MILDEW** mould; blight; rust; must
MILDLY leniently; placidly; suavely
MILIEU environment
bt **MILIUM** millet grass
MILKED emptied; taken advantage of
MILKEN milk-like
MILKER cow-man
MILLED ground; struggled; levigated
MILLER one who grinds corn
MILLET grain
MILORD my lord
MILSEY milk strainer
zo **MILTER** male fish
ar, rl **MIMBAR MIMBER**, pulpit in mosque
MIMING mimicking; aping; acting (theatre)
bt **MIMOSA** plant genus
ck **MINCED** affected; abbreviated; shredded

MINCER mincing machine; (meat)
MINDED heeded; noted; objected
MINDER care-taker; attendant (nurse)
MINGLE blend; mix; join; jumble
MINIFY diminish; depreciate
MINIMA the lowest
MINING burrowing; sapping
MINION a favourite; sycophant
MINISH diminish; reduce; minify
pt **MINIUM** vermilion (colour)
zo **MINNOW** meaker; mennad, fish
MINOAN Cretan
MINTED coined; stamped; invented
MINTER inventor; creator
MINTON china ware
mu **MINUET** courtly dance
MINUTE small; tiny; minikin; record
fr **MIOMBO** woodland (Tanzania)
MIOSIS rhetorical understatement
pl **MIOTIC** eye-pupil contractor
MIRAGE optical illusion (oasis)
MIRING muddying; besmirching
MIRROR exemplar; reflector
ga **MISCUE** (billiards)
ga **MISERE** (solo whist, no tricks) (cards)
MISERY distress; woe; grief; anguish
MISFIT square peg in round hole
MISGET obtain unjustly
MISHAP accident; ill chance
md **MISHMI** vegetable drug
rl **MISHNA** the text of the Talmud
MISKEN to ignore; be unaware (Sc.)
mu **MISKIN** a little bagpipe
MISLAY misplace; lose
MISLED (mislead); deluded; deceived
rl **MISSAL** Mass-book
MISSAY say wrongly; slander
MISSED failed; wanted; needed
MISSEE view erroneously
zo **MISSEL** thrush; storm cock
MIS-SET to arrange unfitly
MISSIS missus; mistress (Mrs)
MISTER ordinary title for man (Mr)
zo **MISTLE** missel-thrush
MISUSE abuse; profane; misapply
zo **MITHAN** Indian ox; gayal
rl **MITHRA** sun-god (Pers.) (later, Roman)
MITRAL like a mitre; somewhat conical
rl **MITRED** wearing mitre (Bishop)
MITTEN a fingerless glove
MIURUS dactylic hexameter
MIXING mingling; jumbling
nt **MIZZEN** aft mast and sail
MIZZLE fine rain; to drizzle; decamp

MIZZLY misty
pc -MNESIC pertaining to memory
MOANED lamented; bewailed;
   deplored
MOATED surrounded by water
   (castles)
MOBBED surrounded by hostile
   crowd
MOBCAP a frilly cap
MOBILE volatile; mercurial; motile
lw MOB-LAW lynch-law
MOCKED derided; jeered; aped
MOCKER scorner; scoffer; taunter
MOCK-UP a non-working model
pt MODENA crimson
MODERN present; current; up-to-
   date
MODEST chaste; unassuming;
   diffident
MODIFY alter; change; vary;
   moderate
MODISH stylish; fashionable; chic
MODIST a follower of fashion
me MODIUS 2 gallons (Roman)
MODOCS Oregon Indian tribe
ar, bd, me MODULE model; proportion length;
   spacecraft
ae, cp MODULE hardware; self-contained
   unit, faculty behaviour; sputnik
ma MODULO remaindering formula
MOFFLE bungle
gl, mn MOGOTE conical hill (karst) (Sp.)
tx MOHAIR hair of the Angora goat
MOHAWK ruffian; N. Am. Indian;
   (ice-skating)
MOHOLE penetration of earth's crust
MOIDER to toil; confuse; spend (Sc.)
MOIETY a half; a share
MOILED drudged; toiled; soiled
MOIRAE the Fates
pl MOLARS grinder teeth of mammals
rl, zo MOLECH MOLOCH, Semitic deity;
   Australian lizard
MOLEST vex; harry; worry; pester
MOLINE mill-stone rynd
ce MOLING laying drains with mole
   plough
rl MOLLAH MULLAH, judge; Moslem
   teacher
MOLTEN melted; liquefied; fused
MOMENT instant; trice; import
MONDAY Solomon Grundy's
   birthday
zo MONERA simple protozoans
MONGER deal; to deal in
MONGOL native of Mongolia
rl MONIAL nun
MONIED rich; opulent

MONIES coins; means; specie
MONISM a doctrine of single reality
MONIST believer in monism
zo MONKEY tailed tree animal (Rhesus)
MONKEY £500; pile-driver; meddle
mu MONODY a dirge
MONOID (versification)
bt MONOSY abnormal condition
MONTEM Eton custom of money-
   raising
mn MONTON ore (Sp.)
mu MONTRE organ stop; ceramic
zo MOO-COW pet word for cow
MOOING lowing; cowtalk
MOONED wandered aimlessly
MOONER listless lounger
MOONET little moon
zo MOORUK Bennett's cassowary
tx MOORVA fibre; bowstring-hemp
MOOTED debated; discussed
MOOTER disputer
MOPING languishing
MOPISH gloomy; spiritless;
   despondent
zo MOPOKE Australian owl
MOPPED swabbed
MOPPET MOPSEY, a kept person;
   popsy
MORALE courageous endurance
MORASS bog; fen; swamp; quagmire
MORBID diseased; vitiated; sickly
tx MOREEN watered woollen fabric
zo MORGAY shark; dog-fish
me MORGEN about 2 acres (0.8 hectare)
MORGUE mortuary (Fr.)
MORIAN a Moor; Moroccan
MORION open helmet
MORKIN dead beast
mn MORLOP jasper
rl MORMON member of sect (Utah)
hd MORNED blunted; dawned
MOROSE sullen; surly; churlish
MORRIS folk dance style
MORROW the next day
MORSAL pert. to cutting edge
MORSED signalled by Morse
MORSEL titbit; piece; fragment
MORTAL human; deadly; fatal
MORTAR trench weapon; cement
md MORULA button-scurvy
rl MOSAIC law; inlaid ornamentation
lw, bt MOSAIC green; symptoms of virus in
   plants
rl MOSLEM Muslim; Mohammedan
rl MOSQUE temple; mesjid
pt MOSTIC maulstick
MOSTLY chiefly; mainly
MOTHER (liquors); dam; generatrix

MOTILE mobile; capable of movement
MOTION proposal; action; impulse
MOTIVE spur; incentive; reason
MOTLEY mixed; clown's costume
zo **MOT-MOT** American bird
MOTORY giving motion
MOTTLE to stain
MOUJIK muzhik; Russian peasant
MOULDY fusty; musty; rusty; fungusy
gl **MOULIN** glacial crevasse
ck **MOULIN** mill (Fr.); grinder
MOUNTY Canadian Mounted Police
zo **MOUNTY** the rise of a hawk
nt **MOUSED** bound with spun-yarn
zo **MOUSER** capable cat
ck **MOUSSE** culinary confection
bt **MOUTAN** tree-peony
MOUTHY ranting; bombastic
nm, zo **MOUTON** sheep; ancient French coin
MOVIES moving pictures (cinema)
MOVING stirring; budging; touching
MOWING grass cutting
tx **MOZING** raising nap (cloth)
MUCAGO mucilage; mucus
ch **MUCATE** MUCITE, mucic acid
MUCHLY rather much
nt **MUCHVA** MASHVA, mini-dhow (E. Africa)
MUCKED muddled; dirtied; spread dung
MUCKER a failure; a fall
MUCKLE much (Sc.)
md **MUCOID** resembling mucus
MUCOSA mucous membrane
md, ps **MUCOUS** mucoid; slimy; viscous
MUDDER muddy course; race-track (racing)
MUDDLE confuse; chaos; derange
MUD-PIE child's inedible confection
MUFFED fumbled and failed
ck **MUFFIN** a winter's delicacy
MUFFLE (furnace); deaden; shroud
MUGGED crammed up; beaten up
zo **MUGGER** Indian crocodile; assailant
bt **MUGUET** lily of the valley
lw **MULIER** wife
MULISH obstinate
rl **MULLAH** (see Mollah); teacher (Moslem)
ck **MULLED** hot; spiced (wine); pondered
bt **MULLEN** mullein plant
MULLER a miller (Sc.)
MULLER heating vessel; pestle
zo **MULLET** genus of fish
hd **MULLET** a star; a rowel

zo **MULLEY** mooly; a cow; hornless
br **MULTUM** adulterant used in brewing
MUMBLE mutter; chew
MUMMER masquerader; actor; histrion
MUMPED nibbled; grinned; chewed
MUMPER a beggar
mn **MUNDIC** iron pyrites
MUNDIL a turban
MUNSHI Eastern teacher
ar **MUNTIN** part of window; glass frame; mullion
MURAGE money for town repairs (Fr.)
MURDER kill; assassinate; slaughter
zo **MURINE** (mice)
MURING immuring; walling up
MURMUR whisper; complain; repine
bt **MURPHY** potato (Irish)
gl **MURREN** a murrain (obs.)
MURREY dark red
zo **MUSANG** East Indian coffee-rat
bt **MUSCAL** (mosses)
bt **MUSCAT** a grape; a wine
pl **MUSCLE** thew; sinew
MUSEUM collection/treasure repository
MUSHED commanded (sled dogs) (forward)
MUSHER snow traveller (Canada)
MUSING ruminating; reflecting
MUSIVE mosaic
go **MUSKEG** swamp; marsh (Canada)
zo **MUSKET** hawk; smooth-bore gun
zo **MUSK-OX** N. American arctic ox
MUSLIM Moslem; Mohammedan
tx **MUSLIN** soft cotton fabric
zo **MUSMON** moufflon; European sheep
MUSNUD Persian throne of state
MUSSAL Indian torch
MUSSED messed; disarranged
zo **MUSSEL** a shellfish
zo **MUSTAC** small tufted monkey
MUSTEE mestee; an octoroon
MUSTER parade; assemble; rally
MUTAGE (checking fermentation)
MUTATE to change
MUTELY dumbly; silently
MUTING guano; silencing; bribing
nt **MUTINY** hijack by crew; riot; revolt
MUTISM dumbness; speechlessness
MUTIVE tending to alter
MUTTER murmur; grumble; maunder
MUTTON proverbially dead
MUTUAL reciprocal; correlative
ar **MUTULE** projection
lw **MUTUUM** loan contract

MUZHIK moujik; Russian peasant
MUZZLE jaw cover (dog)
MUZZLE gun mouth; censor
MYCOID fungus-like
MYELIC pertaining to spinal cord
zo MYELIN fatty material round nerve
pl MYELON spinal cord
zo MYGALE shrew mouse
ch MYOGEN water-soluble muscle
    albumin
md MYOPIA near-sightedness
md MYOPIC short-sighted; purblind
md MYOSIN MYOSIS, disease of the eye
MYRIAD countless; innumerable
    (stars)
bt MYRTLE genus of shrub
bt MYRTUS wax-myrtle
MYSELF reflexive pronoun
MYSTIC occult; recondite; enigmatic
MYTHIC legendary; fictitious;
    fanciful
MYTHUS a myth; a fable
zo MYXINE hag-fish
pl MYXOID mucoid
md MYXOMA a tumour

N

NABBED grabbed; arrested
ck NABKET snuff; small cake (Sc.)
md NAEVUS birth-mark
md NAGANA tsetse fly disease
NAGARI Sanskrit script
nt NAGGAR cargo felucca boat
NAGGED scolded; upbraided;
    pestered
NAGGER a fault-finder
zo NAHOOR sheep (Nepal)
hd, zo NAIANT (swimming)
NAILED caught; secured; exposed
NAILER nail-maker
zo NAKONG water-koodoo (S. Africa)
NAMELY viz, specifically
NAMING christening; nominating
zo NANDOO S. American ostrich; Rhea
NANISM dwarfishness
tx NANKIN nankeen; cotton cloth
rl NANNAR Chaldean moon-god
NANOID dwarf; pigmy
ch NAPALM flammable oil/soap gel
    (warfare)
tx NAPERY household linen
NAPKIN serviette; nappy; diaper
    (ring)
mn NAPPAL soaprock
NAPPED dozed; slumbered
bt NARDOO Australian plant

bt NARDUS mat-grass
bt NARGIL coconut tree; hubble-bubble
md NARIAL NARINE, nasal
NARROW strait; close; contracted
    (bowels); -minded; truncate
zo NARWAL sea-unicorn; whale
mu NASARD organ stop
md NASION part of nose
NASUTE captious; critical
hd NATANT swimming; naiant
NATION people; race; country
NATIVE aboriginal; intrinsic;
    congenial
zo NATRIX genus of snakes
ch NATRON carbonate of soda
NATTER to nag (dial.); to chat,
    complain
ar NATTES surface decoration
bl, bt NATURE the biological world
NATURE character traits
me NAUGHT O; zero; nought; nothing
NAUSEA sea-sickness; disgust; qualm
NAUTCH dancing girl; a dance
nt NAUTIC nautical; naval; maritime
mu NAZARD 3-f organ pitch
zo NEANIC of adolescent period
nv, nt NEAPED aground at low tide
NEARBY adjacent; nigh; at hand
NEARED approached; drew closer
NEARER more adjacent
NEARLY closely; all but; almost
NEATLY smartly; featly; dexterously
bt NEBBUK (crown of thorns)
bt NEB-NEB acacia pods
NERRIS fawn-skin worn by Bacchus
as NEBULA heavy cloud; whirl (stars)
NEBULE nebula; mist; fog
NEBULY wavy
NECKED embraced; hugged;
    beheaded
bt NECRON dead plant material
ck NECTAR ambrosia; honey-sap (juice)
NEED-BE a necessity
NEEDED wanted; lacked; necessitated
NEEDER requirer
to NEEDLE critical
NEEDLY thorny
NEESED NEEZED, sneezed
NEGATE deny; mollify
bt, zo NEKTON swimming water organisms
NEMEAN (lion killed by Hercules)
go NEOGEA neotropical region
NEPALI language (Nepal)
NEPHEW sibling's male child
NERIED sea-nymph
rl NEREUS sea-god
bt NERINE Guernsey lily
zo NERITE mollusc

bt **NERIUM** oleander
bt, ck **NEROLI** oil from orange flowers
NERVAL nervous; sinewy
NERVED fortified; plucky; courageous
NESHEN to soften
NESHKI Arabic script
NESSUS a Centaur
NESTED built a nest
NESTLE snuggle; rest; cherish
NESTOR genus of parrots (NZ)
NETHER lower; under
cy **NETRUM** minute spindle
NETTED reticulated; gained; trapped
bt **NETTLE** to irritate; fret
zo **NEURAD** dorsal
md **NEURAL** (nerves)
NEURIC nervous
NEURIN protein coating; membrane
md **NEURON** nerve cell
pc **NEUROT-** of the nerves (neurotic)
NEUTER neutral; non-partisan; sexless
NEWING yeast; barm
NEWISH somewhat novel
NEW-SAD recently bereaved (Shak.)
me **NEWTON** gravity force
ch **NIACIN** nicotinic acid; B Vitamin
NIBBED complete with nib (pen)
NIBBLE bite; gnaw
NICELY exactly; accurately; adroitly
rl **NICENE** (Nicaea) prayer-book creed (A.D. 325)
NICEST daintiest; choicest
NICETY precision; delicacy
NICHED in a niche or recess
NICHER neigh; snigger
NICKED notched; stolen
nm, mn **NICKEL** 5 cent piece; metal; acoustic delay time
zo **NICKER** a cheat; woodpecker; thief
nt **NICKEY** Manx fishing boat
NIDDER shiver; molest
NIDGED nudged (stone-cutting)
NIDGET a fool
NID-NOD nod repeatedly; (half-asleep)
NIDOSE olfactory
NIELLO engraving; ornamentation
NIFFER exchange (Sc.)
NIFFLE pilfer; steal
NIGGER negro; black
NIGGLE trifle; to be finicky
NIGHLY nearly; adjacent
NIGRIC black
zo **NILGAI** Indian antelope
NIMBLE agile; lively; swift
NIMBLY alertly; briskly; quickly

mt **NIMBUS** a halo; rain cloud
NIMROD a mighty hunter
NINETY cardinal number
NINGAL Nannar's wife
NIPPED pinched; compressed; gripped
zo **NIPPER** tooth (horse); boy (slang); bed-bug
NIPPLE teat; dug; pap; mamilla
NIPPON Japan
rl **NIPTER** feet-washing ceremony
md **NIRLES** herpes; shingles
ch **NITRIC** (nitre); acid
ch **NITRON** reagent for nitric acid
zo **NITTER** bot-fly; body-louse
NITWIT numskull; idiot
NIVOSE 4th French month (Revol.)
nt **NNGGAR** NUGGAR, cargo dhow (Nile)
ga **NO-BALL** (cricket) (penalty)
vt **NOBBLE** dope; lame; cheat
NOBLER more illustrious
NOBODY a nonentity; negative pronoun
ck **NOCAKE** parched corn
NOCENT hurtful; mischievous
zo **NOCTUA** large moth genus
NODDED agreed; auction offer
NODDER a drowsy person
NODDLE the head
NODOSE knotted
NODULE small knot
NOESIS pure knowledge
NOETIC intellectual
me **NOGGIN** small cup; ¼ pint (0.14 litres)
NO-GOOD useless
NOISED reported; rumoured
el **NO-LOAD** normal voltage; speed, but no output
NOMIAL a single term in algebra
NOMISM moral law as basis of conduct
NONAGE immature; minority
ch **NONANE** paraffin hydrocarbon
NONARY group of nine
NON-COM an NCO; under-officer
NON-CON not content
NON-EGO (metaphysics)
NONIUS a graduating instrument
ch **NONOSE** monosaccharide group
ck **NOODLE** simpleton; form of pasta
NOOSED snared; caught; lassooed
NORDIC Scandinavian
gl **NORITE** coarse-grained igneous rock
NORMAL regular; conforming; without deviation; standard
NORMAN of Normandy
hd **NORROY** King at Arms

mn **NOSEAN** a silicate
ga **NO-SIDE** end of a game of Rugby
ar, bd **NOSING** snooping; blunt overhang of
stair, sill, roof
NOSISM speaking of self as regal
'we'
bt **NOSTOC** genus of seaweed
lw **NOTARY** official witness of
documents
NOTICE see; remark; heed;
intimation
NOTIFY warn; advise; apprise
NOTING recording; registering
NOTION idea; belief; theory; concept
NOTOUR notorious (Sc.)
ck **NOUGAT** a sweetmeat
cp **NOUGHT** 0; nought; cypher; zero
condition
NOUNAL (noun); of substantive
NOUSLE to nurse; nuzzle
rl **NOVENA** nine days' devotion
NOVENE by nines
NOVICE tyro; neophyte; probationer
NOWAYS in no way
NOWISE nohow
hd **NOWYED** heraldic branches
NOYADE execution by drowning
(Fr.)
NOZZLE snout; projecting
mouthpiece
NUANCE a subtle distinction
bt **NUBBIN** stunted maize
NUBBLE punch; small lump
NUBBLY bumpy; knotty
NUBIAN of Nubia; Sudanese
NUBILE marriageable
md **NUCHAL** (nape of neck)
NUCLEI cell-centres; cores; kernels
cf **NUCLEO-** of the nucleus (Gr.)
NUCULE a little nut
NUDELY barely; nakedly
NUDGED jogged; poked; pushed
NUDISM NUDIST, naked sun-
worshipping
NUDITY nakedness
zo, nt **NUGGAR** mugger; alligator; dhow
(Nile)
mn **NUGGET** a lump of gold
go **NULLAH** watercourse; ravine (Ind.)
NUMBED torpid; paralysed; dazed
NUMBER count; compute; figure;
identity; amount
tc **NUMBER** code address in network
NUMBLY in a frozen manner
tx **NUMNAH** saddle cloth
NUNCIO Papal representative
NUNCLE mine uncle (Shak.)
tx **NUNOME** mesh fabric

bt **NUPHAR** water-lily
NUPPEN surface droplets glass
technique
nm **NURLED** milled like a coin
NURSED fostered; encouraged
NURSER tender; cherisher
NUTANT nodding
bt, ck **NUTMEG** an aromatic kernel
bt **NUT-OIL** paint ingredient
zo **NUTRIA** the fur of the coypu
NUTTER a nut-gatherer
NUZZER a presentation (India)
NUZZLE nousle; fondle
zo **NYLGAU** nilgai; an Indian antelope
zo **NYMPHA** pupa; chrysalis

O

OAFISH idiotic; dull; doltish
ga **OARAGE** rowing
ga **OARING** sculling
bt **OARIUM** an ovary; ovarium
zo **OARLAP** a distinctive rabbit
OBDUCE draw over
bt, fr **OBECHE** African satin/whitewood
OBELUS mark (†); obelisk
OBERON king of the fairies
OBEYED complied; yielded
OBEYER heeder; minder
rl **OBIISM** West Indian witchcraft
OBITER incidentally
OBJECT protest; demur; goal; intent
cp **OBJECT** purpose; thing; (language)
OBJURE to swear
rl **OBLATE** communion wafer-bread
OBLIGE compel; bind; favour; serve
OBLONG longer than broad
mu **OBOIST** oboe-player
nm **OBOLUS** Charon's ferry fee
OBSESS besiege; beset; haunt
OBTAIN get; win; acquire; attain
zo **OBTECT** of pupae unable to move
OBTEST to beseech; supplicate
OBTUND deaden; blunt
OBTUSE dull; stolid; stupid
ma **OBTUSE** open geometrical angle
OBVERT turn toward; to face
OCCAMY silvery alloy
OCCULT mystic; hidden; obscure
OCCUPY fill; possess; inhabit
zo **OCELLI** peacock's 'eyes'
zo **OCELOT** American leopard
bt **OCHREA** cup-shaped plant structure
O'CLOCK on the hour
OCRACY government
ch **OCTANE** petrol purification figure
as **OCTANS** constellation (South Pole)

me, nv **OCTANT** measuring instrument
mu **OCTAVE** ottava; consisting of eight
pr **OCTAVO** (eight leaves to the sheet)
OCTILE octant; eighth of a circle
ps **OCTODE** a thermionic valve
ch **OCTOSE** monosaccharide group
OCTROI monopoly; trade privilege (Fr.)
OCULAR visible
ar **OCULUS** circular office
ODDITY singularity; strangeness
ODIOUS hateful; detested; obnoxious
ODYLIC mesmeric
OECIST founder of Greek colony
md **OEDEMA** localized dropsy; water-retaining cells; obesity; swollen
OEUVRE complete works; artist, writer
OFF-DAY unlucky occasion; free day
OFFEND affront; insult; trespass
rl, tc **OFFICE** post; function; bureau; (holy); (telephone)
nt **OFFING** outer sea; future
OFFISH haughty; snobbish
gl **OFF-LAP** strata conformation
bd **OFFSET** counter-balance; wall ledge; swan neck pipe; accounts; tax
pr **OFFSET** rubber-to-paper process
OGAMIC ancient Irish script
OGDOAD group of 8
OGHAMS ancient Irish alphabet
ar **OGIVAL** arched
OGLING an amorous advance (eyeing)
OGRESS a monstrous lady; giantess
OGRISH orgreish
ga **OH-HELL** card game like whist
bt **OIDIUM** fungus; vine-mildew
pl **OIL-BAG** oil gland
OIL-CAN oil applier
OILERY oilman's stock
ch **OIL-GAS** inflammable gas
OILING lubricating
OIL-MAN oil-dealer
bt **OIL-NUT** butternut
OIL-RIG boring apparatus for oil
OJIBWA puckered moccasins
OLDEST most senile; eldest
OLDISH somewhat ancient
ch **OLEATE** (oleic acid)
ch **OLEFIN** ethylene hydrocarbon
OLEINE liquid fat
ps **OLEOSE** oily; oleic
lw, nt **OLERON** ancient code of sea laws
to **OLIVER** small tilt-hammer; (Roland)
OLIVET mock pearl
OLIVIL gum from the olive tree

md **OLLAMH** ancient Irish doctor
zo **OMASAL** (cow's stomach)
OMASUM ruminant's third stomach
OMBROS madder
OMEDED predicted; augured; presaged
ck **OMELET** omelette; beaten eggs
OMNIFY to render universal
pg **OMNIUM** multi-projector cinema
zo **ONAGER** wild ass; ghorkhar
ONCOME deluge; approach
mn **ONCOST** extraneous mining charges
ONDINE undine; water-spirit
mt **ONDING** fall of rain or snow
ONE-MAN soloist
ONE-TWO successive punches (boxing)
ONE-WAY (traffic); single route
ONEYER (of uncertain origin)
ONFALL storm; attack; assault
ONFLOW gush; on stream
cp **ON-LINE** computer operation
ON-LINE on course; direct hit
mu **ONRUSH** onset; charge
ON-SIDE correct placing (football) (netball)
ONWARD forward; advancing
zo **ONYMAL** (technical group name)
zo **OOCYST** cyst round gametes in protozoa
zo **OOCYTE** cell in meiosis; forming ovum
OODLES quantities; heaps
bl **OOGAMY** union of un-like-sized gametes
OOGENY embryonic development
OOIDAL egg-shaped
mn **OOLITE** a limestone (ovulites)
gl **OOLITH** spherical concretion
OOLOGY the study of birds' eggs
bt, ck **OOLONG** OULONG, tea
nt **OOMIAK** kayak, Eskimo boat
zo **OORIAL** wild sheep (India)
zo **OOTYPE** oviduct section
OOZING exuding; seeping; percolating
OPAQUE impermeable to light
OPENED undid; disclosed; revealed
OPENER beginner; cutter
OPENLY publicly; above-board
gn **OPERON** genes in chromosome
mn **OPHITE** porphyry
rl **OPHITE** gnostic serpent-worshipper
ch **OPIANE** narcotine
md **OPIATE** a sedative medicine
OPINED supposed; thought; fancied
OPPOSE prevent; hinder; combat
OPPUGN oppose; obstruct; resist

OPTANT volunteer
OPTICS science of light and vision
OPTIME almost a wrangler
OPTING choosing; co-opting
OPTION choice; wish; selection; right
  to buy (Am. football)
bt ORACHE genus of plants; spinach
ORACLE wiseacre; ambiguous
  response
ORALLY by word of mouth
bt ORANGE Citrus aurantium
ORATED harangued; prated; spouted
ORATOR declaimer; spell-binder
ORBATE bereaved; fatherless
pl ORBITA eye-sockets
zo ORCHIC of the testis
bt ORCHID orchis
bt ORCHIL archil; purple dye; a lichen
cf ORCHIO- of the testicle (Gr.)
ORCINE lichen dye
ORDAIN prescribe; enjoin; appoint
ORDEAL test; trial; assay; scrutiny
ar ORDERS decorated columns
ORDURE excrement
OREIDE imitation gold
md OREXIS appetite
md ORGASM sexual climax
el OR-GATE pulse circuit
br ORGEAT liquor (barley)
ORGIES revels; carousals (sexual
  bouts)
ORIENT eastern; the east
bt, ck ORIGAN marjoram (herb)
ORIGIN fount; spring; source; root
pr ORIHON continued folded uncut
  sheet
zo ORIOLE a bird species
rl ORISON prayer; supplication
ORMULU ORMOLU, gilt brass
ORMUZD (Magian system)
ORNATE florid; embellished
ORNERY ordinary; mean; low
mn OROIDE alloy; oreide
ch OROTIC vitamin B-13; growth acid
ORPHAN child who has lost both
  parents
ORPHIC (Orpheus)
bt ORPINE a yellow plant
ORRERY model of solar system
bt ORRICE dried iris root
ORTIVE rising; eastern
zo OSCINE of a sub-order of birds
OSCULE small mouth
OSELLA Doge's medal (Venice)
bt OSIERY osier-bed
rl OSIRIS greatest Egyptian god
mn OSMIUM metallic element
me OSMOLE unit of osmolic pressure

OSMOSE (diffusion of fluids)
cf -OSOPHY belief or doctrine
zo OSPREY sea-hawk; an egret plume
pl OSSEIN bone-cartilage
OSSIFY to become bone-like; harden
  to inflexible
OSTEAL pertaining to bone
OSTENT portent; show; appearance
go OSTIUM an opening; mouth of river
OSTLER stableman; groom
OSTMEN Danish settlers in Ireland
zo OSTREA oyster
md OTALGY earache
zo OTARIA genus of seals
OTIANT idle; resting
OTIOSE at ease; lazy; idle
md OTITIS ear-trouble
mu OTTAVA an octave (It.)
OUSTED deposed; ejected; thrown
  out
OUSTER ejection; dispossession
OUTAGE electrical failure
OUTASK ask for the last time
OUTBAR to shut out
OUTBID offer more; auction; sale
OUTCRY hue; clamour; tumult; bruit
OUTDID excelled; surpassed;
  exceeded
OUTFIT equipment; clothing
OUTING expedition; trip; holiday
ae OUTJET exhaust vent
OUTLAW brigand; bandit; proscribe
OUTLAY expense; disbursement
OUTLET exit; vent; loophole
OUTLIE excel in lying
OUTMAN outnumber
ro OUTPUT production; resulting
  sound; signal
cp OUTPUT information from processor
OUTRUN outstrip; beat; surpass; flat,
  halting terrain; after ski-jump
OUTSET start; beginning; opening
OUTSIT sit longer than
OUTSUM outnumber
OUTTOP over-reach
OUTVIE surpass; out-rival; eclipse
OUTWIT dupe; overreach;
  circumvent
OVALLY elliptically
OVERBY adjacent
OVERDO carry too far
OVERGO exceed
zo OVIBOS musk-ox; buffalo-cow
zo OVISAC (ovary)
bt OVULAR embryonic
zo OWLERY haunt of owls
OWLING smuggling; especially wool
OWLISH as wise an an owl!

OWNING possessing; conceding
ch OXALIC an acid; (spinach)
bt OXALIS wood sorrel
ch OXALYL bivalent acid radical
zo OXBIRD the dunlin
zo OXEOTE rod-shaped
OX-EYED having large eyes
OXFORD (blue); (shoe); (movement)
OXGALL cleaning/painting agent
OXGANG OXGATE, OXLAND, a bovate;
  c.15 ac./6 ha of land (size
  cultivable with one ox)
OXHEAD block-head; dolt (Shak.)
bt OX-HEEL the setter-wort
OX-HIDE leather
ck OXTAIL (soup)
ch OXYGEN principal gas in atmosphere
OXYGON a triangle with 2 acute
  angles
OXYMEL honey and vinegar
zo, ck OYSTER shell; pearl; (prairie)
OZALID copy of engineering drawing
md OZOENA chronic atrophic rhinitis
OZONIC of ozone

P

PACIFY calm; appease; reconcile
nt PACING setting the pace; walking;
  measuring yards; giring against
  wind cycle
PACKED crowded; compressed;
  prearranged fraudulent voting
ce PACKER stower; inflatable rubber
  ring; washer
nt PACKET parcel; bale; a mail vessel
go PADANG scrub heath (Malaya)
PADDED travelled slowly; (cell);
  (protective)
PADDER foot-pad; highwayman
nt PADDLE canoe oar; wade; to propel
  (-steamer); semaphore
zo PADNAG ambling horse
to PADSAW saw blade in toolholder kit
mu PADUAN (Padua); the pavan
cf PAEDIO- of the feet (Gr.)
ck PAELLA rice-seafood dish (Sp.)
cp, pr PAGING marking pages; calling
  (persons); adding data; layout
nm, rl PAGODA pagode; temple; (Ind. coin)
lw PAID-UP shares; capital;
  membership
bt PAIGLE cowslip
PAINED hurt; distressed; grieved
PAINIM (see Paynim); pagan
PAIRED coupled; yoked; mated;
  (voting)

PAKEHA white man (Maori)
PALACE ruler's residence; court
  circles
cf, gl, zo PALAEO- of ancient, prehistoric life
  (Gr.)
zo PALAMA toe-webbing
pl PALATE roof of mouth; taste-buds
PALELY wanly; ashy; pallidly
PALING a fence; blanching
pt PALISH wan; weak colour
PALKEE palanquin (Ind.)
zo PALLAH African antelope
rl PALLAS Athene, goddess of wisdom
PALLED cloaked; covered (coffin);
  lost interest
PALLET straw mattress; makeshift
  bed
PALLID colourless; lifeless
PALLOR paleness
pl PALMAR (hand) palm, sole (hand/
  foot), volar
PALMED concealed; conjured away;
  stolen
rl PALMER pilgrim (with palm leaf)
md PALMUS palpitation; twitching
zo PALOLO edible worm
zo PALPAL PALPED, (antennae-like
  feelers)
zo PALPUS feeler of an insect
PALTER dodge; shuffle; prevaricate
PALTRY mean; petty; despicable
bt, go PAMPAS treeless plains; grasses
  (S.America)
bt, go PAMPER indulge; coddle; humour
ck PANADA bread pulp
PANAMA sun-hat
PANARY store-house for bread;
  pantry
PANDER a procurer; cater to (tastes)
PANDIT pundit; a learned man
PANDUR robber; Austrian soldier
ck PANFRY method of cooking
ck PANFUL filling a pan
PANGED emotionally upset
PANISC Pan as a satyr
PANMUG crockery; butter-pan
mn PANNED yielded
PANNEL rustic saddle
PANNER a nagger; faultfinder (gold)
md PANNUS birthmark; a dressing
nt PANSHI sailing dugout (Bengal)
PANTED gasped; blew; palpitated
zo PANTER a snare; panther
PANTON a special kind of horseshoe
PANTRY food storage closet
PANZER armoured corps (Ger.);
  panser
rl PAPACY (pope); popery

md **PAPAIN** disgestive enzyme
bt **PAPAYA** large sub-tropical fruit; pawpaw
PAPERY resembling paper
PAPISH characteristic of Popes
rl **PAPISM** papal doctrine; authority
PAPIST pro-Pope; Roman Catholic
bt **PAPPUS** hairy tuft
PAPUAN from New Guinea
md **PAPULA** pimple
PAPYRI scrolls of papyrus (Egypt)
PARADE show; display; flaunt
go **PARAMO** wind-swept desert in Andes
PARANG heavy Malay knife
PARAPH a flourish to a signature
PARASE movements (fencing)
PARCAE the Fates
lw **PARCEL** packet; bundle; piece; share; (land)
PARDON remit; condone; forgive
PARDON mercy
PAREIL an equal
PARENT author; producer; cause
ck **PAREVE** made without animal products
PARFAY! by, or in, faith!
PARGET plaster decoration
zo **PARIAH** social outcast
PARIAN (marble); (porcelain)
zo **PARINE** pertaining to titmouse (bird)
PARING rind; shaving; reducing
rl **PARISH** church district
cp **PARITY** equality; parage; check on transfer of data
el **PARITY** space; reflection; symmetry
au **PARKED** (left); (cars)
PARKER park-keeper; (nosey-)
ck **PARKIN** perkin; Lancashire cake
PARLAY expand; exploit
PARLEY confer, discuss; talk
PARODY travesty; burlesque; caricature
PAROLE word of honour
zo **PAROUS** offspring liveborn (mammals)
ar **PARPEN PARPEND, PARPENT,** transverse 2-faced stone in wall
nt **PARRAL PARREL,** collar to prevent spars from slipping from the mast
zo **PARROT** repeat by rote; talking bird
me **PARSEC** interstellar distance unit
PARSED analysed grammatically
PARSEE Persian living in India
rl **PARSON** vicar; clergyman
zo **PARTAN** crab (Sc.)
PARTED left; broke; separated
PARTER distributor; sharer

PARTIM in part
PARTLY not altogether
PARURE set of jewels
rl, ar **PARVIS** court; portico
ga **PASAKA** form of play (pelota)
PASCAL unit of pressure of newton unit
PASSED ignored; spent; elapsed
PASSEE faded (Fr.)
PASSER a passer-by
PASSIM here and there
PASTED basted; gummed
PASTEL crayon; chalk drawing
md **PASTIL** medicated lozenge
rl, zo **PASTOR** shepherd; starling
ck **PASTRY** confiserie
PATCHY unequal standard; mottled
lw **PATENT** proprietary; copyright
PATENT an open fact; truth; (letters-)
PATERA shallow circular dish; ornament
PATHAN tribe of Afghanistan, Pakistan
md **-PATHIC** of diseases
PATHOS deep emotion
nt **PATILE** Ganges barge, India
ar **PATINA** glow given by age; oxidized, lead, bronze effect
rl **PATINE** paten; eucharistic plate
ga **PATLID** stone at start (curling)
PATOIS dialect (Fr.)
PATROL mobile armed guard; police unit
rl **PATRON** customer; supporter; saint
PATTED congratulated; tapped
PATTEN clog (Dutch wooden shoe)
PATTER high speed talk; rain sound
pl **PAUNCH** the belly (obese)
PAUPER indigent person
PAUSAL ceasing; pausing
PAUSED hesitated; halted; tarried
PAUSER a deliberator; a demurer
PAVAGE paving cost
mu **PAVANE PAVAN,** court dance
PAVIER PAVIOR, PAVER, pavement layer
PAVING surfacing (crazy) (street)
PAVISE great shield
PAWING clawing; touching (rudely)
PAWNED pledged; risked; hazarded
PAWNEE N. American Indian tribe
PAWNEE pawnbroker
PAWNER a borrower on security (possessions)
bt **PAWPAW** papaw; a tropical fruit
zo **PAXWAX** tendon; faxwax
nt **PAYANG** fishing boat (Malaya)

PAY-BOX public coin call box; telephone
PAY-DAY day when wages paid
PAYING gainful; punishing; tarring
PAYNIM painim; infidel; heathen
nt, pc **PAY-OFF** payment; denouement; side-benefits; spin-off
PAYOLA bribe to mention on media
PEACHY like a peach
bt **PEACOD** pea-pod
zo **PEAHEN** a peafowl
PEAKED reached highest form
PEALED resounded; reverberated
bt **PEANUT** the ground-nut
mn **PEA-ORE** oxide of iron
bt **PEA-POD** pea seed envelope
PEARLY transparent; translucent
mn **PEBBLE** a stone; an agate
PEBBLY shingly
PECKED struck (birds); nagged (hen-)
zo **PECKER** woodpecker; courage; mouth; beak; penis
cp **PECKER** tape reader sensing voice
zo **PECTEN** bivalve genus; scallop
zo **PECTEN** eye membrane of a bird
PECTIC congealing; gelatinizing
PECTIN (apple jelly)
zo **PECTUS** insect sclerite; vertebrate breast
rl **PEDALE** altar foot-cloth
PEDANT schoolmaster; precise person
bt **PEDATE** divided like a foot
PEDDLE to sell retail; to trifle; to hawk (drugs)
PEDION single-plane crystal
PEDLAR PEDLER, hawker; vendor; bagman
PEELED stripped; skinned; pillaged
ck **PEELER** policeman (Sir Robert Peel); perfect wave (surfing); rind, skin remover
PEEPED chirped; glimpsed; snooped
zo **PEEPER** (chicken); the eye
bt **PEEPUL** sacred tree; Indian bo-tree
PEERER a peeping Tom
PEERIE peg-top (Sc.)
PEEVED annoyed; fretful
zo **PEEWIT** green plover; lapwing
PEGGED fixed; toiled
PEG-LEG wooden leg
PEG-TOP a spinning top
zo **PELAGE** animal fur
PELIKE double-handled Greek vase
PELION and Ossa, mountains
jn **PELLET** small ball or shot; wood cover over screw

PELMET curtain housing
ga **PELOTA PELOTE**, a Basque ball game
PELTER rainstorm; shower of missiles
PELTRY skins with fur on them
pl **PELVIC** (pelvis)
pl **PELVIS** skeletal cavity (hips)
PENCIL light rays; small brush (graphite pen)
PENDED held up; balanced
PENFUL contents of a pen
pl **PENIAL** pertaining to penis; phallic
PENMAN scribe; author; clerk
PENNAL freshman (Ger.); student
PENNED wrote; indited; enclosed
PENNER writer; scribe
nt **PENNON** pennant; flag; streamer
PENSEE thought (Fr.) (literature)
PENSUM an imposition; examination
PENTAD set of five
PENT-UP confined; mewed
PENULT last but one
PENURY need; want; indigence
PEOPLE mob; rabble; populace; nation
PEPITA nugget of gold (Sp.)
bt **PEPLIS** water-purslane
PEPLUM PEPLUS, robe worn by Greek women
bt, ck **PEPPER** pelt with shot; capsicum, (cayenne) condiment
md **PEPSIN** (gastric juice)
PEPTIC digestive
PERDIE! pardieu!
PERDUE perdu; hidden; concealed
PERIOD age; era; term; epoch; stage
PERISH die; wither; expire; pass
PERKED smartened up; received extra benefits; encouraged
ck **PERKIN** perry; see parkin
PERMIT let; grant; sanction; tolerate
zo **PERNIS** honey-buzzard
PERONE fibula
PERRON external stairway
PERSIC Persian
PERSON individual; party; someone
PERTLY impudently; saucily
PERUKE a periwig; a vallancy
PERUSE read; scrutinize; observe
PESADE an equine evolution
nm **PESETA** Spanish money
PESHWA Mahratta chief (India)
PESTER vex; worry; harass; nettle
PESTLE for grinding with mortar
PETARD explosive machine; bomb
PETARY a peat-bog
PETITE small (Fr.); short and trim figure

zo **PETREL** sea-bird
ch **PETROL** gasoline
PETTED fondled; caressed; indulged
PETTLE indulge (Sc.)
PEWTER an alloy of tin and lead
bt **PEYOTE** cactus; source of mescalin
bt **PEZIZA** cup-shaped fungi
PHANIC visible; obvious
PHAROS lighthouse; world wonder (Gr.)
bt, ck **PHASEL** French bean
PHASIS PHASE, a stage of development
zo **PHASMA** leaf insects, etc.
PHATIC of speech as mood implement
ch **PHENIC** carbolic
PHENOL carbolic acid
ch **PHENYL** an organic radical
zo **PHINOC** sea trout
PHLEGM calmness; indifference
md **PHLEME** lancet
bt **PHLEUM** cat's-tail grass, etc.
bt **PHLOEM** bast tissue
md, cf **PHOBIA** morbid fear or aversion (Gr.)
PHOBOS a satellite of Mars
zo **PHOCAL** (seal)
rl **PHOEBE** the moon-goddess
zo **PHOLAS** stone-boring molluscs
PHONED telephoned
PHONEY specious; sham; bogus
cf **-PHONIA** of vocal disorder (Gr.)
PHONIC phonetic
me, ps **PHONON** quantum of thermal energy
md **PHORIA** lack of eye coordination
PHOSSY caused by phosphorus
cf **-PHOTIC** concerning light (Gr.)
me **PHOTON** unit of light energy
mu **PHRASE** idiom; diction; style; theme; motif; melody
bl **PHYLON** PHYLUM, biological group
bt, md **PHYSIC** dose; drug; medicine
cf **PHYSIO-** of the physical, body (Gr.)
ch **PHYTIC** of a cereal acid
PHYTON bud
PIACLE sin, crime
PIAFFE a horse gait (Sp.)
PIAZZA square; market place (It.)
PICARD high shoe (Fr.)
ch **PICENE** coal-tar hydrocarbon
PICKED selected; (pickpockets); taken
ag **PICKER** selector; collector; gatherer (fruit-)
PICKET sharp stake; guard; range-pole; striker at gate; railing (Am. football)

ck **PICKLE** to preserve in spices; jumbled
ro **PICK-UP** person of easy virtue; (motoring)
PICNIC alfresco meal
ch **PICRIC** trinitro-phenol; lyddite
PIDGIN merged version made of two (or more) languages
PIECED mended; joined; augmented
PIECER patcher
PIEDOG PYEDOG, a pariah; outcast
PIEMAN (Simple Simon); meatpies vendor
PIERCE drill; bore; perforate
zo **PIERID** of certain butterfly group
PIFFLE nonsense; worthless task
zo **PIGEON** a town dove; tell tale; sneak
PIGGIN small bowl
zo **PIGLET** PIGLING, a young porker
bt **PIGNON** pine seed
bt, ck **PIGNUT** carrot
PIG-STY pig enclosure
ck **PILAFF** PILAV, rice dish; savoury
pl **PILARY** hairy; comate
zo **PILEUM** top of head in birds
PILE-UP crash (motoring)
bt **PILEUS** mushroom cap
PILFER purloin; filch; steal; rob
PILING amassing; stacking; heaping
ar, mo **PILLAR** post; column; support; rock pinnacle
PILLED black-balled; vetoed; rejected
PILLOW a block; bearing; bed cushion
PILOSE PILOUS, hairy; comate
md **PILULA** PILULE, a small pill
PI-MODE multicavity magnetron operation
md **PIMPLE** a pustule; acne
PIMPLY having pimples
bt **PINANG** betel nut
wv **PINCOP** weft in power loom
PINDAR Greek poet
PINDER pinner; impounder
bt **PINEAL** like a pine-cone
ch **PINENE** terpene
bt **PINERY** hothouse
ro **PINGED** whistled by; bleeped (signalled)
PINGLE dawdle
PINING languishing; losing vigour
PINION feather; cogwheel; disable; bind fast
mn **PINITE** (iolite)
PINKED motoring (petrol effect)
PINNED fastened
PINNER pinmaker; pinder

PINNET pinnacle (Sc.)
PINOLE meal of sorts (USA)
nt PINTLE iron bolt
PINXIT he painted it (artist's name)
PIPAGE pipe-distribution
PIPING boiling; shrill; feeble
PIPKIN boiler; small pot
ck PIPPED pilled; just defeated; de-
stoned
bt PIPPIN apple
PIQUED offended; irritated
ga PIQUET card game; picket
PIRACY buccaneering; (copyright)
PIRATE freebooter; corsai; picaroon
nt PIRAUA PIROGUE, canoe, Atlantic
coast
PIRNIE night cap (Sc.)
bt PISANG plantain; banana
PISCES the fishes (Zodiac sign)
bt PISTIL part of flower
PISTOL a fire-arm
au, mu PISTON part of engine; valve (horn)
rl PITAKA Buddhist scriptures
PITCHY black; dark; tarry
PITHED central nervous system
destroyed
PITHOS round Greek vase
PITIED commiserated
PITIER a compassionate party
PITMAN a miner
to PITSAW large saw
ck PITTED pock-marked; challenged;
de-stoned
PLACED invested; ascribed; put
PLACER auriferous gravel
PLACET Latin affirmation; 'so be it'
PLACID serene; calm; even; tranquil
mu PLAGAL (Gregorian music)
PLAGUE pest; contagion; pester
PLAGUY vexatious; harassing
zo PLAICE flat fish
lw PLAINT lamentation; dirge; wail
zo PLAISE plaice
PLANCH to cover with planks
el, me PLANCK unit of action, one joule
second
PLANED smoothed; (aeroplane)
to PLANER planing machine
as PLANET a celestial body (solar
system)
zo PLANTA vertebrate foot sole
PLAQUE commemorative mark; an
ornament
md PLAQUE destructive coating on teeth
PLASHY sloppy
PLASMA ionised substance at solar
gas state temperature for nuclear
fusion purposes

md PLASMA quartz; blood liquids in
cells
bt PLATAN plane tree
PLATED overlaid; armoured
ce PLATEN the roller of a typewriter;
molten steel plates
zo PLATER race-horse
PLATEY flat
PLAYED sported; trifled; acted
mu PLAYER professional crickets
PLEACH interweave
PLEASE like; prefer; delight; oblige
PLEDGE promise; security for such;
pawn; toast
as PLEIAD a star
zo PLEION flat platelike structure
PLENTY abundance; profusion
PLENUM space; a full assembly
md PLEURA (lungs)
lw PLEVIN assurance
PLEXOR hammer used with
pleximeter
md PLEXUS nerve centre
PLIANT flexible; limber; lithe; facile
to PLIERS PLYERS, pincers for wire
work
PLIGHT promise; dilemma;
predicament
ar PLINTH pedestal
tx PLISSE pleated/woven cloth with
shirred effect
PLONGE superior slope of parapet
PLOUGH plow; furrow; to pluck
zo PLOVER bird
ag PLOWED ploughed; failed
(examination)
PLUCKY courageous; brave; bold
PLUFFY puffy (Sc.)
el, ro, cp PLUG-IN connect; detachable unit
PLUMAE stiff feathers
PLUMED took pride in
PLUMPY plump; fat; burly
PLUNGE dip; dive; sink; souse; (Am.
football)
PLURAL more than one
tx PLUSHY like plush (material)
PLUTUS the god of wealth
to PLYERS pliers
PLYING practising (trade); supplying
PLYING action of ferry boat
PLYING for hire (taxis); thread
twisting
mu PNEUMA breath; spirit; florid
passage
cf PNEUMA- of air, respiration (lung)
(Gr.)
POACHY set and soft
md POCKED pitted; scarred

POCKET pouch; cavity; (pick-); (thief)

PODERE country estate, farm (It.)

to **PODGER** tightening wrench for tubular coupling

bt **PODIAL** stalk-like

zo **PODITE** lobster's limb

bt **PODIUM** pedestal; rostrum; stylobate

gl **PODZOL PODSOL**, leached subpolar strata (Russian)

POETIC lyrical; metrical

POETRY poesy; verse

rl **POGROM** plunder and massacre (Rus.); persecution (of minorities)

POINTE tip of toes (ballet)

nt, rw **POINTS** switch-point, features of horse; score; angles; of compass, 32

POISED suspended in equilibrium

POISER a balancer

POISON venom; evil; kill (-gas) (-pen)

POKING thrusting

POLACK a Pole

ag, go **POLDER** reclaimed; drained land (Holland)

POLICE constabulary

POLICY statesmanship; strategy; plan

POLING scaffolding; punting

POLISH furbish; burnish; lustre

POLISH pertaining to Poland

POLITE courtly; urbane; civil

POLITY the constitution

lw **POLLAM** jurisdiction of Ind. chief

zo **POLLAN** a salmon-type of Irish fish

POLLED cropped; lopped; voted

bt **POLLEN** flower seed; fine bran

POLLER voter; tree-trimmer

md **POLLEX** thumb

POLLUX twin brother of Castor

ck **POLONY** sausage

ch **POLYAD** polygamous element

md, zo **POLYPE** polyp; aquatic animal; growth

POMACE crushed fruit

POMADE perfumed hair unguent

bt **POMELO** a citrus fruit; shaddock

POMMEL part of saddle; belabour

to, bd **POMMEL** flattener mallet (punner); knob; globular boss or knob; drum (American Indians)

mu **POMMER** ancient bassoon (shawn)

POMONA goddess of fruit

POM-POM quick-firing gun battery

POMPON ornament; a tuft

PONCHO cloak (S. America)

PONDER weigh; meditate; ruminate

PONENT western

tx **PONGEE** soft woven silk

rl **PONGYI** Buddhist priest (Burma)

gs, to **PONTEE** pontil; punty

PONTIC (Black Sea)

to **PONTIL** glass-maker's iron rod

PONTON lighter; pontoon

zo **POODLE** curly-haired dog

mu **POOGYE** nose-flute (Ind.)

POOLED shared; amalgamated

le **POOLER** leather worker

POONAC pulp refuse

POOPED overtaken by a wave (from aft)

POORER more impecunious; inferior (quality)

POORLY indisposed; unwell

POPERY Roman Catholicism

POPGUN an air gun of sorts

POPISH of Catholics; denigratory

bt **POPLAR** genus of trees; abele

tx **POPLIN** silk-cotton mix; shiny cotton

POPPED pawned; proposed; exploded

POPPER a pistol; popcorn; amyl nitrate, drug; plug; (angling)

POPPET puppet; head of a lathe

POPPLE to bob about

zo **PORGIE** bream fish

PORING sweating; brooding; studying

PORISM corollary

mn **PORITE** a species of coral

zo **PORKER** young pig

bt **POROID** having obvious pores

bt **POROSE** of pore-pierced cell walls

gl **POROUS** porose; interstitial limestone

bt **PORRET** small onion; leek

PORRON wine bottle with descending spout

PORTAL gate; entry; entrance

nt **PORTED** conveyed

PORTER door-keeper; carrier

PORTLY burly; stout; imposing

POSADA a Spanish inn (hotel)

POSEUR poser; an affected person (Fr.)

POSING feigning; puzzling; posturing

POSNET small bowl

ck **POSSET** a bedtime drink; potion

zo **POSSUM** opossum

POSTAL (order); (Union); (mail)

POSTEA record of subsequent events

POSTED set; stationed; hastened

POSTER bill; placard; advertisement; ball against goal-post (Am. football)

POSTIL marginal note; a homily
br POT-ALE distillery refuse
br POTALE grain refuse
ch POTASH alkali; potassium
bt POTATO murphy; a tuber
POTBOY a junior tapster; barman; bottle-washer
ck POTEEN home-made spirits (Irish)
POTENT efficacious; powerful; cogent
POTHER bother; bristle; fuss; ado
POTION dose; draught; philter
ck POT-LID a cover; stone on tee (curling)
POTMAN barman; general factotum
POTTAH lease (Ind.)
POTTED preserved; abbreviated
POTTER clay craftsman
me POTTLE 4 pints (2.2 litres); a tankard
POTTLE a small basket for fruit
POUDRE powdered (Fr.)
POUFFE a cushion (Fr.)
zo POULPE octopus; poulp
POUNCE jump suddenly; snatch; seize; prey
zo POUNCE claw of a bird of prey
POUNCE fine blotting powder
POURED uttered; flowed; gushed
POURER the lady of the tea-pot
POUSSE bitters added to a drink
POUTED registered displeasure facially
zo POUTER POWTER, pigeon having an inflated breast
POWDER crush; pulverize; sprinkle; ideal light snow surface (skiing)
POW-WOW incantation; conference (American Indian)
PRAISE laud; extol; eulogize; encomium
PRANCE to bound; to spring
ck PRANZO meal (It.)
PRATED orated; gabbled; talked
PRATER a chatter-box
PRAXIS use; practice; an example
PRAYED supplicated; craved; besought
PRAYER petition; entreaty; orison
PREACH teach; exhort; declare
rl PRECIS prayers
PRECIS summary; abstract
PRECUT ready-sliced; -shaped (portions)
PREDAL rapacious; voracious; ravenous
ar PREFAB a prefabricated house
PREFER pick; select; choose; promote

PREFIX appoint beforehand; word; code qualifier
PREPAY pay in advance
cf PRESBY- of old, aged (Gr.)
PRESEE foresee; anticipate; foretell
PRESES chairman (Sc.)
mu PRESTO quickly; (conjuror) (It.)
cf PRETER- beyond
lw PRETOR PRAETOR, Roman judge
PRETTY neat; comely; pleasing
PRETTY the fairway of a golf course
PRE-WAR from before a war
PREYED ravened; ravaged; despoiled
PREYER a plunderer; freebooter
PRICED appraised; valued
PRICEY expensive
PRIDED plumed; arrogated
rl PRIEST pastor; divine; minister
PRIMAL primary; main; first; original
pt PRIMER detonator; pre-paint; text-book
pr PRIMER prayer-book; type of type
bt PRIMET PRIVET, shrub
PRIMLY precisely; formally; demurely
rl PRIMUS bishop (Sc.); first
PRINCE heir to sovereign; ruler; lord
rl PRIORY monastery
PRISED prized; levered; (opened)
PRISMY prismatic
PRISON jail; gaol; quod; restrain
bt PRIVET genus of shrub; primet
PRIZED valued; esteemed
PRIZER an appraiser
ch, tx PROBAN flameproof fabric finish
PROBUD reproductive bodies in cyclo-myaria
PROFIT gain; benefit; advantage
PROKER a poker (dial.)
pl PROLAN mammal pregnancy hormone
zo PROLEG a caterpillar's leg
PROLIX long-winded; verbose
PROMPT urge; incite; quick; apt
cp PROMPT message from system to operator; (theatre) (cues)
PRONTO precipitately; at once!
zo PROPED pseudo-leg
PROPEL hurl; cast; throw; impel
PROPER correct; accurate; seemly
PROSED conversed in lengthy periods
PROSER tedious speaker
PROSIT! here's luck! a toast! (Germ.)
bt PROTEA S. African flowering shrubs
PROTON electrical nucleus
PROVED tested; verified; established

PROVEN proved; justified
PROVER demonstrator; assayer
PRUINA powdery bloom on plant surfaces
PRUNED trimmed; clipped; lopped
bt **PRUNUS** genus of trees and shrubs
nm **PRUTAH** Israeli coin
PRYING peeping; curious; inquisitive
cp **PSEUDO** false; spurious; imitation; a pre-machine code
md **PSORIC** (psora); itchy
PSYCHE maiden beloved by Cupid; soul; mind
cf, pc **PSYCHO-** of mind; psyche (Gr.)
zo **PTERIC** of wing or shoulder
bt **PTERIS** fern genus
zo **PTERNA** heel-pad in birds
PTERON Greek portico
PTOSIS (fallen eyelid)
bt **PTYXIS** leaf-folding in bud
PUBLIC open; common; general
PUCKER wrinkle; crease; furrow
PUDDLE muddy pool; (iron)
PUDDLY dirty; foul; bespattered
PUDEUR sexual modesty (Fr.)
PUEBLO S. American town or village (Sp.)
PUENTE carved trestle table (Spain)
PUFFED fuffed; blown
zo, nt, rw **PUFFER** globe-fish; coastal steam cargo vessel (Sc.) (loco)
zo **PUFFIN** bird; an auk
zo **PUG-DOG** a lap-dog
PUGREE Indian hat scarf
PUISNE inferior in rank
PUKKHA pucka; real (Ind.)
PULING whimpering; whining
PULLED drawn; hauled; extracted
PULLER hauler; an attraction
zo **PULLET** young hen
to **PULLEY** grooved wheel; tackle (crane)
PULL-IN PULL-UP, roadside halt
PULL-ON boxing gloves
PULPED PULPER, mashed; machine-shredded
rl **PULPIT** rostrum; ambo
ck **PULQUE** a Mexican beverage
as **PULSAR** space radio-energy source
PULSED throbbed; vibrated
PULTUN native infantry regiment (Ind.)
PULVIL scented powder
ar **PULVIN** dosseret, supercapital (Byzant.)
nt **PULWAR** sailing dugout, cargo boat Ind.
PUMELO pomelo; shaddock; fruit

bd, mn, gl **PUMICE** spongy lava; powder (pounce) for stencils; -stone
PUMPED forced transfer of liquids, gas; interrogated (tyres) (-dry); exhausted
PUMPER cross-examiner; pump man
PUNCHI Kashmiri people
PUNCHY fat; stocky
ga **PUNCTO** point (fencing); punctual
PUNDIT savant; wiseacre; guru; authority
bt **PUNICA** pomegranate
PUNIER weaker; feebler; smaller
PUNISH correct; chasten; scourge
PUNKAH fan (Ind.)
to **PUNNER** a ram; maul; word-joker
PUNNET basket for fruit
PUNTED betted; kicked
PUNTER gambler
zo **PUPATE** from caterpillar to pupa
zo **PUPOID** like a chrysalis
PUPPED whelped; littered
PUPPET doll; marionette; pawn
rl **PURANA** sacred Sanskrit books
PURDAH curtain; seclusion
PURELY simply; clearly; really
PUREST without blemish
tx **PURFLE** embroider
PURFLY wrinkled
PURGED cleaned; purified; shriven
PURGER an aperient; laxative
PURIFY cleanse; clean
ch **PURINE** uric acid compound, toxin
PURISM precision; nicety; exactness
PURIST stickler for style
PURITY chastity; fineness; simplicity
PURLED curled; swirled; knitted
PURLER a fall; a cropper
PURLIN a roof timber
rl **PURPLE** colour; dye; mollusc; imperial; cardinalate
PURPLE ornate (prose); rhetorical
PURRED curred, (cats or pigeons)
PURSED contracted; wrinkled
nt **PURSER** paymaster; supply chief
PURSUE follow; track; chase; practise
PURVEY sell; cater; retail; procure
· **PUSHED** urged; impelled; jostled
nt, rw **PUSHER** type of plane; thruster; tugboat; locomotive
PUSHER thruster; salesman; street hawker
PUSH-IN gatecrash; struggle; (hockey)
PUSHTU Afghan tongue
bt **PUSULE** small plant vacuole
PUTEAL well-curb
nt **PUTELI** Ganges boat

PUTLOG short board; putlock

ga **PUT-OUT** irritated; thwarted; laid; displayed; dismissed (cricket, baseball)

PUTRID corrupt; rotten; decaying

PUTSCH revolt attempt (Ger.)

ga **PUTTED** took short green shot (golf)

PUTTEE cloth legging

PUTTER a golf club

tx **PUTTOO** goat's-wool cloth

PUZZLE bewilder; enigma; problem

PUZZLE a solver's delight (jigsaw) (crossword-)

bt **PYCNID** (fungus' spores)

mu **PYCNON** a semi-tone

zo **PYEDOG** piedog; a pariah

md **PYEMIA** blood-poisoning

md **PYEMIC** septicaemic

zo **PYGARG** antelope (Herodotus)

zo **PYGARG** osprey or sea-eagle

md **PYKNIC** fat (of persons)

zo **PYLOME** opening in sarcodina

md **PYOSIS** formation of pus

bt **PYRENE** fruit stone

ch **PYRENE** tar product

mn **PYRITE** a shining mineral; (poor man's gold)

md **PYROLA** wintergreen

ch **PYRONE** heterocyclic compound

mn **PYROPE** garnet

PYTHIA Delphic oracle priestess

zo **PYTHON** serpent (slain by Apollo)

md **PYURIA** pus in urine

Q

QIVIUT underneath hair of musk-ox (Inuit)

QUADRA square frame or border

zo **QUAGGA** extinct zebra (S. Africa)

QUAGGY boggy; marshy

zo **QUAHOG** clam (N. America)

QUAICH QUAIGH, drinking cup; tassie (Sc.)

QUAINT droll; fantastic; curious; odd

QUAKED shook; quivered; rocked

QUAKER member of Society of Friends

QUALLY wine that has gone off

QUANTA (plural of quantum) a quantity of anything

QUARRY pit; prey; victim; an arrow

QUARTE guard (fencing)

pr **QUARTO** a size of book

mn **QUARTZ** silica (double refracting)

ps, ch **QUARTZ** crystal with varying polarization

as **QUASAR** far-space radio-energy source

mu **QUAVER** quiver; tremble; vibrate; ⅛ note

bd, nt **QUAYED** having a wharf; jettied

QUBBAH domed tomb (Arabic)

QUEASY squeamish; fastidious

zo **QUEEST** ring-dove

zo **QUELEA** weaver-bird

QUENCH extinguish (fire); slake (thirst)

QUERRY equerry; groom; courtier

zo **QUESAL QUEZAL**, resplendent trogon; brilliant green bird

QUEUED lined up (waited turn)

ck **QUICHE** egg flan with savoury filling

QUIDAM somebody (Lat.)

QUIHYE Anglo-Indian (Bengal)

bt **QUILCH** couch grass

zo **QUILLS** feather pens, porcupine spikes

bt, ck **QUINCE** fruit (jelly)

md **QUINIC** (quinine)

bt **QUINOA** Mexican oats

pg **QUINOL** reducing agent

md **QUINSY** tonsilitis

QUINTA manor, large farm (wine grower's) (Portugal)

ga **QUINZE** card game (of 15)

pr, mu **QUIRED** in quires; sang in harmony

QUIRKY evasive; artful; illusive

bt **QUITCH** couch grass

QUIVER case for arrows; vibrate

nt **QUODDY** open fishing boat (Maine, N. America)

ar, bd **QUOINS** dressed corner stones

ga **QUOITS** ring-throwing game (deck)

lw **QUORUM** sufficiency of attendance

QUOTED referred; repeated; mentioned

QUOTER a citer

QUOTHA forsooth

QUOTUM share; proportion

Q-VALUE the amount of energy produced in nuclear reaction

R

RABATE beat down; abatement

RABATO turned-down collar; rebato (It.)

rl **RABBAN** super-rabbi

cr **RABBET** a groove in a plank

RABBIN Jewish lawyer or rabbi

zo **RABBIT** timid breeder and burrower; weak player; lesser person

me **RABBLE** the mob; iron puddling bar

md, vt **RABIES** canine (human) hydrophobia
bt **RACEME** a cluster
bt, zo **RACHIS** backbone; spine
RACIAL ethnic; colour judgement
RACILY piquantly; spicily; pungently
ga **RACING** speed contest (men, horses, cars, etc.)
RACISM ethnic or colour superiority attitude
RACKED strained; wrestled; stretched; (storage)
RACKER a torturer; storer
RACKET snow-shoe; clamour; (tennis) broad bat; fraud
RACKLE rattle; crackle
cp **RACK-UP** video information; lines ascending
RADDLE twist; red ochre
nt **RADEAU** scow defence ship (N. Amer.)
RADIAL extending outward from a centre
RADIAN an angle of 57.3 degrees
bt **RADISH** plant
mn **RADIUM** metal
bt, md **RADIUS** bone of forearm; half a diameter
RADIUS crane load formula based distance
nt **RADOUB** recaulking of ship's hull
zo **RADULA** mollusc's tongue
RAFALE burst of fire; squall
RAFFED swept; huddled together
nt **RAFFEE** schooner sail
bt **RAFFIA** palm fibre
RAFFLE sweeptstake; draw; lottery
bd, nt **RAFTER** roof-timber; lumberman (river)
RAG DAY students' carnival
tx **RAGBAG** odd scraps of fabric
RAGGED jagged; uneven; torn
RAGGED bullied; persecuted
bt **RAGGEE** Indian millet
RAGGLE notch irregularly; raglet
RAGING wroth; rabid; furious; storm
RAGLAN loose overcoat style
ar, bd **RAGLET** narrow masonry groove
RAGMAN rag-picker
ck **RAGOUT** stew; a spicy mixture
RAG-TAG riff-raff
hd **RAGULY** jagged
RAIBLE rabble (Sc.)
RAIDER invader; plunderer (sudden) (night) (cops)
RAILER scoffer; sneerer
RAISER producer
bt, ck **RAISIN** a dried grape

RAJPUT Royal Hindu
RAKERY debauchery
RAKING inclining; enfilading
RAKISH dissolute; licentious
zo **RALLUS** water-rails; etc.; birds
bt **RAMAGE** boughs of tree
nv **RAMARK** non-directional radio beacon
RAMBLE excursion; stroll; roam (on foot)
zo **RAM-CAT** tom-cat (male)
bt **RAMEAL** branching
bt **RAMENT** bristle-shaped leaflet
RAMIFY branch; divide; sub-divide
RAMISM system of logic
ae **RAMJET** open duct combustion
RAMMED butted; crammed
RAMMEL refuse wood
to **RAMMER** sand-packing hand tool
bt **RAMOON** mulberry (W. Indies)
RAMOUS branched
RAMPED bounded; sprang; sloped
RAMPER race-course rough
RAMROD gun-bore stuffer
bt **RAMSON** hedgerow garlic
bt **RAMULE** small branch
RANCHO ranch; stock farm
RANCID sour; musty; fetid
nt **RANDAN** a row boat
RANDLE plate rack
RANDOM casual; haphazard; fortuitous
cp **RANDOM** numbers production
RANGED extended; disposed
fr **RANGER** forest guard (parks); commando; (free-) rover
zo **RANGIA** a bivalve genus
zo **RANINE** frog-like
RANKER fouler; officer from the ranks
RANKLE resent; remain bitter
RANKLY rampantly; excessively
RANSOM money to free a hostage
RANTAN clatter of pots and pans
RANTER spouter; boisterous preacher
md **RANULA** frog-tongue
bt **RAPHIA** raffia; palm fibre
bt **RAPHIS** crystal in plant cell
mu, rw **RAPIDO** with rapidity; express
RAPIER a thrusting sword
RAPINE pillage; spoliation; plunder; rape
RAPING ravishing; violating
RAPPED tapped; struck
RAPPEE snuff
RAPPEL call to arms
nm **RAPPEN** Swiss centime (coin)

RAPPER knocker; arouser (disasters)

zo **RAPTOR** a bird of prey

RAPTUS trance; seizure

RAREFY attenuate

RARELY seldom; infrequently

RAREST sparsest; thinnest; scarcest

RARITY scarcity; fewness; tenuity

RASANT flanking; raking

RASCAL rogue; scamp; knave; caitiff

ck **RASHER** to thin slice (bacon); more reckless

RASHLY audaciously; recklessly

bd **RASING** razing; levelling; demolishing

RASPED filed; abraded; grated

RASPER scraper; stiff fence

tv **RASTER** beam picture on screen; video signal

bt **RATANY** Peruvian shrub

tx **RATEEN** ratteen; woollen fabric

RATHER sooner; preferably; slightly

RATIFY confirm; endorse; approve

tx **RATINE** rough-surface dress fabric

nt **RATING** tonnage; class; seaman; popularity scale; (rowing)

RATION share; quota; portion

zo **RATITE** flat-breasted

nt, tx **RATLIN** (shrouds)

bt **RATOON** sugarcane sprout

RATRAC snow compressor vehicle for clearing pistes (skiing)

bt **RATTAN** drum-beat; basketry

RAT-TAT postman's knock

RATTED deserted; informed upon

RATTEN stealing non-unionists' tools

RATTER rat-catcher

mu **RATTLE** chatter; vibrate; a herb; baby's toy; (snake); (rarely) percussion

RAUCID raucous; hoarse

RAUCLE rough; fearless (Sc.)

RAVAGE spoil; lay waste; ransack

go **RAVINE** gulch; gulley; gorge; defile

RAVING delirious; ranging; frenzied

RAVISH rape; violate; delight

RAWISH somewhat raw

RAYING radiating; shining

zo **RAY-OIL** ray-fish oil

RAZING overthrowing; rasing

pr **RAZURE** rasure; an erasure

RAZZIA a foray (Algerian); police raid

READER proof corrector; reading book

READER (TV news-); University title

REALIA 3-dimensional exhibits

REALLY truly; verily; actually

lw **REALTY** real estate

REAMED frothed; enlarged; edged

to **REAMER** belling tool (drilled holes)

REAPED acquired; cropped; obtained

ag **REAPER** harvester; a machine; death

REARED erected; educated

REARER up-bringer; guardian (foster-)

REASON logic; rational approach; motive; discuss; intelligence; excuse

REASTY rancid; rotting

REAVED bereaved; robbed

REAVER reiver; freebooter

REAVOW avow again; re-pledge

pr **RE-BACK** to repair spine of book

mn **REBATE** discount; abatement; blunt; freestone

REBATO a ruff; rabato

mu **REBECK** Moorish violin

REBIND refasten

pr **REBITE** engraving; acid process

ck **REBOIL** seethe again; re-heat

au **REBORE** worn-cylinder treatment

REBORN re-incarnated ('born again')

ga **REBOTE** (pelota)

REBUFF snub; repel; repulse

REBUKE upbraid; reprove; chide

REBURY inter again

RECALL revoke; rescind; retract

RECANT adjure; renounce; deny

RECAST compute again

RECEDE ebb; decrease; withdraw

RECENT modern; late; new; novel

RECEPT RECEIPT, having received; obtained

RECESS niche; alcove; nook; interval; adjournment

ck **RECIPE** prescription; formula; cooking

RECITE tell; relate; repeat; recount

RECKED regarded; heeded

RECKON deem; calculate; estimate

rl **RECOAL** refuel (locomotives)

ck **RECOCT** reconcoct; vamp up

RECOIL kick; rebound (gun); shrink

nm **RECOIN** remint

RECORD enter; note; achievement

mu **RECORD** achievement; (disc) evidence

cp **RECORD** archives; memory; filed data

RECOUP indemnify; make good

rl **RECTOR** academic leader; vicar

RECTUM section of intestine above anus

zo **RECTUS** equal-width muscle

md **RECURE** cure again

lw **RECUSE** reject; withdraw statement

pr **REDACT** to reduce; to edit

bt **REDBUD** Judas tree

zo **REDCAP** goldfinch; military policeman

REDDED tidied; arranged (Sc.)

pt **REDDEN** blush; red colour (rouge)

REDDLE raddle; red chalk

ck **RED-DOG** low-grade flour; (Am. football)

lw **REDEEM** ransom; free; retrieve; repay

zo **RED-EYE** rudd; carp

bt **RED-GUM** eucalyptus

RED-HOT extreme

bt **RED-LAC** Japanese wax-tree

bt **RED-OAK** N. American oak

REDOUT fort

mu **REDOWA** Bohemian dance

REDRAW redraft; copy

bt **RED-TOP** kind of grass

REDUCE degrade; curtail; abridge; decrease

REDUCT a diminution in size

REDUIT redoubt; redout; bastion; fort

RED-WUD stark mad (Sc.)

zo **REEBOK** rhebok; S. African antelope

RE-ECHO repeat; reverberate

REECHY REEKIE, smokey (city) (Sc.)

REEDED covered with reeds

bt **REEDEN** (reeds)

RE-EDIT compile new edition

nt **REEFER** wind-jacket; drugged cigarette

nt **REEFER** refrigerated ship

REEKED exhaled; fumed; stank of

REEKIE smoky (city) (Sc.)

REELED staggered; spun; swayed

zo **REELER** the grasshopper warbler

bd, pt **RE-FACE** redecoration (wall); reoppose (ice hockey)

ga **REFAIT** a draw game (Fr.)

pg **REFILL** replenish; film cassette

RE-FIND retrieve

REFINE clarify; purify; cleanse

REFLET iridescent glaze

ae **REFLEX** reactive; introspective; automatic reaction; wing structure

ma **REFLEX** angle greater than ½ circle

REFLOW re-issue

REFLUX ebb; return; redound

REFOLD replicate

lw **REFORM** make; remodel; betterment

REFUEL take in more fuel

REFUGE security; sanctuary; asylum; traffic 'island'

REFUND repay; return; restore

REFUSE veto; decline; deny; trash

REFUTE disprove; confute

REGAIN retrieve; recover; recapture

REGALE feast; entertain; honour

REGALO a gift; a sumptuous repast (Sp.)

REGARD note; watch; repute

REGENT ruling; a ruler during minority

REGIME system; administration; government; diet regimen, rules

REGINA title of queen

REGION province; tract; vicinity

· **REGIUS REGIUM**, appointed by the Crown

lw **REGIVE** restore (title, rights)

pr **REGLET** flat moulding

pr **REGLET** spacing block

REGLOW to recalesce; rekindle

REGNAL during the reign of

REGNUM badge of royalty

REGRET rue; deplore; remorse

lw, rl **REGULA** book of rules

REHASH discuss again; rearrange

pr **REHEAD** apply new heading

md **RE-HEAL** to heal again

RE-HEEL shoe repair

REIGLE a channel or guide

REINED harnessed; restrained; steered

REIVER reaver; robber; freebooter

REJECT jilt; spurn; discard; repudiate

REJOIN respond critically

RE-JOIN link up again

REJOLT a new shock

RELAID (carpets)

RELAIS a rampart walk (Fr.)

ae **RELAND** land again

RELATE tell; recite; narrate; report

RELENT become less severe, harsh

RELIED depended on; confided

RELIEF aid; redress; alleviation

RELIER a trusting person

RELISH appreciate; zest; gusto; taste

RELIVE revive

cp **RELOAD** recharge; refill; system recovery time

RELUME to rekindle

REMADE remanufacture; refashioned

REMAIN persist; tarry; stop; survive

REMAKE make anew; revamp

REMAND send back to custody

REMARK state; comment; observation

REMEDY cure; panacea

zo **REMIGE** large wing contour feather

REMIND rearouse memory

lw **REMISE** release; give back; renewed attack (fencing)

REMISS slack; dilatory; negligent

zo **REMORA** a sucking fish

REMOTE distant; (-control); (space, time, relation)

REMOVE transfer (chattels); relationship

REMOVE dislodge; transport; eject

hd **REMPLI** heraldic colouring

lw **RENAME** change name; re-christen

zo **RENARD** Reynard, a fox

RENATE renewed; born again

RENDER return; assign; supply; restore

RENEGE to revoke (cards); break oath or promise

ck **RENNET** enzyme for cheesemaking

md **RENNIN** gastric juice ferment

RENOWN fame; eminence; repute

RENTAL money paid for house, car, tv

lw **RENTED** hired (tenancy) (contract)

RENTER hires out flats, films, cars, tv

RENTES French Government securities

md **RENULE** small kidney

lw **RE-OPEN** restart (file) (case)

REPACE retrace one's steps; re-measure

REPAID compensated; requited (loans)

REPAIR patch; mend; restore; wend

REPAND bent back

RE-PART share; divide again

ck **REPAST** a meal; victuals; food

lw **REPEAL** annul; rescind; nullify

REPEAT iterate; renew; echo

REPENT beg forgiveness; apologize; rue; regret

REPINE fret; complain; murmur

RE-PLAN re-design; re-arrange

lw **REPONE** re-appoint

REPORT rumour; relate; bang

REPOSE lie; recline; rest

REPOUR re-issue

REPPED ribbed

REPUGN oppose (Shak.)

REPUTE reputation; renown; regard

RESAIL put to sea again

RESALE a second sale

RESCUE release from danger; save

RESEAT repair; change-seating

RESEAU a network (Fr.)

md, sv **RESECT** cut off

bt **RESEDA** mignonette genus

RESELL re-market

RESENT dislike; repel; resist; hate

RESIDE live; dwell; lodge; sojourn

RESIGN relinquish a post; submit

RESILE ability to recover; readjust

RESINY resinous; rosiny

RESIST oppose; thwart; withstand

RESORB swallow up

RESORT recourse; (holiday)

RESTED reposed; quieted; paused

RESTEM force back; recheck

bt **RESTIO** plant genus

RESULT ensue; outcome; sequel; end

RESUME renew; summarize; synopsis

RETAIL sell in a shop; explain

RETAIN hold; keep; reserve; detain

RETAKE recapture

RETARD clog; hinder; impede; check

ch **RETENE** coal-tar constituent

lw **RETENT** assets held back

RE-TEST try again; re-adjust; reset

pl **RETINA** a network of optic nerves; screen of sight

md **RETINE** cancer cell growth inhibitor

RETIRE recede; withdraw; shrink

RETOLD already narrated

RETOOK regained; recaptured

RETORT rejoinder; distilling vessel

bt **RETOSE** reticulated

RETOSS throw again

RETOUR return (Sc.)

RETRAD backward

RETRAL posterior; retrorse

pr **RETREE** paper refuse; wastage

RETRIM embellish; smarten up

RETUND to dull; to blunt

RETURN also re-turn; restore; recur

RETUSE blunt

ar, bd **REVALE** of cornices completed in position

REVAMP renovate; remake

ar **REVEAL** disclose; divulge; unveil; part of jamb

REVERE adore; venerate; honour

REVERS revere; lapel (jacket)

lw **REVERT** return of assets (trusts)

REVERT to previous circumstances

REVERY reverie; dream; trance

REVIEW survey; inspect; journal

REVILE asperse; traduce; defame

REVISE reconsider; improve; correct

REVIVE rouse; invigorate; quicken

REVOKE annul; cancel; quash

REVOLT rebel; nauseate; mutiny

REVVED rotated at speed (motor)

REWARD guerdon; repay; premium

REWOOD afforest

REWORD change the phraseology

REXISM REXIST, Royalist party,
Belgium
RHAGON form of sponge
bt RHAPIS genus of Chinese palms
zo RHESUS bandar; Indian monkey
md RHEUMY watery; rheumatic
bt RHEXIA genus of flowering plants
md RHEXIS rupture of bodily structure
zo RHINAE shark genus
md RHINAL nasal
bt RHIZIC radicle; root-like
ch RHUSMA a depilatory
RHYMED versified
RHYMER versifier
RHYMIC almost poetic
zo RHYSSA ichneumon flies
RHYTHM cadence; metre; symmetry
RHYTON Assyrian drinking vessel
ceramic or metal
ar RIALTO a bridge in Venice
RIANCY gaiety; laughter
RIBALD coarse; rude; gross; lewd
nt, cr RIBAND ribbon (blue-); palisade rail
RIBBED ridged; furrowed
cr RIBBON riband; strip; saw; hand
apparatus (gymn)
mu RIBIBE REBEC, old woman (obs.)
RIBLET rudimentary rib
ch RIBOSE pentose sugar in vitamin B-
2
bt RICCIA a plant genus
RICHEN enrich; enhance
RICHER wealthier
RICHES abundance; affluence
RICHLY opulently; sumptuously
RICKED piled; sprained
fr RICKER thin round timber
RICKLE small pile or rick (Sc.)
RICTAL gaping
RICTUS open mouth
rl RIDDEL altar-curtain
RIDDEN went riding; (bed-); infested
(lice-)
RIDDLE sieve; enigma; rebus
(grate)
RIDEAU curtain (theatre) (Fr.)
RIDGED ribbed; furrowed
RIDING county sub-division (Yorks);
(horse-)
RIEVER reaver; robber; pirate
RIFELY abundantly
pr, to RIFFLE engraving tool; small shallow
rapid (canoeing)
RIFLED pillaged; grooved (gun
barrel)
RIFLER robber; freebooter;
plunderer; soldier
RIFTED cleft; split

nt RIGGED the setout of sailships;
(tackle) (machinery)
RIGGED uniformed; manipulated
(finance); (elections) (markets)
to, pt RIGGER mechanic; fitter; long-haired
brush; (rowing)
nt RIGGER out-rigger (sailing);
equipment (parachuting)
zo RIGGLE sand-eel
cr RIGLET (see reglet); flat piece of
wood
RIGOUR rigidity; austerity; harshness
RIG-OUT complete outfit; uniform
RILING annoying; irritating
RILLED trilled; flowed
go RILLET rivulet; stream
RIMIST writer of doggerel
RIMLET thin rim
RIMMED bordered; edged
ck, to RIMMER pastry cutter
rl RIMMON Syrian god
RIMOSE RIMOUS, gnarled
RIMPLE wrinkle; rumple
to RIMSAW edging saw
mn RIMULA fossil limpets
RINDED peeled
RINDLE gutter; runnel; rine
RINGED encircled
RINGER expert shearer (Australia)
RINKED roller-skated
RINSED laved; cleansed; cleared
RINSER (washing machine)
RIOTED brawled; luxuriated
RIOTER disturber of the peace
nt RIPECK REPECK, RYPECK, punt pole
for mooring
RIPELY maturely
RIPEST mellowest
RIP-OFF overcharging; defrauding;
robbery
RIPPED torn; split; stripped;
vandalized
nt, to RIPPER murderer; saw; cutter;
speedster
pt RIPPLE flax-comb; small wave;
fiddleback (sycamore); finish
RIPPLY rippling
RIPRAP broken stone used for walls
to RIPSAW a ripper
RISALA troop of native cavalry
RISBAN defended ground
ae RISERS parachutists' webbing straps
RISING insurrection; towering
RISKED chanced; ventured (capital)
RISKER gambler; venturer
RISLEY an acrobat
RISQUE indelicate; audacious (Fr.)
RITELY with due rites

RITTER a knight (Ger.)
RITUAL rite; ceremony
go **RIVAGE** the coast; shore; bank (Fr.)
RIVERY riparian; of the shores
bt **RIVINA** the pokeweed genus
RIVING splitting; rending
RIVOSE tabby; furrowed
RIZZER dry in the sun (Sc.)
bt **RIZZER** a red currant (Sc.)
ROAMED ranged; rambled
ROAMER nomad; vagrant; stroller
ROARED bawled; guffawed
zo **ROARER** broken-winded horse
zo **ROBALO** a fish (USA)
ROBBED stole; despoiled; purloined
ROBBER brigand; bandit; burglar
ROBBIN spun-yarn
zo **ROBERD** chaffinch
ROBING attiring; dressing
ROBUST sturdy; vigorous; hale;
  hearty
zo **ROCCUS** striped bass fish
bt **ROCHEA** a plant genus
zo **ROCHET** fish; the roach
rl **ROCHET** bishop's surplice
ROCKED reeled; tottered
ROCKEL a woman's cloak
ROCKER mining cradle; (swivel
  chair); compulsory figure (ice
  skating)
rw **ROCKET** Stephenson's locomotive
  1829
ae, sp **ROCKET** firework; jet transport;
  alarm; salad herb
zo **ROCKIE** rock-linnet
ar **ROCOCO** florid style
bt **RODDIN** rowan-tree (Sc.)
zo **RODENT** gnawing; small mammal
RODING evening flight
gl **ROGGAN** logan; rocking stone
ROILED riled; vexed
ROINEK Boer name for British
  soldier
ROLAND legendary hero
ROLLED trundled; rotated; turned
ROLLER road-levelling vehicle
zo **ROLLER** wave; blue crow; a sect
cp **ROLL-IN** hockey; to garage;
  activating process
cp **ROLL-ON** (ferry); copying file
bd **ROLOCK** brick on edge bond
ROMAIC modern Greek
ROMANT exaggerate; romance
ROMANY gipsy; gipsy language
zo **ROMERO** pilot-fish
rl **ROMIST** papist
ROMPED frolicked; gambolled;
  sported

ROMPER garment; overall costume
mu **RONDEL RONDEAU**, poem, music
  cycle
RONDLE bastion trust
ROOFED covered
ROOFER tiler
ROOKED cheated
ROOKER swindler
ROOKIE recruit
ROOKLE rootle
ROOMED lodged; housed;
  accommodated
ROOMER lodger (in bedsit or
  dormitory)
ROOPIT hoarse; roopy; roupy
ROOTED firmly based (plant)
  (family)
ROOTER grubber; towed scarifier
ROOTLE rookle; poke about like a pig
ROPERY rope walk (factory)
ROPING lassoing
ga **ROQUET** (croquet)
rl **ROSARY** Catholic string of prayer
  beads
ROSCID dewy; roric
ROSEAL rose-like
ROSERY a rose garden
ROSIED adorned with roses
ROSING sprinkling
ROSINY resiny
ROSSER policeman (slang)
bt **ROSTEL** embryo root; radicle
ROSTER duty list; roll of names
bt **ROSULA** small rose
ROTARY rotatory
ROTATE spin; revolve; take turns;
  (wheel on axis)
ROTCHE little auk
ROT-GUT bad liquor
ROTTED disintegrated; decayed
ROTTEN corrupt; rank; moribund
ROTTER a pestilent person
md **ROTULA** knee-cap
ROTUND round; spherical
ROTURE plebeian rank (Fr.)
nm **ROUBLE** 100 kopecks (Russian)
ROUCOU a dye (annatto)
ROUGED powdered (rosy cosmetic)
ROUGET swine-fever
ga **ROUNCE** a pulley; card game
zo **ROUNCY** a nag; a hack
ROUSED ruffled; agitated; provoked
ROUSER a stimulator; inciter
ROUTED fled in disorder; defeated
ROUTED planned itinerary; direction
cp, to **ROUTER** sash-plane; message
  switching selector; plough
ROUTLE grub up; rootle

ROVERY roving; nomadism
ROVING rambling; ranging
ROWING sculling
bt ROYALS (family); of Western Red
  Cedar
bt ROYENA ebony
nt RUA-PET coastal vessel (Siam)
mn RUBACE rock crystal
mu RUBATO change of rhythm
RUBBED wiped; scoured; chafed;
  galled
ga RUBBER coagulated latex; set of 3
  games (cards, sports)
RUBBLE undressed stone
RUBBLY broken
RUBIAN madder colour
RUBIED red as a ruby
RUBIFY to redden
bt RUBIGO mildew, rust (fungi) (rot)
RUBINE crimson dye; rubin
RUB-OFF incidental harm, side-effect
  of an action
pr, rl RUBRIC a heading in red
  (prayerbook)
RUCKLE wrinkle; pucker
nt, ae RUDDER boat guiding device;
  trailing fin on aircraft
RUDDLE red chalk or ochre
zo RUDDOC RUDDOCK, robin redbreast
bt, nm RUDDOC kind of apple; gold coin
RUDELY boorishly; insolently;
  impolitely
RUDEST most savage; crudest
RUEFUL mournful; sad; melancholy
RUELLE a coterie
ga RUFFED trumped; finessed (bridge)
RUFFER comb for flax
zo RUFFIN freshwater perch
RUFFLE a pleated border; disorder
RUFOUS ruddy; florid
RUGATE wrinkled; furrowed
RUGGED ragged; harsh; austere
ga RUGGER Rugby football
to RUGINE surgeon's rasp
mn RUGOSA corals
RUGOSE RUGOUS, RUGATE, wrinkled
RUINED wrecked; destroyed;
  beggared
RUINER demolisher
RULING governing; ascendant
RULLEY a dray
RUMBLE carriage-seat; reverberate
RUM-BUD grog-blossom
zo RUMKIN tailless fowl
bd RUMMEL soakway; dry well; pit
RUMMER drinking glass
RUMOUR report; bruit; hearsay
RUMPLE rimple; crumple; pucker

RUMPUS uproar; disturbance
nt RUM-TUM Thames sculling boat
RUNDLE a ladder-rung; a spoke
RUNKLE wrinkle
go RUNLET RUNNEL, rivulet
nt RUN-MAN naval deserter (obs.)
bt, ck RUNNER rotating part of water wheel
  turbine; (coward); (plant gone to
  seed); (bean)
RUNNER plough guide; timber joists;
  withies; (ski-) (sledge-)
RUNNER racer; messenger
ck RUNNET rennet for cheesing making
RUN-OFF experimental, production-
  line method
RUN-OFF printing batch; drain;
  cattle stealing; abduct; compose
  rapidly; deviate from fixed route
  (horse racing); rainfall course
RUNOFF final contest; election; river
  floodwater
RUN-OUT rope length between
  mountaineers
RUN-OUT cricket; experiment
RUNRIG land tenure (Sc.)
ae, pb RUNWAY track; airfield take-off path
nm RUPIAH (Indonesia)
bt RUPPIA a grass genus
bt RUSCUS butcher's broom
RUSHED dashed; flew; ran; plunged
bt RUSHEN of rushes
RUSHER impetuous person; thruster
zo RUSINE of E. Ind. maned deer
tx, zo RUSSEL woollen fabric, fox
tx, bt RUSSET homespun; apple
le RUSSIA leather
RUSTED oxidized
RUSTIC rural; bucolic; pastoral
RUSTLE quiver; whisper (wind);
  steal
hd RUSTRE heraldic lozenge
gl RUSURE earth-slide
zo RUTELA beetle genus
ch RUTILE an oxide of titanium
RUTTED grooved; furrowed; mated
  (of stags)
RUTTER a chart; trooper
RUTTLE gurgle; rattle (dial.)
bd RYBATE REBATE or jamb store
nt RYPECK RIPECK, REPECK, punt pole

___

S

zo SABALO the tarpon; Atlantic fish
SABIAN star worshipper
bt SABINE plant; the savin; (raped
  women)

SABLED darkened; furred
mu **SACBUT** sackbut; stringed instrument
rl, tx **SACCOS** Oriental vestment
zo **SACCUS** pouchlike structure
SACHEM American Indian chief
SACHET scent bag; tea bag
SACKED plundered; dismissed; (packaged)
SACKER sack-filling machine
pl **SACRAL** (pelvic arch)
SACRED holy; divine; consecrated
pl **SACRUM** a pelvis bone
SADDEN to grieve; depress
SADDLE seat on horseback; -bag; burden; encumber
go, ck **SADDLE** contour formation; butcher's cut
SADISM lustful cruelty
SADIST torturer; tormentor
ag **SAETER SETER**, Norwegian hill farm
SAFARI caravan; expedition
SAFELY securely; surely; reliably
SAFEST surest
SAFETY security; protection; safeguard; (measure); score; snooker (Am. football)
SAGELY wisely; sagaciously
SAGENE fishing net; a network
me **SAGENE** 7 ft (2.1 m) (Russian)
SAGEST wisest
SAGGAR sagger; fire-clay pot
SAGGED drooped; bent
SAGGER clay retort for stoneware
bt **SAGINA** pink genus
zo **SAGOIN** S. American monkey
zo **SAGUIN** capuchin monkey
go **SAHARA** a desert (Africa)
nt **SAILED** departed; cruised
nt **SAILOR** A.B.; tar; seaman
nt **SAIQUE SAIC**, small trading ketch
SAIRLY sorely (Sc.)
zo, ck **SAITHE** ling (fish)
SAKIEH Persian water-wheel
SALAAM salutation (India)
ck **SALAMI** spiced sausage (It.)
SALARY pay; wages; stipend
lw **SALIAN** (Mars); salic; male heirs only
ch, ck **SALIFY** to salten; add salt
go **SALINA** sea-salt lagoon; process
SALINE salty; briny
ck **SALITE** to season with salt
mn **SALITE** monoclinic pyroxene
md **SALIVA** spittle
bt **SALLAL** a fruit
SALLET light helmet
bt **SALLOW** yellow; a willow

ck **SALMIS** game-bird; ragout; salmi; a hash
zo **SALMON** highly prized fish
SALOON meeting room (pub) (dance) (carriage)
bt, ck **SALOOP** a decoction of sassafras
SALTED preserved
SALTEN to preserve; made of salt
SALTER salt-seller
zo **SALTIE** dab (fish)
SALTUS a mental jump
zo **SALUKI** hunting dog (Iran)
SALUTE hail; greet; accost
SALVED soothed; rescued
SALVER a tray
bt **SALVIA** sage
SALVOR a salvage expert
bt **SAMARA** winged fruit
SAMARE old-fashioned jacket
ck **SAMBAL** hot spice (Indonesia)
nt **SAMBAR** dhow
zo **SAMBUR** Indian elk
SAMELY in identical manner; (repeatedly)
SAMIAN of Samos
mt **SAMIEL** Arabian/Saharan hot poison wind
SAMIOT native of Samos
tx **SAMITE** silk
zo **SAMLET** a parr; salmon
SAMOAN native of Samoa
nt **SAMPAN** sanpan; Chinese boat
SAMPLE try; taste; specimen
ck **SAMSHU** rice spirit (China)
bt **SAMYDA** West Indian birch
mu **SANCHO** African guitar
nt **SANDAL** a Barbary vessel; footwear
mn **SANDIX SANDYX**, red lead, vermilion
go, gl **SANDUR** glacial outwash alluvial plain (Iceland)
SANELY rationally
SANEST most intelligent; soundest
bd **SANGAR** stone breastwork; masonry
rl **SANGHA** Buddhist church
md **SANIES** discharge from ulcer
SANIFY to restore to health
SANITY wisdom; normality; lucidity
SANJAK division of a vilayet (Turk.)
SANNOP SANNUP, American Indian; brave
mu **SANTIR SANTUR**, Eastern dulcimer
rl **SANTON** Dervish priest
fr **SAPELE** silky-grained Afr. hardwood
bt **SAPFUL** juicy
bt **SAPIUM** gum-tree
bt **SAPOTA** sapodilla
SAPOUR flavour (savour)

SAPPED undermined (tunnels; explosives); weakened

SAPPER Royal Engineer

rl SAPPHO Greek poetess

bd SAP-ROT dry rot; fungal

zo SAPYGA digger-wasps

zo SARCEL pinion of a hawk's wing

gl SARCEN SARSEN, Stonehenge sandstone; tin worker

zo SARDEL herring type of fish

zo SARGUS fish of mullet type

zo SARLAK sarlac; the yak

SARONG Eastern skirt

zo SARSIA jellyfish

SARTOR a well-dressed person

bd SASHES window-framings; scarves

lw SASINE seizin (Sc.)

rl SASTRA sacred book (Hindu)

nm SATANG Thailand coin

tx SATARA lustred woollen cloth

tx SATEEN fabric

bt SATINE SATIN, wood (hard-)

SATING satisfying; cloying

SATINY glossy

SATIRE irony; ridicule; sarcasm

SATIVE sown

SATRAP Persian provincial governor

SATURN planet; god of agriculture

nt SAUCER a piece of china-ware; flat canoe

zo SAUGER American pike

SAUMUR white wine

zo SAUREL the horse-mackerel

zo SAURIA reptile genus

zo SAURUS lizard-fish genus

SAVAGE barbaric; ferocious; brutal

SAVANT a scientist; professor

ga SAVATE French boxing

bt SAVINE medicinal shrub; red cedar

SAVING preserving; reserves; excepting

bt SAVORY aromatic pot-herb

SAVOUR taste; flavour; odour

SAVVEY nous; commonsense

pr SAW-CUT groove; binder's sewing mark

SAWDER flattery

zo SAW-FLY plant-harmful insect

zo SAW-NEB sawbill

tx SAWNEY complete yarn breakage

SAW-PIT sawing location

to SAW-SET tool for wrenching

SAWYER plank-cutter

tx SAXONY type of flannel

SAYING saw; dictum; adage; proverb

zo SAYNAY a lamprey

SBIRRO Italian policeman

S'BLOOD an imprecation, exclamation (God's blood)

SCABBY rough; itchy; leprous

SCAITH harm; damage (Sc.)

SCALAR magnitude without direction

SCALER climber

to SCALER instrument to register a count

mu SCALES a balance; octaves

vt SCALMA a horse disease

zo SCAMEL bar-tailed godwit

ck, zo SCAMPI prawns (It.)

SCANTY meagre; niggardly; chary; see-through (clothing)

md SCAPHA (helix of ear)

nt SCAPHO sailing cargo ship (Greek)

SCAPUS shaft of column

rl SCARAB sacred sunbeetle; gem (Egypt)

SCARCE rare; infrequent; uncommon

SCARED affrightened; panic-stricken

cr SCARPH to scarf

SCARRY scarred; disfigured

zo SCARUS parrot fish

vt SCATCH a horse-bit

SCATHE injury; damage

SCATTY showery; feather-brained; crazy

zo SCAURY gull (Shetlands)

SCAZON imperfect rhythm

zo SCELIO parasite insects

SCENIC dramatic; theatrical; route

SCHANS fortification (Dutch, Afrikaans)

SCHELM rascal (Boer)

cp SCHEMA diagrammatic representation; data base

SCHEME plan; plot; intrigue; devise

SCHEMY cunningly; devised

me SCHENE 7½ miles (12 km) (Egyptian)

SCHISM a split; discord; dissent

mn SCHIST slaty rock

cf, pc SCHIZO- of split, separate, cleavage (Gr.)

SCHOOL train; educate; academy

mn SCHORL tourmaline

ga SCHUSS unimpeded downhill ski run

nt SCHUYT ketch; sloop; (Dutch)

zo SCIARA gnats and midges

SCIATH Irish wicker shield

SCIENT knowing; aware

bt SCILLA hyacinth

SCLATE slate (obs.)

md SCLERA hard coating

zo **SCLERE** skeletal structure

zo **SCOBBY** chaffinch

SCOGIE a drudge (Sc.)

zo **SCOLEX** a worm

zo **SCOLIA** burrowing insects

zo **SCOLUS** thornlike process in larvae

SCONCE skull; bulwark

SCONCE to fine; wall candle with metal reflector

cf, md **-SCOPIA -SCOPIC, SCOPY,** visual; viewing (suffix)

zo **SCOPUS** genus of wading birds

SCORCH singe; char; parch; scar

mu **SCORED** registered; marked out; (-for orchestra)

SCORER recorder

mn **SCORIA** dross; coarse pumice stone

mn **SCORZA** variety of epidote

ck **SCOTCH** to thwart; cut; wedge; (-tape) (-egg)

zo **SCOTER** a sea-duck

ar **SCOTIA** Scotland; a concave moulding

ck **SCOUSE** meat and vegetable broth (Liverpool); Liverpudlian

SCOUTH scope (Sc.)

SCOUTS boys' brigade; guides; talent spotters

SCOVAN tin lode (Cornish)

SCOVED smeared (dial.)

SCOVEL oven-mop

SCRAMB SCRAMP, snatch; scrape together

SCRAPE grate; abrade; rasp; difficulty

SCRAWL hasty writing (illegible)

SCREAK SCREAM, SCREECH, cry; yell; shriek

SCREED tiresome harangue; a shred; wall-edging; jointless

tc **SCREEN** shroud; cloak; hide; sieve; scan; filter; (print); cinema; tv picture

SCREES stony debris

nt, md **SCREWS** divers' bends, caisson disease; fastening bolts, prison warders (sl.); propellors

SCREWY nefarious; underhand; exacting

SCRIBE writer; notary; scrivener

ga **SCRIME** to fence

SCRIMP to stint

pc **SCRIPT** handwriting; typescript; life-scenario; document; drama

SCRIVE scribe; engrave

zo **SCROBE** groove in mandible

SCROLL roll; list; register; flourish

SCROOP to grate; to crack

pl, zo **SCRUFF** back of neck

SCRUNT miser (Sc.)

SCRUTO theatrical trap

SCUFFY SCRUFFY, unkempt; shabby; seedy

SCULPT to sculpture; carve

SCUMMY covered with scum

zo **SCURFF** bull-trout

md **SCURFY SCURVY,** wasting disease; (sores); lack of Vitamin C

ga **SCURRY SKURRY,** haste; skamper; show jumping

SCUTCH to beat; to comb

hd **SCUTUM** Roman shield

SCUTUM middle noturn sclerite in insects

SCYLLA six-headed monster; (Charybdis)

ag, to **SCYTHE** a reaping implement (death)

S'DEATH an imprecation

zo **SEA-APE** sea-otter

zo **SEA-BAR** tern

zo **SEA-BAT** flying fish

nt **SEA-BOY** sailor lad

zo **SEA-BUN** sea-urchin

SEA-CAP a sponge

zo **SEA-CAT** cat-fish

zo **SEA-COB** a gull

zo **SEA-COW** manatee

zo **SEA-DOG** common seal

zo **SEA-EAR** a mollusc; ormer shell

zo **SEA-EEL** conger

zo **SEA-EGG** sea-urchin

zo **SEA-FAN** a polyp

zo **SEA-FIR** another polyp

zo **SEA-FOX** thrasher shark

rl **SEA-GOD** Neptune

zo **SEA-HEN** guillemot

zo **SEA-HOG** porpoise

SEALED ratified; confirmed; shut; closed

nt **SEALER** seal hunter; vessel

nt **SEAMAN** tar; sailor

zo **SEA-MAT** polyzoa

zo **SEA-MAW** sea-mew

tx **SEAMED** united by sewing; lined

SEAMER seamster

zo **SEA-MEW** a gull

SEA-MUD ooze

SEANCE spiritualism session

zo **SEA-ORB** globe fish

zo **SEA-OWL** lump fish

zo **SEA-PAD** star-fish

bt **SEA-PEA** beach-pea

zo **SEA-PEN** quill zoophyte

zo **SEA-PIE** a seafowl

zo **SEA-PIG** the dugong

zo **SEA-RAT** herring-king; a fish

SEARCH scrutiny; seek; inquire; quest

cp, lw **SEARCH** examine for specified conditions

SEARED cauterized; burnt; scorched

zo **SEA-ROD** a polyp

SEASON time; period; flavour

SEATED sited; established; accommodated

nv **SEA-WAY** steerage way

ch **SEBATE** a fatty compound

bt **SECALE** SEA-KALE, plant

nv **SECANT** (geometrical); cutting

SECEDE withdraw; segregate

SECERN secrete; discriminate

bt **SECKEL** variety of pear

me **SECOHM** electrical unit

me **SECOND** support; assist; inferior

mu **SECOND** melodic interval; lower pitched part

SECRET covert; occult; privy; cryptic

SECTOR an area; a cutting; a zone

cp **SECTOR** part of recorded data block

SECUND unilateral

SECURE get; obtain; safe; firm

SEDATE to calm; tranquillize, staid; placid

SEDENT inactive; still; torpid; sediment

bt **SEDGED** flagged; grassed

rl **SEDILE** seat in chancel

SEDUCE entice; tempt; inveigle

SEEDED planted; placed in tournament

to **SEEDER** seed-drill

SEEING observing; viewing; watching

SEEKER inquirer; searcher

SEELOS series of three gates (slalom skiing)

SEEMED befitted; appeared

SEEMER pretentious person; pretender

SEEMLY proper; becoming; decorous

SEEPED oozed; percolated

SEE-SAW teeter-totter; unbalance; pastime

cp **SEE-SAW** sign reversing amplifier

SEETHE to boil; (-with anger)

bt **SEGGAN** sedge (Sc.)

SEGGAR SAGGER, fireclay pot

SEGHOL Hebrew vowel point

nt **SEINER** net-fisherman

lw **SEISED** possessed of

zo **SEISON** a parasite genus

lw **SEIZED** confiscated; held prisoner; possessed (-by devil)

SEIZER thief; snatcher; grasper

lw **SEIZIN** SEISIN, held in possession

SEIZOR bailiff

hd **SEJANT** sitting upright

SELDOM rarely; hardly ever

SELECT pick; choose; prefer

cp **SELECT** courses of action after test

rl **SELENE** Greek Moon-goddess

SELION a ridge of land

SELJUK dynasty; art; empire (Turk.)

SELLER vendor; hawker; retailer

SELVES individualities

zo **SEMELE** genus of bivalves

SEMESE half-eaten

zo **SEMITA** (sea-urchins)

SEMITE descendant of Shem

SEMMIT undershirt (Sc.)

SEMPLE simple (Sc.)

mu **SEMPRE** in the same style

SENARY six of; half a dozen

SENATE assembly; council

SENDAL thin linen

cp **SENDER** transmitter; despatcher; exchange control

tc **SENDER** signal transmission line

SEND-UP compliment; ridiculing

bt **SENEGA** snake-root; an antidote

SENHOR SENOR, gentleman (Port., Sp.)

SENILE aged; doting; tottering; infirm

SENIOR elder; older; higher; superior

mu **SENNET** trumpet call

SENNIT braided cord; plaited straw

SENORA SENHORA, married lady (Sp., Port.)

SENSED perceived, felt

ga **SENSEI** instructor (judo, karate)

SEN-SEN breath-sweetener

SENSOR small-variation detection device

pc **SENSUM** sense datum

SENTRY sentinel; watchman; guardian

ck **SEPAWN** maize-meal

zo **SEPHEN** sting-ray

zo **SEPIUM** cuttle-bone

cn **SEPMAG** 1-magnetic-soundtrack film

cn **SEPOPT** 1-optical-soundtrack film

md **SEPSIN** a ptomaine

md **SEPSIS** (blood poison); putrefication

SEPTAL partitional (Irish)

SEPTAN weekly

mu **SEPTET** seven part ensemble

md **SEPTIC** rotting; putrid

SEPTON (putrefaction)

bt **SEPTUM** a partition

SEQUEL consequence; upshot; result

nm **SEQUIN** a spangle; Venetian
go **SERACS** postglacial ice pillars (Fr.)
    SERAIL SERAGLIO, SARAY, oriental
    palace; (harem)
nt **SERANG** Lascar boatswain
tx **SERAPE** zarafe; Mexican blanket
rl **SERAPH** six-winged angel
    SERDAB secret chamber (Egypt)
mt **SEREIN** rain from a cloudless sky
mt **SERENA** damp evening air
    SERENE calm; placid; tranquil; clear
cp **SERIAL** a periodical (instalments);
    identity number; in sequence
pr **SERIAN** Chinese; Seric
    SERICA beetle genus
    SERIES sequence; succession; order
ch **SERINE** acid from protein hydrolysis
pr **SERIPH** SERIF, typesetting (sans-)
    SERMON address; homily; discourse
md **SEROON** package of drugs
pl **SEROSA** chorium; connective-tissue
    membrane
md **SEROUS** watery; thin
go **SERTAO** jungle wilderness (N.E.
    Brazil)
zo **SERULA** red-breasted merganser
zo **SERVAL** small African leopard
    SERVED ministered; acted; obeyed
rl **SERVER** salver; waiter; mass R.C.;
    beginner of volley (tennis)
    (squash) etc
bt **SESAME** plant having oily seeds
bt **SESBAN** a marsh plant
bt **SESELI** saxifrage
mu **SESTET SEXTET,** six part ensemble
oc, zo **SESTON** tiny plankton organisms
pr **SET-OFF** compensation; insulation
    SETOSE SETOUS, bristly
    SET-OUT display; layout; basic
    concept
nt **SETTEE** sofa; Mediterranean ship
ga **SETTER** pioneer; placer; (trend-)
    (tennis)
    SETTLE colonize; (pay claims)
    (disputes); mediate
bt **SETULE** small bristle
    SEVERE harsh; cruel; rigorous; plain
ar **SEVERY** part of vaulted ceiling
    SEVRES porcelain (Fr.)
    SEWAGE drainage; effluent; wastes
    SEWING needlework
bt **SEXFID** six-cleft
pc **SEXISM** prejudice; sex
    discrimination
    SEXTAN recurring every sixth day
mu, ga **SEXTET** six part ensemble; team of 6
    ice hockey players
    SEXTIC of the 6th degree

rl **SEXTON** gravedigger
    SEXUAL of sex; sensual
    SHABBY threadbare; paltry; beggarly
    SHADED screened; obscured
as **SHADOW** umbrage; dark; silhouette;
    eclipse; follow secretly
    SHADUF Nile water-raising device
    SHAGGY rugged; rough; uneven;
    unkempt dog (-story)
zo **SHAHPU** Tibetan wild sheep
tx **SHAIRL** Cashmere cloth
    SHAKEN jarred; agitated; moved
rl **SHAKER** religious sect (USA)
md **SHAKES** involuntary trembling;
    (deep sea divers) hand-split
    shingles
tx **SHALLI** Indian cotton stuff
bt **SHALOT SHALLOT,** (onion)
zo **SHAMAH** shama; Indian song-bird
mt **SHAMAL** Mesopotamian summer
    wind
    SHAMAN animist; wizard (Siberia)
    SHAMED abashed; disgraced
le **SHAMMY** shamoy; chamois-leather
zo **SHANNY** blenny fish
mu, nt **SHANTY** hut; hovel; shack; sea chant
    SHAPED moulded; formed; regulated
to **SHAPER** metal-planing machine
    SHARED partook; divided; held in
    common; with joint access
    SHARER participator
nt **SHARPY** oysterman's boat
    SHAVED swindled; smooth-faced
    SHAVEN without hair; shorn; bald
    SHAVER a sharp dealer; a barber
    SHAVIE a trick; a prank (Sc.)
tx **SHAYAK** coarse cloth (Tripoli)
ag **SHEAFY** of sheaves (cereal harvests)
    SHEARS cutters; scissors
    (sheepwool-)
md **SHEATH** scabbard; condom;
    (sanitary-)
    SHEAVE pulley-wheel (on block &
    tackle)
    SHEENY bright; showy; a Jew
nt **SHEERS SHEERLEGS,** a hoisting
    appliance; dipod portable crane
nt, pp, ml **SHEETS** sails; broad cloth; bedding
    (swaddling) (paper) (metal)
me, mn **SHEKEL** Jewish half-crown
    SHELFY shelvy; shallow
    SHELLY abounding with shells
fr **SHELLY** of shell-shake timber
    SHELTA beggars' cant
zo **SHELTY** Shetland pony
    SHELVE put aside; to incline
    SHELVY sloping shallow
bt **SHE-OAK** Australian shrub

SHEPPY sheep-cote (-pen) (Aust.)
SHERIF shereef; Arab title
ck **SHERRY** a wine from Jerez (Sp.)
SHEUCH SHEUGH, ditch; drain;
trench; furrow (Sc.)
SHEWEL scarecrow
SHICER welsher (Australia)
SHIELD shelter; cover; screen; guard
SHIFTY tricky; resourceful;
untrustworthy (eyes)
rl **SHI-ISM** faith of a Moslem sect
(Iran)
SHI-ITE believer in Shi-ism
SHIKAR big game hunting (Ind.)
SHIMMY chemise; a dance
SHINDY trouble; quarrel; spree;
brawl
nm **SHINER** £1; a boot-black
ga **SHINNY SHINTY, SHANDY** bandy ball;
West Highland hockey; turmoil;
kicking sport
SHINTO Japanese ancestor worship
zo **SHIPOV** small sturgeon
SHIPPO Japanese enamel
nt **SHIPPY** ship-shape; in order; tidy
SHIRES the Shires, midland counties
SHIRTY indignant; wroth; angry
mn **SHIVER** tremble; quiver; slate
nv **SHOALY** shallow; shelfy; seabottom
tx **SHODDY** coarse cloth
SHODER goldbeater's packet
mu **SHOFAR** ram's horn trumpet (Heb.)
SHOGUN Japanese C. in C.
SHONKY shocking; twisting;
dishonest
SHOOED drove away
SHOPPY commercial
bd **SHORED** propped; buttressed; braced
nt **SHORER** a support (in dry dock or
ashore)
SHORTS bran; pants
zo **SHOUGH** shaggy dog
SHOULD advised to; ought to; duty
to
SHOVED obtruded; pushed; jostled
to **SHOVEL** clergyman's hat; spade;
upturned tip of ski
SHOVER pusher
mt **SHOWER** distribute liberally; rain;
douche
SHRANK contracted; recoiled
SHRAUM mucus deposit in the eye
SHREWD astute; cunning; wise;
canny
SHRIEK cry; scream; yell; screech
rl **SHRIFT** confession; absolution
zo **SHRIKE** butcher-bird
mu **SHRILL** high; sharp; piping (note)

zo **SHRIMP** small prawnlike crustacean;
young thin child
rl **SHRINE** tomb; reliquary
SHRINK shrivel; contract; decrease in
size; withdraw in fear
zo **SHRITE** missel thrush; bird
rl **SHRIVE** to absolve; pardon
SHROFF Indian banker
nt **SHROUD** winding sheet for the dead
rl **SHROVE** pardoned; (Tuesday)
tx **SHRUFF** dross
SHRUNK contracted
SHUCKS! nonsense!
SHUFTI look! (Arab)
bt **SHUNIS** herb; Scotch lovage
SHYING throwing; withdrawing in
fear (horses)
bc, ch **SIALIC** derivative of neuraminic acid
SICCAN such (Sc.)
SICCAR sicker; sure (Sc.); certain
SICKEN (disgust); languish; become
ill
ag, to **SICKLE** reaping hook
SICKLY faint; unhealthy; morbid
zo **SICSAC** crocodile bird
bt **SICYOS** gourds
rl **SIDDHA SIDDHI**, Buddhist who has
attained perfection
rw **SIDING** train parking track
SIDLED moved furtively; sideways
me **SIEMEN** unit of electrical
conductance
pt **SIENNA** yellow paint; (burnt)
go **SIERRA** mountain range (Sp.)
SIESTA midday nap (Med., Mexico)
zo **SIFAKA** a lemur
SIFFLE to whistle (Fr.)
ag **SIFTED** sieved; separated; sorted;
(winnowed)
SIFTER scrutinizer; analyst
SIGHED breathed heavily, sadly
SIGHER repiner
lw **SIGLUM** seal; mark; initials
ae, nt, rw **SIGNAL** eminent; a sign; lamp; flag;
semaphore; traffic
tc **SIGNAL** call (start or end) code
SIGNED signified; endoresed; agreed;
autographed
SIGNER one who subscribes
lw **SIGNET** a seal; ring with crest (Sc.)
SIGNOR Mr in Italian
SILAGE ensilage; stored fodder
ch **SILANE** silicon hydride
bt **SILENE** bladder-campion
SILENT mute; dumb; taciturn
mn **SILICA** flint; quartz; etc.
SILKED repaired with silk backings
(bks.)

tx **SILKEN** delicate; tender
SILLER silver; money (Sc.)
SILLON a mound in a moat
zo **SILPHA** carrion beetles
nv **SILTED** (waterway) choked with debris
zo **SILURE** cat-fish
fr **SILVAN SYLVAN**, wooded; rustic
ml, nm **SILVER** shining metal; coins; cutlery
SIMBIL African stork
zo **SIMIAL SIMIAN**, ape-like characteristics
SIMILE parable; comparison
ck **SIMMER** a gentle boil; stew
ck **SIMNEL** sweet fruit cake
rl **SIMONY** buying preferment
mt **SIMOON** summer whirlwind Sahara (Arab.)
zo **SIMORG SUMURG**, fabulous Persian bird
SIMOUS snub-nosed; concave
zo **SIMPAI** Sumatra monkey
SIMPER silly affected smile
SIMPLE naive; artless; frank; ingenuous
SIMPLY merely; only; barely; solely
bt **SIMSON** groundsel
SINAIC (Mount Sinai)
ga **SIN-BIN** bench for ice hockey offenders
SINDON a wrapper; winding sheet
SINEWY strong; vigorous; muscular
SINFUL wrong; iniquitous; depraved
SINGED scorched; slightly burnt
mu **SINGER** warbler; songster
cp **SINGLE** choose; select; alone; celibate; unit; score
SINGLY uniquely; individually
mn **SINIAN** Chinese rock formation
SINISM Chinese custom
SINKER a plummet; weight for pets (fishing)
SINNED erred; transgressed
SINNER wrong-doer; transgressor
nt **SINNET SENNET**, braided cordage
mn **SINTER** a siliceous deposit
bt **SINTOC** cinnamon bark
SIOUAN Sioux; American Indian tribe
SIPAHI sepoy; colonial soldier
ck, ce **SIPHON** syphon; atmospheric pressure pump (soda)
SIPING perculating; oozing; leaking
SIPPED (tasted); **SIPPET** (small sop)
SIPPER can **SIPPLE** (sup small drops)
SIRCAR sirkar; Hindu clerk
SIRDAR Egyptian commander
mu **SIRENE** a pitchpipe

SIRING begetting; fathering
as **SIRIUS** the Dog Star
SIRRAH sir, sirree
ck **SIRUPY** like syrup; syrupy
zo **SISKIN** bird; a finch
bt **SISSOO** Indian timber-tree
lw **SISTED** summoned (Sc.)
SISTER nun; nurse; sibling
SITTER painter's patient model
rl **SITULA** bucket-shaped vessel liturgical
zo **SIWASH** N. American Indian; Alaskan dog
SIZING size; weak glue; grading
ck **SIZZLE** fry (frypan)
SKATER one who skates (ice) (rollers)
SKATHE scathe; injury; harm; damage
SKEARY scary; scared
SKEELY skilful (Sc.)
pl **SKELIC** pertaining to skeleton
SKELLY to squint (Sc.)
go **SKERRY** rocky island
SKETCH limn; portray; outline; draught
ct **SKEWER** to impale; kitchen implement
SKIING moving; (jumping) on skis
ck **SKILLY** thin gruel; (porridge)
SKILTS trews; Sc. trousers
SKIMPY scanty; meagre
SKINNY lean; lank; (-dipping) (bathing naked)
zo **SKITTY** water-rail
SKIVED sliced; split
SKIVER split sheep-skin
SKIVIE askew (Sc.)
SKLENT to slant; to split (Sc.)
SKRYER a diviner
mt **SKURRY** scurry (Sc.); breeze; puff
SKYISH ethereal
SLABBY viscous; thick; sloppy
SLACKS women's trousers
SLAGGY (slag); scoriaceous
nt **SLAKED** quenched; water-heated (lime)
SLALOM timed ski-race through 'gates'
SLANGY colloquial
SLAP-UP posh; lavish
SLASHY muddy (Sc.)
nt **SLATCH** fair weather
SLATED abused; upbraided; chided
zo **SLATER** a wood louse
SLAVED drudged
nt **SLAVER** dribble; slave ship

SLAVEY serving wench; skivvy; kitchen maid
SLAVIC Slavonic
SLAYER murderer; killer
tx **SLEAVE** unwrought silk; floss
SLEAZE bribery of MPs
SLEAZY sordid; shabby; disreputable
SLEDGE SLED, snowcart; (-hammer)
SLEEKY of smooth appearance
SLEEPY soporous; drowsy; somnolent
mt **SLEETY** wet and cold; wet snowfall
ae **SLEEVE** arm cover; (wind indicator)
SLEIGH horse- or reindeer-drawn open snow vehicle
zo **SLEUTH** detective; bloodhound
SLEWED swung askew; tipsy
ga **SLICED** chopped; cut; (golf-shot)
ck **SLICER** ham cutter (in shops)
SLICKS (oil spill at sea); treadless tyres (motor-racing)
SLIDER a moveable part
SLIDER hard curving throw (baseball)
SLIEST slyest; most artful; most crafty
SLIGHT scorn; disdain; minimal
SLINKY lean; furtive
md **SLIP-ON** easily put on (clothing); condom
SLIPPY nimble; unstable
SLIP-UP error; mistake
SLITHY lithe and slimy
SLIVER a cut (splinter-thin)
tx **SLIVER** continuous fibre strand
SLOGAN war-cry (Sc.); curt phrase
SLOKEN SLOCKEN, quench with water
SLOPED tilting (ground); walked slowly
SLOPPY maudlin; slipshod
SLOSHY SLUSHY, muddy; boggy; watery; miry
SLOUCH depressed gait (clown); hat on head
go **SLOUGH** deep mud; morass; swamp
SLOUGH a cast skin (snake's)
SLOVAK Slav of Slovakia
SLOVEN slattern; slut
fr **SLOVEN** splintered timber stump
SLOWER not so fast
SLOWLY gradually; tardily; sluggishly
SLUDGE mire; wet refuse
SLUDGY muddy
gl **SLUGGA** subterranean cavity
SLUICE floodgate; wash
SLUICY streaming

SLUING turning round
SLUMPY marshy
ce **SLURRY** to smear; to dirty; cement water mix; (trench)
ga **SLURVE** fast, curved throw (baseball)
SLUSHY swampy; muddy; miry
gl **SLUTCH** sediment; muck; mire
SLYEST sliest; most artful
SMALLS exams; underwear
SMALTO glass; enamel; mosaic fragment
SMARMY oily; ingratiating
SMARTY over-bright youth
SMEARY bedaubed; adhesive; glutinous
zo **SMEATH** aquatic bird; smew
SMEIGH being clever
SMELLY odoriferous
SMILED grinned; simpered
SMILET a little smile
SMIRCH depreciate; foul
SMIRKY smart; smiling
ga **SMITER** slogger; hitter
SMITHY blacksmith's forge
SMOKED ridiculed; fumed; reeked
SMOKER a tobacoo addict
mt **SMOKES** dry season mists, coast of Guinea
SMOOTH level; flatten; suave; bland
SMOUCH smack; to kiss
SMOUSE pedlar (S. Africa)
SMUDGE stain; blot; margin decoration (signwriting)
SMUDGY stained; smeary
SMUGLY primly; neatly; complacently
SMURRY misty (Sc.)
SMUTCH to blacken
SMUTTY sooty; lewd; dirty
zo **SNABBY** chaffinch (Sc.)
zo **SNACOT** pipe-fish
SNAGGY full of troublesome difficulties
SNAKED moved like a snake
SNAPED bevelled
SNAPPY abrupt; noticeable style
SNARED netted; caught
SNARER trapper; hunter; poacher
ga **SNATCH** grab; seize; steal; (weight-lifting)
mu **SNATCH** fragment of song
to **SNATHE** scythe-handle
SNEEZE exhale explosively
SNIFFY disdainful; proud
SNIFTY having a luscious smell
SNIPER concealed marksman; gunman
SNIPPY fragmentary; stingy

SNITCH nose
SNIVEL snuffle; blubber; whine
SNOBBY snobbish; bogus superiority
SNOOTY conceited snob
SNOOZE a nap; doze; siesta; drowse
nt SNOTTY midshipman
SNOUTY protuberant
SNUBBY somewhat snub; rather
  blunt
SNUDGE sneak; miser
SNUFFY irritable; peevish
SNUGLY cosily; comfortably
SOAKED sodden; drenched; steeped
SOAKER confirmed toper; alcoholic
pb SOAKER watertightness plug in roof
SOAPED lathered; shampooed
SOARED aspired; towered; ascended
SOBBED wept; cried
. *lw* SOBEIT if it be so
bt SOBOLE budding/rooting stem
lw SOCAGE tenure of land by service
ga SOCCER association football
SOCIAL genial; civic; civil; festive
SOCKED biffed; whanged; coshed
cp, el, pb SOCKET a cavity; (for a plug); pipe
  joint
lw SOCMAN tenant by socage
SODAIC containing soda
ag SODDED turfed; grassed; gardening
SODDEN soaked; wet; drenched
ch SODION sodium ion
ch SODIUM metallic element
md SODOKU rat-bite fever
SODOMY anal intercourse
SO-EVER indefinite suffix
SOFFET small sofa
ar SOFFIT ceiling; underside of
  architectural element
SOFTEN to weaken resistance; to
  impair strength; make malleable
SOFTER tenderer; milder
SOFTLY pliably; quietly; dulcetly
SOGGED saturated; sopped
SOIGNE well-decorated; carefully
  dressed
SOILED tarnished; smirched
SOIREE evening party (Fr.) (recital)
SOLACE consolation; cheer; relief
zo SOLAND the gannet
mt SOLANO LEVANTER, rainwind (Spain)
SOLDER fusible metallic cement
SOLEIL worsted dress fabric; the sun
  (Fr.)
SOLELY singly; alone; solitarily
SOLEMN august; grave; sad; serious
SOLERA cask; blending of sherry
  vintages
pl SOLEUS a leg muscle

ce SOLING large stones for road bed;
  (-and heeling) (pitching)
el SOLION audio signal detector
mu SOLITO in the usual manner
ar SOLIVE joist; cross-timber
ar SOLLAR SOLLER, upper gallery;
  garret
SO-LONG good-bye
SOLUTE readily soluble substance
SOLVED removed; resolved
SOLVER elucidator; interpreter;
  decoder
SOMALI native (Somalia)
nm SOMALO Somali currency
SOMBRE dismal; gloomy; lugubrious
zo SOMITE body segment
SOMNUS sleep personified
SONANT sounding; resonant
mu SONATA instrumental piece
SONCIE buxom; lucky
tx SONERI cloth of gold (Ind.)
eg SONICS study of mechanical
  vibrations
SONNET a poem of 14 lines
mu SONORE loudly (It.)
SONSIE good natured (Sc.)
SONTAG knitted cap
SOODRA Hindu castle
ck SOOJEE SOUJEE, SUJEE, specially
  fine flour (Ind.)
SOONER earlier; more readily
SOORMA an antimony cosmetic
zo SOOSOO river dolphin
SOOTHE calm; pacific; lull; palliate
SOPHIC teaching wisdom; wise
SOPITE to quash
SOPPED very wet; sogged
SOPPER wet feeder
zo SORAGE phase of hawk's life
ck SORBET water-ice; sherbet (Turk.)
bt, ck SORBIC SORBIN, vitamin C, acid
bt SORBIN mountain ash
SORDES sordor; dregs; filth
mu SORDET a mute for an instrument
SORDID base; vile; ignoble; foul
SORELY grievously; deeply; sadly
SOREST most grievous
SORNER gate-crasher; uninvited
  guest
bt SOROSE clustered
bt, zo SORREL colour; buck
SORROW woe; distress; affliction
SORTED grouped; suited
cp SORTER classifier; arranger; punched
  card machine
SORTIE sally; raid
SOSSLE dabble
as SOTHIC dog-star

SOTNIA Cossack troop
SOTTED drunk; infatuated; out of mind; be-
bt **SOUARI** butter-nut tree of Guyana
SOUCAR Hindu banker/usurer
SOUGHT searched; quested; looked for
SOULED full of feeling
SOUPER (a convert) (drinker)
SOUPLE flail arm
tx **SOUPLE** sericin-content yarn/fabric
SOURCE fount; cause; spring; origin
cp **SOURCE** compiled object program language
SOURER more acid
SOURLY tartly; bitterly
SOUSED SOWSED, soaked; drenched
SOUTAR SOUTER, SOWTER, cobbler; shoemaker
SOVIET Communist Russian council committee
ag **SOWANS** SOWENS, oat husk flummery
zo **SOW-BUG** a millipede
ag **SOWING** planting; disseminating; propagating
SOZZLE sossle; muddle
SOZZLY sloppy
SPACED extended
SPACER distance piece; (typewriter)
SPADED dug
SPADER SPADIX, clay spade; spike
SPAHEE Algerian cavalryman
zo **SPALAX** mole-rats
SPANDY wholly, completely
SPARED saved; refrained; withheld
SPARER economizer
SPARES spare parts; duplicates
SPARGE to sprinkle
SPARKE battle-axe (Spens.)
SPARKS radio operator
mn **SPARRY** (spar); (crystalline)
SPARSE scanty; meagre; thin
SPARTH halberd; mace
zo **SPARVE** hedge-sparrow
bt **SPATHE** flower sheath
vt, md **SPAVIN** a swollen joint
nm **SPECIE** bullion; coin; cash
SPECKY speckled
SPEECH harangue; oration; palaver
SPEEDY prompt; fast; rapid; hasty
mt **SPEISE** cobalt/lead smelting product
mn **SPEISS** metallic dross
SPELIN form of Esperanto
SPENCE buttery; pantry
le **SPETCH** strip of hide

SPEWED spat; vomited
mn **SPHENE** titanite
SPHERE globe; orb; ball; domain
SPHERY spherical; round
rl **SPHINX** man-lion statue
bt **SPICAL** spiky
ck **SPICED** seasoned
SPICER spice-merchant
zo **SPIDER** a weaver of webs; Ariadne; cue support (billiards, snooker)
SPIFFY spruce; smart (slang)
SPIGOT spile; peg for a cask
SPIKED pointed; put out of action
bt **SPIKES** outside nails; shoe grips for track events; grain
SPILTH anything spilt
md **SPILUS** birth-mark; a naevus
md **SPINAL** (back-bone)
SPINED thorny
mn **SPINEL** (corundum)
mu **SPINET** form of harpsichord
SPINNY a small copse
SPIRAL cork-screw; winding (Am. football) (skating) (parachuting)
ar **SPIRED** having a spire; sprouted
nt **SPIRIC** like an anchor-ring
SPIRIT zeal; soul; essence; spook
SPITAL hospital (obs.)
SPITED thwarted; vexed
SPLASH spatter; splurge; a sensation
md **SPLEEN** anger; melancholy
SPLICE to marry; a junction
SPLINE flexible ruler
md **SPLINT** SPLENT, support for broken bone
SPLITS with legs at angle of 180° (gymn.)
SPOFFY officious
SPOKEN told; articulated
zo, ck **SPONGE** porous fibre; cadge; (-cake) (wiper)
SPONGY absorbent
SPOOKY eerie; ghostly
SPOONY weak-minded; amorous
SPOSHY slushy
SPOT-ON accurately placed
SPOTTY speckled
SPOUSE husband or wife
SPRACK sprightly; alert
SPRAID chapped with cold
md **SPRAIN** strain; wrench; injury
SPRANG jumped; leapt; bounded; tea
SPRAWL lounge; spread; straggle
ck, ga, ro **SPREAD** open; broadcast; scatter; savoury paste; banquet; extend; (show-jumping)
SPRENT sprinkled

SPRING well; fount; leap; emanate; coiled energy
SPRING vernal season of new growth
SPRINT running extra spurt
SPRITE elf; fay; pixy; fairy; hobgoblin
SPROUT bud; germinate; shoot; spire
bt SPRUCE fir-tree; neat; trim; finical; furniture from the Baltic (Old English)
SPRUIT water-course (S. Africa)
SPRUNG has leapt; tipsy
SPRUNT sprouted
SPRYER more vigorous
SPUDDY potato-like; chubby; podgy
SPUNGE sponge
SPUNKY mettlesome; spirited
bt SPURGE a plant
bt SPURRY pink weed
SPYING watching secretly; spyism; coding; espionage; (agent)
SQUAIL a disc or counter
SQUALL blast; gust; yell; squeal
bt, zo SQUAMA squame bract; scale
SQUARE fair; just; bribe; adjust; straight; equal oblong; (rowing)
bt, ck SQUASH a gourd; a game; juice; crush
SQUAWK harsh utterance of protest
SQUEAK small creaking sound
SQUEAL cry out in pain; to inform
bt, zo SQUILL hyacinth; shrimp
md SQUINT a strabismus; glance
md SQUIRE landowner; escort; gallant
SQUIRM writhe; twist; wriggle
SQUIRT syringe; spout; eject
STABLE durable; fixed; constant; horse-house
STABLY firmly; steadfastly; securely
bt STACTE myth
to STADDA comb-cutting saw
STADIA a range-finder
STAGED performed (dramatics); deceived
STAGER old hand (theatre)
STAGEY melodramatic
STAITH coaling stage; staithe
STAKED (a claim); wagered
STALAG prisoners-of-war camp (Ger.)
STALER less fresh; older
bt STAMEN stamina; pollen container of flower
tx STAMIN harsh woollen stuff
STANCE position; attitude; station; (sport) (body)
STANCH STAUNCH, firm; stop liquid flow

STANZA verse of poem
md STAPES ear-bones
STAPLE essentials; basic materials; needs; requirements; industries; a clip
tx STARCH for stiffening clothes, etc.
STARCH feature of green plants; (stored sugar)
STARED gazed; glared; gaped
STAREE one who is stared at
STARER beholder
STARRY stellated (eyed)
STARVE famish; lack; deprive
md STASIS static; stable; unchanging state
STATED settled; regular; asserted
nm STATHER ancient Greek gold coin
STATHE landing stage
STATIC motionless; in equilibrium; immobile
cp STATIC dump; rewriting at end of run
STATOR cf. rotor; circuit holder
STATUE image; figurine
STATUS rank; standing; position
cp STATUS situation warning of paper shortage
STAVED burst; delayed
STAVES (staff); rods; sticks
md STAXIS haemorrhage; bleeding
STAYER one with endurance; pacing rider
STAY-IN sit-in demonstration
STAYNE deface; stain (Spens.)
STEADY equable; regular; uniform
STEAMY vaporous; humid; overshoot (golf)
zo STEARE a steer; an ox (Spens.)
STEBOY! go seek (dog talk)
STEELY hard; firm; obdurate
br STEELY of glassy barley grains
STEEPY precipitous
STEEVE to stow; pack closely; (-door)
bt STEGMA small silica-filled cell
STEMMA pedigree; family tree
STENCH fetid; odour; effluent
STEP-IN take control; seize power
go STEPPE Russian plain
STEREO stereotype
cf STEREO- of three dimensions (Gr.)
ch STERIC (atomic arrangement)
ch STEROL solid alcohol
mu STESSA (It.) the same
ck STEWED simmered; seethed
STHENE unit of force
ch STIBIC (antimony)

ga **STICKS** to raise above shoulders; foul (hockey) (lacrosse)
STICKY gummy; adhesive; viscid
STIDDY a forge; smiddy; smithy
STIFLE suffocate; smother; end (project)
STIGMA brand; mark; disgrace
bt, zo **STIGMA** algae 'eye'; spiracle of insect
STILAR (sundial stile)
STILLY calm; tranquil; silent
STILTY stilted; high-hat
ga **STIMIE** stimy (golf) (balls in line)
STINGO strong ale
STINGY near; close; mean; parsimonious
STINTY stinted; limited
bt **STIPEL** stipule
bt **STIPES** stalk; stipe; stem
STIRPS progenitor; ancestor
STITCH sew; twinge (pain, laughter); manipulate
nm **STIVER** Dutch halfpenny coin
STOCKY sturdy; thick-set; robust
STODGE to cram
ck **STODGY** heavy; indigestible; starchy
STOKED fuelled
nt, rw **STOKER** furnace operator (steamship, locomotive etc)
ps, me **STOKES** kinematic viscosity symbol
STOLEN filched; purloined; taken
STOLID obtuse; phlegmatic
bt **STOLON** a runner
STONED lapidated (killed); drugged; drunk
STONER wall builder
ro, tv **STOOGE** a butt; foil; foolish helper
STOORY dusty
bt **STORAX** resinous balsam
STORED garnered; treasured; deposited
STORER hoarder; stocker
STORES emporium; (department-)
STOREY one of many floors
STORGE natural affection (Greek)
STORMY wild; rough; tempestuous
ck **STOVED** dried; baked
STOVER fodder for cattle
STOWED packed; placed
STOWER stevedore; packer
STRAFE punish (Ger.); attack fiercely
mu **STRAIN** exert; race; filter
rw **S-TRAIN** suburban train (Dan., Ger., etc.)
go **STRAIT** narrows; distress; dilemma
nt **STRAKE** (wheel); flanging
STRAND shore; beach; thread; fibre
STRASS flint glass

STRATA layers; beds
go **STRATH** broad river valley (Sc.)
STRAWY straw-like
STREAK stripe; line; run naked
STREAM flow; pour; brook; burn
cp **STREAM** data from resource to controller
STREET town roadway; avenue
STRESS accent; force; urgency; tension
STREWN scattered here and there
STRIAE stripes; streaks
zo, bt **STRICK** screech-owl; flax
STRIDE long step forward; gait; brisk walk
STRIFE discord; conflict; quarrel
bt **STRIGA** bristle; stripe
ga **STRIKE** to hammer; hit (golf, cricket etc.)
STRIKE work stoppage; break camp; drum (gold)
STRING cord; twine; series
STRIPE band; line (military rank)
ck, tx **STRIPY** streaky (bacon); (pyjamas)
STRIVE vie; compete; attempt
el **STROBE** waveform enlargement
STRODE straddled; bestrode
STROKE blow; knock; caress; seizure; apoplexy; oarsman (stern seat); action of strike (golf); clock chime
STROLL ramble; rove; stray
md **STROMA** tissue
zo **STROMB** a gasteropod
STRONG puissant; bold; lusty
STROUT strunt; to strut (obs.)
STROVE vied; toiled; tried; attempted
STRUCK smote; hit; collided
md **STRUMA** goitre; scrofula
STRUNG threaded; filed
STUBBY stocky; blunt; truncated
ar **STUCCO** plaster facing
STUDIO atelier; broadcasting chamber
STUFFY close; fusty; musty; angry
STUMER bouncer; worthless cheque
ga **STUMPS** tree-boles; legs; wickets (cricket)
STUMPY stubby; short and thick
STUPID witless; dull; idiotic; asinine
STUPOR torpor; coma; lethargy
STURDY robust; stalwart; vigorous
STYING penning
STYLAR pillar-like; pointed
STYLED designed; fashioned; (character)
md **STYLET STILETTO**, pointed bristle; dagger; knife

cp, tv **STYLUS** pen; disc needle; torch; stile
ga **STYMIE** (golf); stimy; balls in line
bt **STYRAX** gum plants; storax
STYTHE after-damp
lw **SUABLE** liable to be sued
SUBDUE quell; overpower; tame
lw **SUBFEU** (subinfuedation) (Sc.) tenancy
mu **SUBITO** quickly
lw **SUBLET** make secondary lease
SUBMIT yield; capitulate; acquiesce
SUBORN to bribe; commit perjury
tc **SUBSET** subscriber's phone; part of relay system
ma **SUBSET** subsidiary of mathematics
SUBTLE SUBTLY, sly; crafty; clever manner
SUBULA sharp-pointed organ prolongation
SUBURB city outskirts; (satellite village)
SUBWAY underground passage; metro
mn **SUCCIN** amber (stone)
SUCKED suckled; imbibed via tube; straw
zo, bt **SUCKER** a fish; a shoot; suction pad
SUCKER gullible person
ck **SUCKET** sweetmeat
SUCKLE to wet-nurse
SUDARY a sweat-cloth
SUDDEN abrupt; (unexpected, rapid, happening)
SUDDER chief; supreme (Ind.)
SUEING prosecuting; entreating
SUFFER undergo (pain); endure; tolerate; permit
SUFFIX an affix
rl **SUFISM** Moslem doctrine
SUGARY sweet; honeyed; dulcet
zo **SUIDAE** pigs, hogs; etc.
SUITED contented; dressed
SUITOR wooer; admirer; litigant
mu **SUIVEZ** conductor to follow soloist
SUKAMA native of Tanzania
SULCUS furrow; groove
SULLEN morose; sulky
zo **SULTAN** a fowl; a Moslem ruler, emperor
SULTRY stuffy; oppressive; stifling; (air)
bt **SUMACH** sumak; plant used in tanning
SUMMED counted; added; reckoned
SUMMER season of year
SUMMIT top meeting; peak; zenith; vertex
SUMMON bid; cite; invoke; prosecute

SUMPIT poisoned dart (Borneo)
SUNBOW rainbow
ck **SUNDAE** ice-cream with fruit and syrup
SUNDAY Christian holy day
SUNDER brake; sever; disrupt
bt **SUN-DEW** a bog plant
as **SUN-DOG** a parhelion; mock sun
SUNDRY miscellaneous; various
rl **SUN-GOD** Phoebus; Apollo; Re or Ra
SUN-HAT solar topee (panama)
SUNKEN submerged; engulfed
SUNLIT illuminated by sun
SUNNED exposed to sun; sunbathed
SUNSET sundown
SUN-TAN sun-browned skin; (sun bathing)
SUPERB magnificent; splendid
SUPINE indolent; torpid; inert
ck **SUPPER** evening meal
SUPPLE lithe; pliant; flexible
SUPPLY provide; furnish; grant
bd **SURBED** (stone-laying)
bt **SURCLE** little shoot; sucker
SURELY certainly; positively
SUREST safest; most certain
SURETE crim. investigation service (Fr.)
SURETY bond; guarantee; pledge
SURGED billowed; advanced in mass
zo **SURREY** a fowl; carriage (Amer.)
SURTAX an impost
SURVEY see; review; look; observe
zo **SUSLIK** marmot; ground squirrel
lw **SUSSED** arrested on suspicion
md **SUTILE** wound stitching
SUTLER camp follower; caterer
SUTTEE self-immolation
SUTTLE neat; (tare and tret)
bt, md **SUTURE** stitching thread
SVELTE lissom; slender
SWAGGY bending
SWALED wasted; consumed
SWAMPY marshy; spongy
SWANKY superior; boastful
SWANNY swan-like
SWARAJ home-rule (India)
SWARDY grassy
SWARMY oleaginous; unctuous
SWARTH tawny; apparition
SWASHY squashy; over-ripe
tx **SWATCH** cloth sample; Swiss watch
SWATHE to bind; a bandage
SWATHE harvester's trail
SWATHY like a scythe-cut
SWAYED tottered; unsteady (in wind); persuaded

SWEATY causing sweat; (perspiration)

md SWEENY emaciation; atrophy

SWEEPS jeweller's dust/debris

SWEEPY strutting; wavy

SWERVE deviate; turn aside

SWIM-UP regroup in water for polo etc.

SWINGE to belabour; chastise

SWINGY ice conditions (curling)

SWIPED lashed out; slogged

SWIPER a smiter

ck SWIPES sweeping blows; small beer

SWIPEY mind-blown; fuddled; (shell-shocked)

SWIRLY curly

SWITCH twig; whip; bypass; shunt; control

el SWITCH tap device for electrical circuit

SWIVEL to turn; revolve; rowlock with pivot of oars (rowing)

mn SYCITE fig-stone

md SYCOMA tumour

fr SYLVAN rustic; rural; woodland

cp SYMBOL token; badge; emblem; logo

SYNDAW a plant

bt SYNEMA column of filaments

SYNEPY interjunction

SYNTAX grammatical sequence, structure

cp SYNTAX correct statements in source language

SYNTOL syntagmatic organization lang.

SYPHER to join flush

SYPHON siphon; atmospheric pressure pump (soda)

SYRIAC SYRIAN, of Syria; language

zo SYRINX vocal organ in birds; fistula

mu SYRINX Pan's pipes

SYRTIC like a quicksand

SYRTIS quicksand

ck SYRUPY sirupy; sugary

cp SYSTEM unit formed by connections

SYSTEM rule; method; order; plan (organized)

as SYZGY astronomical conjunction

T

hd TABARD heraldic coat; tunic

TABBED labelled; registered; listed

TABEFY to emaciate

TABLED parliamentary motions; catalogued

TABLER boarder

ma TABLES data; (conversions); (indoor games)

md TABLET flat monument

mu TABRET small tabor

ga TABULA Roman board game; backgammon; corals

nt TACKED attached; stitched; nailed; change of course (sailing)

TACKER he who tacks (nails)

ce, to, nt, TACKLE grapple; challenge; pulley

ga (football)

TACTIC cunning move; finesse

TACTUS sense of touch

zo TAENIA tape-worm; a fillet

TAG-END end of queue; list (last)

TAGGED tabbed; touched; fastened

TAGGER thin metal sheet

TAGGER an appendage (electronic)

ce TAGLIA a hoisting device; tackle (crane)

TAG-RAG and bobtail

zo TAGUAN Malayan flying squirrel

TAIGLE entangle; delay; tarry

TAILED docked; followed

TAILOR clothes maker

zo TAJACU Mexican wild pig, peccary

TAKE-IN a hoax; trick by con-man

TAKE-UP tailor's alterations to clothes

TAKING alluring; attractive; winning

ga TAKRAW 7-a-side field game (S.E. Asia)

lt, me TALBOT luminous energy unit

zo TALBOT hunting dog

nm, me TALENT genius; aptitude

mu TALIAN Bohemian dance

lw TALION retaliation

TALKED discoursed; prated; spoke

TALKER chatterbox; gossip

TALKIE sound film

TALLER higher; sturdier; bolder

TALLOW hard candle fat

rl TALMUD Hebrew Bible

go TALWEG deep valley (Ger.)

ck TAMALE Mexican cornmeal roll

bt TAMANU gamboge tree (E. Ind.)

ck TAMARA mixed spice

mn, bt TAMBAC alloy; also aloes-wood

TAMBOO TABOO, TAMBU, taboo

zo TAMBOR globe-fish

TAMELY meekly; submissively

TAMEST flattest; dullest

tx, wv TAMINE TAMINY, TAMISE, TAMROY, worsted cloth

TAMING domesticating; training

TAMKIN tampion

rl TAMMUZ Syrian sun-god

zo TAMPAN South Afr. venomous tick

TAMPED packed with earth
TAMPER meddle; interfere; screed board
pb **TAMPIN** turning pins; boxwood pipe plug
bt **TAMPOE** an E. Indian fruit
md **TAMPON** medical plug (feminine)
TAMTAM gong of indefinite pitch
TAN-BED bark bed; sunray bed
cp **TANDEM** bicycle for two; two-horse couch; master/slave
TANGED sharply flavoured (smelling); taint suggestion
TANGLE jumble; twisted
rl **TANGLE** Orcadian water-spirit
TANGLY complicated; intricate
zo **TANGUM** Tibetan piebald horse
TANIST land owner (Irish)
TANITE a cement
tx **TANJIB TANZIB**, figured muslin (India)
TANKED stored; fuddled
nt **TANKER** oil-carrying ship (truck)
TANKIA boat population, (Canton)
TANNED browned off; leathered
nm **TANNER** sixpence; leather worker
ch **TANNIC TANNIN**, acid astringent
TANNOY commerical sound systems
zo **TANREC** hedgehog (Madagascar)
rl **TANTRA** Sanskrit holy book
le **TAN-VAT** tub used in tanning
rl **TAOISM TAOIST**, Chinese religion(ist)
TAO-TAI Chinese official
zo **TAPETI** Brazilian hare
to, tv **TAPING** binding; measuring; recording
TAPPED screw-threaded; rapped
rw **TAPPER** rapper (wheels)
au **TAPPET** (motor vehicle); small lever
TAPPIT crested
TARGET shooting butt; production aim
rl **TARGUM** Bible in Chaldee
TARIFF duties on trade; schedule of prices etc.
TARING recording tare allowance
TARMAC road material
TARNAL eternal or infernal
zo **TARPAN** wild horse (Asia)
zo **TARPON TARPUM**, Jew-fish
TARRED macadamized; asphalted
TARSAL (tarsus); (the ankle)
zo **TARSEL** hawk; tiercel
TARSIA marquetry
pl **TARSUS** instep; ankle
nt, tx **TARTAN** chequered fabric (Sc.); ship
md, ck **TARTAR** Turkic people; plaque on teeth; wine cask sauce

TARTLY sharply; pungently; acidly
TASCAL informer's reward
TASKED employed; burdened
TASKER taskmaster; overseer
TASLET TASSET, thigh armour
tx **TASSEL** pendant (often cloth)
TASSET thigh armour
TASTED TASTER, food savoured/ sampler
zo **TATLER** a gossip; sandpiper
tx **TATTED** lace making
tx **TATTER** a rag
TATTIE Indian trellis; tatta
TATTLE prattle; gossip; babble
TATTOO army pageantry; skin decoration
TAUGHT imparted; tutored; coached
as **TAURUS** a sign of the Zodiac; the Bull
TAUTEN stretch; strain
TAUTER tighter
zo **TAUTOG TAWTOG**, blackfish (N. Am.)
TAVERN inn; hostel
TAWDRY gaudy; garish
le **TAWERY** white leather factory
le **TAWING** leather dressing
zo **TAWTOG** tautog
TAXEME linguistic selection
TAXIED ground movement made by aircraft
ch **TAXINE** alkaloid mixture
TAXING accusing; straining; costing
TCHEKA CHEKA, first Soviet Secret Police
TCHICK a click
TEA-BAG tea sachet; tisane
TEA-CUP tea-drinking vessel
TEAGLE a tackle; a hoist
TEAGUE an Irishman
TEAMED associated conjointly
TEA-POT vessel holding tea; (roller skating)
TEA-POY small table for teapot
TEARER render; ripper
TEASED combed; tantalized
bt, tx **TEASEL TEAZLE**, burr plant for nap cloth
TEASER a puzzle; aggravator
TEA-SET dishes for tea service
TEATHE (manure)
TEA-URN a samovar
mt **TEBBAD** Centr. Asian simoon wind
TEBETH Jewish month
ar, bd **TECTUM** covering/roofing structure
TEDDED spread (new-mown hay)
TEDDER a tether; hay-maker
ag **TEDDER** machine to loosen windrows

mu, rl **TE DEUM** thanksgiving; choral	**TERETE** clyindrical
TEDIUM boredom; ennui; monotony	**TERGAL** dorsal
ga **TEEING** golf ball mounting for first drive	**TERGUM** the back
	TERMED terminated; designated
TEEMED full of life; in myriads	*lw* **TERMER TERMOR**, long-term estate holder
TEEMER a producer	
TEEPEE wigwam (N. Amer.)	*zo* **TERMES** white ant genus
zo **TEE-TEE** S. Amer. squirrel monkey	**TERMLY** term by term
TEETER see-saw (USA)	*mt* **TERRAL** land breeze (coast) (Chile, Peru)
TEETHE to grow teeth	
bt **TEGMEN** inner seed coat	**TERREL** a spherical magnet
pr **TEGULA** subtitle (Italian)	**TERRET TERRIT**, harness pad ring
TELARY web-like	**TERROR** awe; dismay; dread; panic
zo **TELEDU** stinkard; Malayan badger	**TESTED** proved; assayed; tried out
TELEGA Russian springless cart	*ga, nm* **TESTER** canopy; time trials (cycling); Henry VIII shilling
TELESM amulet; charm	
rw, ce **TELFER** Telpher monorail; electric hoist	*pl* **TESTIS** male gonad; gland in scrotum
	md **TETANY** muscle spasm; lock jaw
TELLER cashier (bank); narrator; scorer	**TETCHY** testy; peevish
	TETHER tie; fasten; stake
rl **TELLUS** Goddess of Earth (Roman)	**TETRAD** group of four
zo **TELSON** tail segment	*zo* **TETRAO** capercaillie
TELUGA dialect (S. India)	*ch* **TETRYL** yellow detonating compound
ce **TEMOIN** column of earth	
me **TEMPER** mood; tantrum; anneal (steel); mitigate	*md* **TETTER** a rash
	zo **TETTIX** cicada; tree-cricket
rl **TEMPLE** Inns of Court; place of worship; fane; upper head	**TEUTON** ancient German
	zo **TEWHIT** peewit; lapwing
ga **TENACE** (bridge)	**TEXTUS** authoritative version
lw **TENANT** lease-holder	*nm* **THALER** German dollar
TENDED cared for; contributed	**THALIA** comic Muse
nt, rw **TENDER** mild; offer; (loco); (boat); (bar-)	**THANKS** an expression of gratitude
	THATCH roof with straw
md **TENDON** a ligament	**THAWED** melted (ice and snow)
TENNER £10 note	*zo* **THEAVE** ewe of the 1st year
ga **TENNIS** net/ball game	**THEBAN** of Thebes
mu **TENORA** Catalan instrument	*bt* **THECAL** sac-like
ga **TENPIN** of bowling alley	*zo* **THECLA** hair-streak butterflies
zo **TENREC** hedgehog (Madagascar)	*ch* **THEINE** tea alkaloid
TENSED keyed up; taut; stretched	**THEIRS** of them
TENSER under greater strain	*rl* **THEISM THEIST**, one God faith; ditto believer
mu **TENSON TENZON**, song tournament	
md **TENSOR** muscle	*rl* **THEMIS** goddess of law
TENTED probed	*md* **THENAL THENAR**, of palm or sole
TENTER machine attendant	**THENCE** for that reason
TENTER machine operative; females' cardroom	*rl* **THEODY** hymn in praise of God
	THEORY speculation; hypothesis; (idea)
TENUIS voiceless stop consonant	
lw **TENURE** possession; holding	*cf* **THERMO-** of heat (Gr.)
mu **TENUTO** sustained	**THESIS** a theme; a dissertation; essay
bt **TEPARY** hardy Amer. bean	**THETIC** dogmatic (thesis)
TEPEFY to warm	**THETIS** sea-nymph; the sea
gl **TEPHRA** erupted material; solids	**THEWED** trained; muscular
TERAPH Hebrew household god	*tx* **THIBET** heavy woollen fabric
ch **TERBIC** containing terbium	**THIBLE** to make holes
zo **TERCEL** male falcon	**THIEVE** filch; pilfer; purloin; rob
mu **TERCET** triplet	*jn* **T-HINGE** like a cross-garnet
zo **TEREDO** boring worm; ship-worm	

THINLY scantily; sparsely; (spread-)
lw THIRDS widows' rights
THIRST crave; yearn; hanker; desire
THIRTY cardinal number
ar THOLOS THOLUS, domed chamber; cupola (Gr.)
rl THORAH the Pentateuch
THORAL nuptial
md, pl THORAX (chest)
THORNY spiny; prickly; sharp
nc THORON thorium emanation
THORPE a homestead
THOUGH notwithstanding
nt THOWEL thole-pin
THRALL a slave; slavery
THRASH drub; castigate; beat (punish)
THRAVE two stooks (Iceland)
THREAD cord; filament; drift; gist
THREAT menace; intimidation
THRENE a lament (Gr.)
THRESH THRASH, (harvest); drub; trounce
THRICE three times
bt THRIFT frugality; economy; sea-pink
THRILL excite; rouse; electrify
zo THRIPS corn-bugs
THRIVE prosper; flourish
pl, bt, nt THROAT constricted passage (neck); (plants); (sail)
lw, rl THRONE seat of sovereign (power); (bishop's cathedra)
THRONG crowd; flock; congregate
THROVE thrived; prospered
THROWN cast; propelled; flung
zo, vt THRUSH songbird; disease of horses
md THRUSH disease of women
THRUST lunge; stab; attack
THUSLY as follows
THWACK belabour; whack; thump
THWART balk; frustrate; obstruct
mn THYITE pale green clay
md THYMOL oil of thyme
md THYMUS a gland
bt THYRSE panicle
pl, mu TIBIAL leg-bone; flute
TICING enticing; decoying; luring
TICKED clicked; marked; speckled
tx TICKEN thick pillow; mattress linen
pl, el TICKER rhythmic beat (watch) (heart); (telegraph tape)
TICKET voucher; coupon; pass
mn TICKEY coin (S. Africa)
TICKLE gratify; amuse; pleasurable touch
TICKLY ticklish; risky; difficult
TIC-TAC bookie's signalling system

ck TIDBIT TITBIT, beakful (birds); small snack (cocktails)
TIDDER to fondle
TIDDLE to potter; to trifle
TIDIED set in order; shipshape
TIDIER neater
TIDILY methodically; neatly
nt, pr TIED-UP busy; moored; docked (ship); books heading for cover binding
TIEING binding; confining
TIE-PIN ornament for a cravat
me TIERCE 42-gallon (190-litre) cask
mu TIERCE 5-f organ pitch
rw TIE-ROD connecting rod (steam locomotive)
TIE-WIG court-wig
ck TIFFIN Indian lunch; superior snacks
TIGHTS combined stockings and pantie
TILERY tilework; tile factory
bd TILING roofing
ag TILLED cultivated; ploughed
ag, nt TILLER helm; drawer; cultivator; side shoot (grass)
md TILMUS floccillation
TILTED covered with awning; aslant
TILTER tent-pegger; jouster (lancer)
mu TIMBAL tymbal; kettledrum
TIMBER wood; lumber
mu TIMBRE resonance; tone; quality
TIMELY opportune; punctual; apropos
TIME-ON extra time (sports matches etc.)
cp, me TIMING clocking; punctuality measuring device
mu TIMIST timekeeper (metronome)
mn TINCAL TINGAL, TINKAL, crude borax
TIN-CAN food container
TINDAL Lascar bo'sun's mate
bt TINDER touchwood (fire lighting)
zo TINEID (small moths)
TINGED coloured; imbued; flavoured
zo TINGIS an insect genus
TINGLE thrill; small nail
bt TINGUY Brazilian soap-tree
TINIER much smaller
TINKED tinged; tinkled
TINKER bungler; a fish; rubbish man
mu TINKLE make bell-like sound
TINMAN expert in tin production; canning
TINNED preserved
TINNER tin miner
TIN-POT inferior
TINSEL finery; glittering; gaudy
TINTED tinged; imbued (coloured)

TINTER colourist
ga TIP-CAT a children's game
TIP-OFF secret information; betrayal; (basket-ball)
TIPPED overturned; (racing); gratuity given
tx TIPPET garment; small cape
TIPPLE secret (regular) drink
TIP-TOE walk on the toes
TIP-TOP first class
zo TIPULA insect genus; daddy-longlegs
TIRADE diatribe; invective; harangue
TIRING dressing; wearying
TIRLED vibrated; twisted
TIRRET handcuff; manacle; fetter
zo TIRWIT lapwing
ck TISANE herbal drink
md TISSUE web; fabric; series
ck TIT-BIT tidbit; morsel for birds or cocktails
TITHED taxed (church)
TITHER tithe collector
TITLED yclept; inscribed; named
zo TITLER stickle-back
cn TITLER lettering screen
bt TI-TREE the manuka
TITTER giggle; snigger; laugh
TITTLE an iota; small particle
TITTUP canter (horse-riding)
TMESIS rhetorical intersection
tx TOBINE twilled silk
zo TOCSIN an alarm; poisonous serum
TODDLE saunter
TOE-CAP boot-tip
ck TOFFEE 'butter scotch' sweet
lw TOFORE before; heretofore
TOGGED arrayed; dressed up
nt, ae TOGGLE wooden pin; ski lift grip; safety rope device
cp TOGGLE circut based on stable state
TOILED moiled; strove
TOILER labourer; worker; striver
TOILET dress; attire; washroom (W.C.)
tx TOISON a fleece; sheepwool
mu TOLLED rang church bells
TOLLER toll-gatherer (highway taxes) (tollgates)
TOLLER bell-ringer
TOL-LOL goodish
TOLSEY toll-booth; mart
TOLTEC early Mexican
ch TOLUIC TOLVOL, (methyl) benzine
me TOMAND Arabian grain
bt TOMATO red fruit-vegetable
nm TOMAUN Persion gold coin
mn TOMBAC TOMBAK, copper zinc alloy; (bells, gongs)

TOMBED buried and exalted
TOMBIC like a tomb
TOMBOC Javanese weapon
TOMBOY a romping girl; hoyden
zo TOM-CAT male feline
zo TOMCOD a fish
zo TOMIAL TOMIUM, cutting edge of bird's bill
TOMPON inking pad
zo TOMPOT blenny fish
zo TOM-TIT blue tit
mu TOMTOM drum; (N. Amer. Indians)
mu TONADA tune, air (Sp.)
TONAME nickname; byname
TONGAN native of Tonga
TONGUE mouth organ; language; lick; scold
rl TONING intoning (recitative prayers)
TONING tinting; to suit (colours)
TONISH stylish; having 'tone'
ch TONITE an explosive
pl TONSIL throat appendage
bt TOOART Australian eucalyptus
cr TOOLED kitted for production; ornamental style
TOOTED hooted
TOOTER a piper
TOOTHY with teeth too apparent
mu TOOTLE play on the flute
TOO-TOO quite so; super
zo TOPAZA humming birds
TOP-DOG leader; victor
TOPFUL brimming
TOP-HAT topper
TOPHET place of torment (Hebrew)
md TOPHUS (gout)
zo TOPMAE insect labrum surface
nt TOPMAN top sawyer; dominant partner; demolisher
TOPPED surpassed; filled up; (golf)
TOPPER high hat
TOPPLE fall; tumble; collapse; totter
TORERO bull-fighter on foot
TOROID a symmetrical geometrical fig.
TOROSE TOROUS, swelling; protuberant
TORPID inert; numb; lethargic
TORPOR apathy; dullness; dormancy
TORQUE twisting force (motors)
TORQUE collar; necklace
TORRID sultry; scorching; fiery
TORSEL twisted scroll
bt TORULA yeast plant
TOSSED thrown; pitched
TOSSER pitcher; thrower; handy man
TOSS-UP an even chance; spin a coin

T'OTHER the other
TOTING carrying; humping
TOTTED added up
TOTTER topple; reel; rock; stagger
TOTTIE a small tot (rum)
zo **TOUCAN** S. American bird
TOUCHE a palpable hit (fencing)
TOUCHY testy; irascible; petulant
TOUPEE TOUPET, wig; false hair
TOURED journeyed
TOUSED hauled; torn; rumpled
TOUSER a teaser; a worrit
TOUSLE to rumple; ruffle; derange
TOUTED canvassed
TOUTER a tout
nt **TOWAGE** haulage (also by tugs)
TOWARD direction; docile; tractable; apt
TOWERY lofty
zo **TOWHEE** American marsh robin
TOWING dragging; drawing
oc **TOW-NET** water-fauna sample net
zo **TOWSER** a dog
md **TOXOID** detoxified toxin
zo **TOY-DOG** miniature dog
TOYFUL trifling
TOYING dallying; trifling
TOYISH playful; wanton
TOY-MAN a dealer in playthings
ar **TRABAL** beamy
TRABEA Roman consular robe
TRACED trailed; drawn; limned
TRACER investigator; (bullet); artificial isotop; monitor (drawings)
TRADED bartered; vended; sold
TRADER merchant; trafficker
TRAGIC shocking; calamitous
md **TRAGUS** (ear portal)
pc, md **TRANCE** dream state; hypnosis
TRANKA juggler's box
TRAPAN to ensnare; stratagem
TRAPES a slut; a tramp
TRAPPY treacherous
TRASHY rubbishy; worthless
pc, md **TRAUMA** a shock; harsh experience
TRAVEL tour; trip; journey; move; deviation from spin (ice skating)
TRAVIS stable partition
TREATY pact; covenant; alliance
mu **TREBLE** triple; threefold; high voice
TREBLY triply
bt **TREFLE** trefoil; clover
zo **TREMEX** an insect genus
ce **TREMIE** underwater concrete funnel
TREMOR shudder; earth shock (earthquake)

TRENCH deep furrow; groove; -warfare
md **TREPAN** (skull cutting)
TREPAN a cheat; ensnare; trapan
TREPID quaking; trembling; afraid
TRESSY curly
TRIACT having three rays
TRIAGE sorting; classifying state of wounded, injured
lw **TRIALS** performance tests; test cases
TRIBAL clannish
TRICAR motor-cycle
cf **TRICHO-** of the hair (Gr.)
TRICKY intricate; difficult; troublesome
nv **TRICON** on-course signal system
tx **TRICOT** machine-made fabric
bt **TRIFID** three-cleft
ck **TRIFLE** a sweet; gewgaw; daily
zo **TRIGLA** gurnards
TRIGLY dandified
mu **TRIGON** ancient harp; triangle
TRILBY a hat
ch **TRIMER** 3-molecule substance
TRIMLY neatly; compactly; evenly balanced
TRINAL three-fold
zo **TRINGA** sandpiper genus
ro **TRIODE** thermionic valve
ck **TRIOSE** simplest monosaccharide
ga **TRIPLE TRIPLY**, threefold scores (darts) (baseball hit)
TRIPOD three-legged stool or stand
TRIPOS Cambridge examination
zo **TRIPUS** 1 of Weberian vesicles
mu **TRISTE** sad; sorrowful; gloomy
TRITON Neptune's three-pronged fish-spear
zo **TRITON** genus of molluscs
el, ps **TRITON** nucleus of tritium atom
zo **TRITOR** tooth masticatory surface
ch **TRITYL** triphenylmethyl group
rl **TRIUNE** Trinity
TRIVET trevet; small hob; fireside
TRIVIA trivial matters (unimportant)
md **TROCAR** surgical instrument
TROCHE a lozenge; tabloid
zo **TROGON** Central American bird
TROIKA Russian 3-horsed sleigh
TROJAN a champion; a plucky fellow
TROLLY small truck
mu **TROMBA** trumpet (It.)
zo **TROPHI** (insect's mouth)
cf **TROPHO-** of food nourishment (Gr.)
ar **TROPHY** prize; laurels; sculptured arms or armour
TROPIC (Cancer and Capricorn)

md **-TROPIN** benefit of substance on organ
mu **TROPPO** excessively; too much (It.)
ch **TROTYL** explosive
TROUGH groove; trench; furrow; (feeding-)
TROUPE ensemble (circus) (actors)
lw **TROVER** finder (of treasure)
TROWED trusted; believed
to **TROWEL** garden implement
TRUANT shirker; absentee (school)
TRUDGE tramp; plod; march
TRUEST exactest; most veracious
TRUISM axiom; platitude
TRUITE crackled (porcelain)
TRUSTY reliable; staunch; faithful
zo **TRYGON** sting-ray
TRYING irksome; difficult; arduous
TRY-OUT preliminary trial
bt **TSAMBA** black barley ('Tibet)
zo **TSETSE** deadly fly (S. Africa)
TSONGA language (Mozambique)
TSWANA language (Africa)
T-TOTUM teetotum; teetotaller (sl.); abstainer
TUAREG tribe (Sahara)
TUBAGE inserting a tube
TUBBED bathed
TUBFUL the contents of a barrel; (bath)
TUB-GIG Welsh open carriage
TUBING piping
TUBULE small tube
TUCHUN Chinese military governor
TUCKED stuffed; folded; pleated
TUCKER bib; frilling
mu **TUCKET** trumpet-call
TUCK-IN large meal; picnic
TUFFET Miss Muffet's seat; grass
TUFTED tufty; crested
zo **TUFTER** a stag-hound
TUGGED TUGGER, heaved/-er; pulled/-er
TUILLE thigh armour
TULWAR Eastern sabre
bt **TUMBAK** coarse Persian tobacco
TUMBLE trip; stumble; somersault
TUMBLY uneven; unstable
TUMEFY to swell; distend; inflate
md **TUMOUR** morbid swelling
TUMPED hilled (gardening)
ck **TUM-TUM** W. Indian food
TUMULI ancient burial mounds
TUMULT uproar; hubbub; turmoil
gl, go **TUNDRA** subarctic plain (permafrost)
TUNDUN a toy; a bull-roarer
ro, tv **TUNE-IN** find station on waveband
TUNGUS Turanian tribe

ro **TUNING** syntonizing
TUNKER dunker; baptist; the great Dipper
TUNNED casked
TUNNEL underground passage (chunnel)
zo **TUPAIA** tree-shrew (Malay)
bt **TUPELO** gum-tree
zo **TUPPED** butted; rammed; served (ewes)
zo **TUPPER** ram; bricklayer's labourer
zo **TURACO** Afr. plantain-eating bird
TURBAN oriental head-dress (Sikh)
TURBID muddy; cloudy; confused
zo **TURBOT** a flatfish
zo **TURDUS** the thrush
TUREEN a receptacle for soup
TURFED sodded; kicked out
TURFEN (turf); covered with sward
TURGID bloated; tumid; bombastic
md **TURGOR** fullness
bt **TURION** runner; underground shoot
zo, ck **TURKEY** straight talk; poultry
mn **TURKIS** turquoise
cr **TURNED** revolved (-hinged); (lathe)
zo **TURNER** lathe-worker; pigeon
TURN-IN part-exchange deal; bed-time
bt **TURNIP** old-fashioned watch; root
TURN-UP attendance; (trousers); (trumps)
zo **TURNUS** swallow-tail butterfly
to **TURREL** tool used by coopers
ar **TURRET** minaret; small tower (castle)
zo **TURTLE** marine tortoise
TURVES plural of turf; sods (peat) (fuel)
ar **TUSCAN** people; art; architecture (It.)
TUSKAR peat cutter
zo **TUSKED TUSKER**, with ivory tusks; elephant
bt **TUSSAC** a tussock; cushion (grass)
tx **TUSSAH TUSSER**, wild silkworm's silk
md **TUSSIS** a cough
TUSSLE scuffle; wrestle; contend
bt **TUTSAN** a plant
TU-WHIT TU-WHOO, owlish night calls
TUXEDO dinner jacket (USA)
TUYERE a pipe; twyer
zo **TWAITE** species of shad
TWAITE THWAITE, arable acreage
TWEENY very small; maid
TWELVE a dozen
TWENTY a score
TWICER compositor and pressman

bt **TWIGGY** abounding in shoots
(skeletal)
tx **TWILLY** cotton-cleaning machine
tx **TWINED** twisted; meandered
bt **TWINER** climbing plant; cord maker
TWINGE pang; twitch; spasm
TWITCH twinge; jerk
tx **TWITTY** yarns with twisted portions
tx **TWO-PLY** of 2 layers (wood, wool,
etc.)
T'WOULD it would
TWO-WAY (a switch)
TYCOON Japanese prince; oil
magnate (Am.)
zo **TYLOTE** sponge-spicule
mu **TYMBAL** kettledrum; timbal
pr **TYMPAN** printing frame
TYPHON evil genius (Egypt)
md **TYPHUS** gaol fever
TYPIFY categorize; symbolize;
exemplify
pc **TYPIFY** categorizing of persons;
objects; (typewriter)
TYPIST typewriter user
TYRANT autocrat; despot
TYRIAN purple
mn **TYRITE** a mineral
zo **TYSTIE** the black guillemot
mu, zo **TZETZE** Abyssinian guitar

U

zo **UAKARI** S. American monkeys
UBERTY fruitfulness
UBIETY local relation
UBIQUE everywhere
UDMURT native of Central Asia
U-GAUGE laboratory test tube of
glass
UGLIFY to make hideous
UGLILY in an ungainly manner
UGRIAN UGRO Hungaric-Finnic-
Turkic
UGSOME hideous; gruesome
mn **UIGITE** a silicate of aluminium
md **ULITIS** gum inflammation
ULLAGE ULLING, lack of fullness in a
cask
bt **ULMOUS** (elm exudation)
md **ULNARE** cuneiform bone
md **ULOSIS** cicatrization
ULSTER overcoat
ULTIMO last; in last month
ULTION revenge
UMBERY UMBRAL, dark mustard
colour; shade
zo **UMBLES** entrails of deer

UMBRAL shady; darksome
UMBRIL umbrel; helmet vizor
UMLAUT vowel inflection (Ger.)
UMPIRE arbiter; referee; judge
UMWELT one's relationship with the
environment (Ger.)
UNABLE powerless; impotent;
unskilled
UNAWED undismayed; undaunted;
unimpressed
UNBANK (stoking)
UNBEAR to release from burden;
unharness; ungear
UNBELT remove or undo belt,
garment
nt **UNBEND** stand straight; unfasten
sails; cast loose (rope)
UNBEND UNBIND, release from
bondage
UNBENT relaxed; untied
UNBIAS to free from prejudice
nt **UNBIND** release from tether; knots;
set free
nt **UNBITT** (release cable)
UNBOLT unlatch; unlock (doors etc.)
UNBONE remove the bones
UNBOOT to take off shoes, boots
UNBORN non-existent; uncreated
UNBRED of ignoble birth
UNBURY disinter; exhume
UNCAGE release from captivity;
(ideas)
UNCALM to disturb; agitate
UNCAMP dislodge; evict; remove
UNCAPE unhood; disrobe; defrock;
reveal
UNCART unload (at destination)
UNCASE unpack; display; unsheath
UNCATE hooked
UNCIAL a script used in ancient
MSS.
UNCLAD naked; nude
nt **UNCLEW** release guy ropes;
(moorings)
UNCLOG clear drains; unhamper
ag **UNCOCK** make gun safe; remove
stooks (harvesting)
UNCOIF remove cap
nt **UNCOIL** unwind; straighten out;
(snakes); (ropes)
UNCOIN withdraw from currency
mu **UNCOOL** unrelaxed; unpleasant; jazz
UNCORD set free; release knots
UNCORK remove cork from bottle
UNCOWL remove cloak; defrock;
expose
lw **UNCURB** remove restrictions; (legal
obstacle)

UNCURL straighten out (hair); untwist

rl UNDEAN deprive of that office; unfrock

UNDECK divest of ornaments

UNDERN 9 a.m.; the third hour

UNDIES underclothes

UNDINE water-nymph

nt UNDOCK to separate space ships; leave dock

UNDOER subversionary agent

UNDONE unfastened (clothes); yet to be done

UNDUKE deprive of duke's rank

UNDULL sharpen; whet

UNDULY excessively; improperly

UNEASE mental unrest; anxiety

UNEASY restive; disturbed

UNEVEN rugged; rough; odd

UNFACE expose the character within

UNFAIR inequitable; unjust; partial

nt UNFAST insecurely tied

lw UNFEED without fees (salary)

UNFELT callous; insensitive (action)

UNFILE remove from a file

UNFINE shabby

lw UNFIRM weak legally; unsound

UNFIST to release; unhand

UNFOLD spread out; reveal (thoughts)

UNFOOL restore from folly; unhoax

lw UNFREE tied; restricted

nt UNFURL spread out sail; flag; unroll

UNGEAR to unharness; unbear

UNGILD UNGILT, remove the gold

UNGILL release from a gill-net

UNGIRD UNGIRT, release girdle or girth (harness)

UNGLUE unstick; release

UNGOWN disrobe; expel from university

zo UNGUAL UNGUIS, having claws; sharp nails

md UNGULA instrument; cylinder section

UNGYVE unfetter; free (from chains)

UNHAND UNHOLD, cry for release

UNHANG remove from drying line

UNHASP unfasten; (free from a catch)

UNHEAD behead; decapitate

nt UNHELM remove helmet or rudder

UNHEWN rough

UNHIVE deprive of habitation (bees)

UNHOLD UNHAND, cry for release

UNHOLY impious; profane; ungodly

UNHOOK disconnect; release from fastenings

ck UNHUNG (unhanged game meat); (rejected pictures)

UNHURT without injury (personal)

UNHUSK to shell

rl UNIATE Greek Catholic sect

UNIBLE UNIFIC, unifiable

bt UNIOLA American grass genus

UNIPED single-footed

pg UNIPOD single support camera mount

UNIQUE peculiar; sole; unexampled

UNISEX for either; or both sexes together

mu UNISON harmony; concord; accord

UNITAL unique; singular

UNITED combined; coalesced

UNITER joiner; merger

UNJUST biased; partial

UNKENT unknown

UNKEPT independent; discarded; rejected

UNKIND cruel; harsh; unfriendly

UNKING dethrone

UNKINK straighten out; (loosen knots)

UNKNIT unravel interlocked matter

nt UNKNOT untie; unfasten

UNLACE loosen, undo (shoes)

UNLADE discharge cargo; (burdens); unload

UNLAID virginal; untwisted; not allayed

UNLASH let loose; unbind; untie

pr UNLEAD remove lead

. UNLEAL unloyal

UNLENT not loaned

UNLESS if not; except if; when if

UNLIKE dissimilar; different from

UNLIME extract the lime

tx UNLINE remove the lining (clothes)

UNLINK unfasten; undo a chain

el UNLIVE not electrified; safe

UNLOAD unburden; remove from; give vent (feeling)

UNLOCK unfasten; open case

UNLORD deprive of that dignity

UNMADE not manufactured

UNMAKE destroy; dismantle

UNMASK expose; denounce; reveal

UNMEET unworthy; unbecoming

nt UNMOOR release a ship from moorings

UNMOWN uncut grass (lawn)

UNNAIL open by extracting nails

UNOWED not in debt

UNPACK disburden; open; uncover possessions

cp UNPACK recover data from storage

UNPAID still owing; outstanding
UNPICK take apart (clothes)
UNPROP remove a support
UNQUIT not discharged (from profession)
UNREAD not perused; ignorant
UNREAL fantastic; visionary; illusory
UNREEL show; tell a story; (film)
UNREIN slacken the rein
UNREST disquiet; unease; fidgetiness
UNRIPE immature; crude; green
UNROBE deprive of robes of honour
UNROLL open out; uncoil; evolve
UNROOF remove a roof (hurricanes)
UNROOT UPROOT, extirpate; eradicate
mo **UNROPE** release from rope (climbing)
UNROVE UNREEVED, rope freed from pulley, block
UNRULY riotous; turbulent
UNSAFE risky; hazardous; insecure
UNSAID unspoken (hint)
UNSEAM unpick sewing (clothes); rip; tear
UNSEAT to throw a rider; remove an official
UNSEEL to open the eyes
UNSEEN invisible
UNSELF absence of personality
UNSENT not despatched
UNSEWN unstitched
UNSHED retained; kept
nt **UNSHIP** remove part of a machine, mast of ship
UNSHOD barefoot; without shoes
UNSHUT open
UNSOLD not purchased
UNSOWN not propagated
UNSPAR remove spars
UNSPIN unravel
nt **UNSTEP** remove (a mast)
UNSTOP remove stoppage; make workable
UNSUNG forgotten; neglected
UNSURE uncertain
UNTACK disjoin
UNTAME wild; undomesticated
UNTELL never to narrate
UNTIDY slovenly; disorderly
UNTIED undone; unloosed
UNTILE remove tiles from roof
UNTOLD not narrated; numberless; innumerable
UNTOMB exhume
UNTORN unrent
UNTRIM disarray
UNTROD little frequented
UNTRUE false; fallacious; spurious

UNTUCK open bedclothes
UNTUNE disorder settings of a machine
UNTURN untwist; unscrew
UNUSED new; unaccustomed to; left idle
UNVEIL official opening; uncover a statue; reveal
UNWARM chillsome
UNWARY rash; incautious; indiscreet
UNWELL ailing; sick; indisposed
UNWEPT not lamented
UNWILY lacking in craft
UNWIND uncoil; disentangle; relax
UNWIND to show all instructions used
UNWISE indiscreet; imprudent
UNWOOF unweave
UNWORN new; unimpaired
UNWRAP open parcel; uncloak; disclose
UNYOKE release from harness; set free
UPBEAR sustain; elevate
mu **UPBEAT** unaccentuated rhythm
UPBIND confine
UPCAST uptoss; ventilation shaft
gl **UPCAST** upward strata displacement
UPCOIL to coil
cp **UPDATE** bring into line; modernize
UPFLOW upgush (oil)
UPGROW develop; evolve
UPGUSH upflow
UPHILL gradient; sloping; (effort)
UPHOLD advocate; maintain; champion
nt **UPHROE** awning support
UPKEEP maintenance
UPLAND highland
UPLEAN to incline upwards (Austral.)
UPLIFT improvement; moral encouragement
UP-LINE line to London (railway)
UPMOST topmost
UPPERS of shoes (leather); stimulating drugs
UP-PILE accumulate; upheap
UPPING departing suddenly; price raising; (swan-)
UPPISH UPPITY, being over-important; bumptious
UPREAR to raise the backside (horses)
UPRISE to revolt; ascend
UPROAR riot; hubbub; turmoil
UPROOT remove & destroy; (-self from home)

UPRUSH sudden upward surge (air, oil, water)
UPSHOT outcome; issue; result
UPSIDE topside
UPTAKE chimney; speed of learning
UPTILT bend upwards
cp **UPTIME** serviceable time, normal
UPTOWN city centre (if north)
UPTURN create disorder; upheaval
UPWARD ascending; uphill
UPWAYS upward
UPWELL upspring; gush
nt **UNWIND** into the wind; windward
UPWISE top side up
ch **URACIL** pyrimidine; nucleic acid
zo **URAEUM** tail-end of bird
URAEUS serpent emblem (Egypt)
ga **URAKEN** back fist blow (karate)
URANIA Muse of astronomy
URANIC (uranium); celestial
ch **URANIN** yellow dye
URANUS a planet; father of Saturn
ch **URANYL** chemical radical
md **URATES** urine salts
URBANE courteous; polite; affable
URCEUS single-handed jug; urn
zo **URCHIN** hedgehog; brat; gamin
ch **UREASE** enzyme
ch **UREIDE** acid derivative of urea
URESIS passing urine
md **URETER** duct that carries urine
md **URETIC** a medicine
URGENT pressing; imperative
URGING impelling; inciting
URNING consigning to an urn
ch **URONIC** of sugar oxidation compound
zo **UROPOD** abdominal limb
zo **URSINE** bear-like
bt **URTICA** nettle genus
hd **URVANT** turned up
USABLE employable; applicable
rl **USAGER** a religionist
USANCE usury
USEFUL helpful; beneficial
USTION combustion
USURER money-lender; a Shylock
USWARD towards us
UTERUS womb
UTGARD abode of Loki (Scand.)
UTMOST extreme; farthest
UTOPIA a political romance; an ideal society
md **UVEOUS** grape-like
md **UVULAR** (uvula)

V

VACANT void; empty; inane; free
VACATE quit; leave; annul; rescind
VACHER cow-keeper
VACUNA Roman goddess of horticulture
VACUUM void; vacuity; emptiness
VAGARY whim; crotchet; fancy
zo **VAGINA** sexual passage in female
VAGOUS wandering; erratic
VAGUER more indefinite; dimmer
VAIDIC Vedic; (philosophical)
VAILED submitted; tipped
VAILER a yielder
VAINER more conceited; falser
VAINLY ineffectually; proudly
VAISYA (Hindu caste)
rl **VAKASS** Armenian clerical vestment
lw **VAKEEL** Indian attorney
VALETE farewell
VALGUS knock-kneed man; club-foot
ch **VALINE** amino acid
VALING receding, lowering
VALISE portmanteau; holdall
ch,md **VALIUM** tranquillizer
rl,mu **VALKYR VALKYRIES** Odin's Amazons (Wagner)
VALLAR (rampart)
bd **VALLEY** dale; vale; dell; glen; dingle; (roof-edge) tile
VALLUM Roman rampart
VALOUR heroism; courage; prowess
VALUED esteemed; prized; treasured
VALUER appraiser
VALVED having valves
VAMOSE vamoose; to clear out
VAMPED improvised; patched; repaired
mu **VAMPER** a pianist; siren
VANDAL barbarian; destroyer
VANISH fade; disappear; depart
VANITY conceit; egotism; futility
VAN-MAN pantechnicon worker
zo **VANNER** light cart horse
md **VAPORS** vapours; nervous dejection
VAPOUR steam; reek; fume; to boast
VARIED diverse; motley; altered
VARIER an inconsistent person
VARLET scoundrel; rascal; knave
zo **VARMIN VERMIN, VARMINT,** noxious pests (rats)
VARSAL universal
rl **VARUNA** The Creator (Hindu Myth)
go **VARZEA** Amazonian flood plain (Brazil)
VASSAL retainer; dependant; bondman

VASTER on a grander scale
VASTLY spaciously; widely; immensely
md VASTUS a thigh muscle
tx VAT-DYE oxidation of textiles
br VATTED mellowing; maturing
VAULTY arched
VAWARD vanward; in the van
bd V-BRICK perforated instead of cavitied
VEADER Jewish intercalary month
VECTOR data display organism transmitting parasites
ma VECTOR force with thrust, direction, and magnitude
VEDDAH native Cingalese
VEDUTA painting of recognizable scene
nt VEERED changed course; shifted
VEILED concealed; shrouded; glozed
VEINED streaked; variegated; venose
VELARY a sail or awning
bt VELATE enveloped; veiled
mu VELETA waltz
VELITE lightly armed Roman soldier
VELLED removed turf
VELLON Spanish money of account
VELLUM parchment from calf-skin
zo VELLUS downy foetal hair
mu VELOCE very quick
VELOUR velvet
VELURE velvet; smoothing pad
tx VELVET soft silky stuff
VENDED sold; peddled; hawked
VENDEE the buyer; purchaser
lw VENDER VENDOR, one who sells
vt VENDUE auction; poultry disease
VENEER thin surface layer (fine wood); superficial
ga VENERY sport; hunting
ga VENEUR head game-keeper
VENGER AVENGER, wrathful punisher of wrong doer
VENIAL excusable; pardonable
VENITE 95th Psalm
VENNEL an alley-way (Sc.)
pl VENOSE VENOUS, veined
VENTED poured forth; uttered; emitted
md VENTER the abdomen
mu VENTIL (comet valve)
cf VENTRO- ventral from the anterior; stomach, abdomen
zo VENULE blood vessel in chordata
VERANO dry season C. Amer. summer (Sp.)
VERBAL oral; by word of mouth

hd VERDOY charged with heraldic flowers
VERDUN antique rapier (Fr.)
VERGED sloped; inclined; bordered on
me VERGEE about half acre
rl VERGER church caretaker
VERIFY confirm; authenticate; identify
VERILY truly; really; certainly
cn VERITE realism; film documentary technique
VERITY actuality; fact; reality
zo VERMES worms
VERMIL vermilion colour
zo VERMIN noxious animal; rabble
zo VERMIS main part of cerebellum
VERNAL springlike
VERREL ferrule; see virole
hd VERREY vaire; furry
VERSAL universal (Shak.)
VERSED skilled; familiar; accomplished
VERSER versifier; poetaster
mu VERSET prelude
VERSUS against; opposing
VERTEX top; apex; acme; zenith
zo VERVET S. African monkey
md VESICA a bladder; a sac
as VESPER evening star; Venus
nt VESSEL receptacle; utensil
VESTAL chaste (virgins)
VESTED fixed; legalized; established
rl VESTRY sacristy
bt VETCHY (vetch)
VETOED prohibited; banned; forbidden
VETTED carefully examined
VETUST ancient
VEXING annoying; tormenting; trying
VIABLE capable of existence
VIANDS food; provisions
VIATIC (journey)
VIATOR wayfarer
zo VIBRIO spiral bacillus
VICTIM a dupe; martyr; sacrifice
VICTOR conqueror; winner; champion
zo VICUNA cousin of wild llama
VIDAME French noble
VIDEOT media addict (TV)
VIDUAL widowed
mu VIELLE antique viol (Fr.)
VIEWED beheld; surveyed; scanned
VIEWER examiner; inspector
VIEWLY striking
VIGOUR force; energy; manliness

rl **VIHARA** Buddhist temple
nt **VIKING** Norse sea-rover; longshipman
VILELY basely; ignobly; malignantly
VILEST lowest; abject
VILIFY defame; traduce; disparage
md **VILLUS** hair; wool
hd **VILNED** wounded beast
rl **VIMANA** Indian temple
VINAGE wine doctoring
VINERY grape house
VINNEY a blue Dorset cheese
VINOSE VINOUS, concerning wine
VINTED made into wine
VINTRY wine shop; bodega; bistro
mn **VIOLAN** violet blue
bt **VIOLET** a colour; flower
VIOLIN fiddle; instrument with bow
VIRAGO nagging; overbearing woman (shrew)
VIRENT verdant; green; fresh
VIRGIN maiden; damsel; spinster; untouched; (city) fresh
VIRILE manly; robust; masculine
zo **VIRION** mature virus
hd **VIROLE** ferrule; hoop
VIROSE VIROUS, venomous; poisonous
VIRTUE integrity; probity; goodness
VISAED endorsed (passport)
VISAGE face; aspect; countenance
VISCID sticky; glutinous; tenacious
bt **VISCIN** mistletoe fruit substance
bt **VISCUM** mistletoe
md **VISCUS** an entrail; singular form of viscera, innards
rl **VISHNU** The Preserver (Hindu God)
VISIER VIZIER, leading Ottoman minister
VISILE with visual preference
VISION view; foresight; dream; eye sight (tele-)
VISIVE visual
cp **VISUAL** visible; perceptible; data display unit
VITALS essential organs (heart, genitals)
VITRIC glassy
mu **VIVACE** lively
VIVARY VIVARIUM, limited zoo
VIVIFY animate; enliven; quicken
VIZARD mask; visor
VOCULE a feeble cry
VOICED said; declared; uttered
VOICER spokesman
VOIDED evacuated; cancelled
VOIDER shallow basket
hd **VOLANT** flying; nimble; active

mu **VOLATA** rapid phrase (It.)
VOLENT exercising will power (gunfire)
VOLERY flight of birds
ga **VOLLEY** salvo (gunfire); strike with racquet (tennis) (ball game)
cp **VOLUME** book; tome; bulk; mass; magnetic storage; sound
VOLUTE spiral scroll
bt **VOLVOX** freshwater algae
md **VOMICA** an abscess in the lungs
md **VOMITO** yellow fever
rl **VOODOO VOUDOU**, Haitian witchcraft beliefs
VORAGO whirlpool; vortex; gull
hd **VORANT** devouring
VORTEX whirlpool; whirlwind
VOTARY a fan; devotee; zealot
VOTING electing; polling
VOTIVE vowed; devoted
VOULGE ancient pike (weapon) (Fr.)
VOWING pledging; promising
VOYAGE trip; cruise; passage
VOYANT seer with psychic vision
VULCAN god of fire
VULGAR coarse; ordinary; vernacular

W

WABBLE WOBBLE, stand unsteadily
ar **WABBLY** insecure; unstable (construction)
WADDED stuffed; filled
WADDIE Australian war club
WADDLE walk like a duck
WADING walking through water (sea)
tx **WADMAL** thick woollen cloth
lw **WADSET** a mortgage
WAFERY wafer-like
ck **WAFFLE** a grilled pancake
WAFTED floated; waved; beckoned
WAFTER a fan
WAGGED WAGGLE, shook about; (dog's tail); (-a finger)
zo **WAGGEL** great gull
WAGGLE vibrate; oscillate (golf)
rw **WAGGON WAGON**, cart; caravan; railway-
WAGING betting; venturing; conducting
WAG-WIT a would-be wit
rl **WAHABI** Puritan Moslem
WAHINE Maori woman; female surfer (Am.)
WAILED bemoaned; lamented
WAILER howler; weeper
WAITED attended; tarried; lingered

WAITER attendant; servitor; garçon
WAIVED WAIVER, relax the rules;
   release penälty
WAKING arousing from sleep; (-to
   new ideas)
WALING chastising
ce **WALING** trench-timbering plank
WALKED strolled; hiked
WALKER pedestrian; (street-);
   (sleep-); (jay-); frame
WALLAH Government official
   (Indian Raj)
WALLED enclosed
WALLER a wall-builder
WALLET purse; scrip; pouch
WALLEY skating jump
br **WALLOP** to hit; to beat; beer
WALLOW lounge in heat; flounder
   around; grovel
bt **WALNUT** commonest European nut
zo **WALRUS** tusked seal; (morse)
WAMBLE to be queasy
tx **WAMMUS** knitted jacket (USA)
WAMPEE a Chinese fruit
WAMPUM beads used as cash
   (N.Am. Ind.)
WANDER stroll at random; roam;
   (mind-)
bt **WANDOO** Australian white gum
WANGLE to obtain by craft, by
   persuasion
as **WANING** shrinking; ebbing (moon
   phase)
WANKER winder; handyman
WANKLE weak; unstable
WANNED made pale
WANTED needed; lacked; desired
WANTER a requirer; craver
WANTON frisky; uncontrolled;
   frolicsome
zo **WAPITI** stag; American reindeer
zo **WAPPER** gudgeon; ball-on-string
   weapon
zo **WAPPET** yelping cur
mu, vt **WARBLE** cattle tumour; quaver; sing
WAR-CRY slogan
ga **WARDED** guarded; parried (fencing)
WARDEN custodian; protector;
   curator
WARDER turnkey; keeper; jailer
WARIER more cautious
WARILY cautiously; carefully;
   cannily
WARMAN warrior; man-at-arms
WARMER hotter; nearer; (a bribe)
WARMLY earnestly; ardently;
   zealously
WARMTH heat; enthusiasm; fervency

WARM-UP loosening exercises; pre-
   match
WARNED cautioned; notified;
   apprised
WARNER an admonisher
WARPED distorted; perverted; biased
tx, wv **WARPER** a weaver; a twister
WARREN labyrinthine; rabbit
   burrows
WAR-TAX tax to help war
md **WARTED** verrucose
ck **WASABI** Jap. horseradish
WASHED bathed; cleaned (clothes)
pb **WASHER** metal ring; tap root
WASH-IN increase in angle of
   incidence
WASH-UP cleaning dishes
WASTED frittered; squandered
WASTEL a fine sort of bread
WASTER a cudgel; spendthrift;
   chisel; defective brick
WATERY aqueous; dilute; thin;
   insipid
zo **WATTLE** fowl's gills
bt **WATTLE** a acacia; a hurdle
WAULED WAWLED, HOWLED,
   (caterwauled); (street calling)
WAVERY unsteady; tremulous
WAVING undulating; swaying
WAVURE procrastination
WAX-END cobbler's thread
WAXIER more irate
WAXING increasing; growing; (shoe
   polish); (skiing)
WAYLAY to ambush; kidnap; mug;
   rob
WAYOUT advanced; unusual
WEAKEN impair; enfeeble; enervate
WEAKER more dilute; thinner;
   feebler
WEAKLY delicately; infirmly; fraily
WEALTH riches; opulence;
   abundance
WEANED newly independent (baby);
   free; withdrawn
WEAPON instrument of combat;
   (economic)
WEARER bearer; (-of clothing) (-of
   flag)
zo **WEASEL** explosive carnivore
wv, zo **WEAVER** intertwined cloth maker;
   bird
WEAZEN wizened; sharp; shrivelled
   (Sc.)
wv **WEBBED** arachnoid; woven (duck-
   foot)
md **WEB-EYE** a disease of the cornea
pr **WEB-FED** of printing paper by reel

WEDDED married; espoused; spliced
WEDELN S-course downhill ski technique
WEDGED joined; jammed; crowded
WEEDED hoed; (eradicated) (gardening)
to **WEEDER** garden tool; gardener
WEEKLY hebdomadary; a periodical
WEENED imagined; thought
zo **WEEPER** Niobe; a monkey
zo **WEEVER** sting-fish
zo **WEEVIL** a beetle
ps **WEIGHT** moving force needed to overcome inertia
me **WEIGHT** measure of heaviness; load; burden
WELDED joined; metal parts fused in heat (process)
WELKIN sky, clouds; universe (ring)
WELLED poured forth; spouted; gushed
WELTED edged; bordered
WELTER wallow; flounder; heavy
WENDED journeyed; wandered
WENDIC a Sorabian
WESTER to turn westward
WET-BOB Eton aquatic sportsman
zo **WETHER** a castrated ram
WETTER damper; more showery
nt **WHALER** whale-boat
WHALLY having greenish-white eyes
WHATSO of whatever kind
WHEELY circular
WHEEZE puff; blow; ancient joke
WHEEZY asthmatic; whistling mechanical sound
WHELKY rounded; protuberant
WHENCE wherefrom
nt **WHERRY** a liquor; sailing boat
WHEUGH! exclamation of surprise
zo **WHEWER** the widgeon; duck
ck **WHEYEY** of curdfree, watery milk
zo **WHIDAH WHYDAH**, African weaver bird
WHILED of time passing away; beguiled
WHILES meanwhile
WHILLY to cajole; to wheedle
WHILOM formerly
WHILST while
WHIMSY fad; caprice; fancy; crotchet
WHINED WHINER, whimper in complaining tone
bt **WHINNY** horsey greeting; gorse
WHIPPY flexible; springy
WHISHT! hush!
WHISKY colour of Napoleon's white horse

WHITEN blanch; bleach; turn pale
WHITER purer; brighter
WHITES flannel trousers (cricket); (eyes); (eggs)
WHOLLY entirely; fully; utterly
WHOMSO every one whom
WICKED evil; sinful; ungodly; nefarious
bt **WICKEN** mountain ash
bt **WICKER** pliant twig; osier
WICKET small gate; (cricket)
bt **WICOPY** American basswood
WIDELY spaciously; extensively; rifely
WIDEST broadest; remotest
WIELDY manageable
WIFELY of the missus
zo **WIGEON WIDGEON**, duck
WIGGED scolded; reproved; chid
WIGGLE WAGGLE, WRIGGLE, snake-like movement
WIGWAG flag-wag; twist
WIGWAM Indian tent (tepee) (Amer.)
WILDER more impulsive; bewildered
WILDLY fiercely; recklessly; savagely
WILFUL wanton; perverse; obdurate
WILIER craftier; slyer
WILILY artfully; cunningly; insidiously
WILING beguiling; deceiving
lw **WILLED** intended; resolved; bequeathed
WILLER one who decides forcefully
zo **WILLET** North American snipe
bt **WILLOW** a cricket bat tree
WILTED drooped; withered
to **WIMBLE** to drill; gimlet
WIMBLE nimble; active
WIMPLE medieval female headdress; ripple
WINCED flinched; quailed
WINCER a shrinker
tx **WINCEY** winsey; a fabric
WINDED blown; lost breath; caught scent
WINDER to fan; to winnow; a key
WINDLE a spindle; reel
WINDOW lattice; casement
WIND-UP crank a machine for starting; (clock); twist
WINERY where wine is bottled/stored
WINGED alate; rapid; wounded
ga **WINGER** enclosed chair; 'outside' forward (football)
WINKED twinkled; flickered; acquiesced

WINKER horse's blinker
zo, bt WINKLE sea-snail; (periwinkle)
WINNER victor; conqueror; champion
ag WINNOW open-air threshing; separate grain from chaff
tx WINSEY wincey; twilled cotton
WINTER hyemal, viernal; cold season
WINTRY icy; frosty; cheerless
WIPING deterging; rubbing
WIRIER capable of greater strain
WIRILY vigorously; tenaciously
WIRING circuits; telegraphing
WISARD WIZARD, sorcerer; necromancer
WISDOM sagacity; knowledge
WISELY sagely; sensibly; sapiently
WISEST most learned and judicious
WISHED listed; wanted; longed for
WISHER desirer; yearner
WISKET a basket
WISTLY earnestly; attentively
WITHAL together with; likewise
WITHED bound with a withe
WITHER fade; pine; languish
WITHIN not exceeding; indoors
WITH-IT up to date; aware of trends
WITTED alert; wise
zo WITWAL popinjay; woodpecker
WIVELY WIFELY, of a spouse
hd WIVERN WYVERN, winged dragon
WOBBLE wabble; oscillate; vibrate
WOBBLY unstable; unsteady
WOEFUL waeful; tragic; grievous
WOLFER voracious feeder
zo WOLVES predacious animals
zo WOMBAT burrowing marsupial
WONDER marvel; miracle; prodigy; awe
WONING a dwelling
WONTED accustomed; usual
ck WONTON 'Chinese ravioli', cooked in soup
fr WOODED afforested; timbered
WOODEN made of timber; impassive
ac WOOFER bass loudspeaker
WOOING courting; courtship
tx WOOLLY lanate; of wool
WORDED. expressed; phrased
WORKED moiled; strove; slaved
WORKER hand; toiler; operative
WORK-UP rehearsal; exercise; obtaining data, become heated
WORMED crept; insinuated; crawled
zo WORMUL WORNIL, cow maggot
zo WORREL lizard (Eygpt)
WORRIT an annoyance
WORSEN to defeat; to deteriorate

WORSER far worse
WORTHY exemplary; noble; meritorious
WOUNDY excessive; injurious
zo WOU-WOU silver gibbon; wow-wow (Java)
WOWSER kill-joy; fanatical Puritan
WRAITH apparition; ghost; spectre
zo WRASSE prickly fish
WRATHY apt to wrath; choleric
WREATH festoon; garland; chaplet
to WRENCH strain; sprain; twist; spanner
WRETCH villain; vagabond; miscreant
WRIEST most distorted
WRIGHT an artificer; mechanic
WRITER scribe; author; scribbler
WRITHE squirm; wriggle; contort
WUZZLE to jumble (USA)
hd WYVERN WIVERN, heraldic dragon

X

XANADU Kubla Khan's country estate
XANGTI Zeus (Chinese)
cf XANTHO- of yellowness
XENIAL genial; friendly
XENIUM gift; picture of still life
zo XENOPS tree-creeper birds (S. Amer.)
XERXES Persian King; Ahasuerus
X-GUIDE transmission line
XOANON primitive Greek statue
md X-RAYED (Rontgen rays)
ch XYLENE a benzene derivative
mn XYLITE asbestos
XYLOID like wood
bt XYLOMA internally spore-forming body
ch XYLOSE wood sugar
md XYSTER a bone scraper
ar XYSTOS XYSTUS, covered portico (Gr.)

Y

YABBER JABBER, speech (Australian)
zo YAFFLE the green woodpecker
YAGGER pedlar; hawker (Sc.)
rl YAHVEH JAHVEH, JEHOVAH, God of the Hebrews
YAKSKA Hindu gnome
YAMMER whine; blather; grumble
YANKED heaved; pulled up; hauled

YANKEE Northern American
nt YANKEE a specially large jib
YANKER a big lie (Sc.)
ck YAOURT YOGHURT, fermented milk
zo YAPOCK S. Amer. water-opossum
YAPPED yelped
zo YAPPER a yapping dog
YARDED confined
YARNED related; narrated
YARPHA peaty soil (Shetland)
bt YARRAH Australian red gum tree
bt YARROW the milfoil
pp YARYAN soda-recovery method
YAUPON holly (used as tea)
nt YAWING side-to-side movement in
   rough sea
YAWLED howled; cried
YAWNED gaped; oscitated
YCLEPT by name of; called
YEANED YEENED, brought forth
YEARLY annual
YEASTY turbid; frothy; foamy
YELLED bawled; howled; screamed
YELLOW cowardly
YELPED yauped; yapped; barked
YELPER yapper
YEMENI native of Yemen
mn YENITE a silicate of iron
nt YEOMAN a beefeater; farmer; tower
YERKED jerked
bt YER-NUT pig-nut
YES-MAN sycophant; ministerial
YESTER previous; last
YEXING hiccuping
YOGISM a Hindu philosophy
YOICKS! a hunting cry
me YOJANA about 5 miles (8 km)
   (Indian)
YOKING coupling; linking;
   harnessing; binding
ck YOLKED having a yolk; an eggy jolke
YONDER over there
YONKER a stripling
YONNIE pebble (Aus.)
YORKER (cricket)
YORUBA tribe (South Sahara)
YOUTHY young; callow
YOU-UNS you, you ones
YOWLED howled; yelled
zo YOWLEY yellow bunting
rw Y-TRACK reversing lines for trains
ch YTTRIA oxide of yttrium
ch YTTRIC containing yttrium
zo YUCKER American woodpecker
YURROP US word for Europe

Z

ZABIAN Sabian; non-Christian
   gnostic
ZABISM Sabianism
zo ZABRUS beetle genus
ZACCAB Yucatan wall plaster
ZACCHO the base of a pedestal
mn ZAFFER ZAFFRE, cobalt ore
bt ZAMITE fossil-plant
zo ZANDER sander; pike-perch
ZANIES clowns; buffoons
tx ZANTHA knitted fabric
bt ZAPOTE plums (Mexico)
tx ZARAPE SERAPE, Mexican blanket
ZAREBA ZERABA, ZARIBA, fortified
   camp
mn ZARNEC orpiment
ZEALOT fanatic; bigot; partisan
bc ZEATIN adenine derivative
nt ZEBECK Algerian pirate-ship
ZEDONK offspring of zebra (m.) and
   donkey (f.)
zo ZEEKOE SEACOW manatee (S. Africa)
ZEETAK red-coral (S. Africa)
ZEMZEM sacred fountain at Mecca
ZENANA women's quarter (Ind.)
ZENDIK Eastern heretic; magician
ZENITH acme; apex; climax; summit
ZENZIK maths term
mt ZEPHYR the west wind; soft breeze
nm ZEQUIN SEQUIN, gold coin decoration
ZEREBA ZARABA, thorn bush
   stockade
gl, go ZEUGEN table-like masses of rock in
   deserts
ZEUGMA grammatical conjunction
zo ZICSAC sicsac; crocodile bird
ZIG-ZAG alternating turns; hairpin
   bends; horse show
ZILLAH Indian district
ZIMONE (gluten)
ZINCKY like zinc
zo ZINGEL perch; Danube fish
bt ZINNIA a flower
ZIPPED whizzed; encoded
ZIPPER zip-fastener
mn ZIRCON a silicate
mu ZITHER the cithern
zo ZIVOLA yellow-hammer
ZODIAC a heavenly-girdle; the
   ecliptic
ZOETIC vital
ZOMBIE moron; drugged person
ZONARY ZONOID, resembling
   planetary girdle
ZONATE belted
ZONING area allocation; planning

ZONNAR girdle worn in the Levant
ZONULE zonula; small zone
zo ZONURE lizard covered with spikes
zo ZOONAL embryonic
zo ZOONIC zoological
ZOOSIS animal-parasite-caused
  disease
zo ZOO-ZOO wood-pigeon
md ZOSTER shingles
ZOUAVE Algerian soldier
ZOUNDS 'God's wounds' (slang)
Z-SCORE standard; sigma score
  (statistics)

mu ZUFOLO zuffolo; flageolet
ch ZUMATE ZYMATE, a salt of zymic
  acid
ZUNIAN Pueblo-Indian
ZYGITE an oarsman in a trireme
md ZYGOMA the cheek-bone
bl ZYGOSE ZYGOTE, fertilization; spore;
  germ cell
ZYMASE a ferment; an enzyme
rl ZYMITE priest using leavened bread
ch, ck ZYMOID like a ferment; yeasty
ZYMONE insoluble gluten
br ZYTHUM ancient type of beer

SEVEN-LETTER WORDS

A

rl **AARONIC** (Jewish priesthood)
ABACIST an accountant
ABACTOR cattle thief, rustler
ABADDON Apollyon; bottomless pit
zo **ABALONE** mother-of-pearl; oyster
shell
ABANDON joie-de-vivre; forsake;
quit
ABASHED shamed; embarrassed
ABASING degrading; humbling
ABATING mitigating; stopping
ABATTIS military obstacles
ABATURE beast tracks
pg, bt **ABAXIAL** outward rays from stem
ABBOZZO preliminary sketch
tx **ABB-WOOL** warp-yarn
ABDOMEN lower belly
ABDUCED abducted; separated
ABETTED incited; aided; assisted
lw **ABETTER** an abettor; instigator
ABEYANT in abeyance
ABIDING residence; lasting; durable
bt **ABIETIC ABIETIN**, conifers; resin
ABIGAIL serving-girl; Hebe;
waitress
lw **ABIGEAT** cattle theft
ABILITY legal power; wealth; talent
ABIOSIS absence of life
ABIOTIC incompatible with life
lw **ABJUDGE** deprive by law
ABJURED recanted; repudiated
ABJURER forswearer
md **ABLATOR** heat-protection material;
instrument
ABLEISM pro able-bodied
discrimination
md **ABLEPSY** blindness
ABLINGS aiblins; perhaps
ABLUENT detergent
ABOLISH destroy; extirpate;
annul
pc, md **ABOULIA** atrophy of reasoning
ABRADED scraped; worn away
ABRAXAS Gnostic god; amulet
ABREAST side by side
ABRIDGE curtail; epitomize;
summarize
md **ABSCESS** inflamed body tissue
ABSCIND cut off
ABSCISS a geometric line

ABSCOND quit secretly
ABSENCE lack; deficiency; non-
presence
ar, rl **ABSIDAL** apse-like
ck **ABSINTH** liqueur; wormwood
ABSOLVE release; exonerate; shrive
ABSTAIN refrain; desist; avoid
ABUSING perverting, violating
ABUSION deception; disparagement
ABUSIVE ribald; reviling; calumnious
ABUTTAL the boundary of lands
ABUTTED contiguous; bordered on
lw **ABUTTER** neighbour
ABYSMAL fathomless; profound
ABYSSAL bottomless
ACADEMY also academe; institution
ACADIAN Nova Scotian
ACALEPH jelly fish
bt **ACANTHA** prickly plant
md **ACAPNIA** loss of CO_2 in blood
ACARDIA heart-less
zo **ACARIDA ACARINA**, mites; ticks
ACCEDED assented; succeeded
ACCEDER one who concurs
ACCLAIM applaud; applause;
proclaim
lw **ACCOMPT ACCOUNT**, reckon; bill;
statement
ACCRUED resulted; accumulated
ACCURSE curse; condemn; execrate
ACCURST accursed; damned;
diabolical
ACCUSAL an accusation; indictment
lw **ACCUSED** defendant; arraigned
lw **ACCUSER** plaintiff
ch **ACERATE** (aceric acid)
ACERBIC sour; caustic; astringent
bt **ACEROLA** Amer. cherry-like fruit
bt **ACEROSE** acerous; prickly
ACETARY acid pulp
ch **ACETATE** (vinegar)
ch **ACETIFY** acidify
ch **ACETONE** liquid ketone; solvent
ACETOUS also acetose; sour
ACHAEAN of Achaia (Greek)
bt **ACHAENE** seeded fruit
ACHATES a true friend
ACHERON river of woe
ACHIEVE perform; perfect; attain
ck **ACHIOTE** red colouring matter from
seeds
md **ACHOLIA** lack of bile

ACHTUNG beware!; look out! (Ger.)
ACICULA spiked crystals
ACIDITY sourness; tartness
ACIDIZE to add acid
ACIDOID potentially acid (soil)
ACIFORM needle-shaped
ACINOSE ACINOUS, granular
   consistency
ACLINIC no magnetic dip
md ACOLOGY the healing art
rl ACOLYTE also acolyth; assistant
bt ACONITE plant genus; monkshood
zo ACONTIA free threads of anthozea
zo ACOUCHY guinea pig; agouti
lw ACQUEST acquisition
ACQUIRE get; gain; procure; win
pc ACRASIA inability of self-restraint
ACRATIA impotence
ACREAGE area in acres
md ACRISIA therapeutic uncertainty
ACROBAT a tumbler; funambulist
bt ACROGEN (club-moss); (tree-fern)
as ACRONIC non-cosmical (astronomy)
ACRONYM word composed of initials
ACRONYX ingrowing nail
ar ACROTER pinnacle
md ACROTIC superficial
ch ACRYLIC acid, resins for plastics
ACTABLE performable
ACTAMER substance stopping
   bacteria growth
zo ACTINIA (sea-anemones)
ACTINIC chemical ray action (solar)
ACTRESS a lady of parts
ACTUARY statistical expert; registrar
ACTUATE impel; urge; instigate;
   incite
zo, bt ACULEUS sting; prickle
ACUTELY keenly; intensely;
   poignantly
ACYESIS sterility of female
ADACTYL fingerless
ADAGIAL proverbial
mn ADAMANT the diamond; unshakable;
   unyielding
ADAMITE a nudist
ADAPTED conformed; attuned;
   adjusted
ADAPTOR ADAPTER, fitment; joining
   device
bt ADAXIAL axis-face of leaf
ma ADDABLE ADDIBLE, easily joined for
   increase
ADDENDA appendix; augmented
   matter
ADDIBLE addable
ADDLING going rotten; confusing
ADDRESS skill; accost; speech

ADDRESS stance over ball (golf);
   domicile; archery
ADDUCED cited; brought forward;
   alleged
ADDUCER a deducer
ADDULCE to sweeten
ch ADENINE purine derivative
md ADENOID growth in nasal pharynx
md ADENOMA glandular tumour
md ADENOUS ADENOSE, glandular
ADHERED stuck; clung; held; cleaved
ADHERER partisan; ally; parasite
ADHIBIT attach; administer
md ADIPOMA morbid obesity
ADIPOSE fatty; adipous; sebaceous
md ADIPSIA never thirsty
ADJOINT united; connected
ADJOURN suspend; postpone; defer
ADJUDGE condemn; decree; ordain
ADJUNCT a concomitant
ADJURED charged on oath
ADJURER adjuror
ADJUTOR a helper; colleague; ally
nt ADMIRAL highest naval officer
ADMIRED wondered; appreciated
ADMIRER a lover; adorer
ADMIXED adulterated; infused
ADOLODE distillation tester
ADONAÏS Shelley's elegy on Keats
ADONIZE beautify; worship youth
ADOPTED (foster-child);
   appropriated
ADORING worshipping; idolizing
ADORNED embellished; decked
hd ADORSED back to back
md ADRENAL (kidneys); gland
ADULATE flatter; cajole; belaud
ADVANCE to extoll; loan; promote;
   move forward
ADVENED acceded
ADVENER an assentor
ADVERSE contrary; hostile; inimical
ADVISED notified; informed;
   apprised
ADVISER informer; cautioner
ADVISOR advice giver; counsellor
rl ADVOWEE a patron of a benefice
md ADYNAMY weakness
mu, gl, go AEOLIAN aerial; deposits, sanddunes,
   caused by wind
AEOLIST wind-bag
AEONIAN eternal
AERATED gassy
AERATOR soda-water machine
AEROBAT an aerial stunter
md AEROBIA bacteria
md AEROBIC microbial; gymnastic dance
AEROBUS passenger plane

AEROGEL gel containing gas
ch **AEROSOL** sprayed mist
AERO-TOW record heights achieved (gliding)
AETATIS at the age of
AFFABLE benign; gracious, sociable
AFFABLY cordially, courteously
AFFICHE notice; placard
AFFINAL akin; related
AFFINED united; allied; related
AFFIXED attached; appended; annexed
AFFLICT distress; torment; chasten
AFFORCE reinforce
AFFRONT insult; outrage; abuse
AFFUSED sprinkled
AFFYING betrothing
nm **AFGHANI** native (Afghanistan)
AFRICAN of Africa
AGAINST opposite; counter; despite
md **AGALAXY** lack of milk
AGAMIST matrimonial objector
AGAMOUS cryptogamic
mn **AGATINE AGATIZE**, like agate; become agate
AGELESS timeless
AGELONG ancient; antiquated
AGENDUM a business item
md **AGEUSIA** loss of taste
AGILELY, AGILITY gracefully and mentally quick
AGISTER, AGISTOR grazing controller
AGITATE arouse public feeling; shake
mu **AGITATO** spasmodic; restless
zo **AGNATHA** lampreys; hagfish
AGNATIC akin
AGNOMEN added surname
md **AGNOSIA** perceptionlessness
AGONISE AGONIZE, to suffer anguish amid effort
ga **AGONISM, AGONIST** competing; contestant (prot-)
AGRAFFE clasp or hook (armour)
nt **AGROUND** stranded (also figuratively)
bt **AGYNOUS** non-reproductive
AHRIMAN evil spirit (Persian)
AIBLINS ablings; perhaps
AIDANCE help; succour; bounty
AIDLESS unsupported; unbacked; solo
AIGULET aglet; pendant
bt **AILANTO** tree of Heaven
ae **AILERON** wing lateral-control
AILETTE armoured epaulet
AILMENT malady; complaint; disorder

AIMLESS pointless; random; haphazard
AIR BASE strategic air supply point
AIR GLOW atmospheric luminosity
AIR MAIL post carried by air
AIR MARK par avion
AIR RAID attack by aeroplanes
AIR-BATH nudity for health
AIR-BONE hollow bone
ae **AIR-BUMP** sudden jolt during flight
AIRCAST sow seed from the air
tc **AIR-CORE** cable
AIR-FLUE hot air distributor
AIRFOIL aileron
eg **AIR-FUEL** gas–liquid ratio
AIRHEAD unintelligent; vapid; forward supply (airport)
AIRHOLE ventilator; (cavern)
AIRLESS stuffy
AIRLIFT aerial transportation
AIRLINE flight transport company
AIR-LOCK pump flow stoppage
AIRPARK fleet of aeroplanes
AIRPORT aeroplane landing area
AIR-PUMP vacuum maker
zo **AIR-SACS** quill vesicles
ae **AIR-SHED** a hangar
ae **AIRSHIP** dirigible; zeppelin
AIRSIDE post control embarkation areas (airports)
ae **AIRWAYS** airlines
ch **AJACINE** cycactonine acid ester
AJUTAGE vent pipe
bt **AKINETE** oil/food storage cell
ar **ALAMEDA** shaded promenade (Moorish)
A-LA-MODE stylish
A-LA-MORT till death
md **ALANINE** amino acid
bt **ALANTIN** starch
ALARMED shocked; appalled; daunted
ALASKAN (Alaska)
ALASTOR Nemesis
hd **ALBERIA** shield without arms
ch **ALBITIC** (felspar)
ALBORAK Mahomet's mount to heaven
ALBUMEN white of egg
md **ALBUMIN** (endosperm)
ALCAICS Alcaic verse
ALCALDE judge; Spanish mayor
bt **ALCANNA, ALHENNA** henna, dye for hands
ALCAZAR Moorish palace
ALCHEMY alchymy; medieval chemistry
ch **ALCOHOL** pure wine spirit

as **ALCYONE** star in Pleiades
bt **ALECOST** costmary; ale flavouring
ALE-GILL medicated liquor
bt **ALEHOOF** ground ivy
ALEMBIC distilling retort
ALENGTH full length
ALERTER brisker; more wakeful
ALERTLY vigilantly; actively; warily
pc **ALETHIA** inability to forget
ALETUDE fatness; bulkiness
bt **ALEURON** albuminoid
zo **ALE-WIFE** kind of skad; mackerel
bt **ALFALFA** lucerne grass
md **ALGAROT** antimony emetic
ALGATES by all means; always
as **ALGEBAR** the constellation Orion
ALGEBRA number-properties'
  investigation
ALGESIA sensitiveness to pain
ALGIFIC producing cold
ALHENNA henna; alkenna; orange
  dye
sv **ALIDADE** surveyor's sight rule
ALIFORM wing-like
ALIGNED adjusted; regulated; aimed
ALIMENT nutriment; sustenance;
  food
lw **ALIMONY** maintenance
ALIQUOT integral factor
bt **ALKANET** henna dye
rl **ALKORAN** alcoran; the Koran
md **ALLALIA** loss of speech
ALLAYED quieted; alleviated;
  pacified
ALLEGED averred; asserted; declared
mu **ALLEGRO** gaily; cheerful pace
ALLERGY distaste; repugnance
ar **ALLETTE** building wing; buttress
bt **ALL-GOOD** a plant
ALL-HAIL a greeting
ALL-HEAL a panacea; valerian, etc.
nc **ALLOBAR** non-natural-isotope form
  of element
ALLONGE added leaf; lunge
ALLONYM assumed name;
  pseudonym
ALLOWED abated; authorized
ch **ALLOXAN** cyclic ureide
ALLOYED debased; tempered
ALL-PASS phase-shift for any
  frequency
bt **ALLSEED** flax
ALL-TIME unprecedented occurrence
ALLUDED suggested; insinuated;
  hinted
ALLURED enticed; inveigled; decoyed
ALLUVIA waterborne desposit
el **ALL-WATT** induction motor

ro **ALL-WAVE** multi-wave
ALL-WISE of infinite wisdom
ALLYING betrothing; leaguing
nt **ALMADIE** bark canoe
ALMANAC calendar
ALMOIGN charitable endowment
ALMONER giver of alms
ALMONRY almsgiving place;
  cupboard
ALMS-BOX charity receptacle
ALMS-FEE Peter's pence
ALMSMAN receiver of alms
ALNAGER wool inspector
lw **ALODIUM** freehold
md **ALOETIC** purgative
ALOGISM illogical statement
ALONGST along with
mu **ALP-HORN** Swiss cow-horn
ALREADY before; previously
ALSIRAT bridge to paradise
ALTERED modified; transmuted
bt **ALTERNE** sudden plant-life change
bt **ALTHAEA** hollyhock genus
ALTHING Iceland Parliament
mu **ALT-HORN** saxhorn
ALTRICE bird hatching immature
  young
ch **ALTROSE** glucose stereoisomer
mn **ALUMINA** aluminium clay
ALUMINE oxide of aluminium
ALUMING impregnating with alum
ALUMISH resembling alum
ALUMNUS college student
mn **ALUNITE** alum-stone
pl **ALVEARY** hive; ear cavity
ALVEATE to hollow out
bt **ALVEOLA** small cavity
pl **ALVEOLE** tooth socket
bt **ALYSSUM** a rock plant
ch **AMALGAM** mercury alloy
bt **AMANDIN** (almonds)
AMANOUS lacking hands
bt **AMARANT AMARANTH**, a fadeless
  flower
AMASSED heaped; collected
AMATEUR not a professional
AMATIVE loving; lovesome
AMATORY ardent; erotic; passionate
AMAZING astounding; bewildering
AMAZONE riding habit
AMBAGES circumlocution;
  subterfuge
AMBARIE covered howdah
AMBETTI speck-containing glass
AMBIENT encompassing; enfolding
AMBITAL pertaining to skeletal parts
AMBITUS outer edge
AMBLING at an easy gait; sauntering

bt **AMBOYNA** a decorative wood
AMBREIN AMBERGRIS, sea wax used
  in perfumes
AMBROID moulded amber
ga **AMBSACE AMESACE**, double-ace dice
AMBULET small ambulance
bt **AMELLUS** purple star-wort
AMENAGE domesticate; manage
AMENDED emended; ameliorated
AMENING ratifying; sanctioning
AMENITY pleasantness; agreeableness
bt **AMENTAL** bearing catkins
md **AMENTIA** mental deficiency
bt **AMENTUM** a catkin
AMERCED fined
AMHARIC language (Ethiopia)
AMIABLE lovable; benign; winsome
AMIABLY kindly; charmingly
el **AMMETER** ampere meter
ch **AMMONAL** an explosive
ch **AMMONIA** pungent gas
md, pc **AMNESIA** loss of memory
md, pc **AMNESIC** loss of language ability
AMNESTY pardon; absolution;
  oblivion
zo **AMNIOTE** embryo sac classification
AMOEBAN pertaining to amoeba
AMONGST amid; between
AMORIST philanderer
AMOROSA, AMOROSI sweetheart;
  gallants
mu **AMOROSO AMOROUS**, tenderly,
  passionate
bt **AMORPHA** indigo
lw **AMOTION** deprivation
AMPASSY AMPERSAND, the &
AMPHORA two-handled wine jar
AMPLEST most lavish; most copious
AMPLIFY expand; enlarge; augment
md **AMPOULE** container for hypodermic
  dose
AMPULLA glass vial for oil, perfume
AMUSING AMUSIVE, entertaining;
  droll
AMUTTER muttering
ch **AMYLASE** starch-hydrolysing
  enzyme
ch **AMYLENE** amyl
bt, ch **AMYLINE AMYLOID**, starchy cellulose
ch **AMYLOSE** starch constituent
ANABION anabolism-dominated
  organism
bt **ANACARD** cashew-nut
md **ANAEMIA** general debility
md **ANAEMIC** bloodless
ANAGOGUE ANAGOGY, mindless
  interpretation
ANAGRAM word puzzle

ANALECT anthology
ANALGIA analgesia
md **ANALITY** anal libidinous energy
ANALOGY similarity; likeness
ANALYSE examine critically
ANALYST a resolver
ANANICE absolute necessity
ANAPEST poetic metre
ANAPHIA loss of sense of touch
zo **ANAPSID** having roofed skull
ANARCHY chaos; disorder; violence
ch **ANATASE** titanium oxide
md **ANATOMY** a skeleton; dissection
ANATRON glass scum
ANAUDIA loss of voice
zo **ANAXIAL** asymmetrical
zo **ANCHOVY** a small fish
bt **ANCHUSA** alkanet, red dye
ANCIENT antique; pristine ensign
ANCONES ornamental brackets
ANCORAL like an achor; hooked
ANCRESS ANKRESS, female anchorite
mu **ANDANTE** slow; walking pace
ANDARAC a red pigment
ANDRASE male-producing enzyme/
  hormone
ANDROID automaton; robot;
  imitation man
ANDVARI a dwarf (Norse myth.)
ANELACE anlace; a broad dagger
rl **ANELING** annointing with oil
bt, zo **ANEMONE** anemony; windflower
md **ANERGIA** lack of energy
ANEROID a kind of barometer
ANESONE white anise liqueur
bt **ANETHOL** oil of anise
ANEURIA lack of nervous energy
ANEURIN B-group vitamin
ANGARIA war rights
ANGELIC seraphic; cherubic;
  heavenly
ck, mu, nm **ANGELOT** cheese; lute; coin
rl **ANGELUS** a prayer; (bell-ringing)
ANGERED exasperated; enraged;
  roused
ANGERLY angrily; wrathfully
ANGEVIN dynasty of Anjou
ANGIOID like blood/lymph vessel
md **ANGIOMA** dilated-blood-vessel
  tumour
ANGLIFY anglicize, make English
ANGLING hopefully fishing
ANGLIST expert in English
ANGRILY wrathfully, irately
ANGUINE snake-like
ANGUISH agony; distress; rack; pang
ANGULAR sharp cornered
ANIDIAN shapeless

ch **ANILINE** indigo derivative
   ANILITY dotage; senility; imbecility
mu **ANIMATE ANIMATO**, actuate; lively
rl **ANIMISM ANIMIST**, soul as vital
   principle
bt **ANISEED** the seed of the anise
rl, lw **ANNATES** first fruits
bt **ANNATTO** annotto; a reddish dye
zo **ANNELID** worm
   ANNEXED affixed; subjoined;
   attached
   ANNOYED harassed; pestered;
   molested
   ANNOYER an irritator; teaser
   ANNUENT nodding
   ANNUITY a yearly payment
bt **ANNULAR** ring-like growth markings
   ANNULET small fillet round a column
pl, md **ANNULUS** ring; ring-shaped;
   sphincter
bt **ANODERM** skinless
   ANODISE dyeing aluminium
zo **ANODONT** a freshwater mussel
   ANODYNE pain-killer; opiate;
   sedative
pc **ANOESIA** comprehension failure
   ANOESIS state of non-cognitive
   mind
   ANOETIC responds only to emotion
ck **ANOLINI** ravioli
el **ANOLYTE** portion of electrolyte
   ANOMALY irregularity; eccentricity
md **ANOPSIA** blindness; (cataract);
   squint
md **ANOREXY** appetite failure illness
   ANORMAL ABNORMAL, exceptional
md **ANOSMIA** loss of smell power
   ANOTHER one more
   ANSATED with a handle
ch, md **ANTACID** a corrective; neutralizer
as **ANTAPEX** point opposite to apex
zo **ANT-BEAR** American ant-eater
   ANTE-ACT an act preceding
   ANTEFIX ornamental tiling
zo **ANT-EGGS** the pupae of ants
ro, zo **ANTENNA** a feeler
zo **ANT-HILL** a formicary
bt **ANTHOID** flower-like
rl **ANTHONY** saint; piglet
md **ANTHRAX** wool-sorter's disease
bt **ANTICAL** stem/leaf upper surface
ae **ANTICER** anti-icing means
   ANTICOR animal disease
   ANTICUM a front porch
   ANTI-GAS for combating gas
md **ANTIGEN** cause of antibodies
ma **ANTILOG** anti-logarithm
ch **ANTIPYR** formalin

pr **ANTIQUA** printing type
   ANTIQUE archaic; old; ancient
   ANTI-RED anti-communist
ar **ANTISAG** preventing sagging
   ANT-LIKE industrious
zo **ANT-LION** a neuropterous insect
   ANTONYM the opposite of a
   synonym
   ANXIETY ANXIOUS, concern,
   apprehensive
   ANYBODY person unspecified
   ANYWAYS anyhow
   ANYWHEN any old time
   ANYWISE somehow
   APAGOGE APAGOGY, progressively
   absurd
   APANAGE natural attribute;
   perquisite
   APANDRY male impotence
mn **APATITE** lime phosphate
hd **APAUMEE** open hand
   APE-HOOD APELIKE, apishness;
   simian
md **APEPSIA** poor digestion
md **APERTOR** eye-opener; muscle
bt **APETALY** absence of petals
   APHACIA APHAKIA, lensless eye
md, zo **APHAGIA** inability to swallow, feed
md **APHASIA** temporary dumbness
as **APHELIA** maximum distances (earth
   from sun)
md **APHEMIA** loss of speech
   APHETIC APHESIS, vowel curtailment
zo **APHIDES** plant-lice; ants' milchcows
md **APHONIA** loss of voice
   APHONIC speechless
   APHORIA sterility
bt **APHOTIC** able to grow without light
mn **APHRITE** carbonate of lime
md **APHTHAE** ulceration of the mouth
bt **APHYLLY** absence of leaves
   APICIAN epicurean; gastronomic
md **APINOID** clean
   APISHLY monkey-like
   A-PITPAT palpitating
   APLANAT lens lacking spherical
   aberration
md **APLASIA** defective structural growth
   APOCOPE elision; verbal curtailment
bt **APOCYTE** cell-less protoplasm
   APODAL APODOUS, footless
bt **APOGAMY** sex-function loss
   APOGEAN culminating; climactic
bt **APOGYNY, APOGENY** sterility
   APOLOGY excuse; explanation; plea
as **APOLUNE** point in moon satellite
   orbit
   APOSTIL marginal note; postscript

rl **APOSTLE** closest to Jesus; messenger
ma **APOTOME** mathematic difference
mu **APOTOMY** major semitone
APPAREL equipment; attire; vesture
APPEASE pacify; assuage; placate
APPLAUD praise; commend; extol
APPLIED referred; exercised; used
APPOINT nominate; prescribe; enjoin
APPOSED placed side by side
APPOSER an examiner; questioner
APPRISE inform; acquaint; warn
APPRIZE appreciate; appraise
APPROVE ratify; assent; encourage
APPULSE rapprochement
pc **APRAXIA** loss of movement ability
bt, ck **APRICOT** ABRICOCK, fruit (-brandy)
APRONED wearing an apron
APROPOS pertinent; opportune;
timely
ch **APROTIC** high-dielectric solvent
ar, rl **APSIDAL** ABSIDAL, apse (church)
APSIDES perigee and apogee
zo, ar **APTERAL** wingless; end columns
zo **APTERYX** kiwi-bird (New Zealand)
md **APTHOUS** (thrush); ulcerous
APTNESS suitability; felicity
APTOTIC indeclinable
md **APYREXY** absence of fever
APYROUS unchanged by heat
gl **AQUAFER** AQUIFER, permeable strata
zo **AQUARIA** (aquariums)
ch **AQUASOL** sulphonated castor oil
AQUATIC in/of water
AQUEOUS water; humid; damp
AQUILON the north wind
ARABIAN of Arabia
bt **ARABINE** gum arabic
ARABISM Arab idiom
ARABIST Arabic expert
bt **ARACHIS** peanut genus
ARAMAIC Syriac; Aramite
ARAMEAN Chaldaic; Chaldean
ARATION ploughing
ARBITER umpire; judge; referee
ARBLAST crossbow
ARBORED arboured
bt **ARBORET** shrub
bt **ARBUTUS** mountain strawberry
ar **ARCADED** having arched galleries
ARCADIA pastoral country
ARCANUM a mystery; a secret
ARCHAIC Noachian; antiquated
ga **ARCHERY** bowmanship
ARCH-FOE Satan
ARCHING curved; vaulting
ARCHIVE home for public
documents; file
ARCHLET small arch

ARCHWAY gateway; gatehouse
ARC-LAMP carbon-pole-bridge lamp
ARCTOID like a bear
ARCUATE bow-shaped
ARDENCY passion; warmth; fire
ARDUOUS laborious; toilsome
AREFIED withered; arid; parched
ARENOSE sandy; arenaceous
bt **AREOLAR** areolic; cell nucleus
mu **ARGHOOL** Arab reed pipe
ARGOTIC slangy
ARGUING discussing; debating
md **ARGYRIA** silver poisoning
ARGYROL silver antiseptic
ARIDITY dryness; aridness; sterility
mu **ARIETTA** ARIETTE, operatic air
bt **ARILLED** ARILLUS, husk; seed coating
ARISING emerging; originating
tx **ARMHOLE** clothing aperture for arm
hd **ARMIGER** bearer of coat of arms
(crest)
ARMILLA antique bracelet
ARMLESS lacking arms
hd **ARMOIRE** cupboard for coats of arms
ARMORIC Breton dialect
ARMOURY arsenal; magazine
bt **ARNOTTO** annatto; orange dye
AROUSAL awakening; uprising
AROUSED excited; provoked
lw **ARRAIGN** accuse; summon
ARRANGE group; classify; dispose
ARRAYED marshalled; equipped
ARREARS payments overdue
ARRIVAL advent; coming; newcomer
ARRYISH festive; jovial
ARSENAL armoury; depository
ch **ARSENIC** a metallic element
nt **ARTEMON** bowsail on Rome vessel
cf, md **ARTERIO-** ARTERIAL, concerning
arteries
ARTICLE essay; paper; indenture
ARTISAN artizan; workman;
operative
ARTISTE a fine performer
ARTLESS simple; ingenuous; naive
ARTSMAN a craftsman
ARTWORK creative design
ARUSPEX soothsayer; seer; diviner
ASARONE form of camphor
ASBOLIN oil from soot
zo **ASCARID** parasite worm
rl **ASCESIS** self-discipline
ASCETIC austere; rigid; abstemious
ASCIANS equator dwellers
zo **ASCIDIA** molluscs
md **ASCITES** peritoneal fluid collection
md **ASCITIC** dropsical
ASCRIBE attribute; assign; impute

md **ASEPSIS** sterilization
ASEPTIC sterilized
ASEXUAL algamic; sexless
ASHAMED abashed; confused
ck **ASH-CAKE** pastry cooked in ashes
ASH-FIRE chemical operations fire
ASH-HEAP tip for ashes
ASH-TRAY cigarette-butt tray
bt **ASH-WORT** a weed
ASIARCH Asiatic Proconsul
ASIATIC of Asia
ASINEGO ASINICO, a dolt; dunce; dulled
ASININE ass-like; idiotic; obstinate
ASKANCE obliquely; aslant; awry
pc **ASOCIAL** drop-out from society
mn **ASPHALT** bitumen
md **ASPHYXY** suffocation
ASPIRED soared; aimed high; yearned
ASPIRER aspirant; competitor
ASSAGAI ASSEGAY, Zulu spear
zo **ASSAPAN** flying squirrel (N. Amer.)
ASSAULT onset; attack; storm; assail (fencing)
ASSAYED tested; tried; endeavoured
ASSAYER metallurgist; analyst
ASS-HEAD blockhead; Bottom
ASSIZER inspector of weights
lw **ASSIZES** Courts of jurisdiction
lw **ASSIZOR** juror
ASSUAGE allay; pacify; mollify; quell
ASSUMED usurped; feigned; supposed
ASSUMER pretender, arrogant person
ASSURED pledged; guaranteed
ASSUROR ASSURER, underwriter (insurance)
ro **ASTABLE** free-running; self-sustaining
md **ASTASIA** inability to keep erect
ASTATIC unstable; lacking polarity
ASTEISM refined irony
mn **ASTERIA** (sapphire)
zo **ASTERID** star-fish
ASTOUND amaze; daze; stupefy
ASTRAEA Goddess of Justice
ASTRICT restrict; bind
ASTRIDE astraddle
mn **ASTRITE** star-stone
ASTROID star-shaped
ar **ASTYLAR** without columns
ASUNDER apart; divided; divergent
ch, tx **ATACTIC** of random polymer constituents
ATARAXY impassiveness; coolness

ATAVISM ATAVIST, reversion to ancestral type
nt **ATCHEEN** banting, sail dugout (Malaya)
ATEKNIA childlessness
ATELENE amorphous; imperfect
ATELIER studio; sculptor's workshop
ATHALIA saw-fly
ATHANOR alchemist's furnace
ATHEISE ATHEIZE, proselytize unbelief
ATHEISM disbelief
ATHEIST a nullifidian
ATHLETE athleta; a contestant
ATHWART across; askew; aslant
md **ATHYMIA** lack of feeling
md **ATHYMIA** thymus gland deficiency
md **ATHYRIA** absence of thyroid gland
ATOBOMB atomic bomb
ATOKOUS lacking offspring
bt **ATOMATE** covered by small particles
ATOMISM atomic theory
ATOMIST atomic theorist
ATOMIZE vaporize
ATONING expiating; reconciling
ATRESIA failure of opening development
bt **ATROPAL** not inverted; upturned
md **ATROPHY** wasting away
md **ATROPIA** bella-donna
bt **ATROPIN** deadly nightshade
ATTABOY a panegyric (USA)
mu **ATTACCA** continue without break (It.)
ATTACHE important embassy man (-case)
zo **ATTAGAS** a pheasant
ATTAINT corrupt; convicted
ck **ATTELET** ornamental meat skewer
ATTEMPT try; aim; endeavour; effort
ATTICAL classical
ATTINGE touch
ATTIRED garbed; dressed; arrayed
ATTRACT draw; allure; charm; decoy
ATTRIST to sadden
ATTRITE worn by friction; penitent
ATTUNED in harmony
AUBERGE an inn (Fr.)
AUCTION roup; vendue
AUDIBLE able to be heard
AUDIBLY spoken clearly
AUDIENT listening; attentive
AUDILES preference for heard images, stimuli
ma **AUDITED AUDITOR,** books examined; accountant
mn **AUGITIC** (augite); (pyroxene)
AUGMENT amplify; increase; enhance

AUGURAL, AUGURED ominous;
   foretold; portended
pl **AURALLY** concerning the ears; sound
AURATED AUREATE, AUREITY, golden;
   gilded
zo **AURELIA** a chrysalis
rl **AUREOLA AUREOLE,** golden halo
md, bt **AURICLE** ear; heart; leaf base
AURIFIC gold bearing
AURITED having ears
zo **AUROCHS** urus; wild ox;
   (prehistoric)
as **AURORAL** dawn (-Borealis) Northern
   Lights
AUSLAUT final syllable/word sound
   (Ger.)
AUSONIA Italy
AUSPICE augory; omen; portent
AUSTERE severely simple; ascetic
AUSTRAL southern
AUTARCH autocrat; tyrant
AUTARKY national self-sufficiency
AUTOBUS omnibus
AUTOCAR motor car
AUTONYM true name
md **AUTOPSY** post-mortem exam.
AUTOSET quick-levelling in
   surveying
au **AUTO-VAC** vacuum
AUXESIS hyperbole
AUXETIC amplifying
AVAILED answered the purpose;
   helped
AVARICE greed; rapacity; cupidity
lw **AVENAGE** barley-corn rent
AVENGED retaliated; revenged
AVENGER vindicator
md **AVENOUS** lacking veins
AVERAGE mean; moderate; ordinary
AVERNUS infernal regions
AVERRED affirmed; alleged; stated
AVERTED warded off; prevented
AVERTER preventer; diverter
AVIATED AVIATOR, flew; pilot (air
   navigation)
AVICIDE killing of birds
AVICULA kind of pearl oyster
AVIDITY greed; voracity; eagerness
AVIETTE a glider
AVIFORM bird-shaped
bt, ck **AVOCADO** alligator-pear
bt **AVODIRE** African hard-wood
AVOIDED eschewed; annulled;
   eluded
AVOIDER dodger; shunner
lw **AVOWANT** defendant in replevin
AVOWING owning; admitting;
   averring

AWAITED eagerly expected; tarried
AWAKING emerging from sleep;
   arousing
AWELESS without fear
AWESOME full of awe; fearsome
AWFULLY dreadfully; portentously
AWKWARD clumsy; ungainly; inapt
zo **AWL-BIRD** woodpecker
bt **AWL-WORT** an aquatic plant
bt **AWNLESS** beardless
AXIALLY from pole to pole
AXIFORM like a spindle or aborr
zo, bt **AXILLAR** a feather
au **AXLE-BOX** automobile part
AXLE-PIN linch-pin
zo **AXOLOTL** larval salamander
md **AXOTOMY** severing of axon nerve
AZALINE emulsion-sensitizing dye
   mixture
bt **AZAROLE** medlar
ch **AZELAIC** rancid-fat acid
AZILIAN pre-Neolithic
me, nv, as **AZIMUTH** angle over horizon
   (distance)
ch **AZOTITE** nitrous acid
AZOTIZE to nitrogenize
AZOTOUS nitrous
AZTECAN concerning the Aztecs
   (Mexico)
AZULEJO bright-coloured Iberian
   tile
AZUREAN sky-blue
AZURINE azure
mm **AZURITE** copper carbonate
AZYGOUS not in pairs
rl **AZYMITE** Armenian churchman
AZYMOUS unleavened; unfermented

B

rl **BAALISM BAALITE,** of Baal, idolatry
BABASSU oil in shampoo
BABBARI hare
BABBING catching eels (angling)
BABBLED chattered; jabbered
zo **BABBLER** betrayer; talker; thrush
rl **BABIISM** Persian religion
zo **BABUINA** female baboon
BABYISH BABYISM, infantile
   expression
ga **BACCARA BACCARAT,** gambling
   cardgame
BACCARE stand back!
bt **BACCATE** berry-shaped; pulpy
BACCHUS BACCHIC, carousing wine
   god
md **BACILLI** bacteria; microbes

BACK OUT withdraw
fr **BACK-CUT** tree-felling
BACKERS supporters; target background
nt **BACKING** aiding; abetting; retiring; strengthening; (finance); anticlockwise (wind)
BACK-LOG delayed work
BACK-OFF back-out; retire; leave; withdraw
BACK-OUT reversal of missile drill
cr **BACK-SAW** thick-backed saw
BACKSET an eddy
bt **BACTRIS** peach-palm
BADDISH rather bad
BADIAGA small sponge
bt **BADIANE** BANDIAN, aniseed (flavour)
BADNESS depravity; evil; wickedness
BAFFLED foiled; checked; bewildered
BAFFLER thwarter; confounder
BAGASSE refuse sugar stalks
BAGGAGE luggage; belongings
nt **BAGGALA** 2-masted Arab vessel
BAGGING bag-cloth; pouching (theft)
mu **BAGPIPE** windbag instrument, Gr./ Sc.
ce **BAGWORK** bagged concrete, gravel for sea wall
BAHADUR Indian title
lw **BAILAGE** ancient export duty
lw **BAILIFF** land steward; overseer
ag **BAILING** packing (hay bundles)
nt **BAILING** of water (emptying a boat)
ae **BAILING** -out; parachuting (pilots)
lw **BAILING** court release (money pledged)
BAILLIE councillor of Scottish burgh
BAITING taunting; (bear-); angling
el **BAKE-OUT** electrode/valve pre-heating
BALANCE poise; weigh; surplus
zo **BALANUS** crustacean; acorn-shell
ar, bd **BALCONY** hanging porch
BALDEST barest; plainest
BALDING BALDISH, losing head hair
BALDRIC baudric; shoulder-belt
BALEFUL evil; noxious; pernicious
BALKING BAULKING, horse's refusing jump
mu **BALLADE** BALLATA, poetic aria
nt **BALLAST** non-cargo weight (gravel, sand)
ga **BALL-BOY** ball returner (tennis, football)
mu **BALLETT** dance-like vocal composition

BALLING becoming clogged; partying
md **BALLISM** motor nerve disorder
BALLIUM bulwark
ae **BALLOON** hot-air (gas) skycraft
ga **BALLOON** idea tryout; up-hit (cricket)
BALLS-UP muddled (confusion)
BALMIER sweeter; milder; gentler
BALMILY soothingly; tranquilly
md **BALNEAL** spa treatment (mineral)
md **BALNEUM** curative public bath
BALONEY unbelievable nonsense
BALSAMY fragrant; aromatic
BAMBINO a child (It.)
BAMMING hoaxing; cheating
BANABAN Micronesian language
ck **BANBURY** a cake
tx **BANDAGE** wound dressing fabric
tx **BANDANA** colourful silk hankie, tie
BANDBOX hat box, new-clothes box
BANDEAU brow-band
bt **BANDIAN** badiane; aniseed
BANDIED discussed; tossed; agitated
BANDING uniting together; decorative multiwood inlay; border
BANDLET bandelet; a flat moulding
mu **BANDORA** PANDORA, ancient cittern, zither
mu **BANDORE** lute-like plucked continuo
BANDROL banderole; small flag
to **BAND-SAW** saw over wheels
BANEFUL baleful; deadly; venomous
BANGING overwhelming; clattering
BANGLED with bangles
mn **BANK-BAR** mine-shaft lining
ae **BANKING** relying; (financial); earthworks; tilting of aircraft
bt **BANKSIA** dwarf yellow climbing rose
BANNING cursing; proscribing; barring
ck **BANNOCK** oaten-cake (Sc.)
ck **BANQUET** feast; regalement
BANSHEE ghost (Irish)
BANTENG Malayan wild ox
BANTERY mild repartee
BANTING reducing the diet; slimming
nt, zo **BANTING** wild ox (Ind.); atcheen, sail-dugout craft (Malaya)
BANYULS Pyrenean wine
rl **BAPTISM** immersion at christening
BAPTIST member of Protestant sect
BAPTIZE christen
tx **BARACAN** camel-hair cloth
BARBARY a Saracen country (N. Africa)
bt **BARBATE** bearded; awned

BAR-BELL dumb-bell; weight-lifting bar
BARBING shaving; trimming; piercing
BARBOLA modern gesso
bt **BARBULE** small beard on plant
gl **BARCHAN BARCHANE**, windblown deposit
BARCODE lined stockcode label
BARDISH BARDISM, Celtic poetry & its lore
BARDLET BARDLING, young bard (poet)
BAREBOW without sighting or aiming (archery)
BARGAIN chaffer; haggle; compact
BARGING shoving; elbowing; jostling; intrusion of line (yachting)
BARILLA raw seaweed alkali
BAR-IRON malleable iron in bars
le **BARK-BED** tanner's hot-bed
le **BARKERY** tan-house
gl **BARKHAN** lone crescentic sandhill
BARKING peeling; (shins); dog noise
le **BARK-PIT** tan-vat
BARMAID Hebe; tavern server; sleeper
BARMIER flightier; more crazy
BARMKIN outer castle ward
BARNABY the apostle Barnabas
zo **BARNAGH** large whelk
BARNING storing; garnering
zo **BARN-OWL** screech owl; night-bird
BARONET bart; hereditary title; Sir
mu **BAROQUE** 17th cent. style architecture, music
BARRACK army lodgement house; to boo
BARRAGE embankment; barrier; dam
mu **BARRAGE** (artillery fire); guitar chords
BARRENS elevated plateaux (arctic)
BARRICO small keg (Sp.)
BARRIER hindrance; embargo; obstacle
BARRING excluding; banning
hd **BARRULY** heraldic division
BAR-SHOE special horseshoe
BAR-SHOT double connected shot
bt **BARTRAM** the plant pellitory
bt **BARWOOD** red dye-wood
ch **BARYTES** barium sulphate
BARYTIC (baryta)
mu **BARYTON** tenor-bass viol
BASBLEU blue stocking
BASCULE balanced drawbridge; perfect arc of horse jumping

ml **BASE-BOX** metal-plate measurement unit
BASENET bascinet; basnet; a helmet
zo **BASENJI** Congo barkless dog
BASHFUL strikingly modest; shy
BASHING coshing; slugging
BASHLYK Russian hood
BASILAR serving as a basis
BASILIC basilican style
BASINED in a basin
BASINET BASNET, round helmet
zo **BASKING** luxuriating; revelling (-shark)
BASLARD a small dagger
BASSOCK fibre mat
mu **BASSOON** bass oboe
BASTARD illegitimate offspring; spurious
BASTILE castle on wheels
tx, ck **BASTING** coarse stitching; (roasting)
ar **BASTION** outer fortification; stronghold
bt, ck **BATATAS** sweet potatoes; yams
ae, nt **BAT-BOAT** sea plane
nt **BATEELE, BATELO** small dhow
BATEFUL contentious; disputable
ck **BATH BUN** a comestible
BATHING giving/having a bath
BATHMAN attendant
BATH-MAT thick towel-like mat
BATHYAL pert. to deep-sea zone
BATISTE cambric
BATSMAN a cricketer
BATTELS provisions (Oxford)
el, zo **BATTERY** stored electricity; hens
lw **BATTERY** (assault); test group; (baseball)
BATTERY (artillery) gun group unit; site
BATTING quilting; cricket; angling
BATTISH bat-like
BATTLED fought
BATTLER resident at Oxford
go **BATTURE** raised sea/river bed
mu **BATTUTA** 3 bar rhythm beat (It.)
BAUDRIC shoulder sash
BAULKED shield; balked; jibbed
zo **BAUSOND** badger-like
mn **BAUXITE** (aluminium)
BAWCOCK fine fellow
BAWDILY lewdly; obscenely
rl **BAWDKIN BALDACHIN**, canopy
BAWLING shouting; clamouring
BAYONET rifle-dagger
BAY-SALT evaporated sea-water
bt **BAY-TREE** the laurel
bt **BAYWOOD** mahogany
BAY-YARN woollen yarn

BAZIGAR nomadic Ind. gypsy
BAZOOKA anti-tank gun
nt BEACHED aground; on the beach
BEADING narrow moulding
BEADMAN an almsman
BEAKING (cock-fighting)
BEAMILY broad on the beam
BEAMING radiant; gleaming; bright
zo BEAN-FLY a garden pest
BEARDED awned; defied; opposed
zo BEARDIE the whitethroat bird
BEARING (magnetic); (rein); (ball);
wheel bearing
BEARISH uncouth; boorish; rude
BEAR-PIT enclosure for bears
BEASTLY brutal; sensual; bestial
BEATIFY (sainthood); canonize
BEATING chastisement; battering
BEATNIK latter-day Bohemian
BEAUISH foppish
bt BEBEERU greenheart tree
BECAUSE owing to
BECKING servile bowing
bt, tx, bd BEDDING planting out; bedclothes;
foundation; gun mounting
BEDEAUX piece-work system
BEDELRY BEADLERY, street orderlies
BEDEMAN the bead-maker
BEDEVIL bewitch
BEDEWED covered with dew; affused
BEDFAST bed-ridden
BED-GOWN night gown
BED-MATE bed-fellow
BEDOUIN nomadic Arab
BED-POST bedstead support
BED-REST recuperation
gl BEDROCK basic stratum
BEDROOM sleeping apartment
BEDSIDE (table); (lamp); (manner)
md BED-SORE sore from bed-lying
zo BED-TICK bed bug
BEDTIME time to sleep
BEDWARF to belittle; to dwarf
BEDWORK easy toil; copulation
zo BEE-BIRD bee catcher
bt BEECHEN of the beech tree, wood
BEEF-TEA meat-extract drink
BEE-GLUE beeswax
BEE-HIVE home for bees
BEE-LINE straight line
zo BEE-MOTH wax-moth
BEESWAX product of hives
zo BEET-BUG agricultural pest
zo BEET-FLY a dipterous insect
BEETLED speeded along
bt BEE-TREE American linden
BEFFANA befana; Epiphany fairy
BEGGARY mendicancy; indigence

BEGGING soliciting; craving;
imploring
rl BEGHARD BEGUINE, religious order
bt BEGONIA elephant's ear plant
BEGUILE pass pleasantly; amuse
BEGUILE deceive; delude; trick
rl BEGUINE BEGHARD, religious
almshouse
BEHAVED acted correctly
BEHOVED was necessary; befitted
BELATED overdue; retarded
nt BELAYED fastened; held
BELCHED eructated
BELCHER coloured kerchief
BELDAME old hag
BELGIAN of Belgium
BELIEVE credit; opine; accept
BELL-HOP page boy
BELLIED dilated
zo BELLING full and ripe; bellowing; of
deer in rut
BELL-JAR vacuum enclosure
BELL-MAN town crier
BELLONA goddess of War
BELLOWS draught producer (organ)
(forge)
BELOVED dear; darling
BELTANE May Day fire festival
BELTING beating; a belt
BEMUSED confused, bewildered
BENCHED furnished with seating
lw BENCHER senior (Inns of Court)
BENDING curving; flexing; inclining
hd BENDLET small heraldic bend
BENEATH inferior; subordinate;
under
BENEFIC favourable (astrol.)
BENEFIT boon; profit; gain; enrich
BENELUX Belgium, Netherlands and
Luxemburg
BENGALI of Bengal
BENISON benediction
bt BENTEAK Nana-wood
zo BENTHOS ocean-bed organisms
ch BENZENE BENZINE, cleaning solvent;
paint remover
bt BENZOIN resinous incense
ch BENZOLE tar product
ch BENZOYL BENZOIC acid
lw BEQUEST legacy; inheritance
BERATED scolded; nagged; chided
BEREAVE deprive; divest; despoil
zo BERGYLT red sea-fish
BERHYME to lampoon in verse
BERLINE berlin; a vehicle
BERSERK Norse warrior; in a fury
nt BERTHED moored; situated
nt BERTHON collapsible lifeboat

bt **BERTRAM** bastard pellitory
BESEECH implore; entreat; crave
BESHMET grape pulp
BESIDES except; save; moreover
BESIEGE beset; invest; beleaguer
BESPOKE ordered
BEST MAN groomsman (weddings)
BESTIAL brutal; uncivilized
BESTING winning
BETROTH affiance; plight
BETTING wagering; staking
zo **BETTONG** kangaroo rat
BETULIN birch camphor
BETWEEN amid
BETWIXT amidst
BEVATON proton synchrotron
BEWITCH fascinate; enchant; charm
ga **BEZIQUE** card game
BHANDAR store; library (Hindu)
BHISTEE water-carrier (India)
BIALATE with 2 wings
BIARCHY rule by 2 persons
BIASING prejudicing; influencing
BIAXIAL with 2 axes
eg **BIB-COCK** down-curving draw-off
tap
BIBELOT personal trinket, snuffbox,
etui
rl **BIBLIST** zealous Bible quoter
ce **BI-CABLE** multi-line aerial ropeway
mu **BICHORD** doubly strung
to **BICKERN** pointed anvil
BICOLOUR having 2 colours
bt **BICONIC** double-cone-shaped
BICYCLE bike; 2-wheeler
BIDDERY metal alloy
BIDDING enjoining; directing
ck **BIFFINS** dried apples
BIFIDLY cleft
BIFILAR double-threaded
BIFOCAL type of spectacles (twin
lenses)
BIFROST Rainbow Bridge (Norse)
BIG-BORE larger rifles (8 mm)
shooting
nv **BIGELOW** flexible sailing boom
BIGENER cross-breed
BIGGEST largest; greatest
BIGGISH somewhat massive
zo **BIG-HORN** wild sheep
BIGNESS of a size; bulkiness
BIGOTED dogmatic; intolerant
BIGOTRY zealotry; fanaticism
BILBOES bars and shackles
BILGING rubbishing others' remarks
md **BILIARY BILIOUS**, of bile glands
BILKING defrauding; eluding;
cheating

BILLING invoicing (charging);
petting
BILLION a large number
BILL-MAN hedger; pruning hook
BILLOWY roughish
BILOBED double-lobed
cp **BILSTED** mahogany substitute
ck **BILTONG** dried meat (S. Africa)
BIMANAL two-handed
el **BIMETAL** of 2 different metals
ma **BIMODAL** 2 similar frequencies
BINDERY bookbinding
BINDING obligatory; a fillet;
fastening; (boot to ski); books
md **BINDWEB** (nervous system)
BINNING wine storage; (rubbish
bin)
BINOCLE double-telescope
BINOTIC binaural
BIOCIDE plant-life-destroying
substance
BIOGENY life origin science
gl **BIOLITH** rock from living organisms
bl **BIOLOGY** science of life
ec **BIOMASS** population living weight
cp **BIONICS** study of functions of brains
and computers
BIORGAN physiological organ
zo **BIOTAXY** grouping of organisms
zo **BIOTICS** living organisms (viruses,
bacteria)
mn **BIOTINE** (alumina)
mn **BIOTITE** magnesia mica
BIOTOMY vivisection
BIOTOPE uniform habitat
BIOTYPE uniform genetic make-up
BIPEDAL having two feet
BIPLANE 2-winged aeroplane
BIPOLAR with 2 poles
pg **BIPRISM** obtuse-angle prism
BIRCHED beaten with stick or cane
BIRCHEN made of birchwood
BIRDEYE bird's eye
BIRDING snaring
BIRDMAN fowler; single flyer (hang-
glider)
BIRETTA clerical cap
BIRLING whirling; spinning
BIRLINN Gaelic barge
BIRYANI type of pilaw (India)
ck **BISCUIT** thin, hard cookie; ceramic
process
mn, ch **BISMUTH** metal ochre
BISSEXT (leap year)
bt **BISTORT** snakeweed
BITLESS no bit
zo **BITTERN** also bittour
BITTERN brine

BITTERS wormwood-impregnated liquor
BITTILY disjointedly
BITTING harnessing a horse
BITTOCK small bit
zo BITTOUR the bittern
mn BITUMED BITUMEN, bituminous asphalt; pitch
zo BIVALVE a mollusc
BIVIOUS two ways
mo BIVOUAC make-do camp (army)
BIZARRE fantastic; whimsical; strange
BIZONAL double zone ticket
BLABBED babbled; told; revealed
BLABBER sneak; tell-tale; prattler
BLACKED inked; obscured
BLACKEN darken; defame; decry
BLACKER darker; more sullen
BLACKLY sombrely
md BLADDER urine collection organ
BLADING fitting a blade to
BLAMING censuring; reproaching
BLANDLY mildly; benign; affably
bt BLANKET the mullein
nc BLANKET cover (bed, snow); group usage; yacht; surrounder of nuclear reactor core
BLANKLY vacantly
BLARING strident; obvious
BLARNEY whimsical flattery (Irish)
ck BLARNEY yellow Irish cheese
BLASTED withered; blighted; ruined
BLASTER froth-blower; golf
BLATANT obtrusively vulgar
BLATHER BLATTER-BLETHER, to babble
bt BLAWORT harebell
BLAZING flaming; proclaiming
BLEAKER more exposed; barer
BLEAKLY cheerlessly; drearily
md BLEEDER haemophiliac; (baseball)
BLEMISH defect
BLENDED mingled; blent; mixed
ck, to BLENDER mixing device; paint brush of badger hair; (tea)
BLESBOK S. African antelope
BLESSED extolled; glorified; adored
BLETTED decayed
bt BLEWART the germander speedwell
bt BLEWITS mushrooms
BLIGHTY England (soldiers' slang)
BLINDED shuttered; deceived
BLINDER more obtuse; a blinker
BLINDLY ignorantly; heedlessly
BLINKED twinkled; flickered; connived

md, nt BLISTER abraised skin spot; extra hull for stability
BLOATED swollen; distended
zo BLOATER smoked herring
zo BLOBBER BLUBBER, whale or seal fat
BLOCKED obstructed; jammed
ar BLOCKER headstone of column; offensive player (Am. football)
BLOMARY a forge
BLONDIN tight-rope walker
BLOODED foxhunting rite; wounded
bt BLOOMED BLOSSOMED, flowered, throve
tx BLOOMER error; woman's undergarment
bt BLOSSOM bloom; bud; flower
BLOTCHY patchy; smeary
BLOTING drying by smoke
BLOTTED stained; sullied
BLOTTER a blotting pad
zo BLOWFLY blue-bottle
BLOW-GUN blow-pipe
gl, pb BLOWING puffing; disclosing; (glass); surface pits; hollows in sand, soil
BLOW-OUT a spread; banquet; short work-out of horse (racing)
BLOWZED frowsy; slovenly
zo BLUBBER wail; whale fat (blobber)
zo BLUE-CAP a titmouse (bird)
zo BLUE-CAT Siberian cat
zo BLUE-EYE honey-eater bird
bt BLUE-GUM eucalyptus
BLUEING a metal finish; expanding
zo BLUE-JAY North American jay
BLUFFED concealed; spoofed
BLUFFER a deceiver; con-man
BLUFFLY bluntly; frankly; openly
BLUNDER gross mistake; howler
BLUNGER clay-mixer
BLUNTED took the edge off; dulled
BLUNTER more outspoken
BLUNTLY stolidly; obtusely
BLURRED dimmed; obscured
BLURTED uttered abruptly
BLUSHED flushed; coloured
BLUSHET a damsel
BLUSTER turbulence; swagger; storm
nt BOARDED lodged; embarked
BOARDER paying guest
BOARISH swinish; brutal
BOASTED vaunted; bragged; blustered
to BOASTER a broad chisel; a vain proud fellow
BOAT-CAR canal trolley
zo BOAT-FLY water-boatman
nt BOATFUL ship-load
BOATING an aquatic pastime

BOATMAN a rower; an oarsman
BOBBING cheating; curtseying
BOBBING (winter sports); angling
BOBBISH hearty; energetic; uppish
BOB-SLED bob-sleigh
nt BOBSTAY bowsprit stay
BOBTAIL rabble; caudal abbreviation
lw BOCLAND feudal freehold
BODEFUL ominous
bt BOG-BEAN marsh plant
BOGGARD bugbear; scarecrow
BOGGART hobgoblin; spectre
BOGGLED hesitated; vacillated
BOGGLER a waverer; demurrer;
  doubter
BOG-LAND fen; marsh; swamp
bt BOG-MOSS sphagnum
bt BOG-RUSH a sedge
mt BOHOROK Föhn-like winds in
  Sumatra
BOILING enraged; seething;
  pasteurizing
BOLDEST bravest; most valiant
bt BOLETIC fungoid extract
bt BOLETUS fungus genus
BOLIVAR Venezuelan currency unit
nt BOLLARD mooring post; kerb-post
bt BOLLING a pollard; a lopped tree
pl BOLLOCK testicle; nonsense; rubbish
BOLONEY phoney palaver
BOLSTER to support; prop; pillow
BOLTING sifting; swallowing
BOMBARD to pump with projectiles,
  (artillery); drop bombs
mu BOMBARD large leather water bottle;
  jug; larger shawm (bassoon)
BOMBAST fustian; rodomontade
BOMBING blitzing
BOMBOUS rounded, convex
BONANZA stroke of luck
zo BONASUS bison or wild ox
BONDAGE captivity; thraldom;
  helotry
BONDING (Customs); (bricklaying);
  pairing; linking
BONDMAN villein; peon
ga BONE-ACE card game
BONE-ASH burnt bones
gl BONE-BED strata with fossils
zo BONETTA BONITA, tunny fish
BONFIRE a beacon; (Guy Fawkes)
BONNILY handsomely
BOOKFUL theoretical
BOOKING reserving; buying; on
  record; (office)
BOOKISH studious
BOOKLET brochure; pamphlet
BOOKMAN scholar

cp BOOLEAN truth, algebra, and
  calculus system
BOOMING in demand; resounding
nt BOOMKIN short boom overhanging
  the stern
zo BOONDER Rhesus monkey
BOORISH mannerless; clumsy;
  lubberly
BOOSING tippling; bousing
BOOSTED advertised; eulogized
bd BOOSTER output or energy raising
  device; pump; compressor
BOOTING foot-wear; sacking
ga BOOTLEG sell prohibited goods; Am.
  football
BOOZING boosing; toping; getting
  drunk
ch BORACIC a boron derivative
ch BORAZON boron/nitrogen
  compound
BORDAGE feudal tenure
BORDMAN feudal tenant
hd BORDURE heraldic border
BOREDOM ennui; tedium; dullness
ch BORNEOL camphor-yielding
  chemical
mn BORNITE erubiscite; copper ore
BOROUGH electoral division;
  municipality
BORSTAL a reformatory for youth
ck BORTSCH beetroot soup (Rus.)
bt BOSCAGE undergrowth; macchia
  (It.); scrubs; shrubbery
zo BOSHBOK bush-buck
BOSOMED embraced
BOSQUET an arbour
BOSSAGE (projecting stones)
BOSSING controlling; dominating;
  bullying
BOSSISM political dictatorship
BOTANIC botanical; floral
ck BOTARGO special sausage
ck BOTARGO grey-mullet roe
BOTCHED bungled; patched
BOTCHER incompetent worker
BOTTINE small boot
BOTTLED inebriated
BOTTLER person or machine that
  fills bottles
hd BOTTONY heraldic cross
bt BOUCHET a pear
hr BOUCHON hollow watch plug
BOUDOIR a lady's private room
ck BOUILLI BOUILLON, boiled meat
  (broth)
gl BOULDER a large rock
md BOULIMY, BULIMY morbid appetite
BOULTER fishing line

BOULTIN convex moulding
BOUNCED rebounded, bluffed
BOUNCER chucker-out; bad cheque;
(baseball); (cricket)
BOUNDED sprang; limited; bordered
BOUNDER inconsiderate ass
bt BOUQUET nosegay
BOURBON Kentucky corn whisky
mu BOURDON bass stop
BOURDON mule; pilgrim's staff
BOURLAW local jurisprudence
BOURREE lively dance (Fr., Sp.)
BOW-BACK crooked; hog-back
BOW-BENT bent as a bow
BOW-HAND left hand (archery)
BOWLESS no bow
nt BOWLINE a rope; a non-slip knot
BOWLING (bowls); (cricket);
trundling
BOW-SHOT about 80 yards (73 m)
(archery)
BOWSOCK bow cover (archery)
BOX-CALF tanned calfskin
BOX-COAT heavy coat
nt BOXHAUL luffing; sailing to
windward
BOX-IRON heater receptacle
BOX-KITE scientific kite
tx BOX-LOOM multiple-shuttle-box
loom
cr BOX-SLIP boxwood planing face
eg BOX-TOOL single-point lathe cutter
bt BOXWOOD odoriferous shrub; its
wood
BOYCOTT ostracize; refuse to do
business with
BOYHOOD puerility
BRABBLE squabble; a quarrel; broil
bl, nt BRACING strengthening; invigorating
bt BRACKEN brake-fern
BRACKET brace; corbel; a support;
(figure-skating); small ornamental
shelf
bt BRACTED (irregular leaf)
to BRADAWL boring tool
BRAGGED boasted; blustered
rl BRAHMAN BRAHMIN, Hindu priest
BRAIDED plaited; embroidered
nt BRAILED trussed
BRAILLE raised letters
BRAINED brainy; bashed
ck BRAISED stewed
BRAKING retarding
bt BRAMBLE brier-brush
BRAMBLY thorny; prickly
BRANCHY spreading; ramifying
BRANDED marked; disgraced
BRANDLE waver; shake

BRANGLE wrangle; a brawl
zo BRANLIN striped worm
BRANTLE a dance
BRASIER BRAZIER, brass-workers'
charcoal pan; for hot chestnuts
BRASSET casque or helmet
BRATINA loving cup (Russia)
BRATTLE clatter
BRAVADO arrogant bluster; showing
off; dare-devil
BRAVELY gallantly; daringly
BRAVERY valour; heroism
BRAVEST most courageous
BRAVING defying; daring
BRAVOES hired assassins
mu BRAVURA florid virtuoso
performance needed
BRAWLED wrangled; quarrelled
BRAWLER rowdy ruffian
zo BRAWNER boar-meat
BRAYING clamour; pounding
BRAZIER brasier
ce BRAZING soldering; capillary
jointing (metals)
BREACHY unruly
BREADTH broadness; beaminess
BREAKER small water cask
el BREAKER wave; circuit stop;
gyratory or jaw (rocks, cask) (ice)
BREAK-IN interruption; burglary
BREAK-UP disrupt; disillusion
nt BREAMED cleaned of barnacles
BREATHE respire; exhale; express
mn BRECCIA conglomerate
BREEDER (animal husbandry) (sire)
pr BREVIER a size of type
BREVITY terseness; conciseness
ch BREVIUM uranium
br BREWAGE a brew
br BREWERY brewhouse
BREWING plotting; beer-making
zo BRIABOT angler-fish
BRIBERY palm-oil; graft
BRIBING illicit payments for illegal
acts
BRIBRIS Costa Rican Indian
BRICKED blocked completely
BRIDGED spanned; linked; covered;
(loan)
BRIDLED BRIDLER, curbed; checked;
controller
BRIDOON snaffle bit
lw BRIEFED informed; instructed;
courtcase
BRIEFER shorter; more concise
BRIEFLY curtly; pithily; in short
BRIERED set with briars
BRIGADE subdivision of army

BRIGAND bandit; outlaw; freebooter
BRIMFUL almost overflowing
BRIMMED edged
BRIMMER a hat; a full glass
BRINDLE streaky-brown
ck BRINING BRINISH, salting (brackish)
bt, ck BRINJAL egg-plant (Indian)
ck BRIOCHE light pastry (Fr.)
BRISKER sharper; quicker; sprier
ck BRISKET breast of meat
BRISKLY quickly; vivaciously
BRISTLE BRISTLY, (beard); rough
and prickly
BRISTOL (glass); (china)
BRISURE rampart deviation
BRITISH of Britain
BRITTLE easily broken; fragile
BROADEN BROADER, widen; extend;
amplified
BROADLY tolerantly, more liberally
tx BROCADE woven silk
BROCAGE brokerage; brokery
BROCARD maxim or canon; wise
words
tx BROCART gold, silver thread cloth
patterns
BROCKED black and white
zo BROCKET young red deer
BRODKIN a buskin; brodekin
ck BROILED BROILER, flame-cooked;
gridiron
BROKAGE, BROKERY, BROKERAGE
shares sales
BROKING bargaining; negotiating
ch BROMATE a salt of bromic acid
ch BROMIDE a sedative
ch BROMINE a liquid element
md BROMISM state after overdose
pt BROMOIL oil pigment prints
zo BRONCHO unbroken horse
BRONZED tanned
BROODED cherished; meditated
BROOKED allowed; enjoyed; endured
BROOMED swept and dusted
BROTHEL sex-workers' den; bawdy
house
BROTHER sibling; kinsman; friar
BROUGHT conducted; led; fetched
ck BROWNED BROWNER, bronzed;
tanned; gratinated
BROWNIE young girl guide; elfin
BROWSED pastured; grazed;
(bookshop)
zo BRUCHUS pea-beetle
bt BRUCINE nux vomica
ch BRUCITE hydrate of magnesia
BRUISED injured; contused;
pounded

BRUISER a boxer
BRUITED rumoured; noised abroad
zo BRUMMER large fly (S. Africa)
BRUMOUS foggy; wintry
bt BRUNION nectarine
BRUSHED swept; grazed; (hair)
BRUTIFY brutalize; bestialize
BRUTISH BRUTISM, gross; cruel;
savage
md BRUXISM teeth-grinding
zo BRYOZOA incrustations
zo BUBALIS antelope genus
zo BUBALUS buffalo
ck BUBBLED gurgled; burbled;
(boiling); aerated
BUBBLER a cheat
md BUBONIC plague
ch BUBULUM neat's-foot
md BUCCATE with protruding cheeks
BUCCULA double chin
zo BUCEROS rhinoceros horn-bill
gl BUCHITE clay/shale fusion rock
BUCKEEN Irish squireen
bt BUCKEYE horse-chestnut
BUCKING BUCKISH, (horse); boasting;
foppish
BUCKLED BUCKLER, bent in; fastener;
shield; belt
BUCKRAM stiffened cloth
to BUCKSAW frame-saw
BUCOLIC Arcadian; pastoral; rural
ar BUCRANE garlanded ox-skull frieze;
Doric
bt BUDDING germinating; blossoming
nt BUDGERO Bengal boat
BUDGING shifting; stirring
bt BUDLESS barren; sterile
zo BUFFALO cattle-like animal
BUFFING polishing
BUFFOON a rough fool; clown
nt BUGALET square-rigger ship,
Brittany
BUGBEAR bugaboo; hobgoblin;
bogey
bt BUGLOSS borage
bt BUGWORT a plant
to BUHL-SAW spaced-back frame-saw
BUILDED built; erected; raised
BUILDER constructor
BUILD-UP favourable publicity
BUILT-UP urban area; compounded
(timber) (interest)
BULBING BULBOUS, BULGING,
swelling; expanding
bt BULBLET BULBULE, small bulb
zo BULCHIN bull-calf
BULGING protuberant; distended
md BULIMIA rapid over-eating disorder

BULKIER BULKING, more massive;
becoming huge
bt BULLACE wild-plum
rl BULLARY (papal bulls)
BULLATE blistered
zo BULL-BAT night-hawk
zo BULL-BEE stag-beetle
zo BULLDOG college police
zo BULL-FLY gadfly
BULLIED blustered; hazed; (hockey)
BULLIES browbeaters; hectors
BULLING boosting
BULLION uncoined metal
BULLISH obstinate; mulish
zo BULLOCK steer
BULLPEN pitcher's enclosure
(baseball)
zo BULL-PUP young bulldog
bt BULRUSH the reed-mace
BULWARK ship's side
BUMBAZE bamboozle
BUMBOAT refuse and slops removal
boat
bd BUMICKY masonry repair cement
ck BUMMALO Bombay duck (dried fish)
BUMMILY preposterously;
protuberously
BUMMING sodomizing; begging;
loafing
BUMMOCK ale
BUMPERS shock absorbers (cars);
extra portions
BUMPING thumping; jarring;
knocking
BUMPKIN short boom; rustic; swain
BUNCHED clustered; concentrated
BUNDLED packed together closely
BUNGLED BUNGLER, mismanaged;
botcher
nt BUNKAGE coaling charge
BUNKING decamping; sharing
dormitory
zo, tx BUNTING bird; celebration flaglets
nt BUOYAGE placing buoys
BUOYANT light; floating
BUOYING sustaining
zo BUPHAGA beef-eater bird
BURDASH fringed sash
bt BURDOCK dock with prickly head
BURETTE graduated glass tube; phial
BURGAGE tenure in socage
BURGEON to bud; expand rapidly
(status)
BURGESS freeman of a borough
BURGHAL of a borough
BURGHER inhabitant
BURGLAR house-breaker; cracksman
BURGLED stole; robbed

ck BURIDDA Ital. fish stew
BURKING smothering; concealing
bt BURLACE a variety of grape
BURLIER more robust; sturdier
BURLING removing knots
BURMESE (Burma)
BURNING vehement; ardent; fervent
BURNISH polish; furbish; brighten
BURNOUS Arab attire
pc, el BURNOUT excess emotional reaction;
voltage change
bt BUR-REED a plant
bt BURRELL pear; russet cloth
zo BURRHEL wild sheep of Tibet
BURRING raising a ridge
BURROCK small weir
BURSARY educational grant for
students
BURSTER eruptor; exploder; terrorist
cp BURSTER offline separation of
output
BURTHEN burden
bt BUR-WEED a plant
BURYING burial; concealing;
sepulture
zo BUSH-CAT the serval
BUSHIDO Japanese code of chivalry
BUSHING detachable lining
BUSHMAN aborigine
zo BUSH-TIT long tailed titmouse
BUSKING street entertainment;
(begging)
BUSSING conveying; (anti-racialism);
kissing (Am.)
BUS-STOP here by request sign!
zo BUSTARD large bird
BUSTLED BUSTLER, hastened;
(noisily); (ostentatiously); hurrier
BUSY-BEE a finger in every pie
BUSYING meddling; interfering
ch BUTANOL an alcohol
BUTCHER murder; slay; slaughter
ck BUTLERY BOTTLERY, pantry (of
kitchen area)
bl BUTMENT houses' end to end
contact
BUTT-END ditto; fag end (cigarette)
ck BUTTERY larder; cold area in kitchen
BUTTING clash of goats (rutting);
ramming
pl BUTTOCK thigh as sit-upon; backside
BUTTONS BUTTONY, fastening knobs;
(decorative)
ch BUTYRIC rancid
BUVETTE refreshment bar
bt BUXEOUS (box-tree)
BUXOMLY generously breasted
BUYABLE for purchase; available

zo **BUZZARD** rapacious bird
to **BUZZ-SAW** circular saw
BY-AND-BY presently
BYE-ROAD secondary road
BY-GOING passing by
BYRONIC cynical
BYSSINE of flax
BYSSOID fringed
BY-THING a minor detail
BYWONER squatter (S. Africa)

C

CABARET entertainment show (night club)
bt, ck **CABBAGE** green vegetable
CABBALA rabbinic mysticism
CABBLED fragmented
CABEIRI deities of Semitic origin
tx **CABESSE** Indian silk
CAB-FARE money for taxi ride
CABINED confined; cribbed
CABINET governing ministers; chamber; WC
CABINET show case; (furniture)
CABIRIC (nature worship)
CABLING telegraphing
rw, bd **CABOOSE** guard's van; shanty
CAB-RANK row of cars for hire
CA'CANNY work in slow time
md **CACHEXY** morbid state
mt **CACIMBO** heavy mists, low cloud, Angola
CACIQUE cazique; Mexican chieftain
CACKLED CACKLER, a noisy hen
ch **CACODYL** oily compound
CACOEPY false pronunciation
CACOLET mule-chair
CACONYM wrongly derived name
CADAVER corpse; dead body
CADDISH impolite; trickster; impostoring
CADENAS condiment casket
mu **CADENCE** falling tones; flow sequence
CADENCE rhythmical movements
CADENCY regularity of movement
CADENUS Dean Swift
mu **CADENZA** a flourish
CADGING hawking; sponging; soming
CADMEAN (Cadmus); moral victory
ch **CADMIUM** a metal
to **CADRANS** (jewel cutting)
ch **CAESIUM** a metal
CAESURA poetic pause
CAFENET Turkish inn

CAFFEIC CAFFEIN, coffee alkaloid
mo **CAGOULE** waterproof hooded garment
CAINITE (Cain); a Gnostic
nt **CAISSON** floatable, sinkable dock port
CAITIFF knave; miscreant; churl
bt **CAJEPUT CAJUPUT,** pungent oil (tree)
CAJOLED CAJOLER, inveigled; beguiler
bt **CAJUPUT** pungent oil
CALABER squirrel-fur
zo **CALAMAR** cuttle-fish
bt **CALAMUS** dragon's blood palm
pr **CALAMUS** antique Islamic reed pen
mu **CALANDO** diminuendo
CALCIFY turn to lime
CALCINE pulverize by heat
mn **CALCITE** calc-spar
ch **CALCIUM** a metallic element
md **CALCULI** gall-stones
gl **CALDERA** lava collapse crater; steep cliffs
CALDRON cauldron; boiler; kettle
CALECHE a vehicle; calash (Fr.)
CALENDS first of month
CALIBAN a tempestuous monster
CALIBER CALIBRE, diameter of bore gauge; capacity; faculty; talent
ch **CALICHE** sodium nitrate
bt **CALICLE** small cup
CALINDA W. Indian dance
CALIPEE calipash; turtle fat
to **CALIPER** measuring instrument
CALIVER a musket
nt **CALKING CAULKING,** water-proofing hulls
CALL-BOY prompter's attendant; (rent-boy)
pg **CALLIER** photographic ratio
CALLING vocation; profession; trade; game-, dance instructions
CALLOUS insensitive; hard; obdurate
bt **CALLUNA** heather
md **CALMANT** a sedative
CALMING tranquillizing
CALMUCK Kalmuck; Mongolian
md **CALOMEL** mercuric chloride
CALORIC heating
me **CALORIE** unit of heat
ar, rl **CALOTTE** skull-cap; dome
rl **CALOYER** Greek monk
CALTRAP CALTROP, 4-pin spike against cavalry
bt **CALUMBA** climbing plant
CALUMET Indian peace-pipe
CALUMNY slander; aspersion; obloquy

rl **CALVARY** Golgotha (skulls)
crucifixion place
CALVING bringing forth (of cattle)
CALVING icebergs from polar ice
zo **CALYCLE** coral-polyp
bt **CALYPSO** sea nymph; (Odysseus)
CAMAIEU cameo; a monochrome
ar, rl **CAMARIN** chapel behind high altar
(Sp.)
CAMARON freshwater prawn; Sp.
shrimp
CAMBIAL pertaining to cambium
CAMBISM art of exchange; (cambio
It.)
CAMBIST banker; financier
CAMBIUM cellular tissue
tx **CAMBLET** camel-hair cloth
bt **CAMBOGE** gamboge
CAMBREL meat-hook
tx **CAMBRIC** white linen
rl **CAMBUCA** pastoral staff
CAMELOT King Arthur's Court
CAMELRY camel corps
CAMORRA secret society (It.)
bt, mu **CAMPANA** an anemone; bell (It.)
bt **CAMPHOR** aromatic laurel
CAMPING encamping; struggling
bt **CAMPION** plant
nt **CAMSHIP** merchant ship with fighter
aircraft
bt **CAMWOOD** a red wood
mu **CANARIE** triple time dance
ga **CANASTA** two-pack card game
CAN-BANK collection container for
recycling
nv **CAN-BUOY** conical buoy
me **CANDELA** luminous intensity
CANDENT incandescent; glowing
CANDIED CANDIFY, sweetmeat
preserve in sugar
bt **CANDOCK** yellow water-lily
CANDOUR frankness; openness
bt, ck **CANELLA** cinnamon tree (W. Indies)
CANHOOK cask-hook
CANIKEN CANAKIN, small container
CANKERY cankered
tx **CANNELE** horizontally ribbed silk
fabric
CANNERY CANNING, food processing
(factory)
CANNIER more artful, cunning
CANNING preserving; tinning
md **CANNULA** surgical tube
rl **CANONIC** canonical
rl **CANONRY** residence of cathedral
canon
CANOPIC (Canopic case)
as **CANOPUS** star in Argo

CANTARO drinking glass (Spain)
rl, mu **CANTATA** sung mass; choral work
ck **CANTEEN** factory restaurant; cutlery
box; tin
pl **CANTHAL CANTHUS**, corner of the
eye
CANTING hypocritical;
sanctimonious
rw **CANTING** curve adjustment slope
CANTLET CANTLE, fragment; cutting
tx **CANTOON** cotton material
CANTRED hundred; county division
CANTRIP a witch's spell
pt **CANVASS** seek votes (lobby);
(painting)
nt, ga **CANVASS** (sails) (tentcloth)
(flooring)
mu **CANZONE** song or melody
CAPABLE CAPABLY, efficient; able;
competent
CAP-A-PIE from head to foot
CAP-CASE travelling case
zo **CAPELIN** small smelt fish
CAPERED CAPERER, frolicked;
bounded; dancer
cr **CAP-IRON** cutting-iron stiffener
CAPITAL money; main; excellent
nt **CAPITAN** naval officer
CAPITOL Roman temple
CAPORAL shag tobacco
CAPOTED won all tricks at piquet
rl **CAPOUCH** monk's cowl
CAPPING topping; limiting (finance)
ch **CAPRATE** a salt
mu **CAPRICE** whim; light fugue;
(humour)
zo **CAPRINE CAPROIC**, like a goat
ck **CAPRINO** goat-milk cheese
(Argentina)
CAPRONE flavouring oil
CAPSIZE upset; overturn
nt, cp **CAPSTAN** windlass; tape-winder
bt **CAPSULA** seed-vessel; a cap
md **CAPSULE** soluble envelope
ae **CAPSULE** detachable compartment
nt **CAPTAIN** leader; chief; master
CAPTION certificate; title; arrest
CAPTIVE prisoner
CAPTURE take; apprehend; catch
rl **CAPUCHE** a Capuchin's hood
CAPULET father of Romeo's Juliet
bt **CAPULIN** Mexican cherry
CAR PARK parking area
zo **CARACAL** Persian lynx
ar **CARACOL** snail; spiral shell; staircase
zo **CARACUL** Bukhara sheep
ck **CARAMEL** a sweetmeat; caromel
bt **CARANNA** aromatic resin (Amazon)

CARAVAN house on wheels
nt CARAVEL four-masted ship
bt CARAWAY seed; plant; spice
ch CARBIDE (lamp)
CARBINE short rifle
CARCAKE pancake
CARCASE body; bomb; framework
CARCASS a fire-work; shell arch
nm CARDECU French quarter-crown
md CARDIAC (heart); cardial
CARDING combing flax
bt CARDOON artichoke
bt CARDUUS thistle genus
CAREFUL meticulous; heedful; wary
CARGOES argosies
zo CARIAMA bird of prey
zo CARIBOU Arctic reindeer (N. Amer.)
CARIOLE light cart
CARIOUS decayed
rl CARITAS love of God and neighbour
CARKING anxious
bt CARLINE a witch; thistle genus
CARLISM CARLIST, royal faction (Sp.)
CARLOCK motor door; isinglass
CARMINE red pigment
CARNAGE slaughter; butchery
CARNIFY turn to flesh
CARNOSE CARNOUS, fleshy; meatlike
nm CAROLUS sovereign of Charles I
CAROSSE sheepskin or fur rug (S. Africa)
md CAROTID arterial
md CAROTIN carrot pigment, vitamin
CAROUSE revel; feast; tipple
CARPING captious; cavilling; objecting
CARPORT open garage
nt CARRACK armed trading ship; argosy
CARRIED borne; upheld; transported
CARRIER transporter; conveyor
CARRION putrid meat
CARROTY rufous (rufus); colour of carrots
rw CAR-SHED carriage depot for buses, trains
CARTAGE conveyance
CARTING transporting
CARTOON topical sketch
CARVING slicing; cutting; engraving
zo CARVIST hawk on hand
ch CARVONE caraway oil ketone
mu CARYOKE video-led pub singing
bt CARYOTA fish-tail palms
CASCADE waterfall; collar
md CASCARA herbal laxative

CASEASE casein-decomposing enzyme
ck CASEATE CASEOUS, cheese-like
lw CASE-LAW based on judgements
CASEMAN compositor
CASHIER cash desk teller; discharge
CASHING (cheques)
bt, ck CASSADA CASSAVA, tapioca
ga CASSINO CASINO, card game
CASSIUS (purple)
rl CASSOCK a vestment
CASSONE bridal chest (It.)
CASTING rejecting; pitching; (mould); (spell); (roles); angling
CASTLED (chess)
CASTLET small castle
CAST-OFF laid aside
CASTRAL (camp)
CASUIST a quibbler; sophist
CATALAN Catalonian
zo CATALLO hybrid; buffalo and cow
CATALOG university calendar (USA)
bt CATALPA Shawnee-wood
CATAPAN Byzantine governor
CATARRH (inflammation)
CATASTA slave-block
bt CATAWBA Ohio grape
zo CAT-BIRD American thrush
nt CAT-BOAT boat with mast in bow
CAT-CALL derisive yell
CATCHER (base-ball)
CATCHES songs; (fish)
ck CATCHUP CATSUP, KETCHUP, tomato and spices sauce
CATCH-UP draw level; chance-taking
md CATECHU an astringent
CATERED provided for; food obtained
CATERER restaurant meals purveyor
CAT-EYED (night vision)
nt CAT-FALL anchor rope
zo CAT-FISH wolf-fish; nurse-hound
CATHEAD anchor rest
CATHECT to direct feelings
el, pc CATHODE negative electrode; (TV)
nt CAT-HOLE hawser hole
CATHOOD cf. spinsterhood
CATLIKE feline character
zo CATLING small cat; cat-gut
bt CAT-MINT a species of Nepeta
CAT-SALT rough salt
mn CAT'S-EYE a quartz
CAT'S-PAW a dupe; a ripple
zo CATTALO hybrid; buffalo and cow
CATTISH spiteful
nt CATWALK narrow plank bridge
bt CATWHIN needle-gorse

CAUDATE with a tail
bt **CAULINE** stalky
CAULKED rendered watertight
CAULKER a dram; a whopper
bt **CAULOME** all organs of a shoot
CAUSING resulting in; occasioning
CAUSTIC corrosive; mordant
md **CAUTERY CAUTERIZATION,** searing
treatment
CAUTION care; heed; warning
CAVALRY horse-soldiers
CAVEMAN a troglodyte; grotto–
dweller
CAVETTO hollow moulding
zo **CAVIARE** sturgeon's roe
bt **CAYENNE** red pepper
CAZIQUE cacique; West Ind. chief
CEASING desisting; ending; stopping
zo **CEBIDAE** class of monkeys
fr **CEDARED** cedar forest
CEDILLA c like s sign
bt **CEDRELA CEDRINE,** types of cedar
bd, ae **CEILING** upper limit; (room, prices,
flights)
CELADON stoneware (ceramics) (Ch.)
mu **CELESTA** keyboard; bell effects
ch **CELLASE** apricot-kernel enzyme
mu **CELLIST** violoncellist
cy **CELL-SAP** cell fluid constituents
CELLULE small cell
ps **CELSIUS** centigrade heat scale
mu **CEMBALO** It. clavichord,
harpsichord
CENACLE supper-room
CENSING burning incense
CENSION assessment
CENSUAL (census)
CENSURE blame; rebuke; chide
CENTAGE percentage
CENTAUR mythological horse-man
nm **CENTAVO** Portuguese halfpenny
bd, ar **CENTERS** temporary supports (arch,
dome)
ma **CENTILE** scores system below 100
nm **CENTIME** hundredth part of a franc
me **CENTNER** foreign cwt
nc, me **CENTRAD** one hundredth of a radian
CENTRAL mediate; middlemost
CENTRED concentrated; based;
located
CENTRIC central
zo **CENTRON** neuron
pl **CENTRUM** part of spinal vertebra
ga **CENTURY** hundred (years, runs –
cricket)
CERAMIC (pottery)
bt **CERASIN** plum-gum
CERATED waxed

CEREALS edible grass crops;
breakfast food
CEREOUS CERESIN, wax
CEROTIC beeswax extract
CERTAIN assured; infallible;
undeniable
CERTIFY avouch; attest; witness
CERULIN indigo
md **CERUMEN** ear-wax
CERUSED white-leaded
CERVINE (stags)
CESIOUS bluish-grey
CESSING taxing
CESSION relinquishment; surrender
bd **CESS-PIT** midden; sewage tank
zo, md **CESTODA CESTOID,** tapeworm
zo **CETACEA** whales, etc.
CHABLIS white wine
CHABOUK Eastern whip
mu **CHACONY CHACONNE,** slow dance;
repeated theme
CHAFERY welding furnace
CHAFFED bantered; scoffed; derided
CHAFFER haggle; bargain
CHAFING fretting; fuming; rubbing
CHAGRIN vexation; irritation
CHAINED fettered; measured
CHAIRED presided over; carried in
triumph
bt **CHALAZA** the base of an ovule
CHALDEE Chaldean
me **CHALDER** 96 bushels
rl **CHALICE** communion cup; goblet
CHALKED scored; recorded
(blackboard)
tx **CHALLIS** fine silk
md **CHALONE** an internal secretion
CHAMADE invitation to a parley
CHAMBER room; closet; hall; cavity
CHAMFER groove; polish
CHAMLET camlet; camel-hair
zo **CHAMOIS** leather
bt **CHAMPAC** Indian tree; champak
CHAMPED crunched; chewed; bit
CHANCED happened; befell; risked
rl, bd **CHANCEL** clergy's area of church
CHANDOO prepared opium
CHANGED altered; varied; shifted
CHANGER exchanger; shifter
cp, nt, tc **CHANNEL** canal; strait; gutter
mu **CHANSON** song (Fr.)
CHANTED (horse-coping); intoned
rl **CHANTER** a precentor
mu **CHANTER** (bagpipes)
rl **CHANTRY** chapel for mass
CHAOTIC confused; disordered
gl **CHAPADA** tableland in Bahia, Brazil
ck **CHAPATI** unleavened bread (India)

CHAPEAU a hat (Fr.)
CHAPLET garland; wreath; coronal
CHAPMAN pedlar; hawker
CHAPNET CHAPNUT, pewter salt-cellar
CHAPPED seamed; cleft; cracked
CHAPPIE ghost (Sc.)
rl CHAPTER cathedral council; (freemasonry)
CHAPTER a division within history, novel, etc.
CHARACT a character (Shak.)
CHARADE dramatic enigma
CHARGED rushed forward; accused; billed; loaded
zo CHARGER platter; war horse
CHARILY stingily; warily; reluctantly
CHARING drudgery
CHARIOT Roman vehicle
CHARISM sense of power
CHARITY benevolence; alms
CHARLEY night-watchman
CHARLIE pointed beard
CHARMED enchanted; fascinated
CHARMER a siren; beguiler
CHARNEL mortuary; house of the dead
CHARPOY Indian bedstead
CHARQUI dried beef (Peru)
CHARRED scorched; seared; burnt
nt CHARTED tabulated; recorded
CHARTER right; privilege; hire
CHASING engraving; pursuing; hunting
CHASSIS frame-work; base structure of vehicle
CHASTEN correct; punish; humble
CHATEAU country seat
CHATTAH Indian umbrella
CHATTED gossiped; prattled
lw CHATTEL movable property
CHATTER talk; prate; tattle
CHAUVIN French patriot; chauvinism (excessive group loyalty)
CHAWING chewing; munching
ck CHAYOTE custard marrow
CHEAPEN belittle; depreciate; reduce price, quality
CHEAPER not so dear
CHEAPLY inexpensively
CHEATED bobbed; duped; gulled
CHEATER trickster; swindler
CHECHIA Arab skull-cap
CHECKED restrained; hindered; verified
ce CHECKER chess board; to variegate; section leader

CHECK-IN arrival formality (airport, hotel)
ck CHEDDAR a cheese
CHEEKED sauced; was impertinent
CHEEPED chirped
zo CHEEPER young game bird
CHEERED applauded; enlivened
CHEERER vociferous supporter
CHEERIO convivial salutation
zo CHEETAH hunting leopard
zo CHELATE (claw)
zo, bt CHELONE tortoise; shell flower
ck CHELSEA china porcelain; spiralled buns
CHEMISE shift; smock; slip
ch CHEMISM chemical action
CHEMIST chymist; pharmacist; druggist
CHEMOSH a Moabite god
CHENILE fluffy cord
CHEQUER checker; diversify
mt CHERGUI Saharan wind, Morocco
CHERISH to foster; harbour; treasure
CHERMES KERMES, a crimson dye
CHEROOT Burmese or Manila cigar
bt CHERVIL culinary herb
CHESSEL a cheese mould or vat
CHESTED boxed; (flat-)
bt CHESTON a species of plum
CHETNIK guerilla (Croat)
zo CHEVIOT sheep bred on the Cheviots
CHEVRON zigzag badge
CHEWING chawing; munching
CHIANTI Italian red wine
md CHIASMA nerve intersection
CHICANE trick; artifice; (cards); evasion; diversion of circuit turns (motor cycling)
CHICKED sprouted; hatched
CHICKEN young fowl; young person
bt CHICORY salad plant, root (coffee)
CHIDING rating; scolding; blaming
CHIEFLY principally; mainly; mostly
CHIEFRY rent; chief's lands
tx CHIFFON gauzy material
mu, zo CHIKARA Indian guitar; antelope
CHILEAN Chilian; native of Chile
CHILIAD a thousand years
CHILLED discouraged; depressed
CHILLER an iceberg or wet blanket
CHILLUM hookah
zo CHILOMA camel's lip
zo CHIMERA mythical monster; illusion
zo CHIMERA graft; hybrid; fish
rl CHIMERE bishop's robe
mo, gl CHIMNEY funnel; smoke-stack; narrow rock cleft
zo CHINCHA S. American rodent

CHINDIT Burmese guerilla
CHINESE Sinesian
CHINING cutting the backbone
CHINKED jingled; clinked
mt CHINOOK N. American Indian tribe; föhn wind by East Rocky mountains, Canada
CHINSED caulked
CHINWAG chatty conversation
to CHIPAXE light axe
CHIP-HAT hat made of palm leaves
nv CHIP-LOG log-line attachment
CHIPPED chaffed; chopped; cut
CHIPPER lively; twitter; cutter; sculptor
CHIPPIE holed shot (golf); (basket ball)
CHIRPED bird song
zo CHIRPER grasshopper
CHIRRUP bird noise
CHISLEU a Jewish month
CHISLEY gravelly
CHITTER shiver with cold
zo CHITWAH panda; red bear-cat
md CHLORAL a narcotic
ch CHLORIC chlorine derivative
bd, mu, rl CHOIRED in chorus (church)
CHOKING stifling; strangling; coughing
md CHOLEIC of bile
md CHOLERA deadly infectious disease
md CHOLINE B vitamin; organic base
CHOLTRY caravanserai; Eastern inn
CHOOSER a picker; a selector
CHOPINE clog or patten
CHOPPED cut; minced; changed
to, ae, cp CHOPPER cleaver; axe; helicopter; pulsator
CHOPPER high-bouncing ball (baseball)
mu CHORALE choral composition
eg CHORDAL of chords
mu CHORDED strung
CHOREUS a trochee
bt CHORION a membrane
rl CHORIST chorister
md CHOROID eye-membrane
CHORTLE chuckle noisily; exult
ck CHOWDER dish of clams
CHOWTER grumble; croak
rl CHRISOM baptismal cloth
ml CHROMAX iron-based alloys
ch CHROMIC of chromium
ch CHROMYL chrome radical
CHRONIC long continuing; inveterate
nc, ps CHRONON hypothetical particle of time
CHUCKED pitched; tossed; thrown

zo CHUCKIE a chicken
CHUCKLE exult; crow
tx CHUDDAH chudder; cloak or cloth (Ind.)
nv CHUFFED proud; satisfied; steamed
ga CHUKKUR CHUKKA, period of play (polo)
CHUMMED roomed together
ck CHUPATI unleavened bread (Ind.)
rl CHURCHY pious; ritualistic
CHURNED agitated; jostled; upset
CHURRED made deep whirring sound
ck CHUTNEY fruit pickle (Ind.)
ch CHYAZIC (hydro-cyanic)
ch CHYMIFY to digest
CHYMIST CHEMIST, pharmacist
rl CIBORIA canopies
zo CICHLID Tanganyika fish
zo CICONIA storks genus
zo CIDARIS sea-urchins
md CILIARY (eyelashes)
CILIATE with hairs
CIMARRE ceremonial wine vessel (2 handles) (Fr.)
CIMBRIC a language of Jutland-Germanic invaders of Imperial Rome
CIMELIA stored treasures
CIMETER scimitar
CINDERY full of cinders; ashy
ch CINEOLE eucalyptole
md CINEREA nerve tissue
mn CIPOLIN green marble
CIRCEAN of a witch; enchantress; (Circe)
CIRCLED went right round; circumnavigated
CIRCLER CIRCLET, small ring (finger)
cp, el, lw, CIRCUIT judicial itinerary; round
tc, ga tour; racing track; electrical layout; water course; (cars, greyhounds), channel (radio, TV, telex); rotational route; golf; revolution (planetary); turn
mt CIRRATE curly (of clouds)
bt CIRROSE CIRROUS, with tendrils; curls
pt CISSING retreat of paint from surface
CISSOID geometric curve
CISTERN CYSTERN, waterholder; wine cooler (table)
md CISTRON gene (function)
CITABLE quotable
bd CITADEL inner stronghold of city fort
CITADIN alpine races for part-time skiers

lw **CITATOR** a summoner; quoter; speaker

mu **CITHARA** Greek lyre

mu **CITHERN** guitar

CITIZEN burgher; burgess; resident

ch **CITRATE** lemon salts

CITRENE oil of lemons

CITRINE a yellow

mu **CITTERN** cithern; zither

CIVILLY courteously; politely

CIVVIES mufti; civilian clothes

CLABBER thicken

CLACHAN small village (Sc.)

CLACKED clucked; clicked; jabbered

CLACKER clack-valve; football fan's rattle; turnstyle rachet

CLADISM evolutionary classification by common factor

bt **CLADODE** leaflike branch

CLAIMED demanded; insisted; usurped

ga, lw **CLAIMER CLAIMANT,** horse when racing; appellant (court) challenger

CLAMANT insistent crying (demonstration)

CLAMBER climb; scramble

CLAMMED clogged; smeared

CLAMOUR din; uproar; hubbub

CLAMPED clumped; held down

CLAMPER iron patch

CLANGED clashed; pranged

CLANKED clinked; clanged

CLAP-NET bird fowler's net

CLAPPED applauded; shut

CLAPPER tongue of a bell

CLAQUER claqueur; hired applauder

CLARAIN fine coal

CLARIFY make clear; strain; purify

mu **CLARINO** It. trumpet, horn parts; clarionet

mu **CLARION** a shrill trumpet

CLARITY cleanness; distinctness

bt **CLARKIA** a flowering annual

mu **CLASHED** suddenly opposed; cymbals

CLASPED grasped; gripped; fastened

bt **CLASPER** tendril; embracer

CLASSED ranked; grouped; ranged

CLASSER classificationist

CLASSIC first rate; standard; masterly

rl **CLASSIS** assembly or convention

mt **CLASTIC** fragmental; brittle

CLATTER clash; rattle; crash; (breakage)

CLAVATE club-shaped

mu **CLAVIER** keyboard

CLAWING scratching; fawning

CLAYING puddling; purifying

CLAYISH clay-like

CLAY-PIT marl pit

CLEANED purified; washed; scoured

CLEANER dirt remover

CLEANLY spotlessly; adroitly

rl **CLEANSE** wash; purify; (ritual)

CLEAN-UP to tidy; make respectable; purge; cartoon technique; (baseball)

CLEARED acquitted; absolved

CLEARER more obvious; less opaque

CLEARLY distinctly; patently

CLEAVED split; parted; adhered

CLEAVER butcher's chopper

CLEDDYO Celtic sword

CLEMENT merciful; lenient; mild

CLEMMED held fast (crowd, rocks); starving

CLERKLY learnedly; scholarly

nt **CLEWING** coiling; securing

CLICKED found favour; ticked

CLICKER cobbler; compositor

CLICKET knocker; door-latch

mt **CLIMATE** clime; weather

CLIMBED scaled; ascended

bt **CLIMBER** a creeper; mountaineer

CLINKED clanked; jingled (of chains), jailed

CLINKER slag; (ship design)

CLINOID like a bed

CLIPPED shorn; pared; snipped; docked

nt **CLIPPER** schooner; cutter, trimmer

CLIPPIE bus-conductress

ec, mt **CLISERE** climate changes and climaxes

CLITTER clatter

bt **CLIVERS** goose-grass

CLIVITY slope; incline

CLOAKED disguised; concealed; hidden

CLOBBER clothing; cobbler's paste; assault

ar, rl **CLOCHER** belltower (Fr.)

CLOCKED timed; (-in)

CLOCKER time-keeper; clock-watcher

CLODDED clotted; mired

CLOGGED congested; coalesced

CLOGGER clog-maker

CLOSELY intimately; accurately

CLOSEST nearest

CLOSE-UP (to action) (movies); frank

CLOSING conclusion; sealing; clogging; deadline date; (horse-racing)

CLOSURE also cloture; enclosure

bt **CLOT-BUR** the burdock

CLOTHED attired; arrayed; draped

CLOTHES apparel

CLOTTED curdled

CLOTTER to coagulate

CLOTURE closure; conclusion

CLOUDED obscured; blended; dimmed

CLOUTED patched; buffeted

CLOVATE inverse taper

CLOWNED played the fool

CLUBBED coshed; bludgeoned

CLUBBER clubbist; club member

CLUB-LAW might is right

CLUB-MAN member of clubs

CLUCKED clocked; cackled

zo **CLUMBER** a spaniel

CLUMPED in clusters; mustered

CLUMPER to form clumps

rl **CLUNIAC** Benedictine monk

mu **CLUSTER** group; clump; assemble; adjacent notes played together

CLUTTER confused mass

CLYPEAL like a shield; scutate

zo **CLYPEUS** insect's forehead

CLYSMIC cleansing

md **CLYSTER** an injection

COACHED tutored; trained

COACTED compelled; concentrated

COAGENT an associate; colleague

COAKING dowelling

COAL-BED stratum of coal

COAL-GAS extraction from coal

nt **COALING** taking on coal fuel

COALISE COALESCE, come together

COALITE a form of fuel

COAL-PIT mine

ch **COAL-TAR** extraction from bituminous coal

zo **COAL-TIT** a passerine bird

nt **COAMING** raised border surrounding cockpit of kayaks

CO-ANNEX join jointly

COARSEN roughen

COARSER rougher; ruder; cruder

COASTAL COASTER, shorewise, inshore vessel

COASTED free-wheeled (cycles and cars)

COASTER plate for glasses; decanters; bottles

pt, tx **COATING** layer; covering

eg **CO-AXIAL** having common axis

COAXING cajoling; wheedling; (manipulating)

COBBING rounding up swans; picking cherries

bd **COBBING** mixing clay, chalk and straw for walls

COBBLED mended; tinkered; patched

COBBLER shoe repairer; botcher

ce **COBBLES** stones for paving

COBIRON andiron; firedog (open fire place)

COBLOAF crusty loaf

zo **COB-SWAN** male swan

COB-WALL mud-wall

ar **COBWORK** log-house construction

md **COCAINE** drug

zo **COCALON** large cocoon

md **COCHLEA** ear-cavity

ch **COCINIC** cocoa extract

COCKADE badge on 3-cornered hat

pl **COCKEYE** imperfect vision; a squint

ag **COCKING** making hay cocks; stooks; strutting

COCKLED puckered; wrinkled; (like a cockleshell)

COCKLER purveyor of seafood; shell-fish

COCKNEY true Londoner

ae, nt **COCKPIT** cock-fighting arena; enclosure for pilot, kayak canoeist; deck for wounded (Navy)

gl **COCKPIT** sinkhole in karst areas

COCK-SHY coconut shy; target (Aunt Sally)

bt, ck **COCONUT** tropical tree fruit

COCOTTE light of love (Fr.); faithless

ck **COCTILE** baked

COCTION cooking, (con-) result

CODDING fishing; codswallop; nonsense

ck **CODDLED** simmered (eggs); pampered

bt **CODEINE** an alkaloid from opium

mu **CODETTA** rounding off passage (It.)

zo **CODFISH** esteemed food fish

CODICES manuscript books

lw **CODICIL** addition to a will

bt **CODILLA** coarse hemp

CODILLE card-term at ombre

zo **CODLING** young cod

CODLING codlin apple

COELEBS bachelor

md **COELIAC** abdominal

zo **COENURE** young tape-worm

COEQUAL a peer; a compeer

COERCED COGENCE, COGENCY, compelled to; forced to

bl **COEXIST** be coeval; live together

ga **COGGERY COGGING**, cheating at dice

COGNATE related; allied; akin to

bt **COG-WOOD** a Jamaican tree

lw **COHABIT** live together as married

COHERED adhered; cleaved; coalesced
ro **COHERER** early form of detector
COIFFED (hairdressing)
COIGNED billeted (Irish)
COILING entangling; winding up
COINAGE money; specie
COINING minting; counterfeiting
COITION sexual intercourse
lw **COJUROR** witness to credibility
bt **COLA-NUT KOLA-NUT**,
COLD-CUT buffet items; cold lacquer solvent
COLDEST iciest; frostiest
COLDISH chillsome
COLD-PIG cold douche
zo **COLIBRI** species of humming-bird
COLICKY with pains
md **COLITIS** colic; colonic infection
bt **COLLAGE** real objects on art forms
COLLARD cole-wort
COLLATE collect and compare
COLLAUD unite in praising
COLLECT a prayer; assemble; amass
COLLEEN Irish girl
COLLEGE academy; seminary; guild
COLLIDE crash; encounter; clash
nt **COLLIER** miner; vessel
COLLING embracing; necking
COLLOID gelatinous
COLLUDE connive fraud in collaboration
zo **COLOBUS** a monkey genus
COLONEL highest regimental rank
COLOSSI gigantic statues
COLOURS tints, (army flags; sports awards)
COLOURY coloured
COLTISH frisky (of young horses)
zo **COLUBER** a snake genus
COLUMBA holy vessel; (Iona)
COLUMEL a small column
COMBINE unite; blend; coalesce
COMBING breaking into foam; smoothing; (hair); removing wet paint
as **COMBUST** astrological term
COMETIC (comets)
COMFORT console; solace; ease; cheer
COMFORT luxury (furniture; financial)
bt **COMFREY** a plant
COMICAL droll; diverting; farcical
COMITIA assemblies
COMMAND govern; rule; enjoin; decree
COMMARK marches; frontier land

COMMEND laud; praise; eulogize
COMMENT remark; note; criticize
COMMERE a gossip
COMMODE chest of drawers; (portable toilet)
ck **COMMONS** food; fare; non-nobility
COMMOVE agitate
COMMUNE converse; discourse
COMMUNE a self-sufficient group sharing family tasks
COMMUTE exchange; replace; travel
mu **COMPACT** mini-pack; cosmetics; (-disc)
COMPANY society; group; business firm
COMPARE examine for likeness or difference
go, ma **COMPASS** to encircle; scope; magnetic pointer N
COMPERE introducer; leader of an entertainment
COMPETE strive as rival
COMPILE amass; combine; arrange
COMPLEX intricate; complicated
pc **COMPLEX** mental inhibition
COMPLOT conspiracy
nv, ps **COMPOLE** auxiliary magnetic pole
COMPORT behave fittingly; glass stand for syllabub glasses
ar, mu, pt, **COMPOSE** create; assemble;
ck formulate
ag **COMPOST** convert decayed debris to fertility
ck **COMPOTE** dessert of cooked fruit
cp **COMPUTE** reckon; analyse; solve
COMRADE pal; mate; associate
COMTISM COMTIST, (Comte's Positivism)
CONATUS volition; effort; impulse
CONCAVE hollow; scooped; turning inwards; converging
CONCEAL cloak; hide; cover; disguise
CONCEDE yield; allow; grant
CONCEIT vanity; egotism; pride
CONCEPT basic idea expanded
CONCERN trouble; regard; firm
mu **CONCERT** devise; concoct
CONCISE terse; pithy; laconic
CONCOCT plot; hatch; brew
mu **CONCORD** harmony; amity; union
md **CONCUSS** stuns by fall or blow
CONDEMN declare doom; convict; punish
CONDIGN deserved; merited; appropriate
CONDITE to pickle; to preserve
CONDOLE console; share sorrow with sympathy

CONDONE to overlook wrong-doing with apathy; pardon
CONDUCE to lead to desirable result; promote
CONDUCT guide; escort; deportment
mu **CONDUCT** direct a musical performance
CONDUIT passage; pipe; channel; canal
md **CONDYLE** knuckle
bt **CONEINE** coniine; hemlock
ck **CONFECT** a sweetmeat; to prepare
CONFERVA freshwater algae
CONFESS admit; own; disclose; avow
CONFIDE close trust (secrets); depend; rely
CONFINE imprison; limit (of freedom); in bounds
CONFIRM ratify; endorse; re-establish
CONFLUX crowd; confluence of people
CONFORM comply with obedience; similarity
CONFUSE confound; mislead; muddle
CONFUTE disprove; refute; find wrong
CONGEAL make solid (freeze, coagulate)
CONGEST clog; overfill; overpack
CONGIES vitamin-rich rice-cookery water
CONICAL cone-shaped; tapering
bt **CONIFER** evergreen (bearing spores)
CONJOIN unite for link-up; common aim
CONJURE spirit-raising; creating illusions
CONJURY sleight of hand tricks; entertainment
CONKERS chestnuts (challenging game)
CONNATE congenital; innate; inherent
CONNECT couple; conjoin; hyphenate
CONNING studying situation; confidence deception
CONNIVE overlook; permit wrong; abet
CONNOTE imply a logical connection
CONQUER overpower; vanquish
CONSENT concur; agree; assent
CONSIGN despatch; send; trasmit
CONSIST comprised of; made up of
mu **CONSOLE** sympathize (sadness); organ (control point)

CONSOLS government Consolidated Funds
mu **CONSORT** associate with; chamber orchestra; spouse
CONSULT deliberate together; confer
CONSUME devour (eat) (fire); expend
el **CONTACT** get in touch; (communication) (-lens)
CONTAIN include; embody; comprise
CONTEND strive; vie; assert; cope
CONTENT volume; satisfy; mollify; (contained)
ga **CONTEST** struggle; compete (arena)
CONTEXT applicable background situation
CONTORT bend; twist (body) (facts)
CONTOUR outline; height line; profile
el **CONTROL** check; steer; master; (switches)
CONTUSE bruise; crush (physical)
CONVENE assemble; muster; summon
rl **CONVENT** a nunnery
rl **CONVERT** change; alter; transform; win over; after-try (goal) rugby; Canadian football
CONVICT prove guilty; (judge); criminal
CONVOKE summon to a meeting; convene
ck **COOKERY** COOKING, concocting; cuisine
COOLANT liquid or gas preventing overheating
COOLEST most impudent; exciting; least warm
COOLING moderating
COOLISH somewhat cool
COONCAN card game
bt **COONTIE** arrowroot
COOPERY barrel production
COOPING confining; penning
CO-OPTED invited to elected body
bt **COPAIBA COPAIVA**, balsam
zo **COPEPOD** minute water organism
mu **COPERTO** muffled covered drums
ae, nt **CO-PILOT** assistant aviator; partner
COPIOUS abundant; plenteous; ample
COPLAND angular piece of land
ml, pt **COPPERY** copper-coloured
COPPICE spinney; clump of trees; thicket
COPPING catching; arresting; (policeman)
zo **COPULAR** linking; of mating; coupling

md **COPULIN** vaginal secretion
COPYCAT apeing others' ideas
COPYING aping; transcribing
COPYISM copyist's work
COPYIST plagiarist; imitator
bt **COQUITO** palm with edible sap/seeds
nt **CORACLE CURRAGH**, river craft
(Wales)
mu **CORANTO** a running dance
CORBEAU raven-black
CORBEIL sculptured basket
nt **CORBITA** cargo vessel of Imperial
Rome
CORCASS Irish salt marsh
bt **CORCULE** an embryo
CORDAGE rope
bt **CORDATE** heart-shaped
CORDIAL cocktail; hearty; ardent
CORDING cordage; binding
CORDITE a propellant
fd **CORE-BOX** sand-moulding container
zo **CORINNE** gazelle; small deer
bt **CORINTH** a currant
CO-RIVAL competitor
CORKAGE charge for guests' own
wine
CORKING stopping; sealing wine
bottles
CORK-LEG artificial limb
ag, lw **CORNAGE** agricultural land tenure
bt **CORN-COB** spike of maize
md **CORNEAL** (eye-membrane)
mu **CORNETT CORNET**, woodwind 17th c.
zo **CORN-FLY** destructive insect
mo, ar **CORNICE** ledge of snow; a top
moulding
bt **CORNINE** quinine type
CORNING preserving; granulating
CORNISH (Cornwall)
mu **CORNIST** hornist; cornet blower
lw **CORN-LAW** regulating corn trade
ck **CORN-OIL** maize oil
CORN-RIG strip of growing corn
CORNUAL CORNUTE, horny
CORN-VAN winnowing machine
bt **COROLLA** floral whorl
CORONAL circlet; wreath
CORONER official of causes of death
zo **CORONET** a moth; tiara
CORONIS elision; word contraction
CORRECT amend; exact; precise; true
CORRODE destroy slowly (rust)
CORRUPT degraded; depraved;
putrid
tx **CORSAGE** flowery female dress
CORSAIR pirate (Barbary coast)
mn **CORSITE** diorite
CORSLET sleeveless armour

CORSNED an ordeal
ga **CORTADA** shortened; low shot
(pelota)
CORTEGE solemn procession
md **CORTICO-** of outer layer tissue
ar **CORTILE** courtyard
ch **CORUBIN** aluminium oxide
CORVINE like a cow
CORYDON a rustic lover
bt **CORYLUS** hazel
bt **CORYPHA** fan-palm
COSAQUE cracker; bon-bon (Fr.)
COSHERY billeting (Irish)
COSHING bashing; slugging
COSIEST snuggest; warmest
(intimate)
COSMISM COSMIST, of secular
philosophy
COSSACK KHAZAK, cavalryman
(Russian)
bt, ck **COSTARD** apples (and custard)
ar **COSTATE** ribbed construction
COSTING calculation of right sales
price
COSTIVE obstructive; constipated
COSTREL pilgrim's bottle
COSTUME dress; uniform; livery
COTERIE social circle (similar
interests)
COTIDAL contemporaneous tides
zo **COTINGA** chattering birds
COTLAND cottage land
COTTAGE cot; lodge; hut
hd **COTTICE** heraldic barulet
COTTIER Irish tenant
zo **COTTOID** fish genus; miller's thumb
COTTONY downy; nappy
COUCHED expressed; reclined;
(bedded)
COUCHEE soirée; evening reception
(Fr.)
COUGHER splutterer
rl **COULDST** thou could; (prayer form)
gl **COULOIR** cleft; canyon; eroded gully
el **COULOMB** unit of electrical charge
COULTER fore-end of plough
COUNCIL ministry; assembly; diet
lw **COUNSEL** advice; barrister
COUNTED reckoned; relied;
numbered
COUNTER contrary; adverse;
opposed; small chest (Am.
football) (curling)
me, mu **COUNTER** token, meter; table;
(-point) (-foil)
ga **COUNTER-** being against trend; (ice-
hockey)
COUNTRY region; nation; state

COUPLED paired; bracketed; joined
mu COUPLER connector; duplicated
organ controls
mu COUPLET two lines (rhyming)
(musical)
COURAGE pluck; valour; heroism
mu COURANT disseminator; dance form
COURIER messenger; runner
zo COURLAN S. American crane
COURSED hunted; pursued; chased
zo COURSER war-horse; plover
nt COURSES some sails
COURTED wooed; invited; solicited
COURTER a wooer; swain
COURTLY elegant; urbane; debonair
COUTEAU long knife
COUTURE (haute); clothes for the jet-
set
COUVADE a curious custom
COVELET small bay
COVERED enveloped; veiled; spread
zo COVERTS certain feathers
COVER-UP boxing; concealment
COVETED longed for; desired
bt COW-BANE water-hemlock
zo COW-BIRD American cuckoo
zo COW-CALF female calf
COWERED cringed; shrank; crouched
COWHAGE a bean (Hindu)
ck COW-HEEL ox-foot stewed to a jelly
COWHERD a cow tender
COWHIDE leather
mu COW-HORN alphorn; drinking-
bt COW-ITCH cowhage
COW-LICK salt lick, in fields
COWLIKE ruminant; placid
ae COWLING hood
bt COWSLIP paigle
bt COW-TREE moraceous tree
bt COW-WEED herb
COXCOMB conceited fellow; dandy
COYNESS shyness; bashfulness
COZENED deceived; gulled
COZENER white collar bandit
me, ps C-PARITY charge parity (quantum)
CRABBED morose; surly; disparaged
nt CRABBER small open boat
CRABITE fossil crab
bt CRAB-OIL carap-oil
CRACKED crazy; snapped; split;
broke
CRACKER cosaque; biscuit; firework
CRACKLE glazed fissures in china
pc CRACK-UP nervous breakdown;
crash
CRACOWE KRAKOW, pointed shoe
(Poland)
CRADLED nurtured

CRAGGED rugged; jagged
CRAKING cawing
zo CRAMBUS grass moth
CRAMESY crimson
CRAMMED stuffed; studied
CRAMMER intensive teacher;
packer-in
CRAMPED confined; cabined
CRAMPIT curlers' stand
CRAMPON spiked shoe cover
(Alpine)
CRANAGE dockyard crane dues
zo CRANIAL skull
CRANING stretching the neck
md CRANIUM a skull
CRANKED bent; turned; wound
CRANKLE crinkle; wrinkle; a turn
CRANNOG lake dwelling
CRAPING curling
CRAPNEL grapnel; hook
zo CRAPPIE N. Amer. sunfish
CRASHED smashed; shattered; fell
CRASHER (gate-), uninvited guest;
clumsy
CRATING encasing; packaging
CRAVING longing; yearning; desiring
CRAWLED crept; (swimming)
CRAWLER a reptile; a baby's overall
CRAZIER madder
CRAZILY daftly; distractedly
ar CRAZING weak, broken (crazy
pavement)
bd CREAKED grated, squeaked (floor
noise)
ck CREAMED take the best of milk;
foamed
CREANCE hawk-leash line
ga CREASED folded; wrinkled; lined
(cricket)
CREATED originated; formed;
produced
md CREATIN muscular constituent
CREATOR maker; originator;
inventor
CREDENT credulous; trusting
CREEING softening grain
zo, bt, ga CREEPER crawler; ski-aid; plant;
bird; larva of stonefly; bait
(angling); low ball (cricket)
CREMATE reduce to ashes; incinerate
mu CREMONA a violin
bt CRENATE notched
CRENAUX loop-holes
ch CREOSOL (phenol)
CREPANE wound due to brushing
CRESSET beacon; torch
hd CRESTED capped; surmounted;
(badge)

CRETIFY impregnate with lime
CRETISM a falsehood
CRETOSE chalky
mo **CREVICE** fissure; rift; breach
CREWELS embroidery
CRIBBED cradled; plagiarized; cheated
CRIBBLE coarse sieve; a temse
CRICKED sprained
CRICKET a low stool; an insect; 11 a side bat and ball game
CRICOID ring-shaped
lw **CRIMING** making criminal accusations
tx, ck **CRIMPED** CRIMPER, CRIMPLE, corrugated edging (pies); shrunk
CRIMSON blood red colour
CRINGED cowered; fawned
CRINGER a yes-man; sycophant
nt **CRINGLE** cyclet in sail
CRINITE hairy; a fossil
CRINKLE crankle; wrinkle; crimp
mn **CRINOID** fossilized sea-lily
CRINOSE crinite; pilose; hairy
bd **CRIPPLE** disable; impair; hobble
ck **CRISPED** frizzled; toasted; made brittle
CRISPER curler; more friable
CRISPIN the cobblers' saint
CRISPLY briskly
CRIZZEL CRIZZLE, cloudy roughness on glass
zo **CROAKED** uttered; grumbled; decried (frog)
zo **CROAKER** a fish; a pessimist
CROCHET fancy-work
CROCKED blackened; broken down
ar **CROCKET** pinnacle adornment
CROESUS a wealthy man
ag **CROFTER** hill farmer
CROOKED tortuous; awry; bent
CROONED sung (chromatic); lamented
CROONER sentimental singer
CROPFUL full stomach; satiated
CROPPED mowed; reaped; cut
pr, ce **CROPPER** printing machine; heavy fall; steel bar cutter
ga **CROQUET** up to date pall-mall
rl **CROSIER** CROZIER, bishop's crook
hd **CROSLET** crossed cross
CROSSED thwarted; interbred
CROSSLY peevishly; testily; petulantly
mu **CROTALO** Turkish cymbal
CROTTLE lichen-dye
ck **CROUTON** chopped fried bread
to **CROWBAR** lever; jemmy

CROWDED huddled; thronged
mu **CROWDER** Welsh fiddler
zo **CROWGER** striped wrasse; fish
CROWING rejoicing; boasting; cocks
CROWNED honoured; completed; (king)
bt **CROW-TOE** the buttercup
rl **CROZIER** CROSIER, pastoral crook
CRUBEEN cooked pig's trotter (Irish)
CRUCIAL cross-like; critical; decisive
zo **CRUCIAN** goldfish; crusian
CRUCIFY hang to death on cross
mn **CRUCITE** red iron ore
CRUDELY unpolished; roughly
CRUDEST rawest; coarsest
ck **CRUDITY** rawness; immaturity; salad
CRUELER more brutal; harsher
CRUELTY savagery; barbarity
nt **CRUISED** moved watchfully; voyaged
nt **CRUISER** patrol warship; powered yacht
CRUISIE primitive lamp
ck **CRULLER** a cake
ck **CRUMBED** CRUMBLY, friable; fragmented
ck **CRUMBLE** disintegrate, (fruit dish)
CRUMPED artillery; bomb noise; exploded
ck **CRUMPET** hot griddled tea-bun; (love)
ck **CRUMPLE** CRUNKLE, collapse; crimp
md **CRUORIN** haemoglobin
CRUPPER severe fall; saddle-strap
rl **CRUSADE** idealists' campaign
nm **CRUSADO** Portuguese coin
CRUSHED overwhelmed; compressed
CRUSHER pulverizer; chucker-out
zo **CRUSIAN** CRUCIAN, carp; goldfish
CRUSTED hard surface; en- with debris
CRY-BABY a weakling
CRYOGEN a freezing mixture
CRYPTIC hidden; occult; secret
ch **CRYPTON** krypton; a gas
mn **CRYSTAL** cut-glass; quartz; (-gazing)
CRYSTIC pertaining to ice
CSARISM TSARISM, CZARISM, despotic
CTENOID comb-shaped
CUADROS division lines (pelota Sp.)
CUBBING whelping; hunting fox cubs; scouting
CUBBISH ill-mannered
md **CUBEBIN** cubeb extract
CUBICAL cubic
CUBICLE little bedroom
me **CUBITAL** CUBITED, CUBITUS, (cubit c.50 cm)

CUCKOLD husband of loose wife
zo **CUCULUS** cuckoo
bt **CUDBEAR** a lichen; a purple dye
CUDDLED hugged; fondled; caressed
bt **CUDWEED** a plant
CUE-BALL (billiards)
CUFFING scuffling; buffeting
CUINAGE tin stamping
CUIRASS breastplate (armour)
ck **CUISINE** style of cookery
mu **CUIVRES** brass band instruments (Fr.)
CULETTE hip-armour
CULLIED duped; gulled; hoaxed
CULLING gathering; reducing animal population
bt **CULLION** bulbous root
CULPRIT delinquent; offender
rl **CULTISM CULTIST**, ritual supporter
CULTURE arts; enlightenment; customary beliefs
md **CULTURE** clinical lab. cultivation
CULVERT small bridge; (waterway)
bt **CUMQUAT** kumquat; Chinese fruit
mt **CUMULUS** large cloud formation
CUNEATE wedge-shaped
CUNNING crafty; sly; wily; astute
ag **CUP-FEED** seed drill system
bt **CUP-GALL** an oak-gall
ce **CUPHEAD** rivet shape
bt **CUP-MOSS** a lichen
CUPPING blood-letting
mn **CUPRITE** oxide of copper
bt **CUP-ROSE** poppy
ch **CUPROUS** copper compound
CURABLE remedial
CURACAO orange liqueur
CURATOR custodian; keeper; warden
CURBING repressing; restraining
bt **CURCUMA** (arrowroot, etc.)
CURDING coagulating
CURDLED congealed; thrilled
CURE-ALL universal remedy; panacea
md **CURETTE** surgical scraper
CURIOSA collection of exotic objects
CURIOSO unconventional object collector
CURIOUS inquisitive; strange; novel; odd
ga **CURLING** bowls played on ice
nt **CURRAGH CORACLE**, Celtic water craft
bt **CURRANT** ribes; a dried raisin
nt, el, pr **CURRENT** up-to-date; flow (tide); (-account)
ck **CURRIED** spiced Indian food; flattered; groomed

le **CURRIER** leather-dresser
CURRISH doglike snarling; spiteful
CURSING evil invocation of harm; swearing
pr **CURSIVE** running; ongoing; script
CURSORY hasty; superficial; transient
CURTAIL abridge; contract; shorten
CURTAIN window, theatre drapery; (-call)
CURTANA sword of mercy (Coronation)
cp **CURTATE** cut short; reduced; punched
CURT-AXE short broad-sword
CURTEST bluntest; briefest; shortest
CURVATE CURVITY, bending (surface of globe)
CURVING turning; change of direction
ga **CUSHION** pad; pouffe; lining (billiards)
CUSSING cursing; swearing
ck **CUSTARD** milk, egg and vanilla sauce
CUSTODE a watchman; custodian
CUSTODY care; imprisonment; duress
CUSTOMS duties on merchandise
CUSTREL buckler-bearer; a costrel
tx **CUT-AWAY** tailored coat, dress
CUT-BACK decrease of work; retreat
CUT-DOWN reduce; cheapen (prices etc.)
pl **CUTICLE** fingernail skin area
nt **CUTLASS** short broad sword
CUTLERY edged steel tools (knives etc.)
CUTLINE across front wall (pelota)
CUT-OVER attack (fencing)
CUT-RUSH technique (croquet)
CUTTING satirical; sardonic; sarcastic
bt, rw **CUTTING** trough; gap; sproutling
CUTTING tailoring; escaping; ignoring
CUT-WORK type of embroidery
zo **CUT-WORM** caterpillar pest
CUVETTE crucible; trench; cunette
ch **CYANATE CYANIDE, CYANINE**, poison
mn **CYANITE KYANITE**, aluminium silicate
CYCLING CYCLIST, two wheeling, biker
CYCLOID geometric curve
mt, zo **CYCLONE** tornado; hurricane; typhoon; genus, waterfleas
CYCLOPS one-eyed Sicilian giant
CYCLORN a cycle horn

mu **CYMBALO** the dulcimer
CYNICAL disparaging; ironical
bt **CYPERUS** a sedge
bt **CYPRESS CYPRINE**, funereal tree
CYPRIAN CYPRIOT, of Cyprus
md **CYSTINE** calculus growth
md **CYSTOID CYSTOSE**, cystlike
md **CYSTOMA** tumour
ch **CYTIDIN** nucleic acid
bt **CYTISUS** the broom genus
md **CYTITIS** dermatitis
mu **CZARDAS** Hungarian dance
CZARINA TSARINA, empress (Russia)

D

pt **DABBING** daubing; adding oil or
paint
DABBLED sprinkled; meddled; trifled
DABBLER dilettante; trifler
DABSTER an expert; adept
DACOITY DAKOITY, brigandage
DADAISM art movement
DADDLED tottered
DADDOCK the heart of a rotten tree
DAFIEST silliest; maddest; craziest
DAGGING wool clotted with dung,
earth
DAGGING cutting into strips
DAGGLED befouled; smirched
DAG-LOCK hanging lock of wool
DAGONET King Arthur's fool
bt **DAGWOOD** dog-wood; sandwich
nt **DAHABIA** dhow for cargo, Nile
bt **DAHLINE** dahlia starch
DAKOITY DACOITY, brigandage
DALLIED DALLIER, dawdled; trifler;
flâneur
DALRIAD an Ulster Scot
DAMAGED marred; injured; hurt
DAMMING embanking
DAMNIFY DAMNING (injure)
(condemning)
DAMOSEL DAMSEL, maiden; lady
mu **DAMPFER** dampered; mute (Ger.)
DAMPING discouraging; moistening;
lulling
ro, el **DAMPING** decreasing wave motion
DAMPISH moist; dank; humid
DANAKIL nomad fisher tribe
DANCING social rhythmic movement
to music
DANDIFY overdone dress; dandy's
movement
DANDLED fondled
DANELAW DANELAG, Danish East
England

DANGLED DANGLER, suspended,
cause to swing
DANKISH damp and dark
DANTEAN sombre; infernal
DANTIST specialist of Dante's works
bt **DAPHNAL DAPHNIN**, laurels (bay
leaf)
zo **DAPHNIA** water-fleas
DAPIFER meat-bearer; royal
steward
bd **DAPPING** fly-fishing; cement
patterns
DAPPLED variegated grey; (horses)
DARBIES handcuffs
zo **DARCALL** long-tailed duck
zo **DARCOCK** water-rail
DARIOLE rich cake
DARKEST most secret; blackest
DARKISH sombre; gloomy; blackish
DARLING beloved; dear; pet; idol
DARNING mending clothes
ga **DARTING** swift movements;
sprinting
DASHING rushing; impetuous;
spirited
el **DASHPOT** snubber
DASTARD poltroon; coward; craven
DATABLE traceable to epoch; of
friendships
rl **DATARIA** (papal chancery)
bt **DATISCA** hemp
DATIVAL of dative case (grammar)
DAUBERY DAUBING, poor painting;
smearing; graffiti
DAUNTED discouraged; cowed
DAUPHIN king's eldest son (Fr.)
DAWDLED lagged; dallied; tarried
DAWDLER time-waster; laggard
DAWNING day-break; day-spring
DAY-BOOK daily register
mn **DAY-COAL** (upper stratum)
DAY-GIRL non-resident schoolgirl
bt **DAY-LILY** the hemerocallis
DAY-MAID dairy-maid; daily girl
DAY-PEEP dawn
DAY'S-MAN umpire
DAY-STAR the morning star
zo **DAYSURE** a wolf genus
DAY-TIME not night
DAYWORK (paid daily)
DAZZLED dazed by lights; confused
DEAD-END blind street; cul-de-sac;
without future
nt **DEAD-EYE** 3-eyed naval tackle
(pulley)
DEADISH rather moribund; decaying
DEAD-MEN empty bottles
DEADPAN expressionless (facial)

DEAD-PAY (pay drawn; death concealed)
DEAD-SET determined effort
bt **DEAD-TOP** arboreal disease
DEAF-AID hearing device
bt **DEAF-NUT** without kernel
DEALATE divest of wings
ga **DEALING** handling; trading; (card games)
rl **DEANERY DECANAL**, office of dean (university)
DEAREST costliest; closest loved one
DEARNLY secretly; grievously
DEASIUL DEASOIL, opposite of widdershins
DEATHLY mortal; deadly; destructive
DEBACLE fiasco; theatrical ending; rout; stampede
DEBASED DEBASER, degraded; shady dealer
DEBATED DEBATER, deliberated; disputed; arguer
DEBAUCH intemperate sensual action; deprave
DEBITED DEBITOR, DEBTOR, owing; charged with
DEBOUCH emerge into open area
DECADAL DECADIC, units of ten; decimal system
DECAGON ten-sided figure
rl **DECANAL DEANERY**, office of deans
zo **DECAPOD** having ten limbs; (lobster)
DECARCH commander over 10
DECAYED rotted; degenerated; wasted
DECAYER source of decay
DECEASE perish; die; expire; demise
DECEIVE beguile; mislead; overreach
DECENCY propriety; decorum
me **DECIARE** tenth of an are (Fr.)
me **DECIBEL** unit of noise
DECIDED resolute; firm; unwavering
ga **DECIDER** umpire; referee; final contest
ma **DECIMAL** system based on tens, tenths
DECKING ornament; embellishment
DECKLED with edges uncut
cp **DECKLET** record, set of IBM cards
DECLAIM orate; harangue; rant; spout
DECLARE avouch; assert; proclaim
DECLINE refuse; decay; wane; languish
DECODED deciphered
DECODER info. locater/fetcher/solver
DECORUM seemliness; decency

DECOYED allured; snared; inveigled
DECREED ordered; resolved; enacted
DECREET announce court judgement
DECRIAL DECRIER, clamorous censure; vilifier
DECRIED disparaged; traduced
DECROWN discrown; dethrone
DECUMAN main gate; tenth; principal
DECUPLE tenfold
DECURVE straighten
lw **DEDIMUS** judicial commission
DEDUCED inferred; concluded; reasoned
bd **DEDUCTS** calculation (excluding doors, windows etc)
DEEDFUL DEEDILY, manly; valiantly
lw **DEEDING** conveying by deed
DEEMING opining; considering
DEEPEST most profound; lowest
ck **DEEP-FRY** cooking method
DEEP-SEA in deep ocean
DEERITE iron/manganese hydrous silicate
DEFACED DEFACER, disfigured; mutilator
DEFAMED DEFAMER, libelled; slandered; detractor
DEFAULT lapse; financial failure
DEFENCE plea; excuse; protection
DEFIANT provocative; contumacious
DEFICIT shortage
DEFILED DEFILER, polluted; taken; seducer
DEFINED DEFINER, accurately described; clarifier
DEFLATE release air; reduce credit; erode
DEFLECT divert; turn aside
DEFRAUD trick; cheat; deceive
DEFUNCT deceased
DEFYING challenging; flouting
DEGAUSS antimagnetic device
DEGLAZE to clear thick gravy
DEGRADE lower; humble; debase
DEICIDE a god-destroyer
DE-ICING removing ice
rl **DEIFIED DEIFORM**, idolized; godlike
DEIGNED condescended; vouchsafed
rl **DEISTIC** theory of non-active God
DELAYED procrastinated; deferred
DELAYER a cunctator; procrastinator
DELETED expunged; effaced
DELIGHT charm; ravish; joy; ecstasy
DELIMIT fix limits
DELIVER cede; consign; rescue; save
DELOUSE to remove lice
DELPHIC oracular

go **DELTAIC** delta-like
md **DELTOID** a muscle
DELUDED misled; beguiled; gulled
DELUDER deceiver; trickster; hoaxer
DELUGED flooded; inundated; swamped
DELVING digging; excavating
DEMENTI official denial (Fr.)
DEMESNE DOMAIN, lord's land (feudal)
DEMIGOD almost worshipped person
DEMIREP a lady of doubtful virtue
DEMISED bequeathed; willed
DEMODED old fashioned
DEMONIC fiendish; satanic; diabolical
DEMONRY devilry
DEMONYM pseudonym using pop. style
DEMOTIC popular; common
DENDRAL living in trees; arboreal
DENDRON dendrite of nerve-cell
DENIZEN inhabitant; naturalized plant, animal
DENOTED indicated; signified
DENSELY closely; thickly
DENSEST thickest; closest
DENSITY compactness; stolidness
pl **DENTARY** (teeth); dermal bone
DENTATE toothed
DENTELS toothed ornaments
pl **DENTINE** ivory tissue of teeth
DENTING dinting; notching
md **DENTIST** tooth doctor
DENTOID tooth-like
DENTURE false teeth
DENUDED stripped; bared; divested
DENYING controverting; refuting
DEPLANE cf. detrain
DEPLETE to empty; exhaust; drain
DEPLORE lament; grieve; bewail
DEPLUME to pluck
lw **DEPONED** testified
DEPOSAL dismissal; sacking
DEPOSED bore witness; ousted
cp **DEPOSIT** store; lodge; intrust; part payment
DEPRAVE corrupt; debase; vitiate
DEPRESS damp; dishearten; sadden
DEPRIVE strip; rob; divest
DEPUTED delegated; authorized
DERANGE disturb; upset; ruffle
DERATED freed from local taxation
DERIVED deduced; traced; obtained
DERMOID like skin
DERNFUL solitary; mournful
DERNIER final; last (Fr.)
DERRING daring
DERVISH Moslem monk

rl **DESCANT** counterpoint superimposed on melody
DESCEND dismount; alight; drop; sink
DESCENT slope; decline; origin; raid
DESERVE earn; win; merit; justify
DESIRED wanted; solicited; coveted
DESIRER craver; yearner; fancier
DESKILL simplify industrial work
mn **DESMINE** stilbite; zeolitic mineral
DESPAIR hopelessness; despondency
DESPISE disdain; contemn; scorn; scout
DESPITE in spite of; malice
DESPOIL rob; bereave; strip; rifle
DESPOND despair; dejectedness
ck **DESSERT** fruit course; pudding; afters
DESTINY fate; fortune; doom; Kismet
DESTROY devour; demolish; raze
mu **DETACHE** violin bowing technique (Fr.)
DETENTE relaxing political strain
fr **DETERMA** a useful wood from Guyana
lw **DETINUE** writ of distraint
DETRACT defame; disparage; traduce
DETRAIN alight from train
DETUNER jet-engine noise-reduction
bt **DEUTZIA** a white flower
DEVALUE depreciate
DEVELOP grow; unfold; expand
DEVIATE swerve; turn; tack; digress
DEVILED stuffed; seasoned before frying
DEVILET small demon; imp
DEVILRY cruel mischief; diabolism
DEVIOUS wandering; erratic; tortuous
DEVISED contrived; willed; concocted
DEVISEE legatee; inheritor
DEVISER inventor; schemer; planner
DEVISOR testator
DEVOLVE deliver; depute; impose
DEVOTED loving; ardent; attached
DEVOTEE an addict; a fan; zealot
DEW-DROP drop of earth condensation
DEW-FALL aqueous precipitation
DEWLAPT with a dewlap
DEW-POND pond fed by condensation
zo **DEW-WORM** earthworm
md **DEXTRAD** to the right side (body)
DEXTRAL (not left)
DEXTRAN synthetic blood plasma

DEXTRIN starch gum
mn DIABASE variously defined rock type
ga DIABOLO game (devil on two sticks)
DIAGRAM graph; sketch; drawing
DIALECT local parlance; idioms
DIALIST dial-maker
ch DIALIZE separate
DIALLED rang up (telephone call)
ch DIAMINE 2-amino-group compound
mn, hd, ga DIAMOND hard valuable stone;
(cards); lozenge; baseball
bt DIANDER (two stamens)
zo DIAPSID condition of skulls
DIARCHY dual monarchy
DIARIAL DIARIES, daily memoranda
DIARISE DIARIST, to record;
chronicler
cy DIASTER stage in cell-division
bt DIATOMS seaweed
bd DIATONI face-dressed quoins
zo DIAXONE bipolar nerve cell
ch DIBASIC giving two salts
zo DIBATAG N. African gazelle
DIBBING dipping
DIBBLED made hole in the ground
DIBBLER planter
DICE-BOX dice holder
ga DICEING throwing dice; (gambling)
(game)
zo DICERAS clams
mu DICHORD lyre
mn DICKITE hydrated aluminium silicate
bt DICLINY state of sex separation
DICTATE record; command; state
DICTION style; speech; clear
enunciation
DIDACHE apostolic teaching
DIDDLED out-witted; cajoled;
cozened
DIDDLER a cheat; swindler; cajoler
DIE-AWAY languishing; losing sound
DIE-CAST (condenser construction)
DIEDRAL dihedral
DIE-HARD last ditcher; anti-
reformist
ck DIETARY DIETING, system of diet
ck DIETIST DIETITIAN, diet advisor
DIE-WORK die-cutting
DIFFUSE spread; copious; prolix
DIGAMMA obsolete Greek letter
DIGGING delving; excavating
ma DIGITAL integral; decimal; binary
el, cp DIGITAL numeric system data
DIGLYPH grooved face
DIGNIFY ennoble; exalt; grace
DIGNITY majesty; decorum; rank
DIGRAPH (two letters)
DIGRESS deviate; wander; swerve

bt DIGYNIA curious plant; (two pistils)
ch DIKETEN ketene dimer
DILATED enlarged; expatiated
DILATER an expander; amplifier
md DILATOR a muscle
DILEMMA quandary; plight; strait
md DILL-OIL a carminative
DILUENT a diluter; reducer
DILUTED watered; attenuated
DILUTEE unskilled worker
(industrial)
DILUTER thinner
DIMETER (poetry)
DIM-EYED with weak vision; weepy
DIMMING blurring; clouding; dulling
DIMMISH somewhat obscure
DIMNESS vagueness; dinginess
DIMPLED showing dimples
DINETTE a dining compartment
bd DINGING ringing; urging; single coat
stucco walls
zo DINGOES wild dogs of Australia
DINNING advocating clamorously
DINTING denting; striking
rl DIOCESE a bishopric
zo DIOCOEL diencephalon lumen
DIODONE iodine x-ray preparation
bt DIOECIA genus of plants
bt DIONAEA Venus's fly-trap
zo DIOPSIS fly genus
me DIOPTER optical measurement
DIOPTER speculum; theodolite
pg DIOPTRE unit of lens power
DIORAMA panorama
DIORISM definition
mn DIORITE igneous rock
ch DIOXIDE oxygen-based oxide
DIPHONE a shorthand sign
md DIPLOID twin chromosomes
DIPLOMA a certificate
DIPLONT diploid-nuclei-bearing
plant body
DIPOLAR with two poles
DIPPING dibbing; plunging;
immersing
DIPTERA two-winged insect
DIPTOTE noun with 2 cases only
DIP-TRAP bend in a pipe
rl DIPTYCH pictorial altar-piece
DIREFUL calamitous; baleful; awful
DIRKING stabbing
DIRT-BED (quarrying)
DIRTIED soiled; sullied; begrimed
DIRTIER DIRTILY, grubbier; more
soiled; filthily
DIRT-PIE mud-pie
DISABLE unfit; incapacitate; maim
cp DISABLE suppress an interrupt

DISAGIO money-exchange charge
DISALLY separate; sunder
DISAVOW repudiate; disown; deny
DISBAND disperse; disembody
DISCARD cast; reject; abandon
DISCERN espy; perceive;
  discriminate
DISCOID flat like a disc
mu **DISCORD** strife; brawl; animosity;
  dissonance
DISCUSS debate; argue; consume
DISDAIN spurn; contemn; ignore
md **DISEASE** malady; complaint
DISEUSE woman reciter (Fr.)
DISGOWN unfrock (clergy)
DISGUST nausea; aversion; loathing
DISHFUL filling a dish
ck **DISHING** thwarting; preparing food
DISJOIN part; detach; sunder; sever
DISLIKE hate; detest; antipathy
DISMALS unhappy pessimists (anti-
  social)
nt **DISMAST** remove masts (sea battle)
DISMISS cashier; discharge; sack
DISOBEY transgress; disregard;
  infringe
DISPLAY parade, flaunt; show;
  evince
cp, lw **DISPLAY** reveal; put on screen
lw **DISPONE** hand over
DISPORT sport; gambol; frolic;
  wanton
DISPOSE sell; transfer; arrange
DISPUTE argue; wrangle; bicker
DISROBE unrobe; strip; divest; bare
DISRUPT break up; disintegrate
DISSECT anatomize; analyse; cut
DISSENT disagree; differ
DISTAFF staff for holding unspun
  flax
DISTAFF the opposite of spear-side
DISTANT remote; far; aloof; reserved
DISTEND dilate; swell; expand; bloat
DISTENT distended (Spens.)
DISTICH rhyming couplet
zo **DISTOMA** genus of worms
DISTORT pervert; misrepresent
DISTURB molest; confuse; vex;
  annoy
DISUSED obsolete; neglected;
  abandoned
DITCHED fallen into the sea (RAF);
  discarded; failed examination
DITCHER ditch clearer
nt **DITHERY** nervous; agitated;
  tremulous
bt **DITTANY** candle plant
DITTIED DITTIES, sung sea shanties

DIURNAL daily; quotidian; journal
DIVERGE fork; radiate; part
DIVERSE unlike; different; varied
DIVIDED severed; sundered;
  separated
cp, tc **DIVIDER** distributor; apportioner
DIVINER predictor; seer; magician
DIVISOR (arithmetic)
DIVORCE dissever; part; alienate
DIVULGE tell; reveal; disclose; impact
DIVVY-UP provide dividend (on
  profit); divide
DIZENED DIZZIED, DIZZIER, dazed;
  confused
DIZZARD blockhead; idiot
DIZZILY confusedly
rl **DOCETAE** DOCETIC, ungodly heretic
  sect
DOCKAGE dock dues
nt **DOCKING** taking ships into dock;
  curtailing (dog)
DOCQUET DOCKET, list sheet (cargo)
  loads
DODDING lopping tails; polling horns
  (cows, deer)
DODGERY trickery; prevarication
DODGING evading; quibbling
le **DOESKIN** soft leather
DOFFING divesting; putting off
bt **DOG-BANE** plant with a bitter root
DOG-BELT part of dog harness
DOG-BOLT arrow; dog-meal
DOG-CART two-wheeled vehicle
nt **DOG-DAYS** (occur in July and
  August)
DOGEATE office of Doge (Venice)
zo **DOG-FISH** tope; small shark
DOGGING following closely; tailing
DOGGISH rather posh; doglike
DOGHEAD gunlock hammer
nt **DOG-HOLE** BOGHOLE, ship's WC
DOGHOOD cf. manhood
DOGLIKE having canine attributes
DOG-NAIL large nail
bt **DOG-ROSE** wild rose
DOG'S-EAR a fold in a page in a
  book
DOGSHIP of dogs; dogginess
DOG-SICK sick as a dog
le **DOGSKIN** glove leather
bt **DOG'S-RUE** a plant; Scrophularia
as **DOG-STAR** Sirius
zo **DOG-TICK** a parasite
DOGTROT jog
nt **DOG-VANE** wind-vane
bt **DOGWOOD** flowering bush
DOLABRA Roman hatchet
DOLEFUL woe-begone; dismal; rueful

DOLLIED hammered; laundered
DOLLIER an ore-crusher
zo, nt DOLPHIN cetacean; (pilot); a spar
buoy
DOLTISH stupid; stolid; witless
DOMABLE tamable; tractable
DOMICAL dome-shaped
DOMINIE schoolmaster (Sc.)
DOMINUS Master; Lord
DONATOR donor; presenter; giver
DONNING putting on; assuming
DONNISH like a don
DONNISM self-importance
DONSHIP estate of being a don
DOOMING condemning; judging
DOORING door-case
DOORMAT boot-scraping mat
DOORWAY portico
ps DOPPLER change of frequency
(colour, sound) (distance)
ar, rl DOPSKAL font for baptism
zo DORHAWK nightjar
DORMANT quiescent; latent
zo DORMICE sleepy rodents
tx DORNICK DORNOCK, figured linen
rl DORTOUR dorter; dormitory
DOSSIER file of papers; a brief (Fr.)
DOTTARD decayed tree
DOTTIER barmier; more foolish
DOTTING spotting; stippling
zo DOTTREL plover
DOUBLED turned; ran; repeated
DOUBLER duplicator; increaser
DOUBLES two teams of two against
each other (golf, tennis, sculls)
DOUBLET jerkin; one of a pair
DOUBTED distrusted; suspected
DOUBTER an unbelieving Thomas
DOUCELY sweetly
zo DOUCETS DOWCETS, stones of deer
DOUCEUR tip; vail; gratuity
DOUCHED sprayed
DOUCINE ornamental moulding
DOUGHTY valiant, intrepid; dauntless
zo DOUPION double cocoon
DOUREST grimmest; staunchest
vt DOURINE breeding-horse infection
DOUSING dipping; extinguishing;
DOWSING water-divining
DOUTING extinguishing; quenching
zo DOVECOT dove-cote
zo DOVELET young dove
DOVERED slumbered
DOWABLE endowable
DOWAGER widow with a jointure
DOWDILY untidily; slovenly
DOWERED gifted
DOWN-BED feather bed

mu DOWN-BOW playing motion (violin)
DOWNING felling; overcoming
DOWSING water-divining
DOYENNE senior lady
DOZENTH 12th
DRABBER more dingy
DRABBET smocking
DRABBLE befoul; draggle
nt DRABLER additional sail
nm DRACHMA Greek silver coin
bt DRACINA dragon's blood palm
bt DRACINE dracina; a dye
DRACONE nylon/rubber liquids
container
DRACULA Transylvanian vampire
DRAFTED outlined; detached
zo DRAFT-OX draught-ox
DRAG-BAR draw-bar
DRAGGED tugged; hauled; lingered
DRAGGLE bemire; drabble
DRAG-MAN a fisherman
DRAG-NET his net
DRAGOON compel; coerce;
cavalryman
DRAINED filtered; exhausted;
emptied
DRAINER a colander
DRAPERY haberdashery
DRAPIER a Swift 'nom de plume'
DRAPING covering; dressing
DRASTIC severe; forcible; efficacious
DRATTED confounded
DRAUGHT dose; breeze; outline
rw, me DRAWBAR connecting rod; train
couplings; tractive force
DRAWBOY a weaving assistant
DRAWING pulling; sketch; plan
DRAWLED dawdled; droned
DRAWLER monotonous speaker
DRAW-NET bird net
DRAWN-ON printing technique
DRAYAGE charge for a dray
DRAYMAN dray-driver; brewer's
driver
DREADED apprehended; feared
DREADER an alarmist
DREAMED dreamt; imagined
DREAMER visionary; idealist
DREDGED sprinkled
nt DREDGER tea cup with strainer lid;
salt pot; vessel for deepening
waterways
DREEING enduring; bearing (Sc.)
DRESDEN Meissen porcelain
DRESSED cooked; decked; arrayed in
DRESSER kitchen sideboard;
(window-); (attendant)
to DRESSER lead beater

DREULED slavered; dribbled
DRIBBED inveigled; filched
DRIBBLE (football); trickle; drip; ooze
DRIBLET driplet; a small quantity
DRIFTED floated
nt **DRIFTER** wanderer; fishing boat with drift net; amateur aimless wanderer; dilettante
DRILLED trained; perforated; pierced
DRINKER reveller; carouser; toper
DRIP-DRY non-iron fabric
DRIPPED dropped; oozed; trickled
bt **DRIP-TIP** a leaf-point
DRIVE-IN service for motorists
DRIVING dragooning; urging; forcing
mt **DRIZZLE** DRIZZLY, (fine rain)
DROILED toiled tediously
DROLLED jested; clowned
DROLLER farceur; funnier; odder
nt **DROMOND** fast sailing ship
DRONING prosing; humming
DRONISH lazy
DROOLED slavered; dribbled
DROOPED withered; declined
DROPLET a drip; bead of moisture
DROP-NET a fishing-net
cp **DROP-OUT** computer error; failure
ga **DROP-OUT** social non-participant; (dropkick) (Rugby football)
DROPPED dripped; let fall (clanger); quitted
DROPPER end fly of a cast (medicine)
bt **DROSERA** sun-dew
DROSHKY Russian vehicle
DROUGHT aridity; dryness
DROWNED submerged; blotted out; drenched
DROWSED dozed; napped; slept
DRUBBED DRUBBER, thrashed; mauled; beater
DRUDGED DRUDGER, toiled; labourer
md **DRUGGED** stupefied (medicated); lulled
nt **DRUGGER** drogher; small ship
DRUGGET floor covering (over carpet)
rl **DRUIDIC** of Druids (ancient bards)
DRUMBLE to drone
gl **DRUMLIN** long glacially-formed hill
DRUMMED expelled; tapped; played
DRUMMER salesman (USA); drum player
DRUNKEN inebriated; crapulous; tipsy
DRUSIAN Levantine sectarian (Moslem)

DRY-BEAT thrash without bleeding
mn **DRY-BONE** silicate of zinc
el **DRY-CELL** type of battery
nt **DRY-DOCK** (graving-) exposing whole ship
DRY-EYED tearless
DRYNESS aridity; drought; thirst
DRY-PILE voltaic battery
lw **DRY-RENT** (no distress)
DRY-SALT preserve; cure
DRYSHOD with shoes not wet
DUALISE DUARCHY, split in two; dual control
rl **DUALISM** doctrine; Manichaeism
DUALIST DUALITY, twofoldness in universe
DUBBING ennobling; sound translation (films)
DUBIATE DUBIETY, DUBIOUS, doubtful; uncertainty
DUCALLY like a duke in style
DUCHESS consort of a duke
zo **DUCK-ANT** Jamaican termite
DUCKING evading; thrusting under water
DUCTILE tractile; malleable
zo **DUCTULE** narrow-lumen duct
DUDDERY rags; old clo' shop
DUDGEON dagger; sullenness
DUE-BILL accepted debt
DUELIST DUELLED, antagonist; fought for; combated
DUELLER combatant in single fight
DUENESS fitness; propriety; seemliness
DUFFING sham; furbishing up
DUKEDOM duke's realm
DULCIFY sweeten
DULCINE DULCITE, DULCOSE, manna; saccharine
DULLARD stupid fellow; blockhead
DULLEST bluntest; most obtuse
DULLING allaying; benumbing
DULLISH rather dull; somewhat inert
DULNESS dullness; stupidity; apathy
zo **DULOSIS** ant slavery
DUMPING heaping (exporting)
DUMPISH in the dumps
zo **DUN-BIRD** pochard duck
DUNCERY dulness; stupidity
DUNCISH not clever
DUNEDIN Edinburgh (Celtic form); also N.Z.
ck **DUNFISH** cured cod-fish
DUNGEON dark prison; cell
DUNKERS Tunkers; triple baptists
DUNKING jumping to score (basketball)

DUNNAGE packing; baggage; timber
DUNNING debt collecting; fish curing
DUNNISH dirty brown
zo **DUNNOCK** hedge-sparrow
lw **DUODENA** ancient jury
DUOTONE two-colour half-tone printing
pr **DUO-TYPE** 2 like plates for different colours
DUPABLE credulous; gullible
DUPPING opening as a door
DURABLE DURABLY, long lasting; stable
bt **DURAMEN** heart-wood
lw **DURANCE** DURANTE, permanent restraint
ml **DURIRON** acid-resistant iron alloy
bt **DURMAST** an oak
lw **DURSLEY** bloodless blows; assault
DUSKIER more sable or swarthy
DUSKILY DUSKISH, dimly; darkly (twilight)
DUSTBIN garbage receptacle
DUSTIER unswept; flocculent state
DUSTING a beating
DUSTMAN garbage collector
DUSTPAN house-cleaning implement
DUTEOUS DUTIFUL, deferential; respectful
DUUMVIR Roman magistrates
DVORNIK Russian concierge
DWARFED stunted; eclipsed
DWELLED sojourned; abode; inhabited
DWELLER resident; inmate; indigene
DWINDLE diminish; decrease; shrink
DYARCHY duarchy; dual control
pr **DYELINE** document-copying process
bt **DYE-WOOD** (various woods)
DYE-WORK dyeing establishment
DYINGLY in the process of death
DYNAMIC forceful; energetic; mobile
cp **DYNAMIC** influx message handling
DYNASTY family; succession; house
DYSLOGY disapproval; disapprobation
DYSNOMY bad laws
md **DYSOPSY** poor sight
md **DYSURIA** impaired urination
zo **DYTICUS** water-beetles
lw **DYVOURY** bankruptcy

E

EAGERLY avidly; ardently; fervently
zo **EANLING** young lamb
md **EARACHE** a pain in the ear

EARDROP a pendant; earring
md **EAR-DRUM** tympanum
EAR-HOLE aural portal
EARLDOM the seignory of an earl
EARLESS reluctant to hear
EARLIER sooner
EARLOCK love-lock
EARMARK identity cut (sheep, reindeer)
EARNEST serious; steady; persevering
EARNING bread-winning; meriting
EAR-PICK tool for cleaning ears
EARRING pendant; eardrop
EARSHOT hearing distance
el **EARTHED** driven to den (hunting); circuit
EARTHEN (-ware); clay pottery
EARTHLY carnal; mundane; terrestrial
EASEFUL restful; tranquil; contented
EASIEST least difficult; simplest
EAST-END east part of city
EASTERN oriental; auroral
nt **EASTING** east of any meridian
EATABLE edible; succulent; esculent
nt **EBB-TIDE** recede from flood (sea movement)
EBONIST ebony-wood artisan
ch **EBONITE** EBONIZE, artificial ebony; vulcanite
EBRIETY intoxication; intemperance
EBRIOSE EBRIOUS, fond of drink; fuddled
ECBASIS ECBATIC, rhetorical treatment
md **ECCRINE** cell-excretory; glandular
md **ECDEMIC** foreign; not inbuilt
ECDYSIS moulting (feathers); sloughing
ECHAPPE (horse-breeding)
ECHELLE ECHELON, ladder formation; cycling to minimize crosswind
zo **ECHIDNA** ant-eater (Australia)
zo **ECHIMYD** S. American dormouse
ar, zo **ECHINUS** egg and dart moulding; sea urchin
ECHOING resounding; repeating
ECHOISM onomatopoeia
ECHOIST a yes-man
as **ECLIPSE** hide; blot out; surpass; obscuration of sun or moon
ECLOGUE pastoral poem
ec **ECOLOGY** wide environmental studies; (-ist)
ECONOMY thrift; (national) household keeping

bt, ec **ECOTONE** plant-community limit
bt, ec **ECOTYPE** habitat-adapted plants
ECOUTES listening posts (Fr.)
ECSTASY rapture; fervour; delight
ECTASIS mispronunciation
md **ECTHYMA** a rash
md **ECTOPIA ECTOPIC,** dislocation, displaced
zo **ECTOZOA** parasites
ECTYPAL actual copy
ck **ECUELLE** two handled dish with cover
EDACITY greed; voracity; rapacity
EDAPHIC pertaining to soil
EDAPHON soil community of living organisms
bt **EDDERED** a top-pruned hedge
EDDYING swirling; whirling; vortical
mn **EDELITE** a silicate
EDENTAL toothless
EDICTAL laid down; ordered
EDIFICE a stylish building
EDIFIED EDIFIER, spiritually benefited; uplifter
EDITING EDITION, preparing a publication
EDUCATE teach; tutor; school; train
EDUCING extracting; eliciting
EDUCTOR corkscrew
EELBUCK basket-net
zo **EEL-FARE** a young eel
zo **EEL-POUT** blenny
EFFABLE explicable; utterable
EFFACED erased; became inconspicuous
EFFECTS personal estate; theatrical illusions
EFFENDI master; sir; gentleman ('Turk.)
EFFULGE gleam; glisten; coruscate
EFFUSED emanated; diffused
EGALITY parity; equality
zo **EGG-BIRD** tern
bl **EGG-CELL** within an ovum or zygote
EGG-COSY cap for a boiled egg
ck **EGG-FLIP** (-nog); thick alcoholic drink
EGGHEAD intellectual; highbrow
EGOTISM EGOTIST, of hyper self-importance
EGOTIZE (excess of 'I')
EGRETTE (egret); spray of gems; aigrette
pc **EIDETIC** having vivid mental pictures
EIDOLON apparition; phantom
EIRENIC irenic; peaceful
EJECTED threw out; dispossessed

ae **EJECTOR** chucker-out; pilot's safety seat
ch **ELAIDIC ELAIDIN,** of oil products
ELAPSED slid away; passed, of time
ELASTIC ELASTIN, resilient; stretchable; (rubber)
ELATERY elastic force; elasticity
bt **ELATINE** water-wort
ELATING stretching to joy; high spirits
ELATION gratification; exhilaration
hy **ELAULIC** with oil in pipes
mn **ELBAITE** tourmaline variety
ELBOWED thrust aside; nudged
ELDERLY getting on in years
ELEATIC philosophic
ELECTED chosen; picked; preferred
ELECTOR voter; German title
cf **ELECTRO-** (platc); (magnetic); electric
ELEGANT refined; graceful; tasteful
ELEGIAC a lament; dirge
ELEGIST plaintive writer
ELEGIZE lament in writing
zo **ELEIDIN** skin cells substance
FLEMENT part; component; ingredient
ELEVATE elate; raise; hoist; promote
ga **ELEVENS** teams (cricket, football etc.)
ELF-BOLT ELF-SHOT, small arrow; flint head
ELF-LAND fairy-land
ELF-LOCK tangled hair
bt **ELF-WORT** elecampane
ELIDING ELLIPSIS, shortening words
ELIMATE to file; to polish
ELISION suppression of metre (poetry)
bt **ELK-WOOD** umbrella-tree
bt **ELLAGIC** of gall-nuts
ma, as **ELLIPSE** oval; orbit of a comet
me **ELL-WAND** (a yard and a quarter)
ELOGIST ELOGIUM, funeral orator; panegyric speech
rl **ELOHIST** Pentateuch author (O.T.)
ELOINED removed; separated; banished
ELOPING sloping; bolting; decamping
ELUDING dodging; evading; baffling
ELUSION evasion; avoidance
ELUSIVE illusory; deceptive; fugitive
ELUSORY hard to solve; intangible
ELUVIUM detritus from rock weathering
ELYSIAN ELYSIUM, heavenly paradise (Gr.)

zo **ELYTRAL** shield-like

zo **ELYTRON ELYTRUM,** (wing sheath beetles)

EMANANT EMANATE, proceeding from origin

EMARCID wilted

EMBALED packed; bundled

EMBARGO a prohibition; veto

EMBASSY ambassadorial residence

EMBATHE to soak (industrial process)

hd **EMBLAZE** embellish

EMBLEMA inlaid ornament

bt **EMBLICA** Indian tree

md **EMBOLUS** wedge; a clot

EMBOSOM caress

EMBOWED arched

EMBOWER give shelter

EMBRACE hug; welcome; include

EMBROIL involve in dispute, confusion

hd **EMBRUED** ensanguined heraldically

pl, zo **EMBRYON** of an embryo, zygote

EMENDED text corrected

EMERALD smaragdus; brilliant green

EMERGED resulted; appeared from; arose

EMERITI honourably retired

EMINENT exalted; prominent

EMIRATE the domain of emir

EMITRON early UK TV tube

EMITTED circulated; exhaled; gushed

cp **EMITTER** electrode; punched card signal

md **EMMENIA** menstrual flow

pc **EMOTION** moody excitement; strong feelings

pc **EMOTIVE** arousal of reactions

EMPANEL coopt; enrol to a committee

EMPATHY sympathetic reaction of agreement

EMPERIL endanger

EMPEROR head of an empire

EMPIRIC based on practical experience

lw **EMPLEAD** prosecute

EMPLUME to put on feather, apparel, dress

EMPOWER authorize; warrant; allow

EMPRESS female ruler of empire

EMPTIED drained; discharged

EMPTIER remover; less complete

EMULATE to vie; compete; rival

EMULOUS striving to equal

md **EMULSIC** emulsive

ch **EMULSIN** almond ferment

zo **EMU-WREN** an Australian bird

ENABLED authorized; allowed

ENACTED decreed; ordained

lw **ENACTOR** law-maker

ENAMOUR charm; fascinate; enslave

ENCAGED cooped up; in captivity

ENCASED stored in; stowed in

ENCAVED trapped in cave

ENCHANT enamour; bewitch; captivate

ENCHASE set with jewels; engrave

md **ENCHYMA** injection; infusion

ENCLASP embrace; hug; enfold

rl **ENCLAVE** secret meeting (election, Vatican)

ENCLAVE separated zone (land)

lw **ENCLOSE** fence in, claim land

ENCLOSE cover; pack in box (letter)

mt **ENCLOUD** mystify; make obscure

cp, tc **ENCODER** data; official converter (into code)

ENCORED repeated after applause

ENCRUST achieve overlay of sediment; (jewels)

bt **ENDARCH** xylem strand characteristic

ENDEMIC local; indigenous

md **ENDERON** true skin

END-GAME chess; final stage

ENDIRON andiron; firedog

ENDLESS eternal; interminable

ENDLONG not sideways

cp **END-MARK** code conclusion signal

ENDMOST furthest in

END-NOTE footnote; (postscript)

bt **ENDOGEN** botanical growth

ENDORSE assign; ratify

ENDOWED supplied; bequeathed

ENDOWER benefactor; donor

ENDUING imbuing; endowing; providing (finances)

ENDURED ENDURER, stayer; bore suffering

cp **ENDWAYS ENDWISE,** upright; card feed in

ENDYSIS development of new hair/ skin

pr **ENFACED** paper headings

lw **ENFEOFF** assignment

hd **ENFILED** heraldic sword thrust

ENFLESH turn into flesh

ENFORCE compel; oblige; coerce

ENGAGED fiancé; occupied; betrothed; committed

ENGAGER employment agent; fixer

ENGINED powered

ENGLISH of England; language

ENGORGE stuff with food; engulf

ENGRACE bring into favour

ENGRAFT insert; graft
hd ENGRAIL spot with dots
ENGRAIN dye; permeate
ENGRASP clutch; seize
ENGRAVE cut; chisel; carve
ENGROSS monopolize; absorb; copy
ENHANCE to intensify; heighten
ENJOYED ENJOYER, liked;
  appreciator; (gourmet)
ENLACED entwined; spliced
ENLARGE amplify; extend; expand
ENLIVEN wake; arouse; quicken
ENMEWED cooped up in a mews;
  encaged
ENNICHE to enshrine
ENNOBLE exalt; raise; aggrandize
ENNUIED bored stiff
ENODING unknotting
ENOMOTY Spartan band
ENOUNCE to pronounce words
  clearly
ENQUIRE ENQUIRY, ask searching
  questions
cp, tc ENQUIRY search address control for
  terminal
ENRAGED exasperated; incensed
ENRIPEN to mellow; mature
ENROBED attired; invested
ENROUGH to roughen
ag ENSILED stored in a pit; silage
ENSLAVE enthral; captivate;
  subjugate
ENSNARE entrap; allure; inveigle
ENSUING resulting; issuing; accruing
ENSURED made certain; guaranteed
md ENTASIA spasm
ENTASIS architectural swell
ENTENTE understanding; alliance
ENTERED joined; penetrated;
  registered
md ENTERIC typhoid fever
zo ENTERON collenterata body cavity
ENTHEAL divinely inspired
ENTHUSE to spread enthusiasm
ENTICED ENTICER, cajoled, drawn
  into; seducer
ENTITLE permit; qualify; grant
zo ENTOMIC of insects
ENTONIC of high tension
md ENTOTIC (interior of ear)
zo ENTOZOA internal parasites
ENTRAIL interweave; plait
ENTRAIN to board a train
ga ENTRANT who enters profession;
  competitor
ENTREAT beg; implore; importune
pl ENTROPY lost energy and body
  functions

ENTRUST confide; commit to others
ENTWINE weave; interlace; twist;
  (rope)
ENVELOP enwrap; enfold; encase
ENVENOM to poison
ENVIOUS jealous; invidious;
  grudging
ENVYING grudging; coveting
ag, gl EOAPHIC soil-related
EOBIONT stage in creation (nature)
bt EPACRID of heathlike shrubs
EPAGOGE figure of speech
EPARCHY prefecture
EPAULET shoulder-piece
EPAXIAL above the axis
EPEEIST duelling by sword
  (fencing)
EPERGNE ornamental stand
zo EPHEBIC adult; of optimum period
EPHEBUS young Greek citizen
md EPHELIS freckle
zo EPIBOLY overgrowth
bt, ag EPICARP of the rind, skin of fruit
EPICEDE funeral ode
EPICENE common to both sexes
bt EPICHIL orchid labellum end
EPICISM sagas; heroic poems; etc.
EPICIST epic writer
ec EPICOLE harmless parasite animal
EPICURE gourmet; voluptuary
zo EPICYTE ectoplasm cuticular layer
zo EPIDEME wing articulation sclerite
mn EPIDOTE a silicate
EPIGEAL low growing
bt EPIGEAN found on ground
bt EPIGEIC with stolons on soil surface
EPIGENE mineral change
bt EPIGONE a descendant; seed
  container
zo EPIGONE spore-bag
EPIGRAM barbed wisdom
zo EPIHYAL hyoid arch element
EPILATE remove (hair)
md EPILOIA development defect
  affliction
EPIMERE mesothelial-wall zone in
  vertebrates
EPIMYTH moral of story
zo EPIOTIC a bone in vertebrate skull
EPISODE separate event within a
  narrative
ba EPISOME of genetically active
  bacteria
rl EPISTLE lengthy letter (N.T.)
EPITAPH monumental inscription
EPITAXY crystal growth or
  deposition
EPITHEM lotion; poultice

EPITHET a disparaging, abusive description
EPITOME brief summary; abstract
zo **EPIZOAN EPIZOIC, EPIZOON,** parasitic
EPOCHAL of outstanding memorable period
EPOXIDE plastic resin
EPULARY festive
EQUABLE fair; severe; uniform; calm
EQUABLY uniformly; justly
EQUALLY evenly
EQUATED made equal; balanced
go **EQUATOR** Great Circle; tropical centre
EQUERRY court gentleman; adjutant
EQUINAL pertaining to horses
vt **EQUINIA** glanders disease
as **EQUINOX** equality of day and night
md **EQUINUS** hoof-like; foot deformity
EQUITES Roman cavalry, knights (Lat.)
pr **ERASING ERASURE,** obliterating; cancellation
ar, bd **ERECTED ERECTER,** raised; constructed; builder
ERECTOR penis; enlarger
ERELONG before long; later on
ERGODIC probability theory
bt **ERGOTED** afflicted with fungus
ERGUSIA vitamin A
bt **ERICOID** with heather-like leaves
bt **ERINEUM** leafy excrescence
mn **ERINITE** arseniate of copper
ERINOID a plastic material (milk)
ERINYES the Furies
ERISTIC controversial
cf **ERITHRO-** of redness
zo **ERMELIN ERMINED,** fur garment; stoat
hd **ERMINES** white marked spots
ERODENT EROSIVE, gnawing; acid
gl **ERODING EROSION,** denudation; weathering
EROTEME interrogation mark
EROTICA of sex (pornographic)
ERRATIC of no fixed course; inconsistencies
pr **ERRATUM** misprint; mistake; text error
ERUDITE scholarly; learned
ERUGATE smoothed
ERUPTED exploded; ejected
ESCAPED eluded; avoided; leaked
ESCAPER danger dodger
zo **ESCHARA** net-like coral
lw **ESCHEAT** forfeiture; confiscate
ESCRIME fencing; swordsmanship (Fr.)

hd **ESCROLL** heraldic scroll
ESCUAGE feudal tenure
ch **ESCULIN** alkaloid (horse chestnut)
ch **ESERINE** alkaloid (Calabar bean)
ESKIMOS inhabitants of Arctic America
ESOTERY mysticism; necromancy
ESPADON Spanish sword
bt **ESPARTO** exportable grass
mn **ESPINEL** kind of ruby
ESPOUSE to marry; support a cause
ESQUIRE gentleman (bodyguard); shield bearer
ESSAYED wrote serious article
ESSENCE extract; kernel of matter
rl **ESSENES** Jewish sect, fraternity
ESTIVAL of summer
hd **ESTOILE** heraldic star
ESTRADE a dais (Fr.)
lw **ESTREAT** true extract
md **ESTRIOL ESTRONE,** female hormone
ESTUARY river mouth; firth; frith
ETATISM central control (government)
ch **ETCHANT** copper-removing chemical
ETCHING engraving; an impression
ETERNAL endless; perennial; immortal
ETESIAN Levant wind
zo **ETHERIA** river-oyster
ETHICAL conduct conforming to morality
ETONIAN of Eton (College)
mn **EUCLASE** beryl
gl **EUCRITE** coarse-grained igneous rock
EUDOXID monogastric stage in siphonofora
zo **EUGAMIC** of maturity-period
bt **EUGENIA** a large genus of spices
md **EUGENIC** (-s), control of hereditary genes
EUGENIN clove camphor
ck **EUGENOL** item of clove/cinnamon oil
bt **EULALIA** ornamental grass
EULOGIA EULOGIC, praises; laudatory
EUPATHY contentment with moderation
md **EUPEPSY** hearty digestion
EUPHONY melodious sound
EUPHROE ridge-pole
bl **EUPLOID** cell chromosome valve
md **EUPNOEA** free respiration
EURIPUS strait having violent tides
mn **EURITIC** like granite
bt **EURYALE** water-lilies
EUSTYLE columnar building style

EUTERPE muse of music
md **EUTONIA** firmness of tone
EUTROPY variation in chemical compounds
EVACUEE a displaced (rescued) person
EVADING EVASION, EVASIVE, avoiding; dodging
EVENING eventide; night-fall; twilight
lw **EVICTED** dispossessed of house (property)
EVICTOR tenant remover; chucker-out
EVIDENT obvious; patent; manifest
EVIL-EYE a bewitching look
EVINCED manifested; proved
EVIRATE castrate; geld
EVOCATE EVOCATION, to summon spirits
EVOKING rousing; exciting (of memory)
EVOLUTE geometric curve
EVOLVED unfolded; emitted; educed
EWE-LAMB poor man's only possession
EXACTED demanded; levied
EXACTER extortioner
EXACTLY just so; precisely; literally
EXACTOR a tax collector
EXALTED lofty; ennobled; elevated
EXALTER magnifier; extoller
EXAMINE inquire; scrutinize
EXAMPLE model; pattern; sample
md **EXANGIA** blood-vessel
zo **EXARATE** of pupae with free members
EXARCHY a vice-royalty
EXCERPT an extract; cutting; citation
lw **EXCHEAT** escheat; confiscate
EXCISED cut out; removed
EXCITED EXCITER, provoked; stimulant; agitator
el **EXCITON** electron pair in semiconductor
zo **EXCITOR** stimulating to activity
EXCLAIM cry out; utter sharply; vociferate
lw **EXCLUDE** to shut out; bar from; omit
md **EXCRETA** human or animal waste
EXCUSED released; pardoned; condoned
lw **EXECUTE** accomplish; put to death
EXEDRAE halls; recesses
EXEGETE theological exponent
EXERGUE date space on coin
EXERTED strove; applied; used

EXHALED emitted; evaporated; breathed
EXHAUST drain; empty; expend; tire
EXHIBIT display; manifest; evince
EXHUMED disinterred; unearthed
EXIGENT urgent; critical; importunate
EXILIAN exiled Jew
EXILING banishing; proscribing
EXILITY EXILE, period of enforced absence
EXISTED was; lasted; endured; subsisted
EXITIAL destructive to life
zo **EXOCONE** of insect compound eyes
zo **EXODERM** outer cell layer in porifera
EXODIST an emigrant
EXOGAMY outbreeding; beyond tribal group
EXOMION Greek sleeveless vest
EXOTISM EXOTIC, not native; strikingly different
zo **EXOTYPE** a non-heritable creature
EXPANSE wide area (to spread out)
lw **EX-PARTE** prejudiced; biased
EXPENSE cost, outlay; charge; price
EXPIATE atone; sin no more
EXPIRED exhaled; ended; dead
EXPLAIN elucidate; interpret; expound
EXPLODE burst; detonate; discharge
EXPLOIT feat; deed; achievement
EXPLORE search; prospect; examine
EXPORTS outward trade goods (foreign)
EXPOSED EXPOSER, unmasked; open; revealer (nark)
EXPOUND explain; unfold; interpret
EXPRESS explicit; exude; speedy
EXPUNGE erase; abrogate; cancel
EXSCIND cut out; exsect
EXTINCT defunct; obsolete; quenched
EXTRACT decoction; essences; juice
lw **EXTRACT** extort; derive; select; (copy) (spy)
EXTREME utmost; ultimate; excessive
EXTRUDE swelling; push out (unsightly)
EXUDING sweating; oozing; dripping
EXULTED crowed; triumphed; boasted
zo **EXUVIAE EXUVIAL,** of cast-off animal skins
pl **EYE-BALL** the eye itself (orb)
EYE-BATH basin for lotions
EYE-BEAM EYELIAD, a strong glance

nt **EYE-BOLT** (for hooks)
ar **EYE-BROW** a hairy arch; dormer
window
EYE-DROP a falling tear; ciliary
EYE-FLAP blinker (horses)
ar **EYE-HOLE** (peep-hole)
EYELASH cilary hair
EYELESS blind; unobservant
EYESHOT range of vision observed
EYESORE a hideosity
bl **EYESPOT** (peacock's feather);
'stigma' in algae
EYEWASH spoken rubbish; humbug
lw **EZEMENT EAZEMENT**, gymnastics;
legal benefit

F

pg **F NUMBER** relative aperture, stop
zo **FABELLA** sesamoid bone (in
mammals)
FABLING FABULAR, inventing stories
FABRILE (handicraft)
FACE-OFF ball into play (ice hockey
etc.)
mn, pc **FACETED** having differing faces
(gems)
FACETIA facetiousness; witty jokes
wv **FACONNE** woven figurative design
FACTION dissenting clique within an
association
FACTORY works; mill; workshop
FACTUAL real; actual; authentic
FACTURE manufacture;
workmanship
FACULAE large bright areas of sun
photosphere
FACULTY skill; ability; section of
university
FADAISE trivial remark (Fr.)
FADDING shellac lacquering
FADDISH FADDIST, idiosyncratic
craze; follower (diet)
FADDLED trifled (of dilettantes)
cn **FADE-OUT** end of film sequence;
disappear
FADGING suiting; prospering
FAGGERY drudgery
FAGGING domestic slavery in schools
mu **FAGOTTO** musical bundle of wind;
bassoon (It.)
FAIENCE FAYENCE, glazed pottery,
ceramics
FAILING a foible; defect; no pass
(exams)
FAILURE fiasco; non-success; ruin
cp **FAILURE** disruption by defect

FAINING willingly; desiring; wishing
md **FAINTED** swooned; lost
consciousness
FAINTER FAINTLY, weaker; paler;
dimmer
FAIREST most beautiful, attractive
FAIRIES benevolent enchantresses;
pixies; gays
FAIRILY of elf-like, ethereal qualities
FAIRING a present; streamlining
pl **FAIRISH** moderately fair; blondish
(hair)
ga, nt **FAIRWAY** (golf); navigable channel
FALANGE Spanish fascist party
tx **FALBALA** furbelow; pleated lining;
seam
FALCADE (equitation); curvetting
zo **FALCATE FALCULA**, beaked; hooked;
claw
lw **FALDAGE** privilege; right of farming
FALLACY a sophism; mistaken idea;
not so
FALLALS showy trifles (ornament)
FALLING dropping; tumbling; (error)
(loss)
FALLOUT spread of nuclear
radioactivity
FALLOUT secondary result; pollution
nt **FALLUCA** Nile dhow
FALSELY wrongly; untruthfully
FALSEST most disloyal
FALSIES artificial bust; dentures
FALSIFY counterfeit; belie; fake
FALSISH somewhat erroneous
FALSISM obvious falsity
FALSITY fallacy; fabrication
FANATIC bigot; zealot; visionary
FANCIED favoured; imagined;
thought
FANCIER expert; breeder
FANFARE flourish of trumpets
FANGLED newly contrived
FAN-MAIL letters of adulation
FANNING extending; winnowing;
(flames); cowboy's balance tactics
bt **FAN-PALM** the talipot palm
zo **FANTAIL** pigeon; a gas burner
FANTASM spook; phantasm
FANTAST visionary; enthusiast
mu **FANTASY** imaginative idea (arts)
el, me, ps **FARADAY FARADIC**, inductive
electrolysis unit
FARAWAY distant; remote
FARCEUR satirical jester
FARCIFY to burlesque
ck **FARCING** edible stuffing; force-meat
nt **FARDAGE** dunnage; packing (Fr.)
ag **FARMERY** rural homestead

FARMING agriculture; leasing out
FARMOST uttermost; furthest
FARNESS remoteness
FARRAGO a medley; hodge-podge
FARRIER shoeing-smith; a vet
mu **FARRUCA** Andalusian dance
FARTHEL farl; oatcake
FARTHER besides; further; beyond
to **FASCETS** glass-making tools
FASCIAE fillets; name boards
FASCIAL of fasces (Roman emblems)
FASCINE bound brushwood
FASCISM FASCIST, party,
dictatorship (It.)
FASHERY FASHING, annoyance;
bothering
FASHION mode; vogue; style; mould
rl **FAST-DAY** non-eating day
FASTEST swiftest; fleetest; closest
FASTING abstaining from food
FASTISH rather quickly; reckless
FATALLY mortally; calamitously
zo **FAT-BODY** fatty tissue in amphibians
FATEFUL ominous; portentous
FAT-HEAD blockhead; moron; dunce
FATIDIC prophetic; oracular
FATIGUE tire; jade; lassitude
zo **FATLING** young fatted animal
mu **FATLUTE** a broad guitar
pl **FATNESS FATTEST**, of corpulence;
obesity
ck **FAT-RICH** greasy; high caloric (food)
FATTISH rather plump; adipose
FATUITY self-complacency; folly
FATUOUS illusory; imbecile; witless
FAUCIAL pertaining to fauces
ga **FAULTED FAULTY**, mistaken;
displaced
FAVOURS free services; party badges
FAWNING sycophantic; cringing
FAYENCE faience; pottery
FEARFUL dismayed; dire
FEARING dreading; revering; timid
FEASTED caroused; gratified
FEASTER a Lucullus
zo **FEATHER** adorn; quill; (oar)
FEATURE aspect; trait; (film) (press)
FEAZING unravelling
FEBRILE feverish
FECULUM starchy extract
FEDERAL confederated; (state)
FEEDING eating; grazing; providing
food (machine)
lw **FEE-FARM** tenure without fealty
FEELING touching; sensibility;
perception
lw **FEE-TAIL** entailed estate
FEEZING twisting; unscrewing

FEIGNED FEINTED, simulated;
shammed
zo **FELIDAE FELINAE**, the cat genus
FELLING hewing; cutting down
mn **FELSITE** igneous rock
mn **FELSPAR** metamorphic rock
FELTING felt cloth
nt **FELUCCA** Nile, Red Sea lateen
sailboat
bt **FELWORT** mullein
FEMINAL womanly
md **FEMORAL** (thigh)
ga **FENCING** enclosing; evading; sword
duelling
FENDING warding off; averting
zo **FEN-DUCK** shoveller-duck
FEN-FIRE will o' the wisp
mn **FENGITE** alabaster
FENNISH marshy; boggy; swampy
lw **FEODARY** feudal tenure
lw **FEOFFEE FEOFFOR**, receiver; granter
of a fief
FERDWIT a quittance; penalty
FERINGI foreigner (European team)
in India
mu **FERMATA** a pause
ck **FERMENT** inflame; commotion; yeast
ps **FERMION** particle (statistical theory)
ch **FERMIUM** man-made element
bt **FERNERY** fern garden
zo **FERN-OWL** night-jar
FERRARA a sword-blade (It.)
ch **FERRATE** an iron salt
FERRIED transported
FERRIES ferry-boats; air-lift
transport
ch, cp **FERRITE** ferro-magnetic (ceramics)
ch **FERROUS** (iron)
bt **FERRUGO** plant-rust; fungus
mu **FERRULE** protecting cap; shaft of
hunting horn
FERTILE inventive; prolific; fruitful
FERULED caned; punished
FERVENT zealous; ardent; glowing
FERVOUR eagerness; intensity;
ardour
FESTIVE joyous; convivial; gay
FESTOON wreath; garland
bt **FESTUCA** grass genus
FETCHED brought; conveyed;
reached
FETCHER collector; heaver
zo **FETLOCK** a tuft of hair
lw **FEUDARY FEODARY**, rights; medieval
fee
FEUDING quarrelling (ice hockey)
lw **FEUDIST** writer on feudal law
lw **FEU-DUTY** annual payment, fee (Sc.)

FEVERED agitated; febrile
FEWMAND fouling (on a carpet)
FEWNESS paucity; scarcity; sparsity
FEYNESS otherworldliness
FIANCEE betrothed woman
FIBBERY FIBBING, telling lies;
    prevaricating
bc FIBROID FIBROIN, of fibre; cobweb;
    elastic protein
md FIBROMA fibrous tumour
FIBROSE FIBROUS, filamental; stringy
FIBSTER petty liar
md FIBULAR (leg bone)
bt FICARIA celandine
FICTILE plastic; mouldable
FICTION romance; fantasy; invention
FICTIVE imaginative; feigned
FIDALGO Portuguese hidalgo
FIDDLED trifled; meddled
zo FIDDLER a crab; violinist
nt FIDDLEY small finger's work;
    hatchway railing
FIDGETY restless; uneasy; impatient
FIDIBUS taper to light a pipe
FIELDED (cricket); (baseball)
ga FIELDER defender; not batting side
FIERCER more violent
FIERILY vehemently; ardently
ga FIFTEEN a Rugby team
ck FIG-CAKE a sweetmeat
FIGGING dressing up
FIGHTER combatant; warrior
bt FIG-LEAF early dress material
FIGMENT a fabrication
bt FIG-TREE Mediterranean plant
FIGURAL pictorial; figurate
FIGURED computed; depicted
bt FIGWORT a plant
lw FILACER FILAZER, writs and pleas
    officer
zo FILARIA parasitic worms
bt FILBERT hazel-nut
FILCHED FILCHER, stole; pickpocket;
    pilferer
FILEMOT dead-leaf colour
cp FILESET magnetic data; (manicure)
FILIBEG the kilt (Scots' national
    dress)
FILICAL FILICES, the ferns
FILINGS fragments (sawdust, metal)
ck FILLING replenishing; stuffing;
    ballast; putting in
mt FILLING atmospheric pressure in
    depression
FILM-FAN a devotee; star-
    worshipper
FILMING recording in celluloid
pl FIMBRIA brain neural fibre; bundle

FIMETIC foul in thought
FINABLE liable to a fine; amerceable
FINALLY ultimately; lastly;
    eventually
FINANCE money affairs; revenue
zo FINBACK rorqual whale
FINCHED striped; spotted
FINDING verdict; discovering
FINECUT chopped into small pieces
FINESSE subtletly; craft; artifice
zo FIN-FISH finback whale
zo FIN-FOOT tropical bird
· FINGENT moulding
FINICAL fastidious; dainty; faddy
FINICKY niggling; meticulous
zo FINLESS without steering propulsion
FINNACK FINNOCK, white sea trout
FINNISH language; of the Finns
zo FIN-RAYS bony fin supports (fish)
FIN-TOED web-footed
mn FIORITE volcanic residue
FIRE-ARM weapon
FIRE-BAR furnace bar
FIRE-BOX boiler fuel chamber
FIRE-BUG an incendiary
FIREDOG an andiron
zo FIREFLY a luminous beetle
ga FIREMAN fire fighter; pitcher
    (baseball)
FIRE-NEW brand-new (ceramic)
FIRE-PAN brazier; priming pan
FIRE-POT incendiary device
lw FIRMARY tenant's rights
FIRMING confirming; establishing
bd FIRRING wood strips for roof
    boarding
pb FIRRING FURRING encrusting; lathing
rl FISH-DAY Friday
FISHERY fish-breeding station
FISH-FAG wife of gay male
zo FISH-FLY a bait
FISH-GIG fishing appliance
FISH-GOD Dagon (coastal Palestine)
FISHIFY become a fish
FISHILY in a fishy manner
FISHING angling; piscatorial pursuit
FISH-MAW swimming bladder
FISH-OIL nutrient-rich oil
FISHWAY fish-ladder
FISKERY friskiness
ps FISSILE FISSIVE, of spontaneous
    cleavage (nuclear)
gl, ps FISSION FISSURE, rift; fracture; cleft;
    crevice
FISTING pommelling; boxing;
    fisticuffs
FIST-LAW might is right
bd FISTUCA pile-driving machine

bt, md **FISTULA** reed; ulcer
hd **FITCHED FITCHEE**, pointed
zo **FITCHET FITCHEW**, polecat; foumart
FITMENT a fitting (small part of whole)
FITNESS aptness; decency; seemliness
lw **FITTAGE** brokerage
FITTING try on (clothes); appropriate
bt **FITWEED** anti-hysteric plant
FIXABLE securable
FIXEDLY firmly; steadfastly
jn **FIXINGS** fasteners holding joinery
FIXTURE appointment; engagement; (match); building; fitment
FIZZING spluttering; hissing
FIZZLED failed; flopped
FLACCID flabby; loose; limp
FLACKER flutter like a bird
FLAG-DAY charity or national funds day
FLAGGED FLAG-MAN, signalled by flag (motor circuits)
bd **FLAKING** crumbling; peeling
FLAMING blazing fire; glowing
FLAMMED shammed; hoaxed
to **FLAMMER** splitting knife
FLANEUR an idling gossip
rw **FLANGED** having a raised edge; wheel
ga **FLANKED FLANKER**, side by side (wingers)
tx **FLANNEL** woollen garment; persuasion
ae **FLAPPER** emancipated girl; wing adjunct
FLARING funnel-shaped; trousers
FLASHED glistened; sparkled; gleamed
FLASHER would-be wit; male exposed
bd **FLATLET** small flat; dwelling
bd **FLATTED FLATTEN**, of levelling; laid low
FLATTER compliment falsely; cajole
FLAUNTY showy; gaudy
bt **FLAVEDO** yellowness
FLAVIAN (T. Flavius Vespasianus)
bt **FLAVINE** a yellow dye
ch **FLAVONE** yellow plant pigment
FLAVOUR zest; savour; taste; relish; quality
FLAWING cracking; marring
FLAYING skinning; excoriating
FLEABAG sleeping bag
bd **FLEAPIT** dosshouse; shabby theatre
FLECKED FLECKER, dappled; to add spots

FLEDGED chicks ready for flight (birds)
FLEECED FLEECER, sheepshearer; overcharged
FLEEING absconding; retreating
FLEERED mocked; scoffed
FLEERER a derider; flouter
FLEETED flitted; flew; sped
FLEETLY swiftly; nimbly; rapidly
FLEMING native of Flanders (Belgium)
FLEMISH variant of Dutch language
FLENSED skinned (of whale blubber)
FLESHED well-fed; satiated (carnally)
zo **FLESHER** butcher; red-backed shrike
FLESHLY carnal; sensual; fat; obese
bd **FLETTON** pink/yellow indented brick
FLEURET floral decoration; fencing-foil
FLEURON type flower in printing
FLEXILE pliable; pliant; supple
ga **FLEXING FLEXION**, bending (muscles); (archery)
FLEXURE curvature
FLICKED flipped
FLICKER FLICKS, failing light; (movies)
FLIFFIS double somersault; trampoline
FLIGHTY volatile; mercurial; fickle
FLINDER splinter; fragment
ga **FLINGER** hurler; thrower; caster
FLIP-DOG 'feet' of marine divers
FLIPPED boosted; flicked (pages); be enthused
zo **FLIPPER** feet of marine denizen, diver
FLIRTED showed amorous interest
FLITTER change frequently (jobs etc.)
FLOATED drifted (aimlessly); launched; (loan)
pb **FLOATER** indifferent voter; ballcock
FLOCCUS tuft of hair; down
FLOCKED crowded; swarmed; thronged
FLOGGED scourged; lashed; sold (illegally)
pt **FLOGGER** graining brush; whipper; overdoer
FLOODED inundated; swamped (market)
FLOOKAN slimy clay
bd **FLOORED** overthrown; baffled; storeyed
ga **FLOORER** knockdown blow (boxing)

FLOPPED fell; failed (business)
    (show)
FLOPPER faller; failure; splasher
FLOREAL 8th month (Fr.
    Revolution)
FLORIST a nurseryman
FLOROON flower border
FLORUIT a life-time
FLOTAGE buoyancy
FLOTSAM recovered wreckage
FLOUNCE a jerky movement
FLOURED powdered
FLOUTED jeered; insulted
FLOUTER mocker; derider
FLOWAGE flow; current; discharge
FLOWERY florid; ornate; figurative
FLOWING of river; fluent; smooth
ps **FLUENCE** energy (f); particle (f-)
FLUENCY lingual mastery;
    exuberance
FLUEWAY smoke and gas duct
FLUFFED bungled; foozled
FLUIDAL flowing; liquid
FLUIDIC FLUIDLY, of liquids
FLUKILY by a fluke
FLUKING scoring by chance
FLUMMOX perplex; defeat
FLUMPED slumped
FLUNKEY footman; snob; toady
ch **FLUORIC** (fluorine)
FLUSHED blushed; roused; disturbed
zo **FLUSHER** toilet device; emptier;
    butcher bird
FLUSTER agitation; disconcert;
    bustle
zo **FLUSTRA** sea-mat; polyzoa
mu **FLUTINA** accordion
ar **FLUTING** decorative grooving
mu **FLUTIST FLAUTIST**, flute-player
md **FLUTTER** speculation; palpitation
    (heart); wave
el, ps **FLUTTER** undue modulation; scare;
    excitement
go **FLUVIAL FLUVIATILE**, of rivers; soil
    deposits
fd **FLUXIDE FLUXING, FLUXION**, melting;
    welding; fusion
FLYAWAY flighty; impracticability;
    gymnastic move
el, tc **FLYBACK** restart of scanner beam
    cycle
FLY-BILL handbill; poster (advert)
FLY-BOAT canal boat
FLY-BOMB pilotless aerial torpedo
FLY-BOOK (fishing)
FLY-FLAP fly-whisk
FLY-HALF (football)
FLY-LEAF blank page

FLY-LINE fishing line
FLY-OVER road or rail crossing
FLY-PAST flight by aircraft
FLY-RAIL table leaf support
bt **FLY-TRAP** an insectivorous plant
FOALING colt-birth
FOAMING raging; bubbling;
    creaming
FOBBING cheating; tricking
FOCUSED clarity of aim (optics, lens)
FODIENT pertaining to digging
FOE-LIKE hostile; inimical; adverse
FOG-BANK accumulation of fog
FOG-BELL sea warning device
FOG-DUST cloud of groundbait
    (angling)
bt **FOGGAGE** coarse grass
go **FOGGARA** underground water
    channel (Arab.)
FOGGIER FOGGILY, FOGGING, murkier;
    obscurance
nt **FOGHORN** sea warning device
FOGLAMP penetrating headlight
FOGLESS clear
FOG-RING bank of fog
FOGYISH FOGYISM, senile; dull
    notions
FOILING tracery; deer track
ga **FOILIST** fencer
FOINING thrusting; tilting
FOISTED FOISTER, thrust on one;
    imposer; cheat
lw **FOLDAGE** sheep folding rights
FOLDING sheep penning; (clothes);
    bankruptcy
FOLIAGE leafage; boscage
FOLIATE a curve; laminate
FOLINIC acid constituent of folic
    acid
pr **FOLIOED FOLIOLE**, in pages; leaflet
FOLIOSE FOLIOUS, leafy; thin;
    insubstantial
FOLLIES imbecilities; revue show
ch **FOMITES** porous substances
ck **FONDANT** sugar icing (cakes)
    (sweets)
FONDEST dearest; most affectionate
FONDING doting
FONDLED caressed; dandled
FONDLER sugar daddy
FONTEIN spring (Afrikaans)
rl **FONTLET** small font
FOOLERY FOOLING, clowning;
    playing
FOOLISH doltish; stupid; irrational
ae **FOOT-BAR** aeroplane rudder control
FOOTBOY page; bell-hop
ar **FOOTING** walking; basis; foundation

FOOTLED bungled; wasted time ineptly
FOOTMAN servant; lackey; flunkey; (coach)
FOOTPAD highwayman; pickpocket; robber
vt FOOT-ROT disease of sheep
FOOTSIE linked feet; (flirting)
me FOOT-TON a measure of work
FOOTWAY footpath
FOOZLED footled; mishit
FOOZLED deceived; bungled
FOPPERY FOPPISH, affectation; dressy
FORAGED FORAGER, pillaged; plunderer
md FORAMEN a pore
FORAYED raided
FORBADE FORBIDDEN, permission refused
FORBEAR ancestor; refrain; abstain
FORBORE desisted; withheld; shunned
to, md FORCEPS pliers; graspers (surgery)
FORCING plant culture; coercing
FORDING riding, wading across a stream
FORDONE tired out; exhausted
pl FOREARM lower part of arm
hy FOREBAY pipeline head reservoir
FORE-BOW front of saddle
FOREDAY forenoon
nt FORE-END front end; bow
pl FORE-GUT beginning of alimentary canal
FOREIGN alien; exotic; strange
FORELAY ambush
FORELEG front leg
lw FOREMAN boss; overseer; ganger
FORERAN preceded; ushered
FORERUN herald
FORESAW foretold; forecast
FORESAY predict; presage; augur
FORESEE anticipate; forecast
nt FORETOP FOREMAST (part of ship)
FOREVER everlasting; always
lw FORFANG an ancient felony
FORFEIT confiscation; lose rights
FORFEND to avert; ward off
FORGAVE pardoned; absolved
FORGERY counterfeiting
FORGING shaping an imitation; falsifying
FORGIVE pardon; excuse
FORGONE abstained from; past
ck FORKFUL fork load (mouthful)
el FORKING branching; dividing (routes) (circuits)

mu FORLANA FORLANE, old dance (It.)
FORLORN desolate; lost; hapless; scruffy
FORMANT vowel pitch (phonetics)
ch FORMATE a salt from formic acid
FORMICA rigid laminated plastic material
FORMING shaping; moulding
ch FORMOXY organic radical
FORMULA order; ritual; ingredients
FORSAKE abandon; quit; desert
FORSOOK renounced; relinquished
FORTIFY strengthen; brace
FORTLET small redoubt
FORTUNE luck; Kismet; felicity; wealth
FORWARD bold; brazen; despatch
ga FORWARD -gear; front ranker (football)
FORWENT FOREGONE, past; a missed chance
FOUGADE fougasse; mine
tx FOULARD silk
ga FOULING soiling; blocking; agin rules
zo FOUMART the polecat; fitchew
FOUNDED started; established
nt FOUNDER originator; to sink
FOUNDRY (metal casting)
FOURGON baggage wagon
md FOVEATE FOVEOLA, dented; notched
bt FOVILLA pollen; plant seed
FOWLING bird catching; (shooting)
FOWLRUN chicken run; poultry yard
FOX-CASE foxskin
md FOX-EVIL baldness
FOXHOLE safety pit; bivouac (army)
FOXHUNT with horses and hounds
FOXLIKE FOXSHIP, cunning; craftiness
bt FOXTAIL a grass
FOX-TRAP a snare to catch foxes
FOX-TROT ballroom dance step
FRABBIT peevish
FRACHES glass annealing trays
hd FRACTED broken
FRAGILE delicate; infirm; brittle
FRAILTY foible; weakness; infirmity
FRAISED defended by pointed stakes
FRAKTUR German black-letter type
FRAME-UP plot; conspiracy for entrapment
FRAMING putting together; devising
FRANCIC FRANKISH, French culture etc.
FRANION boon companion; paramour
FRANKED exempt; post paid

FRANKLY candidly; openly; unreserved
FRANTIC frenzied; raving; distracted
nt **FRAPPED** bound
FRATCHY quarrelsome
rl **FRATERY** refectory in monastery
FRAUGHT laden; pregnant; surcharged
FRAYING peeling; tattering of clothes
FRAZZLE to make extremely upset; exhausted
FREAKED STREAKED, ran naked; took drugs
pl **FRECKLE** small facial spot (macula)
pl,pt **FRECKLY** FRECKLED, spotted design (skin)
FREEBIE complimentary ticket, meal etc.
FREEDOM liberty; informality; scope
FREEING loosing; liberating
FREEMAN privileged citizen
bt **FREESIA** bulbous plant
FREEWAY bypass; motorway
FREEZER refrigerator
ps **F-REGION** F-LAYER, ionosphere
FREIGHT cargo; burden; burthen
ae **FREMLIN** beery; female gremlin
zo **FRENATE** bristly
FRESHEN refresh; invigorate; revive
FRESHER freshman; less faded
FRESHES a flood; a spate
FRESHET flooding of a river; clear stream
FRESHLY recently; briskly; newly
me **FRESNEL** unit of optical frequency
FRETFUL petulant; testy; fractious
to **FRETSAW** for jigsaw puzzle making
ml,pc **FRETTED** frayed; abraded; sorrowed
pc **FRETTER** one with extreme anxiety
ck,gl **FRIABLE** crumbly; powdery
FRIAGEM wintry spell in Brazil
FRIARLY monkish; unsophisticated
FRIBBLE frivolous; to trifle; totter
ar **FRIEZED** with ornamental border; unshaven
nt **FRIGATE** a patrol warship
bt **FRIJOLE** Mexican bean
FRILLED with decorative collar (ham); (pastor)
FRINGED decorative border (hairstyle)
FRINGES light and dark lines on bordering
FRIPPER second-hand clothes merchant
FRISEUR hairdresser
zo **FRISIAN** Frieslander cattle race

FRISKED gambolled; made personal search
FRISKER a gad-about; a searcher
FRISKET a printing frame
FRISLET small ruffle
FRISURE a crisping of the hair
FRITTED fused; baked
ck **FRITTER** food fried in batter
FRIZING inducing curls; (hairstyle)
pl **FRIZZED** FRIZZLY, curled (hair)
FRIZZLE to fry; to crisp; to splutter
FROCKED wearing a frock; of clergy
bt **FROGBIT** aquatic plant
zo **FROGERY** a frog pool
FROGGED braided
nt **FROG-MAN** special type of diver
bt **FRONDED** leafy
FRONTAL a pediment; head on
FRONTED faced; encountered
FRONTIS front wall of court (pelota)
FRONTON a pelota ground (Sp.)
FROSTED roughened; decorative glass effect
FROTHED foamed; (at the mouth) (beer)
FROUNCE wrinkle; frown
FROWNED scowled; glowered
FROWSTY foul and stuffy
FRUCTED bearing fruit
FRUGGIN oven stirring pole
FRUIBLY do something with enjoyment
FRUITED bore fruit
FRUITER fruit grower
FRUMPED jeered
FRUMPER scoffer; mocker
FRUSTUM a conic section
FRUTIFY fructify; team; produce
FUBBERY deception
FUCATED painted deceptively
bt **FUCHSIA** a flowering shrub
FUCHSIN red fuchsia dye
FUDDLED bemused; fuzzled
FUDDLER drunkard; toper
FUDGING faking; of poor workmanship
FUEHRER German (Nazi) leader
FUELLER stoker; petrol salesman
FUFFING puffing (with exhaustion)
mu **FUGUIST** fugue composer
FULCRUM of leverage; rowing oars
FULGENT dazzling; radiant; brilliant
zo **FULGORA** lantern fly
FULGOUR splendour
tx **FULLAGE** fee for cleansing woollen cloth
tx **FULLERY** a fuller's cloth factory
FULLEST amplest; most exhaustive

FULL-HOT vehement; blazing
FULLING (cloth process)
FULL-PAY salary without deductions
FULMINE FULMINATE, to denounce with thunder
FULNESS FULSOME, plenitude; repletion
FULVOUS FULVID, tawny yellow colour
bt **FUMARIA** FUMARIC, tobacco plant genus
FUMBLED FUMBLER, bungled; groper
ck **FUMETTE** smell of high game
bt **FUMITER** plant genus
FUN FAIR amusement park
bt **FUNARIA** genus of mosses
FUNCTOR performer (of process)
FUNDING obtaining financial resources
mu **FUNEBRE** funeral; march
rl **FUNERAL** interment occasion (burial)
ch **FUNGATE** (fungic acid)
mn **FUNGITE** fossil coral
bt **FUNGOID** FUNGOUS, of fungi
FUNGOUS of fungi; behaving like fungus
pl, bt **FUNICLE** ligature; ovule stalk
FUNKING afraid to take any action
FUNNILY comically; humorously
FURBISH burnish; rub; polish
FURCATE forked
zo, ck **FURCULA** merrythought; wishbone (of chicken)
mu **FURIANT** FURIOSO, quick Czech dance
FURIOUS frantic; raging; frenzied
FURLANA forlana; Venetian dance
tx **FURLING** wrapping; rolling
me **FURLONG** running; horse racing; (201m)
FURMETY FRUMENTY, Elizabethan porridge
FURNACE coal firebox (in steam locomotive); (iron- and steelworks)
FURNISH equip; supply; produce
FURRIER a dealer in furs
pb **FURRING** FIRRING, encrusting pipes and leads
ag **FURROWY** in furrows
FURTHER FARTHER, increase in distance
FURTHER promote; support (cause) (fund)
FURTIVE stealthy; sly; clandestine
FUSCINE FUSCOUS, oil extract; swarthiness
FUSIBLE able to be melted

FUSSIER FUSSILY, more bothered; fidgety
FUSSING bothering; making trouble
FUSS-POT anxious busy-body
FUSTIAN coarse cloth; bombastic
FUSTIER mouldier; mustier
FUTCHEL supporting bar
FUTHORC Runic alphabet
nt **FUTTOCK** ship's timber
FUZZIER curlier; more crinkled
FUZZLED fuddled; inebriated
FYRDUNG whole country military array (Saxons)

G

nt **GABBARD** GABBART, a barge
GABBING gossiping
GABBLED GABBLER, chattered; babbler
GADDING GADDISH, restless roving
ck, bt **GADELLE** currant (Fr.)
GADLING gauntlet spike
GADROON ornamented edge
GADSMAN ploughman
zo **GADWALL** migratory duck
GAFFING fish spearing; gambling
GAGGING preventing speech; silencing
GAGGLED sound of noisy geese
mn **GAHNITE** spinel-group mineral
nt **GAIASSA** cargo felucca, Nile
GAINFUL lucrative; beneficial
GAINING profiting; winning; acquiring
GAINSAY (against); contradict; dispute
GAIRISH garish; gaudy colours
tx **GAITERS** GAMBADOES, mudguards for legs
as **GALACTO-** of constellations; galaxies
GALANTY (shadow pantomime)
GALATEA Pygmalion's statue
tx **GALATEA** cotton fabric
zo **GALEATE** crested
zo **GALEENY** guinea-fowl
GALENIC (lead)
GALERIA ancient Mexican water system
ck **GALETTE** a small gateau; (cream cake)
rl **GALILEE** West porch of cathedral
bt **GALIPOT** pine-resin
GALLANT courtly; valiant; a beau
zo **GALLA-OX** Abyssinian ox
ch **GALLATE** (gallic acid)
nt **GALLEON** carrack; trader (Sp.)

ar **GALLERY** grand corridor; mining
    passage
ga **GALLERY** balcony; (play to-) (tennis)
zo **GALL-FLY** a pest
   GALLICE in French
   GALLING irritating; exasperating
nt **GALLIOT** galiot; brigantine; later,
    barge
ch **GALLIUM** a metallic element
   GALLIZE (wine-making)
bt **GALL-NUT** a pestiferous growth
tx **GALLOON** woven fabric; lace
   GALLOWS for hanging criminals
    (noose)
   GALOCHE GALOSH, rubber over-shoe
   GALUMPH wild price rise (property)
   GAMBADO mud gaiter
   GAMBIAN native of Gambia (W.
    Africa)
bt **GAMBIER** catechu; a dye
mu **GAMBIST** cello player; (viol da
    gamba)
   GAMBLED GAMBLER, hazarded;
    speculator
pt **GAMBOGE** CAMBOGE, yellow gum
ar **GAMBREL** butcher's crook; roof
   GAME-BAG hunter's bag
zo **GAME-EGG** a bad egg
   GAMEFUL sportive; playful
mu **GAMELAN** Indonesian ensemble
   GAME-LEG lameness
   GAMETAL gametic; reproductive
zo **GAMETID** sporont-body bud cell
   GAMMOCK sky-larking; gammon
   GAMPISH bulging; slatternly (Mrs
    G-)
   GANGING grouping; teaming
md **GANGLIA** nerve-centre
   GANGREL vagrant; vagabond
to **GANG-SAW** multiple saw
nt, bd **GANGWAY** ship's ladder; passage;
    scaffolding
   GANOIDS fish of sturgeon type
   GANOSIS reducing shine on marble
wv **GANTREE** loom jacquard frame
   GAPPING opening; cleaving
cp **GARBAGE** litter; unwanted data
ga **GARBAGE** easy goal (basketball); soft
    shot (tennis)
   GARBLED GARBLER, distorted sound,
    meanings
ck **GARBURE** Pyrenean ragout
hd **GARDANT** full-faced
zo **GARFISH** sea-fish; belone
   GARGLED warbled
bt, ga **GARLAND** festoon; sideslip (skiing)
tx **GARMENT** clothing; apparel;
    vestment

ck **GARNISH** adornment (food)
    (ceramics)
   GAROTTE GARROTTE, strangling
    collar
zo **GARPIKE** the garfish
nt **GARUKHA** CARUCA, dhow; Arab
    vessel
nv **GAS-BUOY** lightbuoy; marine
    warning
mn **GAS-COAL** GAS-COKE, anthracite for
    gas
   GASEITY GASEOUS, containing gas
   GAS-FIRE domestic heating unit
   GASHFUL GASHING, mutilated;
    slitting
tx **GASKINS** leggings for warmth
   GAS-LAMP Victorian lighting
   GAS-LIME (gas filtration)
   GAS-MAIN chief gas conduit
   GAS-MASK protection against poison
    gas
   GAS-OVEN gas-fired (kitchen) oven
md **GASPING** spasmodic breathing
   GAS-PIPE gas conduit
   GAS-RING cooking grid
   GASSING loquacity; chattering
   GAS-TANK portable gas cylinder
cf, pl, md **GASTERO-** GASTRIC, of stomach
    (acid)
ar **GATEMAN** GATEWAY, door keeper;
    portal
   GATLING a gun
tx **GAUDERY** GAUDIED, loud coloured
    finery
   GAUDILY ostentatiously; embellished
ck **GAUFFER** GAUFFRE, crimped; wafer
    (Fr.)
rw **GAUGING** measuring widths (rail
    gauge) etc.
bd, to **GAUGING** GAULTER, estimating
    mortar mix; marking timber
   GAULISH of France (Caesar's Gallia)
   GAUMING daubing; smearing
   GAUNTLY lankily; leanly
rw **GAUNTRY** GANTRY, overhead signals
lw **GAVELET** land forfeiture
zo **GAVILAN** species of hawk
mu **GAVOTTE** a country dance
   GAYNESS of homosexuals;
    cheerfulness
   GAYSOME blithe; vivacious; jolly
   GAZEFUL regardant; contemplative
zo **GAZELLE** graceful animal
   GAZETTE journal; newspaper; record
   GEAR-BOX GEARING, varying motor
    wheels
   GEHENNA place of abomination;
    (Hell)

ck **GELABLE GELATIN**, glutinate; jelly
zo **GELDING** castrated stallion
ck, pt **GELIDLY GELLING**, liquid to set jelly
to **GELLOCK** crowbar; gavelock
GEMMATE budding
GEMMERY GEMMARY, collection of
    mounted gems and precious stones
bt **GEMMING GEMMULE**, budding; small
    bud
zo **GEMSBOK** S. African antelope
GENAPPE worsted yarn
GENERAL high officer; over all; (in-)
GENERIC of general features
    classified
rl **GENESIS** starting point; birth of;
    (Bible)
bl **GENETIC** of heredity; chromosomes;
    DNA
zo **GENETTE GENET**, civet
rl **GENEVAN** of Geneva; Calvinist
ck **GENEVER** 'Holland's gin'
bt **GENIPAP** orange-like fruit
bt **GENISTA** broom (bush) (Plantagenet)
bl, pc **GENITAL** of reproductive organs
GENIZAH store-room for ancient
    relics
GENOESE of Genoa
GENTEEL elegant; polite; mincing
bt **GENTIAN** plant genus
GENTILE not a Jew
GENTLER milder; more kindly
GENUINE sincere; authentic;
    veritable
bl **GEOCOLE** soil-dwelling organism
gl **GEODESY** (earth measurements)
go **GEOGONY** (earth formations)
gl **GEOIDAL** globe, earth-shaped
gl **GEOLOGY** history of globe through
    rocks
go **GEONOMY** physical geography
go **GEORAMA** globular map
nm **GEORDIE** miner's lamp; guinea coin
GEORGIC poetic metre (verse form)
bt, gl **GEOTOME** soil-sample taker
bl **GEOXENE** soil-dwelling organism
GERMANE relevant; apposite;
    pertinent
md **GERMULE** a small germ
ck **GERVAIS** cream cheese (Fr.)
pc **GESTALT** total perception; art as
    unity
GESTAPO Nazi secret police
bl, pl **GESTATE** of pregnancy; (womb time)
pc **GESTURE** an act expressing feeling
GETABLE obtainable; procurable
GET-AWAY escape
GETTING acquisition; gaining;
    reaching

ps **G-FACTOR** magnetic energy level
    changes
GHASTLY fearsome; spectral; awful
bt **GHERKIN** small cucumber
GHILGAI Australian dewpond
GHILLIE game-keeper (Sc.)
GHOSTLY weird; spiritual; spectral
GIANTRY large human monsters
as, pl **GIBBOSE GIBBOUS**, convex; of moon;
    humpbacked
ck **GIBLETS** edible internal organs
    (fowls)
GIDDILY whirling around; unsteady
GIFTING endowing; bestowing;
    donating
GIG-MILL nap-raising device
GILBERT magnetic potential
pt **GILDING** enhancing with gold
GILLIAN sweetheart
ma, me **GILLION** 10 to the 9th power
zo **GILL-LID** 'lung cover' of fish
bt, pt **GILVOUS** brownish gold
nt **GIMBALS** compass holder; magnet
    balancer
to, nt **GIMBLET GIMLET**, hand borer
GIMMICK publicity trick
GIN-FIZZ a long drink based on gin
GINGALL swivel gun
ck **GINGERY** hot-flavoured; spicey
tx **GINGHAM** umbrella; gamp; (material)
bt, ck **GINGILI** sesame-oil
mn **GINGING** mine-shaft lining
GIN-MILL off-licence (Amer.)
GINNING cotton making
bt, ck, md **GINSENG** Chinese elixir root
GIN-SHOP gin-palace
GIN-TRAP snare; leg-trap (poachers)
mu **GIOCOSO** jocund; playful (smiling)
    (It.)
GIPPING gutting; cleaning out meat
GIPSIES Romanies; caravanners;
    Zingari
zo **GIRAFFE** long-necked cameleopard
mn **GIRASOL** fire-opal
GIRDING dressing for war (action)
GIRDLED belted (of surround);
    zoned
GIRDLER belt or girth-surround
    maker
GIRLISH childish; young ladyish
zo **GIRROCK** garfish
GIRTHED girdled; bound
GISARME battle-axe; bill; halberd
mu **GITTERN** cither; guitar
zo **GIZZARD** birds' food-grinding organ
GJETOST Norwegian goat's-milk
    cheese
gl, go **GLACIAL** of Ice Age, glaciers

mo, gl, go **GLACIER** slowly moving icefield
GLADDEN delight; gratify; rejoice
GLADDER brighter; more cheerful
GLAD-EYE an invitation
zo **GLADIUS** swordfish
bt **GLADWYN** purple iris
GLAIDIN glutin; (wheat)
GLAIRED varnished
pc **GLAMOUR** illusory fascination
GLANCED glimpsed; bounced away
GLARING obvious; staring fiercely
md **GLASSES** eye-; sun-; (spectacles)
zo **GLAUCUS** genus of molluscs
GLAZIER instals window-glass
ck **GLAZING** glassy; glossy; surfacey
GLEAMED shone; flashed; glinted;
smiled
GLEANED GLEANER, post reaping
(remnants) harvesting
GLEBOUS cloddy, turfy ground
GLEDGED squinted
GLEEFUL gay; lively; hilarious
mu **GLEEMAN** minstrel; chorister
md **GLENOID** of being bled; cupped
GLEYING squinting
ae **GLIDING** non-powered flight
GLIDING skimming; sliding; skiing
GLIMMER soft gleam (light); inkling
(idea)
GLIMPSE glance; hasty look or
impression
GLINTED gleamed; sparkled;
reflected
GLIRINE rodent-like
GLISTEN give sparkling radiance
GLISTER glitter; lustre; sparkle
GLITTER deceptive; ornamental;
sparkle
GLOAMED grew dark
GLOATED exulted; revelled
zo **GLOBARD** a glow-worm
GLOBATE spheroidal
GLOBING encircling
GLOBOID spherical
GLOBOSE round
GLOBOUS globular
GLOBULE corpuscle
GLOOMED made dark, sombre
GLORIED exalted; took pride in
GLORIFY honour; magnify; extol;
bless
GLOSSAL vocabulary; tongue
GLOSSED explained; palliated
GLOSSER polisher; commentator
GLOSSIC phonetic alphabet
md **GLOTTAL GLOTTIC**, phonetical stop
pl **GLOTTIS** larynx; vocal cord
GLOWING vehement; ardent; fervid

GLOZING specious representation
ch **GLUCIDE** saccharin; gluside
ch **GLUCINA** an oxide
GLUCOSE sugar
GLUE-POT gum receptacle
GLUMMER more dismal and dejected
bt **GLUMOUS** husky
GLUTEUS hind-limb muscle in
vertebrates
GLUTTED gorged; surfeited;
crammed
zo **GLUTTON** the wolverine
ch **GLYCINE** amino-acetic acid
pr **GLYPHIC** coded; ideogram; cartouche
GLYPTIC engraved; figured
bt **GMELINA** (verbena)
GNARING snarling; growling
bt **GNARLED GNARRED**, knotty timber
pc **GNASHED** teeth ground in anger
pl **GNATHAL GNATHIC**, of the jaws
GNAT-NET mosquito-net
GNAWING champing; eroding
ck **GNOCCHI** maize/potato dumplings
(It.)
GNOSTIC speculative believer
GOADING inciting; annoying
GO-AHEAD enterprising
GOATISH lustful; satyr-like
GOBBING coal refuse
zo **GOBBLER** turkey-cock
GOBBLER gourmandizer
GOBELIN French tapestry
GODDARD pewter cup
GODDESS female deity
bt **GODETIA** a garden annual
ce **GO-DEVIL** concrete pipeline cleaner
GODHEAD divine nature
GODHOOD state of being god
GODILLE wavy ski-descent technique
GODLESS atheistic; irreligious;
profane
GODLIER more righteous
GODLIKE deific
GODLILY devoutly
GODLING an inferior deity
GODROON gadroon; beading
GODSEND windfall; a crowning
mercy
GODSHIP deification
GODWARD heavenward
GOGGLED lobster-eyed
GOGGLES eye-protectors
GOITRED afflicted with bronchocele
bt **GOLD-CUP** buttercup
zo **GOLDNEY** a bream
ga **GOLFING** playing golf (social
pastime)
GOLIARD wandering jester

zo **GOLIATH** Biblical giant; beetle
GOMBEEN money-lending; usury (Irish)
GOMELIN cotton starch
md **GONAGRA** gout (of uric acid)
nt **GONDOLA** canal boat (Venice); galley
ae, mo **GONDOLA** passenger car of airship, cable funicular
GONGING prelude to speeding fine (USA)
bt **GONIDIA** lichen-moss spores
vt **GONITIS** stifle joint inflammation
zo **GONOPOD** insect reproduction organ
GOOD-BYE adieu
GOOD-DAY conventional greeting
GOOD-EGG cordial approval
GOODISH not so bad
GOODMAN a husband
GOOD-NOW exclamation of wonder
GOONDIE Australian native hut
zo **GOOSERY** cf. swannery
ar **GOPURAN** Hindu gate tower
zo **GORCOCK** red grouse
zo **GOR-CROW** carrion crow
GORDIAN intricate; (knot)
zo **GORDIUS** hair-worm
GORGING cramming; stuffing
zo **GORILLA** largest anthropoid ape
GORMAND gourmand; glutton
GORSEDD Welsh bardic assembly
zo **GOSHAWK** short-winged hawk
zo **GOSLING** a young goose
zo **GOSNICK** small sea-fish; skipper
GOSSIPY chatty; loquacious
GOSSOON a boy (Irish)
pt **GOUACHE** (water-colour painting)
GOUGING scooping out (eyes)
ch **GOULARD** lead acetate
ck **GOULASH** a ragout; (cards)
zo **GOURAMI** tropical fish
GOURMET a dainty feeder; epicure
zo **GOURNET GURNARD, GURNET**, a fish
rl **GOWN-MAN** of university or church
nc, ps **G-PARITY** particle quantum number
GRAB-BAG lucky-dip bag
GRABBED clutched; snatched
GRABBER gripper; pincher
GRABBLE sprawl; grope; paw
GRACILE slender
GRACING honorary adorning
to **GRADINE** sculptor's chisel
GRADING classifying; (quality) (results)
GRADUAL step by step progress
lw **GRAFFER** notary; scrivener
bt **GRAFTED** one plant on to another
GRAFTER financial swindler

bt **GRAINED** pattern of cross-section of wood, marble
GRAINER painter of above (imitator)
zo **GRALLAE** genus of wading birds
GRALLIC stilted
GRAMARY magic; wizardry
GRAMMAR linguistic treatise
zo **GRAMPUS** blunt-headed delphinoid cetacean
GRANARY grain-store
GRANDAD grandpa
GRANDAM a grannie
GRANDEE Spanish nobleman
GRANDER finer; superior; sublime
GRANDLY splendidly; superbly
GRANDMA grandam
GRANGER farm bailiff
gl **GRANITE** coarse, igneous, plutonic rock
GRANNOM grandam
GRANTED ceded; allotted; vouchsafed
lw **GRANTEE** the receiver
GRANTER the bestower
lw **GRANTOR** conveyor
GRANULE small particle
bt **GRAPERY** vinery
cp, pt, pr **GRAPHIC** pictorial, vivid comic strip
nt **GRAPNEL GRAPPLING**-iron (boarding ships)
GRAPPLE close-up fighting grip
GRASPED GRASPER, gripped; understood; clasp
GRASSED informer told police
pr **GRASSER** extra printing hand
GRASSUM a premium
GRATIFY to satisfy; gladden; please
GRATING scratching, rasping sound
pc **GRATING** harsh; offensive; annoying
cp **GRAUNCH** unplanned fault of machine
GRAVEDO cold in the head
GRAVELY seriously; staidly; sober
GRAVEST most serious; very cogent
GRAVIED served with gravy
nt **GRAVING** engraving; scraping
GRAVITA of seriousness
ps **GRAVITY** law of falling weight
GRAVITY seriousness; dignity; importance
pr **GRAVURE** photo printing technique
GRAZIER shepherd
GRAZING animals browsing; glancing blow
GREASED lubricated; oiled (machinery)
GREASER lubricator; machine-minder

GREATER larger; more important
GREATLY notably; immensely
GREAVES leg-armour; old tallow
GREAVES tallow refuse; cracklings
GRECIAN Greek or man of Greece (poet)
GRECISM a Greek expression
GRECIZE to Hellenize
GRECQUE in Greek style; coffee-machine
GREENED hoaxed; duped; cheated
GREENER verdant; easily fooled
GREETED accosted; welcomed
mt GREGALE GREGAL, NE Med. winter wind
rl GREMIAL bishops' pinafore
GREMLIN aerial imp; pilot's illusion
ga GREMLIN unskilled skateboardist
GRENADE hand-bomb
GREY-HEN stone bottle
zo GREY-HEN female grouse
GREYISH grayish
zo GREYLAG wild goose; grey goose
zo GREY-OWL tawny owl
zo GRIBBLE marine borer (crustacean)
GRIDDED marked in squares
ck GRIDDLE circular iron baking plate
GRIDING grating; jarring
GRIEVED lamented; mourned
hd GRIFFIN GRIFFON, mythical dragon-eagle
GRIFFIN greenhorn; a duenna
GRILLED broiled; cross-examined
GRIMACE a moue; facial distortion
GRIMING fouling; soiling
GRIMMER dourer; fiercer; more grisly
pl GRINDER molar tooth; quern; peppermill
GRINNED smiled broadly
md GRIPING causing intestinal pains
GRIPPED seized; held; clutched
GRIPPER a bailiff
GRIPPLE usurious; tenacious
GRIQUAS Dutch half-castes
GRISKIN lean bacon
GRISLED grizzled; grey
ck GRISTLE GRISTLY, cartilage; indigestible (meat)
GRITTED grated; ground
GRITTER road, salt-spreading device
GRIZZLE whimper; gray
zo GRIZZLY grey; a bear
GROANED moaned; bewailed
GROBIAN clumsy lout
GROCERY provision shop
tx GROGRAM fabric of silk and mohair
GROINED thigh cleft; breakwater

GROLIER of book-binding technique
nt GROMMET GRUMMET, rope-ring for mooring
GROOMED made smart, tidy (horses)
GROOVED furrowed channel; rut
GROPING seeking by touch
GROSSER GROSSLY, coarser; rougher; outrageously
lw GROTIAN (legal philosophy)
ga, ck GROUNDS arenas; reasons; dregs
GROUPED GROUPER, graded; arranger
GROUSED GROUSER complained; grumbler
GROUTED filled with cement
GROWING raising; waxing
GROWLED snarled
nt, zo GROWLER a wandering iceberg; dog
GROWN-UP an adult
to GRUB-AXE a hoe
GRUBBED GRUBBER, dug up; investigator
GRUBBLE grope; grabble
GRUDGED envied; resented
GRUFFER surlier; rougher; (voice)
GRUFFLY churlishly; roughly; bluntly
GRUMBLE grouse; complain; repine
nt GRUMMET GROMMET, rope-ring for mooring
GRUMOSE GRUMOUS, clustered; clotted
zo GRUNDEL loach or rock-goby
zo GRUNTER a pig; a gurnet
ck GRUYERE a Swiss cheese
GRYLLID pertaining to crickets
hd GRYPHON GRIFFIN, dragon-eagle
zo GRYSBOK S. African antelope
GUAJIRA peasant dance (Cuba)
zo GUANACO HUANACO, llama genus
bc GUANINE purine base in living tissues
bt GUARANA Brazil cocoa
nm GUARANI (Paraguay)
GUARAPO sweet drink (Peru)
GUARDED wary; watchful; defended
zo GUDGEON an axle; a fish
bt GUELDER rose; snowball tree
zo GUENONS a monkey genus
GUERDON a reward; recompense
zo GUEREZA the Abyssinian monkey
GUERITE watch-tower
GUESSED divined; solved; supposed
GUESSER a conjecturer
bt GUIACUM lignum vitae
GUICHET small ticket window (Fr.)
GUIDING leading; directing; piloting
nm GUILDER Dutch golden coin
GUINEAN (W. African)

tx **GUIPURE** a heavy lace
rl **GUISARD GUIZER,** Christmas mummer (actor)
zo **GULLERY** bird sanctuary; easy deception
go **GULLIED** of water-eroded ravines
go, to **GULLIES** small narrow canyons; knives
GULLING greening; duping
md **GUM-BOIL** inflamed swelling
GUM-BOOT rubber shoe
GUMDROP a confection
bt **GUMMING** fruit-tree disease; cementing
GUMMOUS gummy; mucilaginous
md **GUM-RASH** red gum; strophulus
bt **GUM-THUS** resin from Amer. pine
bt **GUM-TREE** (quandary); (rubber)
bt **GUMWOOD** similar grain to rosewood
nt **GUNBOAT** small warship
nt **GUN-DECK** ships' artillery deck
nt **GUNDELO GUNDELOW,** cargo (felucca) vessel
GUN-FIRE war-sound; ceremonial salute
GUNLOCK firing mechanism
nt **GUNNAGE** (number of guns)
GUNNERY the craft of the artillery
GUNNING shooting
nt **GUN-PORT** port-hole
nt **GUN-ROOM** a mess-room
GUNSHOT distance of effective range
GUN-SITE location of gun
nt **GUNWALE** topmost plank (ship's side)
GURGLED GARGLED, rippling sound; water-warbled
zo **GURNARD** gurnet fish
GUSHING spouting; flowing; effusive
GUSTATE to taste, consume
GUSTILY in gusts; fitfully; breezily
GUTTATE spotted
GUTTING gipping; eviscerating
GUTTLED gulped; swallowed
GUTTULE small drop
GUZZLED ate greedily; swilled; caroused
GUZZLER gourmand
zo **GWINIAD** freshwater salmon
zo **GWYNIAD** small white fish
GYMNAST athlete
zo **GYPLURE** moth sex attractant
GYRATED twirled; span; spun; rotated
el **GYRATOR** component used at microwave frequencies
zo **GYRINID** whirligig beetle
hd **GYRONNY** heraldic triangulation

ae **GYROSYN** flux-gate gyro compass
GYTRASH a ghost

H

bt, zo **HABITAT** natural life-environment
HABITED dressed; attired
HABITUE a frequenter; regular
pr **HACHURE** engraved line; groove
HACKBUT arquebus; musket
HACKING cutting; notching; kicking
cp **HACKING** penetrating computer secrets
HACKLED combed
HACKLER flax-comber
HACKLES feathers; imitation flies (angling)
zo **HACKLET** sea-bird; shearwater gull
HACKLOG chopping block
zo **HACKNEY** horse; cab; trite
to **HACK-SAW** a saw for metal
zo **HADDOCK HADDIE,** (Sc.)
HAFFLED prevaricated
ch **HAFNIUM** metallic element
HAFTING fitting a handle
HAGANAH Jewish militia
nt **HAGBOAT** hull design of sailing vessels
zo **HAGDOWN** shearwater gull
zo **HAGFISH** parasite fish
HAGGADA Jewish commentary
zo **HAGGARD** stackyard; wild falcon
HAGGING HAGGISH, ugly; nagging female
HAGGLED HAGGLER, bargainer
HAGSEED offspring of a witch
HAGSHIP haggishness
bt **HAGWEED** witches' broom (transport)
mt **HAILING** greeting; raining ice
HAIRCUT barber's service
HAIRNET coiffure cover
HAIR-OIL hair dressing
HAIRPIN coiffure; (sharp bend)
HAITIAN native of Haiti
HALACHA HALAKAH, Jewis oral laws
HALBERD HALBARD, pike-axe
HALBERT guard's weapon; pike-axe
zo **HALCYON** kingfisher; calm
bd **HALF-BED** stone laying term
HALF-ONE a golf handicap
HALF-PAY semi-retirement
HALFWAY intermediate position
HALF-WIT nitwit; moron
zo **HALIBUT** the largest flounder
HALIDOM mascot; sanctuary
md **HALITUS** foul exhaled breath

HALLAGE market-hall dues
HALLIER bird net
HALLING national folk dance
(Norway)
HALLION hallyon; hallian; rascal
ch **HALOGAN** salt producer group
HALOGEN one of the 7th-group
elements
HALTING faltering; hesitating
mn **HALVANS** ore-mining refuse
HALVING tieing; bisecting
nt **HALYARD** halliard; running rope
HAMBLED mutilated the foot
zo **HAMBURG** domestic fowl
HAMITIC sons of Ham (of Noah)
tc **HAMMING** overacting; radio hobby
cp **HAMMING** code signal distance error
nt **HAMMOCK** a slung bed
zo **HAMSTER** rodents; (pets)
HAMULAR HAMULUS, small crooked
hook
HANAPER HAMPER, basket-box
(picnic)
HANDBAG women's closed everyday
bag
HANDFUL small amount; difficult
person
HANDIER more manageable (size)
HANDILY conveniently; adjacently
HANDING presenting; delivering
HANDJAR Persian dagger
HANDLED dealt with; manipulated
HANDLER dealer
HAND-OFF self-defence; fending off
a tackle (rugby football)
HANDOUT prepared statement;
sample; advertising material
to **HANDSAW** carpenter's tool
HANDSEL earnest money; a present
tc **HANDSET** telephone receiver and
microphone (mouthpiece)
HANDS-ON direct participation
HANGDOG sullen; morose; abject
HANGING dangling; depending
HANGMAN topsman; public
executioner
HANG-NET vertical net
tx **HANKIES** handkerchiefs
nt **HANKING** coiling ropes; skeining
wool
HANKLED entangled (in coils);
involved
HANSARD Parliamentary Debate
Reports
HANSTER a freeman of a guild
rl **HANUKAH** Jewish feast day
HANUMAN Hindu monkey-god
HAPLESS luckless

HAPLOID single chromosomes
HAPLONT special-nucleus-type plant
mn **HAP'ORTH** halfpenny-worth
HAPPIER pleased; luckier
HAPPILY joyously; blissfully; gaily
HAPPING happening
HARBOUR shelter; haven; asylum
HARDEST densest; firmest; harshest
HARDIER pluckier; braver; tougher
HARDILY stoutly; intrepidly;
resolutely
HARDISH somewhat hard
bt **HARDOCK** harlock; burdock; coarse
weed
gl **HARDPAN** bedrock; level of soil
horizon
HARD-RUN greatly pressed
HARDSET beset by difficulty; hungry
HARDTOP fixed roof on a car
HARD-WON barely victorious
HAREING speeding
md **HARELIP** fissured lip
bt **HARICOT** French bean
HARKING listening; hurrying
bd **HARLING** of steel-clad houses
bt **HARMALA** wild rue
HARMFUL noxious; baneful; baleful
ch **HARMINE** wild rue extract
HARMING molesting; scathing
mu **HARMONY** chord structure
HARMONY amity; agreement; literary
notes
eg, ae **HARNESS** safety gear; (pilots)
ag **HARNESS** fastenings; yoke (horses)
(carts)
HARNESS control and utilize
pc **HARPING** repeating endlessly
mu **HARPIST** minstrel; musician
to **HARPOON** barbed spear on rope
(whaling)
HARRIED harassed; raided; ravaged
zo **HARRIER** hound; hawk; hare courser
HARRIER cross-country runner
HARSHEN stiffen; embitter
HARSHER rougher; severer; sterner
HARSHLY raucously; stridently
mn **HARTALL** orpiment (stone)
cp **HARTLEY** unit of information; bits
me, nc **HARTREE** atomic unit of energy
HARVEST crop; yield; produce
HAS-BEEN diminished fame
ck **HASHING** muddling; mangling;
cooking a medley
pr **HASHIRA** narrow print (Jap.)
ch, md **HASHISH** bhang; the assassin's drug
HASLOCK wool on sheep's throat
rl, tx, bt **HASSOCK** prayer cushion; tuft grass
bt **HASTATE** arrowhead-shaped leaf

HASTIER quicker; rasher; brisker
HASTILY rapidly; hurriedly; abruptly
HASTING ripening early; expediting
HASTLER (turn-spit); cook's help
HATABLE odious; obnoxious
HATBAND ribbon on hat
HATCASE bonnet-box
vt HATCHED new chicken; graduated
cp HATCHEL to heckle; to tease; public speaker
HATCHER plotter; conspirator; information thief
nt HATCHES deck trapdoor
to HATCHET an axe
HATEFUL detestable; execrable; odious
HATLESS bareheaded
HAT-RACK place to hang hat
HAUBERK coat of mail
HAUGHTY arrogant; proud
HAULAGE a charge for conveyance
HAULIER carter
HAULING tugging; drawing; dragging
HAUNCHY with full hips
HAUNTED frequented; followed; (ghost)
HAUNTER frequent visitor; (ghost)
HAURLED dragged; rought-cast
HAUSTUS adult medicine dose
mu HAUTBOY HAUTBOIS, oboe (woodwind)
HAUTEUR disdain; arrogance; loftiness
HAUTPAS a dais
HAVENOT under-privileged
HAW-BUCK a clown
bt HAWKBIT a plant
HAWKING falconry; peddlary; touting
HAWKISM war-minded advice
zo HAWK-OWL snowy owl
HAYBAND hay-rope
HAYCOCK gathered hay in stack
HAYDITE expanded clay (USA)
to HAYFORK farm implement
HAYLOFT part of barn
HAYRICK regular hay pile
bt HAYSEED hick, bumpkin
HAY-TIER hay bundler
HAYWARD a warden
HAYWIRE in confusion
HAZELLY light brown
HAZIEST foggiest; vaguest
HEADILY impetuously; precipitately
HEADING adit; headline; intercepting
HEADMAN chief; boss
HEAD-PIN no. 1 pin (bowling)
HEADWAY progress

bt HEAL-ALL valerian; a panacea
HEALING mollifying; remedying
HEALTHY hygienic; bracing; hale
HEAPING collecting; amassing
lw HEARING audition; trying
HEARKEN listen; attend; heed
HEARSAY rumour; report; gossip
HEARSED put in a hearse
HEARTED emboldened; cheered
HEARTEN encourage; rally; inspire
HEATHEN pagan; paynim; infidel
bt HEATHER ling; erica
HEATING warming; exciting
HEAVERS stevedores; dockyard unloaders
nt HEAVE-TO command: stop!; storm tactic
HEAVIER weightier; denser
HEAVILY ponderously; onerously
HEAVING a rising; hoisting; throwing
HEBAMIC pert. to Socratic method
bt HEBENON hen-bane; poison
HEBETIC occurring at puberty
HEBRAIC Hebrew
HECKLED combed; questioned
HECKLER political enquirer; demonstrator
me HECTARE 100 ares
HECTOID flushed; feverish; hectic
bt HEDEOMA penny-royal
HEDERAL of ivy
bt HEDGING natural garden fence
HEDGING guarding against losses
HEDONIC pleasure-seeking
HEEDFUL mindful; wary; cautious
HEEDING paying attention; regarding
HEELING (cock fighting); (football)
HEFTIER stronger; more vigorous
HEFTILY vigorously; powerfully
rl HEGUMEN Greek abbot
HEIGH-HO exclamation of complaisance
HEINOUS infamous; flagrant; atrocious
HEIRDOM succession
HEIRESS female inheritor
md HELCOID ulcerous
HELIBUS HELICAB, helicopter bus/taxi
HELICAL spiral
HELICES circumvolutions; spirals
HELICON mount of Muses
mu HELICON tuba; sousaphone (brass; wind)
HELIOID like the Sun
ch HELIXIN an ivy extract
pr HELL-BOX receptacle for broken type
HELL-CAT malignant hag

HELLENE Greek
HELL-HAG witch
HELLISH diabolical; infernal; fiendish
nt HELMAGE guidance; steering
md HELOSIS corns in feet
HELOTRY serfdom; bondage;
  (Sparta)
HELPFUL assistant; useful; beneficial
HELPING share; aiding; abetting
HELVING hafting; fitting a handle
mn HELVITE beryllium silicate
mu HEMIOLA HEMIOLIA, rhythmic
  change (Gr.)
zo HEMIONE half-ass; dziggetal
bt, md HEMLOCK poison plant; conine
HEMMING edging; besetting; sewing
bt HENBANE narcotic plant
HENCOOP a fowl abode
HENNAED dyed with henna
HENNERY poultry farm
HENOTIC conciliatory
HENPECK nag; dominate
HENTING final furrow
HENWIFE chicken-girl
HEPARIN anticoagulant
md HEPATIC of liver ailments
HEPTADE seven
ch HEPTANE petrol constituent
HEPTODE type of electric valve
ch HEPTOSE monosaccharide subgroup
HERBAGE pasture
HERBARY herb garden
HERBIST herbalist; collector of
  natural remedies
HERBLET small herb
HERBOUS herbaceous; herbose
HERDING tending; crowding; group
  instinct; driving groups about
HERDMAN herdsman; ranchero
HEREOUT out of this
HERETIC unorthodox; schismatic
HERISSE bristled
HERITOR inheritor
zo HERLING young sea-trout
md HERNIAL (rupture)
HEROINE intrepid damsel
HEROISM valour; bravery; fortitude
HEROIZE lionize
zo HERONRY bird sanctuary
zo HERRING tasty fish
HERSELF reflexive pronoun
HERSHIP cattle-theft (Sc.)
HESSIAN jute fabric; burlage (USA)
mn HESSITE telluride of silver
HETAIRA Greek dancing girl
HEXAGON a six-sided figure
HEXAPLA a Bible edition
HEXAPOD with 6 feet

bt HEXARCH with 6 protoxylem strands
HEXERIS galley with 6 oar banks
HEXONIC chemical base
HEYDUCK Haiduk; Hungarian
HEY-PASS conjuror's command
HIBACHI charcoal brazier (Jap.)
zo HICATEE Central American tortoise
bt HICKORY American nut-bearing tree
zo HICKWAY small woodpecker
as HIDALGO Spanish Don; asteroid
HIDEOUS unshapely; monstrous;
  grisly
HIDE-OUT a cache
HIEMATE hibernate; to winter
HIGGLED negotiated; peddled;
  chaffered
HIGGLER haggler; bargainer; hawker
HIGHBOY TALLBOY, pillar chest of
  drawers
HIGHDAY holiday
HIGHEST tallest; loftiest
HIGHFED pampered
HIGH-HAT high-brow
HIGHLOW sort of shoe
HIGHWAY main road; (-code)
  (-signals)
cp HIGHWAY digital transmission canals
HILDING paltry; base; a deceiver
HILLIER steeper
HILLING earthing
HILLMAN a mountaineer
HILLOCK small hill
HILLTOP summit
HIMSELF reflexive pronoun of 'he'
HINDBOW saddle cantle; equestrian
zo HIND-GUT posterior of alimentary
  canal
zo HINNIED WHINNIED, greeting of a
  horse
HINTING implying; suggesting
HIP-BATH portable sitting bath
HIP-BELT swordbelt
md HIP-GOUT sciatica
HIP-KNOT gable ornament
HIP-LOCK wrestling trick
HIPPING grieving; glooming
HIPPOID like a horse
HIP-ROOF a type of roof
HIPSHOT dislocated hip
HIPSTER clothes held by a belt
HIRABLE for hire; leasable
zo HIRCINE goatish
HIRSUTE hairy; rude
HIRUDIN anticoagulant chemical
  from leeches
HISKING breathing heavily
HISSING audible disapproval
ch HISTONE simple-protein group

HISTORY chronicle; annals; account
HISTRIO histrion; an actor
HITCHED caught; fastened; attached
HITTING smiting; striking; succeeding
HITTITE ancient Near-Eastern people
zo HIVE-BEE honey-bee
HOARDED garnered; amassed; secreted
HOARDER miser; husbandman
zo HOATZIN S. American bird
HOAXING duping; gammoning
HOBBISH clownish
HOBBISM a moral philosophy
HOBBIST follower of Hobbes
HOBBLED hoppled; tethered
HOBBLER horse-soldier
HOBLIKE boorish; clownish
HOBNAIL boot-nail
HOBOISM vagrancy (USA)
HOCK-DAY old English festival
HOCKLED houghed; hamstrung
HODADDY incompetent surf boarder
ck HOE-CAKE Indian meal cake
HOE-DOWN American folkdance
HOGBACK ridge; eskar
ag HOGCOTE pig-sty (America)
HOGGERS miner's leg-wear
HOGGING bending
HOGGISH swinish; sordid; greedy
HOG-HERD swineherd
HOG-MANE clipped mane
bt HOG-PLUM tropical tree
tx HOGSKIN pigskin; leather
HOGWASH swill; pig food
bt HOGWEED cow parsnip
HOISTED raised; heaved
HOISTER an elevator; lift
HOITING capering
HOLDALL a pack; luggage
lw HOLDING tenure; company finance
HOLDING climb-grip; horse-race conditions
HOLIDAY festival; vacation; free day
HOLIEST most sacred
tx HOLLAND coarse linen
ch HOLMIUM metallic element
bt HOLM-OAK evergreen oak
HOLSTER leather pistol case
rl HOLY-DAY feast day; sacred day
HOMAGER a vassal
HOMBURG gentleman's hat
HOME-BOY of home town; (-street kid)
HOMELOT home-plot
zo HOMELYN spotted ray
HOMERIC of Homer; grandiose

HOMINID man (ancient and modern)
HOMONYM equivocation
HONESTY best political creed
HONEYED flattering; sweet
HONITON centre for lace
HONKING (motoring); (geese)
HONOURS of university degree; court cards
HOODING covering; blinding
HOODLUM hooligan; rowdy; mobster
HOOFING walking
HOOGAAR cutter rigger pleasure boat (Dutch)
HOOKING ensnaring; bending; (polo)
HOOKPIN floor nail
bt HOOP-ASH nettle-tree
HOOPING binding; encircling
HOOTING decrying; booing
HOP-BACK brewer's vessel
bt HOPBIND HOPBINE, hop stem
HOPEFUL eager; expectant; confident
mn HOPEITE hydrated zinc phosphate
zo HOP-FLEA a parasite
HOPKILN an oast
HOPLITE Greek heavy-armed soldier
HOP-OAST hop-kiln
ga, rw HOPPERS a game; gravel spreaders
HOPPING leaping; (netball fault)
HOPPLED hobbled; tethered
HOPPLES hobbles; rope shackles
HOP-POLE husbandry implement
bt HOP-TREE American shrub
bt HOP-VINE hopbind
HOP-YARD hop-garden
bt HORDEIN HORDEUM, barley genus
HORDING crowding; herding; amassing
HORIZON where sea meets sky
md HORMONE gland secretion
HORNBAR crossbar
zo HORN-BUG stag beetle
lw HORNING debtor's summons
HORNISH ungual
HORNITO volcanic smoke-hole
bt HORN-NUT a water-plant
zo HORN-OWL tufted owl
HORRENT bristling
HORRIFY appal; terrify; alarm; shock
rl HOSANNA beatific invocation
HOSEMAN fireman
HOSIERY stock of stockings
HOSPICE home for terminally ill patients
HOSTAGE personal pledge (prisoner)
HOSTESS woman giving hospitality
HOSTILE inimical; opposed; (-bid)
HOSTLER ostler
HOTFLUE drying room

HOT-FOOT in haste
HOT-HEAD impetuous; rash
HOTNESS fieriness; ardency;
  fervency
HOT-SPOT internal combustion
HOTSPUR impetuous
HOTTEST most vehement
HOT-TROD Border pursuit
HOT-WALL (fruit culture)
nt **HOUARIO** pleasure sail boat
  (Mediterranean)
zo **HOUBARA** ruffed bustard
HOUGHED hockled; hamstrung
HOUNDED pursued; harassed; dogged
HOUSAGE storage fee
ce **HOUSING** saddle-cloth; sheltering;
  protective cover (machinery)
HOVERED vacillated; lingered
HOVERER waverer; flutterer
HOWBEIT nevertheless
HOWDY-DO ado; fuss; commotion
HOWEVER notwithstanding
HOWLING dreary; lamenting; wailing
zo **HUANACO GUANACO**, llama (Andes)
HUDDLED heaped; piled; mixed
HUDDLER bungler; confused
  cogitator
HUELESS colourless
HUFFILY petulantly; angrily; irritably
HUFFING puffing; swelling;
  (draughts)
HUFFISH hectoring; furious
ck **HUFFKIN** hot larded bread bun
  (Eng.)
HUGGING clasping; embracing;
  necking
HUKILAU Polynesian party
HULKING big and clumsy
HULLING husking; shelling
HUMANLY ethically; rationally
HUMBLED abashed; humiliated
HUMBLER an abaser; mortifier
HUMBUZZ a bull-roarer
HUMDRUM commonplace; prosaic
rl **HUMERAL** Jewish shoulder-veil
pl **HUMERUS** shoulder bone
hd **HUMETTE** heraldic fesse
HUMIDLY damply; dankly
HUMMING bumming; droning
HUMMOCK hommock; hillock
HUMORAL vapourish
bt, br **HUMULIN HUMULUS**, hop extract
HUNCHED bunched; crooked
HUNDRED cantred; county division
HUNGRED hungry; famished
HUNKERS the hams; haunches
HUNTING blood sport; searching;
  chase

el **HUNTING** of thermostat temperature
HURDLED enclosed with a wattle
  fence
HURDLER racing jumper
HURDLES 10 obstacles to overcome
  per event
HURLING casting; flinging; pitching
HURLING ancient form of hockey
HURRIED scurried; accelerated; ran
HURRIED cursory; superficial
HURRIER hastener; quickener; urger
HURTFUL noxious; baleful;
  detrimental
HURTLED whizzed; crashed
HURTOIR a bumper
HUSBAND male spouse; breadwinner
HUSHABY lullaby
HUSHING repressing; calming
zo **HUSKIES** Eskimo dogs; toughs
HUSKING removing husks
HUSSIES worthless women
HUSSITE (John Huss); Moravian
HUSTING an assembly; a council
HUSTLED bustled; elbowed
HUSTLER rent boy
HUSWIFE hussif; housewife
HUTCHED cooped; boxed; confined
HUTMENT a hut
HUTTING temporary building
HYALINE glassy
mn **HYALITE** clear opal
HYALITH dense black Bohemian
  glass; dark sealing wax
HYALOID vitreous
HYDRANT fire-plug
ch **HYDRATE** hydride; hydrous
HYDRIAD water-nymph
HYDROID hydra-like
HYDROUS containing water
HYGEIAN hygienic
HYGIENE sanitary science
vt **HYGROMA** fluid-filled swelling
HYLOIST materialist
HYMNARY hymn-book
HYMNING lauding
HYMNIST hymn-writer
HYMNODY hymn-singing
HYODONT pig-toothed
nc **HYPERON** cosmic-ray particle
zo **HYPNODY** larval resting period
HYPNOID resembling sleep
HYPOGEA cellars; basement
zo **HYPOPUS** cheesemites
HYPPISH hippish; depressing
zo **HYPURAL** below the tail
zo **HYSTRIX** the porcupine

I

IAMBICS classic verse metre
IAMBIZE satirize; versify
IBERIAN Spanish and Portuguese
ICARIAN of Icarus; rash;
  adventurous
go ICEBELT region of ice
ICEBERG floating ice mass
zo ICEBIRD little auk
nt ICEBOAT ICE-FOOT, with sled hull
go ICE-FALL ICE-FLOE, calving of a
  glacier
ICE-FERN with frosty encrustations
ICE-HILL slalom; tobogganing slope
ICEPACK polar glacial barrier
ICEPAIL for chilling wine
ICE-RINK skating rink (natural ice)
mn ICE-SPAR ryacolite
ICHABOD calamity (Heb.)
ICHNITE fossil footprint
ICHTHYS (fish); Christian symbol
ICINESS chilled drinks
pl, pu ICINESS frigidity; personality
md ICTERIC ICTERUS, of jaundice
ICTINUS designer of the Parthenon
IDALIAN sacred to Venus
IDEALLY perfectly; for best result
IDIOTCY IDIOTIC, imbecility; witless;
  fatuous
IDOLISM IDOLIST, of fan club
IDOLIZE venerate; adore (as fan)
IDYLLIC pastoral; poetic
IGNEOUS volcanic in origin
IGNITED lit; kindled; inflamed
IGNITER primer; detonator
IGNITOR electrode of ignition
IGNOBLE dishonourable; low; base
IGNOBLY infamously; unworthily
IGNORED disregarded; neglected
IGOROTE Filipino
gl IJOLITE coarse-grained igneous rock
md ILEITIS ileum inflammation
ILL-BRED poorly brought up
ILLEGAL unlawful; illegitimate; illicit
ILLEISM too much 'he'
ILL-FAME of bad repute
ILLICIT forbidden; banned;
  prohibited
ILLNESS malady; disease; ailment
ILL-TIME mistime
ILL-TURN unkindly act
ILL-USED badly treated
ILL-WILL enmity; odium; spite;
  malice
mn ILVAITE hydrous iron silicate
IMAGERY fanciful concept
IMAGINE dream; think; suppose

IMAGING imagining
rl IMAMATE the parish of a Moslem
  Imam (priest)
IMBIBED IMBIBER, swallowed; toper
IMBOUND impound
bt IMBREKE houseleek
IMBROWN embrown; tan
IMBRUED drenched; soaked; stained
IMBRUTE to brutalize
IMBUING pervading; drenching
IMBURSE financing services in
  advance
IMITATE copy; ape; mimic;
  counterfeit
IMMENSE titanic; colossal; boundless
IMMERSE plunge into; souse;
  engross
IMMORAL against code of conduct;
  vicious
IMMURED shut up; imprisoned
IMPALED fenced in; speared through
  (executed)
IMPASSE deadlock; no escape from
IMPEACH charge with official
  misconduct
IMPEDED hindered; obstructed
IMPERIL endanger; hazard;
  jeopardize
IMPETUS momentum
zo IMPEYAN Indian pheasant
IMPFING crystallization technique
IMPIETY iniquity; profanity
IMPINGE to touch upon; infringe
IMPIOUS irreverent; ungodly
IMPLANT to graft; infuse; instil
IMPLATE to cover with metal;
  sheathe
IMPLIED understood; insinuated
IMPLORE entreat; crave; adjure
IMPORTS inward-bound trade goods
IMPOSED forced; misled
IMPOSER impostor; charlatan
IMPOUND confine; confiscate
IMPRESS stamp; mark; imprint
  respect
IMPREST cash from pressgang
  enrolment
- IMPRINT impress; fix on the mind
IMPROVE armed; ameliorate; raise
cp IMPULSE stimulus; urge to action;
  short signal
IMPUTED attributed; implied
IMPUTER ascriber
IN-AND-IN overly inbred
INANELY vapidly; stupidly
INANITY fatuity; emptiness
INAPTLY untimely; unsuitably
INBEING inherence

INBOARD within the ship (including motor); oar handle

INBOUND inward bound; ball thrown into play (basketball)

INBREAK inburst

INBREED mate with relative

INBURST break in; irruption

INCENSE holy smoke; to enrage; anger

INCHEST embox; encase; (jewels)

INCHING moving gradually

INCHPIN deer's sweetbread

mu **INCIPIT** here begins (Lat.); identifying reference with first bars

INCISED cut; engraved

INCISOR cutting tooth

INCITED roused; fomented; egged

INCITER agitator; agent provocateur

INCIVIL uncivil; impolite

hd **INCLAVE INCLEAVE**, dovetail joint design

INCLINE gradient slope; prefer (opinion)

INCLUDE embody; comprise; contain

INCOMER new arrival; invader; infiltrator

pc, rl **INCUBUS** incumbrance; dead weight; intercourse with devil

rw **INCURVE** circumference of decreasing circle

ml **INCUSED** stamped, hammered; code

ch **INDICAN** a glucoside or acid

ma **INDICES** maths terms; plural of index

INDICIA indications

lw **INDITED INDICTED**, formal accusation

lw **INDITER** legal accuser; prosecuting party

pc **INDOLES INDOLENT**, disposition (anti-effort)

INDOORS within house

INDRAFT INDRAUGHT, inflow of manpower, wind power

ae, zo **INDRAWN** retracted (aircraft wheels during flight); (claws)

INDUCED impelled; prompted; effected

INDUCER persuader; instigator

INDUING ENDUING giving moral strength

INDULGE gratify; humour; pamper

INDWELL of aboriginal inhabitants

el **INEARTH** inter; bury; return contact

INEPTLY not professionally; pointlessly

ps **INERTIA** stationary state (overcome by movement)

INERTLY sluggishly; torpidly

INEXACT unexact; incorrect; faulty

INEYING inoculating; grafting; immunity

lw **INFANCY** stage of the child (birth–18)

INFANTA princess (Spain)

INFANTE prince (Spain – second son)

md **INFARCT** coronary thrombosis; blood stoppage

INFAUST cursed as was Dr Faustus

INFERNO INFERNAL, of hell, heating, destruction

rl **INFIDEL** non-adherent to majority faith

ga **INFIELD** land nearest mansion; (cricket)

INFIXED positioned; fastened; (radar)

md **INFLAME** excite; kindled; body infection sign

INFLATE expand; distend (balloon) (economy)

INFLECT vary pitch (linguistics) (curves)

INFLICT power causing others to suffer

rl **INFULAE** priestly badges

INFUSED inspired; instilled; inculcated

INFUSER a coffee machine; tea-maker

INGENUE naive girl

md **INGESTA** food

INGLOBE ENGLOBE, encircle; ensphere

INGOING direction entering; joining; enrolling

bd **INGOING** visible frame of door, window

INGRAIN root deeply; instil

bd, ar **INGRESS** entrance; portal

IN-GROUP influential, dominant elite

INHABIT dwell; occupy

INHALED breathed in

INHALER respirator

INHERIT acquire by bequest

cp **INHIBIT** ban; prohibit; restrain; warn

INHUMAN merciless; cruel

INHUMED interred; buried

cp **INITIAL** first steps; pre-sign; acronym

INJURED offended; marred; maltreated

INJURER abuser; impairer

INKATHA Zulu loyalist movement

INKHORN portable inkpot

INKLING hint; suggestion; innuendo

INKNEED knock-kneed
INKWELL ink-cup
INLACED enlaced; entwined
INLAWED cf. outlawed
INLAYER cabinet-maker; mosaic
decorator
ck INMEATS offal; innards
ga INNINGS batting turn (baseball;
cricket)
INNUENT of significance; allusion;
slight of character
IN-PHASE (electrical)
cp IN-PLANT automatic data handling
lw INQUEST judicial inquiry
INQUIRE enquire; ask; interrogate
INQUIRY ENQUIRY, (information);
investigation
cp INQUIRY access to programs
INSHOOT pitch to batter (baseball)
INSHORE close to the beach
INSIDER in the know; (-trading,
dealing)
INSIGHT vision; perception
INSINEW innerve; invigorate
INSIPID tasteless; vapid; flat; tedious
INSOOTH in truth
INSPECT supervise; investigate
INSPIRE animate; inflame; imbue
INSTALL instal; instate; induct;
invest
INSTANT current; urgent; prompt
INSTATE install; inaugurate;
introduce
INSTEAD in place of; in lieu
INSULAR of islander; narrow-
minded
md INSULIN (diabetes treatment)
INSURED risks covered against loss
INSURER insurance underwriter
INSWEPT narrowed
INTEGER whole; a whole number
INTENSE acute; vehement; extreme
INTERIM pause; provisional
md INTERNE inmate; boarder; (doctor)
mu INTONED INTONER, chanted; pitched
mu INTRADA entry; preliminary piece
(It.)
mu, rl INTROIT opening anthem (mass)
INTRUDE trespass; butt in
md INULASE an enzyme
INURING enuring; habituating
INUTILE useless (Fr.)
INVADED violated; entered; occupied
INVADER aggressor; raider; attacker
INVALID null and void; infirm; weak
INVEIGH revile; reproach; upbraid
INVERSE reciprocal; inverted
hd INVEXED arched

INVIOUS impassable; untrodden
INVITED offered; requested; bid
INVITER welcomer; enticer; allurer
INVOICE sales note (commercial); bill
INVOKED adjured; implored;
besought
INVOKER summoner; conjuror
INVOLVE implicate; entangle;
embrace
INWARDS internally; to inside
(direction)
tx INWEAVE of woven pattern (cloth)
INWHEEL circling tactics (military)
tx INWOVEN patterns intertwined
(cloth)
md IODIZED treated with iodine
ch, ps IONIZED converted into ions
pc IPSEITY essence of the self
IRACUND irascible; petulant; angry
IRANIAN Persian
IRENICS pacifist theology
IRICISM Irish (Celtic) phrasing
ch IRIDIUM metallic element
IRIDIZE make iridescent
IRISHRY Irish people
IRKSOME tiresome; tedious
IRONIES unexpected contradictions
IRONING flattening; (-out faults)
IRONIST writes dramatic incongruity
ISAGOGE introduction; handbook
ch ISATINE ISATIN, indigo; woad colour
zo ISCHIUM pelvic bone in tetrapods
ISERINE titanic steel
bt ISIDIUM excrescence on lichen
ISLAMIC Mohammedan; Moslem
ISLEMAN islander
ISMATIC faddish; fond of isms
gl ISOBASE land-depression line
ISOBATH under-sea contour
ISODOMA form of masonry
ISODONT uniform teeth
bt ISOETES quill-worts
bt, zo ISOGAMY union of equal gametes
ISOGENY similar origin
ISOGRAM map line linking like
places
ISOHYET (seasonal) rainfall map
ISOLATE insulate; segregate;
dissociate
nc, ps ISOMERS of same weight molecules
mt ISONEPH equal-cloudiness line
mt ISONETH cloud map
ISONOMY equal rights
lw ISONYMY paronymy; equal
zo ISOPODA crustaceans
mn ISOPYRE impure opal
nc ISOSPIN quantum isotopic spin
mt ISOTACH equal wind-speed line

ISOTAXY polymerization characteristic
ISOTONE stable nucleus (atom)
ch ISOTOPE allied element
nc ISOTRON isotope-separating device
pr ISOTYPE picture writing
bc ISOZYME like/unlike enzyme form
ISRAELI Jew (Israel)
hd ISSUANT issuing
ISSUING emanating; proceeding
go ISTHMUS narrow land joining masses
ITACISM Greek egotism
ITALIAN of Italy
pr ITALICS sloping letters
ITCHING skin irritation; restless desires
ITEMIZE note particulars in detail
ITERACY ITERANT, repetition; repeating
ITERATE recapitulate an argument
pl, zo IVORIED with teeth or tusks
bt IVY-BUSY Bacchus's bush
md, vt IXIODIC infested with ticks
mn IXOLITE fossil resin

J

JABBING prodding; stabbing; injecting
zo JACAMAR tropical kingfisher
zo JACCHUS marmoset
bt, mn JACINTH hyacinth; a gem
zo, nt JACKASS donkey; bird; schooner
mn JACKBIT blast-hole drill end
zo JACKDAW a daw
JACKING lifting; abandoning; pulling off
ga JACKPOT poker; total prize; gambling
to, zo JACKSAW metal saw; goosander
nt JACK-TAR a sailor
JACOBIN French revolutionary
nm JACOBUS James (Latin form) coin
tx JACONET muslin
JADEDLY of tiredness; worn out
mn JADEITE a silicate
JADOUBE adjust chesspiece on square
JAGGERY palm sap sugar
JAGGING notching; carousing
JAGHIRE land revenues (Hindu)
JAHVIST scriptural writer
ga JAI-ALAI pelota court, festival
JAILING gaoling; imprisoning
JAINISM an Indian religion
md JALAPIN a purge

ga JAMBONE (cards on table, euchre)
tx JAMDANI JAMDARI, flowery figured muslin
tx JAMEWAR goat hair cloth
JAMMING rock climbing; becoming wedged
JAMMING interference in radio reception
JAMRACH animal mart
JAMSHID King of the genii
JANEITE fan of Jane Austen (writer)
JANGADA timber raft
JANGLED jingled; discordant sound
JANGLER wrangler; petty disputant
JANITOR doorkeeper; (caretaker)
JANIZAR JANISSARY, Turkish palace-guard
ck JANNOCK BANNOCK, scone-like cake
JANNOCK straightforward
JANTILY jauntily; airily; finically
JANTING jaunting; rambling
JANUARY 1st month
tx JAP-SILK a thin kind of silk
mn JARGOON a gem; zircon
JARKMAN begging letter writer
JARRING discordant; grating; clashing
bt, ck JASMINE fragrant flower; (tea)
mn JASPERY JASPOID, like jasper
JAUNTED took a pleasure trip
ga JAVELIN hurling-, spear field event
md JAWBONE Samson's lethal weapon
zo JAW-FOOT maxilliped
JAW-HOLE a sink
nt JAW-ROPE sailing tackle
JAY-WALK careless road-walking, crossing
JAZZING making garish imitations
JEALOUS envious; covetous; resentful
pl JECORAL pertaining to the liver
zo JEDCOCK JUDCOCK, jack snipe
JEERING derision; taunting; scoffing
md JEJUNUM digestive organ
JELLIED congealed
JELLIFY to become gelatinous
JEMIMAS elastic-sided boots; galoshes
lw JEOFAIL an oversight
JEOPARD to hazard; to endanger
JERKING JERK-OFF, spasmodic motion
ch JERVINE white hellebore alkaloid
bt JESSAMY jasmine; a dandy
hd JESSANT heraldic uprising
JESTFUL humorous; witty; sportive
JESTING joking; quipping
nt JETTIED with landing pier (harbour)

nt **JETTIED JUTTED** (-out); breakwater
JETTING spouting (fountains);
emitting
mn **JEWELRY JEWELLERY**, gems, trinkets
bt **JEW'S-EAR** edible fungus
JEZEBEL a flagrant courtesan
JIBBING balking; shying
nt **JIB-BOOM** triangular bowsprit sail
JIB-DOOR flush (fire-proof) door
JIGAJOG JIGJOG, feet movement
(horse)
md **JIGGERS** tropical foot complaint
JIGGING shaking (drinks); dancing
ma **JIGGING** (machines)
JIGGISH frivolous; frolicsome
JIGGLED joggled; wriggled
JILTING discarding; rejecting lovers
JIMCROW of black segregation
(Amer.)
JIM-JAMS nervous apprehension
JINGLED jangled; tingled
JINGLET sleigh-bell clapper
JINKING dodging; twisting
el **JITTERS** fear; distortion
JITTERY nervy; agitated; dithery
JOBBERY financial cheating
conspiracy
JOBBING doing small jobs
JOBLESS unemployed
JOCULAR jokey; jolly; cheerful
JOGGING shaking movement;
stimulation
JOGGING slow running exercise
JOGGLED jostled; shook
bd **JOGGLES** stone jointing
JOG-TROT easy running pace
lw **JOINDER** united action
JOINERY carpentry
JOINING uniting; linking; connecting
JOINTED articulated
to **JOINTER** smoothing plane
JOINTLY in concert; unitedly
bd **JOISTED** floor laying; roof making
JOLLIER merrier; more genial
JOLLIFY celebrate; carouse
JOLLILY heartily; mirthfully
JOLLITY joviality; hilarity; frolic
JOLTING jerking; shaking
JONGLER a wandering minstrel
bt **JONQUIL** narcissus
JOOKERY jokery; trickery
JOTTING memorandum; reference
note
JOUNCED shook; jolted
JOURNAL diary; newspaper; log
JOURNAL spindle bearing; gazette
JOURNEY jaunt; excursion; travel
JOUSTED tilted

JOYANCE gaiety; festivity
JOY-RIDE a trip for pleasure
J-STROKE to correct trim (kayaking)
JUBILEE (fiftieth) anniversary
rl **JUDAISE JUDAIST**, practises Judaism
rl **JUDAISM** Jewish doctrine and rites
rl **JUDAIZE** enforce Jewish religious
rules
zo **JUDCOCK JEDCOCK**, jack snipe
JUDGING trying; deeming;
estimating
JUFFERS square timber
JUGATED coupled; yoked; (con-)
verbs
JUGGING imprisoning; stewing
JUGGINS a simpleton
JUGGLED manipulated; balanced;
swindled
JUGGLER thrower and catcher;
(performer)
pl **JUGULAR** main veins in the neck
zo **JUGULUM** breast/neck region in
birds
ga **JUJITSU JUJUTSA**, Japanese defence
art
mu **JUKE-BOX** a pay-record player
ga **JUKSKEI** horse-shoe throwing (S.
Africa)
JUMBLED disordered; confused
JUMBLER a muddler
JUMPING leaping; bounding
(equestrians)
JUMPING sudden change;
(conclusions)
JUMP-OFF beginning point
JUNCATE JUNKET, picnic; spree
(party)
JUNCOUS rush-like
bt **JUNIPER** coniferous tree; gin-berry
mn **JUNKING** coal-cutting process
JUNKING discarding as worthless
JUNKMAN second-hand dealer
JUPETTE short petticoat
JUPITER a planet
lw **JURALLY** lawfully; legally
JURY-BOX where jury sits
lw **JURY-MAN** juror
JUSSIVE imperative
JUSTICE equity; fairness;
impartiality
JUSTIFY vindicate; exonerate; excuse
pr **JUSTIFY** adjust text
JUTTING projecting; beetling
JUVENAL JUVENILE, a youth
bt **JUWANZA** camel-thorn
zo **JYNGINE** a wryneck bird family

K

KABADDI 12-a-side field game (Far East)

rl KABBALA CABBALA, Jewish oral tradition

KACHINA doll (Amer. Indian)

ck KADAYIF baklava-type pastry (Turk.)

rl KADDISH Jewish funeral prayer

ck KAKAVIA fish soup; cooking pot (Gr.)

KAKODYL cacodyl; noisome liquid

KALENDS 1st day of Roman month

KALMUCH Calmuck; Mongolian

KAMERAD COMRADE! surrender call (German)

zo KAMICHI Brazilian tropical bird

KAMPONG (Malay) court-yard

KANAGAI lacquer work (Japan)

mn KANDITE kaolin minerals group

ml KANTHAL high-resistivity alloy

KANTIAN (Kant); Kantist

KANTISM a philosophy

KAPITIA lacquer (Sri Lanka)

zo KARAGAN Russian fox

rl KARAITE strict Jewish sect

bt KARATAS W. Indian pineapple

KARTING GOKART, primitive motor racing

mu KARYOKE CARYOKE, video-led pub singing

tx KASHGAR white silky Asian wool

KATHODE negative electrode

mn KEATITE synthetic silica form

KECKLED CACKLED, noise of hens (laying)

nt KEDGING warping; moving ships by rope

bt KEDLACK wild mustard

KEEKING PEEPING, prying; spying

KEELAGE harbour tax

nt, zo KEELING codling (codfish); heeling over

nt KEELMAN bargee (skipper or crew)

nt KEELSON keel-plate; (foundation plate)

KEENING wailing; mourning

KEEPING holding; maintaining; conforming

KEEP-NET live fish storage (angling)

KEEVING (fermentation)

zo KEITLOA S. African rhinoceros

KELKING beating; thrashing

KENNING range of vision; knowing

KENOSIS KENOTIC, denial of godhood

KENTISH of West Kent

ch KERASIN brain-substance cerebroside

md KERATIN (horn and hair)

ar KERFING curving bullnose stairs

rl KERMESS Dutch fair

KERNING granulating

KERNISH clownish

mn KERNITE sodium borate

zo KESTREL a falcon

ck KETCHUP a sauce (tomato)

md KETOSIS fat-metabolism toxaemia

KEYBOLT part of lock

KEYCOLD cold as a key

KEYED-UP tense with suspense

KEYHOLE orifice for key

mu KEYNOTE which sets tone

KEY-RING key holder

KEY-SEAT a groove

KEYWORD word showing topic discussed

cp KEYWORD retrieval; significant entry

rl KHALIFA KHALIF, CALIF, Mohammed's representative on earth

mt KHAMSIN hot wind of the Sahara

KHANATE khan's jurisdiction

KHEDDAH enclosure; (elephant hunting)

KHEDIVA wife of a khedive

KHEDIVE chancellor-viceroy of Egypt, 19th C.

rl KHOTBAH KHUTBAH, Moslem prayer and service

KIBBLED fine-ground in a hand mill

KIBBUTZ communal farm (Israel)

KIBITKA Russian vehicle

KICKING spurning; punting

ga KICK-OFF start of play (football)

KIDDIES kids; small youngsters

KIDDING bluffing; joking; jesting

bt KIDDING replanting riverbanks

zo KIDLING young kid-goat; infant

KIDSKIN goat leather

KIKUMON imperial crest of Japan

zo KILLDEE N. Amer. ring plover

nt KILLICK KILLOCK, small stone anchor

KILLING slaying; butchering; tiring

KILL-JOY a sourpuss; puritan

KILN-DRY desiccate; dry in kiln

el KILOVAR volt-ampères unit

tx KILTING wearing national costume (Sc.)

KINDEST most benevolent; helpful

KINDLED set ablaze; incited

KINDLER lighter; an igniter; pyromaniac

KINDRED related; kin; of groups

md KINESIA motion sickness

KINETIC force in motion
bt KINETIN plant growth substance
bt KINGCUP marsh marigold
KINGDOM monarchy; realm;
   dominion
zo KINGLET golden-crested wren
KING-PIN head of organization
KINKING twisting; looping
KINLESS without kindred
KINSHIP relationship
KINSMAN of same family; clan
KIP-SHOP bawdy house; brothel
KIPSKIN sleeping bag
KIRGHIZ of Central Asia (Turkic)
bt KIRIMON KIKUMON, a
   chrysanthemum
KIRTLED wearing a petticoat
KIRUNDI language of Burundi
   (Africa)
KISSING lips touching lovingly
KISSING bowl by jack; bussing
ck, nt KITCHEN cook-house; galley
ga KITCHEN shuffleboard (court arca)
mu KITHARA ancient lyre (Gr.)
KLICKED CLICKED, fell in love;
   (doors)
gl KLIPPEN hill-top outliers
KLISMOS revived ancient chair (Gr.)
ck KLODNIK iced beetroot soup (Pol.)
KNABBED gnawed; bitten
KNACKER cat's meat purveyor;
   slaughterer of horses
KNAPPED snapped; nibbled
KNAPPER flint worker
KNAPPLE snap; nibble
KNARRED knotted
KNAVERY roguery; trickery; fraud
KNAVISH rascally; fraudulent
KNEADED massaged; mixed
KNEADER dough-mixer
md KNEECAP knee-pan
KNEELER prayer cushion; hassock
bd KNEELER pad-stone; kneestone; skew
   table, panel
mu KNELLED tolled (church bells)
KNESSET Israeli Parliament
KNIFING stabbing
tx KNITTED (garments) of wool stitch
KNITTED joined; contracted;
   contrived
KNITTLE a draw-thread
KNOBBED with protruberance
KNOBBLE small boss; handle
KNOBBLY irregular; with knobs on
KNOCKED buffeted; rapped; hit
KNOCKER door rapper; (waker up)
ga KNOCK-ON ball falling forward
   (football)

KNOCK-UP practice game (tennis)
mu KNOLLED pealed (church bells)
bt KNOPPER gall-nut
KNOTTED tied; kinked; entangled
KNOW-ALL a wiseacre
KNOW-HOW technical expertise
KNOWING canny; shrewd; astute
pl KNUCKLE clenched fist; (-duster)
KNUCKLE threaten; (-under); submit
bd KNUCKLE pinholes in a hinge
KOFTGAR metal inlayer (Hindu)
bt KOLA-NUT cola-nut
KOLKHOZ Soviet collective farm
pc KOLYTIC inhibitory processes,
   hindering (Gr.)
KOMATIC long Eskimo sledge
KORANIC (Koran)
KOUMISS fermented mare's milk
KOWTOWED made obeisance
KREATIN creatin; muscle constituent
KREMLIN citadel (Moscow)
KRIMMER grey lambskin fur
KRISHNA an incarnation of Vishnu
KRUPSIS a theological doctrine
KRYPTOL electrical resistant
ch KRYPTON gaseous element
mu KUH-HORN Alpine horn
bt KUMQUAT Chinese citron
KURBASH Arab hippo-hide whip
KURDISH (Kurd)
KURHAUS spa pavilion (Ger.)
KURSAAL the pump-room of a spa
KUWAITI native of Kuwait
KYANISE rot-proofing of timber
mn KYANITE aluminium silicate

L

LABARUM symbolical banner
LABIATE lip-like
LABROSE thick-lipped
bt LACCATE as if varnished
LACCINE (shellac)
LACEMAN lace-dealer
zo LACERTA lizard genus
bt, zo LACINIA leaf incision; maxilla lobe
LACK-ALL destitute
LACKING needing; wanting
LAC-LAKE lac dye
LACONIC concise; pithy; curt; terse
LACQUER varnish
LACTASE lactose-dissolving enzyme
ch LACTATE (lactine); to suckle; milk
   salt
ck LACTEAL LACTEAN, of milk
ch LACTONE hydroxy acid anhydride
LACTOSE LACTINE, a sugar in milk

bt **LACTUCA** lettuce genus
LACUNAE gaps; blanks; chasms
LACUNAL discontinuously
LACUNAR (panelled ceiling)
md **LADANUM** resinous extract
LADINOS Judeo-Spanish Sephardim
ck **LADLING** serving with deep-bowled
spoon
zo **LADY-BUG LADY-FLY**, insect
zo **LADY-COW LADYBIRD**, red-cased
beetle
LADY-DAY 25 March
LADYISH LADYISM, of affected
gentility
LAETARE 4th Sunday in Lent
LAGGARD sluggard; lazy-bones
bd **LAGGING** dawdling; insulation cover
ga **LAGGING** order of play in billiards
LAGOTIC rabbit-eared
rl **LAICIZE** commit to laymen
LAIRAGE cattle depot yard
nt **LAKATOI** large sailing raft (Papua)
LAKELET pool; mere; pond
rl **LAKSHMI** wife of Vishnu
LALIQUE artistic glassware
LALLANS Lowland Scottish dialect
LALLING repetition of a sound
rl **LAMAISM LAMAIST**, of Tibetan
Buddhism
LAMBADA fast erotic dance (Brazil)
LAMB-ALE shearing feast
LAMBENT softy radiant
me **LAMBERT** unit of brightness
LAMBING giving birth
zo **LAMBKIN** baby lamb
LAMBOYS armoured kilts
zo **LAMELLA** thin plate or scale
pl **LAMETER LAMIGER**, a cripple
LAMETTA metal foil
LAMINAL LAMINAR, in plate form
LAMMING thrashing
ch **LAMPATE** a salt
zo **LAMPERN LAMPREY**, eel-fish
zo **LAMP-FLY FIRE-FLY**, illuminated flies
LAMPING ultraviolet detection
LAMPION fairy lamp
LAMP-LIT artificially illuminated
LAMPOON a satirical article
zo **LAMPREY** eel-fish
LANATED woolly
mu **LANCERS** cavalry; a dance
LANCING piercing; cutting
go **LAND-ICE** fresh water; inland, ice
LANDING disembarking; floor; (fish)
mu **LANDLER** Tyrolean waltz; folk song
(Ger., Austrian)
LANDMAN country dweller
LANDTAG Federal parliament (Ger.)

LAND-TAX type of impost
zo **LANGAHA** snake (Madagascar)
mn **LANGITE** copper sulphate
me **LANGLEY** unit of radiation
LANGREL chain-shot
hd **LANGUED** heraldic tongue
LANGUET tongue-shaped
LANGUID LANGUOR, listless; lassitude
LANIARY slaughter-house
LANIARY canine tooth
LANIATE tear in pieces
LANKIER taller and thinner
md **LANOLIN** wool grease; ointment
bt **LANTANA** verbena; herb
LANTERN hand lamp
LANYARD LANIARD, sailor's uniform
rope
LAO-THAI language of Laos
LAOTIAN native of Laos
gl **LAPILLI** volcanic stones; cinders
LAPPING covering exposed copper
(over-)
LAPPING how cats and dogs drink
LAPPISH of Lapland; Saami
ck **LAPSANG** for afternoon tea (China)
LAPSING slipping; failing
LAPUTAN visionary
zo **LAPWING** peewit
LAPWORK overlapping work
lw **LARCENY** theft, pilfering
bt **LARCHES** conifers
LARDING smearing with lard
LARD-OIL a lubricant
ck **LARDOON LARDON**, strip of bacon
LARGELY greatly; abundantly
LARGESSE bounty; alms; gift
LARGEST most capacious; biggest
LARGISH somewhat extensive
mu **LARIGOT** 6-f organ pitch
LARIKIN LARRIKIN, hooligan
(Australia)
LARKING having fun; pranking
LARMIER drip-stone; corona
mn **LARNITE** orthosilicate of calcium
zo **LARVATE** larval; masked
ck **LASAGNE** flat pasta dish (It.)
LASHING whipping; scourging;
upbraiding
LASHKAR LASCAR, N. W. Indian
tribe
eg **LASKETS GASKETS**, anti-leak sealing
LASSOED LASSOES, steer-catching
noose rope
LASTAGE ballast; fishing dues
LASTING abiding; enduring; durable
tx **LASTING** strong twill cloth
bt **LATAKIA** Syrian tobacco
LATCHED fastened; locked; secured

LATCHES door bolts; lock systems
LATCHET shoe-fastening
zo **LATCHET** sapphirine gurnet
zo **LATEBRA** an egg cavity
LATENCE suspended activity
LATENCY force in suspense
LATERAL side by side
cp **-LATERAL** beside; parallel; (bi-) joint
rl **LATERAN** papal palace; church (-councils)
cr **LATHING** lathe workmanship; carving
LATRANT barking
LATRINE camp privy; toilet
LATROBE a form of stove
cp **LATTICE** grid form; network
LATVIAN Lettish; of Latvia
LAUDING extolling; praising
LAUGHED expressed amusement (-at)
LAUGHER game won by a wide margin
LAUNDER wash; ore trough
LAUNDRY the wash
bt **LAURELS** bay leaf crowns of victory
mn **LAURITE** a sulphide
LAUWINE LAVINE, avalanche
LAVOLTA an old dance
zo **LAVROCK** LARK, a song bird
lw **LAW-BOOK** case book (common law)
LAW CALF ditto bound in calf leather
LAWLESS wild; rebellious; disorderly
lw **LAW-LORD** House of Lords' judge
LAW-LORE in a lawyer's library
lw **LAW-SUIT** case in court
md **LAXATOR** a muscle
LAXNESS slackness; negligence
mo **LAYBACK** rock-climbing technique
nt **LAY-DAYS** harbour days; cargo lading
LAYERED stratified
LAYETTE infant's outfit
LAYLAND pasture land
bt **LAYLOCK** lilac
nt **LAY-LORD** civil lord
LAYOUTS aerial somersaults (skiing)
LAZARET hospital
md **LAZARLY** of Lazarus the leper; leprous
LAZIEST most sluggish; idlest
LAZY-BED potato-bed
L-DRIVER learner driver
ch, ps **LEACHED** elements filtered from a mix
LEADING metal roof or cover
LEADING high-ranking; famous; guiding

mu **LEAD-OFF** opening; overture; departure
ga **LEAD-OUT** well-positioned player
LEAFAGE foliage; boscage
bt **LEAF-BED** gemma
LEAF-FAT fat in layers
LEAFING leaf-growth; (gold-)
pt **LEAFING** floating of metal particles
pr **LEAFLET** PAMPHLET, hand-out; advert
ga **LEAGUED** LEAGUER, placed in groups
LEAKAGE divulgence (secrets); liquid loss
LEAKING liquid oozing out, escaping
LEANDER Hellespont swimmer (Gr.)
LEANEST thinnest; lankiest
LEANING penchant; bias; relying
LEAPING jumping; springing
LEARNED erudite, scholarly
LEARNER pupil; tyro; student
LEASHED bound; under control
LEASING falsehood; letting
LEASOWE a pasture
LEATHER tanned animal skin; to thrash
lw **LEAVING** resigning; departing; donating
LECTERN LETTERN, reading desk
LECTION a reading
LECTUAL necessitating bed-rest
LECTURE reproof; rebuke; discourse
md **LEECHED** healed
bt, ck **LEECHEE** LYCHEE, Chinese fruit
nt **LEEFANG** jib sheet
nv **LEEMOST** most leeward
LEERILY wideawake; sly; fly
LEERING ogling
nt **LEE-SIDE** LEE-GAGE, sheltered side
nv **LEE-TIDE** tide with the wind
nv **LEEWARD** down wind
LEFT-ARM cricket
LEGALLY legitimately; licitly
lw **LEGATEE** inheritor of legacy; bequest
LEG-BAIL (absconding)
LEGGATT thatcher's wooden mallet
mu **LEGGERO** light and easy (It.)
LEGGERS barge-pushers
LEGGING a gaiter
LEGGISM black-leggism
zo **LEGHORN** straw hat; fowl
LEGIBLE readable
LEGIBLY clearly written
LEG-IRON ankle to wall fetter
lw **LEGITIM** Bairn's Part
LEGLESS apodal
LEG-PULL a draw; a joke; a hoax
ga **LEG-SIDE** right-handed cricketer's bat side

ga **LEG-SLIP** fielding position (cricket)
LEGTRAP (cricket)
bt **LEGUMEN** vegetable casein; pulse
LEISTER fishing spear (Ice.)
LEISURE restful ease
LEMMATA logical premises
zo **LEMMING** Arctic rodent
LEMNIAN (Lemnos)
nm **LEMPIRA** coin, Honduras
LEMURES spirits in the Roman
household
LENDING loaning; advancing
LENGTHY extended; protracted
LENIENT mild; clement; merciful
md **LENTIGO** a rash; freckle
bt **LENTISK** mastic tree
LENTOID lens-shaped
LENTOUS viscous; tenacious
zo **LEONERO** puma-hunting dogs
as **LEONIDS** meteor shower
LEONINE like a lion
zo **LEOPARD LIBBARD**, the spotted tree
cat
LEOTARD one-piece, stretch costume
md **LEPROMA** leprous swelling
md **LEPROSE** scurfy
md **LEPROSY LEPROUS**, a disease
bt **LEPTOME** phloem elements
LESBIAN female homosexual
LETCHED percolated; filtered
LET-DOWN an avoidable failure
LETHEAN oblivious
LETTERN LECTERN, reading desk
LETTING preventing; hindering
LETTISH Latvian; Lettic
bt **LETTUCE** salad plant
md **LEUCINE** (decomposition)
mn **LEUCITE** volcanic rock
md **LEUCOMA** wall-eye
LEUCOUS albino
md **LEVATOR** a muscle
mt **LEVECHE** dry S. W. wind in Spain
LEVELER leveller
LEVELLY evenly; horizontally
LEVERED raised; lifted
zo **LEVERET** young hare
rl **LEVITIC** of Levites (Hebrew priests)
LEVYING collecting; exacting
LEXICAL alphabetically arranged
LEXICON dictionary
LIAISON co-ordination; intrigue
bt **LIANOID** ground-rooted climbing
plant
gl **LIASSIC** geological formation
LIBERAL bounteous; generous
LIBERTY freedom; emancipation
LIBRARY collection of books
(Public-)

cp **LIBRARY** software; routes
LIBRATE to balance; poise; oscillate
LICENCE permission; excess; warrant
LICENSE to permit; allow; authorize
zo **LICH-OWL SCREECH OWL**, night bird
of prey
rl **LICH-WAY LYCH-WAY**, funeral path
to church
LICITLY lawfully; legally;
legitimately
LICKING a thrashing; a beating
LICKING sucking from the tongue;
tasting
LIE-ABED a sluggard
LIFT-BOY LIFTMAN, elevator operator
LIFTING raising; elevating; stealing
(shop-)
md **LIGATED** bandaged
LIGHTED lit; ignited; illumined
LIGHTEN enlighten; alleviate; ease
LIGHTER barge; brighter; igniter
LIGHTLY buoyantly; airily; joyfully
LIGNIFY become woody
bt **LIGNINE** woody fibre
mn **LIGNITE** brown coal
LIGNOSE cellulose
LIGROIN paraffin
bt **LIGULAR** strap-shaped
LIKABLE attractive; lovable; amiable
LIKENED resembled; compared
bt **LILY-PAD** water-lily leaf
ma **LIMAÇON** heart-shaped curve
LIMBATE bordered; edged
LIMBING dismembering
zo **LIMBOUS** overlapping
tx **LIMBRIC** plain-weave cotton cloth
LIME-LIT illuminated
LIME-PIT limestone quarry
LIMINAL almost conscious
LIMITED restricted; circumscribed
LIMITED liability company, Ltd
LIMITER restraining factor; agent;
signal
LIMNING water-colour painting
mn **LIMNITE** iron ore
md **LIMOSIS** abnormal hunger
LIMPING halting; walking lamely
zo **LIMPKIN** tropical crane
md **LINCTUS** soothing syrup
LINEAGE ancestry; extraction; race
LINEATE lined; (paper) (graphs)
ga **LINEMAN** railwayman; marker
(football)
ga **LINE-OUT** for throw-in (football)
LINGUAL of the tongue, language
LINKAGE cross-cultural mergings
ma **LINKAGE** in mechanics, and
mathematics

pl **LINKAGE** genetics (genes and chromosomes)

ps **LINKAGE** analog; magnetic flux in coils

LINKBOY relay torchbearer (Olympic)

LINKING connecting; joining; merging

ga **LINKMAN** go-between; midfield (football)

bt **LINNEAN** floral classification

pt **LINOXYN** dried film of linseed oil

zo **LINSANG** Indian civet cat; fox

bt **LINSEED** flax-seed

hd **LIONCEL** small lion

zo **LION-CUB** baby lion

zo **LIONESS** lady lion

LIONISM LIONIZE, to build up a person's importance

LIP-BORN hearsay; not genuine

ch, pl **LIPIDIC** of fats, waxes in cells

LIPPING uttering impudent remarks

LIQUEFY melt to liquid state

LIQUEUR a distilled cordial

bt **LIRELLA** ridged apothecium

LISPING speaking with a lisp

LISSOME svelte; lissom; agile

LISTFUL attentive; heedful

LISTING tabulation; choosing

LITERAL verbatim; prosaic exactness

ch **LITHATE** (lithium)

LITHELY actively; pliantly

LITHIUM metallic element; salts

ch, pc **LITHIUM** anti-psychotic drugs

LITHOID stone-like

LITOTES (figure of speech)

LITTERY covered with litter

LITUATE forked

rl **LITURGE** leader in public worship

rl **LITURGY** ritual

LIVABLE habitable

LIVENED cheered up; enlivened

bt **LIVE-OAK** American oak

LIVERED lily-livered; cowardly

LLANERO S. American plain dweller

LOADING cargo; lading; charging

tc **LOADING** distance versus power loss

LOAFING loitering; idling

LOAMING earthing

LOANING lending; advancing

LOATHED hated; detested

LOATHER an abhorrer

LOATHLY reluctant; unwilling; hateful

LOBBIED sought votes

LOBBIES vestibules (in Parliament)

ga **LOBBING** pitching; throwing a ball

LOBCOCK lubber; clumsy fellow

pl, zo **LOBELET** small protrusion; leg

bt **LOBELIA** a flower genus

zo **LOBIPED** having extended feet

zo **LOBSTER** a decapod (10 feet) crustacean

LOBULAR LOBULUS, lobed (ears) etc.

zo **LOBWORM LUGWORM**, sea-bait

LOCALLY in the vicinity

LOCANDA rough Italian doss-house

LOCATED placed; fixed; found

LOCATOR finder

LOCKAGE canal dues; water losses

LOCKIAN (Locke's philosophy)

LOCKING grappling; securing

LOCKIST philosopher

md **LOCK-JAW** tetanus

LOCK-MAN in charge of lockgates (canals)

lw **LOCK-MAN** Under-Sheriff (Isle of Man)

LOCK-OUT exclusion of employees

cp, el **LOCK-OUT** activation of hardware unit

tx **LOCKRAM** coarse linen

LOCULAR cell-like

LOCULUS small cell

bt **LOCUSTA** carob-tree

LODGING abode; accommodation

LOFTIER of greater eminence

LOFTILY arrogantly

LOFTING raising; lifting

ac **LOGATOM** artificial testing word

LOG-BOOK motorcar documentation

nt **LOG-BOOK** official daily record

nt **LOG-CHIP LOG-SHIP**, speed recorder

ga **LOGGATS** (ninepins)

nt **LOGGING** recording

LOG-HEAD a blockhead

LOG-HEAP log-pile; wood-pile

LOGICAL reasonable; deductive; sensible

cp **LOGICAL** entities as appearing to user

nt **LOG-LINE** speed-measuring line

LOGOGEN exact words for clear speech

nt **LOG-REEL** for winding in log-line

LOG-ROLL pulling strings (influence)

bt, pt **LOGWOOD** red dye; openfire wood

rl **LOLLARD** religious sect

LOLLING lounging; (tongue)

bt **LOMARIA** ferns

LOMBARD a banker; a money lender

LONG-AGO remote in time

LONGBOW for medieval archery

LONGEST most protracted

ga **LONG-HOP** (cricket)

LONGING eager desire; yearning

LONGISH somewhat long
ga LONG-LEG (cricket)
pt LONG-OIL high-oil-content varnish
LONG-RUN record amount (theatre shows)
LOOBILY lubberly; clumsily
LOOKING watching; scanning; searching for
LOOKING with threatening eyes
LOOKOUT duty seaman; watcher; sentinel
LOOKOUT panorama point; gazebo
LOOK-SAY word recognition
LOOK-SEE glance; hasty visit
LOOMING coming into sight, approaching
zo LOONING cry of the loon bird
zo LOOPERS (moth caterpillars)
LOOPING circling; knotting; bypassing
LOOPING coloured thread in glass
LOOSELY vaguely; diffusely; slackly
LOOSING relaxing; releasing
LOOTING pillaging; stealing; (war)
LOPPING amputating; curtailing; (trees)
LORDING bossing others
LORELEI a Rhine maiden; rock
LORGNON an eye-glass (magnifying)
LORIMER LORINER, bridle; harness maker
LOTTERY draw (chance); (lots)
LOTTING allocating; cataloguing
LOUDEST showiest; noisiest
ck LOUKOUM LOKUM, Turkish delight
LOUNGED reclined; lolled
LOUNGER flâneur; loafer; idler
LOURING threatening; menacing
LOUSILY despicably; uselessly; badly
LOUTISH clumsy; uncouth; oaflike
LOVABLE amiable; charming; winsome
LOVE-ALL no score (tennis)
bt LOVEMAN a plant
LOVERED having a lover
LOW-BORN of humble birth
LOW-BRED poorly reared
LOWBROW unintellectual
LOWDOWN rascally
LOWERED threatened; frowned
au LOW-GEAR low speed machine
LOWLAND netherland
LOW-LIFE in poverty; degradation; crude
LOWLILY humbly; meekly
LOWNESS dejection; depression
LOW-TECH absence of technology
LOW-TIDE when tide is out

LOXOTIC oblique; distorted
LOYALLY faithfully; devotedly
LOYALTY fealty; fidelity
hd LOZENGE a rhomb; diamond-shaped
LOZENGE a throat pastille
LOZENGY pertaining to above
LUBBARD LUBBER, clumsy fellow
zo LUCANUS stag beetle (insect)
ar LUCARNE LUTHERN, dormer window
LUCENCE LUCENCY brightness; radiance
ag LUCERNE clover for fodder
LUCIDLY clearly; simply; exactly (style)
LUCIFER Satan; a match
LUCIGEN powerful oil lamp
LUCKIER more fortunate
LUCKILY happily; fortunately
nt LUFFING turning toward wind
LUGGAGE baggage; impedimenta
LUGGING tugging; dragging; hauling
LUGMARK earmark
nt LUGSAIL 4-cornered sail
zo LUGWORM lob-worm
LUK-CHIN hybrid Chinese
LULLABY soporific song
LULLING soothing; waning; subsiding
md LUMBAGO muscular rheumatism
md LUMINAL narcotic drug
LUMPIER bumpier; more awkward
LUMPING accepting without satisfaction
LUMPING mixing together for sales; lots
LUMPING laying ready-made rail track
LUMPISH dull; heavy
LUMP-SUM cash down payment
LUNATIC maniac; crazy; insane
ar LUNETTE half-moon; small window
LUNETTE bastion; watch glass; ornament
LUNULAR crescent (moon) shaped
bt, br LUPULIN LUPULUS, extract of hop plant
LURCHED pitched; lurked; shifted
zo LURCHER a lurker; dog
LURKING skulking; awaiting
LUSHING swilling; toping
LUSTFUL lascivious
LUSTIER stronger; sturdier
LUSTILY vigorously
LUSTING desirous
LUSTRAL (purification)
LUSTRUM period of 5 years
LUTEOUS fulvous; tawny
LUTETIA old name for Paris

LUTHERN lucarne; dormer-window
mu LUTHIER lutemaker (and viols) (Fr.)
zo LUTRINE (otter)
LUXATED dislocated
LYCHNIC (vespers, Greek church)
bt LYCHNIS campion plants
bt LYCOPOD a moss
zo LYCOSID wolf spider
LYDDITE a high explosive
md LYING-IN maternity confinement
LYINGLY falsely; mendaciously
pt LYMNATO spray-gun decorating
technique
zo LYNCEAN lynx-eyed; cat's night-
sight
LYNCHED victim of mob-law
LYNCHET unploughed strip
LYRATED lyre-shaped
mu LYRICAL musically poetic

M

MACABRE gruesome; grisly
zo MACACUS baboon
MACADAM road material (asphalt)
zo MACAQUE monkey
bt MACCHIA MAQUIS, scrub; Resistance
(Fr.)
pt MACCHIA first sketch of painting
(It.)
MACE-ALE spiced ale
mn MACERAL elementary coal
constituent
MACHAIR low-lying ground (Gael.)
MACHETE West Indian knife
MACHINE complicated device
MACKITE asbestos plaster
tx MACRAME corded fringe; lace
(Arab)
md, pc MACRONT post-schizogony stage
nt MACSHIP merchant ship (helicopter
carrier)
MACULAE dark sun-spots
MACULAR of body tissue spots
MAD-BRED passionately conceived
MADDEST craziest
MADDING raging; distracted
MADEIRA a wine; a cake
MADLING a lunatic
MADNESS mania; delirium; frenzy
MADONNA Our Lady
zo MADOQUA Abyssinian antelope
mn MADRIER mine-plank
bt MADRONA MADRONO, evergreen tree
(USA)
bt MADWEED black horehound
MADWORT mugwort; cure for rabies

mu MAESTRO eminent conductor
(orchestra)
MAESTRO N.W. wind
(Mediterranean)
MAFFICK rejoice riotously
MAFFLED muddle-headed
MAGALOG magazine-mail-catalogue
MAGENTA purple aniline dye
MAGGOTY grub-ridden (inedible
meat)
MAGICAL talismanic; supernatural
MAGINOT French defensive line
MAGNATE wealthy, influential
businessman
MAGNETO a generator in a car
el MAGNETO- recording disc; tape
(-phone)
MAGNIFY praise; enlarge; augment
bt MAHALEB cherry (Arab.)
MAHATMA adept in esoteric
Buddhism
rl MAHDISM restoration of faith (Islam)
rl MAHDIST of Mahdism; Mahdi
supporter
ga MAHJONG Chinese game
MAHOUND Moslem evil spirit
zo MAHSEER Indian river fish
MAIL-BAG post sack
MAIL-CAR postal van
MAILING posting
MAIL-VAN post vehicle
MAIMING mutilating; crippling
lw MAINOUR stolen property
nt MAINTOP part of rigging
MAISTER maestro; master
bt MAIZENA maize-meal
MAJESTY grandeur; magnificence
MAJORAT primogeniture (Fr.)
bt MALACCA cane
md MALACIA pathological tissue
softening
mn MALACON variety of zircon
MALAISE unease; disquiet
md MALARIA fever
MALAYAN of Malaysia; citizen;
language
MALEFIC maleficent; baneful;
noxious
MALICHO villainy
MALISON a curse; malediction
zo MALLARD wild duck
vt MALLEIN glanders inoculum
md MALLEUS ear bone
MALLING MAULING, biting; injuring
MALMSEY canary wine
ch MALTASE an enzyme (glucose-
splitting)
MALTESE native or language of Malta

br **MALTING** brewing
br **MALTMAN** maltster
ch **MALTOSE** sugar-extracting enzyme
ck **MALTOSE** barley starch sugar
pl **MAMELON MAMMARY**, rounded; glands
zo **MAMMATE** breasted mammals
MAMMOCK shapeless mass; (mangle flat)
MAMMOSE like a bosom
pl **MAMMOTH** elephantine; colossal
zo **MAMMOTH** hairy, extinct elephants
pl **MAMMULA** small protuberance; nipple
MANACLE handcuff; shackle; fetter
MANAGED contrived; administered
MANAGER controller; director
zo **MANAKIN MANIKIN**, small bird; dwarf
zo **MANATEE** sea-cow; dugong
ck **MANCHET** small French loaf
MANCHOO MANCHU, Chinese dynasty
rl **MANDALA** mystic cosmos symbol
MANDATE trust territory; authorization
bt **MANDIOC MANIHOC**, cassava (tapioca) shrub
mu **MANDOLA** mandora; guitar
MANDREL lathe-head
MANDRIL mandrel; spindle
ae **MANETON** heavy gripping pinch-bolt
zo **MANGABY** monkey (Madagascar)
MANGLED laundered; spoiled by bad work
MANGLER indifferent carver (worker)
bt **MANGOLD** mangel-wurzel
MANHOLE underground-channel exit
MANHOOD man's ideal
me **MAN-HOUR** unit of work
MAN-HUNT search for fugitive
bt **MANIHOC MANIHOT, MANDIOC**, cassava manioc shrub
nm **MANILIO** arm-ring; copper coin
MANILLA cheroot; cigar
ga **MANILLE** a card value
lw **MANIPLE** handful; scarf
MANITOU Great Spirit
MANKIND blot on creation
MANLIKE as a man
mn, nt **MAN-LOCK** air lock for pressure changes
MAN-MADE hand-made
MANNING providing a crew
MANNISH masculine
bt **MANNITE** manna-sugar
ch **MANNOSE** a hexose
nt **MAN-ROPE** handrail
ar **MANSARD** two-slope roof

MANSION residence; house
MANTLED cloaked; disguised
MANTLET cloak; testudo
MAN-TRAP snare for trespassers
MANUALE case for papyrus rolled text
MANUMIT free from slavery
ag **MANURED** land spread with droppings
ag **MANURER** cultivator (machine)
MANX-CAT tailless, from Isle of Man
MAPPERY MAPPING, surveying; delineating
MAPPIST cartographer artist
ar, rl **MAQSURA** VIP's concealment in mosques
zo **MARABOU** adjutant stork
zo **MARACAN** parrot
mu **MARACAS** Cuban instrument
MARATHI Mahratta language
ar, ck **MARBLED** veneer grain (marble, cheese)
MARBLER stone-slab decorator
ga **MARBLES** friezes in stone; balls game
mu **MARCATO** as indicated previously (It.)
MARCHED movement of troops on foot
MARCHEN folk-stories
MARCHER border-defender
go **MARCHES** borderland territories
md **MAREMMA** marsh; malaria
mn **MARGODE** bluish stone
bt **MARGOSA** Indian tree
zo **MARIKIN** marmoset
mu **MARIMBA** kind of xylophone
nt **MARINER** sailor; seafarer
zo **MARIPUT** civet cat
pc **MARITAL** of husband and wife relationship
zo **MARKHOR** wild goat
MARKING branding; labelling
MARLINE rope
nt **MARLING** binding
mn **MARLITE** variety of marl
MARLPIT clay-pit
zo **MARMOSE** opossum
MARPLOT spoil-sport
MARQUEE large tent
MARQUIS French nobleman
MARRANO Jew converted to Christianity
MARRIED spliced; wedded
MARRING spoiling; interrupting
MARROWY full of marrow
MARSALA a light wine
MARSHAL arrange; harbinger; officer

MARTEXT careless preacher
MARTIAL warlike; military
MARTINI rifle; cocktail
mn **MARTITE** variety of haematite
hd, zo **MARTLET** house martin (bird)
MARXIAN according to Marx's theories
MARXISM MARXIST, the idea; communist
MARYBUD marigold
MASCARA eye shading (cosmetics)
MASCLED net-like
hd **MASCULE MASCULY**, lozenge-shaped
ck **MASHING** rendering mushy
MASHLIN MASHLUM, mixed grain
ck **MASH-TUB** where malt processed
MASKING disguising; hiding; revels
cp **MASKING** bit pattern
MASONIC of freemasons; fraternity
bd, ar **MASONRY** stone work (construction)
md **MASSAGE** kneading body and muscles
cp **MASSAGE** manipulate figures, data
md **MASSEUR MASSEUSE**, physiotherapist; osteopath
MASSING assembling; accumulating, heaping
MASSIVE bulky; weighty; ponderous
MASSORA Biblical references
MASTABA Egyptian tomb
MASTERY skill; supremacy
MASTFUL full of beech-nuts
bt **MASTICH** gum; mastic
zo **MASTIFF** large strong dog
nt **MASTING** system of masts
md **MASTOID** nipple-shaped
md **MASTOID** bone behind ear
MATADOR bull-fighter
MATADOR a domino game
MATCHED tallied; harmonized
MATCHES contests; lucifers
to **MATCHET MACHETE**, cutlass
MATELOT a sailor (Fr.)
MATERIA as substance
MATINAL MATINEE, early theatre show
MATRASS chemical retort
bt **MAT-REED** reed-mace
cp **MATRICE MATRIX**, (dieplate); key
nt **MATROSS** assistant gunner
md **MATTERY** purulent; pus discharge
MATTING floor cover; silver technique
to **MATTOCK** pick-adze for roots and stiff ground
MATTOID cogenital idiot
MATURED experienced; ripened; payable

MAUDLIN drunk and silly
ga **MAULING** tearing flesh; attacking (rugby)
MAUNDER move idly; mutter drivel
rl **MAURIST** a Benedictine monk
MAWASHI silk cummerbund belt of sumo wrestler
MAWKISH squeamish
bt **MAW-SEED** poppy-seed
zo **MAW-WORM** tape-worm
pl **MAXILLA** upper jaw bone
MAXIMAL greatest; upper limit
MAXIMED proverbial
MAXIMUM greatest quantity, value etc.
MAXIMUS senior (of a group)
el **MAXWELL** unit of magnetic flux
zo **MAY-BIRD** wood-thrush
MAY-DAY *M'aider* International 'Help' Call
MAY-DAY 1 May, Spring Labour day
bt **MAY-DUKE** cherry
MAY-GAME May day sport
MAY-LADY May-queen
bt **MAY-LILY** spring flower
MAY-MORN start of May celebrations
MAYORAL of the town mayor; official
MAY-POLE ribboned for folk dancing
MAY-TIME of hawthorn and spring revels
bt **MAY-WEED** camomile flower
bt **MAZAGAN** bean
MAZARIN deep blue
MAZDEAN godlike
MAZEFUL intricate, labyrinthine
mu **MAZURKA** Polish country dance
ga **MAZURKA** ice-skating jump
MAZZARD skull; cherry
MEADOWY pasturable
MEAL-ARK meal-chest
MEALMAN grain merchant
MEANDER aimless wandering river course
MEANING purport; import; signifying
md **MEASLED** spotted
md **MEASLES** spotty diseases; tapeworms
ma, pr **MEASURE** unit of amount or dimension
MEASURE estimate; regulate; mark out
zo **MEAT-FLY** blow-fly or other parasite
MEAT-TEA consommé of meat base
MEAT-TUB for preserved or pickled meat

MECCANO do-it-yourself construction kit
MECHLIN lace
md MECONIC (opium)
rl MEDALET small medal
MEDDLED interfered; muddled
MEDDLER busybody
MEDIACY dispute-solving process ·
mu MEDIANT a tone
MEDIATE negotiate a settlement (claims)
md MEDICAL concerning doctors' treatments
md MEDINAL soporific drug
pl MEDIOLA bone in cochlea (ear)
md MEDULLA marrow; pith; inner core of organ
zo MEDUSAE Gorgons; hydrozoans
MEDUSAN (petrifying, of gorgons)
zo MEERKAT mongoose (S. Africa)
MEETING encounter; conference; (sport)
cp MEGABIT one million binary digits
MEGAERA one of the Furies
me MEGA-ERG a million ergs
MEGAFOG multiple foghorn
zo MEGAPOD having large feet
MEGARON ancient Gr. house
MEGASSE megass; cane residue
me MEGATON measure of explosive force
vt MEGRIMS giddiness; staggers
MEIOSIS hyperbole; cell division in gametes
MEISSEN (Dresden china)
MELANGE medley; farrago; jumble
MELANIC black
md MELANIN black skin pigment
md MELASMA black spots
bt MELILOT sweet-scented clover
mu MELISMA melodic ornamentation
bt MELISSA herb; balm
mn MELLITE honey-stone
MELLOWY mellow; soft; unctuous
mu MELODIC tuneful; harmonious
MELROSE honey of roses
MELTING from solid to liquid; fusion
pl MEMBRAL concerning limbs, body
MEMENTO keepsake; souvenir
MENACED alarmed; frightened
MENACER threatener; intimidator
MENDING repairing; amending
MEN-FOLK in contrast to women
pl MENINGE of brain, spinal membranes
MENIVER miniver; white fur
ch MENTHOL peppermint camphor
MENTION remark; state; cite; declare

fr MERANTI Malayan hardwood
MERCERY haberdashery
MERCIES small fortunate circumstances
as MERCURY planet; Hermes (messenger)
ch, cp MERCURY quicksilver; acoustic delay
MERGING absorbing; blending; uniting
cy MERISIS cell-division size increase
MERITED deserved; earned; incurred
zo, ck MERLING the whiting (fish)
MERMAID sea woman with fish tail
MERRIER more cheerful; festive
MERRILY joyously; blithely; happily
MESHING netting
mt MESOBAR region of normal atmospheric pressure
MESODIC (intermediate system)
MESOPIC night vision
bt MESOPOD central-stipe fungus fruit
zo MESOTIC paired cartilage in birds
MESSAGE despatch; missive; errand
tc MESSAGE information to be transmitted
rl MESSIAH MESSIAS, heavenly saviour
MESSING muddling; communal feeding
ck MESS-TIN a soldier's canteen food-dish
MESTINO MESTIZO, half-caste Sp. Indian
zo METAGON cytoplasmic particle; amoeba
zo METAZOA multicellular animals
ch, mm METHANE marsh-gas; firedamp
pm METHOIN anticonvulsant chemical
METOCHE an architectural interval
as METONIC lunar cycle of 19 years
METONYM attribute representing a thing
METOPIC superficial
md METOPON opium-based drug
zo METOTIC behind auditory vesicle
zo METOVUM nutrition-surrounded ovum
METRICS versification; mensuration
ma METRIFY metricate; decimalize
METRIST a ballad-monger
METTLED high-spirited
MEWLING squalling
MEXICAN citizen of Mexico
MEXICAN wave, ripples in crowds; statistics
bt MEZQUIT MESQUIT, a Mexican tree
md MIASMAL airborne infection
MIAUING mewing
MIAULED caterwauled

MICELLA foundation structure of cell walls
ch MICELLE aggregate of molecules
MICHING pilfering
md MICROBE germ; bacillus
me MICROHM electrical resistance
MIDDEST middlemost
MIDGARD cf. Asgard (Scand.)
MID-HOUR crossword combination
MIDI-BUS medium-sized bus
MID-IRON golf-club
MIDLAND some way from the coast
MID-LIFE halfway to death
MIDMOST middlemost; central
MID-NOON midday
MIDRASH Jewish commentary
md MIDRIFF diaphragm; garment
nt MIDSHIP middle of ship
bd MIDSPAN between beam support
MIDWIFE birth assistant
mn MIEMITE limestone
MIGRANT nomad; wandering; roving
MIGRATE annual transit of birds (reindeer)
MILDEST calmest; blandest
MILDEWY mouldy; musty; rusty
MILEAGE distance travelled
bt MILFOIL the yarrow
md MILIARY a fever
MILITIA citizen army
MILK-BAR snack bar
MILKMAN milk distributor
MILK-RUN routine round
MILKSOP effeminate fellow
MILL-COG water-wheel tooth
MILL-DAM mill reservoir
MILLIAD 1000 years
me MILLIER a thousand kilos (2204 lbs)
MILLING struggling; grinding
MILLION 1,000,000
nm MILLREA MILLREIS, Port., Brazilian coins
MILTING spawning
MILVINE (kite family)
MIMESIS MIMETIC, MIMICRY, imitative miming
bt MIMULUS musk plant
rl MINARET prayer tower (mosque)
MINCING grinding; affecting; -words
MINDFUL heedful; wary; attentive
MINDING attending to; objecting to
pc MINDSET imprinted, accepted attitudes
mn MINERAL planetary substance
rl MINERVA Pallas Athene (Gr.)
MINETTE biotite-orthoclase lamprophyre
MINEVER MINIVER, plain white fur

MINGLED joined; associated; jumbled
MINGLER a mixer; blender; compound
MINIATE to paint red
MINIBUS bus for a dozen or so
MINICAB private hired car
MINIKIN small pin; pet; favourite
MINIMAL MINIMUS, smallest (youngest son)
MINIMUM least quantity
MINIOUS vermilion
MINIVER plain white fur
zo MINORCA a fowl
rl MINSTER cathedral; monastery church
MINTAGE coinage; mint dues
MINTING coining; inventing
MINTMAN coiner
ma MINUEND number to be diminished; subtraction
MINUTED briefly recorded
MINUTIA detailed detail (trivial)
MIOCENE geological period
MIOLNIR Thor's hammer
MIRACLE prodigy; supernatural event
MIRADOR balcony; viewpoint (Sp.)
ck MIRATON beef/onion stew (Fr.)
MIRBANE (bitter almonds)
MIRIFIC marvellous; wondrous
MISBORN of illegitimate, improper origin
MISCALL revile; with abusive title
MISCAST actor in unsuitable role
MISCITE misquote; mislead
MISCOPY reproduce falsely
ga MISCUED wrong aim (snooker; billiards)
MISDATE put wrong date on
MISDEAL faulty card distribution
MISDEED fault; crime; trespass
MISDEEM judge wrongly
MISDOER delinquent; malefactor
MISDONE ill-done
MISDRAW draft badly
MISERLY parsimonious; niggardly
MISFALL mishap; misadventure
cp MISFEED hopper fault (punched cards)
MISFIRE fail to go off; (firearm)
MISGAVE filled with doubt
MISGIVE mistrust; doubt
rl MISHNAH MISHNIC, Jewish oral law
MISKICK (football) misdirections
MISLAID temporarily lost
MISLEAD dupe; delude; hoodwink
MISNAME misterm; miscall
MISPLAY foozle

MISRATE rate erroneously
MISREAD read incorrectly
MISRULE anarchy; chaos; riot
MISSAID incorrectly stated
MISS-HIT cricket
MISSILE bullet; projectile
MISSING lost; lacking; absent
MISSION trust; errand; embassy
MISSISH girlish; affected
MISSIVE missile; letter; message
MISSUIT not harmonize
MISTAKE err; error; fault; oversight
MISTELL misstate; misrepresent
MISTILY hazily; obscurely
MISTIME judge occasion poorly
mt MISTRAL a cold N. or N.W. wind (Fr.)
MISUSED abused; squandered
rl MITHRAS MITHRA, Persian/Roman god
MITOGEN MITOSIS, somatic cell division
MITRATE mitre-shaped
cr MITRING carpenters' wood joint
MIXABLE can be blended or united
MIXEDLY with mixed feelings
MIXED-UP confused; disordered; hotch-potch
MIXTION gold-leaf fixative
MIXTURE combination formula; rigid blend
mt MIZZLED mist-and-drizzled
rl MJOLNIR MIOLNIR, Thor's hammer (Norse)
MOABITE a tribe (in modern Jordan)
MOANFUL mournful; grievous
MOANING deploring; repining
MOBBING crowding around
MOBBISH tumultuous; disorderly
MOBILES free-hanging ornaments
MOB-RULE lynch law (Mafia dominance)
MOBSMAN well-dressed swindler
MOBSTER gangster; hoodlum; ruffian
MOCKADO ancient woollen fabric; tawdry
MOCKERY scorn; derision; ridicule
MOCKING taunting; jeering
mn MOCK-ORE a zinc ore
MOCK-SUN a parhelion
MODALLY conditionally
MODESTY chastity; propriety
MODICUM small quantity
mu MODINHAR Portuguese popular song
MODISTE dressmaker
MODULAR MODULUS, factor of a function

bd, el MODULOR proportional units (buildings)
zo MODWALL bee-eater (bird)
ga MOEBIUS aerial somersault (skiing)
MOELLON masonry-filling
MOFETTE (earth-fissures)
MOHICAN Algonquin Indian
mn MOHSITE titanite of iron
nm MOIDORE Portuguese gold coin
MOILING toiling; drudging
MOINEAU bastion (Fr.)
MOISTEN damp; add water
mn MOLASSE sandstone
zo MOLE-RAT a rodent
nt MOLETTA MULETTA, fishing boat (Port.)
MOLIMEN strenuous effort
MOLLIFY pacify; alleviate; soothe
MOLLINE emollient base
zo MOLLUSC (snail; cuttlefish; octopus)
MOLOSSI (3 long syllables)
MOMENTA masses having velocity
ch MONACID with one hydroxyl group
ch, cp MONADIC single operand process
MONARCH ruler of Kingdom, Empire
zo MONAXON of one axis only
MONEPIC comprising one word
zo MONERAL MONERON, protozoans
MONERGY saving money and energy
MONEYED rich; wealthy; opulent
MONEYER coiner
MONGREL mixed breed
MONIKER nickname
MONITOR overseer; mentor; adviser
nt MONITOR big-gun naval craft
cp MONITOR radio deviation censor; nozzle
rl MONKERY MONKISH, monastic; monk-like
zo MONKEYS non-human primates; scamps
MONKISH monastic
MONOCLE eye-glass
MONODIC monotonous and mournful
zo MONODON narwhal
bt MONOGYN type of plant
ch MONOMER single-molecule substance
MONONYM MONOMIAL, single-term name
MONOPOD single-foot chair; table (Roman)
md MONOTIC affecting 1 ear only
MONSOON MAVSIM, Indian rainy season
MONSTER abnormal; horrifying; huge (ogre)

MONTAGE film editing
MONTANT fencing term
MONTERO horseman-cap (Sp.)
MONTHLY menses
MONTOIR mounting-stone (Fr.)
zo MONTURE saddle-horse (Fr.); mount
MOOCHED loitered; mouched
MOOCHER thief; aimless wanderer
MOODILY morosely; capriciously
lw MOOKTAR Indian lawyer
MOOLVEE doctor of Moslem law
zo MOONEYE lake fish
MOONING day-dreaming
MOONISH fickle; variable
MOONLIT visible in moonlight
MOON-MAD moonstruck
MOON-SET the setting of the moon
MOORAGE anchorage
zo MOORHEN water-hen
MOORING boat tie-up
ar, rl MOORISH MORESQUE, Arab décor
(Morocco)
MOOTING suggesting; debating
lw MOOTMEN debating law students
MOPPING dabbing; wiping
gl MORAINE glacial debris; pile-up
pc MORALLY of right, ethic conduct
MORASSY marshy; swampy; boggy
mu MORBIDO of gloom; disease; dire
situation (It.)
MORDANT biting; caustic; (style)
mu MORDENT a trill
bt, ck MORELLO sour red cherry
mu MORENDO dying; slowing down (It.)
ar MORESCO MORESQUE, Moorish art
design
bt MORICHE American palm
bt MORINGA Malay tree
MORISCO Moorish; moresco
MORLING dead sheep or its wool
zo MORMOPS repulsive-looking bats
MORNING dayspring; daybreak
MOROCCO goatskin leather
MOROSIS feeble-mindedness
md MORPHEW scurf
MORPHIA opium extract
bl MORPHIC form and structure; shapes
MORRION open helmet
MORSURE the act of biting
pc MORTIDO death wish; energy
(Thanatos)
MORTIFY putrefy; fester; corrupt
MORTIFY bodily self-denial;
humiliate
cr MORTISE and tenon joint; door lock
lw, rl MOSAISM MOSAIC, of Moses
ck MOSELLE MOSEL, light wine
(Germany)

MOTHERY MOTHERLY, maternally;
protective
MOTTLED variegated; spotted
pt MOTTLER brush for graining,
marbling
MOTTOES pithy maxims
MOUCHER skulker
zo MOUFLON wild sheep
MOUILLE liquid tone
MOULAGE casting footprints
MOULDED kneaded; shaped
MOULDER metal-caster; crumble
MOUNDED banked; fortified
MOUNTED on horseback; ascended;
framed
MOUNTER climber
MOURNED grieved; keened; wailed
MOURNER bewailer
ck MOUSAKA moussaká; Gr. dish
MOUSING cat-work
MOUTHED orated; chewed
MOUTHER stump-orator; ranter
MOVABLE portable; mobile
ag MOW-BURN slash-burn (field
clearance)
ar MOZARAB Christianized Arab (Sp.)
art
rl MOZETTA cardinal's cape
MUCKING dung-raking; seeking
scandal
md MUD-BATH skin, health treatment
nt MUD-BOAT dredger
MUD-CART night-soil pick-up
service
MUD-CONE mud volcano
MUDDIED fouled; dirtied; soiled
MUDDING smearing with mud
MUDDLED misused; confused;
fuddled
MUDDLER mixer; fuddler
zo MUD-FISH the bow-fin
MUD-FLAT low-tide bank
MUD-HOLE waterside residence
MUD-LARK to play in/with mud
mn MUDLINE water/slurry division
line
MUD-SCOW (dredging)
cr MUD-SILL tide mud level; soleplate
MUD-WALL soil embankment
bt MUD-WORT aquatic plant
rl MUEDDIN MUEZZIN, Moslem prayer-
caller
MUFFING botching; fluffing;
bungling
MUFFLED wrapped; deadened;
dulled
tx MUFFLER silencer; scarf
MUFFLON MOUFLON, wild sheep

MUGGARD sullen; displeased
zo **MUGGENT** wild freshwater duck
MUGGING ruffianly street assault
MUGGINS simpleton; a juggins
MUGGISH damp and warm
MUGIENT bellowing like cattle
bt **MUGWORT** wormwood plant
MUGWUMP independent politician; idiot
MULATTO with black and white parentage
ag **MULCHED** applied compost dressing on soil
MULCTED fined; swindled
nt **MULETTA MULETTO**, fishing boat (Port.)
MULETTE Portuguese sailing vessel
bt **MULLEIN** yellow plant
MULLING warming and spicing
MULLION munnion; uprt. window bar
mn **MULLITE** aluminium silicate
MULLOCK rubbish; dirt
MULTURE grain grinding
MUMBLED muttered
MUMBLER indistinct articulator
nc **MU-MESON** elementary particle
MUMMERY MUMMING, pantomiming; merrymaking
MUMMIED embalmed; caused to shrivel
MUMMIFY make a mummy
MUMMOCK ragged coat
MUMPING mockery; begging tricks
MUMPISH dull; sullen
MUNCHED crunched; chewed
MUNCHER a masticator
MUNDANE worldly; secular; temporal
MUNDIFY cleanse; purify
bt **MUNJEET** Siberian madder
MUNNION a mullion
MUNTING a door upright
zo **MUNTJAK** barking deer
ar **MUQARNA** stalactite decoration; arabesque
zo **MUREXAN MURICES**, Tyrian purple (shellfish) dye
ch **MURIATE** hydrochloric
MURKIER more overcast
MURKILY duskily; luridly; darkly
vt **MURRAIN** cattle disease
mn **MURRINE** fluorspar
MURRION morion; helmet
bt **MUSCARI** grape hyacinth
mn **MUSCITE** fossil moss
MUSCLED muscular
bt **MUSCOID** moss-like
MUSEFUL pensive; meditative

MUSETTE refreshments haversack (cyclists)
MUSHING dog-sleighing
MUSICAL tuneful; harmonious
zo **MUSIMON** moufflon
MUSK-BAG perfume sachet
zo **MUSK-CAT** civet cat
MUSKILY like musk
zo **MUSK-RAT** the musquash
MUSROLE nose-band of a bridle
zo **MUSTANG** wild horse
bt **MUSTARD** sinapis
zo **MUSTELA** weasel
MUSTILY sourly; acridly; frowsily
MUSTING growing mouldy and rank
MUTABLE changeful; fickle; unstable
MUTABLY variably; inconstantly
md **MUTAGEN** mutation producer
MUTANDA things to be altered
MUTTONY resembling mutton
MUZZILY confusedly; dizzily
MUZZLED forcibly restrained
md **MYALGIA** cramp
md **MYALGIC** tense; stiff
MYALISM W. Ind. magic cult
zo **MYARIAN** (mussels)
bt **MYCELIA** mushroom spawn
zo **MYCETES** howler monkeys
md **MYCOSIS MYCOTIC**, fungoid growth (infection)
MYELOID marrow-like
md **MYELOMA** bone-marrow malignancy
vt **MYIASIS** parasitism by fly lavae
zo **MYLODON** extinct sloth
md **MYOCELE** muscle hernia
zo **MYOCOEL** coelomic space in myotome
zo **MYOCYTE** ectoplasm layer of protozoa
zo **MYODOME** eye-muscle chamber
MYOGRAM (muscular movement)
md **MYOLOGY** (muscles)
zo **MYOMERE** somite muscles
zo **MYONEME** ectoplasm fibril in protozoa
zo **MYOTOME** muscle merome
md **MYOTOMY** dissection
MYOXINE pertaining to doormice
MYRINGA ear-drum
bt **MYRRHIC MYRRH**, labdanum and resin scent
MYRRHIN MYRRHOL, extract and oil
MYSTERY a craft; enigma
MYSTICS a sect
MYSTIFY nonplus; perplex; bewilder
MYTHIST a recorder of legends
zo **MYTILUS** mollusc genus; mussels
zo **MYXOPOD** a protozoan

N

NABBING grabbing; seizing
NACARAT bright orange-red colour
NACELLE body of aeroplane
NACODAH Arab sea-captain
mn **NACRITE** pearl-like
mn **NACRITE** clay mineral
NACROUS pearly
md **NAEVOID** (birthmark)
NAEVOUS freckled
NAFFING make oneself a fool
NAGGING incessant scolding
NAIADES water nymphs
NAILERY nail factory
NAILING spiking; fastening
NAIL-ROD nail material
NAIVELY artlessly; candidly
NAIVETE ingenuousness
NAIVETY unaffected simplicity
NAKEDLY uncovered; starkly
zo **NAMAQUA** African dove
zo **NANDINE** civet cat (W. Africa)
tx **NANKEEN** buff coloured cloth
  (Nankin)
NAOLOGY study of church buildings
mn **NAPHTHA** rock-oil
NAPLESS threadbare
NAPPING dozing; snoozing; unalert
ga **NAPPING** horse's refusal to perform
pc **NARCISM NARCISSISM**, self-love
  (Gr.)
md **NARCOMA** narcotics coma
md **NARCOUS NARCOSE**, stupor-inducing
bt **NARDINE** spikenard
NARGILE Eastern pipe; hubble-
  bubble
NARRATE chronicle; describe; report
rl **NARTHEX** church porch with lean-to
  roof
zo **NARWHAL** sea-unicorn; whale
zo **NASALIS** proboscis monkey
NASALLY through the nose
mu **NASARDE** organ stop
NASCENT natal; originating;
  incipient
md **NASITIS** nasal inflammation
NASTIER more disagreeable
NASTILY offensively; nauseously
NATTERY peevish; captious
NATTIER French blue; smarter
NATTILY neatly; sprucely
NATURAL an idiot; normal; inherent
NATURED temperamentally disposed
NATUREL unadulterated
NAUGHTY forward; perverse
NAUPEGY ship-building
zo **NAUPLII** crustaceans

nt **NAUTICS** art of navigation
zo **NAUTILI** cephalopods with
  chambered shells
NAVARCH an admiral (Greek)
NAVARHO aircraft navigation system
ck **NAVARIN** mutton/vegetable stew
bt **NAVETTE** rape plant
NAVVIES labourers; canal diggers
NAVY-CUT rope-bound tobacco
  sliced
NAYWORD by-word; watch-word
NAZIISM German national socialism
NEAD-END show end
md **NEALOGY** embryology
NEAREST closest; stingiest
NEARING approaching; drawing nigh
NEATERY place to buy meat (17th c.)
NEATEST sprucest; tidiest; trimmest
NEATNIK anti-beatnik
NEBULAE gaseous matter
NEBULAR cloudy; vague; hazy
ar **NECKING** embracing; an annulet
NECKLET small necklace
NECKTIE cravat
bt **NECTARY** honey-gland
NEEDFUL essential; vital; requisite
NEEDIER rather worse off
NEEDILY necessitously
NEEDING wanting; lacking
NEEDLED pierced; sown;
  embroidered
NEEDLED persuaded against will
NEEZING NEESING, sneezing
NEGATED denied; mollified
NEGATER computer inverter
el **NEGATON** negative electron
cp **NEGATOR** NOT element; reverse
  binary
lw **NEGATUR** it is denied
NEGLECT disregard; omission
NEGLIGE loose attire; negligee
NEGRESS NEGROID, woman
NEGRITO pygmy (Polynesia)
NEGROID negro-type
bt **NEGUNDO** box-elder
zo **NEIGHED** whinnied call (of horse)
NEITHER not either; not the one
bt **NELUMBO** water-lily; lotus
ps **NEMATIC** with parallel orientation
NEMESIC retributive; final
  judgement
NEMESIS goddess of vengeance
NEMORAL arboreal
gl **NEOCENE** geological epoch
gl **NEOCENE** rock formation
mn **NEOLITE** silicate of aluminium
NEOLITH 'stone-ager' slang epithet
NEOLOGY (new terms); rationalism

NEONATE reborn; immaturity; new
ideas
NEORAMA interior view of building
zo **NEOTENY** larval-character retention
zo **NEOTYPE** evolution within species
NEOZOIC geological system
md **NEPHRIA** Bright's disease
pl **NEPHRIC** of the kidney
pl **NEPHRON** excretory unit in kidney
NEPOTIC favouring the family
as **NEPTUNE** sea-god; planet
mn **NEREITE** fossil centipede
nt **NERITIC** of shallow coastal waters
bt **NERVATE** veined
md **NERVINE** nerve tonic
NERVING summoning resolution
NERVOSE having nerves
NERVOUS sensitive; timid; fearful;
tense
pl **NERVOUS** neural system; neuronal
bt **NERVULE** vein in leaf
zo **NERVURE** vein in insect wing
NESIOTE living on an island
NEST-EGG cash savings
NESTING nidification (birds); home-
making
cp **NESTING** instructional loops
NESTLED cherished; lay close
NESTLER a snuggler; cuddler
ga **NETBALL** 7-a-side; like basketball
ga **NET-CORD** divides the tennis court
NETSUKE Japanese fastening
NETTING wall or curtain of net; trap
NETTLED stung; fretted; irritated
NETTLER a provoker
tx **NETWORK** mesh; cord; fabric;
curtain
NETWORK social, influential contacts
cp, tc **NETWORK** chain series; data
transmission
md **NEURINE** nerve-matter
NEUROID nerve-like
md **NEUROMA** tumour
NEURONE nerve cell
NEUROSE veined
zo **NEURULA** stage of embryo
development
ec **NEUSTON** water-surface animals
NEUTRAL unbiased; indifferent
nc **NEUTRON** uncharged particle
mt **NEVADOS** mountain wind, Andes, S.
America
NEW-BORN just hatched
NEWCOME recently arrived
NEW-LAID fresh eggs
NEW-MADE novel; fresh; neoteric
NEWNESS novelty
NEWSBOY paper seller

NEWSMAN reporter
gl **NIAGARA** waterfall; torrent (N.
America)
NIBBLED lightly chewed
NIBBLER dainty feeder
NIBLICK a golf club
NICKING stealing; notching
NICTATE wink
NIDGING stone dressing
bt **NIGELLA** love-in-a-mist
NIGGARD a miser; covetous; sparing
NIGGLED trifled
NIGGLER fuss-pot
NIGHTED benighted
NIGHTIE nightdress; robe de nuit
NIGHTLY every evening
mn **NIGRINE** an ore of titanium
NIGRITE insulating material
NILLING unwilling
NILOTIC of the river Nile
NIMBLER more agile; quicker;
swifter
NIMIETY excessiveness
ml **NIMONIC** high-temperature-work
alloy
ga **NINE-PIN** skittle
NIOBEAN (Niobe); lachrymose;
tearful
ch **NIOBIUM** metallic element
bt **NIPBONE** herb comfrey
to, zo, pl **NIPPERS** pincers; crabs' claws;
youth
NIPPIER quicker; more agile
NIPPING biting; pinching; fleeing
NIRVANA peace in unity with
creation
rl **NIRVANA** liberation from desires
NITENCY effort; brightness
NITHING poltroon; idiot
ch **NITRATE NITRIDE**, nitrogen salts
ch **NITRIFY** convert to nitre
ch **NITRILE** alkyl cyanide
ch **NITROUS NITROSE**, of nitrogen
rl **NJORTHR** a Vanir (Norse god)
NOACHIC of Noah's time
NOBBLED stole; tampered with a
horse
NOBBLER confederate; doper
pc **NOBLESS** noblesse oblige; nobility
attitudes
NOBLEST most illustrious
NO-CLAIM (insurance)
zo **NOCTUID** nocturnal moth
zo **NOCTULE** bat (night-flyer)
mu, rl **NOCTURN** psalm service; (-al) of
night
NOCUOUS harmful; noxious; baleful
NODATED knotted

NODDING (auction); unwary; nutation
as **NODICAL** (ecliptic point)
NODULAR (intersections)
NODULED knotted
NODULUS small knop
NOEMICS intellectual science
NOETIAN a dogmatic theologian
NOGGING brick and wood-work
NOISILY rowdily; loudly; uproariously
NOISING bruiting; rumouring
NOISOME noysome; disgusting
NOMADIC wandering; migratory
NOMANCY divining; (chiro-) healing
NOMARCH frontier province governor, Gr.
NOMBLES entrails of deer
NOMBRIL escutcheon centre
NOMINAL titular; ostensible
NOMINEE prospective candidate
NON-ACID alkali
NON-AGED under 18; minor (USA)
NONAGON nine-sided figure
NONPLUS perplex; astound; bewilder
NON-SKID steady grip tyres
NONSTOP uninterrupted (cinema); (chatter)
bt **NONSUCH** fodder plant
lw **NON-SUIT** no case
NON-TERM vacation
NONUPLE 9-fold
pc **NOOLOGY** psychology
NOONDAY 12 o'clock midday
NOONING siesta
NOOSING lassoing; snaring
NORFOLK loose jacket; turkey
cp **NOR-GATE** logic with binary digits
NORIMON Japanese palanquin
NOR-LAND north country
mt **NORTHER** north wind (USA)
NORWICH school of painting
NOSE-BAG horse's lunchbox
NOSEGAY bouquet
NOSE-LED befooled
pl **NOSTRIL** nose passage
NOSTRUM panacea; medicine; (Mare-) sea
NOTABLE remarkable; memorable
NOTABLY conspicuously; notoriously
zo **NOTAEUM** bird's back
NOTAGEA Australian region
NOTANDA memoranda
NOTCHED inscribed; scored; nicked
NOTCHEL to repudiate
NOTCHER marker; scorer
ce **NOTCHER** steel flange stripper (machine)

NOTEDLY markedly; particularly
NOTELET small note
mu **NOTE-ROW** TONE-ROW, 12-note octave
NOTHING nihil; zero; naught
NOTHOUS spurious; bastard
tx **NO-THROW** barely twisted silk thread
ga **NO-THROW** foul (football, cricket)
NOTICED observed; heeded; marked
NOTITIA a catalogue
NOUMENA opp. to phenomena
NOURISH cherish; foster; encourage
NOVALIA reclaimed land
NOVELLA NOVELETTE, short novel, story
NOVELTY new; unusual; knick-knack
NOWHERE address unknown
NOXIOUS hurtful; nocuous; baneful
bl, nc **NUCLEAL** NUCLEAR, of nucleus
bl, nc **NUCLEIC** NUCLEIN, central cell; (-protein)
nc **NUCLEON** proton; neutron; isospin
nc **NUCLEOR** core; kernel; centre
bl, nc **NUCLEUS** essence of being; comet-head
ch, nu **NUCLIDE** atom isotope of nucleus
NUDGING elbowing; jostling
NULLIFY annul; rescind; revoke; repeal
NULLITY invalidity; noughtiness
ma, rl **NUMBERS** amounts; biblical book
NUMBING deadening; paralysing
NUMBLES entrails of deer
ma **NUMERAL** NUMERIC, digit; figure; character
NUMMARY numismatics
NUNATAK projecting rock (Eskimo)
NUN-BUOY conical buoy
NUNDINE market day (Roman)
NUNHOOD nunation
rl **NUNNERY** convent
NUNNISH sisterly; conventual
NUPTIAL conjugal; bridal; hymeneal
NURAGHE Sardinian fort
NURLING milling an edge
NURSERY infants' room; care centre
bt, fr **NURSERY** plants; tree-propagation area
ga **NURSERY** handicap; 2-year old; horserace
NURSING fostering; developing
NURTURE upbringing; sustenance
bt **NUT-BUSH** hazel
bt **NUT-GALL** dyestuff source
NUT-HOOK crooked stick
ck **NUT-LOAF** NUT-MEAT, vegetarian rissole/meal
ck **NUT-MEAL** nut-flour rissole

bt **NUT-PINE** food-producing tree
NUTTING gathering nuts
bt **NUT-TREE** hazel
bt **NUT-WOOD** panel wood
NUZZLED nestled; cuddled
zo **NYCTALA** genus of owls
NYMPHAL NYMPHLY, NYMPHIC,
    maiden-like

O

OAFLIKE doltish; stupid; idiotic
bt **OAK-BARK** could be cork
bt **OAK-FERN** 3-branched polypody
bt **OAK-GALL** tree excrescence
bt **OAK-LEAF** colonel's decoration
bt **OAKLING** young oak
OARFISH ribbon-fish
nt **OARLOCK** rowlock
nt,ga **OARSMAN** sculler; (rowing) (racing)
ck **OAT-CAKE** Scottish delicacy
ck **OAT-MALT** malt from oats
ck **OATMEAL** meal from oats (porridge)
    (Sc.)
OBCONIC funnel-shaped
OBDUCED drawn over; covered
OBDURED hardened; inured
OBELION part of skull
OBELISK monolith; memorial pillar
pr **OBELISK** printer's dagger (†)
OBELIZE mark as spurious
OBESITY corpulence; fatness
OBEYING submitting; complying
OBITUAL funereal
OBLIGED favoured; forced to;
    constrained
OBLIGEE under bond to recompense
OBLIGER favourer; lender; helper
lw **OBLIGOR** bond giver
OBLIQUE askew; crooked; aslant
OBLOQUY calumny; censure; odium
OBOLARY poverty-stricken
OBOVATE OBOVOID, egg-shaped
OBSCENE repulsive; lewd; indecent
OBSCURE abstruse; indistinct;
    hidden
OBSEQUY funeral ceremony etc.
OBSERVE mark; notice; espy; remark
OBTRUDE thrust; disturb; interfere
nm **OBVERSE** head side (coin); truth
OBVIATE get round; preclude
OBVIOUS evident; patent; palpable
mu **OCARINA** Sicilian keyless oval flute
md **OCCIPUT** back of head
OCCLUDE absorb; include
OCEANIC of oceans
OCEANID ocean nymph

OCEANUS ocean god
zo **OCELLAR** ocellate; with 'eyes'
OCELLUS single eye; a spot
zo **OCELOID** spotted leopard; jaguar
    (cat)
OCHROID pale yellow
OCREATE wearing boots/leggings
OCTAGON 8-sided figure
OCTAPLA eight-fold text
OCTAVUS eighth (Latin)
mu **OCTETTE OCTET,** 8 instrumentalists
OCTOBER 10th month
bt **OCTOFID** eight segments
zo **OCTOPOD** eight-footed
zo **OCTOPUS** cephalopod with 8
    suckered arms
OCTUPLE eightfold
ch **OCTYLIC** (organic radicle)
OCULATE eyed
md **OCULIST** eye doctor
OCYPETE one of the Harpies
ODALISK concubine of Sultan;
    whore
ODD-BALL eccentric; peculiar person
cp **ODD-EVEN** street numbers; parity
ODDMENT remnant; something left
    over
ODDNESS oddity; eccentricity
ODFORCE mesmeric force
zo **ODONATA** dragonflies
ODONTIC pertaining to teeth
ODORANT odorous; fragrant
ODORINE a bone distillate
ODOROUS fragrant; also smelly
ODYSSEY wandering; quest; saga
    (Odysseus/Ulysses)
md **OEDEMIA** overweight; palsy;
    liquescent
pc **OEDIPUS** a child's parental complex
ck **OENOMEL** wine and honey
me **OERSTED** magnetic field intensity
OESTRUM frenzy; on heat; rut
OESTRUS ESTRUS, gadfly; ovarian
    cycle
mu **OFF-BEAT** unconventional; advanced
lw **OFFENCE** insult; outrage; crime
OFFERED proffered; tendered;
    essayed
OFFERER a bookie; volunteer
OFFHAND casual; impolite;
    (volleyball)
OFFICER commissioned office holder
    (army)
nt,cp **OFF-LINE** off-course; off-centre
OFF-LINE impromptu; off-cue
OFF-LOAD unload; discharge; cargo
OFF-PEAK at time of least demand
ga **OFF-ROAD** dirt-track motor racing

OFF-SCUM offscouring; cleansing
ga OFF-SIDE fault (football)
OFFWARD leaning overboard; departing
OGHAMIC Irish (Celtic) style script
OGREISH like an ogre
OGYGIAN prehistoric; primeval
OIL-BATH bicycle accessory
zo OIL-BIRD the guacharo
OIL-CAKE cattle food
OIL-GOLD (gold leaf)
OIL-MEAL ground linseed cake
OIL-MILL oil factory
bt OIL-PALM oil source
OIL-SHOP lubricatorium
tx OILSILK oil-impregnated fabric
OILSKIN waterproof garment
OIL-SUMP drainage cavity in motor
OIL-WELL petroleum well
OJIBWAY Algonquin Indian
OLDNESS senility
OLDSTER middle-aged
OLD-TIME old fashioned; quondam
ch OLEFINE hydrocarbons
OLIGIST haematite
OLITORY (kitchen-garden)
OLIVARY olive shaped; oval
mn OLIVINE chrysolite
OLYMPIC of Olympus; Games
OLYMPUS abode of the gods
OMENING auguring; presaging
pl OMENTAL OMENTUM, of peritoneum
OMICRON Greek short 'o'
OMINOUS portentous, inauspicious
OMITTED left out; neglected; dropped
OMNEITY state of including all things
OMNIBUS public bus; compendium; for all
OMNIFIC all-creating
ONANISM self-pleasuring
ONCOSTS extras; overhead costs
ONCOTIC osmotic pressure of colloids
ONDATRA musk-rat
ONE-EYED round-eyed; a cyclops
ONEFOLD single
pc ONEIRIC pertaining to dream
ONENESS unity; concord
ONEROUS burdensome; weighty
ONESELF me, you or anybody
ONE-STEP a dance
ONE-TIME former; previous
ONGOING continuous event (course)
mn ONICOLO cameo-onyx
bt ONOCLEA fern genus
ONOLOGY prattle

ONSHORE landbased (services)
md ONYCHIA a whitlow
ONYMIZE categorize
ONYMOUS identified; not anonymous
bl OOCYTIN substance in spermatozoa
zo OOECIUM brood pouch
OOGRAPH ovum-drawing device
OOLITIC granular
zo OOLOGIC (birds' eggs)
bt OOLYSIS conversion to leaf
OOMETRY egg measurement
bt OOPHYTE gametophyte
OOPLASM central cytoplasm in oomycetes
zo OOSPORE fertilized ovum
zo OOTHECA egg-carrying structure
zo OOZOOID zooid arising from ovum
OPACITY opaqueness; obscurity
OPACOUS opaque, untransparent
OPALINE opalescent
OPALIZE make opaque
OPEN-AIR outdoor (activity)
ro, lw OPEN-END radio contract; of contracts
OPENING vacancy; opportunity; chance
pg, pl OPENING aperture; breach; orifice
ga OPENING ceremony; first gambit (chess)
OPEN-JAW air ticket (two routes)
cp, ma OPERAND sum to be worked on
OPERANT a worker; artisan; employee
md OPERATE drive (machine); apply surgery
OPEROSE OPEROUS, laborious; tedious
nt OPETIDE spring-tide
zo OPHIDIA snakes
zo OPHIURA starfish
OPIATED drugged
ch, md OPIATES OPIOIDS, classes of drugs
OPINANT of opinion
OPINING a notion; supposing
OPINION conception; idea; conjecture
OPORICE preserved fruit
zo OPOSSUM a marsupial
OPPIDAN town boy (Eton)
OPPOSED combated; competed
OPPOSER rival; resister
OPPRESS persecute; crush; maltreat
md OPSONIC OPSONIN, germ-resistant blood
OPTICAL of vision
zo OPTICON brain zone in insects
OPTIMUM best value
OPULENT wealthy; affluent

bt **OPUNTIA** cactus family
OPUSCLE opusculum; a small work
rl **ORAISON** orison; a prayer
ORALITY oral eroticism; oral disorder
ORARIAN coastal
rl **ORARION ORARIUM**, clerical stole
ORATING speech-giving; declaiming
ORATION speech; harangue; address
rl **ORATORY** eloquence; chapel
ORATRIX lady speaker
ORBIFIC world-creating
as **ORBITAL** encirclement course; elliptic
pl **ORBITAL** of the eye; sphere of influence
pl, ps, ch **ORBITAL** bony cavity; molecular
ORBLIKE globular; spherical; earth shape
ORCHARD garden of fruit-trees
ORDERED regulated; commanded
ORDERLY methodical; soldier-servant
ga **ORDINAL** figure (ice)-skating penalty
ma **ORDINAL** numerical order (rank)
rl **ORDINAL** RC book of forms of services
rl **ORDINEE** newly ordained (deacon, priest)
OREADES mountain nymphs
ORECTIC pert. to desire/satisfaction
ORGANIC vital; radical; fundamental
ORGANIC natural farming (no chemicals)
ORGANON ORGANUM, enquiry; dissertation
mu **ORGANRY** organ music
ORGIAST a Bacchanalian extremist
ORIENCY brightness of sunrise; colour
ORIFICE aperture; vent; pore
ORIFORM mouth-shaped
ORIGAMI paper cut-out, fold designs (Jap.)
bt **ORLEANS** cloth; plum
OROGENY (mountain formation)
OROLOGY mountain lore
OROTUND full voiced
ORPHEAN enchantingly musical
ORPHEUS made music sweet and low
ORPHISM cult of Bacchus
ORPHREY embroidered border
mn **ORTHITE** allanite
ORTHROS morning service (Greek)
zo **ORTOLAN** garden bunting
ck **ORVIETO** a white wine (It.)
OSCHEAL of the scrotum
zo **OSCINES** singing birds

OSCULAR (kissing)
OSCULUM exhalant aperture in porifera
OSIERED made with reeds
OSMANLI of the Turkish Ottoman dynasty
OSMATIC having olfactory organs
ch **OSMIOUS** containing osmium
mn **OSMOSIS** diffusion balance of dissolved minerals
bt **OSMOTIC** diffusible respiration
bt **OSMUNDA** royal fern
OSSELET morbid growth
OSSEOUS bony
OSSICLE small bone
md **OSSIFIC** bony
OSSUARY charnel-house
OSTEOID like bone (material)
OSTERIA hostelry (It.)
rl **OSTIARY** church janitor
bt **OSTIOLE** spore-door
md **OSTIOMA** bone tumour
md **OSTITIS** inflammation
zo **OSTRICH** also estrich
md **OTALGIA** ear-ache
zo **OTARINE** referring to seals
zo **OTIDINE** pertaining to bustards
md **OTOCYST** auditory vesicle
md **OTOLITH** ear-stone
md **OTOLOGY** ear science
OTTOMAN Turk; sofa; divan
OURSELF our kingly self
OUSTING ejecting; evicting; dislodging
OUT-BACK one from the interior (Australia)
OUTBRAG out-boast
OUTBURN burn away
OUTCAST pariah; exile
OUTCOME issue; sequel; upshot
OUTCROP geological fault
OUTDARE outventure
OUTDONE surpassed; eclipsed
OUTDOOR open air
OUTEDGE farthest extremity
OUTFACE to brave criticism
OUTFALL the place of discharge
OUTFLOW outlet
OUTFOOT out-pace; outsail
OUTGATE exit
OUTGAZE look longer than
OUTGIVE surpass in liberality
OUTGOER opposite of incomer
OUTGONE over-reached; went beyond
OUTGROW get too old for
OUTGUSH outpour; outwell
nt **OUTHAUL** a rope

OUTHIRE to let out

OUTJEST write dictionary definitions

OUTLAND foreign

OUTLASH sudden outburst

OUTLAST survive; outlive; outwear

OUTLEAP sally attack from besieged town

gl **OUTLIER** outcrop of rocks

OUTLINE draft; sketch; profile

OUTLINE précis; synopsis; description

OUTLIVE survive

OUTLOOK prospect; future; view

OUTMATE overmatch; checkmate

OUTMOST furthest outward

OUTMOVE out-manoeuvre

OUTNAME surpass in reputation

OUTNESS externality; objectiveness

OUTPACE outrun

OUTPART remote part

ga **OUTPEER OUTPLAY**, prove superior to rival

nt **OUTPORT** ship's gun-port (shutters)

OUTPOST detached fort; look-out point

OUTPOUR stream; spout

OUTPRAY surpass in prayer

OUTRAGE wanton mischief; abuse

OUTRANK precede

OUTRASE exterminate; destroy

OUTRIDE win horse race

ga **OUTROAR** competing football-team fans

OUTROOT uproot; eradicate garden weeds

ga **OUTRUSH** besieged; make a foray

OUTSAIL win yacht race

OUTSELL succeed in America

pr **OUTSERT** extra outside binding leaf

OUTSHOT a projection

OUTSIDE external; exterior; superficial

OUTSIZE extra big (clothing)

OUTSOAR fly higher than high

OUTSOLD sold out; no more stock

OUTSOLE outer sole of shoe

OUTSPAN to unyoke

OUTSTAY stay longer than

OUTSTEP overstep

OUTTALK continue talking endlessly

OUTTURN output; production; delivery

ga **OUTTURN** ball throw (rugby football)

OUTVIED surpassed; exceeded

OUTVOTE get majority

OUTWALK outpace

OUTWALL outer wall

OUTWARD ostensible; apparent

OUTWEAR last longer; outlast

OUTWELL gusher (oil)

OUTWENT outstripped; overtook

ga **OUT-WICK** shot on other stone (curling)

OUTWIND unwind; extricate

OUTWING out-flank (battle)

OUTWORE lasted longer than

ar **OUTWORK** redoubt; bastion

OUTWORN worn out

pl **OVARIAN** of the ovary

OVATION enthusiastic applause

zo **OVEN-TIT** willow-warbler

OVERACT act too much

OVERALL protective garment

OVERARM bowling (cricket)

OVER-ATE surfeited

OVERAWE intimidate; daunt; cow

OVERBID succeed at auction

OVERBUY buy too much

OVERDUE in arrears; outstanding; (debt)

OVERDYE dye too deeply

OVEREAT gourmandize

OVEREYE flirt openly

OVERFAR too far

OVERFLY soar beyond; fly over

OVERLAP one extending over another

tc **OVERLAP** dialling; fax-scan faults

tc **OVERLAY** bedcover; spread across

tc **OVERLAY** multiple-store program

OVERLIE to smother

OVERMAN foreman; manager; umpire

OVERMAN to employ too many

OVERPAY pay too much

OVERPLY over-exert

OVERRAN outran; invaded

pr **OVERRUN** swarm; infest; printing

OVERSAW superintended

OVERSEA foreign

OVERSEE superintend

pr **OVERSET** carried over (bookkeeping)

OVERTAX tax too highly

OVERTLY openly; publicly; patently

OVERTOP surpass

zo **OVICELL** brood-pouch in ectoprocta

OVICIDE killing of sheep

OVIDIAN narrative verse form

md **OVIDUCT** ovary passage

OVIFORM oval

OVIFORM OVOIDAL, egg-shaped; oval

OVOLOGY all about eggs

bt **OVULARY** (seed)

mm **OVULITE** fossil egg

OWENITE of cooperative ideals (R. Owen)

OWL-EYED global eyes; alert
OWL-LIKE as wise as an owl
ga **OWN-GOAL** scoring for opponents
(fault)
ch **OXALATE** of oxalic acid
mn **OXALITE** oxalate of iron
ch **OXAMIDE** oxalic acid amide
bt **OXHEART** kind of large sweet cherry
ch **OXIDANT** combustive agent
ch **OXIDASE** enzyme
ch **OXIDATE OXIDIZE**, to rust (of iron)
ch **OXIMIDE** oxamic acid compound
OXONIAN of Oxford
OX-STALL home for non-bulls
ch **OXYACID** proton-giving hydroxide
ae **OXYDANT** oxygen component in
rocket
OXYNTIC secreting acid (of stomach
glands)
md **OXYOPIA** acute vision
ch **OXYSALT** containing oxygen
OXYTONE accented syllable
ch **OZONIDE** explosive organic
compound
ch **OZONIZE OZONOUS**, charge with
ozone

P

PABOUCH oriental slipper
PABULAR yielding food
PABULUM aliment; fodder;
nutriment
PACABLE appeasable
PACATED calmed; quieted; pacified
PACEMAN runner; fast bowler
(cricket)
ga **PACHISI** pachesi; Indian
backgammon
bt **PACHYMA** fungus genus
PACIFIC peaceful; tranquil; irenic
PACKAGE bale; bundle; parcel;
(holiday)
cp **PACKAGE** multipurpose programs'
set
go **PACK-ICE** icy-sea barrier (Arctic)
PACKING packeting; stowing;
crowding
PACKMAN peddler; hawker; tallyman
zo **PACKWAX** tendon in animals' necks
PACKWAY bridle path (for
horsemen)
PACTION a pact; covenant; bond
PADDING stuffing
PADDLED dabbled; propelled
zo, nt **PADDLER** canoeist; wader; steamship
zo **PADDOCK** frog or toad

PADDOCK puddock; field
PADELLA small lamp
PADISHA Persian title
PADLOCK durable, portable lock
PADRONE employer (Iberia, It.)
PAD-TREE harness frame
rl **PAENULA** chasuble (church
vestment)
PAEONIN red colouring matter
PAGEANT historic spectacle; display
show
PAGINAL (pages)
PAHLEVI pehlevi; early Persian
dialect
PAILFUL the contents of a bucket
PAILLON metal backing
PAINFUL grievous; vexatious; sore
PAINING afflicting; tormenting;
aching
PAINTED limned; bedizened; daubed
PAINTER artist in colour; depictor
nt **PAINTER** R.A.; mooring rope
PAIRING matching; mating; MPs'
voting
tx **PAJAMAS PYJAMAS**, slumber wear
PAKFONG PAKTONG, silver
(Germany)
PALABRA wordy discussion
PALADIN knight errant, crusader
zo **PALAMAE** toe-webbings
md **PALATAL** of the palate (tasting)
PALAVER parley with chieftains
br **PALE-ALE** type of brew
PALEOUS like chaff
PALETOT loose overcoat
PALETTE artist's board; (pelota)
zo **PALFREY** saddle-horse
md **PALINAL** retrogressive
zo **PALLIAL** (mantle of mollusc)
PALLING covering; surfeiting
zo **PALLIUM** brain-shell of mollusc;
mantle of bird
rl **PALLIUM** archbishops' mantle (pall)
ga **PALLONE** ball game (It.)
ar **PALMARY** worthy; capital decoration
zo **PALMATE** web-footed
bt **PALMERY** palm-house
PALMING sleight of hand; (trick)
PALMIST hand-reader; fortune teller
PALM-OIL bribery
cp **PALM-TOP** a hand-held computer
bt **PALMYRA** East Indian palm
PALOOKA incompetent boxer;
simpleton
md **PALPATE** touch gently (medical)
PALSHIP comradeship
md **PALSIED** of palsy (paralysis,
tremors)

PALUDAL marshy; malarial; fenny
mt PAMPERO cold S.W. squall
(Argentina)
PANACEA universal remedy
PANACHE plume; self-esteem
rl PANAGIA all holy; an ornament
ck, ae PANCAKE fried batter; flat landing
rl PANDEAN of Pan, god of Nature
(Gr.)
PANDECT digest of Roman Law
zo PANDION osprey genus
zo PANDORA (her fateful box); sea
bream
mu PANDORA BANDORA, plucked lyre;
zither
mu PANDORE a lute
PANDOUR Hungarian soldier; robber
mu PANDURA Neapolitan guitar
rl PANEITY state of being bread
PANFISH small non-commercial food
fish
gl, go PANGAEA sial; primeval single
landmass
PANGANI East African ivory
PANGING paining; causing anguish
PANICKY jumpy; nervous; fearful
bt PANICLE a small web
bt PANICUM millet-grain
PANIKIN tin mug
nt PANJANG sampan, Malaysia
PANNADE curveting
PANNAGE swine food
tx PANNIER 2 bread-baskets; hooped
skirt
mn, pg PANNING gold washing; photo-
spanning
PANNOSE like felt
PANOCHA coarse sugar (Mexico)
PANOPLY complete armour
mu PAN-PIPE piped wind instrument
PANSIED with pansies
zo PANTHER leopard
PANTHOS Divinity made manifest
PANTIES undies
PANTILE S-shaped roof tile
PANTING palpitating; desirous
PANTLER butler
mu PANTOUM Malayan quatrain
PANURGE a Rabelaisian rascal
PANURGY skill in work
rl PAPALLY popishly (ceremoniously)
PAPBOAT small feeding vessel for
infants
PAPERED sand-papered
PAPERER paperhanger
PAPHIAN (worship of Venus)
zo PAPILIO butterfly
md PAPILLA nerve extremity

PAPMEAT soft food
PAPOOSE North American Indian
infant
PAPPING feeding with pap
PAPPOSE pappous; downy
bt PAPRIKA red pepper (Hungarian)
PAPULAE dermal gills in
echinodermata
md PAPULAR pimply
bt PAPYRUS sedge; scroll
PARABLE allegorical similitude
PARACME decline; decadence
PARADED displayed; vaunted
PARADOS rampart
PARADOX surprising statement
PARAGON model of perfection
PARAMOS semi-tundra (Andes)
PARAPET rampart
PARASOL sunshade
ck PARBAKE bake partially
ck PARBOIL boil partially
PARCHED scorched; dried; shrivelled
PARDIEU in truth
PARDINE like a leopard; spotted
bt PAREIRA drug (Brazilian plant)
bt PARELLA PARELLE, PERELLE, litmus
lichen
PARERGY subsidiary work
md PARESIS paralysis
md PARETIC partially paralysed
ck PARFAIT cold egg/whipped cream
dessert
PARGING pargeting; external
decorative plaster work
gs PARISON intermediate glass shape
PARITOR beadle; apparitor
PARKING lodging; collecting
PARLOUR the Mayor's 'front room'
PARLOUS perilous; difficult;
precarious
PARODIC (parody); farcical
md PAROTIC auricular
md PAROTID PAROTIS, salivary gland
PARQUET wooden flooring; stalls of
theatre
PARRIED avoided; warded off;
fended
PARSING grammatical exercise
bt PARSLEY a culinary herb
ck, bt PARSNIP root vegetable
PARTAKE to share; participate
PARTIAL biased; restricted; fond
ga PARTIDO 15-point limit (pelota)
lw PARTIES social; political; legal
PARTING division; separating;
breaking
mu PARTITA notation scores
bt PARTITE partially parted

zo **PARTLET** a ruff; a collar; a hen
PARTNER colleague; associate; buddy
md **PARULIS** gumboil
PARVENU upstart
rl **PARVISE** porch; church garden
PARVULE tiny pill
PASCHAL (Easter)
PASCUAL grazing; pasturing
PASGANG striding technique (skiing)
PASQUIL PASQUIN, lampoon, satire
PASSADE sword thrust
PASSADO equestrian exercise
lw **PASSAGE** clause; context; law
mu **PASSAGE** extract (music, literature)
PASSAGE corridor; alley; voyage
hd **PASSANT** walking
PASSING brief; transient; exceeding
PASSION ardour; fervour; wrath
PASSIVE patient; submissive; inert
PASS-KEY a master-key
PASSMAN of examinations
(university)
PASSOUT ice-skating movement
pr **PASTE-IN** late correction, insert
PASTERN (fetlock); part of horse's
foot
pr **PASTE-UP** extended arrangement of
proof sheets
ck **PASTIES** patties; pies
PASTIME recreation; sport; diversion
PASTING cementing; gumming
PASTOSE painted thickly
PASTURE herbage; meadowland
nt **PATACHE** fishing boat from Malaysia
nt **PATAMAR** coasting vessel; dhow;
India
ga **PATBALL** tennis of sorts
PATCHED repaired clumsily
PATCHER repairer; botcher
zo, pl **PATELLA** limpet; kneecap
PATELLA saucer; shallow dish
PATHWAY footway; track; trail;
(garden)
md **PATIENT** steadfast; calm; (hospital-)
PATNESS quick in the uptake
ga **PATOLLI** Aztecs' board game
hd **PATONCE** heraldic curved cross
PATRIAL racial; national
PATRICO gipsy priest; patercove
PATRIOT staunch non-cosmopolitan
rl **PATRIST** a theologian
PATROON American proprietor
PATTERN design; model; sample
PATTERN exemplary (ideal)
ck **PATTIES** pasties; pies
ck **PATTING** tapping; stroking; (butter-)
PATTRAS wooden wall-plug
PAUCITY fewness; exiguity; lack

rl **PAULINE** (St Paul); sect
PAUNCHY obese; stout
PAUSING halting; wavering; tarrying
PAVIOUR pavement layer
PAWLATA method of righting a
kayak
PAWNING pledging; hypothecating
PAYABLE due for payment
PAYBILL cheque; order to pay
PAYBOOK record of wages (military)
PAYCOCK vain husband of Juno
PAYDIRT alluvial deposit
PAYLIST PAYROLL, of employees
PAYLOAD amount of cargo permitted
PAYMENT financial transaction
PAYNISE to preserve wood
PAYROLL paylist
PAYSAGE landscape (painting) (Fr.)
PEACHED divulged
PEACHER an informant
PEA-COAT pea-jacket
zo **PEACOCK** pavonine
zo **PEACRAB** small crustacean
zo **PEA-FOWL** a species of Pavo genus
PEAKING reaching full performance
nt **PEAKING** sail raising
PEAKISH off colour; sickly
PEALING bellringing; resounding
PEANISM song of praise or triumph
PEARLED made success as oyster
nt **PEARLER** fishing boat (Japan)
tx **PEARLIN** lace made of silk thread
PEASANT rustic; swain; farm
labourer
PEASCOD Tudor genitals' protector;
pod
PEA-SOUP London fog
PEAT-BED damp moss
PEAT-BOG Irish fuel source
PEAT-HAG peat-hole
PEAVIES lumbermen's levers
PEBBLED shingled
zo **PEBRINE** silk-worm disease
PECCANT sinning; guilty; criminal
zo **PECCARY** S. American pig
PECCAVI confession of error
PECKING picking up; striking;
(-order)
PECKISH hungry
bt **PECTASE** gel-forming plant enzyme
PECTATE PECTOSE, gelatinous
ck, bt **PECTINE** jelly from apple acid
PECTOSE carbohydrate plant
constituent
PEDDLED retailed; trifled
PEDDLER hawker; huckster
PEDESIS molecular vibration
bt **PEDICEL PEDICLE,** small stalk

PEDLARY hawking; (street) selling
gl, ag PEDOCAL calcium rich zonal soil
PEDRAIL tracked vehicle
PEELING excoriating; skinning
PEELITE follower of Sir R. Peel
PEENING hammer-blow metal-
  working
PEEPING snooping; peering
PEERAGE Debrett; rank of peer
PEERESS consort of a peer
PEERING prying; peeping; gazing
PEEVISH querulous; snappish
zo PEEWEEP peewit; pewit
PEGASUS winged horse of the
  Muses
as, zo PEGASUS (fish); constellation
PEGGING fastening; (croquet)
PEGWOOD clock-hole cleaning sticks
PEHLEVI PAHLEVI, Persian dialect
PELAGIC (deep sea)
zo PELAMID bonito; mackerel type
PELASGI Greek tribe
zo PELICAN genus of birds
md PELIOMA livid spot
PELISSE fur-coat
PELLAGE duty on skins
PELOPID a son of Pelops
md PELORIA PELORIC, abnormalism
nv PELORUS pivoted dial
PELOTON bunch of racing cyclists
PELTAST soldier with buckler
PELTATE shield-like
PELTING raining; pouring; throwing
PENALLY by way of punishment
PENALTY handicap; retribution
ga PENALTY free kick; throw (-goal)
PENANCE punishment; humiliation
PENATES Roman household gods
PEN-CASE pen-holder
PENDANT an ornament; pennant
PENDENT hanging; dangling
PENDING awaiting decision
PENEIAN (river Peneus in Vale of
  Tempe)
zo PEN-FISH sparoid fish
ag PENFOLD PINFOLD, cattle enclosure
zo PENGUIN Antarctic sea-bird
PENICIL paint-brush
PEN-NAME pseudonym; nom de
  plume
nt PENNANT a long streamer
zo PENNATE Penguin genus of birds
PENNIED having a cash asset
nm PENNIES pence
PENNILL stanza (Eisteddfod)
PENNINE magnesium/aluminium
  silicate
PENNING inditing; cooping

PENSILE pendulous; suspended
PENSION retirement income; (social)
PENSION annuity; boarding house
PENSIVE meditative; thoughtful
PENTACT five-rayed
ch PENTANE (paraffin)
bd PENTICE pent-house; a sloping roof
  or weather cover
PENTODE pentone; wireless adjunct
ch PENTOSE a form of sugar
bt PENTZIA S. African shrub
ck PENUCHE type of fudge
PENWORK drawings; calligraphy
PENWORK on japanned lacquer
  furniture
PEONAGE PEONISM, agricultural
  slavery
bt PEONIES PAEONIES
PEOPLED inhabited; populated
mn PEPERIN volcanic tufa
PEPPERY irascible; choleric
PEP-PILL stimulant
md PEPSINE an enzyme
PEP-TALK encouragement
md PEPTICS digestion
ch PEPTIDE protein-breakdown
  substance
md PEPTONE digestive product
PERBEND bonding stone
PERCALE woven cambric
PERCASE perhaps
PER-CENT out of 100
PERCEPT that which is perceived
PERCHED roosted; settled
zo PERCHER candle; rooster
zo PERCINE like a perch; percoid
PERCOCT well cooked
zo PERCOID perch-like
PERCUSS strike; tap
PERDURE endure; persist
PEREGAL fully equal
zo PEREION thorax of crustacea
bt PERELLE PARELLE, PARELLA, lichen
mu PERFECT complete; faultless; pitch
PERFIDY betrayal; treachery
PERFORM fulfil; act; execute; effect
PERFUME scent; aroma; fragrance
PERFUSE sprinkle; bedew; permeate
PERGOLA PERGULA, garden arbour
PERHAPS aiblins; peradventure
PERIAPT amulet; charm; talisman
mn PERIDOT green jewel; olivine
PERIGREE point nearest to earth of
  other orbits
ro PERIKON detector
PERIQUE Louisiana tobacco
PERIWIG peruke
PERJURE forswear

lw **PERJURY** false testimony
PERKIER more irrepressible
PERKILY saucily; jauntily; airily
PERKING peering; smartening up
bd, mn **PERLITE** in sandless gypsum plaster
gl **PERLITE** vitreous rock
gl **PERMIAN** geological era
PERMUTE commute; change
zo **PEROPOD** rudimentary leg
zo **PERORAL** surrounding the mouth
vt **PEROSIS** slipped tendon
PERPEND ratiocinate; cogitate
PERPEND bonding stone
PERPLEX puzzle; nonplus; embarrass
PERRIER catapult; a table water
PERSEID a meteor from Perseus
PERSEUS slew Medusa; a
constellation
PERSIAN Iranian
PERSIST persevere; continue; last
PERSONA (grata); actor's mask
PERSPEX a glazing material
PERTAIN to relate to; concern
PERTURB disturb; agitate; disquiet
PERTUSE riddled; bored
PERUSAL careful reading
PERUSED read; studied; examined
pr **PERUSER** a scrutineer of pages
PERVADE perfuse; impregnate;
imbue
PERVERT deviate; lead astray
rl **PESHITO** Syriac Testament
PESKILY annoyingly
PESTLED pounded in a mortar
PETASUS Mercury's winged cap
PETERED pottered; exhausted;
(cards)
bt **PETIOLE** leaf-stalk; pedicle
cr **PETRAIL** heavy framing beam
PETRARY catapult for stones
PETREAN stony
PETRIFY stupefy; dumbfound; stun
rl **PETRINE** according to St Peter
PETROUS rocklike
PETTILY meanly; trivially
PETTING fondling; canoodling
PETTISH peevish; fretful; querulous
bt **PETUNIA** a flower
mn **PETZITE** silver/gold telluride
rl **PEW-RENT** rent paid for use of pew
PEWTERY (pewter)
nm **PFENNIG** German copper coin
md **PHACOID** lenticular
PHAETON sky-hog; four-wheel
carriage
zo **PHAETON** boastwain-bird
PHALANX compact body
pl **PHALLIC PHALLUS**, penis, symbol

PHANTOM spectral; illusive; ghost
PHARAOH ancient Egyptian ruler
PHARATE of development phase in
insects
md **PHARYNX** upper part of gullet
tc, tv **PHASING** correcting screen picture
of facsimiles
bt **PHELLEM** tissue external to
phellogen
ch **PHENATE** (phenol)
ch **PHENOIC** carbolic
PHIDIAS Greek sculptor
PHILTRE PHILTER, love potion
bt **PHLOEUM PHLOEM**, bark fibre
zo **PHOCINE** of seals
PHOEBUS Apollo; the sun
zo **PHOENIX** date palm; fabulous bird
PHONATE to utter inarticulately
PHONEME relevant sound
(linguistics)
PHONICS harmony; phonetics
PHONING telephoning
PHONISM synesthesia; noises off
zo **PHORESY** transport by clinging to
animal
pg **PHOTICS** science of light
pg **PHOTISM** colour sensation
pg **PHOTOMA** hallucinated flash of light
zo **PHRAGMA** septum or partition
PHRASED expressed; styled
PHRASER phrase-monger
PHRATRY tribal subdivision
md **PHRENIC** diaphragmatic
PHYSICS a science
bt **PHYTOID** plant-like
mu **PIACERE** at pleasure
PIAFFER a horse gait
mu **PIANINA** small piano
mu **PIANISM** musical technique
mu **PIANIST** an expert on the ivories
mu **PIANOLA** self-playing piano
nm **PIASTRE** coin (Egypt)
mu **PIBROCH** a tune; bagpipe (Sc.)
PICADOR mounted bull-fighter
PICAMAR tar extract
lw **PICCAGE** pitch-money
mu **PICCOLO** small flute
PICEOUS pitch-black
to **PICKAXE** pointed chopper
PICKING petty larceny; choosing
PICKLED preserved
PICK-OFF automation device
bt **PICOTEE** carnation
PICOTTE little lace loop
PICQUET piquet; card game
ch **PICRATE** an explosive; lyddite
bt **PICRINE** foxglove·extract
mn **PICRITE** olivine; peridot

PICTISH Celtic
PICTURE portrait; drawing; imagine
zo PIDDOCK mollusc
PIEBALD PYEBALD, motley (horses)
PIECING patching; uniting
PIERAGE pier tolls
PIERCED transfixed; impaled
PIERCER borer; gimlet; drill
PIERIAN (Muses); (of Pieria)
PIERROT an entertainer
PIETISM sanctimoniousness
rl PIETIST religious sect
zo PIEWIFE lapwing
el PIEZOID crystal blank
mu PIFFERO oboe; organ-stop
PIFFLED chattered; drivelled
zo PIG-DEER invented animal
PIGEYED with small eyes
PIGGERY pig-sty
PIGGING living higgledy-piggledy
PIGGISH hoggish; swinish; messy
PIGHTLE small enclosure
PIG-IRON iron ingots
PIG-LEAD cast lead
PIGMEAN of pygmies; Lilliputian
pt PIGMENT paint; colour; tincture
PIGMIES PYGMIES, diminutive
   Africans
bt PIGNONS fir-cone seeds
le PIGSKIN (leather); (saddle)
PIGTAIL plait of hair
PIG-WASH hog-wash
ck PIKELET PIKELIN, small crumpet, tea
   cake
PIKEMAN turnpike gatekeeper
mn PIKRITE igneous rock
PILCHER a scabbard
PILEATE cap-shaped
lw PILFERY petty theft; larceny
PILGRIM palmer; devotee; wayfarer
bt PILKINS pill-corn; oats
PILLAGE rifle; sack; ravage; loot
PILLBOX concrete defensive
   emplacement
PILLBOX medicine box; hat (ladies,
   pages)
PILLING blackballing (vetoing
   membership)
PILLION saddle, 2nd rider's seat
PILLORY expose to ridicule
PILLOWY yielding; soft
PILOTED steered; conducted; guided
ar PILOTIS building on columns
zo PILTOCK coalfish
PILULAR (pills)
bt, ck PIMENTA PIMENTO, red capsicum
PIMPLED blotched (skin)
zo PINBONE hipbone of quadruped

PIN-CASE pin etui
to PINCERS pliers
PINCHED gripped; purloined
zo PINCHER sea fish
PINCHES wee drams; nips
PINDOWN children in punishment
   room
PINE-OIL oil from resin
bt PINETUM plantation of pine-trees
PIN-FIRE (cartridge)
zo PIN-FISH a scaly fish; sailor's choice
PINFOLD cattle pound
PINGING bullet noise (rifle)
pt PINGUID greasy; unctuous
PINHEAD top of a pin; minute
PIN-HOLD pin-housing
PINHOLE tiny aperture
vt PINK-EYE a horse disease
PINKING scalloping; knocking
PINKISH somewhat pink
nt PINNACE a man-of-war's boat
bt PINNATE pennate; feathered
PINNING making fast
zo PINNOCK tom-tit
bt, zo PINNULA PINNULE, branchlet; small
   feather
zo, tx PINTADO guinea-fowl; chintz, 18th
   c.
zo PINTAIL a duck
me PINT-POT vessel holding pint
PIN-WORK (flexing flax)
PIONEER forerunner; initiator
PIONEER 1st bowler; pilot
PIOUSLY devoutly; religiously
PIP-EMMA p.m. (signalling)
PIPERIC peppery
PIPETTE graduated tube
bt PIPLESS seedless
bt, ck PIPPING piling; de-seeding
PIQUANT stimulating; caustic; tart
PIQUING irritating; nettling
nt PIRAGUA a dug-out canoe
PIRATED plundered; marauded
PIRATIC infringing; piratical
lw PISCARY fishing rights
PISCINA PISCINE, swimming pool
   (Sp., Fr.)
zo PISMIRE an ant; emmet
nm PISTOLE Spanish golden coin
PITAPAT in a flutter; raindrops
PITCHED flung; tossed; planted; cast
ga PITCHER eared jug; thrower
   (baseball)
mn PITCOAL from underground
PITEOUS woeful; sorry;
   compassionate
PITFALL a trap; snare; danger
PIT-HEAD top of coal mine

PITHILY tersely; concisely; briefly
PITHING extracting the marrow
bt PITH-RAY root or stem cell sheet
PITIFUL humane; lenient; wretched
PIT-MIRK dark as pitch (Sc.)
PITTING striving; seed removal
bd PITTING plaster-blowing technique
PITTING setting one against another
PITTITE playgoer (in the pit)
md PITUITA PITUITE, phlegm
PITYING commiserating
PIVOTAL axial
PIVOTED hinged; centred on
PIXY-LED bewildered
PLACARD bill; poster; notice
PLACATE conciliate; appease
md, rl PLACEBO fake drug; prayer (mass)
PLACING identifying; assigning
PLACKET slit; pocket
zo PLACODE platelike structure
PLACOID scaly
PLACULA small plate; plaque
PLAGUED persistently annoyed
PLAGUER a vexatious person
tx PLAIDED wearing tartan (Scots)
PLAINER clearer; more obvious
PLAINLY simply; clearly; candidly
tx PLAITED folded; woven·
tx PLAITER an interlacer; interweaver
PLANARY as foundation; flat; level
PLANCHE body position (gymnastics)
fr PLANCON octagonally hewn log
PLANING smoothing; aeroplaning
PLANISH to hammer smooth
bd PLANKED floorboards laid
PLANNED sketched; schemed
PLANNER a projector; designer
PLANTAR (sole of foot)
PLANTED instilled; inculcated; sown
PLANTER settler; grower
zo PLANULA embryo protoplasm
PLANXTY Welsh lament
PLASHED splashed; dabbled
PLASMIC proto-plasmic
bl PLASMID of cytoplasmic structure
ch PLASMIN fibrin-destructive blood item
PLASMON flour-like food
PLASTER sinapism; daub; stucco
PLASTIC elastic; pliable; yielding
zo PLASTID living cell
bt PLATANE plane-tree
ma PLATEAU flattened graphic curve
go PLATEAU high tableland; stand on plinth
ch PLATINA platinum
PLATING sheathing

ga PLATOON army squad; sports team
PLATTED plaited; weaved
PLATTER wooden plate
PLAUDIT applause; approbation
PLAY-BOX theatre seat
PLAYBOY man of pleasure
ga PLAYDAY sports day
PLAYFUL frolicsome; joker
PLAYING acting; competing; romping
ga PLAY-OFF repeat match after a tie
ga PLAY-OUT finish the game
PLAYPEN children's play enclosure
lw PLEADED entreated; argued
lw PLEADER barrister; advocate
PLEASED delighted; contented; obliged
PLEASER charmer; gratifier
PLEATED platted; interlaced
mu PLECTRE plectrum; plectron
PLEDGED pawned; engaged
PLEDGEE pawnbroker
PLEDGER pawnbroker's customer
md PLEDGET lint compress
PLEIADS the Pleiades; 7 stars in Taurus
PLENARY in full; complete; entire
PLENISH provide; equip
PLENIST spacious materialist
zo PLEOPOD fin-paws of whale
PLEROMA abundance; fullness
bt PLEROME centre of apical meristem
md PLEURAL (lungs)
zo PLEURON shell extension
PLEXURE weaving; texture
PLIABLE tractable; supple
PLIABLY flexibly; lithely
PLIANCY flexibility
PLICATE folded; plaited
PLIFORM in the form of a fold
PLIMMED swollen
PLODDED toiled; drudged
PLODDER steady worker
PLOPPED plumped
PLOSIVE phonetic sound-group
PLOTFUL full of schemes
PLOTTED planned; schemed
nt PLOTTER intriguer; conspirator; radar
PLOW-BOY ploughboy
ag PLOWING PLOUGHING, furrowing
PLOWMAN ploughman, (lunch)
PLUCKED failed examination; pulled
PLUCKER feather remover
PLUGGED plodded; shot; sealed
PLUGGER stopper
PLUMAGE plumery; feathers
PLUMBED measured; made vertical

PLUMBER lead-worker; water-system worker
ch PLUMBUM PLUMBIC, of lead
bt PLUMCOT plum-apricot
PLUMERY display of plumes
PLUMING self-congratulation
PLUMIST feather-dresser
PLUMMET lead bob
PLUMMET fall headlong downwards
PLUMOSE plumous; feathery
PLUMPED fell suddenly
PLUMPER chubbier; fatter; stouter
PLUMPLY roundly; fully
bd PLUMULE plumula; bud
PLUNDER loot; spoil; pillage; booty
PLUNGED dived; gambled heavily
PLUNGER part of a pump
PLUNKET blue colour
zo PLUTEUS pelagic larval form
PLUVIAL rainy; humid
PLUVIUS Jupiter
PLY-WOOD laminated wood
bt POACEAE the grasses
POACHED trespassed; stabbed; (eggs)
POACHER thief; setter of snares
zo POCHARD a duck
pr POCHOIR stencil colour process
md POCK-PIT pox-mark
md PODAGRA gout
PODALIC pertaining to feet
PODDING producing pods
PODESTA Italian magistrate
zo PODITIC (crab's leg)
PODRIDA Spanish stew
zo POE-BIRD tui; parson bird; (NZ)
POEISIS creation
POETESS lyrical lady
POETICS criticism of poetry
POETIZE versify
lw POINDED pounded; distrained
POINTED acute; sharp; keen; significant
POINTEL pencil; spike; stylo
zo POINTER indicator; hunting dog
POISING balancing; loading
POITREL horse-armour
nt POLACCA FALLUCA, sailing vessel
nt POLACRE Mediterranean dhow
mu POLACKA polonaise (Polish dance)
POLAIRE ancient leather book-satchel
POLARIS guided missile
el POLARON trapped electron
POLDERS reclaimed land
to POLE-AXE poll-axe
zo POLE-CAT civet
POLEMIC controversial; contentious
POLENTA Italian maize porridge

POLICED regulated
POLIGAR S. Ind. village chieftain
POLITER more courteous or civil
POLITIC statesmanlike; discreet
zo POLLACK sea-fish; pollock; chub
POLLARD stag after casting his antlers
zo POLLARD lopped; bran; the chub
POLLCAP capping municipal spending
POLLENT strong; mighty; puissant
POLLING voting; lopping (trees)
tc, bt POLLING multidrop network act
POLL-MAN pass-man (Cam.)
POLL-TAX capitation tax
POLLUTE contaminate; defile
POLOIST polo player
POLONYM joint-authorship name, work
bt POLSTER lichen moss on glacial rock
zo POLSTER glacier mouse (Scand.)
POLYACT rayed
POLYGON angular figure
bt POLYGYN plant genus
ch POLYMER complex compound
POLYOPY multiple vision
ch POLYOSE polysaccharide
zo POLYPOD many-footed
zo POLYPUS sea-anemone; coral
zo POLYZOA barnacles
ch POMATUM POMADE, an ointment
bt, ck POMELOE POMERANCE, shaddock citron
bt POMEROY the king-apple
zo POMFRET a fish
POMMAGE crushed apples
POMMARD a Burgundy wine
zo POMPANO edible fish (N. Amer.)
bt POMPION pumpkin
bt POMPIRE an apple
mu POMPOSO with due pomp
POMPOUS self-important; grandiose
bt PONCEAU poppy; poppy-coloured
PONDAGE water in a pond
PONDING collecting into a pond
mt PONENTE W. wind, Mediterranean (It.)
zo PONGIDS long-armed gibbons (apes)
PONIARD dagger
PONTAGE bridge toll
rl PONTIFF high priest; pope
PONTINE Roman marsh
PONTOON bridge of boats; card game
POOH-BAH a pluralist
POOLING merging; combining
POOPING (following sea)
POOR-BOX alms for the poor
POOREST most necessitous; neediest

POOR-LAW charity provisions
bt POPCORN parched maize
rl POPEDOM papality
POP-EYED with protruding eyes
ck POPOVER Amer. 'Yorkshire pudding'
POPPIED drowsy; slumbrous; narcotic
POPPING exploding; darting eyes; (-in)
POPPING surface pitting; uncorking
POPPLED rippled; bubbled
POP-SHOP soda-fountain bar
POPULAR commonly liked; (prices)
bt POP-WEED bladder-wort
PORCATE ridged
zo PORCINE piggy; swinish; suiform
PORIFER a sponge
ck PORK-PIE type of hat; meat in pastry
md POROSIS bone formation
md POROTIC (porosis); callous
ch PORPHIN pyrrole/methene nucleus
PORRECT erect; extended
md PORRIGO dandruff
nt PORTAGE conveying boats overland
nt PORT-BAR harbour bar; (sand spit)
PORTEND foretell; augur; bode
PORTENT an evil omen; presage
PORTICO porch; stoa; colonnade
PORTIFY aggrandize
PORTING PORTAGE, conveying; carrying
PORTION bit; part; share; division
pr PORTRAY depict; describe (art) (words)
zo PORZANA water-rail; crake
mu POSAUNE German trombone
POSITED affirmed; postulated
mu POSITIF small choir organ (Fr.)
POSSESS own; hold; keep; control
POSTAGE mail carriage fee
POST-BAG sack for letters
POST-BOX letter-box
POST-BOY mail collector
POST-DAY day for sending/getting mail
POSTEEN Kashmir sheepskin coat
POSTERN back-door; small gate
POSTFIX affix; suffix; append
POSTING mailing; recording
POSTMAN letter carrier
POSTURE pose; attitude; position
POST-WAR since hostilities ended
POTABLE drinkable; liquid
POTAGER porringer; soup-bowl
zo POTAMIC pertaining to rivers; (hippo-)
POTANCE part of a watch

POTARGO a pickle
ch POTASSA potash
POTATOR an imbiber; toper
pp POTCHER paper-pulp machine
hd POTENCE heraldic gibbet
hr POTENCE inverted clock
ch POTENCY effectiveness; strength
POT-HEAD dunderhead
POTHEEN home-distilled spirits (Irish)
ck POT-HERB herbal cookery flavouring
gl POT-HOLE earth cavity (water-course)
POT-HOOK kettle-holder (fireplace)
POTICHE porcelain vase
ce POT-LIFE period in pot etc.
ck POT-LUCK makeshift meal; make-do
POTOROO rat kangaroo
POT-SHOP pub; off-licence
POT-SHOT random round; sly remark
ck POTTAGE nourishing thick soup; (mess)
POTTERY ceramics (factory)
POTTING preserving; shooting; (plants)
zo POUCHED bagged; marsupial
zo POULARD plump hen; pullet
zo POULTRY fattened fowls
POUNCED with claws; sprang; swooped
me POUNDAL unit of force
md POUNDED struck; to crush; (heartbeats)
POUNDER weight of projectile (gunnery)
POUNDER grinder; pestle; hand-mill
POURING streaming; gushing; (rain)
POUTING sulking; grimacing; (displeasure)
POVERTY want; penury; indigence
POWDERY pulverous; floury; dusty
POWERED engined
PRAESES academical disputers
PRAETOR Roman magistrate
go PRAIRIE treeless grassy lands
PRAISED lauded; glorified
PRAISER laudator; extoller; eulogizer
PRAKARA temple passage (India)
PRAKRIT Sanskrit and allied languages
ck PRALINE chocolate sweetmeat
PRANCED strutted; bounded; (horses)
PRANGED bombed heavily; struck
PRANKED played comic tricks
PRANKER practical joker
bt PRATIES potatoes (Irish)

PRATING babbling; boasting
PRATTLE idle chatter
rl PRAYING addressing God; entreating
PREACHY tediously didactic
rl PREBEND canon's stipend
PRECEDE herald; usher; introduce
PRECEPT behest; maxim; rule; canon
lw PRECIPE writ
PRECISE exact; accurate; finical
PREDATE ante-date
PREDIAL (farm estate)
PREDICT foretell; calculate future
PREDONE completed in advance
PREDOOM judge in advance of facts
PRE-ECHO prior sound from record defect
cp PRE-EDIT run of input data, records
PREEMPT appropriate in advance
PREENED tidied up
PREFACE preamble; prologue
PREFECT French magistrate; monitor
PREFINE limit; delimit
PREFORM form beforehand
PREFORM larger moulding composition
ck PREHEAT heat (oven) up for use
rl PRELACY episcopal church government
rl PRELATE church dignitary
PRELECT discourse; lecture; address
PRELIMS introductory features of book
PRELIMS examinations
mu PRELUDE preface; exordium
PREMIAL at a premium
PREMIER first; principal; P.M.
PREMISE antecedent proposition
PREMISS logical premise
PREMIUM bounty; fee; reward; bonus
lw PRENDER right of seizure
md PREORAL in front of the jaw
PREPAID paid in advance
PREPARE make ready (for process, action)
md PREPUCE foreskin; penile cover
zo PREPUPA insect larval stage
PRESAGE foretell; predict; prophesy
PRESEEN foreseen
PRESELL promote products in advance
PRESENT here; now; existing; current
PRESENT exhibit; proffer; gift
PRESIDE officiate; direct; control
PRESSED urged; crushed; encroached

PRESSER squeezer (clothes-)
mu PRESSEZ increase speed (Fr.)
md PRESSOR causing arterial pressure rise
PRESTER medieval king; (priest-king)
PRESUME assume; suppose; reckon
PRETEND feign; simulate; claim (title)
PRETEST pre-examine; check; control
PRETEXT excuse; plea; cloak
PRETONE (accented syllable)
PRETZEL crisp biscuit
PREVAIL dominate; win; succeed
PREVENE precede
PREVENT hinder; hamper; thwart
PREVIEW foresee
PREVISE forewarn; foresee
PREWARN give notice of
PREYFUL predatory
PREYING plundering; wasting; robbing
rl,pl PRIAPUS god of procreation; (erection)
PRICING costing; valuing; rating
PRICKED spurred; punctured; bored
PRICKER prickle; light horseman
PRICKET early candlestick
zo PRICKET a young buck
bt PRICKET stone-crop
bt PRICKLE to prick; a thorn
PRICKLY spinate; spicate
PRIDIAN of yesterday
PRIDING valuing; esteeming highly
PRIDWIN King Arthur's shield
PRIGGED filched; purloined; nabbed
PRIGGER thief; pincher
rl PRIMACY leading archbishopric
PRIMAGE a lading charge
PRIMARY main; first; pristine; initial
zo,rl PRIMATE genus of apes; archbishop
PRIMELY originally; excellently
PRIMERO card game
ck PRIMEUR early wine (Beaujolais) (Fr.)
bt PRIMINE outer husk
pt PRIMING (powder); first coat
PRIMMED formed precisely
bt PRIMULA primrose genus
PRINKED pranked; all dressed up
PRINKER (dressed showily)
PRINTED published; pressed; issued
PRINTER typographer
PRISAGE a levy on wines
bt PRISERE primary succession
PRISING forcing open; levering
zo PRISTIS saw-fish

PRITHEE I pray thee
PRIVACY seclusion; solitude; retreat
PRIVATE soldier; personal; unofficial
PRIVILY privately; confidentially
PRIVITY secrecy; cognizance
PRIZING appreciating; valuing
md PROBANG whalebone swab
lw PROBATE proof of a will
PROBING scrutinizing; testing;
  sifting
PROBITY proved integrity; sincerity
PROBLEM enigma; query;
  conundrum
bt PROCARP female organ in
  rhodophyta
PROCEED advance; continue; act
PROCESS operation; course; progress
cp PROCESS method; patterning of data
lw PROCTOR university official
PROCURE get; obtain; induce
PROCYON lesser Dog-star
PRODDED goaded; shoved; poked
PRODDER inciter; stimulator
PRODIFY modify production car
  (motor racing)
mu PRODIGY marvel; wonder; (infant)
PRODUCE engender; show; bring
  forth
cp, ck PRODUCT arithmetic; concoction
PRODUCT staple; yield; commodity
PROFACE May it profit you!
PROFANE desecrate; secular
PROFESS own; aver; proclaim
PROFFER offer; tender; volunteer
bd PROFILE outline view; biography
PROFUSE lavish; prodigal; copious
PROGENY offspring; issue; young
PROGGED begged; prodded;
  (proctored)
PROGRAM programme; syllabus
PROJECT propel; contrive; jut
PROLATE extended
zo PROLEGS legs of caterpillars
ch PROLINE protein cleavage product
PROLONG protract; lengthen; sustain
md PROMINE cancer-cell growth
  stimulant
PROMISE pledge; engage; stipulate
PROMOTE further; sponsor; organize
PRONAOS temple porch
PRONATE face or palms downwards
PRONELY lying down
PRONGED fork-like; bifurcated
zo PRONOTA beetles' backs
PRONOUN word for known person,
  thing
PROOFED PROVEN, tried, tested
md PROOTIC an ear-bone

PROPALE to disclose
PROPANE paraffin gas
PROPEND to favour; lean forward
ch PROPENE propyl alcohol
PROPHET seer; augur; preacher
PROPINE pledge; guarantee
ch PROPINE methyl acetylene
ae PROPJET a turboprop aircraft
PROPOSE suggest; intend; purpose
PROPPED shored; strutted;
  supported
PROPUGN vindicate; defend
PRORATE assess pro rata
md PRORSAD prorsal; anterior
PROSAIC unexciting; dull; humdrum
PROSIFY turn into prose
PROSILY unimaginatively
PROSING talking tediously
PROSODY (harmonious writing)
PROSPER thrive; flourish; succeed
PROTEAN in many guises
PROTECT shield; defend; ward
PROTEGE trusted nominee
ch PROTEID complex essential food
ch PROTEIN dietetic energy component
PROTEND hold out; extend
PROTEST expostulate; exclaim;
  object
PROTEUS sea-god of Carpathian
  Sea
ch PROTIUM hydrogen isotope
PROTYLE hypothetical nucleus
PROUDER more arrogant and
  haughty
PROUDLY majestically; imperiously
PROVANT of inferior quality
PROVERB saw; adage; epigram;
  maxim
PROVIDE supply; produce; survey
PROVINE (vine culture)
cp PROVING truth; fault-testing
  program
lw PROVING establishing; trying; trial
PROVISO a condition
PROVOKE infuriate; enrage; rouse
rl PROVOST magistrate
PROWESS valour; skill; dexterity
PROWLED slunk; roved; roamed
PROWLER stealthy stalker
PROXIME nearest
PROXIMO next month
PRUDENT wise; cautious; frugal
PRUDERY mock modesty
PRUDISH very formal; puritanical
bt PRUNING lopping; clipping;
  trimming
md PRURIGO an itch
ch PRUSSIC acid; a cyanide

PRY-OVER Canadian canoe sideways movement
PRYTANY Athenian Council division
PRYTHEE I pray thee
PSALTER psalm book; rosary
PSCHENT royal crown of ancient Egypt
md **PSOATIC** (tenderloin)
PSYCHAL spiritualistic
PSYCHIC not based on materialism
cl **PSYCHRO-** of coldness (Gr.)
md **PTARMIC** sneezing mixture
md **PTERION** (craniology)
PTEROMA Greek peridrome; side-wall
zo **PTEROPE** flying fox; fruit-bat
md **PTOMAIN PTOMAINE** toxic poison
md **PTYALIN** (saliva)
PUBERAL of age
PUBERTY the generative age
PUBLISH announce; disclose; blazon
gs **PUCELLA** wine-glass top opener
PUCELLE Joan of Arc
zo **PUCERON** plant louse
PUCKERY wrinkled
PUCKISH impish; mischievous
PUCK-OUT free hit by defenders (hurling)
PUDDING fruity farinaceous food
PUDDLED stirred up the mud
PUDDLER iron-worker
PUDENCY modesty; bashfulness
PUEBLAN Mexican aborigine
pc **PUERILE** child-like, irresponsible acts
le **PUERING** skin-steeping/softening
PUFF-BOX powder compact
PUFFERY PUFFING, overdone advertisement
PUFFIER more swollen (skin)
PUFFILY bombastic; conceited
PUFF-OUT breather pause; exhale (smoke)
PUGMILL clay mill
pl **PUG-NOSE** boxer's flattened nose
bt **PULIALL** pennyroyal herb
nt **PULLIES** pulley-wheels (block/tackle)
PULLING towing; drawing back; extract
PULLING (weapon) (votes) (punches) (oars)
rw **PULLMAN** luxury railway carriage
PULL-OUT extensible; withdrawal; quit
ck **PULPIFY** make mash; purée
PULPOUS like pulp
PULSATE throb (rhythm); vitality

pl **PULSING** heart beats; vibration
el **PULSION** electric waves; surges
ck **PUMMAGE** crushed apples (cider)
PUMPAGE the amount pumped
PUMPING extracting information
PUMPING syphoning liquids
ga **PUMPING** to vary weight (skateboards)
bt **PUMPKIN** pumpion; quashey; a gourd
au **PUMP-ROD** part of engine
PUNCHED perforated; struck
PUNCHER a bruiser; cattle drover
PUNCH-UP fist-fight (boxing)
zo **PUNCTUM** marking dot; tiny aperture
PUNGENT acrid; caustic; tart
PUNJABI an Indo-Aryan language
PUNNING play on word similarities
PUNSTER a maker of puns
PUNTING gambling against banker
PUNTING poling a punt forward
ga **PUNTING** football pool chancing
zo **PUPATED** formed a chrysalis
rl **PURANIC** (Brahmin scriptures)
mn **PURBECK** Dorset stone
ar **PURFLED** decorated
PURFLEW wrought border
PURGING cleaning up; pruning
PURITAN religious bigot
PURLIEU slum; environs
PURLINE timber-work
PURLING rippling
PURLOIN steal; pilfer; filch
PURPLED dyed purple; imperial
md **PURPLES** livid spots
PURPORT significate; state intent
PURPOSE aim; reason for action
zo, hd **PURPURA** Tyrian heraldic purple
PURRING curring; (feline felicitude)
PURROCK PADDOCK, witch's cat
PURSING wrinkling
PURSUED continued; hunted; practised
lw **PURSUER** plaintiff (Sc.)
PURSUIT chase; search; hobby
ga **PURSUIT** track-cycling start-points
PURVIEW extent; scope; range
PUSHFUL enterprising; self-assertive
PUSH-OFF leave hastily; forced departure
ga **PUSHPIN** a child's game
au **PUSH-ROD** auto engine part
PUSTAKA Indonesian magic book (on bark)
md **PUSTULE** a pus-pimple
go **PUSZTAS** Hungarian open plain
bt **PUTAMEN** fruit-stone; husk

md **PUTAMEN** lenticular nucleus
bd **PUTLOGS** horizontal bearers
(scaffolding)
PUTRIFY rot; decay; decompose
PUTTIED fixed with putty
PUTTIER glazier
PUTTIES leg-wear; puttees
PUTTING (golf); (the weight)
zo **PUTTOCK** kite; buzzard
PUTWITH acknowledgement,
addenda for book
PUZZLED perplexed; mystified
PUZZLER poser; riddler
md **PYAEMIA** blood-poisoning
md **PYAEMIC** suffering from pyaemia
mn **PYCNITE** topaz
bt **PYCNIUM** spermogonium in
uredinales
zo **PYEBALD PIEBALD**, 2 colours (horses)
PYE-BOOK rules to determine Easter
date
PYGMEAN PIGMEAN, dwarfish
PYGMIES negrillos; negritas; 1.5 m.
tall
tx **PYJAMAS PAJAMAS**, nightwear
zo **PYLORIC** of stomach-intestine entry
md **PYLORUS** an outlet
rl **PYRAMID** triangular on a square;
tomb
cy **PYRENIN** paranuclein
md **PYRETIC** fever-reducer
PYREXIA PYREXIC, of fever
mn **PYRITES PYRITIC**, flints
md **PYROGEN** fever inducer
md **PYROSIS** indigestion; heartburn
md **PYROTIC** caustic; burning
PYRRHIC victory at great cost
ch **PYRROLE** coal-tar constituent
bc **PYRUVIC** of an α-keto acid
PYTHIAD a period
PYTHIAN oracular
bt **PYXIDIA** capsules

Q

el **Q-FACTOR** efficiency, reactive circuit
me, nc **Q-FACTOR** ditto electrical
components
zo **QUABIRD** night heron
QUACKED boasted; practised
quackery
QUACKLE CAKKLE, croak; quack
(ducks)
pr **QUADRAT** filling piece in printing
QUADREL square tile
QUADRIC four-sided, oblong shape
QUAFFED tippled; swilled; caroused

QUAFFER deep drinker; soaker; toper
zo **QUAHAUG** American clam
QUAILED flinched; cowered;
blenched
rl **QUAKERS QUAKERY, QUAKERISM**, a
sect
QUAKING shaking; quivering
QUALIFY entitle; regulate; dilute
QUALITY trait; attribute; grade
bt **QUAMASH** camass lily
zo **QUANACO** S. American llama
to **QUANNET** flat file
cf **QUANTAL** small changes, amounts
QUANTIC algebraic function
QUANTUM a sufficiency; elemental
unit
el, nc **QUANTUM** radiant energy; theory
QUARREL wrangle; brawl; bicker
QUARREL cross-bow bolt; diamond
pane
QUARTEN every fourth day
ma **QUARTER** one fourth; district; mercy
mu **QUARTET** 4-part music
mn **QUARTZY** of quartz silicon
as **QUASARS** quasi-stellar radio sources
QUASHED rendered void; nullified
bt **QUASHEY** pumpkin; a gourd
bt **QUASSIA QUASSIN**, bitter, tonic
QUATERN a quarter; 4-pound loaf
QUAVERY tremulous; quivery;
tottery
QUAYAGE quay dues
QUEACHY bog-like; unsteady;
yielding
QUEENED played the queen
QUEENLY regal
QUEERED put at a disadvantage
QUEERER odder; rummier; stranger
QUEERLY quaintly; whimsically
QUELLED crushed; allayed; quenched
QUELLER subduer; represser
bt **QUERCUS** oak
QUERELA complaint
lw **QUERENT** inquirer; plaintiff
QUERIED doubted; challenged
QUERIST questioner; interrogator
QUERLED twirled
QUERNEL oaken
QUESTED sought; requested
QUESTER a seeker; searcher;
candidate
QUESTOR Roman treasury official
nm, zo **QUETZAL** resplendent trogon
QUIBBED quipped; sneered
QUIBBLE prevaricate; cavil; trifle
QUICKEN revive; rouse; expedite
QUICKER faster; more swiftly
QUICKIE a fatuous film

QUICKLY rapidly; speedily; pronto
QUIDDIT a quibble
QUIDDLE to potter
QUIETED calmed; assuaged; mollified
QUIETEN lull; allay; pacify; soothe
QUIETER more placid or secluded
QUIETLY peacefully; serenely
QUIETUS discharge; death
QUILLED pleated; crimped
QUILLER adept at paper-filigree art
QUILLET a quibble; a furrow
QUILLON part of a sword-guard
QUILTED padded; tufted
QUILTER coverlet maker
ma QUINARY in fives (biquinary= 2×binary)
bt QUINATE five-leafed
bt, md QUININE bitter (tonic water)
zo QUINNAT king salmon
ch QUINONE (benzene)
QUINTAD pentad
me QUINTAL a hundredweight
me QUINTAL 100 kilograms weight
md QUINTAN recurring ague
nm QUINTAR (Albania)
mu QUINTET 5-part music
ma QUINTIC QUINTUS, of the fifth degree
QUIPPED quibbled; taunted
QUIRING singing in unison
QUISCHE be still; calm; be silent
QUITTAL repayment; requital
QUITTED abandoned; forsook; left
vt QUITTER shirker; horse ulcer; deserter
vt QUITTOR foot cartilage suppuration
QUI-VIVE alert; on the look-out
QUIXOTE a chivalrous Don
QUIZZED queried; bantered; chaffed
QUIZZER questioner; a joker
bt, ck QUODLIN CODLING, cooking apple; boy
QUONDAM former
QUOTING citing; pricing
QUOTITY quantity

R

RABBANA raffia matting (Madagascar)
RABBITY petty; rabbit-like
RABBLER puddler; iron-worker
RABBONI Jewish title
RABIDLY frantically; maniacally
md RABIFIC causing hydrophobia
RABINET ancient gun
RABIOUS raging mad
zo RACCOON N. American racoon

RACE-CUP a trophy
bt RACEMED clustered
ch RACEMIC acid from grapes
RACEWAY sluice
RACKETS raquet and ball game in court; (squash)
mu RACKETT woodwind, 'sausage bassoon'
RACKETY bobbery; clamorous
RACKING decanting; straining
ga RACQUET RACKET, (tennis, badminton)
RADDLED interwoven; infested
zo RADDOCK RUDDOCK, robin red-breast
md RADIALE radiocarpal bone
RADIANT beaming; effulgent; shining
RADIATE sparkle; glitter; emit
RADICAL essential; root; basic change
RADICAL Liberal; molecular atoms
ga RADICAL exacting skateboarding
bt RADICEL small root of seedling
RADICLE root; corm; rootlet
RADIOED transmitted by wireless
RADULAR rasping; rough
RAFFING sweeping; snatching
RAFFISH rakish; dissipated
RAFFLED notched; (lottery)
RAFFLER lottery organizer
RAFT-DOG iron clamp
RAFTING raft-work
RAG-BOLT iron holdfast
bt RAG-BUSH heathen shrine
RAG-DUST rag refuse
RAGEFUL angered; wroth; ireful
RAG-FAIR old clothes sale
RAGGERY rags collectively
RAGGING boisterous pranks; rampaging
RAGGING teasing; students' stunts
tx RAGSHOP used clothes junk shop
mu RAGTIME syncopation with rhythm (jazz)
hd RAGULED jagged
bt RAG-WEED RAGWORT
tx RAG-WOOL shoddy
bd RAGWORK mason's work with stones
RAIDING foraying; pillaging
rw RAILBUS bus-engine railway coach
rw RAILCAR self-propelled rail coach
RAILING fencing; nagging; rating
to, rw RAILSAW portable saw
rw RAILWAY RAILROAD, iron road (trains)
RAIMENT garb; vesture; apparel
RAINBOW water-refracted sunlight

RAINING pouring; showering
mt RAINMAP weather chart
RAISING growing; erecting; lifting
RAISING levying; (old) pipe-making
RAKE-OFF share of crooked profits
RALLIED recovered; reformed
RALLIES bouts; jamborees
zo RALLINE waterbirds
rl RAMADAN RAMAZAN, month of fasting
RAMBADE boarding platform
RAMBLED sauntered; maundered
RAMBLER footpath, pleasure walker
bt RAMBLER climbing rose; long-winded
bt, ck RAMEKIN RAMSKIN, cheese savoury
bt RAMENTA scales on ferns
bt RAMEOUS RAMULOUS, branching out
RAM-HEAD iron lever; a cuckold
RAMLINE guide line in ship-building
RAMMING thrusting; forcing
zo RAMMISH of ram; strong-scented
RAMPAGE wild uncontrolled behaviour
hd RAMPANT exuberant; rearing stance
bd RAMPART fortified wall; bastion
bt RAMPICK RAMPIKE, tree-stump; log
RAMPING creeping; climbing; bounding
bt RAMPION campanula
bt, ck RAMSKIN RAMEKIN, cheese savoury
RAMSONS garlic, broad-leaved
bt RAMULUS small branch
RANCHED (stock farming)
RANCHER stock-breeder
RANCOUR deep-seated enmity
RANGERS National Parks' patrol men
hd RANGIER scythe
RANGING ranking; roving; extending
zo RANIDAE the frogs
RANKEST coarsest; most rancid
RANKING grading; ranging
RANKLED festered; smouldered
RANSACK rummage; pillage; plunder
RANTING orating; declaiming; raving
zo RANTOCK goosander
bt RAPE-OIL cole-seed oil
nt RAPFULL full of wind
RAPHAEL an archangel; a painter
bt RAPHIDE plant-cell crystal
RAPIDLY speedily; swiftly; despatch
RAPPING knocking; hitting; beating
fd RAPPING mould pattern loosening
pc RAPPORT harmony; understanding
RAPTURE ecstasy; beatitude; bliss
ck RAREBIT Welsh cheese savoury

nt RASCONA sail cargo boat, Venice
mn RASHING thin layer of shale/poor coal
zo RASORES gallinaceous birds
RASPING grating; abrading
mu RASTRUM a music-pen
RATABLE taxable; assessable
RATABLY by rate
RATAFIA almond-flavoured biscuit
mu RATATAT drumming
RATCHED stretched; racked
RATCHEL ratchil; loose stones
RATCHET pawl; toothed bar
RAT-HOLE retreat for rat
zo RATITAE (ostriches, emus, kiwis)
nt RATLINE RATLING, rigging ladder step
RAT-RACE career competition
RAT-TAIL tapering
tx RATTEEN twilled wool
RATTERY apostasy
RATTING quitting; abandoning
RATTLED clattered; shaken
RATTLER snake
bt RATTOON young sugar-cane
RAT-TRAP bicycle pedal
RAUCITY hoarseness
RAUCOUS harsh; noisy
RAUNCHY male ruggedness; strength
RAVAGED laid waste; devastated
RAVAGER despoiler; plunderer
RAVELIN part of a fort
RAVENED preyed; plundered
RAVENER ravager; devourer
RAVINED gullied
ck RAVIOLI small filled pasta cases (It.)
RAWBONE gaunt, lean person
RAWCOLD damp and cold
RAWHEAD bughead; devil; scarecrow
RAWHIDE untanned skin
RAWNESS immaturity; callowness
nt RAWPORT porthole for an oar
RAYLESS dark
REACHED attained; arrived; stretched
REACHER stretcher
REACTED took violent action
nc REACTOR atomic power generator
READIED prepared
READIER prompter; more glib
READILY willingly; cheerfully
READING recital; version; studying
READMIT glove used when reading
cp READ-OUT transfer of data
READ-OUT data display on screen
ch REAGENT active agent
REAGREE reconcile
mn REALGAR red arsenic

REALIEN objects for study; teaching aids
REALISM natural limits accepted
REALISM naturalism in art
REALIST a facer of facts
REALITY actuality; truth; verity
REALIZE convert into cash
REALLOT re-assign
REALTOR estate agent (USA)
REAMING enlarging a hole
REANNEX claim back; reunite
REAPING harvesting
RE-APPLY repeat a process
RE-ARGUE rediscuss a matter
REARING breeding; lifting; raising
REARISE reascend
REARMED re-equipped
RE-AROSE got up again
ps REAUMUR scale of temperature
REAVING bereaving; ravaging
REAWAKE rouse again
REBATED blunted; diminished
REBIRTH renascence
REBLOOM impossible action
REBOANT resounding; reverberating
REBORED facelift for gun-barrel
REBOUND bounce back; recoil
ga REBOUND regain the ball (basketball)
REBUILD REBUILT, re-erected
REBUKED chided; upbraided
REBUKER reproacher; gainsayer
RECEDED retreated; withdrew
RECEIPT a recipe; formula; quittance
RECEIVE welcome; acquire; get
RECENCY newness
RECITAL concert; narration
RECITED RECITER, narrated; narrator
RECLAIM rescue; salve; regain
RECLASP refasten
RECLINE lean; lie; rest; repose
RECLOSE fail to keep open
RECLUSE sequestered; a hermit
RECOAST coast back
RECOUNT tell; relate; enumerate
hd RECOUPE heraldic division
RE-COVER cover anew
RECOVER rally; revive; retrieve
RECROSS go back over
RECRUIT enlist; novice
RECTIFY amend; correct; redress
RECTION grammatic influence
rl RECTORY rector's benefice
zo RECTRIX steering feather
RECURVE concave; backwards
zo RED-BIRD bull-finch
RED-BOOK a register
nm RED-CENT copper cent
RED-CLAY raddle; reddle

REDCOAT a soldier
REDCOCK incendiary fire
mn RED-CRAG Pliocene rock
zo RED-DEER the common stag
REDDEST ultra-radical
REDDISH colour; rubicund; Titian
zo RED-DRUM RED-BASS, fish
REDEYED needing sleep
zo RED-FISH Pacific salmon
RED-HAND (Ulster)
zo REDHEAD red-haired; a duck
REDLEAD oxide as orange pigment
zo REDLEGS purple sandpiper
REDNESS ruddiness
REDORSE reverse of dorsal
REDOUBT fort
REDOUND conduce; lead; tend
zo REDPOLL linnet
REDRAFT revised copy
REDRAWN drawn again
REDRESS remedy; reparation
REDRIVE drive back
bt RED-ROOT buckthorn
RED-SEAR to break when too hot
zo RED-SEED small crustaceans
REDSKIN N. American Indian
zo RED-TAIL N. American buzzard
RED-TAPE bumbling officialdom delays
REDUCED curtailed; abridged; (prices)
REDUCER contractor; diminisher
RED-WEED the poppy
zo REDWING fieldfare
bt REDWOOD sequoia tree
tx, ar REEDING combing (yarns); moulding
nt REEFING shortening sail
REEKING fuming; smoking
REELING staggering; vacillating
nt REEMING caulking
RE-ENTRY regress; return
RE-EQUIP rearm
RE-ERECT rebuild
nt REEVING (passing a rope)
REFEOFF reinvest in a fief
REFEREE umpire; arbitrator; judge
REFINED highly cultivated
REFINER purifier; clarifier
REFLAME flare up again
REFLECT mirror; muse; meditate
REFORGE fashion anew
REFRACT to bend at an angle
REFRAIN chorus; forgo; abstain
REFRESH invigorate; revive; brace
REFUGED took sanctuary
REFUGEE a displaced person
REFUSAL declination; denial

REFUSED declined; denied; vetoed
REFUSER repudiator
REFUTED disproved; confuted
REFUTER rebutter
REGALED entertaining sumptuously
REGALIA insignia of royalty
REGALLY royally
nt **REGATTA** waterborne competitions
REGENCY rule of a stand-in (heir)
ar **REGENCY** fashions and of arts
REGIBLE governable
REGIMEN regulation; diet
REGNANT ruling
REGORGE vomit
REGRADE re-assess
REGRANT grant again
bd **REGRATE** retail; treating hewn stone
REGREET welcome again
pc **REGRESS** return; revert to
   (hypnosis)
REGULAR steady; systematic; normal
gn **REGULON** enzyme-production gene
as **REGULUS** star in Leo
ma **REGULUS** line set in ruled surface
REIGNED ruled; administered
REINING curbing; restraining
REINTER to bury again
zo **REIT-BOK** S. African buck
REJOICE revel; exult; gladden
cr **REJOINT** make a new joint
RELAPSE revert; backsliding
RELATED akin; connected; recited
RELATER gives an honest account
cp, lw **RELATOR** linkup factor; informant
RELAXED loosened; slackened;
   abated
ro **RELAYED** transmitted
RELEASE set free; emancipate;
   liberate
RE-LEASE lease again
RELIANT confident; self-assured
RELIEVE release; allay; assuage
RELIEVO rilievo; in relief
RELIGHT rekindle; reignite
rl **RELIQUE** a holy relic (Fr.)
RELIVED lived again
RELUMED rekindled
RELYING depending; trusting
REMAINS (literary productions)
REMAINS evidence of past history
lw **REMANET** delayed lawsuit
REMERGE merge again
zo **REMIGES** flight feathers
zo **REMIPED** oar-shaped feet
lw **REMISED** released; surrendered
REMNANT residue; odd lot; fragment
REMODEL refashion; remake;
   redesign

REMORSE anguish; compunction
REMOTER farther off
REMOULD shape anew
zo **REMOUNT** a fresh horse
REMOVAL euphemism for murder
REMOVED dislodged; abstracted
REMOVER homestead shifter
REMPHAN Israelitish idol
RENAMED rechristened
RENDING ripping; tearing; severing
RENEGED denied; revoked
RENEWAL refreshment; extension
RENEWED repeated; rejuvenated
RENEWER renovator
RENT-DAY time to pay or flit
RENTIER estate or fund holder
RENTING letting; leasing
RENUENT nodding
ga **RENVERS** half-pass in horse-dressage
REORDER bid again; repeat request
REPAINT (a golf ball); a fresh coating
REPAPER (a palindrome); redecorate
mu **REPIANO REPIENO**, all performers
   (It.)
REPINED fretted; murmured; envied
REPINER plaintive person
REPIQUE (piquet)
REPLACE reinstate; refund
REPLAIT refold
REPLETE crammed; fraught
lw **REPLEVY** to bail
REPLICA a copy; duplicate; model
REPLIED answered; folded back
REPLIER respondent
REPLUME to preen
REPOINT sharpen; accentuate
bd **RE-POINT** restore brickwork joins
REPONED replaced; relied
REPOSAL rest; sleep; ease
REPOSED settled; reclined
REPOSER slumberer
REPOSIT replace item in right place
REPRESS crush; check; restrain
REPRINT a subsequent edition
lw **REPRISE** repeat of music, song;
   estate charge; (fencing)
REPRIVE deprive (obs.)
REPROOF censure
REPROVE chide; upbraid
zo **REPTANT** creeping; reptilian
zo **REPTILE** crocodile; snake
REPULSE rebuff; deter; reject
REPUTED alleged; deemed; reckoned
REQUEST demand; entreat; solicit
rl **REQUIEM** a mass
REQUIRE want; lack; desire; need
REQUITE repay; reward; avenge
rl **REREDOS** altar screen

RESCIND revoke; quash; cancel
mu **RE-SCORE** try again
RESCUED freed; liberated
RESCUER deliverer; saviour
lw **RESEIZE** (legal confiscation)
RESERVE withhold; restraint
RESERVE set aside (for future) (land)
RESHAPE remould; remodel
lw **RESIANT** resident
RESIDED abode; inhered
RESIDER sojourner; dweller
RESIDUE remainder; dregs
RESILED showed ability to recover
RESOLVE determine; resolution
RESOUND reverberate; extol; echo
RE-SOUND reconsult; second opinion
RESPEAK repeat; reply
RESPECT revere; honour; esteem
RESPIRE breathe; inhale
RESPITE reprieve; pause; rest
RE-SPOKE reiterated; maintenance
  (bicycle)
RESPOND answer; accord; tally; react
ar **RESPOND** pillar set under arch
ar **RESSAUT** a projection
RESTANT persistent; remaining
RESTART return to paid work
cp **RESTART** recommence re-run
RESTATE re-assert; recite
lw **RESTAUR** claim for indemnity
REST-DAY the Sabbath
RESTFUL tranquil; quiescent; irenic
RESTING reposing; relaxing; leaning
RESTIVE refractory; obstinate
RESTOCK replenish
RESTORE reinstate; repair; heal
RE-STORE return to store
mn **RESUING** pre-mining technique
RESUMED renewed; continued
rl **RESURGE** rise again
RETABLE altar shelf for candles
RETAKEN recaptured
RETAKER recaptor
RETENUE self-control
RETIARY net-like, (gladiator)
RETICLE small net; reticule
md **RETINAL** RETINA, of eyes and sight
RETINOL resin oil; vitamin A
RETINUE suite; escort; bodyguard
zo **RETIPED** having veined feet
RETIRAL withdrawal; departure
RETIRED left; retreated; secluded
RETOUCH re-engrave; revise
RETRACE return by the same road
RETRACT adjure; recant; withdraw
RETREAD repair of a tyre
RETREAT recede; asylum; refuge
lw **RETRIAL** repeating court case

RETRUDE to thrust back
RETRUSE abstruse; hidden; occult
RETTERY flax mill
RETTING prepared flax
RETYRED renewed motor tyre
  surfaces
REUNIFY rejoin
REUNION social gathering
REUNITE reconcile; recombine
REURGED entreated again
REUTTER repeat; reiterate
REVALUE re-assess
REVELRY carousal; debauch; orgy
REVENGE requite; retaliate; vindicate
REVENUE income; return; reward
nt **REVENUE** (-man) (-cutter) ship
REVERED honoured; worshipped
REVERER venerator
REVERIE dreaminess; trance; vision
REVERSE backwards; setback;
  backspin
REVERSE misfortune; opposite;
  turnround
ga **REVERSI** a counter-game
REVERSO left-hand page of a book
hd **REVESTU** heraldic squaring
REVILED aspersed; vilified; abused
REVILER a despiser; contempt
  spreader
REVISAL revision; reviewal
REVISED amended; altered
REVISIT return to the same place
REVISOR editor; checkman
REVIVAL comeback; repeat; recall
rl **REVIVAL** religious reawakening
REVIVED quickened; resuscitated
REVIVER invigorator; rouser
lw **REVIVOR** renewed action
REVOKED reneged; repealed;
  quashed
REVOLVE rotate; spin; whirl; circle
REVVING spinning at speed
REWAKEN re-arouse
REWRITE recall; transcribe; revise
cp **REWRITE** return data to former
  location
zo **REYNARD** the fox
RHAETIC Ladino; Latin-Swiss
pl **RHAGADE** RHAGOSE, spongy wet skin
  crack
bt **RHAMNUS** buckthorn, etc.
bt **RHATANY** Peruvian shrub
RHEMISH (Rheims)
RHENISH (Rhine) (wine)
ch **RHENIUM** metallic element
zo **RHESIAN** RHESUS, sacred monkey
  (India)
zo **RHIZOTA** small aquatic animals

bt **RHIZOTE** rooted
RHODIAN RHODESIAN, (Cecil
  Rhodes)
ch **RHODIUM** hard white metal
bt **RHODORA** rhododendron
RHOMBIS RHOMBUS, oblique
  parallelogram
md **RHONCUS** harsh bronchial-tube
  sound
zo **RHOPODE** a marine invertebrate
bt, ck, cp **RHUBARB** pudding plant; statists'
  talk; rubbishy argument
RHYMING versifying
RHYMIST ballad-monger
RHYNCHO snouted; (rhinoceros)
nt **RIB-BAND** shipbuilding technique
RIBBING lampooning; ridiculing
nt, bd **RIBBING** corrugation frame
tx **RIBBONS** decorative bands (medals
  etc.)
mu **RIBIBLE REBEC** (forerunner of
  violin)
RIBLIKE lying like slats
bt **RIBSTON** pippin; an apple
RICASSO part of rapier-blade
zo **RICE-HEN** American fowl
bt **RICINUS** castor-oil plant
RICKERS tree stems for spars
md **RICKETS** softness of the bones
RICKETY shaky; unstable; feeble
RICKING wrenching; spraining
RICKSHA jinricksha; carriage
ck **RICOTTA** bland creamy It. cheese
RIDABLE rideable
RIDDING freeing; banishing; clearing
RIDDLED full of holes
RIDDLER propounder of riddles
RIDE-OFF bumping and pushing
  (polo)
RIDERED stakes laid across bars
mu **RIDOTTO** musical entertainment (It.)
zo **RIETBOK** rietboc; reedbuck (S.
  Africa)
to **RIFFLER** curved file
RIFLING spiral grooving; ransacking
nt **RIFTING** riving; cleaving; splitting
gs **RIGAREE** broken design band; collar
nt **RIGGING** ropes, lines (masts, sails)
RIGGING fraudulent accounting,
  deals
RIGHTED redressed; rectified;
  adjusted
RIGHTEN set right; adjusted
RIGHTER redresser of wrongs
RIGHTLY properly; correctly
RIGIDLY inflexibly; staunchly
RIG-VEDA Vedic doctrine (India)
RIKSDAG Swedish Parliament

RILIEVO bas-relief
RILLING flowing; purling; rippling
RIMFIRE a cartridge
RIMLESS unframed
RIMMING making a border or edge
RIMPLED wrinkled; rumpled
ar **RINCEAU** vine-foliage moulding
  motif
RINDING peeling; excoriating
fr **RING-DOG** used for hauling timber
RINGENT irregular and gaping
zo **RINGHAL** spitting cobra
RINGING resounding
RINGLET circlet
RINGMAN Zulu chief
RING-NET butterfly-net
to **RING-SAW** scroll-saw
ga **RINKING** roller-skating; ice-skating
RINSING cleansing
mn **RIOLITE** silver selenide
RIOTING disorder; lawlessness
RIOTOUS turbulent; tumultuous
RIPCORD parachute release cord
mu **RIPIENO** supplementary
RIPOSTE lightning repartee;
  (fencing)
RIPPING splendid; tearing
RIPPLED purled; rilled
to **RIPPLER** comb for flax
RIPPLET tiny ripple
zo **RIPSACK** Californian whale
RIPTIDE fast flowing current
RISIBLE laughable; droll; absurd
RISIBLY amusingly; farcically
RISKIER more hazardous
RISKING venturing; chancing;
  hazarding
ck **RISOTTO** Italian rice dish
ck **RISSOLE** an entrée
RISTORI woman's jacket
zo **RITTOCK** tern
RIVALRY emulation; competition
RIVERET small river; stream; rivulet
RIVETED fastened
RIVETER clincher
RIVIERA fashionable resort
RIVIERE a necklace of jewels
RIVULET stream; brook; riveret
hd **RIZOMED** heraldic grains
ROADBED road foundation
ROADCAR rural streetcar
ROAD-HOG a motor pest
ROADING team racing
ROADMAN road repairer
ROAD-MAP plan of road network
ROADWAY highway; turnpike;
  autobahn
ROAMING roving; wandering

ROARING bellowing; shouting; bawling
ck ROASTED cooked in oven or embers
ROASTED cross-questioned; parched
ck ROASTER micro-oven; (pig, fowl etc.)
ROBBERY piracy; spoliation; pillage
ROBBING stealing; depriving; theft
zo ROBINET chaffinch
bt ROBINIA acacia
ROCK-CAM cam on rocking shaft
zo ROCK-DOE chamois
zo ROCK-EEL slippery customer
ROCKERY rock garden
ROCKIER more unstable
ROCKILY reeling; tottery
ROCKING lulling; staggering
mn ROCK-OIL petroleum; naphtha
sp ROCKOON balloon/rocket technique
mn ROCK-TAR petroleum
pb RODDING piping; drain-cleaning
RODLIKE cylindrical
ROD-LINE fishing line
RODOMEL roses and honey
ROD-RING (fishing-rod)
RODSTER an angler
zo ROE-BUCK male roe-deer
zo ROE-DEER small deer species
ROGALLO delta-shaped hang-glider
ROGUERY knavery; fraudulence
ROGUISH arch; wanton; puckish
ROILING rilling; angering
vt ROINISH ROINOUS, mangy; spotty
ROISTER to bluster; swagger; bully
ROKEAGE parched Indian corn
ROKELAY short cloak; roguelaure
ROLLICK frolic
ROLLING trundling; wallowing; lurching
ck ROLLMOP cured spiced herring
nt ROLL-OFF car ferry; primitive file
ae ROLL-OUT launching a new aircraft
ROLLTOP desk with sliding slats cover
ga ROLLWAY an incline, indoor bowls
ROMAIKA modern Greek dance
ROMAINE cos; firm-leafed lettuce
ROMANCE love story; (love affair)
ROMANCE ROMANIC, Latin-based tongue
ROMAUNT romance (exaggeration)
mn ROMEINE (antimony and lime)
mn ROMEITE antimonite of calcium
ROMMANY ROMANY, gipsy; (-language)
ROMPERS children's overalls
ROMPING frolicking; capering
ROMPISH frisky; sportive; frolicsome

zo RONCHIL ronquil; a N. Pacific fish
mu RONDEAU verse with a refrain
mu RONDENA Andalusian serenade
RONDEUR rounded contour; shape
md RONGEUR surgical forceps
zo RONQUIL ronchil, sea-fish
RÖNTGEN (X-rays)
ROOFING materials for roof
ROOFLET small roof
ROOF-TAX community tax
ROOINEK a Englishman (S. Africa)
zo ROOKERY (rooks); (seals)
ROOKING defrauding; fleecing
ROOK-PIE unsavoury dish
ROOMAGE stowage
ROOMFUL quantity of roses
ROOMIER more extensive
ROOMILY spaciously
ROOMING shared lodging
ROOSTED perched; slept
zo ROOSTER chanticleer; cock
ROOTAGE manner of rooting
bt ROOTCAP tip at end of root
ROOTERY pile of stumps
ROOTING eradicating; implanting
ROOTLED rummaged; dug
bt ROOTLET radicle; a root fibre
ROPALIC club-shaped
ROPEWAY aerial transport
zo RORQUAL a whale
mu ROSALIA progressive melody
ROSATED crowned with roses
ROSEATE rosy; blushing
bt ROSEBAY willow-herb
to ROSE-BIT (for countersinking)
bt ROSE-BOX a plant
bt ROSE-BUD what Citizen Kane said
zo ROSE-BUG rose-chafer
ROSE-CUT (diamond-cutting)
bt, ck ROSE-HAW ROSE-HIP wild rose fruit
ROSELET ermine's summer fur
zo ROSELLA a parakeet
bt ROSELLE rose-mallow
md ROSEOLA a rash
bt ROSE-RED deep-red (of roses)
ROSETTA inscribed (-lingual) stone
tx ROSETTE coloured cloth; a favour
ROSETTE party election badge
ROSIEST most blushing; reddest
ROSINED resined; gingered up
ROSLAND moorland
ck ROSOLIO raisin brandy
ROSSING bark removal
nt ROSTRAL Roman bow-beak (rammer)
ROSTRUM platform; pulpit; a beak
ROSULAR (leaves in clusters)
zo ROTALIA foraminifers

ROTATED revolved; spun; twirled
ROTATOR a rotor
zo ROTCHET red gurnard
zo ROTCHIE little auk; sea-dove
ROTELLA round shield
zo ROTIFER an animalcule
ROTODIP car-painting technique
ROTONDE ruff; cope (Fr.)
ROTTING decaying; fooling
me ROTTOLO Levantine weight
md ROTULAR (patella)
ROTUNDA circular building
ROUCHED puckered
ROUELLE wheel-like amulet
ROUERIE debauchery
ROUGHED rasped; (horse-shoes)
ROUGHEN scarify; coarsen
ROUGHER ruder; harsher; coarser
ROUGHIE hoodlum; hooligan
ROUGHLY boisterously; crudely
ROUGH-UP violent fight
ROUGING painting with rouge
ck ROULADE rolled meat
ROUNDED curved; turned
ROUNDEL a Norman shield; a ballad
ROUNDER more like a circle
ROUNDLY boldly; openly; plainly
ROUND-UP cowboys' work; rodeo
   show
hd ROUSANT starting up
ROUSING stimulating; brisk; lively
ROUSTER vagrant; vagabond
ROUTIER long-distance delivery-man
ROUTIER armed brigand (Fr.)
cp ROUTINE workstyle; regularity
   system
ROUTING utterly defeating; furrows
cp ROUTING itinerary; transmissions
ROUTISH clamorous; disorderly
ROWABLE a truly oarful state
nt ROWBOAT oars-boat
ROWDIER more uproarious or
   rampant
ROWDILY turbulently; noisily
nt ROWLOCK oarlock (rowing)
bd ROWLOCK bricklaying pattern
ROWPORT oar-hole
ROYALLY regally; imperially
ROYALTY author's perquisite
ROYNISH roinish; mangy
zo ROYSTON hooded crow
bt ROZELLE hibiscus
RUB-A-DUB beat of drum
mn RUBASSE Ancona ruby
RUBBING brass/stone tracing
   (brasses, tombstones)
RUBBING abrasion; chafing; erosion
RUBBING friction; massage (-down)

RUBBISH litter; trash; worthless
RUB-DOWN aphrodisiac
md RUBELLA German measles
RUBIATE madder
RUBICAN roan
mn RUBICEL variety of ruby
RUBICON boundary; fateful river
RUBIFIC making red
RUBIOUS ruby-red
RUBYING reddening
RUCHING a plaited frilling
RUCKING creasing; ruffling
RUCKLED wrinkled; rucked
RUCTION uproar; turmoil;
   disturbance
RUDDIED reddened
RUDDIER rosier; more rubicund
RUDDILY glowingly
tx RUDDLED interwoven; ochred
zo, bt RUDDOCK robin; apple
RUDERAL waste growth
bt RUE-WORT herb of grace
RUFFIAN desperado; apache; rascal
RUFFING trumping; ruffling
RUFFLED disordered; agitated
RUFFLER a bully
tx RUGGING heavy napped cloth
RUINING wrecking; demolishing
RUINOUS pernicious; calamitous
RULABLE allowable; governable
RULLION veldt-shoe; virago
RUMBLED reverberated
RUMBLER tum; (record-deck
   chafing)
RUMINAL of cud chewer; ruminant
RUMMAGE search; ransack
RUMMIER stranger; droller; quainter
RUMMILY oddly; whimsically
RUMNESS queerness; oddity
RUMPLED rimpled; crushed
RUM-SHOP a tavern
RUNAWAY fugitive; deserter;
   renegade
RUNDLED rounded like a rung
RUNDLET small barrel; runlet
RUN-DOWN exhausted; weak;
   anaemic
RUN-DOWN tracked to lair
RUN-LINE factory production;
   (stadium)
ce RUNNERS timber sheet piles
   (excavation)
RUNNING managerial; organizing
nt RUNNING sailing downwind; in order
RUN-OVER continuation over (body)
RUPTION eruption
RUPTIVE ruptile; liable to snap
RUPTURE fracture; breach; rift

RURALLY rustically
RUSALKA water-nymph (Rus.)
RUSHING dashing; careering; flying
RUSH-MAT reed pad
bt RUSH-NUT edible tuber
RUSSETY reddish-brown
RUSSIAN of Russia
RUSSIFY to enforce Russian style
bt RUSSULA red fungus
RUSTFUL rusty
RUSTICA ancient Rom. manuscript
  style
RUSTIER less practised
RUSTILY fustily; mustily
RUSTING oxidizing
RUSTLED stirred
RUSTLER cattle-thief
hd RUSTRED lozenge-shaped
RUTHFUL compassionate
nv RUTTIER routier; bearings chart
RUTTING grooving; furrowing;
  pairing
RUTTISH lustful; of mating season
  (deer)
me, nc RYDBERG atomic ionizing energy
  unit
zo RYE-MOTH a harvest pest
zo RYE-WOLF (German folk lore)
zo RYE-WORM larva of rye-moth

S

rl SABAISM SABEISM, Chaldean star
  worship
SABAOTH armies (Heb.)
SABBATH day of rest
zo SABELLA sea-worms
SABREUR user of sabre (fencing)
SABRING cutting with a sabre
SABURRA grittiness of the tongue
pl SACCADE rapid eye movement
  (dreams)
mu SACCADE sudden check
zo SACCATA molluscs
SACCATE sack-like
SACCULE small pouch
SACELLA altars; sanctuaries
SACKAGE pillage
mu SACKBUT dulcimer trombone
SACKFUL bagful
SACKING looting; plundering
rl SACRIST sacristan; a sexton
SADDEST most dismal and
  depressing
SADDLED loaded; hampered
SADDLER a saddle maker (horses)
SAD-EYED mournful

SADIRON box-iron; flat-iron
SADNESS sorrowfulness; melancholy
bt SADTREE night jasmine
mn SADWARE pewter dishes; plates etc.
SAFFIAN (tanned skins)
bt, ck SAFFRON plant; a colour; flavour
SAGAMAN a bard; narrator of sagas
tx SAGATHY woollen stuff
SAGESSE wisdom (Fr.)
ck SAGGARD box for baking porcelain
SAGGING drooping; sinking; failing
as SAGITTA arrow; star in Great Bear
zo SAGOUIN capuchin monkey
bt SAGUARO giant cactus
mn SAHLITE augite
SAIL-ARM (windmill)
nt SAILING voyage with wind
zo SAIMIRI squirrel monkey
SAINTED canonized
SAINTLY holy; devout; religious
rl SAIVISM worship of Siva
SALABLE saleable; vendible
SALADIN a Sultan (Crusades)
SALAMBA fishing device (Manila)
zo SALAMIS insect genus
SALCHOW skating jump
mu SALICET soft tone organ stop
bt, md SALICIN willow extract (aspirin)
SALIENT projecting front-line sector
SALIERE salt-cellar (Fr.)
bt SALIGOT water caltrops
lw SALIQUE SALIC, male succession law
pl, ch SALIVAL SALIVARY, of mouth
  enzymes
SALLIED when besieged attacked
pt, md SALLOWY yellowish (jaundice)
SALMIAC sal-ammoniac
ch SALMINE fish-testicle protamine
zo SALPIAN ascidian
md SALPINX Eustachian tube
bt SALSAFY oyster plant saxifrage root
bt SALSIFY purple goat's beard root
bt SALSOLA glass-wort
SALTANT dancing; leaping
bl SALTANT suddenly developed
  variant
SALTATE to dance; leap; jump; skip
SALT-BOX salt cellar
SALT-CAT pigeon medicine
SALTERN salt factory
SALTIER saltire
SALTING sea-marsh; pickling; curing
SALTIRE St Andrew's cross
SALTISH brackish; briny
SALT-PAN evaporating pan
SALT-PIT open salt mine
SALUTED honoured; kissed; greeted
SALUTER that which salutes

SALVAGE rescue; compensation
SALVETE greetings to new members
SALVING healing; restoration
SAMADHI broken; mind/body link in yoga
zo **SAMBHUR** Indian stag
SAMBUCA SAMBUKE, ancient harp
SAMIOTE native of Samos (Gr.)
mu **SAMISEN SHAMISEN**, Japanese lute
SAMNITE Sabine tribe (It.)
ck **SAMOGON** illicit vodka (Russia)
bt **SAMOLUS** primrose genus
SAMOVAR Russian tea-urn
zo **SAMOYED** arctic people; sledge dog
SAMPLED tried; tasted
SAMPLER needlework; pattern picture
ce **SAMPLER** soil, sand crusher for testing
SAMSARA transmigration; reincarnation
SAMSHOO rice spirit (China)
SAMURAI Japanese military class
rl **SANCTUM** a refuge; a shrine
rl **SANCTUS** a hymn
SANDBAG ballast; defence; weapon
SAND-BAR estuarine barrier
SANDBED a mould
rw **SANDBOX** on loco for slippery rails
bt **SANDBOX** for wet ink; tree (W. Indies)
SAND-BOY a happy lad
zo **SANDBUG** digger wasp
bt **SANDBUR** a weed
zo **SAND-DAB** plaice
zo **SAND-EEL** small fish
bt **SANDERS** red sandal-wood
zo **SAND-FLY** a biting midge
SANDING burying oysters (in moisture)
jn, pt **SANDING** smoothing; flattening down
SANDISH gritty; friable
SANDJET sand-blast
zo **SAND-LOB** lug-worm
SANDMAN children's sleep-giver
SAND-PIT source of sand
zo **SAND-RAT** the camass rat
SANHITA Vedic hymns
bt **SANICLE** healing plant
SANKHYA Hindu philosophy
zo **SAPAJOU** S. Amer. spider-monkey
zo **SAPERDA** boring beetles
SAP-HEAD (fortification)
md **SAPHENA** prominent vein
SAPIENT wise; sage; clever; astute
SAPLESS dry; not juicy
bt **SAPLING** young tree

zo **SAPLING** young greyhound
SAPONIN soapwort extract
SAPPHIC SAPPHO, stanzas; lifestyle
bt **SAPPING** draining juices; undermining
SAPROBE plant growing in foul water
ck **SAPSAGO** a green Swiss cheese
bt **SAPWOOD** the alburnum
SARACEN Arab; Selçuk Turk
SARAFAN Russian gala-dress
SARAWAK glossy yellow cane
SARCASM irony; satire; ridicule
SARCELE partly cut through
bt **SARCINA** fungoid plant
md **SARCINE** (muscular tissue)
SARCODE protoplasm
SARCODY conversion to fleshlike state
SARCOID flesh-like
md **SARCOMA** tumour; skin cancer
SARCOUS fleshy
mu **SARDANA** folk dance (Catalan)
zo **SARDINE** fish; (pilchard)
nt **SARDINE** sea-boat (Portugal)
mn **SARDIUS** sard; a quartz
zo **SARGINA** mullet (fish)
zo **SARIGUE** opossum (Brazil)
SARKING roof sheathing
bt **SARMENT** a runner; filiform stem
tx **SARPLAR** sarpler; packing cloth
tx **SARSNET** fine woven silk
SARTAGE forest clearing
SASHERY dress bands; court orders
SASHING framework for windows
zo **SASSABY** tsessebe; hartebeest
SASSING (-out); ascertaining
SATANIC infernal; diabolical; abuse
SATCHEL small sack or container
SATIATE glutted; to cloy; to gorge
SATIETY surfeit; over-gratification
tx **SATINET** thin satin
SATIRIC sarcastic; ironical; mordant
SATISFY gratify; requite; settle
SATRAPY stand-in governorship
bt **SATSUMA** Japanese pottery; citrus fruit
tx **SATTARA** ribbed woollen material
tx **SATTEEN** ratteen; thick woollen fabric
rl **SATYRAL SATYRIC**, satyr; woodland goat-god of lustful revelling
SATYRUS orang-utan (wild-man)
SAUCIER ruder; more impudent
SAUCILY pertly; flippantly; pungently
SAUCING sassing; seasoning
SAUNTER dawdle; stroll; dally

zo **SAURIAN** lizard; reptile; crocodile
zo **SAUROID** reptilian; (dino-)
ck **SAUSAGE** minced meat inside skin
hd **SAUTOIR** diagonal ribbon
SAVABLE SAVEABLE, salvageable
SAVAGED attacked brutally
go **SAVANNA** treeless plain
ck **SAVARIN** syrup-soaked yeast cake
SAVE-ALL an economizer
ck **SAVELOY** red smoked pork sausage
SAVIGNY red Burgundy wine
SAVINGS 'nest-egg'; reserve cash
rl **SAVIOUR** Messiah; Redeemer
ck **SAVOURY** piquant, stimulating dish
zo **SAW-BACK** a caterpillar
zo **SAWBILL** goosander; merganser
SAWBUCK sawhorse
SAWDUST carpentry by-product
to **SAWFILE** triangular file
zo **SAWFISH** serrated-proboscis fish
zo **SAWHORN** an insect
SAWMILL lumber factory
zo **SAWWHET** Acadian owl
bt **SAWWORT** a plant
mu **SAXHORN** brass wind instrument
SAXONIC of Saxony, Germany
tx **SAY-CAST** coarse part of wool, from
tail
tx **SAYETTE** serge; woollen yarn
SCABBED worthless; black-listed
SCABBLE SCAPPLE, (stone-dressing)
md **SCABIES** itch; mange; parasitic mite
md **SCABRID SCABROUS**, skin scabs
SCADDLE skaddle; hurtful; impish
mn **SCAGLIA** Italian calcareous rock
SCALADE scaling ladder (Fr.)
SCALADO escalade assault (It.)
SCALARY stepped like a ladder
SCALDED immersed in boiling
water
SCALDIC (Norse eddas, sagas)
SCALENE irregular triangle
mn **SCALING** removal of loosened rock
SCALING evaluation; measurement
bd **SCALING** ladder; (siege-ladder)
SCALING fish scales etc.
SCALING ornament; overlapping
circles
SCALLED scurfy; scabby
zo, ck **SCALLOP** shellfish; baking mould
SCALLOP pilgrim badge; (border)
(pattern)
zo **SCALOPS** American shrew-moles
SCALPED head-skin removed as
trophy
SCALPED speculators' quick profits
md **SCALPEL** surgeon's dissecting knife
SCALPER hair-raising savage

SCAMBLE SHAMBLE, SCRAMBLE,
mangle
zo **SCAMMEL** bar-tailed godwit
SCAMMUM geometrical figure
SCAMPED skimped
SCAMPER scurry; run; hasten
SCANDAL disgrace; infamy; discredit
bt **SCANDIX** Venus' comb
SCANNED scrutinized; perused
tv **SCANNER** television or radar beam
md, cp **SCANNER** (medical) sampling device
SCANTED limited; stinted
SCANTLE cut into small pieces
SCANTLY scantily; niggardly
SCAPNET minnow-net
SCAPPLE stone-dressing
md **SCAPULA** shoulder blade
SCARCER rarer; less plentiful
SCARFED (timber joint)
SCARIFY to scratch; to harrow
SCARING affrighting; daunting
SCARLET bright orangish red
SCAROID like parrot fish
SCARPED made precipitous
SCARRED disfigured
SCARVES kerchiefs; cravats
SCATHED injured; damaged; hurt
ag **SCATTER** disperse; strew; sow seed
cp **SCATTER** distributing data within
store
to **SCAUPER** engraver's tool
SCENERY prospect; view; landscape
SCENTED perfumed; smelt;
suspected
SCEPSIS philosophic doubt
SCEPTIC skeptic; a doubter
SCEPTRE royal staff; power
tx **SCHAPPE** spun silk
zo **SCHELLY** white fish
SCHEMED plotted; planned;
contrived
SCHEMER intriguer; plotter
SCHEPEN magistrate (Dutch)
mu **SCHERZO** playfully
SCHESIS habitude; wont
SCHETIC constitutional; habitual
bt **SCHINUS** mastic-tree
to **S-CHISEL** well-boring cutter
mu **SCHISMA** tonal difference
SCHLICH ore slime
SCHLOSS castle; ancient seat (Ger.)
SCHMUCK unsophisticated person;
idiot
SCHNAPS SCHNAPPS, akvavit
SCHOLAR student; pupil; disciple
SCHOLIA marginal notes
mn **SCHORLY** tourmaline
md **SCIATIC** affecting the hip

SCIBILE knowable
SCIENCE knowledge; reduced to system
zo SCINCUS lizard; skink; a saurian
mu SCIOLTO with abandon
bt SCIRPUS bulrush genus
SCISSEL SCISSIL, metal clippings
SCISSOR to cut
zo SCIURUS squirrel genus
md SCLERAL hard; ossified
bt SCLERIA sedges
bt SCOBINA ends of grass
SCOFFED mocked; jeered; derided
SCOFFER a taunter; ridiculer
SCOLDED chided; nagged; rebuked
SCOLDER railer; upbraider
mn SCOLITE fossil worm
zo SCOLLOP scallop
zo SCOMBER mackerel genus
SCOONED skimmed; glided
nt SCOONER a schooner
SCOOPED hollowed out; dredged
zo SCOOPER a water-fowl; the avocet
SCOOTED bolted; squirted
SCOOTER ice-boat; toy; light motorcycle
SCOPATE brush-like
SCOPTIC bantering; jesting
zo SCOPULA small tuft of hairs
SCORIAC ashy
mn SCORIAE volcanic ashes
SCORIFY reduce to ashes
SCORING recording points, runs etc.
SCORING scratching; making marks
SCORNED disdained; spurned
SCORNER contemner; flouter
to SCORPER a gouge
zo SCORPIO (Zodiac); scorpion
rl SCOTICE in Scottish
SCOTISM doctrine of Duns Scotus
rl SCOTIST a theologian
md SCOTOMA blind spot
md SCOTOMY dizziness
SCOURED made searching survey
SCOURED vigorously cleansed
SCOURER scrubber; polisher; scraper
SCOURGE lash; chastise; plague
SCOUTED made an intensive search
SCOUTER stone flaker
SCOWLED registered displeasure
SCRAGGY lean and lanky
SCRANCH SCRUNCH, grinding noise
SCRANNY lean and spare
SCRAPED erased; rubbed; rasped
to SCRAPER plane
SCRAPER miser; fiddler; scourer
vt SCRAPIE nervous sheep disease
SCRAPPY fragmentary; incomplete

SCRATCH lacerate; zero handicap
SCRATCH withdraw from contest
cp SCRATCH reusable tape; (-an income)
SCRAWLY scribbled; ill-formed script
SCRAWNY raw-boned
SCREECH shrill sound; owl call
SCREEVE to write begging letters
SCREWED twisted; tipsy; bored
SCREWER screw-driver; extortioner
SCRIBAL clerical
SCRIBED wrote; recorded; marked
to SCRIBER engraving tool
SCRINGE CRINGE, FLINCH, grate
zo SCRITCH SCREECH, a thrush
SCROGGY having thick undergrowth
SCROOGE scrudge; squeeze
SCROTAL of the scrotum
zo SCROTUM testicle sac in mammals
SCROUGE squeeze; to crowd
SCRUBBY stunted; squabby
SCRUFFY unkempt; untidy; uncouth
SCRUNCH CRUNCH, crush; (-dry)
SCRUNCH for tousled -look hair-style
me SCRUPLE honesty; 20 grains Troy wt
SCRYING crystal gazing
nt SCUDDED ran before the wind
SCUDLER scullion; kitchen boy
ag SCUFFLE struggle; a hoe
SCULLED rowed gently
nt SCULLER rowed water taxi
SCULPIN sea-fish; dragonet; bull-head
zo SCUMBER fox-dung
SCUMBLE overlay painting
SCUMMER a skimmer of scum
SCUPPER vent; annihilate
SCUPPET SCOPPET, scoop; shovel
SCURRIL SCURRIT, foul-mouthed rogue
md SCURVEY vitamin-deficiency disease
SCUTAGE feudal tax
SCUTATE like a shield
SCUTTER scurry
nt SCUTTLE (coal); hatchway; sink
zo SCYMNUS ladybirds; sharks
SCYPHUS a large drinking-cup (Gr.)
bt SCYPHUS podetium end widening
SCYTALE secret message (Gr.)
zo SCYTALE coral snake
SCYTHED mowed; cut
SCYTHIC Scythian (of Ukraine)
SEA-BANK protective bank
zo SEA-BASS marine fish
bt, zo SEA-BEAN small univalve shell

zo **SEA-BEAR** seal; polar bear
SEA-BEAT lashed by the waves
bt **SEA-BEET** rare vegetable
bt **SEA-BELT** fucus plant
zo **SEA-BIRD** aquatic bird
nt **SEA-BOAT** manageable at sea, stable
SEA-BORN produced by the sea
zo **SEA-CALF** common seal
nt **SEA-CARD** compass card
zo **SEA-CLAM** a bivalve
mn **SEA-COAL** cash
zo **SEA-COCK** gurnard; a valve
nt **SEA-COOK** marine father
zo **SEA-COOT** exotic ocean bird
zo **SEA-CORN** spawn
zo **SEA-CRAB** ocean crustacean
zo **SEA-CROW** cormorant
zo **SEA-DACE** bass
zo **SEA-DOVE** little auk
zo **SEA-DUCK** cider-duck
SEA-FIRE phosphorescence
zo **SEA-FISH** cod and others
mn **SEA-FOAM** meerschaum
SEA-FOLK sailors
zo **SEA-FOOD** fish as food
SEA-GAGE depth gauge
SEA-GATE harbour bar
SEA-GIRT insular
SEA-GOWN dress worn at sea
zo **SEAGULL** marine bird
SEA-HAIR sea-mist
SEA-HALL hall below the sea
zo **SEA-HARE** mollusc
zo **SEA-HAWK** a skua
bt **SEAHOLM** sea-holly
bt **SEAKALE** a cruciferous plant
SEA-KING a viking
bt **SEA-LACE** (scaweed)
ce **SEALANT** adhesive compound;
   plastic coating
zo **SEA-LARK** the dunlin
SEA-LEGS ability to balance at sea
nt **SEALIKE** shipshape; spirits up
zo **SEA-LILY** sea-urchin
nt **SEA-LINE** horizon; sky-line
zo **SEALING** culling
zo **SEA-LION** large seal
SEAL-OFF closure
zo **SEA-LUCE** hake
SEA-MAID mermaid
zo **SEA-MALL** sea-gull
nv **SEA-MARK** spar; buoy; light
me **SEA-MILE** 1853m or 2000 yards
SEAMING sewing together; scarring
zo **SEA-MINK** whiting
zo **SEA-MONK** monk-seal
bt **SEA-MOSS** seaweed
to **SEAM-SET** tinman's punch

SEA-OOZE soft mud
SEA-PASS passport
zo **SEA-PEAR** sea-squid
zo **SEA-PECK** the dunlin
zo **SEA-PERT** the opah fish
zo **SEA-PIKE** pike
bt **SEA-PINK** the thrift
zo **SEA-PORK** an ascidian
SEAPORT harbour for large ships
bt **SEA-REED** mat grass
SEARING cauterizing
SEA-RISK marine hazard
zo **SEA-ROLL** sea-cucumber
SEA-ROOM manoeuvre space
zo **SEA-ROSE** sea-anemone
zo **SEA-RUFF** sea-bream
mn **SEA-SALT** cookery condiment
SEASICK mal-de-mer
SEASIDE beach
zo **SEA-SLUG** a nudibranch
SEASONS climate and growth; (-of
   events)
SEA-TANG sea-tangle-weed
SEATING (bums on seats) (capacity)
zo **SEA-TOAD** angler fish
SEA-TOST common or garden tost
SEA-TURN a gale from the sea
SEAVIEW glimpse of the briny
SEA-WALL retaining wall
SEA-WANE wampum
SEAWARD toward the sea
bt **SEA-WARE** seaweed; sea-wreck
bt **SEAWEED** tangle; algae
zo **SEA-WHIP** a zoophyte
zo **SEA-WIFE** wrasse; mermaid
SEA-WING a sail
SEA-WOLD imaginary tract
zo **SEA-WOLF** wolf fish; pirate
zo **SEA-WORM** marine annelid
ch **SEBACIC** fatty acid
SEBILLA wooden bowl (meals)
SEBUNDY SEPOY, Indian soldier
SECANCY intersection
SECEDED withdrew; separated
SECEDER separationist
bt **SECHIUM** gourds
SECLUDE segregate; isolate
mu **SECONDO** bass of duet
SECONDS imperfect items; (stale);
   rejects
SECONDS deputies; assistants; extras
SECONDS time units; (boxing)
   (duelling)
SECRECY privacy; stealth; reticence
SECRETE hide; conceal; cache; yield
SECTANT geometric figure
SECTARY sectarian
SECTILE sliceable

SECTION portion; division; segment;
  (cross-); (-leader); (maps)
cp **SECTION** part of magnetic tape block
SECTIST dissenter
SECTIVE divisible
SECULAR of the world; lay; temporal
SECURED obtained; ensured;
  fastened
SECURER protector; guardian; safer
rl **SEDILIA** altar seats
SEDUCED enticed; led astray
SEDCUCER a libertine
SEEABLE visible
zo **SEE-CAWK** the American skunk
SEED-BAG germ-pouch
SEED-BED plantation
bt **SEED-BUD** germ of the fruit
SEED-COD seed-basket; husk
SEEDFUL promising; hopeful
SEEDILY shabbily
SEEDING (tournaments); sowing
SEED-LAC dried resin
bt **SEED-LOP** seed container
SEED-OIL linseed oil
SEEKING inquiring; questing
SEELING closing the eyelids
SEEMING specious; guise; apparent
SEEPAGE leakage; oozings
SEETHED boiled; soaked
SEETHER boiling pot
bt **SEGGROM** ragwort
SEGMENT a portion; section of a
  whole
cp **SEGMENT** redivide into chapters
SEINING netting fish
lw **SEISING** taking possession
SEISMAL seismic; (earthquake)
mt **SEISTAN** Persian summer north
  wind
zo **SEISURA** Australian fly-catchers
zo **SEIURUS** wagtail genus
SEIZING (ropes); grappling; binding
lw **SEIZURE** grasp; legal confiscation
md **SEIZURE** stroke; attack; theft
hd **SEJEANT** seated
zo **SELACHE** shark
ch **SELENIC** (selenium)
SELFBOW of single yew, archery
SELF-FED automatic feeding
SELFISH egotistical; mean;
  ungenerous
SELFISM me first and me only
SELFIST egoist
bt **SELINUM** milk-parsley
SELLING vending; hawking;
  betraying
SELTZER mineral water
SELVAGE selvedge; border

SEMATIC significant
SEMEION metrical mark
zo **SEMI-APE** a lemur
SEMI-GOD demi-god
SEMILOR imitation gold
SEMINAL rudimentary; original
SEMINAR special study occasion
zo **SEMIPED** prosody; a half-foot
SEMIPED verse, metre
SEMI-RAG paper with some rag
  content
SEMITIC Jewish; Hebrew
SENATOR a counsellor
SENATUS governing body
bt **SENCION** groundsel
SENDING despatching; forwarding
SEND-OFF farewell party
SENECAN style of philosophy of
  Seneca
bt **SENECIO** ragwort
zo **SENEGAL** African fire-bird
SENIORY council of elders
SENSATE sensible
SENSILE sensitive
SENSING understanding; feeling
SENSING perceptual awareness
SENSION perception
SENSISM sensualism
SENSIST sensationalist
md **SENSORY** nerve system
SENSUAL voluptuous
zo **SEPIARY** relating to cuttlefish
zo **SEPIOID** ink producers
zo **SEPIOST** cuttle-bone
SEPPUKU hara-kiri (Jap.)
SEPTATE partitioned
SEPTIME fencing posture
SEQUELA a consequence
SEQUELA abnormal, chronic
  condition
SEQUENT following; succeeding
bt **SEQUOIA** Californian red-wood
SERAPIS Apis; goddess of fertility
SERBIAN of Serbia; Yugoslav
SERENED tranquillized
SERENER calmer; more placid
bt **SERENOA** dwarf-palms (Florida)
SERFAGE serfdom; slavery
SERFDOM villenage; thraldom
SERIATE in series; serial
tx **SERICIN** silk
SERICON alchemic red
zo **SERIEMA** cariama; (heron)
SERIFIC silk-producing
bt **SERINGA** flowering shrub
zo **SERINUS** canary genus
zo **SERIOLA** amber fish
SERIOUS grave; sedate; staid

SERMENT oath
zo, mu SERPENT snake; old bassoon
md SERPIGO ring-worm
zo SERPULA sea-worms
SERRATE serrous; notched
SERRIED at close interval
zo SERRULA comblike ridge on
chelicerae
zo SERTOLI of seminiferous tubule cells
bt SERTULE collection of plants
SERVAGE servitude; enthralment
SERVANT retainer; henchman;
menial
SERVIAN Serbian; Serb
SERVICE duty; performance; utility
rl, mu SERVICE Anglican worship and
music
ga SERVICE start of rally; (squash)
(tennis)
SERVICE maintenance; employment
SERVICE military-; public-; social-;
tip
SERVILE fawning; sycophantic;
slave-like
rl SERVING ministering; (tennis)
SERVITE mendicant monk, 13th
cent.
bt SESAMUM sesame genus
SESOTHO Basuto language (S.
Africa)
bt SESSILE (no stalk)
lw SESSION meeting; assize; sitting
cp, tc SESSION open-time transmission
SESTINA sestine; verse (Fr.)
SESTOLE sextuplet
bt SETARIA spiky grasses
ar SET-BACK check; reverse; recess
SET-DOWN a rebuff
mu SETLESS no score; tennis
mu SETTIMA interval of a seventh
mu SETTIMO a seventh (It.)
SETTING appointing; congealing
SETTLED fixed; paid; sank; serene
SETTLER colonizer; arbitrator
bt SETWALL valerian
SETWORK (boat-building); (plaster)
SEVENTH ordinal number
SEVENTY cardinal number
SEVERAL sundry; diverse; various
SEVERED cut; rent; divided
SEVERER stricter; simple
zo SEVRUGA caviare-fish
nt SEWED-UP stranded
bt SEXFOIL six-leafed plant
SEXLESS of inteterminate gender
SEXTAIN (six lines)
nm SEXTANS Roman bronze coin
nt SEXTANT optical instrument

pp SEXTERN quire of 6 sheets
SEXTILE planet aspect
zo SEXUALE sexually reproducing being
SHABASH bravo! (Pers.)
SHACKED tramped; hibernated
SHACKLE manacle; gyve; bond;
fetter
zo SHADFLY May-fly
SHADIER more dubious
SHADILY umbrageously
zo SHADINE American sardine
SHADING screening; tinting
SHADOOF water-raising device (Nile)
SHADOWY obscure; dim; gloomy
SHAFTED handled; hafted
SHAGGED shaggy; rough; rugged
zo SHAHEEN peregrine falcon
SHAITAN Satan (Arabic)
SHAKE-UP upheaval; reorganization
SHAKILY insecure; precariously
SHAKING quaking; jarring; jolting
bt SHALLON an edible fruit
nt SHALLOP rowing boat; skiff; gun-
boat
nt SHALLOP fishing boat; tender
bt SHALLOT small type of onion
zo SHALLOW superficial; rudd-fish
SHAMBLE shuffle along
SHAMING humiliating; abasing
SHAMMED simulated; feigned
SHAMMER impostor; malingerer
SHAMPOO hair-washing
SHANDRY rickety conveyance (Irish)
SHANGIE shackle (Sc.)
rl SHANGTI Chinese for God
SHANKED (golf); shin; legged
zo, bt SHANKED shanks's pony; stem
SHAPELY finely formed
SHAPING moulding; fashioning
zo SHARDED beetle-winged
SHARING apportioning; dividing
SHARKED cheated; duped; gulled
SHARKER shark-hunter
SHARPED tricked; defrauded; duped
SHARPEN strop; point; whet
SHARPER a trickster; cheat; rogue
nt SHARPIE oyster boat, New England
SHARPLY keenly; acutely; tartly
rl SHASTER Hindu Bible
rl SHASTRA sacred Hindu book
SHATTER splinter; disrupt; smash
SHAVIAN (Bernard Shaw)
SHAVING slicing; pairing; grazing
SHEAFED bundled in sheaves
SHEARED reaped; cut through
SHEARER clipper; reaper; cutter
SHEATHE encase; cover
SHEATHY like a scabbard

SHEAVED collected in sheaves
SHEBANG store; saloon
nt **SHEBECK CHEBEK, XEBEC,** mixed rig boat
SHEBEEN Irish whiskey shop
SHEDDER emitter; diffuser
SHEERED moved away
SHEETED covered with sheets
bt **SHELLAC** resin lac
SHELLED bombarded; husked
SHELLER huller; shucker
SHELTER screen; asylum; refuge
zo **SHELTIE** Shetland pony
SHELVED put aside; pigeonholed
SHELVES ledges
SHEPPEY sheep-cote
SHERBET a cooling drink
SHEREEF an amir; emir
lw **SHERIAT** Islamic law
lw **SHERIFF** county officer
SHEWING showing; demonstration
SHIFTED changed; altered; quitted
SHIFTER remover; contriver
SHIITES Persian sectarians
SHIKARI hunter (India)
SHIMMED wedged
SHIMMER gleam; glisten; glimmer
SHINGLE style of hair cutting
gl **SHINGLE** pebbles on sea shore
bd **SHINGLE** wooden roof tiles
SHINGLY pebbly
SHINING resplendent; coruscating
SHINNED climbed
nt **SHIP-BOY** sailor's solace
SHIPFUL boat-load
cr **SHIPLAP** rebate-cut sheathing boards
nt **SHIP-MAN** a sailor
SHIPPED embarked; (oars)
SHIPPEN sheep-pen; stable
SHIPPER exporter
SHIPTON a prophetess
SHIP-WAY (dry dock)
SHIRKED evaded; avoided; scamped
SHIRKER malingerer; dodger
zo **SHIRLEY** bull-finch
bt **SHIRLEY** poppy
SHIRRED puckered
SHIRTED wearing a shirt
bt **SHITTAH SHITTIM** acacia; (Tabernacle wood)
SHIVERY brittle; chilly
SHIZOKU Japanese gentry
SHOALED became shallow
nt **SHOALER** coasting-vessel
SHOCKED offended; surprised
SHOCKER sensational novel
SHOE-BOY a shiner

SHOEING farrier's work
SHOE-PEG a nail
SHOE-TIE shoe-lace
SHOGGED jolted; jogged
SHOOING scaring away
SHOOKED packed
SHOOTER marksman; sniper
ga **SHOOTER** goal scorer (netball, football)
SHOPBOY assistant; errand boy
SHOPMAN shop/factory foreman
SHOPPED imprisoned; framed
SHOPPER peripatetic buyer
SHORAGE landing charge
SHORING props; buttressing
el **SHORTED** circuit fault
SHORTEN abbreviate; abridge; curtail
SHORTER briefer; terser; curter
SHOTGUN light sporting gun
ga **SHOT-PUT** putting the weight (sport)
SHOTTED loaded
SHOTTEN dislocated; curdled
pc **SHOULDS** internalized demands
SHOULDS acceptable behaviour
SHOUTED yelled; bawled; roared
SHOUTER crier; vociferator
SHOVING propelling; pushing; jostling
SHOW-BOX presentation carton
SHOW-END (roll of cloth)
SHOWERY pluvial
SHOWILY ostentatiously; flashily
SHOWING representation; displaying
SHOWMAN exhibitor; actor-manager; artiste
SHOW-OFF play for admiration; swank
SHREDDY ragged; fragmentary
SHRILLY piercingly; sharply; high-toned
SHRINAL sacred; hallowed
SHRINED enshrined
SHRIVEL to dry up; parch
rl **SHRIVEN** given absolution
rl **SHRIVER** a confessor; absolver
SHROUDS winding sheets
nt **SHROUDS** mast to ship's sides' rigging
SHROUDY giving shelter
bt **SHRUBBY** full of shrubs
SHUCKER husker; huller; sheller
SHUDDER shake; quiver; shiver
SHUFFLE mix; cavil; quibble; (cards)
SHUNNED avoided; eluded
SHUNNER eschewer; evader
SHUNTED put in siding
SHUNTER a railway-man
SHUT-EYE sleep; a nap

nt **SHUT-OFF** turn off (steam)
SHUT-OFF stoppage; isolated
ga **SHUT-OUT** no score for opponent (sport)
bd, pg **SHUTTER** window aperture cover
SHUTTLE sliding thread-holder
ae, rw **SHUTTLE** service (space, chunnel)
SHYLOCK rapacious usurer
SHYNESS bashfulness; coyness
SHYSTER rascally lawyer
zo **SIAMANG** Malay gibbon
md **SIAMESE** joined, before birth
SIBILUS sibilant rhoncus
SIBILUS (nasal) phonetics
SIBLING one's brother or sister
SIBSHIP brothers and sisters of one family
SICCATE desiccate; dry; parch
SICCITY aridity; dryness
nt **SICKBAY** hospital ward
md **SICKBED** in-patient at home
SICKEST very poorly
SICKISH unwell; out of sorts
SICKLED with sickle
SICK-PAY wages during illness
SIC-LIKE such like
SIDEARM sword or bayonet
SIDEBOX (theatre)
SIDECAR cocktail (motorcycle)
SIDECUT branch canal; not off the grand joint (butchers' meat)
SIDE-OUT loss on a service
ga **SIDEOUT** losing a rally (tennis)
SIDE-ROD coupling rod (steam locomotive)
SIDLING edging away
el, me **SIEMENS** electrical conductance unit
SIENESE of Sienna
mn **SIENITE** syenite; hornblende
SIFFLED whistled
SIFFLET small whistle
SIFTING scrutinizing; sorting; sieving
SIGHFUL grievous
SIGHING lamenting; repining
SIGHTED seen; viewed; glimpsed
SIGHTER a trial shot
SIGHTLY handsome
SIGMATE (sigma)
SIGMOID curve of beauty
nt, tc **SIGNALS** lights; sounds; radio flags
SIGNATE designate
SIGNIFY indicate; betoken; portend
SIGNING subscribing; gesturing
SIGNORA an Italian lady
SIGNORY seigniory; overlordship
rl **SIKHARA** spire of Indian temple

SIKHISM monotheistic sect
SILENCE quiescence; dumbness
SILENUS foster-father of Bacchus
tx **SILESIA** cotton fabric
ch **SILICIC** (silica)
bt **SILICLE** broad pod
ch **SILICON** an element
bt **SILIQUA** seed vessel
me **SILIQUE** carat
SILKIER more lustrous
SILKING silk chiffon
pt **SILKING** books on paint lining
SILKMAN silk-mercer
zo **SILLAGO** a fish genus
SILLERY a white wine
SILLIER more witless
SILLILY inanely; foolishly; ineptly
ch **SILOXEN** polymerized silicon analogue
go **SILTING** depositing mud
zo **SILURUS** cat-fish
SILVERN of silver
SILVERY bright; clear; sweet
SIMARRE a cymar; a costume
SIMILAR alike; analogous; twin
SIMILIA similes; metaphors
SIMILOR semilor; imitation gold
zo **SIMIOUS** ape-like; simian
SIMPLER herbalist; plainer; easier
tc **SIMPLEX** one-way circuit flow
SIMPLEX centre shafted putter (golf)
bt **SIMPSON** groundsel
SIMULAR counterfeit; feigned
SIMURGH fabulous bird (Pers.)
bt **SINAPIS** sinapin; mustard
SINBORN illegitimate
SINBRED raised to vice
SINCERE true; genuine; honest
SINEWED powerful; vigorous
SINGING the vocal art
el **SINGING** oscillation transmission
SINGLED selected; separated
SINGLES tennis; reeled silk
SINGLET undervest
SINGULT a sob; a sigh
ma **SINICAL** of sine (trigonometry)
SINKAGE excess margins of headings
nt **SINKING** foundering; declining
jn **SINKING** greater screw cavity
SINLESS innocent; blameless
SINNING transgressing
SINOPIA red pigment
SINOPIS sinople; sinoper
SINSICK repentant
SINSYNE since (Sc.)
SINUATE insinuate; curved
SINUOUS sinuose; winding

SINWORN fabulous monster
SIPPING supping
zo SIREDON larval salamander
zo SIRENIA sea-cows
zo SIRGANG green jackdaw
SIRLOIN surloin
mt SIROCCO SCIROCCO, hot African desert wind
SISTINE SIXTINE, (Vatican chapel)
lw SISTING summoning (Sc.)
mu SISTRUM holy rattle (Egypt)
md SITFAST ulcer
SITHENS since; after that
zo SITTINE (nut-hatches)
SITTING session; incubating; bent-knee stance (fencing)
SITUATE permanently fixed
rl SIVAITE follower of Siva
SIXFOLD 6 times as much
SIXTEEN age of sweetness
SIZABLE of a size; bulky
SIZZLED frizzled
SJAMBOK S. Afr. rawhide whip
zo SKEETER mosquito
SKELDER swindle
SKELLUM a rascal; scamp; scoundrel
SKELTER skedaddle
SKEPFUL basketful
SKEPTIC sceptic; doubting
SKETCHY vague; incomplete
SKEWGEE crooked; skewed
SKIDDED scotched; slipped
SKIDLID crash helmet
SKID-PAN motorists' training ground
mu SKIFFLE folk-song and jazz
SKI-JUMP skiing slide
SKILFUL dexterous; adept; expert
SKI-LIFT cable or funicular lift
SKILLED expert; artful; adroit
SKILLET iron cooking pot
SKIMMED glided; grazed
zo SKIMMER scoop; bird
SKIMPED stinted
SKINFUL amount of drunkenness
SKINKER tapster; barman
SKINNED peeled; fleeced
SKINNER a furrier
SKIPPED omitted; jumped
nt SKIPPER a captain on board
nt SKIPPET seal-box; boat
SKIRLED shrieked shrilly
bt SKIRRET water-parsnip
SKIRTED bordered
SKIRTER a dodger
SKI-SUIT winter-costume
SKITTER glide; skim
SKITTLE bowl out; knock down

SKIVING leather splitting; work dodging
SKULKED lurked
SKULKER a shirker; malingerer
zo SKULPIN sea-fish
SKYBLUE azure
SKYBORN heaven-born
SKYHIGH excessively elevated
nt SKYHOOK overhead crane
zo SKYLARK the laverock
SKYLINE horizon; sea-line
nt SKYSAIL sail above royal
tx SKYTEEN satin weave shirting
SKYWARD heading upward
SLABBED cut into thick slices
SLABBER slobber; dribble; slaver
SLACKED eased off
SLACKEN relax; mitigate; abate
SLACKER skulker; sluggard; idler
SLACKLY negligently; laxly
SLAINTE! Good health! (Irish)
SLAKING quenching; allaying
SLAMKIN a slut; loose gown
SLAMMED banged
SLANDER malign; traduce; obloquy
SLANGED abused; vituperated
SLANKET strip of land; slang
SLANTED sloped; tilted
SLANTLY slantwise; atilt; obliquely
SLAPPED smacked; spanked
SLAPPER slap-up affair
SLASHED gashed; cut
to SLASHER cutting tool
SLASHER violent attacker (films)
SLATHER lots of
SLATING roofing; reprimand; abusing
SLATTER wasteful; slovenly
bd SLATTER slater; tile mason
SLAVDOM Slavs collectively
SLAVERY serfdom; thraldom; bondage
SLAVING drudging; moiling
SLAVISH servile; obsequious
SLAYING destroying; despatching
SLEAVED not spun; raw
SLEAVED separated; divided
SLEDDED travelled across snow
SLEDGED sledded; mushed
SLEEKED glided; smoothed
SLEEKEN to smooth
to SLEEKER slicker
SLEEKLY fair spoken; glossily; silky
cr, rw SLEEPER track bed; overnight (train)
ga SLEEPER slumberer (bowling)
SLEEPER honeycomb wall; valley
bd SLEEPER board (roof) earstud
mt SLEETED rained and snowed

SLEIDED unwoven; sleaved
SLEIGHT dexterity; skill; adroitness
SLENDER frail; slim; slight
nt **SLEWING** rotatory roll of crane, ship
SLEYING swinging askew
SLICING severing; (golf)
SLICKER smarter; more deft
SLIDDER to slither; slip; slide
SLIDING a lapse; varying
SLIMILY viscously; muddily
SLIMMER more slender; lankier
SLIPPED conveyed secretly
SLIPPER steel cradle; mule
SLIPWAY (shipbuilding)
SLITHER slide about
SLITTED slashed; split
to **SLITTER** a cutter
SLOBBER slabber; dribble; slaver
SLOCKEN slake; quench
SLOE-GIN pleasant drink
SLOGGED hit hard
SLOGGER mighty smiter
SLOPING inclined; declinous;
  oblique
SLOPPED spilt
SLOTTED grooved
SLOTTER to foul; filth
SLOUCHY slackly
SLOUGHY swampy; miry; queachy
SLOVENE language, people of
  Slovenia
SLOWEST dullest; tardiest
SLOWING delaying; retarding
SLUBBER to scamp; slabber
nt **SLUDGER** sewage dumping; bum
  boat
to **SLUDGER** sandpump; hole cleaner
SLUGGED bashed; coshed
SLUGGER big hitter (baseball)
SLUICED drenched; flushed
SLUMBER sleep; repose; doze
SLUMGUM honey and wax polish
SLUMMER slum visitor
SLUMPED fell heavily
SLUNKEN shrivelled
mu **SLURRED** sullied; disparaged
ce, mn **SLUSHER** scraper (USA)
SLUTCHY residual; mucky
SLYNESS sliness; craft; cunning
SMACKED slapped; spanked
SMACKER a resounding kiss
mn **SMARAGD** the emerald
SMARTED endured sharp pain
SMARTEN brighten; quicken
SMARTER brisker; sprucer
SMARTLY promptly; readily; alertly
SMASHED disrupted; broken;
  drunk

SMASHER blow; fine thing;
  (argument)
SMASH-UP a crash; raid; gangsters
SMATTER slight superficial
  knowledge
SMEARED daubed; contaminated
tc **SMEARER** overshoot-cancelling
  circuit
ps **SMECTIC** with parallel-oriented
  atoms
SMEDDUM energy; powder
SMELLED had an odour; smelt
pl **SMELLER** nose; proboscis
SMELTER ore worker; iron furnace
zo **SMERLIN** loach fish
SMICKER to smirk; ogle; leer
SMICKET a smock
SMICKLY amorously
SMIDGEN a bittock; a trifle
SMILING smirking
SMIRKED simpered
SMITING striking; buffeting; hitting
SMITTEN afflicted; chastened
SMITTLE to infect
SMOKIER reekier
SMOKILY fumily
SMOKING bloating; quizzing
SMOLDER smoulder
SMOOTHE palliate; flatter; flatten
SMOTHER stifle; suppress
SMOUSER pedlar (S. Africa)
SMUDGED blurred; blotted
SMUDGER plumber
SMUGGLE convey secretly; snuggle
SNABBLE snaffle; plunder; eat
SNAFFLE a bit; appropriate; filch
SNAGGED snaggy
to **SNAGGER** a cutter
nt **SNAKING** rope-winding
SNAKISH reptilian; serpentine
SNAPING bevelling
SNAPPED caught; broke;
  photographed
zo **SNAPPER** a turtle
SNARING entrapping; catching
SNARLED entangled; complicated
zo **SNARLER** growler; grumbler; dog
SNATCHY irregular
SNEAKER soft-soled shoe
SNEAKER short drink
SNECK-UP go hang!
zo **SNEDDEN** sand-eel
SNEERER derider; taunter
SNEEZED snorted violently
SNICKER snigger; giggle
SNIFFED snuffed; inhaled
SNIFFLE snuffle
SNIFTER dram; radio-detector

SNIGGER snicker; giggle
SNIGGLE ensnare
SNIPING shooting from ambush
SNIPPER a tailor
SNIPPET a cutting
SNIRTLE snigger
SNOODED wearing a fillet
ga SNOOKER potting game; pool
SNOOPER a nosy Parker
SNOOZER a daydreamer
nt SNORKEL breathing pipe (U-boat)
SNORTER a fast one (cricket)
nt SNOTTER bowsprit housing
SNOUTED with snout
SNOW-BOX (stage snowstorm)
SNOW-FED (streams)
zo SNOW-FLY a stone-fly
SNOW-ICE frozen slush
SNOW-MAN snowball in human form
zo SNOW-OWL the great white owl
SNUBBED deliberately slighted
SNUBBER shock absorber
SNUFFED sniffed
SNUFFER a snuff taker
md SNUFFLE nasal catarrh
SNUGGLE smuggle; cuddle; fondle
SNUGIFY to make cosy
SNUZZLE nuzzle
SOAKAGE absorption
SOAKING drenching; steeping;
   imbruing
SO-AND-SO a vague definition;
   (derogatory)
SOAP-BOX orator's platform
SOAPING flattering; lathering
SOAP-PAN soap boiler
hd SOARANT heraldic flying
ae SOARING airborne on upward
   currents
SOARING (gliding) (eagle) (at zenith)
SOARING mental uplift; aspiring
SOBBING lamentation; ululation
SOBERED enjoyed morning after
SOBERLY staidly
bt SOBOLES botanical suckers
SOCAGER socage tenant
lw SOCCAGE land tenure
SOCIETY company; sodality; élite
zo SOCKEYE Pacific salmon
SOCKING beating; throwing
mn SODA-ASH impure sodium carbonate
SODDING turfing
SOFA-BED day-bed; divan; ottoman
SOFTEST gentlest; easiest
SOFTISH yielding; compliant
SOGGING saturating
SOIGNEE admirably turned out (Fr.)
bt SOILING replacing topsoil; (re-)

SOILING dirtying; staining;
   tarnishing
SOILURE pollution
SOJOURN visit; tarry; remain; abide
lw SOKEMAN tenant by socage
SOLACED consoled; comforted
bt SOLANUM night-shade genus
ar SOLDIER warrior; man-at-arms
bd SOLDIER brick as vertical support
SOLICIT importune; canvass; crave
SOLIDLY compactly; firmly; densely
SOLIDUM complete sum
nm SOLIDUS 's' for shilling
zo SOLIPED not cloven-hoofed
mu SOLOIST lone musician
bt SOLOMON wisdom personified; (seal)
SOLONIC wise like Solon
zo SOLPUGA a spider genus
SOLUBLE capable of solution
SOLVEND a substance to be dissolved
SOLVENT able to pay all debts
SOLVING elucidating; unravelling
SOMATIC corporeal; bodily
SOMEHOW in one way or another
SOMEONE unspecified person
SOMNIAL dreamy
bt SONCHUS sow-thistle genus
zo SONDELI Indian musk-rat
SONGFUL full of glee
SONGMAN balladmonger
SONLESS defiliated
rl SONNITE SUNNITE, orthodox Moslem
SONSHIP cf. daughterdom
SOOPING sweeping ice away
   (curling)
SOOTHED assuaged; pacified; cajoled
SOOTHER diplomatist; mollifier
SOOTHLY truly
SOOTING (sparking plugs)
SOOTISH like soot
SOPHISM a fallacy; specious
   argument
SOPHIST captious reasoner
bt SOPHORA pagoda tree
SOPIENT a soporific
SOPPING soaking; steeping
mu SOPRANO female treble
SORBENT an absorbent
SORBIAN SORBISH, Slavonics in
   Saxony
SORBILE that can be sipped/drunk
bt SORBINE sorbate extract
bt SORBITE sweet berry
ch SORBOSE keto hexose
SORCERY witchcraft; enchantment
mu SORDINA damper pedal on piano
mu SORDINO bowed/wind instrument
   mute

mu **SORDONO** (oboe)
SOREHON Irish tenure
bt **SORGHUM** sugar-cane
SORICID like a shrew
SORITES syllogistic argument
SORNING obtruding; sponging on
md **SOROCHE** altitude sickness (Andes)
SORORAL sisterly
bt **SOROSIS** mulberry type of fruit
SOROSIS woman's club
SORRILY meanly; pitiably
cp **SORTING** disposing; classifying
SORTING sequence; order
mu **SOSPIRO** a breathing rest
SOSTRUM life-saving reward (Gr.)
SOTTING tippling; toping; boozing
SOTTISE blundering act (Fr.)
SOTTISH besotted; foolish
ck **SOUBISE** onion sauce
ck **SOUCHET** boiled fish
ck **SOUFFLE** frothy egg-dish
md **SOUFFLE** blowing sound over heart
SOULFUL spiritually emotional
nt **SOUNDED** vibrated; tested
SOUNDER (Morse)
zo **SOUNDER** boar; herd of swine
SOUNDEX consonant-based coding
system
SOUNDLY thoroughly; validly
SOUPCON a suspicion; a taste (Fr.)
SOUREST most acid; rankest
SOURING acidulating
SOURISH tart; acetous; acrid
bt **SOUROCK** sorrel
bt **SOURSOP** American custard apple
SOUSING pickling; drenching
rl **SOUTANE** cassock
mu **SOUTENU** sustained; smooth flow
(Fr.)
SOUTHER south wind
SOUTHLY southerly
SOU'WEST S.W.
SOVKHOZ state-owned farm
(U.S.S.R.)
SOWBACK gravel ridge
bt, ck **SOYBEAN** protein-rich Asiatic
legume
SOZZLED sossled; tipsy; fuddled
SPACIAL extensive; commodious
SPACING arranging intervals
to **SPADDLE** spittle; small spade
SPADING digging
SPADONE double-handed sword
SPAEMAN diviner (Sc.)
SPAIRGE sparge; sprinkle
SPALING a bracing; cross-band
SPALLED chipped; splintered
SPANCEL cow-hobble

SPANDAU German light machine
gun
SPANGLE glittering disc
SPANGLY sparkling
zo **SPANIEL** fawning; mean
SPANISH Iberian
SPANKED slapped; speeded
nt **SPANKER** a sail
SPANNED measured; embraced
SPANNER monkey-wrench
SPARELY sparingly; charily
SPARGED sprinkled; sprayed
SPARGER sprinkler; diffuser
SPARING frugal; parsimonious
SPARKED played the gallant
SPARKLE coruscate; twinkle
SPAROID like sea bream
SPARRED disputed; wrangled; boxed
SPARRER boxing partner
zo **SPARROW** a small finch
SPARSIM here and there (Lat.)
SPARTAN austere; hardy; undaunted
tx **SPARVER** type of bed curtain
SPASTIC spasmodic
SPATHED ensheathed
SPATHIC laminated; foliated
SPATIAL spacial; wide; spacious
SPATTER asperse; besprinkle; splash
ch **SPATTLE** SPADDLE, mouth enzymes
SPITTLE saliva
md **SPATULA** a blade; a small spade
zo **SPATULE** (tail feather)
SPAWLED slavered
SPAWNED deposited eggs
zo **SPAWNER** female fish
SPAYING gelding
SPEAKER (House of Commons)
SPEARED lanced; pierced; impaled
SPEARER spearman
SPECIAL distinctive; particular
SPECIES group; genus; class; kind
SPECIFY definite; indicate; detail
SPECKED spotted; speckled
SPECKLE small speck or stain
SPECTRA (spectrum); images
SPECTRE apparition; spook;
hobgoblin
SPECULA mirrors; reflectors
SPEEDED ran; hastened; executed
SPEEDER pace-maker
SPEED-UP accelerate
SPELDER a splinter; chip
SPELEAN troglodytic
SPELLED charmed; entranced; spelt
SPELLER spelling book
ml **SPELTER** solder alloy; zinc
compound
SPENCER butler; jacket

nt **SPENCER** gaff-sail
SPENDER prodigal; wastrel; waster
SPERKET spirket; harness hook
SPEWING vomiting
md **SPHACEL** gangrene
SPHENIC wedge-like
SPHERAL ball-like; globular
SPHERED englobed
SPHERIC spherical
SPHYRNA hammer-headed sharks
SPICATE SPICOSE, prickly
ck **SPICERY** of various spices
SPICILY pungently; piquantly
SPICING seasoning; varying
SPICOUS SPINATE, thorny
SPICULA spike ear
bt **SPICULE** small pine
zo **SPIDERY** thin of legs and web
SPIEGEL steel alloy
bt **SPIGNEL** baldmoney; a plant
SPIKING impaling; transfixing
bd **SPILING** building-piles
gl **SPILITE** fine-grained igneous rock
SPILLED spilt; wasted; slopped
nt **SPILLER** reefing rope; surfing
ga **SPILLER** slow, even wave; (bowling)
SPILLER lucky strike; oil gusher
md **SPILOMA** birthmark; a naevus
bt, ct **SPINACH** vegetable
bt **SPINATE** spiky; spicate
SPINDLE axis; arbor
SPINDLY fusiform; slender
SPINNER a bait; textile operator
SPINNEY spinny; copse
SPINODE cusp in a curve
SPIN-OFF chance; side effect; product
bt **SPINOSE** spinous; thorny
bt **SPINULA** spicule
bt **SPINULE** small spine
bt **SPIRAEA** a plant genus
SPIRANT fricative consonant; a sibilant
SPIRING tapering; sprouting
mu **SPIRITO** SPIRITOSO, spirited
SPIRITY mettlesome; alcoholic
SPIRKET sperket; harness hook
SPIRTLE to spin; to spurt
zo **SPIRULA** cephalopods; cuttlefish
SPITBOX a cuspidor
SPITING grudging; thwarting
ck **SPITTED** transfixed
zo **SPITTER** young deer
SPITTLE small spade; saliva
zo **SPIZINE** (buntings; finches)
SPLASHY wet and muddy
SPLAYED sloped; slanted
SPLEENY ill-humoured; fretful

md **SPLEGET** a swab
SPLENIC spleeny; fretful; melancholy
nt **SPLICED** main brace; hit
tx **SPLICED** married, interwoven
nt, cp **SPLICER** joiner (ropes) (tapes)
md **SPLINTS** surgical appliances
SPLODGE daub; patch
SPLODGY stained; blotched
SPLOTCH smear; stain
SPLURGE rowdiness
SPLURGY boisterous; spend freely
SPODIUM ivory-black
SPOFFLE to bustle; to fuss
SPOILED pillaged; ruined; marred
SPOILER plunderer; bungler
rl **SPOLIUM** church property
SPONDEE poetic foot (2 long syllables)
md **SPONDYL** a vertebra; a joint
SPONGED deleted; purged; moistened
SPONGER a parasite; sorner
SPONSAL (marriage)
nt **SPONSON** protecting bracket
SPONSOR guarantor; a surety
SPOOFED hoodwinked; hoaxed
SPOOLED wound on spools (films)
SPOOMED scudded before the wind
SPOONED hit into the air; courted
SPOONEY love-sick
SPOORER tracker; detective
bt **SPOROID** sporous; sporelike
SPORONT stage in protozoa life history
SPORRAN kilt-pouch
SPORTED wore; trifled; romped
SPORTER jester; player
bt **SPORULE** small spore
SPOTTED spied; detected; pied
nt **SPOTTER** sharp-sighted look-out
rw **SPOTTER** (train-); (talent-)
ga **SPOTTER** assistant to gymnast
SPOUSAL nuptial; matrimonial
SPOUTED orated; spirted; pawned
zo **SPOUTER** declaimer; whale
SPRAYED sprinkled; spurned; affused
SPRAYER water cart; town cleansing
bt **SPRAYER** fountain; flow aimer (garden)
bt **SPRAYER** (crops-) (fruit-)
SPRAYEY branching
SPREAGH plunder (Sc.)
SPRIGGY full of sprigs
SPRIGHT sprite; a spirit; a ghost
SPRINGE spring trap; a gin
SPRINGY vernal; elastic

SPRINTS bicycle wheels
SPRUCED smartened up; prinked
SPRUNNY spruce; a sweetheart
SPRYEST spriest; gayest; pertest
SPUMING spumous; frothy; foamy
ck SPUMONE ice-cream in varied layers (It.)
SPUN-HAY twisted hay
SPUN-OUT long drawn
zo SPUR-DOG a shark
zo SPURIAE bastard quills
SPURNED rejected; scouted; contemned
SPURNER a disdainer
SPURRED goaded; impelled; galloped
SPURRER inciter; instigator
bt SPURREY a plant
SPURTED gushed; sprinted
SPURTLE spurt; spirtle
SPURWAY bridle-path
SPUTNIK earth satellite (Rus.)
SPUTTER splutter
nt SPY-BOAT vessel for secret agents
SPY-HOLE peep-hole; Judas' hole
SPYNDLE unit of length of jute/flax yarn
SQUABBY squaddy; squat; tubby
zo SQUACCO crested heron
SQUAILS form of table bowls (19th cent.)
SQUALID sordid; unclean; filthy
SQUALLY gusty; blustering
SQUALOR dirtiness; foulness
zo SQUALUS shark
SQUARED adjusted; tallied; bribed
SQUARED oar-blades (rowing) (circle)
SQUASHY pulpy; soft
SQUATTY squabby; clumsy
SQUEAKY clean; more than true
SQUEASY scrupulous; squeamish
SQUEEZE compress; crush; pinch; nip
ga SQUEEZE (money); block players
SQUEEZY congested; squashy
SQUELCH crush; suppress; (wet noise)
SQUIFFY tipsy; inebriated; sozzled
SQUINCH small stone arch; tight squeeze
SQUINNY to look asquint; meagre
SQUIRED escorted
bt SQUITCH quitch-grass
rl SRADDHA Hindu devotional offerings
STABBED wounded; pierced
to STABBER awl; marlinspike
STABLED stalled; horses

STABLER stable-keeper
mu STABLES a trumpet call (cavalry)
bt STACHYS hedge-nettle genus
STACKED piled; (cards)
STACKER washer-up (kitchen)
STACKER haymaker; storeman
cp STACKER punched-cards receptacle
STADDLE crutch; support
STADIUM arena; running track
STAFFED manned by
STAGERY scenic exhibition
STAGGER astound; lurch; reel; sway
STAGGER (time-); (hours)
STAGING a structure; producing
STAIDLY steadily; sedately; soberly
STAINED foxed; tarnished; sullied
STAINER a dyer
STAITHE coaling stage
STAKING hazarding; wagering
STALDER cask rack; horizontal bar (gymnastics)
STALELY mustily; effetely; insipidly
STALEST most trite
bt STALKED with peduncle
STALKER stealthy sportsman
STALLED fatted; lost speed
ml STALLOY silicon-content steel
STAMINA endurance; vitality; vigour
tx STAMMEL rough red cloth
STAMMER stutter
STAMNOS Greek urn
STAMPED impressed; crushed; branded
STAMPER ore crusher
STAND-BY a reserve
STANDER provider; candidate (elections)
STAND-IN deputy; substitute
STAND-TO military readiness
STAND-UP well fought
zo STANIEL STANNEL, kestrel bird
STANINE statistical unit
STANNIC (of tin)
ch STANNUM tin, metallic element
zo STANYEL windhover
STAPLED connected together
STAPLER a dealer; clipping machine
STARCHY stiff; formal; precise
STARDOM film eminence
STARING glaring; gaping; prominent
STARKEN stiffen; make obstinate
STARKLY completely; absolutely
STARLET junior actress
STAR-LIT almost invisible
STARRED shone; bespangled
STARTED winced; roused; began
ck STARTER first course; foretaste
STARTER (self-); also ran (horses)

STARTLE alarm; frighten; surprise
START-UP of a business, refinery
STARVED famished; emaciated
STASIMA choral odes (Gr.)
hd **STATANT** standing
STATELY lofty; magnificent; imposing
bt **STATICE** sea-lavender
STATICS conditions for equilibrium
STATING narrating; affirming
rw, ag **STATION** train-; bus-; stockfarm
STATION petrol-; office; status
cp **STATION** network computer terminal
STATISM policy; art of government
STATIST statistical expert
STATIVE fixed; standing still
el, me **STATOHM** obsolete electrostatic unit
STATUED with statues
STATURE natural height
lw **STATUTE** an enactment; decree
STAUNCH stanch; trusty; steadfast
STAVING delaying; broaching
STAYING enduring; detaining; abiding
STAY-PUT semi-permanent
STEALER purloiner; peculator
STEALTH furtiveness; secrecy
ck **STEAMED** cooked in vapour
nt **STEAMER** cooking vessel; ship
ch **STEARIC** of candle grease
STEARIN fat; wax; stearic acid
STEELED hardened; nerved
STEEPED soaked; drenched
STEEPEN to make steep
STEEPER soaking vat
rl **STEEPLE** a spire
STEEPLY almost sheer; abruptly
STEERED conned; controlled; directed
STEERER pilot; guide; director
STEEVED packed closely
STELENE pillar-like; columnar
STELLAR astral; starry
STEMLET small stalk
STEMMED compressed
jn, bd **STEMPLE** crossbeam
nt **STEMSON** jointing timber
STENCHY odoriferous
STENCIL pattern plate
STENGAH whisky and soda (Malay)
STENODE supersonic heterodyne receiver
tx **STENTER** fabric-sketching machine
STENTOR a loud speaker
STEP-INS elastic-held shoes; underwear
STEPNEY spare-wheel; (born at sea)
STEPPED paced; walked; fixed

STEPPER horse with high action
STEPSON spouse's earlier product
STERILE barren; germ-free; acarpous
zo **STERLET** sturgeon
md **STERNAL** (breast-bone)
STERNER harsher; more austere
STERNLY severely; strictly; dourly
nt **STERN-TO** in reverse; backwards
md **STERNUM** breast-bone
ch **STEROID** sterol compound
STEROLS cholesterols (universal)
md **STERTOR** noisy breathing
STETSON a hat (USA)
nt **STEVING** stowing
STEWARD seneschal; bailiff
nt **STEWARD** airline; purser (ship); agent
STEWARD (horse-racing) (rally); waiter
ck **STEW-CAN STEW-POT**, cooking vessel
STEWING simmering; worrying
md **STHENIA** strength
STIBIAL (antimony)
ch **STIBINE** antimony hydride
ch **STIBIUM** antimony
• **STICHIC** rhythmic
STICHOS a line of verse
STICKER last ditcher; adherent
STICKLE a rapid in a stream
STIFFEN harden
STIFFER more rigid; harder; primmer
STIFFLY rigidly; firmly; starchy
STIFLED suffocated; smothered
STILLED hushed; calmed; distilled
STILLER pacifier
STILTED pompous; bombastic
ck **STILTON** a cheese
STIMIED obstructed; (golf)
STIMULI incentives; spurs
zo **STINGER** insect organ; injects poisons
nt **STINGER** pontoon; lay barge
STINKER despicable person
STINTED restricted; rationed
STINTER pincher; restrainer
bt **STIPATE** crowded
STIPEND salary; emolument
STIPPLE to make dots
md **STIPTIC** astringent
bt **STIPULA STIPULE**, leaf appendage
STIRPES forefathers; races
STIRRED roused; incited; bustled
STIRRER thriller; agitator; disturber
STIRRUP foot-holder for rider; pump; cup
STIVING stewing
nt **STOAKED** choked; stopped

STOCKED stored; saved; hoarded
STOCKLI pommel horse; gymnastics
STOICAL passionless; unfeeling
STOKING adding fuel
ck STOLLEN sweet German currant
bread
pl STOMACH digestive organ
STOMACH to brook; to resent
STOMACH desire for courage
md STOMATA breathing pore
bt STOMIUM fern-sporangium-wall part
STONIED astonished; amazed
STONILY obdurately; unrelentingly
STONING pelting; (fruit)
STOOGED loitered; filled in time
STOOKED set up in sheaves
STOOKER harvest worker
STOOMED fermented
STOOPED condescended; swooped
STOOPER bender
nm STOOTER Dutch silver coin
STOPGAP locum tenens
STOPING series of ledges
STOPPED restrained; repressed;
closed
STOPPER STOPPLE, restraint; a
centre-back (soccer)
STORAGE space; safe-custody
STORAGE warehouse facilities
el STORAGE accumulator cell
cp STORAGE memory system
(computer)
STORIED legendary; fabled
STORIES floors; tales
STORING garnering; hoarding
STORMED assaulted; raved; raged
STORMER blusterer
STOTTER rebound; a bounce (Sc.)
STOUTEN hearten; cheer
STOUTER more corpulent; braver
STOUTLY sturdily; stalwartly; robust
STOVING a heat treatment
STOWAGE packing; loading
STOWING arranging; packing
STRAIKS wheel-plates; strakes
STRANGE unfamiliar; abnormal;
exotic
STRAPPY strong; fit; many straps
gl STRATUM rock formation
mt STRATUS cloud formation
STRAWED strewed
STRAYED erred; roved; deviated
STRAYER wandered; vagrant
ck STREAKY striped; bacon with fat
STREAMY well watered
STRELLI parallel bars (gymnastics)
STRETCH reach; strain; expand;
(baseball)

mu STRETTO quick and sharp (It.)
STREULI backward roll to handstand
STREWED strewn; scattered
STRIATE streaky; scratched
STRIDOR harsh noise
zo STRIGES the owl genus
STRIGIL skin-scraper
STRIKER (industrial action)
STRIKER blacksmith's assistant
ga STRIKER firing-pin; batsman
(cricket)
mu STRINGS viol family instruments
STRINGY filamentous
STRIOLA small/weak stria; scratch
STRIPED streaked
STRIPES tiger; denoting military,
naval rank
STRIP-IN recombining photo
material
STRIVEN strove; struggled; tussled
STRIVER emulator; trier; competitor
STROBIC rate of turning; spinning
STROCAL glass-maker's shovel
STROKED rubbed gently; (rowing)
STROKER rubber; soother
STROPHE a stanza; verse; (Gr.)
ck STRUDEL Austrian thin-dough
pastry
STUBBED blunted; obtuse;
extirpated
bt STUBBLE corn stumps
STUBBLY like stubble; unshaven
STUCKLE clump of sheaves
STUCK-UP arrogant; pompous
STUDDED (shirts); (nails)
STUDDLE a trestle
STUDENT pupil; scholar; philomath
STUDIED conned; pondered; worked
STUDIER student; scrutinizer
STUFFED padded; crowded; rammed
STUFFER packer; crammer
STUMBLE trip; slip; blunder; lurch
STUMBLY apt to stumble
STUMMED fortified; doctored
STUMMEL tobacco pipe (Ger.)
STUMPED at a loss; (cricket)
STUMPER wicket-keeper; difficult
problem
STUMPER heavy walker; tree-cutter
STUNNED unconscious after blow,
fall
STUNNED dumbfounded; amazed
STUNNER an astonisher; stupefier
STUNTED dwarfed; pygmean; runty
STUPEFY bemuse; dope; benumb
STUPENT struck with stupor
STUPOSE tufted; scaly; matted
zo STURNUS starling genus

STUTTER stammer; hesitant utterance
STYGIAN infernal; black; murky
STYLATE styloid; like a style or pen
STYLING naming; designating
STYLISH modish; chic; elegant
STYLIST fine writer
STYLITE pillar-dweller
STYLIZE to make average
STYLOID pen-like
STYMIED stimied; obstructed; (golf)
md STYPSIS use of styptics
md STYPTIC stiptic; astringent
SUASIVE urbane; agreeable
SUASORY convincing
SUAVELY pleasantly; blandly
SUAVITY affability; sweetness
SUBACID rather acid
SUBADAR Mogul governor
SUBARID slightly arid
nt, ce SUB-BASE (submarines); road undersurface
mu SUBBASS low organ note
SUBBING acting as substitute; subediting
zo SUBCOXA segment of primitive leg in insects
rl SUBDEAN under-dean
SUBDUAL conquest; subjugation
SUBDUCE withdraw
SUBDUCT subtract
SUBDUED piano; routed; worsted
SUBDUER queller; vanquisher
SUBEDAR native captain
SUBEDIT (edit)
SUBERIC of cork
bt SUBERIN cork-cell fatty mixture
SUBFUSC subfusk; dusky
SUBGENS sub-clan
SUBGOAL intermediary goal or achievement
SUB-HEAD sub-title
lw, mu SUBJECT thesis; topic; subservient; conquer; impose; grammar; (fugue)
SUBJOIN append; affix; postfix
SUBLATE carry off; take away
SUBLIME exalted; lofty; superb
bt SUBNUDE almost leafless
SUBOVAL almost ovate
lw SUBPENA subpoena; writ
SUBRENT sublet
ch SUBSALT below the salt
SUBSIDE sink; ebb; wane; abate
SUBSIDY a grant; dole; monetary aid
SUBSIGN undersign
bd SUB-SILL steel window-level wall covering

SUBSIST live; exist; endure
SUBSOIL the under-soil
SUBSUME include as comprehended
SUBTACK an under-lease (Sc.)
SUBTEND embrace; enfold
SUBTILE subtle; cunningly devised
SUBTLER wilier; craftier
SUBTYPE subdivision
SUBURBS outlying districts
SUBVENE aid; support
SUBVERT overthrow; ruin; corrupt
SUCCADE candied fruit
SUCCEED follow; prosper; win
SUCCESS prosperity; victory; triumph
bt SUCCISE ending below abruptly
SUCCOSE sappy
SUCCOUR aid; help; support; foster
SUCCUBA battering demons; spirits
SUCCULA capstan; winch
SUCCUMB yield; submit; die; capitulate
SUCCUSS to shake suddenly
SUCKING absorbing; imbibing
SUCKLED nursed
SUCKLER an infant; a suckling
SUCROSE cane sugar
SUCTION vacuum-filling
SUDANIC group of languages (Sudan)
SUDORAL sweaty; perspiring
SUFFETE Punic official
SUFFICE to content; be enough; avail
SUFFUSE diffuse; blush; overspread
SUGARED candied; sweetened
SUGGEST hint; insinuate; propose
nt SUGGING sea-rocked when stranded
SUICIDE taking one's own life; felo-de-se; self-destruction
SUIFORM pig-like; swinish
tx SUITING pleasing; according
SULCATE grooved; furrowed
SULKIER more sullen
SULKILY morosely; sullenly; surlily
SULKING glowering
SULLAGE dross; scum
SULLENS morose; temper; the sulks
SULLIED tainted; tarnished; defamed
ch SULPHUR brimstone
bt, zo SULTANA raisin; marsh bird
mt SUMATRA Malaccan summer squall
SUMLESS beyond count
SUMMARY epitome; abstract; digest
cp SUMMARY report
lw SUMMARY to be done without delay
SUMMERY summerlike; hot weather
SUMMING summary; adding; counting

SUMMIST writer of a compendium
lw **SUMMONS** writ; citation
mn **SUMPERS** cut holes (shaft sinking)
zo **SUMPTER** pack-horse
SUN-BATH outdoor near-nudity
SUNBEAM ray from the sun
SUNBEAT struck by the sun's rays
zo **SUNBIRD** humming bird
SUNBURN tan; browned skin
SUNCLAD radiant
bt **SUNDARI** hardwood tree (Borneo)
SUNDAWN dawn-light
SUNDIAL stylish timepiece
SUNDOWN sunset
bt **SUNDROP** primrose (Amer.)
zo **SUNFISH** shark
SUN-KIST kissed by the sun
SUN-LAMP ultra-violet ray
SUNLESS cloudy; overcast
SUNLIKE solar
SUNMYTH a solar myth
SUNNING sun-bathing
SUNNITE orthodox Muslim
SUNRISE dawn; cock-crow
bt **SUNROSE** sunflower
as **SUNSPOT** solar phenomenon
SUNWARD towards the sun
SUNWISE clock-wise
SUPPING eat evening meal
SUPPLED made pliant
SUPPORT prop; uphold; assist;
  position on arms (gymnastics)
SUPPOSE surmise; fancy; deem
SUPREME dominant; paramount
zo **SURANAL** above the anus
SURBASE cornice; base moulding
SURCOAT coat worn over chain mail
SURDITY lack of resonance; deafness
SURFACE exterior; superficies
SURFARI safari in search of good
  surfing
SURFEIT excess; plethora; cloy;
  gorge
SURFING to plane on forward
  portion of wave on a surfboard
SURFMAN skilled swimmer
SURGENT swelling; heaving
SURGEON who treats people by
  operation
md **SURGERY** cutting into bodies
SURGING billowing regularly
SURGING regular increase of power
SURGING Faradayism; (running)
SURLIER more churlish and crusty
SURLILY gruffly; sullenly; morosely
ck **SURLOIN** sirloin beef
SURMISE conjecture; suppose;
  imagine

SURNAME cognomen
SURPASS excel; exceed; outdo
SURPLUS residuum; balance; excess
lw **SURSIZE** feudal penalty
SURTOUT overcoat
SURVIVE outlive; endure; outlast
SUSCEPT parasite's host
SUSPECT doubtful; mistrust; distrust
SUSPEND hang; postpone; relieve
SUSPIRE sign; yearn; breathe
SUSTAIN uphold; bear; endure
SUTLERY sutler's occupation
SUTLING commissariat (Turk.)
SUTURAL sewn; seamy; stitched
SUTURED sewn together
SWABBED washed; mopped
SWABBER scrubber; mopper-up
SWABIAN (South German)
SWADDLE swathe, wrap; bind
SWAGGED sagged; leant
SWAGGER strut; ruffle; boast
SWAGING assuaging; mitigating
mt **SWAGING** metal-rod tapering
SWAGMAN burglar
SWAHILI East African language
SWALING wasting; consuming;
  burning
go **SWALLET** underground stream
zo **SWALLOW** voracity; engulf; absorb
SWAMPED overwhelmed; inundated
SWANKED boasted; bragged
SWANKIE swipes; thin beer
SWANPAN Chinese abacus
SWAPPED bartered; exchanged
SWARAJI home rule (India)
SWARDED grassy; turfy
SWARFED fainted; swooned;
  dwalmed
SWARMED thronged; teemed;
  clustered
SWARTHY tawny; swart; dark
SWASHED blustered; swanked
SWASHER swash-buckler
SWATTED hit with a fly swat
SWATTER fly-killer
SWAYING governing; oscillating
SWEALED guttered like a candle
SWEARER blasphemer
SWEATED drudged; perspired;
  reeked
SWEATER a pullover; jersey
SWEDISH (Sweden)
SWEEPER road cleaner; artist brush
SWEEPER defensive (soccer, hockey)
SWEETEN to palliate; dulcify
SWEETER more fragrant
SWEETIE sweetmeat; confectionery
SWEETLY dulcetly; fragrantly

SWELLED inflated; heaved; bulged
zo **SWELLEL** American squirrel
SWELLET rush of water in a mine
SWELTER perspire; sweat
SWELTRY sultry; oppressive
SWERVED deviated; turned aside
SWERVER curve-swinger
SWIFTER faster; nimbler; quicker
SWIFTLY rapidly; promptly; suddenly
SWIGGED drank deep; quaffed
SWILLED rinsed; washed; boozed
SWILLER copious absorber
zo **SWIMMER** water-spider
SWINDLE fraud; dupe; cheat
SWINERY piggery
SWINGED beaten up; punished
SWINGEL SWINGLE, flail
SWINGER disco dancer; pendulum
SWINGER wife-swapper; trench bar
SWINGER a wielder
SWINISH hoggish; suiform
SWINKED drudged; moiled; toiled
SWIPING slogging; lashing out
SWIPPLE at a loose end
SWIRLED whirled; eddied
SWISHED flogged
SWISHER a wielder of the birch
SWISHER shot for goal (basketball)
SWITHER hesitate; doubt; fright
SWITZER Swiss bodyguard; a Swiss
SWIZZLE a mixed drink
SWOLLEN distended; enlarged; bloated
SWOONED fainted; swarfed; dwalmed
SWOOPED caught on the wing
SWOPPED swapped; bartered
SWOTTED studied hard
SYBOTIC pertaining to swineherd
md **SYCOSIS** barber's itch
mn **SYENITE** Egyptian granite
SYLPHID small sylph; fairy
ch **SYLVINE** potassium chloride
ch **SYLVITE** potassium chloride
zo **SYMBION** symbiotic organism
SYMPTOM indication (of illness)
bt **SYNACMY** floral maturity
md **SYNAPSE** nerve junction
rl **SYNAPTE** Greek litany
SYNAXIS an assembly for worship
bt **SYNCARP** multiple fleshy fruit
SYNCHRO transformer for transmitting
SYNCHRO right-angular
SYNCOPE contraction; collapse
SYNERGY co-operation
SYNESIS harmonious construction

bt **SYNNEMA** erect bunch of hyphae
md **SYNOCHA** fever
SYNOCIL a growth on sponges
rl **SYNODAL** bishop's benefit
SYNODIC (synod); conventional
SYNONYM a word of similar significance, meaning
zo **SYNOTUS** long-eared bat
md **SYNOVIA** lubrication
SYNTONY wireless tuning
bt **SYRINGA** mock-orange
SYRINGE a squirt; to spray
md **SYSTOLE** contraction of the heart
ar **SYSTYLE** a stylish portico
ar **SYSTYLE** type of colonnade

T

TABANAC French white wine
zo **TABANUS** horse-fly or gad-fly
tx **TABARET** satin striped silk
md **TABELLA** lozenge
md **TABETIC** consumptive
TABIDLY tabific; tabetic
TABINET curtain material
TABLEAU vivid picture (Fr.)
TABLIER apron; chess-board
TABLING setting down in order
md **TABLOID** multum in parvo
TABOOED banned; barred; accursed
mu **TABORER** drummer
mu **TABORET** small drum
TABULAR listed; tabulated; catalogued
cp **TABULAR** program language
nc **TACHYON** fast-moving particle
TACITLY noiselessly implied
TACKILY stickily; adhesively
TACKING stitching; fastening
nv **TACKING** zigzag course against wind
TACKLED seized; grappled with
pt **TACK-RAG** dust/grit remover
TACTFUL diplomatic and sensitive
TACTICS cunning moves
TACTILE tangible; perceptible
TACTION sense of touch; contact
ch, ps **TACTOID** double-reflecting droplet
TACTUAL tactile; palpable
zo **TADORNA** duck genus
zo **TADPOLE** embryonic frog
TADZHIK Central Asian people
mn **TAENITE** iron-nickel solution
tx **TAFFETA** wavy fabric
tx **TAFFETY** taffeta; lustrous silk
TAGALOG language (Philippines)
bt **TAGETES** French marigolds
TAGGERS thin sheet iron

TAGGING following; tailing; tacking
TAGMEME smallest meaningful speech unit
vt **TAGSORE** sheep disease
vt **TAGTAIL** worm; parasite
lw **TAILAGE** entail
TAILCAP leather fold on book spine
TAILEND fag-end
TAILING following; a winter sport
lw **TAILZIE** deed of entail
TAINTED infected; stained; sullied
TAIPING Chinese rebel
ae **TAKE-OFF** a burlesque; ascent from earth
ga **TAKE-OFF** a stroke (golf) (croquet)
TAKE-OUT withdraw; (insurance)
lw **TAKE-OUT** courtship; (patents) (export)
TAKINGS cash receipts
TAKOURA golf-like game (Morocco)
ar **TAKSPAN** pine-roof shingles
TALARIA Mercury's winged sandals
mn **TALCITE** nacrite
TALCOSE a talc
TALEFUL newsy
TALIPED club footed
md **TALIPES** slub-foot
bt **TALIPOT TALIPAT**
bt **TALIPUT** fan-palm
TALKIES talking films
TALKING prating; discoursing
TALLAGE ancient tax
TALLBOY chest of drawers
TALLEST loftiest; highest
TALLIED agreed; correspond; fitted
TALLIER tally-keeper
TALLISH rather tall; of good height
TALLITH praying mantle (Heb.)
TALLOWY fatty
TALLY-HO hunting call
TALONED with claws
TAMABLE docile; tractable
zo **TAMANOA** ant-eater
zo **TAMARIN** S. American monkey
TAMASHA entertainment (India)
mu, tx, ar **TAMBOUR** drum; embroidery; vestibule; dome-(holding walls)
mu **TAMBURA TANPURA**, long Indian lute
mu **TAMBURO** It. small snare drum
TAMILIC TAMULIC, Tamil language (Sri Lanka)
TAMMANY corrupt political organization, USA
TAMPING (blasting)
TAMPION also tompion; a stopper
TANADAR Hindu police officer
zo **TANAGER** American finch
zo **TANAGRA** finches

TANAGRA terracotta ware
TANGENT meeting but not intersecting
mu **TANGENT** a clavichord; tongue
TANGENT squaring the circle
bt **TANGHIN** poison tree (Madagascar)
TANGING twanging; flavouring
TANGLED jumbled; matted; twisted
ga **TANGRAM** Chinese jigsaw
TANKAGE storage
TANKARD drinking vessel
TANKCAR tanker; oil-tank
TANKING waterproofing a basement
TANLING sun-bather
TANNAGE tanning materials
ch **TANNATE** a salt of tannic acid
le **TANNERY** leather factory
le **TANNING** leathering
ch **TANNINS** organic compounds for ink and leather – T for two
TANRIDE riding school
to **TANSPUD** bark-peeling tool
mu **TANTARA** fanfare
TANTITY tantamount
TANTIVY coach horn call; (hunt)
zo **TANTONY** smallest pig in litter
TANTRUM temper; petulance
TANYARD tanning place
TAPBOLT screw bolt
TAPERED conical; pointed
md **TAPETUM** (retina)
bt **TAPIOCA** cassava
TAPLASH stale swipes
TAPPING broaching; screwcutting
TAPROOM bar
bt **TAPROOT** main sustenance root
TAPSTER bartender
TARACEA inlaid wood (Spanish style)
mu **TARAGOT** Transylvanian clarinet
TARBUSH tarboosh; fez; Muslim cap
TARDIER slower; later; slacker
TARDILY slowly; reluctantly
TARDIVE tardiness; lateness
TARNISH sully; soil; stain
TARRACE volcanic earth
TARRIED loitered; lingered; sojourned
lw **TARRIER** dawdler; estate register
TARRING covering with bitumen
zo **TARROCK** arctic tern
zo **TARSIER** lemur; the malmag
nt **TARTANE** coastal trader, Mediterranean
TARTARY Tartarus; nethermost hell
TARTISH somewhat sharp
ck **TARTLET** small tart; (sweetmeat)
TASHRIF respect; compliment (Ind.)

TASKING taskwork; drudgery; toiling
TASTIER choicer; more succulent
TASTILY artistically; with gusto
TASTING relishing; enjoying; gustation
TATARIC Mongolian, Turkish, etc.
zo **TATOUAY** armadillo; peba; tatou
TATTERY in rags; not riches
TATTING lace work
TATTLED gossiped; chatted; prated
TATTLER tale-bearer; a wag
TAUNTED derided; flouted; scorned
TAUNTER mocker; upbraider; reviler
TAURIAN (bulls)
TAURIDS meteoric shower
ch, md **TAURINE** ox extract; amino acid
TAUTEST tightest; tensest
TAXABLE rateable; inescapable
TAXCART small farm cart
TAXFREE scot-free
TAXICAB hire car for lower price
ae **TAXI-ING** runway movements
TAXI-MAN cab driver
ck **TEA-CAKE** scone or bun for tea
TEACHER master; tutor; pedagogue
TEACH-IN active seminar discussion
TEACHTA member of parliament (Irish)
TEA-COSY pot warmer
TEA-GOWN long afternoon dress
TEA-LEAD (tea-chest linings)
bt **TEA-LEAF** blade of tea
TEAMING grouping; selecting
md **TEARBAG** lachrymal gland
TEARFUL maudlin; weeping; Niobean
ch **TEAR-GAS** riot repellant; eye irritant
TEARING rending; raving; raging
bt **TEA-ROSE** tea-scented rose
TEARPIT a lachrymal depression
TEA-SHOP shop serving tea
TEASING tantalizing; plaguing
TEATHED manured by livestock
TEA-TIME 4/5 o'clock
TEA-TRAY on which tea carried
bt **TEA-TREE** Asian camellia; shrub
TECHILY fretfully; peevishly
TECHNIC technique; technical
zo **TECTRIX** a wing or tail feather
TEDDING spreading; bedding
TEDESCO German (It.)
TEDIOUS wearisome; hum-drum
TEEBEAM rolled steel; concrete flow
TEEIRON golf club (driver)
TEEMFUL prolific; swarming
TEEMING fruitful; abundant
TEENAGE thirteen to nineteen
TEENING troubling; provoking

TEGULAR of tiles
mn **TEKTITE** non-volcanic natural glass
TELAMON statue supporting masonry
TELECAR mobile telegraph office
TELEOST osseous
TELERGY telepathy
mn **TELESIA** sapphire
TELLING effective; informing
el **TELPHER TELFER**, electric traction
TEL-QUEL exchange rate
TELSTAR television satellite
TEMENOS temple precinct (Gr.)
TEMPEAN delightful; (Vale of Tempe)
TEMPERA oilless paint; distemper
TEMPEST hurricane; typhoon; gale
lw **TEMPLAR** student of law
TEMPLED in a temple
to **TEMPLET** template; jig
TEMPTED allured; tried; solicited
TEMPTER a decoy; an enticer
TENABLE maintainable; rational
TENANCY tenure
TENDING tendentious; trending
bt **TENDRIL** twining shoot
zo **TENERAL** immature
TENFOLD decuple
zo **TENIOID** like tapeworms
TENONED mortised
to **TENONER** tenon cutter
TEN-PINS cf. nine-pins
TENSELY tautly; tightly
TENSEST stiffest; most emotional
TENSILE ductile
TENSION strain; stress; exigency
TENSITY tenseness; urgency
TENSIVE intensive
TENTBED canopied bed
TENT-FLY part of tent
TENTFUL tent fully occupied
TENTGUY tent-rope; not its occupant
TENTING camping
TENTORY the awning of a tent
TENTPEG TENTPIN, used to secure a tent
TENTURE wall hangings
TENUATE thin; attenuate
TENUITY rarity; thinness
TENUOUS diffused; slender
nt **TEPUKEI** Polynesian sail canoe
TEQUILA fermented sap drink (Mex.)
ch **TERBIUM** a metallic element
bt **TERCINE** seed-coat
bt **TEREBIC** (turpentine)
zo **TEREBRA** Roman ram; ovipositor
zo **TEREKIA** sandpiper genus

hd **TERGANT** recursant
zo **TERGITE** back of an anthropod
lw **TERM-FEE** periodic payment
TERMING naming; denominating
rw **TERMINI** boundaries; stations
zo **TERMITE** white ant
TERNARY in threes
bt **TERNATE** three-leafed
TERNERY tern breeding ground
TERNION (twelve pages)
ch **TERPENE** terebene
ar **TERRACE** raised level (vines)
TERRACE continuous house row
go **TERRAIN** geological features
gl **TERRANE** area covered by certain rock
TERRENE terrestrial; earthy
zo **TERRIER** fine fighter
lw **TERRIER** tarrier; register
TERRIFY alarm; appal; dismay
TERRINE earthenware cooking dish
TERSELY concisely; briefly; laconically
TERSION wiping
zo **TERTIAL** wing feather
TERTIAN on alternate days
TESSERA mosaic block
lw **TESTACY** testate
lw **TESTATE** leaving a will
TEST-BAN nuclear weapons agreement
bt **TESTBED** for horticultural experiments
cp **TESTBED** software for program testing
nm **TESTERN** testril; a sixpence
TESTIER more irritable or irascible
TESTIFY affirm; avow; depose; depone
TESTILY peevishly; petulantly
TESTING proving; trying
nm **TESTOON** Henry VIII shilling
nm **TESTRIL** a tester; a sixpence
zo **TESTUDO** tortoise; early tank
md **TETANUS** lock-jaw disease
TETRACT having four rays
TETRODE a thermionic valve
ch **TETROSE** monosaccharide
TEXTILE woven fabric
TEXT-MAN a quoter
rl **TEXTUAL** valid; literal; written source
TEXTURA medieval handwriting
pr **TEXTURA** Gothic dark type
TEXTURE a web; structure; fabric
THALIAN comic; theatrical
THALLUS a stem formation
gl **THALWEG** longitudinal river profile

THANAGE thanedom (Scottish rank)
THANATO- of death (instinct) (Gr.)
THANKED gratefully acknowledged
THAWING melting; dissolving
THAYYAM board game with sticks (Ind.)
md **THEATRE** operations; drama
md **THEBAIA THEBAIN**, opium
THEBAIC Theban
bt **THECATE** sheathed; encased
bt **THECIUM** spore-case
mu **THEORBO** lute with 11 strings
THEOREM logical proposition
md **THERAPY** curative art
THEREAT on that account
THEREBY in consequence
THEREIN inside that
THEREOF about that
THEREON upon that
THERETO in addition
md **THERIAC** alleged antidote
THERMAE public steam baths (Roman)
THERMAL thermic; warm
THERMIE heat-calory unit (Fr.)
THERMIT incendiary mixture
THERMOS flask
zo **THEROID** animal-like
THESEUS slew Minotaur in Labyrinth
THESPIS founder of Greek drama
THEURGY miracle making
ch **THIAMIN** B vitamin
THICKEN condense; coagulate; curdle
THICKER closer; duller; muddier
THICKET underwood
THICKLY solidly; densely; closely
nm **THICKUN** £1; a sovereign
THIEVED stole; peculated; purloined
THIGGED cadged; begged
THIGGER threatening beggar; sorner
zo **THILLER** wheel-horse; shaft-horse
nt **THIMBLE** iron rope ring; sleeve piece
tx **THIMBLE** fingertip sewing shield
THINKER cogitator; (Rodin)
THINNED attenuated; reduced
THINNER slimmer; slighter; (paint)
pt **THINNER** solvents; (turpentine)
THIRSTY dry; parched; craving
bt **THISTLE** emblem of Scotland; weed
THISTLY overgrown with thistles
THITHER to there; yonder
THOLING enduring; yielding
rl **THOMISM** doctrine of Thomas Aquinas
nc **THORIDE** radioactive isotope
mn **THORITE** thorium silicate
ch **THORIUM** a metallic element

THOUGHT solicitude; concern; care
THOUGHT concept consideration
THOUING treating with familiarity
THRATCH gasp for breath (Sc.)
THREADY filamentous
THREAVE 24 sheaves
THRIFTY frugal; economical; thriving
THRIVED waxed; luxuriated
THRIVER prosperer
THROATY guttural (sounds)
THRONAL like a throne
THRONED exalted
THROUGH clear; unobstructed
THROWER caster; hurler; heaver
ga **THROW-IN** football
THRUMMY shaggy cloth; fringed
THUGGEE practice of thugs, assassins
mn **THULITE** Norwegian rock
ch **THULIUM** a metallic element
THUMBED beckoned for a lift
THUMPED struck heavily; drubbed
THUMPER whacker; wammer
THUNDER denounce; rumble
THURIFY to cense frankincense
THWAITE reclaimed land
bc **THYMINE** of animal nucleoprotein
md **THYMOMA** tumour in thymus
el **THYRITE** voltage-rise limiting device
md **THYROID** shield-like gland
bt **THYRSUS** branched inflorescence
THYSELF reflexive pronoun of deity
TIARAED wearing a tiara, mini-
  coronet
TIBETAN of Tibet
mu **TIBICEN** flute player
TICKING bedding material; marking
TICKLED titillated; amused
TICKLER enlivener
zo **TIDDLER** small fry
TIDERIP rough water
TIDEWAY a channel
TIDIEST neatest; sprucest
TIDINGS news; intelligence; message
TIE-BACK window drape fastener
TIE-BEAM rafter retainer
nt **TIE-LINE** ship's mooring rope
cp **TIE-LINE** channel link
zo **TIERCEL** male hawk
TIERCET triple rhyme
tx **TIFFANY** gauze; thin silk
bt **TIGELLA** short stem
TIGHTEN increase the strain
TIGHTER more compact; closer
TIGHTLY tautly; tensely
bt **TIGLINE** croton oil
zo **TIGRESS** fierce female tiger
TIGRINE marked like a tiger
TIGRISH fierce

cy **TIGROID** of nerve-cell granules
TILBURY dog-cart
mn **TILE-ORE** copper ore
TILE-RED brownish-red
TILLAGE cultivation
TILLING husbandry
TILLITE till; boulder clay
bt **TILSEED** seed of sesamum indicum
TILTING jousting; forging
ga **TILTING** slanting; twist throw
  (bowls)
ck, mu **TIMBALE** a fowl dish; kettle-drum
mu **TIMBREL** tambourine
TIMEFUL seasonable; timely
TIME-GUN parting shot
TIME-LAG an interim; delay
TIME-OFF leisure break; free period
ga **TIME-OUT** entertainment; sports
  news
TIMIDLY fearfully; diffidently
bt **TIMOTHY** cat's tail grass
mu **TIMPANI** kettle drums; percussion
zo **TINAMOU** S. American quail
zo **TINCHEL TINCHIL** deer culled
TINDERY inflammable
nt **TIN-FISH** torpedo
TINFOIL leaf aluminium
TINGING ringing; tinking
TINGLED thrilled; smarted
TINIEST smallest; puniest;
  microscopic
TINKLED rang; clinked
TINKLER small bell
TIN-MINE Cornish hole
TINNING covering with tin
zo **TINNOCK** blue tit
TINSICA cartwheel and half-twist
TINSICA somersault (gymnastics)
TIN-TACK tack of/for tin
TINTAGE colouring; shading
pt **TINTERS** stainers; dyers
TINTIES coloured films
TINTING tingeing
TINTYPE ferro-type
TINWARE tin pots
ml **TIN-ZINC** metal finish
TIPCART rubbish barrow
TIPPING hinting; donating
TIPPLED drank deep
TIPPLER steady drinker
TIPSIFY inebriate
TIPSILY drunkenly
TIPSTER racing tout
TIPTOED walked warily
md **TIQUEUR** person suffering from tic
mu **TIRASSE** pedal coupling
TIRLING quivering; vibrating;
  twisting

TISSUED woven; variegated
TITANIA fairy queen
TITANIC gigantic; colossal
TITHING township
zo TITLARK meadow pipit
pr TITLING title pages
zo TITLING hedge sparrow
zo TITMICE TITS, birds
TITOISM political practice
ch TITRATE (volumetric analysis)
TITTUPY frisky
TITULAR nominal
TIVERED marked with ochre
TOADIED cringed; truckled; fawned
TOADIES sycophants
TOASTED lightly grilled
TOASTER toast maker
TOBACCO insidious narcotic
TOBASCO red pepper
TOBYMAN highwayman
mu TOCCATA a touchy composition
TODDLED strolled; meandered
TODDLER a tiny tot
TOE-HOLD foot grip for climber
TOENAIL horn on foot digits
TOFTMAN a cottager
TOGGERY raiment
TOILFUL wearisome
TOILING moiling; labouring; snaring
TOKENED spotted; marked
TOLLAGE dues
TOLLBAR toll-gate
lw TOLLING knelling; annulling
TOLLMAN toll-gatherer
ch TOLUENE methyl benzene
zo TOMALLY lobster liver
ch TOMATIN tomato antibiotic
TOMBOLA a form of lottery
go TOMBOLO sand, shingle bar (beach)
TOMFOOL buffoon
bt TOMOSIS disease of cotton plant
TOMPION inking pad; clockmaker
TONGUED possessing a tongue
TO-NIGHT night of this day
TONNAGE amount of tons
au TONNEAU back-seat part of motor-
car
TONSILE clippable
TONSURE shaving; (shorn)
TONTINE co-operative loan
bd,cr,jn TOOLBOX container for toolkit
TOOLING (bookbinding); driving
TOOTHED dentate; serrated edge
ar TOOTHED (saw-); (dog-)
bd TOOTHER projecting horizontal brick
TOOTING prying; hornblowing
mu TOOTLED played the flute
TOPARCH a Greek governor

TOPBOOT boot with high top
TOPCOAT overcoat
TOP-EDGE smooth gilded upper
book edge
TOPFULL brimming over
TOPHOLE first-rate; best quality
bd TOP-HUNG of top-hinged window-
sash
TOPIARY ornamental clipping
TOPICAL local; particular; allusive
zo TOPKNOT plume or crest of feathers
TOPLESS without a lid; bare-
bosomed
nt TOPMAST elevated mast
TOPMOST highest
TOPONYM topographical name
cr TOPPING upper layer (decor);
splendid
ga TOPPING beheading; hitting top of
ball
TOPPLED tumbled down
nt TOPSAIL part of rigging
TOPSIDE the upper part
TOPSMAN bailiff; public hangman
TOPSOIL planting earth
ga TOPSPIN rotary motion of ball in
play
TORBITE peat fuel
TORCHER torch-bearer; linkman
TORCHON geometric lace
zo TORGOCH a species of char
TORMENT rag; rack; plague; harry
md TORMINA griping pains
TORNADO cyclone; hurricane;
typhoon
TORNOTE with blunt extremities
zo,nt TORPEDO ray fish; the tin fish
TORPENT torpid; inert
TORPIFY benumb
hd TORQUED wreathed
TORREFY parch; roast; scorch
TORRENT stream; flood; current
TORSADE twisted scroll
TORSION twisting force
TORSIVE spiral
mn TORSTEN an iron ore
hd TORTEAU red circlet
TORTILE coiled; wreathed
TORTIVE twisted; tortile; tortuous
zo TORTRIX a moth genus
TORTURE torment; agony; pang
zo TORULUS antenna socket
TORVOUS grim; stern in aspect
TORYISM Conservatism
TOSSILY perty
TOSSING flipping; heaving
TOSSING throw a coin; a caber; one's
head

TOSSING twisting and turning; shaking

TOSS-POT toper; quaffer; drinker

TOTALLY wholly; entirely; completely

TOTEMIC (totems); emblematic

TOTTERY shaky; unsteady

TOTTING adding up

TOUCHED sympathetic; impinged

TOUCHED made body contact; handled

TOUCHED emotionally moved; aroused

TOUCHER confidence trickster

ga **TOUCHER** bowls; snooker; billiards

TOUGHEN indurate; harden

TOUGHLY stubbornly; tenaciously

zo **TOURACO** African bird

TOURING journeying

TOURISM co-ordinated travel

TOURIST tripper; excursionist

TOURNEY tournament

TOUSING teasing; worrying

TOUSLED unkempt; in disarray

TOUTING seeking custom

TOWARDS in direction of

nt **TOWBOAT** tug

TOWERED with towers

TOWIRON whaling toggle-iron

nt **TOWLINE** tow rope

TOWNISH urban

TOWPATH boat-haulage path

nt **TOWROPE** boat-haulage rope

md **TOXEMIA** blood poisoning

md **TOXEMIC** septicaemic

TOXICAL poisonous

zo **TOXODON** extinct rhinoceros

TOYSHOP plaything emporium

TOYSOME playful

bt **TOYWORT** shepherd's purse

TRACERY ornamental stonework

md **TRACHEA** wind-pipe

TRACING a copy; traversing

TRACKED trailed; traversed

TRACKER a sleuth

TRACTOR agricultural field vehicle

TRADE-IN part exchange

TRADING commerce; barter

TRADUCE misrepresent; libel; slander

TRAFFIC communications; movement

TRAFFIC flow of social intercourse

TRAFFIC transport; trade; exchange

TRAGEDY drama; calamity

TRAIKET worn out (Sc.)

TRAILED followed; dragged; dogged

TRAILER towed vehicle; follower

TRAILER tracker; preview (play, film)

cp **TRAILER** signal of filed data

TRAINED proficient; skilled

TRAINEE man under instruction

TRAINER a coach

TRAIPSE to tramp

TRAITOR quisling; betrayer

TRAJECT ferry; project

TRAMCAR passenger carriage on lines

TRAMMEL bird-net; compass; hamper

TRAMPED walked; trudged

TRAMPER vagrant; stroller; hiker

TRAMPLE crush; spurn; squelch

TRAMPOT socket for a spindle

rw **TRAMWAY** street railway; (factory)

TRANCED in a dream; enraptured

TRANCHE slice; book-edge; life aspect

hd **TRANGLE** small band

TRANKUM a gew-gaw

TRANNEL wooden rail

TRANSIT conveyance; passage

bd,nt **TRANSOM** window beam; stem of yacht

TRANTER pedlar

TRAPEZE swinging cross-bar aloft

TRAPEZE daring circus gymnastics

TRAPPED adorned; caught

TRAPPER setter of snares

TRASHED lopped; crushed; hindered

TRAVAIL toil; labour; affliction

TRAVERS equestrian dressage act

nt **TRAWLED** fished

nt **TRAWLER** fishing boat

TREACLE molasses; dark syrup

TREACLY viscous and sweet

TREADER trampler

TREADLE pedal

TREASON treachery; disloyalty

TREATED entertained; doctored

TREATER negotiator

TREBLED tripled; threefold

TREEING cornering

ar **TREFOIL** (clover)

el **TREGOHM** million megohms

bt **TREHALA** Turkish manna

TREKKED migrated

TREKKER (ox-wagons, S. Africa)

TRELLIS lattice work

TREMBLE quiver; shake; oscillate

TREMBLY tottery; unsteady

mu **TREMOLO** trembling; shaking; vibrato

TRENDED tended; inclined; gravitated

TRENDLE a roller
rl **TRENTAL** 30 masses
zo **TREPANG** sea-slug
TRESSED curled
TRESSEL trestle; a movable framework
TRESTLE wooden construction support for tables, bridges, scaffold
ce **TRESTLE** ropeway bridges
TREVISS cross-beam
lw **TRIABLE** (jurisdiction)
ch **TRIADIC** trivalent
zo **TRIAENE** spicule in porifera
bt **TRIARCH** with 3 xylem strands in stele
nt **TRIATIC** jumper stay
TRIAXON with three axes
TRIBADE lesbian
TRIBBLE paper drying frame
to **TRIBLET** a goldsmith's mandril
TRIBUNE Roman magistrate; platform
TRIBUTE tax; impost; toil; offering
md **TRICEPS** extensor muscle
zo **TRICHAS** American warblers
nt **TRICING** hauling; clewing
TRICKED defrauded; hoaxed
TRICKER trickster
TRICKLE drip; ooze; percolate
TRICKLY trickling
TRICKSY artful; deft
TRICORN three-cornered
TRIDARN having three tiers
TRIDARN Welsh drying cupboard
TRIDENT Neptune's sceptre
TRIDUAN every third day
TRIDUUM period of three days
TRIFLED dallied; toyed; played
TRIFLER philanderer; idler; fribbler
bt **TRIFOLY TREFOIL**, leaf grouping
TRIFORM triple form
TRIGAMY cf. bigamy
TRIGGED skidded; obstructed
TRIGGER firing catch (gun); (-happy)
TRIGGER activate; detonate
TRIGGER switching device; bistable circuit
TRIGLOT in three languages
TRIGONE triangular area
TRIGRAM a triphthong; a trigraph; 3 letter sequence
md **TRILABE** surgical fork
ar **TRILITH** stone doorway
TRILLED warbled; quavered
TRILOGY a series of three linked books
zo **TRIMERA** type of beetle

TRIMMED clipped; balanced; rebuked
cr **TRIMMER** fishing float; beam joists
TRIMMER shearer; timeserver
el **TRIMMER** trimming capacitator
TRINARY ternary; threefold
TRINDLE trundle; trickle
TRINGLE curtain rod (Fr.)
rl **TRINITY** unit of 3
TRINKET small ornament
TRINKLE trickle or tinkle
TRIOLET poetic stanza
md **TRIONAL** hypnotic drug
as **TRIONES** 7 stars in Ursa Major
pg **TRIPACK** 3-emulsion-base process
TRIPARA woman giving birth 3 times
TRIPERY tripe-booth
TRIPLED trebled
TRIPLES series of midair jumps (skating)
mu **TRIPLET** three of a kind; (birth)
TRIPODY verse measure of 3 feet
TRIPOLI polishing powder; diatomite
bt **TRIPOLY** Michaelmas daisy
TRIPPED erred; slipped; stumbled
TRIPPER excursionist; dancer
TRIPSIS shampooing; pulverizing
nt **TRIREME** a galley
TRISECT cut into three
TRISEME (tribrach)
md **TRISMUS** lock-jaw; tetanus
md **TRISOMY** genetic basis of syndrome
TRISULA Siva's trident
TRITELY jejunely; hackneyed
TRITIUM very rare isotope of hydrogen
bt **TRITOMA** red-hot poker
mu **TRITONE** dissonant interval
TRIUMPH exultation; success; ovation
TRIVIAL trifling; slight; paltry
TRIVIUM grammar, logic and rhetoric
zo **TROCHAL** wheel-shaped
TROCHEE long and short foot metre
zo **TROCHUS** gastropod genus
TRODDEN trampled
TROGGIN pedlary
TROLAND unit of illuminance (optics)
TROLLED sang; fished
TROLLER fishing style
TROLLEY truck; metal pulley
TROLLOL sing; troll; trill
TROLLOP a slattern; a slut
TROMLET side pommel horse (gymnastics)

TROMMEL coal sieve with rotary screen
TROMPIL blast regulating device
TRONAGE wool-tax
TROOPED thronged; (the colours)
nt TROOPER mounted man; ship
TROPHIC (nutrition)
TROPICS (Cancer and Capricorn)
md TROPINE constituent of atropine
TROPISM enforced turning movement
TROPIST figurative speaker
TROTTER pig's foot; (globe-); horse
TROUBLE disturb; worry; trial; dolour
TROUNCE to larrup; castigate
TROUPER strolling player
md TROUSSE set of instruments
TROWING trusting; believing
TRUANCY vagrancy
TRUCAGE counterfeiting a picture
TRUCKED bartered; trafficked
TRUCKER exchange agent; driver
TRUCKLE roller; yield; submit
TRUDGED walked wearily; tramped
TRUDGEN a swimming stroke
bt TRUFFLE an edible fungus
TRUMEAU part of a wall
TRUMPED deceived; ruffed
mu TRUMPET proclaim; blazon; instrument
TRUNCAL main; principal
zo TRUNCUS main blood vessel
TRUNDLE wheel; truck; to roll
TRUNDLE spool of golden thread
TRUSSED bound; tied up
TRUSTED credited; confided
TRUSTEE guardian; fiduciary
TRUSTER an optimist; creditor
lw TRYABLE triable (law courts)
zo TRYPETA boring flies
md TRYPSIN pepsin
md TRYPTIC peptic; digestive
nt TRY-SAIL part of rigging
TRYSTED rendezvoused; appointed
TRYSTER tryst convener; go-between
TSANTSA head-shrinking technique
TSARINA Empress of Russia
TSARISM of the tsar (czar)
TSARIST Russian royalist
T-SQUARE draughtsman's tool
TSUKPIN Proa canoe, Micronesia
TSUNAMI seismic sea wave tremor, Japan
zo TUATERA tuatara; NZ lizard
mn TUBBING mine shaft lining; bathing
zo TUBBISH rotund; tub-like

zo TUB-FISH sapphirine gurnard
mu TUBICEN trumpeter
TUB-SIZE strengthening dip for handmade paper
TUBULAR hollow; fistular; capillary
TUCK-BOX for schoolboys' treats, delicacies
TUCKING cramming; folding; gathering
TUCK-OUT gorge of eating; blow-out
TUESDAY a weekday
mn TUESITE slate-pencil material
TUFTING knotting (carpets); adorning
nt TUGBOAT ship-towing craft
TUGGING lugging; pulling; hauling
nm TUGHRIK (Mongolia)
TUITION instruction; education
TULCHAN spoof calf
TULLIAN Latin style of M. Tullius Cicero
TUMBLED rumpled; fallen; twigged
zo TUMBLER pigeon; glass; acrobat; lock system
TUMBREL tumbril; two-wheeled cart
TUMIDLY pompously; turgidly; puffily
bt TUMPING stamping (after planting)
TUMULAR heaped
TUMULUS burial mound
TUNABLE melodious; musical
TUNABLY harmoniously
bd TUNDISH wine funnel; flue; condensation collector
TUNEFUL musical; dulcet
bt TUNG-OIL wood-oil
zo TUNICIN animal cellulose
TUNICLE small tunic
TUNMOOT village council
TUNNAGE (and poundage) wine tax
TUNNERY tunny-netting area
TUPPING hammering; butting
TURACIN carmine
zo TURAKOO gaudy bird; plantain-eater
TURBARY turf digging rights
TURBINE rotary engine
TURDINE thrush-like
TURFING laying turf; swarding
TURFITE racing fan
TURGENT swelling; distended; tumid
mn TURGITE a form of haematite
TURKISH of Turkey; language
TURKMEN Turkic people
TURMOIL tumult; ado; hubbub
TURNCAP chimney cowl
TURNERY lathe work
TURNING flexure; spinning; fermenting

TURNKEY prison warder
TURN-OUT parade; clearout; tidying
TURNPIN TAMPIN, boxwood roller (USA)
TURN-UPS trouser leg folds
bt **TURPETH** purgative plant
TURTLER turtle-hunter
ar **TUSKING** projecting stones (toothing)
TUSSIVE afflicted with a cough
TUSSLED struggled; fought; battled
TUSSOCK tuffet; tuft
tx **TUSSORE** coarse silk
TUTAMEN a protection; a defence
TUTANIA Britannia metal; alloy of copper, calamine, antimony, tin (1770)
TUTELAR protective
TUTENAG a Chinese alloy; zinc
TUTORED taught; educated; instructed
TUTULUS Etruscan head-dress
mn **TUT-WORK** excavation piece work
TWADDLE verbiage; balderdash; prattle (sl.)
mu **TWANGED** played the banjo
TWANKAY green tea
TWANKED twanged; twangled
TWEAKED twitched; pinched
TWEEDLE (fiddle); wheedle
TWEENIE maid; diminutive
ac **TWEETER** loudspeaker
mu **TWELFTH** ordinal number; mutation stop organ
to **TWIBILL** mattock; axe
TWIDDLE twist; tweedle
TWIGGED understood; observed (sl.)
TWIGGEN of wicker
TWINGED twitched; pained
TWINING twisting; meandering; coiling
TWINKLE wink; glimmer; scintillate
TWINNED two at a time
TWINSET matching sweater and cardigan
TWINTER beast, two winters old
au **TWIN-TOP** (motoring)
TWIRLED span; rotated; whirled
TWIRLER spinner; twister
TWISTED spun; contorted; tangled
TWISTER a puzzle; cheat; tornado
TWISTLE twist; a wrench (Sc.)
TWISTOR computer memory device
TWITTED reproached; rallied; taunted
TWITTEN by-lane
TWITTER an upbraider; chirp; palpitate

TWIZZLE turn and twist; a step-dance on one spot; jig
TWO-FOLD double
pr **TWO-LINE** size of printing type; whip (parliamentary)
TWONESS doubleness
TWOSOME a couple
mu **TWOSTEP** a dance
TWO-TIME double-cross
tc **TWO-WIRE** (AC or DC) transmit and receive channel
TYCHISM theory based on chance
pt **TYING-IN** tubular scaffolding, interior grip
nt **TYING-UP** mooring a vessel; securing
pr **TYING-UP** binding; setting book bands
zo **TYLARUS** padded hoof
TYLOPOD camel-footed
md **TYLOSIS** eye-trouble
md **TYLOTIC** eye-inflammation
md **TYMPANA** ear-drums
md **TYMPANY** turgidity; flatulence
TYNWALD parliament (Isle of Man)
pr **TYPE-BAR** a line of type
md **TYPHOID** a fever
mt **TYPHOON** cyclone; hurricane
TYPICAL emblematic; characteristic
TYPONYM type-name
TYRANNY despotism; iron rule
TZARINA Tsarina (Russia)
TZIGANE gipsy (Hungary)

U

UBEROUS fruitful
lw **UDALLER ODALLER,** freehold
UDARNIK 'shock' worker (Rus.)
mu **UKULELE** Hawaiian guitar
mn **ULEXITE** sodium calcium borate
ULLALOO Irish lament
pl **ULNARIA** arm-bones
md **ULONCUS** swollen gums
ULULANT wailing; sobbing
ULULATE howl; hoot
ULYSSES Odysseus; a wanderer
UMBERED tinged with brown colour
UMBONAL protuberant
UMBONES bosses on shields
UMBONIC humpy
UMBRAGE shade; resentment
UMBRERE helmet visor
UMBRIAN of Umbria province (It.)
zo, pt **UMBRINE** fish; darkish brown
UMBROSE shady; umbrageous
ga **UMPIRED** refereed; arbitrated
UMPTEEN more than ten

UNACTED never staged
UNAGING remaining youthful; immortal
UNAIDED single-handed
UNAIRED stuffy; unventilated; hidden
rl UNALIST holding one benefice
UNAPTLY not à propos
UNARMED defenceless
UNASKED gratuitously; unrequested
UNAWARE ignorant; uninformed
ga UNBATED unblunted point (fencing)
UNBAYED opened up
UNBEGUN not started
UNBLIND restore vision
UNBLOCK to clear; (cards)
UNBLOWN not sounded; in the bud
UNBORNE not carried
UNBOSOM freely disclose
UNBOUND loose; limitless
UNBOWED unsubdued
UNBRACE relax; free from tension
UNBRAID disentangle
UNBRUTE domesticate; tame
UNBUILD destroy (a house)
UNBUILT not yet constructed
UNBURNT unconsumed
UNCAGED released; freed
UNCANNY eerie; weird; mysterious
UNCARED untended; unheeded
UNCASED taken out; displayed
UNCEDED not transferred or granted
UNCHAIN free; let loose; unfetter
UNCHARM unspell; exorcise
UNCHARY heedless; not frugal
UNCINAL hook-shaped
md UNCINUS small hook
UNCIVIL incivil; impolite
UNCLASP unfasten; disconnect
UNCLEAN foul; dirty; leprous
UNCLEAR confused; unintelligible
UNCLING unclasp; disengage
UNCLOAK disrobe; unveil; unmask
UNCLOSE open; babbling
UNCLOUD free from obscurity
UNCOUTH boorish; rustic; rough
UNCOVER lay open; disclose
UNCROSS straighten (the legs)
UNCROWN dethrone
rl UNCTION an anointing
UNCULAR avuncular
md, ck UNCURED unremedied; unpreserved
UNDATED unrecorded; timeless
UNDEIFY remove a god
ck UNDERDO cook insufficiently
UNDERGO experience; bear; suffer
UNDIGHT to undress

UNDOING opening; unravelling; ruining
UNDRAPE strip; uncover
UNDRAWN not delineated
UNDREAM abandon a scheme, fantasy
UNDRESS disrobe; casual wear
UNDRIED wet; green
UNDYING immortal; continuing
UNEARTH disclose; reveal; discover
UNEATEN not consumed
UNEQUAL varying; not uniform
UNEXACT INEXACT, inaccurate
UNFADED remaining fresh; unwithered
UNFENCE remove a hedge
UNFILED unsorted reports; unrasped
UNFITLY unsuitably; improperly
UNFIXED unsettled; unsecured
UNFLESH reduce to a skeleton
UNFLUSH lose colour
UNFOUND still lost; not met with
rl UNFROCK deprive of office
UNFUMED not fumigated
el, mn UNFUSED unmerged; (unsafe)
UNFUZED shells unset for gunnery
UNGIVEN not conceded
UNGLAZE remove the glass
UNGLOVE bare the hand
UNGLUED unstuck
UNGODLY sinful; impious; profane
UNGUARD leave defenceless
md UNGUENT an ointment
zo UNGULAR (hoof; nails; etc.)
UNGYVED unfettered
UNHANDY awkward; clumsy
UNHAPPY sad; grievous; sorrowful
bt UNHARDY irresolute; delicate
UNHASTY slow; deliberate
UNHEARD inaudible; obscure
UNHEEDY careless; rash
UNHINGE to unsettle; derange
UNHIRED not engaged
UNHITCH loosen; unfasten
UNHIVED driven from shelter
UNHOARD dissipate; spend
UNHOPED unexpected
UNHORSE force to dismount
UNHOUSE evict
UNHUMAN not of mankind
UNIAXAL on one plane; uniaxial
UNICATE to make as one
UNICITY uniqueness; city sprawl
zo UNICORN a fabulous animal; oryx
UNIDEAL realistic; prosaic
UNIFIED united; merged
UNIFIER amalgamator; merger
bt UNIFOIL bearing only one leaf

UNIFORM consistent; steady; standard
ma UNITAGE of measurement
UNITARY (method); integral
UNITATE remainder after division
UNITERM key-word graphic index system
cp UNITERM information retrieval
UNITING combining; concerting
UNITION conjunction
UNITIVE harmonizing
UNITIZE to treat as one unit
UNJOINT separate; individualized
UNKEMPT uncombed; rough
UNKNOWN nameless; anonymous
UNLACED not done up; untied
nt, rw UNLADED UNLADEN, unloaded (of cargoes)
UNLATCH unlock; open
UNLEARN to forget
UNLEASH remove all constraint
UNLEAVE strip of leaves
UNLEVEL uneven; rough
UNLIMED freed from lime
UNLINED (paper); unruled
UNLIVED bereft of life (Shak.)
UNLOUSE unleash from restraints
UNLOVED disliked; unrequited
UNLUCKY ill-starred; hapless
UNLUSTY weak; infirm; sickly
UNLUTED unglued; uncemented
UNMANLY effeminate; cowardly
UNMARRY divorce
UNMATED single; unconsummated
UNMEANT not intended
UNMETED not measured
UNMEWED set free; released
UNMIXED pure; unadulterated
UNMORAL immoral; licentious
UNMOULD change the form of
UNMOVED impassive; serene; quiet
UNNAMED anonymous
UNNERVE frighten; intimidate
UNNOBLE ignoble; unworthy
UNNOTED unremarked
UNOFTEN infrequently
UNOILED free from lubrication
UNORDER countermand
UNOWNED unacknowledged
UNPAGED unnumbered (of prelim. pages)
UNPAINT remove paint
UNPANEL remove from committee
UNPAVED uncobbled (streets)
UNPENAL without penalty
UNPERCH dislodge; unroost
UNPLAIT unbraid; unravel
UNPLUMB not vertical

UNPLUME pluck
UNQUEEN dethrone; expose
UNQUIET unease; restless; noisy
UNQUOTE end quotation
UNRAKED untilled
UNRATED unvalued; unregarded
UNRAVEL disentangle; solve
UNREADY irresolute; slow
nt UNREEVE withdraw a rope
ck, pl UNRISEN unbaked; flaccid
UNRIVET undo; loose; detach
UNROYAL unkingly; not in lineage
UNRULED uncontrolled; unlined
UNSATED rapacious; not satisfied
rl UNSAVED lost; condemned
zo UNSCALY without fish scales
UNSCREW untwist; unfasten
UNSEXED undetermined or castrated
UNSHORN unshaven; unclipped
UNSHOWN not exhibited; hidden
UNSIGHT lose sight of; (cricket)
UNSIZED not stiffened; ungraded
UNSLING release from slings
UNSLUNG not projected
UNSOLID fluid; unsubstantial
UNSOUND erroneous; defective
UNSPENT unexhausted; still moving
UNSPIED unobserved; undetected
UNSPIKE pull put prickles
UNSPILT not shed; not slopped
UNSPLIT undivided
UNSTACK disperse; dishevel
UNSTAID unsteady; unstable
UNSTATE deprive of dignity
UNSTEEL soften; disarm
UNSTICK ungum; tear free
UNSTRAP loosen
UNSTUCK loosened; dished
UNSWEAR recall an oath
UNSWEET inharmonious; acid
UNSWEPT unbrushed
UNSWORN not on oath
UNTAKEN left; relinquished
UNTAMED savage; barbaric
UNTAXED not charged
UNTHINK dismiss from the mind
UNTILED detesselated
UNTIRED unwearied
UNTOOTH extract
UNTRIED inexperienced; new
UNTRULY falsely; erroneously
UNTRUSS take apart; dissect
UNTRUTH lie; imposture; error
ro, mu UNTUNED not set to play
UNTWINE untwist; unravel
UNTWIST disentangle
UNTYING unknotting
UNURGED unsolicited

UNUSUAL bizarre; queer; odd; rum
UNVEXED unharassed; untroubled
UNVOWED not bound by oath
UNWAGED unsalaried
UNWAYED trackless
UNWEARY unspent; unflagging
UNWEAVE unplait
UNWHIPT unbirched
UNWIRED unstrung
UNWITCH uncharm; unspell
UNWITTY lacking humour; prosaic
UNWOOED uncourted; unsolicited
UNWOUND untwined; uncoiled
UNWOVEN not made into cloth
UNWRUNG untwisted; undrained
UNYOKED freed (of oxen)
UNZONED unpartitioned (area)
UPBRAID rebuke; chide; taunt
UPENDED stood on end
UPFIELD cricket
UPGRADE promote
UPHEAVE lift up; raise
UPHOARD secrete; amass; garner
go **UPLYING** elevated ground
UPRIGHT vertical; honest; just
UPRISEN ascended
UPSHIFT change gear
bt **UPSHOOT** a sprout; result
UPSIDES horses exercising together
UPSTAGE theatrical; steal attention
bt **UPSTART** parvenu; meadow saffron
UPSURGE upswell
ga **UPSWEEP** woman's coiffure
UPSWELL upsurge; crowds; tide
UPTIGHT unduly inhibited
UP-TRAIN train to London
UPWARDS upward; upwardly
md **URAEMIA** kidney disease
mn **URALITE** fireproof material
URA-NAGE rear throw (judo)
URANIAN astronomical
ch **URANIDE** element beyond
  protactinium
mn **URANITE** a green uranium ore
ch **URANIUM** metallic element
ch **URANOUS** containing uranium
zo **URETHRA** urinary duct
URGENCY importunity; stress
URICASE uric acid salt
ch **URIDINE** crystalline nucleoside
hd **URINANT** bent fish
md **URINARY** of the bladder/urine
md **URINATE** to pass body water
zo **UROCYON** American grey fox
pl **UROCYST** the bladder
zo **URODELA** newts and salamanders
md **UROLOGY** study of urinary tract
md **UROSOME** caudal segment

zo **URSINAL** ursine; bearish
bt **URTICAL** (nettles)
USELESS vain; bootless; abortive
USHERED introduced; foreran;
  heralded
USITATE usually; customary
USUALLY normally; generally
USURPED arrogated; seized; assumed
USURPER a dictator
UTENSIL implement; vessel
md **UTERINE** of the uterus
UTILISE utilize; employ; apply
UTILITY usefulness
UTOPIAN imaginary; chimerical;
  ideal
UTOPISM unpractical hopefulness
UTOPIST optimist; visionary
md **UTRICLE** small cell or bladder
UTTERED issued; pronounced; said
UTTERER promulgator; (counterfeit)
UTTERLY absolutely; completely
md **UVEITIS** eye congestion
UXORIAL dotingly fond of a wife

V

VACANCY job, place available
VACATED left; abandoned
VACATOR a quitter
lw **VACATUR** annulment
md **VACCINE** anti-disease extract
VACHERY cow-house; dairy
VACUATE make a vacuum
VACUIST vacant believer
VACUITY emptiness; a void
VACUOLE minute cavity
VACUOUS void; unfilled
VAGITUS cry of a newborn child
VAGRANT vagabond; nomad; tramp
VAGUELY dimly; indefinitely
VAGUEST most uncertain
VAILING veiling; tipping
VAINEST most conceited
VALANCE draped border
ch **VALENCE VALENCY**, combining
  power; compatibility of elements
bt **VALERIC** derived from valerian
VALIANT intrepid; gallant; doughty
VALIDLY with legal force
VALINCH cask tap
VALLARY (rampart)
VALLATE cup-shaped
bt **VALONIA** acorn-cup (Levant)
bt **VALSOID** with perithecia in circle
VALUING esteeming; appraising
VALVATE valvular
VALVLET valvula; small valve

VALVULA cerebellum process in fish
zo VALVULE valvula; small valve
VAMOOSE to retire
VAMOSED decamped
mu VAMPING patching; bewitching
mu VAMPING simplified reissuing
zo VAMPIRE blood-sucker; a bat
VAMPLET spear buckler
ch VANADIC of vanadium
ch VANADYL electrolyte cation
VANDYKE lace collar
zo VANESSA butterfly genus (Swift)
VAN-FOSS a moat
bt VANILLA orchid; a flavour
VANNING mining; transporting
zo VANSIRE mongoose (Madagascar)
ga VANTAGE (tennis); advantage
VANTAGE sighting point
VANWARD vanguard; ahead
VAPIDLY inertly; insipidly; languidly
md VAPOURS nervous malady
VAPOURY hypochondriac
VAQUERO S. Amerian cow-puncher
zo VARANUS monitor lizard
VAREUSE seaman's jersey, jacket
VARIANT different; diverse
VARIANT differing version
VARIATE to vary; altered form
md VARICES knotted veins
VARIETY diversity; assortment
VARIETY music hall; revue
md VARIOLA smallpox
bl VARIOLE pitted (of skin, stem)
VARIOUS sundry; several; numerous
zo VARMINT vermin
VARNISH to gloss over; palliate
VARSITY university
VARVELS vervels; rings on a hawk
VARYING differing; deviating;
altering
VASTATE make immune
VASTEST bulkiest; greatest
rl VATICAN papal capital
VATTING mixing wines; customs
VAUDOIS Waldensian of Swiss
canton
ar VAULTED arched; sprang; (of ceiling,
roof)
ga VAULTER bounder (athletics)
VAUNTED boasted; bragged
VAUNTER braggart; boaster
VAVASOR titled landowner
VECTION porterage; convection
VEDANGA Veda commentary
VEDANTA Veda philosophy
VEDETTE vidette; mounted scout
nt VEERING shifting; changing; varying;
wind moving clockwise

bt, ck VEGETAL of vegetable, plant
VEHICLE car; conveyance; art form
rl, tx VEILING covering; concealing;
cloth
md VEINAGE VEINOUS, of the vein
system
md VEINING pattern of veins
pl VEINLET VEINULE, smaller vein
pl VELAMEN membrane; of palate
VELARIA Roman amphitheatre
awnings
zo VELIGER larval stage of mollusca
VELLING cutting turf
VELLUMY like vellum
tx VELOURS plush fabric
ck VELOUTE creamy meat sauce
VELVETY smooth
VENALLY mercenary
VENATIC sporting
zo VENDACE a lake fish
VENDING selling; bartering
ck VENISON deer meat
VENOMED poisoned
VENTAGE escape hole
VENTAIL helmet visor
VENTING releasing; uttering;
emitting
VENTOSE windy; breezy
VENTOSE Republican month (Fr.)
VENT-PEG a plug for a cask (wine)
pl VENTRAD VENTRAL, VENTRIC,
abdominal
VENTURE to undertake (risks); dare
ae VENTURI convergent/divergent duct
ar VERANDA VERANDAH, roofed open
gallery
bt, ck VERBENA VERVAIN, herbal tea
VERBIFY VERBALIZE, express
thoughts
VERBILE VERBOSE, loquacious;
wordy
bt VERDANT VERDURE, green growth
lw VERDICT decision; finding;
judgement
mn VERDITE green S. Afr. rock
VERGENT VERGING, bordering;
adjacent
VERGLAS thin ice or frost layer
VERIEST absolute; truest
VERISMO expressionist objectivity
(art)
VERITAS French shipping register
VERMEIL a glaze; ormolu
zo VERMIAN wormlike
pt VERMILY VERMILION, red pigment
VERNANT VERNATE, of spring; to
flourish
VERNIER measuring device

md **VERONAL** an opiate
bt, md **VERRUCA** a wart; foot ailment
VERSANT conversant; familiar
ch **VERSENE** sodium versenate
VERSIFY VERSING, relate in rhyme
ma **VERSINE** function of an angle
VERSION an account; interpretation
VERSUAL paragraphic
VERSUTE crafty; wily
md **VERTIGO** dizziness; giddiness
hd **VERULED** ringed
hd **VERULES** concentric rings
bt, ck **VERVAIN VERBENA**, herbal tea
VERVELS varvels; rings on a hawk
md **VESANIA VERSANIC**, insanity; psychoses
pl **VESICAL VESICLE**, bladder-like cavity
zo **VESPINE VESPOID**, wasplike
VESTIGE footprint; trace; remains
VESTING fabric for vests; investing
zo **VESTLET** a sea-anemone
VESTRAL (vestry)
VESTURE clothing; garment; dress
VETERAN experienced; seasoned (war-)
VETERAN pre-1918 used cars (crocks)
bt **VETIVER** a fragrant grass
VETOING prohibiting; barring; banning
VETTING examining; checking
VETTURA Italian cab
VEXILLA processional banners
VIADUCT raised road
VIARIAN wayfarer
md **VIBICES** feverish spots
VIBRANT resonant; undulous
VIBRATE oscillate; quiver; sway
mu **VIBRATO** tremolo
md **VIBRION** mobile bacterium
VICEROY king's deputy
VICIOUS depraved; sinful; defective
VICTORY success; mastery; triumph
VICTRIX a lady winner
VICTUAL provide provisions
VIDENDA things to be seen
VIDEOCY media addiction (TV)
VIDETTE vedette; mounted scout
VIDIMUS an inspection; summary
VIDUOUS widowed
VIEWING surveying; scanning; eyeing
tx **VIGONIA** llama wool fabric
VILAYET Turkish province
VILLAGE hamlet; thorpe
VILLAIN miscreant; rascal; rogue
VILLEIN serf; villager
VILLINO small villa in a park

VILLOSE VILLOUS, shaggy; hairy
mu **VILUELA** ancient Spanish lute
VIMINAL of twigs
VINALIA Roman wine festival
VINASSE wine dregs
VINCULA chains; (prisoners); brackets
ma **VINCULA** similarly treated terms
VINEGAR fermentation acid; sour wine
VINGT-UN card game
VINTAGE season's yield of wine (harvest)
VINTAGE year of an extra fine wine
VINTAGE cars of 1919–30
VINTNER wine-seller
mn **VIOLANE** violet-blue diopside
VIOLATE outrage; break; profane
VIOLENT fierce; vehement; furious
bt **VIOLINE** poisonous extract
mu **VIOLINO** ancient high-pitched viol (It.)
mu **VIOLIST** viola player
mu **VIOLONE** ancient double-bass (It.)
mt **VIRAZON** sea breeze, Chile, Peru
mu **VIRELAY VIRELAI**, medieval roundelay (Fr.)
VIRGATE wand-like; slender and straight
me **VIRGATE** a quarter of a hide
VIRGULE small rod; a comma
md **VIROSIS** viral infection
VIRTUAL almost entirely; de facto
pg **VIRTUAL** image by light-convergences
cp **VIRTUAL** environment for code data
VISAGED of face; aspect; appearance
VIS-A-VIS face to face
md **VISCERA** internal organs
VISCOUS sticky; glutinous; tenacious
mn **VISEITE** zeolite
VISIBLE patent; evident; apparent
VISIBLY obviously; manifestly
VISITED stayed; chastised; afflicted
VISITOR visiter; a caller
VISORED masked; helmeted
VITALLY essentially; (-necessary)
ck **VITAMIN** vital organic compound (diet)
VITIATE to spoil; impair; debase
VITRAIL stained-glass window
mn **VITRAIN** a type of coal
md **VITREUM** eye-fluid
VITRICS VITRIFY, glassmaking; glazing
VITRINE glass show case
ch **VITRIOL** sulphuric acid
VITRIOL virulent speech; feeling

VITRITE black glass
bt VITTATE with longitudinal stripes
VITULAR (calf); (veal)
VIVENCY existence
zo VIVERRA civet genus
VIVIDLY animatedly; brilliantly
VIVIFIC enlivening
VOCABLE call-able
VOCALIC concerning, containing vowels
VOCALLY by voice, speech, song
VOCODER synthetic speech device
VOCULAR vocal
mn VOGLITE uranium ore
VOICING expressing
VOIDING ejecting; emptying
VOIVODE VAIVODE, Hungarian, Polish, Romanian governor
VOLABLE nimble-witted; volatile
mu VOLANTE Sp. vehicle; fast and light (It.)
VOLCANO eruptive mountain
VOLSUNG Odin's grandson
el, me VOLTAGE amount of volts
VOLTAIC galvanic
VOLUBLE having the gift of the gab
VOLUBLY glibly; fluently
VOLUMED bulky
VOLUMEN rolled papyrus text
VOLUSPA song of the sybil (Scand.)
VOLUTED with spiral scroll
md VOMITUS vomited matter
VORLAGE forward leaning position (skiing)
VOTABLE enfranchised
VOUCHED warranted; attested
lw VOUCHEE warrantee
VOUCHER a witness; a pass
VOWELLY full of vowels
VOYAGED cruised; traversed
VOYAGER ocean traveller
rl VULGATE authentic Latin Bible
VULPINE foxy; cunning
zo VULTURE carrion-eating bird
zo VULTURN Australian turkey

W

WADABLE fordable
WADDING stuffing; non-edible filling
WADDLED walked like a duck
WADDLER wobbly walker
to WAD-HOOK an extractor
tx WADMOLL woollen cloth
lw WADSETT a mortgage

lw WAFERED sealed; secured
WAFTAGE transportation
WAFTING floating; airing; beckoning
WAGERED hazarded; risked; staked
WAGERER a better
WAGGERY sportive merriment
WAGGING swaying (flags) (dogs)
WAGGISH droll; facetious; jocular
WAGGLED wiggled
WAGONED carted; transported
WAGONER cart-driver
WAGSOME whimsical; witty
zo WAGTAIL bird; joinery
bt WAGWANT totter-grass
rl WAHABEE primitive Moslem
WAILFUL mournful; sorrowful; grievous
WAILING bemoaning; lamenting
WAINAGE transport
WAISTED narrowed
WAISTER whaling greenhorn
WAITING attendance; biding; tarrying
WAIVING relinquishing; remitting
WAKEFUL alert; wary; vigilant
WAKEMAN a watchman
WAKENED stimulated; excited
WAKENER a rouser; knocker-up
WALKING pedestrianism; hiking; rambling
WALK-OUT industrial strike; protest
bt WALLABA timber tree (Guyana)
zo WALLABY kangaroo-like animal
WALLACH Wallack; a Wallachian
md WALL-EYE eye condition
WALLING wall material
WALLOON Belgian (French-speaking)
bt WALL-RUE a fern
WALTZED danced (Viennese style)
WALTZER ballroom athlete
WAMBLED rumbled
WAN-EYED languid; sad
WANGHEE a cane; a stick
WANGLED acquired by craft
WANHOPE despair
bt WANHORN a plant
WANNABE aspiring to be liked
WANNESS pallor; paleness
WANNISH sickly
WANTAGE deficiency; lack
WANTING absent; desiring; needing
WANTWIT a numbskull; nitwit
zo WAPACUT American snowy owl
bt WARATAH Australian shrub
WARBLED trilled (bird-song)
zo WARBLER crooner, bird
WARBLES saddle-sores; tumours

WARDAGE watch-tax
WARDING repelling; fending; guarding
WARD-WIT warder's quittance
WAREFUL wary; cautious; vigilant
WARFARE strife; hostilities
WARHEAD explosive part of missile
WARHOOP war-cry; slogan
WARIEST most circumspect
WARISON a reward; a gift
WARLIKE belligerent; martial
WARLOCK wizard (devil's own)
WARLORD Junker militarist
WARMEST keenest; most ardent
WARMING heating
WARNING caution; notification; omen
WARPATH hostile expedition
WARPING twisting; distorting (the mind)
WARPING expansion of wood
nt WARPING docking by ropes (ships)
WARRANT authorize; justify
WARRANT police permission; guarantee
WARRING contending; striving
WARRIOR veteran fighter
WAR-RISK (insurance)
WAR-SCOT war-tax; a levy
nt WARSHIP battleship, etc.
WARSONG song on martial theme
zo WART-HOG an African ungulate
WARTIME during hostilities
WARWORN battle-weary
WASH-DAY laundry day
WASHING ablution; rinsing
ga, rw WASHOUT sports; track; unusable (rain)
ga WASHOUT failure; fiasco (bowling)
WASHTUB (mobile) bath; (clothes)
zo WASP-FLY fly resembling wasp
WASPISH resentful; irritable
WASSAIL carolling outside houses
WASSAIL festival; punch (drink)
WASTAGE dissipation; debris
WASTING emaciation
WASTREL waif; a dud
WATCHED guarded; tended; noted
WATCHER observer; (bird-); overseer
WATCHET light blue
WATERED wavy; moistened; sprinkled
WATERER irrigator
WATTLED (hurdles); (cocks-comb)
WAULING howling; caterwauling
WAVELET a ripple
WAVERED faltered; swayed
WAVERER hesitator

nt WAVESON flotsam; floating wreckage
ps WAVICLE quantum mechanical entity
bt WAX-BEAN butter-bean
zo WAXBILL (weaver-bird)
WAX-DOLL poupée (Fr.)
WAX-JACK sealing wax taper stand
zo WAX-MOTH (a bee scourge)
bt WAX-PALM wax-producing tree
bt WAX-TREE American gamboge tree
zo WAXWING a crested bird
WAXWORK wax statue counterfeiting life
WAYBILL a list (transport)
WAYGONE exhausted; wayworn
WAYLAND a legendary smith
WAYLESS pathless; trackless
WAY-MARK direction pointer; sign
WAY-POST guide-post
WAYSIDE of the roadside
WAYWARD froward; wilful; unruly
WAYWISE directional capacity
WAYWORN exhausted; spent
WEAKEST puniest
WEALDEN WEALD, old woodland (Kent, E. Sussex)
WEALTHY opulent; affluent; rich
WEANING ending milk-child stage
WEARIED fatigued; jaded; careworn
WEARIER more jaded and tired
WEARILY tediously
WEARING exhausting
WEARISH withered; washy
WEAR-OFF effect decreasing gradually
WEAR-OUT to become worn and torn
md WEASAND windpipe; throat
WEATHER climate; endure; overcome
tx WEAVING interlacing threads (cloth)
nt WEAVING zigzag course; (pattern)
WEBBING hempen fabric
md WEB-EYED filmy-eyed
WEB-FOOT characteristic of aquatic birds
WEBSTER a weaver
WEB-TOED frog-footed
WEDDING nuptials; espousal; marriage
WEDGING timber joint; doorstop jamb
WEEDING eliminating; purging
WEDLOCK BEDLOCK, matrimony; marriage
rl WEE-FREE church group (Sc.)
WEEKDAY WORKDAY, (not Sunday)
WEEKEND Saturday and Sunday
WEENING thinking; imagining
WEEPING sobbing; crying; bewailing

zo, ck **WEEVILY** maggoty; meat infestation
WEFTAGE texture
pc **WE-GROUP** in-group; elitism
WEIGHED pondered; pressed;
(anchor)
WEIGHER weighing machine
WEIGH-IN pre-contest weight check
WEIGHTY ponderous; onerous; grave
WEIRDER more fantastic
WEIRDLY eerily; uncannily
WELADAY LACKADAY, alas!
WELCHER welsher; absconding
bookie
WELCOME salutation; greeting
WELDING welded joint
WELFARE comfort; prosperity; weal
WELLING springing; gushing
WELL-MET all hail! welcome!
WELL-OFF well-to-do; prosperous
WELL-SET firmly set
WELL-WON honestly gained
WELSHED betrayed
WELSHER absconding bookie
WELTING shoe-edging
WENDING wandering; strolling
WENDISH WEND (Baltic) dialect
mn **WENLOCK** limestone
WENNISH cyst-like
WERGILD WERGOLD, blood money
(Scand.)
rl **WERWOLF WEREWOLF**, wolfman
(Scand.)
WEST-END stylish city district
WESTERN occidental; democratic
WESTING westerly; wind
nt **WET-DOCK** dock where ship can float
WETNESS dampness; humidity
WET-SHOD with wet feet
WETTEST supersaturated
WET-TIME wages for rainy days
WETTING moistening; drenching
WETTISH rather rainy
fr **WETWOOD** high-water-content wood
WHACKED beaten; defeated; smitten
WHACKED exhausted
WHACKER of large size; formidable
WHALERY port and factory base for
whaling
WHALING whale-fishing; thrashing
bt **WHANGEE** bamboo cane
WHAPPED struck; fluttered
nt **WHARFED** brought to jetty
WHARVES quays; docks
WHATNOT small, 3-shelf stand
WHATSIT unspecified; forgotten item
bt **WHEATEN** of wheat
WHEEDLE to coax; to cajole
WHEELED with wheels

zo **WHEELER** shaft-horse; cyclist
WHEELER wheelwright
WHEEZED breathed asthmatically
WHEEZLE whaizle; whaisle; obtain
WHELKED ridged; shell-like
ornamentation
zo **WHELPED** littered; gave birth to
brood
WHEREAS in view of fact that
WHEREAT thereupon
WHEREBY through which
WHEREIN within which
WHEREOF whence
WHEREON upon which
WHERETO to which
WHETHER if; in the case of
zo **WHETILE** woodpecker
WHETTED stimulated; urged
WHETTER a sharpener
WHEWING whistling with surprise
WHEYISH like whey
WHEY-TUB cream-tub
WHIFFED puffed
WHIFFER a puffer
WHIFFET whipper-snapper
mu **WHIFFLE** whistle; flute; prevaricate
WHILERE while here; recently
WHILING loitering; passing the time
WHIMPER whine; cry; moan
WHIMPLE WIMPLE, pointed
headdress
WHIMSEY WHIMSY, a caprice;
crotchet
WHINING complaining; snivelling
WHIPCAT a tailor
WHIPPED lashed; beaten; thrashed
WHIPPER a flagellant
zo **WHIPPET** greyhound; small tank
zo **WHIP-RAY** a sea-fish
to **WHIPSAW** frame-held narrow saw
WHIP-TOP whipping top
WHIRLED span; spun; revved
WHIRLER a whirligig
WHIRRED WHURRED, rotated rapidly
WHIRRET WHERRIT, vex; a blow
WHISHED WHIZZED, hurtled
WHISKER facial hair (man, cat etc.)
WHISKET a basket
WHISKEY (Irish), **WHISKY** (Scotch)
WHISKEY light dog-cart
WHISPER murmur; disclose
nt, mu **WHISTLE** bosun's pipe; tin; police
WHISTLY silently
WHITELY palely; pallidly
WHITEST purest; lightest
WHITHER to which place
zo **WHITING** whitewash; a fish
WHITISH near white

md **WHITLOW** an abscess on finger or toe
WHITSUL curds and whey
rl **WHITSUN** Whitsuntide; Pentecost
WHITTAW a saddler
WHITTLE shawl; to cut; pare
WHIZZED tore through the air
WHIZZER a fast one; motorist
ga **WHIZZER** form of arm-lock wrestling
WHOEVER anyone at all
WHOLISM in entirety; holistic
WHOMMLE confusion; overwhelm
WHOOBUB hubbub
WHOOPED hooted; yelled; shouted
WHOOPEE a joyous cry; a revel
zo **WHOOPER** the hooper swan
WHOPPED beat; defeated
ga **WHOPPER** whacker; very large
WHORLED spiral; convoluted
ga **WICKING** cannoning when curling
(bowls)
WICKIUP shelter (Amer. Indian)
WIDENED extended; broadened
WIDENER an enlarger; a reamer
zo **WIDGEON** migratory duck
WIDOWED bereaved; viduous
WIDOWER bereaved husband
WIELDED handled; plied; governed
WIELDER a controller; user
bt **WIGGERS** dandelion
WIGGERY creations with false hair
WIGGING a scolding; reprimand
WIGGLED waggled
WIGGLER a wriggler
WIGLESS deperuked
zo **WILD-ASS** the onager
zo **WILDCAT** speculative; strike (indust.)
WILDEST most turbulent and rash
bt **WILDING** growing wild; crab-apple
WILDING city youth rampaging
WILDISH rather wild
bt **WILD-OAT** youthful crop
WILIEST craftiest; pawkiest
WILLING devising; agreeing;
consenting
zo **WILLOCK** young guillemot
WILLOWY slender; pliant
WILSOME wilful; stubborn; wayward
WILTING drooping; fading
bt **WIMBERY** whortleberry
WIMBLED drilled; bored
zo **WIMBREL** whimbrel; small curlew
WIMPLED puckered; wrinkled
WINCHED hoisted; hauled up
WINDAGE clearance
WINDBAG a would-be orator
zo **WIND-EGG** an addled egg
WIND-GUN air-gun
WINDIER breezier; more alarmed

pc **WINDIGO** Red Indian hunter
syndrome
WINDILY breezily; panic-struck
WINDING tortuous; changing;
scenting
WINDROW hay or peat in rows
WINDSOR Royal House; dynasty
WINEBAG wine-skin; a tippler
WINEFAT a vat
bt **WINESAP** American winter apple
WING-ICE (ice on aircraft)
WINGING flying; wounding
zo **WINGLET** bastard wing
au **WINKERS** flashing lights
WINKING nictitating; conniving at
WINNING first; successful; acquiring
WINSOME childish; engaging;
seductive
WINTERY WINTRY, hibernal; cold
WIPE-OUT exterminate; slaughter
tc **WIPE-OUT** intense interference
ga **WIPE-OUT** fall into wave (surfing)
ml **WIREBAR** copper in tapered ingots
WIREMAN linesman
WIREWAY telpherage; aerial
transport
WIRIEST leanest; toughest
WISE-GUY clever trickster; smart
Alec
WISHFUL desirous; eager and
anxious
WISTFUL pensive; meditative;
yearning
zo **WISTITI** marmoset
WITCHED bewitched; charmed
bt **WITCHEN** mountain ash; rowan
WITHERS (horse's neck)
bt **WITHIES** willow twigs
WITHOUT outside; except; lacking
WITLESS indiscreet; thoughtless
WITNESS attest; testimony; see
WITTIER droller; more facetious
WITTILY jocularly; humorously
WITTING wotting; knowing
zo **WITWALL** golden oriole
WIZENED shrivelled; wimpled
WOBBLED swerved; staggered;
quavered
mu **WOBBLER** unsteady singer; rocker
ga **WOBBLER** erratic fast glide (curling)
WOESOME WOEFUL, sorrowful;
grievous
zo **WOLF-DOG** fierce guard-dog
WOLFISH rapacious; ravenous
WOLFKIN young wolf
WOLF-MAN werewolf
WOLF-NET large fishing net
ch **WOLFRAM** tungsten

WOLSUNG grandson of Odin
WOMANLY feminine
WONGSHY yellow dye (Chinese)
zo **WOOD-ANT** the red ant
WOODCUT a print from a wooden block
rl **WOOD-GOD** sylvan deity; Pan
WOODMAN a forester
bt **WOODNUT** hazel-nut
bt **WOOD-OIL** balsam
zo **WOOD-OWL** brown owl
ch **WOOD-TAR** a distillate
mn **WOOD-TIN** tin-stone
WOOLDED roped; lashed
WOOLDER lashing stick
zo **WOOLFAT** lanolin
WOOLLEN of wool
WOOLMAN wool dealer
WOOLSAW evil spirit (C. American)
tx **WOOLSEY** a dress material
WOOMERA spear, throwing stick (Aust.)
bt, ch **WOORALI WORRARA**, curare (arrow) poison
WORDILY verbose; prolix; garrulously
WORDING phrasing; expressing
WORDISH wordy; loquacious
WORKBAG lady's sewing bag
WORKBOX box of work materials
WORKDAY M., T., W., Th., Fr.
WORKING fermenting; drudging
WORKMAN a toiler; operative
WORK-OUT gymnastic exercise
WORKSHY allergic to labour
WORLDLY earthy; secular; mundane
WORMING (rope); squirming
WORN-OUT exhausted
WORRIED harassed; bothered; troubled
WORRIER a worrit; a hector
WORSHIP adoration; idolize; venerate
WORSTED wool yarn
WOULD-BE aspiring
WOULDST (thou) would
WOUNDED injured; hurt; damaged
WOUNDER a pain-giver
WRANGLE bicker; brawl
WRAPPED covered; swathed; wound
WRAPPER envelope; scarf
WREAKED inflicted; (vengeance)
WREAKER an avenger
WREATHE entwine; to garland
WREATHY twisty; interlaced
WRECKED shattered; ruined; destroyed
WRECKER saboteur; blighter

zo **WREN-TIT** Californian bird
WRESTED wrenched; forced; pulled
WRESTER a twister
WRESTLE grapple; strive; contend
WRIGGLE worm; squirm; writhe
WRIGGLY tortuous; sinuous
WRINGER a mangle
WRINKLE crinkle; pucker
bd, cr **WRINKLE** unglued fault in veneer
WRINKLY creased; ruffled
WRITE-UP flattering notice
WRITHED squirmed; wriggled
WRITING calligraphy; penmanship
WRITING literature; (desk); (paper)
cp **WRITING** electronic, fax, computer
WRITTEN inscribed; indited, forever
WRONGED maltreated; oppressed
WRONGER a wrong-un; evil-doer
WRONGLY falsely; unjustly
WROUGHT worked; effected
zo **WRYBILL** a New Zealand plover
zo **WRYNECK** (woodpecker)
WRYNESS irony; twisted humour; crooked
mn **WUSTITE** cubic iron oxide
zo **WYANDOT** Iraquoian Indian; fowl
bt **WYCH-ELM** witch-elm

X

ch **XANTHIC XANTHIN**, acid; yellow extract
XANTHOS colour of Greek chariot horses
zo **XENURUS** genus of armadillos
md **XERASIA XEROSIS**, hair disease; dry scalp
md **XERODES XEROTIC**, body dryness
zo **XIPHIAS** sword-fish genus
as **XIPHIAS** a Southern constellation
XIPHOID ensiform
ch **XYLENOL** monohydric phenol
XYLOLIN wood pulp fabric
bt **XYLOPIA** bitter plants

Y

YACHTED cruised
YACHTER yachtsman
rl **YAHWISM** worship of Jehovah
rl **YAHWIST** Jehovist
YAKAMIK S. Amer. bird
bt **YAMADOU** nutmeg oil
YANKING jerking; heaving; hauling
YAPPING yelping; yauping
YAPSTER a barking dog

nt, me **YARDAGE** sail dues (yachting); distance
nt **YARD-ARM** end of sail-support spar
YARDING enclosing
ag, rw **YARD-MAN** (farm-); (railway-)
YARNING tale-spinning; narrating
YARRING snarling
YASHMAK Moslem woman's double veil
YATAGAN Turkish curved knife
YAUPING yelping
YAWLING howling; screaming
YAWNING gaping; gasping; yawing
YEANING lambing; bring forth young
YEARNED desirous; grieved
YEGGMAN criminal tramp (USA)
zo **YELDRIN** yellow bunting
YELLING howling
vt **YELLOWS** an animal disease
YELLOWY yellowish; sallowy
YELPING yauping; yapping
YERKISH lingo for chimpanzees
YEW-TREE (bow-wood; archery)
YEZIDIS devil worshippers
YIDDISH Jewish dialect
YIELDED rendered; resigned; conceded
YIELDER capitulator; abdicator
YODELER Tyrolese singer
YOGHURT fermented milk
YOICKED chanted Lappish motifs
zo **YOLDING YOLDRIN**, yellow-hammer
zo, ck **YOLK-SAC** within the white of an egg
YORKIST (War of Roses)
YOUGHAL needle-point lace
YOUNGER not so old
YOUTHLY YOUTHFULLY, immature
YOWLING howling; bawling
ch **YPERITE** poison gas
ch **YTTRIUM** a metallic element
YULE-LOG midwinter feast of light (Scand.)
mn **YU-STONE** high-quality jade

Z

bt **ZALACCA** dragon's blood palm
ZAMARRA sheepskin jacket (Sp.)
zo **ZAMOUSE** W. African ox
ZANELLA umbrella fabric
bt, ck **ZANONIA** cucumber
rl **ZANSHIN** awareness; alertness (Jap.)
ZANYING fooling
ZANYISM buffoonery
mu **ZAPATEO** shoe dance (S. Amer.)

ZAPHARA sky blue dye used in pottery
mn **ZARNICH** realgar; orpiment
ZEALFUL eager; keen; enthusiastic
ZEALOUS fervent; ardent; extreme
zo **ZEBRASS** a cross-breed; zebra and ass
zo **ZEBRINE ZEBROID**, of zebra type
zo **ZEBRULA** (zebra and horse)
bt **ZEDOARY** aromatic root
ZEMSTVO Russian local assembly
mn **ZEOLITE** aluminium silicate
ZEROING concentrating firepower
cp **ZEROIZE** to reset a meter to zero
ZESTFUL piquant; eager; keen
ZESTING flavouring; relishing
ZETETIC a seeker; a Pyrrhonist
nc **ZEUGITE** nuclear-fission cell
mn **ZEUXITE** a silicate of aluminium
ZIMOCCA bath-sponge
ZINCALI ZINGARI, gipsies
ch **ZINCATE** zinc oxide
ZINCIFY coat with zinc
mn **ZINCITE** red zinc ore
ZINCODE positive pole electrode
mn **ZINCOID ZINCOUS**, of zinc (metal)
ZINGARI (cricket); gipsies (It).
ZIONISM Jewish Nationalism
ZIONIST who supports free Israel
ZIPCORD parachute release cord
zo **ZIPHIUS** swordfish genus
ZIPPING pinging; whizzing; fastening
mu **ZITHERN ZITHER**, plucked strings (board)
mu **ZITHERN CITHARA**, hand-held lyre
bt **ZIZANIA** aquatic grasses; (rice)
zo **ZOARIUM** polyzoan
ar **ZOCCOLO** square base
ZOILEAN supercritical
ZOILISM carping criticism
ZOILIST a caviller
mn **ZOISITE** a silicate; an epidote
ZOLAISM Zola's excessive naturalism
go **ZONALLY** of divisions, sectors, areas
go **ZONULAR** belted; girdled; divisions
ZONULET a small girdle
zo **ZONURUS** saurian (reptile) genus
zo **ZOOECIA** polyp cells
zo **ZOOGAMY** of reproduction; sex
zo **ZOOGENY ZOOGONY**, zoological origins
zo **ZOOIDAL** animal-like
mn, zo **ZOOLITE ZOOLITH**, fossil animal
zo **ZOOLOGY** study of animals
pg **ZOOMING** flying low; closing in (films)
ZOONITE articulated segment

ZOONOMY natural laws
ZOOPERY experimenting on lower
   animals
ZOOTAXY systematic zoology
ZOOTOMY animal anatomy
md **ZOPISSA** pitch used medicinally
mn **ZORGITE** a metallic ore
zo **ZORILLA** ZORRINO, American skunk
ZOTHECA alcove (Gr.)

mu **ZUFFOLO** Italian flute
mn **ZUNYITE** orthosilicate of aluminium
mn **ZURLITE** a Veruvian mineral
zo **ZYGAENA** a shark genus
bt, zo **ZYGOSIS** ZYGOTIC, uniting as zygote
ch **ZYMOGEN** a fermentor
md **ZYMOSIS** inflammation
md **ZYMOTIC** bacteriological
ch **ZYMURGY** fermentation

EIGHT-LETTER WORDS

A

zo **AARDVARK** antbear (S. Afr.)
rl **AARONITE** Hebrew priest
ABACTION cattle-theft; rustling
ABACULUS counting-frame; tavola
ABAMPERE absolute electromagnetic unit
bd **ABAMURUS** buttress; wall support
ABAPICAL distant from opposite pole
ABASHING humiliating; shaming
ABATABLE reducible; alleviable
ABAT-JOUR skylight; reflector
ABATTOIR slaughter-house
rl **ABAT-VOIX** canopy over pulpit
rl **ABBATESS** abbess; Lady Superior
rl **ABBATIAL** under abbey control
bt **ABDALAVI** Egyptian musk melon
ABDERIAN given to laughter
ABDERITE a Thracian; Democrites
ABDICANT renouncing; an abdicator
ABDICATE resign; cede; renounce
rl **ABDITORY** secret repository
ar, rl **ABDOCULE** shrine between 2 columns
md, pc **ABDUCENS** outward movement
ABDUCENT retracting; separating
lw **ABDUCTED** removed; taken by fraud
md **ABDUCTOR** kidnapper; a muscle
rl **ABELIANS ABELITES**, sect practising marriage chastity (Abel)
bt **ABELMOSK** Syrian mallow
zo **ABERDEEN** a terrier; (-Angus) beef breed
ABERRANT abnormal; rambling
ABERRATE deviate; diverge; wander
ABERRING straying; digressing
lw **ABETMENT** aiding and abetting
ABETTING conniving; encouraging
ABEYANCE suspension; dormancy
ABEYANCE cessation; contemplation
ABHORRED hated; loathed; detested
ABHORRER Tory nickname, A.D. 1680
ABIDANCE abode; dwelling; habitation
ABIOGENY spontaneous generation
ABJECTLY servilely; despicably
ABJURING apostasy; forswearing
md **ABLATION** removal; attrition
ABLATIVE the sixth case in Latin

rl **ABLEGATE** a Papal envoy
ABLENESS ability; skill; vigour
md **ABLEPSIA** ablepsy; blindness
ABLOCATE hire; lease; let
rl **ABLUTION** purification; baptism
ABLUVION water-deposited detritus
ABNEGATE deny; adjure; renounce
ABNODATE untie; remove the knots
ABNORMAL odd; irregular; monstrous
ABOCOCKE peaked cap of 15th century
zo **ABOMASUS** abomasum; cow's stomach
ABORTING miscarrying; frustrating
md **ABORTION** a premature expulsion of a foetus; hideosity
ABORTIVE premature; broken off
ABRADANT disintegrator; scraper
ABRADING grinding; abrasing; fraying
ABRASION surface wound; attrition
ABRASIVE scratchy; gritty; rough
ABRIDGED epitomized; curtailed
ABROGATE cancel; repeal; quash
ABRUPTED rent; torn asunder
ABSCISSA an axial line in geometry
ABSENTED played truant
ABSENTEE deliberate duty dodger
ABSENTLY dreamily; inattentively
bt **ABSINTHE** wormwood; French liqueur
ABSOLUTE pure; despotic; supreme
ABSOLVED acquitted; excused
ABSOLVER a pardoner; forgiver
ABSONANT irrational; discordant
ABSONOUS incongruous; out of tune
ABSORBED imbibed; preoccupied
ABSTERGE purge; wipe away
ABSTRACT summarized gist; theoretical
ABSTRUSE recondite; occult; obscure
ABSURDLY irrationally; foolishly
ABUNDANT profuse; plentiful; copious
ABUSABLE improper usage; violable
bt **ABUTILON** plant genus; the jute
ar **ABUTMENT** an arch support; adjacency
lw **ABUTTALS** estate boundaries
ABUTTING bordering; alongside

ACADEMIC scholastic; literary
zo ACALEPHA hydrozoa (jellyfish)
bt ACANTHUS a 'capital' plant
ACARDIAC heartless
zo ACARIDAE mites; ticks; etc
bt ACARPOUS sterile; barren
zo ACAUDATE tailless; acaudal
bt ACAULOUS acauline; stalkless
ACCEDING complying; consenting
rl ACCENSOR R. C. candle-trimmer
ACCENTED stressed; emphasized
zo ACCENTOR the hedge-sparrow
mu ACCENTOR leading singer
ACCEPTED received; acknowledged
ACCEPTED admitted; entered for
race
lw ACCEPTER ACCEPTOR, recipient;
official
ACCIDENT mischance; mishap;
fortuity
ACCLINAL sloping; atilt
ACCOLADE act of knighting; award
ACCOLENT neighbour; borderer
hd ACCOLLED collared
ACCORDED harmonized; granted
ACCOSTED hailed; solicited boldly
ACCOUNTS recorded transactions
ACCOUNTS newspaper reports;
hearsay
ACCOUTRE dress in military array
ACCREDIT authorize; empower;
entrust
ACCRUING accumulating; resulting
ACCURACY precision; exactness;
truth
ACCURATE correct; unerring
ACCURSED execrable; doomed
lw ACCUSANT informer; accuser
ACCUSING charging; impeaching
ACCUSTOM habituate; familiarize
ACELDEMA the field of blood
(Hebrew)
ACENTRIC out of centre
zo ACEPHALA oyster genus
ACERBATE exasperate; embitter
ACERBENT caustic; astringent
ACERBITY bitterness; sour taste
ACERVATE clustered
ACESCENT turning sour
ch ACETATED (acetic acid)
bt ACHENIUM single-seeded fruit
me ACHERSET 8-bushel measure
bt ACHEWEED gout-weed
ACHIEVED won; attained; perfected
ACHIEVER a performer; an executant
bt ACHILOUS lipless
mn ACHIRITE dioptase
mn ACHROITE tourmaline

ACHROMAT colour-blind individual;
lens
bt, zo ACICULAE spikes and prickles
ACICULAR needle-shaped
ch ACIDIFIC producing acid
ACIDNESS bitterness; tartness
md ACIDOSIS acidity
ACIERAGE steel electro-plating
ACIERATE turn into steel
zo ACNESTIS part of spine
ACOEMETI religious community
bt ACONITIC (wolf's-bane, monk's-
hood)
bt ACORN-CUP acorn top, case
md ACOUSTIC relating to sound
ACQUAINT notify; apprise; teach
ACQUIRED scrounged; won;
procured
zo ACRIDIAN locust
ACRIDITY pungency; harshness
ACRIMONY sharpness of temper
ACRITUDE corrosive quality
ACROATIC esoteric; (oral instruction)
ch ACROLEIN acryl aldehyde, propenal
ACROLITH statue with wooden body
ACROMIUM ventral process
zo ACROSOME head of sperm
ACROSTIC word puzzle in verse
md ACROTISM lack of pulsation
ACTINISM effect of light rays
ch ACTINIUM radio-active element
zo ACTINOID star-shaped
ACTIVATE to move to activity
ACTIVELY energetically; sedulously
ACTIVISM practical idealism
ACTIVIST production promoter
(indust.)
ACTIVITY pastime; happening
ACTIVITY quick movement
ACTUALLY really; as a fact
ACTUATED influenced; set in
motion
ACUITION mental, physical keenness
bt ACULEATE spiky; pointed
pt ACUTANCE clarity of enlargement
ADAMITIC Adamic; nudistic
ADAPTING adjusting; suiting
ADAPTIVE adaptable; conformable
ADDEEMED adjudged; considered
ADDENDUM adjunct; appendix
zo ADDER-FLY dragonfly
ADDICTED wont; prone; inclined
cp ADDITION accession; summation
ck, ch, ps ADDITIVE an added substance
hd ADDORSED back to back
md ADDUCENT retracting (muscles)
ADDUCING citing; alleging
pl ADDUCTOR a muscle

md **ADENOIDS ADENITIS,** inflammation of nasal glands
ADEPTION attainment; perfection
ADEQUACY sufficiency; fitness
ADEQUATE suitable; condign
ADHERENT adhesive; partisan
ADHERING sticking to; supporting
ADHESION coalescence; attachment
rw **ADHESION** railways on easy inclines
ADHESIVE tenacious; gummy
bt **ADIANTUM** maidenhair fern
md **ADIPOSIS** fat-deposit illness
ADJACENT contiguous; close by
ADJOINED connected; neighbouring
ADJUDGED awarded; deemed
lw **ADJURING** charging on oath
ADJUSTER arranger; fitter
ADJUTAGE tubular connection
ADJUTANT assistant; regimental officer
zo **ADJUTANT** Indian scavenging stork
ADJUTRIX lady help
md **ADJUVANT** helping; intensifier
pc **ADLERIAN** of human inferiority
ADMIRING respecting; marvelling
ADMITTED included; conceded
ADMIXING mingling with
ADMONISH warn; reprove; exhort
bt **ADNATION** length attachment of organs
ADOPTING choosing; embracing
ADOPTION formal acceptance; (child)
ADOPTIVE selective
ADORABLE reverential; venerable
ADORABLY worshipfully; devotedly
ADORNING embellishing; decking
md **ADRECTAL** adjacent to the rectum
ADROITLY dexterously; adeptly
ADSCRIPT conscript; postscript
ADSORBED condensed
mn **ADULARIA** moonstone
ADULATED lauded; flattered
ADULATOR scyophant; yes-man
ADULTERY extra-marital cohabitation
bt **ADUNCATE** hooked
md **ADUSTION** cauterization
ADVANCED in the van; lent; progressed
ADVANCER promoter
ADVENING acceding
ADVERTED drew attention to
ADVISING counselling; notifying
ADVISORY advice service offer
ck **ADVOCAAT** egg-yolk liqueur (Dutch)
ADVOCACY defence; support
lw **ADVOCATE** barrister; recommend
rl **ADVOWSON** patronage of benefice

md **ADYNAMIA** loss of vitality
ADYNAMIC slack; lifeless; listless
md **AEGROTAT** academic certificate
AERARIAN voteless Roman freeman
AERATING charging with gas
AERATION gasification
AERIALLY ethereally
AERIFIED inflated
AERIFORM unsubstantial
AEROBICS gymnastics with music
bt **AEROCYST** seaweed air cell
AERODART dart dropped by airman
ae **AERODYNE** aircraft
AEROFOIL lifting surface (gliding)
AEROGRAM wireless message; letter
mn **AEROLITE AEROLITH,** meteoric stone; meteorite
AEROLOGY meteorology
AERONAUT airman; balloonist
AEROSTAT barrage balloon
bt **AESCULIN** horse-chestnut extract
AESTHETE professes beauty lover
AESTIVAL estival (summer)
md **AFEBRILE** unaccompanied by fever
AFFECTED moved; unnatural; insincere
md **AFFERENT** conducting inwards
AFFIANCE confidence; betroth
AFFINAGE metal refining
AFFINING refining; purifying
AFFINITY relationship; attraction
AFFIRMED confirmed; ratified
rl **AFFIRMER** testifier; a Quaker
AFFIXING attaching; connecting
AFFLATUS inspiration; ecstasy
AFFLUENT flowing with wealth
AFFORDED bore the cost easily; gave
fr **AFFOREST** convert into forest
AFFRIGHT sudden tremor; frighten
hd **AFFRONTE** confronting
rl **AFFUSING** spraying; bedewing
rl **AFFUSION** baptismal sprinkling
AFTER-ALL in conclusion
AFTER-WIT wisdom after the event
bt **AGAL-WOOD** aloes-wood
bt, ck **AGAR-AGAR** seaweed; edible gel
zo **AGASTRIC** stomachless
mn **AGATIZED** turned into agate
AGEDNESS antiquity; senility
AGENBITE remorse
AGENESIS imperfect development
AGENTIAL acting through an agent
AGERASIA healthy-looking elder
AGGRIEVE give sorrow; injure
AGIOTAGE (stock jobbing)
lw **AGISTAGE** tax on pasturage
AGITABLE excitable; tremulous
AGITATED roused; instigated

AGITATOR agent provocateur
AGLIMMER shimmering
zo AGLOSSAL tongueless
md AGLOSSIA tongueless; inarticulate
lw AGNATION male descent
AGNOSTIC humanist; positivist
AGONIZED tormented
md AGRAPHIA inability to write
AGRARIAN of farming, land, rural
AGREEING matching; tallying
mu AGREMENT adornment (Fr.)
bt AGRESTAL weedlike
bt AGRIMONY liverwort
AGRONOMY scientific farming
md AGRYPNIA insomnia
md AGUE-CAKE a tumour
bt AGUE-TREE sassafras tree
md AHEDONIA depressive listlessness
ce, ag A-HORIZON podsol; uppermost of
soil layers
zo AIGRETTE egret's plume
AIGUILLE spire; peak; rock-drill
ae AILERONS wing brake flaps
(gliding)
AILLETTE ailette; epaulet
AIR-BORNE no earthly connection
AIR-BRAKE brake operated by air
AIR-BRICK ventilating brick
AIRBRUSH fixative spray
AIR-BUILT chimerical; baseless
AIRCRAFT flying machines
ar AIR-DRAIN an airspace
AIR-DRAWN imaginary; visionary
zo AIREDALE terrier
AIRFIELD landing ground
AIR-FLEET unified collection of
aeroplanes
mn AIR-FLOAT sand-shaking process
zo AIRFRAME fuselage
AIRGRAPH air mail letter; microfilm
AIRINESS lightness; gaiety
AIR-LINER commercial passenger
plane
AIR-PILOT a flyer; a navigator
AIRPLANE aeroplane
AIRPOISE aneroid barometer
AIR-POWER air war potential
AIRSCREW propeller
AIRSHAFT ventilation shaft
AIRSPACE supra-construction; of
territory
AIRSPEED rate relative to airflow
(gliding)
AIR-STOVE heating apparatus
AIRSTRIP landing ground
mn AIR-SWEPT dry grinding process
AIRTIGHT impermeable to air
AIRTRUNK ventilating shaft

md AKINESIA muscular weakness/
paralysis
ALACRITY briskness; agility;
readiness
ALARM-GUN signal of distress
ALARMING calling to arms; ominous
ALARMIST Jeremiah; panic-monger
zo ALBACORE ALBICORE, tunny-fish;
species of thynnus
ALBANIAN of Albania
ALBINESS female albino
ALBINISM deficiency of pigment
mu ALBORADA folk music (Sp.)
bt ALBURNUM sap-wood
ALCAHEST alkahest; alchemists'
solvent
zo ALCATRAS ocean birds; pelican
ALCHEMIC relating to alchemy
ch ALDEHYDE a volatile liquid
ALDERMAN a civic dignitary
ch ALDOLASE an enzyme
ALEATORY depending on dice
ALEBENCH alehouse bench
ALEBERRY hot ale with sops
ALEHOUSE (no spirit licence)
ALEMBDAR Sultan's standard-
bearer
ALE-STAKE an alehouse sign
bt ALEURONE a protein in seeds
ALFRESCO in the open air
ALGERINE Algerian; pirate
ALGIDITY chilliness
bt ALGOLOGY the study of seaweeds
ALGONKIN Canadian Indian
ALGORISM the decimal system
ALGRAPHY aluminium printing
ALHAMBRA Moorish palace
ALICANTE Spanish red wine
ALIENAGE estrangement
ALIENATE transfer; estrange
pc ALIENISM study of insanity
pc ALIENIST mental specialist
ALIGHTED stepped off; descended
ALIGNING adjusting; dressing
ar ALIGNING straight lines; common
cause
ALIQUANT a remainder
zo ALITRUNK winged segment
ALIZARIN madder; synthetic dye
ch ALKAHEST ALCAHEST, solvent
ALKALIES caustic bases
ch ALKALIFY ALKALIZE, neutralize an
acid
ch ALKALINE salty
md ALKALOID active part of a drug
ALKERMES a crimson cordial
ch ALLANITE cerium silicate
ALLAYING stilling; mitigating

ch **ALL-BURNT** rocket-fuel exhaustion point
ALL-CLEAR end of danger
ALLEGING asserting as a fact
ALLEGORY parable; metaphor
ALLELULA alleluyah; halleluiah
ALLERGIC antipathetic
hd **ALLERION** heraldic beakless eagle
ga **ALLEY-WAY** board-game
ALL-FIRED infernal; hell-fired
ALL-FOURS (cards); mode of progress; crawling
ALLIANCE union by treaty; coalition
ALLIGATE to bind together
ALLOCATE allot; assign; share
ALLODIAL freehold; not feudal
lw **ALLODIUM** freehold estate
bt **ALLOGAMY** cross-fertilization
md **ALLOPATH** user of healing drugs
cy **ALLOSOME** non-typical chromosome
ALLOTTED meted; assigned; dispensed
ALLOTTEE shares received
ALLOTYPE varying type specimen
ALL-OUTER extremist; zealot
ALLOWING conceding; admitting
ml **ALLOYAGE** the alloying of metals
ALLOYING blending; debasing
bt **ALLSPICE** Jamaica pepper
ALLUDING hinting; insinuating
ALLURING enticing; tempting
ALLUSION hint; reference
ALLUSIVE relative; innuent
ALLUSORY symbolical; figurative
ALLUVIAL sedimentary
ALLUVION alluvial land
ALLUVIUM water-borne silt
as **ALMAGEST** astronomical problems
ALMIGHTY all-powerful; omnipotent
ALMSDEED act of charity
ALMSGATE (where alms were given)
ALOMANCY divination by salt
md **ALOPECIA** baldness; fox-evil
ALPHABET order or list of letters
ALPHA-RAY a radio-active ray
ck **ALPHENIC** white barley-sugar
ALPINIST mountaineer
mn **ALQUIFOU** Cornish lead ore
zo **ALSATIAN** sheep-dog
rl **ALTARAGE** altar offerings
ALTERANT production of change
ALTER-EGO second self
ALTERING varying; changing
ALTERITY being otherwise
ALTERNAT precedence by rotation
bt **ALTHEINE** asparagine
ALTHOUGH notwithstanding
ch **ALTINCAR** unrefined borax

ae **ALTITUDE** height; eminence; (aircraft, gliders) data
mu **ALTO-CLEF** C on 3rd line of staff
ALTRUISM devoted to others' welfare
ALTRUIST philanthropist
mn **ALUMINIC** containing aluminium
ch **ALUMINUM** aluminium
ch **ALUNOGEN** aluminium sulphite
ALVEATED hollowed out; saucer-shape
ALVEOLAR speech sound; honeycomb-like
ALVEOLUS alveole; tooth socket
zo **AMADAVAT** a weaver-bird
AMANDINE sweet almond ointment
mn **AMANDOLA** green marble
ch **AMANITIN** poison in fungi
bt **AMARACUS** marjoram
bt **AMARANTH** love-lies-bleeding
AMASSING piling up; accumulating
AMAZEDLY confusedly; dazedly
ch **AMBERITE** smokeless explosive
AMBITION desire; aspiration
pc **AMBIVERT** one turned both ways
AMBLYGON obtuse-angled
AMBREADA spurious amber
ch **AMBREATE** salt of ambreic acid
AMBROSIA food of the gods; bee-bread
nm **AMBROSIN** Milanese coin
AMBULANT peripatetic; hiking
AMBULATE saunter; walk; stroll; hike
AMBUSHED attacked in surprise trap
AMENABLE liable; pliant; subject
AMENABLY docilely; responsively
AMENDING rectifying; correcting
AMERCING fining; mulcting
AMERICAN Yankee
mn **AMETHYST** anti-inebriation jewel
mn **AMIANTUS** fibrous asbestos
AMICABLE friendly; neighbourly
AMICABLY benignly; peacefully
nt **AMIDMOST** in the very centre
AMITOSIS constriction-division of nucleus
cy **AMITOTIC** characterized by amitosis
zo **AMMODYTE** sand-eel
ch **AMMONIAC** of nature of ammonia
AMMONITE explosive
zo **AMMONITE** spiral fossil
ch **AMMONIUM** base of ammonia
md **AMNIOTIC** a membrane
AMOEBEAN alternately answering
AMOEBEUM poetic dialogue
zo **AMOEBOID AMOEBOUS**, of protozoan structure
AMORETTO cupid; a lover

lw **AMORTIZE** transfer property
AMOUNTED reached; rose; resulted
mn **AMPELITE** anti-pest earth
zo **AMPHIBIA** amphibians
bt **AMPHIGEN** a lichen-like plant
zo **AMPHIONT** a zygote; an egg-shell
AMPHORAL like a two-handled vase
md **AMPHORIC** hollow sounding
AMPULLAR like a two-handled flask
AMPUTATE lop; prune; sever
AMULETIC like an amulet; charming
AMURCOUS foul with dregs
AMUSABLE capable of enjoyment
AMUSETTE light field gun (salutes)
pl **AMYGDALA** limbic system
ch **AMYLASES** diastase enzymes
ANABASIS epic of 10,000 mercenary
Greeks (Xenophon)
mt **ANABATIC** hot-air convection winds
md **ANABOLIC** body-building
zo **ANACONDA** python (S. America)
md **ANACUSIA** total deafness
mt **ANAFRONT** frontal-zone warm-air
rise
ANAGLYPH a cameo; stereoscopic
ANAGOGIC mystical; allegorical
ANAGRAPH catalogue; inventory
ANALECTS collection of literary
fragments
ANALEMMA pedestal of sundial
md **ANALEPSY** recurring epilepsy
ANALOGIC analogous; alike; akin
ANALOGON similarity; synonym
ANALOGUE corresponding part
ANALYSED examined
ANALYSER scrutator; analyst
ANALYSIS opposite of synthesis
ANALYTIC inductive
md **ANANDRIA** lack of maleness
pl **ANANGIAN** lacking vascular system
ANAPAEST a reversed dactyl
ANAPHASE nuclear division stage
rl **ANAPHORA** rhetorical repetition
ANARCHIC lawless and turbulent
md **ANASARCA** dropsy
rl **ANATHEMA** excommunication
md **ANATOMIC** internal
ANCESTOR forefather; forebear
ANCESTRY lineage; descent
ANCHORED fixed securely
rl **ANCHORET** anchorite; hermit
md **ANCONEAL** relating to the elbow
ANDERSON steel air-raid shelter
1940
mn **ANDESINE** felspar; andes
mn **ANDESITE** igneous rock, Andes
ANDIRONS fire-dogs
ANDORRAN (Andorra)

bc **ANDROGEN** male hormone
ANECDOTE a chatty relation
ac **ANECHOIC** echoless
md **ANEURISM** dilated artery
md **ANEURYSM** abnormal enlargement
ANGEL-BED open bed without posts
bt **ANGELICA** plant; Californian wine
ANGERING inflaming; infuriating
rl **ANGLICAN** Church of England
ANGLOMAN anglo-maniac
ANGRIEST exceedingly irate
lt, me **ANGSTROM** light wave-length unit
ANGULATE angular
gl **ANHEDRAL** allotriomorphic
md **ANHYPNIA** insomnia
pc **ANICONIA** lack of mental energy
ANIENTED annulled
ANIMALLY beastly
ANIMATED enlivened
ANIMATOR a rouser
rl **ANIMETTA** cloth for chalice
md **ANIRIDIA** absence of iris
ANISETTE liqueur from aniseed
md **ANISOPIA** unequal vision
ANNALISE record historical events
ANNALIST writer of annals
ml **ANNEALED** tempered steel
zo **ANNELIDA** worms
ANNEXING attaching; taking over
ANNOTATE add notes to;
commentate
ANNOUNCE pronounce; proclaim
ANNOYING irritating; vexatious
ANNUALLY yearly; every year
ANNULARY ring bearing (fourth
finger)
ANNULATE dividing into rings
ANNULLED rendered void; abolished
ANNULLER a voider
zo **ANNULOSE** annular; ringed
ANODISED treated electrically
rl **ANOINTED** consecrated; Messiah
zo **ANOPLURA** parasitic lice
md **ANOREXIA** loss of appetite
ANORTHIC oblique angled (crystals)
pl **ANOVULAR** eggless
ANSERINE gooselike; stupid; silly
ANSWERED solved; responded;
refuted
md **ANTALGIC** anodyne; pain-killer
zo **ANT-EATER** ant-bear, etc.
ANTECEDE precede
ANTEDATE anticipate
ANTEFIXA ornamental tiling
zo **ANTELOPE** deer
ANTENATI born before a given date
zo **ANTENNAE** feelers; aerials
ANTENNAL relating to the above

el **ANTENODE** (maximum displacement)
ANTEPORT outer gate or harbour
ANTERIOR prior; before
ANTEROOM antechamber
ANTHELIA luminous rings around sun
pl **ANTHELIX** antihelix; part of the ear
bt **ANTHEMIS** plant genus; camomile
bt **ANTHERAL** (pollen bearing anthers)
bt **ANTHESIS** full bloom
zo **ANTHOZOA** sea-anemones; corals
cf **ANTHROPO-** related to man
md **ANTIACID** antacid medicine
ANTI-ARMY pacifist
md **ANTIBODY** a counteractive
ANTICIZE to play antics
bt **ANTICOUS** centripetal
ANTIDOTE counter-measure
gl **ANTIDUNE** sandhill, dune
zo **ANTIGENY** sexual dimorphism
ANTI-ICER anti-freeze
ANTILOGY contradiction; antinomy
ANTIMASK grotesque interlude
ch **ANTIMIST** preventing misting up
mn, ch **ANTIMONY** stibium; a white metal
ANTINAZI anti-Hitlerite
ro **ANTINODE** radio term
lw **ANTINOMY** legal contradiction
ANTINOUS ideal of youthful beauty
ANTIPHON anthem; alternate chanting
ANTIPODE Australia (down under)
ANTIPOLE South Pole (down under)
ANTIPOPE opposition pope; (Avignon)
ANTIQUED simulated parchment
md **ANTISERA** antibiotics
ANTISPIN assisting recovery from spin
rl **ANTISTES** chief priest or prelate
ANTI-TANK (guns, mines, etc.)
ANTITYPE typical example
ANTLERED furnished with antlers
ANTRORSE up-turning
ANYTHING an unspecified object
ANYWHERE an undefined locality
AORISTIC indefinite as to time
md **AORTITIS** inflammation of artery
APAGOGIC reducing to an absurdity
md **APELLOUS** without a skin
md **APERIENT** a laxative; an opening
APERITIF a cocktail
pg **APERTURE** gap; hole; lens
md **APEX-BEAT** heartbeat visibility point
APHANITE hornblende, quartz, etc.
as **APHELION** max. earth–sun distance
zo **APHIDIAN** (green-fly)
bt **APHLEBIA** lateral fern outgrowth

md **APHONOUS** voiceless; dumb
APHORISM a maxim; a saw
APHORIST a writer of adages
APHORIZE define briefly
pc **APHRENIA** without mind
md **APHTHOUS** ulcerous
zo **APIARIAN** concerning bees
APIARIST a bee expert
APICALLY topmost; at the apex
APLASTIC not easily moulded
nt **APLUSTRE** ornament on stern
APNEUSIS state of maintained inspiration
APOCONYM foreshortened word-name
md **APOCRINE** of gland-cell breakdown
APODOSIS consequent clause
APOGAEIC (apogees and aphelions)
APOGRAPH a copy; transcript
APOLLYON the destroying angel
APOLOGIA vindication; formal defence
APOLOGIA excuses
APOLOGUE moral fibre; allegory
ar **APOPHYGE** base of column
md **APOPLEXY** loss of mental control
md **APOSITIA** aversion to food
rl **APOSTASY** renunciation of faith
APOSTATE a renegade
md **APOSTEME** apostume; an abscess
APOTHEGM sententious maxim
APPALLED terrified; dismayed
APPANAGE territorial dependency
APPARENT obvious; evident; palpable
APPEALED implored; entreated
APPEALER a suppliant; invoker
APPEARED emerged; dawned; arrived
APPEASED soothed; allayed; mollified
APPEASER pacifier; tranquillizer
lw **APPELLEE** defendant in an appeal
APPELLOR prosecutor
APPENDED subjoined; attached
md **APPENDIX** supplement; addendum
APPESTAT appetite controller
APPETENT desirous; solicitous
APPETITE craving; longing; hunger
APPETIZE to create a desire
APPLAUSE praise; laudation
APPLE-PIE dessert; orderly; (bed!)
APPLE-PIP apple-seed
bt **APPLIQUE** applied work
APPLYING employing; requesting
APPOSITE fit; suitable; pertinent
APPRAISE set a value to; rate; survey
APPRISED informed; notified; told

APPRIZED appreciated; valued
APPROACH advance; resemble; avenue
APPROVAL approbation; sanction
APPROVED commended; ratified
APPROVER ratifier; king's evidence
tx **APRES-SKI** Alpine late party; (dress)
APRON-MAN a mechanic
zo **APTEROUS** wingless
APTITUDE natural ability; talent; faculty
md **APYRETIC** feverless
md **APYREXIA** intermittent fever
AQUACADE musical water show
AQUALUNG diver's oxygen pack
AQUARIUM tanks of aquatic animals
AQUARIUS water-carrier (zodiac)
AQUASTAT boiler temperature regulator
AQUATINT a print; (engraving on copper)
pg **AQUATONE** photo printing process
AQUEDUCT artificial water channel
AQUIFUGE (clay strata) low permeability
AQUILINE like an eagle; hooked
gl **AQUITARD** slow permeability strata
AQUOSITY sloppiness
zo **ARACHNID** spider; mite or scorpion
ARAINGEE gallery of a mine
ARAMAISM an Aramaic idiom
zo **ARANEOUS** araneose; cobwebby
zo **ARAPUNGA** the bell-bird; campanero
ARBALIST arbalest; cross-bow
ARBITRAL arbitrational
bt **ARBOREAL** tree-like
ARBORETA shrubberies
ARBORIST tree expert; herbalist
ARBOROUS woody; arboreal
ARBOURED with shady bowers
bt **ARBUSCLE** dwarf tree
bt **ARBUSTUM** copse; shrubbery
bt **ARBUTEAN** (strawberry tree)
ARCADIAN pastoral; rustic
ARCATURE a small arcade
ARCHAEAN geologically remote
ARCHAISM an archaic expression
ARCHAIZE employ archaisms in speech
ARCHDUKE a princely title
ARCHICAL chief; primary
ARCHIVAL documentary
ARCHIVES record office; records
ARCHLIKE arcuate; iridian
mu **ARCHLUTE** double-stringed lute
ARCHNESS roguishness
ARCHPOET Poet Laureate
ARCHWISE bowed

as **ARCTURUS** Bear-guard; star in Boötes
ar, bd **ARCUATED** built on arches
ARDENTLY fiercely; zealously
AREFYING withering; desiccating
bt **ARENARIA** sandwort; chickweed
AREOLATE divided into small areas
bt **ARESCENT** drying
bt **ARGEMONE** silver-weed
ARGENTAN German silver
ARGENTIC argental; silvery
ch **ARGENTUM** silver; Ag
pl **ARGINASE** enzyme
ARGONAUT (golden fleece)
ARGOSIES richly laden vessels
ARGUABLE debatable
ARGUFIED wrangled
ARGUMENT discussion; an abstract
ARGUTELY keenly; shrewdly; piercing
rl **ARIANISE** convert to Arianism
rl **ARIANISM** doctrine of Arius
ARIDNESS dryness; sterility
bt **ARILLARY** (exterior coating of a seed)
nt **ARISINGS** irregularities after refit
bt **ARISTATE** awned; bearded
ARMAMENT munitions; arms; guns
ARMARIAN monastic librarian
ARMARIUM scroll; book cupboard
ARMATURE armour; rotor of dynamo
ARMCHAIR chair with arm rests
rl **ARMENIAN** of Armenia; Christian sect
ARMIGERO esquire; armour-bearer
ARMILLET small bracelet; armlet
rl **ARMINIAN** (opposed to Calvinism)
hd **ARMORIAL** relating to coats-of-arms
hd **ARMORIST** expert in heraldry
ARMOURED plated
ARMOURER artificer; manufacturer
tx, rl **ARMOZEEN ARMOZINE**, taffeta or silk, used for clerical gowns
AROMATIC fragrant; pungent
AROUSING stirring
mu **ARPEGGIO** harplike chord
ARQUEBUS heavy musket
ARRANGED settled; grouped
ARRANGER planner; orchestrator
ARRANTLY infamously; notoriously
ARRASENE Arras embroidery
ARRAUGHT taken by force
ARRAYING disposing; adorning
ARRESTED halted; seized; captured
lw **ARRESTER** an apprehender
ga **ARRIMADA** front wall shot (pelota)
ARRIVING reaching; attaining; landing

ARROGANT haughty; overbearing
ARROGATE usurp; assume
hd **ARRONDEE** segmented heraldic cross
pl **ARSEHOLE** the anal orifice
ch **ARSENATE ARSENITE**, arsenical salts
ARSONIST ARSONITE, felon who deliberately sets fire to property
ARTEFACT man made, modified object
md **ARTERIAL** (arteries); (roads)
gl **ARTESIAN** well water-table pressure
ARTFULLY craftily
lw **ARTICLED** bound by agreement
ARTIFACT product of primitive art
ARTIFICE stratagem; trick; device
ARTISTIC tasteful; aesthetic
ARTISTRY vocation; workmanship
ARUSPICE haruspex; soothsayer
ARUSPICY divination by augury
zo **ARVICOLA** vole genus
mn **ASBESTIC** made of asbestos
ASBESTOS incombustible material
ASCENDED rose; mounted
pr **ASCENDER** part of letters in printing
bt **ASCIDIUM** bottle-like appendage
ch **ASCORBIC** acid; vitamin C
ASCRIBED attributed; assigned
md **ASEMASIA** symbol-blindness
ga **ASHIKUBI** ankle kick (karate)
ga **ASHIWAZA** leg throwing (judo)
ASH-LEACH tub for washing wood-ash
ASH-PLANT ash sapling; walking stick
ASH-STAND ash-tray
ASHY-GRAY ashy in colour
bt **ASPARTIC** obtained from asparagus
ASPERATE to roughen
rl **ASPERGES** ceremonial sprinkling
ASPERITY harshness; sourness; acerbity
ASPERSED sprinkled; slandered; abused
bt **ASPHODEL** a lily; a daffodil
md **ASPHYXIA** suffocation; pulse failure
ASPIRANT suitor; candidate
ASPIRATE to emphasize the 'h' sound
ASPIRING longing; hoping; soaring
bt **ASPOROUS** without spores
ASPORTED stolen away
ASSAILED assaulted; attacked; vilified
ASSAILER aggressor; invader; traducer
ASSAMESE native of Assam; (language)

ASSARTED grubbed up trees and bushes
ASSASSIN a thug primed with hashish
ASSAYING testing; analysing
ASSEMBLE convene; muster; congregate
ASSEMBLY parliament; synod; meeting
ASSENTED agreed; concurred
ASSENTER assentor; approver
ASSERTED maintained; averred
ASSESSED taxed; rated; appraised
lw **ASSESSOR** tax-master; valuer
ASSIETTE oblong dish; dinner plate (Fr.)
nm **ASSIGNAT** paper currency, Fr. Rev.
ASSIGNED allotted; specified
ASSIGNEE a recipient
ASSIGNOR transferer of an interest
zo **ASSINEGO** small donkey; fool; dolt
ASSISTED aided; abetted; sustained
ASSIZING assessing; regulating
ASSONANT harmonious; rhythmical
mu **ASSONATE** correspond in sound
ASSORTED mixed; varied; classified
ASSUAGED allayed; abated; appeased
ASSUAGER mitigator; alleviator
ASSUMING arrogant; presumptuous
ASSURANT holder of insurance policy
ASSURING affirming; pledging
ASSYRIAN a descendant of Shem
zo **ASTACIAN** shellfish; lobster type
zo **ASTERIAS** starfish genus
pr **ASTERISK** printers' mark (*)
as **ASTERISM** small cluster of stars
ASTERNAL not joined to breastbone
as **ASTEROID** minor planet; star-shaped
ASTHENIA lack of vitality; debility
md **ASTHENIC** feeble; weak
zo **ASTOMATA** an order of infusoria
ASTOMOUS astomatous; mouthless
ASTONIED astounded; stunned; dazed
ASTONISH amaze; startle; surprise
ASTRINGE constrict; constrain
ASTUNNED astonished; mazed; dazed
ASTUTELY cunningly; craftily
md **ASYSTOLE** heart failure
md **ATABRINE** quinine type
ATARAXIA stoical indifference
ATHEIZED converted to disbelief
ATHELING Anglo-Saxon noble
ATHENIAN a Greek (Athens)
zo **ATHERINE** fish genus; mullets; smelts
md **ATHEROMA** disease of arteries

ATHLETIC strong; vigorous; sinewy
ATLANTES male supporting figures
go ATLANTIC western ocean
ATLANTIS lost continent
ATMOLOGY science of vaporization
ATOMICAL atomic; minute
ATOMIZED vaporized
ATOMIZER a spray
ATONABLE expiable; amendable
ATREMBLE dithering
ATROCITY a cruel barbarous act
ATROPHIC emaciated; withered
md ATROPINE bella-donna
md ATROPISM illness due to atropine
bt ATROPOUS upturned; erect
lw ATTACHED fond; bound; arrested
ATTACKED assaulted; set about
ATTACKER assailant; invader;
  violater
ATTAINED achieved; secured; won
ATTENDED served; escorted;
  hearkened
ATTENDER attendant; close listener
ATTENTAT attempted assassination
ATTESTED invoked; endorsed
ATTESTOR attester; a witness
ATTICISM witty remark; Attic salt
ATTICIZE to use Athenian idioms
ATTINGED touched lightly; affected
ATTIRING arraying; adorning; robing
ATTITUDE pose; posture; opinion
ATTORNED transferred loyalty
lw ATTORNEY lawyer; solicitor
ATTRITED worn away; abraded;
  erased
mn ATTRITUS a grade of coal
mu ATTUNING harmonizing
ATYPICAL not conforming
AUBUSSON style of carpet
AUCUPATE to go bird-catching
AUDACITY boldness; effrontery;
  daring
AUDIENCE formal interview; listeners
AUDITING examining accounts
AUDITION vocal test; also sound tests
AUDITIVE audible
md AUDITORY sense of hearing
AUGURATE foretell by divination
AUGURIAL ominous
AUGURIES prognostications; portents
AUGURING presaging; prophesying
AUGUSTAN (Emperor Augustus)
AUGUSTLY majestically; imposingly
AULARIAN member of an Oxford
  Hall
AURELIAN (Emperor Aurelius);
  philosophy
rl AUREOLED in a halo

bt AURICLED eared
bt AURICULA the primula
AURIFORM ear-shaped
md AURILAVE ear-washing instrument
AUROREAN rosy; dawning; (aurora
  borealis)
AURULENT golden
AUSONIAN Italian
AUSTRIAN of Austria
md AUTACOID a hormone; a chalone
AUTARCHY autocracy; absolutism
AUTARKIC self-sufficient
pc AUTISTIC withdrawn
AUTOBAHN fast motorway
AUTOCADE motor cavalcade
bt AUTOCARP self-fertilized fruit
AUTOCODE computer operation
  procedure
rl AUTOCRAT absolute ruler
zo AUTOCYST parasite-formed
  membrane
AUTO-DA-FE Inquisition burnings
AUTO-DYNE frequency stabilizer
bt AUTOGAMY self-fertilization
AUTOGENY spontaneous generation
ae AUTOGYRO a type of aircraft
AUTOLOGY the study of self
AUTOMATA automatons; robots
AUTOMATH a self-taught man
AUTONOMY self-government
md AUTOPSIA autopsy; post-mortem
AUTOPTIC seen with one's own eyes
AUTOSLED snow vehicle
cy AUTOSOME non-sexual chromosome
AUTOTOMY amputation; cell division
AUTOTYPE carbon copy process
AUTUMNAL peculiar to the autumn
ch AUTUNITE phosphate of uranium
AUXILIAR subsidiary; assisting
cy AUXOCYTE cell with meiosis
AVAILING profiting; sufficing; using
hd AVELLANE heraldic cross of filberts
AVENGING vindicating; retaliating
AVENTAIL visor; opening in a helmet
lw AVENTURE fatal accident
AVERAGED equated; proportional
ck AVERCAKE oatcake
AVERMENT affirmation
AVERNIAN Plutonic; infernal
AVERRING declaring; alleging
hd AVERSANT heraldic reversal
AVERSELY unwillingly; reluctantly
AVERSION dislike; hatred; allergy
AVIARIST keeper of caged birds
AVIATING flying
AVIATION travel by air
zo AVIFAUNA local birdlife
AVOIDING eschewing; shunning

AVOIDISM trouble evasion
AVOUCHED guaranteed
AVOWABLE affirmable; declarable
AVOWABLY deposably; admittedly
AVOWANCE avowel; confession
AVOWEDLY openly; frankly
AWAITING abiding; expecting
AWAKABLE not dead-asleep
AWAKENED spurred; stimulated
AWAKENER a rouser
AWANTING wanting; lacking; absent
AWARDING decreeing; bestowing
AWEARIED jaded; spent; worn
nt AWEATHER the weather-side
AXE-HELVE handle of an ax
mn AXE-STONE jade
bt AXILLARY (armpit); branch angle
AXIOLOGY theory of value
AXIOTRON value with controlled
  stream
AXLETREE spindle
AXOIDEAN axial
AXOPLASM material around axon
AZOTIZED nitrogenized
AZULEJOS glazed blue-white tiles
  (Port.)

B

zo BABAKOTO a large lemur
BABBLING prattling; gossiping
BABELDOM state of confusion
zo BABIRUSA pig deer of Sri Lanka
BABISHLY childishly
BABOODOM realm of red tape
BABOOISM plethora of verbiage
BABOUCHE oriental slipper
BABY-FACE term of endearment
BABY-FARM baby-boarding house
BABYHOOD state of infancy
ga BACCARAT a card game
BACCHANT bacchanalian
BACHELOR a degree-man; unmarried
  man
md BACILLAR like bacilli
md BACILLUS rod-like organism
md BACHACHE persistent vertebral pain
BACKAWAY retreat; withdraw
BACK-BAND cart-saddle band
lw BACKBEAR poacher stealing venison
BACK-BITE to speak evil; asperse
BACK-BOND conditional deed
pl BACKBONE reliability; spine
BACK-CAST anglers' thrust
  (fishing)
BACK-CHAT impertinent rejoinder
hr BACK-COCK pendulum bracket

BACKCOMB reverse combing
  (coiffeur)
BACKDATE retrospective (cheques)
BACK-DOOR clandestine; furtive
BACKDOWN retire; resign; withdraw
BACK-DROP drop scene
lw BACK-DUTY unpaid tax
BACK-FALL a wrestling throw
BACKFIRE create reverse effect
BACKFIRE a blow back (motoring)
BACKFIST a punch (karate)
BACK-FLAP folding shutter
hy BACK-FLOW reverse liquid flow
jn BACK-FOLD foldable part of shutter
eg BACK-GEAR lathe speed-reducer
ga BACKHAND negative compliment;
  (tennis)
ga BACK-HEEL wrestling throw; football
bd BACKINGS furring strips on joints
BACKINGS financial support; data
BACKINGS picture mounts (framing)
bd BACK-IRON fireplace heat reflector
BACK-KICK violent engine reversal
BACK-KICK gun recoil; horse
  bucking
BACKLASH political counter-reaction
BACKLASH whipping; gear wear
BACKMOST hindermost
BACKPACK rucksack; snail's burden
eg BACK-RAKE surface/base relation
BACK-RENT dues
tx BACK-REST loom bar
BACK-ROOM behind the scenes
BACKSEAT rear in bus, car, theatre
BACKSIDE posterior; buttocks;
  behind
ga BACKSPIN rotary motion of ball
nt BACKSTAY mast-, stern-, sides-
  support
BACK-STEP cycle mounting step
BACKSTOP armature-travel-limit
  relay
ga BACKSTOP manor fence; screen;
  (baseball)
eg BACK-WALL conductor; photovoltaic
BACKWARD retarded; reluctant
BACKWARD unadvanced; in reverse
nt BACKWASH backward current; wake
BACKWASH after suction (air
  current)
BACKWASH aftermath of event
  (results)
tc BACK-WAVE spacing wave
BACKWORK non-mining colliery
  activity
zo BACKWORM filanders; hawk-disease
BACONIAN (Bacon); inductive
md BACTERIA fungoid growths

zo **BACTRIAN** two-humped camel
BACULINE rod-like
mn **BACULITE** fossil cuttlefish
BADGERED pestered; worried
BADGERLY grey like a badger
BADIGEON sculptor's cement
BADINAGE persiflage; chaff
BADLANDS arid, gullied, highland
(Nevada)
tx **BAFFETAS** Indian muslin
BAFFLING defeating; hoodwinking
zo **BAGHEERA** the black panther (India)
mu **BAGPIPER** a bagpipe player
BAGUETTE baton-like crustbread
(Fr.)
lw **BAILABLE** able to be bailed
BAIL-BALL cricket ball bail high
BAIL-BOND security for appearance
lw **BAIL-DOCK** room at Old Bailey
lw **BAILMENT** delivery of goods in trust
lw **BAILSMAN** guarantor of bond
BAKELITE a plastic material
ck **BAKEMEAT** pastry; pies
BAKSHISH discount; commission; tip
BALANCED in equilibrium
BALANCER acrobat, tumbler
mn **BALANITE** fossil barnacle
BALCONET miniature balcony
zo **BALDCOOT** baldicoot; coot; monk
BALDHEAD no hair apparent
bt **BALDMONY** gentian
md **BALDNESS** alopecia
zo **BALD-PATE** species of wild duck
BALDRICK shoulder belt
BALE-FIRE signal-fire; funeral pyre
BALESTRA lunge (fencing)
tx **BALK-BACK** fibrous-back cloth
BALK-LINE baulk-line (billiards)
BALLADER ballad-monger
BALLADRY patriotic or epic verse
gl **BALL-CLAY** fine-textured detrital
clay
BALL-COCK stopcock in a cistern
BALLIAGE an export duty
BALLISTA ancient catapult
BALLONET small balloon; gas bag
BALLOTED drew lots for; voted
to **BALL-PANE** part flat, part globular
BALLROOM location for stately
measures
BALLYHOO bunkum; false fame
BALLYRAG bullyrag; torment
BALMORAL bonnet; boot; petticoat
md **BALNEARY** of spa treatments
BALOTADE an equine feat
BALSAMIC soothing; demulcent
ar **BALUSTER** supporting column
BANALITY triviality; triteness

BANDAGED surgically bound
BANDANNA Indian silk kerchief
BANDEAUX hair-bands or fillets
el **BAND-EDGE** between 2 defined
limits
ar **BANDELET** bandlet
BANDEROL bannerol; small banner
zo **BANDFISH** long lean fish
BANDITTI bandits; robbers; outlaws
el **BAND-PASS** free for specific currents
mu **BANDSMAN** musician in a band
BANDSTER sheaf-binder
BAND-STOP attenuating specific
currents
BANDYING tossing about
bt **BANEWORT** deadly nightshade
am **BANG-BANG** serco control
mechanism
BANGSTER bully; victor
BANGTAIL square-cut tail
BANISHED expelled; outlawed
BANISTER baluster; stair railings
mu **BANJOIST** fretful player
BANKABLE receivable at a bank
BANK-BILL note of exchange
BANK-BOOK depositor's account
book
BANK-NOTE promissory note
BANK-RATE Bank of England rate
BANKRUPT insolvent; broke
BANKSMAN overseer at pit-mouth
(coal)
ce **BANKSMAN** driver's help
BANLIEUE environs of a town (Fr.)
BANNERED beflagged
BANNERET knighthood
BANNEROL banderol; small banner
BANTERED railed; chaffed
BANTERER joker; jester
BANTLING young child; bratling
zo **BANXRING** insect-eating squirrel
BAPHOMET Templar's idol
rl **BAPTIZED** immersed
tx **BARATHEA** woven fabric
BARBACAN barbican; outer defence
BARBARED shaved; shorn
BARBARIC foreign; savage; Hunnish
bt **BARBATED** bearded; awned
ck **BARBECUE** out-door grill
bt **BARBERRY** thorny shrub; berberry
BARBETTE armoured defence
ar **BARBICAN** BARBACAN, gun-port in
wall; outer defence of castle
mu **BARBITON** antique form of lyre
to **BAR-CRAMP** plank-gluing bar
BARDLING bardlet; poetaster;
rhymster
BAREBACK unsaddled

lw **BAREBOAT** chartering contract
BAREBONE (Parliament); lean; thin
BAREFOOT bootless
BARESARK without shirt of mail
BARGEMAN barge owner; bargee
BARGHEST a dog-like goblin
BARILLET watch-spring case
mu **BARITONE** (between tenor and bass)
BARKMILL bark-crusher
bt **BARNABAS** cornflour
zo **BARNACLE** a twitch; cirriped; goose
BARN-DOOR a farm portal
BARNEKIN outermost castle ward
BARNYARD the rooster's realm
mt **BAROGRAM** record of atmospheric
pressure from barograph
BAROLOGY the science of weight
bt **BAROMETZ** a fern
BARONAGE cf. peerage
BARONESS wife or widow of baron
BARONIAL noble and spacious
ps **BAROSTAT** pressure device
BAROUCHE four-wheeled carriage
BAR-POSTS supports of field-gate
tx **BARRACAN** material of camel-hair
BARRACKS the soldier's home
BARRANCO barranca; deep gorge
lw **BARRATOR** encourager of litigation
rl **BARRATRY** traffic in church offices
BARRENLY sterilely; unfruitfully
hd **BARRULET** horizontal heraldic bar
to **BAR-SHEAR** bar-cutter
BARTERED exchanged commodities
BARTERER a dealer
BARTIZAN small overhanging turret
mn **BASALTIC** allied to basalt
mn **BASANITE** touchstone; flinty slate
BASCINET helmet of 15th century
ga **BASEBALL** national game (USA)
BASEBAND frequency modulation
BASE-BORN of low parentage
BASE-BRED of low breeding
BASELESS lacking any foundation
me **BASE-LINE** a surveyor's base
BASEMENT floor below ground level
BASENESS vileness; meanness
BASE-PAIR complementary acid
bases
BASE-RICH iron-rich soil
mu **BASE-VIOL** bass-viol; violoncello
BASHLESS unashamed; undaunted
ch **BASICITY** ratio of acid to base
ch **BASIFIER** an alkali
rl **BASILIAN** monk of St Basil
rl **BASILICA** church
BASILICA public hall (Roman)
BASILING grinding to an angle
zo **BASILISK** dragon; lizard; cannon

BASINFUL bowlful
zo **BASIPHIL** attracted to basic dyes
BASKETED hampered
BASKETRY wickerwork
BASOPHIL attracted to basic dyes
BASQUINE Basque outer petticoat
mu **BASS-DRUM** deep-noted drum
mu **BASSETTE** tenor or small bass viol
mu **BASS-HORN** deep-toned bassoon
BASSINET wickerwork perambulator
mu **BASS-TUBA** euphonium
mu **BASS-VIOL** base-viol; violoncello
bt **BASSWOOD** (N. Amer.)
BASTAARD Dutch half-breed (S.
Afr.)
BASTARDY illegitimacy
BASTERNA mule-borne litter
BASTILLE old castle; state prison
BATAVIAN native of Batavia;
(Indonesian)
BATELESS irrepressible
BATHABLE washable
BATHETIC anticlimatic; bombastic
BATHMISM inherent divergence
zo **BATHORSE** pack-horse
BATH-RAIL side-grip
BATHROOM tub- and wash-room
BATSWING flat gas flame;
flittermouse
nt **BATTENED** dependent; doors secured
BATTERED pounded; shattered
BATTLING striving; warring
mu **BATUCADA** batuque; dance (Brazil)
rl **BAUDEKIN** silk brocade; canopy
BAUDRONS Scottish name for the cat
BAULKING BALKING, checking;
refusal (horse-jumping); jibbing
BAVARIAN of Bavaria
BAWDRICK baldrick; shoulder belt
BAYADERE Indian nautch girl
BAYARDLY blindly
bt **BAYBERRY** war-myrtle
bt **BDELLIUM** aromatic gum-resin
nt, ce **BEACHING** running ashore; loose-
graded stones
ae, nt **BEACONED** aircraft guided; seamarks
lit
BEADLERY beadle's jurisdiction
rl **BEAD-ROLL** names for masses
BEADSMAN almsman
bt **BEAD-TREE** the azedarac
tx **BEADWORK** ornamental, with
coloured glass beads on cloth
BEAGLING hare-coursing on foot
with dogs
nt **BEAK-HEAD** head; (ship's WCs)
nt **BEAK-HEAD** ramming projection
(Roman)

BEAKIRON bickern; anvil point
zo **BEAM-BIRD** spotted flycatcher
lt **BEAM-EDGE** searchlight angle
lt **BEAM-FLUX** total light flux
el **BEAM-TRAP** beam-catching
   electrode
bt **BEAM-TREE** a hardwood tree
BEAN-KING king of the revels
BEARABLE tolerable; supportable
BEARABLY endurably; moderately
bt **BEARBIND** bearbine; bindweed
BEARDING meeting face to face
BEAR-HERD bear-keeper
BEARINGS sense of direction
BEARLIKE rude and rough; ursine
bt **BEAR'S-EAR** primula auricula
BEARSKIN headgear of the Guards
BEARWARD bear-leader; Arcturus
zo **BEASTIES** small animals
BEASTISH brutal; animal
BEATIFIC ecstatic; rapturous
BEAT-NOTE rhythmic accentuation
BEAUFREY beam or joist
BEAUPERE father in-law (Fr.)
BEAUTIES lovelies
BEAUTIFY adorn; array; garnish
BEAVERED covered with beaver fur
BECALMED motionless; tranquillized
ck **BECHAMEL** savoury sauce (white)
BECHANCE befall; accidentally
BECKONED nodded; called; invited
BECOMING befitting; graceful
nt **BECUEING** anchor dragging on rocks
BECURLED with ringlets
BEDABBLE dabble; sprinkle
BEDAGGLE drag through the mire
BEDARKEN obscure; eclipse
BEDASHED bespattered
BEDAUBED smeared; plastered
BED-CHAIR bed back-rest
BEDECKED robed; embellished
bt, zo **BEDEGUAR** a rose scourge
rl **BEDESMAN** see beadsman
bt **BEDEWEEN** the birch tree
BEDEWING sprinkling
BED-GOING retiring
pt **BEDIMMED** tarnished; lights lowered
BED-LINEN sheets, etc.
BEDMAKER college servant
BEDPLATE foundation plate
eg **BEDPLATE** engine-frame base
BED-QUILT an overlay
BEDRENCH saturate; immerse; soak
BEDSTAFF cudgel; truncheon
BEDSTEAD a framework for a bed
BEDSTOCK part of bed (gardening)
bt **BEDSTRAW** a plant
BED-TABLE table for use in bed

BEDUCKED soused
BEDUSTED smothered with dust
BEDWARDS on the way to bed
bt **BEE-BREAD** pollen collected by bees
ck **BEECH-OIL** beechnut oil
zo **BEE-EATER** a bird
BEEFIEST heftiest; lustiest
bt **BEEFWOOD** an Australian wood
BEER-PUMP beer-pull, spout
BEERSHOP inn; alehouse; tavern
BEESWING dregs of port
BEETLING overhanging; projecting
bt **BEETRAVE** beetroot
bt **BEETROOT** beetrave
BEFITTED suitable; becoming;
   worthy
BEFLOWER cover with flowers
BEFOGGED dimmed; confused
BEFOOLED deluded; hoaxed; gulled
BEFOULED polluted; begrimed
BEFRIEND favour; patronize; aid
BEFRINGE adorn with fringes
BEFURRED covered with fur
BEGETTER a sire; father
BEGGABLE borrowable
BEGGARED rendered penniless
BEGGARLY paltry; mean; abject
BEGINNER tyro; novice; neophyte
BEGIRDED belted
BEGIRDLE encompass; encircle
BEGOTTEN born; produced
BEGREASE lubricate
BEGRIMED soiled; grubby
BEGRUDGE envy
BEGUILED deluded; diverted
BEGUILER cheat; deceiver
BEHAVING comme il faut
BEHEADAL an execution
BEHEADED decapitated
zo **BEHEMOTH** Job's hippopotamus
BEHOLDEN grateful; indebted
BEHOLDER observer; surveyor
BEHOVING being necessary
pc **BEINNESS** acceptedness socially
BEKISSED smothered in kisses
BELABOUR to thrash and whack
BELACING adorning with lace
BELAMOUR a gallant; a fair lady
BELATING being late
BELAUDED eulogized
nt **BELAYING** fastening
BEL-CANTO refined singing
   technique
BELCHING eructating
BELFRIED having belfries
rl **BELFRIES** steeples; watch-towers
BELIEVED credited; fancied
BELIEVER theist; devotee; pietist

BELITTLE disparage; deprecate
bt BELLBIND BELL-BINE, bindweed
zo BELL-BIRD New Zealand bird
nt BELL-BUOY the sailor's warning
BELLCOTE small belfry
BELLOWED roared; bawled
BELL-PULL bell-rope
el BELL-PUSH push-button bell switch
BELL-ROPE a ringer of clangers
BELL-TENT conical canvas tent
bt BELLWORT a campanula
BELLYFUL a bun in the oven
BELLY-GOD greedy; epicure;
  gourmand
BELLYING swelling; billowing
BELONGED owned by; pertained
BELOVING loving; fond; doting
eg BELT-FORK belt-transfer prongs
eg BELT-SLIP pulley-face belt slippage
BELZEBUB Beelzebub; satan; the
  devil
BEMASKED wearing a mask
BEMIRING soiling
BEMOANED bewailed; lamented
BEMUDDLE mess up
BEMUFFLE take a wrap for warmth
bd BENCHING extended seating; berm-
  ledge
ce BENCHING over ditch; manhole of
  iron
BENDABLE not rigid; over-bearing
nt BENEAPED aground at low tide
BENEDICK newly married man
rl BENEDICT an orderly saint
BENEFICE church living
BENIGNLY kindly; benevolently
BENITIER holy water vessel
BENJAMIN gum; overcoat
BENOTING noting fully
eg BENT-TAIL having a bent shank
BENUMBED torpid
ch BENZOATE a salt
BEPEPPER shoot repeatedly
BEPESTER annoy persistently
BEPITIED commiserated
BEPLUMED with plumes
BEPOMMEL belabour
BEPOWDER pulverize
BEPRAISE laud
BEPUFFED flattered with hot air
mu BEQUADRO natural (It.)
lw BEQUEATH of bequest, legacy (will)
BERATING scolding
ch BERBERIN barberry extract
bt BERBERRY the barberry
BERCEUSE cradle lullaby; song (Fr.)
BERDACHE Indian transvestite
BEREAVED bereft; widow; widower

bt, ck BERGAMOT herbal perfume; (tea)
mn BERGMEHL crystalline earth
BERGMOTE a miner's court
BERHYMED celebrated in verse
md BERI-BERI a tropical disease
BERNOUSE burnouse; Arab mantle
BERRYING producing berries
BERTHAGE dock fees
nt BERTHING docking
BESCRAWL scribble
BESCREAM yell the house down
BESCREEN shelter
BESEEMED befitted
BESEEMLY becoming; fit; suitable
BESETTER an assailant
BESHADOW overshadow
bt BESIDERY variety of pear
BESIEGED beleaguered; encircled
BESIEGER an investor
BESILVER electro-plate
BESLAVED enslaved
BESLAVER slobber
BESLIMED bemired
BESMIRCH besmutch; beslime
BESNOWED snowed up
BESOILED defiled; dirtied
BESORTED suited; fitted
BESOTTED drunk; crapulous;
  inebriated
BESOUGHT entreated; implored
BESOULED endowed with a soul
BESPICED highly seasoned
BESPOKEN made to order
BESPREAD broadcast; disseminate
BESSEMER a steel process
BESTIARY book about beasts
BESTOWAL gift; grant; distribution
BESTOWED gave; presented; awarded
BESTOWER donor; feoffer
BESTREAK mark with streaks
BESTREWN scattered; dispersed
BESTRIDE astride
BESTRODE traversed; mounted
mn BETAFITE hydrous uranium
BETAKING removing to; applying to
BETA-RAYS radium-rays
BETATRON electron speeding
  machine
BETEARED tearful; bedimmed
bt BETEL-NUT areca nut palm
BETIDING happening; befalling
BETONGUE scold; rail; nag
BETOSSED thrown about
BETRAYAL breach of trust; treachery
BETRAYED ensnared; beguiled;
  deceived
BETRAYER seducer; a Judas; traitor
BETTERED ameliorated; improved

bt **BETULINE** birch camphor
BEVELLED basiled; on the slant; smoothed, rounded
BEVERAGE drink; potion; potation
hd **BEVILLED** sloping lines
BEWAILED lamented
BEWARING minding; avoiding
lw **BEWIGGED** wearing a wig (law courts)
BEWILDER perplex; confuse
BHEESTIE Hindu water-carrier
ag **B-HORIZON** lower level of soil
BIANCONI Irish car
BIATHLON skiing and shooting; running and swimming trophies
ck **BIBATION** tippling; a drink
BIBLE-BOX container for Bible
rl **BIBLICAL** scriptured
BIBULOUS over-indulgence in alcohol
eg **BIB-VALVE** disc-closed draw-off tap
BICAUDAL with two tails
BICKERED squabbled
BICOLOUR of two colours
ps **BICONVEX** lens
BICRURAL two legged
bt **BICUSPID** having two cusps
BICYCLED cycled
BIDDABLE worth bidding for (auction)
BIDENTAL with two teeth
BIENNIAL once in two years
BIER-BALK right of way for funerals
BIFACIAL doublefaced
bt **BIFEROUS** two crops each year
bt **BIFIDATE** cleft in twain
BIFORATE having two pores
lw **BIGAMIST** husband of two or more wives
lw **BIGAMOUS** situation of plural marriage
bt **BIGAROON** white-heart cherry
BIG-BONED bony; osseous
BIGGONET cap; deerstalker
bt **BIGNONIA** plant genus
BIJOUTRY bijouterie; trinkets
bt **BIJUGATE** twin
BIJUGOUS paired
BIJWONER squatter (S. Africa)
BILABIAL with both lips (phonetic)
nt **BILANDER** Dutch barge
bt **BILBERRY** blueberry
md **BILEDUCT** a canal
BILL-BOOK account book
BILLETED quartered
BILLETEE person billeted
zo **BILLFISH** lake fish (N. Amer.)
pr **BILLHEAD** letterhead; printing

to **BILLHOOK** hedge-cutting tool
BILLIARD- for a special green smooth cloth-covered table
BILLOWED surged; swelled (waves)
nt **BILLY-BOY** bluff-bowed ketch
BILLY-CAN bush teapot (Aust.)
BILOBATE with two lobes
BIMANOUS two-handed
md **BIMANUAL** done with both hands
BIMARINE between two seas
BIMENSAL every other month
BIMESTER two-month term
BIMIRROR slightly inclined mirror pair
nt **BINABINA** canoe (S. Pacific)
BINAURAL adapted for two ears
BINBASHI Turkish army officer
bt **BINDWEED** bearbine; convolvulus
nt **BINNACLE** mounting for ship's compass
ma **BINOMIAL** two-term system
ch **BINOXIDE** a peroxide
pm **BIO-ASSAY** drug-power test on animals
BIOBLAST parturient protoplasm
BIOCYTIN vitamin in yeast
BIOGENIC produced by living organisms
cn **BIOGRAPH** bioscope; cinema; zoetrope
BIOLYTIC destructive to life
bl **BIOMETER** life-measuring instrument
BIOMETRY life mensuration
bl **BIONOMIC** ecological
BIOPHORE minute growth-capable particle
zo **BIOPLASM** protoplasm
BIOSCOPE early cinematograph
BIOSOPHY made of life
BIPAROUS twin-producing
BIPENNIS two-edged battle-axe
BIQUARTZ saccharimeter analyser
zo **BIRADIAL** part radial, part bilateral
BIRAMOUS double-branched
BIRCHING corporal punishment
BIRD-BATH garden ornament
BIRD-BOLT blunt arrow
BIRDCAGE prison for birds; mini-aviary
BIRD-CALL bird song
BIRD-EYED quick-sighted; eagle-eyed
zo **BIRD-LICE** avian irritants
BIRDLIKE aviform
BIRDLIME sticky stuff for catching birds
BIRDSEED aviary food

BIRD'S-EYE of avian view
BIRD-SONG warbling of birds
lw **BIRRETUM** judge's black cap
BIRTHDAY an anniversary
BIRTHDOM privilege of birth
BISCAYAN Basque
BISCOTIN sweet biscuit
mu **BISCROMA** demisemiquaver
ma **BISECTED** halved angles (geometry)
BISECTOR an equal divisor
BISERIAL in two series
bt, zo **BISETOSE** double-bristled
BISEXUAL hetero- and homosexual
vt, zo **BISHOPED** horse ailment
ga **BISHOPED** bishop's conquest (chess)
pl, zo **BISMATIC** with two nipples
nt **BISQUINE** fishing lugger (Fr.)
tc **BISTABLE** with 2 stable states
rd **BISTATIC** transmitter/receiver apart
md **BISTOURY** surgical knife
pr **BITING-IN** acid process (etching)
BITINGLY acidly; mordantly
BITMAKER lorimer; loriner
BITMOUTH bit of a bridle
to **BITSTOCK** carpenter's brace
nt **BITTACLE** compass housing
BITTERED of acid flavour; distressed
BITTERLY acrimoniously
ch **BIVALENT** diatomic valency
BI-WEEKLY periodically
zo **BIZCACHA** chinchilla, rodent
BLABBING telling; tatling; weeping
BLACK-ART necromancy
ae **BLACK-BOX** computer control unit; flight recorder
zo **BLACKCAP** a warbler
zo **BLACK-FLY** turnip-flea
bt **BLACK-GUM** N. American tree
BLACKING boot-polish; black-listing
BLACKISH somewhat dark
BLACKLEG non-participant in works' strike
BLACKLET speck of dust
BLACK-NEB beak of crow, crane etc.
BLACKOUT loss of consciousness
BLACKOUT darkened city (war)
BLACKPOT coarse ceramic
BLACK-ROD Usher to House of Lords
mn **BLACK-WAD** ore of manganese
md **BLADDERY** of the gall, urine bladder
BLAMABLE censurable
BLAMABLY reprehensibly
BLAMEFUL culpable
BLANCARD bleached woven cloth
BLANCHED deprived of colour
BLANCHER white-washer
BLANDEST smoothest; mildest

BLANDISH flatter; coax; cajole
BLANKEST most vacant
BLANKING off-putting; frustrating
bt **BLASTEMA** an off-shoot
BLASTING detonating; cursing
BLAST-OFF launching of rocket
bl **BLASTULA** embryonic cell
BLATANCY obtrusive vulgarity
zo **BLAUWBOK** antelope (S. Africa)
hd **BLAZONED** decorated with
BLAZONER a broadcaster
BLAZONRY heraldic painting
BLEACHED blanched
BLEACHER colour extractor
BLEAKEST coldest; barest; chilliest
BLEAKISH cold and cheerless
BLEATING sheep calls (blethering)
BLEEDING blood-letting; gluing; separation of liquids
BLENCHED flinched; paled
BLENDING intermingling; harmonizing
zo, bt **BLENHEIM** spaniel; apple; plane
rl **BLESSING** divine favour; boon; gain
BLETTING decaying
BLIGHTED mildewed
BLIGHTER pestilent fellow
BLIMPERY blatant reactionary; obstinacy
BLINDAGE art of camouflage
BLINDERS BLINKERS, eye directors (horses)
BLINDEST most ignorant and heedless
ce **BLINDING** hoodwinking; (light); mat; mathers; sight-losing
BLINKARD a blinker or winker
BLINKERS vision restrictors (horses)
BLINKING ignoring; winking; gleaming
BLISSFUL rapturous; ecstatic
md **BLISTERY** swollen; vesicated; painful
BLITHELY joyously
BLITHEST merriest
BLITZING terror bombing (Blitzkrieg – Ger.)
BLIZZARD violent (arctic) snowstorm
ck **BLOATING** smoking (curing) fish
BLOATING inflating; swelling
nt **BLOCKADE** hostile closure of ports as act of war
BLOCKING obstructing; shaping; angling tool
BLOCKISH like a blockhead
BLOCK-OUT defensive trick (baseball)
pb **BLOCK-TIN** pure tin
BLODWYTE penalty for bloodshedding

BLONCKET gray
md BLOOD-HOT body temperature
(37°C/98.6°F)
BLOODIED stained with gore
BLOODILY sanguinely
BLOODING fox-hunting rite
BLOOD-RED a gory hue
BLOOD-TAX conscription
BLOOD-WON dearly bought
BLOOMERS garments; blunders
BLOOMERY forge for smelted iron
BLOOMING flourishing
BLOSSOMY full of blossom
BLOTCHED pimpled; maculose
BLOTTING drying-up; leaving
smudges
bt BLOWBALL dandelion head
zo, gl BLOWHOLE a whale's nostril; vent in
cavern roof with fountain
BLOWLAMP intense local-heat
apparatus
BLOWMILK skim-milk
BLOWPIPE a tube; blow-gun
BLUDGEON truncheon; heavy stick
BLUDGEON to assault with violence
BLUE-BACK the field-fare
zo BLUEBIRD dreambird; warbler (Am.)
BLUE-BOOK Parliamentary report
BLUECOAT Christ's Hospital
schoolboy
BLUE-EYED innocent; promising
zo BLUE-FISH mackerel
BLUE-FUNK alarm and despondency
BLUEGILL common Amer. sunfish
lw BLUEGOWN King's bedesman,
almsman
BLUEJOHN decorative fluorspar
BLUENESS of colour; of
despondency
zo BLUENOSE Nova Scotian whale
md BLUE-PILL mercurial pill
zo BLUE-POLL salmon type
zo BLUE-WING a duck
BLUFFEST most outspoken
BLUFFING acting deceptively
BLUISHLY rather blue
BLUNGING puddling clay
BLUNTING dulling; benumbing
BLUNTISH not sharp
BLURRING indistinct; confusion
BLURTING uttering hastily
BLUSHFUL modest
BLUSHING flushing; reddening,
milky effect; lacquer
BLUSTERY stormy
nt BOARDING embarking; lodging
zo BOARFISH red and silver fish
BOASTFUL vaunting

BOASTING bragging; bucking;
crowing; stone surfacing
BOATABLE navigable
zo BOATBILL a heron
to, nt BOATHOOK grasping pole
ga, nt BOATRACE oars, sailing contest
BOATROPE a painter
BOBBINET netted lace
zo BOBOLINK the rice-bird
BOBOLYNE fool (16th c.)
zo BOB-WHITE American partridge
br BOCK-BEER dark beer
zo BOCKELET a hawk
lw BOCKLAND freehold land
BODEMENT a presentiment
BODILESS incorporeal
BODLEIAN (Oxford Library)
BODY-LINE bowling at batsman;
(penalty); (cricket)
zo BODY-WALL perivisceral cavity wall
bt, ck BOGBERRY cranberry
mn BOG-EARTH peat
BOGEYISM frightfulness
BOGEYMAN hobgoblin
BOGGLING wavering; havering
bt BOG-WHORT whortleberry
BOHEMIAN unconventional
BOISERIE wood panelling (Fr.)
BOLD-FACE brazen
BOLDNESS courage; audacity
BOLIVIAN (Bolivia)
zo BOLL-WORM cotton-worm; weevil
nt BOLT-BOAT cobble
BOLT-HEAD a matrass
BOLT-HOLE escape hole
nt BOLT-ROPE rope round sail
nt BOMBARDA a polacre brigantine (It.)
mu BOMBARDA euphonium (brass band)
mu BOMBARDE organ stop (16 ft)
BOMB-FREE no raiders
ch BOMBIATE a bombic salt
pr BOM-PROOF book-club advance copy
BONA-FIDE in good faith
BONDAGER helpful event
lw BOND-DEBT bond-held debt
BONDMAID slave
lw BONDSMAN surety; bondman
md BONEACHE a pain
BONECAVE (prehistoric bones)
ag BONEDUST fertiliser
BONE-IDLE a good-for-nothing;
shirker
BONE-LACE bobbin-lace
BONELESS spineless
BONHOMIE geniality
BONIFACE an innkeeper
BONING-IN peg-lining
BONNETED with hat or hood

BONSENSE opposite of nonsense
BONSPIEL curling match
zo **BONTEBOK** S. African antelope
BOOBYHUT covered sleigh
BOOBYISH idiotic
BOOBYISM stupidity
BOOHOOED lamented loudly
BOOKCASE shelved case
BOOK-CLUB literary association
BOOK-DEBT outstanding account
BOOKLESS unlearned
BOOKMARK book-marker
BOOKMATE schoolfellow
BOOKNAME nonce name
BOOK-OATH Bible oath
BOOK-REST bed or table lectern
BOOKSHOP voluminous emporium
BOOKWORM avid reader
BOOSTING advertising, pushing
BOOTHOSE spats
BOOTIKIN leggings
BOOTJACK a boot remover
BOOTLACE shoestrings
BOOTLAST boot/shoe makers' model
BOOTLESS unavailing; barefoot
BOOTLICK a lickspittle
BOOT-TREE (for a shapely boot)
BORACHIO leather wine bag
ch **BORACITE** magnesium borate
BORDEAUX claret
BORDERED edged
BORDERER border dweller
lw **BORDLAND** reserved domain land
BORD-LODE timber carrying
bt **BORECOLE** winter cabbage
BOREHOLE geological research site;
   (well); (irrigation); (oil)
zo **BOREWORM** teredo
BORROWED assumed; hypothesized
BORROWER cadger
go **BORSTALL** hill road
bt **BOTANIST** plant studier
BOTANIZE pick flowers
BOTCHERY patchwork
BOTCHING clumsy repair work
BOTHERED plagued
ck **BOTTLING** preserving; storing in a
   bottle
nt **BOTTOMED** constructed (keels);
   butted; fathomed
BOTTOMRY loan secured by ship
md **BOTULISM** form of poisoning
BOUDERIE pouting; petulance
BOUDEUSE sofa with adjustable
   back-rest
BOUFFANT puffed out
ck **BOUILLON** broth; soup
BOUNCING resilient; fraud (of

cheques); playing ball down
   (netball)
BOUNDARY limit; (cricket)
BOUNDING leaping; bordering
bt **BOUNTREE BOURTREE**, the elder
tx **BOURETTE** tufted waste-silk yarn
bt **BOURTREE** the elder
BOUTIQUE trendy fashionable shop
mu **BOUZOUKI** Greek mandolin
BOVIFORM ox-like
BOW-BRACE archer's string-guard
BOW-DRILL rotary drill
nt **BOW-GRACE** a fender
BOWINGLY subserviently;
   courteously
nt **BOW-PIECE** bow-chaser; (gun)
BOWSIGHT adjustable aimer
   (archery)
nt **BOWSPRIT** a spar forward beyond
   the bows
BOX-DRAIN enclosed drain
bt **BOX-ELDER** ash-leaved maple
el **BOX-FRAME** 1-piece traction-motor
   frame
BOX-LOBBY passage in theatre
bd **BOX-PLATE** web-plate steel
BOX-PLEAT a double fold
bt **BOX-THORN** a shrub
BOYISHLY puerilely
BOY'S-PLAY a prank; trifling
zo **BRACCATE** with feathered feet
BRACELET a handcuff; ornament
BRACHIAL belonging to the arm
BRACKISH somewhat salt (of water)
bt **BRACTEAL** leaf formation
BRADBURY £1 note (obs.)
BRADSHAW railway guide
BRADYPOD a sloth
nt **BRAGAGNA** felucca, Adriatic
BRAGGART boaster
BRAGGING vaunting
nt **BRAGOZZI** luggers, Venice
BRAIDING plaiting; (ribbon); (sword)
BRAIDISM hypnotism
nt **BRAILING** hauling in; trussing
BRAIN-FAG nervous exhaustion
BRAINING dashing out the brains
BRAINISH brain-sick; furious
md **BRAINPAN** part of the skull
ck **BRAISING** a form of cookery
rw **BRAKE-MAN** a controller;
   (bobsledding)
rw **BRAKE-VAN** the guard's domain
BRAMBLED overgrown
BRANCARD horse-borne litter; float;
   platform vehicle
BRANCHED forked; ramified
zo **BRANCHER** young bird

BRANDIED laced with brandy
BRANDING stigmatizing; marking
BRANDISE a trivet
BRANDISH flourish; wave; shake
BRAND-NEW unused; branded
BRANGLED wrangled
zo BRANTAIL the redstart; a warbler
zo BRANT-FOX a kind of small fox
BRASSAGE cost of mintage
BRASSARD an armlet
BRASSART arm armour
BRASS-HAT big-wig; officer
bt BRASSICA the cabbage genus
bt BRASSOCK field mustard
BRATLING small brat; youngster
bd BRATTICE BRETTICE, (partition)
ch BRAUNITE manganese oxide
BRAWLING drunken disorder
BRAZENED shameless
BRAZENLY impudently; boldly
BRAZENRY effrontery
bt BRAZILIN a red dye
BREACHED violated; (pact); tore
open
BREACHES gaps; pact-violations
bt BREAD-NUT a fruit
BREAKAGE rupture; fracture
BREAKING smashing; infringing
BREAK-OUT escape; epidemic; war;
molten metal
nt BREAK-OUT canoeing off course
BREAKVOW a perjurer
BREAMING cleaning ship's bottom
BREASTED confronted
BREATHED exhaled; respired
BREATHER a respite
BREECHED put into trousers
BREECHES pantaloons
ps BREEDING lineage; begetting;
nuclear transformation
cn BREEZING of unclear photo image
BRELOGUE watch-chain ornament
BRENNAGE an ancient tribute
zo BREPHNIC neanic; of adolescent
period
BRETHREN brotherly group; kindred
bd BRETTICE BRATTICE, partition
BREVETCY nominal rank
rl BREVIARY prayer-book, R.C.
lw BREVIATE epitome; a brief
zo BREVIPED short-legged
zo BREVIPEN short-winged
BREWSTER brewer; maltster
BRIAREAN many handed
BRIBABLE venal; corrupt
BRICK-AXE 2-bladed brick-dressing
axe
BRICKBAT half-a-brick (thrown)

BRICKING building; wrecking
BRICK-RED dark orange-red
BRICK-TEA tea in blocks
BRIDE-ALE ale at a marriage
BRIDE-BED marriage-bed
mo BRIDGING joining up; loan; rock
chimney climbing technique
BRIDLING controlling; scorning;
ruffling
BRIEFING giving final instructions
BRIEFMAN brief compiler
BRIGADED combined
BRIGHTEN clarify; illumine
BRIGHTLY brilliantly
BRIGUING canvassing
BRIMLESS rimless
BRIMMING full; verging
mu BRINDISI It. toast; drinking song
BRINDLED streaky brown
BRINEPAN BRINEPIT, salt extraction
by evaporation
BRINGING conveying; fetching
BRISANCE shattering effect
BRISKING quickening
BRISKISH rather spry
zo BRISLING small sardine or sprat
BRISTLED ruffled
ck BRITTLED (cooking venison)
BROACHED pierced
BROACHER first proposer
to BROAD-AXE heavy axe
BROADEST vastest; amplest
BROADISH rather broad
BROCADED embroidered
BROCATEL coarse brocade
bt, ck BROCCOLI green cauliflower
BROCHURE pamphlet; leaflet
BRODEKIN buskin; half-boot
ck BROILING grilling
BROKENLY disconnectedly
BROKERLY mean (of brokers)
bt BROMELIA the pineapple
ch BROMELIN proteolytic enzyme
md BROMIDIC dull; calming
ch BROMIZED made to smell
pl BRONCHIC (windpipe)
BRONZIFY make into bronze
pt BRONZING metallic-lustre-giving
mn BRONZITE lustrous diallage
BROODING pondering; incubating
zo BROOD-SAC cockroach egg chamber
BROOKING bearing; enduring
mn BROOKITE crystalline titanium oxide
BROOKLET streamlet
BROOMING sweeping; breaming
ce BROTHERS male siblings; rope or
chain sling
BROUGHAM one-horsed carriage

BROUHAHA fuss and bother
BROWBEAT bully; overbear; haze
BROWLESS shameless
BROWNING tanning; rifle
mu **BROWNING** song variations
BROWNISH somewhat sunburnt
rl **BROWNIST** Congregationalist (now URC)
BROW-POST a main beam
BROWSICK dejected; melancholy
BROWSING grazing; casual reading
BRUISING inflicting tissue injury
BRUMAIRE November (Fr. Rev. cal.)
BRUNETTE dark hair and eyes
el **BRUSH-BOX** brush-holding container
BRUSHING sweeping, skirmishing; brisk
BRUSH-OFF curt rebuff; (lacrosse)
BRUSSELS (carpets); (sprouts)
BRUSTLED crackled; bullied
BRUTALLY ferociously; ruthlessly
BRYOLOGY study of mosses
ch **BRYONINE** extract of bryony
BUBBLING boiling; frothing; cheating
bd **BUBBLING** surface film effect (defect)
ck **BUCCANED** (smoked meat)
BUCCINAL like a trumpet
zo **BUCCINUM** a whelk
fr **BUCHERON** Canadian forest worker
bt **BUCKBEAN** a water-plant
mt **BUCKETED** rode or rained furiously
zo **BUCKHORN** deer horn
BUCK-JUMP quick plunging leap
BUCKLING curling; fastening
ck **BUCKLING** pickled fish
bt **BUCKMAST** beech-mast
ag **BUCKRAKE** tractor transport attachment
BUCKSHEE gratuity; commission; free
BUCKSHOT large shot
BUCKSKIN soft yellow leather
BUCRANIA ornamental ox-skulls
rl **BUDDHISM BUDDHIST**, religion founded by Sakyamuni *c*.500 BC
BUDDLING ore washing
BUDGEREE good (Australian)
BUDGETED made provision
BUFFCOAT a jacket (former regiment)
BUFFERED cushioned; shielded
BUFFETED struck; clouted
mn **BUFONITE** toadstone
BUHL-WORK inlaid tortoiseshell
BUILDING erecting; pile; structure
BULGARIC Bulgarian

BULKHEAD water-tight wall in ships; water tank cover
nc **BULK-TEST** radiation test sample
BULL-BEEF coarse beef
zo **BULL-CALF** male calf
BULLDOZE to raze; intimidate; coerce
BULLETIN official report
zo **BULL-FROG** North American frog
rw **BULLHEAD** rail-type
ar **BULLNOSE** rounded edge
BULLRING Spanish arena
BULL'S-EYE glass window; sweet
bt **BULLWEED** knap-weed
bt **BULLWORT** bishop's-weed
BULLYING BULLYISM, browbeating; tormenting
BULLYRAG BALLYRAG, to badger; intimidate
bt **BULRUSHY** full of rushes
zo **BUMMALOE** Bombay duck (fish)
BUMMAREE fish vendor; money-lender
nc **BUNCHING** clustering; grouping; velocity modulation
BUNDLING hurrying; packaging
BUNDLING offering intimate hospitality
BUN-FIGHT tea party
BUNGALOW one-storeyed house
BUNGHOLE hole in a cask
BUNGLING awkward; clumsy
BUNGVENT spile-hole in bung
BUNKERED coaled; in difficulties
md **BUNODONT** a dental malady
nt **BUNTLINE** a sheet
nt **BUOYANCY** specific lightness; floatability
BURBERRY a waterproof
BURDENED laden; overloaded
BURGANET BURGONET, Burgundian helmet
BURGLARY felony at night
BURGLING stealing; robbing
BURGRAVE German governor
BURGUNDY French wine
BURINIST engraver
mu **BURLETTA** burlesque; comic operetta
BURNOOSE Arab cloak
bt **BURNT-EAR** corn-disease
BURROWED excavated; tunnelled
BURROWER a rabbit
nt **BURR-PUMP** large pump
md **BURSALIS** a muscle
md **BURSITIS** bursa inflammation
BURSTING exploding; rending
zo **BUSH-BABY** night-ape (S. Africa)
BUSH-BRED reared in back country
zo **BUSHBUCK** antelope (S. Africa)

BUSHELER a clothes-repairer (USA)
bt BUSH-ROPE a liana; a creeper
BUSH-VELD bush country (S. Africa)
BUSINESS stage-craft; occupation; commerce
BUSKINED booted
BUSYBODY officious person
BUSYLESS being idle
BUSYNESS state of being busy
BUTCHERY slaughter; massacre
BUTCHING being tough; lesbian
ck,ga BUTTERED of teacake; missed a catch
to BUTTERIS BUTTRICE, farrier's (horse-shoeing) knife
BUTTONED fastened
ar,bd BUTTRESS extra wall, roof support
ch BUTYRATE salt of butyric acid
ck BUTYROUS buttery; oleaginous; greasy
BUZKASHI equestrian team game (Japan)
BY-BIDDER auction-bid encourager
BYCOCKET peaked cap (15th cent.)
BY-CORNER odd corner
BY-DESIGN spin off
nt BY-LANDER BILANDER, coastal hoy (ship)
BY-MATTER something incidental
BY-MOTIVE unavowed motive
BY-PASSED avoided
BYRONISM Lord Byron's phrase
BY-SPEECH casual speech
BY-STREET side street
BY-STROKE sly stroke
BY-THE-BYE by the way

C

bt,fr CAATINGA thorn forest of N.E. Brazil
CABALISM CABALIST, of cliques in politics
CABALLED CABALLER, intrigue of schemers
CABBAGED filched; purloined; stole
CABBLING smashing into small pieces
CABIN-BOY waits on ship's passengers
nt CABINING allotting cabins; sorting in groups
CABIRIAN fire-worshipper (Lemnos)
rw CABLE-WAY funicular railway; rope-linked
hd CABOCHED CABOSHED, neck-less head
CABOCHON gem without facets

CABOODLE the whole lot
CABOTAGE coasting trade
CABRIOLE leap; furniture
CAB-STAND taxi rank
zo CACHALOT the sperm whale
md CACHEMIC unhealthy
CACHEPOT ornamental flower-pot cover
CACHESEX miniwear for beach
md CACHEXIA severe emaciation
mu CACHUCHA Spanish dance
md CACHUNDE aromatic medicine
zo CACKEREL a species of fish
CACKLING gossiping; chattering; (hens)
CACODOXY erroneous opinion
CACOLOGY bad pronunciation
pc CACOSMIA aversion to smells
CADASTRE a survey of land
mu CADENCED modulated; rhythmical
bt CADILLAC a pear; motor car
CADUCEUS Mercury's wand
CADUCITY frailty; transitoriness
bt CADUCOUS early falling (leaves)
CAERLEON King Arthur's residence
CAESIOUS blue-grey
CAESURAL (metric pause)
ch CAFFEINE coffee alkaloid
CAGELING a bird in a cage
CAJOLERY persuading; coaxing
CAKESHOP (confectionery)
mu CAKE-WALK pre-ragtime plantation dance (USA)
bt CALABASH gourd
bt CALADIUM plant genus
zo CALAMARY cuttlefish, squid
bt CALAMBAC aloes-wood
mn CALAMINE zinc ore
bt CALAMINT aromatic plant
mn CALAMITE tremolite
CALAMITY disaster; affliction
zo CALANDER a lark
zo CALANDRA grain-weevil
zo CALANGAY white cockatoo
CALATHUS work-basket
CALCEATE shod; to shoe
mn CALCEDON opaline quartz
CALCINED reduced to quick-lime
CALCINER high-temperature heat device
mn CALC-SPAR calcite
mn CALC-TUFF a limestone
bd,me CALCULON size of brick
ma CALCULUS mathematical system
CALENDAR almanac; roster list
CALENDER hot-rolling machine
CALFLESS spindle-shanked
CALF-LOVE an early attachment

CALF-SKIN binding leather
CALIBRED bored; gauged
CALIDITY warmth; fervency; ardency
CALIDUCT a heating pipe
rl **CALIFATE CALIPHATE**, Islamic
  rulership
CALIPASH calipee; green turtle fat
me **CALIPPIC** (Metonic cycles)
bt **CALISAYA** Peruvian bark
rl **CALIXTIN** Hussite
mn **CALLAITE** turquoise
zo **CALL-BIRD** a decoy
CALL-GIRL prostitute
mu **CALLIOPE** muse of epic poetry;
  organ
to **CALLIPER** a measuring device
CALL-LOAN cash on demand
CALL-NOTE bird-call
pl **CALLOSUM** left-right brain link
md **CALLOUSE** wart; hardening of skin
CALL-OVER a roll-call; betting odds
  on horses
CALMNESS placidity; tranquillity
CALORIST a heat theorist
ml **CALORIZE** aluminium-spray steel
  surfaces
CALOTYPE talbot-type
bt **CALTROPS** a plant
ps **CALUTRON** electromagnetic separator
  of images
CALVERED crimped; pickled
bt **CALVILLE** an apple
bt **CALYCINE** cuplike
zo **CALYCOID** cup-like animal structure
zo **CALYMENE** trilobite genus
bt **CALYPTRA** a covering
bt **CAMASSIA** kind of hyacinth
CAMATINA acorns for tanning
CAMBERED slightly arched
mu **CAMBIATA** changed, device in
  counterpoint (It.)
ch **CAMBOGIA** gamboge gum
gl **CAMBRIAN** Welsh; era
CAMELEER camel driver
zo **CAMELEON** chameleon
CAMELINE camlet; camel hair
CAMELISH obstinate
bt **CAMELLIA** an evergreen
ar **CAMERATE** to build arch shape
tx **CAMISADE CAMISADO**, night attack
  with white shirts over armour
tx **CAMISOLE** short bodice (fem.
  underwear)
rl **CAMISTER** a clergyman
bt, ck **CAMOMILE** soothing herbal flowers
CAMPAIGN military operation; the
  countryside
CAMP-FIRE for outdoor warmth

ch **CAMPHENE** camphine; camphor
CAMP-SHOT a pile revetment
au **CAM-SHAFT** pan of machinery
CAMSTONE whitening for doorsteps
CAM-WHEEL off-centric oval
  mechanism
CANADIAN Canuck
bt **CANAIGRE** Texan dock (plant)
ce, cp **CANALIZE** make into a canal; direct
  flow
CANARESE natives of Canara
mu **CANARIES** triple tune, old dance
bt **CANASTER** a kind of tobacco
rl **CANCELLI CANCELLO**, lattice-work in
  choir, chancel, of church
zo **CANCRINE** crab-like
md **CANCROID** like cancer
CANDIDLY frankly; sincerely; naively
CANDYING preserving in sugar
CANE-HOLE trench for sugar canes
CANE-MILL sugar crushing mill
CANEPHOR basket-bearing figure
CANEWARE yellowish stoneware
  dishes
CANICULA the dog-star; Sirius
CANISTER a tin; tea chest; case-shot
md **CANITIES** whiteness of the hair
CANKERED corroded; infected
ch **CANNABIN** cannabic extract
bt **CANNABIS** hemp; bhang
CANNIBAL anthropophagite
CANNIKIN pannikin; a billy
CANNONED (billiards); collided
CANNULAR tubular
CANOEIST canoe paddler
CANON-BIT cannon-bit; (horse-bit)
rl **CANONESS** lady canon; a beneficiary
rl **CANONIST** ecclesiastical expert
rl **CANONIZE** besaint
lw, rl **CANON-LAW** ecclesiastical law
CANOODLE caress; fondle
CANOPIED with an awning
CANOROUS tuneful; musical;
  melodious
CANTERED galloped easily
to **CANTHOOK** lumberman's lever
rl **CANTICLE CANTICUM**, chant or song
bd **CANTLING** brick-firing course
CANTONAL referring to a district
CANTONED divided into cantons
rl **CANTORIS** of the precentor
CANZONET air or song
CAPACITY volume; capability;
  faculty; motor power in terms of
  cylinder size
CAPE-CART two-wheeled vehicle
  (SA)
md **CAPELINE** bandage; lady's wrap

CAPELLET enlarged hock
CAPERING frolicsome frisking
bt CAPER-TEA black tea
zo CAPIBARA CAPYBARA, Brazilian
rodent
CAPITANO a head-man
bt CAPITATE growing to a head
CAPONIER gallery in a fort
CAPONISE castrate; geld; emasculate
CAPOTING winning all tricks at
piquet
CAP-PAPER wrapping or writing
paper
CAPRIOLE equestrian jump
CAPRIPED goat-footed
ch CAPROATE a butyric salt
ch CAPRYLIC normal; acidic
eg CAP-SCREW nutless screw-bolt
bt CAPSICUM red pepper; chilli
mn, bd CAPSTONE fossil sea-urchin; a
coping, wall ridge
CAPSULAR in capsule form
CAPTIOUS hypercritical; censorious
CAPTURED caught; arrested
CAPUCCIO a hood or cowl
rl CAPUCHIN CAPUCINE, hooded cloak
zo CAPUCINE hooden monkey; pigeon
CARABINI CARBINES, short rifle
zo CARACARA Brazilian carrion-hawk
ar CARACOLE spiral staircase
zo CARACOLE equestrian turn; shell
CARACOLY alloy of gold and silver
nt CARACORE patrol sail boat,
Indonesia
zo CARAPACE tortoise shell; etc.
bt CARAP-OIL crab-wood oil
nt CARAVELA CARAVELLE, CARAVEL,
CARVEL, lateen; atlantic rig (Sp.,
Port.)
ch CARBOLIC phenol
CARBOLOY carbide alloy for cutting
tools
ch CARBONIC of carbon
ch CARBONYL metal/carbon-monoxide
product
CARBURET impregnant with carbon
CARCAJOU wolverine or glutton
CARCANET collar of jewels
bt CARDAMOM aromatic spice (India)
CARD-CASE a receptacle
CARDIACE heart-shaped jewel
CARDIGAN knitted woollen jacket
rl CARDINAL member of Vatican
Council
rl CARDINAL principal; short cloak
CARDIOID heart-shaped curve
md CARDITIS inflammation of heart
nt CAREENED laid on one side

CAREENED caressed; fondled
CAREERED raced; rushed; dashed
CAREFREE joyous
CARELESS heedless; remiss;
incautious
CARESSED fondled; embraced;
petted
CAREWORN grief-stricken
zo CARGOOSE crested grebe
zo CARIACOU Virginian deer
CARIBBEE a Caribbean
bt CARICOUS like a fig
mu CARILLON a unit (ringing) of church
bells
bt CARINATE keel-shaped
bt CARL-HEMP female hemp plant
CARNAGED slaughtered; butchered
CARNALLY of the flesh; sensuously
bt CARNAUBA Brazilian palm
CARNEOUS fleshly
CARNIFEX public executioner
CARNIVAL revelry; masquerade
CAROLINE time of King Charles
mu CAROLLED sung (as choral group)
me CAROTEEL East Indian weight
CAROTENE vitamin A
CAROUSAL CAROUSED, feasted,
drunkenly; held orgies, noisily
CAROUSEL tournament; tourney
CAROUSER a reveller
CARPETED a covered floor; rebuked
CARRIAGE passenger coach;
deportment
CARRIERS hauliers; containers
CARRIOLE open carriage; sledge
CARRYING transporting; conveying
CART-LOAD a measure of capacity
rl CARTOUCH CARTOUCHE, hieroglyph
(Eg.)
CARUCAGE tax on ploughs
CARUCATE (plough-land)
md, bt CARUNCLE CARBUNCLE, fleshy
excrescence; wart; outgrowth on
seeds
CARYATIC (Caryatides)
ar, rl CARYATID a lady supporter (ancient
Gr.)
bt CARYOKAR butter-nut tree
ck CASANOVA loves all; type of salad
CASCABEL swell on cannon's mouth
CASCADED fell in torrents
CASCALHO diamond-bearing earth
CASEMATE armoured chamber
CASEMENT hinged window
CASE-SHOT short range ammunition
zo CASE-WORM caddis-worm
CASHMERE silky goat's hair
CASKETED enshrined; coffined

mu **CASSETTE** container; reel of taped music

bt **CASS-WEED** shepherd's purse

bt **CASTANEA** chestnut-tree

CASTANET a chestnut-like dance clapper

CASTAWAY wrecked; rejected (Crusoe)

CAST-IRON rigid; inflexible

CASTLERY feudal castle control

CASTLING (chess)

CASTRATE geld; emasculate

mu **CASTRATO** high voiced singer

CASTWORK moulded parts of a silver object

CASUALLY by chance; fortuitously

CASUALTY of accident; death; wounded

CATACOMB cave sepulchre

ch **CATALASE** hydrogen-peroxide-decomposing enzyme

CATALYST CATALYSE, (unchanged substance assisting chemical action)

CATAPULT a pellet projector

md **CATARACT** waterfall; eye trouble

nt **CAT-BLOCK** anchor-tackle

CATCH-ALL general jumble container

bt **CATCHFLY** certain plants

CATCHING infectious; charming

CATCH-PIT sump; matter-retaining catchment

CATEGORY order; class; division

CATENARY like a chain

bt **CATENATE** chain-like

ma **CATENOID** catenary revolution surface

CATERESS lady provider

ck **CATERING** of food and entertainment

rl **CATHEDRA** bishop's throne

CATHETUS perpendicular line

CATHEXIS concentration of psychic energy

CATHISMA part of the psalter

el **CATHODAL** negative electrode

el **CATHODIC** produced by cathode reaction

rl **CATHOLIC** universal; liberal; Roman church

CATILINE daring conspirator

CATODONT teeth on lower jaw only

el **CATOLYTE** electrolyte next to cathode

CATONIAN resembling Cato; severe

CATOPSIS morbid keen-sightedness

bt **CAT'S-FOOT** ground ivy

bt **CAT'S-TAIL** the reed mace

CAT-STICK tip-cat's stick

CAUDATED having a tail; tailed

bt **CAUDICES** stems of trees

bt **CAUDICLE** an orchid stalk

CAUDILLO leader (Sp.)

ar, ck **CAULCOLE** Corinthian cabbage

ck **CAULDRON** bowl-shaped cooking pot

bt **CAULICLE CAUDICLE,** small stalk

nt **CAULKING** filling in cracks

CAUSALLY resultantly; productively

CAUSERIE gossip; small talk

CAUSEUSE settee for two

CAUSEWAY roadway over wet ground

CAUTIOUS wary; discreet; watchful

CAVALIER romantic; daring; royalist; beau; earth platform

mu **CAVATINA** short simple air

CAVATION excavation

lw **CAVEATED** warned by writ

lw **CAVEATOR** deliverer of writs

zo **CAVE-BEAR** extinct animal

CAVERNED hollowed out

CAVESSON horse-breaking appliance

zo **CAVICORN** hollow-horned

CAVILLED objected; carped; criticized

CAVILLER captious critic

CAVORTED pranced

bt **CELERIAC** turnip-rooted celery

CELERITY rapidity; swiftness; speed

CELIBACY the unmarried state

CELIBATE unwed

CELLARER wine steward; Simon

CELLARET small wine container; ornamented wooden chest

CELLULAR honeycombed; alveolated

CEMENTED glued; united; stuck

CEMETERY burial ground; necropolis

CENATION supping

rl **CENOBITE** religious order

CENOTAPH a monument; memorial

gl **CENOZOIC** era of mammals

CENSORED blue-pencilled

CENSURED reprimanded; rebuked

bt **CENTAURY** rose-pink flower

CENTERED localized

md **CENTESIS** puncturing a cavity

me **CENTIARE** a square metre

me **CENTIBAR** measurement of pressure

CENTOISM literary patchwork

CENTOIST platitudinarian

ce **CENTRING** football kick; temp. dome or arch support

CENTROID centre of gravity

CENTUPLE a hundredfold

CENTURIA division of 100 horsemen (Roman)

md **CEPHALGY** headache

md **CEPHALIC** remedy for head-pains
CEPHALIN phosphatide substance in brain
CERAMICS pottery
bt **CERASINE** plum gum
zo **CERASTES** a horned snake
mn **CERATITE** species of ammonite
CERATODE horny structure
CERATOID ceratose; horny
rl **CERBERUS** watch-dog of Hell
bt, ag **CEREALIA** of corn types and grasses
ch **CEREALIN** a bran extract
pc **CEREBRAL CEREBRIC**, of the brain; ingenious
CEREBRIN something in the brain
md **CEREBRUM** part of the brain
CEREMENT shroud dipped in wax
CEREMONY prescribed formality
el **CERESINE** refined ozocerite
bt **CERNUOUS** drooping
pg **CERTINAL** a phenol developer
CERULEAN sky-blue
CERULEIN olive-green
mn **CERUSITE** white lead
CERVELAT saveloy; pork-brain sausage
pl **CERVICAL** of the neck of womb
md **CESAREAN** childbirth by operation
CESSPOOL drainage pit; midden
md **CESTODES** tapeworm
zo **CETACEAN** whale or dolphin
bt **CETERACH** fern; cryptogam
zo **CETOLOGY** natural history of cetaceans
bt **CETRARIA** lichen; Iceland moss
mu **CHACONNE** slow courtly dance
CHADBAND a canting hypocrite
CHAFEWAX sealing-wax officer
CHAFFERY haggling; bargaining
CHAFFING bantering; scoffing
CHAFFRON horse armour
CHAINAGE measure of length or steel tape
CHAINING restraining; fettering
CHAINLET small chain
ag **CHAINMAN** survey team member; axeman (USA)
CHAIR-BED convertible contraption
CHAIRING carrying in triumph; (meeting)
CHAIRMAN president of meeting
CHALDAIC Babylonian
me, mn **CHALDRON CAULDRON**, 25 cwt (1270 kg) of coal; portable cauldron; truck-load in mines
CHALICED cup-like
bd **CHALKING** writing in chalk; break up of pigmented films

CHALKPIT a quarry
zo **CHALONIC** inhibitory, depressive
CHAMBREL horse's hind leg joint
CHAMFRON horse's head armour
CHAMORRO native; language (Guam, Marianas)
CHAMPFER bevelled angle on a surface
CHAMPING chewing; gnawing; biting
CHAMPION defender; hero; victor
lw **CHANCERY** court of justice (civil)
CHANCING risking; happening
CHANDLER candle-maker; supplies dealer
CHANFRIN fore-part of horse's head
CHANGE-UP let-up; slow pitch throw (baseball)
CHANGING altering; varying
rl **CHANTING** intoning; reciting; (choral)
ck **CHAPATTY CHUPATTY**, unleavened bread (Ind.)
CHAPBOOK book hawked by chapmen
CHAPELET stirrups and leathers
rl **CHAPELRY** chapel district
CHAPERON to escort (for single ladies)
ar **CHAPITER** capital of a column
rl **CHAPLAIN** a sky-pilot; padre; priest to service groups
fr **CHAPLASH** yellow-brown durable wood
CHAPLESS without a lower jaw
CHAPPING cleaving
ar **CHAPTREL** arch-supporting capital
CHARCOAL charred wood
CHARGING rushing; costing; enjoining
CHARISMA magnetic personality; grace
CHARLIES night watchmen
bt **CHARLOCK** wild mustard
CHARMING fascinating; captivating
CHARRING scorching; toasting
CHARTING mapping; recording; planning
CHARTISM CHARTIST, of suffrage reform
CHASSEUR light-armed soldier; (hunter)
CHASTELY virtuously; modestly
CHASTISE flog; castigate; discipline
CHASTITY sexual abstinence
rl **CHASUBLE** vestment over alb
CHATELET small castle
CHATONES ornamental nailhead
CHATTELS miscellaneous property

CHATTING friendly conversation
CHATWOOD fuel; ducal mansion
mu **CHAUNTER** note-piece (bagpipes)
CHAUSSES trunk-hose; leg-armour
bt **CHAY-ROOT** Indian red dye
CHEATERY fraud; deception
CHEATING knavery; duping; (card-sharper)
nt **CHEBACCO** fishing boat (N. America)
CHECHAKO tenderfoot (Alaska)
cp **CHECKBIT** binary check digit
CHECKERS a draughts game
CHECKING reproving; impeding
CHECKOUT departure formality
CHEEKING saucy behaviour
CHEEPING piping; chirping
CHEERFUL merry and bright
CHEERILY joyfully; gaily; blithely
CHEERING applause; comforting
zo **CHELIFER** book-scorpion
CHELLEAN early Palaeolithic
zo **CHELONIA** tortoises and turtles
ch **CHEMICAL** substance of chemistry
md **CHEMOSIS** eye-disease symptom
CHEMURGY applied organic chemistry
CHENILLE cord with short threads of silk, wool
CHERUBIC angelic
CHERUBIM a celestial spirit
zo **CHESHIRE** cheese; fading cat
CHESSMAN a piece in chess
CHESTING encasing; boxing
bt **CHESTNUT** old joke; conker
CHEVEREL CHEVERIL, kid-skin; flexible
CHEVERET small table (English)
mu **CHEVILLE** bridge of a violin
CHEVYING chasing, pursuing
CHIASMUS inverse parallelism
CHIASTIC crossed
CHICANED cheated; tricked
CHICANER a swindler; artful dodger
CHICKING hatching; sprouting (plants)
bt **CHICK-PEA** edible pealike seed
CHIEFAGE capitation; poll tax
lw **CHIEFRIE** small feudal rent
CHILD-BED in labour; confinement
CHILDISH puerile; infantile
CHILDREN family juniors; kids
CHILIASM doctrine of millennium
CHILIAST believer in that doctrine
CHILLIER cooler; colder
CHILLING discouraging; depressful; freezing; (damage); (wine)

CHILTERN (stewardship by the hundred)
CHIMAERA fabulous monster; illusion
zo **CHIMAERA** graft; hybrid; fish
CHIMERIC fanciful; delusive
CHINAMAN Chinese; left hander's googly (cricket)
CHINAMPA floating garden
CHIN-CHIN a toast
CHINKING jingling; tinkling sound
CHINOITE green mineral
CHINREST violin
vt **CHINSCAB** a sheep-disease
CHINSING caulking
zo **CHIPMUCK CHIPMUNK**, ground-squirrel
CHIPPING chaffing; chopping; fracturing
CHIPSHOT golf
md **CHIRAGRA** gout in the hands
CHIRPING cheeping
CHIRRING cooing; curring; purring
CHIT-CHAT small talk
CHIVALRY gallantry
md **CHLOASMA** a skin disease
ch **CHLORATE** salt of chloric acid
ch **CHLORIDE** compound of chlorine
ch **CHLORINE** a yellow gas
mn **CHLORITE** olive-green mineral
ch **CHLOROID CHLOROUS**, of chlorine
zo **CHOANATA** vertebrates; (nasal-oral)
mn **CHOANITE** fossil sponge
CHOICELY discriminately; exquisitely
rl **CHOIR-BOY** in church choir
CHOIRING singing in unison
CHOLERIC irascible; testy; petulant
CHOLIAMB iambic metre
md **CHONDRAL** cartilaginous
md **CHONDRIN** gelatinous liquid
CHOOSING selecting; picking
CHOP-CHOP hurry; (army)
CHOPNESS kind of spade
CHOPPING and changing; veering; cutting with axe; shortening stride (running)
ck **CHOP-SUEY** a succulent Chinese dish
mu **CHORAGIC CHORAGUS**, musical production
mu **CHORALLY** sung by choir or chorus
zo **CHORDATA** vertebrates, etc.
mu **CHORDING** stringing; time-spaced tonal effect
CHORIAMB iambic metre
bt **CHORISIS** separation
ag **C-HORIZON** soil level
CHORTLED chuckled loudly

CHORUSED concerted; in unison
CHOUSING swindling
ck, zo **CHOW-CHOW** ginger chutney;
    Chinese dog
ck **CHOW-MEIN** Chinese dish
CHRESARD plant water supply in
    earth
rl **CHRISMAL** (consecrated oil)
rl **CHRISTEN** baptize
ga **CHRISTIE CHRISTIANIA**, ski turn
CHRISTIE position for skateboard
    riding
ch **CHROMATE** salt of chromic acid
ch **CHROMIUM** a metallic element
bt **CHROMULE** colouring matter
ch **CHRYSENE** coal-tar component
CHTHONIC subterranean
CHUCKIES a game with pebbles
CHUCKING throwing; hurling; pat on
    chin
CHUCKLED laughed privately
CHUFFILY clownishly; churlishly
CHUMMAGE chamber-fellowship
CHUMMERY friendship; intimacy
CHUMMING sharing accommodation
CHUMMING ground bait for angling
CHUMP-END the buttocks; thick-end
CHURINGA Australian amulet
CHURLISH surly and sullen
CHURNING agitating; rotating;
    foaming
CHUTZPAH bold, impudent (Jew.)
md **CHYLIFIC** producing chyle
CHYMICAL chemical
ch **CHYMOSIN** gastric enzyme, rennin
CIBATION feeding
rl **CIBORIUM** eucharistic vessel
md **CICATRIX** a scar
CICERONE guide (tourism)
CICISBEI sword-knots
CICISBEO philanderer
CICURATE to tame
CIDER-CUP a beverage
CIDERIST cider-maker
CIDERKIN inferior cider
CILIATED with eyelashes
bt **CILIFORM** (fine filaments)
mu **CIMBALOM** Hung. concert dulcimer
CIMBRIAN a German tribe
mn **CIMOLITE** fuller's earth
cn **CINCHING** tightening roll of film
md **CINCHONA** Peruvian bark (quinine)
CINCTURE girdle; belt
CINDROUS ashy
cn **CINEFILM** moving-picture film
cn **CINERAMA** wide-screen film
CINERARY cindery
CINEREAL like ashes

CINGULUM band; zone; belt
mn **CINNABAR** dragon's blood
bt **CINNAMIC** cinnamon type
bt **CINNAMON** a spicy bark
CIPHERED written in code
CIRCAEAN infatuating (Circe)
as **CIRCINUS** the Compasses
    (constellation)
ae **CIRCLING** moving around in circles
CIRCUITY circuitous indirect
    approach
CIRCULAR round; printed leaflet
bt **CIRRHOSE CIRRHOUS**, terminating in
    a tendril or curl
zo **CIRRIPED** a barnacle
CISELEUR engraver; chaser
CISELURE chased metal-work
bt **CISTELLA** capsular shield
CISTVAEN stone tomb
CITATION mention in despatches
CITATORY citing; summoning
CITREOUS citric; lemon-flavoured
CITRININ bacteriostat
CITY-BRED raised in town
zo **CIVET-CAT** muskily perfumed
    carnivore
CIVETING scenting with civet
CIVILIAN non-military
CIVILIST civil law expert
CIVILITY politeness; courtesy
CIVILIZE reclaim from barbarism
CLACK-BOX valve container
CLACKING clicking; jabbering
ar **CLADDING** metal-surfacing coins;
    extra wall or roof surfaces; siding
    (USA)
bt **CLADONIA** reindeer moss
ml **CLAGGING** adhesion of blacking
CLAIMANT assertor of claims
CLAIMING demanding; arrogating
CLAMANCY urgency; exigency
ck **CLAM-BAKE** clam dish (Am.)
CLAMMING daubing; clogging;
    stickiness
CLAMPING fastening
mu **CLANGING** resounding; arousing
CLANGOUR din and noise; clamour
    (crowd)
CLANGOUS resonant
CLANKING metallic clashing noise
CLANNISH tribal; cliquish
CLANSHIP loyalty; sodality
CLANSMAN one of a clan
CLAP-DISH wooden platter
CLAPOTIS increasing pressure of
    larger waves breaking on sea wall
CLAPPING applauding; (–in jail)
CLAP-SILL frame of lock-gates

CLAP-TRAP speciosity; theatrical
CLAQUEUR hired applauder
CLARENCE four-wheeled cab
mu **CLARINET** reed instrument
mu **CLARSACH** Gaelic small Celtic harp
CLASHING colliding; jarring;
differing
CLASHING unmatching colours
CLASPING fastening; grasping;
hugging
eg **CLASP-NUT** split/lathe nut
CLASSIER superior; loftier; finer
CLASSIFY arrange; tabulate
CLASSING grading; grouping;
ranging
CLASSMAN a graduate
CLASS-WAR social enmity
(Marxism)
CLAUDIAN (Roman Emperors)
CLAUSURE closure; stoppage
CLAVATED with knobs on
mu **CLAVECIN** harpsichord
CLAVIARY index of keys
md **CLAVICLE** collar-bone
CLAVIGER clubman; key-man
CLAWBACK a sycophant
md **CLAW-FOOT** foot deformity
md **CLAW-HAND** hand deformity
CLAWLESS no claws
CLAWSICK foot-rot
CLAY-COLD lifeless
mn **CLAY-MARL** chalky clay
CLAY-MILL clay mixing mill
CLAYMORE Scottish broad-sword
bt **CLAYWEED** coltsfoot
eg **CLEADING** coffer dam; lock-gate
boarding
CLEANING washing; purifying;
clearing
CLEANISH rather clean
CLEANSED purged; purified
CLEANSER a detergent; purifier
CLEARAGE removal
CLEAR-CUT sharply outlined
CLEAREST plainest; purest
CLEARING meadow in forest;
banking
CLEARING emptying; tidying up
CLEAVAGE fracture; bosom;
separation
bt **CLEAVERS** goose-grass
CLEAVING splitting; riving
CLEAVING clinging; uniting;
adhering
zo **CLECKING** a brood; a clutch
bt **CLEMATIS** traveller's joy, etc.
CLEMENCY clemence; leniency;
mercy

CLENCHED clinched; gripped
CLERICAL priestly; secretarial
CLERKAGE clerical work
CLERKDOM babooism
CLERKERY accountancy
CLERKISH somewhat learned
mn **CLEVEITE** Norwegian pitchblende
CLEVERER more astute; abler
CLEVERLY dexterously; adroitly
CLICKING progressing satisfactorily
CLIENTAL dependent
CLIENTED supplied with clients
CLIMATIC due to climate
mo **CLIMBERS** undersurfaces for skis for
uphill; ascenders (social-)
CLIMBING scrambling; scaling
heights
CLINCHED CLENCHED, held fast;
agreed on
CLINCHER decisive reply
bt **CLINGING** embracing tenaciously
md **CLINICAL** casework; analytic
CLINKING jingling (coins, keys etc.)
CLIPPERS CLIPPING, trimming
(shearing) (toenails) (haircutting)
CLIQUISH CLIQUISM, clannish;
exclusiveness (interests)
ec, mt **CLISSERE** climate changes and
climaxes
zo **CLITELLA** bands of worms
bt **CLITHERS** burweed
CLITHRAL completely roofed
pl **CLITORIS** female erectile tissue
CLOAKAGE disguise; pretext
CLOAK-BAG portmanteau
CLOAKING hiding; veiling; screening
CLOCHARD tramp (Fr.)
CLOCKING checking in; timing
CLODDING clotting
CLODDISH boorish; rustic
CLODPATE dolt; blockhead
CLODPOOL dullard; clotpoll
CLOGGING coalescing; impeding
rl **CLOISTER** an ambulatory; veranda
CLOSE-CUT close-bodied; cropped
CLOSEOUT collapse of surfing wave
CLOSETED secluded
CLOTHIER cloth merchant; tailor
CLOTHING garments; dress; draping
CLOTPOLL CLODPATE, fathead; idiot
CLOTTING coagulating; curdling
CLOUDAGE cloudiness
CLOUDERY cloudage
CLOUDILY mistily
CLOUDING obscuring; dimming
CLOUDLET a little cloud
ar **CLOURING** chisel indentations on
walls

CLOUTING patching; buffeting; clothing
CLOVERED in clover
CLOWNERY buffoonery; burlesque
CLOWNING playing the fool; jesting
CLOWNISH ungainly; rude; boorish
CLOYLESS insatiable
CLOYMENT a surfeit; a glut
CLOYSOME palling
CLUBBING combining; bludgeoning
CLUBBISH rustic; congenial
CLUBBISM the club system
CLUBBIST frequenter of clubs
CLUB-FIST large heavy fist
md CLUBFOOT taliped
nt CLUBHAUL tacking
CLUB-LAND (Pall Mall, etc.)
bt CLUB-MOSS lycopodium
CLUB-ROOM a meeting room
bt CLUB-ROOT a plant disease
bt CLUB-RUSH bulrush
CLUCKING fowl hen-talk
CLUELESS without a trace
CLUMPING (bootmaking); bunching
CLUMSIER more awkward
CLUMSILY maladroitly
zo CLUPEOID like a herring
bt CLUSTERY in clusters or bunches
CLUTCHED caught; gripped; clasped
CLYFAKER a pickpocket
CLYPEATE like a shield; oscutate
COACHBOX driver's seat
zo COACH-DOG Dalmatian; (spotted)
COACHFUL full inside
COACHING tutoring; driving; training; racing
COACHMAN a coachee
COACTING alliance; working together
COACTION compulsion; coercion
COACTIVE working in unison
COAGENCY joint action
md COAGULUM a blood clot
cp, tc COALESCE merge; unite; amalgamate
zo COALFISH black-backed cod
COAL-HOLE small coal-cellar
COAL-MINE coal-pit
nt COAL-SHIP a collier
COALWORK a colliery
nt COAMINGS raised work
COARSELY crudely; churlishly
COARSEST roughest; grossest
COARSISH rather coarse
CO-ASSUME agree
nt COASTING of navigation; free wheeling
COAT-LINK two buttons and a link
COBALTIC rather blue
COBBLING shoe-repairing

mn COBCOALS cobbles
rl CO-BISHOP joint bishop
mn COBSTONE large rounded stone
COBWEBBY araneous
bt COCCAGEE cider apple
md COCCIDIA parasites
bt COCCULUS narcotic plant
COCHLEAN COCHLEAR, spiral (of seashell); twisted pattern
COCKADED with rosette (on hat) (vanity)
zo COCKATOO crested parrot
COCKAYNE cocaigne; land of plenty
COCK-BEAD hanging decorative bead; moulding on edges of drawer fronts
nt COCK-BILL (anchor-dropping)
nt COCK-BOAT cog; lifeboat; tender
COCK-CROW dawn
COCKERED pampered
zo COCKEREL young cock
md COCK-EYED asquint; crooked
COCKLING puckering; wrinkling
COCKLOFT top loft; (highest perch)
COCKSHOT COCK-SHY, random shot fired
COCK-SHUT eventide; twilight; curfew
COCKSPUR Virginian hawthorn
COCKSURE determinedly certain
zo COCKTAIL mixed (coloured) drink; beetle
bt COCOA-NUT seed of cacao (chocolate) tree
COCOBOLO hard wood used for knife handles
bt, ck COCOYAMS product of Ghana
COCTIBLE able to be cooked
CODDCELL single electric cell
ck CODDLING pampering; indulging; (egg)
CODIFIED CODIFIER, systematized; sorted; a compiler; collator
tx CODPIECE Tudor genitals protector
nt CODSHEAD type of yacht
CO-EDITOR joint editor
COENZYME a fellow enzyme
COERCING compelling; curbing
COERCION force; constraint
COERCIVE repressive; compulsive
COESTATE union of estates
COEXPAND dilate simultaneously
COEXTEND march together
COFFERED COFFERER, packed in a box; sluice treasurer (safe-keeper)
COFFINED sealed; enclosed in box (funeral)
COGENTLY forcibly; potently

COGITATE ponder; meditate; ruminate
lw **COGNIZEE** fine receiver
lw **COGNIZOR** exacter of a fine
COGNOMEN the surname
lw **COGNOSCE** give judgment
lw **COGNOVIT** acceptance of claim
COGWHEEL spur-wheel
COHERENT connected; consistent; logical; comprehensible
COHERING adhering; uniting
COHESION congruity; adhesion
COHESIVE sticky; gummy
ch **COHOBATE** distil
COIFFEUR hairdresser
COIFFURE hairstyle; (wig)
COINCIDE happen simultaneously
CO-INHERE exist together
COINLESS impecunious; broke
COISTRIL a groom; see coystrel
COKE-OVEN coal carbonization process
COKERNUT coconut
COLANDER perforated bowl
COLATION filtration
COLATURE straining
COLDNESS frigidity
COLD-SETT Smith's chisel
COLDSHUT casting imperfection
pr **COLD-TYPE** printing
bt, ck **COLE-RAPE** kohlrabi; cabbage-turnip
bt **COLESEED** cabbage seed
COLESLAW cabbage salad
bt **COLEWORT** young cabbage
COLISEUM Roman ruin
ch **COLLAGEN** gelatine
ga **COLLAPSE** breakdown; subside; faint; fall; tactic
COLLARED pressed; caught
rl **COLLARED** necked shirt; band (dog-)
COLLARET small neck of garment; neck band
COLLATED collected; assembled
cp **COLLATOR** codifier; interpolator; verifier; assembler
COLLEGER Eton scholar
COLLETIC sticky; mucilaginous
COLLIDED crashed; encountered
COLLIERY coal-mine
COLLOGUE plot; confer
COLLOIDS the gummy sector of life (gelatin starch, paste); clay particles; smallest matter
COLLOQUY dialogue; conversation
COLLUDED acted in collusion
COLLUDER conspirator; plotter
COLLYING fouling
COLONIAL colonist

COLONIST a settler in the colonies
COLONIZE establish a colony
md **COLOPEXY** abdominal operation
COLOPHON publisher's tally mark
COLORATE coloured; dyed
bt **COLORINE** madder extract
COLOSSAL gigantic; titanic
COLOSSUS Apollo's statue
md **COLOTOMY** removal of colon
COLOURED specious; painted; tinged
COLSTAFF carrying pole
mn **COLUMBIC** containing niobium
COLUMNAR in columns
COLUMNED having pillars
COMATOSE lethargic; drowsy
COMATOUS sleepy; torpid
COMBINED united; coalesced
COMBINER a merger; blender
COMBLESS lacking comb or crest
COME-BACK repartee; return to fame
COMEDIAN actor; player; performer
COMEDIST writer of comedy
COME-DOWN humiliation; anti-climax
COMELILY attractively; gracefully
COMETARY planetarium; orrery
COMING-IN entrance; income
COMITIAL relating to assemblies
COMMANDO special raiding force
mu **COMMATIC** staccato; concise
COMMENCE initiate; begin; originate
COMMERCE barter; trade; traffic
COMMIXED blended; combined
COMMONED held in common
COMMONER not a nobleman
COMMONEY a playing-marble
COMMONLY usually; frequently
lw **COMMONTY** common land
COMMUNAL public
COMMUNED held private converse
COMMUTED exchanged; altered; bussed
COMMUTER season ticker holder
COMPAGES a complex structure
COMPARED likened
COMPETED strove; emulated
COMPILED amassed; composed; set in order
cp **COMPILER** literary hack; editor; computer program
COMPLAIN grumble; grouse; repine
COMPLETE ended; perfect; fulfil
COMPLICE to aid a crime
COMPLIED met; yielded; fulfilled
COMPLIER an active agent
rl **COMPLINE** evening service (Catholic)
hd **COMPONED** heraldic squares

COMPOSED calm; invented; produced

mu COMPOSER a creator; writer

mu COMPOSTO compounded; medley

COMPOUND combine; agree; mingle

COMPRESS abridge; condense; bandage

lw COMPRINT pirate

COMPRISE include; embrace; contain

COMPTOIR cash-desk

COMPUTED calculated; rated

COMPUTER actuary; reckoner

lw CONACRED sub-let

md CONARIAL CONARIUM, of the pineal gland

CONATION volition

CONATIVE endeavouring

CONCAUSE secondary cause

CONCAVED hollowed

CONCEDED granted; allowed; yielded

CONCEDER a donor; relinquisher

CONCEIVE imagine; think; fancy; plan

CONCEIVE become pregnant

mu CONCERTO orchestral work

CONCETTO a right merry conceit

mn CONCHITE fossil shell

CONCHOID shell-like curve

CONCLAVE synod; assembly; council

CONCLUDE close; terminate; infer

CONCOURS celebratory occasion; (fair)

CONCRETE not abstract; solid; cement

CONDENSE compress; solidify; shorten

CONDENSE steam change

ck CONDITED pickled; preserved

CONDOLED sympathized; commiserated

CONDONED pardoned; forgave

CONDUCED aided; led; promoted

CONE-GEAR variable-speed belt drive

CONFALON gonfalon; banneret

bt CONFERVA a seaweed

CONFETTI rice, petals thrown (wedding)

CONFIDED entrusted; hoped; relied

CONFIDER entruster of secrets

CONFINED limited; shut-up; restrained

CONFINED secluded for childbirth

CONFINER imprisoner

CONFLATE collect; assemble

CONFLICT combat; clash; discord

CONFOUND put to shame; refute; confuse

CONFRERE colleague; companion

CONFRONT to face a challenge

CONFUSED muddled disorder

CONFUTED overwhelmed by facts

CONGENER an affinity

CONGIARY Roman gift of wine

CONGRESS meeting for legislation etc.

CONGRESS representative assembly (Am.)

md CONICINE hemlock

CONICITY conicalness

bt CONIFERS (fir or pine) evergreens

CONIFORM conical

CONJOINT associated; connected

CONJUGAL matrimonial

CONJUNCT concurrent; united

lw CONJURED bound by oath; juggled

CONJURER CONJUROR, magician; juggler; wizard; marabout

mu CONJUSTO with gusto

CONNIVED overlooked; permitted

CONNIVER confidence man; accessory

CONNOTED included; implied

CONOIDAL almost conical

CONOIDIC conoidal

CONQUEST victory; subjugation

ck CONSERVE preserve; maintain

CONSIDER contemplate; regard; ponder

CONSOLED solaced; assuaged; cheered

CONSOLER a comforter; soother

CONSOMME clear soup

bt CONSOUND herb comfrey

CONSPIRE plot; intrigue; machinate

CONSTANT unchangeable; perpetual

CONSTRUE translate; interpret

CONSULAR Foreign Office service

CONSUMED eaten; used up; destroyed

CONSUMER customer; eater

lw CONTEMPT disdain; scorn; (–of court)

CONTENTS materials contained (written)

CONTINUE endure; extend; persist

mu CONTINUO harmonized keyboard accompaniment

pr CONTLINE intervening space

CONTRACT agreement; abridge

mt CONTRAIL condensation trail

CONTRARY otherwise; opposite

cp, el, pg CONTRAST difference; clash; comparison

CONTRITE penitent; repentant; humble

CONTRIVE bring about; scheme
CONTUSED bruised; crushed; knocked
CONUSANT knowing; cognizable
CONVENED called together; gathered
CONVENER summoner
CONVERGE approach; incline
CONVERSE talk; parley; reciprocal
CONVEXED vaulted
CONVEXLY in convex form
CONVEYED delivered; imparted
CONVEYER mechanical moving belt
CONVEYOR carrier (haulage)
CONVINCE persuade; satisfy; prove
CONVOKED convened; mustered
CONVOLVE roll together
CONVOYED escorted; guarded
CONVULSE writhe; agitate; perturb
CONY-SKIN rabbit-skin
CONY-WOOL rabbit's fur
mt COOEEING hailing in Australia
ck COOK-ROOM cook-house
ck COOK-SHOP eating-house
COOLNESS indifference; frigidity
COOPERED barrels constructed, repaired
CO-OPTING adding to a committee
CO-OPTION without election
zo COPEPODA water-boatmen; crustacea
md COPHOSIS deafness
COPHOUSE tool-house
md COPOPSIA eye-strain
ch COPPERAS sulphate of iron
COPPERED covered with copper
COPULATE unite; couple; mate
COPYBOOK exercise book; example
lw COPYHOLD land held under manorial records
COQUETRY flirtation; philandery
COQUETTE courtesan; jilt
COQUILLE conch-shaped guard of epée (fencing)
mn CORACITE uraninite
CORACOID like a crow's beak
CORANACH a dirge
bt CORDATED heart-shaped
le CORDINER CORDWAINER, leather worker (Sp.)
el, tc, cp CORDLESS without plug-in connection
le CORDOVAN CORDWAIN, goatskin leather of Cordoba (Spain)
tx CORDUROY ribbed cloth
CORD-WOOD firewood; tinder wood
CO-REGENT joint ruler
CORE-SAND linseed moulding mixture
CORK-SOLE inner shoe-sole

bt CORK-TREE cork-oak (quercus suber)
zo CORKWING a sea-fish
bt CORKWOOD balsawood (USA)
ck CORN-BALL pop-corn; maize
bt CORN-BIND convolvulus
ck CORNCAKE Indian meal cake
CORNEOUS horny
CORNERED brought to bay; controlled
CORNETCY rank of a cornet (army)
bt CORNFLAG gladiolus
CORNICLE a little horn
zo CORNICLE honeydew tube in aphids
CORNIFIC horn-producing
CORNLAND grain-land
CORNLOFT granary
ck CORNMEAL coarse maize flour
CORN-MILL a grinder; quern
bt CORN-MINT calamint
zo CORN-MOTH a pest
CORN-PIPE straw-pipe
ck CORN-PONE bread (Indian corn)
CORN-RENT rent paid in corn
CORNUTED with horns
CORN-WAIN farm-cart; (haywain)
nt COROCORE Malay boat
bt COROLLET a floret
CORONACH coranach; a lament
md CORONARY crown-shaped, heart artery
CORONATE crowned
ch CORONIUM gaseous element
zo CORONOID CORACOID, of a crow's beak
bt CORONULE downy tuft on seeds
CORPORAL bodily; material; an N.C.O.
rl CORPORAS fine linen
CORRIDOR passage-way; gallery
CORRODED eaten away; rusted; eroded
CORSELET corslet; leather cuirass
CORSICAN of Corsica; (Napoleon)
md, bt CORTICAL outer tissue (brain), bark (tree)
pm CORTISOL adrenal hormone extract
CORUNDUM emerald; ruby; sapphire
nt CORVETTE sloop; convoy escort; naval
CORYBANT priest of Cybele
CORYMBUS top-knot
mu CORYPHEE ballet-dancer
zo CORYSTES masked crab
COSECANT an inverse sine
lw COSENAGE COSINAGE, cousinhood; a writ
COSHERED pampered; coddled

COSHERER (free board and lodgings)
COSINESS snugness
COSMETIC a beautifier
COSMICAL relating to the universe
COSSETED petted; fondled; caressed
COSTATED ribbed
COST-BOOK account book
COST-FREE free of charge
COSTLESS without price; free
COSTLIER more expensive; dearer
bt COSTMARY aromatic plant
COST-PLUS of contracts
COSTUMED garbed; dressed; robed
COSTUMER costumier; dressmaker
CO-SURETY joint security
COTCHELL privately sold timber
tx COTELINE ribbed muslin
lw CO-TENANT joint tenant
COTHOUSE a cottar's house
mu COTILLON cotillion; round dance
COTQUEAN a womanly man
zo COTSWOLD sheep
COTTABUS wine-throwing contest
COTTAGED covered with cottages
COTTAGER small holder
COTTONED attracted to; understood
COTYLOID cup-shaped
hd COUCHANT reclining
md COUCHING removing cataract
COUGHING a raucous noise
COULISSE theatrical side-scene
bt COUMARIC from Tonka beans
bt COUMARIN a scent
COUNTESS wife of earl or count
COUNTING reckoning; enumerating
COUNT-OUT adjournment; boxing
COUPELET cabriolet
mu, rw COUPLING linking; a link; mating
COURANTE French dance; a paper
mu COURANTO musical piece
COURSING racing; chasing; pursuing
lw COURT-DAY sessions-day
COURTESY polished manners
COURTIER courtesy personified
COURTING wooing; soliciting;
inviting
ck COUSCOUS a millet dish (N. Africa)
COUSINLY friendly
COUSINRY kin; relations
COUTILLE material for corsets
ch COVALENT bond: 1 electron to 2
atoms
lw, rl COVENANT contract; bond; pact
COVENTRY ostracism (sent to–)
COVERAGE protection; insurance
COVER-ALL an overlay; genital
protection
COVERCLE a lid

COVERING protecting; including; roof
COVERLET bed cover; counterpane
COVERLID coverlet
COVERTLY surreptitiously;
insidiously
COVETING acquisitiveness
COVETOUS avaricious; rapacious
COVINOUS collusive; fraudulent
COWARDLY timidly; cravenly
mu COWBELLS alpine percussion
bt COWBERRY whortleberry
COWERING crouching; cringing
bt COWGRASS meadow trefoil
COWHIDED whipped
COWHOUSE a byre; milking-shed
COW-LEECH cow doctor
(veterinerary)
CO-WORKER fellow toiler
zo COWPILOT West Indian fish
bt COWPLANT plant (Sri Lanka)
COW-THIEF a rustler
bt COW-WHEAT annual plant
md COXALGIA hip disease
COXINESS conceit; bumptiousness
nt COXSWAIN steersman; cox
COYSTREL COYSTRIL, COISTRAL, a
groom; a knave
COZENAGE deception; deceit; fraud
COZENING cheating; swindling
CRABBING peevish criticism;
grousing
bt CRABTREE crab-apple
bt CRABWOOD S. American tree
md CRAB-YAWS foot disease
CRACKING distilling, splitting
CRACK-JAW difficult to pronounce
CRACKLED crepitated
CRACKNEL a biscuit
CRACK-POT a maniac; crazy
CRACOWES pointed shoes
CRADLING timber framework; goal
pass (lacrosse)
CRAFTIER slyer; more cunning
CRAFTILY shrewdly; pawkily
CRAGSMAN rock-climber
CRAM-FULL no more room
CRAMMING stuffing; tutoring
CRAMOISY CRIMSON, CREMOSIN,
blood red
CRAMPING restraining; impeding
CRAMPONS mountaineering spiked
boots
zo CRANE-FLY daddy-longlegs
zo CRANIATE vertebrates with skull
CRANKING winding; turning; twisting
eg CRANK-PIN link; crank/connecting
rod
CRANNIED full of chinks

CRANNIES nooks; fissures
CRASHING blundering; clashing; colliding
CRATCHES mangers; swollen pastern
CRAVENLY cowardly
md **CRAW-CRAW** tropical skin disease
zo **CRAWFISH CRAYFISH**, langouste
CRAWLING on all fours; creeping; paint cracking, cissing
CRAWLWAY high duct, man-size
CRAYONED drawn with chalk
CRAZIEST maddest; most idiotic
CREAKING grating
CREAMERY milk-bar; dairy
CREAMING foaming; mantling
CREAM-NUT Brazil nut
CREAM-POT cosmetic container
CREASING folding
ck, md **CREATINE** gristle on meat; chemical in muscle
CREATING begetting; fashioning
CREATION the universe; cosmos; product
CREATIVE inventive; productive
CREATRIX a designing lady
CREATURE term of contempt
rl **CREDENCE** belief; credit; reliance; sacrament table
rl **CREDENDA** articles of faith
CREDENZA low cupboard on floor
CREDIBLE trustworthy; believable
CREDIBLY conceivably
CREDITED trusted; accepted
CREDITOR a lender; mortgagee
CREEPING crawling; cringing; stealing
CREMATED reduced to ashes
CREMATOR incinerator
CREMORNE French-window bolt
CREMOSIN crimson; cramoisy
CRENATED notched
CRENELET small loophole
CRENELLE arrow hole; loophole
CREOLIAN of CREOLES
ch, md **CREOSOTE** tar product; wood seasoning
CREPANCE brushing, grooming of horses
md **CREPITUS** lung-rattle
CRESCENT Turkish emblem; moon
CRESCIVE growing; increasing
CRESTING topping; surfing; decorating; coloured identity of arrow (archery)
CRETATED chalked
CRETONNE patterned cloth
nm **CREUTZER** Austrian copper coin
CREVASSE fissure in glacier

CREVICED rent; cracked; flawed
CRIBBAGE card game
CRIBBING shift lining; copying
CRIBBLED sifted; riddled
CRIBRATE perforated
CRIBROSE full of holes
ce **CRIB-WORK** a form of structure; bridge foundation
zo **CRICETUS** genus of rodents
CRIMEFUL criminal; wicked; culpable
lw **CRIMINAL** felon; convict; illegal
CRIMPAGE press-gang work
ck **CRIMPING** plaiting; pattern on pastry
CRIMPLED curled
CRINATED hairy
CRINGING fawning; crouching; servile
CRINKLED wrinkled; corrugated
CRIPPLED disabled; impaired;
- maimed
CRISPATE curly
CRISPING crimping; twisting; waving
CRISTATE crested; tufted
CRITERIA standards of judgement
bt **CRITHMUM** the samphire
CRITICAL crucial; fault-finding; serious
nc **CRITICAL** nuclear transformation; chain reaction
CRITIQUE literary notice
CROAKING woeful; sound (frogs)
CROCEOUS yellow; like saffron
CROCKERY earthenware
CROCKING blackening with soot
mn **CROCOITE** chromate of lead
ag **CROFTING** farming; hill-farming
CROMLECH ancient stone circle
mu **CROMORNA** organ-stop
CROODLED cowered
CROOKING bending; inflecting
mu **CROONING** warbling; chromatic singing
CROPPING harvesting; lopping; cutting
CROP-SICK sick of a surfeit
CROSS-BAR transverse bar
CROSSBIT cheated
CROSS-BOW a weapon
ck **CROSS-BUN** hot cross-bun
to **CROSS-CUT** short cut; large saw
CROSSING a ford; traversing
hd **CROSSLET** small heraldic cross
au **CROSS-PLY** standard flexible-tread
pr **CROSS-ROW** the alphabet
CROSS-SEA choppy tide versus wind
CROSS-TIE railway sleeper

CROSSWAY by-way
mu CROTALUM castanet; small bell
mu CROTCHED forked
CROTCHET whimsey; fancy; conceit
bt CROTONIC (croton-oil)
bt CROTTLES lichens used for dyeing
CROUCHED cringed; fawned; truckled
CROUPADE equestrian feat
CROUPIER a raker of shekels; (casino)
md CROUPOUS croupy; hoarse coughing
md CROW-BILL forceps
CROWDING urging; pressing; swarming
bt CROWFOOT buttercups (ranunculus)
CROWMILL crow-trap
CROWNING a coronation
CROWNING (-mercy) completing
CROWNLET small crown
to CROWN-SAW circular saw
bt CROW-SILK aquatic plant
CRUCIATE cruciform
CRUCIBLE melting pot
CRUCIFER cross-bearer
rl CRUCIFIX religious emblem
ck CRUDITES raw-vegetable salad
CRUELEST most ruthless; harshest
nt CRUISING voyaging; sailing
nt CRUISING zigzag patrolling
CRUMBING covering with crumbs
CRUMBLED disintegrated; crushed
CRUMENAL a purse
CRUMPLED ruffled; rumpled; wrinkled
CRUNCHED munched
CRUSADED campaigned for Holy Land
CRUSADED undertook reforming activities
CRUSADER valiant reformist
CRUSHING subduing; overpowering
CRUSTILY morosely; sullenly
bt CRUSTOSE uninterrupted crust
CRUTCHED on crutches
zo CRUTCHET the perch, fish
nm CRUZEIRO Brazil currency unit
mm CRYOLITE a transparent stone
ps CRYOSTAT low-temperature thermostat
el CRYOTRON small electronic switch
ma CUBATION CUBATURE, determination of cubic contents
md CUBEBINE a carminative
CUBIFORM cubical
CUBOIDAL cube-like
CUCHILLA uplands (S. Amer.)
bt CUCUMBER a creeping plant

ch CUCURBIT distilling vessel
CUDDLING fondling; petting; hugging
CUFFLINK wrist adornment (shirt)
CUL-DE-SAC dead-end; blind alley
CULINARY au cordon bleu
CULLYING imposing on
CULLYISM being a simpleton
CULPABLE censurable; blameworthy
CULPABLY guiltily; sinfully
CULTRATE knife-like
CULTURAL of group norms; of the arts
CULTURED intellectual; refined
CULVERIN a cannon
CUMBERED hampered; clogged
gl CUMBRIAN of Cumbria (Cumberland)
CUMBROUS unhandy; clumsy
CUMULATE a mass; collect
CUMULOSE heaped
CUNABULA a cradle; incunabula
CUNABULA books prior to A.D. 1500
CUNARDER a Cunard steamship
CUNEATED wedge-shaped; cuneiform
CUNIFORM Assyrian writing, etc.
CUPBOARD a repository
eg CUP-CHUCK bell-chuck on lathe
CUPIDITY covetousness; avarice; desire
CUP-JOINT male/female pipe joint
CUPREOUS like copper
ch CURARINE curari extract
CURARISE to poison with curari
zo CURASSOW S. American turkey
CURATIVE healing; restorative
CURATORY remedial; antidotal
. CURBLESS without restraint
CURB-ROOF bent roof
zo CURCULIO corn-worm; weevil
CURDLING congealing; thickening
CURLICUE a fantastic curl; pig's tail
CURLIWIG a curved piece
CURRENCY coin; flow; circulation
CURRICLE two-wheeled chaise
ck CURRYING Indian cooking; seasoning
CURRYING combing, brushing horses; (-favour)
CURSEDLY as deserving a curse
lw CURSITOR Chancery writ writer
zo CURSORES running birds
CURTNESS abruptness; terseness
CURTSIED made obeisance (women)
CURVATED curved; bent
CURVITAL not straight
CUSPIDAL pointed
CUSPIDOR a spittoon

CUSTOMED specially made to order
CUSTOMER purchaser; client; patron
lw **CUTCHERY** Indian court
CUT-GLASS art glassware
rl **CUTHBERT** Northumbrian apostle
CUT-PRICE bargain offer; cheap
CUTPURSE pickpocket
CUT-UNDER (fencing)
nt, ce **CUTWATER** prow; wedge shape of
stone piers; breakwater
ch **CYANOGEN** poisonous gas
md **CYANOSIS** skin disease
md **CYANOTIC** (blue jaundice)
bt **CYCLAMEN** primrose family
CYCLE-CAR side-car (motorbike)
ch, ps **CYCLICAL** of circle; ring of atoms
mt **CYCLONIC** like a hurricane
zo **CYCLOPIA** one median eye (cyclops)
CYCLOPIC gigantic; monstrous
CYCLOSIS circulation; cell
movement
cp **CYLINDER** closed tube (combustion)
(expansion) (gas) (steam); data
store
ce **CYLINDER** solid roller; monolith,
bored piles
ar **CYMATIUM** cyme; a moulding
md **CYNANCHE** sore throat
CYNICISM misanthropy
CYNOSURE centre of attraction
CYRENAIC of Cyrene
CYRILLIC (Slavic alphabet)
md **CYSTICLE** small cyst
md **CYSTITIS** inflammation of bladder
CYTISINE laburnum alkaloid
CYTOLOGY study of cells
ch **CYTOSINE** nucleic acid hydrolysis
zo **CYTOSOME** cell cytoplasm
CYTOZOIC intra-cellular; living in a
cell
CZECHISH characteristic of Czechs

D

DABBLING meddling; trifling; ducks
feeding
zo **DAB-CHICK** grebe; diving bird
md **DACRYOMA** defective tear duct
md **DACRYOPS** eyelid cyst
DACTYLAR (finger); (toe)
DACTYLIC (verse)
DADDLING tottering locomotion
ga **DADDLUMS** form of skittles
ar **DADO-RAIL** edge of border panelling
DAEDALUS human glider
DAEMONIC diabolical; satanic
bt **DAFFODIL** Lent lily

DAFTNESS lunacy; stupidity
DAGGERED stabbed
DAGGLING trapesing
tx **DAG-SWAIN** coarse woollen fabric
nt **DAHABIAH DAHABIEH**, state barge of
Nile
DAINTILY delicately; elegantly
ag **DAIRYING** supplying milk
DAIRYMAN dairy keeper; milkman
DALESMAN northern English dale
dweller
DALLYING trifling; delaying; fondling
DALMAHOY bushy bob-wig
rl **DALMATIC** long white vestment
DAMAGING injuring; impairing
DAMASKED variegated
DAMASKIN Damascus sword
tx **DAMASSIN** damask cloth
DAMBOARD draughtboard
bt **DAME-WORT** dame's violet
DAMNABLE pernicious; execrable
DAMOCLES his sword was a hanger
DAMPENED moistened; discouraged
DAMPNESS humidity
mn **DANALITE** iron/beryllium silicate
ar **DANCETTE** Norman zigzag moulding
DANDIEST neatest; eye-catching
DANDLING fondling; caressing
md **DANDRUFF** scurf
DANDYISH foppish
DANDYISM elegance in attire
DANDYIZE dress ostentatiously
DANE-GELD tribute paid to Danes by
Anglo-Saxons
DANELAGH Danish England (A.D.
878)
bt **DANE-WEED** a plant
bt **DANE-WORT** dwarf elder
DANGLING hanging by a thread
DANSEUSE ballerina
DANUBIAN (Danube)
zo **DAPEDIUS** ganoid fish
mn **DAPHNITE** iron-rich chlorite
DAPPERLY in neat, spruce style
DAPPLING with patches of shade
DARING-DO derring-do; act of high
daring, mischief
DARINGLY intrepidly; bravely
DARKENED obscured; clouded
DARKNESS night; ignorance
DARK-ROOM a developing locality
DARKSOME mysterious; dismal
DASTARDY cowardice; base timidity
zo **DASYURES** Australian marsupials
DATELESS immemorial; timeless
DATE-LINE where East meets West
bt, rl **DATE-PALM** Biblical palm
bt **DATE-PLUM** persimmon

bt **DATE-TREE** (many varieties)
mn **DATOLITE** a silicate
ch **DATURINE** thorn-apple alkaloid
DAUBSTER poor painter
DAUGHTER person's female child
DAUNTING intimidating; dismaying
DAUPHINE dauphin's wife
mn **DAVY-LAMP** miner's safety lamp
DAWDLING dallying; lagging; trifling
DAYBREAK dawn; dawning; day-spring
DAY-DREAM reverie; visionary scheme
pc **DAYDREAM** mental meandering
DAYLIGHT illumination
DAYSHIFT working period (industrial)
DAY-SIGHT night-blindness
DAY-TO-DAY of successive days; programme
DAY-WOMAN daily cleaner; charlady
DAZZLING bewildering; confusing (light)
DEAD-BEAT exhausted
DEAD-BORN still-born
DEADENED retarded; benumbed
DEAD-FALL animal trap
DEAD-FIRE death omen
DEAD-HEAT equal winners
DEADLIER more malignant
DEAD-LIFT (no leverage or help)
DEADLINE a boundary; time-limit
DEADLOCK no compromise; impasse
DEAD-LOSS complete loss
DEAD-MEAT meat for market
DEADNESS inertness; inertia
DEAD-PULL dead-lift
nt **DEADRISE** design of rise from ship's bottom
DEAD-ROPE fixed rope in dead-eye
DEAD-SHOT unerring marksman
DEAD-WALL windowless wall
mt **DEAD-WIND** calm
DEAD-WOOD decayed or useless wood
DEAD-WORK unprofitable work
bt **DEAD-WORT** species of elder
DEAFENED stunned
DEAF-MUTE deaf and dumb
md **DEAFNESS** hard of hearing
zo **DEAL-FISH** a thin fish
rl **DEANSHIP** offfice of dean
DEARNESS costliness; tenderness
DEARNFUL solitary; mournful
DEATH-BED place of dying
DEATHFUL fateful; moribund
bt **DEBARKED** tree with bark removed
DEBARRED excluded; prohibited

DEBASING degrading; vitiating
DEBATING discussing; disputing
DEBILITY functional weakness
DEBITING charging
DEBONAIR genial; cheerful; merry
DEBOUCHE emerge from narrow to wider place
DEBTLESS owing naught
DEBUNKED shown up
DEBUTANT a starter
DECADENT degenerate
me **DECAGRAM** 10 grams
ae **DECALAGE** wing chords angle
DECAMPED sloped off; fled; bolted
DECANTED poured out
DECANTER glass wine bottle
zo **DECAPODA** prawns, lobsters, crabs
DECAYING rotting; declining; ebbing
DECEASED dead; departed; defunct
DECEIVED beguiled; duped; gulled
DECEIVER impostor; trickster
DECEMBER 10th Roman month
bt **DECEMFID** ten-cleft
DECEMVIR Roman magistrate
DECENTLY in fitting good taste
lw **DECERNED** judged; decreed
pm **DECICAIN** local anaesthetic
DECIDING settling; resolving
bt **DECIDUAL** able to be cast off (leaves)
me **DECIGRAM** one-tenth of gram
DECIMATE kill one in ten
DECIPHER decode
cp **DECISION** verdict; firmness; chosen action
DECISIVE final; conclusive
ga **DECKGAME** shipboard game
nt **DECK-HAND** seaman
DECK-LOAD deck-cargo
DECLARED said; announced; averred
DECLINED pined; sank; shunned
DECLINER a refuser
DECLUTCH gear-changing (motoring)
DECOCTED boiled down; concentrated
DECODING deciphering
DECORATE deck; embellish; garnish
DECOROUS proper; befitting; seemly
DECOYING luring; enticing; inveigling
DECREASE minimize; reduce; curtail
DECREPIT broken down
rl **DECRETAL** a Papal decree
DECRYING disparaging; vilifying
DECUPLED tenfold
DECURION controller of ten
DECURVED straightened; (unbent)
DEDENDUM wheel/cylinder radial distance

DEDICATE devote; consecrate; assign
DEDUCING inferring; drawing; deriving
DEDUCTED subtracted; withdrawn
lw **DEEDLESS** without document of legality
lw **DEED-POLL** a legal instrument
lw **DEEMSTER DEMPSTER**, Manx judge
DEEP-DYED extreme; rascally
DEEPENED became more mysterious
DEEP-LAID cunning; intricate
DEEP-MOST uttermost
DEEPNESS profundity
DEEP-READ scholarly
to **DEERFOOT** leathercraft
bt **DEER-HAIR** heath club-rush
DEER-HERD a herd of deer
DEER-LICK salt lick
DEER-NECK scraggy
DEER-PARK paddock enclosure, zoo
DEERSKIN leather
DEFACING disfiguring; marring; spoiling
DEFAMING slandering; traducing
DEFEATED frustrated; overthrown
DEFECATE purge; empty bowels
DEFECTOR deserter; traitor
DEFENCED fortified; walled; covered
DEFENDED warded off; shielded
DEFENDER protector; advocate
DEFERRED postponed; adjourned
DEFERRER a procrastinator
DEFIANCE a challenge; provocation
DEFILING polluting; corrupting
DEFINING explaining; specifying
DEFINITE precise; exact; certain
DEFLATED punctured; of economics
DEFLEXED relaxed of muscles
DEFLEXOR metal outrigger (hang gliding)
DEFLOWER deprive of virginity; rape
DEFOREST clear of trees
DEFORMED disfigured; misshapen
DEFORMER destroyer of symmetry
DEFRAYAL payment
DEFRAYED met the cost; paid
DEFRAYER liquidator; settler
DEFTNESS adroitness; dexterity
pc **DEFUSION** breakup of balance
DEGRADED reduced in rank
DEGREASE remove the grease
DEHORNED dodded (cattle)
DEIFICAL making divine
DEIFYING exalting to Godship
DEIGNING condescending; vouchsafing
DEISHEAL clockwise
DEJECTED downcast; chapfallen

DEJECTLY gloomily; dolefully
DEJEUNER breakfast; lunch (Fr.)
ps **DEKATRON** cold cathode sealing tube
DELAYING retarding; hindering
DELECTUS classical anthology
DELEGACY spreading responsibility
DELEGATE appoint in one's stead
DELEGATE official conference attendee
DELETING obliterating; effacing
DELETION erasure; expunction
DELETIVE delible
DELETORY erasive; blotting
DELIBATE cleanse mouth between tastings
DELICACY consideration; tact; relish
DELICACY a (luxury) edible
DELICATE dainty; frail; slight
DELIMING hide lime-salt removal
DELIRIUM mental aberration; mania
DELIVERY rescue; distribution; (childbirth)
DELOUSED cleared of vermin
DELPHIAN oracular
zo **DELPHINE** dolphin
DELUBRUM shrine; sanctuary
DELUDING duping; gulling; misleading
DELUGING pouring; inundating
DELUSION fallacy; imposture
DELUSIVE deceptive; fallacious
DELUSORY illusory; deceitful
DEMAGOGY popular oration technique
DEMANDED queried; exacted; claimed
DEMARCHE ultimatum; counter-stroke
DEMEANED degraded; behaved
DEMENTED daft; crazy; deranged
md **DEMENTIA** insanity; lunacy
bt **DEMERARA** brown sugar
DEMIBAIN sit-bath
DEMI-FOND motor-paced cycle race
DEMIJOHN super flask in basket
DEMILUNE ravelin; fortification
DEMISING bequeathing; devising
DEMISSLY humbly
au **DEMISTER** windscreen condensation preventive
DEMI-TINT a shade
mu **DEMI-TONE** semitone
DEMITTED dismissed; resigned
DEMIURGE Plato's world-maker
DEMI-VOLT an equestrian trick
zo **DEMI-WOLF** progeny of dog and wolf
DEMOBBED demobilized; discharged
DEMOCRAT upholder of democracy

DEMOLISH destroy; raze; dismantle
DEMOLOGY social statistics
DEMONESS a diabolical lady
DEMONIAC possessed; infernal
DEMONISM Satanic cult
DEMONIST devil worshipper
DEMONIZE turn into a devil
DEMONOMY dominion of devils
DEMPSTER see deemster
DEMURELY gravely; sedately;
  modestly
DEMURRED hesitated; wavered;
  paused
lw **DEMURRER** a plea; objector
DEMYSHIP an Oxford scholarship
nm **DENARIUS** former English penny; d
DENATURE denaturalize
bl **DENDRITE** receptor; neuron
mn **DENDROIT** tree-like fossil
DENEGATE deny; contradict; refute
DENEHOLE shaft cut in chalk
DENIABLE controvertible; refutable
DENOTATE denote, signify
DENOTING indicating; designating
DENOUNCE impeach; censure;
  threaten
md **DENTAGRA** toothache
DENTATED with teeth; notched
ar **DENTELLE** tooth-like decoration or
  edging
zo **DENTICLE** small projection; teeth in
  fish
DENTIZED toothed
gl **DENUDATE** strip bare; divest; erosion
DENUDING the soil (by erosion,
  chemicals)
DEPARTED left; gone away;
  withdrew
DEPARTER metal refiner
DEPENDED relied on; trusted factor
DEPICTED described; limned;
  portrayed
DEPICTOR painter; artist
DEPILATE remove hair
DEPLETED emptied; drained
DEPLORED lamented; bewailed;
  grieved
DEPLOYED extended; unfolded
DEPLUMED plucked
lw **DEPONENT** a witness
lw **DEPONING** testifying under oath
DEPORTED expelled; banished
DEPORTEE person forcibly removed
DEPOSING ousting former ruler
DEPRAVED corrupt; vicious;
  profligate
DEPRAVER vilifier; reprobate
DEPRIVED robbed; dispossessed

DEPRIVER a despoiler; brigand
DEPUTING authorizing; charging
DEPUTIZE delegate; act for another
rw **DERAILED** off the lines
rw **DERAILER** train-wrecker
DERANGED disordered; insane; mad
DERATING reducing liability
DERATION to end limits of purchase
DERBY-DAY in June (horse race)
DERBY-DOG also ran
DERELICT abandoned; deserted;
  ruin
DERIDING mocking; lampooning
DERISION laughing stock; mockery
DERISIVE scoffing; ridiculous
DERISORY scornful; contemptuous
DERIVATE a derivative
DERIVING deducing; tracing;
  obtaining
md **DERMATIC** relating to the skin
DEROGATE disparage; detract
DESCRIBE portray; narrate; tell
DESCRIED observed; espied;
  discerned
DESERTED forlorn; left; abandoned
DESERTER quitter; renegade;
  turncoat
DESERVED justified; merited; earned
DESERVER meritorious person
DESIGNED projected; invented; drew
DESIGNER schemer; contriver
DESILVER extract silver from
DESIRING craving; wanting
DESIROUS covetous; eager; longing
DESISTED stopped; ceased; forbore
DESK-WORK clerical work
DESOLATE solitary; deserted
DESPATCH DISPATCH, expedite; send
DESPISAL contempt; scorn
DESPISED disdained; ignored;
  scouted
DESPISER scorner; contemner
DESPITED vexed; offended; teased
DESPOTAT territory under despot
DESPOTIC tyrannical; arbitrary
DESTINED ordained; fated
zo **DESTRIER** second charger
pc **DESTRUDO** desire for death,
  destruction
DETACHED isolated; disengaged
DETAILED particularized; recounted
DETAILER enumerator; narrator
DETAINED delayed; restrained; held
lw **DETAINER** withholder of goods
DETECTED found out; unmasked
DETECTOR detecter; discoverer
DETERGED cleansed; wiped
DETERRED prevented; hindered

DETESTED odious; abominated; loathed
DETESTER abhorrer
DETHRONE depose; discrown
DETONATE explode violently
DETONIZE fulminate
DETRITAL (detritus); residual
gl **DETRITUS** disintegrated material; eroded
DEUCE-ACE a throw at dice
DEUCEDLY confoundedly
ch **DEUTERON** charged particle
zo **DEUTOVUM** development stage in acarina
DEVALUED depreciated
pc **DEVIANCE** differing from norms
DEVIATED swerved; strayed; veered
DEVIATOR a wanderer
DEVILDOM kingdom of hell
DEVILESS demoness
DEVILISH fiendish; malignant; diabolic
DEVILISM devil worship
DEVILKIN imp
ck **DEVILLED** highly seasoned; curried
DEVISING scheming; bequeathing
DEVISING producing (entertainment)
lw **DEVOLVED** transferred; handed over
gl **DEVONIAN** of county; era
DEVOTING dedicating; consecrating
DEVOTION zeal; piety; attachment
DEVOURED bolted; consumed; gobbled
DEVOURER absorber; destroyer
DEVOUTLY earnestly; piously; holily
bt **DEWBERRY** the bramble
DEWINESS precipitation
DEW-POINT a critical temperature
mn **DEWSTONE** a limestone
ch **DEXTRINE** starch gum
DEXTRONE synthetic blood
ch **DEXTROSE** glucose sugar
DEXTROUS dexterous; skilful
DEZINKED freed from zinc
mn **DIABASIC** greenstone type
md **DIABETES** sugar sickness
md **DIABETIC** of diabetes
DIABLERY diablerie; impishness
DIABOLIC satanic; demoniac; fiendish
DIACETYL colour/flavour constituent in butter
bt **DIACHYMA** cellular tissue
zo **DIACOELE** 3rd brain ventricle in craniata
rl **DIACONAL** concerning deacons
DIACTINE having two rays
bt **DIADELPH** twin
DIADEMED crowned

md **DIADEXIS** disease mutation
DIADOCHI ancient governors (Gr.)
DIAGLYTH an intaglio; carved gem
md **DIAGNOSE** identify
DIAGONAL cross-tie
DIAGRAPH drawing instrument
mn **DIALLAGE** monoclinic pyroxene
DIALLAGE rhetorical argument
tc **DIALLING** selecting telephone numbers
DIALOGIC in dialogue form
cp, tc **DIALOGUE** two talking; two-way exchange
md **DIALYSED DIALYSER**, of kidney-cleaning process
ch, md **DIALYSIS DIALYTIC**, filtration of body salts; unbracing
DIAMANTE artificial glitter stones
ma **DIAMETER** line halving a circle
bt **DIANDRIA** two-stemmed plants
DIANODAL traversing a node
bt **DIANTHUS** carnations, pinks, etc.
mu **DIAPASON** concord of sounds
zo **DIAPAUSE** life-cycle stage in insects
mu **DIAPENTE** interval of a fifth
tx **DIAPERED** clothed with nappy
tx **DIAPHANE** transparent-woven silk
DIAPHONE electrical fog-signal
mu **DIAPHONY** part-writing based on plainsong
DIARIZED recorded in a diary
DIASPORA Jew dispersion
mn **DIASPORE** aluminium hydrate
DIASTASE malt sugar
DIASTEMA tooth-gap in jaw; stage of protoplasm
md **DIASTOLE** heart dilatation
ar **DIASTYLE** proportion in colonnades
ch **DIATOMIC** (two atoms)
mu **DIATONIC** natural scale
DIATRIBE stream of invective; tirade
DIBBLING planting
DIBSTONE stone used in a game
cy **DICARYON** simultaneously dividing nuclei
mn **DICE-COAL** small coal
bt **DICENTRA** bleeding-heart
DICE-PLAY dicing
ch **DICHLONE** chemical fungicide
md **DICHOTIC** contrasting ear stimulation
DICHOTIC doubled; twinned
DICHROIC double refraction
DICKERED bargained
DICLINIC crystalline shape
ch **DICLORAN** chemical fungicide
md **DICROTIC** double pulsation
DICTATED bid; prescribed; ordained

DICTATOR autocrat; despot; tyrant
bt DICYCLIC with 2-whorled perianth
DIDACTIC instructive; moral; directive
DIDACTYL with all hind-foot toes separate
zo DIDAPPER dabchick; grebe
DIDDERED couldn't decide; dithered
DIDDLING cheating; trifling; dawdling
bt, zo DIDYMATE in pairs; twins
ch DIDYMIUM a rare metal
bt DIDYMOUS growing in pairs
DIEGESIS explanation; narrative
bt DIELYTRA the bleeding-heart
DIE-STOCK die-holder
DIETETIC (food regime)
DIFFERED disagreed; diverged; varied
DIFFRACT break; refract
DIFFUSED disseminated; spread
bd DIFUSER a spray; a damper for chimney or ducts
mn DIGENITE cubic copper sulphide
DIGESTED classified; codified; arranged
ch DIGESTER an industrial 'cooker' (chemical)
DIGGABLE suitable for spade work
DIGGINGS (gold); archaeological
bt DIGITATE having five leaflets
el DIGITRON numerical read-out glow tube
zo DIGITULE fingerlike process
bt DIGONOUS with two angles
bt DIGYNIAN DIGYNOUS, flowers having cleft styles
DIHEDRAL angle between planes
DIHEDRON geometric figures
el DIHEPTAL of 14 in number
gn DIHYBRID from parents different in 2 aspects
ch DIKETONE CO–group-containing compound
DILATANT swelling; elastic
DILATING expanding; stretching
md DILATION distention; amplification; by stimulation
DILATIVE expansive
DILATORY tardy; dallying; lagging
DILIGENT busy; industrious; assiduous
DILLY-BAG for billycan (Australian)
DILUTING attenuating; weakening
DILUTION watering; reducing
DILUVIAL alluvial
DILUVIUM glacial or flood deposit
ch DIMEDONE alcohol-detecting reagent

zo DIMEGALY with different-sized spermatozoa
DIMERISM duplex arrangement
DIMEROUS in two parts
DIMETRIC tetragonal
DIMINISH cut; abate; lessen; curtail
DIMPLING smiling
zo DIMYARIA molluscs
DINAMODE unit of work, metre-ton
DINARCHY dual control
DINER-OUT a table companion
DING-DONG hammer and tongs; church bells
nt DINGHIES small boats
DINGIEST dullest; dirtiest
zo DINORNIS moa-bird, N. Zealand
DINOSAUR of extinct reptile community
rl DIOCESAN a bishop's council
DIOGENIC (Diogenes); cynical outlook on life
mn DIOPSIDE augite
DIOPTASE copper silicate
DIOPTRIC (refraction of light)
DIORAMIC of small tableaux exhibition
mn DIORITIC (igneous rock, diorite)
DIOSCURI Castor and Pollux
zo DIPCHICK DABCHICK, grebe
DIPHASIC in two phases
DIPHENYL coal-tar chemical
md DIPLEGIA paralysis
el DIPLEXER two-way transmitter
DIPLOGEN deuterium; heavy hydrogen
DIPLOMAT ambassador; envoy
md DIPLOPIA double vision
cy DIPLOSIS chromosome doubling
zo DIPNOOUS having lungs and gills
DIPROTON two-proton system
bt DIPSACUS the teasel
md DIPSOSIS morbid thirst
zo DIPTERAL with two wings
zo DIPTERAN a fly
ar DIPTEROS (double peristyle)
DIPTYCHA writing tablets
DIRECTED addressed; enjoined
DIRECTLY expressly; soon; forthwith
DIRECTOR manager; controller
DIRENESS horror; calamity
pl, md DIRHINIA of both nostrils
DIRIGENT directing
DIRTIEST filthiest; most sordid
DIRTYING fouling; soiling
DISABLED incapacitated; crippled
DISABUSE enlighten; undeceive
ch DISACRYL acrolin polymer
DISADORN deprive of ornament

DISAGREE differ; vary; deviate
DISALLOW reject; forbid; disclaim
DISANNEX surrender former gains
DISARMED subdued; stripped
DISARRAY disorder; undress
DISASTER calamity; catastrophe
lw DISBENCH of judges (unseat)
DISBOSOM reveal
DISBURSE expend; spend
DISCIPLE learner; follower; pupil
DISCLAIM disown; reject; renounce
DISCLOSE reveal; tell; betray
DISCOUNT allowance; forestall;
  deduct
DISCOVER detect; espy; divulge
ch DISCRASE a silver salt
DISCREET circumspect; prudent
DISCSEAL form of valve
DISEASED indisposed; unhealthy;
  sickly
DISENDOW deprive of endowments
rl DISFROCK expel from clergy
lw DISGAVEL a change in tenure
DISGORGE surrender; eject; vent
DISGRACE ignominy; dishonour
DISGUISE conceal; mask; cloak
DISHEVEL disarray
DISHORSE unhorse
DISINTER exhume; unbury
DISINURE render unfamiliar
zo DISIPPUS an American butterfly
DISJOINT dislocate
DISLEAVE deprive of leaves
DISLIKED detested; hated; loathed
DISLODGE evict; eject; oust
DISLOYAL false; perfidious
DISMALLY drearily; dolefully
DISMAYED terror-struck; appalled
DISMOUNT alight; descend; unhorse
DISORDER confusion; turbulence
DISOWNED repudiated; denied
DISPATCH despatch; expedite; send
DISPATHY antipathy; allergy
DISPENSE administer; dispence
DISPERSE scatter; diffuse; dispel
cp DISPERSE redistribute data
DISPIRIT discourage; dishearten
DISPLACE remove; discharge; oust
DISPLAIT untwist; unravel
DISPLANT uproot; eradicate
DISPONED disposed
lw DISPONEE DISPONER, (conveyance of
  property in legal form)
lw DISPONGE DISPUNGE, expunge
rl DISPOPED deprived of popedom
lw DISPOSAL right of bestowing
DISPOSED inclined; arranged; biased
DISPOSER administrator

DISPROOF refutation; rebuttal
DISPROVE confute; refute
DISPUNGE disponge; expunge
DISPUTED contested; wrangled
DISPUTER arguer; debater
. DISQUIET to vex; unease; anxiety
DISRATED reduced in rank;
  degraded
DISROBED divested; denuded
DISROBER raiment remover
DISSEVER cut in two; rend
DISSOLVE loosen; liquefy; end
DISSUADE deter; disincline
zo DISTALIA 5 bones in tetrapod limb
DISTANCE interval; space; outstrip
DISTASTE aversion; antipathy
mn DISTHENE cyanite; kyanite
DISTINCT definite; clear
DISTITLE deprive of right
zo DISTOMUM liver-fluke parasite
DISTRACT divert; harass; bewilder
lw DISTRAIN seize for debt
DISTRAIT absent-minded
DISTRESS anguish; suffering; worry
DISTRICT territory; region; quarter
DISTRUST discredit; doubt; suspect
DISTUNED put out of tune
DISUNION breach of concord
DISUNITE separate; disrupt
DISUNITY isolation; dissension
DISUSAGE disuse; desuetude
DISUSING abandoning
DISVALUE underrate; disprize
DISYOKED untrammelled
zo DITCH-DOG dead dog
DITCHING excavating; clearing
bt DITHECAL with two spore-cases
rl DITHEISM DITHEIST, co-existence of
  a good and an evil god
DITHERED hesitated
DITOKOUS having twins
mn DITROITE coarse-grained alkali/
  syenite rock
DITTY-BAG sailor's kit-bag
DITTY-BOX sailor's treasure-box
md DIURESIS increased urination
md DIURETIC urination stimulant
DIVAGATE digress; wander
ch DIVALENT bivalent
DIVE-BOMB aerial attack
DIVERGED deviated; digressed;
  veered
DIVERTED distracted; amused
DIVERTER an entertainer
DIVESTED stripped; deprived; bared
DIVIDEND interest; share; profit
ce, nv DIVIDERS drawing, measuring
  instrument

DIVIDING cleaving; parting
bt DIVI-DIVI pods used in tanning
DIVINELY heavenly; exquisitely
DIVINIFY treat as divine
rl DIVINITY deity; theology
DIVINIZE deify
DIVISION category; army unit
DIVISIVE dissentient; discordant
DIVORCED forced assunder
DIVORCEE person divorced
DIVORCER divorcing person
DIVULGED communicated; revealed
DIVULGER betrayer of secrets
DIZZYING confusing
rl DOCETISM doctrine of a sect
rl DOCETIST a 2nd-century heretic
DOCHMIAC Greek metrical foot
DOCILITY pliance; tameness
DOCIMACY metallurgy
nt DOCKYARD naval establishment
DOCTORAL (doctor)
md DOCTORED treated; doped
DOCTORLY scholarly
DOCTRINE dogma; creed; tenet
lw DOCUMENT writing; record; writ,
  account
DODDERED quaked; tottered
DODDERER senile senior
ch DODECANE paraffin
DODIPOLL dolt; numbskull
DODONIAN oracular
DOGBERRY ignorant parish official
bt DOG-BRIER dog-rose
DOG-CHEAP bargain price
DOG-EARED crinkled corner
DOGESHIP chief Venetian office
DOG-FACED unprepossessing
DOGGEDLY obstinately; stolidly
DOGGEREL bad verse
DOGGONED confounded
bt DOG-GRASS couch grass
DOG-HOUSE kennel
DOG-LATIN barbarous Latin
DOG-LEECH a vet
DOGMATIC dictatorial; arbitrary
bt DOG'S-BANE a poisonous plant
DOG'S-BODY utility man
DOG-SLEEP cat-nap
DOG'S-MEAT offal
DOG'S-NOSE beer and gin
DOG-TIRED spent
ar DOG-TOOTH a Norman moulding
DOG-TRICK a currish wile
nt DOG-WATCH short ½ watch
DOG-WEARY exhausted
bt DOG-WHEAT dog-grass
zo DOG-WHELK kind of mollusc
DOLDRUMS calm zone; depression

gl DOLERITE medium-grain-size
  igneous rock
DOLESOME dismal; rueful
bt DOLICHOS hyacinth bean
DO-LITTLE lazy-bones
DOLLARED flush; wealthy
DOLLED-UP dressed showily
DOLLHOOD dollship
DOLLY-MOP handled mop
DOLLY-TUB washing tub
mn DOLOMITE magnesian limestone
mu DOLOROSO pathetically
DOLOROUS sorrowful; dolesome
DOMAINAL DOMANIAL, (landed
  estate); (scope)
DOMELIKE dome shaped
lw DOMESMAN judge; umpire
DOMESTIC household; maid
DOMICILE habitation; residence
mu DOMINANT prevailing; ruling; 5th
  note of scale
DOMINATE control; override
DOMINEER to hector; to sway
DOMINION sovereignty
DOMINIUM ownership
DOMINOES hooded capes; a game
DONATING giving; bestowing
DONATION presentation; offering;
  alms
rl DONATISM a Christian cult
DONATIVE gratuity; benefice;
  largesse
lw DONATORY recipient of land
DOOLTREE duletree; the gallows
bt DOOM-PALM Egyptian palm
DOOMSDAY domesday (Book)
DOOMSDAY end of the world
DOOMSMAN domesman; judge
DOOR-BELL a ringer
DOOR-CASE door framework
DOOR-KNOB a handle
DOORLESS without portal
DOORNAIL considered as dead
DOOR-POST regarded as deaf
DOOR-SILL lower framework
DOOR-STEP slice of bread (slang)
DOOR-YARD an enclosure
DORICISM Doric in expression
DORMANCY abeyance; latency
zo DORMOUSE somnolent rodent
zo DORR-HAWK night jar
zo DORSALIS dorsal organ artery
md DOSOLOGY science of doses
DOTATION donation; dowry
DOTINGLY stupidly; fondly
zo DOTTEREL a plover
DOUANIER custom-house officer
  (Fr.)

DOUBLETS Tudor dress; (dice)
DOUBLING folding; running
nm **DOUBLOON** Spanish guinea
DOUBLURE book-binding
DOUBTFUL uncertain; ambiguous
DOUBTING distrusting; querying
DOUBTIVE questionable; dubious
DOUCHING spraying
DOUGHBOY American infantryman
DOUGHNUT a confection
bt **DOUM-PALM** doom-palm
DOURNESS obstinacy; grimness
DOVECOTE pigeon house
DOVE-EYED meek-eyed
DOVELIKE gentle; innocent
DOVESHIP qualities of a dove; (man of peace)
DOVETAIL a joint; synchronize
DOWDYISH rather slovenly
DOWDYISM shabbiness
DOWELLED pinned together
DOWEL-PIN a fastening
DOWERING endowing; bequeathing
DOWFNESS lethargy; dullness
DOWNBEAR depress
mu **DOWN-BEAT** descending stroke (conductor); gloomy; relaxed; informal
DOWNBORE discouraged
DOWNCAST dejected
DOWNCOME sudden fall
DOWNFALL debacle; ruin
nt **DOWNHAUL** a sheet
DOWNHILL a declivity
DOWNLAND hilly pasture land
rw **DOWN-LINE** (railways)
DOWNPIPE rainwater runaway
DOWNPOUR continuous heavy rain
DOWNRUSH downward draught
pc, cp, tc **DOWN-TIME** depression; machine inoperable
DOWNTOWN business centre
DOWNTROD trampled; tyrannized
DOWNWARD descending
bt **DOWNWEED** cotton weed
rl **DOXOLOGY** hymn of praise
DOZINESS drowsiness
tx **DRABBETT DRABETTE**, twilled linen used for smocks
DRABBISH slatternly; dowdy
DRABBLED fouled with mire
nt **DRABBLER** a sail extension
bt **DRACANTH** gum; tragacanth
DRACONIC (Draco); severe
DRAFTING sketching; drawing up; conscripting; formulating
DRAFTING technique of cycling, driving

DRAG-BOLT draw-bar
DRAGGING tugging; tedious; pulling; forbidden footwork (netball); (motor racing)
DRAGGLED wet and dirty
DRAG-HOOK a connection
DRAG-HUNT foxing the hounds with a scented trail
DRAGOMAN guide; interpreter
zo **DRAGONET** small dragon; a fish
hd **DRAGONNE** heraldic lion-dragon
DRAG-SHOE a brake
DRAINAGE sewage system
DRAINING emptying; exhausting
DRAMATIC theatrical; powerful voice
DRAMMOCK drummock; skilly; gruel (Sc.)
DRAM-SHOP shebeen; illicit bar
DRAUGHTS a game
DRAUGHTY inconveniently airy
DRAWABLE representable
DRAWBACK detriment; defect
DRAWBOLT coupling pin
DRAWBORE carpentry
DRAWGATE sluice gate
DRAW-GEAR harness; railway coupling
DRAWLING droning
DRAW-LINK a couple
DRAW-WELL deep well
DREADFUL frightful; dire; horrific
DREADING fearing; awing
DREAMERY reverie
DREAMFUL fanciful; dreamy
DREAMILY vaguely
DREAMING imagining
DREARILY gloomily; dismally
ce **DREDGING** deepening; sprinkling; underwater excavation
DREGGISH foul with lees
DRENCHED saturated; inundated
DRENCHER a soaker
DRESSAGE training of horses competition
md, bd **DRESSING** alignment; draping; binding; finishing stonework
ck **DRESSING** putting on apparel (–room); (salad–)
DRIBBLED slobbered; footwork with ball
ga **DRIBBLER** (baby); footballer
DRIBBLET a small drop
nt **DRIFTAGE** leeway
DRIFT-ICE polar ice; iceberg
DRIFTING passively awaiting events
DRIFT-NET drifting herring net
DRIFT-WAY cattle-road; leeway
to **DRILL-BOW** a boring device

DRILL-BOX seed-box
DRILLING training; perforating
DRINKING imbibing; carousing
ae **DRIP-FLAP** part of balloon
ck **DRIPPING** pork or suet fat spread; running tap
DRIVABLE condition of road for traffic
DRIVEWAY DRIVE, private access road
DRIZZLED rained softly
DROGHING coastal trade, W. Indies
DROILING drudging; loitering
DROLLERY buffoonery; waggery
DROLLING jesting; clowning
DROLLISH fairly facetious
DROMICAL (race-course)
zo **DRONE-FLY** drone-bee
DROOLING slavering; slobbering
DROOPING withering; languishing
DROP-DOWN short first title in book
DROP-GOAL two points
au **DROPHEAD** convertible automobile
DROPKICK football
zo **DROPPING** spoor of animals; sheldrakes (flock)
DROPPING letting fall; releasing; abandoning
DROP-RIPE fruits ready to fall
DROPSHOT tennis
DROP-SLIP book stockist's order
DROPWISE in drops
bt **DROPWORT** meadow-sweet
DROTCHEL idle wench; slut
DROUGHTY thirsty; arid
DROWNING submerging; overwhelming
DROWSILY sleepily
DROWSING dozing
DRUBBING beating; mauling
DRUDGERY slavery; ignoble toil
DRUDGING moiling; plodding
DRUDGISM menial occupation
md **DRUGFAST** drugproof; immune
DRUGGING inducing stupor
DRUGGIST chemist; chymist
DRUIDESS lady soothsayer
DRUIDISM Celtic cult
DRUMFIRE continuous fire
zo **DRUMFISH** North American fish
DRUMHEAD (service; court-martial)
DRUMMING vibrating
DRUNKARD toper; dipsomaniac
zo **DRY-BIBLE** cattle-disease
DRY-CLEAN without using water
DRY-FLIES artificial gnats as bait (angling)
DRY-GOODS drapery
DRY-PLATE photographic plate

DRY-POINT engraving needle
DRY-STEAM (no unevaporated water)
DRY-STONE (no mortar used)
DRY-STOVE hot-house
DUALIZED halved; split in twain
DUBITATE to doubt; to vacillate
nm **DUCATOON** scudo; silver coin
ck **DUCHESSE** a table-cover; potato dish
zo **DUCKBILL** platypus; duck-mole
DUCK-DIVE swimming-dive
pr **DUCK-FOOT** lowered inverted commas
zo **DUCK-HAWK** marsh-harrier
DUCK-HOOK very low stroke to left (golf)
zo **DUCKLING** young duck
zo **DUCK-MOLE** duckbill
DUCKPINS variation of ten-pin alley
DUCK'S-EGG a zero (cricket)
DUCK-SHOT pellets for wild fowl
bt **DUCK-WEED** a water weed
md **DUCTLESS** endocrine gland
DUELLING DUELLIST, fighting in single combat
DUELSOME prone to duelling
mu **DUETTINO** short duet
mu **DUETTIST** a performer
DUKELING a petty duke
DUKERIES ducal country seats
DUKESHIP ducal rank
mu **DULCIANA** (It.) soft organ stop
mu **DULCIMER** stringed cimbalom (Hung.)
DULCITOR saccharine; sweetener
DULE-TREE DOOL-TREE, the gallows
DULL-EYED lacking expression
DULL-HEAD a dolt
DULLNESS dulness; apathy
DUMB-BELL no ringing tone
DUMB-CAKE (baked on St Mark's Eve)
bt **DUMB-CANE** (causing dumbness)
DUMBNESS muteness
DUMB-SHOW pantomime
DUMMERER bogus mute
DUMOSITY prickliness
ck **DUMPLING** pudding
DUNCEDOM the class of dunces
zo **DUN-DIVER** goosander
DUNGAREE Indian cloth; overalls
DUNG-FORK a gardening implement
DUNG-HILL cock's castle
DUNG-MERE DUNG-YARD, manure pit
pl **DUODENAL DUODENUM**, first of the small intestines
DUOLOGUE two in conversation; a debate
el **DUOPHASE** choke-use in valve circuit

ps **DUPLEXER** two channel multiplexer
(radar)
DURATION indefinite length of time
DUSKNESS twilight
DUST-BALL horse disease
DUST-CART rubbish conveyor
DUST-COAT light house-coat
DUST-HOLE ash-bin
gl **DUSTWELL** dust in glacial hollow
DUTCHMAN Hollander
DUTIABLE subject to customs
DUTY-FREE off-shore transit
purchases
DWARFING stunting; overshadowing
DWARFISH pygmy; undersized; tiny
md **DWARFISM** growth-hindering
condition
DWELLING domicile; habitat
DWINDLED declined; shrank
DYE-HOUSE where dyeing is done
DYE-STUFF dye material
DYEWORKS coloration factory
ps, mu **DYNAMICS** masses in motion;
gradations (loud, soft) in music
DYNAMISM DYNAMIST, theory of
imminent energy
DYNAMITE powerful explosive
nt **DYNASHIP** modern automaton
sailing ship
DYNASTIC in succession
DYNATRON electrical oscillation
md **DYSBASIA** walking difficulty
md **DYSCHROA** skin disease
DYSGENIC detrimental to the race
DYSLALIA over-age baby talk
DYSLEXIA reading learning difficulty
mn **DYSLUITE** manganese ore
mn **DYSODILE** lignite
md **DYSOPSIA** dimness of sight
md **DYSOREXY** depraved appetite
DYSPATHY antipathy
md **DYSPEPSY** indigestion
DYSPHONY difficulty of speaking
md **DYSPNOEA** difficulty in breathing
md **DYSTOCIA** difficult birth-labour
mn **DYSTOMIC** (imperfect fracture)
md **DYSTONIA** impaired muscle tone

E

zo **EAGLE-OWL** great horned owl
zo **EAGLE-RAY** devil-fish
EAR-BORED (for ear-rings)
EARPHONE a receiver
zo **EAR-SHELL** a sea-shell
EARTH-BAG sandbag
EARTH-FED earthly contented

zo **EARTH-HOG** aardvark
EARTHING burrowing; burying
bt **EARTH-NUT** pig-nut, peanut
bt **EARTH-PEA** hog peanut
EAR-TO-EAR a definite distance
lw **EASEMENT** relief; privilege; right of
passage
EASINESS facility; comfort; quiet
EASTERLY oriental
EASTLAND the Orient
EASTMOST farthest east
EASTWARD toward the rising sun
tx **EASY-CARE** minimal-creasing fabrics
EAU-DE-NIL dull green colour (Nile)
EAU-DE-VIE brandy; akvavit; (vodka)
EBENEZER memorial stone; chapel
rl **EBIONIZE** EBIONISM, EBIONITE,
Jewish-Christian sect that upheld
the Mosaic laws
ch **EBLANINE** volatile crystal
EBONIZED blackened
EBURNEAN EBURNINE, like ivory
zo **ECAUDATE** tailless; Manx
rl **ECCLESIA** an assembly; a church
ECCYESIS external foetus
development
ch **ECGONINE** coca-base alkaloid
ECHINATE prickly; bristled
mn **ECHINITE** fossil sea-urchin
zo **ECHINOID** like a sea-urchin
bt **ECHINOPS** globe thistle, etc.
zo **ECHIODON** sand-eel type
ECHOLESS no repetition
md **ECLAMPSY** epilepsy
ECLECTIC derived from selected
sources
as **ECLIPSED** obscured; disgraced
ECLIPTIC a great circle
mn **ECLOGITE** crystalline rock
zo **ECLOSION** emergence from egg case
pc **ECMNESIA** loss of short items of
memory
ec **ECOCLINE** variations based on
unalike habitats
ECONOMIC frugal; thrifty; careful
ECOPHENE physiologically habitat-
affected type
bt **ECOSTATE** ribless
ECPHASIS explicit declaration
pc **ECPHORIA** establishing memory
trace
md **ECRASEUR** surgical instrument
ECSTATIC rapturous; beatific
zo **ECTOCYST** outer cyst layer;
exoskeleton
md **ECTODERM** outer skin, also of embryo
bt **ECTOGENY** pollen effect on female
plant organs

zo **ECTOLOPH** mammalian tooth edge
zo **ECTOZOAN** an external parasite
rl **ECUMENIC** promoting universal
   Christian unity
EDACIOUS greedy; voracious
EDDERING making up fences
EDDY-WIND back draught
zo **EDENTATA EDENTATE**, animal lacking
   front teeth
EDGE-BONE aitch bone; rump bone
EDGELESS blunt
EDGE-RAIL an iron rail
to **EDGE-TOOL** cutting tool
EDGEWAYS EDGEWISE, sideways
EDGINESS angularity
EDIFYING enlightening; instructive
EDITRESS woman editor
EDUCABLE teachable
EDUCATED instructed; taught; literate
EDUCATOR tutor
EDUCIBLE show from various
   evidence
EDUCTION extraction; deduction
bt **EEL-GRASS** grass-wrack
EEL-SPEAR fisherman's fork
zo **EELWORMS** plant-parasites;
   nematodes
EERINESS weirdness; creepiness
EFFACING expunging; deleting;
   erasing
EFFECTED accomplished; executed
EFFECTOR effecter; creator; doer;
   realizer
pl **EFFECTOR** active organ cells
EFFERATE irritating person
EFFERENT conveying outward
EFFICACY production power
EFFIGIAL relating to images
EFFIGIES images; likenesses; guys
EFFLUENT a stream; outflow; with
   sewage
EFFLUVIA noxious exhalations
EFFULGED shone in radiant
   splendour
EFFUSING emanating; pouring
EFFUSION unrestrained expression of
   words, feelings
EFFUSIVE emotionally
   demonstrative; gushing
EFTSOONS soon after; again
EGESTING discharging
EGESTION excretion
bt **EGG-APPLE** brinjal; aubergine
EGG-DANCE ancient blindfold hop
pt **EGG-GLAIR** pre-gilding eggwhite
   surface
EGG-GLASS sand-glass
bt **EGG-PLANT** brinjal; aubergine

EGG-SHELL thin porcelain; paint
ck **EGG-SLICE** frying spatula
EGG-SPOON small pointed spoon
EGG-TOOTH knob on chick's beak
EGG-WHISK wire brush
bt **EGLATERE** eglantine; sweetbriar
pc **EGO-ALIEN** refusal to accept self
EGOISTIC self-assertive; self-
   contained
pc **EGOMANIA** self-preoccupation
pc **EGOPATHY** aggressive; boasting
md **EGOPHONY** a pleurisy symptom
EGOTIZED self-conceited
EGRESSED departed; left
EGYPTIAN (Egypt); gipsy; tiny peg
EIGHTEEN 1½ dozen
EIGHTHLY an ordinal number
EJECTING rejecting; cashiering
EJECTION discharge; dismissal
EJECTIVE expulsive; emissive
ch **ELAIDATE ELAIODIC**, castor-oil
   derivative
ELANCING darting; casting;
   launching
zo **ELAPHINE** like a stag
ELAPHURE a deer
ELAPSING slipping away
ELAPSION lapse; interval
ELASTICS pack-opening bands
   (parachuting)
ELATEDLY in high spirits
ch **ELATERIN** cucumber extract
ELBOWING jostling; nudging
ELDER-GUN pop-gun
ELDORADO land of fabulous wealth
ELECTING choosing; preferring
ELECTION freewill; choice;
   acceptance
ELECTION voting for candidates,
   parties
ELECTIVE selective; preferential
el **ELECTRET** permanently polarized
   material
ELECTRIC stimulating
ELECTRON (negative electricity)
ELECTRUM silver and gold alloy
ELEGANCE refinement; taste; grace
ELEGANCY beauty of propriety
ELEGANTE lady of fashion
ELEGIAST sorrowful bard
ELEGIZED lamented in verse
ELENCHIC elenctic; refutatory
ELENCHUS a sophism
pr, zo **ELEPHANT** size of paper; mammoth
bt **ELEUSINE** tropical grass
ELEVATED high; exalted; dignified
ELEVATOR a lift; animator; tail plane
   flap; (wrestling)

ELEVENTH ordinal number; (last hour)
ELF-ARROW flint arrow-head
ELF-CHILD a changeling
ELICITED deduced; extracted; evoked
ELIDABLE suppressible
ELIGIBLE fit; fully qualified
ELIGIBLY desirably; worthily
ELIMATED polished; smoothed
ELINGUID tongue-tied
ELLIPSIS gap; omission; hiatus
ELLIPTIC oval
ELOCULAR without partitions
ELOINING banishing
ELONGATE stretch; extend; lengthen
ELOQUENT fluent and impressive
ELSEWISE otherwise; differently
ELUDIBLE avoidable; escapable
mn **ELVANITE** crystalline rock
ELVE-LOCK elf-lock
ELVISHLY mischievously; impishly
ELYDORIC oil and water-colour
zo **ELYTRINE** (beetle wing material)
EMACIATE waste away; decline; pine
EMANATED derived from; originated
EMBALING bundling; packing
EMBALMED cleansed body (Egypt)
EMBALMER preserver; mortician
EMBANKED mounded
EMBARKED ventured; undertook
nt **EMBARKED** entered a ship
EMBARRED encaged; shut in
EMBATTLE draw up for battle
nt **EMBAYING** enclosing in a bay
EMBEDDED firmly established
EMBEZZLE appropriate; peculate
EMBITTER exacerbate; exasperate
EMBLAZED displayed; bedecked
EMBLAZON blaze; adorn; embellish
EMBODIED incorporated; integrated
EMBODIER codifier; merger
EMBOGGED mired; bogged
EMBOGUED emptied; discharged; fell
EMBOLDEN encourage; reassure; impel
md **EMBOLISM** intercalation; obstruction
mn **EMBOLITE** a silver ore
EMBOLIUM narrow corium strip in hemiptera
EMBORDER adorn with a border
EMBOSSED ornamented in relief
EMBOSSER a craftsman
EMBOTTLE to bottle
EMBOWING arching; vaulting
EMBRACED embodied; clasped; hugged
lw **EMBRACER** corrupter of a jury
EMBRONZE fashion in bronze

EMBRUTED brutalized
EMBRYOUS inaugural
EMBUSSED loaded on a bus
EMENDALS repair-work
EMENDATE to correct; to rectify
EMENDING amending; reforming
EMERGENT pressing; urgent
EMERGING issuing; arising
EMERITED put on retired list
EMERITUS retired with honour
EMERSION reappearance; emergence
md **EMETICAL** ejective
EMIGRANT distant home seeker
EMIGRATE migrate; remove
EMINENCE distinction; celebrity
EMINENCY a title
EMISSARY envoy; spy; agent
EMISSILE capable of being emitted
EMISSION discharge; ejection
EMISSIVE emanative; expulsive
md **EMISSORY** a duct; channel
EMITTING issuing; delivering
rl **EMMANUEL** Immanuel; Messiah
EMMARBLE enmarble; petrify
EMMEWING confining; penning
EMPACKET to pack up
EMPALING IMPALING, transfixing
EMPARKED enclosed
EMPATRON patronize
EMPAWNED pledged
EMPHASIS stress; force; accent
EMPHATIC definite; positive; earnest
EMPLANED boarded an aeroplane
EMPLOYED at work; occupied
EMPLOYEE a wage earner; hand
EMPLOYER the boss
EMPLUMED plumed
EMPOISON embitter; envenom
EMPORIUM large store; mart
EMPTYING exhausting; discharging
md **EMPTYSIS** haemorrhage
EMPURPLE to dye
EMPUZZLE mystify; bewilder; nonplus
EMPYREAL ethereal; aerial; sublime
EMPYREAN highest; heaven
EMULATED vied; strove; competed
pc **EMULATOR** rival; copyist; bridging device
EMULGENT flowing; oozing
EMULSIFY liquate; blend
EMULSINE a fermented mixture
EMULSION milky liquid
EMULSIVE milk-like
ENABLING empowering; allowing
ENACTING decreeing; ordaining
ENALLAGE change of tense, etc.
hd **ENALURON** heraldic bordure

ENARCHED like a rainbow
ENCAGING confining; immewing
bd ENCALLOW brick claypit surface
   mould
ENCAMPED pitched; settled
ar ENCARPUS festoon of fruit
ENCASHED realized; cashed
ENCASING boxing; packing
bd ENCASTRE end-fixed, of a beam
ENCAVING hiding in a cave
ENCHARGE to trust
ENCHASED decorated
ENCHISEL to chisel
ENCHORIC demotic
ENCIRCLE encompass; hem; environ
ENCLISIS ENCLITIC, (grammatical
   accentuation)
ENCLOSED wrapped; enveloped
ENCLOSER fencer of land
ENCLOTHE to clothe
ENCOFFIN prepare for burial
ENCOLLAR encircle
ENCOLOUR tinge
ENCOLURE horse's mane
ENCOMIUM panegyric; eulogy
ENCORING calling for a repeat
ENCRADLE lay in a cradle
mn ENCRINAL ENCRINIC, (fossilized sea-
   lilies)
ENCROACH trench; intrude; infringe
ENCUMBER burden; clog; obstruct
ENCURLED interlaced
ENCYCLIC Catholic circular
md ENCYSTED enclosed in a wart or
   shell
ENDAMAGE cause loss; spoil
ENDANGER hazard; imperil;
   jeopardize
ENDEARED beloved; made fond
ENDEMIAL locally prevalent
ENDENIZE naturalize
md ENDERMIC (through the skin)
bt ENDOCARP inner coat of fruit
zo ENDOCYST inner membrane
zo ENDODERM inner skin
ENDOGAMY tribal intermarriage
pl END-ORGAN receptor, motor nerve
ENDORSED ratified; approved
ENDORSEE the assignee
bt ENDOSARC endoplasm
zo ENDOSOME protozoa nuclei central
   mass
ENDOWING presenting; bequeathing
bt ENDOZOIC living inside animal
pr ENDPAPER link between cover and
   book
zo END-PLATE muscle motor-nerve
   ending

el END-PLATE type of electrode
ENDURING lasting; persisting
mu ENERGICO with vitality
ENERGIZE animate; excite; force
ENERVATE weaken; sap; relax
ENFEEBLE debilitate; paralyse
ENFETTER manacle; shackle
ar ENFILADE to rake; gunfire volley in
   battle; doors in sequence
ENFOLDED clasped; enclosed
ENFORCED compelled; obliged
ENFORCER active agent; rules
   referee; cop; pressurizer
ENGAGING winning; charming
ENGENDER produce; beget
ENGILDED gilt
ENGINEER scheme; a sapper; (civil);
   mechanic; fitter; contriver
ENGINERY implement of war
ENGINING contriving; racking
ENGIRDED encircled
ENGIRDLE encompass; encircle
hd ENGLANTE heraldic acorns, etc.
ENGORGED glutted
hd ENGOULED heraldic absorption
ENGRAVED scribed; chiselled; cut
ENGRAVER carver; sculptor
ENGROOVE cut a furrow
ENGULFED devoured; overwhelmed
ENHANCED heightened; raised
ENHANCER augmenter
ENJOINED commanded; directed
ENJOINER prohibiter
ENJOYING appreciating; delighting
   in
ENLACING encircling; entwining
ck ENLARDED basted with fat
ENLARGED dilated; expanded
ENLARGER an amplifier
ENLISTED enrolled; engaged
ENMESHED entrapped; caught
ENNEADIC nine of
ENNEAGON nine-sided polygon
ENNEATIC ninth
ENNOBLED made illustrious
ENORMITY atrocity; depravity
ENORMOUS vast; monstrous; gigantic
ENQUIRED inquired; investigated
ENQUIRER a snooper; questioner
ENRAGING maddening; exasperating
ENRAVISH enrapture; entrance
ENRICHED endowed; adorned
ENRICHER a fertilizer
ENRIDGED furrowed; corrugated
ENRINGED encircled
ENROBING dressing
ENROLLED registered; recorded
ENROLLER inscriber

ENROOTED firmly fixed; established
ck ENSALADA onion/tomato salad (Sp.)
ENSCONCE protect; hide; harbour
mu ENSEMBLE all together
ENSHIELD guard; screen
ENSHRINE treasure; cherish
ENSHROUD veil; mask; conceal
ENSIFORM like a sword
ENSIGNCY rank of ensign
ENSLAVED in bondage; enthralled
ENSLAVER captor; subjugator
ENSNARED trapped; inveigled
ENSOULED animated
ENSURING guaranteeing; safe-
   guarding
ENTAILED settled on heirs
ENTAILER a deviser
ENTANGLE mat; ravel; implicate
zo ENTELLUS sacred monkey
ENTERING penetrating; noting
ps ENTHALPY thermodynamic property
ENTHRONE install; exalt; elevate
ENTHUSED became ardent
ENTICING alluring; coaxing
ENTIRELY fully; perfectly
ENTIRETY aggregate; completeness
ENTITLED styled; dubbed;
   empowered
ENTOMBED buried; interred
zo ENTOMOID like an insect
ENTOPTIC inner vision
zo ENTOZOIC ENTOZOON, of internal
   parasites
mu ENTR'ACTE an interval
md ENTRAILS internal parts; offal
ENTRANCE entry; to ravish
ENTREATY urgent request; petition
ck ENTREMET sweet dish
ENTRENCH fortify; encroach
ENTREPAS an amble (Fr.)
ENTREPOT emporium; transit depot
ENTRESOL mezzanine storey
ENTWINED woven; plaited; twisted
md, pc ENURESIS incontinence
ENVEIGLE inveigle; lure; seduce
ENVELOPE a cover; surround;
   dirigible gasbag (airship)
cp, tc ENVELOPE pre- and suffix data code
   signals
ENVIABLE most desirable
ENVIABLY covetously; grudgingly
ENVIRONS suburbs; vicinity
ENVISAGE to face; to consider
zo ENZOOTIC (localized disease)
EOLIENNE dress material; silk and
   wool
EOLIPILE experimental flask
gl EOLITHIC pre-paleolithic

EPAGOGIC inductive
zo EPALPATE no feelers
EPANODOS rhetorical recapitulation
EPENDYMA spinal cord epithelium in
   vertebrates
EPENETIC laudatory
zo EPHEMERA may-flies; etc.
EPHESIAN debauchee; (Ephesus)
md EPIBLAST outer skin
bt EPICALEX outer calyx
EPICERIE grocery; spices (Fr.)
zo EPICOELE cerebellum ventricle in
   craniata
md EPICOLIC (abdomen over colon)
bt, zo EPICOTYL axis of feather or seedling
cy EPICRINE type of secretion gland
EPICYCLE circulating circle
md EPIDEMIC locally prevalent
mn EPIDOTIC (vitreous ore)
zo EPIGAMIC appealing to opposite sex
bt EPIGEOUS low growing
EPIGRAPH motto; inscription
md EPILEPSY fits
EPILOGIC concluding
EPILOGUE farewell speech
hd EPIMACUS heraldic griffin
zo EPIMERAL (segment above joint)
EPIMERON posterior of sclerites in
   insects
mn EPIMORPH crystal natural cast
bt EPINASTY curvature
pc EPINOSIC advantage by illness
zo EPIORNIS extinct bird (Madagascar)
rl EPIPHANY 6 January
md EPIPHORA streams of tears
bt EPIPHYTE (mistletoe, orchids), non-
   parasitic cohabiting plant
bt EPIPLASM residual cytoplasm in
   ascus
EPIPLOCE rhetorical climax
zo EPIPODIA lateral foot lobes in
   gastropoda
EPIPOLIC fluorescent
zo EPIPROCT plate over insect anus
zo EPIPUBIC before or above pubis
lt EPISCOPE projection lantern
rl EPISCOPY superintendence; search
EPISEMON city badge (Gr.)
EPISODAL digressive; accidental
EPISODIC incidental; subordinate
bt EPISPERM outer seed cover
bt EPISPORE outside spore-wall layer
EPISTLER letter-writer; scribe; Paul
EPISTOME face/mouth region in
   various creatures
ar EPISTYLE the architrave
EPITASIS climax; culmination
bt EPITHECA diatom cell valve

EPITONIC overstrained
EPITRITE metrical foot
EPITROPE rhetorical concession
zo EPIZOITE sedentary attached animals
zo EPIZOOTY animal epidemic
EPLICATE unplaited
EPONYMIC yclept; named after
EPOPOEIA epic poetry
mn EPSOMITE Epsom salts
md EPULOTIC cicatrizing
EQUALISE equalize; even
EQUALITY uniformity; sameness
EQUALLED rivalled
EQUATING balancing
EQUATION allowance for inaccuracy
EQUIFORM of equal shape; similar
EQUIPAGE outfit; effects; train
EQUIPPED accoutred; armed
EQUITANT riding astraddle
ERASABLE effaceable
ERASTIAN follower of Erasmus
ERECTILE capable of elevation
ERECTING raising; building
bd ERECTION structure; edifice;
building; (penile)
EREMETIC hermit-like; solitary
md ERETHISM acute irritation
EREWHILE formerly
zo ERGATOID like a worker insect
ERGONOMY physiological distinction
of functions
bl ERGOSOME unit of cell-protein
synthesis
bt ERGOTINE ERGOTIZE, ERGOTISM,
parasitical, poisonous fungus
bt ERIGERON flea-bane genus
mn ERIONITE uncommon zeolite
hd ERMINOIS heraldic fur
EROTICAL amatory; amorous; (Eros)
ERRANTLY like knights of old
ERRANTRY rambling; roving
ERRORIST fallacious fellow
ERUCTATE belch
ERUGATED wrinkled; corrugated
bt ERUMPENT breaking out
ERUPTING casting out
gl, md ERUPTION outburst; volcanic;
suppuration; boil
ERUPTIVE explosive
zo ERYCINIA insect genus
bt ERYSIMUM hare's ear, etc.
md ERYTHEMA a skin disease
ERYTHRON red blood cell
ESCALADE ESCALADO, attack by
means of scaling ladders
ESCALATE increase in scope
zo ESCALLOP scallop; a bi-valve
ck ESCALOPE boneless meat slice

ESCAPADE prank; adventure; frolic
ESCAPADO desperado; on the loose
ESCAPING evading; eluding
ESCAPISM ESCAPIST, the quest of a
mental anodyne
ck ESCARGOT edible snail
ck ESCAROLE dark green salad plant
ESCARPED steeply sloped
ESCHEWED shunned; avoided
ESCHEWER non-joiner; loner
ESCORTED attended; conducted
lw ESCOTTED taxed; maintained
ESOTERIC secret; mysterious
ESPALIER trellised trees
bt ESPARCET sainfoin
ESPECIAL particular; special
bt ESPIBAWN ox-eye daisy
bt ESPIOTTE species of rye
ESPOUSAL betrothal
ESPOUSED married
ESPOUSER wooer
md ESPUNDIA S. Amer. skin infection
ESQUIRED promoted to esquire
(adjutant)
ESSAYING attempting; endeavouring
ESSAYISH experimental
ESSAYIST a scribe; writer
ESSAYKIN short essay
ESSENCED perfumed
ESSENISM Essene doctrine
gl ESSEXITE alkali-gabbro igneous rock
ESSOINED excused for absence
lw ESSOINER attendance excuser
mn ESSONITE yellow garnet
hd ESSORANT heraldic wings
mu ESTAMPIE Fr. instrumental dance
form
ESTANCIA cattle ranch, S. America
ESTEEMED held in high regard
ESTEEMER valuer; admirer
ch ESTERASE ester-hydrolysing enzyme
ESTHESIA ESTHESIS, sensitivity
cf -ESTHESIC of sensibility
ESTHETIC aesthetic; perceptive
ESTIMATE appraise; calculate
nt ESTIVAGE method of ship loading
ESTIVATE pass the summer
ESTONIAN of Estonia (Baltic republic)
lw ESTOPPED impeded; barred
lw ESTOPPEL a plea
lw ESTOVERS timber supplies
ESTRANGE alienate; disaffect
zo ESTRIDGE ostrich down
ESTROGEN female genital hormone
ESTUANCE heat, warmth
ESURIENT greedy; hungry
ps ETA-MESON zero spin elementary
particle

ETA-PATCH balloon patch
ETCETERA etc; etc.
ETEOSTIC a chronogram
ETERNITY perpetuity
ETERNIZE immortalize
ETHEREAL airy; heavenly; celestial
ch **ETHERENE** etherine; a gas
ETHERISM effects of ether
md **ETHERIZE** to gas
ch **ETHEROLE** a light oil
ETHICIST moralist
ETHIOPIC Abyssinian; Ethiopian
ETHNARCH Greek governor
ETHNICAL of mankind (cultural,
    linguistic groupings)
pc **ETHOGRAM** behaviour pattern
pc **ETHOLOGY** cultural customs; animal
    behaviour in wild
ch **ETHYLENE** carburetted hydrogen
ETIOLATE to blanch
ETIOLOGY study of causes
mu **ETOUFFEZ** (Fr.) stuff it down;
    dampen
ETRURIAN ETRUSCAN, of Etruria
ETYPICAL exceptional; aberrant
bt **EUCALYPT** eucalyptus
EUCARPIC with vegetative and
    reproductive organs
bt **EUCHARIS** Amazon lilies, etc.
EUCTICAL supplicatory
EUCYCLIC made up of matching
    successive whorls
EUGENICS eugenism
EUGENIST (race culture)
EUGUBINE (bronze tablets)
bl **EUKARYON** higher-organism nucleus
EULACHAN candle-fish oil
EULOGIST panegyrist
EULOGIUM laudatory speech;
    encomium
EULOGIZE extol; applaud; flatter
zo **EUMERISM** aggregation of like parts
md **EUMYDRIN** atropine-like medicament
zo **EUNICEAE** a worm genus
bt **EUONYMIN EUONYMOUS,** spindle-tree
    extract
bt **EUPATORY** hemp agrimony
EUPATRID Athenian aristocrat
md **EUPEPSIA** good digestion
EUPEPTIČ highly digestible
EUPHONIA smooth enunciation
EUPHONIC harmonious; felicitous
mu **EUPHONON EUPHONIUM,** brass
    instrument
EUPHORIA satisfaction of the artist
md **EUPHRASY** the eye-bright plant
EUPHUISM bombastic diction
EUPHUIST affected speaker; pedant

EUPHUIZE over-emphasize
cy **EUPLOIDY** polyploidy involving
    exact haploid multiples
EUPYRENE typical, of spermatozoa
EUPYRION a quick match, etc.
EURASIAN European-Asiatic
ch **EUROPIUM** metallic element
EURYTHMY symmetry; regularity
rl **EUSEBIAN** (Eusebius)
zo **EUSOCIAL** division of labour
    (insects)
EUTECTIC easily melted
zo **EUTHERIA** genus of mammals
EUTHROPY good digestion
pc **EUTHYMIA** tranquillity; relaxed state
mn **EUXENITE** uncommon rare-element
    mineral
pm **EVACUANT** purgative; laxative
EVACUATE quit; abandon; forsake;
    empty
EVADIBLE escapable; evasible
EVANESCE disappear; vanish
EVASIBLE avoidable; elusory
EVECTION convection
EVEN-DOWN downright
EVENFALL twilight
EVENNESS levelness; regularity
rl **EVENSONG** end of day service
EVENTFUL full of incident; stirring
EVENTIDE evenfall; evening
EVENTUAL last; ultimate; final
EVERMORE always; eternally
EVERYDAY usual; common; routine
EVERYONE everybody
EVERYWAY in all ways
EVICTING expelling; ousting
EVICTION dispossession
EVIDENCE testimony; witness
EVILDOER malefactor; criminal
EVILNESS malignity; depravity
EVINCING demonstrating; exhibiting
EVINCIVE indicative
EVITABLE avoidable; escapable
lw **EVOCATOR** a summoner
EVOLVING on-going evolution
EXACTING enforcing; critical; rigid
EXACTION extortion; tribute
EXALTING extolling; honouring
EXAMINED inquired; studied
EXAMINEE candidate
EXAMINER scrutinizer; inspector
EXAMPLAR model; exemplar; pattern
md **EXANTHEM** surface rash
EXCAVATE delve; dig; scoop
EXCEEDED surpassed; capped;
    excelled
EXCEEDER outdoer; surpasser
EXCEPTED excluded; omitted

EXCEPTOR objector; abstainer
EXCERNED excreted; exuded
EXCESSED exceeded
EXCESSES surpluses; over the limits; orgies
cp **EXCHANGE** barter; commute; transaction
EXCISING cutting out
EXCISION extirpation; amputation
EXCITANT a stimulant
EXCITING rousing; inciting; inflaming
EXCITIVE provocative
EXCITRON mercury-arc rectifier
EXCLUDED banned; barred; vetoed
EXCURSED digressed; wandered
EXCURSUS supplemented treatise
EXCUSING remitting; condoning
EXECRATE curse; detest; abhor
EXECUTED beheaded; achieved
lw **EXECUTER EXECUTOR**, testamentary agent; deed drafter
EXEGESIS explanatory discourse
EXEGETIC elucidative
EXEMPLAR pattern; examplar; model
EXEMPTED excused; released
EXEQUIAL funereal
EXEQUIES obsequies; funeral rites
EXERCISE use; task; drill; exert
EXERGUAL date space on coin
EXERTING striving; wielding
EXERTION effort; strain; attempt
EXERTIVE labouring; toilsome
EXHALANT exhalent; evaporative
EXHALING breathing; emitting
EXHORTED encouraged; warned
EXHORTER incitor; adviser
EXHUMATE disinter; exhume
EXHUMING digging up
EXIGEANT exacting; importunate
EXIGENCY exigence; urgency
EXIGIBLE able to be levied
EXIGUITY scantiness; fineness
EXIGUOUS tiny; diminutive; minute
bt **EXINTINE** floral membrane
EXISTENT extant; living
EXISTING being; continuing
ps **EXITANCE** (luminous); (radiant)
EX-LIBRIS (book-plate)
EXOCHITE outer layer of fucales macrosporangium
zo **EXOCOELE** portion of coelenteron
zo **EXOCRINE** of gland secretion; duct-carried
pc **EXOGAMIC** of marriage outside social group
EXOPHAGY selective cannibalism
EXORABLE not relentless; lenient

rl **EXORCISM EXORCIST, EXORCIZE,** deliverance from evil spirits
EXORDIAL introductory
EXORDIUM the beginning; preamble
EXOSMOSE diffusion
bt **EXOSPORE** outer layer of spore wall
bt **EXOSTOME** part of ovule
EXOTERIC openly professed; superficial
EXOTHERM heat liberator
ba **EXOTOXIN** bacterium-released toxin
EXPANDED stretched; dilated
el, cp **EXPANDER COMPANDOR,** with built-in volume compressor
EXPECTED awaited; forecast
EXPEDITE hasten; accelerate
EXPELLEE expelled; dismissed; sacked
EXPENDED consumed; money used
EXPERTLY dexterously; adroitly
EXPIABLE atonable
EXPIATED made reparation
EXPIATOR indemnifier
EXPIRANT a dying person
EXPIRING at death's door
EXPLICIT clearly stated; categorical
EXPLODED burst; repudiated
EXPLODER a machine
EXPLORED scrutinized; plumbed
EXPLORER investigator
ma **EXPONENT** an executant; idea supporter; power
EXPORTED shipped; sent abroad
EXPORTER foreign trader
EXPOSING exhibiting; revealing
EXPOSURE disclosure; revelation
EXPUGNED overcome; conquered
EXPUNGED erased; deleted
EXTENDED stretched; protracted
EXTENDER dilator; expander
pl **EXTENSOR** joint muscle
EXTERIOR outer; outward
EXTERNAL outer; foreign; exotic
EXTOLLER eulogizer
EXTORTED wrested; extracted
EXTRADOS convex surface of vault
EXTRUDED pointed outwards; visible
EXULTANT triumphant; jubilant
EXULTING crowing; rejoicing
EXUVIATE moult; shed a skin
EYEGLASS monocle
EYEPIECE telescope lens
EYESALVE eyewash; ointment
EYESIGHT vision
zo **EYE-STALK** eye-bearing stalk in crustacea
md **EYESTONE** optical adjunct
EYE-TO-EYE vis-à-vis; face to face

EYETOOTH a canine tooth
EYEWATER tear; lotion

F

FABLIAUX French metrical tale
FABULIST an Aesop
FABULIZE narrate a romance
FABULOUS super; better than real
mu FABURDEN plainsong with simple
  harmony
md FACE-ACHE neuralgia
FACE-CARD court card
cp FACE-DOWN submissive; of punch
  cards
FACELESS lacking a physiognomy
FACE-PACK cosmetic
FACETIAE witticisms; pleasantries
FACETING cutting facets
FACIALLY superficially; externally
FACILITY dexterity; readiness;
  address
FACINGLY oppositely
FACTIOUS turbulent; riotous
FACTOTUM general assistant; dog's
  body
FACULOUS spotted
FADDLING trifling; playing
FADEAWAY old soldier; screwball
  (baseball)
FADELESS imperishable; enduring
FADINGLY decreasingly; vapidly
bt FAE-BERRY fea-berry; gooseberry
mu FAGGOTED bundled (firewood); of
  bassoon
FAGOTING a kind of embroidery
cp FAIL-SAFE automatic close-down
  device
cp FAIL-SOFT slowdown device
FAINTEST barely perceptible;
  dimmest
FAINTING swooning
FAINTISH giddy; languid
FAIR-COPY correct copy
FAIR-HAND freehand
FAIRINGS small porcelain ornament
  (Ger.)
FAIRINGS first milk after calf-birth
nt FAIR-LEAD a rope-guide
FAIRNESS honest dealing; equity
FAIR-PLAY justice; impartiality
FAIRYDOM fairyland
FAIRYISM enchantment
FAITHFUL leal; loyal; steadfast
FAKEMENT makeshift; swindle
FAKIRISM mysticism; poverty
FALCATED like a sickle

FALCHION short curved sword
FALCONER a hawker
zo FALCONET small hawk; cannon
FALCONRY hawking
FALDERAL meaningless refrain
FALDETTA hood and cape (Malta)
ga FALL-AWAY rocket launching pad; to
  pass (ball games)
FALL-BACK reserve; retreat;
  (wrestling)
FALL-DOWN inadequacy; failure
FALLIBLE capable of errors
FALLIBLY erroneously
FALLOWED (field) ploughed but not
  sown
FALL-TRAP a snare
mu FALSETTE FALSETTO, shrill and
  unnatural tone of voice
pr FALSTAFF fat face
FALTERED wavered; hesitated
FAMELESS undistinguished
FAMILIAL common to a family
FAMILIAR unceremonious; intimate
rl FAMILIST (16th-century sect)
FAMISHED anhungered; starved
FAMOUSLY remarkably; eminently
FAMULIST magician's attendant
FAN-BLAST forced delight
FANCIFUL whimsical; capricious
FANCYING preferring; (love);
  imagining
mu FANDANGO Spanish national dance
FANFARON swaggering bully;
  braggart
FANGLESS toothless; (without
  venom)
FANLIGHT lunette; window over
  doorway
mu FANTASIA musical medley
FAN-WHEEL ventilating device
me FARADAIC FARADIZE, FARADISM, of a
  farad
FARCICAL ludicrous; absurd; droll
vt FARCY-BUD glanders
FARDELED in bundles
FAREWELL adieu; good-bye; parting
FAR-FLUNG widely disseminated
FARINOSE mealy; floury
FARMABLE cultivatable
FARMYARD rooster's realm
FARRIERY veterinary work
FARROWED littered
FAR-SPENT well advanced
FARTHEST ultimate; yondmost
nm FARTHING four a penny (d)
FASCHING winter masquerade season
  (Ger.)
FASCICLE a cluster

zo **FASCIOLA** narrow band of colour
FASCIOLE ciliated spines in spatangoidea
FASCISTI Italian fascists
FASCISTS opponents of socialism
FASHIOUS vexatious; provocative
mn **FASSAITE** monoclinic pyroxene
FASTBALL pitch at full speed (baseball)
FASTENED secured; bound; tied
FASTNESS a stronghold; security
FATALISM FATALIST, (belief in the inevitable)
FATALITY a calamity; disaster
FATHERED adopted; begat; sired
FATHERLY paternal; benign
FATHOMED comprehended; plumbed
FATIGUED weary; jaded; tired
FATTENED overfed
FATTENER a fat producer
FAULTFUL defective
FAULTILY imperfectly
FAULTING accusing
FAUTEUIL arm-chair; stall
zo **FAUVETTE** garden warbler
FAVONIAN (west wind)
FAVOURED encouraged; approved
FAVOURER patron; supporter
mn **FAYALITE** an iron ore
bt **FEABERRY** faeberry; gooseberry
FEARLESS intrepid; undaunted; heroic
FEARSOME dread; awe inspiring
FEASIBLE FEASIBLY, workable; achievable; possibly
rl **FEAST-DAY** a festival
FEASTFUL sumptuous; luxurious
FEASTING banqueting; carousing
FEAST-WON (elections) bribed by feasting
FEATEOUS dexterous; deft
FEATHERY with plumes; golf-shot (raising soil); oar-stroke (spray)
FEATNESS adroitness; neatness
FEATURED details, items, actors shown
FEBRIFIC causing fever
FEBRUARY month of expiation
FECKLESS inefficient; spiritless
FECULENT muddy; turbid; fetid
FEDERACY confederacy; alliance
FEDERARY a confederate
FEDERATE league together
FEEBLISH weakish
el **FEEDBACK** sound; energy phenomenon
cp **FEED-BACK** reaction report
FEED-HEAD cistern of a boiler

FEED-PIPE water-pipe
FEED-PUMP a force-pump
pg **FEER-TYPE** positive process
FEETLESS footless; apodal
FEIGNING counterfeiting; shamming
FEINTING pretending; misleading
mn **FELDSPAR** felspar
FELICIDE cat-killing
FELICITY happiness; bliss; blessedness
FELINITY cattishness
FELLABLE capable of being felled
FELLAHIN Egyptian peasants
FELLATIO oral penis stimulation
FELLNESS ruthlessness; ferocity
FELLOWED matched
FELLOWLY companionable
FELLSIDE mountain side
lw **FELO-DE-SE** suicide
mn **FELSITIC** like porphyry
mn **FELSTONE** (quartz and felspar)
FELTERED matted together
FELTMARK imprint left in papermaking
FELTSIDE smooth side of roll of paper
bt **FELTWORT** the mullein
FEMALITY feminality
FEMERELL louvre or ventilator
FEMICIDE lady-killing
FEMININE female; effeminate; tender
FEMINISM (women's rights)
FEMINIST advocate of feminism
FEMINITY womanliness
FFMINIZE to make effeminate
bt **FENBERRY** cranberry
FENCEFUL affording defence
FENCE-OFF exclude; preliminary bout (fencing)
ch **FENCHONE** dicyclic ketone
FENCIBLE a home guard
FENESTER FENESTRA, a window
zo **FEN-GOOSE** greylag goose
FENTHION chemical insecticide
bt **FENUGREC** sort of clover
lw **FEOFFING** granting fief, feudal rights
FERACITY fecundity; fruitfulness
rl **FERETORY** shrine for relics
FERINELY wildly; savagery
bt **FERN-SEED** spores
bt **FERNSHAW** a thicket of ferns
FEROCITY cruelty; savagery
FERREOUS of iron
FERRETED unearthed
FERRETER ferret-like investigator
FERRETTO for colouring glass
nt **FERRIAGE** ferry charge

FERRITES ferro magnetic materials (ceramics)
FERRITIN liver protein
FERRULED tipped
FERRYING transporting
FERRY-MAN Charon (river Styx)
FERULING caning (as punishment)
FERVENCY ardour; devotion; eagerness
FERVIDLY hotly; zealously; with heat
FESTALLY joyously; jovially; merrily
md **FESTERED** rankled; turned septic
FESTIVAL mirthful; an occasion
FETCHING attractive; bringing
bt **FETERITA** dwarf sorghum
FETISHES charms; talismans; amulets
FETTERED shackled; manacled
FETTLING conditioning
bt **FEVERFEW** a febrifuge
FEVERING agitating; heating
FEVERISH inconstant; sultry
FEVEROUS restless; excited
FEWTRILS trifles (dial.)
FIBERKIE fluff on a blanket
bt **FIBRILLA** a filament
FIBROGEN protein
FIBROSIS fibrous growth
md **FIBROTIC** of fibrosis
FIBULATE tell fibs, untruths
pl **FIBULATE FIBULOUS**, of real leg-bones
mu **FIDDLING** playing the violin (folk occasions)
FIDELITY faithful honesty; reliability
FIDGETED worried; fretted; chafed
mu **FIDICULA** small lute
FIDUCIAL honesty in money transactions
FIELD-BED camp-bed
FIELD-DAY tactical exercise
FIELD-GUN mobile gun
FIELDING cricket
FIENDISH malicious; devilish
FIERCELY zealously; vehemently
FIERCEST most ferocious
FIERY-HOT blazing; impetuous
FIERY-NEW brand-new
nt **FIFE-RAIL** belaying pin rack
FIFTIETH ordinal of fifty
bt **FIG-APPLE** a coreless apple
zo **FIG-EATER** garden warbler
FIGHTING contention; strife; faction
zo **FIG-SHELL** a univalve shell
FIGULATE moulded
mn **FIGULINE** potter's clay
FIGURANT male ballet dancer

FIGURATE of determinate form
FIGURIAL represented by a figure
FIGURINE small statuette (Fr.); Oscar (prize)
FIGURING calculating; symbolizing
FIGURIST one skilled in figures
FILAMENT slender thread
FILATORY spinning machine
FILATURE the reeling of silk
FILCHING pilfering; purloining
zo **FILE-FISH** a sea-fish
FILIALLY like a son or daughter
FILIATED adopted; amalgamated
bt **FILICORD** fern-like plant
FILIFORM thread-like
FILIGREE metal lacework designs
rl **FILIOQUE** (clause in Nicene creed) concerning status of God's son
FILIPINO (Philippines)
ck **FILLETED** meat, fish less the bones
FILLIBEG a kilt (Sc.)
FILMGOER a frequenter of cinemas
FILM-STAR popular actor/actress
ga **FILOPINA PHILOPINA**, a nut-game
FILTERED percolated; strained
FILTHIER grubbier
FILTHILY dirtily
FILTRATE filtered solution
FINALISM conclusiveness; purposeful; teleology (ends)
FINALIST in the last round
FINALITY kismet; eventuality
FINANCED capitalized
FINDABLE discoverable
FINE-DRAW invisible mending
FINELESS endless; unlimited
FINENESS purity
FINE-SPUN elaborated
FINESSED acted artfully
FINESSER crafty person
FINGERED handled
FINGROMS woollen cloth
FINISHED ended
FINISHER final blow
FINITELY within limits
FINITUDE limitation
FINNESKO shoe made from reindeer skin
zo **FINNIKIN** crested pigeon
bt **FINOCHIO** sweet fennel
zo **FINSCALE** rudd, fish
zo **FIN-WHALE** rorqual
FIREARMS offensive weapons
ar **FIREBACK** ornamental heat refraction plate
FIRE-BALL explosive-like outbreak
FIRE-BARS furnace bars
FIRE-BOAT fire-fighting steamboat

FIREBOMB incendiary missile; grenade
mn **FIRECLAY** used for fire-bricks
FIRECOCK hydrant connexion
FIREDAMP explosive gas in mines
FIRE-EYED with fiery eyes
FIREFLAG flash of lightning
FIRE-GIRL woman fire fighter
FIRE-HOOK demolition hook
FIRE-HOSE portable piping
FIRE-KILN an oven
FIRELESS showing no flames
FIRELOCK antique musket
FIRE-PLUG valve in a water-main
nt **FIRESHIP** incendiary ship
FIRESIDE the hearth
FIRE-STEP firing-step (warfare) trench
zo **FIRETAIL** the redstart
FIRETRAP (no means of escape)
FIREWARD towards the fire! (as seaward)
bt **FIREWEED** a plant
FIREWOOD chopped sticks
FIRMLESS wavering; unstable
FIRMNESS solidity; resolution
FIRST-AID emergency help
FISHABLE capable of being fished
FISH-BALL fish-cake
FISHBEAM beam of special form
FISH-CAKE fish-ball
FISH-COOP box used for ice-fishing
FISh-GLUE an adhesive; isinglass
zo **FISH-HAWK** the osprey
FISH-HOOK barbed hook
FISH-MEAL fodder; fertilizer
FISH-POND fish storage tank
FISh-ROOM part of ship
FISH-SKIN fish epidermis
FISHTAIL a gas jet; jewellery
FISH-WEIR a fishgarth
FISH-WIFE fish vendor
FISSIPED cloven hoof
FISSURED cleft; cracked
FISTIANA boxing annals
bt **FISTINUT** pistachio nut
FISTULAR tubular
FITFULLY spasmodically; inconstantly
FIVEFOLD 500%
FIVELEAF cinquefoil
FIXATION cast-iron attitudes, opinions
pc **FIXATION** obsessive attachment
pg **FIXATIVE** a stabilizer; adhesive; gum
FIXATURE hair cream
FIXIDITY permanence; constancy
FIZZLING sizzling

FLABBILY limply; weakly
FLAGGING naval fore to aft celebration
FLAGGING becoming exhausted; weakening
FLAGGING denoting winner of horse races, Olympics
FLAGRANT notorious wrongdoing
nt **FLAG-SHIP** leading ship; with flag officer
zo **FLAG-WORM** green gentle
FLAMBEAU a lighted torch
FLAMELET small flame
mu **FLAMENCO** folk dance, music (Sp.)
zo **FLAMINGO** long-legged waterbird
FLAMMING deluding
FLAMMULE pictorial Japanese flame
hd **FLANCHED** heraldic term; flanged
FLANERIE lounging (Fr.)
FLANKING bordering; touching
ck **FLAP-JACK** cookie; compact
FLAPPING flopping; waving; shaking
FLASHILY transiently; gaudily
FLASHING bursts of light; signals; lightning
nt **FLAT-BOAT** invasion landing-craft
zo **FLAT-FISH** flounder, sole, dab, plaice etc.
FLAT-FOOT fallen arches; (of policemen)
FLAT-IRON smoothing iron
FLATNESS monotony; depression
FLAT-RACE not a steeplechase
FLATTERY insincere compliment
FLATTEST dullest, lowest; very level
FLATTING a process
FLATTISH comparatively level
FLATWISE not edgewise
zo **FLAT-WORM** tape worm
FLAUNTED vaunted; paraded
FLAUNTER ostentatious person
mu **FLAUTATO** FLAUTANDO, flute-like effect from violins (It.)
mu **FLAUTIST** FLUTER, flute player
FLAWLESS perfect; without blemish
FLAX-COMB a heckle
bt **FLAX-LILY** New Zealand flax
FLAX-MILL a factory
bt **FLAX-SEED** linseed
bt **FLAX-TAIL** the reed-mace
bt **FLAX-WEED** FLAX-WORT, plants of doubtful provenance
bt **FLEA-BANE** flea-discouraging plant
FLEA-BITE an inconvenient trifle
FLEAKING reed covering under thatch
bt **FLEA-WORT** a plant
FLECKING dappling

FLECTION flexion; bending
FLEECING shearing; swindling
FLEERING mocking; taunting
FLEETEST fastest; swiftest
FLEETING transient; passing; brief
FLENCHED fists as for punching
FLENSING removing skin (whaling)
zo **FLESH-FLY** blow-fly; bluebottle
FLESHING tights; scraping leather
FLESHING add colour to portraits; filling
FLESHPOT stock-pot; good living; night life
FLETCHED feathered (arrows)
ga **FLETCHER** and bow-man (archery)
FLEXIBLE FLEXIBLY, pliant; tractable; not rigid
FLEXUOSE FLEXUOUS, winding; wavering; curving; elastic
FLIC-FLAC back handspring (gymnastics)
FLICKING flipping
mu **FLICORNO** brass band instruments including sax-like instrument (military) (It.)
FLIGHTED took wing
FLIMFLAM humbug; nonsense
FLIMSIES carbon copies
FLIMSILY unsubstantially
FLINCHED winced; shrank back
FLINCHER shrinker; coward
FLINDERS fragments; flitters
FLINGING hurling; casting; pitching
FLINTIFY turn into flint
FLIPFLAP an entertaining device; scenery; theatre
cp, el **FLIPFLOP** walking noise; two state circuit
FLIPPANT pert; saucy; glib
FLIPPERS swim fins of seal and surfer
FLIPPING flicking
FLIRTING philandering; (fan)
FLIRTISH somewhat coquettish
FLITTERS vagrant non-rent payers
FLITTING hastening; leaving hurriedly
bt **FLIXWEED** a hedge plant
lw **FLOATAGE** FLOATSAM, FLOTSAM, shipwrecked goods
md **FLOATERS** 'flying flies' in the eye
FLOATERS markers; inconstants, voters
FLOATING circulating; wafting
FLOATING sideways movement (basketball)
FLOCCOSE tufted
FLOCCULE small tuft of wool

FLOCK-BED bed stuffed with flock
FLOCK-GUN dry spray for textile finishes
FLOCKING congregating; crowding
FLOGGING a chastisement
FLOODING inundating; swamping
FLOOD-LIT illuminated
FLOOKING cross vein or fissure
FLOORAGE floor space
FLOORING material for floors
FLOORMAN bookies' runner at races
mn **FLOPGATE** diverting materials moving gate
FLOPPILY limply; flaccidly
FLOPPING falling; collapsing (exhaustion)
FLORALLY with flowers
tx **FLORENCE** wine; cloth
FLORIAGE blossom
zo **FLORICAN** Indian bustard
FLORIDLY ornately; exuberantly
bt **FLORIGEN** hypothetical hormone
bt **FLOSCULE** a floret; a bloom
nt **FLOTILLA** small fleet
FLOUNCED threw oneself about
zo **FLOUNDER** struggle; a fish
FLOURING reducing to powder
mu **FLOURISH** prosper; wave; fanfare
FLOUTING showing off; exhibiting oneself
FLOUTING mocking conventional behaviour
FLOWERED blossomed
FLOWERED peak of artistic endeavour
FLOWERER plant flowering periodically
cp **FLOW-LINE** production, transport diagram
FLUENTLY volubly; easily
mu **FLUE-PIPE** organ pipe (without reed)
FLUFFING muffing
ps **FLUIDICS** science of liquid tube flow
FLUIDIFY fluidize
FLUIDITY fluidism; liquidity
FLUMMERY a drink; humbug
.ch **FLUORIDE** tooth protector
ch **FLUORINE** a gas
mn **FLUORITE** fluorspar
FLUOROUS derived from fluor
FLURRIED agitated; disconcerted
FLUSHING blushing; colouring
FLUSTERY confused; agitated
md **FLUTTERY** flapping; oscillating; (pulse)
FLUXIBLE fusible
FLY-BLOWN shopworn; stale; dated; mouldy

FLY-BOARD container for artificial flies (angling)
FLY-MAKER (fishing)
FLYPAPER a fly-trap
FLY-SHEET handbill; broadside
FLY-WATER an arsenical solution
FLY-WHEEL a conserver of momentum
bt **FOAL-FOOT** colt's foot
FOCALIZE conveying/focus
pg **FOCUSING** correcting perspectives
FODDERER cattle-feeder
FOG-BOUND wrapped in mist
FOGEYDOM senility
FOGGIEST most obscure; murkiest
FOG-SMOKE thick fog
FOILABLE able to be frustrated
FOILPLAY fencing
FOILSMAN fencer
FOLDEROL refrain of old song
FOLDLESS uncreased
FOLD-YARD cattle enclosure
FOLIATED leafy
FOLIATED laminated; process
bt **FOLICOLE** feeding on leaf material
lw **FOLKLAND** common land
FOLK-LORE legendary traditions
FOLKMOTE assembly of freemen
mu **FOLK-SONG** traditional song
FOLK-TALE fairy story
FOLKWAYS group tradition
pl, bt **FOLLICE** small secreting cavity; pod
FOLLOWED imitated instructions given
FOLLOWED tracked; pursued
FOLLOWER partisan; adherent; copier
FOLLOW-ON giving second innings to opponents with lower score (cricket); strongly delivered bowl
FOLLOW-UP second stage support
FOMENTED growth promoted; treated by heat
FOMENTER agitator; agent provocateur
FONDLING a beloved one
FONDNESS affection; predilection
md **FONTANEL** a cavity
FONTANGE wire cap-frame
FOOD-CARD a rational requirement
FOODLESS lacking sustenance
FOOLSCAP paper, 17 × 13½ inches
FOOL-TRAP snare for simpletons
FOOSLING bungling
ga **FOOTBALL** national sport
FOOT-BATH bath to ease feet
FOOT-FALL footstep; tread
FOOTGEAR shoes and stockings

vt **FOOT-HALT** a sheep disease
go **FOOT-HILL** mini relative of mountain
FOOTHOLD support niche
FOOT-IRON carriage step; fetter
FOOTLESS with nothing to stand on
FOOTLING trifling; trivial; trumpery
FOOT-MARK foot-print
FOOT-MUFF foot-warmer
FOOT-NOTE an addendum
FOOT-PACE slow rate of progression
FOOTPATH pedestrian way
FOOT-POST pedestrian messenger
FOOT-RACE running match
nt **FOOT-ROPE** rope along a yard
me **FOOT-RULE** a 12-inch measure
FOOT-SLOG march; walk; tramp; hike
FOOTSORE with aching feet
FOOTSTEP footfall
FOOTWEAR foot-gear
FOOTWORK movement (sport)
FOOTWORN feet feeling over-used
FORAGING ravaging; searching
pl **FORAMINA** openings; orifices
FORAYING plundering; raiding
FORBORNE refrained; spared
FORCEDLY compulsorily; unnaturally
FORCEFUL coercive
FORCIBLE cogent
FORCIBLY violently
FORDABLE crossable wetshod
FORDOING ruining; exhausting
FOREBEAR ancestor; forefather
FOREBODE prognosticate; portended
nt **FORE-BODY** forward part of ship
FORECAST prediction; prognosis
FOREDATE antedate
nt **FOREDECK** in the bows
FOREDONE overpowered
FOREDOOM predestinate
FOREDOOR front door
FORE-EDGE front edge of book
FOREFEEL sense in anticipation
FOREFELT anticipated
nt **FOREFOOT** foremost end of keel
FOREGIFT lease premium
FOREGOER vor-trekker; precursor
FOREGONE already decided
FOREHAND cf. backhand
FOREHEAD brow; audacity; metope
nt **FORE-HOOK** strengthening piece
FOREKNEW foresaw
FOREKNOW know already
FORELAID previously arranged
go **FORELAND** headland; bluff; cape
FORELAND lend in anticipation
FORELENT previously loaned
FORELOCK sometimes a quiff

nt **FOREMAST** forward lower mast
FOREMEAN intend
FOREMOST in the van; leading
FORENAME home name, not
  surname
FORENOON from sunrise to noon
lw **FORENSAL FORENSIC**, of law–court
  procedure
FOREPART the beginning
nt **FOREPEAK** (in the bows)
FOREPLAY precopulation frolic
FOREPLAN to scheme
ce **FOREPOLE** tunnel cutter
FORE-RANK front rank
FORE-READ prognosticate
FORE-RENT rent due before reaping
FORESAID previously mentioned
nt **FORESAIL** one of various sails
FORESEEN expected; anticipated
FORESEER prophet
nt **FORESHIP** fore-part of ship
FORESHOW introductory frolic;
  portend
FORESIDE front side
FORESTAL concerning forests
nt **FORESTAY** part of rigging
FORESTER woodsman
FORESTRY arboriculture
FORETELL predict; augur
FORETIME the past; days of yore
FORETOLD presaged; warned
FOREWARD the van; the front
FOREWARN caution; admonish;
  advise
FOREWENT foregone; by-gone
FOREWIND favouring breeze
FOREWISH look foward to
FOREWORD preface; prologue
nt **FOREYARD** (yard on foremast)
FORGEMAN at blacksmith's
  workshop
FORGIVEN condoned; absolved
FORGIVER pardoner; remitter
FORGOING preceding
FORKEDLY furcated
FORKHEAD (knuckle-joint)
FORKLESS not branching
zo **FORKTAIL** salmon; kite; crow
ch **FORMALIN** an antiseptic
FORMALLY precisely; ceremoniously
ar **FORMERET** wall rib in medieval vault
FORMERLY ci-devant; whilom
FORMLESS shapeless; chaotic
FORMULAE sets of symbols
FORMULAR prescribed; formal
ar **FORMWORK** shuttering (concrete
  mould)
FORRADER further forward (slang)

FORSAKEN left; abandoned;
  renounced
FORSOOTH in truth; indeed
FORSPEAK forbid; bewitch
FORSPEND exhaust; squander
FORSWEAR deny upon oath; abjure
FORSWINK exhaust; wear out
FORSWORE FORSWORN, pledged
  falsely; recanted
ar **FORTRESS** castle; citadel
FORTUIST believer in chance
FORTUITY luck; accident
FORTUNED presaged
ga **FORWARDS** onward; football players
mu **FORZANDO** emphatically (It.)
FOSSDYKE Roman earthwork
  (Lincs.)
FOSSETTE dimple
zo **FOSSORES** burrowers
FOSTERED brought up; cherished
FOSTERER a nurse
FOSTRESS foster-mother
nt **FOTHERED** stopped a leak
FOUGASSE land-mine
zo **FOUL-FISH** fish when spawning
FOUL-HOOK not hooked in gills
FOULNESS dirt; grossness; scurrility
FOUL-PLAY unfair action
ml **FOUNDERY** foundry
FOUNDING establishing; endowing
FOUNTAIN jet of water
FOUNTFUL full of springs
FOURBALL four singles match (golf)
hd **FOURCHEE** cross
FOURFOLD quadruple
FOURLING one of a quadruplet
FOURNEAU explosion chamber (Fr.)
ga **FOURSOME** four together (golf,
  bridge)
FOURTEEN twice seven
FOX-BRUSH a trophy of the chase
FOX-CHASE hunting
FOX-EARTH reynard's home
bt **FOXGLOVE** digitalis
bt **FOXGRAPE** variety of grape
zo **FOXHOUND** hunt dog
FOXINESS craftiness; slyness
zo **FOX-SHARK** thresher shark
FOX-SLEEP pretended sleep
FRACTION part; particle; fragment
FRACTURE break; rift; fissure
bt **FRAGARIA** the strawberry
FRAGMENT shard; scrap; remnant
FRAGRANT odoriferous; redolent
FRAILISH somewhat weak; delicate
FRAMABLE can be framed
to **FRAME-SAW** Italian saw
bt **FRANCATU** russetin apple

ch **FRANCIUM** heaviest alkali metal
lw **FRANK-FEE** tenure in fee-simple
FRANKING remitting postage
FRANKISH (Frank); proto-French
FRANKLIN old English freeholder
FRAPPAGE sharp slapping
nt **FRAPPING** binding; lashing
zo **FRASLING** the perch
FRAUDFUL dishonest; knavish
FRAULEIN German spinster
ch **FRAXININ** extract from ash bark
bt **FRAXINUS** ash-tree genus
FREAKFUL FREAKISH, capricious; abnormal; erratic
pl **FRECKLED** with natural speckled skin
FREEBORN neither vassal nor slave
FREE-CITY independent town
FREE-COST cost free
FREED-MAN emancipated slave
FREEHAND without instrumental aid
lw **FREEHOLD** held in fee-simple
FREE-LOVE promiscuity
FREENESS freedom; liberty
FREE-PORT (duties not levied)
mu **FREE-REED** vibrating reed
FREE-SHOT legendary hunter
FREE-SOIL (no slavery)
FREE-TRIP complimentary tour
FREE-TRIP trip-close mechanisms
FREE-WILL voluntary; spontaneous
FREEZE-UP immobility; infrozen
FREEZING congealing; chilling
md **FREMITUS** palpable vibration
FRENETIC frenzied; distracted
zo **FRENULUM** a butterfly's bristle
FRENZIED maddened; furious
FREQUENT oft repeated; recurrent
FRESCADE a cool walk
FRESCOED painted on plaster
FRESCOER a washy painter
FRESHISH almost fresh
FRESHMAN first year student
FRESH-NEW unpractised
FRETTING worrying; fuming; abrading
FRETWORK interlaced ornament
FREUDIAN psycho-analytic
FRIATION crumbling
FRIBBLED frivolled; tottered
FRIBBLER trifler
FRICTION attrition; abrasion; sliding; rolling
ps **FRICTION** kinetic; coefficient (dynamic, static)
FRIENDED befriended; well-disposed
FRIENDLY kind; favourable; amicable (society); (match)

FRIESIAN FRISIAN, of Friesland, Netherlands
FRIGHTED affrighted; dismayed
FRIGHTEN alarm; scare; intimidate
FRIGIDLY coldly; icily
FRILLING edging material
FRINGENT FRINGING, encircling; bordering; tasselating
FRIPPERY fallals; old clothes
FRISETTE artificial curl
FRISKFUL lively; sportive
FRISKILY briskly; wantonly
FRISKING capering; skipping; romping
FRISKING rapid search for arms on person
gs, ml **FRITTING** pasty condition of powdered ore
FRIZETTE see frisette
FRIZZLED curled; fried
tx **FRIZZLER** hairdresser; cloth-worker
FROCKING coarse jean
zo **FROG-FISH** angler-fish
FROGGERY an abode of frogs
zo **FROGLING** tadpole
zo **FROG-SPIT** froth-fly
FROMWARD away from
FRONDAGE leafage
bt **FRONDENT FRONDOSE, FRONDOUS**, leafy
FRONTAGE building line
FRONTATE widening like a leaf
FRONTIER boundary; border; march
FRONTING facing; opposing
FRONTLET fillet or browband
ar **FRONTOON** a pediment
FROSTILY frigidly; icily; freezingly
FROSTING icing
FROTHERY mere froth; foam
zo **FROTH-FLY** numerous parasites
FROTHILY verbosely
FROTHING bubbling
FROTTAGE coin-rubbing; erotic stimulation
FROTTEUR performer of frottage
FROU-FROU flounced petticoat
FROUNCED plaited hair
FROWNING glowering; scowling
FRUCTIFY to make fruitful; teem
FRUCTOSE fruit sugar
FRUGALLY economically; thriftily
FRUITAGE crop; harvest; produce
bt **FRUIT-BUD** flower to be fruit
FRUITERY fruit-loft
zo **FRUIT-FLY** a pest
FRUITFUL productive; fecund; prolific
FRUITING bearing fruit

FRUITION fulfilment; realization
FRUITIVE enjoying; gratifying
bt **FRUITLET** a small fruit
FRUMENTY porridge of sorts
FRUMPING insulting; flouting
FRUMPISH old-fashioned; ill-natured
bt **FRUSTULE** shell of a diatom
ch **FUCHSINE** magenta; rosaniline
hydrochloride; dye
mn **FUCHSITE** green muscovite
FUDDLING making drunk or
confused
FUELLING taking in fuel
FUGACITY instability; uncertainty
mu **FUGHETTA** (It.) a little fugue
FUGITIVE volatile; vagabond; refugee
FUGLEMAN exemplary soldier
bt **FULCRATE** with supports
FULGENCY effulgence; brilliance
FULGURAL (lightning); flashy
FULL-AGED of mature age
FULL-BACK (football)
FULL-BUTT head-on crash
FULL-EYED with prominent eyes
FULL-FACE cf. profile
FULLNESS fulness; repletion;
profusion
nt **FULL-ROLL** swell and yawing;
croquet shot
pr **FULL-STOP** end of a period
FULL-TIME normal working hours
FULL-WAGE wireless rectifier
FULMINED fulminated; thundered
FULMINIC explosive; detonative
FUMARASE catalysing enzyme
FUMAROLE volcanic smoke hole
FUMATORY fumigating chamber
FUMBLING clumsy; groping
FUMELESS smokeless
bt **FUMEWORT** the fumitory plant
FUMIGANT fume-producing; incense
FUMIGATE disinfect by smoke
FUMITORY fumewort
FUMOSITY smokiness; flatulence
FUNCTION duty; power; office
cp **FUNCTION** purpose; meeting;
instruction
FUNDABLE able to be financed
FUNDLESS broke
FUNEBRAL FUNEREAL, sombre;
woeful
FUNERARY mournful; dismal
FUNGIBLE interchangeable
FUNK-HOLE coward's corner
FURBELOW puckered flounce
FURCATED forked; branching
FURCULAR fork-shaped
ch **FURFURAL** fural solvent

ch **FURFUROL** organic liquid
FURIBUND raging; furious; frenzied
FURLOUGH leave of absence
FURMENTY see frumenty
FURRIERY the fur trade
FURROWED corrugated; ploughed
FURTHEST most distant; remotest
md **FURUNCLE** a boil
FURY-LIKE furious; violent; frantic
ar **FUSAROLE** a classic moulding
FUSELAGE body of aircraft
FUSEL-OIL malodorous spirit
FUSIFORM spindle-shaped
FUSILIER armed with flint-lock
muskets
bt **FUSTERIC** a yellow dye
FUSTILUG fat unwieldy person
FUTILELY unavailingly; ineffectually
FUTILITY uselessness; vanity
FUTURELY in time to come
FUTURISE anticipate; antedate
FUTURISM art movement
FUTURIST (Biblical prophecies)
FUTURITY future time; the hereafter;
gamble on future commodities
bt **FUZZ-BALL** puff-ball fungus
FUZZLING confusing; intoxicating

G

GABARAGE packing cloth
GABBATHA Pilate's judgement seat
GABBLING chattering; jabbering
GABIONED with gabions
ar **GABLE-END** part of house silhouette
GADABOUT roving busybody
GADHELIC Gaelic Celt language
GADLINGS steel spikes
GADZOOKS a mild expletive
GAGGLING noise of geese; cackling
GAG-TOOTH projecting tooth
mu **GAIEMENT** in lively style
GAIETIES vivacities; jollities
GAIGEOUR a wager, bet
GAINABLE procurable; attainable
GAINLESS unprofitable; bootless
GAINSAID contradicted; denied
zo **GAIR-FOWL** GARE-FOWL, great auk
ch **GALACTAN** anhydride of galactose
md **GALACTIA** excess of milk
as **GALACTIC** of galaxies (Milky Way)
bt **GALACTIN** sap of cow tree
GALALITH material made from milk
bt **GALANGAL** spicy tropical plant
GALATIAN inhabitant of Galatia
mn **GALAXITE** rare form of spinel
bt **GALBANUM** a gum

bt **GALBULUS** fleshy-scaled strobilus
GALEATED floral helmet
GALENISM Dr Galen's principles
GALENIST one of his followers
mn **GALENITE** sulphide of lead
GALENOID (galenite)
mn **GALERITE** fossil sea-urchin
GALILEAN of Galileo; of Galilee
md **GALL-DUCT** body channel
nt **GALLEASS GALLIASS**, galley-galleon trader (W. Europe)
GALLIARD gay fellow; brisk; a dance
GALLICAN of Gaul; later of France
GALLIPOT a glazed pot; artist's pot; apothecary's pot
nt **GALLIVAT** Malay pirate ship
GALLIZED (wine production)
GALLOPED rode at a gallop
GALLOPER mounted orderly
zo **GALLOWAY** a hardy horse
el **GALVANIC** variable pulsating current (Galvani)
GAMBESON GAMDISON, doublet worn under armour
GAMBLING playing recklessly
bt **GAMBOGIC** of gamboge, yellow; gum
tx **GAMBROON** twilled linen cloth
GAMEBIRD bird to be shot at
zo **GAMECOCK** fighting cock
lw **GAME-LAWS** hunting regulations
GAMENESS courage; endurance
GAMESOME sportive; playful
GAMESTER a gambler
zo **GAMMARUS** genus of crustaceans
ck **GAMMONED** pickled ham; bamboozled
GAMMONER cook; practical joker
GAMOBIUM sexual generation in metagenesis
GAMODEME permitted close marriage
zo **GAMOGONY** sporogony; gamete formation
rl **GANG-DAYS** (Rogation week)
GANGETIC (River Ganges)
GANGLAND criminal resort
GANGLING slender, awkward in movement
pl **GANGLION** cyst on tendon; nerve centre
GANGLION a focus of strength; energy
pc **GANGRENE** fatal blood poisoning
GANGSMAN foreman of a team
GANGSTER desperado; ruffian
rl **GANGWEEK** (Rogation week)
mn **GANISTER** sandstone; fire-brick
zo **GANNETRY** haunt of solan geese
nt **GANTLINE** rope for sails/clothes

GANYMEDE cupbearer to Zeus
GAOLBIRD habitual criminal; old lag
GAPINGLY widely open
GARBAGED worthless writing; household waste
GARBLING distorting the facts
nt **GARBOARD** plank next to keel
bt **GARCINIA** plant genus; mangosteen
GARDENER a cultivator
bt **GARDENIA** sub-tropical shrub; flower
zo **GARE-FOWL** gair-fowl; great auk
zo **GARGANEY** sea-duck
GARGLING warbling; throat cleansing
GARGOYLE grotesque gutter-spout
GARISHLY gaudily; showily; tawdrily
bt **GARLICKY** like garlic
GARNERED harvested; stored
GARRETED with watch-towers
GARRISON an armed force
GARROTTE strangle; throttle
zo **GARRULUS** crow genus; jay
GARTERED with socks well up
GASALIER hanging pendant for gas
pt **GAS-BLACK** carbon-black pigment
GAS-GAUGE (for testing pressure)
GASIFORM gaseous
GAS-LIGHT 19th-cent. lighting
GAS-METER (for measuring volume)
GAS-MOTOR a gas engine
GASOGENE aerating; apparatus
GASOLINE rectified petrol; fuel
GAS-STOVE cooking stove
GASTIGHT air-tight
zo **GASTRAEA** primordial organism
zo **GASTRULA** embryonic cup
GAS-WATER (coal-gas purification)
GAS-WORKS a source of illumination
GATE-BILL GATE-FINE, university penalty for lateness
GATEFOLD folded insert in a book
GATELESS without a gate
GATE-POST gate supporter
md **GATE-VEIN** portal vein
GATHERED collected; acquired
GATHERER gleaner; collector; fruit picker
GAUDY-DAY colourful festival (-ing)
GAUDYING making merry
GAUNTLET iron glove; (run the=)
lw **GAVELMAN** tenant in gavelkind
GAVELOCK crowbar; javelin
GAWNTREE barrel stand; gantry
GAZETTED published; recorded
ck **GAZPACHO** Andalusian cold soup
GAZUMPED thwarted by gazumper
GAZUMPER raiser of agreed selling price

au **GEAR-CASE** part of auto works
ch **GEGENION** simple ion
GELASTIC risible
GELATINE an animal jelly
GELATION solidification by cold
GELIDITY extreme cold
GEMATRIA a cabbalistic method
bt **GEMINATE** in pairs
as **GEMINIDS** meteoric shower
GEMINOUS double
bt **GEMMATED** budded
GEMMEOUS gemlike
mu **GEMSHORN** an organ stop
GENDARME armed policeman (Fr.)
GENDERED begat; sired; bred
GENE-FLOW gene-mix within
populations
GENERALE general principle
GENERANT a cause of production
GENERATE originate; beget; produce
GENEROUS munificent; liberal
GENESIAC (Genesis)
GENETICS study of heredity
GENETRIX GENITRIX, a mother,
female parent
GENEVESE of Geneva, Genevan
GENIALLY heartily; cordially; jovially
zo **GENITALS** reproductive organs
GENITIVE possessive case
GENITURE birth; procreation
GENOCIDE racial extermination
gn **GENOMERE** hypothetical gene
constituent
cy **GENOSOME** chromosome part
GENOTYPE individual's genetic
constitution
GENTILIC tribal; non-Jewish
ec **GEOBIONT** soil organism
bt **GEOCARPY** underground fruit
ripening
GEOCLINE cline across organism's
range features
GEODESIC GEODETIC, of earth
measurements
GEOGNOST student of geognosy
gl **GEOGNOSY** petrography
GEOGONIC (formation of the earth)
GEOLATRY earth-worship
GEOMANCY a form of divination
GEOMETER a mathematician
GEOMETRY mensuration
bt **GEONASTY** groundward curvature
GEONOMIC (physical laws)
GEOPHAGY earth-eating
gp **GEOPHONE** portable shock-wave
recorder
bt **GEOPHYTE** subterranean-budding
plant

GEOPONIC agricultural; husbandry
GEORDIES Tynesiders
GEORGIAN period; Caucasian;
(Georgia)
GEOSCOPY observational knowledge
GEOTAXIS gravity-stimulated
movement response
ch **GERANIOL** perfumery ester
constituent
bt **GERANIUM** showy pink flower
GERMANIC Teutonic
GERMCELL gamete
GERMINAL sprouting; French
month
md **GEROCOMY** regime for the aged
GERONTIC of individual's senescent
period
ch **GESTAGEN** hormone promoting
pregnancy
GESTURAL gesticulating
GESTURED acted; posed; signalled
GHANAIAN native of Ghana
GHETTOES Jewish quarters
zo **GHORKHAR** Asiatic wild ass; onager
GHOSTING pattern staining; stand-in
authorship
GHOULISH gruesome; fiendish
GIANTESS colossal lady
GIANTISM hugeness
GIANTIZE play the giant
mn **GIBBSITE** aluminium-hydroxide
constituent of bauxite
GIBINGLY scornfully; mockingly
GIB-STAFF water-gauge; pole
GIDDIEST most thoughtless
GIDDYING making dizzy
GIFTLING a small present
GIGANTIC enormous; elephantine
GIGGLING tittering; sniggering
GIG-LAMPS carriage lamps;
spectacles
zo **GILLAROO** species of trout
bt **GILLENIA** rose genus
zo **GILL-FLAP** a membrane
GILT-EDGE aureate; (securities)
zo **GILT-HEAD** sea-bream
zo **GILT-TAIL** species of worm
GIMCRACK a gewgaw; jimcrack
GIMLETED holed; bored
GINGERLY cautiously; warily
md **GINGIVAL** relating to the gums
zo **GIN-HORSE** mill-horse
GIN-HOUSE cotton factory
ck **GIN-SLING** a short drink (Singapore
cocktail)
GIPSYDOM gipsy life
GIPSYISM cheating; flattery
bt **GIRASOLE** sunflower

GIRDLING encompassing; surrounding
GIRLHOOD juvenile femininity
GIRONDIN moderate republican
GIRTHING saddling; girdling
nt **GIRT-LINE** rigging line
GIVEABLE bestowable; presentable
GIVE-AWAY unintended disclosure
GLABRATE GLABROUS, smooth; without hair or down
GLACIATE freeze; polish by ice
GLADDEST very cheerful; merriest
GLADDING rejoicing; delighting; elating
GLADIATE sword-shaped
bt **GLADIOLE** sword-lily
bt **GLADIOLI** plural of gladiolus
GLADNESS joy; joyfulness; cheer
GLAD-RAGS party frocks
GLADSOME pleasurable; pleasant
GLAIRING varnishing
GLAIROUS viscous
GLANCING glimpsing; ricocheting
GLANDAGE feeding on acorns
vt **GLANDERS** a horse disease
md **GLANDULE** small gland
GLAREOUS glairous; viscous
GLASSEYE a horse disease
GLASSFUL a measure of content
GLASSILY in a vitreous manner
GLASSING glazing
GLASSITE one of a Scottish sect
gs **GLASS-POT** (used for melting glass)
bt **GLAUCIUM** the yellow poppy
md **GLAUCOMA** an eye-disease
GLAUCOUS a sea-green colour
GLEAMING resplendent; radiating
GLEANING harvesting; culling; picking
GLEDGING squinting
GLEESOME frolicsome; hilarious; lively
gl **GLEISOIL** poor-drainage-influenced soil type
bt **GLIADINE** yellow extract
GLIBNESS gift of the gab
GLIMPSED viewed hurriedly; glanced
GLINTING gleaming
cy **GLIOSOME** cytoplasmic granule
GLISSADE a glide on a glacier
zo **GLISSAUN** the coal-fish
GLOAMING dusk; twilight
GLOATING revelling; crowing; exulting
GLOBATED spherical
GLOBULAR spheric; round
GLOBULET round particle
md **GLOBULIN** (a blood constituent)

GLOOMILY despondently
GLOOMING obscuring; depressing
GLORIANA Queen Elizabeth I
rl **GLORIOLE** a halo; saintly aura
bt **GLORIOSA** a lily
GLORIOUS illustrious; noble; eminent
GLORYING exulting; boasting
bt **GLORY-PEA** an Australian pea
GLOSSARY explanatory vocabulary
GLOSSILY smoothly; sleekly
zo **GLOSSINA** the tsetse fly
GLOSSING commenting; polishing
GLOSSIST annotator; glossarist
GLOWERED scowled; frowned
GLOW-LAMP incandescent lamp
zo **GLOW-WORM** a beetle
bt **GLOXINIA** flowering plant
md **GLUCAGON** hormone increasing blood sugar
GLUCINUM white metal; beryllium
ch **GLUCONIC** acid derived from glucose
ch **GLUCOSID** sugar compound
GLUE-LINE dielectric heating
GLUMMEST gloomiest; very morose
GLUMNESS sulkiness; depression
GLUMPISH sullen; splenetic; moody
md **GLUTAEUS** posterior muscle
ch **GLUTELIN** water-insoluble protein
ch **GLUTENIN** wheat glutelin protein
GLUTTING sating; saturating; cloying
GLUTTONY voracity; greed
ch **GLYCEROL** glycerine
ch **GLYCOGEN** animal starch
GLYCONIC kind of verse
GLYPTICS gem engraving
GNARLING gnawing
GNARRING snarling; growling
GNASHING grinding the teeth
GNATHISM (jaw measurement)
zo **GNATHITE** insect mouth-part
zo **GNATLING** small gnat
zo **GNAT-WORM** larva of gnat
GNOMICAL of dialling
nt **GNOMONIC** of shadow casting; (sundial) (suncompass)
bt **GOA-CEDAR** a cypress
GOAL-LINE back-line (football)
GOAL-POST (football)
GOATHERD goat-minder
zo **GOATLING** small goat
zo **GOAT-MOTH** fabulous insect
GOATSKIN skin of goat
bt **GOAT'S-RUE** a plant
GOBBLING guzzling; turkey-noise
GODCHILD protégé
GOD'S-ACRE a graveyard
GODSMITH idol maker

GOD-SPEED a benediction
mn GOETHITE a hydrated iron oxide
GOFFERED crimped
GO-GETTER pushing person
GOGGLING rolling the eyes
GOINGS-ON unexpected, strange happenings
md GOITERED GOITROUS, afflicted with the goitre
bt GOLD-DUST a plant
GOLDENLY splendidly; aureately
zo GOLDFISH a carp
GOLD-FOIL GOLDLEAF, thin gold
GOLD-LACE sumptuary decoration
GOLDLESS destitute of gold
bt GOLD-LILY the yellow lily
GOLD-MINE source of wealth
GOLD-RUSH prospector's scramble
GOLD-SIZE a varnish
GOLD-WIRE thread gold
GOLD-WORK replacement teeth; dental bridges
GOLF-CLUB striker rod; association
rl GOLGOTHA place of a skull (crucifixion)
GOLLYWOG doll (black native)
GOLOSHES GALOSHES, rainproof overshoes
GOMARIST opponent of Armenians
GOMBROON Persian pottery
md GONALGIA pain in the knee
GONENESS that sinking feeling
GONFALON a banner
bt GONGYLUS (seaweed)
bt GONIMIUM lichen thallus cell
zo GONOCOEL gonad cavity
zo GONOCYTE sexual cell in porifera
zo GONODUCT genital products duct
GONOPORE reproductive elements opening
zo GONOSOME repro. individuals in animal colony
zo GONOTOME embryo somite
GOOD-DOER benefactor; patron
GOOD-FOLK the fairies
GOOD-LACK expression of pity
GOODLIER more excellent; fairer
GOODNESS kindness; beneficence
GOODWIFE a term of respect
GOODWILL benevolence; an asset
ga GOOGLIES bouncing cricket bowling
GOOSE-CAP a silly person
ga GOOSE-EGG a 'duck'; zero; no score (cricket)
GORGEOUS splendid and showy
zo GORGONIA corals
GOSPODAR Slav governor
GOSSAMER filmy cobweb

GOSSIPED chatted; tattled
GOSSIPRY small talk; intimacy
GOURMAND glutton; epicurean
bt GOUTWEED goutwort
GOVERNED controlled; ruled; swayed
GOVERNOR regulator; guardian
GOWNSMAN cf. townsman (university)
GRABBING snatching; clutching
nt GRABLINE lifeline on a lifeboat
GRACE-CUP loving cup
GRACEFUL elegant and easy
zo GRACILIS land-vertebrate thigh muscle
mu GRACIOSO Spanish clown; graciously
GRACIOUS dignified; polite; benign; charming
GRADATED stages of change
GRADATIM step by step
me, rw GRADIENT slope; incline; variable quantity ratio
el GRADIENT rate of change of potential in volts per metre
GRADUAND about to be a graduate
GRADUATE pass; proportion; divide
GRAECISM a Greek idiom
GRAECIZE to turn into Greek
GRAFFITI (ancient) wall scribblings
GRAFFITO two-colour plaster layers
GRAFTING implanting one stem into another plant
GRAINAGE duties on grain
bd, zo GRAINING imitating wood or marble using paints etc.; a fish
GRAIN-TIN melted tin
zo GRALLINE (wading birds)
zo GRALLOCK entrails of deer
GRAMARYE necromancy; magic
GRANDDAD grandfather
GRANDEST most magnificent; noblest
GRANDEUR pomp; splendour; majesty
GRANDSON son's son
mn GRANITIC of granite
GRANTING conceding; conferring
GRANULAR in grains
GRAPHICS art of drawing
mn GRAPHITE blacklead
GRAPHIUM a style (for writing)
GRAPPLED seized; grasped; clutched
GRASPING gripping; avaricious
GRASSING turfing; laying low
bt GRASS-OIL an essential oil
GRATEFUL thankful; beholden
bt GRATIOLA hedge hyssop
GRATUITY tip; bonus; pourboire

lw **GRAVAMEN** principal charge
GRAVELLY full of gravel
GRAVITAS weight of dignity
ps **GRAVITON** quantum of gravitation (hypothetical)
GRAY-EYED grey-eyed
zo **GRAYLING** freshwater fish
mu **GRAZIOSO** gracefully (It.)
GREASILY unctuously
GREASING lubricating; corrupting
GREATEST largest; biggest; bulkiest
GRECIZED Hellenized
GREEDILY voraciously; eagerly
GREENERY verdure; foliage
zo **GREEN-FLY** a pest
GREENING hoaxing
GREENISH somewhat green
ck **GREEN-TEA** for Chinese meals
GREETING cheerful welcoming message
lw **GREFFIER** notary (Channel Isles)
GREMLINS malignant aerial imps
ga **GREYCING** greyhound racing
GREYNESS grayness
ro **GRIB-BIAS** adjustment
GRIDIRON a grill; squared plan; map; traffic system
GRIEVOUS burdensome; heinous
ck **GRILLADE** grilled meat (Fr.)
GRILLAGE a cross-beam construction
GRILLING broiling; interrogating
GRIMACED smirked
GRIMALDI prince of clowns (It.)
GRIMMEST sternest; dourest
GRIMNESS fierceness; dourness
GRIMOIRE ancient handbook of black magic
GRINAGOG someone who is always smiling
GRINDERY shoemakers' materials
GRINDING pulverizing; crushing
GRINNING smiling broadly
GRIPEFUL distressing; colicky
GRIPPING holding tight; clutching
GRISELDA a very patient lady
GRISEOUS grey; grizzled
GRITTING grating; grinding; abrading
GRIZZLED grey; grumbled
GROANFUL mournful; lugubrious
GROANING moaning; complaining
GROGGERY a dram-shop; liquor-shop
nt **GROGGING** adding water to rum
GROG-SHOP pub; bar
pl, ar **GROINING** where thighs meet; intersecting vaults
bt **GROMWELL** a plant

GROOMING making neat and tidy; appearance
GROOMING (of horses); fur picking (animals)
GROOVING furrowing; scoring
zo **GROSBEAK** a finch
nm **GROSCHEN** Austrian coin
GROTTOES caves
GROUNDED on the ground
GROUNDER low ball at baseball
GROUPING arranging; disposing
GROUSING grumbling
GROUTING filling in with concrete
GROWABLE cultivatable
GROWLERY a private den
GROWLING grumbling; snarling
GRUBBIER dirtier
GRUBBING digging up
GRUBBLED groped
GRUDGING envying; coveting
GRUESOME horrible; grisly; grim
GRUMBLED complained; repined
GRUMBLER grouser
GRUMNESS surliness; dourness
zo **GRUMPHIE** a sow
bt **GRUNDSEL** groundsel
zo **GRYSBOCK** steinbock (S. Africa)
zo **GUACHERO** oil-bird (S. Amer.)
ch **GUAIACOL** an odorous liquid
bt **GUAIACUM** resinous lignum vitae
GUANCHOS natives of Canary Islands
mu **GUARACHA** a Cuban dance
GUARANTY basis of security
hd **GUARDANT** facing
GUARDFUL wary; cautious
GUARDIAN warden; protector
GUARDING watching; defending
GUBBINGS wild Devonians
GUELPHIC of Hanoverian royal family; (the Georges)
GUERILLA GUERRILLA, irregular warrior
zo **GUERNSEY** a garment; a cow
GUESSING imagining
GUGGLING gurgling
GUIDABLE readily conducted, led
GUIDANCE direction; government
GUILEFUL crafty; insidious
GUILTILY criminally; culpably
bt **GUIMAUVE** marsh-mallow
GUJARATI language (Bombay)
nm **GULCHING** pre-rock-fall sound
bt **GULF-WEED** tropical seaweed
GULLIBLE easily deceived
GULLIVER Swift traveller
GULLYING making a watercourse
GULOSITY voracity
GUMPTION shrewd sense; nous

bt **GUM-RESIN** gamboge
nt **GUNDALOW** weighted felucca sail barge, New England
GUN-LAYER who prepares guns for firing
GUNMETAL alloy; copper and tin
GUN-REACH gunshot; range; (target distance)
GUNSMITH gun-maker
GUNSTICK ramrod
GUNSTOCK part of gun
GUNSTONE stone projectile
GURGLING purling; rippling
GURKHALI language (Nepal)
GUSTABLE tasty; savoury
GUTTATED sprinkled; bedewed
GUTTERED of roof drainage run-off
GUTTLING gorging; swallowing
GUTTURAL throaty
GUYANESE (Guyana; S. Amer.)
GUZZLING swilling; tippling; quaffing
GYMNASIC of Gymnasium College levels
GYMKHANA equestrian competitions meeting
GYMNICAL athletic
zo **GYMNOTUS** electric eel
bt **GYNANDER** a plant
GYNANDRY male characteristics of the female
GYNARCHY female government
GYNECIUM women's quarters
bt **GYNERIUM** pampas grass
mn **GYPSEOUS** (gypsum)
GYPSYISM Romany, gypsy lore, language
GYRATING spinning; rotating; whirling
GYRATION rotation; revolution
GYRATORY circling; revolutionary
ae **GYRODYNE** speedy helicopter
GYROIDAL spiral; winding
mn **GYROLITE** hydrated calcium silicate
ae **GYROPTER** helicopter
nt **GYROSTAT** gyroscope compass housing

H

mu **HABANERA** Cuban dance with singing
lw **HABENDUM** descriptive clause
HABITANT inhabitant; native
HABITING dressing; arraying
HABITUAL customary; usual; wonted
HABITUDE customary manner
pr **HACHURES** shaded height;

indications by pen hatchings
HACIENDA estate or ranch (S. Amer.)
zo **HACKBOLT** great shearwater gull
ga **HACK-LINE** of curling (bowls on ice)
tx **HACKLING** strands separating flax
HAEMATIC acting on the blood
md **HAEMATIN** (haemoglobin)
bt **HAGBERRY** bird-cherry
rl **HAGGADAH** HAGGADIC, Rabbinical commentary on O.T.
HAGGLING chaffering; bargaining
bt **HAGTAPER** the mullein
HAILSHOT small shrapnel shot
HAILSHOT coastal patrol warning: stop!
tx **HAIRCORD** kind of carpet
HAIR-LACE hair ribbon
HAIRLESS bald
HAIRLINE a fine line
mu **HAIRPINS** colloquial; diminuendo and crescendo signs
mn **HAIR-SALT** epsomite
HAIRWORK work done with hair
zo **HAIRWORM** freshwater worm
pg **HALATION** photographic defect
HALENESS robustness; health
HALF-BACK (football)
HALF-BOOT (halway to the knee)
HALF-BRED mongrel
el **HALF-CELL** electrode with electrolyte contact
HALF-COCK gun, using safety lever setting
HALF-DEAD almost dead
nt **HALF-DECK** half length deck
HALF-DONE incomplete; under-done
HALF-FACE the profile
HALF-HALT equestrian exercise
HALF-INCH map scale
ps **HALF-LIFE** radio-activity period
pr **HALF-LINE** light-shading technique
HALFLING a youth
nm **HALF-MARK** old coin, value 33p
HALFMAST a sign of mourning (flag salute)
HALF-MILE athletics
HALF-MOON a semicircle; demilune
HALF-NOTE a semitone
HALF-PASS two-step for horses
HALF-PAST HALF-HOUR, clock time
HALF-PIKE short pike
nt **HALF-ROLL** light swell; croquet shot
nt **HALF-SEAS** half-drunk; half-storm
ar **HALF-SPAN** lean-to; half-arch
HALF-SUIT body armour
HALF-TIDE neither in nor out
HALF-TIME an interval

HALF-TINT intermediate tint

pr HALF-TONE a printing process

zo HALICORE dugong; sea-cow

zo HALIOTIS mother-of-pearl shell

HALL-DOOR front door

nt HALLIARD HALYARD, rigging ropes; lines for sails

HALL-MARK a guarantee

HALLOOED shouted

HALLOWED reverenced; sanctified

HALTERED roped; tethered

zo HALTERES balancing wings

HAMBLING mutilating the foot

HAMIFORM hook-shaped

ck, rl HAMINDAS egg/peppers/onion casserole (Jew.)

HAMMERED expelled from Stock Exchange

HAMMERER hammer-man; smith

HAMPERED impeded; packed; clogged

HANDBALL an old pastime; 11 a side field game

mu HANDBELL one rung by hand

HANDBILL anouncement; broadcast

HANDBOOK a manual

HANDCART transport to hell

HANDCUFF manacle; fetter; restrict in baseball

HANDFAST hold; custody; betroth

HANDGEAR (manual control)

mo HANDGRIP HANDHOLD, climbing

mu HAND-HORN with only harmonic series (valveless)

HANDICAP penalty; allowance

HANDLESS awkward

HANDLINE line without a rod

HANDLING manipulation

HANDLIST convenient list

wv HANDLOOM for home weaving

HAND-MADE product of home industry

HANDMAID Abigail (maid-servant)

HANDMILL home corn-grinder

HANDPICK select carefully

HANDPOST finger-post; guide

HANDRAIL support

HAND-SALE handshake deal

HANDSOME generous; good-looking

HAND-WORK sloyd; handicrafts

HANDYMAN jack-of-all-trades

HANGABLE dependable; suspensible

HANGER-ON parasite; retainer

mn HANGFIRE explosive-detonation delay

md HANGNAIL agnail

zo HANGNEST a bird

HANGOVER after-alcohol reaction

HANKERED coveted; longed; yearned

zo HAPLODON mountain beaver

cy HAPLOSIS chromosome halving

HAPPENED chanced; occurred; befell

bt HAPTERON of plant attachment organs

HAQUETON padded jacket

HARA-KIRI ritual shame suicide (Jap.)

HARANGUE tirade; declaim

HARASSED wearied; persecuted

HARASSER a guerilla; annoyer; molester

HARDBACK book published in stiff covers

HARDBAKE cookery and baking techniques

bt HARDBEAM horn beam

HARD-CASH ready money

bd HARD-CORE unwavering resistance; stone fillers, essence of construction

HARDENED inured; obdurate

ch HARDENER toughener

bt HARD-FERN the northern fern

bt HARD-HACK steeple-bush

HARDIEST most robust; boldest

HARDNESS most solid firmness

HARDSHIP injustice; tribulation

nt HARDTACK ship's biscuit

cp HARDWARE ironmongery; computers and equipment etc.

bt HARDWOOD close-grained timber

bt HAREBELL hairbell; campanula

HAREFOOT swift of foot

bt HAREHUNE horehound

HAREPIPE a snare

bt HARE'S-EAR a yellow flower

HARLEIAN a literary society

HARLOTRY prostitution

HARMLESS innocuous; inoffensive

mu HARMONIC concordant; consonant; tone

HARMONIE windband (Ger.)

nt HARPINGS battens

HARRIDAN gaunt old woman; vixen

HARROWED lacerated; tortured; torn

HARROWER sensationalist

HARRYING harassing; raiding; vexing

bt HARTWORT plant; seseli type

bt HASTATED spear-shaped

HASTENED expedited; urged

HASTENER urgent reminder

bt HASTINGS early peas

HATBRUSH brush for hats

HATCHERY incubator

HATCHETY sharp featured

HATCHING plotting; shading; breeding

nt **HATCHWAY** deck opening
HATEABLE odious; detestable
HATSTAND like a hatrack; but different
zo **HATTERIA** tuatara; lizard (NZ)
HAT-TRICK 3 times (a winner); successful
HAUNCHED in squatting position
HAUNTING frequenting; obsessing
hd **HAURIANT** (fish on end)
HAURLING dragging; trailing
HAUSFRAU housewife (Ger.)
mu **HAUTBOIS** Fr. 'high (tone) wood', Italianized as oboe
HAVANNAH HABANA, (Cuban) cigar
HAVELOCK white cover for cap
HAVOCKED devastated; ruined
HAWAIIAN of Hawaii island group
zo **HAWFINCH** grosbeak
HAWK-BELL small bell on hawk's foot
HAWK-EYED lynx-eyed
zo **HAWK-MOTH** genus of moth
bt **HAWK-WEED** genus of weed
bt **HAWTHORN** the may
md **HAY-FEVER** pollen allergy
HAY-FIELD meadow
HAY-KNIFE stack-cutter
HAY-MAKER a swipe
ag **HAY-STACK** (thatched) hay storage pile
HAZARDED imperilled; ventured
HAZARDER a gambler; speculator
zo **HAZEL-HEN** ruffled grouse
bt **HAZEL-NUT** filbert
HAZINESS uncertainty; vagueness
md **HEADACHE** occipital disorder
HEADACHY off colour
HEAD-BAND book top; fillet
nt **HEAD-BOOM** jib-boom
nt **HEADFAST** mooring rope
HEADGEAR head-dress
HEAD-HOLD HEAD-LOCK, (wrestling)
HEADIEST most exhilarating
HEADLAMP (motor-car)
HEADLAND cape; promontory; ness
HEADLESS decapitated
HEADLINE newspaper superscripture
HEADLONG precipitately; steep; hasty
HEAD-MAIN main water supply
HEAD-MARK outstanding feature
md **HEAD-MOLD** skull; a moulding
HEADMOST most advanced
HEAD-NOTE introductory note
nt **HEAD-PUMP** latrines pump in bow of ship
HEAD-RACE lead to water-wheel; power

HEAD-RENT payment for use of a head
HEAD-REST a support
HEAD-RING Kaffir coiffure
bd, me **HEADROOM** ceiling clearance height
nt **HEADSAIL** set forward of mast (sailing)
HEADSHIP supreme authority
HEAD-TIRE head-dress
HEAD-WIND a contrary wind
HEAD-WORD title word
HEAD-WORK intellectual labour; sport
HEALABLE remediable; curable
HEARABLE audible
HEARTILY cordially; sincerely; warmly
HEARTLET small heart
bt **HEART-ROT** central decay
bt **HEATHERY** heathy; heath-clad
zo **HEATH-HEN** black grouse
bt **HEATH-PEA** legendary plant
HEAT-SPOT a freckle
me **HEAT-UNIT** lot of hot air
HEAT-WAVE calorific undulation
HEAVENLY celestial; seraphic
HEAVIEST most ponderous
HEBDOMAD a group of seven
HEBETANT making blunt; dulling
HEBETATE to dull; stupefy
HEBETUDE dullness; stupidity
HEBRAIST HEBRAISM, HEBRAIZE, of Hebrew customs and literature
HECATOMB sacrifice of 100
HECKLING interrupting, arguing against speaker
zo **HECKYMAL** blue tit
HECTORED boasted; swaggered
HECTORER brawler; bully; braggart
HECTORLY insolent; domineering
zo **HEDGEHOG** 'Mr Prickles'
HEDGEHOP a low flight
zo **HEDGEPIG** young hedgehog
bt **HEDGEROW** bushy boundary
HEDONICS HEDONISM, HEDONIST, 'pleasure is the highest good' doctrine
HEEDLESS regardless; rash
HEELBALL black wax
pr **HEEL-NICK** cut-out portion of movable type
HEFTIEST sturdiest; beefiest
HEGELIAN (process of the spirit)
HEGEMONY leadership
rl **HEGUMENE** prior
HEIGHTEN enhance; raise
lw **HEIRLESS** lacking heirship; no heir
HEIRLOOM family jewel

lw **HEIRSHIP** inherent right
md **HELCOSIS** ulceration
md **HELCOTIC** ulcerous
HELIACAL (sunlight)
HELICOID spiral
mn **HELIODOR** S. Afr. yellow beryl
md **HELIOSIS** sunstroke
zo **HELIOZIA** protozoa
ae **HELIPORT** helicopter airfield
HELLBENT reckless
HELLBORN HELLBRED, of satanic
    origin
HELLENIC Grecian
HELL-FIRE Satan's illumination
HELL-GATE approach to inferno
zo **HELL-KITE** bird of ill-omen
HELLWARD devilish progress
HELMETED double-domed
zo **HELMINTH** a worm
HELMLESS rudderless
HELMSMAN steersman
HELOTAGE HELOTISM, slavery;
    bondage; servitude; serfdom
HELPLESS impotent; weak;
    powerless
HELPMATE wife; partner
HELPMEET helpmate; helper
HELVETIA Switzerland
HELVETIC Swiss
mn **HEMATITE** haematite
zo **HEMIGALE** Malayan civet
mu **HEMIOLIA** HEMIOLA, HEMIOLIC,
    change of rhythm in ratio 2 to 3
zo **HEMIONUS** dziggetai
md **HEMIOPIA** faulty vision
zo **HEMIPODE** sort of quail
zo **HEMIPTER** cicada or bug
zo **HEMISOME** symmetrical half of
    animal
bt **HEMP-PALM** a pretend plant
bt **HEMP-SEED** flaxseed
HENCHMAN servant; page; valet
bt **HENEQUEN** HENEQUIN, sisal hemp
HEN-HOUSE coop
HEN-HUSSY a cotquean
HEN-MOULD black spongy soil
HEN-PARTY ladies' gossip group
HEN-ROOST poultry park
HEN-WOMAN hen-wife
mn **HEPATITE** barium sulphate
HEPATIZE of the liver function
md **HEPATOMA** liver tumour
HEPTAGON 7 sided figure
HEPTARCH ruler of a heptarchy
HERALDED proclaimed; blazoned
hd **HERALDIC** HERALDRY, armorial
    bearings and ceremonial orders
HERBAGED grass-covered

bt **HERBARIA** hortus siccus
bt **HERBELET** small herb
HERBLESS lacking vegetation
rl **HERCULES** strong man of labours
HERD-BOOK cattle stud-book
HERDSMAN cow-puncher
HEREAWAY hereabouts
HEREDITY inherent propensity
HEREINTO into this
HERESIES schisms
HEREUNTO unto this
HEREUPON upon this; then
HEREWITH by saying this
HERISSON spiked obstruction
HERITAGE patrimony; legacy
HERMETIC air-tight; mystic; occult
md **HERNIOID** ruptured; hernial
zo **HERNSHAW** heronshaw; handsaw
HEROICAL intrepid; valiant; epic
HEROICLY dauntlessly; daringly
HEROIZED lionized; idealized
HEROSHIP heroism (the Argonaut)
md **HERPETIC** of shingles (herpes)
HERTZIAN (low frequency waves)
mn **HERTZITE** galena
HESITANT vacillating; doubtful
HESITATE pause; waver; demur
as, nt **HESPERUS** the evening star; a wreck
HEXAGRAM Solomon's seal
HEXAPLAR sextuple
HEY-GO-MAD joyous interjection
HIBERNAL wintry
bt **HIBISCUS** tropical mallow
zo **HICCATEE** Cen. Amer. tortoise
HICCOUGH hiccup
HICCUPED belched politely
zo **HICKWALL** small woodpecker
HIDDENLY privily; furtively; covertly
HIDE-ROPE a reim (S. Afr.)
md **HIDROSIS** sweat
HIELAMAN native shield (Aust.)
rl **HIERARCH** chief priest
rl **HIERATIC** priestly
HIERONYM sacred name used as
    surname
HIGGLING haggling; chaffering
HIGH-BALL whisky and soda
HIGHBORN of noble birth
HIGHBRED not a hybrid
HIGHBROW so-called intellectual
HIGH-HUNG elevated
HIGH-JUMP athletics; dismissal
HIGHLAND where the heart is;
    (cattle)
HIGH-LIFE the jet set
rl **HIGH-MASS** special service
HIGHMOST topmost
mo **HIGHNESS** royal rank; altitude

HIGHROAD thoroughfare; main street
HIGH-SPOT climax
HIGH-TIDE floodtide
HIGH-TIME almost overdue
bt **HIGTAPER** the mullein
HI-JACKED transport passengers forcibly seized
HI-JACKER aerial super-pirate
HILARITY gaiety; jollity; merriment
HILL-FOLK hillmen; Covenanters
HILL-FORT stronghold; fastness
HILLOCKY hummocky
HILLSIDE a declivity
HINDERED delayed; thwarted; impeded
HINDERER obstructionist; opposer
HINDMOST last; posterior
HINDUISM doctrine and rites
HINGEING depending on
HINNIBLE ability to neigh or whinny
HIP-JOINT with-it nightclub
HIREABLE on hire
HIRELESS wageless
HIRELING mercenary
HIRPLING running lamely
HIRRIENT trilling sound
HIRUDINE like a leech
HISPANIC Spanish
md **HISTIOID** resembling tissue
HISTORIC authentic; genuine; famous
HISTRION play-actor
HITCHING fastening; attaching
HITHERTO till now
HIVELESS not a single skep
zo **HIVE-NEST** multiple bird's nest
zo **HOACTZIN** hoatzin; S. Amer. bird
HOARDING storing; treasuring; fence
HOARSELY discordantly; raucously
HOASTMAN member of a guild
HOBBLING walking lamely; limping
HOBBYISM HOBBYIST, cult of favourite pursuit
HOCKCART (last harvest load)
bt **HOCKHERB** a mallow
HOCKLING mowing
HOCK-TIDE harvest festival
HOCUSSED pocussed; dopey; drugged
nt **HOG-FRAME** (shipbuilding)
zo **HOGGEREL** sheep of second year
HOGMANAY New Year's Eve party (Sc.)
HOG-REEVE medieval parish officer
bt **HOG'SBEAN** henbane
ga **HOG-SCORE** block line on a curling rink
HOGSHEAD large cask of beer, wine

zo **HOGSTEER** wild boar
ac **HOHLRAUM** black-body radiator cavity
HOISTING raising; lifting; elevating
HOISTWAY trap-door
HOLDBACK check; retainer
bd **HOLDFAST** catch; grip; anchor spike with eye for joinery
HOLDINGS stock possessed by library
bt **HOLEWORT** moschatel
rl **HOLINESS** sanctity; devoutness
HOLLANDS genever gin
HOLLOAED shouted
HOLLOWED excavated; scooped
HOLLOWLY insincerely; vacantly
bt **HOLOGAMY** mature-cell fusion
ps **HOLOGRAM** laser optical imaging
zo **HOLOPTIC** side eyes meeting
zo **HOLOZOIC** eating other organisms
rl **HOLYROOD** holy cross; Palace (Edinburgh)
HOLY-WEEK the week before Easter
rl **HOLY-WRIT** the Scriptures
HOMAGING paying respects
HOMEBIRD stay-at-home
HOMEBORN native; domestic
HOMEBRED natural; unpolished
HOME-FARM nearest fields to farmhouse
HOMEFELT inward; private
HOMEGOER anti-social recluse
HOMELAND native land
HOMELESS on the streets
HOMELIKE not ornate
HOME-MADE better-tasting
HOME-RULE autonomy
HOMESICK nostalgia
HOMESPUN rough worsted
HOMEWARD return journey
HOMEWORK out of school task
lw **HOMICIDE** man-slaughter
HOMILIST sermonizer
bt **HOMOBIUM** alga/fungus association
zo **HOMODONT** teeth all alike
tc **HOMODYNE** (wireless telephony)
bt **HOMOGAMY** hermaphroditism
HOMOGENY similarity of nature
HOMOLOGY affinity of structure
HOMONYMY (similar-sounding words)
HOMOSOTE material for walls of huts
HOMOTYPE HOMOTYPY, structural affinity
HONDURAN (Honduras)
HONESTLY uprightly; sincerely
bt **HONE-WORT** herb parsley-piert
zo **HONEY-BAG** nectar sac of bee
zo **HONEY-BEE** nectar-sucker

bt **HONEYDEW** tobacco; melon
bt **HONEYPOT** a grape (S. Afr.)
HONORARY gratuitous; unpaid
HONOURED respected; revered
HONOURER venerator
HOODWINK befool; cheat; delude
HOOFMARK imprint of animal
zo **HOOK-WORM** a parasite
HOOLIGAN ruffian; rascal; bully
HOOP-IRON iron band on cask
cp **HOOT-STOP** audible stop signal
HOOT-TOOT toot-toot!; motor horn signal
HOPELESS despairing; despondent
HOPINGLY thinking wishfully
HOPPLING hobbling
HORATIAN (Horace)
bt **HORMESIS** non-toxic organism stimulus
zo **HORNBEAK** garfish
bt **HORNBEAM** a tree
zo **HORNBILL** picarian bird
zo **HORNFISH** garfish
HORNFOOT hoofed
HORNGATE gate of dreams
mn **HORN-LEAD** chloride of lead
HORNLESS dodded
mu, nt **HORNPIPE** air; dance; sailors'
ar **HORNWORK** outer ramparts; bastions
bt **HORNWORT** water-plant
HOROLOGY works on clocks
HOROPTER normal combined vision
HORRIBLE revolting; fearful; dire
HORRIBLY hideously; appallingly
HORRIDLY foully; alarmingly
HORRIFIC terrific; awful; frightful
HORSE-BOX van for horses
HORSE-BOY stable-boy
HORSE-CAR a carriage
zo **HORSE-FLY** large blood-sucking fly
HORSE-HOE a harrow
HORSEMAN rider; equestrian
HORSE-WAY road or track
HOSE-PIPE a duct
HOSE-REEL firefighting equipment
HOSPITAL an almshouse
HOSPODOR GOSPODAR, Slav governor
HOSTELRY inn; tavern
HOT-BLAST pre-heated air
ck **HOTCHPOT** farrago; mixture; medley
HOTELIER hotel-keeper
HOTHOUSE greenhouse
HOT-PLATE a heating appliance
HOT-PRESS a machine
HOT-SHORT brittle
bt **HOTTONIA** water-violet
HOT-WATER trouble

HOUGHING ham stringing
HOUNDING pursuing; tracking; trailing
HOUR-HAND time indicator
HOUSE-BOY serving lad
zo **HOUSE-DOG** watch dog
zo **HOUSE-FLY** musca domestica
lw **HOUSE-TAX** a levy
HOVELLED meanly housed
HOVELLER longshoreman
HOVERING in suspense; maintaining a fixed observation level above earth
mn **HOWIEITE** triclinic hydrous silicate
HOWITZER short cannon
HUCKSTER underhand dealer, rogue, advertiser
HUDDLING cowering in mass
HUDIBRAS political satire by S. Butler
HUGENESS bulk; immensity; vastness
rl **HUGUENOT** French Protestant
zo **HUIA-BIRD** New Zealand bird
HUMANELY mercifully; benignly
HUMANISM HUMANIST, HUMANITY, pragmatism; human interests; rhetoric
HUMANIZE enlighten; civilize
HUMATION burial
HUMBLING abasing; shaming
HUMEFIED moistened
HUMIDIFY to dampen
HUMIDITY moisture content in air
HUMILITY humbleness; meekness
HUMMOCKY hillocky
HUMORISM facetiousness; jocularity
HUMORIST jester; merryman
HUMOROUS witty; droll; comical
HUMOURED indulged; pampered
zo **HUMPBACK** a whale; road-bridge
HUMPLESS no depression here
HUMSTRUM humdrum; monotonous
HUNG-BEEF dried beef
HUNGERED famished; hankered
HUNGRILY cravingly; with appetite
HUNKERED squatted
HUNTRESS female hunter; lioness
HUNTSMAN chasseur
HURDLING (athletics)
zo **HURLBONE** a horse bone
HURRYING urging; speeding
HURTLESS uninjured; innoxious
HURTLING whizzing
HUSHED-UP undisclosed
HUSH-HUSH very secret
HUSH-MUSH highly confidential
HUSKIEST very hoarse

HUSTINGS electioneering platform
HUSTLING bustling; jostling; elbowing
HUTCHING cooping
HUZZAING shouting with joy
mn, bt **HYACINTH** a gem; flower
md **HYALITIS** optic inflammation
md **HYBODONT** irregular teeth
md **HYDATISM** a watery sound
HYDATOID aqueous
zo **HYDRANTH** nutrition polyp
HYDRATED combined with water
HYDROFIN high speed motor-boat
ch **HYDROGEL** water soluble colloid
ch **HYDROGEN** gaseous element
zo **HYDROIDS** animal growths on seaweed
HYDROMEL watered honey
zo **HYDROMYS** water-rats, etc.
HYDROPIC thirsty
md **HYDROPSY** dropsy
HYDROSOL colloidal solution
zo **HYDROZOA HYDROIDS**, jelly fish
ch **HYDRURET** hybrid
HYGIENIC salubrious; healthy
HYLICISM materialism
HYLICIST a philosopher
zo **HYLOBATE** a gibbon
HYLOZOIC materialistic
HYMENEAL conjugal; matrimonial
HYMENEAN nuptial; bridal
bt **HYMENIUM** part of fungus
rl **HYMN-BOOK** for singing praises
zo **HYOIDEUS** nerve branch in vertebrates
md **HYOSCINE** poisonous alkaloid
HYPALGIA insusceptibility
zo **HYPAXIAL** below the axis
sp **HYPERGOL** rocket fuel
HYPERION a Titan
md **HYPHAEMA** interior eye bleeding
pr **HYPHENED HYPHENIC**, linked; jointed
md **HYPNOSIS** hypnotism
HYPNOTIC mesmeric; sleep-inducing
zo **HYPOARIA** brain lobe in fish
HYPOBOLE form of argument
zo **HYPOCONE** molar cusp
bt **HYPODERM** cell layer under epidermis
HYPOGEAL underground
HYPOGEAN subterranean
mn **HYPOGENE** rock formation
ar, mn **HYPOGEUM** underground gallery, vault, or mine
zo **HYPOHYAL** hyoid arch element
zo **HYPOMERE** mesothelial wall zone
zo **HYPONOME** water escape funnel

HYPOSMIA dimished smell sensitivity
HYPOTHEC mortgage house; debt security
gl **HYPOZOAN HYPOZOIC**, below the limit of life
md **HYSTERIA** nervous disorder
HYSTERIC hysterical; in a fit

I

zo **IANTHINA** purple sea-snails
md **IATRICAL** medical
IBSENISM of Henrik Ibsen's works
ICE-BLINK a reflection; mirage
ICE-BOUND immobilized by ice
ICE-BROOK frozen brook
ICE-CREAM the content of a cornet
ICE-FIELD glacier terrain
ICE-FLOAT sea ice-floe
ICE-HOUSE ice storage building
ICE-LEDGE en route for Everest
ICE-PLANT crystalline snow as flower
ICE-SHEET glacial arctic regions
ICE-WATER Amer. national drink
ICE-YACHT for sailing on sea ice
md **ICHOROUS** like ichor
zo **ICHTHINE** (fishes' eggs)
ICHTHYIC fishlike
ICTERINE yellow
IDEALISM transcendency
IDEALIST visionary
IDEALIZE attribute perfection to ideals
IDEATING fancying
IDEATION conception
IDEATIVE imaginative
IDENTIFY recognize; integrate
IDENTITY individuality; sameness
IDEOGRAM ideograph; logo; picture word (cp. Chinese)
IDEOLOGY metaphysics
IDIOTISH doltish; fatuous; inane
IDIOTISM imbecility; inanity
IDIOTIZE ridicule; befool
IDLEHOOD idleness
IDLENESS dolce far niente
mn **IDOCRASE** silicate of lime
IDOLATER a heretic
IDOLATRY image worship
IDOLIZED idolised
IDOLIZER a fan
rl **IGNATIAN** (St Ignatius)
IGNITING kindling; inflaming
IGNITION firing; lighting
el **IGNITRON** mercury arc rectifier
IGNOMINY public disgrace; obloquy

IGNORANT uninstructed; unaware
IGNORING disregarding; overlooking
ILLATIVE deducive; grammatical case
  (direction to)
ILL-BLOOD enmity; discord; rancour
ILL-FATED calamitous; unlucky
ch ILLINIUM metallic element
ILL-TIMED ill-judged
ILL-TREAT maltreat
ILLUDING creating illusions;
  deceiving
ILLUMINE enlighten; irradiate
ILLUMING elucidating
ILL-USAGE harsh treatment
ILLUSION delusion; dream; fantasy
ILLUSIVE ILLUSORY, deceptive;
  fugitive; hallucinatory
ILLYRIAN of Illyricum; of Dalmatian
  coast (Croatia)
mn ILMENITE titanate of iron
zo IMAGINAL relating to an image
IMAGINED fancied; thought
IMAGINER dreamer
IMBECILE idiot; moron
IMBEDDED firmly fixed
IMBELLIC pacific; unwarlike
IMBIBING absorbing; swallowing
pg IMBITION dye transfer
IMBOWING arching
IMBRUING drenching
IMBRUTED degenerated
IMBUMENT deep tincture
IMBURSED supplied with cash
IMITABLE easy to forge
IMITANCY mimicry
IMITATED parodied; aped
IMITATOR copy-cat; impersonator
IMMANENT inherent; innate
IMMATURE unripe; crude; untimely;
  undeveloped
IMMERGED IMMERSED, submerged;
  soused; plunged; inundated
IMMERSED held under water
  (baptism)
IMMINENT impending; perilous
IMMOBILE still; motionless; static
IMMODEST bold; indelicate; coarse
IMMOLATE sacrifice; surrender
IMMORTAL imperishable; deathless
IMMUNITY privilege; freedom
IMMUNIZE exempt
IMPACTED collided; struck
IMPAIRED enfeebled; blemished
IMPAIRER saboteur; marrer
IMPALING transfixing
IMPALMED grasped; handled
IMPANATE to sandwich
IMPARITY inequality; disproportion

IMPARKED enclosed
IMPARLED conversed; discussed
IMPARTED communicated; divulged
IMPARTER bestower; donator
IMPASTED kneaded
IMPAWNED pledged; mortgaged
IMPEDING obstructing; thwarting;
  personal foul in water polo
IMPELLED urged; induced; drove
IMPELLER instigator; inciter;
  centrifugal pump
IMPENDED threatened; hovered
IMPENNED enclosed; encompassed
IMPERIAL shorn beard; a goatee
IMPERIUM sovereignty
md IMPETIGO an eruption
IMPIERCE bore; drill; penetrate
mn IMPINGER dust-measuring device
IMPISHLY mischievously; wantonly
IMPLATED sheathed
IMPLEACH interweave
IMPLEDGE pawn; hypothecate
IMPLICIT tacit; implied; inferred
IMPLORED entreated; craved
IMPLORER supplicant; petitioner
IMPLUMED plucked
IMPLUNGE immerse; dive
IMPLYING indicating; connoting
IMPOCKET filch; steal
IMPOISON envenom; infect
IMPOLDER reclaim from sea
  (Holland)
IMPOLICY inexpedience
IMPOLITE positively rude; insolent
lw IMPONENT a backer; imposer; con-
  man
lw IMPONING wagering; betting
IMPORTED conveyed; denoted
IMPORTER foreign dealer
IMPOSING impressive; stately
IMPOSTOR IMPOSTER, trickster
IMPOTENT non-erectile; unable
IMPRIMIS in the first place
IMPRISON incarcerate; immure
IMPROPER unseemly; indelicate
IMPROVED bettered; amended
IMPROVER developer; rectifier
IMPUDENT saucy; shameless
IMPUGNED gainsaid; contradicted
IMPUGNER attacker; assailant
IMPUNITY exemption; immunity
IMPURELY unchastely; licentiously
IMPURITY an adulterant
IMPUTING charging; insinuating
INACTION inertia; sloth; indolence
INACTIVE idle; torpid; supine
INAQUATE turn into water
INARABLE unfit for tillage

INASMUCH because
INAURATE gild
INBONDED brick-laying technique
INCAGING confining; mewing
INCANTON merge into a canton
INCARNED incarnated
hd **INCENSED** inflamed; enraged
INCENSOR incense burner
INCEPTOR beginner; inaugurator
bd **INCERTUM** early rubble-filled
   masonry
INCHMEAL gradually
INCHOATE begun; immature;
   incipient
cp **INCIDENT** episode; event; fracas;
   breakdown
INCIRCLE encircle; encompass
INCISELY clear cut; acutely
INCISING scribing; engraving
INCISION cut; gash; slit
INCISIVE trenchant; sarcastic
INCISORY sharpness
INCISURA body notch; scar
pl **INCISURE** a cut; wound
INCITANT stimulant; provocative
INCITING goading; arousing;
   spurring
INCIVISM lack of communal spirit
INCLINED disposed; biased; tilted
INCLINER sloping dial
INCLUDED contained; embodied
INCOMING entrance; arrival
INCOMITY incivility; rudeness
INCREASE aggravate; augment
INCREATE create within
INCUBATE hatch
bt **INCUBOUS** (leaf formation)
zo **INCUDATE** characteristic of rotifera
INCURRED contracted; ran into
INCURVED bent
INCUSING stamping
INCUSSED forged; struck
INDAGATE investigate
ch **INDAMINE** used in dye-making
INDEBTED under obligation
INDECENT unbecoming; coarse
INDENTED notched; toothed
INDEVOTE disloyal; unloving
INDEVOUT irreverent; impious
INDEXING compiling an index
nt **INDIAMAN** trading ship
INDICANT symptomatic
INDICATE show; suggest; denote
INDICTED impeached; charged
INDICTEE a defendant
INDICTER an accuser
INDIGENE a native; aboriginal
INDIGENT poor; needy; necessitous

INDIRECT devious; tortuous; oblique
   grammar (speech)
INDITING dictating; writing; penning
INDOCILE intractible; stubborn
INDOLENT lazy; sluggish; inert
INDUCING actuating; urging; causing
rl **INDUCTED** invested; installed
INDUCTOR officiating minister
INDULGED gratified; humoured
INDULGER favourer
ch **INDULINE** a dye
INDURATE harden; inure
zo **INDUSIAL** (caterpillar skins)
bt **INDUSIUM** skin or cover
INDUSTRY trade; assiduity; diligence
bt **INDUVIAE** withered leaves
INEDIBLE uneatable
INEDITED unpublished
INEQUITY injustice; unfairness
bt **INERMOUS** no prickles
INERTION sluggishness; indolence
INEXPERT unskilled; unversed
INFAMING defaming; discrediting
INFAMIZE publicly brand with
   infamy
INFAMOUS vile; notorious; heinous
INFANTLY childishly; infantile
INFANTRY foot-soldiers
INFECTED tainted; corrupted;
   disease-ridden
INFECTER carrier of disease
INFECUND sterile; barren; unprolific
INFERIAE Roman sacrifices
INFERIOR poor; subordinate;
   mediocre
INFERNAL diabolical; fiendish;
   satanic
INFERRED deduced; argued;
   surmised
INFESTED overrun; thronged; beset
INFILTER permeate; seep
INFINITE boundless; unlimited
mu **INFINITO** perpetual
INFINITY immensely
INFIRMLY irresolutely; feebly
INFLAMED exasperated; infuriated
INFLAMER agent provocateur
INFLATED distended; bloated;
   swollen
INFLATOR air-pump
INFLATUS inspiration
INFLEXED bent inwards
INFLOWED ran in
INFLUENT a tributary
INFOLDED embraced
INFORMAL unconventional; simple
INFORMED told; apprised; notified
INFORMER a sneak

INFRA-DIG beneath one's social standing
INFRA-RED beyond red in spectrum
INFRINGE violate; transgress
INFRUGAL prodigal; extravagant
INFUMATE to smoke
INFUSING inculcating; inspiring
INFUSION instillation; introduction
INFUSIVE penetrative
zo **INFUSORY** protozoic
INGENIUM bent of mind
INGROOVE engroove; furrow
INGROWTH opposite of outgrowth
INGUINAL (between thighs)
md **INHALANT** a vapourizer
INHALING breathing
INHERENT innate; congenial
INHUMING burying; interring
INIMICAL allergic; hostile; contrary
INIQUITY vice; sinfulness; offence
INITIATE a novice; start; inaugurate
INJECTED forced in; introduced
md **INJECTOR** kind of pump, syringe
INJURING damaging; maltreating
INKINESS state of being inky
INKMAKER squid
INKSTAND ink-holder
mm **INK-STONE** sulphate of iron
INLANDER not an islander
lw **INLAWING** clearing of attainder
INLAYING ornamenting
INNATELY instinctively; naturally
INNOCENT guileless; blameless; sinless
INNOVATE make changes; alter; new
INNUENDO an insinuation
INORNATE plain
ch **INOSITOL** yeast growth agent
INQUIRED asked; investigated
INQUIRER questioner; scrutineer
nt **INRIGGED** with rowlocks on gunwhale
INSANELY crazily; deliriously
INSANITY dementia; mania; lunacy
INSCIENT ignorant; illiterate; unread
cp **INSCRIBE** dedicate; engrave; imprint; rewrite data
INSCROLL write on a scroll
INSEAMED marked by a seam
INSECTED segmented
INSECURE uncertain; hazardous
INSERTED introduced; injected
INSETTED implanted
INSHADED tinted
INSHRINE enshrine; dedicate
INSIGNIA badges; emblems; tokens
INSISTED persisted; maintained; urged

INSITION ingraftment
INSNARED entangled; caught; ginned
INSNARER trapper
INSOLATE dry in the sun
INSOLENT contumacious; hubristic
md **INSOMNIA** sleeplessness
INSOMUCH so that
INSPIRED inhaled; animated
INSPIRER spiritual leader
INSPIRIT enhearten; infuse
INSTABLE unstable; transient
INSTANCE specify; occurrence; incident
INSTANCY urgency; solicitation
INSTATED established
INSTINCT natural propensity
INSTREAM to flow
INSTRUCT edify; direct; enjoin; order
INSTYLED entitled; named; yclept
lw **INSUCKEN** milling restriction
INSULATE isolate; enisle
INSULTED affronted; outraged
INSULTER taunter; abuser; offender
INSURANT policy holder
INSURING assuring; underwriting
INTAGLIO opposite to cameo
INTARSIA pictorial inlay
INTEGRAL whole; entire; complete
INTENDED betrothed; meant; purposed
INTENDER activator; planner
INTENTLY with fixed attention
INTERACT interplay of various similar factors
tc **INTERCOM** two-way communication system
INTEREST concern; attention
INTERIOR indoors; within
INTERLAY insert
INTERMIT suspend
INTERMIX blend; commingle
INTERNAL domestic; within; inside
INTERNED confined; imprisoned
INTERNEE arrested alien
INTERPOL international criminal police
INTERRED buried; inhumed; entombed
INTERREX a regent; protector
INTERTIE connecting piece
cp, mu, tc **INTERVAL** gap; pause; (music); interim, specific time period
INTER-WAR of period between wars
bt **INTEXINE** pollen cover
INTIMACY INTIMITY, extreme closeness; familiarity
INTIMATE declare intentions in advance

INTONATE intone
INTONING chanting
INTRADOS lower surface of arch
INTREPID dauntless; doughty; daring
INTRIGUE cabal; interest; conspiracy
INTROMIT insert; admit
INTRORSE facing inwards
INTRUDED butted in; thrusted
INTRUDER trespasser; interloper
INTUBATE insert a tube
INUNDANT overflowing;
   overwhelming
INUNDATE flood; swamp; deluge
INURBANE rude; uncouth;
   discourteous
INURNING putting in an urn
INUSTION a branding
INVADING violating; raiding;
   entering
INVARIED set; constant; uniform
INVASION foray; attack; assault
md **INVASIVE** aggressive; intrusive
   (tumours); (epidemic)
INVECKED INVECTED, scalloped
hd **INVECTED** engrailed
INVEIGLE entice; wheedle; decoy;
   lure
INVEILED veiled
INVENTED devised; created;
   fabricated
INVENTOR innovator; contriver
el **INVERTER** conversion device
cp **INVERTER** sign reverser; negative
   binary signal
INVESTED arrayed; indued; beset
INVESTOR buyer; purchaser
INVITING attractive; alluring
INVOCATE adjure; invoke; beseech
INVOICED billed; charged
INVOKING conjuring; summoning
INVOLUTE spiral
INVOLVED complicated; complex
INWALLED enclosed
INWARDLY privily; secretly
INWORKED inset
ch **IODAZIDE** iodine azide
md **IODIZING** with iodine effect
ch **IODYRITE** iodide of silver
mu **IOLANTHE** a fairy; an opera
IONICIZE Grecianize
IONIZING electrolysing
IOTACISM excessive use of 'I'
pc **IPSATIVE** reflected, measured against
   self
IREFULLY angrily; furiously
IRENICAL tranquil; pacific
IRENICON peace propaganda
md **IRIDITIS** eye inflammation

IRISATED like a rainbow
IRISCOPE spectroscope
IRISHISM Celtic expression,
   humorous
IRISHMAN (Ireland)
bt **IRONBARK** eucalyptus
nt **IRONCLAD** metal-hulled warships
mn **IRON-CLAY** yellow iron ore
IRONGREY a colour
IRONICAL satirical; sarcastic; derisive
ch **IRON-SAND** firework mixture
IRONSICK rusty and leaky
IRONSIDE a Cromwellian
IRONWARE ironmongery
bt **IRONWOOD** tough timber
IRONWORK smithery
IRRIGATE supply with water;
   moisten
IRRISION derision; banter
IRRITANT annoying; exasperating
IRRITATE gall; nettle; provoke
bt **IRRORATE** as if dew-covered
IRRUPTED burst in; invaded; raided
ISABELLE yellowish grey
ISAGOGIC introductory
zo **ISENGRIM** a fabulous wolf
rl **ISLAMISM** Mohammedanism
rl **ISLAMITE** worshipper of Allah
rl **ISLAMIZE** proselytize
ISLANDED isolated
ISLANDER not an inlander
ISLESMAN (from the Hebrides)
mt **ISOBARIC** (equal barometric
   pressure)
ISOCHEIM line indicating equal
   winter temperatures
zo **ISOCHELA** equal-jointed chela
ISOCHORE gas pressure and
   temperature
ISOCORIA equal size of eye pupils
ISOCRYME line indicating equal
   winter temperatures
rl **ISODICON** short anthem
bd **ISODOMON ISODOMUM,** masonry
   composed of uniform blocks
ISOGONAL equi-angular
ISOGONIC (equal magnetic angles)
el **ISOLATED** solitary; (fever epidemic);
   (sheltered); (prison); (hermit)
el **ISOLATOR** device for 2-way
   microwave flow
ch **ISOLOGUE** like/unlike compound
ch **ISOMERIC ISONYMIC,** different
   properties of similar compounds
md **ISOPATHY** homeopathy
ISOPLETH map showing weather
   constituents
ch **ISOPRENE** synthetic rubber

ISOSTASY equal-pressure-caused equilibrium
mt **ISOSTERE** atmospheric volume line
ISOTHERE (equal summer heat)
ISOTHERM line of equal heat
ISOTONIC having equal tension
nc **ISOTOPES** nuclides of similar number but different mass
ISOTOPIC of isotopes
ISSUABLE distributable
ISSUANCE delivery
go **ISTHMIAN** of an isthmus, narrow neck
ITALIOTE a Greek colonist in Italy
zo **ITCH-MITE** burrowing insect
ITERANCE repetition
ITERATED repeated; recapitulated
ITHURIEL cherub; guardian angel
bt **IVORY-NUT** a palm-nut

J

JABBERED gabbled; chattered
JABBERER wind bag
JACKAROO greenhorn squatter (Aust.)
JACKETED having a paper cover
zo **JACKFISH** pike
nt **JACK-FLAG** smaller than ensign
JACK-FOOL perfect fool
JACK-HIGH raise car level with jack (tool)
bt **JACKWOOD** jaca-tree
nt **JACKYARD** uppermost short extension to main-mast
JACOBEAN (James I)
JACOBITE partisan of James II
wv **JACQUARD** loom mechanism
JACULATE to throw; to dart
JAGGEDLY raggedly; unevenly
JAILBIRD old lag; often convicted
JALOUSIE Venetian blind
JAMAICAN of Jamaica
JAMBEAUS leggings
JAMBOREE Boy Scouts' rally, frolic, carousal
JAMBOREE hand with 5 highest trumps (cards)
JAMPANEE chair carrier
JANGLING wrangling
md **JANICEPS** 2-headed monstrosity
JANUFORM double-faced; of doorways
JAPANESE of Japan
JAPANNED varnished; enamelled
JAPANNER a shoeblack

JAPAN-WAX lacquer from sumac tree berries
JAPHETIC Armenian alphabet
bt **JAPONICA** Japanese quince
zo **JARARAKA** poisonous snake
mn **JAROSITE** iron-potassium sulphate
mn **JASPONYX** an onyx
md **JAUNDICE** bile-obstruction disorder
JAUNTIER more sprightly
JAUNTILY debonairly
JAUNTING an outing
JAVANESE an Indonesian
zo **JAVELINA** wild boar
JAW-LEVER veterinary instrument
pl **JAW-TOOTH** a molar
JEALOUSY anxiety caused by rivals
tx **JEANETTE** coarse cloth
JEBUSITE a Canaanite
rl **JEHOVIST** Hebrew theologian
JELLYBAG a strainer
fr **JELUTONG** pale Malayan hardwood
zo **JENTLING** Danube chub
JEOPARDY danger; peril; hazard; risk
JEREMIAD lamentation
JEROBOAM super wine bottle
nt **JERQUING** customs searching
JERRICAN 5-gallon (22 litres) petrol tin
JEST-BOOK collection of jokes
rl **JESUITIC** JESUITRY, of Jesuit Order
JET-BLACK deepest black
JET-CRAFT JET-PLANE, jet-propelled aircraft
nt **JETTISON** throw overboard
JETTYING projecting
JEWELLED set with gems
JEWELLER a craftsman with gems
JEWISHLY judaical
mu **JEW'S-HARP** small mouth instrument
JICKAJOG a shake; a push
JIGGERED flabbergasted
JIGGLING wriggling; joggling
JIGMAKER a tool-maker
JINGLING tinkling; rhyming
JINGOISH super-patriotic
JINGOISM ultra-patriotism
JOBATION a tedious scolding
JOCKEYED jostled; outwitted; set aside
JOCKEYED race-horse ridden by –
JOCOSELY facetiously; joyously
JOCOSITY sportiveness; fun
JOCUNDLY mirthfully; waggishly
JODHPURS riding breeches
JOGGLING shaking; jostling; elbowing

nm **JOHANNES** old Portuguese gold coin
pr **JOIN-HAND** connected script
vt **JOINT-ILL** umbilicus disease
bd **JOINTING** finishing joints between
   timber/bricks
JOINT-OIL synovia
lw **JOINTURE** a settlement (estate)
JOISTING fitting with laths
JOKINGLY in jest; hilariously
JOLLIEST very merry and bright
JOLT-HEAD dunderhead; simpleton
JONGLEUR juggler (Fr.)
mu **JONGLEUR** wandering minstrel
bt **JORDANON** faintly varied breeding
   race
JOSTLING pushing; hustling;
   crowding
JOUNCING shaking; jolting (slang)
JOUSTING a tourney; simulation of
   middle-aged knights
JOVIALLY festively; blithely
JOVIALTY merriment; conviviality
JOYFULLY rapturously; gladly
JOYOUSLY blissfully; happily
ae **JOYSTICK** aeroplane control lever
JUBILANT triumphant; exulting
JUBILATE celebrate; rejoice
rl, lw **JUDAICAL** Jewish
rl **JUDAISED** conformed to Mosaic law
rl **JUDAISER** opponent of St Paul
JUDGMENT sentence; decree; award
JUDICIAL legal; legitimate; sagacious
JUGGLERY manual dexterity
JUGGLING conjuring; swindling
JUGO-SLAV Yugoslav
ck **JULIENNE** sliced vegetables (soup)
JUMBLING confusing; mixing
JUMP-SEAT collapsible seat
bd, rw **JUNCTION** union; coalition;
   coupling; (-pipe); (-box of circuits)
   (railway)
JUNCTURE exigency; moment of
   crisis; joined speech sounds
JUNKBALL slow, breaking pitch
   (baseball)
JUNKETED feasted; caroused
JUNK-RING piston-packing
JUNONIAN queenly
gl **JURASSIC** geological period
lw **JURATORY** comprising an oath
lw **JURISTIC** legal jurisdictive
nt **JURYMAST** temporary mast
JUSTLING jostling; jolting
JUSTNESS equity; impartiality
JUVENILE young; puerile; adolescent

K

KAILWIFE scold; cabbage seller
KAILYARD KALEYARD, kitchen garden
KAKEMONO Japanese picture
KAKIEMON style of pottery (17th c.)
pc **KAKOSMIA** abnormal reaction to
   smell
md **KALA-AZAR** black fever
KALAMDAN Persian writing case
tx **KALAMKAR** Indian printed cotton
KALENDAR calendar; almanac
bt **KALERUNT** cabbage stalk
KALEVALA Finnish epic
mn **KALINITE** alum
KALIYUGA Hindu mythological era
KALOLOGY science of beauty
KALOTYPE early photograph
KAMADEVA Indian Eros
KAMIKAZE suicide bomber plane
   (Jap.)
KANARESE language (Mysore,
   India)
tx **KANDAHAR** East Indian wool
zo **KANGAROO** marsupial (pouched)
rl, mu **KANTIKOY** religious dance
KARELIAN of Karelia (N & E of
   Ladoga and East Finland)
cy **KARYOTIN** nuclear reticulum
   substance
KASHMIRI people and language
   (Kashmir)
bl **KATABION** katabolic-predominant
   organism
KATAKANA Japanese script
bt **KAURI-GUM** a resin (Aust.)
KAYMAKAM Turkish governor
nt **KECKLING** binding rope
ck **KEDGEREE** a breakfast dish of rice,
   egg, fish
nt **KEEL-BOAT** type of yacht
nt **KEEL-HAUL** (punishment)
KEENNESS acuity; astuteness
KEEPSAKE memento; relic
el **KENETRON** large vacuum diode
ro **KENOTRON** wireless valve
KERASINE KERATOSE, horn
md **KERATOMA** skin tumour
KERCHIEF a head cover
KERMESSE annual fair in Low
   Countries; also circuit road racing
   events
bt **KERN-BABY** harvest image
bt **KERNELLY** full of seeds
mn **KEROSENE** paraffin
ch **KETOXIME** ketone reaction product
pr **KEYBLOCK** printing
mu **KEYBOARD** clavier, piano, organ

cp, tc **KEYBOARD** type, digit, encoder;
 enigma; typewriter
cp, tc **KEYBOARD** systematic select-
 mu **KEY-BUGLE** Kent bugle
 bt **KEY-FRUIT** ash, sycamore, etc.
 bd **KEYING-IN** bonding a brick wall
 KEY-MONEY levy on a tenant
 KEYPLATE keyhole escutcheon
 cp **KEYPUNCH** punch-card recording
  system
 ar **KEYSTONE** main arch support
 mu **KHOROVOD** Russian round dance
  with singing
 KIBITZER critical observer (USA)
 KICKABLE suitable for booting; (ball)
 KICK-DOWN switch
 KICKSHAW a fallal
 KID-GLOVE soft delicate glove
 mn **KIEFEKIL** meerschaum
 KIELBASA smoked Polish sausage
 KILL-CROP a changeling
 zo **KILLDEER** American plover
 KILL-TIME a pastime
 KILN-HOLE mouth of kiln
me, cp **KILOBITS** one thousand binary digits
 me **KILODYNE** 1000 dynes; units of force
 me **KILOGRAM** 1000 grams, weight
 KILOMEGA one thousand million
  (10^9)
 me **KILOWATT** 1000 watts
 KINDLESS unnatural; merciless
 KINDLIER more forbearing
 KINDLING animating; tinder
 KINDNESS benevolence; generosity
 KINEMICS gestural expression
 KINESICS gestural body movements
 KINETICS dynamics
 zo **KINGBIRD** American fly-catcher
 zo **KING-CRAB** tropical crab
 zol **KINGFISH** the opah
 KINGHOOD sovereignty
 KINGLESS republican
 KINGLIKE truly regal
 KINGLING ruler of petty state
 KINGPOST principal strut and
  support for rigging (gliding/hang-)
 KINGSHIP kingcraft
 KINGWANA language
 bt **KINGWOOD** ebony (S. Amer.)
 zo **KINKAJOU** raccoon; honey-bear
 KINSFOLK kindred; relations
 KIPPERED cured ·
 KIRIKANE gold-foil application (Jap.)
 rl **KIRKYARD** graveyard (Sc.)
 zo **KIROUMBO** tropical bird
 ga **KISS-CURL** stymie in ice curling
 bt **KITEFOOT** a tobacco plant
 KITTENED had a kitty litter

KITTLISH ticklish
KLYSTRON electron converter
KNABBING gnawing
KNACKISH knavish
KNAPPING flint breaking
KNAPSACK haversack; rucksack
bt **KNAPWEED** bachelor's buttons
KNEADING dough work
KNEE-DEEP KNEE-HIGH, nearly thigh-
 high
bt **KNEEHOLM** knee holly
KNEELING kotowing; worshipping
mu **KNEE-STOP** organ lever
rl **KNELLING** tolling; church bells
KNICKERS knickerbockers (men)
KNICKERS undergarments (women)
KNIFE-BOY kitchen scullery lad
KNIGHTED now Sir
KNIGHTLY courtly
bt **KNIT-BONE** herb comfrey
KNITTING uniting; interlacing
KNITWEAR reticulated fabric
KNOCKING rapping; hitting;
 motoring
KNOCK-OUT K.O.; defeat of boxer
KNOTLESS free from ties
KNOTTIER more intricate
tx, pt **KNOTTING** securing; entangling;
 (carpets); (nauti-knots); dissolved
 shellac
KNOTWORK ornamental work
KNOUTING scourging with knotted
 rope
KNOWABLE ascertainable; scibile
KNOW-ALLS wiseacres
KNUCKLED yielded; jointed
ar **KNULLING** fluting and reeding
mt **KOEMBANG** fohn wind, Java
KOFTGARI KOFTWORK, inlaying steel
 with gold
rl **KOHELETH** Preacher (Solomon)
mn **KOHINOOR** famous diamond
bt **KOHLRABI** cole-turnip
zo **KOLINSKY** Siberian mink
KOMITAJI Balkan guerilla band
KONISTRA orchestra of a Greek
 theatre
KOORBASH KOURBASH, whip made
 from rhino hide
KORFBALL 12-a-side field game
 (handball)
KOTOWING making obeisance
nm **KREUTZER** small Austrian copper
 coin
KUKUKUKU people (New Guinea)
KURVEYOR transport rider (S. Afr.)
KUTTROLF Waldglas vessel with
 curved neck (Ger.)

ch **KYANIZED** cyanized
md **KYLOSSIS** club-foot
md **KYPHOSIS** vertebral deformity

L

ch **LABDANUM LADANUM** opium
LABELLED directed
bt **LABELLUM** lower petal
LABIALLY lipwise
LABIATED lipped
pc **LABILITY** quick emotional variations
LABOURED strove
LABOURER a toiler
ck **LABSKAUS** meat/vegetable stew
  (Scand.)
LABURNIC derived from laburnum
bt **LABURNUM** flowering tree
bt **LACE-BARK** bark of a tree
LACE-BOOT (no buttons)
bt **LACE-LEAF** aquatic plant
LACERATE tear
zo **LACEWING** an insect
LACEWORK decoration
LACE-YOKE needlework
LACHESIS one of the Fates
LACING-IN attaching end-boards to
  book body
LACK-A-DAY sorrowful exclamation
LACKEYED valeted
LACONISM brevity; pithiness
ga **LACROSSE** a Canadian game
LACRYMAL LACRIMAL, tearful
LACTEOUS milk-like
LACTIFIC milk producing
bt **LACTUCIC** (lettuce)
LACUNOSE pitted; furrowed
LADDERED (stockings)
ck **LADLEFUL** soup measure
LADYBACK tandem cycle
zo **LADYBIRD** a helpful beetle
bt **LADY-FERN** tall slender fern
LADY-HELP distressed gentlewoman
LADYHOOD gentility
LADYLIKE well-bred; delicate
LADYLOVE a sweetheart
LADYSHIP a title for dame, wife of
  lord, knight
LAGTHING Norwegian Upper House
  (Parliament)
LAICIZED opened to the laity
bd **LAITANCE** milky mortar scum
LAKE-LIKE merely?
LALLYGAG necking (USA)
zo **LAMANTIN** the manatee
rl **LAMASERY** Tibetan monastery
LAMBDOID lambda-shaped (Gr.)

LAMBENCY play of light
LAMBLIKE gentle; meek
zo **LAMBLING** lambkin
LAMBSKIN soft fleece
LAME-DUCK President without
  power (USA)
LAMELLAR of thin plates
LAMENESS halting; crippledness
LAMENTED deeply regretted
LAMENTER deplorer; bewailer
LAMINARY in thin plates
LAMINATE in layers
LAMPHOLE sewer lighting shaft
LAMP-POST support for drunk
LANCEGAY a kind of spear
zo **LANCELET** primitive vertebrate
nt **LANCHANG** lugger sailboat (Malaya)
zo **LAND-CRAB** land-dwelling
  crustacean
nt **LANDFALL** landslip; sighting of land
LAND-FISH fish out of water
LAND-GIRL wartime farm help
zo **LAND-HERD** a herd of animals
LANDLADY boarding-house boss;
  rentier
LANDLESS without land (tenure)
LANDLINE overhead cable
LANDLOCK protect from wind and
  sea
LANDLORD mine host; house or
  estate owner
LANDMARK notable event;
  conspicuous feature; boundary
  stone
LANDMINE parachuted bomb
LANDNAMA Domesday Book (Ice.)
zo **LANDRAIL** corncrake
LAND-ROLL clod-crusher
LAND-SHIP a tank
LANDSLIP landslide
LANDSMAN antithesis of seaman;
  farmer
LAND-TURN land-breeze
nt **LANDWARD** in the direction of land;
  sea-breeze
LANDWEHR German militia
LAND-WIND off-shore wind
LANGLAUF cross-country skiing
  (Ger.)
LANGRAGE grape shot
zo **LANGSHAN** black Chinese hen
LANGSYNE time long past
cp **LANGUAGE** diction; vernacular;
  digital codes
LANGUISH pine; droop; decline
LANIATED torn to pieces
LANKIEST leanest
LANKNESS length without breadth

zo **LANNERET** small falcon
LANOLINE wool fat
LANTHORN hornsided lantern
LAP-BOARD board used by tailors
LAPELLED with lapels; (coat collar)
LAPIDARY stone-cutter
LAPIDATE pelt with stones
LAPIDIFY turn into stone
LAPIDIST stone-worker
mn **LAPILLUS** fragment of lava
LAP-JOINT an overlapping joint
LAPPETED with flaps
LAPSABLE terminal; transient
LAPSTONE (used by a shoemaker)
nt **LARBOARD** port side
LARCENER a thief; pilferer
LARDERER a store keeper
LARGESSE liberality; generosity
bt **LARKSPUR** a delphinium
LARRIKIN Australian hooligan
zo **LARVATED** masked
md **LASER-RAY** searing ray
nt **LASH-DOWN** secure firmly
LASHINGS an abundance; great
   quantity
LASSLORN jilted
pr **LAST-FOLD** last folded sheet in a
   book
LATCH-KEY domestic open sesame
LATENESS tardiness
LATENTLY inherently; not obvious
mn **LATERITE** brick-clay
LATHERED soapy; larruped
LATHWORK lath and plaster
LATINISM Latin idiom
LATINIST Latin scholar
LATINITY purity of Latin style
LATINIZE make like Latin
go, nt **LATITUDE** width; scope; laxity
LATITUDE north and south parallels
LATTERLY more recently; lately
LATTICED cross-barred
LAUDABLE praiseworthy; honourable
LAUDABLY commendably
md **LAUDANUM** an opiate
LAUGHING riant
LAUGHTER convulsive merriment
LAUNCHED hurled; began; initiated
gl **LAURASIA** primeval northern
   landmass
LAUREATE crowned with laurel
LAVA-LIKE hard and full of holes
LAVATION washing; purification
LAVATORY a wash-house; W.C.
bt **LAVENDER** greyish blue
zo **LAVEROCK** skylark
LAVISHED spent; squandered
LAVISHLY prodigally; wastefully

LAWFULLY legally; justly; validly
lw **LAWGIVER** a legislator; a Solon
LAWMAKER an M.P.
LAWYERLY verbose
LAXATION relaxation; slackness
md **LAXATIVE** colonic purgative
LAY-ABOUT lazy; good for nothing
rl **LAY-CLERK** a responder
rl **LAY-ELDER** Presbyterian elder
gl **LAYERING** strata process;
   horticultural
LAYSTALL refuse heap
LAYSTOOL table for newly printed/
   clean paper
rl **LAZARIST** R.C. missionary
LAZARONE Neapolitan beggar
LAZINESS inertness; slackness
mn **LAZULITE** a blue stone
mn **LAZURITE** lapis lazuli constituent
gl, mn **LEACHATE** extraction of salt in
   solution
gl **LEACHING** making an alkali; rain-
   aided descent of soluble topsoil
   minerals
LEAD-MILL lapidary's plate
nt **LEADSMAN** a lead-swinger
LEAF-LARD leaf-fat lard
LEAFLESS destitute of leaves
bt **LEAFSCAR** a mark
LEAGUING confederating; coalescing
pr **LEANFACE** narrow-width type
LEANNESS thinness; gauntness
LEAPFROG play; overtake; location
cp **LEAPFROG** of memory programs
LEAP-YEAR a year of 366 days
LEARNING scholarship; erudition
LEASABLE able to be let
LEASHING binding; securing
LEATHERN made of leather
LEATHERS protective paramilitary
   uniform (baseball); (hockey);
   (motor/motorcycle racing)
LEATHERY tough
ck **LEAVENED** baked with yeast;
   modified; tempered
LEAVINGS (left overs); residue;
   relics; departures
LEBANESE a native of Lebanon
bt **LECANORA** lichen; manna
LECITHIN egg tissue
LECTURED reprimanded; chided
LECTURER an expositor
LED-HORSE spare horse
nt **LEE-BOARD** anti-drift device
md **LEECHING** doctoring
nt **LEEFANGE** sheet guide
nt **LEE-SHORE** windward shore
LEFT-HAND sinister

LEFTWARD to the left
LEFT-WING (politics)
LEGACIES bequests; gifts
lw **LEGALISM** adherence to law
LEGALIST stickler for law
LEGALITY lawfulness
LEGALIZE authorize; sanction
lw **LEGATARY** powers of a legatee
LEGATINE of official deputy
LEGATION later an embassy
LEG-BREAK crooked course bowling
(cricket)
LEGERITY lightness
bt **LEGUMINA** pods
bt **LEGUMINE** nitrogenous proteid
LEMONADE a soft drink
zo **LEMUROID LEMURINE**, monkey-like
LENDABLE loanable
LENGTHEN extend; elongate; protract
LENIENCE LENIENCY, mildness;
clemency; mercifulness;
forbearance
LENINISM LENINIST, follower of
Lenin
LENITIVE mitigating; sedative
pg **LENS-HOOD** light-shield
mu **LENTANDO** slowing up
bt **LENTICEL** cell-formation
gl **LENTICLE** lenslike mass; glass door
of grandfather clock
bt **LENT-LILY** daffodil
nt **LEPALEPA** dugout outrigger sail
canoe (New Guinea)
md **LEPEROUS** leprous
zo **LEPIDOID** ganoid; scaly
bt, zo **LEPIDOTE** with scalelike hairs
zo **LEPORINE** like a hare
LESSENED diminished; decreased
LETHARGY dullness; apathy; oblivion
pr **LETTERED** with degree, diploma;
printed
LETTERER sports award winner
(USA)
mn **LEUCITIC** containing volcanic ore
md **LEUCOSIS** pallor; albinism
LEVANTED decamped; welshed
LEVANTER N. African wind
LEVELING LEVELLING, smoothing
over; reduction to intake capacity
LEVELLED flattened; raged;
demolished
LEVELLER ultra-republican, 1649
LEVERAGE mechanical advantage
LEVERING exerting pressure
LEVIABLE taxable; imposable
LEVIGATE to smooth; to polish
LEVIRATE Hebrew marriage custom
LEVITATE cause to float

LEVITIES frivolities; flippancies
LEVOLOSE fruit sugar
LEWDNESS licentiousness
LEWDSTER a profligate
pc **LEWINIAN** field theory; life-space;
group dynamics
ch **LEWISITE** poison gas
rl **LIBATION** offering of sacred drink
(wine)
LIBATORY oblatory
LIBELLED slandered; defamed
LIBELLER lampooner; calumniator
LIBERATE set free; emancipate
LIBERIAN (Liberia)
LIBRATED balanced
mu **LIBRETTO** words of musical play,
opera
LICENSED authorized; allowed
LICENSEE holder of a licence
LICENSER licence issuer
bt **LICHENIC** made from lichen
LICHENIN moss starch
rl **LICHGATE LYCHGATE**, gate for a
hearse
LICHWAKE post-funeral party
tx **LICKER-IN** toothed carding roller
bt **LICORICE** liquorice
LIEGEMAN vassal; henchman
nt **LIFEBELT LIFEBOAT**, marine
lifesaving equipment
nt **LIFEBUOY** floating navigation marker
lw **LIFEHOLD** lease for life
LIFELESS dull; inanimate; extinct
LIFELIKE as if living
LIFELINE vital cord
LIFELONG till death
LIFE-PEER (not hereditary)
nt **LIFE-RAFT** (for shipwreck)
LIFE-RATE (life insurance)
lw **LIFE-RENT** rent during lifetime
LIFE-SIZE full scale
LIFE-TIME from birth to death,
(actuarial); life-time of particle
until recombination in a charge
LIFE-WORK reason for a career
LIFTABLE capable of elevation
LIGAMENT binder; tendon
ps **LIGASOID** gaseous/liquid colloidal
system
md **LIGATING** binding; bandaging
LIGATION a fastening
mu **LIGATURE** bandage; band
LIGHTFUL cheery; happy; radiant
LIGHTING illuminating; kindling
LIGHTISH not heavy; fickle
tv, cp **LIGHT-PEN** photo electric torch for
screens
gl **LIGNEOUS** previously of trees; (coal)

mn **LIGNITIC** (lignite; brown coal)
LIGULATE straplike
mn **LIGURITE** pea-green gem
LIKEABLE pleasant enough
LIKENESS resemblance; similarity
LIKENING comparing
LIKEWAKE LICHWAKE, post-funeral
party
LIKEWISE also; moreover; besides
bt **LILACINE** extract of lilac
LILLIPUT miniature
LILY-IRON harpoon for swordfish
bt **LILY-STAR** feather-star
zo **LIMACOID** like a slug
LIMATION filing; polishing
LIMATURE filings
bt **LIMA-WOOD** Peruvian red-wood
LIME-FREE clear of calcium
LIME-KILN a furnace
LIMERICK verse often perverse
LIME-SINK a depression
bt **LIME-TREE** linden tree
LIME-TWIG a snare
LIME-WASH whitewash
bt **LIMEWORT** lychnis viscaria
LIMITARY finite; bounded
LIMITING confining; restricting
mn **LIMONITE** haematite ore
md **LINAMENT** bandage material
mn **LINARITE** a lead compound
LINCHPIN keeps the wheel on
md **LINCTURE** linctus; medicine
LINEALLY in a direct line
LINEARLY directly
pr **LINE-FEED** counting control device
LINE-FISH fish taken on a line
zo **LINELLAE** filament system in
sarcodina
ga **LINESMAN** referee's assistant
(football)
zo **LING-BIRD** meadow-pipit
LINGERED lagged; delayed; tarried
LINGERER dawdler; loiterer; (ma–)
tx **LINGERIE** ladies' underwear
LINGUIST seldom tongue-tied?
LINIMENT embrocation
LINNAEAN of Linnaeus; (botanical)
LINOLEUM lino; floorcloth
pr **LINOTYPE** type-setting machine
LINSTOCK flame-holder
LIONIZED heroized
md **LIPAEMIA** fatty blood
gl **LIPARITE** rhyolite; granitic lava rock
LIPIODOL X-ray-opaque substance
LIPO-GRAM (letter omission)
bt **LIPOSOME** fatty/oily globule
LIPSTICK a cosmetic
LIQUABLE fusible; fluent

LIQUATED liquefied
LIQUIDLY smoothly; fluidal
ch **LIQUIDUS** solidification temperature
line
LIQUORED in drink; tipsy
LIRIPOOP hood; trick; nincompoop
LIROCONE floury; powdery
LISTENED hearkened; attended;
heard
LISTENER eavesdropper
LISTLESS languid; apathetic; torpid
LITERACY ability to read and write
LITERARY erudite; scholarly
LITERATE learned; studious
LITERATI writers; critics;
intelligentsia
LITEROSE bookish
mn **LITHARGE** lead oxide
LITHERLY mischievous; lazy
lw **LITIGANT** engaged in a lawsuit
lw **LITIGATE** to go to law
LITTERED scattered; strewn;
deranged
LITTLE-GO examination (Camb.)
go **LITTORAL** a coastal strip
LITURATE blurred; spotted
rl **LITURGIC** ritualistic
LIVEABLE habitable; of a residence
LIVE-AXLE driving axle
LIVE-BAIT living worms for
fishermen
LIVELILY vivaciously; briskly; alertly
bt **LIVELONG** lasting; the orpine
LIVENING cheering up; animating
el, rw **LIVE-RAIL** power track
LIVERIED in uniform
LIVERIES garbs; uniforms
pt **LIVERING** thickening of paints,
varnish
md **LIVERISH** bilious; testy
LIVE-WELL kind of aquarium
LIVE-WIRE human dynamo
LIVIDITY discoloration
LIVINGLY lively; energetically;
agilely
ch **LIXIVIAL** residual
ch **LIXIVIUM** lye; residuum
nt **LOAD-LINE** Plimsoll's loading mark
on ships' sides
LOANABLE available for borrowing
LOAN-WORD borrowed word
LOATHFUL abhorrent; detestable
LOATHING hating; antipathy
LOBBYING endeavouring to influence
LOBBYIST pressurist (parliamentary)
ch **LOBELINE** monoacidic alkaloid
LOBLOLLY gruel; lout; attendant
md **LOBOTOMY** brain surgery

LOCALISM provincialism
LOCALITY situation; district; spot
LOCALIZE assign to a place
LOCATING positioning; fixing
cp **LOCATION** film-setting; place;
 information storage site
LOCATIVE grammatical case of place
 (Lat.)
LOCHLANN Irish word for
 Scandinavian
LOCKFAST firmly fastened
LOCK-GATE (on canal or river)
LOCKLESS without a lock
LOCK-SILL threshold of a lock
LOCKSMAN a turnkey
LOCKSPIT digging mark
LOCK-WEIR weir with lock
bt **LOCULATE LOCULOSE, LOCULOUS,**
 divided internally into cells
LOCUTION diction; phrase
rl **LOCUTORY** place for conversation
nt **LODESMAN** pilot
as **LODESTAR** pole-star
LODGINGS digs; accommodation
LODGMENT occupation; golf
bt **LODICULE** grass stamen scale
nt **LOG-BOARD** rough log
LOG-CABIN timber hut
nt **LOG-CANOE** dugout
nt **LOG-GLASS** timing device
LOGICIAN one skilled in logic
LOGICIZE deduce from reasoning
LOGISTIC transport problems
LOGOGRAM puzzle in verse
LOGOTYPE twin letters in printing
nt **LOG-SLATE** recording slate
LOITERED lingered; tarried
LOITERER an idler; flaneur
LOKWEAVE carpet-splice
rl **LOLLARDY** Lollard doctrine
LOLLIPOP sweet; (traffic sign)
LOLLOPED lounged; lurched
bt **LOMENTUM** branching fruit
mn **LOMONITE** a zeolite
LONDONER citizen of capital
LONENESS seclusion; solitude
LONESOME solitary
nt **LONGBOAT** naval lifeboat (sail),
 tender
ae **LONGERON** main spar of aeroplane
LONGEVAL long lived
LONG-FIRM swindling company
LONGHAND handwriting
LONG-HAUL long distance; lengthy
 time
zo **LONG-LEGS** flying daddy (- -); flying
 insect
bt **LONG-MOSS** tillandsia

nt **LONG-SHIP** Viking sailing vessel
ga **LONG-SLIP** (cricket fielder)
LONGSOME tiresome; tedious;
 irksome
LONG-SPUN protracted; extended
LONG-STOP (cricket)
LONG-TAIL not docked
LONG-TERM far seeing
LONGUEUR tedious patch, padding in
 literature
LONGWAYS lengthways
LONGWISE in extenso
bt **LONICERA** honey-suckle genus
LOOKER-ON spectator; observer
mt **LOOM-GALE** minor gale
LOOP-HOLE gun port in castle;
 (escape)
lw **LOOP-HOLE** legal evasion clause
LOOP-LINE alternative, passing track
cp **LOOP-STOP** program stopper
LOOSE-BOX a stall for horses
md **LOOSENED** undone; relaxed;
 slackened
md **LOOSENER** a laxative
LOP-EARED with drooping ears
gl **LOPOLITH** lens-shaped igneous
 intrusion
LOP-SIDED unbalanced; biased
LORD-LIKE haughty; imperious
LORDLING a would-be lord
md **LORDOSIS** spinal curvature
LORD'S-DAY Sunday
LORDSHIP title; domain of peerage
LORICATE to encrust
zo **LORIKEET** Australian parrot
LOSINGLY wastefully
LOTHARIO a libertine; a filly-buster
LOUDNESS uproar; clamour;
 resonance
LOUNGING reclining; lolling; idling
zo **LOVEBIRD** a budgerigar
LOVEKNOT a tangle
LOVELACE a libertine
LOVELESS passionless; frigid
LOVELIES beauteous damsels
LOVE-LIFE romance
LOVELILY delectably; enchantingly
LOVELOCK a manly curl
LOVELORN jilted
LOVE-NEST romantic abode
LOVESICK languishing
LOVESOME adorable
LOVESUIT courtship
LOVINGLY affectionately; fondly
LOWERING depressing; threatening
nt **LOW-WATER** at the ebb (tide)
LOYALIST patriot; faithful follower
LUBBERLY clumsily; maladroit

LUCIDITY clearness; luminosity
LUCKIEST most fortunate; happiest
LUCKLESS singularly unfortunate
ga LUCKYBAG LUCKYDIP, a bran tub
with hidden gifts
LUCULENT translucent; lucid; clear
LUCULLUS an epicure
gl LUGARITE rare analcite–gabbro form
LUKEWARM tepid
LUMBERED rumbled along
LUMBERER woodman
LUMINANT shining; radiant
LUMINARY a heavenly body
LUMINATE illuminate; brighten
LUMINOUS phosphorescent; lucent
zo LUMPFISH a sea fish
LUNARIAN a moon observer
LUNATION a lunar month
LUNCHEON midday repast
LUNCHING eating in early afternoon
LUNGEING fencing; horse training
zo LUNGFISH queer fish
LUNGLESS not breathing
bt LUNGWORT a lichen
LUNIFORM moon-shaped
LUNULATE like a crescent
LUPERCAL Roman festival
ch LUPININE lupinus-seed alkaloid
bt LUPINITE a bitter extract
br LUPULONE soft hops resin
LURCHING stumbling; rolling
LUSCIOUS rich in flavour
LUSTIEST beefiest; heftiest; sexiest
LUSTRATE polish; cause to shine
tx LUSTRING silk cloth
LUSTROUS shining; luminous
bt LUSTWORT the sun-dew
LUTATION sealing (fastening)
documents
ch LUTECIUM a metallic element
mu LUTENIST a lute player
bt LUTEOLIN yellow dye
LUTETIAN of Paris
rl LUTHERAN Protestant
LUTIDINE bone–oil/coal–tar
constituent
LUXATING displacing
LUXATION dislocation
LUXMETER illuminance
measurement device
LUXURIES unnecessary pleasures
LUXURIST an indulger
LYCHGATE hearse gateway to
churchyard
bt LYCOPODE yellow powder
md LYMPHOID of lymph (from –gland)
LYNCHING mob law
LYNCH-LAW short-shrift

LYNX-EYED can see like a cat
ch LYOLYSIS acid/base formation
process
zo LYRE-BIRD Australian bird
LYRICISM of lyric composition
ch LYSERGIC L.S.D. acid; (dream-
trances)
bl LYSOSOME sac of hydrolytic
enzymes
bl LYSOZYME bacteriolytic enzyme

M

rl MACARIAN blessed
rl MACARISM a beatitude
rl MACARIZE to bless
ck MACARONI fop; food (pasta)
ck MACAROON almond biscuit
MACASSAR hair oil
MACERATE harass; to steep; to rot
MACHINAL mechanical
MACHINED turned on a machine
MACHINER factory operative
(worker)
zo MACKEREL cloud pattern; fish
zo MACRANER large male ant
zo MACROPOD long-legged
zo MACROPUS kangaroo genus
MACULATE to spot; to stain
MADDENED infuriated; incensed
md, pc MADHOUSE bedlam; lunatic asylum
mu MADRIGAL pastoral glee; part song
MAECENAS rich art patron
MAENADIC bacchanalian
mu MAESTOSO majestically
MAFFLING a simpleton
MAGAZINE depot; store; periodical;
feeder (gun) (slides)
MAGDALEN home for repentants
mu MAGGIORE It. major, greater
MAGICIAN wizard; marabout
MAGIRICS the culinary art
md MAGISTER master; doctor
MAGNADUR ceramic magnet/
insulator material
md MAGNESIA a medicine
ch MAGNESON magnesium reagent
el MAGNETIC attracted to poles
el, ps MAGNETON constant of M,
movement of an eletron
MAGNIFIC splendid; majestic
bt MAGNOLIA a flowering tree
zo MAGOT-PIE magpie
rl MAHADENA Hindu god, Siva
MAHARAJA Indian rajah
bt MAHOGANY tropical tree
MAIDENLY virginal; demure

MAIDHOOD girlhood; virginity
MAIEUTIC delivering; evolving
MAILABLE postable
nt **MAIL-BOAT** a packet
MAIL-CART post wagon
MAIL-CLAD armour-plated
MAIL-DRAG mail-coach
nt **MAIN-BOOM** part of sailing ships
nt **MAIN-DECK** part of sailing ships
MAINLAND continent
nt **MAINMAST** MAINSAIL, chief rigging
   units
cp **MAIN-PATH** main course; written
   routine
nt **MAINSTAY** supporting brace
   (mainmast)
MAINTAIN support and care; assert;
   hold
nt **MAINYARD** part of rigging
MAJESTIC imperial; august; regal
MAJOLICA artificial pearls (Majorca)
MAJORATE army rank; attain age of
   18
MAJORITY overwhelming proportion
MAKEBATE quarrel-maker
MAKELESS matchless
MAKIMONO Japanese picture
MALACOID soft-bodied
md **MALADIES** disorders; ailments
MALAGASH MALAGASY, of
   Madagascar
zo **MALAMUTE** Arctic sledge dog
MALAPERT saucy; impertinent;
   flippant
MALAPROP muddled misuse of
   words
md **MALARIAL** (malaria)
gl **MALCHITE** malachite; diorite rock
md **MAL-DE-MER** sea-sickness
bt **MALE-FERN** common lowland fern
MALEFICE evil deed; enchantment
MALENESS having male physical
   characteristics
lw **MALETOLT** MALETOTE, illegal
   exaction
MALIGNED traduced; slandered
MALIGNER defamer; reviler; abuser
MALINGER feign illness
MALLEATE to soften (using hammer,
   mallet)
mn **MALMROCK** sandstone
MALODOUR a smell; stench
MALT-DUST malt grains
ch **MALTHENE** asphaltic bitumen
   constituent
MALT-KILN MALT-MILL, comprise
   malt factory
MALTREAT abuse; hurt; harm; injure

MALTSTER malt-maker
zo **MALT-WORM** a tippler; weevil
md **MALUNION** improper bone-knitting
ck **MAMALIGA** maize-meal porridge
MAMBRINO source of Don Quixote's
   helmet
MAMELUKE Turkic military dynasty
   in Egypt; Caucasian slave
MAMMALIA breast-suckling
   animals
MAMMARED stammered
zo **MAMMIFER** a mammal
md **MAMMILLA** a nipple
tx **MAMMODIS** Indian muslin
MANACLED shackled; fettered
MANAGING controlling; contriving
MAN-CHILD a boy
MANCIPLE a steward; purveyor
MANDAEAN Babylonian sect
lw **MANDAMUS** a writ
bt **MANDARIN** official; orange; language
MANDATOR responsible entrustor;
   administrator
bt **MANDELIC** bitter almond extract
zo **MANDIBLE** a jaw of insect
MANDINGO tribe (South Sahara)
bt **MANDIOCA** cassava; manioc
mu **MANDOLIN** a guitar
MANDORLA oval panel
bt **MANDRAKE** white bryony
zo **MANDRILL** a baboon
zo **MAN-EATER** cannibal; tiger
MANELESS without a mane
MANELIKE like a mane; (of lion,
   horse)
MANFULLY boldly; courageously
zo **MANGABEY** Malagasy monkey
MANGANIN copper-base alloy
MANGCORN (many corn) mixed
   grain crop
MANGLING calendering; mutilating
MANGLING drying cloth by squeezer
   rollers
MANGONEL a ballistic machine
bt **MANGROVE** a tree
MAN-HATER allergic to man
MAN-HOURS labour measure
MANIACAL raving; frenzied; lunatic
bt **MANICATE** hairy
rl **MANICHEE** of God and Devil sect
MANICURE hand, finger nails beauty
   care
nt **MANIFEST** invoice of ship's cargo
MANIFEST evince; clear; obvious
MANIFOLD multiplied; numerous
MANNERLY of good address
MANNIKIN manikin; dwarf
ch **MANNITOL** hexahydric alcohol

bt **MANOCYST** receptive papilla in oomycetes
nt **MAN-OF-WAR** warship
MANORIAL referring to a manor
eg **MANOSTAT** pressure-constancy device
MAN-POWER male potential (labour reserve)
MAN-SIZED of adult dimensions
MANTELET small cloak
hd **MANTIGER** heraldic term
MANTILLA hanging lace and comb hair style (Sp.)
MANTISSA decimal part of logarithm
cp, ma **MANTISSA** number with floating point
MANTLING blushing; flushing; suffusing
MAN-TO-MAN close, confidential; intimate; frank
MANUALLY by hand
zo **MANUCODE** bird of paradise
MANURING fertilizing
MANUTYPE hand-painted
zo **MAORI-HEN** the weka
MAQUETTE mock-up model, sketch (Fr.)
zo **MARABOUT** Indian stork
rl **MARABOUT** Moslem priest or wizard
ml **MARAGING** steel-hardening heat treatment
MARASMUS emaciation
MARATHON long-distance race
MARAUDED roved; plundered; pillaged
MARAUDER raider; bandit; outlaw
nm **MARAVEDI** small Spanish copper
MARBLING form of décor
mu **MARCANDO** with precision
MARCHING bordering; foot slogging
MARGARIC pearly
MARGARON a fatty substance
pr **MARGINAL** in the margin; slight amount
pr **MARGINED** edged; bordered
MARGRAVE German prince
bt **MARIGOLD** orange flower
sv **MARIGRAM** tidal-height record
ck **MARINADE** steeping liquor
ck **MARINATE** steep in liquor; preserve
MARITIME marine; naval; nautical
bt **MARJORAM** aromatic plant
MARKEDLY unmistakably; eminently
MARKETED sold; vended
MARKSMAN crack shot
nt **MARLINED** twined with twine
mn **MARLITIC** (clay)
zo **MARMOSET** American monkey

tx **MAROCAIN** fine-rep dress fabric
MARONITE Jewish sect
MAROONED left on desert island
MAROQUIN morocco leather
MARQUESS a marquis
MARQUISE marchioness
MARRIAGE wedlock; espousal
MARRYING wedding; uniting
ch **MARSH-GAS** methane
zo **MARSH-HEN** moorhen
zo **MARSH-TIT** blackheaded tom-tit
bt **MARTAGON** turk's cap lily
MARTELLO circular tower
mu **MARTENOT** electronic keyboard
MARTINET a disciplinarian
MARTYRED died for their faith
bt **MARYGOLD** MARIGOLD, flower
zo **MARY-SOLE** a flat-fish
mu **MARZIALE** martial (It.)
ck **MARZIPAN** a sweetmeat of almonds
MASCARON grotesque head as decoration
MASORITE a theologist
MASSACRE pogrom; carnage
MASSAGED kneaded; rubbed
rl **MASS-BELL** serving bell
rl **MASS-BOOK** R.C. missal
pl **MASSETER** a jaw muscle
md **MASSEUSE** a manipulator
mn **MASSICOT** lead oxide
MASSORAH Hebrew tradition
MASTERED conquered; overcame; learned; competent
MASTERLY expertly; dexterously
MASTHEAD head of (esp.) lower mast
pr **MASTHEAD** newspaper heading
md **MASTITIS** breast inflammation
nt **MASTLESS** dismasted; steam-diesel-powered vessels
zo **MASTODON** early mammoth
nt **MASTSHIP** masts, timber carrier vessel
ch **MASURIUM** a metallic element
MATADORE bull-fighter; domino game
zo **MATAMATA** S. Amer. river tortoise
MATCHBOX chez Lucifer
cp **MATCHING** equalling; suiting; comparing records; matchboard
ck **MATELOTE** fish/wine stew (Fr.)
MATERIAL stuff; essential; relevant
MATERIEL equipment (Fr.)
MATERNAL motherly
MATESHIP comradeship
bt **MAT-GRASS** weavable reeds
MATHESIS mathematics; learning
MATHILDA army tank (obsolete)

MATRONAL motherly; sedate
MATRONLY elderly
MATTERED signified; imported
ce **MATTRESS** stuffed base of bed; concrete base (slabs)
md **MATURANT** a cataplasm
md **MATURATE** to poultice
MATURELY acting on experience and maturity
MATURING ripening; mellowing
MATURITY repayment date (insurance policies)
MATURITY fullness of age; ripeness
to **MAUNDRIL** a pick-axe
ch **MAUVEINE** synthetic dyestuff
MAVERICK unbranded animal
MAXIM-GUN single-barrelled machine gun
MAXIMIST a dealer in old saws
MAXIMIZE raise to maximum (prices, production)
bt **MAY-APPLE** N. American fruit
bt **MAY-BLOBS** marsh marigold
bt **MAY-BLOOM** hawthorn
MAYORESS wife of mayor
MAY-QUEEN spring deity
ck **MAZARINE** deep blue; flat plate within a dish; cake
MAZDAISM Zoroastrianism
MAZINESS perplexity; haziness
zo **MAZOLOGY** a zoological science
mu **MAZOURKA** mazurka; Polish folk dance
MEAGRELY scantily; sparsely; meanly
MEAL-POCK MEAL-POKE, beggar's meal bag
MEALTIME breakfast, lunch or dinner
zo **MEALWORM** one infesting flour
MEAN-BORN of humble origin
MEANNESS sordidness; paltriness
MEANTIME meanwhile
MEASURED meted; ascertained; steady
MEASURER computer; gauger
ck **MEAT-BALL** rissole; mini-hamburger
ck **MEATLESS** of vegetarian foods
MEAT-RACK hooked storage facilities
MEAT-SAFE storage cupboard
MECHANIC artisan; fitter
bt, zo **MECONATE MECONINE, MECONIUM,** opium; poppy-juice; foetal intestine contents
MEDALIST a prize winner
MEDALLIC relating to medals
MEDDLING interfering; intruding
MEDIATED intervened; reconciled

MEDIATOR an intercessor; arbitrator
MEDICATE to doctor; to dose
MEDICEAN (Medici of Florence)
md **MEDICINE** the curative art
MEDIEVAL (Middle Ages)
MEDIOCRE middling; ordinary
rl **MEDITATE** deep reflection; focus; spiritual exercise
bt **MEDULLAR** pithy (heart)
bt **MEDULLIN** lilac cellulose
MEEKENED became gentle
MEEKNESS submissiveness; humility
MEETNESS fitness; propriety
el **MEGALINE** magnetic flux unit
MEGALITH stone monument
zo **MEGALOPS** last larval stage in crabs
zo **MEGAPODE** mound bird
MEGATRON light-house valve
MEGAVOLT million volts
MEGAWATT million watts
mn **MEIONITE** a silicate
bt **MEIOTAXY** whorl development failure
ch **MELAMINE** organic compound
MELANISM black coloration
mn **MELANITE** black garnet
MELANOMA pigmented mole
MELANOUS dark-visaged
zo **MELANURE** sea-bream
MELIBEAN alternately responsive
mn **MELILITE** complex mineral
MELINITE a high explosive
MELLIFIC honeyed
MELLOWED matured; ripened; enriched
MELLOWLY sweetly; melodiously
mu **MELODEON** harmonium
mu **MELODIST** song and tune maker; composer
mu **MELODIZE** render harmonious
MEMBERED having limbs
bt, zo **MEMBRANE** tissue wall; tent roof; film (surface)
MEMORIAL relic; monument; memento
MEMORIZE learn by heart
MEMPHIAN MEMPHITE, of Memphis (Egypt)
MEMSAHIB white lady (India)
MENACING threatening; intimidating
MENDABLE repairable
zo **MENHADEN** American herring
mn **MENILITE** brown opal
md **MENINGES** brain membranes
MENISCAL MENISCUS, crescent-shaped type of lens
MENOLOGY calendar of saints
zo **MENOPOME** mud-devil

MENSURAL measurable
MENTALLY intellectually
MEPHITIC noxious; pestilential
MEPHITIS an exhalation; miasma
MERCABLE saleable; vendible
MERCHAND to traffic; to trade
MERCHANT trader; dealer; monger
MERCIFUL humane; clement; lenient
MERCURIC mercurial; quick witted;
  changeable
MERCYISM rumination; infantile
  regurgitation
bt MERICARP seed carpel
go MERIDIAN great circle; noon
go MERIDIAN longitude line through
  terrestrial poles
ck MERINGUE eggwhites and sugar cake
zo MERIONES Can. jumping mouse
MERISTEM formative tissue
zo MERISTIC segmented
MERITING deserving; earning
bt MEROGAMY individualized-gamete
  union
md MEROSMIA smell sense deficiency
zo MEROSOME a segment; a somite
mn MEROXENE biotite class
zo MEROZOON protozoon fragment
MERRYMAN mountebank; jester
md MESCALIN alkaloid 'truth drug'
MESDAMES ladies
MESHWORK network; reticulation
mn MESITITE a carbonate
MESMEREE one mesmerized
MESMERIC hypnotic
bt MESOCARP central carpel
md MESODERM inner skin
mn MESOLITE needlestone
zo MESOMERE muscle-plate zone in
  vertebrates
zo MESOSOMA abdomen division in
  arachnida
MESOTRON electron-directing device
mn MESOTYPE zeolitic mineral
gl MESOZOIC Triassic period
bt MESQUITE African thorn-bush
MESSIDOR 19 June – 18 July (Fr.)
MESSMATE table companion
MESSROOM forces' dining room
MESSUAGE premises and garden
METACISM excess of 'M'
zo METACONE cusp of mammal molar
el, ps METADYNE generator, converter
METALLED plated; macadamized
  roads
ch METALLIC compound of metals;
  lustrous; harsh
METALMAN metal-worker
zo METAMERE similar body segment

mn METAMICT glassy amorphous state
METAPHOR allegory; image;
  (comparison)
zo METASOMA abdomen part in
  arachnida
zo METASOME mid-body of cyclops
METATOME an architectural space
METAYAGE produce sharing (Fr.)
zo METAZOAN METAZOIC, METAZOON,
  multi-cellular construction of an
  animal
METECORN a corn issue
METEORIC transient; dazzling;
  flashing
METERAGE measurement
me METEWAND METEYARD, yard-stick
ch METHANOL methyl alcohol
METHINKS I think
METHODIC systematic; orderly
METHYLAL chemical solvent
ch METHYLIC (methyl)
md METHYSIS drunkenness
METONYMY a trope
ME-TOOISM alsoiology
md METOPISM (frontal suture)
ch METOPRYL anaesthetic
METRICAL rhythmic
bt MEZEREON aromatic shrub
MIASMATA nauseous exhalations
zo MICRANER small male ant
ps MICROBAR unit of pressure
zo MICROBIC microbial
zo MICROZOA animalculae
bl MICRURGY cell-study technique
pl MIDBRAIN sight and hearing
MIDDLING mediocre; medium;
  average
MIDFIELD players (cricket, lacrosse)
MIDNIGHT 24.00 hours
MIDPOINT central position (place,
  opinion)
MIDRANGE average distance
  achieved
nt MIDSHIPS on bow-aft line, in the
  beam
MIGHTILY vigorously; potently
md MIGRAINE the vapours
MIGRATED left; moved
MIGRATOR emigrant; nomad; rover
MILANESE (Milan)
MILDEWED mouldy; musty; rusty
MILDNESS gentleness; blandness
MILEPOST milestone
MILESIAN early Irish race
MILITANT eager to fight; warring
MILITARY martial; soldierly; warlike
MILITATE oppose; contend; fight
MILK-MAID dairy-maid

bt **MILK-TREE** the messaranduba
MILK-WALK milk delivery route (locally)
MILK-WARM tepid
bt **MILK-WEED** the sow-thistle
bt **MILK-WORT** flowering plant
as **MILKY-WAY** our galaxy group
MILL-HAND factory operative
MILLIARD a thousand millions
MILLIARE thousandth of an are (Fr.)
me **MILLIBAR** unit of barometric pressure
gp **MILLIGAL** 1000th of a gal
lt **MILLILUX** unit of illumination intensity
MILLINER bonnet-maker
MILLPOND reservoir for working millwheel
MILLRACE actuating stream
MILLTAIL (used) water past mill-wheel
jn **MILLWORK** mill machinery; prefabricated joinery
MILTONIC (of Milton's writings)
mn **MIMETITE** lead compound
MIMICKED aped; took off; imitated
MIMICKER impersonator; mime
MINATORY menacing; threatening
ck **MINCE-PIE** fruit-filled tart (Christmas)
MINDLESS stupid; heedless
MINGLING mixing; blending
MINIATED illuminated
bd **MINIBORE** (central heating); small-bore piping
MINIFIED depreciated
MINIMIZE treat slightingly
MINISTER servant; pastor; succour
MINISTRY agency; cabinet
rl **MINORITE** Franciscan friar
MINORITY the smaller number
MINOTAUR half man, half bull
MINSTREL ballad-monger
nm **MINTMARK** identification mark
mu **MINUETTO** MINUET, triple-time dance (Fr.)
MINUTELY particularly; exactly
MINUTEST smallest; tiniest
MINUTIAE small details
MINUTING recording; noting
zo **MIRE-CROW** black-headed gull
ck **MIREPOIX** vegetable bed for braised meats
MIRINESS muddiness; swampiness
mu **MIRLITON** Fr. kazoo, hum-through toy
MIRRORED reflected
MIRTHFUL festive; jocund; vivacious

MISAIMED ill-directed
MISAPPLY pervert; misuse; abuse
MISARRAY disarray; disorder
MISBEGOT shapeless
pr **MISBOUND** pages in wrong order
MISCARRY expulsion of a foetus
MISCARRY failure to execute a plan
ch **MISCELLA** oil/solvent solution
MISCHIEF injury; harm; hurt; trouble
MISCHOSE made wrong choice
MISCIBLE mixable
MISCLAIM claim in error
MISCOUNT reckon wrongly
MISCUING faulty move (billiards, snooker)
MISDATED wrong date ascribed
MISDEALT uneven dealing of cards
MISDOING wronging; offending
MISDOUBT to be wrong in doubting
MISDRAWN wrong file or information extracted
cp **MISENTER** enter facts wrongly (book-keeping)
MISENTRY erroneous record
mu, rl **MISERERE** Catholic repentance anthem
ar, rl **MISERERE** curiously decorated under-seats (choir-stalls)
MISFAITH distrust; perfidy; wrong reliance
MISFEIGN failure to disguise
MISFIELD failure to stop batsman's score
MISFIRED faulty gun shot
MISGUIDE lead astray
bt **MISGRAFT** fail to graft plant correctly
MISHEARD wrongly heard
mu, ck **MISHMASH** jumble; hotchpotch
rl, lw **MISHNAIC** MISHNOTH, (Jewish Oral Laws)
MISINFER deduce erroneously
MISJUDGE misconstrue; mistake
MISLABEL address incorrectly
MISLAYER untidy person
bt **MISLETOE** MISTLETOE, parasitic plant
MISLIKED disapproved; disliked
MISMATCH out-class
MISNAMED wrong appellation
MISNOMER incorrect appellation
MISOGAMY hatred of marriage
MISOGYNY hatred of women
MISPLACE displace; mislay
lw **MISPLEAD** win case for opponent
pr **MISPOINT** punctuate improperly
pr **MISPRINT** typographical error
MISPRISE to mistake

MISPRIZE slight; undervalue; belittle
MISQUOTE cite erroneously
MISRATED rated erroneously
MISRULED governed badly
MISSABLE not necessary or desirable
to attain
MISSERVE serve unfaithfully
MISSHAPE to deform
MISSPEAK utter wrongly
MISSPELL write wrong
MISSPELT an error in orthogaphy
MISSPEND squander; misuse
MISSPENT wasted; dissipated
MISSTATE state falsely
MISTAKEN in error; wrong; incorrect
MISTEACH teach wrongly
MISTHINK think ill of
MISTIMED chronologically erroneous
MISTITLE use wrong title
MISTRAIN to educate amiss
MISTRESS lady of the house
lw **MISTRIAL** (jury fail to agree)
MISTRUST want of confidence
mu **MISTUNED** discordant
MISTUTOR educate wrongly
MISUSAGE abuse; perversion
MISUSING misapplying; profaning
MISVOUCH to bear false witness
MISWRITE write incorrectly
MISYOKED unevenly matched (2
plough-horses)
MITCHELL hewn Purbeck stone
MITHRAIC (Mithras)
MITIGANT alleviating; lenitive
MITIGATE lessen; allay; assuage
MITTENED wearing mitts (fingerless
gloves)
lw **MITTIMUS** a writ
mt **MIZZLING** ceasing to rain; drizzling
MNEMONIC sound association
(memory aid)
MOBILITY readily mobile; uncertain
MOBILIZE gather armies, manpower,
for war
MOBOCRAT demagogic speaker
zo **MOCCASIN MOCASSIN**, leather shoe;
venomous snake
MOCKABLE ridiculous; derisive
MODALISM Sabellian doctrine
MODALIST theorist
MODALITY logical custom; sensory-
system
MODELLED fashioned; designed
MODELLER copyist; plastic planner
MODERATE so-so; fair; pacify;
mollify
mu **MODERATO** at moderate pace
MODESTLY decently; unobtrusively

MODIFIED altered; varied; changed
MODIFIER moderator
mu **MODINHAR** Portuguese popular song
MODIOLAR like a bushel measure
zo **MODIOLUS** central pillar of cochlea
MODISHLY foppishly; fashionable
MODULATE regulate; harmonize
MOFUSSIL rural districts (Hindu)
rl **MOHARRAM** Mohammedan fast
MOIDERED spent; toiled
MOISTFUL damp; humid
MOISTURE humidity
ch **MOLALITY MOLARITY**, mole/solvent
solution ratio
MOLASSES treacle
MOLE-CAST a molehill
ch **MOLECULE** group of atoms
MOLE-EYED having small eyes
MOLE-HILL miniature mountain
tx **MOLE-SKIN** strong cotton fustian
MOLESTED troubled; pestered
MOLESTER an annoyer; harasser
rl **MOLINIST** a Jesuit
MOLLIENT assuaging; softening
zo **MOLLUSCA** invertebrates
ch **MOLYBDIC** (molybdenum)
MOMENTLY every moment
MOMENTUM impetus; impulsive
weight
rl **MONACHAL** monastic
MONANDRY (one husband only)
MONARCHY royal family in kingdom
rl **MONASTIC** a monk
MONAURAL uni-aural; one ear only
mn **MONAZITE** a phosphate
MONDAINE woman of fashion
MONETARY financial; (money-wise)
MONETIZE manufacture money from
gold
MONEYBOX cash-box
MONGERED dealt in
zo **MONGOOSE** cobra-killing ichneumon
MONISTIC single-minded
lw **MONITION** a summons
MONITIVE warning
MONITORY cautionary
MONITRIX woman instructor
MONKEYED played about with
zo **MONKFISH** angler-fish
rl **MONKHOOD** monastic state
zo **MONK-SEAL** kind of sea creature
MONNIKER sobriquet; nickname
pg **MONO-BATH** developing/fixing
solution; for single person only
au **MONOBLOC** integral cylinder casting
bt **MONOCARP** an annual plant
MONOCLED wearing an eye-glass
MONOCRAT autocrat

zo **MONOCULE** one-eyed animal
zo **MONOCYTE** uninuclear leucocyte
MONODIST writer of dirges
zo **MONODONT** having a single tooth
MONOGAMY (one wife)
bt **MONOGERM** seed producing single seedling
MONOGONY asexual reproduction
MONOGRAM interwoven initials
MONOGYNY (one wife)
MONOLITH stone monument
MONOLOGY soliloquizing
MONOMIAL expressed by one term
MONOPODE single-footed
MONOPOLY exclusive privilege
MONOPTIC with one eye; monocular
rw **MONORAIL** single-rail system
MONOTINT picture in one colour
MONOTONE unvaried tone
MONOTONY dull uniformity; tedium
pr **MONOTYPE** printing machine
MONSIEUR a Frenchman
MONTANIC mountainous
MONTEITH punch-bowl; kerchief
MONTEURS artificial flower makers
MONTICLE hillock; molehill
MONUMENT a memorial; cenotaph; beacon
MOOCHING loitering
MOONBEAM a lunar ray
MOONCALF monster; dolt
MOON-EYED purblind
MOONFACE a round face
MOONLESS (a dark night)
MOONLING born last day of month and moon
nt **MOON-SAIL** a small sail
bt **MOONSEED** climbing plant
MOONSHEE Moslem linguist
pr **MOONTYPE** embossed lettering
bt **MOONWORT** a fern
MOON-YEAR lunar year
zo **MOORCOCK** red grouse
zo **MOORFOWL** moorcock
zo **MOORGAME** grouse
zo **MOORHAWK** marsh harrier
go **MOORLAND** moreland; peaty soil
bt **MOORWHIN** a genista
bt **MOORWORT** marsh andromeda
MOOTABLE debatable; doubtful
MOOT-CASE a moot-point
MOOT-HALL judgement hall
MOOT-HILL a rendezvous
MOPE-EYED myopic; purblind
MOPISHLY gloomily; dejectedly
MOQUETTE a carpet (Fr.); of coarse wool and linen
MORALIST virtuous man

MORALITY ethics; virtue
MORALIZE philosophize on morality
MORATORY of moratorium agreement to delay
rl **MORAVIAN** of Moravia; Hussite sect
MORBIDLY unhealthily
md **MORBIFIC** causing disease
MORELAND moorland
MOREOVER besides; also; likewise
ar **MORESQUE MOORESQUE**, arabesque decorative style
MORIBUND decaying; dying
bt, zo **MORILLON** grape; duck
zo **MORMYRUS** Egyptian pike
MOROCCAN (Morocco)
MOROLOGY foolish talk
MOROSELY sullenly; sourly
mn **MOROXITE** a phosphate
MORPHEAN sleepy; dreamy
MORPHEMA minimal meaningful linguistic unit
MORPHEUS god of sleep
md **MORPHINE** morphia
MORTALLY fatally; deadly
bd **MORTARED** of gunfire; solid brickwork
lw **MORTGAGE** loan on house security
cr **MORTISED** wood-joint; door lock
gl **MORTLAKE** ox-bow (ex-river, lake)
zo **MORTLING** morling; dead sheep
lw **MORTMAIN** inalienable property
MORTUARY charnel house; morgue
le **MOSLINGS** curried leather
zo **MOSQUITO** an insect
MOSS-BACK a Rip van Winkle character (USA)
MOSS-CLAD mossy
go **MOSSLAND** peat-land
bt **MOSS-PINK** a phlox
bt **MOSS-ROSE** house plant
bt **MOSS-RUSH** bog plant
MOTHBALL naphthalene; anti-moth
MOTHERED adopted
MOTHERLY parental; tender
MOTILITY movement; mobility
MOTIONAL of parliamentary motion (debate)
MOTIONED gestured; proposed
MOTIONER a mover; proposer of motion
MOTIVATE actuate; impel; induce
MOTIVITY power of energizing
MOTOR-BUS coach
MOTOR-CAR automobile
MOTORIAL motory; giving motion
MOTORING travelling by car
MOTORISE equip with motors
MOTORIST car driver

rw **MOTORMAN** chauffeur; one-man-
train driver
MOTORWAY fast main road
MOTTLING variegating
MOUCHING slouching; skulking
zo **MOUFFLON** wild sheep
MOULD-BOX box for casting
MOULDING shaping; fashioning
MOULINET drum of capstan
MOULTING shedding feathers, fur
MOUNDING banking
MOUNTAIN a light wine; peak
MOUNTANT photographic paste
MOUNTIES R. Can. Mounted Police
MOUNTING surround for a picture
MOUNTING ascending; copulating
MOUNTING sword movement (army)
MOURNFUL lugubrious; grievous
MOURNING lamenting; sorrow
bt **MOUSE-EAR** a herb
ck **MOUSSAKA** aubergine dish of
minced meat, eggs etc. (Gr.)
MOUSSEUX sparkling frothy wine
(Fr.)
ck **MOUTHFUL** pithy statement; tasty
snack
MOUTHING con molta espressione
MOVABLES personal belongings;
chattels, furniture
MOVELESS fixed; stationary
MOVEMENT motion; speed; crusade
mu **MOVEMENT** part of a musical work
MOVINGLY affectingly; eloquently
MOWBURNT (hay)
MUCCHERO rose and violet infusion
bt **MUCEDINE** a fungus
MUCHNESS almost abundance
bt **MUCILAGE** gum
zo **MUCIVORA** insects
MUCKERED made a muck of
MUCK-HEAP midden
MUCK-HILL dung-hill
MUCK-RAKE dig up dirt
bt **MUCK-WEED** white goosefoot
zo **MUCK-WORM** a miser; a grub
md **MUCOCELE** mucus accumulation
MUCOSITY mouldiness
MUCULENT slimy; viscous
bt **MUDARINE** an extract
MUDDLING confusing; deranging
MUDDYING miring
MUDGUARD a screen
gl **MUDSTONE** argillaceous sedimentary
rock
MUD-VALVE of drainage
MUFFLING noise deadening;
shrouding
MUG-HOUSE ale-house

MUHARRAM a Moslem month
bt **MULBERRY** a fruit-tree
MULCHING fertilizing
MULCTING fining; amercing
zo **MULE-DEER** N. American deer
MULETEER mule-driver
bt **MULEWORT** a fern
MULISHLY obstinately; stubbornly
MULTEITY multiplicity
MULTIFID many cleft
MULTIPED with many feet
cp **MULTIPLE** factor; combined units;
paralleling
ma, cp **MULTIPLY** increase; augment; spread
bd **MULTI-PLY** more than 3 ply (-wood)
MUMBLING muttering incoherently
MUMMYING embalming (ancient
Egypt)
MUNCHING chewing; masticating
MUNERARY donative
lw, bd **MUNIMENT** title-deed; stronghold
MUNITION military stores;
equipment
ga **MUNSHETS MUNSHITS**, stick and hole
field game
MURALLED painted on a wall
MURDERED assassinated; slain
MURDERER a Cain
mn **MUREXIDE** a crystal
MURIATED soaked in brine
ch **MURIATIC** hydrochloric
MURICATE prickly; thorny; spiky
MURIFORM like a wall
MURKSOME darksome; obscure
MURMURED complained; repined
MURMURER grumbler; grouser
mn **MURRHINE** (fluor-spar)
bt **MUSCADEL** muscatel
bt **MUSCATEL** grape; wine
MUSCULAR brawny; sturdy;
powerful
MUSELESS uncultured
bt, ck **MUSHROOM** upstart; blewit; edible
fungus
mu **MUSICALE** private recital
mu **MUSICIAN** instrumentalist
MUSINGLY in contemplative fashion
MUSK-BALL perfumed sachet
zo **MUSK-CAVY** a rodent
zo **MUSK-DEER** Cent. Asian ruminant
zo **MUSK-DUCK** Muscovy duck
MUSKETRY rifle-shooting
bt **MUSK-PEAR MUSK-PLUM**,
odoriferous fruits
bt **MUSK-ROSE** rambling rose
bt **MUSK-WOOD** musky tree
tx **MUSLINET** coarse muslin
zo **MUSQUASH** musk-rat

MUSTACHE moustache
bt MUSTAIBA Brazilian hardwood
MUSTERED assembled; gathered
MUTACISM mytacism
MUTATION discontinuous variation
MUTENESS dumbness
bt MUTICATE without a point
zo MUTICOUS lacking defence
structures
MUTILATE maim; dismember
MUTINEER insurgent crew member
nt MUTINIED rebelled; revolted
MUTINOUS seditious; unruly;
turbulent
MUTTERED mumbled; whispered
MUTTERER grumbler; grouser
MUTUALLY reciprocally
MUZZLING restraining (jaws);
silencing (opinion)
bt MYCELIUM mushroom spawn
md MYCETOMA a foot disease
zo MYCETOME special insect organ
md MYCODERM fungoid pellice
MYCOLOGY study of fungi
md MYELITIS spinal disease
zo MYLODONT (extinct sloth)
gl MYLONITE compact streaky rock
zo MYOBLAST embryonic-muscle cell
md MYOGENIC of spontaneous muscle
contraction
md MYOGRAPH recording machine
MYOMANCY divination by mice
md MYONOSUS MYOPATHY, muscular
disease
zo MYOPHORE muscle-connected
structure
cy MYOPLASM contractile part of
muscle cell
md MYOSITIC MYOSITIS, muscular
inflammation
bt MYOSOTIS the forget-me-not
pl MYOTASIS muscular tension
pl MYOTONIA excessive muscle rigidity
zo MYRIAPOD centipede
MYRIARCH a commander
MYRICINE (bee's wax)
MYRMIDON desperate ruffian
bt MYRRHINE myrrh (gum and
ladanum mix)
ch MYRTENOL myrtle oil monoalcohol
MYSTICAL enigmatical; occult
MYSTIQUE reverence for cleverness/
skills
MYTACISM excess of 'M' in
speaking
MYTHICAL legendary; fabulous
zo MYTILITE fossil mussel
MYTILOID mussel-like

md MYXEDEMA severe depression of
nervous system activity
zo MYXOPODA protozoans

N

NACREOUS pearly; iridescent
bd NAILABLE material that tolerates
nails
NAIL-FILE manicurist's implement
NAILHEAD visible outer portion of
nail
ar NAILHEAD early English
embellishment
NAIL-HOLE surface depression after
hammering
bt NAILWORT whitlow grass
tx NAINSOOK jaconet muslin
hd NAISSANT issuing from; parentage
NAMEABLE identifiable
NAMELESS obscure; inglorious
NAMESAKE having identical name
md NANOSOMA dwarfism
ch NAPHTHOL coal-tar constituent
NAPIFORM turnip-shaped
nm NAPOLEON nap; 20 francs
mn NAPOLITE volcanic substance
md NARCEINE opium extract
bt NARCISSI flowers
md NARCOSIS stupefaction; stupor
NARCOTIC anodyne; sedative; opiate
NARGHILE hookah-pipe
zo NARICORN horny beak
NARIFORM beak-like
NARRATED recited; related;
recounted
NARRATOR story-teller; historian
NARROWED contracted; cramped
NARROWER closer; nearer
NARROWLY nearly; barely; scarcely
NASALITY nosiness
NASALIZE enunciate nasally
NASCENCY growth; production
zo NASICORN horn-beaked
NASIFORM nose-shaped
ec NATALITY population's increase
ability
zo NATANTES water-spiders
NATANTLY buoyantly
NATATION swimming
NATATORY of aquatic habits
NATHLESS nevertheless
NATHMORE never more
NATIONAL public; general; racial
NATIVELY by birth; naturally
NATIVISM doctrine of genetics
versus experience

NATIVITY birth; Christmas; base of horoscope
NATTERED chatted
NATTIEST neatest; smartest
NATURISM nature worship
NATURIST practiser of nudism
nt **NAUMACHY** a sea-fight
zo **NAUPLIUS** larva of crustaceans
nt **NAUSCOPY** ship-sighting
NAUSEANT disgusting; revolting
NAUSEATE to sicken
nt **NAUSEOUS** offensive; repulsive
nt **NAUTICAL** marine; maritime; naval
zo, nt **NAUTILUS** cephalopod with chambered shell; diving bell
nt **NAVALISM** sea power
nt **NAVARCHY** admiralship
nt **NAVICERT** naval permit
NAVICULA incense-boat
nt **NAVIFORM** art; boat-like
nv **NAVIGATE** voyage; cruise; steer; pilot
nt **NAVY-BLUE** dark blue
NAZARENE of Nazareth
rl **NAZARITE NAZIRITE**, early Christian sect
NAZIFIED Hitler-minded
NEALOGIC adolescent
NEARCTIC N. of N. America
NEARHAND nigh; nearly
NEARNESS propinquity; closeness; togetherness
NEAR-SIDE left side looking forward
NEATHERD cow-herd
NEATNESS spick and span; dexterity
as **NEBULIUM** questionable element
NEBULOSE NEBULOUS, nebular; cloudy; hazy; misty; obscure
NECKATEE kerchief; scarf
NECKBAND collar
ck **NECKBEEF** coarse flesh
NECKLACE rivière
rl **NECKWEAR** scarves; ties; dog-collar
NECROPSY post-mortem
md **NECROSIS** mortification; death
NECROTIC moribund
NECTARED honeyed
zo **NECTOPOD** swimming appendage
NEED-FIRE fire by friction (Scouting)
NEEDLESS unnecessary; superfluous
NEEDLING embroidering; sewing
NEGATING denying; disclaiming
NEGATION denial; refusal; confute; absence
cp **NEGATION** mirror-wise; reversal of digits
pg **NEGATIVE** right of veto; not; (photo)

el **NEGATRON** thermionic tube
NEGLIGEE loose apparel
NEGRITOS pygmies (Malay)
NEIGHING whinnying; horse language
NEMALINE fibrous
mn **NEMALITE** hydrate of magnesia
zo **NEMATODA** eel worms
zo, md **NEMATOID** like a thread; internal parasite
zo **NEMERTEA** worms
NEMOROSE growing in groves
NEMOROUS woody
bt **NENUPHAR** water-lily
zo **NEOBLAST** large amoeboid cell
NEOCRACY rule by upstarts
NEO-LATIN modern Latin
NEOLOGIC of adding new words to language (neologisms)
pm **NEOMYCIN** antibiotic
md **NEONATAL** of newborn infants
zo **NEOPHRON** genus of vultures
NEOPHYTE novice; tyro; proselyte
NEOPLASM new tissue
NEPALESE a native of Nepal
md **NEPENTHE** drug causing oblivion
mn **NEPHRITE** jade
NEPHROID kidney-shaped
md **NEPHROMA** kidney tumour
zo **NEPIONIC** of embryonic period
NEPOTISM favouritism of family
NEPOTIST favours relatives
NERONIAN concerning Emperor Nero
NERVE-WAR cold war
NESCIENT NESCIOUS, ignorant; unlettered; unaware; agnostic
NESISTOR bipolar-field-dependent transistor
zo **NESTLING** young bird
NETHINIM temple servants (Heb.)
NETTLING irritating; provoking
md **NEURALGY** neuralgia
NEURAXIS spinal cord-brain axis
md **NEURITIS** nerve inflammation
NEURONAL concerning the neuron
zo **NEUROPIL** brain nerve fibre maze
NEUROSAL neurotic; temperamental
md **NEUROSIS** nervous disease
NEUROTIC highly strung
nc **NEUTRINO** subatomic particle
gl **NEVADITE** rhyolite; acid lava
NEWBLOWN just blossoming
NEWCOMER late arrival
NEW-MODEL Cromwell's army (Civil War)
NEWS-HAWK journalist; reporter
NEWS-REEL cinematic news

NEWS-ROOM incoming news; room where news is prepared
NEXTNESS nearest proximity
NIBBLING consuming tiniest morsels
NIBELUNG a Rhine gnome
NICENESS politeness; precision; choice
NICKELIC of nickel
NICKNACK a trifle; gewgaw
NICKNAME a monniker; sobriquet
el, ps, ml **NICKROME** alloy for electrical heating elements
ch **NICOTINE** tobacco constituent
NIDERING rascal; coward
ck **NIDOROSE** NIDOROUS, smelling of cookery
zo **NIDULANT** NIDULATE, nestling, birdling
NIELLURE metal-work
NIFFNAFF a trifle; nicknack
NIFLHEIM region of mist (Teutonic)
NIGERIAN of Nigeria
NIGGLING finicking; trifling
NIGHNESS nearness; proximity
NIGHTCAP cap or drink; horsehood (baseball)
NIGHT-DOG nocturnal venatic hound
zo **NIGHT-FLY** nocturnal moth
NIGHT-HAG a witch
zo **NIGHT-JAR** night-churr; goat-sucker
NIGHTMAN watchman
NIGHT-OWL who stays out late
NIHILISM extreme negation (doctrine)
NIHILIST Russian revolutionary (Tsarist era)
NIHILITY nothingness
cp **NINE-EDGE** feeding in punch cards
zo **NINE-EYES** lampreys
NINEFOLD 9 times
NINEPINS skittles
NINETEEN cardinal number
NINEVITE of Nineveh
bt **NISBERRY** naseberry; medlar
bt **NITIDOUS** lustrous; shining; reflecting
ch **NITRATED** (nitric acid)
ch **NITROGEN** an inert gas
NITROLIC acid
NITROXYL halogen/metal-attached radical
NIVATION snow-caused erosion
NOACHIAN (Noah); archaic; bygone
NOBBLING doping; injuring; swindling
ch **NOBELIUM** man-made element
NOBILITY distinction; aristocracy
NOBLEMAN a peer

NOBLESSE obliges all; (nobility)
zo **NOCTILIO** bat-genus
NOCTUARY night record
mu **NOCTURNE** NOTTURNO, serenade; lyrical; (It.) night scene
NODECUSP intersection of orbits
bt **NODIFORM** knots on stems
NODOSITY an entanglement
NODULOSE knotty; nodulous
NOEMATIC NOETICAL, intellectual; mental; thoughtful
ck **NOISETTE** small round piece of meat etc.
NOMADISM of regular seasonal migration
NOMADIZE migrate with flocks
NOMARCHY provincial rule
NOMINATE designate; name; appoint
NOMISTIC lawful
NOMOGENY life origin
ce **NOMOGRAM** alignment chart; diagram
NOMOLOGY psychology
lw **NON-CLAIM** failure to claim (insurance)
ch **NON-CREEP** smooth flow additive
NON-ELECT not of the elect
NONESUCH without parallel; paragon
rl **NON-JUROR** (Jacobite clergy)
ch **NONMETAL** negative-ion former
NON-MORAL amoral
NON-NASAL (phonetics)
NON-PARTY independent
NON-RIGID limp
NONSENSE balderdash; inanity; trash
md **NON-TOXIC** not poisonous
NON-UNION not accepting trades unions
NOONTIDE midday
NORMALCY regularity; standard
NORMALLY usually; ordinary
NORSEMAN NORTH-MAN, (Viking) Scand.
NORTHERN of the north
NORTHING distance northward
NORWEYAN Norwegian (Shak.)
NOSEBAND part of bridle
ae **NOSE-DIVE** a sudden plunge
zo **NOSE-LEAF** a bat appendage
NOSELESS non-nasal
NOSE-RING bull's ornament
md **NOSOLOGY** NOSONOMY, classification of diseases
md **NOTALGIA** backache
NOTANDUM a memorandum
NOTARIAL clerical
NOTATION system of figures
NOTCHING nicking; scoring

NOTEBOOK jotting pad
NOTELESS insignificant; petty; trivial
NOTICING observing; remarking
NOTIFIED made known; apprised
NOTIONAL fanciful; imaginative
zo **NOTORNIS** coot, (extinct) NZ
mu **NOTTURNO** NOCTURNE, night serenade; lyrical (It.)
ag **NOTWHEAT** of cereals without beard forms
NOUMENAL not phenomenal
NOUMENON a definite conception
rl **NOVATIAN** puritanical sect
lw **NOVATION** debt transference
NOVELESE inferior-novel language style
NOVELISH resembling a novel
NOVELIST author of romances; fiction
NOVELIZE to spin yarns, tell tales
NOVEMBER eleventh month
NOVENARY nine collectively
NOVERCAL like a step-mother
lw **NOVERINT** a writ
NOWADAYS in these days; at present
mt **NUBECULA** cloudiness
NUBILITY marriage
mt **NUBILOSE** NUBILOUS, cloudy; overcast
bt **NUCAMENT** a catkin
bt **NUCELLUS** nucleus of ovule
NUCIFORM nut-like
ch **NUCLEASE** nucleic-acid-hydrolisis enzyme
NUCLEATE having a nucleus
NUCLEOLE small nucleus
bl **NUCLEOME** protoplast's nuclear substance
bt **NUDATION** stripping area of plants
NUDISTIC scantily attired
NUGATORY ineffectual; futile; bootless
NUISANCE pest; annoyance; bother
NUMBERED reckoned; computed; limited
NUMBERER counter; numerator
NUMBNESS torpor; stupefaction
NUMERARY of numerals
NUMERATE as literate, but in numbers
NUMEROUS plentiful; manifold; frequent
NUMMULAR numismatic
NUMSKULL blockhead; dunce
NUPTIALS a marriage (occasion)
NURIMONO lacquer-ware (Jap.)
NURSLING an infant; child
NURTURED brought up; tended

NUTARIAN nut-eater
ma **NUTATION** nodding; Euler's angles showing position of body around a point
NUT-BROWN colour of ale
zo **NUTHATCH** small bird
NUTHOUSE lunatic asylum
ck **NUTMEGGY** of nutmeg flavour etc. as spice
NUTRIENT nourishing; alimental
NUT-SCREW monkey wrench
NUTSHELL receptacle for small amount
NUZZLING nestling
bt **NYMPHAEA** water-lilies
NYMPHEAN NYMPHISH, maidenly; like a nymph
NYSTATIN antifungal antibiotic

O

bt **OAK-APPLE** wen on oak tree
OAK-PAPER a wall paper
bt **OAT-GRASS** sort of straw
OATHABLE capable of being sworn
OBDUCING enveloping; covering
OBDURACY stubbornness; callousness
OBDURATE harsh; hardened; inflexible
OBEDIENT dutiful; submissive
OBEISANT reverencing; respectful
pr **OBELIZED** marked as spurious (†)
OBERHAUS upper house (Ger.)
OBITUARY list of the dead
OBJECTED protested; interposed
OBJECTOR opposer; heckler
OBLATION an offering; libation
rl **OBLATORY** of divine bread
lw **OBLIGANT** bound by contract
OBLIGATE oblige; pledge; mortgage
mu **OBLIGATO** obbligato; of special import
OBLIGING gratifying; constraining
OBLIQUED slanted
zo **OBLIQUUS** obliquely placed muscle
OBLIVION forgetfulness; (nepenthe)
zo **OBLONGUM** wing-vein cell coleoptera
OBSCURED eclipsed; clouded; dimmed
OBSCURER a concealer; hider
OBSERVED saw; remarked; obeyed
OBSERVER spectator; commentator
OBSESSED besieged; beset; haunted
mn **OBSIDIAN** volcanic rock
OBSOLETE discarded; archaic; effete

OBSTACLE hindrance; barrier; check
OBSTRUCT block; clog; impede; choke
OBTAINED got; won; earned; acquired
OBTAINER procurer; achiever
OBTRUDED thrust out; assertive
OBTRUDER importunate gate-crasher
OBTUNDED blunted; deadened
OBTURATE to close up; seal; shut
OBTUSELY stolidly; stupidly
OBTUSION bluntness
OBVERTED faced; confronted
OBVIATED avoided; prevented
bt **OBVOLUTE** wavy; enfolded
rl **OCCAMISM OCCAMIST**, doctrine of Occam
OCCASION create; event; incident
OCCIDENT the west
as **OCCLUDED** eclipsed; hidden
OCCLUSOR a shutter; valve
OCCULTED one eclipsed by another
OCCULTLY by secret (planetary) forces
OCCUPANT holder; tenant; resident
OCCUPIED engaged; employed
OCCUPIER inhabiter
OCCURRED chanced; happened; befell
OCEANIAN (Oceania)
mn **OCEANITE** basaltic igneous rock
zo **OCELLARY OCELLATE**, with spots like eyes; leopard-like genus
OCHEROUS yellow
zo **OCHIDORE** shore-crab
md **OCHLESIS OCHLETIC**, illness due to overcrowding
bt **OCHREATE** sheathing
OCHREOUS yellowish
mn **OCHROITE** cerite
OCTAPODY verse of 8 feet
OCTARCHY government by 8
mu **OCTOBASS** lower than double bass cello
OCTONARY referring to 8
zo **OCTOPODA** sub-order of molluscs
OCTOROON one-eighth negro blood
mu **OCTUPLET** (eight notes)
OCULARLY visibly; demonstrably
ODIOUSLY hatefully; offensively
ODOGRAPH distance and course meter
ODOMETER mileage recorder
md **ODONTIST** dentist
ODONTOID toothlike
md **ODONTOMA** tooth tumour
bt **OENANTHE** water dropwort
OENOLOGY study of wine

OERLIKON light A.A. gun
OESTROUS female reproductive cycle
ga **OFF-BREAK** of erratic bowling (cricket)
ga **OFF-DRIVE** batsman's stroke (cricket)
OFFENDED violated; affronted
OFFENDER transgressor; delinquent
OFFERING tendering; proposing
OFFICIAL functional; authorized
pr **OFFPRINT** a reprint; copy
OFFSHOOT branch outwards; new direction
OFFSHOOT scion; extension of company; gutter; water run-off
OFFSHORE non-domestic (banking etc.)
OFF-STAGE behind the scenes; unrecorded
OFF-WHITE variation shade
OFT-TIMES frequently; repeatedly
me **OHMMETER** (resistance)
OILCLOTH linoleum
OIL-FIELD oil well area
OIL-FIRED boiler; furnace
md **OIL-GLAND** secreting gland
OILINESS greasiness; lubricity
OILING-IN pre-painting surface preparation
OIL-PAPER transparent paper
OIL-PRESS olive squeezer
OILSKINS weatherproof garments
OILSTONE whetstone; sharpening stone; hone
md **OINTMENT** an unguent
fr **OITICICA** oil from nut tree (Brazil)
OLD-TIMER old-stager
OLD-WORLD antiquated
bt **OLEANDER** an evergreen
bt **OLEASTER** wild olive
OLEFIANT oil producing
pg **OLEOBROM** developing process
zo **OLEOCYST** oil-containing diverticulum
bt **OLEOSOME** cell fat inclusion
me **OLFACTIE** odour intensity unit
bt **OLIBANUM** frankincense
OLIGARCH one of power-sharing few
zo **OLIPHANT** elephant (obs.); cup made of ivory-tusk (medieval)
bt, ck **OLIVE-OIL** food oil of purity
rl **OLIVETAN** a Benedictine
OLYMPIAD period of 4 years
OLYMPIAN godlike
ga **OLYMPICS** competitive games, athletics
OMELETTE beaten-egg dish

OMISSION oversight; failure; disregard
OMISSIVE exclusive; neglectful
OMITTING missing; skipping; dropping
zo **OMMATEUM** compound eye
OMNIFORM of all shapes; protean
md **OMOHYOID** (shoulder-blade)
md **OMOIDEUM** pterygoid bone
md **OMOPLATE** shoulder-blade
md **OMPHALIC** (navel)
OMPHALOS boss on a shield; hub
ONCE-OVER comprehensive glance
bt **ONCIDIUM** orchid genus
md **ONCOLOGY** science of tumours
ONCOMING approaching
md **ONCOTOMY** cutting a tumour
ONE-HORSE poorly equipped
ONE-SIDED partial; biased
ONE-TRACK single interest or file
zo **ONISCOID** like a woodlouse
ONLINESS managing independently, alone
ONLOOKER spectator (match) (occasion)
mn **ONOFRITE** a mercury salt
ONOMANCY divination
ONRUSHES onsets
ONTOGENY development during individual life history
ONTOLOGY metaphysics
zo **ONYCHIUM** pulvillus in insect
zo **ONYMATIC** genetic
bt **OOGONIUM** algae/fungi female sex organ
zo **OOKINETE** vermiform stage in protozoa
OOLOGIST collector of bird's eggs
zo **OOSPHERE** an egg
zo **OOTOCOUS** oviparous
OPALESCE to be iridescent
OPALIZED make like an opal
mn **OPENCAST** excavating surface coal
OPEN-EYED watchful; alert; awake
OPENNESS frankness; sincerity
ar **OPEN-WELL** uncovered well
OPEN-WORK metal/lace pattern
OPERA-HAT a gibus
rw,md **OPERATED** as service (trains etc.); - on (as patient)
OPERATIC in opera style
OPERATOR service organizer; businessman
OPERATOR factory machinist; artisan; hand-
mu **OPERETTA** light, humorous musical
zo **OPHIDIAN** reptilian
zo **OPHIDION** conger eel

zo **OPHIURAN** starfish
OPIFICER artificer
OPINABLE conjecturable
OPIUM-DEN centre for drug addicts
bt **OPOPONAX** a perfume; a gum
OPPILATE block up; obstruct
zo **OPPONENS** muscle related to digits
OPPONENT foe; rival; antagonist
OPPOSING resisting; withstanding
OPPOSITE contrary; adverse; inimical
OPPUGNED contested; fought
OPPUGNER adversary; competitor
OPTATIVE optional; elective; voluntary
OPTICIAN spectacle-maker
OPTIMACY the nobility
OPTIMISM hopefulness
OPTIMIST a sanguine person
OPTIMIZE take a bright view
OPTIONAL left to choice; discretional
OPTOGRAM image of object seen on retina
OPULENCE wealth; affluence; profusion
OPULENCY riches; possessions
OPUSCULE a small work
ORACULAR portentous; ominous
ORANGERY orange garden
ORANGISM of Ulster Protestantist power
mn **ORANGITE** thorium silicate
mu **ORATORIO** sacred musical drama
ORATRESS a woman orator
ORCADIAN (Orkney Islands)
bt **ORCHANET** alkanet
ORCHESIS art of dancing
rl **ORDAINED** invested as priest; enacted
rl **ORDAINER** bishop; assigner; prescriber
ORDERING disposing; directing
rl **ORDINAND** candidate for orders
rl **ORDINANT** a prelate
ORDINARY a dinner; usual; customary
ORDINATE methodical; orderly
ORDINATE vertical axis on two dimensional graph
ORDNANCE war material (national)
ORDNANCE survey; mapping (national)
tx **ORGANDIE** figured muslin
ORGANIFY add organic matter
ORGANISM living structure
mu **ORGANIST** a player
ORGANIZE frame; constitute; construct

ORICHALC imitation gold

ORIENTAL of matters, cultures in the East

ar,bd **ORIENTED** lined up; on course

ORIGINAL authentic; an eccentric; new approaches

ORILLION a bastion

ORINASAL mouth and nose sound

ORNAMENT embellishment; decoration

ORNATELY elaborately; in florid style

zo **ORNITHIC** referring to birds

zo **ORONASAL** of mouth and nose

ORPHANCY orphanhood

ORPHANED parentless

ch **ORPIMENT** sulphurous yellow pigment; (arsenic sulphide)

tv **ORTHICON** type of camera tube

ORTHODOX true; conventional; correct

ORTHOEPY correct pronunciation

mn **ORYCTICS** fossils

ch **ORYZENIN** rice glutelin protein

zo **OSCININAN** (singing birds)

OSCITANT drowsy; yawning

OSCITATE to gape

OSCULANT kissing

OSCULATE to buss

zo **OSETROVA** sturgeon; caviar

OSMAZOME meat extract

tx **OSNABURG** coarse linen

ac **OSOPHONE** headphone for the deaf

OSSIANIC (Ossian)

OSSIFIED turned into bone

ck **OSSOBUCO** stew of veal with bone, wine (It.)

md **OSTEITIS** bone inflammation

md **OSTEOZOA** the vertebrata

bt **OSTERICK** bistort plant

mu **OSTINATO** recurrent theme

OSTIOLAR cellular

OSTRAKON engraved pottery shard (Gr.)

OTAHEITE Malay apple (Pacific)

zo **OTOCONIA** concretions in mollusca

OTOLITHS tiny calcium crystals (in ear)

md **OTORRHEA** discharge from ear

md **OTOSCOPE** ear examiner

md **OTOSCOPY** ear examination

mu **OTTAVINO** It. small flute, piccolo

zo **OUISTITI** marmoset

OUTBLUSH outflush

nt **OUTBOARD** external, portable, boat motor

OUTBOUND outward bound

OUTBRAVE defy; dare; challenge

OUTBREAK fray; riot; broil; revolt

OUTBURST eruption; ebullition

OUTCASTE rejected; casteless Hindu

OUTCLASS excel; outvie; surpass

OUTCROSS (cross-breeding)

OUTDARED defied; flouted

OUTDATED outmoded; old-fashioned

OUTDOING surpassing; outstripping

OUTDOORS not at home; fresh airing

OUTDWELL outstay

OUTFACED braved

OUTFIELD (cricket); nearer to the boundaries

OUTFLANK asssault from side or rear

OUTFLASH outshine

OUTFLING sharp retort

OUTFROWN show the greater dissatisfaction

OUTGOING expenditure; outlay

pc **OUT-GROUP** the excluded ones; pariahs

OUTGROWN become too constricting

OUTGUARD outpost

OUTGUIDE file marker for removed entries

OUT-HEROD be bigger stinker

OUTHOUSE shed; shack; shanty; barn

OUTLAWED beyond the pale

OUTLAWRY exile; banishment

ga **OUTLEAPT** higher than competitors sprang

OUTLEARN excel in learning

OUTLINED delineated; sketched

OUTLIVED outlasted

OUTLYING far; remote; distant

OUTMARCH walk until drop

OUTMODED out of fashion

OUTPACED over-run; run faster

cp **OUT-PLANT** system with remote data terminals

OUTPOINT win (sport)

OUTPOWER overpower; vanquish

OUTRAGED insulted; maltreated

OUTRANGE extend further

OUTREACH exceed; surpass

OUTREIGN sit on throne longer

OUTRIDER mounted attendant

OUTRIGHT at once; utterly

OUTRIVAL excel; outvie; beat

lw **OUTROPER** kind of bailiff

OUTSCOLD upbraid excessively

OUTSCORN despise; disdain; contemn

OUTSHINE eclipse; overshadow

OUTSHONE outrivalled

OUTSIDER not a favourite; onlooker; as alien

OUTSIDES backs or three quarters (rugby football)

OUTSIGHT outlook
OUTSKIRT border
OUTSLEEP perchance to outdream
OUTSLEPT snored longer than
OUTSLIDE slide better than everyone else
OUTSMART diddle; outwit; overreach
OUTSPEAK speak boldly
OUTSPENT over tired
OUTSPOKE bad English
OUTSPORT outdo in sport
OUTSTAND resist; withstand
OUTSTARE look longer than
OUTSTOOD withstood
OUTSTRIP outrun; undress faster
OUTSWEAR collect cursing prize
OUTSWELL overflow
OUT-TO-OUT overall measurement
OUTVALUE appraise too highly
OUTVOICE talk down
OUTVOTED won election
OUTVOTER imaginary elector
OUTWARDS externally
OUTWATCH peer superiorly
OUTWEARY bore stiff
OUTWEIGH exceed in value; offset; overbalance
zo **OVARIOLE** egg-tube in insects
zo **OVARIOUS** consisting of eggs
zo **OVEN-BIRD** a tree-creeper
OVER-AGED disqualified by age
tx **OVERALLS** garments
OVERARCH overhang
OVERAWED quelled; intimidated
OVERBEAR overwhelm; domineer
OVERBODY head, shoulders and breast
OVERBOIL let kettle blow top
OVERBOLD impudent; presumptuous
OVERBOWL cricket
OVERBRIM overflow
OVERBUSY officious
OVERCAME vanquished; subdued
mt **OVERCAST** lowering; cloudy
OVERCOAT winter topcoat
OVERCOME defeat
OVERCROW to insult; exult; brag
OVERDATE post-date
OVERDONE exaggerated
OVERDOSE too many pills
OVERDRAW take too much from bank
OVERDREW exaggerate in drawing
OVER-FACE requiring horse to jump beyond its limits
OVERFALL tidal effect
OVERFEED glut; cloy; satiate
OVERFILL flood

OVERFISH trawl too many
OVERFLOW overrun; inundate; swamp; annex (space)
tc, cp **OVERFLOW** reserve circuits; excess (location); (audience)
gl **OVERFOLD** inverted strata
OVERFOND doting
OVERFULL too full
OVERGAZE look over
OVERGIVE give lavishly
OVERGROW grow excessively (overgrown)
OVERHAND throwing; hand higher than shoulder
OVERHANG jut; impend
OVERHAUL repair; overtake; examine
OVERHEAD aloft
OVERHEAR eavesdrop
OVERHEAT scorch
OVERJUMP neglect; pass by
OVERKILL excess of casualties (nuclear war)
OVERKIND indulgent
OVERKING control lesser kings
OVERKNEE (above the knee)
OVERLADE overburdened
mn, gl, tx **OVERLAID OVERLAIN**, smothered; with decorative layers, (jewellery; gems)
OVERLAND cross-country
OVERLEAF on the next page
OVERLEAP skip
OVERLIVE outlive; survive
OVERLOAD encumber
OVERLOCK lock up too much
OVERLONG too long
OVERLOOK to slight; connive; condone
OVERLORD feudal superior
OVERMOST highest; topmost
OVERMUCH in excess
OVERNEAT finicky
OVERNICE fastidious
OVERPAID given excessive wages
OVERPASS traffic routing
OVERPLAY gambling
OVERPLUS remainder; surplus
OVERRAKE to sweep over like a wave
OVERRATE esteem too highly
OVERRIDE trample; quash; annul; exhaust a horse
OVERRIPE passé; past the prime
OVERRULE prevail; repudiate; rescind
OVERSEAM a seam
OVERSEAS abroad
OVERSEEN observed; overlooked
OVERSEER superintendent; foreman

OVERSELL make excess profits
OVERSEWN sewn over the edge
OVERSHOE a galosh (waterproof)
OVERSHOT beyond the target; went too far
nt **OVERSIDE** when water floods into a ship
OVERSIZE outsize; exaggerated
OVERSKIP leap-over; overtip
OVERSLIP pass without notice
ga **OVERSMAN** umpire (cricket)
OVERSOLD sales exceeded stocks
OVERSOUL divine being
ga **OVERSPIN** of twisted bowling (cricket)
OVERSTAY remain too long
OVERSTEP exceed; transgress
OVERSWAY overrule
OVERTAKE catch up with and pass
OVERTASK overtax; overtoil
bd **OVERTILE** imbrex; (It.); (Sp.)
OVERTILT upset
OVERTIME extra-pay and -play hours
OVERTOIL overexert
mu **OVERTONE** harmonic; partial tone, vibrating body
OVERTRIP be tripped by tripwire
mu **OVERTURE** offer; proposal; prelude (opera)
OVERTURN cause revolution
OVERVEIL overmantel; covering
OVERVIEW an inspection
OVERWASH glacial formation
OVERWEAR outdoor clothing
OVERWEEN to be conceited
OVERWIND overtax clock-mechanism
OVERWISE too clever by half
OVERWORK excess toil
tx **OVERWORN** exhausted by above; threadbare
zo **OVIPOSIT** lay an insect's eggs
OWL-LIGHT dusk to darkness
OXIDABLE oxidizable
ch **OXIDATOR** source of oxidation
OXIDIZE OXIDIZER, combined with oxygen; oxidizing agent
zo **OX-PECKER** African bird
bt **OX-TONGUE** a plant
OXYGONAL having acute angles
OXYMORON bitter-sweet
zo **OXYTOCIC** causing muscle contraction
md **OXYTOCIN** pituitary hormone strengthening uterus, mammary glands
OZOKERIT waxen material
ch **OZONIZED** converted to ozone

ch **OZONIZER** oxygen-to-ozone converter

P

PABULARY alimentary
PABULOUS nourishing
PACHYOTE thick-eared
PACHYPOD thick-footed
PACIFIED calmed; lulled; assuaged
PACIFIER tranquillizer; conciliator
PACIFISM PACIFIST, refusal to participate in armed warfare
PACKETED made into a parcel
PACK-LOAD load for an animal
PACK-MULE beast of burden
PADDLING walking in shallow water
nt **PADDLING** canoeing; of side wheelers
bt **PADELION** lady's mantle
PADELOUP inlaid leather book decoration
PADISHAH Turkish title; sultan; supreme ruler
PADSTONE kneeler; template
PADUAKAN coasting ketch (Celebes)
tx **PADUASOY** corded silk
ga **PAGANICA** feather filled leather ball
PAGANISH heathen
PAGANISM of polytheistic religions
PAGANIST follower of above
PAGANIZE proselytizing others to this
pr **PAGINATE** to number the pages
mn **PAGODITE** pagoda-stone
zo **PAGURIAN** (hermit-crabs)
gl **PAHOEHOE** ropy or cordel lava (Hawaii)
PAILLONS spangles (Fr.)
PAINLESS pangless
PAINTBOX box of colours
pt **PAINTING** a picture; limning; coating; application of paints
pt **PAINTOUT** test of pigment
PAIR-WISE in pairs
zo **PALAMATE** web-footed
PALATIAL royal; magnificent; stately
PALATINE with royal privileges
zo **PALEBUCK** the oribi
PALE-FACE white man among Red Indians
PALENESS wanness
PALESTRA wrestling school
bt **PALIFORM** stake-shaped
PALILOGY repetition
PALINODE recantation
bd **PALISADE** fortified paling enclosure

ga **PALISADE** horse-jumping obstacle
PALLIATE extenuate; mitigate; gloss
PALLIDLY palely; wanly
ga **PALL-MALL** ancient croquet
PALMETTE palm-leaf decor
bt **PALMETTO** fan-palm; hat
zo **PALMIPED** web-footed
PALMITIN natural oil fat
PALM-WINE fermented palm juice
zo **PALOMINO** cream coloured horse
with light-coloured mane and tail
(Sp.)
PALPABLE perceptible; evidently
PALPABLY obviously; tangibly
zo **PALPACLE** tentacle in siphonophora
PALPATED handled; felt
pl **PALPEBRA** eyelid
zo **PALPIFER** lobe of maxilla
zo **PALPLESS** absence of palpi
zo **PALPOCIL** sense hairlet in
coelenterata
PALSTAFF PALSTAVE, Celtic stone
axe
PALSYING paralysing
PALTERED shuffled; quibbled
PALTERER dodger; prevaricator
PALUDINE marshy
md **PALUDISM** malaria
PALUDOSE boggy
pm **PAMAQUIN** synthetic antimalarial
drug
PAMPERED coddled; humoured
PAMPERER over-indulgent person
PAMPHLET a broadsheet; brochure
rl **PANAGHIA** bishop's pendant
ae **PANCAKED** landed flat
PANCARTE royal charter
PANCHEON earthenware pan
md **PANCREAS** sweetbread
bt **PANDANUS** (screw-pines)
PANDEMIC epidemic in an area
PANDERED appeased others' desires
ck **PANDOWDY** apple-charlotte dessert
PANEGYRY eulogy; encomium;
adulation
PANELESS no glass
PANELLED (walls; a jury)
to **PANEL-SAW** a cutting tool
zo **PANGAMIC** of indiscriminate mating
zo **PANGOLIN** scaly ant-eater
PANICKED terrorized; affrighted
bt **PANICLED** in clusters
PANIONIC (Ionian people)
zo **PANMIXIA** cessation of natural
selection
PANNIKEL brain-pan; skull
PANNIKIN small vessel
PANOPTIC all seeing

PANORAMA extensive view
PANOTYPE antique photograph
mu **PANPIPES** a scale of wood pipes
PANSOPHY all wisdom
ar,rl **PANTHEON** complete mythology;
burial place of monarchs
mu **PANTONAL** synthesis of keys; atonal
PANURGIC skilled in all craft
PAPABILE suitable for papal/other
office
mt **PAPAGAYO** northerly wind (Mexican
plateau)
rl **PAPALISM** popery
rl **PAPALIST** an R.C.
rl **PAPALIZE** proselytize (R.C.)
PAPERBOY newsagent's delivery
boy
PAPERING wall and house-
decorating
zo **PAPILLAE** nipples
PAPILLAR warty
rl **PAPISHER** a papist
rl **PAPISTIC** popish
ck **PAPPADAM PAPPADUM**, Indian bread
wafer
PAPULOSE pimply
PAPYRINE like paper
rl **PARABEMA** Byzantine sacristy
PARABLED used a parable
PARABOLA a conic section
PARABOLE similitude
PARACHOR molecular volume
zo **PARACONE** molar cusp in mammals
PARADIGM example; model;
grammar pattern
PARADING displaying; flaunting
PARADISE Heaven; Eden; Elysium;
oasis; open court; atrium
mn **PARAFFIN** an oil
ch **PARAFORM** fumigant; formaldehyde
PARAGOGE literal addition
PARAGRAM a pun
zo **PARAGULA** region of insect head
zo **PARAKEET** paroquet; small parrot
PARAKITE tailless kite
PARALLAX alternation; displacement
PARALLEL side by side
PARALOGY false reasoning
PARALYSE benumb; deaden;
unnerve
zo **PARAMERE** an antimere
PARAMOUR a lover; mistress
bt **PARANEMA** paraphysis
PARANGON matchless jewel
md **PARANOEA PARANOIA**, chronic
monomania; hallucination
zo **PARAPSID** reptile skull condition
zo **PARAPSIS** (thorax)

ch **PARAQUAT** weedkiller toxic to
humans
me **PARASANG** about 4 miles (Pers.)
rl **PARASEVE** Jewish Saturday night
PARASHOT an anti-parachutist
zo **PARASITE** a sycophant; toady
ac **PARASTAT** gramophone record
cleaner
PARATYPE not the type specimen
PARAVAIL inferior; cf. paramount
nt **PARAVANE** minesweeping aid
pg **PARAXIAL** near to axis
lw **PARCENER** co-heir
PARCHING scorching; drying
rl **PARCLOSE** screen
PARDONED excused; absolved
rl **PARDONER** sells papal indulgences
PARENTAL affectionate; fatherly
mu **PARERGON** subsidiary work (Gr.)
PARGETED decorated exterior house-
walls
PARGETER plasterer; artist-modeller
PARHELIA mock suns (illusory)
pl **PARIETAL** walls of anatomical cavity
pl **PARIETES** of organ cavities; skull
PARISIAN (Paris)
mn **PARISITE** a marble
PARLANCE mode of speech
mu **PARLANDO** articulation in singing
mu **PARLANTE** crisp (piano playing)
PARLAYED conferred; discussed
PARMESAN a cheese
PARODIED took off; burlesqued
PARODIST burlesqued in literature,
on stage
PARONYME similar-sounding word
zo **PAROQUET** small parrot; parakeet
md **PAROSMIA** smell sense abnormality
rl **PAROUSIA** second Advent
md **PAROXYSM** fit; convulsion
PARROTER copyist
PARROTRY servile imitation
PARRYING warding; frustrating
PARSONIC like a parson
PARTAKEN consumed
PARTAKER sharer; partner
PARTERRE (flower beds, etc.)
ground floor; stalls; auditorium
PARTHIAN (Parthia)
PARTIBLE divisible
lw **PARTIBUS** marginal note
PARTICLE an atom; scrap; fragment
PARTISAN firm adherent to a faction
PARTNERS couples (dancing)
(wedded); associates
mu **PART-SONG** glee; for several parts
PART-TIME works for part of day
only

PARTYISM party loyalty
PASCUAGE grazing
PASCUOUS growing in pastures
PASHALIK pasha's jurisdiction
PASILALY universal speech
PASSABLE tolerable, up to standard
PASSABLY acceptably; reasonably
zo **PASSAGER** free tripper (falconry)
PASSBOOK identity documents; pay;
bankbook
PASSCODE secret entry requirement
PASSER-BY street pedestrian on his
way
zo **PASSERES** perching birds (genus)
PASSLESS trackless; without pass,
identity
rl **PASSOVER** Jewish festival
PASSPORT document of nationality,
identity; visas
PASSROLL stroke in croquet
PASSWORD secret watchword for
entry
PASTICHE comic imitation,
entertainment
md **PASTILLE** medicated lozenge
PASTORAL rustic
PASTORLY pastorlike; priestly
ck **PASTRAMI** smoked/sun-dried
seasoned meat
ck **PASTRIES** confectionery
PASTURED grazed
zo **PATAGIUM** wing membrane
PATCHBOX for decorative black spots
PATCHERY botchery
PATCHING repairing; cobbling
pl **PATELLAR** of the knee-cap
PATENTED protected by law
PATENTEE to whom a patent is
granted
PATENTOR the Patent Office; issuer
PATERERO PEDERERO, ancient swivel
gun (Sp.)
PATERNAL fatherly; parental
PATHETIC sad; grievous; emotional
PATHLESS no beaten track
zo **PATHOGEN** disease-causing parasite
PATIENCE cards; an opera
ec **PATOCOLE** forest-floor animal
hd **PATONCEE** heraldic cross
ec **PATOXENE** accidental forest-floor
animal
PATRONAL condescending
nt **PATTAMAR** large 3-masted dhow
(East India)
PATTENED wearing clogs
PATTERED falling rain; children's
feet
PATTERER with flowing salestalk

ck **PATTY-PAN** baking dish
PATULOUS spreading
PAULDRON a shoulder plate
PAUNCHED obese
PAVEMENT footway; sidewalk
PAVILION large tent; canopy; sports house
PAVILLON grand opening of horns, bells (Fr.)
PAVISADO galley defence
PAVONINE like a peacock
PAWNSHOP pawnbroker's pledged goods shop
PAYCLERK employee charged with paying
PAYPHONE public coin callbox; telephone
PAYSHEET list of wages owed
PEACEFUL placid; serene; pacific
PEACHERY a hothouse
zo **PEACHICK** young peafowl
PEACHING divulging; informing
PEAGREEN a colour
el **PEAK-LOAD** maximum activity
mn **PEARL-ASH** potash
md **PEARL-EYE** cataract
PEARLIES coster's buttons
PEARLING diving for pearls
ml **PEARLITE** iron/steel microconstituent
mn, bd **PEARLITE** granules of volcanic glass, insulation aggregate
bt **PEARMAIN** an apple
bt **PEASECOD** pea-pod
mn **PEASTONE** limestone
PEAT-MOOR peat-bog
bt **PEAT-MOSS** sphagnum
PEAT-REEK peat smoke
PECCABLE weak; frail; erring
PECCANCY sinfulness; offence
PECTINAL like a comb
PECTORAL breast-plate
PECULATE embezzle; steal; purloin
PECULIAR odd; singular; unusual
PECULIUM prerogative; privilege
PEDAGOGY instruction
ag, gl **PEDALFER** cyclist; iron-clay rich zonal soil
PEDALIAN referring to feet
PEDALIER pedal keyboard
PEDALITY foot measurement
PEDALLED worked by foot
PEDALLER PEDALFER, cyclist
PEDANTIC finical; exact; precise
PEDANTRY priggishness; conceit
PEDDLERY hawking
PEDDLING retailing; trifling
PEDERERO paterero; swivel gun (Sp.)

PEDESTAL plinth; base
md **PEDIATRY** childish diseases
md **PEDICURE** foot treatment
PEDIGREE lineage; stock; genealogy
PEDIMENT portico decoration
zo **PEDIPALP** whip-scorpion
zo **PEDIREME** a crustacean
PEDOLOGY study of soil
bt, pl **PEDUNCLE** stalk; nerve fibre stalks in brain
PEEK-A-BOO punching cards with identity code
PEEK-A-BOO children's frolic
PEEP-HOLE chink for illicit observation
PEEP-O'-DAY dawn
PEEP-SHOW galanty-show
PEERLESS unrivalled; matchless
zo **PEESWEEP** peewit
zo **PEETWEET** spotted sandpiper
PEGAMOID imitation leather
PEGASEAN (Pegasus)
PEIGNOIR loose wrapper
PEINTURE special consistent use of paints
PEJORATE deteriorate
zo **PEKINESE** small pug-nosed dog
PELAGIAN (deep sea)
PELARGIC stork-like
PELASGIC early Grecian
PELERINE a tippet or cape
md **PELLAGRA** acute anaemia
PELLICLE thin skin or crust
PELL-MELL rapidly; in disorder; confusedly
PELLUCID transparent; vitreous; clear
bt **PELORISM** abnormality
PELTATED shield-shaped
PELT-WOOL wool from a hide
ck **PEMMICAN** dried meat/berry food
PENALIZE handicap; punish
PENCHANT inclination; turn; bent
PENCRAFT penmanship
PENDENCE suspense
PENDENCY indecision
PENDULUM swinging weight
zo **PENELOPE** currasow-bird (S. Amer.)
PENITENT contrite; repentant
nt **PENJAJAP** square-lug trade vessel (Malaya)
PENKNIFE pocket-knife
PENNORTH a pennyworth
zo **PENNY-DOG** a kind of shark
PENOLOGY prison management
PENSTOCK duct to waterwheel
PENTACLE five-pointed star
PENTAFID cleft in five

PENTAGON five sided figure
mn **PENTELIC** (marble)
ch **PENTOSAN** polysaccharide
bd **PENT-ROOF** lean-to; sloped roof
as **PENUMBRA** partial shadow; (partial solar eclipse)
PENWIPER rag for pen user
PENWOMAN lady journalist; author
PEOPLING populating
mn **PEPERINO** granular tufa
PEPPERED hit with shot
PEPTOGEN PEPTONIC, digestive principle; digestive
PEPYSIAN (Samuel Pepys) (diary)
PERACUTE very sharp or violent
PERCEIVE apprehend; discern; descry
PERCHING roosting
hd **PERCLOSE** screen; railing
mu **PERDENDO** dying away
PERDURED endured; lasted
PERFORCE of necessity; forcibly
PERFUMED scented; odoriferous
PERFUMER perfume seller
PERFUSED sprinkled; bedewed
nt **PERIAGUA** dug-out canoe, W. Indies (Sp.)
pl **PERIANAL** anal/rectal region
bt **PERIANTH** floral envelope
bt **PERIBLEM** portion of apical meristem
bt **PERICARP** seed-vessel
rl **PERICOPE** scriptural passage
md **PERICYTE** small-blood-vessel cell
bt **PERIDERM** outer bark
bt **PERIDIUM** outer wall of fungus fruitbody
as **PERIGEAL PERIGEAN**, of moon's orbit nearest to the earth
bt **PERIGONE** perianth
PERILLED endangered; risked
PERILOUS hazardous; risky; parlous
as **PERILUNE** point in lunar satellite orbit
PERIODIC at stated intervals
PERIOTIC around inner ear
PERIPETY climax; solution
PERIPLUS circumnavigation
zo **PERISARC** chitinous layer in hydrozoa
PERISCII polar people
PERISHED decayed; died; expired
ch **PERISSAD** (odd atomic valency)
el **PERITRON** special cathode-ray tube
PERJURED perfidious; forsworn
PERJURER false witness
gl **PERKNITE** coarse-grained igneous rock

mn **PERLITIC** vitreous obsidian
ec **PERMEANT** highly mobile animal
PERMEATE penetrate; percolate; seep
PERMUTED changed; transmuted
lw **PERNANCY** rent in kind
PERNETTI kiln support
ch **PEROLENE** heat exchange organic fluid
bt **PERONATE** with thick-sheathed stipe
md **PERONEAL** (fibula)
zo **PERONEUS** fibula or leg muscle
PERORATE declaim; harangue
ch **PEROXIDE** a bleacher
bd **PERPENDS** face joints, corners (brick)
PERRUQUE peruke; a wig
PERSICOT peach cordial
bt **PERSIMON** date-plum
PERSONAL distinctive; individual
PERSPIRE sweat
PERSUADE induce; sway; entice
PERTHITE potassium/sodium-felspar intergrowth
PERTNESS sauciness; flippancy
PERTUSED punched
PERUSING reading; scrutinizing
PERUVIAN (Peru)
bt **PERUVINE** Peruvian balsam
PERVADED permeated; diffused
PERVERSE stubborn; vexatious
PERVIOUS porous; permeable
zo **PESSULUS** osseus trachea band in birds
PESTERED plagued; harassed; worried
PESTERER tormentor; teaser
PESTLING pounding; abrading
bt **PETALINE** (petal)
PETALISM banishment; ostracism
mn **PETALITE** silicate of alumina
bt **PETALODY** stamen-to-petal transformation
bt **PETALOID** petal-shaped
bt **PETALOUS** having petals
ga **PETANQUE** of boule (French bowls)
md **PETECHIA** tiny haemorrhage spot
PETERING calling at cards
PETERING collapsing, drying (of machines)
PETERMAN a fisherman
bt **PETIOLAR** having a leaf-stalk
PETITION supplication; ask; beseeching
PETITION of right demand of Govt.
PETITORY of petitioning; demanding
PETRIFIC turning to stone
PETRONEL horse pistol
zo **PETROSAL** otic-fusion bone

PETTIFOG quibble over details
PETULANT irritable; querulous; testy
mn PETUNTSE china clay
mn PETWORTH variety of marble
PEWTERER worker in pewter
bt PEZIZOID like cup-shape apothecium
md PHAKITIS eye inflammation
pl PHALANGE finger-bone
PHANTASM spectre; chimera
PHANTASY airy speculation; fancy
PHARISEE formalist
PHARMACY drug-store
zo PHEASANT a game bird
bt PHELLOID plant-surface cell crust
PHENETIC maximum observable
similarity
mn PHENGITE species of mica
PHENOLIC plastic mould
bt PHIALIDE flask-shaped sterigma
PHIALLED filled small one-dose flask
tx PHILABEG PHILIBEG, the kilt
zo, mu PHILOMEL the nightingale; unit of
melody (Shak.)
md PHLYCTEN nodule on conjunctiva
zo PHOCENIC (dolphins)
PHONATED gurgled
PHONE-BOX public telephone; call
box
PHONEMIC phoneme minimal unit of
speech in language
PHONETIC vocal
pl PHORESIS ion passage through
membrane
bt PHORMIUM New Zealand flax
ch PHOSGENE poisonous gas
PHOSPHAM ammonia compound
ch PHOSPHOR morning star; Venus;
fluorescent substance
zo PHOTOGEN phosphorescent organ
PHOTOPIC normal daylight vision
md PHOTOPSY an eye trouble
PHRASING expressing; uttering
bt PHRYGANA scattered thorn scrub
(Greece)
PHRYGIAN a Montanist
md PHTHISIS consumption
PHYLARCH Greek tribal leader
md PHYLAXIS body defence against
infection; protection
PHYLETIC tribal
mn PHYLITTE clay state
bt PHYLLARY bract outside capitulum
zo PHYLLIUM leaf insects
PHYLLODE a form of leaf
bt PHYLLODY PHYLLOID, leaf-like
structure
bt PHYLLOME foliage
PHYSALIA Portuguese man-of-war

bt PHYSALIS Cape gooseberry
zo PHYSETER sperm whale
PHYSICAL material; corporeal;
tangible
PHYSIQUE bodily structure
bt PHYTOMER phyton; plant unit
bt PHYTOSIS vegetable parasites
zo PHYTOZOA sea anemones, etc.
PIACULAR atrociously bad
mu PIANETTE small piano
bt PIASSABA PIASSAVA, Brazilian palm;
fibre for ropes and brooms
PIAZZIAN like a piazza
PIBLOKTO culture syndrome
(Eskimos)
zo PICARIAN (woodpeckers)
fr PICAROON small hooked pulling pole
PICAROON pirate; rogue
PICCADIL high collar
zo PICIFORM woodpecker type
zo PICKEREL pike; dunlin
PICKETED enclosed; guarded
PICKLING preserving
PICKLOCK master (skeleton) key
PICK-ME-UP a cordial; stimulant
PICKWICK a club
mn PICOTITE a spinel
PICTURED described; represented
PIECENER a piecer; joiner of threads
PIECRUST tart pastry
gl PIEDMONT zonal character at foot of
mountain
PIEDNESS spotted diversity
bd PIEDROIT pier without cap or base
PIERCING keen; shrill; acute
PIERHEAD jetty
PIERIDES the nine Muses
PIFFLING trifling; peddling
PIGEONED fleeced; swindled
PIGEONRY pigeon loft
PIG-FACED swine-visaged
mn PIGOTITE aluminium compound
PIGSTIES pig-pens
PIGSWASH swill; hogwash
PIKEHEAD head of a pike
ar PILASTER square column
zo PILCHARD sea-fish
PILEATED capped
bd PILE-WORK foundation of piles
zo PILE-WORM teredo; boring worm
PILE-WORN threadbare
bt PILE-WORT celandine
PILFERED filched; peculated
PILFERER thief; purloiner
zo PILIDIUM larval form of nemertea
PILIFORM slender as a hair
PILING-UP accumulating to surfeit
PILLAGED ransacked; looted

PILLAGER plunderer; rifler; robber
PILLARED columnar
bt PILLCORN oats
PILLOWED cushioned
bt PILLWORT a plant
PILOSELY hairily
PILOSITY hairiness
nt PILOTAGE harbour pilot's fee
ac, nt PILOTING directing; guiding;
    steering
mn PIMELITE aluminium silicate
nc PIMPLING fuel can surface swelling
PINACOID crystalline structure
nt PINAFORE apron; ship of line
    (Gilbert-rigged)
bt PINASTER the cluster-pine
cp PINBOARD bagatelle; plugboard
    (cordless)
PINCE-NEZ eye-glasses
PINCHERS pincers; pliers
nv PINCHING nipping; being frugal;
    sailing too close to the wind
el, ps PINCH-OFF breakdown point in field
    transmissions
PINDAREE Mogul freebooter
PINDARIC in the style of Pindar
PINE-CLAD crowned with pines
bt PINE-CONE fir-cone
PINE-WOOD deal
PINE-WOOL fibrous substance
PING-PONG table tennis
cp PINGPONG twin-tape multiple
    recording
PININGLY longingly; languishingly
PINIONED bound; shackled
PINK-EYED having small eyes
bt PINK-ROOT a vermifuge
PINKSTER Whitsuntide; a pink
    flower
PINMAKER who makes pins
PIN-MONEY an allowance
PINNACLE apex of tower decoration;
    zenith; crown
PINNATED feathered
bd PINNINGS different coloured stones
    set in rubble wall
zo PINNIPED fin-footed; a seal
PINOCHLE card game (USA)
PINOLEUM wood and canvas
    sunblind
bt PINPATCH periwinkle
PINPOINT locate exactly
PINTABLE bagatelle gambling
hr PIN-WHEEL firework; clock part
PINWHEEL revolving coloured wheel
    on stick
bt PIONNATE fungal spore layer
PIPE-CASE pipe-holder

mn PIPE-CLAY a kaolin-like clay
zo PIPE-FISH sea-horse type
w PIPELINE cross-country oil-lead
PIPERACK storage for tobacco
    smoker
ck PIPERINE pepper concentrate
PIPE-ROLL Great Roll of Exchequer
bt PIPE-TREE the lilac
PIPE-WINE wine from the cask
mn PIPE-WORK a pipe-vein of ore
bt PIPEWORT pepperwort
PIQUANCY pungency; raciness
PIRATING illegal action at sea;
    (radio)
PIRATING infringing a copyright
PIRIFORM pearshaped
PISCATOR Izaak Walton; fisherman
PISCINAL (fishpond)
zo PISIFORM fishlike
mn PISOLITE coarse oolite
bt PISTACIA the pistachio-tree
PISTOLET small pistol
PITCHING flinging; casting; lurching
PITCH-OUT (baseball)
mn PIT-FRAME framework round
    mine
zo PITHECUS an ape
PITHLESS lacking energy; sapless
PITIABLE arousing pity or contempt
PITIABLY deplorably; movingly
PITILESS merciless; ruthless
PITTACAL a blue dye
PITTANCE dole; small allowance
pl PITUITAL (pituitary gland)
PITYROID branlike
PIVOT-GUN swivel-gun
PIVOTING moving around; hingeing
PIVOT-MAN key-man
PIXY-RING fairy-ring
PLACABLE relenting; forgiving
PLACATED pacified; appeased
PLACEMAN office-holder
PLACENTA the afterbirth
PLACIDLY serenely; tranquilly;
    calmly
PLAGIARY literary theft
PLAGUILY pestiferously
PLAGUING tormenting; pestering
lw PLAINANT plaintiff
PLAITING pleating; braiding
PLANCHED planked
PLANCHET disc; a blank
PLANETIC planetary; revolving
PLANGENT resounding;
    reverberating
PLANKING flooring; putting down
zo PLANKTON drifting organic life
PLANLESS unsystematic; aimless

PLANNING scheming; plotting; devising

bt **PLANTAIN** banana-like fruit; a weed

PLANTING inculcating; inserting

bt **PLANTLET** a small shrub

bt **PLANTULE** embryo of a plant

zo **PLANULAR** (embryo of hydrozoa)

PLASHING dabbling; splashing

bd **PLASHING** hurdle-making process

ps **PLASMOID** characteristic plasma section

ar **PLASTERY** plasterwork

ch **PLASTICS** industrial synthetic resins; organic polymer materials

PLASTRON breastplate (fencing)

bd **PLATBAND** impost; lintel; projecting; moulding

PLATEFUL a meal

md **PLATELET** blood corpuscle form

rw **PLATFORM** party policies; raised level

ch **PLATINIC** (platinum)

ch **PLATINUM** metallic element

PLATONIC philosophical; (-friendship)

PLATTING plaiting; weaving

zo **PLATYPUS** duck bill

zo **PLATYSMA** dermal musculature

PLAUSIVE applauding

PLAYABLE stageable drama, music, pageant

PLAYBILL programme

PLAYBOOK book of rules; log (Am. football); script

PLAYBOOK book of dramas

PLAY-DEBT gambling debt

PLAYGOER stage fan

PLAY-MARE hobby-horse

PLAYMATE sportive companion

PLAYSOME frolicsome; wanton

PLAYTIME recreation

PLEACHED interwoven; plaited; matted

PLEADING arguing; disputing

PLEASANT welcome; delectable

PLEASING grateful; charming

PLEASURE indulgence; gladness; joy

PLEATING folding

PLEBEIAN popular; vulgar; ignoble

mu **PLECTRUM** plucking quill for lute, lyre, mandolin, banjo

PLEDGING plighting; pawning

as **PLEIADES** group of 7 stars

rl **PLENARTY** (benefice)

PLEONASM verbosity

PLEONAST a sprouter; demagogue

PLESSITE entectic intergrowth in meteorites

PLETHORA super abundance; surfeit

md **PLEURISY** lung inflammation

md **PLEXITIS** nerve plexus inflammation

PLIANTLY easily bent; flexibly

PLICATED folded; involved; intricate

PLIGHTED betrothed; promised

PLIGHTER one who pledges

PLIMMING becoming plump

PLIMSOLL rubber shoe; ship's load line

gl **PLIOCENE** a geological strata

el **PLIOTRON** hot-cathode vacuum tube

PLODDING slow but sure

PLOPPING dropping into water

PLOTTING conspiring; contriving; planning

nt **PLOTTING** demonstrating movements (radar)

PLOUGHED furrowed; failed exam

PLOUGHER husbandman; persister

PLUCKILY courageously; valorously

gl, mu **PLUCKING** glacial theft and misplacement of rocks; stripping; (examination); (strings)

el **PLUGGING** stopping; blocking; core; inserting a lead

el **PLUGMOLD** duct for laying cables; raceway (Amer.)

PLUG-UGLY thug; street ruffian; fister; slasher

cp **PLUGWIRE** two live sockets (also earth) circuits

mn, bt **PLUMBAGO** graphite; blue or violet flower

pb **PLUMB-BOB** test for vertical alignment

PLUMBEAN leaden; dull; heavy

PLUMBERY lead work

nt **PLUMBING** sounding for depth of ocean

bd **PLUMBING** water piping system

bd **PLUMBING** heating; sanitation

md **PLUMBISM** lead poisoning

ck **PLUMCAKE** fruit cake (Christmas) (wedding)

ck **PLUMDUFF** plain flour pudding with raisins/currants

zo **PLUMELET** downy feather

zo **PLUMIPED** feathered feet

PLUMMING sinking a shaft

PLUMPEST fattest

PLUMPING going all out

zo **PLUNGEON** a sea-bird

PLUNGING immersing; ducking

PLURALLY more than once

PLUTONIC infernal; dark; igneous

PLUVIOUS rainy; pluvial; humid

bd **PLYMETAL** metal-faced plywood

POACHING stabbing; trespassing (It.)
ck POACHING hunting unlawfully;
(eggs)
POCHETTE POCHETTO, pocket wallet;
book; violin; kit (Fr., It.)
POCKETED stolen; concealed; filched
md POCKMARK a scar
bt POCKWOOD a hard wood
md PODAGRAL PODAGRIC, gouty
md PODALGIA neuralgia in foot
zo PODARGUS genus of nocturnal birds
to PODAUGER grooved auger
PODIATRY chiropody; foot care
md PODISMUS spasm of foot
bt PODOCARP stalk to a carpel
zo PODOMERE limb segment in
arthropoda
PODOSOMA leg-bearing segments in
acarina
POEMATIC poetical; lyric; metrical
POETICAL imaginative; rhyming
POETIZED versified
POIGNANT acutely painful; caustic
POIGNARD small dagger
lw POINDING distraining
POINTING directing; aiming;
indicating
bd, mu POINTING exposed mortar treatment;
allocation of syllables to notes
POISONED corrupted; envenomed
POISONER who gives poison
POLARITY united opposites
POLARIZE magnetize
ga POLE-JUMP assisted leap
nt POLEMAST (without a topmast)
POLEMICS controversies
as, nv POLE-STAR Polaris; a lode-star
POLICIES lines of conduct;
insurance–
POLICING maintaining public order
POLISHED smooth; burnished
POLISHER shoe or furniture shiner
POLITELY courteously; urbanely
POLITICO opportunist politician
POLITICS art of government
to POLL-ADZE blunt-headed adze
POLL-BOOK register of voters
vt POLL-EVIL bursa inflammation in
horse
pl POLLICES thumbs or great toes
bt POLLINAR covered with pollen
zo POLLIWOG POLLYWOG, tadpole;
children's rag doll (Moorish)
POLLSTER opinion taker
POLLUTED contaminated; filth-laden
POLLUTER defiler; contaminator
zo POLOCYTE polar body
POLONIUM radio-active element

POLTROON coward; dastard; craven
bt POLYARCH of many-stranded stele
zo POLYAXON having many axes
zo POLYCARP gonad form in
urochorda; (philosophy)
POLYFOIL circular ornamentation
POLYGAMY POLYGYNYplurality of
wives just then
POLYGLOT in several languages
POLYGRAM many sided figure
POLYMERS POLYMERY, organic,
synthetic resins; rubbers
bt POLYMERY whorl of many members
md POLYOPIA multiple vision
POLYPARY hard covering of polyps
zo POLYPIDE compound polyzoan
POLYPODE having many feet
bt POLYPODY a fern
zo POLYPOID POLYPOUS, resembling
polyps; octopus type
pg POLYPOSE multi-pose portrait
POLYSEMY multi meanings of word,
root
ch POLYSOME cluster of ribosomes
cy POLYSOMY multiple-chromosome
state
POLYTENE identical chromatids
(genes)
POLYTERM unit concept heading
POLYTYCH many-leaved ancient
book
POLYTYPE cast of an engraving
md POLYURIA excessive urine secretion
zo POLYZOAN colony of polyzoa
zo POLYZOIC zoolatrous; sporozoic
zo POLYZOON barnacle type
POMANDER perfumed ball
POMIFORM like an apple
bt POMOLOGY apple culture
POMPEIAN of Pompeii
PONDERAL ascertained by weight
PONDERED meditated; thought
PONDERER cogitator; ruminator
bt POND-LILY inhabitant of lily-pond
bt POND-WEED aquatic plant
bt POND-WORT water-soldier plant
PONTIFEX a Roman pontiff
rl PONTIFIC of a bishop; papal
PONTINAL bridging
PONY-SKIN soft hide
PONY-TAIL hairstyle for girls and
youths
POOH-POOH sneer at; deride
POOL-ROOM billiard-room
bt POONSPAR an Indian tree
POOR-JOHN salted hake
lw POOR-LAWS former legislation
concerning paupers

POORNESS poverty; indigency
POOR-RATE a tax
POPE-JOAN a card game
rl POPELING a would-be pope
zo POPE'S-EYE fatty gland
rl POPESHIP popehood
POPINJAY parrot; coxcomb; fop
rl POPISHLY in popish style
md POPLITIC (knee joint or ham)
zo POPODERM dermal layer of hoof
POPPLING bubbling
POPPY-OIL slow-drying paint
  ingredient
POPULACE rabble; mob; masses
POPULATE propagate
bt POPULINE aspen bark extract
POPULOUS thronged; crowded;
  dense
zo PORIFERA the sponges
PORIFORM like a pore
PORISTIC porismatic; inferential
PORK-CHOP meat of pig
zo PORKLING young pig; piglet
zo POROCYTE tube-pierced cell in
  porifera
bt POROGAMY pollen-tube entry in
  micropyle
POROROCA tidal bore wave, Amazon
POROSITY porousness
POROTYPE a reproduction
mn PORPHYRY igneous rock
zo PORPOISE sea-hog
PORRIDGE Scotch oatmeal dish;
  prison sentence (sl.)
PORTABLE easily carried
mu PORTANDO carrying the voice;
  singing (It.)
PORTERLY coarse; vulgar
rl PORTESSE a breviary
PORTFIRE an igniter
nt PORTHOLE gun-port; scuttle; ship's
  window
PORTIERE doorway curtain
mn PORTLAND (stone; cement)
nt PORTLAST gunwale
lw PORTMOTE court held in port
nt PORTOISE gunwale
nv PORTOLAN old grid charts
PORTRAIT likeness; representation
PORT-ROPE rope for porthole lid
rl PORTUARY portable breviary
POSEIDON sea-god; Neptune
POSHTEEN sheepskin coat
POSINGLY so as to puzzle
POSITING postulating; affirming
POSITION spot; post; locality
mu POSITIVE actual; real; true; small
  organ

nc POSITRON radioisotope decay
  product
md POSOLOGY science of quantity
POSSIBLE feasible; likely
POSSIBLY practicably
POSTABLE mailable
nt POSTBARK mailboat
POST-BILL placard
POST-CARD card sent by post
POST-DATE future date on a cheque
POST-FACT a later occurrence
POST-FREE postage paid
POSTICHE counterfeit; coil of false
  hair; wig
POSTIQUE added ornament
POSTLUDE conclusion
POST-NATI born after a certain date
POST-NOTE promissory note
POST-OBIT payable after death
POST-PAID prepaid
POSTPONE defer; adjourn; shelve
POST-TEST final examination
POST-TIME hour of despatch
POST-TOWN district mail office
POSTURAL body position, reflexes,
  attitudes
POSTURED posed
POSTURER acrobat
cf,ec -POTAMOUS living in streams
POTATION drinking bout
bt POTATOES edible tubers
POTATORY draughty
POT-BELLY a paunch
POTENTLY forcibly; powerfully
POTHERED bothered; harassed
POT-HOUSE drinking booth
POTLATCH custom of giving presents
  (N. Amer. Indian)
POT-METAL lead and copper alloy
bt POT-PLANT (grown in a pot)
ck POT-ROAST braised meat
POTSHARD POTSHARE, broken pieces
  of earthenware; potsherd
ck POT-STICK stirring stick
ck POT-STILL for distilling spirits
mn POTSTONE soapstone
POTTERED spent time aimlessly
POTTERER desultory worker
zo POTTOROO rat kangaroo
POTULENT rather tipsy
POUCHING pocketing
bt POUCHONG black tea
POULAINE long pointed shoe
POULTICE a cataplasm
POUNCING sudden onset
POUNDAGE discount; taxation
POUNDING bruising; braying;
  hammering

POWDERED sprinkled
POWERFUL potent; puissant
POWERGAS coal-gas
pt POYOK-OIL W. African drying oil
ce, mn POZZOLAN volcanic dust; hydraulic cement; fly-ash (It.)
lw PRACTICE profession; normal method, conduct
PRACTICK practical training
PRACTISE work repeatedly for proficiency
PRACTISE perpetuate; pursue activities
PRACTIVE practised; adept; dexterous
lw PRAECIPE writ or instruction
lw PRAEFECT magistrate
PRAISING lauding; exalting; eulogizing
PRANCING bounding; capering
PRANDIAL concerning dinner
ae PRANGING crash-landing; bombing
PRANKING of practical jokes; frolicking
PRANKISH freakish; impish
nt PRATIQUE clearance certificate
PRATTLED babbled; chattered
PRATTLER chatterbox
PREACHED proclaimed; exhorted
PREACHER pastor; divine; declarer
PREAMBLE an introduction; preface
PREBOUND (books) in a library binding
PRECEDED anticipated; headed; led
PRECINCT a close; enclosure
PRECIOUS dear; prized; treasured
PRECLUDE shut out; obviate; debar
PRECURSE a prognostication
PREDABLE raptorial; predacious
PREDATED antedated
PREDATOR carnivorous (preying) plunderer
PREDELLA altar decoration; stool
PRE-ELECT choose beforehand
zo PREENING smartening (self, dress); trim feathers
PRE-ENTRY prior to joining (formalities)
PRE-EXIST of an earlier life
PREFACED introduced by
PREFACER preface writer
PREFINED limited beforehand
PREFIXED anticipated; put before
PREGNANT mother-to-be; prolific; suggestive
mn PREHNITE silicate of alumina
PREJUDGE condemn unheard
PRELUDED prefaced; started

PRELUDER prelude player
PREMIANT incentive
PREMIATE to reward
PREMIERE first performance
PREMISED introduced
lw PREMISES a messuage
md PREMOLAR bicuspid tooth
PREMORSE ending abruptly
PRENASAL in front of your nose
PRENATAL before birth
PRENOMEN Christian name
PREORDER arrange beforehand
PREPARED provided; planned; made
PREPARER arranger
PREPENSE premeditated
PREPUBIC prepubertal; preadolescence
PRESAGED foreboded; foretold
PRESAGER seer; soothsayer
PRESBYTE a far-sighted person
PRESCIND cut off; distract
PRESENCE mien; demeanour; company
PRESERVE conserve; defend; keep
PRESIDED controlled; officiated
PRESS-BED collapsible bed
PRESS-BOX reporter's box
PRESSING urgent; importunate; vital
PRESSION compression
PRESSMAN journalist
PRESSURE straits; urgency; stress; preparation for attack (fencing)
PRESTIGE reputation; fame; renown
cp PRESTORE deposit data temporarily
PRE-STUDY con; cogitate; ponder
PRESUMED surmised; thought
PRESUMER conjecturer
PRETENCE cloak; mask; guise
PRETERIT the past tense
PRE-TRIAL court case dry run
PRETTIFY beautify; adorn
PRETTILY neatly; daintily
PREVIOUS antecedent; prior; former
PREVISED foreseen
md PRIAPISM chronically erect penis
PRICKING inciting; spurring; needlepoint decoration; perforating
PRICKLED minor pain sensation (needle)
PRIDEFUL haughty; scornful
rl PRIEDIEU folding stool; praying desk
PRIESTLY sacerdotal
PRIGGERY super-respectability
PRIGGING larceny; pinching
PRIGGISH conceited; prim; affected
PRIGGISM coxcombry; pedantry
zo PRIMATES monkeys; archbishops

PRIMEVAL antediluvian; pristine
PRIMMING decking; pranking
PRIMNESS formality; demureness
bt **PRIMROSE** flower; a badge
PRINCELY regal; stately; lavish
PRINCEPS of first-rank status
PRINCESS king's daughter
PRINCOCK a prig; coxcomb
PRINKING strutting; pranking
PRINTIES concave circles; ovals cut
in glass
PRINTING typography
cp **PRINTOUT** reproduction of stored
information
rl **PRIORATE** office of prior
rl **PRIORESS** lady prior
PRIORITY precedence
PRISMOND prismatic
PRISONED incarcerated; gaoled
PRISONER captive
PRISTINE original; ancient
PRIZEMAN a winner
zo **PROATLAS** bone between skull and
vertebra
PROBABLE credible; likely
PROBABLY maybe; peradventure
PROBATOR examiner; approver
pm **PROCAINE** crystalline solid
PROCEEDS results; produce
lw **PROCHEIN** next; nearest
PROCINCT complete preparation
PROCLAIM bruit; trumpet; blazon
PROCURED got; obtained; acquired
PROCURER provider of women and
other services
PRODDING goading
PRODIGAL wasteful; reckless; lavish
PRODITOR traitor
PRODROME preliminary treatise
PRODUCED created; caused; made
PRODUCER generator; manufacturer
PROEMIAL introductory
PROFANED violated; debased
PROFANER blasphemer; desecrater
PROFILED outlined; drawn;
described in brief
PROFITED benefited; gained
PROFITER PROFITEER (speculator)
(contriver)
PRO-FORMA advance checking for
confirmation
PROFOUND deep; abysmal; occult
PROGERIA stunted; dwarfism; early
senility
PROGGING begging food
zo **PROGONAL** of genital ridge portion
PROGRESS advancement; growth
PROHIBIT inderdict; forbid; ban

md **PROLAPSE** anatomical slippage
PROLIFIC productive; fertile; fecund
PROLIXLY at great length
PROLOGUE dramatic preface; poem
PROLONGE rope; rings and toggle
ml **PROMETAL** heat-resistant cast iron
PROMISED guaranteed, engaged
PROMISEE assured person
PROMISER PROMISOR, assuror;
warranter; pledger; stipulator
PROMOTED elevated; preferred
PROMOTEE advanced person
PROMOTER active agent
PROMPTED suggested
PROMPTER encourager; souffleur
(theatre)
PROMPTLY readily; quickly
PROMULGE announce; publish
PRONATED naturally leaning
forwards, downwards
md **PRONATOR** an arm-muscle
PRONG-HOE a gardening tool
zo **PRONOTUM** prothorax notum in
insects
zo **PRO-NYMPH** a stage of insect life
PROOFING making waterproof
PROOFING establishing alcohol
quantity in spirits
ch **PROPANOL** propyl alcohol
ch **PROPENOL** allyl alcohol
PROPENSE inclined; disposed
PROPERLY correctly; formally;
exactly
PROPERTY quality; wealth; chattels
bt **PROPHAGE** inactive bacteriophage
cy **PROPHASE** mitosis/meiosis early
stage
PROPHECY forecast; divination
PROPHESY to prognosticate; foretell
bt **PROPHYLL** bracteole
PROPLASM mould; matrix
PROPOLIS beeswax
PROPOSAL suggestion; tender (offer)
PROPOSED suggested; meant
marriage; planned
PROPOSER mover; instigator
PROPOUND advocate; enunciate
PROPPAGE support
PROPPING shoring up
PROPRIUM self-hood; egotism
PROPYLON temple gateway
PRORATED assessed
PROROGUE adjourn; defer; postpone
PROSAISM prose writing
PROSAIST prosy person
PROSEMAN writer of prose
zo **PROSODUS** canal in porifera
PROSPECT aspect; outlook; survey

bt **PROSPORY** sporangia formation
pl **PROSTATE** male gland near bladder
PROSTYLE pillared portico
PROTASIS maxim; prologue
PROTATIC introductory
ch **PROTEASE** protein enzyme
PROTEGEE a ward
ch **PROTEIDS PROTEINS**, albuminoids
zo **PROTELES** the aard-wolf
ch **PROTEOSE** protein derivative
zo **PROTHECA** coral calyx rudiment
bt, zo **PROTISTA** organisms
PROTOCOL treaty; draft agreement
tc, tv **PROTOCOL** etiquette; precedence;
information flow
PROTOPOD early abdominal phase in
insects
mm **PROTOSET** mine rescue equipment
zo **PROTOZOA** early life forms
PROTRACT draw out; prolong; delay
PROTRUDE bulge; jut; project
PROVABLE demonstrable
PROVABLY verifiably
PROVIANT provender; fodder;
provisions
PROVIDED if in that case; supplied
PROVIDER donor; furnisher; caterer
PROVINCE department; tract
PROVINED (vine culture)
PROVISOR purveyor; treasurer
PROVOKED exasperated; stung;
vexed
PROVOKER inciter; annoyer; offender
PROWLING roving for prey; slinking
PROXIMAL adjoining; adjacent
PRUDENCE discretion; judiciousness
PRUINOSE PRUINOUS, powdery;
mealy
bt **PRUNELLA** self-heal plant
bt **PRUNELLO** dried plum
PRURIENT interested in the obscene
md **PRURITIS** persistent severe itching
PRYINGLY inquisitively; curiously
rl **PSALMIST** poet; psalm writer
rl **PSALMODY** psalms collectively
mu **PSALTERY** stringed instrument
mn **PSAMMITE** sandstone
md **PSELLISM** stammering
zo **PSITTACI** the parrot tribe
PSYCHICS mental phenomena
PSYCHISM spiritualism
PSYCHIST psychologist
zo **PTEROMYS** flying squirrel
zo **PTEROPOD** class of molluscs
zo **PTEROTIC** skull ear-wall bone
zo **PTERYLAE** clump of feathers
zo **PTILINUM** cephalic sac in dipters
zo **PTILOSIS** plumage

md **PTOMAINE** organic poison
md **PTYALISM** salivation
PUBCRAWL round all the taverns
PUBLICAN pub manager; collector of
tribute
PUBLICLY open to all
PUCELAGE virginity
bt **PUCKBALL** puffball
PUCKERED wrinkled; crinkled
mn **PUDDLING** clay/iron refining process
PUDICITY modesty
bt **PUFF-BALL** lycoperdon (mushroom)
zo **PUFF-BIRD** S. American bird
PUFF-PUFF onomatopoeic
locomotive
PUG-FACED monkey-faced
PUGGAREE scarf round helmet
PUGILISM prize-fighting
PUGILIST a pug; a boxer
PUISSANT powerful; forcible
PULINGLY fretfully; whiningly
PULLBACK a restraint
to **PULL-LIFT** chain or rope-operator
pulling device
PULLOVER jersey; sweater
md **PULMONIC** consumptive
PULPITER preacher
PULPITUM stone screen in major
church
PULSATOR vibrator
PULSIFIC throbbing
pl **PULVINAR** a cushion; brain fibres in
visual sector
bt **PULVINUS** swollen leaf base
PUMICATE polish; make smooth
PUMP-DALE water trough
PUMP-ROOM mineral spring at spa
PUMP-WELL water pumped from
well
PUNCHEON steel tool; large cask
PUNCHING perforating; striking
PUNCTATE pointed
PUNCTUAL punctilious; timely
PUNCTURE a hole; perforate; prick
PUNGENCE acridness
PUNGENCY keenness; acuteness
PUNINESS feebleness; frailty
PUNISHED chastised; penalized
PUNISHER disciplinarian
PUNITIVE punishing; penal
PUNITORY corrective
PUNTILLA lace-work
PUNTSMAN poleman on a river punt
zo **PUPARIAL PUPIFORM, PUPARIUM**,
pupa; a chrysalis
zo **PUPATION** incubation
PUPILAGE wardship; minority
PUPILARY in statu pupillari

PUPILATE having a central spot
zo PUPIPARA viviparous inspects
PUPPETRY puppet-show; finery
PUPPYISH of a young wag; conceited
PUPPYISM dog-like loyalty, affection
PURBLIND dim-sighted
PURCHASE buy; procure; leverage
PURENESS purity; chastity
PURFLING embroidering
PURIFIED ceremonially cleansed
PURIFIER refiner
md PURIFORM resembling pus
PURISTIC scrupulously stylish
lw PURPARTY share of an estate
PURPLING dyeing with purple
PURPLISH somewhat purple
PURPOSED resolved; meant;
    intended
PURPURIC madder-purple
PURSEFUL enough to fill a purse
PURSE-NET purse with strings
PURSLANE salad herb
PURSUANT conformably
PURSUING prosecuting; chasing
md PURULENT suppurating
PURVEYED procured; retailed
PURVEYOR caterer
rl PUSEYISM of Pusey; Tractarianism
rl PUSEYITE high-church doctrinaire
PUSHBALL a great ball game
PUSHBIKE pedal bicycle
PUSHCART barrow; handcart; (street
    sales)
PUSHOVER easy success; easily
    conned victim
cp, rw PUSHPULL parallel amplifiers; two-
    way train
zo PUSS-MOTH large hairy moth
bt PUSS-TAIL a bristle grass
bt, zo PUSSY-CAT willow-catkin
zo PUSSYCAT domestic feline pet
md PUSTULAR pimpled
PUTATION computation; sum
PUTATIVE reputed; alleged
bt PUTCHOCK root used for incense
pr PUT-TO-BED stopped press
PUTTYING cementing glass panes
    with putty
PUZZLING bewildering; perplexing
cy PYCNOSIS staining-matter
    shrinkage
md PYELITIS kidney pelvis inflammation
md PYOGENIC pus-producing;
    (inflammation)
pl PYRAMIDS elevated medulla nerves
    (ear)
PYRAMOID of pyramid form
ch PYRAZOLE heterocyclic compound

bt PYRENOID refractive protein mass
bt PYRENOUS globular; nucleiform
md PYREXIAL feverish
ch PYRIDINE organic compound
PYRIFORM pear-shaped
PYRITIZE turn into pyrites
mn PYRITOUS like pyrites
PYROGRAM mechanical firework
PYROLOGY blowpipe analysis
zo PYROSOMA luminous animalculae
PYROSTAT a thermostat
nc PYROTRON thermonuclear device
mn PYROXENE augite
ch PYROXYLE gun-cotton
PYRRHOUS reddish
PYTHONIC oracular; of Delphi
bt PYXIDATE having a lid
bt PYXIDIUM lidlike capsule

Q

QUABLING tropical fish
QUACKERY charlatanism; humbug
QUACKING boasting; duck-talk
QUACKISH somewhat bogus
QUACKISM medical pretence
QUACKLED almost choked
nm QUADRANS Roman farthing
nv QUADRANT quarter-circle; for
    sun-sighting
QUADRATE square; to agree
QUADRIGA four-horsed chariot
QUADROON (quarter negro blood)
mn QUADRUNE gritstone
QUAESITA to be decided on later
QUAESTOR treasurer
QUAFFING swallowing; imbibing
QUAGMIRE a bog; swamp
QUAGMIRY yielding; boggy
QUAILING flinching; blenching
QUAINTER odder; stranger
QUAINTLY whimsically; fancifully
QUAKERLY soberly
QUALMISH squeamish; queasy
bt QUANDANG Australian peach
QUANDARY dilemma; predicament
QUANTIFY determine quantity
QUANTITY measure; amount; bulk
QUARRIED stone hewn from the
    rocks
QUARRIER quarryman
QUARRIES arrows; panes of glass
QUARRIES animals hunted; targets
    shot at
me QUARTERN a gill (liquid); 4 lb (1.8
    kg) loaf
QUARTERS living places

as **QUARTILE** planetary aspect; point of quarter division
bt **QUARTINE** a seed covering
QUASHING annulling; crushing
md **QUASSINE QUASSITE**, extract of quassia, a febrifuge
QUATERON a quadroon
ga **QUATORZE** 14; a count in piquet (cards)
QUATRAIN four line stanza
mu **QUAVERED** of musical notation
QUAVERED QUIVERED; shook; vibrated
QUAVERER a warbler
QUAY-WALL harbour-wall
QUEASILY squeamishly
QUEBRADA a ravine (Sp.)
zo **QUEEN-BEE** ruler of hive
QUEENDOM queenly state
QUEENING playing the queen
QUEENLET a petty queen
QUEEREST quaintest; oddest
QUEERING spoiling; disarranging
QUEERISH rather strange
mn **QUELLERZ** limonite
QUELLING crushing; subduing; curbing
QUENCHED extinguished; (fire); (appetite); (thirst)
QUENCHER a long drink; thirst or fire subduer
QUENELLE forcemeat
bt **QUERCITE** acorn extract
QUERLING twirling
QUERYING challenging; inquiring
QUESTFUL adventurous
QUESTING seeking; searching
QUESTION interrogation; catechize
QUESTMAN authorized inquirer
QUEUEING lining up; taking one's turn
QUIBBLED evaded the question
QUIBBLER prevaricator
QUICKEST speediest; fastest
QUICKIES quickly done films; drinks, etc.
bt **QUICKSET** living plant
QUIDDANY a dish of quinces
vt **QUIDDING** spitting out chewed food
QUIDDITY captious question; quibble
QUIDDLED wasted time; pottered
QUIDDLER a trifler
QUIDNUNC tattler; know-all
QUIESCED silenced; subsided
QUIETAGE tranquillity
QUIETEST calmest
QUIETISE pacify
QUIETISM placidness

QUIETIST a mystic
QUIETIVE sedative
QUIETUDE rest; repose
QUILLING crimping; goffering; decorating surface of glass with coloured glass ribbons (Amer.)
QUILL-NIB penpoint
QUILTING of eiderdown coverings
mu **QUINABLE** interval of a fifth
fr **QUINCUNX** plantation of 5 trees
ga **QUINIEZA** pelota with bets
ga **QUINTAIN** balanced tilting beam
QUINTILE aspect of the planets
mu **QUINTOLE** five-stringed viol
QUIPPING taunting; jesting
QUIPPISH sarcastic
QUIRINAL Italian Court
QUIRINUS defied Romulus
QUIRITES Roman citizens
QUIRKING twisting
QUIRKISH evasive
QUISLING traitor; betrayer
QUIT-RENT rent in lieu of service
QUITTING deserting; ratting; hiatus; (golf)
QUIXOTIC QUIXOTRY, romantic and absurd notions and actions
QUIZZERY ridicule
QUIZZIFY hoax; puzzle
QUIZZING bantering; chaffing
QUIZZING asking questions (of knowledge)
QUOTABLE citable
QUOTIENT how many times
QUOTIETY proportionate frequency

R

RABATINE turned-down collar
RABBETED grooved
RABBINIC Hebrew language, etc.
RABBITER rabbit catcher
RABBITRY enclosure for rabbits
RABIDITY of rabies; raving madness
RABIETIC of rabies; maniacal; demented
ga **RACE-CARD** record of runners, horse races
ga **RACEGOER** watcher of winners
bt **RACEMOSE RACEMOUS**, in clusters
bt **RACEMULE** small bunch
bt **RACHILLA** leaf-rib
md **RACHITIC RACHITIS**, of rickets
RACIALLY pertaining to race (mixed)
RACINAGE acid technique for leather twig effects
RACINESS piquancy

RACKETED made noisy
RACKETER dishonest business man
rw **RACK-RAIL** (cogwheel) mountain track
RACK-RENT highest the market will fetch
RACK-TAIL part of clock
rw **RACK-WORK** rack and pinion locomotive
ck **RACLETTE** Swiss melted cheese
RACOVIAN Polish Socinian
RADARMAN radar petty officer R.N.
el **RADECHON** mesh-grid storage tube
RADIALLY like spokes of a wheel
as, ps, el, **RADIANCE** effulgence; lustre; energy
me in watts per steradian per m² directional intensity
RADIANCY brilliancy; glitter; sheen
RADIATED shone; sparkled
RADIATOR heating apparatus
RADICANT taking root
RADICATE to plant; emplant
bt **RADICOSE** having a large root
bt **RADICULE** a small root
RADIOING transmitting by wireless
zo **RADIOLUS** part of a feather
zo **RADULATE** (rasping tongue)
RAFFLING lottery for an article or articles
zo **RAFT-DUCK** black-headed duck
RAFTERED timbered
nt **RAFT-PORT** (timber loading)
RAFT-ROPE thickish piece of string
RAFTSMAN castaway
RAGABASH ragamuffin
RAGGEDLY in tatters
RAGINGLY furiously; rabidly
RAGNAROK twilight of the gods (Norse mythology)
RAG-PAPER high-quality paper
mn **RAGSTONE** impure limestone
RAG-WHEEL polishing wheel
rw **RAILHEAD** a terminus
RAILLERY banter; chaff; ridicule
rw **RAILROAD** railway; forceful insistence; overhead serve (tennis); (bowls)
RAINBAND band in solar spectrum
zo **RAINBIRD** Jamaican bird
RAINCOAT waterproof
RAINDROP single drop of rain
RAINFALL shower
RAINLESS state of drought
RAINPOUR downpour
bt **RAINTREE** S. American tree
gl **RAIN-WASH** gravity/rain soil creepage
RAISINEE a confection

RAKEHELL a rip; debauchee
RAKISHLY set at an angle
RAKSHASA Hindu ghoul
RALLYING reuniting; gathering; track and trek events; cycling; motor racing
RAMAYANA Indian epic poem
RAMBLING roaming; wandering
RAMBOOZE a cordial
bt **RAMBUTAN** Malayan fruit tree
bt **RAMENTUM** brown scale on ferns
bt **RAMICOLE** living on twigs
RAMICORN horny sheath
RAMIFIED diverse
RAMIFORM like a branch
RAMPAGED romped; rioted; gambolled
RAMPANCY excessive prevalence
RAMPSMAN highwayman
RAMRODDY stiff
mn **RAMSHORN** an ammonite
RAMULOUS ramulose; branching
zo **RANARIUM** frog aquarium
RANCHERO cow-puncher
RANCHING cattle-raising
RANCHMAN stockbreeder
RANCIDLY fustily; mustily; sourly
RANDOMLY at a venture; fortuitously
zo **RANGIFER** a reindeer
zo **RANIFORM** froglike
RANKLING festering; smouldering
RANKNESS overgrowth; exuberance
RANSOMED redeemed; released; purchased; (release money)
RANSOMER liberator; indemnifier
RAPACITY greed; avarice; voracity
RAPE-CAKE cattle fodder
bt **RAPE-SEED** (hence colza oil)
RAPHANIA ergotism; blight
bt **RAPHANUS** radish
RAPHIDES crystals in plants
RAPIDITY celerity; despatch; speed
RAPPAREE Irish robber; bandit
zo **RAPTORES** birds of prey
RAPTURED ravished; ecstatic
RAQUETTE (pelota); (racket)
RAREFIED tenuous
RARENESS infrequency; scarceness
RARERIPE early ripe; untimely
RASCALLY knavish; roguish; dishonest
RASHLING reckless fellow
RASHNESS foolhardiness; unwariness
RASORIAL scratching
RATAPLAN beat of drum
RATCHETY jerky
wv **RATCHING** yarn-tightening process

RATEABLE assessable
RATE-BOOK book of valuations
zo **RAT-GOOSE** brent goose
RATHRIPE early ripe
RATIFIED confirmed; endorsed
RATIFIER approver; authorizer
RATIONAL reasonable; judicious; sane
RATIONED on an allowance
RAT'S-BANE rat poison
zo **RATSNAKE** rat-killing snake
RAT'S-TAIL tapering
RATTINET a woollen stuff
RATTLING quick; lively; clattering
RAVAGING despoiling; plundering
to **RAVEHOOK** ripping iron
RAVELLED entangled; untwisted
RAVENING plundering; devouring
RAVENOUS starving; voracious
RAVINGLY with fury; frantically
RAVISHED enchanted; charmed
RAVISHER abductor
RAW-BONED gaunt
REABSORB soak up again
REACCESS fresh approach
REACCUSE indict again
nv **REACHING** extending; attaining; sailing, wind abeam
ch **REACTANT** substance involved in chemical reaction
REACTION counter-measure; recoil
REACTIVE capacity to react
READABLE well written; good style
READABLY clearly; legibly
tc **READ-HEAD** of tape recorder, cassette
cp **READ-HEAD** electro-magnetic pickup
READJUST reset; modify
READ-ONLY on loan; unalterable
READ-RATE speed of reading
cp **READ-TIME** access to screen; delay
REAFFIRM swear on oath; state anew
pc **REAGENCY** reflex influence; reaction
REALISED felt; understood; comprehended
REALLEGE assert a 2nd time
REALNESS actuality; verity; fact
REANOINT relubricate
REANSWER reply again
REAPPEAR turn up again
REAR-LINE behind the army
REARMING re-equipping
REARMOST last; ultimate
REAR-RANK back line
REARWARD rearguard
REASCEND climb again
REASCENT a further climb
REASONED argued; disputed

REASONER debater
REASSERT re-affirm
REASSESS re-impose; revalue
REASSIGN give different job to
REASSURE console; comfort
REATTACH refix
REATTAIN get again
REAVOWED said so again
REBATING deducting from
REBELLED revolted; mutinied
REBELLER a rebel; insurgent
REBELLOW re-echo
REBITING re-engraving
ch **REBOILER** vessel at still bottom
REBRACED restrengthened
REBUFFED repulsed; snubbed
REBUKING chiding; carpeting
REBURIED re-interred
REBUTTAL refutation; retort
REBUTTED confuted; refuted
lw **REBUTTER** a legal reply
RECALLED revoked; annulled; denied
RECANTED retracted; abjured
RECAPTOR one who retakes
RE-CASING rebinding of book in original cover
RECEDING retreating; ebbing
RECEIVED got; allowed; welcomed
lw **RECEIVER** a recipient; receptionist; (bankruptcy); (telephone); (stolen goods)
RECENTLY lately
RECEPTOR sensory organ; nerve transmitter
RECESSED dimpled; secluded
RECESSES niches; vacations
RECESSUS a recess; a niche
RECHAMPI gold ornamentation on chair frames
RECHARGE attack anew; reload
RECISION cutting back; pruning
RECITING rehearsing; relating
RECKLESS heedless; rash; headstrong
zo **RECKLING** weakest in a litter
RECKONED considered; judged
RECKONER calculator; computer
RECLINED leant; lay; reposed
RECLINER a reclining dial
RECLOSED shut again
RECLOTHE provide new garments
RECOALED refilled the bunkers
RECOILED retreated; reacted
RECOILER flincher
RECOINED minted afresh
rl **RECOLLET** Franciscan monk
RECOLOUR repaint
RECOMMIT refer again; re-entrust

RECONVEY transfer back
lw RECORDED entered; minuted
mu, lw RECORDER flageolet; judge
el, mu RECORDER permanent sound
   receptor
RECOUPED regained
RECOURSE reference; resort; refuge
lw RECOURSE right to demand
   compensation
RECOVERY convalescence; revival;
   body renewal; return (rowing)
lw RECOVERY to regain possession
RECOVERY economic upturning
RECREANT craven; apostate
RECREATE reproduce with exact
   resemblance
el RECTIGON thermionic gas diode
rl RECTORAL duties of an incumbent
.   rector
RECTORAL ditto of university
   rector
RECUBANT recumbent
RECUMBED reclined; reposed
RECURRED remembered; repeated
RECURVED bent back
rl RECUSANT Elizabethan R.C.
REDACTOR editor
REDARGUE to refute; disprove
zo RED-BELLY terrapin; char
bt RED-CEDAR pencil-wood
mn RED-CHALK reddle
mn RED-CORAL living coral
RED-CROSS humanitarian
   organization
lw REDDENDA rent clauses
lw REDDENDO (vassal's duties)
REDDENED blushed; flushed
mn RED-EARTH reddish loam
REDEEMED ransomed; freed;
   retrieved
REDEEMER liberator; saviour
REDELESS unwise; ill-advised
REDEMAND request again
lw REDEMISE reconveyance
REDENTED indented
REDEPLOY movement of army;
   industrial
RED-FACED florid; rubicund
REDIGEST reduce to form again ➛
REDIRECT re-address
REDITION return
REDIVIDE re-allot
RED-METAL a copper alloy
REDNOSED nose red with cold
REDOLENT aromatic; fragrant
REDOUBLE a bridge call
REDRIVEN herded back again
zo REDSHANK red-legged sandpiper

RED-SHIRT follower of Garibaldi;
   athlete (USA)
RED-SHORT brittle
RED-STAFF millstone trimmer
REDUBBER old clothes merchant
REDUCENT reducing
REDUCING curtailing; abating
zo REDUVIUS predacious bug
RE-DYEING recolouring
RE-ECHOED reverberated; repeated
mu REED-BAND clarionets, etc.
zo REED-BIRD bobolink
REEDLESS no rush
zo REEDLING bearded titmouse
bt REED-MACE cat's tail
mu RED-PIPE an organ pipe
mu REED-STOP an organ stop
zo REED-WREN greater reedwarbler
nt REEF-BAND strip of canvas
REEF-KNOT secure flat knot
nt REEF-LINE a rope
REELABLE able to be wound in
REEL-LINE fishing line
REEL-SEAT reel housing on rod
RE-EMBARK get back in a boat
RE-EMBODY reform into a body
RE-EMERGE come out again
RE-ENLIST sign on again
RE-EXPORT ship out again
REFASTEN refix
REFERRED attributed; assigned
REFERRER enquirer
REFIGURE present anew ➛
REFILLED replenished
REFINERY purification plant
REFINING purifying
REFITTED re-equipped
REFLEXED curved back
REFLEXLY reactively
REFLOWED ebbed
REFLOWER bloom again
REFLUENT flowing back
REFOREST plan anew
REFORGED kept signing false name
REFORMED remodelled; restored
REFORMER innovator
REFRAMED re-modelled; traduced all
   over again
REFREEZE make icebound again
REFRINGE infringe
REFUGIUM locality remaining
   unchanged despite climatic
   alteration
REFUNDED reimbursed; repaid
REFUNDER one who pays back again
REFUSING declining; repudiating
REFUTING gainsaying; rebutting
REGAINED retrieved; recaptured

REGALIAN regal; sovereign
REGALING faring sumptuously
REGALISM sovereignty
REGALITY royalty
REGARDED noticed; heeded; gazed
REGARDER observer; watcher
REGATHER recollect
REGICIDE killer of a king
REGILDED made golden once more
REGIMENT organize; a military unit
REGIONAL topographical
REGIONIC local
cp, mu **REGISTER** record; chronicle; fit; list;
    filed data storage; range or
    compass of voice, instruments,
    organ stops
REGISTRY labour agency
sv **REGLETTE** measuring tape scale
REGNANCY predominance;
    supremacy
REGOLITH mantle rock; topsoil
zo **REGORGED** of chewing the cud
REGRATED furnace fire area renewed
REGRATER boiler maker
REGROUND knives resharpened
REGROWTH new growth
REGULATE adjust; control; arrange
REGULIZE readjust
REHANDLE start again from
    beginning
REHASHED restyled
REHEARSE recapitulate
ce **RE-HEATED** warmed up again;
    superheated
ce **REHEATER** part of steam or
    compressed air machines
REHOUSED given new homes
REIGNING prevailing; governing
RE-IGNITE rekindle
REIMBODY re-incorporate
REIMPORT bring back
REIMPOSE retax
REINCITE reanimate
REINDEER Father Christmas's sleigh
    steeds
md **REINFECT** spread disease again
REINFORM renotify
REINFUND pour in again
REINFUSE reanimate
REIN-HOOK bearing-rein hook
REINLESS unchecked
REINSERT put in again
REINSMAN accomplished driver
REINSURE make doubly certain
REINVENT create anew
REINVEST put money in again
REINVITE bid home again
pr **REISSUED** revalidated; reprinted

REJECTED excluded; rebuffed
REJECTOR decliner; rejecter
el **REJECTOR** impedance of circuit (due
    to overloading)
REJOICED exulted; gloried; delighted
REJOICER reveller; merry-maker
REJOINED knit together; reunited
REJUDGED re-examined;
    reconsidered
REKINDLE arouse anew; relight
RELANDED came down twice
RELAPSED retrogressed
RELAPSER backslider
RELATING narrating; telling
RELATION connection; kinsman;
    (harmony)
cp, mu **RELATIVE** comparative; kinsman;
    parallel common key-signature
lw **RELATRIX** female informant
RELAXANT a loosener
RELAXING slackening; unbending
ro **RELAYING** transmit programmes
RELEASED emancipated; freed
RELEASEE discharged person
RELEASER releasor; liberator
RELEGATE consign; transfer ⏤
RELESSEE releasee
lw **RELESSOR** releaser
RELEVANT applicable; apt; pertinent
RELIABLE trustworthy; trusty; safe
RELIABLY dependably
RELIANCE confidence; trust
lw **RELICTED** left bare
RELIEVED palliated; soothed; eased
RELIEVER mitigator; assuager
RELIGION faith
RELISHED appreciated
RELISTEN hear once more
RELIVING experiencing again
RELOADED ready to fire again
RELUCENT transparent; shining
RELUMINE rekindle
REMAINED left over; stopped
REMAKING rebuilding
REMANENT remaining
REMANNED provided with a new
    crew
REMARKED said; declared;
    mentioned
REMARKER commentator; observer
REMARQUE marginal etching
REMEDIAL curative; healing
REMEDIED repaired; rectified
REMEMBER recall; recollect
REMIFORM oar-shaped
REMINDED brought to notice
REMINDER keepsake; souvenir
lw **REMISING** releasing

REMISSLY negligently; slackly
REMITTAL surrender; remittance
REMITTED relaxed; forgave
REMITTEE consignee
REMITTER pardoner; remittor
REMODIFY remodel
ck **REMOLADE** salad dressing
REMOLTEN remelted
REMOTELY faintly
REMOVING dislodging; abstracting
REMURMUR complain again
RENAMING rechristening
RENDERED translated; gave
RENDERER supplier; assignor
RENDIBLE able to be torn; note not
renderable; degradable
gl **RENDZINA** intrazonal dark soil on
chalk (Poland)
➟**RENEGADE** RENEGADO, RENEGATE,
quisling; apostate; runagate;
traitor; recreant; rebel
ga **RENEGING** revoking agreement;
(cards)
RENEWING renovating; rejuvenating
RENIDIFY build a new nest
RENIFORM kidney-shaped
RENITENT allergic; resistant
RENOUNCE disclaim; forsake;
abjure
RENOVATE renew; repair; refresh
RENOWNED famous; eminent
RENOWNER swaggerer; braggart
RENTABLE leasable
RENTERER invisible mender
RENT-FREE living without paying
rent
RENT-ROLL list of tenants
RENUMBER put new numbers on
RENVERSE inverted; reverse
REOBTAIN get again
REOCCUPY move back in
REOPENED no longer shut
REOPPOSE not capitulate
REORDAIN refrock the defrocked
REORIENT arising again
REPACIFY calm down again
➟ **REPAGULA** egg-protection bodies
REPAIRED redressed; went
REPAIRER restorer
REPARTEE witty retort; riposte
REPASSED went by twice
REPASTED fed
REPAYING refunding
REPEALED rescinded; annulled
REPEALER abrogator; revoker
REPEATED iterated; echoed
tc **REPEATER** a watch; transmission
channel amplifier

REPELLED repulsed; checked;
rebuffed
REPELLER deterrer; rejecter
REPENTED truly contrite; rued
rl **REPENTER** penitent person; (sect)
REPEOPLE repopulate
REPERTOR a finder
REPERUSE read again
REPETEND recurring decimal
REPINING fretting; murmuring
REPLACED reinstated; restored
REPLACER a substitute
REPLEDGE swear again
lw **REPLEVIN** a legal action
REPLUNGE dive again
REPLYING answering
REPOLISH shine up again
lw **REPONING** replacing
REPORTED communicated; related
REPORTER announcer; journalist
REPOSING reclining; resting
REPOSURE repose; peace,
tranquillity
REPOTTED (gardening)
REPOUSSE embossed
REPRIEVE respite; pardon; acquit
RE-PRIMER recapping machine
REPRISAL retaliation; revenge
REPROACH reprimand; upbraid
REPROVAL admonition; censure
REPROVED blamed; rebuked; chided
REPROVER reprehender
REPRUNED lopped again
zo **REPTILIA** snakes and crocodiles, etc.
REPUBLIC democratic state
➟ **REPUGNED** resisted; opposed
REPUGNER a rebel
REPULPIT restore a preacher
REPULSED checked; refused;
rebuffed
REPULSER repeller
REPURIFY purify again
REPUTING esteeming
REQUIRED wanted; demanded;
lacked
REQUIRER exactor; claimant
REQUITAL recompense; punishment
REQUITED reciprocated
REQUITER avenger
rw **RE-RAILED** got back on track
lw **REREFIEF** an under-fief (Sc.)
REREWARD rear-guard
REROOFED given new roof
RESAILED sailed again
RESALUTE put hand to head again
mu **RE-SCORED** rearranged
RESCRIBE rewrite
RESCRIPT edict; decree

RESCUING extricating; liberating

RESEARCH scientific enquiry

RESEATED given chair again

lw **RESEIZED RESEIZER**, legal seizure of disseized property

RESEMBLE liken; compare; collate

RESENTED strongly objected; resisted

RESENTER an injured party

RESERVED shy; distant; unsociable

RESERVER withholder

RESETTER jeweller; repairer

RESETTLE repopulate

mt **RESHABAR** dry wind in Near East

RESIANCE residence

cp **RESIDENT** occupier; dweller; agent; routine

ps **RESIDUAL** left over; difference between observation and true value

RESIDUUM residue; surplus; excess

RESIGNED abdicated; relinquished

RESIGNEE he who becomes resigned

RESIGNER renouncer; quitter

RESILING applying resilience in recoil

RESINATA RESINATE, Greek resinous white wine

RESINIFY RESINIZE, to make resinous

RESINOUS olfactory quality (pine, pitch)

RESISTED withstood; repelled; opposed

RESISTER opposer

el **RESISTOR** non-conductor

RESMOOTH smooth again

RESOLDER solder again

RESOLUTE steadfast; staunch

RESOLVED determined; settled

mu **RESOLVER** solver; mediator; catalyst; chord

RESONANT resounding; sonorous

RESONATE re-echo; vibrate

RESORBED absorbed

ch **RESORCIN** crystalline phenol

RESORTED betook; repaired; flew

RESORTER frequenter

RESOURCE expedient; means; natural wealth; ingenuity

RESOWING broadcasting again

RESPECTS compliments

RESPIRED exhaled

RESPITED postponed; reprieved

RESPOKEN repeated

RESPONSE answer; reply; rejoinder

RESTATED reaffirmed

REST-CURE convalescence

RESTLESS agitated; turbulent; uneasy

RESTORED returned; renewed; cured

RESTORER reviver; healer

RESTRAIN check; curb; suppress

RESTRICT limit; confine; hamper

RESTRIKE lay down work a second time

RESTRING tennis racket; violin

RESULTED caused; followed; ensued

RESUMING renewing; continuing

RESUMMON call again

RESUPINE lying on the back

RESURVEY review

RETAILED gossiped; peddled

RETAILER not a wholesale merchant

hd **RETAILLE** divided twice

RETAINED detained; kept; withheld

RETAINER henchman; lackey; servant

RETAKING recapturing

RETARDED slowed up; delayed

RETARDER hinderer; obstructionist; hardening reducing admixture

md **RETENTOR** retaining muscle

zo **RETEPORE** a coral

RETICENT taciturn; reserved; quiet

RETICULE lady's workbag; graticule; linked webs

hd **RETIERCE** heraldic arrangement

zo **RETIFERA** the true limpet

RETIFORM meshed; reticulated

ch **RETINENE** rhodopsin; pigment of retina (eye)

mn **RETINITE** obsidian; amber

RETINOID resin-like

zo **RETINULA** pigmented cells

RETIRING unobtrusively withdrawing from service

hd **RETORTED** rejoined; replied

RETORTER responder

RETOSSED thrown back

RETRACED returned by same route

lw **RETRAXIT** loss of action

RETRENCH curtail; economize

RETRIEVE recover; regain; rescue

RETROACT oppose

RETRORSE bent back

RETRUDED thrust back

RETRYING attempting again

RETUNDED blunted

RETURNED rendered; reverted

RETURNER remitter; (reappeared)

REUNITED rejoined

RE-UPTAKE reabsorption of a substance

REURGING pressing on again

mn **REUSSITE** magnesium compound

REVALUED re-assessed

REVAMPED repatched

REVANCHE revenge (Fr.)
REVEALED disclosed; published
REVEALER betrayer; divulger
REVEHENT taking away
REVEILLE trumpet-call; dawn
REVELLED wantoned; feasted
REVELLER carouser
REVENANT returned from the dead;
   ghost
REVENGED requited; repaid
REVENGER vindicator
REVEREND respectful epithet
REVERENT submissive; humble
REVERING venerating; honouring
REVERIST a dreamer
REVERSAL complete change
REVERSED subverted; overthrew
lw REVERSER mortgager of land
REVESTED reappointed
REVETTED faced with masonry
REVIEWAL a reconsideration
REVIEWED revised; edited; surveyed
REVIEWER an inspector; critic
REVILING aspersing; maligning
REVISING checking; amending
REVISION re-examination
REVISORY correctional
REVIVIFY reanimate; revive
REVIVING renewing; rousing
REVOKING repealing; quashing
REVOLTED felt disgust
REVOLTED rebelled
REVOLTER guerilla; partisan
REVOLUTE rolled back
REVOLVED rotated; wheeled; circled
REVOLVER a firearm
md REVULSOR h. and c. apparatus
REWARDED decorated; requited
REWARDER guerdon giver
REWORDED redrafted
zo RHABDITE rod-like structure
zo RHABDOID spindle-shaped body
md RHABDOME lens supporter
RHAETIAN (Rhaetia) Latin-Swiss
   linguistic area, population
md RHAGADES fissures of the skin
bt RHAGODIA grapelike genus
ch RHAMNOSE methyl-pentose
RHAPSODE rhapsodist
mu RHAPSODY rambling composition
RHEOBASE minimal electrical
   response stimulus
RHEOCORD resistance wire
ps RHEOLOGY formation of matter
RHEOSTAT (variable resistance)
RHEOTOME a switch
RHETORIC florid oratory
zo RHINIDAE sharks

md RHINITIS nasal inflammation
zo RHINODON immense shark
bt RHIZANTH flowering root
bt RHIZOGEN parasite plant
zo RHIZOMYS genus of mole-rats
zo RHIZOPOD locomotive protozoa
ch RHODANIC rose-red colour
zo RHODEINA goldfish
ch RHODEOSE isomer of rhamnose
zo RHODITES genus of gall-flies
ch RHOEADIC (poppy extract)
RHOMBOID quadrilateral figure
ml RHOMETER molten-metal impurity
   measurer
md RHONCHAL bronchial
md RHONCHUS a raâle
RHOPALIC a hexameter
nv RHO-THETA distance/bearing
   navigation system
bt, md RHUBARBY cathartic
mm RHYOLITE a quartz
RHYTHMIC harmonious; metric;
   lilting
RHYTHMUS rhythm; cadence; verse
RIBALDRY RIBAUDRY, irreverent
   jesting; obscenity
RIBBONED striped; streaked
bt RIB-GRASS ribwort
RIB-NOSED like a baboon
RIBOSOME nuclear source of protein
   synthesis
RIB-ROAST beat soundly
zo RICE-BIRD the bobolink
nt RICEBOAT backward-sailing river
   craft (Burma)
RICE-DUST rice-meal
RICE-GLUE a cement
RICE-MEAL oriental flour
RICE-MILK milk with rice
RICHNESS wealth; opulence;
   affluence
zo RICINIAE mites; ticks, etc.
RICINIUM Roman mantle
RICK-RACK openwork edging
RICKSHAW Indian or Chinese
   vehicle
RICOCHET rebound
mm RICOLITE ornamental stone
RIDDANCE deliverance; release
RIDDLING perforating; sieving
RIDEABLE broken in
RIDICULE deride; lampoon; mock
RIFENESS prevalence
RIFFRAFF sweepings; refuse; rabble
RIFLEMAN modern musketeer
RIFLE-PIT short trench
RIGHTFUL genuine; true; lawful
RIGHTING doing justice; rectifying

RIGIDITY stiffness; tautness;
  contraction (muscle); social
  strictness
RIGORISM austerity
RIGORIST a martinet
RIGOROUS inflexible; severe; harsh
RILL-MARK corrugation
RIMIFORM having a rim
RIMOSITY roughness
RIMULOSE fissured
RIND-CALL defect in timber; (callus)
RING-BARK make a circular cut
zo **RING-BILL** ring-necked duck
RINGBOLT embedded ring
vt **RINGBONE** exostosis on horse foot
  bones
RINGBONE callus on pastern
RING-DIAL portable sundial
zo **RING-DOVE** cushat; wood-pigeon
tc **RINGDOWN** operator-signalling
  method
RING-GOAL a ball game
RINGLETY with ringlets
RING-LOCK a puzzle lock
RING-MAIL chain armour
RING-NECK ring-plover
RING-ROAD by-pass
nt **RING-ROPE** a cable rope
RING-SIDE close to the scene
zo **RING-TAIL** hen-harrier
RING-TIME time for marriage
RING-WALL ring fence
RINGWISE experienced; of boxing
vt **RINGWOMB** incomplete cervix
  dilatation
RING-WORK mail construction
md **RING-WORM** skin disease; fungoid
ps **RIOMETER** ionosphere absorption
  measurer
RIPARIAN riparial; riverbanks
RIPENESS maturity; mellowness
RIPPLING flax cleaning
RISE-WOOD tinderwood; hedge
  cuttings
RISKIEST most reckless
RISORIAL ludicrous
mu **RITENUTO** restrained; slower tempo
RITUALLY ceremoniously
RIVALISE compete
RIVALITY equality in rank
RIVALLED emulated; vied; matched
RIVER-BED a channel
RIVER-GOD tutelary deity
zo **RIVER-HOG** the capybara
RIVERINE riparian
RIVER-MAN river-liver
zo **RIVER-PIE** water-ousel
RIVETING clinching

RIVULOSE wavy; rivose
RIXATION brawl; quarrel
RIZZERED salted and sun-dried
ROAD-BOOK guide-book; route; list;
  itinerary
ROADLESS unwayed
ROAD-POST signpost
ROADSIDE footpath; wayside
ROADSMAN road repairer
ROADSTER coachdriver; cycle
bt **ROAD-WEED** plantago
ROAD-WORK highway repairs
ROAN-TREE rowan tree; mountain
  ash
ROASTING parching; bantering
ROBURITE an explosive
ROBUSTLY lustily; stoutly; sturdily
ROCAILLE scroll ornament
bt **ROCCELLA** dyers' lichen
mn **ROCK-ALUM** alum stone
ROCKAWAY American carriage
zo **ROCK-BIRD** a pigeon
ck **ROCK-CAKE** small, hard bun
bt **ROCK-CIST** a plant
zo **ROCK-COOK** rock-fish
mn **ROCK-CORK** asbestos
zo **ROCK-CRAB** stony crustacean
ROCK-DOVE pigeon nesting on rocks
ROCKETED shot away
ROCKETER a high flier
ROCKETRY science of rockets
ROCK-FIRE firework mixture
zo **ROCK-FISH** wrasse, bass, etc.
zo **ROCK-GOAT** ibex
zo **ROCK-HAWK** merlin
mn **ROCK-HEAD** bed-rock
ROCK-HEWN cut from rock
zo **ROCK-LARK** rock pipit
bt **ROCK-LILY** (various types)
zo **ROCK-LING** cod; haddock
bt **ROCK-MOSS** lichen
bt **ROCK-ROSE** member of rock garden
mn **ROCK-RUBY** a garnet
mn **ROCK-SALT** native salt
zo **ROCK-SEAL** common seal
mn **ROCK-SOAP** a kind of bole
mn **ROCK-WOOD** ligniform asbestos
ROCK-WORK a rockery
zo **ROCK-WREN** stone-preferring bird
zo **RODENTIA** rats; mice; squirrels
RODOMONT vain boaster; braggart
me **ROENTGEN** unit of radiation
mn **ROE-STONE** oolite
ROGAILLE decorative work with
  rocks, shells
ROGATION litany; supplication
zo **ROITELET** kinglet; gold-crest
ROLLBACK price legislation

ROLL-CALL a check of all present
ck **ROLY-POLY** rolled suet and jam
    pudding
ROMANCED economized the truth
ROMANCER tall tale teller
ROMANESE Wallachian language
ROMANIAN RUMANIAN, of Romania
rl **ROMANISH** Catholic
rl **ROMANIST** R.C.
rl **ROMANIZE** Latinize; convert
ROMANSCH Swiss dialect
ROMANTIC quixotic; fanciful
rl **ROME-SCOT** Peter's pence
ROMEWARD verging on Romanism
zo **RONCADOR** Pacific fish
RONDELET form of poem
RONDELLE ladder rung
ROOD-ARCH (over rood-screen)
ROOD-BEAM beam supporting rood
zo **ROODEBOK** bush-buck
ROOD-LOFT gallery over screen
ROOD-TREE Holy-rood; the cross
ROOFLESS open for the rain
ROOF-RACK automobile baggage
    holder
ROOF-TREE a beam
ROOSTING perching; lodging
ROOT-BEER dandelion ale
ROOT-CROP (esculent roots)
ROOT-FAST firmly rooted
ROOT-FORM shape of a root
bt **ROOT-HAIR** delicate filament
bt **ROOT-KNOT** an abnormality
bt **ROOT-LEAF** a leaf that roots
ROOTLESS footloose
ROPE-PUMP (by an endless rope)
ROPE-WALK shed for spinning ropes
ROPE-YARN manilla; hemp; sisal,
    etc.
ROPINESS stringiness
ROQUETED (croquet)
bt **RORIDULA** sundew plants
RORULENT dewy
ROSARIAN sect
ROSARIUM rose garden
mn **ROSASITE** copper/zinc carbonate
bt **ROSE-BUSH** where the rose thorns
bt **ROSE-DROP** rose-flavoured orange
ROSEFISH redfish; Atlantic food fish
ROSE-GALL an excrescence
ROSE-HUED rosy
ROSE-KNOT a rosette
mn **ROSELITE** cobalt arseniate
bt **ROSEMARY** aromatic plant
ROSE-PINK sentimental
md **ROSE-RASH** German measles
bt **ROSE-ROOT** herbaceous plant
bt **ROSE-TREE** a standard rose

ROSETTED wearing a rosette (party
    colours)
bt **ROSEWOOD** Brazilian timber tree
zo **ROSE-WORM** a caterpillar
ROSINESS rubicundity
ROSINING impelling; hustling
ROSIN-OIL a lubricant
zo **ROSMARUS** walruses, etc.
ROSOGLIO red wine of Malta
ROSTRATE beaked
ROSTROID like a rostrum
bt **ROSULATE** having rosetted leaves
ROSY-DROP a grog blossom
zo **ROSY-WAVE** a moth
zo **ROTALIAN** ROTALINE, protozoan
ROTALITE fossil rotalian
ROTARIAN (Rotary Club)
ROTATING spinning; turning
ROTATION revolution; series
ROTATIVE in succession
ROTATORY circulatory
ROT-GRASS butterwort
zo **ROTIFERA** animalculae
ROTIFORM wheel-shaped
ROT-STEEP cotton purification
ROTTENLY putridly
bt **ROTTLERA** dye yielding plant
ROUGHAGE fibre food to keep
    regular
ROUGH-DRY not ironed
ROUGH-HEW back formation from
    rough-hewn
ROUGHING (ice-nails)
ROUGHISH rather boisterous
ROULEAUX bundles of fascines
ROULETTE a game of chance
ROUND-ALL acrobatic feat
ROUND-ARM (bowling)
ROUNDERS a game; 9-a-side
    forerunner of baseball (UK)
ROUNDING encircling
ROUNDISH not quite spherical
ROUNDLET a small circle
nt **ROUND-TOP** masthead platform
ROUTEING selecting a route
ROWDYISH riotous; noisy
ROWDYISM turbulence; brawling
ROWELLED spurred
ROXBURGH a book-binding
ROYALISM ROYALIST, king-supporter
ROYALIZE become a king
RUBBISHY trashy
zo **RUBECULA** robin redbreast
RUBEDITY ruddiness
mn **RUBELIAN** magnesia mica
RUBEZAHL mountain imp (Ger.)
RUBIANIC madder-coloured
RUBICUND ruddy; florid

ch **RUBIDIUM** metallic element
RUBIFORM like a ruby
RUBRICAL marked in red
RUBSTONE whetstone
zo **RUBY-TAIL** cuckoo-fly
bt **RUBY-WOOD** red sandalwood
zo **RUCERVUS** East Indian deer
RUCKLING crumpling; creasing
RUCKSACK knapsack
RUDDLING marking with ochre
RUDENESS unmannerliness
RUDENTED ornamented
RUDIMENT first principle; embryo
RUEFULLY sorrowfully; regretfully
RUFFLING disturbing; agitating
RUGGEDLY jaggedly; unevenly
RUGOSELY wrinkly
RUGOSITY roughness
RUINABLE of delicate virtue
RULE-CASE a printing tray
RULE-WORK tabulation
RULINGLY dominantly
RUMANIAN ROMANIAN, of Romania
RUM-BARGE a warm drink
RUMBLING noise from stomach
zo **RUMINANT** chewing the cud
RUMINATE meditate; muse; ponder
RUMMAGED ransacked; rifled
RUMMAGER searcher
RUMOURED bruited; reported
RUMOURER a gossip; tattler
RUMPLESS having no tail
RUMPLING puckering; rimpling
RUM-SHRUB an odd decoction
nt **RUNABOUT** vagabond; convenient
motorcar; motorboat
RUNAGATE renegade; vagabond
RUNMAKER cricket
RUNNER-UP second
RUNOLOGY rune-craft
RUNRIDGE open-field husbandry
RUN-ROUND railway shunting
zo **RUPICOLA** cocks of the rock
RURALISM country life
RURALIST country bumpkin
RURALITY ruralness
RURALIZE rusticate
RUSH-HOUR commuter-time
RUSHLIKE reedy; weak
RUSH-LINE football
zo **RUSH-TOAD** the natterjack
RUSTICAL rustic; sylvan
RUSTLESS stainless
RUSTLING cattle lifting
zo **RUST-MITE** gall-mite
bt **RUTABAGA** Swedish turnip; swede
RUTHLESS pitiless; barbarous
RUTILANT shining

RUTILATE emit rays of light
bt **RYE-GRASS** fodder grass
RYOT-WARI RYOT-WARY, land tenure
(Ind.)

S

SABAEISM star worship
bt **SABBATIA** gentian
rl **SABBATIC** holy rest day; or year off
SABBATON armoured boot
zo **SABELINE** sable type of skin
ch **SABINENE** terpene derivative
SABLIERE sand-pit
SABOTAGE wanton destruction
SABOTEUR a wrecker
SABOTIER a wearer of wooden shoes
bt **SABULOSE** growing in sandy places
SABULOUS sandy; gritty
SACCATED pouched
SACCULAR baggy; saclike; vesiculate
zo **SACCULUS** a small sac or cyst
rl **SACELLUM** makeshift altar
SACK-RACE race run in sack
SACREDLY divinely; holily
rl **SACRISTY** the vestry
SADDENED mournful; downcast
SADDLERY horse furniture
SADDLING loading
rl **SADDUCEE** Jewish ritualist
SADFACED gloomy; depressed
SAFENESS security; trustiness
SAFFRONY saffron coloured
ch **SAFRANIN** saffron dye
SAGACITY wisdom; shrewdness
SAGAMORE American Indian chief
zo **SAGE-COCK** American grouse
SAGENESS sapience; sagacity;
wisdom
mn **SAGENITE** crystals of rutile
bt **SAGE-ROSE** an evergreen
SAGINATE pamper; fatten
SAGITTAL like an arrow
bt **SAGO-PALM** food-giving tree
bt **SAGUINUS** marmoset
SAHIB-LOG Europeans
zo **SAIBLING** the char
SAILABLE navigable
nt **SAIL-BOAT** yacht
zo **SAIL-FISH** basking shark
nt **SAIL-HOOP** mast-hoop
SAILLESS steam-driven
SAIL-LOFT (where sails are made)
nt **SAIL-PLAN** layout of sails
nt **SAIL-ROOM** storage place for sails
nt **SAIL-YARD** spar for sails
bt **SAINFOIN** a fodder-plant

SAINTISH rather saintlike
SAINTISM sanctimoniousness
SALACITY lustfulness
bt SALADING salad vegetables
ck SALAD-OIL vegetable oil for dressing
SALARIED receiving wages
SALEABLE marketable
SALEABLY vendibly
SALE-ROOM auction room
SALESMAN persuading to buy
SALE-WORK work carelessly done
SALICINE extract of willow bark
SALIENCE prominence
SALIFIED made into salt
SALINITY saltiness
SALITRAL saltpetre mine
md SALIVANT SALIVARY, SALIVATE, of saliva
SALLYING dashing out
zo SALMONET young salmon
SALOPIAN from Shropshire
ck SALPICON Spanish savoury dish
bt SALSILLA edible tuber
bt SALT-BUSH Australian plant
mn SALT-CAKE sulphate of soda
SALT-COTE salt-pit
SALT-FOOT (below the salt)
ck SALTJUNK former ships' supplies
ck SALTLESS without the savour
gl SALT-LICK animals' balancer source
SALT-MINE mine of rock salt
SALTNESS salinity
SALT-WELL salt spring
SALT-WORK salt factory
bt SALT-WORT (several species)
SALUTARY beneficial
SALUTING greeting; hailing
SALVABLE rescuable
SALVAGED saved
bt SALVINIA genus of ferns
ch SAMARIUM spectroscopic metal
bt SAMAROID (winged fruit)
rl SAMAVEDA Veda with chants
bt SAMBUCUS honeysuckle type
SAMENESS monotony; similarity
bt SAMPHIRE a herb
tx SAMPLARY test of pictorial sewing
ck SAMPLING selection; tasting; matching value
SANATION a cure
SANATIVE healing
SANATORY curative; remedial
el SANATRON valve circuit
rl SANCTIFY make holy; hallow
SANCTION ratification; approve
SANCTITY holiness; godliness
mn, bt SANDARAC realgar; resin

SANDARIC N. Afr. resin for map varnishes
SAND-BALL pumice soap
SAND-BAND protecting band
go, nv SAND-BANK a shoal
SAND-BATH household pets' toilet
zo SAND-BEAR Indian badger
zo SAND-BIRD sandpiper
zo SAND-COCK redshank
zo SAND-CRAB the lady crab
zo SAND-DART a moth
SAND-DUNE a ridge of drifted sand
SANDEVER SANDIVER, glass scum in state of fusion
zo SAND-FISH dry land fish
mn SAND-FLAG a sandstone
zo SAND-FLEA chigoe or jigger
ch SAND-HEAT heat of sand-bath
SAND-HILL mound of sand
ga SAND-IRON niblick; golf club
zo SAND-LARK a wading bird
zo SAND-MOLE S. African rodent
zo SAND-PEEP American stint
SAND-PUMP (rock drilling)
bt SAND-REED a shore grass
SAND-REEL a windlass
SAND-ROLL a casting
SAND-SHOT small shot
zo SAND-STAR starfish
SAND-TRAP sand eliminator
zo SAND-WASP the digger-wasp
SAND-WELD silica fusing
ck SANDWICH a snack between slices
ga SANDWICH rubber-layered ping-pong bat
ce SANDWICK vertical sand drain construction
zo SAND-WORM lob-worm; lug-worm
bt SAND-WORT genus Arenia
SANENESS sanity; mental equilibrium
SANGAREE W. Indian drink
SANGLANT bleeding
zo SANGLIER wild boar
rl SANGRAAL holy grail
SANGREAL sangraal
SANGUIFY to make blood
SANGUINE optimistic; hopeful
mn SANIDINE potassium feldspar
SANITARY hygienic; healthful
pr SANSERIF serifless type face
SANSKRIT ancient Indian language
bt SANTALIC (sandal-wood)
SANTALIN red dye
bt SANTALUM sandal-wood genus
ch SANTONIN wormwood
SAP-GREEN yellow green
SAPIDITY tastiness

SAPIENCE wisdom; sagacity; intellect
bt SAPINDUS the soapberry
zo SAPI-UTAN wild ox (Celebes)
SAPONIFY convert into soap
SAPONINE soapwort extract
mn SAPONITE hydrous silicate of
magnesium
SAPOROUS tasty; piquant (savour)
mn SAPPHIRE blue, green or red gem
SAPPHISM lesbianism; (Sappho)
md SAPREMIA blood poisoning
gl SAPROPEL stagnant water sediment
fr SAPSTAIN fungus-caused
discoloration
bt SAPUCAIA Brazil nut-tree
SARABAND Spanish dance
SARATOGA American travelling
trunk
zo SARCELLE a teal
tx SARCENET sarsenet; woven silk
bt SARCINIC fungoid
md SARCITIS eye inflammation
bt SARCOCOL gum Arabic
zo SARCODIC protoplasmic; resembling
flesh
md SARCOSIS a tumour
md SARCOTIC generating flesh
zo SARDELLE herring-like fish
SARDONIC ironical; cynical
mn SARDONYX variety of onyx
SARGASSO sea of seaweed
SARPLIER packing cloth
SARRASIN a portcullis
bt SARRIZIN buckwheat
SARSENET sarsenet; woven silk
SASH-DOOR door having panes of
glass
SASSANID a Persian ruler
mn SASSOLIN native boracic acid
zo SASSOROL rock-pigeon
go SASTRUGI hard wind-ridges on
winter snow surface (Russia)
SATANISM devil worship
SATANITY devilry; diablery;
(witchcraft)
SATELESS insatiable
SATHANAS Satan
SATIABLE appeasable
SATIATED glutted; gratified
SATIRIST lampoonist; ironic writer
SATIRIZE ridicule
SATRAPAL province of a satrap
SATURANT saturating
SATURATE soak; drench
SATURDAY Jewish sabbath
zo SATURNIA a moth genus
SATURNIC (lead poisoning)
bt SATYRIUM orchid genus

SAUCEBOX impudent fellow
SAUCEPAN cook-pot
SAUCISSE powder bag for use in
mines
mu SAUDADES Port. 'remembrance of
past' pieces
mn SAURODON fossil fish
bt SAURURUS pepper plants
SAUTERNE white wine (Fr.)
mu SAUTILLE rebounding violin
technique (Fr.)
hd SAUTOIRE heraldic ribbon
SAVAGELY barbarously; inhumanly
SAVAGERY ferocity; brutality
SAVAGING maltreating
SAVANNAH savanna; a treeless plain
SAVEABLE rescuable; salvable
SAVINGLY thriftily; frugally
SAVOURED tasted
SAVOURLY well seasoned
SAVOYARD Gilbert and Sullivan
operas enthusiast
md SAWBONES a surgeon
zo SAW-FLIES boring insects
to SAW-FRAME blade holder
bt SAW-GRASS a marsh grass
SAW-HORSE cradle for sawing logs
SAW-TABLE boring table
SAW-WREST a saw-set
SAXATILE rock-inhabiting
zo SAXICAVA mollusc genus
zo SAXICOLA the stone-chats
bt SAXICOLE growing on rocks
SAXONDOM Anglo-Saxon world
SAXONISM a Saxon idiom
SAXONIST Saxon scholar
gl SAXONITE coarse-grained igneous
rock
SCABBARD sheath
ce SCABBING worn road surface;
fretting; working non-strikers
SCABBLED rough hewn; scappled
bt SCABIOSA teasel plants
bt SCABIOUS plant; scabby
zo SCAB-MITE a parasite
SCABROUS rough; rugged
bd SCAFFOLD temporary structure for
construction also ski-jumps
SCALABLE climbable; measurable
zo SCALARIA ladder-shells
SCALAWAG scallywag; scamp
SCALDING injuring with boiling
water
SCALDINO Italian brazier
SCALENUM scalene triangle
pl SCALENUS a muscle
SCALIOLA imitation marble
bt SCALLION shallot; leek

bd **SCALLOPS** short withies (thatching willows)
SCALPING selling tickets at surcharge
SCALPING removing skin from skull
SCAMBLED mauled; mangled
SCAMBLER gate-crasher
bt **SCAMMONY** convolvulus
SCAMPING shirking; skimping
SCAMPISH knavish; rascally
SCANDENT climbing
ch **SCANDIUM** a metal
md **SCANNING** scrutinizing; viewing (tests)
cp **SCANNING** action of a scanner
SCANSION rhythm
SCANTIES light attire
SCANTILY meagrely; sparingly
SCANTING stinting
SCANTLED in small pieces
SCANTLET a small pattern
zo **SCAPANUS** shrew-moles
SCAPHISM a Persian torture
mn **SCAPHITE** fossil ammonite
zo **SCAPHIUM** beetle genus
SCAPHOID boat-shaped
SCAPPLED rough hewn; scabbled
SCAPULAR (shoulder-blade); scarf
zo **SCARABEE** scarab; beetle
SCARCELY hardly; barely
SCARCITY dearth; rarity; lack
SCARE-BUG a bugbear
SCARFING uniting timber
SCARF-PIN male decoration
zo **SCARIDAE** parrot-fish
SCARIOUS dry; scaly
zo **SCARITID** (carabid beetles)
SCARLESS unwounded; unscathed
zo **SCARN-BEE** dung-beetle
bd **SCARPHED** (a timber joint)
SCARRING wounding; injuring
SCATCHES stilts
SCATHING bitterly severe; caustic
SCATHOLD open pasture ground
SCATLAND peat and pasture land
SCATTERY dispersed
SCAVENGE to collect/eat refuse
mn **SCAWTITE** calcium silicate/ carbonate
SCELERAT villain
zo **SCELIDES** the hind-legs
SCENARIO plan of a play
SCENE-MAN scene shifter
SCENICAL scenic; dramatic
zo **SCENT-BAG** animal's pouch
SCENT-BOX perfume pack
SCENTFUL highly odoriferous
SCEPTRAL regal

SCEPTRED kingly (isle)
SCHEDULE catalogue; inventory; list
SCHEDULE programme; timetable; (to-) punctuality
SCHELLUM rascal; rogue
SCHEMING planning; intriguing
SCHEMIST projector; astrologer
md **SCHEROMA** dryness of the eye
SCHILLER bronze lustre
mn **SCHISTIC** laminated; slaty
pc **SCHIZOID** tendency to dementia
zo **SCHIZONT** trophozoite ready to reproduce
SCHLAGER duelling sword (Ger.)
SCHMALTZ grease (Ger.); sentimental
SCHMELZE enamel (Ger.)
SCHNAPPS akvavit; firewater
bt **SCHOENUS** a sedge genus
nt **SCHOKKER** fishing vessel, Holland
SCHOLION SCHOLIUM, marginal note in old classics
SCHOOLED disciplined; trained
SCHOONER large drinking glass
nt **SCHOONER** fore-and-aft rigged ship
md **SCIAGRAM** X-ray picture
md **SCIATICA** neuralgia
SCIENTER knowingly; deliberately
SCIENTLY fully aware
SCILICET to wit; namely
SCIMITAR curved sword
zo **SCINCOID** pertaining to the skink
SCIOGRAM radio photograph
SCIOLISM superficiality
SCIOLIST a know-all
SCIOLOUS shallow; skin-deep
SCIOPTIC (camera obscura)
md **SCIRRHUS** cancerous tumour
SCISSILE able to be cut
SCISSION division
to, rw **SCISSORS** acrobatic feat; forfex; cutters; secateurs; crossing
SCISSURA fissure; cleft
SCISSURE rupture division
zo **SCIURINE SCIUROID,** rodent mammals
md **SCLERITE** hardened tissue
SCLEROID ossified
md **SCLEROMA** sclerosis
SCLEROUS bony
SCOFFING deriding; taunting; jeering
SCOFF-LAW contemptuous to law
SCOLDING nagging; chiding; rating
zo **SCOLEINA** earth-worms, etc.
zo **SCOLOPAX** woodcock genus
zo **SCOLYTUS** destructive beetle
bd **SCONTION** inside quoin
SCOONING skimming

SCOOPING ladling
SCOOP-NET a hand-net
SCOOTING decamping
bt SCOPARIA sweet bromweed
SCOPEFUL with wide prospect
zo SCOPIDAE African wading birds
zo SCOPIPED having brushy feet
SCORCHED parched; charred
SCORCHER road-hog
mu SCORDATO out of tune
SCORIOUS ashy; clinkery
SCORNFUL mocking; insolent
SCORNING spurning; scouting
zo SCORPION stingtail
SCOTCHED wounded; blocked
SCOT-FREE untaxed
SCOTOPIC night vision
SCOTSMAN Scot
SCOTTICE in Scottish manner
SCOTTIFY Caledonianize
SCOTTISH Scots
SCOURAGE refuse water
SCOURGED chastised
SCOURING scurrying; scrubbing
SCOUTING rejecting; scorning
SCOUT-LAW Scout Code
SCOWLING glowering; frowning
SCRABBLE scribble; scrawl
SCRAGGED strangled; throttled
SCRAGGLY rough-looking
ck, mo SCRAMBLE hurry; strife; clamber;
(eggs); (code); (jumble); (Amer.
football)
ae SCRAMJET spacecraft
nt SCRAN-BAG food sack
SCRANNEL squeaking; slender;
meagre
SCRAPING abrading; rasping
SCRAPPED discarded; fought
SCRAPPLE to grub about; scrabble
SCRATCHY ragged; sketchy
SCRATTLE to scuttle
SCRAWLED scribbled
SCRAWLER slovenly writer
SCREAMED yelled; cried; squalled
zo SCREAMER tropical bird; monkey;
human offspring
SCREECHY shrill and harsh
SCREENED veiled; hidden; sieved
SCREEVER begging-letter writer
SCREWING exacting; twisting;
racking
to SCREW-KEY a spanner
bt SCREW-POD screw-bean
SCRIBBET painter's pencil
SCRIBBLE scrawl; write
SCRIBING recording
SCRIBISM Jewish literature

SCRIGGLE wriggle
SCRIMPED stinted
SCRIMPLY miserly
SCRINIUM scroll/relic container
SCRIPTOR ancient book-copier,
handwriter
SCRIVANO Italian clerk
SCRODDLE to variegate
md SCROFULA the king's evil
SCROGGIE full of brushwood
SCROLLED convoluted
SCROOPED grated; cracked
SCROUGED squeezed
SCROUGER a whopper
SCROUNGE acquire by stealth; cadge
SCRUBBED scoured
ch SCRUBBER charlady; removal of gas
impurities
bt SCRUB-OAK stunted oak
SCRUPLED hesitated; wavered
SCRUPLER demurrer; doubter
SCRUTINY close inquiry; search
SCUDDICK scuttock; a trifle; a
shilling
SCUDDING speeding
le SCUDDING pre-tanning hide
treatment
SCUFFLED tussled
SCUFFLER brawler
SCULLERY room for washing dishes
SCULLING rowing
SCULLION dish-washer
SCULPSIT he engraved it
SCULPTOR image maker
SCUMBLED painted over
SCURRIED scampered; hastened
SCURRIES pony races
SCURRILE scurrilous
SCURVILY basely; shabbily
SCUTCHED separated
SCUTCHER hedger
zo SCUTELLA sea-urchin genus
SCUTIFER shield-bearer
zo SCUTIPED having scaly shanks
SCUTTLED ran; bolted; scampered;
sabotaged
SCUTTLER ship-sinker
SCUTTOCK see scuddick
gl SCYELITE coarse-grained igneous
rock
SCYTHIAN (Scythia)
zo SCYTODES a genus of spiders
zo SEA-ACORN a barnacle
zo SEA-ADDER stickle-back
bt SEA-APRON a seaweed
zo SEA-ARROW flying squid
SEA-BEACH seashore
zo SEA-BEAST a sea monster

bt **SEA-BELLS** bindweed
nv **SEA-BOARD** the coast
nt **SEA-BORNE** shipped
zo **SEA-BRANT** brent goose
zo **SEA-BREAM** mackerel type
nv **SEA-CHART** marine map
nt **SEA-COAST** seashore
nt **SEA-CRAFT** seamanship
bt **SEA-DAISY** the lady's cushion
zo **SEA-DEVIL** ray; angel-fish
zo **SEA-DRAKE** sea-crow
zo **SEA-EAGLE** the osprey
nt **SEA-FARER** voyager; sailor
nt **SEA-FIGHT** marine engagement
SEA-FRONT shore promenade
SEA-FROTH foam
nv **SEA-GATES** (tidal basin)
nt **SEA-GAUGE** ship's draught
nt **SEA-GOING** deep water line ship
zo **SEA-GOOSE** a dolphin
bt **SEA-GRAPE** glasswort
bt **SEA GRASS** the thrift
SEA-GREEN marine colour
bt **SEA-GROVE** under-water grove
bt **SEA-HEATH** beach plant
bt **SEA-HOLLY** the eryngo
zo **SEA-HORSE** the walrus
zo **SEA-HOUND** dog-fish
zo **SEA-JELLY** sea-blubber
zo **SEA-LEECH** an annelid
zo **SEA-LEMON** a doridoid mollusc
SEA-LEVEL mean tide level
zo **SEA-LOACH** a gadoid fish
zo **SEA-LOUSE** a parasite
SEAL-PIPE a dip pipe
SEAL-RING signet ring
SEAL-SKIN pelt; fur
zo **SEA-LUNGS** a comb-jelly
bt **SEAL-WORT** Solomon's seal
SEAMANLY seamanlike
nv **SEA-MARGE** seashore; tide-line
zo **SEA-MELON** sea-cucumber
SEAMIEST most sordid
SEAMLESS in one piece
zo **SEA-MOUSE** the dunlin; a worm
SEAM-RENT a tear at the seam
SEAMSTER one who sews
SEA-NYMPH an Oceanid
bt **SEA-ONION** a squill
zo **SEA-OTTER** marine otter
bt **SEA-OXEYE** seashore plant
zo **SEA-PEACH** sea-squirt
zo **SEA-PERCH** bass
mu **SEA-PIECE** seascape; poem; song; music
SEA-PLANE hydroplane; floatplane
bt **SEA-PLANT** a seaweed
SEA-POWER strategic

zo **SEA-PURSE** eggcase of skate
zo **SEA-QUAIL** the turnstone
SEA-QUAKE marine earthquake
zo **SEA-RAVEN** cormorant
SEARCHED quested; probed; sought
SEARCHER inquirer; examiner
SEA-REEVE customs officer
SEARNESS dryness; sereness
zo **SEA-ROBIN** gurnard fish
nt **SEA-ROVER** pirate; pirate ship
SEARWOOD dry wood
SEASCAPE marine view, painting
zo **SEA-SHARK** man-eater shark
zo **SEASHELL** marine shell
SEASHORE the beach
zo **SEA-SHRUB** a sea-fan
zo **SEA-SNAIL** the periwinkle
zo **SEA-SNAKE** sea-serpent
zo **SEA-SNIPE** sandpiper
SEASONAL not always available
SEASONED matured; inured
ck **SEASONER** a relish; strong flavouring
zo **SEA-SQUID** cuttlefish
SEA-STICK herring cured at sea
zo **SEA-SWINE** porpoise
SEAT-BACK loose cover
zo **SEA-TENCH** black sea-bream
bt **SEA-THONG** cord-like seaweed
SEAT-LOCK a catch
SEAT-MILE transport statistic
SEAT-RAIL a crosspiece
zo **SEA-TROUT** saltwater trout
zo **SEAT-WORM** pin-worm
SEA-WATER brine
zo **SEA-WOMAN** mermaid; dugong
SEA-WRACK coarse seaweed
bt **SEBESTAN** SEBESTEN, tree with plumlike fruit
SEBUNDEE Indian militia-man
bt **SECAMONE** shrubby climber
to **SECATEUR** pruning shears
SECEDING withdrawing; retiring
SECERNED secreted
SECESHER a secessionist
SECLUDED aside; shut off
zo **SECODONT** with cutting teeth
SECONDED aided; transferred
SECONDER supporter; abettor
SECRETED cloaked; concealed
bc **SECRETIN** secretion-stimulating hormone
SECRETLY privily; covertly
SECTATOR an adherent
SECTORAL in a sector
bd **SECTROID** space between groins
SECUNDUM according to (Latin)
SECURELY fast; safely

SECURING acquiring; getting
SECURITE an explosive
SECURITY safety; surety; pledge; secrecy
cp SECURITY protection from risks of data losses
SEDATELY calmly; seriously; soberly
md SEDATIVE tranquillizing; soothing
lw SEDERUNT court session (Sc.)
zo SEDGE-HEN marsh-hen
rl SEDILIUM chancel seat
SEDIMENT lees; dregs; grounds
SEDITION treason; mutiny; rebellion
SEDUCING enticing; inveigling
SEDUCTOR tempter; corrupter
SEDULITY assiduity; diligence
SEDULOUS industrious; busy
SEECATCH Alaskan male seal
zo SEED-BIRD water-wagtail
SEED-CAKE caraway cake
bt SEED-COAT husk
bt SEED-CORN corn for sowing
bt SEED-DOWN down on cotton, etc.
zo SEED-FISH spawn; roe
zo SEED-FOWL grain-fed bird
SEED-GALL plant disease
bt SEED-LEAF a cotyledon
SEED-LEAP seed-basket
SEEDLESS pipless
SEEDLING young plant
bt SEED-LOBE seed-leaf
SEED-PLOT a hot-bed
SEEDSMAN dealer; sower
zo SEED-TICK a parasite
SEEDTIME sowing season
SEED-WOOL cotton-wool and seeds
vt SEEDY-TOE a horse disease
zo SEER-FISH SEIR-FISH
SEERSHIP talent of foretelling
SEESAWED oscillated
SEETHING boiling
hd SEGREANT rampant and salient
SEIGNEUR lord of the manor
SEIGNIOR seigneur; feudal lord
oc SEINE-NET long shallow net
zo SEIR-FISH seer-fish
SEIZABLE apprehendable
zo SEIZLING the carp
bt SEJUGOUS (six pairs of leaflets)
SEKITORI sumo wrestler
zo SELADANG Malayan tapir; bison
ar SELAMLIK men's quarters (Turk.)
nt SELANDER post-Roman trireme, Mediterranean
SELECTED chosen; culled; preferred
cp SELECTOR picker and chooser; specified conditions finder

tc SELECTOR electromagnetic switching device
ch SELENATE a selenic salt
ch SELENIDE a compound
mn SELENITE gypsum
ch SELENIUM a chemical element
SELF-BORN self-begotten
SELF-ENDS endpaper leaves in books
bt SELF-HEAL burnet saxifrage
SELF-HELP unaided effort
SELFHOOD conscious personality
SELFLESS unselfish
SELF-LIKE indulgence
SELF-LIKE twin
SELF-LOVE wrapped up in self
SELF-MADE independent
SELFMADE hermaphrodite solves chess problem
SELFNESS egotism
SELF-PITY sorriness for self
SELFSAME identical; equivalent
SELF-SOWN plant from windblown seed
SELF-WILL obstinacy
SELF-WISE self-conceit
SELLABLE saleable; marketable
SELVAGEE untwisted rope
SELVEDGE woven border
cp SEMANTIC significant; expressive; symbol-meaning link
SEMBLANT resembling; like
SEMESTER period of six months
SEMI-ACID half-acid
go SEMI-ARID between desert and savannah
rl SEMI-BULL a papal bull
SEMI-COPE outer monastic garment
SEMI-DOME half-dome
SEMI-FLEX to half bend
SEMI-MUTE half deaf
SEMINARY academy; college; school
SEMINATE propagate; sow
SEMINOLE American Indian tribe
SEMI-NUDE barely clothed
mm SEMI-OPAL half-opal
SEMI-OPEN sport
SEMIOTIC sign language
SEMI-OVAL half-oval
SEMI-PULP ground-wood impurities in paper
SEMI-RING half-circle
SEMITAUR half-bull, half-man
SEMITISM Hebrew idiom
SEMITIST Hebrew scholar
mu SEMITONE musical interval
ck SEMOLINA SEMILINO, granules of flour; manna; grits
mu SEMPLICE simply

SEMPSTER seamstress
nm **SEMUNCIA** Roman coin
SENARIUS verse of six feet
SEND-DOWN expel; rusticate
zo **SENG-GUNG** Java badger
bt **SENGREEN** the houseleek
SENILITY dotage; old age
SENNIGHT a week
gl **SENONIAN** geological formation
SENORITA Spanish young lady
SENSEFUL judicious; rational
SENSIBLE intelligent; wise; discreet
SENSIBLY sagaciously; sanely
SENSIFIC exciting
SENSUISM sensuality
SENSUIST amorist; materialist
SENSUOUS carnal; voluptuous
SENTENCE doom; maxim; clause
SENTIENT perceptive; aware of; alert
SENTINEL sentry; watchman; warder
cp **SENTINEL** signal ending tape
    recording
SENTRIES watchers; guards
SENTRY-GO sentry duty
bt **SEPALINE** (leaf of calyx)
bt **SEPALODY SEPALOID,** reversion of
    petals to sepals
SEPALOUS sepaline
SEPARATE sort; divorce; sever
cn **SEPDUMAG** 2-magnetic-sound-track
    film
cn **SEPDUOPT** 2-optical-sound-track
    film
zo **SEPIACEA** cuttlefish
zo **SEPIIDAE** cephalopods
SEPIMENT hedge; boundary
mn **SEPTARIA** turtle-stones
bt **SEPTATED** divided into cells
mu **SEPTETTE** (seven performers)
bt **SEPTFOIL** the tormentil
SEPTUARY group of seven
bt **SEPTULUM** small cell
SEPTUPLE sevenfold
SEQUENCE continuity; series
mu **SEQUENZA** repetition in higher key;
    hymn for mass; solo pieces (It.)
SERAFILE serrefile
SERAGLIO Ottoman sultan's palace
SERAPHIC angelic; sublime
rl **SERAPHIM** celestial being
bt **SERAPIAS** genus of orchids
mu **SERENADE SERENATA,** Nachtmusik
    (Ger.); piece for woodwind in
    several movements
SERENELY tranquilly; calmly;
    placidly
SERENEST calmest; most tranquil
SERENISE glorify

SERENITY peacefulness; quiet
SERGEANT serjeant
tx **SERGETTE** thin serge
SERIALLY consecutively
SERIATIM in regular order
SERICATE silky; downy
mn **SERICITE** potash mica
SERIFORM Chinese writing
mu **SERINGHI** Indian viol
SERJEANT sergeant
rl **SERMONER** preacher
SERMONET short address
rl **SERMONIC** admonitive
md **SEROLOGY** study of blood, serum
md **SEROSITY** (exuding serum)
zo **SEROTINE** species of bat
to **SERPETTE** pruning knife (Fr.)
me **SERPLATH** 80 stone (Sc.)
bt **SERPOLET** wild thyme
zo **SERRANUS** perch; bass
SERRATED notched; like a saw
zo **SERRATUS** a thorax muscle
zo **SERRIPED** with serrated feet
SERVIENT subordinate; slavish;
    abject
SERVIOUS obsequious; sycophantic
SERVITOR waiter; henchman
md **SESAMOID** (toe bones)
nm **SESTERCE** Roman 2d. coin
mu **SESTETTE** sextet
mu **SESTOLET** sextuplet
SET-ASIDE reserve(d)
SETIFORM bristly
SET-PIECE stage scene; battle
SETTLING colonizing; deciding;
    fixing
SETULOSE prickly; spinate; spicate
SEVERELY rigorously; strictly
SEVERING disrupting; sundering
SEVERITY harshness; austerity
zo **SEWELLEL** mountain beaver
SEWERAGE drainage
SEWER-GAS bad smell
SEXAGENE angle of 60 degrees
SEXANGLE a hexagon
SEXOLOGY study of sex and
    sexuality
mu **SEXTETTE** sextet
mu **SEXTOLET** sextuplet; group of 6
    notes
SEXTUPLE sixfold
SEXUALLY in a sexual way
mu **SFORZATO** emphatically
SGABELLO stool or bench (It.)
SHABBIER more ragged
SHABBILY despicably; meanly
SHABRACK saddle-cloth
SHACKING sharing digs, lodgings

SHACKLED fettered; manacled
zo **SHAD-BIRD** American snipe
bt **SHAD-BUSH** the June-berry
bt **SHADDOCK** grapefruit
SHADEFUL umbrageous
zo **SHAD-FROG** jumping frog
SHADIEST most obscure
SHADOWED followed; obscured
SHAFTING of propeller drive;
  copulation
SHAGGING of intercourse; exhausting
SHAGREEN sharkskin and rayfish tea
  caddies; untanned leather (Persia)
SHAKE-OUT return to normal;
  economics
tx **SHALLOON** woollen fabric
SHAMANIC magical
SHAMBLES slaughter-house; ruin
SHAMEFUL humiliating; heinous;
  base
SHAMMING feigning; counterfeiting
bt **SHAMROCK** Irish emblem
SHANGHAI kidnap
SHANKING mishitting at golf
SHANTIES sea songs; huts
tx **SHANTUNG** coarse silk
SHAPABLE fashionable
SHARKING of commercial scoundrel
SHARP-CUT clearly defined
SHARPING tricking
SHARP-SET keen
ck **SHASHLIK** grilled lamb on skewer
SHATRANJ board game for two, like
  chess
SHATTERY brittle; rickety
zo **SHAW-FOWL** a wappenshaw fowl
SHEADING district, Isle of Man
SHEALING SHEILING, shepherds'
  shelter
zo **SHEARHOG** shorn sheep
SHEARING clipping; shaving; fleecing
SHEARMAN cloth-cutter
SHEATHED encased; sheeted
bt **SHEA-TREE** butter tree
SHEAVING collecting; harvesting
SHEDDING discarding; diffusing
SHEEP-DIP cleansing pool
zo **SHEEPDOG** shepherd's flock-director
zo **SHEEPFLY** a parasite
SHEEPISH shy; timid
SHEEP-PEN an enclosure
SHEEP-RUN tract of pasture
SHEERING moving aside
nt **SHEER-LEG** a crane spar
ce **SHEETERS** steel poling boards for
  trenches
pr **SHEET-FED** separate-sheet printing
SHEETING cloth for sheets

bd **SHEETING SHEATHING,** vertical
  boards with struts for trenches
SHEKINAH Divine Aura
zo **SHELDUCK** female sheldrake
SHELL-GUN a cannon
SHELL-ICE (no water below it)
SHELLING bombarding; husking
SHELL-OUT spend cash; pay for (sl.)
SHELTERY affording shelter
SHELVING sloping; shelves
SHEMITIC Semitic; (Shem)
SHEPHERD a swain; shove; impede,
  shoulder (Australian football)
SHERATON furniture designer
SHIELDED sheltered; screened
SHIELDER projector
SHIFTILY deceitfully; evasively
SHIFTING moving; varying; changing
SHILLALY Irish blackthorn cudgel
nm **SHILLING** a bob
SHIMMING wedging
md **SHIN-BONE** the tibia
SHINGLED bobbed
md **SHINGLES** herpes
SHINNING climbing
SHIPLESS without boats
nt **SHIPLOAD** a full cargo
SHIPMATE fellow seaman
SHIPMENT embarkation
nt **SHIPPING** freighting; seaborne craft
SHIP-TIRE head-dress
zo **SHIP-WORM** the teredo
nt **SHIPYARD** building yard
SHIREMAN sheriff
SHIRKING evading; scamping
tx **SHIRTING** material for shirts
SHIVAREE mock serenade; charivari
SHIVERED shattered; quaked;
  trembled
SHOALING thronging
zo **SHOCK-DOG** a poodle
SHOCKING offensive; outrageous
zo **SHOEBILL** whale-headed heron
SHOEHORN footwear aid
SHOELACE a latchet
SHOELESS barefoot
SHOGGING shaking; jogging
SHOGUNAL (of Japanese C. in C.)
SHOOTING a game-preserve;
  slaughter-sporter
SHOOTOUT police versus gangsters
SHOP-BELL bell at shop door
SHOPGIRL shop assistant
SHOPLIFT pilfer; rob a store
SHOPPING purchases
SHOPWORN faded
zo **SHORLING** newly shorn sheep
SHORTAGE deficiency; lack

pr **SHORT-AND** the ampersand; &
SHORT-CUT (tobacco); a quick way
SHORT-LEG (cricket)
md **SHORT-RIB** a false rib
SHOT-BELT bandolier
SHOT-FREE Scot free; untaxed
SHOT-HOLE hole for explosives
SHOT-SILK iridescent silk
SHOTTING loading with shot
SHOULDER carry; hump; a
prominence
SHOUTING cheering; crying; calling
SHOW-BILL a show-card
SHOW-CARD card of patterns
SHOW-CASE display case
SHOW-DOWN cards on the table
SHOWERED bestowed liberally
SHOW-ROOM display salon
SHOW-YARD (horses and cattle)
SHRAPNEL a projectile
SHREDDED cut into strips
SHREDDER machine for shredding
SHREWDLY sagaciously; astutely
SHREWISH vixenish
SHRIEKED yelled; squealed; cried
SHRIEKER screamer
SHRIEVAL (sheriff)
SHRILLED squeaked; piped
SHRIMPED went fishing for shrimps
SHRIMPER boat or catcher
SHRINKER (head-); psychiatrist
SHRIVING absolving; pardoning
SHROUDED veiled; hidden; screened
SHROVING Shrove-tide festivity
SHRUGGED uplifted
SHUCKING husking; stripping
SHUCKING SHACKING, sharing a
shelter
SHUFFLED (cards); evaded
SHUFFLER palterer; quibbler
SHUNNING avoiding; evading
SHUNPIKE a byroad
SHUNTING switching railway cars
SHUTDOWN closure
SHUTTING fastening; barring
SHWANPAN Chinese abacus
SIBERIAN of Siberia
mn **SIBERITE** red tourmaline
SIBILANT hissing; buzzing
SIBILATE to hiss
SIBILOUS sibilant
SIBYLLIC oracular; prophetic
SICANIAN Sicilian
SICELIOT a Greek in Sicily
SICILIAN (Sicily)
SICK-CALL doctor's visit
SICKENED languished; ailed; wearied
SICKENER a cause of disgust

nt **SICK-FLAG** quarantine-flag
SICKLIED pallid; wan
SICKLILY languidly
SICK-LIST register of patients
SICKNESS malady; disease; illness
md **SICK-ROOM** patients' room
SICULIAN early Sicilian
SIDE-ACHE side stitch or pain
SIDE-ARMS sword or bayonet
ro **SIDEBAND** close frequencies
tc **SIDEBAND** signal for close
transmission
au **SIDE-BEAM** (above crank-shaft)
SIDE-COMB ornamental comb
SIDE-DISH subsidiary, extra dish
mu **SIDE-DRUM** snare-drum; small drum
SIDELINE subsidiary activity
SIDELING sideways; sloping
SIDE-LOCK a curl
SIDELONG obliquely
SIDE-NOTE marginal note
as **SIDEREAL** of interval between 2
transits
mn **SIDERITE** ironstone
SIDE-SEAT seat not in front
SIDE-SHOW raree show at fair,
circus, amusement park
SIDE-SLIP a skid; descending
technique (skiing)
rl **SIDESMAN** deputy churchwarden
SIDE-STEP evade
SIDE-SWAY wind-caused side
movement of frame
SIDETONE telephony
SIDE-VIEW profile
SIDEWALK pavement; footway
SIDEWAYS crabwise
SIDE-WIND undue influence
pr **SIDE-WIRE** wire-staple stitching
SIEGE-GUN heavy gun
SIFFLEUR whistler
SIFFLING whistling
bt **SIGATOKA** fungal banana disease
SIGHTERS first six arrows on target
(archery)
SIGHTING spotting; aiming; viewing
SIGMATIC (sigma)
SIGNABLE able to have a name
written on
SIGNALLY eminently; notably
SIGNIEUR seignior; feudal lord
SIGNLESS making no sign
SIGN-POST modern milestone
bt **SIKYOTIC** plasma-fusing parasitic
SILENCED stilled; hushed
SILENCER (cars, guns, etc.)
SILENTLY mutely; dumbly;
taciturnly

ch **SILICATE** silicon compound
ch **SILICIDE** silicon-content compound
SILICIFY make into silica
mn **SILICITE** labradorite
ch **SILICIUM** silicon
bt **SILICOLE** plant on silica-rich soil
ch **SILICONE** organo-silicon compound
bt **SILICULA SILICULE**, seed vessel
tx **SILKENED** made glossy
SILK-MILL cloth factory
zo **SILK-REEL** spool for silk
zo **SILKWORM** source of silk
ck **SILLABUB** syllabub; a drink; jelly
sweetmeat
SILLADAR Indian cavalryman
pl **SILLY-HOW** a caul; foetal membrane
bt **SILPHIUM** rosin-weed
mn,gl **SILURIAN** rock formation; geological
era
SILURIST a Silurian
SILVANUS a forest-god
SILVERLY like silver
bt **SIMARUBA** quassia; bitterwood
SIMILIZE find similarities; compare
SIMMERED boiled gently
rl **SIMONIAC** one guilty of simony
SIMPERED smiled fatuously
SIMPERER smirker
SIMPLIFY make plain and easy
SIMPLING gathering herbs
SIMPLIST herbalist
SIMULANT like unto
SIMULATE pretend; imitate; sham
rl **SINAITIC** (Mount Sinai)
md **SINAPISM** mustard plaster
pl **SINCIPUT** the skull
SIN-EATER (a Welsh custom)
SINECURE salary for no work
SINEWING strengthening
SINEWOUS strong; vigorous
mu **SINFONIA** a symphony
SINFULLY unrighteously; naughtily
SINGABLE vocable
SINGEING scorching; searing
SINGERIE monkeys represented as
human
SINGLING selecting; picking
mu **SING-SONG** community singing
SINGULAR peculiar; unique; quaint
SINICISM a Chinese custom
ch **SINIGRIN** black-mustard-seed
glucoside
SINISTER evil; unlucky; baneful
gl **SINK-HOLE** a vent; swallow hole; pot
hole in depression
SINN-FEIN Irish home-ruler
SINOLOGY Chinese lore
SINOPHIL lover of China

SINUATED insinuated; wound
SINUSOID geometric curve
SIPHONAL working on the siphon
principle
SIPHONED extracted to a lower level
SIPHONET aphid cornicle
SIPHONIC working on the siphon
principle
ch **SIPYLITE** niobite of erbium
zo **SIRENIAN** mermaid-like sea mammal
SIRENIZE entice; allure
md **SIRIASIS** sunstroke
SIRVENTE troubadour's song
zo **SISCOWET SISKIWET, SISKOWET,**
variety of trout from Lake
Superior
SISTERLY affectionate; sororal
SISYPHUS stone-roller
md **SITOLOGY** dietetics
SITTYBUS papyrus-roll title label
SITUATED placed; located; sited
SITZ-BATH hip-bath
nm **SIXPENCE** a tanner
SIXPENNY worth sixpence
SIXTIETH ordinal number
SIZEABLE of some bulk
SIZINESS adhesiveness
SIZING-UP estimation; rapid
evaluation
SIZZLING hissing; seething; frying
SKEAN-DHU Highland dirk
SKELETAL like a skeleton
SKELETON outline; nucleus; cadre
SKETCHED drafted; depicted; drew
SKETCHER delineator
SKEWBACK an abutment
SKEWBALD piebald
SKEWERED impaled
SKEWNESS deviation of curve of
frequency distribution
md **SKIAGRAM** X-ray photograph
el **SKIATRON** type of cathode-ray
tube
SKIDDING side-slipping
SKILLESS maladroit; artless
SKILLING outhouse; bay of a barn
SKIM-MILK weightwatcher's drink
SKIMMING scan superficially
SKIMMITY a burlesque
SKIMPING scamping; stinting
SKIN-DEEP superficial
SKINLESS flayed
SKINNING flaying
bd **SKINTLED** of irregularly laid
brickwork
SKIN-WOOL wool from dead sheep
SKIPETAR an Albanian
zo **SKIP-JACK** upstart; click-beetle

nt **SKIPJACK** sail cargo boat, Chesapeake, N. America
SKIPPING leaping; bounding; hopping
mu **SKIRLING** bagpipe music
SKIRMISH contest; brush; fray
SKIRTING bordering
SKITTISH mettlesome; fickle
ga **SKITTLES** ninepins
zo **SKUA-GULL** the great skua
SKULKING lurking; slinking
SKULL-CAP the sinciput
zo **SKUNKISH** like a skunk
SKURFING SKURFER, skateboarding
SKYLIGHT glazed hole in roof
rl **SKY-PILOT** aviator; padre
SKYSCAPE cloud painting
pg **SKY-SHADE** lens; hood
SLABBING cutting into slabs
nt **SLABLINE** a running rope
SLACKING relaxing; loosening
SLAMMING banging
SLANGILY colloquially
SLANGING vituperating
SLANTING sloping; tilting; oblique
SLAP-BANG violently
SLAP-DASH carelessly; rashly
ck **SLAPJACK** flapjack; pancake
SLAPPING large; strong; spanking
SLASHING showy; severe; gashing; swing of ice hockey stick
to **SLATE-AXE** a seax
SLATTERN slovenly person
SLAVERED dribbled
SLAVERER driveller; idiot
SLAVONIC (Czechs; Poles; etc.)
SLEAVING separating
SLEDDING sled-transport
SLEDGING sleighing
SLEEKING gliding; smoothing
SLEEPFUL somnolent
SLEEPILY drowsily
SLEEPING dormant; slumbering
mt **SLEETING** rain, snow and hail
SLIDABLE capable of sliding
SLIGHTED insulted; peeved
SLIGHTLY slenderly; faintly; scantily
SLIGHTLY superficial
SLIME-PIT pit of viscous mire
SLIMMING banting; reducing; dieting
SLIMNESS craftiness; artfulness
SLINGING throwing; flinging; tossing
SLINKING skulking; lurking; sneaking
nt **SLIP-DOCK** slipway
nt **SLIP-KNOT** sailor's device
SLIPOVER sleeveless sweater

SLIPPERY evasive; shifty; elusive
SLIPPING tripping; erring; sliding
SLIP-RAIL form of gate (Australian)
rw **SLIP-ROAD** minor by-pass; siding
SLIPSHOD down at heel
SLIPSLOP jejune; trash; slovenly
SLIPWARE lead-glazed earthenware with relief slip pattern
SLITHERY slimy; deceitful
SLITTING splitting
SLIVERED cut into strips
SLOBBERY moist
SLOGGING smiting
SLOP-BOWL slop-basin
SLOP-DASH weak cold tea
SLOP-PAIL household bucket
SLOPPING spilling
SLOPSHOP (ready-made clothes) R.N.
SLOPWORK slovenly work
SLOTBACK (Am. football)
SLOTHFUL idle; dronish; dilatory
SLOTTERY squalid; dirty
SLOTTING grooving
SLOUCHED bent; depressed
SLOUGHED cast off
SLOVENLY negligently; unkempt
SLOVENRY slovenliness; disorder
SLOWBACK lazy lubber
SLOW-DOWN ca' canny; reduce capacity
SLOWNESS tardiness; sluggishness
zo **SLOW-WORM** limbless lizard
SLUBBING twisting
SLUGFEST high scoring (baseball)
SLUGGARD laggard; lounger; slacker
SLUGGING slogging
SLUGGISH slothful; inert
mu **SLUG-HORN** a trumpet
SLUICING flushing
SLUMBERY somnolent; soporous
SLUMMING visiting slums
SLUMPING falling heavily
tx **SLURGALL** knitted-fabric fault
SLURRIED smeared
SLURRING disparaging
SLUTTERY of prostitutes
SLUTTISH dirty; slovenly
SLY-BOOTS a wag
zo **SLY-GOOSE** the sheld-duck
SMACKING tasting of; slapping
bt **SMALLAGE** wild celery
SMALL-ALE (no hops)
SMALLEST minutest; tiniest
SMALLISH on the small side
md **SMALLPOX** variola
mn **SMALTINE SMALTITE**, cobalt-arsenic compound

SMARTING stinging; rankling
SMASH-HIT popular song; musical
SMASHING shattering (blow); excellent
SMATCHET person of no importance
SMEARING daubing; begriming
mn **SMECTITE** fuller's earth
SMELLING redolent; scenting
SMELTERY foundry
SMELTING producing metal
SMIRCHED soiled; clouded
SMIRKING simpering
SMITCHEL a particle
SMITHERY a smiddy; a smithy
SMITHING iron-working
SMOCKING pleating
SMOKABLE fumable
rw **SMOKE-BOX** of steam locomotive
ck **SMOKE-DRY** cure; bloat (of fish)
SMOOTHED palliated; levelled
SMOOTHEN to allay; mollify
SMOOTHLY suavely; blandly
mu **SMORZATO** diminuendo
SMOTHERY stifling; stuffy
SMOULDER hangfire
SMOULDRY slow burning
SMUDGING blotting
nt **SMUG-BOAT** smuggling boat
SMUGGLED brought in illegally
SMUGGLER a night-owler
SMUGNESS self-satisfaction
bt **SMUTBALL** a fungus
SMUTCHED blacken with soot
ck **SNACK-BAR** buffet
SNAFFLED purloined; filched
nt **SNAGBOAT** (removing snags)
SNAGGING lopping trees
SNAILERY small farm
zo **SNAKE-EEL** sinous fish
pt **SNAP-LINE** chalked-string design marker
SNAPPING biting; breaking; cracking
SNAPPISH short-tempered
cp **SNAPSHOT** amateur photograph; store data for correcting errors
SNAP-VOTE sudden vote
bt **SNAP-WEED** balsams, etc.
SNARLING entangling (traffic hold-ups)
SNATCHED plucked; clutched; wrested
SNATCHER grasper; grabber
SNATTOCK fragment
SNEAK-CUP insidious scoundrel
SNEAKING telling; secret; slinking
SNEERING taunting; jeering; mocking

SNEEZING sudden, involuntary, explosive expiration
SNICKING cutting; nicking
SNIFFING inhaling drugs; dogs detecting same
SNIGGLED snared
SNIPPETY fragmentary
SNIPPING shearing; clipping
SNIP-SNAP smart sharp dialogue
SNITCHER handcuff; informer
SNIVELLY whining
SNOBBERY tuft-hunting
SNOBBISH feeling superior
SNOBBISM aping gentility
SNOBLING a little snob
SNOGGING illicit intercourse
SNOOPING furtive enquiry; prying
SNOOZING dozing; drowsing
SNORTING puffing
bt **SNOWBALL** guelder-rose
zo **SNOWBIRD** American finch
SNOWBOOT long boot; galosh
SNOWCAPT crowned with snow
SNOWCOLD cold as snow
bt **SNOWDROP** first sign of spring
SNOW-EYES snow goggles
SNOWFALL frozen precipitation
SNOWLIKE cold, white and soft
SNOWLINE line of perpetual snow
rw **SNOWSHED** railway protection
SNOWSHOE wide-framed shoe for walking on snow
SNOWSLIP avalanche
SNOWSUIT winter garments
SNUBBING checking a rope
SNUBBISH petulant
SNUB-NOSE short nose
SNUFFBOX collector's item
SNUFFERS candle trimmers
SNUFFLED obstructed nasal air intake
SNUFFLER one who snuffles
md **SNUFFLES** infantile breathing noise
SNUGGERY cosy quarters
SNUGGLED cuddled
SNUGNESS warmth and comfort
SOAKAWAY dry well; rummel; pit
SOAPSUDS froth on soapy water
SOAP-TEST (for hardness of water)
bt **SOAP-TREE** a Chilean tree
SOAPWORK soap factory
bt **SOAPWORT** a genus of plants
SOBERIZE to calm down
SOBRANJE Bulgarian tobacco
SOBRIETY dispassion; temperance
SOB-STORY false, pathetic tale
SOB-STUFF synthetic emotion
SO-CALLED incorrectly known as

SOCIABLE companionable
SOCIABLY friendlily
SOCIALLY gregariously
SOCIETAL of society; social in nature
SOCINIAN a polemic theologian
SOCKETED shanked
lw **SOCMANRY** feudal tenure
SOCRATIC (Socrates)
SODA-LIME soda and quicklime
mn **SODALITE** a soda compound
SODALITY comradeship; association
ch **SODAMIDE** ammonia-sodium
   compound
SODA-SALT baking ingredient
SODDENED saturated; drenched
SOFTBALL rounders; derivative of
   baseball
SOFTENED mollified; melted;
   assuaged
SOFTENER mitigator; mollifier
SOFT-EYED compassionate
SOFTLING weakling
SOFTNESS tenderness
SOFT-SHOE light tap-dancing
SOFT-SOAP flattery
cp **SOFTWARE** computer programs,
   subroutines
bt **SOFT-WOOD** sap-wood
SOILLESS untarnished
SOIL-PIPE drain-pipe
SOLACING consoling; comforting
SOLANDER case for prints
bt **SOLANINE** an alkaloid
md **SOLANOID** potato-shaped
SOLARISM solar myths
SOLARIST mythologist
SOLARIUM suntan parlour
SOLARIZE injure by sun's rays
zo **SOLASTER** starfish
SOLATIUM compensation
bt **SOLDANEL** blue moonwort
SOLDERED cemented
SOLDERER a joiner of metals
SOLDIERY the military
SOLECISM incongruity; impropriety
SOLECIST SOLECIZE, breaches of
   manners or syntax
SOLEMNLY gravely; formally; staidly
SOLENESS singleness
mn **SOLENITE** fossil razor-shell
tc **SOLENOID** switch based on copper
   coil
mu **SOLFAISM SOLFAIST,** use of sol-fa
   for sight-reading songs
SOLIDIFY harden; congeal; petrify
md **SOLIDISM SOLIDIST,** medical theory
   of diseases
SOLIDITY compactness

SOLITARY lonely; single; remote
SOLITUDE isolation; seclusion
SOLLERET foot armour
lw **SOLONIAN** (Solon, a lawgiver)
SOLSTICE an ecliptic point
SOLUTION release; elucidation
SOLUTIVE loosening
SOLVABLE explainable; resolvable
SOLVENCY all debts payable
zo **SOMACTID** bony fin rod in fish
SOMATISM a doctrine
SOMATIST materialist
SOMATOME homologous segment
SOMBRELY gloomily; darkly; gravely
SOMBRERO broad-brimmed hat (S.
   Amer.)
SOMBROUS gloomy; sombre; doleful
SOMEBODY more than a nobody
SOMEDEAL in some degree
SOMESUCH similar
SOMETIME formerly; once
SOMEWHAT more or less
SOMEWHEN some time or other
SOMNIFIC inducing sleep; soporific
mu **SONATINA** short sonata
zo **SONG-BIRD** warbler
mu **SONG-BOOK** collection of songs
mu **SONGFORM** ternary; (3 sections)
mu **SONGLESS** not in good voice
mu **SONGSTER** vocalist
SON-IN-LAW daughter's husband
SONOBUOY underwater noise-fixing
   equipment
mu **SONORITY** resonance
mu **SONOROUS** melodious; audible
SOOTHING pleasing; calming; lulling
SOOTHSAY foretell; augur; predict
SOPHERIM Hebrew scribes
SOPITION lethargy
SOPOROUS drowsy; somnolent
bt **SORALIUM** group of soredia in lichen
ch **SORBITOL** hexahydric alcohol
SORCERER wizard; magician
SORDIDLY ignobly; basely; meanly
bt **SOREDIUM** a brood-bud
SOREHEAD disgruntled person
SORENESS regret; rancour
zo **SORICINE** (shrew-mice)
SORORATE marriage of widower to
   dead wife's sister
SORORISE be a sister to
SORORITY women's club (Amer.
   university)
ch **SORPTION** absorption, adsorption,
   etc.
SORROWED grieved; lamented; wept
SORROWER mourner; repiner
SORTABLE befitting; suitable

SORTMENT assortment; distribution
SOTADEAN satirical and malicious
SOTERIAL about salvation
SOUCHONG black China tea
SOUGHING moaning; sighing
rl **SOUL-BELL** dying funeral bell
SOULLESS dull; spiritless
rl **SOUL-SCOT SOUL-SHOT,** requiem fee
SOUL-SICK morally diseased
SOUND-BOW part of a bell
nt, me **SOUNDING** swinging the lead;
     determination of sea depths and
     speed in knots of vessel
SOUR-BALL tart hard spherical sweet
mu **SOURDINE** a muffler; sordet
bt **SOUR-DOCK** sorrel
SOUR-EYED morose
SOURNESS tartness; asperity
SOUR-PUSS a kill-joy
SOUTHERN of the south
as **SOUTHING** of star crossing meridian
SOUTHING maintaining direction
     towards the south
SOUTHPAW boxer's stance in ring
SOUVENIR memento; relic; keepsake
bt **SOW-BREAD** a tuber
SOW-DRUNK beastly drunk
bt **SOYA-BEAN** protein/oil plant
     (Manchuria)
SOZZLING getting fuddled
SPACE-AGE era of astronautics
SPACE-BAR typewriter gadget
SPACEMAN astronaut
SPACIOUS vast; roomy; ample; wide
ga **SPADILLE SPADILIO,** ace of spades in
     ombre and quadrille
SPADROON double-handed sword
SPAGIRIC chemical
SPALLING stonework fragmentation
SPALPEEN scamp; rascal (Ir.)
ar **SPANDREL SPANDRIL,** triangular
     space beside an arch
md **SPANEMIA** anaemia
SPANGLED glittering
SPANGLER sparkler
SPANIARD an Iberian
SPANKING dashing; open-hand
     striking
SPANLESS immeasurable
me **SPAN-LONG** 9 inches (22 cm)
SPANNING bridging; extending
SPAN-ROOF roof with eaves
SPARABLE shoe nail
nt **SPAR-DECK** the upper deck
SPARE RIB a piece of pork
. **SPARGING** sprinkling
zo **SPAR-HAWK** sparrow-hawk
SPAR-HUNG (with fluorspar)

SPARKFUL lively; gay
SPARKING playing the gallant
SPARKISH well-dressed; airy
mn **SPARKLER** a diamond
SPARKLET charge of gas
zo **SPARLING** a smelt
SPARRING boxing
SPARSELY thinly; meagrely
SPARSILE scanty; infrequent
bt **SPATHOSE SPATHOUS,** foliated or
     lamular
zo **SPATHURA** humming-birds
SPAVINED (leg swelling)
SPAWLING slobbering
SPAWNING putting forth eggs
SPEAKING hailing; addressing
SPEARING lancing
SPEARMAN he who spears
cp **SPECIFIC** distinctive; peculiar;
     particular; absolute address
SPECIFIC qualifier per unit mass for
     physical property
SPECIMEN sample; type; exemplar
SPECIOUS plausible; ostensible
SPECKING staining
SPECKLED variegated
SPECTRAL ghostly; spooky
SPECTRAL of spectrum or of
     monochromatic radiation; of
     separation of wavelengths
SPECTRUM (colour bands); of
     refracted light waves
SPECULAR reflective
SPECULUM a mirror
SPEEDFUL speedy; hasty; impetuous
SPEEDIER faster; quicker
SPEEDILY with rapidity
SPEEDWAY racing track; specially
     built light racing vehicles
bt **SPEKBOOM** S. African shrub
SPELDING SPELDRIN, SPELDRON,
     dried haddock; fish split and dried
     in the sun
SPELLING charming
SPEND-ALL spendthrift
SPENDING exhausting; squandering
SPERABLE hopeful
bt **SPERGULA** spurry; sandweed
SPERM-OIL whale by-product
bt **SPHAGNUM** bog-moss
zo **SPHECIUS** digger-wasps
SPHENOID wedge-shaped
SPHERICS spherical geometry
SPHEROID almost a sphere
SPHEROME cell-inclusion causing oil
     globule
SPHERULE small globe
mn **SPHRAGID** ochreous clay

md **SPHYGMIC** pulsative
mu **SPIANATO** smoothed out evenness (It.)
SPICATUM herring-bone work
mu **SPICCATO** rapid detached notes (violin)
SPICE-BOX condiment-holder
SPICEFUL aromatic
bt **SPICKNEL** baldmoney plant
SPICULAR spiky; pointed
bt **SPICULUM** small spike
SPIFFING delightful
bt **SPIGELIA** worm-grass; pink-root
bt **SPIKELET** unit of grass inflorescence
ga **SPILIKIN** spillikin; splinter of wood
SPILLING upsetting; shedding
SPILLWAY overflow
zo **SPILOTES** a snake genus
SPINDLED tapering
mu **SPINETTO** It. spinet (harpsichord type)
bt **SPINIFEX** porcupine grass
md **SPINITIS** spinal fever
SPINNERY spinning mill
SPINNING whirling; twirling
SPINSTER unmarried woman
SPINSTRY spinning industry
zo **SPIRACLE SPIRICLE**, breathing-hole; pore
SPIRALLY whorled
mn **SPIRIFER** fossil brachiopod
SPIRITED sprightly; alert
SPIRITUS aspiration; breathing
SPIRTING spurting; sprinting
SPITBALL illegal pitch in baseball
SPIT-CURL soap-lock
SPITEFUL vindictive; malicious
SPITFIRE fighting aircraft; irascible
SPITTING piercing
SPITTOON a cuspidor; receptacle
SPLASHED spattered
SPLASHER ornamental nameplates
nt **SPLASHER** protecting paddle-box; mudguard
rw **SPLASHER** locomotive driving wheels
SPLATTER to splash
SPLAYING sloping
SPLEENED angered
SPLENDID lustrous; refulgent
md **SPLENIAL** splint-like bone
zo **SPLENIUM** posterior bend of commissure
pl **SPLENIUS** a neck muscle
SPLICING joining; binding
SPLINTER fragment; cleave
SPLITTER separator
SPLOTCHY unevenly daubed

SPLUTTER a bustle; a stir
SPOFFISH fussy; officious
SPOILFUL wasteful; rapacious
SPOILING marring; vitiating
SPOLIARY Roman mortuary
SPOLIATE plunder; pillage
SPOLVERO perforation cartoon technique
SPONDIAC metre of drinking songs (spondees)
bt **SPONDIAS** hog-plums, etc.
pl **SPONDYLE** a vertebra
SPONGING cadging; sorning
SPONSION sponsorship
SPONTOON kind of halberd
SPOOFING bluffing
SPOOKISH ghostly
cp **SPOOLING** winding on reels (cinema), (fishing), (recording)
SPOONFUL a bite
SPOONILY amorously
SPOONING courting
SPORADIC scattered; irregular
zo **SPOROSAC** a gonophore
SPORTFUL frolicsome; jocose
SPORTING generous
SPORTING romping; displaying
SPORTIVE wanton; hilarious
SPOT-BALL billiards
SPOTLESS pure; untainted
pt **SPOTTING** observing; raining; appearance of defect, disease; choosing correct moment to jump (parachuting)
SPOUTING orating; gushing
SPRACHLE SPRACKLE, to clamber up with difficulty
SPRAGGED scotched up
SPRAINED overstrained
SPRAINTS dung of an otter
SPRAWLED straggled; spread
SPRAWLER lounger
SPRAYING atomizing
ag, ce, rw **SPREADER** extender; distributor; disperser; trench strut
SPRIGGED adorned with sprigs
SPRINGAL catapult; youth
SPRINGAR Norw. folkdance
mu, zo **SPRINGER** arch support; ornamental short note; spaniel dog
SPRINKLE bedew; perfuse
SPRINTED speeded; spurted
SPRINTER racer
cp **SPROCKET** a cog; (film); (tape)
SPRUCELY neatly; tidily
SPRUCIFY to smarten
SPRUCING refurbishing
SPRUNTED sprang; sprouted

ce **SPUDDING** lifting potatoes; enlarging hole with piles
SPUNYARN loosely twisted rope
SPUR-GALL wound with a spur
SPUR-GEAR gear wheels
SPURIOUS bastard; faked
SPURLESS without incentive
zo **SPURLING** the smelt
SPURNING disdaining; scouting
SPURRIER spur-maker
SPURRING inciting
SPURRITE carbonate/silicate of calcium
SPURTING gushing
SPURTLED showered
SPY-CRAFT secret service
SPY-GLASS a telescope
SPY-MONEY pay to secret agent
SQUABBED stuffed; crashed
SQUABBLE wrangle; brawl; printing
SQUAB-PIE pigeon-pie
SQUADDED grouped
SQUADRON military grouping
ch **SQUALENE** symmetrical triterpine
SQUALLED yelled; cried
SQUALLER screamer; informer
zo **SQUALOID** like a shark
zo **SQUAMATA** reptile genus
SQUAMATE SQUAMOID, scale-like
zo **SQUAMOSE SQUAMOUS,** scaly
SQUAMULA SQUAMULE, a small scale
SQUANDER dissipate; lavish; fritter
SQUARELY evenly; quadrilaterally
SQUARING adjusting; regulating; resetting; blade turning (rowing)
SQUARISH not quite square
rl **SQUARSON** squire-parson
SQUASHED compressed; squeezed
SQUASHER suppresser
SQUATTED cowered; crouched; sat
SQUATTER settler without title
SQUAWKED squalled
SQUAWMAN transvestite wife (N. Am. Indian)
SQUEAKED shrilled
SQUEAKER informer
SQUEALED squalled
SQUEEGEE rubber mop
SQUEEZED crushed; constricted
SQUEEZER playing card
SQUEGGER self-quenching circuit
SQUIBBED wrangled
SQUIGGLE squirm; wriggle
SQUILGEE squeegee
SQUINTED peered with narrowed/ crossed eyes
SQUIREEN a petty squire
SQUIRELY gallantly

SQUIRING escorting
SQUIRMED wriggled
zo **SQUIRREL** plume-tailed rodent
SQUIRTED ejected; gushed
SQUIRTER a syringe
STABBING piercing; thrusting
STABLING accommodation for horses
STABLISH establish
mu **STACCATO** abruptly
STACKING piling
STADDLED supported
STAFFING providing personnel
STAFFMAN right-hand man; assistant
vt **STAG-EVIL** horse disease
zo **STAGGARD** 4-year-old stag
STAGGERS giddiness
bt **STAGHORN** large fern
STAGNANT motionless; inert
STAGNATE become dull
md **STAHLIAN STAHLISM,** medical theory
STAINING sullying; discolouring
STAIR-ROD carpet retainer
STAIRWAY a staircase
STAKE-NET fishing net
STALKING approaching prey warily
STALLAGE street traders' stall rent
STALL-FED luxuriously nurtured
STALLING losing speed when flying; to remain motionless (basketball)
zo **STALLION** male horse
STALLMAN stall-holder
STALWART resolute; sturdy; valiant
bt **STAMENED** having stamens
STAMINAL constitutional; vigorous
STAMPEDE panic; rush; flight
STAMPING pounding; impressing
STANCHED staunched; stopped
STANCHER a tourniquet
STANCHLY steadily; staunchly
ce **STANDARD** banner; colours; size; quantity; U-shaped metal casting
STANDARD normal; plant with treelike stem
STANDARD (street or house lamp)
STANDING rank; duration; status; (-order)
STAND-OFF (Rugby football)
STAND-PAT decline to budge
STANHOPE dog-cart
zo **STANK-HEN** moorhen
ch **STANNANE** tin hydride
STANNARY tin mine
ch **STANNATE** a salt
STANNINE a tin alloy
STANNITE sulphostannate of copper/iron
STANNOUS containing tin

STANZAIC (stanzas)
bt STAPELIA milkweed plants
STAPLING sorting; binding
STARCHED formal; stiff
STARCHER stiffener
STARCHLY rigidly; punctiliously
STAR-DUST cosmic dust
STARE-CAT over-inquisitive
neighbour
zo STAR-FISH an echinoderm
STAR-FORT angular redoubt
STAR-GAZE astronomize
STARLESS lacking stars
STAR-LIKE stellate
as STARLING small heavenly body
zo STARLING ring of piles; bird
zo STAR-NOSE N. American mole
STAROSTA Polish noble
STAROSTY life-estate
bt STAR-REED Peruvian plant
STARRING taking the lead
ck STARTERS introductory meal course
STARTFUL skittish; jumpy
STARTING beginning; (post); (price)
STARTISH nervous; fearful; scared
STARTLED affrighted; dumbfounded
STARTLER a shock; a rouser
STAR-TURN revue or circus act
STARVING famished; hungry
bt STARWEED star-shaped plant
bt STARWORT aster genus
rl, mu STASIMON choral ode
STATABLE declarable; affirmable
STATEDLY regularly
STATICAL in equilibrium; restful
STATUARY sculpture
STATURED full grown
nt STAYBAND mast hoop to take stay
wires
STAY-BOLT a holdfast
STAY-LACE corset cord
nt STAYSAIL triangular upper mainsail
(schooner)
STEADIED supported; upheld
STEADILY constantly; firmly
STEADING farm out-houses
STEALING filching; purloining
STEALTHY clandestine; furtive; sly
STEAM-GUN steam-propelled firearm
ck STEAMING evaporatng; reeking;
cooking
nt STEAM-TUG steam-driven boat
STEANING well-shaft lining
zo STEAPSIN fat-digesting enzyme
STEARATE a fatty acid
STEARINE tallow; suet; etc.
mn STEATITE soapstone
md STEATOMA wen or tumour

STEELING hardening; bracing;
nerving
STEEL-PEN a nib
STEENING well-shaft lining
STEEPING soaking; macerating
STEEPLED having a thick spire
nt STEERAGE third class at sea
STEERING directing; piloting;
guiding
STEEVING stowing
zo STEINBOK African antelope
STEINGUT lead glazed earthenware
(Germ.)
ce STEINING process of well-lining
STELLARY starry
STELLATE radiated
zo STELLION a lizard
mn STELLITE zeolitic mineral
nt STEM-HEAD bow-post (forward end)
bt STEM-LEAF part of plant
STEMLESS no stalk
STEMMING techniques of stopping
and turning (skiing)
zo STENLOCH overgrown coalfish
STENOSED contracted
STENOSIS constriction
STEP-DAME step-mother
STEP-GIRL doorstep cleaner
STEPOVER wrestling manoeuvre
STEPPING pacing; working; chorus
dancing; (stones); (netball)
STEPWISE photocopying method
zo STERCOME faecal matter in
sarcodina
bt STEREOME mechanical plant tissue
bt STERIGMA fungal-spore-bearing
hypha
STERLING genuine; pure; pound
nt STERNAGE steerage
zo STERNITE part of an insect
STERNWAY backward movement
md STEROIDS bile acids; vitamin D
hormones; saturated hydrocarbons
rl STIBBLER clerical locum tenens
STIBNITE antimony compound
mu STICCADO xylophone
STICKBOY oddjobs boy (ice hockey)
STICKING adhering; fixing; piercing
STICKJAW toffee
STICKLED interposed; obstructed
STICKLER purist over trifles
STIFF-BIT horse's bit
STIFFISH rather tight
STIFLING suffocating; muffling
rl STIGMATA bearing crucifixion marks
ch STILBENE S-diphenylethylene
mn STILBITE zeolitic mineral
bt STILBOID having stalked spore-head

STILETTO small dagger; high heel
br **STILLAGE** cask-storing platform
STILLING calming; distilling; ceramics
STILLION stand for a cask
STIMMUNG tone; atmosphere, mood (Ger.)
STIMULUS spur; incitement; goad
STINGILY parsimoniously; miserly
STINGING pricking; wounding
zo **STING-RAY** a fish
zo **STINKARD** teledu; badger
STINKPOT night-soil pot
STINKPOT grenade; hand-bomb; insult
STINTING limiting; pinching
STIPPLED dotted
STIPPLER engraver
zo, bt **STIPULAR** STIPULED, having pin-feathers; (leaf lobe)
STIRLESS quiescent; still; dull
STIRRING rousing; exciting; lively
STITCHED united; sewn
STITCHEL a hairy wool
STITCHER seamstress
ga **STOCCADE** STOCCADO, thrust in fencing
STOCKADE palisaded defence
STOCKIER stouter built
STOCKILY thickset
STOCKING footwear; storing
STOCKISH stupid; blockish
STOCKIST a tradesman
STOCKMAN herdsman
ck **STOCKPOT** soup, stew of the day
STOICISM imperturbation
STOLIDLY impassively; obtusely
mn **STOLZITE** lead tungstate
md **STOMATIC** mouth medicine
zo **STOMIDIA** disc apertures in actinaria
STONE-BOW (for shooting stones)
zo **STONE-FLY** a lure for trout
mn **STONE-OIL** petroleum
STONEPIT quarry
STOOGERY clownish fraudulence
STOOKING corn gathering
STOOLING ramifying
STOOMING fermenting
STOOPING condescending; bending
STOP-BATH developing accessory
STOP-BUTT safety bank behind targets
pb **STOP-COCK** regulating valve; cistern system
STOP-CODE colours of traffic lights
cp **STOP-CODE** emergency stop signal
STOP-OVER intermediate landing
STOPPAGE a deduction of pay

STOPPING a filling; checking
STOPPLED corked
ga **STOP-SHOT** stroke in croquet, snooker
rw **STOP-TIME** deceleration time (trains)
STORABLE tolerates being stored
STORMILY angrily; tempestuously
STORMING assaulting; ranting
STORYING narrating
md **STOVAINE** an anaesthetic
nt **STOWAWAY** secret passenger
STOWDOWN arrange cargo
STRADDLE bracket; striddle
STRAGGLE stray; digress; wander
STRAIGHT direct; honest; upright
STRAINED stressed; exerted; taxed
STRAINER a filter; percolator
STRAITEN confine; perplex; constrict
STRAITLY narrowly; closely
bt **STRAMMEL** straw
STRANDED driven ashore; aground
STRANGER odder; quainter; alien
STRANGLE choke; suppress; smother
STRAP-OIL a thrashing
STRAPPED secured; stropped
STRAPPER harness-maker
STRATEGY military art
STRATIFY laminate (plywood)
bt **STRATOSE** of well-defined layers
STRATULA thin rock layer
STRAW-HAT Panama headgear
STRAYING roving; deviating; erring
STREAKED variegated; striped
STREAKER dare-naked runner
STREAMED flowed; poured; gushed
STREAMER a pennant; wind-drift indicator (parachuting)
STREAMER ecliptic corona; wet fly (angling)
STRELITZ Muscovite militia-man
STRENGTH power; vigour; might
STREPENT noisy; strident
zo **STREPERA** crow-shrikes
STREPHON love-sick swain
STRESSED emphasized; accented
STRESSOR factor of stress
STRETCHY elastic
STREWING scattering; broadcasting
STRIATED furrowed; streaked
md **STRIATUM** brain ganglion
STRICKEN afflicted; smitten; struck
STRICKLE a template
STRICTLY exactly; literally; severely
STRIDDEN strode
STRIDDLE straddle; bracket
STRIDENT harsh; grating; creaking
STRIDING bestriding; stalking
STRIGATE striped; variegated

STRIGGED with fruit stalks removed
zo **STRIGINE** owl-like
zo **STRIGOPS** owl-parrots
bt **STRIGOSE STRIGOUS**, bristly; setous; aciform; setiform
bd **STRIKING** impressive; forcible; breaking camp; removal of support structure
mu **STRINGED** (rackets; billiards)
STRINGER horizontal tie rod; binder; surfboard slat
STRINKLE sprinkle sparingly
STRIPING making stripes
STRIP-OFF dismantling; undressing
STRIPPED deprived; naked; fleeced
STRIPPER pillager; peeler; husker
zo **STROBILA** tape-worm
bt **STROBILE** hardened catkin
STROKING (rowing); caressing
STROLLED sauntered; wandered
STROLLER actor; vagrant
zo **STROMBUS** wing shells, etc.
STRONGLY forcibly; mightily
ch **STRONTIA** strontium oxide
mu **STROPHIC** choral ode for turning chorus (Gr.)
STROPPED (razors) sharpened
tc **STROWGER** relay selectors in telephone exchanges
STRUGGLE wrestle; strive; contend
mu **STRUMMED** vamped
bt **STRUMOSE** with cushion-like swellings
md **STRUMOUS** scrofulous
STRUMPET trollop; fly-by-night
zo **STRUTHIO** ostrich genus
STRUTTED braced
STRUTTER proud walker
STUBBING uprooting
STUBBLED bristly
STUBBORN refactory; wilful; perverse
STUB-IRON (used for gun-barrels)
STUB-NAIL short thick nail (boots)
STUCCOED plastered
STUDBOLT headless bolt
STUD-BOOK pedigree book
STUDDING putting in studs
STUD-FARM (horse breeding)
STUDIOUS diligent; scholarly
zo **STUD-MARE** breeding mare
STUDWORK form of brickwork
STUDYING conning; learning
STUFFING cramming; taxidermy
STULTIFY deaden; dull the mind
STUMBLED tripped; lurched
STUMBLER blunderer
STUMMING fermenting

STUMPING (cricket); nonplussing
STUNDISM STUNDIST, (Russian dissenters)
STUNNING dazing; marvellous
nt **STUNSAIL** studding-sail
STUNTING dwarfing; performing
zo, bt **STUPEOUS** with matted hair
STUPIDLY doltishly; senselessly
STUPRATE to ravish
STURDILY stoutly; stalwartly
zo **STURGEON** caviare fish
zo **STURNOID** (starlings)
SUASIBLE persuasible
SUBACRID pungent
SUBACUTE slightly blunt; dull
SUB-AGENT an underling
SUBAHDAR Indian captain
sv **SUBCHORD** way-measuring chord length
SUB-CLASS subdivision
zo **SUBCOSTA** primary wing vein in insects
SUBCRUST layer between pavement and foundation
SUBDUING overpowering; mastering
SUBDUPLE ratio of one to two
zo **SUBDURAL** under dura mater
SUB-ENTRY subdivision
SUB-EQUAL nearly equal
SUBERATE compound derived from cork
SUBERECT half upright, half nodding
SUBERINE compound derived from cork
bt **SUBEROSE** somewhat gnawed
SUPEROUS corky texture
bd **SUB-FLOOR** basic underfloor; blind or rough floor base
bt **SUB-FLORA** floral division
bd **SUBFRAME** fixing for cladding
zo **SUBGALEA** parastipes in insects
SUB-GENUS subdivision
as **SUB-GIANT** bright star
ce **SUB-GRADE** lower division; original natural road surface; strata
SUB-GROUP subsidiary part
SUB-HUMAN almost human
md **SUBHYOID** under the tongue
zo **SUB-IMAGO** a state of change
zo **SUBIMAGO** stage in mayfly life history
SUB-INDEX index within an index
pr **SUBITISE** not counting dots
SUBLATED taken away
SUB-LEASE an underlet
SUBLIMED exalted
SUBLUNAR under the moon

SUBMERGE plunge; drown; flood
SUBMERSE duck; douse; dive
SUBNASAL under your nose
bt **SUBNODAL** below a node
SUBORDER subdivision; sub-genus
SUBORNED bribed; led astray
SUBORNER perjurer; false witness
SUBOVATE almost egg-shaped
lw **SUBPOENA** writ of attendance
SUBPOLAR adjacent to polar sea
eg **SUBPRESS** die set; punch and die
  unit
SUBPRIOR prior's deputy
SUBRIGID fairly stiff
SUBSERVE help forward; promote
SUBSIDED sank; abated; waned
SUBSOLAR under the sun
SUBSONIC slower than sound
SUBSTAGE microscopic device
SUBSTYLE line on sundial
SUBSUMED logically included
SUBTENSE chord of an arc
SUBTEPID lukewarm
SUBTITLE secondary title
SUBTLETY cunning; artfulness
mu **SUBTONIC** leading note of scale
SUBTOPIA suburban ideal
SUBTRACT withdraw; deduct; take
SUBTRIBE section of a tribe
SUBTRIST somewhat sad
SUBTUTOR under-master
SUBULATE awl-shaped
SUBURBAN built-up area
  surrounding a city
SUBURBIA the suburbs
SUBVENED relieved; subsidized
SUBZONAL below the belt
SUCCINCT concise; compact; terse
SUCCINIC derived from amber
rl **SUCCUBUS** night demon; intercourse
  with the devil
SUCHLIKE in such manner; similar
SUCHWISE in like manner
zo **SUCKERED** arms of an octopus
SUCKLING unweaned child
md **SUDAMINA** sweating fever
SUDANESE (Sudan)
SUDARIUM sweat room of Roman
  bath
SUDATION perspiration
SUDATORY connected with sweating
SUDDENLY hastily; abruptly; quickly
SUFFERED underwent; allowed; bore
SUFFERER victim; martyr
SUFFICED satisfied; was adequate
SUFFIONI volcanic fumes
SUFFIXED added; subjoined;
  appended

SUFFLATE inflate; blow up
SUFFRAGE vote; prayers;
  intercession
SUFFRAGO hock joint
SUFFUSED permeated; overspread
rl **SUFISTIC** (Moslem pantheism)
SUGARING sweetening
SUICIDAL self-destructive
zo **SUILLINE** of the pig family
SUITABLE appropriate; convenient
SUITABLY fittingly; aptly
SUITCASE portable oblong bag
ck **SUKIYAKI** Jap. meat/vegetable dish
SULCATED grooved; furrowed
zo **SULCULUS** siphonoglyph of anthozoa
SULLENLY morosely; gloomily
SULLYING smirching
ch **SULPHATE SULPHITE**, sulphur
  compounds
ch **SULPHONE** hexavalent sulphur
  compound
SULPHURY containing sulphur
SULTANIC despotic
SULTANRY Sultan's dominion
cp **SUM-CHECK** digit produced by
  summation check
SUMERIAN pre-Babylonian
SUMMERED passed the summer
SUMMONED bid; cited; arraigned
SUMMONER invoker; prosecutor
SUMPITAN Malay blow-pipe gun
SUN-BLIND window-shade
SUNBURNT tanned; bronzed
SUNBURST dazzling gleam
SUNCRACK a fissure
SUNDERED parted; severed; broken
SUNDRIED dehydrated
SUNDRIES miscellanea; odds and
  ends; extras on bill or in scores
SUNLIGHT illumination from Helios
rl **SUNNITES** orthodox Moslems
SUNPRINT photograph
SUNPROOF fadeless
SUNSHADE a parasol
SUNSHINE solar illumination
SUNSHINY sunny
as **SUNSPOTS** regions of cool gas as
  dark patches
mn **SUNSTONE** feldspar
SUPERADD increase the total
SUPERBLY magnificently; gorgeously
pc **SUPER-EGO** conscience
ro **SUPERHET** (wireless oscillations)
rl **SUPERIOR** senior by rank; (larger,
  finer than); boss; head of a
  monastery
SUPERMAN fictional Herculean hero
SUPERNAL celestial; heavenly

SUPERTAX a gross imposition
SUPINATE bring palm upward
SUPINELY inertly; languidly
SUPPLANT displace by intrigue
SUPPLIAL provision; provenance
SUPPLIED bestowed; furnished; gave
SUPPLIER contributor; provider
SUPPOSAL supposition; conjecture
SUPPOSED assumed; opined;
 imagined
SUPPOSER surmiser; thinker;
 imaginer
SUPPRESS quell; check; smother
SURBASED (pedestal moulding)
SURCEASE cessation
bt **SURCULUS** a botanical sucker
SURENESS certainty; infallibility
SURETIES sponsors
SURFACED smoothed
zo **SURF-BIRD** plover; sandpiper
nt **SURF-BOAT** shallow-draught boat
zo **SURF-DUCK** the scoter
pc **SURGENCY** hypothesized personality
 trait
md **SURGICAL** chirurgical
zo **SURICATE** the meercat
SURMISAL surmise; assumption
SURMISED took for granted
SURMISER conjecturer; supposer
SURMOUNT overcome; surpass; scale
zo **SURMULOT** brown rat
SURNAMED having as family name
rl **SURPLICE** linen vestment
SURPRISE shock; bewilder; astound
lw **SURREBUT** rebut a rebuttal
pl **SURRENAL** above the kidneys
SURROUND encircle; hem; beset;
 loop
ma **SURSOLID** fifth power
SURVEYAL review; scrutiny;
 prospect
SURVEYED scrutinized; scanned
SURVEYOR inspector; land measurer
SURVIVAL an outliving; relic
SURVIVED outlasted; endured;
 outlived
SURVIVOR who lives through
SUSPENSE uncertainty; indecision
SUSPIRAL breathing-hole
SUSPIRED sighed
SUSURRUS whispering; muttering;
 rustling
SUZERAIN paramount ruler
SWABBING mopping
SWADDLED swathed; wrapped
rl **SWADDLER** a Methodist (nickname)
SWADESHI Indian boycott
SWAGGING sagging

SWAGSHOP where trash is sold
SWAINING lovemaking; courting
SWAINISH boorish; rustic
SWAMPING overwhelming;
 inundating
bt **SWAMP-OAK** semi-tropical tree
mn **SWAMP-ORE** bog-ore
SWAN-HERD tender of swans
SWANKING bragging
SWAN-LIKE as a swan
SWAN-MARK identification mark
bd **SWAN-NECK** curved; S-bend;
 handrail
zo **SWANNERY** nesting area, home for
 swan colony
SWANNING moving around aimlessly
SWAN-SHOT buck-shot
SWAN-SKIN soft flannel
SWAN-SONG last act or appearance
SWAPPING bartering
SWARDING turfing
SWARMING (bees, mosquitoes);
 (crowding)
SWASHING splashing
nv **SWASHWAY** navigable channel
SWASTIKA Nazi emblem; triskele
SWATHING wrapping; binding
SWATTING killing flies
SWEALING melting; singeing
SWEARING profaneness; avowing
SWEATILY laboriously
pt **SWEATING** toiling; extorting;
 perspiration; separation in paint;
 gloss
SWEAT-OUT plastic defect due to
 moisture
SWEEPING comprehensive; extensive
SWEEP-NET fishing gear
to **SWEEP-SAW** curved-cut saw
bt **SWEET-BAY** the tree laurel
bt **SWEET-GUM** a gum tree
bt **SWEETING** sweet apple; dearest one;
 beloved
SWEETISH rather sweet
SWEET-OIL olive oil
bt **SWEET-PEA** an attractive flower
bt **SWEET-SOP** an evergreen shrub
SWELLDOM fashionable world
SWELLING bombastic; dilating
SWELLISH foppish
SWELL-MOB thieving gang
SWERVING deviating; diverging
SWIFTEST fastest; fleetest
zo **SWIFTLET** (bird's nest soup)
SWIGGING quaffing; drinking
SWILLING rinsing; toping
SWIMMING waterborne mobility
 knack

SWIMSUIT bathing costume
SWINDLED defrauded; cheated
SWINDLER sharper; trickster
bt **SWINE-OAT** a coarse oat
vt **SWINE-POX** disease of pigs
SWINE-STY a pig-sty
SWINGING vibrating; dangling
SWINGLED flailed
SWINGMAN both guard and forward (baseball)
SWINKING drudging; moiling; toiling
SWIRLING twirling; gyrating; eddying
SWISHING birching; caning; chastising
SWISHING noise of winds, rushing water, dresses
rw **SWITCHED** changed choice, track; shunted
el, cp **SWITCHED** (-on); controlled (flow of electricity, traffic etc.)
SWITCHEL treacle beer
md **SWOONING** fainting; dizziness; a syncope
mu **SWOOPING** descending in a rush (tempo)
SWOPPING exchanging; bartering; (duplicates)
SWORD-ARM right arm
SWORD-CUT a wound
SWORD-LAW violence
SWOTTING studying hard
SYBARITE a voluptuary
SYBOTISM pig culture
bt **SYCAMINE** mulberry tree
bt **SYCAMORE** species of maple
bt **SYCONIUM** figlike fruit
mn **SYENITIC** (syenite)
SYLLABIC in syllables
SYLLABLE to utter
SYLLABUB sillabub; a drink; jelly sweetmeat or glass to hold it
SYLLABUS an abstract; summary; programme of education
SYLPHISH SYLPHINE, fairylike
SYMBATIC of partly-like polymorphism types
SYMBOLIC emblematic; representative
SYMMETRY harmony; regularity
SYMMORPH similar notion
SYMPATHY fellow-feeling; affinity
SYMPHILE guest species among insects
mu **SYMPHONY** unison of sound
zo **SYMPHYLA** an insect genus
cy **SYMPLAST** multinucleate cell variety
SYMPLOCE rhetorical repetition

SYNACRAL (common vertex)
md **SYNALGIA** sympathetic pain
zo **SYNANCIA** fish genus
zo **SYNAPSID** reptile skull condition
zo **SYNAPTIC** of nerve-cell contact
bl **SYNAPTON** model imitating living matter
SYNARCHY joint rule
SYNASTRY stellar coincidence
SYNCLINE geological basin
mu **SYNCOPAL SYNCOPIC**, syncopation rhythm
cy **SYNDESIS** fusion of chromosomes
SYNDETIC linking together
md **SYNDROME** concurrence; illness (AIDS)
md **SYNECHIA** an eye-disease
SYNEDRAL (angularity)
zo **SYNERGIC** working together
lw **SYNGRAPH** signed deed
md **SYNOCHAL** feverish
rl **SYNODIST** member, attender at Synod
SYNOMOSY sworn brotherhood
SYNONYME SYNONOMY, alternative word with similar meaning
SYNOPSIS abstract; short outline
SYNOPTIC comprehensive
md **SYNOVIAL** (synovia)
SYNTAXIS syntax; grammar; mode of thinking; expression
md **SYNTEXIS** emaciation
pc **SYNTONIA** reactiveness to environment, surroundings
mu **SYNTONIC** intense sharp
md **SYNTONIN** acid albumin
SYPHERED flush jointed
md **SYPHILIS** sex-transmitted venereal disease
rl **SYRIARCH** a chief priest
md **SYRIGMUS** noises in the ear
SYSTASIS political union
md **SYSTEMIC** pertaining to the system
SYSTOLIC contractive
SYZYGANT (quadratic function)
SZLACHTA Polish landowner

T

hd **TABARDER** a herald
mn **TABASHIR** mostly silica
tx **TABBINET** damask-like fabric
zo **TABBY-CAT** a mouser
tx **TABBYING** watered fabric process
md **TABITUDE** emaciation; atrophy
TABLEAUX theatrical pageants (Fr.)
TABLE-CUT flat-faced

TABLEDEX co-ordinate book index for computers
TABLEFUL filling a table
TABLEMAT plate underlay
ar **TABLINUM** room by atrium (Roman)
TABOOING prohibiting; banning
mu **TABORINE** tabor; tambourine
mu **TABORING** drumming
rl **TABORITE** extreme Hussite
tx **TABOURET** embroidery frame; drum shaped stool
cp **TABULATE** enumerate; classify; list; group totals for items
bt **TACAHOUT** a leaf gall
TAC-AU-TAC (fencing)
pt **TACHISME** spilling, smearing painting technique
el **TACITRON** type of thyratron
TACITURN mute; reticent; silent
TACKLING harnessing; dealing with; challenging (football)
pr **TACKMARK** dot(s) used in 'work and turn' system
TACTICAL strategic
TACTLESS insensitive; indiscreet
zo **TAENIDIA** thickenings of eudotrachea
TAENIOID ribbonlike
nt **TAFFRAIL** tatereel; stern-rail
ch **TAGILITE** copper phosphate
zo **TAGMOSIS** grouping of somites
TAIGLING entangling
TAILBACK retreating (Am. football)
TAILBACK long queue; dawdling cars on holiday
pr **TAILBAND** decorative back-cover band
TAIL-BOOM an aeroplane spar
TAILCOAT formal jacket
TAIL-EDGE lower edge
mu **TAILGATE** trombone technique
TAILINGS mining refuse
TAILLESS Manx; without end
TAILORED cut to figure
TAILRACE (mill stream)
TAILROPE guide-rope
TAINTING corrupting; sullying
TAINTURE taint; stain; blot
cp **TAKE-DOWN** dismantle prior to next job; hold after fall-back (wrestling)
TAKE-DOWN order to secretary; disrobe
TAKE-OVER acquire control
TAKER-OFF mimic; quantity surveyor
TAKINGLY captivatingly; winningly
cy **TALANDIC** of rhythmic changes in cell
rl **TALAPOIN** Buddhist monk

TALENTED accomplished; gifted
TALESMAN a juror
TALISMAN charm; amulet
TALKABLE conversable
ae, ro **TALK-DOWN** landing technique
TALLNESS height; loftiness
TALLOWED fattened; of candle wax
TALLOWER tallow-chandler
TALLYING recording; agreeing
TALLYMAN pedlar
rl **TALMUDIC** (the Talmud)
zo **TAMANDUA TAMANOIR**, arboreal ant-eater
bt **TAMARACK** American larch
bt **TAMARIND** tropical tree
bt **TAMARISK** evergreen shrub
TAMEABLE submissive; docile
TAMELESS intractable; wild
TAMENESS dullness; monotony
TAMPERED interfered; machinated
TAMPERER meddler; schemer; plotter
TANAISTE deputy premier (Irish)
TAN-BALLS (refuse bark)
TANGENCY TANGENCE, state of contact
TANGIBLE tactile; positive; corporeal
TANGIBLY palpably; obviously
TANGLING complicating; matting
TAN-HOUSE tan-bark store
lw **TANISTRY** Irish land tenure
le **TANNABLE** able to be cured
TANNADAR Indian policeman
TAN-STOVE used for tan-bark
ch **TANTALUM** metallic element
TANTALUS spirit-stand
zo **TANTICLE** stickleback
TANTRISM Indian doctrine
TANTRIST a devotee
TANZIMAT Turkish reform bill
TAPADERA leather stirrup guard
TAP-DANCE toe-tapping dance
TAPE-LINE tape measure
TAPERING slightly conical; pointed
TAPESTRY woven work
zo **TAPEWORM** a parasite
zo **TAPIROID** like the tapirs (S. America)
bt **TARA-FERN** bracken (NZ)
TAR-BLACK coal-tar product for earthed posts
TARBOOSH a fez; red hat (Moslem)
TARGETED aimed on target guns
rl **TARGUMIC** (Bible in Aramaic)
TARIFFED dutiable; taxed
tx **TARLATAN** muslin; tarletan
mu **TAROGATO TARAGOT**, Transylvanian clarinet

TARPEIAN (Roman rock)
bt **TARRAGON** savoury herb
TARRYING awaiting; loitering; halting
zo **TARSIPED** kangaroo-footed
zo **TARSIPES** small marsupial
ck **TARTARIC** wine incrustation; (-acid), sauce ingredient
ck **TARTARIN** carboxylic acid (food, medicines)
ch **TARTARUM** compound of above
TARTARUS sunless abyss
TARTNESS sharpness; piquancy
ch **TARTRATE** a tartar salt
TARTUFFE a hypocrite
ce **TARVIATE** of tar/stone surfacings
md **TAR-WATER** an infusion
TASKWORK piece-work
TASTABLE savoury; palatable
TASTE-BUD sensory bud on tongue
TASTEFUL discriminative; elegant
TATTERED in rags; rent
TATTLERY idle gossip
TATTLING chatting; prattling
TATTOOER TATTOOED, skin artist
TAUNTING deriding; flouting; reviling
TAUROCOL bull's glue
TAUTENED tightened; stretched
TAUTNESS strain; tenseness
TAVERNER inn-keeper
TAWDRILY gaudily; garishly; flashily
TAXATION imposition; levy; toll
TAXIARCH Greek commander
TAXIRANK cab queue
bt **TAXODIUM** swamp-cyprus
TAXOLOGY TAXONOMY, classification
TAXPAYER one liable for taxation
TEA-BOARD tea-tray
TEA-BREAK refreshment pause (industrial)
TEA-CADDY small tea box
TEA-CHEST box of tea
TEACHING instructing; enlightening; explaining
cp **TEACHING** hardware for storage; display, response
TEA-FIGHT a bun-worry
TEA-HOUSE oriental pleasure dome
TEAMSTER waggoner; drayman
TEAMWISE harnessed together
TEAMWORK cooperation
TEA-PARTY (Boston 1773)
TEA-PLANT source of tea
TEARDROP a tear
md **TEARDUCT** lachrymal duct
TEARLESS unfeeling
TEA-SPOON kitchen measurement

TEA-TABLE where tea is served
TEATHING fertilizing
TEA-TOWEL towel for drying dishes
TECHNICS doctrine of arts
zo **TECTARIA** shellfish
TECTONIC constructive
ar, gl **TECTONIC** of roofing, folds, faults
TEENAGER youngster
TEETHING dentition
TEETOTAL abstinence from alcohol; dry
TEETOTUM small top
pl **TEGUMENT** the skin
zo **TEGUMERE** portion of tegumant in somite
TELALGIA distant pain
TELAMONE carved male figure as support
zo **TELARIAN** web-spinner spider
bt **TELEBLEM** membrane of hyphae in agarics
TELECAST televised
TELECINE TV cine film projector
TELEFILM television film
TELEGONY hereditary influence
tc **TELEGRAM** a wire, cablegram message
TELEMARK ski turn on slope; paddle stroke (canoe)
bl **TELEOSIS** purposive development
TELESTIC ending
tv, tc **TELETEXT** graphics, documents sent by television system
TELETRON TV cathode ray tube
TELETYPE teleprint (Telex)
tv **TELEVIEW** watch television programmes
tv **TELEVISE** to broadcast
ar, bd **TELLTALE** revealer; indicator; earthquake indicator; glass in shifting wall; sneak; tin (squash rackets)
TELLURAL earthy
ch **TELLURIC** (tellurium)
TELONISM last letters of author's name; pseudonym
TELOOGOO Dravidian dialect
TELOTYPE printed telegram
TEMERITY rashness; audacity
TEMEROUS reckless; bold; foolhardy
TEMPERED toughened; moderated
cp **TEMPLATE** a pattern; a jig; similar pattern identifier
pl, md **TEMPORAL** secular; transient; of cortex area of the temples; of the head; of time
TEMPTING alluring; inveigling
TENACITY adhesiveness; cohesion

TENAILLE a rampart
TENANTED occupied; dwelt
TENANTRY the tenants
TENDANCE attendance; care; attention
TENDENCY bias; drift; inclination
TENDERED offered; estimated
TENDERLY leniently; gently; softly
rl **TENEBRAE** shades; R.C. evening service
TENEMENT a flat or house-block
TENESMUS ineffectual evacuation straining
TENONING mortising
to **TENON-SAW** metal-backed saw
mu **TENORIST** a tenor
mn **TENORITE** oxide of copper
md **TENOTOMY** tendon-cutting
TENSIBLE tensile; ductile
zo **TENTACLE** a feeler
TENTERED stretched
zo **TENTILLA** branches of a tentacle
TENTWORK embroidery
bt **TENTWORT** a fern
TEOCALLI Mexican temple
TEPEFIED warmed up
mn **TEPHRITE** andesite
TEPIDITY lukewarmness
TERAPHIM Hebrew idols
TERATISM being a foetal monstrosity
TERATOMA foetal tumour
ch **TEREBENE** (turpentine)
zo **TEREDINE** teredo; boring worm
zo **TERGETIC** dorsal
TERMATIC an artery
bt, md, tel, **TERMINAL** binding screw; oil-; air-;
cp end of line; (illness); growing point
TERMINAL telephone; tele printer, (plug)
lw **TERMINER** a determination
rw **TERMINUS** the end of a line
TERMLESS boundless; openness
TERRACED having or being in terraces
zo **TERRAPIN** tortoise
bd **TERRAZZO** mosaic in cement; terrace
TERRIBLE formidable; dire; gruesome
TERRIBLY frightfully; awfully
TERRIFIC horrific; dreadful
TERTIARY third in order
TERTIATE triplicate
TERYLENE man-made cloth
mu **TERZETTO** a trio
TESSELLA TESSERAE, small tiles for paving
TESSERAL tesselated; tiled

TESSULAR like dice; cubes
lw **TESTABLE** can be proved; bequeathable
zo **TESTACEA** animals with shells
zo **TESTACEL** a little shell
lw **TESTAMUR** a certificate
lw **TESTATOR** will-maker; devisor
lw **TESTCASE** sample legal decision
pl **TESTICLE** male gonad
ch **TESTTUBE** laboratory vessel
TESTWISE by testing; test experience
md **TETANISE** cause spasms (tetany)
TETANOID convulsive
TETCHILY peevishly; testily
TETHERED restricted; tied; fastened
ch **TETRADIC** fourfold
TETRAGON quadrangle
ch **TETRALIN** organic solvent
rl **TETRAPLA** Bible in four versions
TETRAPOD four-footed
TETRARCH Roman governor
bt **TETRARCH** with 4 xylem strands
zo **TETRAXON** having 4 axes
pm **TETRONAL** hypnotic/sedative drug
TEUTONIC Germanic
TEXT-BOOK a manual
TEXT-HAND large script
tx, wv **TEXTRINE** textile
pr **TEXT-TYPE** type for bookprinting
TEXTUARY authoritative
rl **TEXTUIST** text reciter
bt **THALAMIA** layers of cells
pl **THALAMIC** of the brain
THALAMUS an inner room; brain
ch **THALLIUM** metallic element
rl **THANATOS** god of death (Gr.) (instinct)
THANEDOM thane's jurisdiction; earldom
THANKFUL grateful; beholden
THANKING acknowledging gratefully
THATCHED covered with straw
THATCHER straw-roof craftsman
rl **THEARCHY** theocracy; priestly government
THEIFORM like tea
THEMATIC dissertative
THEOCRAT divine ruler
THEODICY a philosophy
THEOGONY (genesis of the gods)
rl **THEOLOGY** divinity
THEORIES speculations; hypothesis
THEORIST conjecturer
THEORIZE postulate
THEOSOPH inspired person
THERBLIG division of movement
THEREFOR for that purpose
mu **THEREMIN** electronic instrument

THEREOUT therefrom
md **THERIACA** an opiate
THERMALS reflected solar heat; ascending air currents (gliding)
ps **THERMION** ion from incandescent matter
ch **THERMITE** incendiary mixture
THESPIAN of acting (trouper)
THEURGIC magical
THEWLESS weak; frail; feeble
ch **THIAMIDE** amide compound
THIAMINE vitamin B-1
ch **THIAZINE** heterocyclic compound
ch **THIAZOLE** pyridine-like liquid
THICKEST densest; closest
THICKISH rather thick
zo **THICKNEE** the stone curlew
THICKSET closely planted; heavily built (human)
THIEVERY larceny
THIEVING purloining; filching
THIEVISH sly; stealthy
THIGGING begging
cp **THIN FILM** glass-plate memory storage
THINGAMY thingumabob; whatsitsname
THINKING ruminating; cogitating
THINNESS attenuation; emaciation
THINNEST lankiest; leanest
THINNING reducing; diminishing
THINNISH meagre; spare
ch **THIO-ACID** hydroxyl-replaced acid
THIOCTIC lipoic acid
ch **THIOPHEN** coal-tar constituent
ch **THIOPHIL** with affinity for sulphur
ch **THIOUREA** thiocarbamide; bismuth reagent
lw **THIRLAGE** milling rights
THIRSTED craved; yearned; longed
THIRTEEN the baker's dozen
THISNESS individuality
md **THLIPSIS** compression
THOLE-PIN rowlock
rl **THOMEANS** Malabar Christians
THORACIC (thorax)
zo **THORNBUT** turbot
bt **THORNSET** beset with thorns
THOROUGH complete; perfect
THOUSAND M; mille
THRALDOM slavery; bondage
nt **THRANITE** trireme rower
zo **THRAPPLE** windpipe; thropple
THRASHED drubbed
zo **THRASHER** fox-shark; thrush
THREADED strung on a line; sewn
THREADEN made of thread
THREADER loom-shuttle worker

THREATEN menace; intimidate
bd **THREE-PLY** threefold; triple; treble; of wooden sheets
mu **THRENODY THRENODE**, lamentation for the dead (Fr.)
ag **THRESHED** beat out grain; (-out), discussed
THRESHEL a flail for harvesting
zo **THRESHER** mocking-bird
THRESTLE three-legged stool
THRIDACE lettuce juice
THRILLED agitated; stirred; excited
THRILLER a gripping story
THRIVING flourishing; prospering
THROBBED pulsated; beat; palpitated
md **THROMBIN** blood clotting enzyme
md **THROMBUS** blood-clot
THRONGED crowded; flocked
THRONING enthroning
zo **THROPPLE** windpipe; thrapple
zo **THROSTLE** missel thrush
THROTTLE garrote; strangle; stifle
THROWING casting; hurling; slinging
THROW-OUT rejected product
THRUMMED strummed
mu **THRUMMER** vamper
THRUSTED intruded; drove; pushed
THRUSTER reckless rider
THUDDING reverberating
THUGGERY THUGGISM, brutality; violence; criminal assault
THUMBING fingering
THUMB-NUT screwed by hand
THUMBPOT small flower pot
THUMPING enormous
THUNDERY gloomy; frowning
rl **THURIBLE** incense censer
rl **THURIFER** incense bearer
THURSDAY one of the weedays
THUSWISE like so
THWACKED thumped; belaboured
THWARTED frustrated; balked
THWARTER obstructionist
ch **THYROXIN** hormone; iodine containing amino acid
THYRSOID (Bacchus's ivied staff)
md **TIBIALIS** tibial muscle
TICK-BEAN horse bean
TICKETED labelled
TICKLING titillation of the body
TICKLISH sensitive to such touch; critical
bt **TICK-SEED** coreopsis
TICK-SHOP (goods on credit)
TICK-TACK signalling system (racing)
TICK-TICK TICK-TOCK, watch or clock

nt **TIDEGATE** TIDE-LOCK, dock
TIDELESS not rising/falling
TIDEMARK low or high water border
TIDEMILL sea-operated mill
TIDESMAN customs officer
TIDE-WAVE tidal wave
TIDINESS neatness; trimness
ga **TIE-BREAK** extra play for winning
points; (sports finals, matches)
TIED-DOWN involved; restricted;
busy
bt **TIGELLUM** first bud on a stem
bt **TIGELLUS** an internode
zo **TIGER-CAT** margay; ocelot
TIGERISH ferocious
TIGERISM voracity
TIGHT-WAD a miser
TILE-KILN tile factory
TILLABLE arable; cultivable
TILLERED produced offshoots
nt **TILT-BOAT** boat with roof; covered
excursion boat, Thames
TILT-YARD jousting place
TIMBERED wooded
TIME-BALL time signal
TIME-BILL timetable
TIME-BOMB explodes by time-fuse
TIME-BOOK works record
TIME-CARD a register
TIME-FUSE time-fuze
TIMELESS untimely
TIME-WORK rate of pay
TIMEWORN decayed; weatherbeaten
TIMIDITY fearfulness; shyness
nt **TIMONEER** helmsman
TIMONIST misanthrope
mu **TIMOROSO** hesitatingly; timidly
TIMOROUS fearful; pusillanimous
md **TINCTURE** tinge; solution
bt **TINE-TARE** the vetch
TINEWALD TYNEWALD, Manx
Parliament
TINGEING colouring
TINGLING thrilling
TINGLISH sensation
hr **TING-TANG** two-note clock
TINKERED botched
TINKERLY clumsily
TINKLING clinking
md **TINNITUS** ringing in the ears
TINPLATE covered in tin
TINSELLY tawdry
TINSMITH tin worker
mn **TINSTONE** cassiterite
mn **TINSTUFF** tin ore
TINTAMAR confused noise
TINTLESS colourless
pr **TIPPED-IN** inserted by use of gum

TIPPLING drinking to excess; toping;
soaking
lw **TIPSTAFF** court officer
zo **TIPULARY** (crane-flies)
TIRELESS inexhaustible
TIRESOME tedious; fretful
TIRONIAN (Roman shorthand)
TISSUING interweaving soft material
(paper)
TITANESS giantess
ch **TITANIAN** (titanium)
mn **TITANITE** sphene
rl **TITHABLE** subject to tithes
TITHONIC actinic
TITIVATE smarten oneself up to
impress
pr **TITLE-CUT** title-page woodcut
decoration
zo **TITMOUSE** a small bird
ch **TITRATED** solution added from
burette
ga **TIT-TAT-TO** a game; criss-cross
TITTERED giggled
zo **TITTEREL** whimbrel; curlew
TITTERER sniggerer
TITTUPPY frisky; lively
TITUBANT stumbling
TITUBATE stagger
TITULARY nominal; titular
TIVERING marking sheep
ga **TLACHTLI** Mexican court game like
baseball
zo **TOAD-FISH** the sapo
bt **TOAD-FLAX** snapdragon
bt **TOAD-PIPE** a horsetail
TOAD-SPIT cuckoo-spit
TOADYING fawning
TOADYISH sycophantic
TOADYISM obsequiousness
TOBOGGAN (toboggin; taboggin) long
light sled for snow transport
md **TOCOLOGY** obstetrics
TODDLING strolling aimlessly
TOGETHER in unison
TOHU-BOHU desolation; confusion;
chaos; (Heb.)
TOILETTE ceremonial wear (Fr.)
TOILLESS workless
TOILSOME arduous; laborious
TOILWORN fatigued; tired; weary
md **TOKOLOGY** tocology
bt **TOKONOMA** flower alcove in a house
(Jap.)
TOLBOOTH a toll-booth
TOLERANT forbearing; liberal
TOLERATE suffer; brook
TOLEWARE japanning on tinplate
(Amer.)

me **TOLL-DISH** (used in mills)
TOLLETAN of Toledo wares (swords) (steel)
TOLL-GATE high-road entry fees office
TOLTECAN early Mexican
TOMAHAWK war hatchet (of N. Am. Indians)
zo **TOMALLEY** lobster-liver
bt **TOMATOES** love apples
TOMBLESS no tomb
md **TOMENTUM** a downy covering
to **TOMMY-BAR** small lever
TOMMY-GUN a handy weapon
TOMMY-ROT balderdash; nonsense
zo **TOM-NODDY** puffin; a dolt
md **TOMOGRAM** X-ray photograph
TOMORROW the following day
TOMUNDAR Baluchi chief
mn **TONALITE** ingeous rock
mu **TONALITY** pitch
TONE-DEAF unmusical
TONELESS unmusical
nt **TONGKANG** ketch; lighter; (Singapore)
TONGUING barking; licking
md **TONICITY** healthiness; possessing tone
mu **TONOTOPY** concerning pitch of a tone
md **TONSILAR** (tonsils)
rl **TONSURED** clerical; shaven
bt **TOONWOOD** Indian red wood
TOOTHFUL a short drink
ar **TOOTHING** decorative indenting of bricks
md **TOOTH-KEY** forceps
mu **TOOTLING** playing the flute
TOPARCHY small state control
TOPAZINE (topaz)
TOP-BOOTS longish boots
ag **TOP-DRESS** to manure
TOP-HEAVY tipsy; ill-proportioned
TOP-LEVEL TOPNOTCH, excellent
TOP-LOFTY bombastic
ma, pc **TOPOLOGY** of distorted space; a child's outlook
TOPOLOGY an aid to memory
TOPONOMY TOPONYMY, topical terminology
zo **TOPOTYPE** specimen from original locality
TOPPLING falling
TOP-PROUD very proud
zo **TOP-SHELL** a mollusc
nt **TOPSIDES** above waterline; upper works of ship
TOP-STONE a finial

TORCHERE ornamental lampstand
TORCHING night fishing
md **TORCULAR** a tourniquet
TOREADOR bullfighter
TOREUTES an artist in metal
TOREUTIC chased metalwork
md **TERMINAL** colicky
mt **TORNADIC** (tornadoes); very stormy
zo **TORNARIA** larval form of balanoglossida
nt **TOROIDAL** like an anchor-ring
TOROSITY muscularity
zo **TOR-OUZEL** the ring-ousel
TORPIDLY apathetically; dully
TORQUATE collared
TORSHENT youngest child (USA)
ck **TORTILLA** maize cake; omelette (Sp.)
lw **TORTIOUS** injurious
zo **TORTOISE** terrapin
TORTUOSE TORTUOUS, twisted; winding; wreathed; deceitful
TORTURED agonized; racked
TORTURER tormentor
TORULOID TORULOSE, somewhat cylindrical
TOTALITY full amount; sum
ma **TOTALIZE** to tote; to add up
rl **TOTEMISM** of creatures depicting family or clan
TOTITIVE (no common factor)
TOTTERED reeled; staggered
TOUCHILY peevishly; petulantly
TOUCHING concerning; pathetic
TOUCHPAN priming pan
TOUGHEST most stubborn
TOUGHISH stiffish; leathery
TOURELLE slender tower
TOURNURE turn; contour; curver
TOUSLING ruffing; rumpling
TOWARDLY toward; docile; tractile
TOWERING soaring; mounting
TOWN-HALL council offices
TOWNLAND a township
TOWNLESS without a town
TOWNSHIP a municipality
TOWNSMAN urbanite
TOWN-TALK local gossip
md **TOXAEMIA** blood-poisoning
TOXICANT poisonous
TOXICITY poisonousness
TOYISHLY playfully
pl **TRACHEAL TRACHEAN,** (windpipe)
md **TRACHOMA** eye disease
mn **TRACHYTE** volcanic rock
TRACKAGE towing; traction
ce **TRACKING** spooring; trailing; liner of surface ways; horizontal progress during free fall (parachuting)

TRACKMAN (railroad track)
TRACKWAY path or open road
TRACTATE a treatise; a tract
TRACTILE ductile; tractable
TRACTION attraction; towage; hauling
TRACTIVE pulling
TRACTORY drawing; pulling
TRACTRIX geometrical curve
TRADEFUL commercial
TRADITOR traitor; quisling; renegade
TRADUCED defamed; slandered
TRADUCER calumniator; libeller
TRAGICAL calamitous; disastrous
zo TRAGOPAN Chinese pheasant
TRAGSITZ suspended alpine rescue stretcher (Ger.)
TRAILING hauling; dragging
TRAIL-NET a trawl
TRAINING drilling; schooling
rw TRAIN-OIL railway lubricant
TRAIPSED trudged to little purpose
TRAKENER cross country obstacle (steeple-chasing)
TRAMPING trudging; hiking
TRAMPLED trod under foot
TRAMPLER grape-treader
rw TRAMROAD tramway
pc TRANCING of semi-conscious; visions; ecstasy
TRANGRAM trinket; souvenir; knick-knack
TRANQUIL placid; calm; serene
TRANSACT negotiate; conduct; enact
bt TRANSECT belt of vegetation for study
ar,rl TRANSEPT cross-aisle; (church)
TRANSFER make over; exchange; send; move across
cp TRANSFER convey; copy; control; data; peripheral
TRANSFIX penetrate; perforate; impale
TRANSHIP change conveyance
TRANSIRE customs pass
TRANSMIT despatch; forward; remit; broadcast
cp TRANSMIT send data, information to other location
TRANSOME TRANSOM, cross beam; fanlight
TRANSUDE to sweat
tc TRANSVAR power-transfer coupler
ga TRAP-BALL an old game
TRAP-DOOR door in the floor
TRAPESED traipsed; tramped
TRAPEZIA trapeziums
TRAP-FALL a trap

mn TRAPPEAN (traprock)
TRAPPING snaring
rl TRAPPIST Cistercian monk
mn TRAPPOUS like traprock
gl TRAP-TUFA TRAP-TUFF, igneous rock
TRASHERY rubbish; balderdash
TRASHILY in a rubbishy way
zo TRASLING freshwater perch
mu TRAVERSA TRAVERSO, transverse flute (It.)
TRAVERSE crossing or lateral movement; grid survey
TRAVERSE sideways or diagonal climb (mountaineering)
TRAVESTY a burlesque; parody; (of sex)
TRAWLING fishing towing a submerged net
ga TRAY-TRIP a draughts game
TREACLED (moth catching)
TREADING trampling; pacing; stepping
TREADLED TREADLER, pedalled; bicyclist
TREASURE preserve; hoard; garner
TREASURY money/gold office; repository
TREATING entertaining; dealing
TREATISE written discourse; essay
TREBLING doing 3-fold
TRECENTO 14th-century Italian art
TREE-CALF leather binding
zo TREE-CRAB (lives on coconuts)
zo TREE-DOVE Indian pigeon
bt TREE-FERN tropical fern
zo TREE-FROG many species
TREELESS lacking forest cover
TREE-NAIL long wooden pin
TREKKING migrating; hiking
mu TREMANDO tremulously
zo TREMATIC of gill-clefts
TREMBLED quivered; shook; quaked
TREMBLER vibrator; oscillator
bt TREMLELA jelly-like fungi
TRENCHED encroached; furrowed
TRENCHER wooden platter
TRENDING inclining; tending
md TREPHINE cutting tool
bl TREPHONE cell-breakdown substance
cy TREPTION environment-change response
TRESPASS sin; walk on others' land
TRESPOLO spindly three-legged table (It.)
hd TRESSURE heraldic border
tx TREVETTE loop-pile wire knife
TREWSMAN (wearing trews)
TRIADIST composer of triads

TRIALISM (body, soul and spirit)
TRIALITY threeness
ma, mu TRIANGLE flogging frame; three-sided figure; metal percussion
ar, rl TRIAPSAL church with three apses
TRIARCHY rule of three
TRIARIAN of the third rank
gl, mn TRIASSIC geological formation; era
cy TRIASTER mitotic figure
TRIAXIAL having three axes
ch TRIAZOLE heterocyclic compound
ch TRIBASIC with three hydrogen atoms
TRIBELET a small tribe
zo TRIBONYX genus of water-hens
TRIBRACH three short syllables
TRIBUNAL court of justice
TRIBUTED contributed
TRIBUTER piece-work miner
md TRICHINA parasitic worm
mn TRICHITE hairlike fibre
zo TRICHODA hairy infusoria
zo TRICHOID hairlike
md TRICHOMA hair disease
bt TRICHOME hairy outgrowth
mu TRICHORD three-stringed lyre
TRICKERY chicanery; deception
TRICKILY artfully; cunningly
TRICKING duping; gulling
TRICKLED oozed; percolated
TRICKLET small rill
TRICKSEY wily; pretty
TRICOLOUR flag of France
TRICORNE three-cornered hat
ga TRICTRAC variety of backgammon
TRICYCLE three-wheeled bicycle
zo TRIDACNA genus of molluscs
TRIFLING toying; trivial; paltry
TRIGAMMA wing-vein feature in lepidoptera
gn TRIGENIC controlled by three genes
TRIGGING stopping; skidding
zo TRIGLOID gurnard genus
TRIGLYPH Doric ornamentation
TRIGNESS trimness; neatness
ma TRIGONAL TRIGONIC, triangular
ma TRIGONON a triangle
TRIGRAPH a triphthong
TRILEMMA (three alternatives)
mu TRILLING quavering; warbling
TRILLION million³ (GB) million² (USA)
bt TRILLIUM a lily genus
bt TRILOBED trilobate
nt TRIMARAN racing yacht between two outriggers
ch TRIMERIC of 3 times molecular weight

TRIMETER (versification)
ce TRIMMERS rib holes for structure
ck TRIMMING decorating; adjusting; extra delicacies; (barber)
TRIMNESS neatness; tidiness
TRIMURTI Hindu Trinity
zo TRINGINE TRINGOID, of sandpipers
TRINODAL treble-jointed
TRINQUET small covered court (pelota)
rl TRIODION Greek prayer-book
TRIOLEIN fatty oil
TRIP-BOOK (fishing records)
TRIPEMAN tripeseller
mn TRIPHANE spodumene
TRIPLANE an aeroplane
TRIPLING trebling
mn TRIPLITE a phosphate
cy TRIPLOID with triple chromosomes
TRIPODAL tripedal; three-footed
hd TRIPPANT heraldic trotting
TRIPPING lapsing; dancing; felling
TRIP-SLIP tram ticket (USA)
TRIPTANE trimethyl butane
TRIPTOTE having 3 cases only
rl TRIPTYCH painted screen
nt TRIP-WIRE obstacle; brake
TRISEMIC iambic
TRISKELE swastika
cy TRISOMIC of 3-chromosome type
TRISTFUL sorrowful; dejected; doleful
TRITICAL trite; common; hackneyed
TRITICUM wheat, etc.
TRIUMVIR one of three (Rome)
TRIUNITY trinity
TRIVALVE with three valves
TROCHAIC of TROCHEE (verse), long and short syllables
zo TROCHITE sea-urchin's joint
md TROCHLEA a cartilage
TROCHOID cycloid
pc TROILISM sexhibitionism
mn TROILITE nonmagnetic iron sulphide
TROLLING singing; spinning; towing metal bait (angling)
TROLLOPY slatternly
TROMBLON fire-arm support
mu TROMBONE a brass musical wind instrument with slide valve
zo TROOPIAL American starling
TROOPING collecting; parading
md TROPHESY indigestion
TROPHIES emblems of victory
TROPICAL figurative; fervid
ga TROTTING of horse- and sulky-racing
TROTTOIR side-walk (Fr.)
TROUBLED incommoded; vexed

TROUBLER disturber; pest
TROUNCED thrashed; castigated
zo **TROUPIAL** American song-bird
TROUSERS TROWSERS, hose; legwear
TROUTING fishing for trout
zo **TROUTLET** small trout
TROUVERE French lyric poet
TRUANTLY lazily; evasively
TRUCKAGE cost of conveyance
TRUCKING bartering; hawking;
  haulage
TRUCKLED cringed; yielded; stooped
TRUCKLER servile agent
TRUDGEON a swimming stroke
TRUDGING foot-slogging
TRUE-BLUE conservative partisan
TRUE-BORN TRUE-BRED, legitimate
bt **TRUE-LOVE** sweetheart; a herb
TRUENESS honesty; accuracy;
  veracity
TRUMPERY rubbish; trash; trifling
ga **TRUMPING** ruffing; (cards) bridge
bt **TRUNCATE** lop; shorten; reduce;
  prune
cp **TRUNCATE** suppress insignificant
  digits
TRUNDLED rolled; bowled; revolved
TRUNDLER barrow-mover; slow
  bowler
TRUNKFUL enough to fill a trunk
TRUNNION gun support
TRUSSING binding; fastening
TRUSTFUL confiding; trusty
TRUSTILY faithfully; staunchly
TRUSTING relying on; believing
md **TRYPTONE** pancreatic ferment
TRYSTING rendezvousing; meeting
TUBE-FORM tubular
md **TUBERCLE** tumour
bt **TUBEROSE** Mexican lily
bt **TUBEROUS** potato-like growth
TUBE-WELL artesian well
zo **TUBICOLE** caddis-worm
TUBIFORM tubular
zo **TUBIPORE** a coral
pp **TUB-SIZED** dipped and strengthened
  (handmade paper)
TUBULATE formed of tubes
TUB-WHEEL flat water-wheel
bt **TUCKAHOE** edible fungus
TUCKSHOP sweet-shop
zo **TUCOTUCO** small rodent
TUG-OF-WAR rope sport
ae **TUG-PLANE** gliders
zo **TUKUTUKU** tucotuco; rodent (SA)
TULA-WORK niello work
TUMBLING falling; tripping
TUMEFIED swollen; distended

TUMIDITY bombast; pomposity
TUMOURED distended; enlarged
TUMP-LINE carrying strap
TUMULATE make a barrow
TUMULOSE tumulous; many mounds
TUN-BELLY pot-belly
TUNELESS unharmonious; unmusical
ch **TUNGSTEN** same as wolfram
ch **TUNGSTIC** (tungsten)
zo **TUNICARY** ascidian; sea-squirt
zo **TUNICATE** coated; a mollusc
ro **TUNING-IN** adjusting to listen
TUNISIAN (Tunis)
TURANIAN family of languages
ch **TURANOSE** disaccharide
TURBANED wearing a turban
TURBIDLY disorderly; opaquely
md **TURBINAL** scroll-like bone
ae **TURBO-JET** gas engine
TURCOMAN TURKOMAN, Turk of Asia
TURF-CLAD grassy
TURF-MOSS boggy land
TURGIDLY in grossly swollen style
TURLOUGH shallow pool (Irish)
bt, ck **TURMERIC** yellow dye; hot spice;
  ingredient of curry
zo **TURNAGRA** thrush (NZ)
TURNCOAT renegade
TURNCOCK water-man
TURNDOWN fold down; reject
nt **TURNMARK** logline mark
ck **TURNOVER** a pasty; volume of sales;
  deliver; transfer
TURNOVER (leaf); generation and
  loss of cells; running with ball
  (basketball)
TURNPIKE toll-gate; a road
TURN-SICK giddy
TURN-SKIN a werewolf
bt **TURNSOLE** sunflower
TURNSPIT kitchen-boy
TURRETED having little towers
TUSSOCKY tufty
TUTELAGE guardianship; charge; care
TUTELARY protective
TUTORAGE instruction
TUTORESS governess
TUTORIAL educational
TUTORING teaching
TUTORISM education; coaching
TWADDLED gabbled
TWADDLER tattler; chatter-box
TWEAKING twisting
TWEEDLED fiddled
TWEELING twilling
to **TWEEZERS** forceps
pr **TWELVEMO** 4 times folded for 12
  leaves

pr **TWENTYMO** paper folded into 20 leaves
TWIDDLED twisted
TWIDDLER thumb-twirler
TWIGGING understanding
TWILIGHT dusk
TWILLING weaving
pr **TWINBATH** 2-solution processing method
TWIN-BORN contemporaneous
TWINGING twitching
TWINKLED sparkled
TWINKLER a star
zo **TWINLING** twin lamb
tc **TWINPLEX** radio-telegraph system
pr **TWINWARE** paper-holding system for offset
TWIRLING revolving; whirling
TWISTING writhing; contorting
TWITCHED jerked; snatched
TWITCHER angle trowel; involuntary jerker
TWITTING upbraiding; taunting
TWO-EDGED double-cutting
TWO-FACED false; double-dealing
TWO-LAYER twin-ply paper/board
TWOPENNY cheap; worthless
el **TWO-PHASE** with 2 equal alternating voltages
TWO-PIECE costume; suit
TYCHONIC astronomic; (Tycho Brahe)
pl **TYMPANIC** like a drum; middle ear bone
md **TYMPANUM** eardrum
TYNEWALD Manx Parliament
TYPE-CAST single-character actor
TYPE-HIGH standard height
zo **TYPHLOPS** earthworms, etc.
mt **TYPHONIC** cyclonic
TYPIFIED exemplified; symbolized
TYPIFIER prototype
mn **TYPOLITE** fossil footstep
TYPOLOGY types and their classification
TYPORAMA facsimile
ch **TYRAMINE** amino-ethyl benzene
TYROCINY pupilage
TYROLEAN TYROLESE, of Tyrol (the Alps)
mn **TYROLITE** Tyrol sandstone
TYRONISM apprenticeship
ch **TYROSINE** precursor of amino acid
TYRRANIC despotic; autocratic
TYRTAEAN (warlike verse)
TZAREVNA TZARITSA, TSARINA, Empress of Russia

U

UBIQUITY omnipresence
UDOMETER rain gauge
UGLIFIED made hideous
UGLINESS repulsiveness; unsightliness
mn **UINTAITE** variety of natural asphalt
md **ULCERATE** cause or form an ulcer
ULTERIOR remote; hidden; indirect
ULTIMATE furthest; final; eventual
ULTIMITY last consequence
ULTRAISM extreme views
ULTRAIST extremist
ULULATED howled; yowled; lamented
bt **UMBELLAR** form of inflorescence
UMBONATE having a boss
UMBRATIC shadowy; shady; obscure
UMBRELLA a gamp; collapsible shade
zo **UMBRETTE** African heron
UMBRIERE vizor of helmet
UMPIRAGE arbitration; adjudication
UNABASED not degraded; unashamed
UNABATED undiminished; persistent
UNADORED unloved; unvenerated
UNAFRAID bold; valiant; undaunted
UNAIMING purposeless; random
UNALLIED alone; separate; isolated
UNAMAZED composed; unruffled
UNAMUSED not entertained; bored
UNARGUED not disputed
UNATONED not expiated
UNAVOWED unconfessed; secret
UNAWARES suddenly; unexpectedly
UNBACKED unaided; unassisted
UNBAGGED trouserless; let loose
UNBANDED disbanded; disembodied
UNBANNED permitted; unrestricted
UNBARBED unshaven; pointless
UNBARKED stripped of bark
UNBARRED unfastened; opened
UNBATHED untubbed
UNBEATEN untrodden; undefeated
UNBEDDED uprooted
UNBELIEF incredulity; scepticism
UNBENIGN malignant; malevolent
UNBEREFT not bereaved; unspoiled
UNBIASED impartial; unprejudiced
UNBIDDEN spontaneous; unsolicited
rl **UNBISHOP** deprive of a bishopric
UNBLAMED uncensured; unrebuked
UNBLOODY not cruel
UNBOILED raw
UNBOLTED unfastened; unbarred
UNBOUGHT not bribed; incorrupt
UNBOYISH sedate; unchildish

UNBRACED relaxed; unsupported
UNBREECH debag
UNBREWED pure; genuine
UNBRIBED not corrupt
UNBRIDLE free from restraint
UNBROKEN inviolate; continuous
UNBUCKLE unfasten; unclasp
UNBUNDLE unpack
UNBURDEN disclose; reveal
UNBURIED uninterred
UNBURNED uncharred
UNBURROW to ferret out
UNBUSIED free at that moment; unhurried
UNBUTTON unfasten a jacket etc.
UNCAGING releasing; liberating
UNCALLED not awakened
UNCAPPED his cap doffed
UNCARTED unloaded
UNCAUGHT still free
UNCHASTE impure; lewd
UNCHEERY dull; gloomy
UNCHEWED not masticated
UNCHIDED unrebuked
rl **UNCHURCH** excommunicate
UNCIATIM ounce by ounce
UNCIFORM hook-shaped
zo **UNCINATA** marine worms
UNCINATE hooked
UNCLENCH UNCLINCH, open the hand
nt **UNCLEWED** unwound
UNCLOSED open; ajar
UNCLOTHE undress
UNCLUTCH let go of something held
UNCLUTCH release the clutch of a car
UNCOILED unwound
UNCOMBED unkempt
UNCOMELY lacking grace
UNCOMMON odd; rare; strange
UNCOOPED set free
UNCORDED unbound
UNCORKED ready to pour
rw, el **UNCOUPLE** disconnect
rl **UNCOWLED** unveiled; dismonked
UNCTUOUS greasy; oily; fulsome
UNCULLED unpicked
UNCURBED licentious; loose; unbridled; unchecked
UNCURLED straightened
UNCURSED not execrated
UNDAMPED not put out, of fires
UNDASHED undaunted; undismayed
UNDEFIED unchallenged
UNDEFINE make indefinite
UNDENTED smooth
UNDERACT perform inadequately
lw **UNDER-AGE** not adult; immature

UNDERARM (bowling); underside of arm
UNDERBID offer less
UNDERBUY haggle the price downward
UNDERCUT tenderloin; buy below price
UNDERDID economized effort; below standard
UNDERDOG lower-class individual
UNDERFED starved of nourishment
UNDERLAP extend below
UNDERLAY foundation
lw **UNDERLET** sublet
UNDERLIE below the surface
nt **UNDERMAN** operate with insufficient crew
UNDERPAY remunerate inadequately
UNDERPIN support
UNDERSAY minimize essentials in report
UNDERTOW tidal current below surface
UNDEVOUT behaving irreligiously
UNDIMMED untarnished
pc **UNDINISM** urophilia; erotic effect of urine
UNDINTED undismayed by difficulties
UNDIPPED unbaptized; sheep uncleansed
UNDOCKED dogs, horses retaining their tails
nt **UNDOCKED** ships waiting to enter harbour
UNDULANT wavy, of the sea
UNDULATE UNDULOUS, of wavy movement; vibrate
UNEARNED free; gain without work
UNEASILY anxiously; nervously
UNELATED modestly content
UNENDING everlasting; ceaseless
UNENVIED viewed with complacency
UNERRING certain; sure; exact
UNESPIED not observed
UNEVENLY ruggedly; unequally
lw **UNEXEMPT** liable
UNEXPERT unskilled
UNFABLED of real true-life events
UNFADING everlasting; constant
UNFAIRLY dishonestly; falsely
UNFASTEN open; let loose
UNFAULTY free from blemish
UNFEARED not held in awe
UNFELLOW expel from a society
UNFENCED not enclosed; open
UNFETTER unchain; unshackle
UNFILIAL undutiful

UNFILLED empty
UNFILMED not photographed
UNFLOWER deflower (of virginity)
UNFLUENT tongue-tied
UNFOILED not baffled
UNFOLDED deployed; disclosed; unwrapped
UNFORCED freely agreed to; natural
UNFORGED not counterfeited
UNFORMED shapeless; not yet composed
UNFOUGHT uncontested
UNFOULED clean; unsullied
UNFRAMED of pictures; not 'set-up' by police, gangsters
UNFROZEN uncongealed
UNFRUGAL prodigal; lavish; wasteful
UNFUELED unfuelled
UNFUNDED floating; unmonied
UNFURLED displayed
UNGAINLY uncouth; clumsy
UNGEARED unharnessed; without gear system
UNGENTLE rude; rough
UNGIFTED without talent
UNGILDED plain
UNGILLED (free fish from net)
UNGIRDED beltless; unenclosed
UNGIVING rigid
UNGLAZED paneless; without window glass
UNGLOVED barehanded
UNGOWNED unrobed
UNGRACED awkward
UNGROUND not milled
zo **UNGUICAL** (snail, claw, hoof)
UNGUIDED unregulated
UNGUILTY innocent; unproven
zo **UNGULATA** hoofed mammals
zo **UNGULATE** having hoofs
UNGUMMED unstuck; not sealed
UNHACKED not notched
UNHANDED let go; released
UNHANGED not dependent; not executed
UNHARMED scatheless; immune
UNHASPED unlatched
UNHEATED cold; without heating
UNHEDGED hedgeless; without a border
UNHEEDED disregarded
UNHELPED unassisted
UNHEROIC timid; shrinking
UNHINGED unsettled
UNHIVING unhousing
UNHOODED bareheaded; (exposed)
UNHOOKED unfastened
UNHOOPED (casks and barrels)

UNHORNED uncuckolded
UNHORSED dismounted
UNIAURAL monaural; single ear
UNIAXIAL having a single axis
ch **UNIBASAL** having a single base
UNICYCLE acrobat's cycle
UNIFYING uniting; merging
bt **UNILOBAR UNILOBED**, having one lobe
UNIMBUED not saturated
UNIMODAL only one mode; single 'peak' effect
UNINURED not hardened
UNIONISM combination; alliance
UNIONIST confederate; conservative; (Ulster)
mn **UNIONITE** lime silicate
zo **UNIPOLAR** of one-process nerve cells
UNIQUELY peculiarly; exceptionally
UNIQUITY singularity
mu **UNISONAL** harmonious
UNITEDLY jointly; concertedly
UNITIZED treated as a unit
zo **UNIVALVE** a mollusc
UNIVERSE the world
UNIVOCAL unanimous
rw **UNJOINED** uncoupled; separated
UNJOYFUL dull; mirthless; downcast
UNJOYOUS gloomy; melancholy; glum
UNJUDGED awaiting verdict
UNJUSTLY prejudicially; unfairly
UNKINDLY unfriendly; harshly
UNLACING unloosing
UNLADING unloading
UNLAVISH sparse; frugal
UNLAWFUL illegal; illicit
UNLEARNT forgotten
UNLIKELY improbable; risky
UNLIMBER get into action
UNLINEAL not in succession
UNLOADED discharged
UNLOCKED open
UNLOOKED unheeded
UNLOOSED slackened
UNLOOSEN set free
UNLORDED not raised to peerage
UNLORDLY undignified
UNLOVING passionless
UNMANNED in absence of crew
UNMAPPED uncharted
UNMARKED unobserved
UNMARRED unsullied
UNMASKED exposed; unveiled
UNMELTED undissolved
UNMILKED fat-uddered
UNMILLED unground
UNMISSED good riddance

UNMOANED not lamented
UNMODISH out of fashion
UNMOVING motionless; impassive
UNMUDDLE coordinate
UNNEEDED superfluous
UNNERVED frightened
UNOPENED closed
UNPACKED taken out of wrappings
UNPACKER parcels, freight worker
UNPAIRED singly
UNPATHED trackless
UNPAWNED not pledged
UNPEELED with skin intact
UNPEGGED not stabilized
UNPENNED released
UNPICKED not selected
UNPLACED not in the first three
UNPOETIC prosaic
UNPOISED out of balance
UNPOSTED not advertised widely
UNPRICED without price-tag;
  unvalued
UNPRIEST de-frock (unfrock)
lw **UNPROVED** untested in law court
UNREAPED not harvested
UNREASON lack of sense
UNREELED unwound
UNREINED unbridled
UNREPAID not requited
UNRIDDLE solve; unravel; decipher
nt **UNRIGGED** dismantled; of sailing
  vessel
UNROLLED spread out
UNRUFFLE fail to disturb
UNSADDLE remove saddle from
UNSALTED without salt preservative
rl **UNSAYING** recanting
UNSEALED not yet closed; still open
UNSEATED unhorsed; fell off;
  expelled
UNSEEDED not sown; unselected
  (tennis)
UNSEEING blind
UNSEEMLY unbecoming
UNSETTLE unhinge; disturb
UNSEXUAL without sexual
  implications
UNSHADED exposed
UNSHAKEN unworried; undisturbed;
  firm
UNSHARED undivided
UNSHAVED not yet shaved
UNSHAVEN uncouth; of vagabond
UNSHELVE to act at once
UNSHROUD to unveil; to make public
UNSHRUNK unwashed as yet
UNSIFTED not yet sorted out
UNSINGED of the hair, unscorched

UNSLAKED unquenched (of lime)
ck **UNSMOKED** untreated; uncured
UNSMOKED cigar, cigarette
  unfinished
UNSMOOTH rough
UNSOAPED unwashed
pc **UNSOCIAL** shy; hermit-like; reserved
el **UNSOCKET** disconnect
UNSOILED still clean
UNSOLVED of enigma (puzzle) so far
UNSORTED not yet sorted
UNSOUGHT not looked for
UNSPIKED with barbs removed
UNSPOILT natural
UNSPOKEN agreed, but not
  mentioned
UNSPRUNG ready-set trap
UNSTABLE inconstant existence
UNSTATED not mentioned
UNSTAYED unrestrained
UNSTEADY vacillating
UNSTITCH unsew
UNSTORED not warehoused
UNSTRUNG remove strings
UNSTRUNG loosened; relaxed
UNSUCKED full, erect
UNSUITED unbecoming
UNSURELY of uncertainty
UNSWATHE unwrap (a small baby)
UNSWAYED unaffected by argument
UNTANGLE unravel confusion
UNTANNED not sunburnt (pale)
UNTAPPED problem not answered;
  discussed
UNTAPPED room free from listening
  microphone
ck **UNTASTED** new wine, cheese etc.
UNTAUGHT uninstructed; illiterate
UNTENDED neglected
UNTENDER of harsh manner
UNTESTED unproved
UNTETHER release; untie a knot
UNTHAWED still frozen
UNTHORNY smooth
UNTHREAD disentangle
UNTHRONE oust from royal rule
ga **UNTHROWN** still on horseback
  (rodeo)
UNTIDILY disorderly
UNTILLED left land fallow
UNTIMELY premature
lw **UNTINGED** uncoloured; innocent
UNTIRING unwearied
rl **UNTITHED** 10% tax not paid
UNTONGUE to extract the tongue;
  torture
UNTOWARD rude perverseness
UNTRACED no records found

UNTRUCED without truce
UNTRUSTY unfaithful
UNTUCKED half undressed
UNTUFTED hairless
UNTURFED expelled from horse racing
UNTURNED left untouched
UNTWINED not twisted together (rope)
UNVALUED worth uncalculated
UNVARIED monotonous
UNVEILED made open; disclosed
UNVEILER revealer
UNVENTED unuttered; unreleased
UNVERSED unskilled
UNVIZARD unhelm
UNVOICED not spoken; mute
UNWAITED unattended
UNWALLED not enclosed
UNWARILY rash; reckless
UNWARMED unheated
UNWARNED unadmonished
nt **UNWARPED** flat; original dry wood
UNWASHED dirty
UNWASTED made use of
UNWEANED suckling child
UNWEDDED unwed
UNWEEDED overgrown
UNWIELDY ponderous
UNWILFUL weakminded; docile
UNWILLED involuntary
UNWISDOM folly; fatuity
UNWISELY irrationally
UNWONTED unusual
UNWOODED treeless
UNWORDED silent
UNWORMED with worms removed
UNWORTHY undeserving
UNYOKING unharnessing; freeing
UPCAUGHT caught up
UPCOMING impending; ascending
UPHEAVAL earthquake; extreme change
UPHOLDER supporter
UPLIFTED elevated; exalted
UPPERCUT boxing blow
UPPER-TEN the aristocracy
UPRAISED lifted
UPRIDGED in ridges
UPRISING insurrection
UPROOTED eradicated
UPSTAIRS among the gentry
lw **UPSTAYED** upheld
UPSTREAM against the current
UPSTROKE alternates with downstroke
UPTHRUST upheaval
UPTOSSED upchucked

UPTURNED inverted
UPWAFTED borne aloft
UPWARDLY in ascending direction
mn **URALITIC** (uralite)
URBANISM changing to big-city styles
URBANITY suaveness; courteousness
URBANIZE make urban
bt **URCEOLUS** floral envelope
ch **URETHANE** ethyl carbamate
URGENTLY momentously; pressingly
UROBILIN bile/urine pigment
zo **UROCHORD** (sea-squirt)
zo **UROCHROA** humming-birds
zo **UROCISSA** Asiatic magpie
zo **URODAEUM** urinary duct in cloaca
zo **UROESTON** a tail bone
zo **UROMERIC** (tail-piece)
md **UROSCOPY** urine examination
zo **UROSTEGE** a snake's scale
zo **UROSTYLE** lengthy tail
zo **URSIFORM** like a bear
rl **URSULINE** a nun (St Ursula)
zo **URTICANT** irritating; stinging
URTICATE to sting; cause a rash
USEFULLY advantageously
USHERDOM schoolmastery
USHERING heralding; introducing
bt **USTILAGO** genus of fungi
USTULATE scorched
lw **USUFRUCT** temporary possession
USURIOUS at high interest
USURPING arrogating; assuming
UTILIZED employed; used
UTOPIAST (Utopia)
UTRIFORM bottle-shaped
UTTEREST furthest; remotest
UTTERING disclosing; issuing
UXORIOUS wife-loving

V

VACATING quitting; annulling
VACATION intermission; recess; holiday
md **VACCINAL** pertaining to vaccine
md **VACCINIA** cow-pox
VAGABOND VAGRANT, tramp; thief
rl **VAGANTES** itinerant clerics
VAGARIES whims; caprices; crotchets
ec **VAGILITY** power of movement
bt,pl **VAGINANT** VAGINATE, sheathing
bt **VAGINULA** sheath of seta in bryophyta
md **VAGOTOMY** division of vagus nerves
VAGRANCY itinerance of the homeless

VAINNESS vanity; conceit; inanity
VALENCED decorated; draped
tx **VALENTIA** woven material
bt **VALERIAN** all-heal; medicinal plant
VALETING personal attendance
rl **VALHALLA** palace of Norse gods
VALIANCE bravery; intrepidity
VALIANCY courageousness; chivalry
VALIDATE confirm; legalize
VALIDITY soundness; justness;
aptness within limits
rl **VALKYRIE** Norse warrior angels
VALLANCY large wig
VALLATED cup-shaped;
circumvallated
VALORIZE make a currency reform
VALOROUS intrepid; bold; heroic
VALUABLE precious; costly;
expensive
VALUATOR appraiser; assessor
VALVELET small valve
VALVULAR containing valves
VAMBRACE arm-armour
VAMOOSED decamped; skedaddled
VAMPIRIC extortionate, of vampires
VAMPLATE hand-guard of lance
ch **VANADATE** vanadium salt
ch **VANADIUM** metallic element
ch **VANADOUS** of divalent vanadium
VANDALIC of Baltic raiders
VANDYKED indented; notched
VANGUARD forefront; front line
ck **VANILLIC** flavoured with vanilla
VANILLIN compound from vanilla
pods
VANISHED disappeared; dissolved
VANISHER absconder
VANQUISH overpower; rout; subdue
VAPIDITY insipidity
VAPORIZE turn into gas
VAPOROSE unsubstantial; gaseous
VAPOROUS unreal; steamy
VAPOURED evaporated; peevish
VAPOURER boaster; vaunter;
braggart
VAQUERIA cattle ranch
zo **VARANOID** lizardlike
mt **VARDARAC** mistral wind
(Macedonia)
cp **VARIABLE** mutable; fickle; mercurial;
(field)
VARIABLY changeably; fitfully
VARIANCE discord; strife; dispute
VARIANCE average of deviation
squares
VARIANCE discrepancy; deviant
human behaviour
VARIATED altered; variegated

VARIATIM variations; in different
ways
zo **VARICORN** a horned beetle
md **VARICOSE VARICOUS,** permanently
dilated (veins)
VARIETAL mutative; subgeneric
VARIFORM protean; diverse
md **VARIOLAR** pox-marked
VARIORUM commentated edition
el **VARISTOR** 2-electrode semi-
conductor
VARLETRY the rabble; the crowd
rl **VARTABED** Armenian priest
md **VASALIUM** vascular tissue
md **VASCULAR** vessels; ducts, etc.
bt **VASCULUM** specimen-box
mn **VASELINE** petroleum jelly
md **VASIFORM** like a duct
VASSALED enslaved
VASSALRY bondage; feudal system
VASTNESS immensity; spaciousness
mn **VATERITE** polymorph of calcium
carbonate
VATICIDE murder of a prophet
pp **VAT-SIZED** with sizing added to
pulp
ar, bd **VAULTAGE** arched work
ar, bd **VAULTING** leaping; bounding;
competition event (gymn.); cross-
arched ceiling
VAUNTERY boastfulness; arrogance
VAUNTFUL ostentatious; swaggering
VAUNTING bragging; crowing
VAUNTLAY a dog in challenging
mood
lw **VAVASORY** (land tenure)
VAVASOUR feudal tenant
md **VEALSKIN** a skin-disease
rl **VEDANTIC** (Hindu philosophy)
VEGETATE to sprout; (secluded life)
VEHEMENT impetuous; ardent
VEILLESS open to view; undisguised
bt **VEINLESS** lack of venation
VELARIUM awning; canopy
VELATION mystery; concealment
VELATURA picture glazing (It.)
VELLEITY volition; inclination
hd **VELLOPED** heraldic wattles
nt **VELOCERA** multi-rigged coaster (It.)
VELOCITY swiftness; rapidity; rate
el **VELODYNE** tachogenerator
ro **VELOGRID** a grid in a wireless valve
VELVERET ersatz velvet
VELVETED like velvet
VENALITY mercenariness;
corruptness
bt, zo **VENATION** veins as a whole
VENATION hunting; pursuit of game

VENDETTA a blood feud; vengeance
VENDIBLE marketable; disposable
VENDIBLY saleably
VENEERED overlaid; disguised
VENENATE poisonous; poisoned;
  toxic
VENERATE esteem; respect; revere
md **VENEREAL** venusian; sexual diseases
VENETIAN (Venice)
VENGEFUL vindictive; retributive
VENIABLE pardonable
VENIALLY excusably; trivially
md **VENOMING** poisoning (snake bite)
VENOMOUS venemous; poisonous
VENOSITY full-bloodedness
VENOUSLY veined
go,gl **VENT-HOLE** blowhole; spouter
md **VENTOUSE** vacuum-traction birth
VENT-PLUG barrel-peg
VENTURED hazarded; dared
VENTURER speculator; adventurer
VENUSIAN pertaining to Venus, love
  goddess
VERACITY truth; truthfulness
VERANDAH covered balcony
ch **VERATRIC** hellebore extract
bt **VERATRUM** hellebore, etc.
VERBALLY orally; by word of mouth
VERBATIM word for word
VERBIAGE verbosity; prolixity
VERDANCY greenness
VERDERER forest-keeper
VERDITER green pigment
VERGENCE turning the eye
VERGENCY border; verge
hd **VERGETTE** heraldic pallet
VERIFIED confirmed; authenticated
VERIFIER corroborator
VERJUICE sourjuice
VERMINLY verminously
VERMOUTH wine flavoured with
  wormwood
VERNICLE miraculous imprint
VERONESE (Verona)
bt **VERONICA** speedwell plants
md **VERRUGAS** Peruvian skin disease
VERSABLE reversible
VERSELET VERSICLE, brief ode
pl **VERTEBRA** segment of the spine
VERTICAL upright; erect;
  perpendicular
VERTICES summits; apices; zeniths
bt **VERTICIL** a whorl
VESICANT blistering
VESICATE to blister
md **VESICULA** a pustule
VESPIARY wasp's nest
VESTIARY a wardrobe

rl **VESTMENT** garment; robe; dress
VESTUARY vestiary
VESTURAL (robe; clothing)
rl **VESTURER** vestment keeper
VESUVIAN fusee; fuzee
VEXATION affliction; torment;
  worry
zo **VEXILLAR** feathery
VEXILLUM a banner; Roman
  standard
VEXINGLY provokingly; annoyingly
me **VIAMETER** an odometer
rl **VIATICUM** Eucharist
VIBRATED quivered; oscillated
VIBRATOR a trembler; buzzer
el **VIBRATOR** device for producing
  A/C
VIBRISSA whisker; bristle
bt **VIBROGEN** cellular tissue
el **VIBRONIC** electronic vibrations
bt **VIBURNUM** guelder-rose
rl **VICARAGE** vicar's house
VICARIAL substituted
VICARIAN deputy
rl **VICARIUS** a vicar
rl **VICE-DEAN** a canon
VICE-KING regent; viceroy
VICENARY based on twenty
VICHYITE supporter of Vichy France
VICINAGE VICINITY, neighbourhood;
  proximity
VICTORIA a vehicle
VICTRESS woman conqueror; victrix
VICTUALS provisions; sustenance
VIDENDUM thing to be seen
VIDEOTIC addicted to media (TV)
VIETMINH Vietnam Communist
VIEWABLE able to be seen
VIEWLESS vistaless
VIEWSOME panoramic
VIGILANT circumspect; alert; wakeful
VIGNERON wine-grower (Fr.)
VIGNETTE character sketch
mu **VIGOROSO** forcibly
VIGOROUS lusty; powerful; virile
VIHYLITE plastic glass
VILENESS baseness; depravity; vice
VILIFIED slandered; defamed;
  decried
VILIFIER traducer; maligner
VILIPEND disparage; calumniate
VILLADOM suburban villas
VILLAGER dweller in village
VILLAINY depravity; fraud; rascality
vt **VILLITIS** coronet inflammation in
  horse
VINCIBLE conquerable;
  surmountable

VINCULUM bond of union; link; chain
VINE-CLAD covered with vines
VINE-GALL vine disease
zo **VINE-GRUB** a parasite
VINE-LAND grape acreage
bt **VINEYARD** grape plantation
VINOLOGY art of wine making
VINOSITY wine flavour
VINTAGER grape gatherer
VINTNERY the wine trade
VIOLABLE transgressive
VIOLATOR ravisher; debaucher
VIOLENCE brute force
zo **VIPERINE** venomous
VIPERISH malignant
VIPEROUS treacherous
VIREMENT bookkeeping transfer
mu **VIRGINAL** early form of spinet
VIRGINAL (spinster)
bt **VIRGINIA** tobacco; creeper
VIRIDIAN bluish-green colour
mn **VIRIDINE** green variety of andalusite
VIRIDITY verdure; greenness
VIRILISM male characteristics in woman
VIRILITY manhood; energy; manliness
md **VIROLOGY** virus diseases
VIRTUOSE expert in art
VIRTUOSO connoisseur; expert
VIRTUOUS upright; moral; chaste
VIRULENT bitter in enmity; toxic
zo **VISCACHA** pampas hare
md **VISCERAL** abdominal
VISCOUNT title of peerage
VISIGOTH Spanish Goth
VISIONAL illusory; chimerical
VISITANT guest; frequenter
VISITING inspecting; haunting; calling
VITALISM VITALIST, hypothetical vital principle
VITALITY vigour; life; energy
VITALIZE animate; quicken
VITELLIN a protein in egg
VITELLUS the yolk of an egg
VITIATED impaired; spoilt; debased
VITIATOR a pervert
zo **VITICIDE** a vine pest
md **VITILIGO** patchy skin depigmentation
VITREOUS glassy
VITULINE (veal)
VIVACITY sprightliness; liveliness
zo **VIVARIUM** small zoo
VIVA-VOCE orally
VIVIDITY vividness; clarity; lucidity

VIVIFIED quickened; enlivened
bt **VIVIPARY** manner of bud/seed production
md **VIVISECT** operate on the living
VIXENISH quarrelsome; snappish
VIZERATE viziership
mu **VOCALISE** wordless composition (Fr.)
mu **VOCALIST** singer
VOCALITY utterableness
VOCALIZE voice; articulate
VOCATION profession; calling; pursuit
VOCATIVE (invocation); a case
mn **VOGESITE** hornblende-lamprophyre
VOIDABLE able to be annulled
VOIDANCE evasion; annulment
VOIDNESS nullity; emptiness
mn **VOIGTITE** form of mica
VOLATILE lively; fickle; changeable; unstable
cp **VOLATILE** memory lost; without power
VOLCANIC eruptive
VOLITANT able to fly
VOLITION freewill; choice; purpose
VOLITIVE wishful
VOLLEYED (tennis)
VOLPLANE glider
VOLSUNGS Norse legendary leaders
VOLTAISM galvanism
mn **VOLTZITE** zinc sulphide
mn **VOLULITE** petrified shell
VOLUMIST an author
VOLUTION convolution; spiral
md **VOLVULUS** stoppage
VOMITING ejecting
md **VOMITION** sickness
VOMITIVE vomitory
md **VOMITORY** an emetic
VORACITY rapacity; greed
mu **VORSPIEL** prelude; overture (Ger.)
VORTEXES whirlpools; vortices
go **VORTICAL** eddies; maelstroms
VOTARESS lady devotee
VOTARIST adherent; votary; zealot
VOTIVELY by way of vow
VOUCHING warranting; backing
VOUSSOIR arch stone
VOWELISM use of vowels
VOWELIST user of vowels
VOWELLED with vowels
VRAICING gathering seaweed (Ch. Is.)
VULCANIC volcanic
VULGARLY commonly; boorishly
md **VULSELLA** forceps

W

WABBLING wobbling
WADDLING walking like a duck
WAFERING sealing a letter (early days)
WAGE-FUND (a theory)
WAGELESS unpaid
WAGERING betting; laying; staking
WAGE-WORK paid work
WAGGLING swaying
WAGGONER wagoner
WAGGONET wagonette
WAGONAGE cost of transport
WAGONFUL load
WAGONING carting
WAGON-LIT sleeping car (Fr.)
zo **WAHDEROO** langur monkey
WAILMENT lamentation
WAINBOTE timber for carts
WAINROPE cart-rope
WAINSCOT panelling
bt **WAIT-A-BIT** (various shrubs)
WAITRESS a female waiter
nt **WAKA-TAUA** Maori war canoe (New Zealand)
WAKENING rousing; stimulating
mu **WALDHORN** hunting horn (Ger.)
WALHALLA VALHALLA, palace of Norse gods
WALKABLE within walking distance
WALK-MILL hammer-mill (blacksmith)
WALK-OVER easy victory
zo **WALLAROO** large kangaroo
WALL-EYED glaring; fierce
WALL-GAME Eton football
nt **WALL-KNOT** Turk's head
bt **WALL-MOSS** stonecrop
zo **WALL-NEWT** lizard; gecko
WALLOPED WALLOPER, thrashed; slogger
WALLOWED WALLOWER, floundered in mud
bt **WALL-TREE** fruit tree against sunny garden wall
bt **WALL-WORT** dwarf-elder
WALOGLAS WEALDGLASS, green glass process (Ger.)
WALTZING dancing
WAMBLING rumbling
WANDERED strayed; roamed
WANDERER rambler; nomad
WANGLING winning by craft
WANTLESS fully satisfied; abundant
WANTONED frolicked
WANTONLY sportively; capriciously

WAPPENED tearful; beaten; wearied; done in
WAPPERED blinked
WARBLING gurgling; birdsong; trifling
WAR-DANCE tribal ceremony
WARDCORN castle guard
WARDENRY warden's district
WARDMOTE court of inquiry
WARDROBE clothes closet
nt **WARD-ROOM** mess-room
WARDSHIP guardianship
WARE-ROOM show-room
WARFARER combatant
WAR-FIELD battle-field
zo **WAR-HORSE** a charger
WARINESS alertness; craftiness
WARM-DOWN relaxing after exertion
WARMNESS warmth; ardour
WARPAINT battle make-up
WAR-PLANE fighting aircraft
WAR-PLUME plume de guerre
WARPROOF valorous
zo **WARRAGAL** the dingo dog (Australia)
WARRANTY authority
WARRENER warren keeper
WARTLESS smooth-skinned
bt **WARTWEED WARTWORT**, spurge used for curing warts
WAR-WEARY tired of fighting
WAR-WHOOP a war-cry
WASHABLE easily washed (clothes)
WASHBALL soap-ball
WASHBOWL washbasin
pt **WASH-COAT** pre-treatment primer
mn **WASH-DIRT** process
WASHLAND between river and flood
WASH-ROOM ablution room
WASTEFUL prodigal; improvident
WASTEWAY overflow weir; spillway
WATCHBOX sentry box
WATCHDOG guard (dog)
WATCHFUL vigilant; alert; wary
WATCHING wakefulness; vigil
WATCH-KEY antique implement
WATCHMAN a look-out; custodian
WATER BAR water or flood excluder
WATERAGE transport dues
WATER-BED with water-filled mattress
zo **WATER-BUG** various types
WATERCAN watering-can for plants
zo **WATER-DOG** water spaniel
zo **WATERFLY** aquatic insect
zo **WATER-FOX** the carp
WATER-GAS illuminating gas
WATER-GOD Neptune

zo **WATER-HEN** moorhen
WATER-ICE a confection
WATERING diluting; irrigating
WATERISH insipid; moist; damp
WATERLOG saturate
WATERMAN ferryman; turncock
bt **WATER-POA** species of grass
WATERPOT watering can
WATER-RAM hydraulic ram
zo **WATER-RAT** water vole
zo **WATER-RUG** water spaniel
WATER-TAP spigot
go **WATERWAY** a canal
me **WATT-HOUR** measure of work
WATTLING plaiting; hurdling
WAVEBAND group of wavelengths
WAVEFORM characteristic of
radiowave
WAVELESS calm; undisturbed;
serene
WAVELIKE undulating; rippling
WAVE LINE stream line
WAVE-LOAF a wave-offering
WAVERING tottering; vacillating
WAVEROUS fluctuating; unsteady
el **WAVETAIL** fall in voltage of a
unidirectional impulse
WAVE-TRAP maritime hazard
el **WAVETRAP** interference reducer for
radios
WAVEWORN of coastal rocks
WAVINESS wave-like line drawing
WAXCLOTH oil-cloth
WAXLIGHT a taper
WAX-PAPER stencil paper
bt **WAX-PLANT** honeywort
WAXWORKS an exhibition (wax
statues)
mn **WAY-BOARD** thin stratum
bt **WAYBREAD** common plantain
WAYFARER traveller; pedestrian
WAYGOING departing
WAYGOOSE a printer's festivity
WAYLAYER interceptor; lurker
WAYLEAVE right of way
WAYMAKER a precursor
me **WAYMETER** pedometer
WAY-SHAFT engine shaft
bt **WAYTHORN** buckthorn
WEAKENED debilitated; enfeebled
WEAKENER enervator
WEAK-EYED needing glasses
WEAKLING delicate creature
WEAKNESS feebleness; frailty
WEANLING newly weaned
WEAPONED armed
WEARABLE fit to be worn
WEARIFUL wearisome; tedious

WEARYING tiring; fatiguing
WEED-HOOK garden tool
WEEDLESS well weeded
bd **WEEPHOLE** small drain hole for
water
zo **WEEVILED** infested with weevils
lw **WEIGHAGE** a toll on laden trucks
WEIGHING balancing; pondering
WEIGHOUT prior to boxing,
wrestling, (horse racing)
WEIGHTED given extra weight (horse
racing)
mn **WEISSITE** iolite
WELCOMED greeted; hailed; saluted
WELCOMER polite host; receptionist
WELDABLE fusable
WELD-IRON wrought iron
eg **WELDMENT** welded assembly
WELLADAY alas; alackaday
WELLAWAY everything going
splendidly
nt **WELL-BOAT** fishing boat
WELL-BORN of noble birth
WELL-BRED of good stock
WELLCURB ring of masonry
nt **WELL-DECK** space above cargo hold
WELLDOER a benefactor
WELL-HEAD source of a spring
ar, bd **WELL-HOLE** ventilation spaces
WELL-KEPT carefully tended
WELL-KNIT compact; sturdy
WELLNIGH nearly; almost
WELL-READ learned; scholarly
WELL-SEEN experienced; skilful
WELLSIAN (H. G. Wells)
WELL-TO-DO prosperous; affluent
WELL-WORN threadbare; shabby
WELSHING absconding; reneging
WELSHMAN a man of Wales
WELTERED wallowed; floundered
WEREGILD compensation for
homicide
zo **WEREWOLF** a changeling
rl **WESLEYAN** (John Wesley)
WESTERLY in westward direction
WESTWARD toward the west
ar, rl **WESTWORK** W. end of Carolingian,
Romanesque church
WET-NURSE breast-giver
WET-ON-WET short-interval spray-
painting
WHACKING astounding; a beating
WHALEMAN Jonah
WHALE-OIL oil from blubber of
whale
bt **WHANGEE** bamboo cane
WHANGING whacking; beating
WHARFAGE dock dues

WHARFING using a wharf (for
cargoes)
nt **WHARFING WHARVES**, existence of
jetties
WHATEVER anything which
zo **WHEATEAR** fallowfinch
zo **WHEAT-EEL** a wheat disease
zo **WHEAT-FLY** a pest
WHEEDLED coaxed; cajoled;
inveigled
WHEEDLER sycophant; fawner; toady
WHEELAGE a toll
WHEELING cycling; turning; twirling
WHEELMAN cyclist
mn **WHEEL-ORE** bournonite
WHEEL-TAX carriage tax
WHEEZILY asthmatically
WHEEZING breathing heavily
WHELPING littering; mothering
(dogs)
WHENEVER at any time that
WHEREOUT out of which
WHEREVER to whatever place
WHETTING sharpening
WHEY-FACE pale face
WHIFFING puffing
WHIFFLER prevaricator
WHIGGERY WHIGGISH, WHIGGISM,
liberalism
zo **WHIMBREL** wimbrel; curlew
WHIMSIES notions; caprices; fancies
WHIM-WHAM a gadget
zo **WHINCHAT** singing bird
WHINNIED neighed
WHINNOCK a milk-pail
WHINYARD sword; dirk
WHIPCORD string; material
WHIPHAND advantage over; control
WHIPLASH crack of whip
WHIPPING lashing; castigating
WHIPSTER whippersnapper
WHIPTAIL slender tail
WHIRLBAT cestus
WHIRLING gyrating; rotating
WHIRRING spinning; twirling;
turning
gl **WHISKERS** cats; minute single
crystals
WHISKERY with whiskers, bristles
WHISKING brushing lightly
mu, nt **WHISTLED** piped; (by mouth);
signalled attention
rw **WHISTLED** of steam locomotives,
warning or starting
zo **WHISTLER** broken-winded horse
zo **WHITE-ANT** a termite
WHITE-ARM arme blanche
WHITE-BOY Irish white-shirt

WHITE-HOT hotter than red-hot
WHITE-LIE an evasion
WHITEMAN of European ancestry
WHITENED WHITENER, blanched;
bleacher
WHITE-OUT open space in display
texts
WHITE-OUT snowblindness; loss of
orientation in arctic regions
WHITEPOT a confection
zo **WHITLING** sea trout; bull trout
WHITSOUR summer apple
WHITSTER a whitener
WHITTLED pared; cut; trimmed
WHITTLER reducer; trimmer (wood)
zo **WHITTRET** the weasel
WHIZZING speeding
WHODUNIT a crime novel
WHOMEVER whomsoever
WHOOPING yelling; hooting
WHOPPING beating; colossal
WHURRING a spinning sound
WICKEDLY evilly; atrociously
WICKERED chairs etc. made of osiers
WIDE-EYED afraid; gullible
pp **WIDELINE** vertical mark in
papermaking
WIDENESS breadth; width
WIDENING extending; broadening
WIDOWING bereaving
WIELDING brandishing; plying
WIFEHOOD wivehood
WIFELESS unmarried
WIFELIKE wifely
WIG-BLOCK wigmaker's block
WIGGLING wriggling
WIGMAKER perukist
hd, zo **WILDBOAR** Richard III's badge; hog;
swine
WILD-BORN not born indoors
zo **WILD-DUCK** mallard and others
WILD-FIRE sheet lightning
WILDFIRE wind-blown forest fire
zo **WILD-FOWL** untamed birds
WILD-LAND uncultivated soil
WILDNESS savageness; recklessness
WILD-WOOD forest
WILFULLY obstinately; deliberately
WILINESS craftiness; artfulness
mt **WILLIWAW** westerly blasting wind
(Straits of Magellan)
bt **WILLOWED** full of willows
WIMBLING boring
WIMPLING rippling
WINCHMAN windlass operator
lw **WIND BILL** guarantee
mu **WIND-BAND** instrumental ensemble
WINDERED fanned; blown

lw **WINDFALL** fruit from trees; legacy
WIND-GALL puffy swelling
nl **WINDLASS** a winch; capstan
WINDLESS calm, still; winded (lungs)
WINDMILL wind-driven machine
WINDOWED fenestrated
WINDPIPE the access to lungs; trachea
nt **WIND-PUMP** small windmill
nt **WIND-ROSE** the nautical chart compass
bd **WINDSAIL** rotating ventilator funnel
WINDSCAB snow surface crust; skiing
WIND-SEED carried by the wind
nt **WINDWARD** toward the wind, (course)
WINE-CASK barrel for wine
WINELESS without wine
WINE-RACK wine-bottle storage unit
WINESKIN bag for wine
WINGBACK half back (Amer. football)
zo **WING-CASE** horny cover of wing (beetles)
zo **WINGLESS** flightless bird; apterous
WING-LOCK wrestlers' hold
ae **WINGOVER** aerobatic, gliding manoeuvre
nt **WING-SHOT** threatening, flying shot
ag **WINNOWED** sifted grain (threshed)
WINNOWER chaff remover
WINTERED hibernated
WINTERLY every winter; wintry
WIREDRAW wire-making process
WIRE-HEEL a foot disease
WIRELESS radio
pp **WIREMARK** horizontal mark in papermaking
WIREROPE tightrope; circus stay
pp **WIRESIDE** underside of paper
zo **WIRE-WORM** a centipede
pp **WIRE-WOVE** (glazed writing paper)
WIRINESS toughness
WISEACRE a simpleton
WISELING wiseacre
mn **WISERITE** manganese carbonate
WISHBONE merrythought; frame of racing cars; T formation (Amer. football)
WISH-WASH weak drink; dishwater; undrinkable
bt **WISTARIA** a climbing plant
bt **WITCH-ELM** variety of elm tree
WITCHERY fascination; sorcery
WITCHING enchanting; charming
WITHDRAW retire; recall; retract

WITHDREW retreated; departed
WITHERED faded; shrunk; drooped
bt **WITHE-ROD** American shrub
WITHHELD kept back; detained
WITHHOLD restrain; reserve
bt **WITHWIND** bindweed
WITTOLLY complacently
WIVEHOOD wifehood
WIVELESS wifeless
WIZARDLY magically
WIZARDRY sorcery; necromancy
WIZENING withering
WOAD-MILL dye-extracting mill
WOBEGONE woebegone; calamitous
WOEFULLY sorrowfully; tragically
zo **WOLF-FISH** catfish
WOLF-SKIN wolf pelt
WOMANISH effeminate
WOMMERAH stick for spear-throwing
WONDERED speculated; marvelled
WONDERER conjecturer; ponderer
WONDROUS marvellous; miraculous
WONTLESS unaccustomed; unused
ch **WOOD-ACID** acetic acid
bt **WOODBIND** WOODBINE, wild honeysuckle
zo **WOODBIRD** forest denizen
zo **WOODCHAT** shrike; woodpecker
mn **WOOD-COAL** charcoal; lignite
zo **WOODCOCK** bird allied to snipe
zo **WOOD-DOVE** stockdove
vt **WOOD-EVIL** cattle disease
WOOD-HOLE woodstore
zo **WOOD-IBIS** tantalus; stork
WOOD-KERN Irish outlaw
WOODLAND forest land
zo **WOODLARK** forest bird
WOODLESS treeless
zo **WOOD-LICE** wood-beetles
bt **WOOD-LILY** lily of the valley
nt **WOODLOCK** to stop
zo **WOOD-MITE** a beetle
lw **WOODMOTE** forest court
WOODNOTE bird call
mn **WOOD-OPAL** silicified wood
WOOD-PULP cellulose
mn **WOODROCK** asbestos
bt **WOODROOF** WOODRUFF, a plant
WOOD-SEAR WOOD-SEER, WOOD-SERE, insect; cuckoo-spit; season
WOOD-SHED store for wood
nt **WOODSKIN** Guyana canoe
WOODSMAN a woodcutter
WOOD-SOOT charcoal soot
zo **WOOD-TICK** death-watch beetle
bt **WOOD-VINE** clematis
zo **WOODWALE** WOODWALL, golden oriole; green woodpecker

WOODWARD forest keeper
mu WOODWIND section of orchestra
WOODWORK carpentry
zo WOOD-WORM a grub
zo WOOD-WREN willow-warbler
WOOINGLY enticingly
WOOLBALL roll of yarn
WOOLDING binding
WOOL-DYED dyed in the wool
WOOLFELL skin with wool on it
WOOL-MILL cloth factory
WOOLPACK 240 lb. of wool
WOOLSACK Lord Chancellor's seat
WOOLWARD wearing wool
tx WOOLWORK wool-embroidery
WORD-BOOK dictionary; vocabulary
WORDLESS at a loss to speak
WORDLESS without language; silent; dumb
WORD-PLAY punning; repartee
WORKABLE feasible
WORKADAY prosaic; ordinary
WORKBOOK duties of staff for the day
WORKCARD report on work, defects, results
WORKFOLK toilers
WORKGIRL female employee
pr WORKMARK title letter and catalogue number
WORKROOM crafts workplace
WORKSHOP tool workroom
WORM-BORE damage by worms to books, furniture
WORMCAST thrown by worms
WORMGEAR gear wheels, etc.
WORM-HOLE track of woodworm
zo WORMLIKE vermicular
bt WORMSEED santonica
bt WORMWOOD absinthe; vermouth
WORRICOW hobgoblin
WORRYING harassing; fretting; chafing
WORSENED deteriorated
WORSTING besting; defeating
WORTHILY deservedly; meritoriously
mn WORTHITE silica compound
WOUNDILY excessively; hurtful
WOUNDING injuring
WRACKFUL ruinous; destructive
WRACKING gathering seaweed
WRANGLED brawled; bickered
WRANGLER disputant
zo WRANNOCK the wren
WRAPPAGE a wrapper
WRAPPING enclosing; muffling
WRATHFUL irate; incensed; wroth
WRATHILY indignantly; furiously

WRAULING caterwauling
WREAKFUL revengeful; angry
WREAKING inflicting; punishing
WREATHED garlanded; festooned
WREATHEN entwined
WRECKAGE crash-debris
WRECKING sabotaging; destroying
WRENCHED twisted; strained; wrung
WRESTING extorting; forcing; usurped
WRESTLED strove; grappled
ga WRESTLER master of wrestling bouts
WRETCHED miserable; paltry; sorry
WRICKING spraining; straining
WRIGGLED squirmed
WRIGGLER shuffler
bt WRIGHTIA tropical climber
pc WRINGING twisting wrists; (emotional stress)
WRINGING squeezing out water (laundry)
WRINKLED furrowed; creased; rumpled
WRISTLET band for wrist-watch
WRIST-PIN connecting pin of bracelet
WRITE-OFF total loss (disaster) (insurance)
WRITHING snake-like wriggling; squirming
WRONGFUL injurious; unjust; unfair
WRONGING violating; maltreating
mn WURTZITE sulphide of zinc

X

ch XANTHATE a salt
XANTHEIN yellow colour
XANTHENE chemical dye
XANTHIAN from Xanthus
XANTHINE yellow dye
mn XANTHITE yellow idocrase
bt XANTHIUM a plant
md XANTHOMA skin disease
XANTHOUS yellowish
zo XANTHURA American jay
bt XENOGAMY cross-fertilization
mn XENOLITE aluminium silicate
zo XENOPHYA foreign particles
mn XENOTIME yttrium phosphate
zo XENURINE armadillo-like
md XERANSIS dryness
md XERANTIC exsiccant
ec XEROCOLE animal living in dry place
bt XEROSERE dry-land succession
XESTURGY process of polishing
XILINOUS of cotton

zo **XIPHIOID** like a swordfish
bt **XYLOCARP** hard woody fruit
XYLOIDIN starch/nitric acid
  explosive
XYLONITE form of celluloid
pr **XYLOTYPE** wood engraving; print

Y

YACHTING ice, ocean, or lake
  pastime
YAHOOING howling and yelping
YAMMERED lamented; whined
mn **YANOLITE** axinite
pr **YAPPEDGE** overlapping bookcover
gl, mo **YARDANGS** overhanging rock ridges
  (Central Asia)
me **YARDLAND** 30 acres (12 hectares)
YARDSMAN scorer (Canadian
  football)
me **YARDWAND** vardstick
zo **YARWHELP** bar-tailed godwit
YATAGHAN long Turkish dagger
zo **YEANLING** eanling; a lamb
YEAR-BOOK voluminous annual
zo **YEARLING** one year old animal
YEARLONG twelve months
YEARNFUL mournful; distressing
YEARNING longing; craving;
  desirous
zo **YELDRING YELDROCK,** yowley;
  yorling; yellow-bunting
YELLOWED dyed yellow
YEOMANLY loyally supportive
YEOMANRY smallholder; attendant of
  sovereign
YEOMANRY signaller; chartman
  (navy); territorial (army)
YIELDING submitting; affording;
  bearing
YODELLED sang in alpine voice
YOGEEISM abstract meditation
YOICKING chanting (Lapland style)
YOKELESS unbound; at liberty
YOKEMATE the other ox of the
  plough
YOKE-TOED pair-toed
zo **YOKOHOMA** a breed of fowls
YONDMOST farthest; uttermost
YOUNGEST most youthful
YOUNGISH somewhat juvenile
YOURSELF reflexive pronoun
YOUTHFUL boyish; puerile; fresh
ch **YTTERBIA** oxide of ytterbium
mn **YTTERITE** gadolinite
ch **YTTRIOUS** containing yttrium
YUGOSLAV Jugo-Slav (South Slav)

YULETIDE Christmas; Noel; winter
  solstice
YUZBASHI Captain of 100 men
  (Turk.)

Z

zo **ZALOPHUS** seal genus
mu **ZAMBOMBA** Spanish instrument
ZAMINDAR zemindar; tax-collector
mu **ZAMPOGNO** Italian bagpipe
ZANTIOTE native of Zante
mn **ZARATITE** nickel compound
mu **ZARZUELA** Spanish operetta
ZEALLESS slack; apathetic
ZEALOTRY fanaticism; fervour;
  ardour
nm **ZECCHINO** sequin (Venice)
ZEGIDINE silver drinking cup
  (Hung.)
ZELANIAN (New Zealand)
ZEMINDAR Indian tax collector
ZENITHAL culminating; crowning
mn **ZEOLITIC** (felspar)
ZEPPELIN airship
bt **ZERUMBET** East Indian drug
ZETICULA a small room
zo **ZIBELINE** like a sable
ar, rl **ZIGGURAT** Sumerian temple
bd, rl **ZIGGURAT** ancient Eg. stepped
  pyramid
ZINCKIFY cover with zinc
bt **ZINGIBER** ginger, etc.
ZINNOBER vermilion pigment
ZIONWARD to Jerusalem (temple
  Sion)
zo **ZIPHIOID** like a swordfish
mn **ZIRCONIA** zirconium oxide
bt **ZIZYPHUS** jujube tree
zo **ZOANTHUS** sea-anemone
as **ZODIACAL** of signs of the Zodiac
ZOETROPE early form of cinema
ZOIATRIA veterinary surgery
mo **ZOLOTNIK** Russian weight
bt **ZONATION** occurrence in bands
ZONELESS beltless
zo **ZOOBLAST** animal cell
ch **ZOOCHEMY** animal chemistry
zo **ZOOECIUM** wall/chamber of
  polyzoan individual
ZOOGENIC generative
md **ZOOGLOEA** colony of bacteria
md **ZOOGRAFT** grafting tissue
ZOOLATER animal worshipper
ZOOLATRY animal worship
mn **ZOOLITIC** (fossilized animals)
ZOOMANCY divination

ZOOMETRY animal mensuration
ZOOMORPH animal in decorative art
zo **ZOONITIC** articulated
ZOONOMIA animal physiology
zo **ZOOPHAGA** carnivorous animals
ZOOPHILY love of animals
zo **ZOOPHYTE** plantlike animal
md **ZOOSCOPY** seeing snakes, etc.
md **ZOOSPERM** male seed-cell
bt **ZOOSPORE** animated spore
md **ZOOTOMIC** (vivisection)
ZOOT-SUIT long coat and tight trousers

ZOPFSTIL pig-tail style (Ger.)
zo **ZOPILOTE** turkey-buzzard
ck **ZUCCHINI** green squash, marrow (It.)
ZUGZWANG compulsive move to disaster (chess)
ck **ZWIEBACK** biscuit rusk
mn **ZYGADITE** aluminium compound
md **ZYGODONT** (molar teeth)
cy **ZYGONEMA** zygotene phase of meiosis
cy **ZYGOTENE** 2nd stage of meiotic prophase
ZYMOLOGY study of fermentation and enzymes

PENGUIN ONLINE

READ MORE IN PENGUIN

In every corner of the world, on every subject under the sun, Penguin represents quality and variety – the very best in publishing today.

For complete information about books available from Penguin – including Puffins, Penguin Classics and Arkana – and how to order them, write to us at the appropriate address below. Please note that for copyright reasons the selection of books varies from country to country.

In the United Kingdom: Please write to *Dept. EP, Penguin Books Ltd, Bath Road, Harmondsworth, West Drayton, Middlesex UB7 0DA*

In the United States: Please write to *Consumer Services, Penguin Putnam Inc., 405 Murray Hill Parkway, East Rutherford, New Jersey 07073-2136.* VISA and MasterCard holders call 1-800-631-8571 to order Penguin titles

In Canada: Please write to *Penguin Books Canada Ltd, 10 Alcorn Avenue, Suite 300, Toronto, Ontario M4V 3B2*

In Australia: Please write to *Penguin Books Australia Ltd, 487 Maroondah Highway, Ringwood, Victoria 3134*

In New Zealand: Please write to *Penguin Books (NZ) Ltd, Private Bag 102902, North Shore Mail Centre, Auckland 10*

In India: Please write to *Penguin Books India Pvt Ltd, 11 Community Centre, Panchsheel Park, New Delhi 110017*

In the Netherlands: Please write to *Penguin Books Netherlands bv, Postbus 3507, NL-1001 AH Amsterdam*

In Germany: Please write to *Penguin Books Deutschland GmbH, Metzlerstrasse 26, 60594 Frankfurt am Main*

In Spain: Please write to *Penguin Books S. A., Bravo Murillo 19, 1°B, 28015 Madrid*

In Italy: Please write to *Penguin Italia s.r.l., Via Vittorio Emanuele 45/a, 20094 Corsico, Milano*

In France: Please write to *Penguin France, 12, Rue Prosper Ferradou, 31700 Blagnac*

In Japan: Please write to *Penguin Books Japan Ltd, Iidabashi KM-Bldg, 2-23-9 Koraku, Bunkyo-Ku, Tokyo 112-0004*

In South Africa: Please write to *Penguin Books South Africa (Pty) Ltd, P.O. Box 751093, Gardenview, 2047 Johannesburg*

READ MORE IN PENGUIN

LANGUAGE/LINGUISTICS

Language Play David Crystal

We all use language to communicate information, but it is language play which is truly central to our lives. Full of puns, groan-worthy gags and witty repartee, this book restores the fun to the study of language. It also demonstrates why all these things are essential elements of what makes us human.

Swearing Geoffrey Hughes

'A deliciously filthy trawl among taboo words across the ages and the globe' *Observer*. 'Erudite and entertaining' Penelope Lively, *Daily Telegraph*

The Language Instinct Stephen Pinker

'Dazzling . . . Pinker's big idea is that language is an instinct, as innate to us as flying is to geese . . . Words can hardly do justice to the superlative range and liveliness of Pinker's investigations' *Independent*. 'He does for language what David Attenborough does for animals, explaining difficult scientific concepts so easily that they are indeed absorbed as a transparent stream of words' John Gribbin

Mother Tongue Bill Bryson

'A delightful, amusing and provoking survey, a joyful celebration of our wonderful language, which is packed with curiosities and enlightenment on every page' *Sunday Express*. 'A gold mine of language-anecdote. A surprise on every page . . . enthralling' *Observer*

Longman Guide to English Usage
Sidney Greenbaum and Janet Whitcut

Containing 5000 entries compiled by leading authorities on modern English, this invaluable reference work clarifies every kind of usage problem, giving expert advice on points of grammar, meaning, style, spelling, pronunciation and punctuation.

READ MORE IN PENGUIN

REFERENCE

The Penguin Dictionary of Troublesome Words Bill Bryson

Why should you avoid discussing the *weather conditions*? Can a married woman be celibate? Why is it eccentric to talk about the aroma of a cowshed? A straightforward guide to the pitfalls and hotly disputed issues in standard written English.

Swearing Geoffrey Hughes

'A deliciously filthy trawl among taboo words across the ages and the globe' Valentine Cunningham, *Observer*, Books of the Year. 'Erudite and entertaining' Penelope Lively, *Daily Telegraph*, Books of the Year.

Medicines: A Guide for Everybody Peter Parish

Now in its seventh edition and completely revised and updated, this bestselling guide is written in ordinary language for the ordinary reader yet will prove indispensable to anyone involved in health care: nurses, pharmacists, opticians, social workers and doctors.

Media Law Geoffrey Robertson QC and Andrew Nichol

Crisp and authoritative surveys explain the up-to-date position on defamation, obscenity, official secrecy, copyright and confidentiality, contempt of court, the protection of privacy and much more.

The Penguin Careers Guide
Anna Alston and Anne Daniel; Consultant Editor: Ruth Miller

As the concept of a 'job for life' wanes, this guide encourages you to think broadly about occupational areas as well as describing day-to-day work and detailing the latest developments and qualifications such as NVQs. Special features include possibilities for working part-time and job-sharing, returning to work after a break and an assessment of the current position of women.

READ MORE IN PENGUIN

REFERENCE

The Penguin Dictionary of the Third Reich
James Taylor and Warren Shaw

This dictionary provides a full background to the rise of Nazism and the role of Germany in the Second World War. Among the areas covered are the major figures from Nazi politics, arts and industry, the German Resistance, the politics of race and the Nuremberg trials.

The Penguin Biographical Dictionary of Women

This stimulating, informative and entirely new Penguin dictionary of women from all over the world, through the ages, contains over 1,600 clear and concise biographies on major figures from politicians, saints and scientists to poets, film stars and writers.

Roget's Thesaurus of English Words and Phrases
Edited by Betty Kirkpatrick

This new edition of Roget's classic work, now brought up to date for the nineties, will increase anyone's command of the English language. Fully cross-referenced, it includes synonyms of every kind (formal or colloquial, idiomatic and figurative) for almost 900 headings. It is a must for writers and utterly fascinating for any English speaker.

The Penguin Dictionary of International Relations
Graham Evans and Jeffrey Newnham

International relations have undergone a revolution since the end of the Cold War. This new world disorder is fully reflected in this new Penguin dictionary, which is extensively cross-referenced with a select bibliography to aid further study.

The Penguin Guide to Synonyms and Related Words
S. I. Hayakawa

'More helpful than a thesaurus, more humane than a dictionary, the *Guide to Synonyms and Related Words* maps linguistic boundaries with precision, sensitivity to nuance and, on occasion, dry wit' *The Times Literary Supplement*

READ MORE IN PENGUIN

DICTIONARIES